SOCIAL PSYCHOLOGY

SOCIAL PSYCHOLOGY

2025 Release

David G. Myers

Hope College

Jean M. Twenge

San Diego State University

Mc Graw Hill

SOCIAL PSYCHOLOGY, 2025 RELEASE

This book is printed on acid-free paper.

1 2 3 4 5 6 7 8 9 LWI 30 29 28 27 26 25

ISBN 978-1-266-58046-8 (bound)
MHID 1-266-58046-8 (bound)
ISBN 978-1-264-74814-3 (loose-leaf)
MHID 1-264-74814-0 (loose-leaf)

Executive Portfolio Manager: *Jason Seitz*
Senior Product Development Manager: *Dawn Groundwater*
Marketing Manager: *Isfa Syed*
Content Project Managers: *Traci Vaske, Vanessa McClune*
Manufacturing Project Manager: *Laura Fuller*
Content Licensing Specialist: *Sarah Flynn*
Cover Image: *insta_photos/Shutterstock; fizkes/Shutterstock*
Compositor: *Aptara®, Inc.*

All credits appearing on page or at the end of the book are considered to be an extension of the copyright page.

Library of Congress Cataloging-in-Publication Data

Names: Myers, David G., author. | Twenge, Jean M., 1971- author.
Title: Social psychology / David Myers, Hope College, Jean M. Twenge, San Diego State University.
Description: 2025 release. | New York, NY : McGraw Hill LLC, 2025. | Includes bibliographical references and index.
Identifiers: LCCN 2024035312 (print) | LCCN 2024035313 (ebook) | ISBN 9781266580468 (hardcover) | ISBN 9781264748143 (spiral bound) | ISBN 9781264765560 (ebook) | ISBN 9781264746774 (ebook other)
Subjects: LCSH: Social psychology.
Classification: LCC HM1033 .M944 2025 (print) | LCC HM1033 (ebook) | DDC 302–dc23/eng/20240808
LC record available at https://lccn.loc.gov/2024035312
LC ebook record available at https://lccn.loc.gov/2024035313

mheducation.com/highered

DGM

For Nelson Black, with gratitude for his 1979 invitation to become a McGraw Hill author

JMT

For my parents: Stephen and JoAnn Twenge

About the Authors

Since receiving his University of Iowa PhD, David G. Myers has professed psychology at Michigan's Hope College. Hope College students have invited him to be their commencement speaker and voted him "outstanding professor."

Photo by Steven Herppich, courtesy Hope College Public Relations.
For more information or to contact David Myers, visit davidmyers.org. David Myers

With support from National Science Foundation grants, Myers' research has appeared in some three dozen scientific periodicals, including *Science,* the *American Scientist, Psychological Science,* and the *American Psychologist*.

He has also communicated psychological science through articles in four dozen magazines, from *Today's Education* to *Scientific American,* and through his 18 books, including *The Pursuit of Happiness* and *How Do We Know Ourselves? Curiosities and Marvels of the Human Mind.*

Myers' research and writings have been recognized by the Gordon Allport Prize, by an "honored scientist" award from the Federation of Associations in the Brain and Behavioral Sciences, and by the Award for Distinguished Service on Behalf of Personality-Social Psychology.

He has chaired his city's Human Relations Commission, helped found a center for families in poverty, and spoken to hundreds of college and community groups. In recognition of his efforts to transform the way America provides assistive listening for people with hearing loss (see hearingloop.org), he has received awards from the American Academy of Audiology, the Hearing Loss Association of America, and the hearing industry.

David and Carol Myers have three children and one grandchild.

Photo by Sandy Huffaker, Jr.
For more information or to contact Jean Twenge, visit www.jeantwenge.com. Sandy Huffaker, Jr.

As Professor of Psychology at San Diego State University, Jean M. Twenge has authored more than 180 scientific publications on generational differences, cultural change, social rejection, digital media use, gender roles, self-esteem, and narcissism. Her research has been covered in *Time, Newsweek, The New York Times, USA Today, U.S. News and World Report,* and *The Washington Post,* and she has been featured on *Today, Good Morning America, CBS This Morning, Real Time with Bill Maher, Fox and Friends, NBC Nightly News, Dateline NBC,* and National Public Radio.

Dr. Twenge has drawn on her research in her books for a broader audience, including *Generations: The Real Differences between Gen Z, Millennials, Gen X, Boomers and Silents—and What They Mean for America's Future* (2023) and *iGen: Why Today's Super-Connected Kids Are Growing Up Less Rebellious, More Tolerant, Less Happy—And Completely Unprepared for Adulthood* (2017). An article by Dr. Twenge in *The Atlantic* was nominated for a National Magazine Award, and she posts updates and analyses on the Generation Tech Substack. She frequently gives talks and seminars on generational differences to audiences such as college faculty and staff, parent-teacher groups, military personnel, camp directors, and corporate executives.

Jean Twenge grew up in Minnesota and Texas. She holds a BA and MA from the University of Chicago and a PhD from the University of Michigan. She completed a postdoctoral research fellowship in social psychology at Case Western Reserve University. She lives in San Diego with her husband and three daughters.

Brief Contents

Olha Romaniuk/Getty Images

SDI Productions/Getty Images

Ingram Publishing/Getty Images

Table of Contents

Mike Kemp/Blend Images/Getty Images

tetmc/iStock/Getty Images

Part Two: Social Influence

Ronnie Kaufman/Blend Images

kali9/Getty Images

Guide to Diversity, Equity, and Inclusion

More than almost any other discipline, social psychology shines its light on our human kinship as members of one human family *and* on our diversity. We are so much alike in how we think about, influence, and relate to one another. Yet we differ in gender identity, sexual orientation, race, culture, income, religion, and abilities.

The 2025 release of *Social Psychology,* therefore, has whole chapters devoted to our diversity in (and attitudes regarding) gender, culture, and race, and to how we can transform diversity-related conflicts into equitable and inclusive human connections. As this guide illustrates, the psychology of human diversity, equity, and inclusion also weaves throughout the text. Moreover, this is a *global* text, as we draw on the whole world of psychology for our worldwide readers. As humans we are all alike. Cut us and we bleed. Yet how richly diverse are the threads that form the human fabric.

Chapter 1 Introducing Social Psychology

- "What Is Social Psychology?," shows that social psychology is enjoying accelerated growth in China, Hong Kong, India, Japan, and Taiwan.
- Figure 1, Social Psychology Is…, demonstrates that social psychology is the scientific study of social influence (culture) and social relations (prejudice), among other topics.
- "Social Influences Shape Our Behavior" notes that emotional expressiveness hinges on one's culture and ethnicity; the power of the situation influences different countries' views on same-sex relationships; body-shape preference depends on when and where people live; and focusing on one's personal needs, desires, and morality or one's family, clan, and communal groups depends on being a product of individualistic or collectivistic societies.
- "The Ethics of Experimentation" observes that 15% of Ukrainian survey respondents declared themselves "religious" while under Soviet communism, but 70% declared themselves "religious" in the post-communist era.
- The section on "sampling" notes that most participants are from WEIRD (*W*estern, *E*ducated, *I*ndustrialized, *R*ich, and *D*emocratic) cultures, which represent only 12% of humanity.

Chapter 2 The Self in a Social World

- "Spotlights and Illusions" discusses research on how being in the minority (race, gender, or nationality) in a group raises an individual's awareness of how they differ, and when the topic of race comes up in a discussion, those in the minority feel an uncomfortable amount of attention directed their way.
- "At the Center of Our Worlds: Our Sense of Self" presents research showing that the threat of negative academic-ability stereotypes for racial minority students or women causes "disidentification," which can lead them to shift their interests elsewhere.
- "Self and Culture" presents individualism and collectivism, with definitions, examples of each, the cultures that tend to be collectivistic/individualistic, within-culture individualism/collectivism, and political viewpoints.
- "Growing Individualism Within Cultures" has examples of cultural and time period differences in child naming practices and song lyrics.
- "Culture and Cognition" has examples of collectivists focusing on objects and people in relationship to one another and their environment, and individualists focusing more on one feature.
- The same section presents the cultural differences in the sense of belonging, and how the desire for harmony in collectivistic countries led to the higher likelihood of following COVID-19 mandates.
- "Culture and Self-Esteem" discusses the different ways individualists and collectivists view happiness and self-esteem.
- "Explaining Positive and Negative Events" discusses research on how collectivists are less likely to self-enhance.
- The "Inside Story: Hazel Markus and Shinobu Kitayama on Cultural Psychology" is a personal account of the professors' observations of the differences in teaching in collectivistic and individualistic cultures.
- Self-presentation differences in collectivistic and individualistic cultures are discussed, with examples of Asian countries focusing on group identity and restrained self-presentation.

Chapter 3 Social Beliefs and Judgments

- "The Psychology of Conspiracy Theories" discusses research showing that people who believed in COVID-19 conspiracy theories were more likely to be prejudiced against people of Asian descent.
- Cultural differences and similarities regarding the fundamental attribution error are covered. Research shows that the attribution error exists across all cultures, but people in Eastern Asian cultures are somewhat more sensitive than Westerners to the importance of situations.

- "Getting from Others What We Expect" presents a research study on self-fulfilling prophecies where a person anticipated interacting with someone of a different race. When they were led to expect that that person disliked interacting with someone of the first person's race, the first person felt more anger and displayed more hostility toward their conversation partner.

Chapter 4 Behavior and Attitudes

- Research shows that self-described racial attitudes provide little clue to behaviors in actual situations. Many people *say* they are upset when someone makes racist remarks; yet when they hear racist language, many respond with indifference.
- "Role-Playing" includes a quotation from African American abolitionist, orator, and writer Frederick Douglass on the transformation over time in the disposition of the woman he had been sold to.
- In "Evil and Moral Acts," the Rwandan genocide is illustrated, showing that cruel acts tend to breed even crueler and more hate-filled attitudes.
- In the same section, the example is given of how, during the Russia-Ukraine war, Russian soldiers made Ukrainians lie on their stomachs before executing them so as not to see the victims' faces.
- The facial feedback effect is illustrated in a photo of employees of Air Nippon Airways biting wooden chopsticks, which caused them to inadvertently smile.

Chapter 5 Genes, Culture, and Gender

- This chapter presents many worldwide examples about culture and gender.
- In the chapter's introduction, the role of gender in the military in different cultures is discussed.
- In "How Are We Influenced by Biology?" the discussion focuses on (with many examples) how people from different cultures are more alike than different: "We're all kin beneath the skin."
- "Genes, Evolution, and Behavior" presents how evolutionary psychology highlights our universal human nature, while cultures provide the specific rules for elements of social life.
- "Terms for Studying Sex and Gender" discusses gender fluidity and nonbinary identity, along with an explanation of transgender identity.
- "Focus on: The Cultural Animal" presents Roy Baumeister's research on the importance and advantages of human culture.
- "Cultural Diversity" discusses how migration and refugee evacuations are mixing cultures more than ever and that cultural diversity surrounds us.
- "Norms: Expected Behavior" discusses how every culture has its own norms, including: individual choices; expressiveness and punctuality; rule-breaking and rule-following; and personal space. It also includes "Research Close-Up: Passing Encounters, East and West," with research on the differences in pedestrian interactions in both the U.S. and Japan.
- "Cultural Similarity" discusses "an essential universality" across cultures, including norms for friendship; personality dimensions; social beliefs; and status hierarchies.
- In the above section, the six universal dimensions of moral beliefs are presented. These moral values influence a culture's social norms and laws and may explain subcultural differences.
- "Gender Roles Vary with Culture" reports on the differences between cultures in attitudes about whether both spouses should work.
- "Gender Roles Vary Over Time" reports that trends toward more gender equality appear across many cultures, with women increasingly being represented in the legislative bodies of most nations, but that many gender differences persist.
- "Social Dominance" presents statistics and research on worldwide attitudes that men are more socially dominant than women; the percentage of women legislators worldwide; and the worldwide disparity between men's and women's wages.
- The section above also discusses how, across cultures, masculinity is seen as something that must be earned and defended.
- In "Sexuality," the percentages of same-sex marriages in several countries are given.
- The concluding section of this chapter discusses how biology and culture interact.

Chapter 6 Conformity and Obedience

- In "What is Conformity?," the differences between collectivistic and individualistic attitudes about conformity are discussed.
- In "Behavior and Attitudes," a photo illustrates a technique used by a White South African torturer during the apartheid era.
- In the above section, an example is given of French villagers protecting Jewish people from the Nazis during World War II.
- In "The Power of Social Norms," research showed that people predicted they would be upset by witnessing a person making a racial slur, but they exhibited indifference when actually witnessing that event.
- Research is presented in "Cohesion" on how people within an ethnic group may feel "own-group conformity pressure." Blacks who "act White" or Whites who "act Black" may be mocked for not conforming to their own ethnic group.
- The subsection "Culture" in the section "Who Conforms?" reports that in collectivistic cultures, conformity rates are higher than in individualistic cultures. There may be biological wisdom to cultural differences in conformity: Groups thrive when coordinating their responses to threats. An example shows the differences between individualistic and collectivistic cultures' responses to the COVID-19 pandemic.
- A margin note quotes a Native American prayer: "Great Spirit, grant that I may not criticize my neighbor until I have walked for a moon in his moccasins."

- "Asserting Uniqueness" discusses how people become keenly aware of their differences when they are in the minority (Black woman in a group of White women, a gay person in a group of straight people, a minority group amid a majority group).

Chapter 7 Persuasion

- The chapter introduction gives examples of the power of persuasion helping to change attitudes around equality: Americans electing a Black president twice, and the majority of Americans now supporting same-sex marriage.
- In "How Old Are They?," Figure 6 shows the generation gap in U.S. attitudes toward same-sex marriage in 2023.
- A new feature titled "The Psychology of Misinformation" shows how debunking and "pre-bunking" can combat misinformation, including misinformation leading to polarization and division among citizens.

Chapter 8 Group Influence

- "Social Loafing in Everyday Life" presents research on social loafing in varied cultures, with examples of communist and noncommunist collectivistic cultures. People in collectivistic cultures exhibit less social loafing than do people in individualistic cultures.
- The May 2020 police killing of George Floyd and the resulting peaceful daytime protests and nighttime violence are discussed in "Deindividuation: When Do People Lose Their Sense of Self in Groups?"
- "Group Size" gives the example of historic lynchings where, the bigger the mob, the more its members lost self-awareness and were willing to commit atrocities.
- In "Group Polarization Experiments," an experiment is presented: When prejudiced students discussed racial issues together, their prejudice increased. When unprejudiced students discussed racial issues together, their prejudice decreased. Group polarization also occurs when people share negative or positive impressions of an immigrant group.
- In "Group Polarization in Politics," Figure 9, A Polarizing Society, illustrates the polarization between U.S. White Democrats and White Republicans when answering the question "Discrimination is the main reason why Black people have worse jobs, income, and housing."
- "The Influence of Individual Group Members" cites Martin Luther King, Jr., Susan B. Anthony, Nelson Mandela, Rosa Parks, and Greta Thunberg as having had the power to influence change.
- "Focus On: Transformational Community Leadership" gives the example of transformational leadership by the owners and editors of the newspaper on Bainbridge Island, WA, during World War II, who spoke out against the removal and interment of Japanese Bainbridge Island residents.
- A photo of the Washington, D.C., statue of Martin Luther King, Jr., illustrates transformational leadership.

Chapter 9 Prejudice

- This chapter is dedicated to better understanding issues of diversity, equity, and inclusion.
- In the chapter introduction, statistics are presented on an increase in antisemitic incidents in the U.S. in 2022; increasing hate crimes against Jewish people in Germany; research showing that bias against overweight people is the one type of prejudice that has *not* declined since 2007; and the prevalence of anti-immigrant prejudice in several countries.
- The targets of prejudice in the U.S. cluster into three categories: marginalized groups, unconventional groups, and privileged or conservative groups.
- When stereotypes are overgeneralized or negative, prejudice often follows.
- An example of discrimination is given of Australian bus drivers allowing Whites to ride for free 72% of the time and Blacks to ride for free 36% of the time when they did not have money to pay for the ride.
- A study is presented where applicants for a vacant apartment were discriminated against or not discriminated against depending on whether their names were associated with White, Muslim, or Black groups. Other studies show that stereotypically Black names lead to more discrimination.
- Research studies show that only a minority of people discriminate.
- Gendered wording in job ads sustain gender inequality.
- The Implicit Association Test (IAT) is described and discussed.
- When same-sex marriage was legalized in U.S. states, implicit prejudice against gays and lesbians declined in those states. Nationwide figures of declining same-sex implicit prejudice are given.
- In "Is Racial Prejudice Disappearing?," positive movement in attitudes is reported: Support for White and Black children going to school together has risen to 90%; U.S. adults' approval of Black people and White people marrying each other has risen to 94%; scores on both explicit and implicit tests of racial prejudice declined between 2007 and 2020; and overt racial prejudice has declined in Britain.
- In the same section, however, research is given on the recent increase in reported U.S. hate crime incidents; the 29% of White Americans agreeing that the country needs to "protect and preserve its White European heritage"; and the White misperception of the Black-White wealth race gap and the chances lower-income Black Americans will move up the economic ladder.
- In "Displays of Racial Prejudice and Discrimination," several examples are given: Results from the IAT show that subtle prejudice persists; racial prejudice can appear indirectly, such as White Americans judging Black neighborhoods and schools as impoverished, crime-ridden, and dirty; employment discrimination; favoritism; interactions with police both in the United States and the U.K.; and patronizing behavior.

- In "The Impact of Racial Prejudice," experiments are presented on how images of Black men holding a harmless object induced White people to shoot, and how Whites primed with a Black face caused them to think "guns." Police killings of Black Americans are discussed.
- In "Gender Prejudice," gender stereotypes are discussed with examples, such as women being more agreeable than men, and characters in popular children's TV shows being treated more positively for gender-stereotypical behavior.
- In "Sexism: Benevolent and Hostile," Figure 1, Changing Gender Attitudes from 1958 to 2020, is presented.
- Gender attitudes often mix "benevolent sexism" and "hostile sexism."
- In "Gender Discrimination," research shows there is bias against women in salaries, teaching evaluations, and group discussions.
- Sexual assault and sexual harassment are discussed, with the example of Harvey Weinstein; a poll reporting that 81% of U.S. women had experienced sexual harassment in their lifetime; one-third of U.S. women reporting having experienced unwanted sexual advances at work; and 1 in 3 women worldwide having experienced sexual assault or partner violence.
- Figure 2, Sex Ratio at Birth, 2017, shows countries where there are an unusually high number of boy versus girl births, indicating that selective abortions have influenced the number of boys and girls born.
- In "LGBTQ+ Prejudice," it is reported that in many countries, same-sex relationships are a criminal offense. But cultures vary in their views of homosexuality: 94% in Sweden say homosexuality should be accepted by society, while only 9% agree in Indonesia.
- Support for same-sex relationships is now very high: In the U.S., it has risen from 27% in 1996 to 71% in 2023. In the U.K., it has risen from 10% in 1987 to 78% in 2023.
- Examples of discrimination against LGBTQ+ people are given: job discrimination; verbal and physical harassment, with 3 out of 4 LGBTQ+ students reporting being verbally harassed at school, and one-third physically harassed; rejection, with one in 3 U.S. transgender adults saying their families are unsupportive of their gender identity, and 1out of 4 U.S. gay and lesbian adults and 81% of bisexual adults are not "out" to the most important people in their lives.
- Research is presented on how, when U.S. states do not have gay-lesbian hate crime and nondiscrimination protection, LGBTQ+ people experience substantially higher mood disorder rates. When states implement non-discrimination policies, LGBTQ+ youth suicide decreases afterward.
- It is reported that the suicide rate among U.S. gay and lesbian teens is at least 3 times higher than the general rate for U.S. teens. Half of U.S. transgender teens and young adults have attempted suicide.
- Three experiments are discussed that confirm the toxicity of gay stigma, and the benefits of its removal.
- In "Social Inequalities: Unequal Status and Prejudice," experiments confirm the idea that stereotypes of Black people and women help rationalize the inferior status of each.
- "The Authoritarian Personality" presents the finding that those with an authoritarian personality react negatively to ethnic diversity and are more likely to express prejudice against transgender individuals.
- "The Inside Story: Sohad Murrar on Pro-Diversity Social Norms" presents research on undergraduates showing that emphasizing that pro-diversity attitudes are the social norm resulted in improved pro-diversity attitudes and behaviors up to 12 weeks later, and led to minority students' well-being and grades improving over that time.
- Examples are given of how conformity maintains gender prejudice.
- There is discussion of the media phenomenon of "fat-shaming," especially of celebrities, and how this can cause women to have more anti-fat prejudice, at least implicitly.
- "Socialization" ends with a message of hope that prejudice can diminish, as it has in the case of same-sex marriage.
- "Systemic Supports" reports on how social institutions can bolster prejudice. Several examples are given: banks denying mortgages to unmarried women and ethnic minority applicants; lenders charging Black and Latino homebuyers higher interest rates than Whites, or rejection of their mortgage applications.
- In the above section there is discussion of how the media can also strengthen stereotypes.
- "Frustration and Aggression: The Scapegoat Theory" discusses how White Americans' frustration during economic downturns led to scapegoating, resulting in lynchings in the past, and to pronounced prejudice between 1964 and 2012.
- The key term "realistic group conflict theory" is presented and discussed, with examples from around the world.
- "Social Identity Theory: Feeling Superior to Others" discusses the influence of evolution on humans forming groups. As a result, people categorize, identify, and compare. The example is given of how the online group Nextdoor enabled unconscious bias due to neighbors posting about seeing a "suspicious" Black person in a primarily White neighborhood. Nextdoor developed a new protocol where users must identify the specific behavior that made the person seem suspicious. This reduced racial profiling by 75%.
- Ingroups, outgroups, and ingroup bias are discussed. Ingroup bias leads to favoritism and sometimes unintended discrimination.
- Prejudice is greater among those who are low or slipping on the socioeconomic ladder and among those whose positive self-image is threatened.

- "Motivation to Avoid Prejudice" discusses how motivations can lead people to want to avoid prejudice, but automatic (unintentional) prejudiced responses still occur. Research examples are presented of interventions to break "the prejudice habit." Encouragement is given to the reader to become aware of their knee-jerk presumptions or feelings.
- Own-race bias is presented, including discussion of the outgroup homogeneity effect. Figure 4, The Own-Race Bias, shows how Blacks and Whites more accurately recognize faces of their own race.
- In the U.S., 74% of Blacks (who are the racial minority) see their race as "being extremely or very important to how they think of themselves," compared with only 15% of Whites.
- Research is presented showing that distinctive cases fuel stereotypes.
- "Group-Serving Bias" discusses how attribution errors can bias people's explanation of group members' behaviors. Disadvantaged groups and groups that stress modesty exhibit less of group-serving bias. Egotistical groups react to threats with group-serving bias and hostility.
- "Discrimination's Impact: The Self-Fulfilling Prophecy" presents Gordon Allport's research from his book *The Nature of Prejudice*.
- "Stereotype Threat" presents research on the effects of stereotype threat involving racial stereotypes and stereotypes about women.
- In "The Inside Story: Claude Steele on Stereotype Threat," Steele discusses his experiments on stereotype threat, and how the researchers were able to eliminate underperformance by making the task irrelevant to stereotype. Tactics on reducing stereotype threat are discussed, with several research examples given.

Chapter 10 Aggression

- The chapter introduction gives the staggering worldwide numbers of those killed in genocides throughout the past and present centuries, including in the Russia-Ukraine war. Bullying is also discussed, with 1 out of 5 U.S. high school students having been bullied in school in 2019.
- "What Is Aggression?" reports that some have recommended abandoning the term "microaggressions" and substituting it with "inadvertent racial slights."
- It is reported that male-on-male aggression may be particularly common in more traditional cultures with less gender equality—perhaps one reason why countries with less gender equality have higher violent crime rates.
- Research shows that people with mental illnesses are more likely to be the victims of violence than to be the perpetrators.
- "Displacement Theory" reports that outgroup targets are especially vulnerable to displaced aggression.
- "The Inside Story: Brett Pelham on Growing Up Poor in the 'Culture of Honor'" is presented where Pelham writes about growing up in the deep South in a "culture of honor," with its associations with inequality, aggression, and prejudice.
- In "Pornography and Sexual Violence," the "rape myth" is discussed, and studies are presented that show that men who consume more sexually explicit and sexually violent media are more likely to be involved in dating violence and sexual violence. Men are more likely to send sexist jokes to women if they play a video game with sexualized female characters.
- The massacres in Rwanda, of Europe's Jewish people during World War II, and the U.S.'s indigenous population are discussed as examples of group/social influence amplifying aggression. Another example is given of the White man who killed 10 Black people at a Buffalo supermarket in 2022, and the online material that influenced him to do so.

Chapter 11 Attraction and Intimacy

- "How Important Is the Need to Belong?" discusses the effects of ostracism and rejection. Prejudice can feel like rejection, which is another reason to work to reduce prejudice based on group membership.
- "Mere Exposure" reports on an experiment where attitudes toward transgender people became more positive after reading stories with accompanying pictures about transgender individuals.
- The above section reports that there is a negative side to the mere exposure effect: wariness of the unfamiliar, which may explain the automatic, unconscious prejudice people often feel when confronting those who are different. Infants as young as 3 months exhibit an own-race preference.
- "Who Is Attractive?" covers how the definition of attractiveness changes depending on the culture or time period. Additionally, research shows that attractiveness does not influence life outcomes as much in cultures where relationships are based more on kinship or social arrangement than on personal choice. Despite cultural variations, there is strong agreement within and across cultures about who is and who is not attractive.
- Evolution explains why males in 37 cultures prefer youthful female characteristics that signify reproductive capacity.
- "Dissimilarity Breeds Dislike" reports that whether people perceive those of another race as similar or dissimilar influences their racial attitudes.
- "Variations in Love: Culture and Gender" discusses the differences between cultures in the concept of romantic love and the cultural variation in whether love precedes or follows marriage. Passionate love has become the basis of marriage in the United States (and tends to be emphasized more in cultures in which relationships are more easily broken.
- Figure 5, Romantic Love Between Partners in Arranged or Love Marriages in Jaipur, India, shows love growing in arranged marriages and love declining in love marriages over more than 10 years of marriage.

- "Divorce" discusses what predicts a culture's divorce rates. Individualistic cultures have more divorce than do communal cultures. Individualists expect more passion and personal fulfillment in marriage.

Chapter 12 Helping

- The chapter opens with the example of the altruism of Scottish missionary Jane Haining, the matron at a school for 400 mostly Jewish girls. On the eve of World War II, her church ordered her to return home. She refused, knowing the girls needed her. She was eventually betrayed for working among the Jewish people and later died in Auschwitz.
- "The Reciprocity Norm" reports that people in Asia, for whom social ties and the reciprocity norm are stronger than for North Americans, are more likely to refuse a gift from a casual acquaintance to avoid the perceived need to reciprocate.
- "The Social-Responsibility Norm" presents research that shows that in relatively collectivist India, people support the social-responsibility norm more strongly than in the individualistic West.
- "Focus On: The Benefits—and the Costs—of Empathy-Induced Altruism" includes the fact that empathy-induced altruism improves attitudes toward stigmatized groups.
- "Assuming Responsibility" discusses how, when university students predicted they would respond with moral courage to sexist remarks or a racial slur, few did so.
- In the same section, the importance of training programs such as "Bringing in the Bystander" is discussed. These can change attitudes toward intervening in situations of sexual assault, harassment, or bullying.
- The same section gives the example of the death of George Floyd, where bystander nonintervention was evident as three police officers stood by and watched but did nothing. Active bystandership training may be a key part of police reform.
- "Similarity" asks the question "Does similarity bias extend to race?" When norms for appropriate behavior are well-defined, Whites don't discriminate; when norms are ambiguous or conflicting, and providing help is more difficult or riskier, racial similarity may bias responses.
- "Who Will Help?" reports that status and social class affect altruism. Researchers found that less privileged people are more generous, trusting, and helpful than more privileged people. People lower in social status show more reaction in brain areas linked to sensitivity to others.
- "Teaching Moral Inclusion" discusses countering ingroup bias by personalizing and broadening the range of people whose well-being should concern us. It includes examples of rescuers of Jewish people in Nazi Europe, leaders of the antislavery movement, and medical missionaries who were morally inclusive. Moral exclusion justifies all sorts of harm, from discrimination to genocide.

Chapter 13 Conflict and Peacemaking

- "The Fundamental Attribution Error" presents research on how, when Muslims have killed Americans, Western media attributed the killing to evil dispositions. But when an American soldier killed 16 Afghans, it was explained that he had several stresses in his life that caused him to snap.
- "Appealing to Altruistic Norms" gives the example of the 1960s struggle for civil rights for Black Americans, in which many marchers willingly agreed, for the sake of the larger group, to suffer harassment, beatings, and jail.
- "Competition" provides research on how terrorist bombings in London increased anti-Muslim and anti-immigrant sentiments. While perceived threats feed prejudice and conflict, prejudice also amplifies the perception of a threat.
- "What is just?" is discussed in "Perceived Injustice." Collectivist cultures define justice as equality or need fulfillment. Western capitalist nations define justice and equality as equity.
- Several international examples are given of how the fundamental attribution error, evolving motives, competition, perceived injustice, misperception, mirror-image perceptions, and the "evil leader-good people" illusion have caused war and conflict between nations.
- In the section "How Can Peace Be Achieved?," the subsection "Contact" reports that conflict can be avoided by contact, through which proximity can boost liking. The example is given of how blatant racial prejudice declined in the U.S. following desegregation.
- The same section cites research showing that in 94% of studies, increased contact predicted more tolerance and decreased prejudice. This is especially so for majority group attitudes toward minorities, and especially true in individualistic cultures. Contact between groups reduced prejudice when people perceived high levels of threat or discrimination. The same holds true with the other-race effect and online exposure.
- Examples are given of how more contact predicts decreased prejudice: straight people with gays, lesbians, and transgender people; with immigrants; with Christians and Muslims; with Catholic and Protestant Irish teens; with White and Black roommates; and intergenerationally. Research shows that even indirect contact through reading or imagination, or having a friend with an outgroup friend, can reduce prejudice.
- "Does Desegregation Improve Racial Attitudes?" presents evidence that affirms that desegregation can improve racial attitudes through friendship and equal-status contact.
- "When Desegregation Does Not Improve Racial Attitudes" covers how, despite desegregation, people tend to stay with others like themselves.
- "Research Close-Up: Relationships That Might Have Been" presents research by Nicole Shelton and Jennifer Richeson describing how social

misperceptions between White and Black students can stand in the way of cross-racial friendships.

- "The Inside Story: Nicole Shelton and Jennifer Richeson on Cross-Racial Friendships" is their first-person account of their research on pluralistic ignorance during interracial interactions.
- "Common External Threats Build Cohesiveness" discusses how, when a person perceives discrimination against their racial or religious group, it causes them to feel more bonded with their group. Research is presented on how, when two groups face a common threat, their perceived differences diminish. Examples are given of Black and White Americans, Israelis and Palestinians, and the unification of Ukrainians when Russia invaded.
- "Superordinate Goals" gives the example of lessened tension when Muslims and Christians worked together digging drainage ditches.
- "Cooperative Learning Improves Racial Attitudes" reports on research that shows that working together on interracial "learning teams" caused members to have more positive racial attitudes. The "jigsaw classroom" technique is presented where children were assigned to racially and academically diverse six-member groups.
- "Focus On: Branch Rickey, Jackie Robinson, and the Integration of Baseball" tells the story of Jackie Robinson, the first African American since 1887 to play Major League baseball, and Major League executive Branch Rickey, who wanted to integrate baseball. Rickey's tactics were to create a perception that change is inevitable, establish equal-status contact with a superordinate goal, puncture the norm of prejudice, and cut short the spiral of violence by practicing nonviolence.
- "Group and Superordinate Identities" discusses ethnic and national identities and how people reconcile and balance those identities. This section covers the debate over the ideals of multiculturalism versus colorblind assimilation. A possible resolution to this debate is "diversity within unity."
- In the "Mediation" section, diversity training is discussed, accompanied by a photo "Communication facilitators work to break down barriers, as in this diversity training exercise. In work organizations, too, diversity training can improve attitudes."

Chapter 14 Social Psychology in the Clinic

- In the discussion of depression, research is presented on how individualist cultures stress the individual's responsibility for success, while collectivist cultures are less tied to guilt and self-blame over perceived personal failure.
- "Loneliness" reports that the number of one-person U.S. households increased from 5% in the 1920s to 28% in 2019, and Canada, Australia, and Europe have experienced a similar growth in one-person households.
- "Poverty, Inequality, and Health" discusses research on the negative health effects of living in poverty and experiencing inequality.

Chapter 15 Social Psychology in Court

- The chapter begins with the story of the shooting of Michael Brown by police officer Darren Wilson in Ferguson, Missouri, and the subsequent grand jury decision not to indict Wilson. The possible reasons: Eyewitness testimony varied; Wilson was White, Brown was Black; and the jury included three Blacks and nine Whites.
- "When Eyes Deceive" discusses eyewitness cross-racial misidentification and its effects. The case of African American Richard Anthony Jones is presented as an example of eyewitness misidentification. It is reported that 42% of 375 convictions overturned by DNA evidence in the U.S. involved cross-racial misidentification.
- Cross-race bias is presented as an influence on eyewitness testimony. Eyewitnesses are more accurate when identifying members of their own race than members of other races.
- In "Minimizing False Lineup Identifications," the case of African American Troy Davis is discussed, where police influenced eyewitnesses' recollections.
- "Similarity to the Jurors" covers a great deal of research on discrimination against African Americans in the U.S. justice system.
- When a defendant's race fits a crime stereotype, mock jurors offer more negative verdicts and punishments. White jurors who espouse nonprejudiced views are more likely to demonstrate racial bias in trials in which race issues are not blatant.
- In 83,924 cases in Florida between 2012 and 2015, Black defendants were 4 to 10% more likely than White defendants to receive a jail sentence, even when controlling for type of crime and previous convictions.
- A U.S. Sentencing Commission analysis of criminal convictions between 2007 and 2011 found that Black men received sentences 20% longer than those of White men in cases with the same seriousness and criminal history.
- Judges were 25% less likely to show Black (versus White) defendants leniency by giving a sentence shorter than suggested by federal sentencing guidelines.
- In South Carolina, sentences for Black juveniles were more punitive than those for White juveniles, especially in counties with larger Black populations and larger populations of adolescents, creating a heightened perception of threat.
- Blacks were sentenced to 68% more prison time than Whites in first-degree felony cases in Florida, even when factors such as the defendant's prior criminal record and the severity of the crime were equal.
- In one Florida county, sentences were three times as long for Black defendants as for White defendants convicted of armed robbery.
- A photo is presented from the trial of George Zimmerman who fatally shot Trayvon Martin. Polls showed that 73% of Blacks believed Zimmerman would have been arrested sooner if Martin had been

White, a view shared by only 35% of non-Blacks. His verdict of not guilty was viewed as dissatisfactory by 86% of Blacks and 30% of Whites.

- Blacks who kill Whites are more often sentenced to death than Whites who kill Blacks. Compared with killing a Black person, killing a White person is 17 times as likely to lead to execution.
- Two studies show that harsher sentences were given to those who looked more stereotypically Black. Given similar criminal histories, Black and White inmates in Florida received similar sentences, but within each race, those with more "Afrocentric" facial features were given longer sentences.
- Among Blacks convicted of murdering White victims over a 20-year period in Philadelphia, defendants whose appearance was more stereotypically Black were more likely to be sentenced to death.
- Black defendants with more stereotypically Black names received longer sentences.
- "Jury Selection" presents research that shows that jurors who believe myths about rape are significantly less likely to vote to convict an accused rapist.
- "Group Polarization" presents research showing that compared with Whites who judge Black defendants on all-White mock juries, those serving on racially mixed mock juries enter deliberation expressing more leniency, exhibit openness to a wider range of information, and think over information more thoroughly.

Chapter 16 Social Psychology and the Sustainable Future

- "Displacement and Trauma" discusses how the frequent result of climate change is increased poverty and hunger, earlier death, and loss of cultural identity.
- "Climate and Conflict" presents the findings of 60 quantitative studies that revealed conflict spikes throughout history and across the globe in response to climate events. The researchers' conclusion: Higher temperatures and rainfall extremes, such as drought and flood, predicted increased domestic violence, ethnic aggression, land invasions, and civil conflicts. They project that a 2-degree Celsius temperature rise—as predicted by 2040—could increase intergroup conflicts by more than 50%.
- "Incentives," reports that Europe leads the way in incentivizing mass transit and bicycle use; small vehicles incentivized by high fuel taxes have closed many city center streets to car traffic; drivers pay congestion fees when entering the heart of a city; and many German cities have "environmental zones" where only low CO_2 cars may enter.
- "Are Wealthier Countries Happier?" contains Figure 7, National Wealth and Well-Being, which shows life satisfaction across 132 countries.
- "Income Inequality" discusses the growth of worldwide income inequality and its negative results.
- "Research Close-Up: Measuring National Well-Being" discusses the worldwide efforts to measure and improve subjective well-being.

A Letter from the Authors

We humans have a very long history, but social psychology has a very short one—barely more than a century. Considering that we have just begun, the results are gratifying. What a feast of ideas! Using varied research methods, we have amassed significant insights into belief and illusion, love and hate, conformity and independence.

Much about human behavior remains a mystery, yet social psychology now offers partial answers to many intriguing questions:

- How does our thinking—both conscious and unconscious—drive our behavior?
- What leads people sometimes to hurt and sometimes to help one another?
- What creates social conflict, and how can we transform closed fists into helping hands?

Answering these and many other questions—our mission in the pages to come—expands our self-understanding and sensitizes us to the social forces that work upon us.

We aspire to offer a text that

- is solidly scientific and warmly human, factually rigorous, and intellectually provocative,
- reveals important social phenomena, as well as how scientists discover and explain them, and
- stimulates students' thinking—their motivation to inquire, to analyze, and to relate research to what's happening in their lives and in the world.

We cast social psychology in the intellectual tradition of the liberal arts. By the teaching of great literature, philosophy, and science, liberal arts education seeks to expand our awareness and to liberate us from the confines of the present. By focusing on humanly significant issues, we aim to offer social psychology's big ideas and findings and to do so in ways that stimulate all students. And with close-up looks at how the game is played—at the varied research tools that reveal the workings of our social nature—we hope to enable students to think smarter.

To assist the teaching and learning of social psychology is a great privilege but also a responsibility. So please: Never hesitate to let us know how we are doing and what we can do better.

David G. Myers
Hope College
www.davidmyers.org
@DavidGMyers

Jean M. Twenge
San Diego State University
www.jeantwenge.com

Preface

***Social Psychology* introduces students to the science of *us*:** our thoughts, feelings, and behaviors in a social world. By studying social psychology, students learn to think critically about everyday behaviors, and they gain an appreciation for how we view and affect one another. Paired with McGraw Hill Education Connect, a digital assignment and assessment platform that strengthens the link between faculty, students, and coursework, instructors and students accomplish more in less time. Connect Psychology is particularly useful for remote and hybrid courses, and includes assignable and assessable videos, quizzes, exercises, and interactivities, all associated with learning objectives. Interactive assignments and videos allow students to experience and apply their understanding of social psychology to the world with stimulating activities.

Social Psychology's conversational voice allows students to access and enjoy this relatively young and exciting science. In *Social Psychology*, students find scientific explorations of love and hate, conformity and independence, prejudice and helping, persuasion and self-determination.

Social Psychology focuses on how people view, affect, and relate to one another. Beginning with its chapter-opening stories, the text relates the theme of the chapter to the human experience. The cutting edge of social psychological research is also at the forefront, with more than 450 new or updated citations since the last release.

The Research Close-Up feature remains a mainstay in this release, offering comprehensive looks at social psychology research around the world, ranging from "On Being Nervous About Looking Nervous" in Chapter 2, to "Misperception and War" in Chapter 13. Research Close-Ups provide students with accessible examples of how social psychologists employ various research methods from naturalistic observation to laboratory experiments to the harvesting of archival and internet data.

Other engaging and instructive features retained in the new 2025 Release are:

- the Focus On feature, an in-depth exploration of a social psychology research topic with real-world implications. This release has two new Focus On features: One on the psychology of conspiracy theories (Chapter 3) and another on misinformation and how it can be debunked (Chapter 7);
- the Inside Story feature in which famous researchers in their own words highlight the interests and questions that guided, and sometimes misguided, their findings. For example, Chapter 5 offers an essay by Alice Eagly on gender similarities and differences;
- the chapter-ending Concluding Thoughts section on the essence of the chapter that engages students with thought-provoking questions and personal reflections on the chapter. For example, the Concluding Thoughts section in Chapter 16, Social Psychology and the Sustainable Future, considers the question "How does one live responsibly in the modern world?"

Much about human behavior remains a mystery, yet social psychology can offer insight into many questions we have about ourselves and the world we live in, such as:

- How do our attitudes and behavior feed each other?
- How do we decide what to believe, and what not to?
- How do the people around us influence our behavior?
- What leads people to love and help others or to hate and hurt them?

Investigating and answering such questions is this book's mission—to expand students' self-understanding and to reveal the social forces at work in their lives. After reading this book and thinking critically about everyday behaviors, students will better understand themselves and the world in which they work, play, and love.

Students Study More Effectively with Connect® and SmartBook®

McGraw Hill's **Connect** is a digital assignment and assessment platform that strengthens the link between faculty, students, and course work, helping everyone accomplish more in less time. *Connect for Social Psychology* includes assignable and assessable videos, quizzes, exercises, and interactivities, all associated with learning objectives. Interactive assignments and videos allow students to experience and apply their understanding of psychology to the world with stimulating activities.

Evergreen

Content and technology are ever-changing, and it is important that you can keep your course up to date with the latest content, assessments, and accessibility. That's why we want to deliver the most current and relevant content for your course, hassle-free.

Social Psychology uses an Evergreen delivery model, which is a product delivery model and experience that provides customers with the most relevant and up-to-date content, tools, and accessibility. Engage students and freshen up assignments with up-to-date coverage of select topics and new questions, all without having to switch editions or build a new course.

Mc Graw Hill | SMARTBOOK®

McGraw Hill **SmartBook** helps students distinguish the concepts they know from the concepts they don't, while pinpointing the concepts they are about to forget. SmartBook's real-time reports help both students and instructors identify the concepts that require more attention, making study sessions and class time more efficient.

SmartBook is optimized for mobile and tablet use and is accessible for students with disabilities. Contentwise, it has been enhanced with improved learning objectives that are measurable and observable to improve student outcomes. SmartBook personalizes learning to individual student needs, continually adapting to pinpoint knowledge gaps and focus learning on topics that need the most attention. Study time is more productive, and, as a result, students are better prepared for class and coursework. For instructors, SmartBook tracks student progress and provides insights that can help guide teaching strategies.

Writing Assignment

Available within McGraw Hill Connect®, the Writing Assignment tool delivers a learning experience to help students improve written communication skills and conceptual understanding. Assign, monitor, grade, and provide feedback on writing more efficiently and effectively.

McGraw Hill GO

McGraw Hill GO is an easy-to-use, quick-to-set-up eBook+ that lives within the Learning Management System (LMS). GO equips instructors and students with essential course materials: trusted, assignable content and auto-graded chapter questions that sync directly into the LMS. GO makes it easier to keep up with student progress and direct attention where it matters.

Powerful Reporting

Whether a class is face-to-face, hybrid, or entirely online, McGraw Hill Education Connect provides the tools needed to reduce the amount of time and energy instructors spend administering their courses. Easy-to-use course management tools allow instructors to spend less time administering and more time teaching, while reports allow students to monitor their progress and optimize their study time.

- The **At-Risk Student Report** provides instructors with one-click access to a dashboard that identifies students who are at risk of dropping out of the course due to low engagement levels.
- The **Category Analysis Report** details student performance relative to specific learning objectives and goals, including APA learning goals and outcomes and levels of Bloom's taxonomy.
- The **SmartBook Reports** allow instructors and students to easily monitor progress and pinpoint areas of weakness, giving each student a personalized study plan to achieve success.

Critical Thinking Assignment

Guiding students through the critical reading of current academic and clinical research is facilitated in Connect with our Critical Thinking Assignment tool. Critical Thinking Assignment (formerly Power of Process) has been redesigned for an improved user experience and enhanced accessibility (now compliant with WCAG standards). Over 50 new research articles were added as part of our summer 2025 Evergreen release. Updated functionality supports additional workflows with the following benefits:

- Supports up to two documents for comparing/contrasting
- Side-by-side display of the document and the question for students
- Ability to leave written or audio feedback for students at an assignment-level or question-level
- Ability to create rubrics or use an MH rubric
- Inclusion of a wizard to guide students through the questions

Application-Based Activities

Application-Based Activities are interactive, scenario-based exercises that allow students to apply what they are learning through role-playing in an online environment. Each scenario is automatically graded and built around course learning objectives. Feedback is provided throughout the activity to support learning and improve critical thinking. Topics include "Ethics in Research" and "Types of Love."

NewsFlash

Located in Connect, NewsFlash is a multi-media assignment tool that ties current news stories, TedTalks, blogs, and podcasts to key psychological principles and learning objectives. Students interact with relevant news stories and are assessed on their ability to connect the content to the research findings and course material. NewsFlash uses expert sources to cover a wide range of topics including: emotion, personality, stress, drugs, COVID-19, disability, social justice, stigma, bias, inclusion, gender, LGBTQ, and many more.

Instructor Resources

The resources listed here accompany *Social Psychology,* 2025 Release. Please contact your McGraw Hill representative for details concerning the availability of these and other valuable materials that can help you design and enhance your course.

Instructor's Manual Broken down by chapter, this resource provides chapter outlines, suggested lecture topics, classroom activities and demonstrations, suggested student research projects, essay questions, and critical thinking questions.

Test Bank and Test Builder This comprehensive Test Bank includes more than multiple-choice and approximately essay questions. Organized by chapter, the questions are designed to test factual, applied, and conceptual knowledge. New to this release and available within Connect, Test Builder is a cloud-based tool that enables instructors to format tests that can be printed and administered within a Learning Management System. Test Builder offers a modern, streamlined interface for easy content configuration that matches course needs, without requiring a download. Test Builder enables instructors to:

- Access all test bank content from a particular title
- Easily pinpoint the most relevant content through robust filtering options
- Manipulate the order of questions or scramble questions and/or answers
- Pin questions to a specific location within a test
- Determine your preferred treatment of algorithmic questions
- Choose the layout and spacing
- Add instructions and configure default settings

PowerPoint Slides The PowerPoint presentations, WCAG compliant, highlight the key points of the chapter and include supporting visuals. All of the slides can be modified to meet individual needs.

Remote Proctoring & Browser-Locking Capabilities Remote proctoring and browser-locking capabilities, hosted by Proctorio within Connect, provide control of the assessment environment by enabling security options and verifying the identity of the student. Seamlessly integrated within Connect, these services allow instructors to control the assessment experience by verifying identification, restricting browser activity, and monitoring student actions. Instant and detailed reporting gives instructors an at-a-glance view of potential academic integrity concerns, thereby avoiding personal bias and supporting evidence-based claims.

Polling Every learner has unique needs. Uncover where and when you're needed with the new Polling tool in McGraw Hill Connect®! Polling allows you to discover where students are in real time. Engage students and help them create connections with your course content while gaining valuable insight during lectures. Leverage polling data to deliver personalized instruction when and where it is needed most.

Supporting Instructors with Technology

With McGraw Hill Education, you can develop and tailor the course you want to teach. Easily rearrange chapters, combine material from other content sources, and quickly upload content you have written, such as your course syllabus or teaching notes, using McGraw Hill Education's **Create.** Find the content you need by searching through thousands of leading McGraw Hill Education textbooks. Arrange your book to fit your teaching style. Create even allows you to personalize your book's appearance by selecting the cover and adding your name, school, and course information. Order a Create book, and you will receive a complimentary print review copy in 3 to 5 business days or a complimentary electronic review copy via email in about an hour. Experience how McGraw Hill Education empowers you to teach your students your way (http://create.mheducation.com).

Trusted Service and Support

McGraw Hill Education's Connect offers comprehensive service, support, and training throughout every phase of your implementation. If you're looking for some guidance on how to use Connect, or want to learn tips and tricks from super users, you can find tutorials as you work. Our Digital Faculty Consultants and Student Ambassadors offer insight into how to achieve the results you want with Connect.

Integration with Your Learning Management System

McGraw Hill integrates your digital products from McGraw Hill Education with your school learning management system (LMS) for quick and easy access to best-in-class content and learning tools. Build an effective digital course, enroll students with ease and discover how powerful digital teaching can be.

Available with Connect, integration is a pairing between an institution's LMS and Connect at the assignment level. It shares assignment information, grades and calendar items from Connect into the LMS automatically, creating an easy-to-manage course for instructors and simple navigation for students. Our assignment-level integration is available with Blackboard Learn, Canvas by Instructure, and Brightspace by D2L, giving you access to registration, attendance, assignments, grades, and course resources in real time, in one location.

Taking Sides: Clashing Views in Social Psychology

This debate-style reader both reinforces and challenges students' viewpoints on the most crucial issues in *Social Psychology*. Customize this title via **McGraw Hill Create**® (http://create.mheducation.com).

Chapter-by-Chapter Changes

The research on social psychology is ever increasing. Not only does the 2025 Release incorporate the latest research and scholarship, it also reflects current social and cultural trends. Below are listed the major additions and changes to the 2025 Release.

Chapter 1 Introducing Social Psychology

- New U.S. Capitol riot example of constructing social reality
- Updated statistics on being safer on commercial airline flights than driving a car
- Updated number of social media platform users and hours per day spent
- New example of the I-knew-it-all-along phenomenon and hindsight bias
- New research example on how random assignment can eliminate extraneous factors in research
- Updated statistics and discussion of the need for replication in research

Chapter 2 The Self in a Social World

- New research on the spotlight effect and the illusion of transparency
- New quotation about how selves are created in relationships
- Updated statistics on "self" appearing in book and article summaries on PsycInfo®
- New research on the effects of a negative self-schema and the sense of self
- Term "Upward social comparison" introduced in discussion of the use of social media
- Updated statistics on growing individualism within cultures
- New example of the planning fallacy
- New COVID-19 example about predicting behavior
- More research on the positive and negative effects of high and low self-esteem
- Expanded discussion of the benefits of self-compassion
- Expanded discussion of narcissism
- Additional research examples of self-serving bias
- New research on unrealistic optimism
- New research on the false consensus effect
- New research on self-handicapping
- New research on the relationships of those low in self-monitoring

Chapter 3 Social Beliefs and Judgments

- New research on the power of political partisanship
- New example of snap judgments of others
- Expanded discussion of confirmation bias, with new political and COVID-19 examples
- New feature box titled "The Psychology of Conspiracy Theories"
- New research examples of the availability heuristic
- Added research on counterfactual thinking
- New research examples of biased perceptions in politics and sports
- New study presented on political belief perseverance
- New figure on belief perseverance
- New research example of the reconstruction of past attitudes
- New research example of the attribution error
- New discussion and research on perspective and situational awareness

Chapter 4 Behavior and Attitudes

- New research on how attitudes do not necessarily predict behavior
- Added research example of the theory of planned behavior
- New research on how bringing attitudes to mind can lead to consistency of behavior
- New research on how role-playing can lead to a positive impact on behavior
- New Russia/Ukraine war example of the attitudes-follows-behavior phenomenon
- New research on cognitive dissonance, with several new examples
- Additional research on conspiracy beliefs often being caused by selective exposure
- New research on how facial expressions and body postures influence emotions
- New research on how affirming personal values can lead to less cheating

Chapter 5 Genes, Culture, and Gender

- Updates on women and transgender people in the military
- Updated and revised discussion on how to define sex categories in women's sports
- Updated statistics on number of U.S. transgender adults
- New research on the effects of high and low testosterone prenatally and in childhood
- Addition of new key term and definition: *cisgender*
- New research on gender and mating preferences
- Expanded discussion and new research on epigenetics
- Expanded discussion of social norms restricting behaviors in individualistic and collectivistic cultures
- Added research examples of peer-transmitted culture affecting behavior
- New material on the six universal dimensions of moral beliefs
- Updated discussion on how gender roles vary over time, with updated statistics
- New statistics on the incomes of women and men
- Many new research examples on gender differences

Chapter 6 Conformity and Obedience

- New research on how to reduce dislike and conflict by synchronization of movement
- New examples of social media and conformity in the mass spread of harmful behavior
- New material on Milgram's experiments and their effects on participants
- New Russia/Ukraine war example in the discussion on depersonalization
- Added example of group size and social media
- New example of how those with higher-status influence others in their group
- New example of the effects of prior commitment on behavior
- New example of conformity to social norms in collectivistic countries during COVID-19
- New research on working-class and middle-class backgrounds and collectivism/individualism
- Added research examples of persuasion messages producing reactance
- New research example of people asserting uniqueness

Chapter 7 Persuasion

- Updated statistics on support for same-sex marriage
- Updated statistics on Americans' attitudes to climate change
- Updated figure on the percentage of American adults who worry about global warming
- Addition of Eagly's and Chaiken's Elaboration Likelihood Model

- Several new examples of "nudging" with the peripheral route to persuasion
- New examples of the influence or lack of influence of the communicator of a message
- New example of perceived trustworthiness of the communicator leading to positive results
- New discussion of social media influencers
- Added research examples of similarity and storytelling leading to persuasion
- Added research on how discussing possible solutions can be persuasive
- New research on political "poison parasite ads" and persuasion
- New feature box titled "Misinformation: Can Inoculation and Debunking Help?"
- New research examples on teaching counterargument
- New discussion on laws banning targeted children's advertising and the effects of advergames

Chapter 8 Group Influence

- New Simone Biles Olympics example in the discussion of the presence of others
- New statistics on deaths as a result of deindividuation at the U.S. Capitol riot
- Updated research on positive deindividuation experiences
- Many new examples of what factors increase deindividuation, including social media
- Many new examples of the effects of group polarization in politics, online, and in society
- Updated figure on polarizing society

Chapter 9 Prejudice

- Updated statistics on rising U.S. antisemitic incidents and rising hate crime in Germany
- Updated statistics on prejudice against immigrants in several countries
- Updated statistics on U.S. liberals' and conservatives' dislike for each other
- New discussion of the finding that targets of prejudice in the U.S. cluster into three categories
- New examples of how discrimination affects Black Americans
- New research on percentage who discriminates against others
- Expanded discussion about the Implicit Association Test (IAT)
- Updated statistics on U.S. adult approval of interracial marriage
- New research on Whites' misperception of the race gap in wealth
- New research on the effects of gender-stereotypical behavior on girls
- New research on female/male hiring, salaries, teaching evaluations, and performance
- Updated statistics on China's boy vs. girl births; India's "Save the girl child" campaign
- New statistics on employment discrimination against transgender people
- Updated U.S. and U.K. statistics on support for same-sex marriage
- Updated statistics on verbal and physical harassment of LGBTQ+ students
- Updated statistics on number of transgender adults having unsupportive families
- New statistics on attempted suicide by U.S. transgender teens and young adults
- Many new research examples of what causes prejudice
- Expanded discussion of left-wing authoritarianism
- New research on the other-race effect causing less socialization
- Update on number of U.S. gay, lesbian, or bisexual people
- New research on the just-world phenomenon, earnings, and competency
- New research on stereotype threat and older adults

Chapter 10 Aggression

- Updated numbers on assault, partner violence, murder with/without gun, bullying
- Included number of people killed in Ukraine/Russia war
- New research shows that aggression can be cold, calculated, and controlled
- Many new research examples expand the discussion of the influences on aggression
- New figure on temperature and incidents of violent crime
- Expanded discussion and new research on laws restricting gun ownership
- Expanded discussion of the risk of violence in a home with a gun
- Updated figure on weapons used to commit murder in the U.S.
- Updated statistics on people viewing, and people feeling addicted to, pornography
- New research on aggression and social media challenges and violent video gaming
- Expanded discussion of violence resulting when people are radicalized, fused with a group, and feel it is morally justified
- New research showing death-penalty states have higher murder rates
- New discussion of peer mediation and anti-bullying training in schools

Chapter 11 Attraction and Intimacy

- Expanded discussion and new research on the effects of social isolation and ostracism
- Many new research examples of the effects of mere exposure and similarity
- New research on the desire for, perception of, and effects of attractiveness
- Updated statistics on PsycInfo® articles covering positive and negative emotions
- New research on the reward theory of attraction
- New research on attachment styles
- New research on the benefits of self-disclosure
- New material on maintaining romantic/marriage relationships; some causes of divorce
- Updated figure on marriage and happiness

Chapter 12 Helping

- New research on people's beliefs about helpfulness
- New research on men's willingness and ability to help their wives and other women
- Additional research on what motivates people to help those outside their circles
- New research on higher empathic concern leading to adherence to health guidelines
- New example and research on bystander inaction
- New research on internalizing positive messages reducing bullying in schools
- New examples and research on when people are more likely to help others

Chapter 13 Conflict and Peacemaking

- Updated statistic on world spending on arms and armies
- "Dunbar's number" introduced
- New research example of the effects of appealing to altruistic norms
- New research on the COVID-19 pandemic leading to desire for authoritarian leadership
- New research on the persistence of mirror image perceptions and political polarization
- New Russia/Ukraine example of the "evil leader-good people" perception
- New research on "we-are-good/they-are-bad" thinking
- Several added research studies on the positive effects of contact between groups

- New example of people uniting under threat
- New example of the positive effects of discussing superordinate goals
- New discussion of colorblind assimilation or a multicultural approach
- New material on the use of mediators to resolve conflicts

Chapter 14 Social Psychology in the Clinic

- Updated statistics on U.S. young people experiencing depression
- New material on hindsight in the aftermath of violence incidents
- New figure on evidence-based practice in clinical decision making
- Expanded discussion and research on the experience and health outcomes of depression
- New research material on the decline of social engagement in several countries
- New research examples about relationships/social connectedness and physical health
- Added research on income inequality leading to more deaths from COVID-19

Chapter 15 Social Psychology in Court

- New research on mistaken eyewitness identification and resulting years of incarceration
- New research on effective questioning and identification techniques for investigators
- Expanded discussion and research on jury instructions and jury behavior and beliefs
- New research on what can cause more guilty verdicts and longer sentences

Chapter 16 Social Psychology and the Sustainable Future

- Updated statistics on rising sea and air temperatures
- Updated figure showing rising global temperatures
- Updated figure showing receding Arctic ice sheets
- Updated reporting on the rising cost of climate events
- New research on young adults' anxiety about climate change
- New photo of images of flooding in the Northeast U.S. in 2023
- New research on the negative effects of rising temperatures
- Updated findings on evidence of climate change in climate science publications
- New research on Americans' opinions about climate scientists and climate change
- New research on consensus, education, interventions, and social norms
- New examples of emerging technologies that help combat climate change
- New research on developing nations being most effected by climate change
- Updated figure titled "Has Economic Growth Advanced Human Morale?"
- Expanded discussion on income and happiness
- New example of how information on well-being leads to sustainable decisions
- New discussion on the need for governments and corporations to change laws/practices

Acknowledgments

Although only two names appear on this book's cover, the truth is that a whole community of scholars have invested themselves in it. Although none of these people should be held responsible for what we have written—nor do any of them necessarily agree with everything said—their suggestions made this a better book than it could otherwise have been.

This 2025 Release still retains many of the improvements contributed by the dozens of consultants and reviewers who assisted with prior version, and now we extend our thanks to these esteemed colleagues who contributed their wisdom and guidance for this one:

Michael Accardo, Hofstra University
Karen Bedell, University of Michigan-Flint
Tyler Graff, Brigham Young University
Zachary Hohman, Texas Tech University
Linda Isbell, University of Massachusetts Amherst
Lynda Mae, Arizona State University
Christina Pedram, Arizona State University
Mark Pezzo, University of South Florida St. Petersburg
David Ward, Arkansas Tech University

Hope College, Michigan, has been wonderfully supportive of these successive editions. Both the people and the environment have helped make the gestation of *Social Psychology* a pleasure. At Hope College, poet Jack Ridl helped shape the voice you will hear in these pages. And Kathryn Brownson did online research, proofed, and edited the manuscript and art, searched for fugitive citations, helped select photos, and managed the workflow.

At San Diego State, colleagues including David Armor, Jeff Bryson, Thierry Devos, David Marx, Radmila Prislin, Dustin Thoman, and Alison Vaughn shared their knowledge of teaching social psychology. Social psychology friends and co-authors also provided insight, including W. Keith Campbell, Jody Davis, Julie Exline, Jeff Green, Benita Jackson, Tim Kasser, Sonja Lyubomirsky, and Kathleen Vohs.

At McGraw Hill, executive portfolio manager Jason Seitz envisioned this new release and supported its author team. Dawn Groundwater commissioned and oversaw its creation. With diligence and sensitivity, our editor and "product developer" Thomas Finn expertly guided, developed, and deftly edited the book into a more modern and even more readable new release. Peter de Lissovoy fine-tuned the final manuscript. Sandy Wille coordinated the transformation of our manuscript into your finished book.

After hearing countless dozens of people say that this book's supplements have taken their teaching to a new level, we also pay tribute to the late Martin Bolt (Calvin College) for pioneering the extensive instructor's resources with their countless ready-to-use demonstration activities and to Jon Mueller (North Central College) as author of the instructor's resources for the eighth through tenth editions. To all in this supporting cast, we are indebted. Working with all these people has made the creation of this book a stimulating, gratifying experience.

David G. Myers
davidmyers.org

Jean M. Twenge
jeantwenge.com

Introducing Social Psychology

Yellow Dog Productions/Lifesize/Getty Images

CHAPTER 1

What is social psychology?

What are social psychology's big ideas?

I knew it all along: Is social psychology simply common sense?

Research methods: How do we do social psychology?

Concluding Thoughts: Why we wrote this book . . . and a preview of what's to come

There once was a man whose second wife was a vain and selfish woman. This woman's two daughters were similarly vain and selfish. The man's own daughter, however, was meek and unselfish. This sweet, kind daughter, whom we all know as Cinderella, learned early on that she should do as she was told, accept poor treatment and insults, and avoid doing anything to upstage her stepsisters and their mother.

But then, thanks to her fairy godmother, Cinderella was able to escape her situation for an evening and attend a grand ball, where she attracted the attention of a handsome prince. When the love-struck prince later encountered Cinderella back in her degrading home, he failed to recognize her.

Does this seem hard to believe? The folktale demands that we accept the power of the situation. In the presence of her oppressive stepmother, Cinderella was humble and unattractive. At the ball, Cinderella felt more beautiful — and walked and talked and smiled as if she were. In one situation, she cowered. In the other, she charmed.

The French philosopher-novelist Jean-Paul Sartre (1946) would have had no problem accepting the Cinderella premise. We humans are "first of all beings in a situation," he wrote. "We cannot be distinguished from our situations, for they form us and decide our possibilities" (pp. 59–60, paraphrased).

WHAT IS SOCIAL PSYCHOLOGY?

Define social psychology and explain what it does.

social psychology
The scientific study of how people think about, influence, and relate to one another.

Social psychology studies how situations influence us, with special attention to how people view and affect one another. *More precisely, it is the scientific study of how people think about, influence, and relate to one another* (**Figure 1**).

Social psychology lies at psychology's boundary with sociology. Compared with sociology (the study of people in groups and societies), social psychology focuses more on individuals and performs more experiments. Compared with personality psychology, social psychology focuses less on differences among individuals and more on how people, in general, view and influence one another.

Social psychology is a young science. The first social psychology experiments were reported a little more than a century ago, and the first social psychology textbooks did not appear until approximately 1900 (Smith, 2005). Not until the 1930s did social psychology assume its current form. Not until World War II did it begin to emerge as the vibrant field it is today. And not until the 1970s and beyond did social psychology enjoy accelerating growth in Asia – first in India, then in Hong Kong and Japan, and, in the last few decades, in China and Taiwan (Bernardo & Liu, 2018; Haslam & Kashima, 2010).

Social psychology studies our thinking, influences, and relationships by asking questions that have intrigued us all. Here are some examples:

- *Does our behavior depend more on the situation or on how we interpret it?* Our interpretations matter. Social beliefs can be self-fulfilling. For example, happily married people will attribute their spouse's acid remark ("Can't you ever put that where it belongs?") to something external (*"He must have had a frustrating day."*). Unhappily married people will attribute the same remark to a mean disposition (*"Geesh, what a hostile person!"*) and may respond with a counterattack. Moreover, expecting hostility from their spouse, they may behave resentfully, thus causing the hostility they expect.
- *Would people be cruel if ordered?* How did Nazi Germany conceive and implement the unconscionable slaughter of 6 million Jews? Those evil acts occurred partly because thousands of people followed orders. They put the prisoners on trains,

FIGURE 1
Social Psychology Is . . .

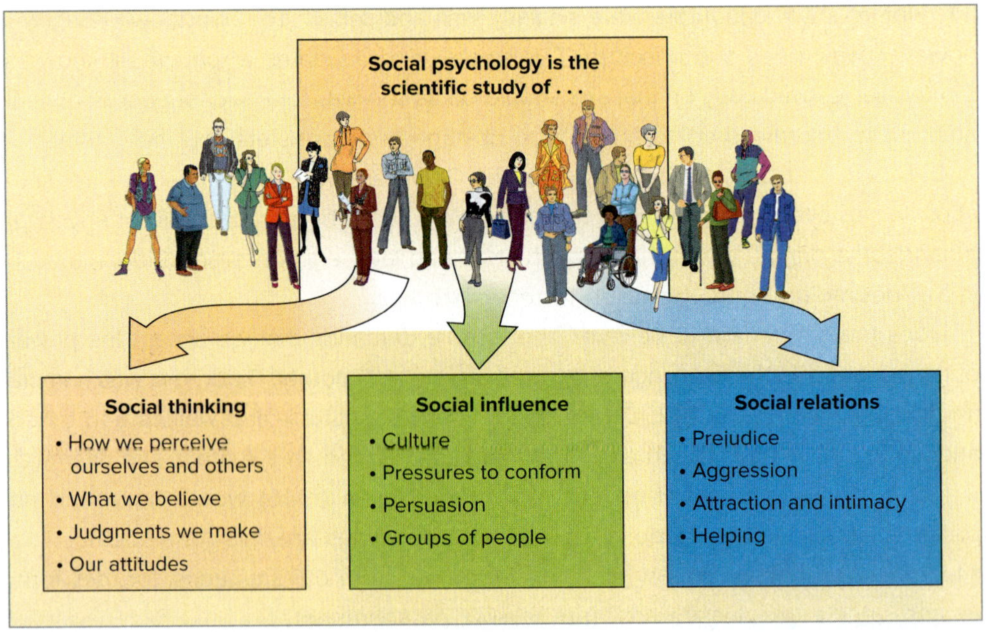

herded them into crowded "showers," and poisoned them with gas. How could people engage in such horrific actions? Were those individuals normal human beings? Stanley Milgram (1974) wondered. So he set up a situation in which people were ordered to administer increasing levels of electric shock to someone who was having difficulty learning a series of words. Nearly two-thirds of the participants fully complied.

- *To help? Or to help oneself?* As bags of cash tumbled from an armored truck one fall day, $2 million was scattered along a Columbus, Ohio, street. Some motorists stopped to help, returning $100,000. Judging from the $1,900,000 that disappeared, many more stopped to help themselves. (What would you have done?) When similar incidents occurred several months later in San Francisco and Toronto, the results were the same: Passersby grabbed most of the money (Bowen, 1988). What situations trigger people to be helpful or greedy? Do some cultural contexts – perhaps villages and small towns – breed less "diffusion of responsibility" and greater helpfulness?

Tired of looking at the stars, Professor Mueller takes up social psychology.

These questions focus on how people view and affect one another – and that is what social psychology is all about. Social psychologists study attitudes and beliefs, conformity and independence, love and hate.

WHAT ARE SOCIAL PSYCHOLOGY'S BIG IDEAS?

Identify and describe the central concepts behind social psychology.

In many academic fields, the results of tens of thousands of studies, the conclusions of thousands of investigators, and the insights of hundreds of theorists can be boiled down to a few central ideas. Biology offers us natural selection and adaptation. Sociology builds on concepts such as social structure and organization. Music harnesses ideas of rhythm, melody, and harmony.

Similarly, social psychology builds on a short list of fundamental principles that will be worth remembering long after you forget the details. Our short list of "great ideas we ought never to forget" includes the points shown in **Figure 2,** each of which we will explore further in chapters to come.

We Construct Our Social Reality

People have an irresistible urge to explain behavior. We want to understand why people do what they do to make behavior seem orderly, predictable, and controllable. You and I may *react* differently to a situation because we *think* differently. How we react to a friend's insult depends on whether we attribute it to hostility or to a bad day.

A Princeton-Dartmouth football game famously demonstrated how we construct reality (Loy & Andrews, 1981). The game lived up to its billing as a grudge match; it was rough and dirty. A Princeton All-American was gang-tackled, piled on, and finally forced out of the game with a broken nose. Fistfights erupted, with injuries on both sides. The game hardly fit the Ivy League image of gentility.

Not long afterward, two psychologists, one from each school, showed game films to students on each campus. The students played the role of scientist-observer, noting each infraction as they watched and who was responsible for it. But they could not set aside their loyalties. The Princeton students, for example, saw twice as many Dartmouth violations as the Dartmouth students saw.

Decades later, a study found the same effect as people watched videos of a protest. Those who disagreed with the protesters' views were much more likely to describe them as

FIGURE 2
Some Big Ideas in Social Psychology

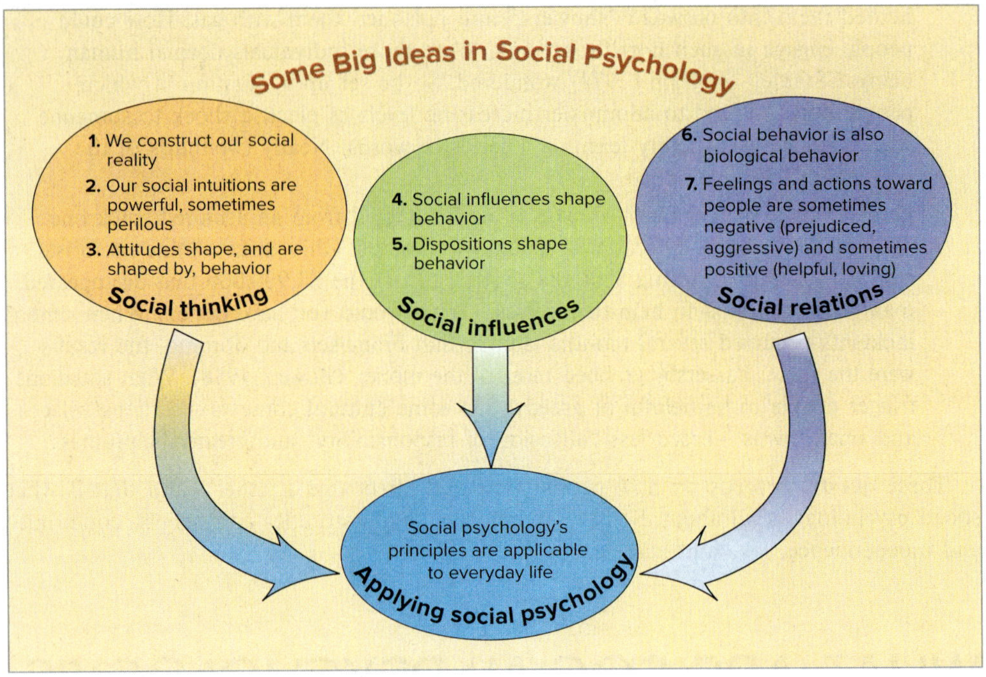

"blocking access" to a building or "screaming" at others than those who agreed with the protesters' views (Kahan et al., 2012). A year after the January 6, 2021 attack on the U.S. Capitol by Trump supporters, 85% of Democrats believed the demonstrators were trying to overthrow the government – compared to only 18% of Republicans (De Pinto, 2022). The conclusion: There is an objective reality out there, but we always view it through the lens of our beliefs and values.

We are all intuitive scientists. We explain people's behavior, usually with enough speed and accuracy to suit our daily needs. When someone's behavior is consistent and distinctive, we attribute that behavior to their personality. For example, if you observe someone making repeated snide comments, you may infer that they have a nasty disposition, and then you might try to avoid them.

Your beliefs about yourself also matter. Do you have an optimistic outlook? Do you see yourself as in control of things? Do you view yourself as relatively superior or inferior? Your answers influence your emotions and actions. *How we construe the world, and ourselves, matters.*

Our Social Intuitions Are Often Powerful but Sometimes Perilous

Our instant intuitions shape fears (*Is flying dangerous?*), impressions (*Can I trust him?*), and relationships (*Does he like me?*). Intuitions influence presidents in times of crisis, gamblers at the table, jurors assessing guilt, and personnel directors screening applicants. Such intuitions are commonplace.

Indeed, psychological science reveals a fascinating unconscious mind – an intuitive backstage mind – that Freud never told us about. More than psychologists realized until recently, thinking occurs offstage, out of sight. Our intuitive capacities are revealed by studies of what later chapters will explain: *automatic processing, implicit memory, heuristics,* instant emotions, and nonverbal communication. We think on two levels – "intuitive" and "deliberate" (Kruglanski & Gigerenzer, 2011); some call these *System 1* and *System 2.* A book title by Nobel laureate psychologist Daniel Kahneman (2011) captures the idea: We do *Thinking, Fast and Slow.*

Intuition is huge, but intuition is also perilous. For example, as we cruise through life, mostly on automatic pilot, we intuitively judge the likelihood of events by how easily they come to mind. We carry readily available mental images of plane crashes. Thus, most people fear flying more than driving, and many will drive great distances to avoid risking the skies. Actually, we have been, mile per mile over the last 10 years, 595 times safer on a commercial flight than in a car, reports the National Safety Council (2023).

Even our intuitions about ourselves often err. We intuitively trust our memories more than we should. We misread our own minds; in experiments, we deny being affected by things that do influence us. We mispredict our own feelings – how bad we'll feel a year from now if we lose our job or our romance breaks up, and how good we'll feel a year from now, or even a week from now, if we win our state's lottery. And we often mispredict our own future. When selecting clothes, people approaching middle age will still buy snug ("I anticipate shedding a few pounds"); rarely does anyone say, more realistically, "I'd better buy a relatively loose fit; people my age tend to put on pounds."

Our social intuitions, then, are noteworthy for both their powers and their perils. By identifying our intuition's gifts and pitfalls, social psychologists aim to fortify our thinking. In most situations, "fast and frugal" snap judgments serve us well. But in others, in which accuracy matters – such as when needing to fear the right things and spend our resources wisely – we had best restrain our impulsive intuitions with critical thinking. *Our intuitions and unconscious information processing are routinely powerful and sometimes perilous.*

Social Influences Shape Our Behavior

We are, as Aristotle long ago observed, social animals. We speak and think in words we learned from others. We long to connect, to belong, and to be well thought of. In one study, University of Texas students wore recording devices that periodically listened in on their lives. Even on weekdays, almost 30% of the students' time was spent talking to other people (Mehl & Pennebaker, 2003). Now, of course, much of that communication takes place electronically. Instagram has 1.4 billion users worldwide, and the average 18-year-old in the United States spends nearly 3 hours a day sending texts (Twenge, 2023). Relationships are a big part of being human.

As social creatures, we respond to our immediate contexts. Sometimes the power of a social situation leads us to act contrary to our expressed attitudes. Indeed, powerfully evil situations sometimes overwhelm good intentions, inducing people to accept falsehoods or comply with cruelty. Under Nazi influence, many decent people became instruments of the Holocaust. Other situations may elicit great generosity and compassion. After major natural disasters, affected regions are often overwhelmed with donated items and offers of assistance.

The power of the situation also appears in widely different views of same-sex relationships. Tell us whether you live in Africa or the Middle East (where people overwhelmingly oppose such relationships) or in western Europe, Canada, the United States, or Australia/New Zealand (where most support them), and we will guess your attitude. We will become even more confident in our guess if we know your educational level, the age of your peer group, and the media you watch. Our situations matter.

Our culture helps define our situations. For example, our standards regarding promptness, openness, and clothing vary with our culture.

- Whether you prefer a slim or a voluptuous body depends on when and where in the world you live.
- Whether you are expressive or reserved, casual or formal, hinges partly on your culture and your ethnicity.
- Whether you focus primarily on yourself – your personal needs, desires, and morality – or on your family, clan, and communal groups depends on how much you are a product of modern Western individualism.

Social psychologist Hazel Markus (2005) summed it up: "People are, above all, malleable." Said differently, we adapt to our social context. *Our attitudes and behavior are shaped by external social forces.*

Personal Attitudes and Dispositions Also Shape Behavior

Internal forces also matter. We are not passive tumbleweeds, merely blown this way and that by the social winds. Our inner attitudes affect our outer behavior. Our political attitudes influence our voting behavior. Our attitudes toward alcohol influence our susceptibility to peer pressure to drink alcohol. Our attitudes toward the poor influence our willingness to help them. (Our attitudes also *follow* our behavior, which means we often believe strongly in what we have committed ourselves to or suffered for.)

Personality dispositions also affect behavior. Facing the same situation, different people may react differently. Emerging from years of political imprisonment, one person exudes bitterness and seeks revenge. Another might seek reconciliation and unity with their former enemies. *Attitudes and personality influence behavior.*

Social Behavior Is Biologically Rooted

Twenty-first-century social psychology provides us with ever-growing insights into our behavior's biological foundations. Many of our social behaviors reflect deep biological wisdom.

Everyone who has taken introductory psychology has learned that nature and nurture together form who we are. Just as the area of a rectangle is determined by both its length and its width, biology and experience both shape us. As *evolutionary psychologists* remind us, our inherited human nature predisposes us to behave in ways that helped our ancestors survive and reproduce. We carry the genes of those whose traits enabled them to survive and reproduce. Our behavior, too, aims to send our DNA into the future. Thus, evolutionary psychologists ask how natural selection might shape our actions when dating and mating, hating and hurting, and caring and sharing. Nature also endows us with an enormous capacity to learn and to adapt to varied environments. We are sensitive and responsive to our social context.

If every psychological event (every thought, every emotion, every behavior) is simultaneously a biological event, then we can also examine the neurobiology that underlies social behavior. What brain areas enable our experiences of love and contempt, helping and aggression, and perception and belief? Do people who are shy (versus more socially secure) react differently seeing a friendly face? How do brain, mind, and behavior function together as one coordinated system? What does the timing of brain events reveal about how we process information? Such questions are asked by those in **social neuroscience** (Cacioppo & Cacioppo, 2013; Cikara & Van Bavel, 2014; Tremblay et al., 2023).

social neuroscience
An interdisciplinary field that explores the neural bases of social and emotional processes and behaviors, and how these processes and behaviors affect our brain and biology.

Social neuroscientists do not reduce complex social behaviors, such as helping and hurting, to simple neural or molecular mechanisms. Each science builds upon the principles of more basic sciences (sociology builds on psychology, which builds on biology, which builds on chemistry, which builds on physics, which builds on math). Yet each discipline also introduces new principles not predicted by the more basic sciences (Eisenberg, 2014). Thus, to understand social behavior, we must consider both under-the-skin (biological) and between-skins (social) influences. Mind and body are one grand system. Hormones affect how we feel and act: A dose of testosterone decreases trust, and a dose of oxytocin increases it (Bos et al., 2010). Feeling left out elevates blood pressure. Social support strengthens the disease-fighting immune system. *We are bio-psycho-social organisms.* We reflect the interplay of our biological, psychological, and social influences. That is why today's psychologists study behavior from these different levels of analysis.

Social support and love impact both the mind and the body, leading social psychologists to consider bio-psycho-social effects.
Cade Martin/UpperCut Images/Getty Images

Social Psychology's Principles Are Applicable in Everyday Life

Social psychology has the potential to illuminate your life, to make visible the subtle influences that guide your thinking and acting. It also offers many ideas about how to know yourself better, how to win friends and influence people, and how to transform closed fists into open arms.

Scholars are also applying social psychological insights. Principles of social thinking, social influence, and social relations have implications for human health and well-being, for judicial procedures and juror decisions in courtrooms, and for influencing behaviors that will enable an environmentally sustainable human future.

As but one perspective on human existence, psychological science does not answer life's ultimate questions: What is the meaning of human life? What should be our purpose? What is our ultimate destiny? But social psychology does give us a method for asking and answering some exceedingly interesting and important questions. *Social psychology is all about life – your life: your beliefs, your attitudes, your relationships.*

The rest of this chapter takes us inside social psychology. Let's first consider how social psychologists' own values influence their work in obvious and subtle ways. And then let's focus on this chapter's biggest task: glimpsing how we *do* social psychology. How do social psychologists search for explanations of social thinking, social influence, and social relations? And how might we use these analytical tools to think smarter?

Throughout this book, a brief summary will conclude each major section. We hope these summaries will help you assess how well you have learned the material in each section.

SUMMING UP: What Are Social Psychology's Big Ideas?

Social psychology is the scientific study of how people think about, influence, and relate to one another. Its central themes include the following:

- How we construe our social worlds.
- How our social intuitions guide and sometimes deceive us.
- How our social behavior is shaped by other people, by our attitudes and personalities, and by our biology.
- How social psychology's principles apply to our everyday lives and to various other fields of study.

I KNEW IT ALL ALONG: IS SOCIAL PSYCHOLOGY SIMPLY COMMON SENSE?

Explore how social psychology's theories provide new insight into the human condition.

Social psychological phenomena are all around you; thus, many of the conclusions presented in this book may already have occurred to you. We constantly observe people thinking about, influencing, and relating to one another. It pays to discern what a facial expression predicts, how to get someone to do something, or whether to regard someone as a friend or foe. For centuries, philosophers, novelists, and poets have observed and commented on social behavior.

Does this mean that social psychology is just common sense in fancy words? Social psychology faces two contradictory criticisms: first, that it is trivial because it documents the obvious; second, that it is dangerous because its findings could be used to manipulate people.

In the "Persuasion" chapter, we explore the second criticism. Here, let's examine the first criticism.

Do social psychology and the other social sciences simply formalize what any amateur already knows intuitively? Writer Cullen Murphy (1990) took that view: "Day after day social scientists go out into the world. Day after day they discover that people's behavior is pretty much what you'd expect." Nearly a half-century earlier, historian Arthur Schlesinger, Jr. (1949) reacted with similar scorn to social scientists' studies of American World War II soldiers. Sociologist Paul Lazarsfeld (1949) reviewed those studies and offered a sample with interpretive comments:

1. Better-educated soldiers adjusted less easily than did less-educated soldiers. (Intellectuals were less prepared for battle stresses than were street-smart people.)
2. Southern soldiers coped better with the hot South Sea Island climate than did Northern soldiers. (Southerners are more accustomed to hot weather.)
3. White low-ranking soldiers were more eager for promotion than were Black low-ranking soldiers. (Years of oppression take a toll on achievement motivation.)
4. Southern Black soldiers preferred Southern to Northern White officers. (Black soldiers had more experience interacting with Southern officers.)

As you read those findings, did you agree that they were basically common sense? If so, you may be surprised to learn that Lazarsfeld went on to say, "*Every one of these statements is the direct opposite of what was actually found.*" In reality, the studies found that less-educated soldiers adapted more poorly. Southerners were not more likely than northerners to adjust to a tropical climate. Black soldiers were more eager than White soldiers for promotion, and so forth. "If we had mentioned the actual results of the investigation first [as Schlesinger experienced], the reader would have labeled these 'obvious' also."

One problem with common sense is that we invoke it after we know the facts. Events are far more "obvious" and predictable in hindsight than beforehand. When people learn the outcome of an experiment, that outcome suddenly seems unsurprising – much less surprising than it is to people who are simply told about the experimental procedure and the possible outcomes (Slovic & Fischhoff, 1977). After more than 800 investigations of this tendency to retrofit our prior expectations, **hindsight bias** (also called the *I-knew-it-all-along phenomenon*) has become one of psychology's best-established phenomena (Roese & Vohs, 2012).

hindsight bias
The tendency to exaggerate, after learning an outcome, one's ability to have foreseen how something turned out. Also known as the *I-knew-it-all-along phenomenon.*

Likewise, in everyday life, we often do not expect something to happen until it does. *Then* we suddenly see clearly the forces that brought the event about and feel unsurprised. Moreover, we may also misremember our earlier view (Blank et al., 2008; Nestler et al., 2010). Errors in judging the future's foreseeability and in remembering our past combine to create hindsight bias.

Thus, after elections or stock market shifts, most commentators find the turn of events unsurprising: "The market was due for a correction"; "2016 was a 'change election,' so it makes sense that Donald Trump won." As the Danish philosopher-theologian Søren Kierkegaard (1844) put it, life is lived forwards but "can only be understood backwards."

If hindsight bias is pervasive, you may now be feeling that you already knew about this phenomenon. Indeed, almost any conceivable result of a psychological experiment can seem like common sense – *after* you know the result.

You can demonstrate the phenomenon yourself. Take a group of people and tell half of them one psychological finding and the other half the opposite result. For example, tell half as follows:

> Social psychologists have found that, whether choosing friends or falling in love, we are most attracted to people whose traits are different from our own. There seems to be wisdom in the old saying "Opposites attract."

Tell the other half:

> Social psychologists have found that, whether choosing friends or falling in love, we are most attracted to people whose traits are similar to our own. There seems to be wisdom in the old saying "Birds of a feather flock together."

Ask the people first to explain the result. Then ask them to say whether it is "surprising" or "not surprising." Virtually all will find a good explanation for whichever result they were given and will say it is "not surprising."

Indeed, we can draw on our stockpile of proverbs to make almost any result seem to make sense. Should we "keep our eye on the prize" or "our nose to the grindstone"? Can we "not teach an old dog new tricks" or are we "never too old to learn"? Is "he who hesitates lost" or should we "look before we leap"?

If a social psychologist reports that separation intensifies romantic attraction, John Q. Public responds, "You get paid for this? Everybody knows that 'absence makes the heart grow fonder.'" Should it turn out that separation *weakens* attraction, John will say, "My grandmother could have told you, 'Out of sight, out of mind.'"

If you hear that similar people are attracted to one another ("birds of a feather flock together"), it may seem like common sense. But so does the reverse idea, that "opposites attract."
kiuikson/Shutterstock

Karl Teigen (1986) must have had a few chuckles when he asked University of Leicester students to evaluate actual proverbs and their opposites. When given the proverb "Fear is stronger than love," most rated it as true. But so did students who were given its reversed form, "Love is stronger than fear." Likewise, the genuine proverb "He that is fallen cannot help him who is down" was rated highly; but so too was "He that is fallen can help him who is down." Our favorites, however, were two highly rated proverbs: "Wise men make proverbs and fools repeat them" (authentic) and its made-up counterpart, "Fools make proverbs and wise men repeat them."

Hindsight bias creates a problem for many psychology students. Sometimes results are genuinely surprising (for example, that Olympic *bronze* medalists take more joy in their achievement than do silver medalists). More often, when you read the results of experiments in your textbooks, the material seems easy, even obvious. When you later take a multiple-choice test on which you must choose among several plausible conclusions, the task may become surprisingly difficult. "I don't know what happened," the befuddled student later moans. "I thought I knew the material."

The I-knew-it-all-along phenomenon can have unfortunate consequences. It is conducive to arrogance – an overestimation of our own intellectual powers. Moreover, because outcomes seem like they should have been predictable, we are more likely to blame decision-makers for what are in retrospect "obvious" bad choices than to praise them for good choices, which also seem "obvious."

When a manager at a Virginia Walmart opened fire in the employee break room just before Thanksgiving in 2022, he killed four employees and wounded three others before taking his own life. Co-workers said the shooter had anger issues, had a habit of asking co-workers if they liked guns, and claimed that if he were ever fired he would seek revenge so "people will remember my name." After the shooting, several employees filed a lawsuit alleging that Walmart should have known the manager was dangerous (Heim et al., 2022).

But what seems clear in hindsight is not always clear before a tragic event. Most people who have anger issues or engage in revenge fantasies will never become mass shooters. Although these were troubling signs, they are much more obvious as warning signs in hindsight than they were before the shooting occurred.

We blame not only others but also ourselves for "stupid mistakes" – perhaps for not having handled a person or a situation better. Looking back, we see how we should have handled it. "I should have known how busy I would be at the semester's end and started that paper earlier." "I should have realized sooner that he was a jerk." But sometimes we are too hard on ourselves. We forget that what is obvious to us *now* was not nearly so obvious at the time.

"It is easy to be wise after the event."

—Sherlock Holmes, in Arthur Conan Doyle's story "The Problem of Thor Bridge," 1922

Physicians who are told both a patient's symptoms and the cause of death (as determined by autopsy) sometimes wonder how an incorrect diagnosis could have been made. Other physicians, given only the symptoms, do not find the diagnosis nearly so obvious (Dawson et al., 1988). Would juries be slower to assume malpractice if they were forced to take a foresight rather than a hindsight perspective?

What do we conclude – that common sense is usually wrong? Sometimes it is. At other times, conventional wisdom is right – or it falls on both sides of an issue: Does happiness come from knowing the truth or from preserving illusions? From being with others or from living in peaceful solitude? Opinions are a dime a dozen. No matter what we find, there will be someone who foresaw it. (Mark Twain jested that the biblical Adam was the only person who, when saying something, knew that nobody had said it before.) But which of the many competing ideas best fits reality? Research can specify the circumstances under which a commonsense truism is valid.

"Everything important has been said before."

—Philosopher Alfred North Whitehead, address to the British Association for the Advancement of Science, 1916

The point is not that common sense is predictably wrong. Rather, common sense usually is right – *after the fact.* We therefore easily deceive ourselves into thinking that we know and knew more than we do and did. And that is precisely why we need science to help us sift reality from illusion and genuine predictions from easy hindsight.

SUMMING UP: I Knew It All Along: Is Social Psychology Simply Common Sense?

- Social psychology is criticized for being trivial because it documents things that seem obvious.
- Experiments, however, reveal that outcomes are more "obvious" *after* the facts are known.
- This *hindsight bias* (the I-knew-it-all-along phenomenon) often makes people overconfident about the validity of their judgments and predictions.

RESEARCH METHODS: HOW DO WE DO SOCIAL PSYCHOLOGY?

Examine the methods that make social psychology a science.

We have considered some of the intriguing questions social psychology seeks to answer. We've also explored how "common sense" can't reliably answer these questions. So how can we answer social psychology's questions by more scientific means? Let's consider how using scientific methods can help us understand our social world.

"Nothing has such power to broaden the mind as the ability to investigate systematically and truly all that comes under thy observation in life."

—Marcus Aurelius, AD 161–180, *Meditations*

Forming and Testing Hypotheses

As we try to understand human nature, it's often useful to organize our ideas and findings into theories. A **theory** is *an integrated set of principles that explain and predict observed events.* Theories are scientific shorthand.

theory
An integrated set of principles that explain and predict observed events.

In everyday conversation, "theory" often means "less than fact" – a middle rung on a confidence ladder from guess to theory to fact. Thus, people may dismiss Charles Darwin's theory of evolution as "just a theory." Indeed, noted Alan Leshner (2005), chief officer of the American Association for the Advancement of Science, "Evolution *is* only a theory, but so is gravity." People often respond that gravity is a fact – but the *fact* is that your keys fall to the ground when dropped. Gravity is the theoretical explanation that accounts for such observed facts.

To a scientist, facts and theories are apples and oranges. Facts are agreed-upon statements about what we observe. Theories are *ideas* that summarize and explain facts. "Science is built up with facts, as a house is with stones," wrote the French scientist Jules Henri Poincaré, "but a collection of facts is no more a science than a heap of stones is a house" (1905, p. 101).

hypothesis
A testable proposition that describes a relationship that may exist between events.

Theories not only summarize but also imply testable predictions, called **hypotheses.** Hypotheses serve several purposes. First, they allow us to *test* a theory by suggesting how we might try to falsify it. Second, predictions give *direction* to research and sometimes send investigators looking for things they might never have considered. Third, the predictive feature of good theories can also make them *practical.* A complete theory of aggression, for example, would predict when to expect aggression and how to control it. As pioneering social psychologist Kurt Lewin declared, "There is nothing so practical as a good theory."

For humans, the most fascinating subject is people.

Warren Miller

Consider how this works. Suppose we observe that people who steal property or attack others often do so in groups or crowds. We might therefore theorize that being part of a crowd, or group, makes individuals feel anonymous and lowers their inhibitions. How could we test this theory? Perhaps we could ask individuals in groups to administer punishing shocks to someone who wouldn't know who was actually shocking them. Would these individuals, as our theory predicts, administer stronger shocks than individuals acting alone?

We might also manipulate anonymity: We could predict that people will deliver stronger shocks if they were wearing masks and were thus more anonymous. If the results confirm our hypothesis, they might suggest some practical applications. Perhaps police brutality could be reduced by having officers wear large name tags and drive cars identified with large numbers or by videotaping their arrests. Sure enough, all of these have become common practice in many cities.

But how do we conclude that one theory is better than another? A good theory

- effectively *summarizes many observations,* and
- *makes clear predictions* that we can use to
  - confirm or modify the theory,
  - generate new research, and
  - suggest practical applications.

When we discard theories, it is not usually because they have been proved false. Rather, like old cars, they are replaced by newer, better models.

Sampling and Question Wording

Let's now go backstage and see how social psychology is done. This glimpse behind the scenes should help you understand the research findings discussed later. Understanding the logic of research can also help you think critically about everyday social events and better comprehend studies you see covered in the media. In this section, we'll consider two issues: Who participates in the research and what questions we ask them.

SAMPLING: CHOOSING PARTICIPANTS

One of the first decisions that researchers must make is about their samples – the people who will participate in their studies. It is usually not possible to do a study on everyone in a population, so researchers study only part of the population, called a *sample.* Ideally, researchers want to get a sample that is representative of the population, called a **random sample** – *one in which every person in the population being studied has an equal chance of inclusion.* With random sampling, any subgroup of people – blondes, joggers, liberals, women – will tend to be represented in the sample in the same proportion they are represented in the total population.

random sampling
Survey procedure in which every person in the population being studied has an equal chance of inclusion.

Very few psychology studies can obtain a random sample of the world population. For one thing, most psychology studies are conducted in Western, industrialized nations (Henrich et al., 2010), so they might not be representative of other nations. Even random samples of the population within one country are difficult and time-consuming to obtain. Instead, many psychology studies rely on college students or people who are paid to

Exit polls require a random (and therefore representative) sample of voters.
Steve Debenport/Getty Images

participate in online studies (Anderson et al., 2019; Walters et al., 2018). These populations may differ in important ways from a truly representative sample. However, results from these samples often replicate (get the same results) when performed with nationally representative samples (Yeager et al., 2019).

Nonrandom sampling causes the most problems when the sampling is skewed by participants' interest in the topic or other factors that might strongly affect the outcome (White & Bonnett, 2019). If you ask fans at a soccer game, "What is your favorite sport?" their answers probably won't represent that of the national population. If you poll your Instagram followers, the responses will not be representative of the population of all Instagram users. That's for two reasons: Your followers are not a random sample of the population, and those who bother to respond to the poll are likely not a random sample of your followers. If you post a poll about cats, the cat-lovers and the cat-haters might be most likely to respond, leaving out everyone in the middle and biasing the results.

A sample can also be unrepresentative if few people respond to a poll – known as having a *low response rate* – and the people who do not respond differ in important ways from those who do. Some have speculated that this was why polls did not predict the 2016 presidential election as accurately as past elections: Response rates to telephone polls, once at 36%, dropped to 6% by the late 2010s (Kennedy & Hartig, 2019). Fortunately, this issue of response rate is not as common in the studies we will discuss here, as most psychology studies have higher response rates than telephone polls.

sample size
The number of participants in a study.

It's also important to obtain a sufficient number of people for the study, known as **sample size.** The size of the sample determines how closely the results are likely to resemble the whole population, no matter the size of the population (Smith, 2017). For example, using a sample size of 1,200 randomly selected people means we can be 95% confident we are describing the entire population's opinions plus or minus 3 percentage points or less (this range is called the *margin of error*). Imagine a huge jar filled with millions of beans, 50% red and 50% white. If you randomly sample 1,200 beans, you will be 95% certain to select between 47% and 53% red beans. If you take out fewer beans (and thus have a smaller sample size), the margin of error will be larger. If your sample size is 100 beans, for example, you can be 95% confident that the actual percentage of red beans is between 40% and 60% – a much wider margin than with 1,200. Similarly, a social psychology study using 1,200 participants is more reliable than a study using 100 participants (Stanley et al., 2018). Social psychology studies have improved their sample sizes in recent years, with more studies including a larger number of participants (Sassenberg & Ditrich, 2019).

ASKING THE RIGHT QUESTIONS

Researchers must also make sure that they have constructed their surveys or questionnaires in a way that doesn't bias responses. For example, the order of questions on a survey can have a surprisingly big impact.

The precise wording of questions may also influence answers. If you ask "Don't you agree that the voting age should be lowered to 16 because many 16-year-olds are responsible and informed?" more people will agree than if you ask, "Do you think 16-year-olds should have the right to vote?" When Americans are asked if climate change was occurring, 74% agreed, but when asked if global warming was occurring, only 68% of people agreed (Schuldt et al., 2011).

Survey wording is a very delicate matter. Even subtle changes in the tone of a question can have marked effects (Krosnick & Schuman, 1988; Schuman & Kalton, 1985). "Forbidding" something may be the same as "not allowing" it. But in 1940, 54% of Americans said the United States should "forbid" speeches against democracy, and 75% said the United States should "not allow" them. Even when people say they feel strongly about an issue, a question's form and wording may affect their answer.

Order, response, and wording effects enable political manipulators to use surveys to show public support for their views. Consultants, advertisers, and physicians can have similar disconcerting influences upon our decisions by how they **frame** our choices. No wonder the meat lobby objected to a U.S. food labeling law that required declaring ground beef, for example, as "30% fat," rather than "70% lean, 30% fat." "Gun control" efforts gain more public support when framed as "gun safety" initiatives, such as requiring background checks (Steinhauer, 2015). Many people who don't want to be "controlled" do support "safety."

Framing research also has applications in the definition of everyday default options. Without restricting people's freedom, thoughtfully framed options can "nudge" people toward beneficial decisions (Benartzi & Thaler, 2013):

SRC's Survey Services Laboratory at the University of Michigan's Institute for Social Research has interviewing carrels with monitoring stations. Staff and visitors must sign a pledge to honor the strict confidentiality of all interviews.
NORC at the University of Chicago

- *Opting in or out of organ donation.* In many countries, people decide, when renewing their driver's license, whether they want to make their body available for organ donation. In countries where the default option is *yes* but one can opt out, nearly 100% of people choose to be donors. In the United States, Britain, and Germany, where the default option is *no* but one can opt in, approximately 1 in 4 chooses to be a donor (Johnson & Johnson, 2003).
- *Opting in or out of retirement savings.* For many years, U.S. employees who wanted to defer part of their compensation to a 401(k) retirement plan had to elect to lower their take-home pay. Most chose not to do so. A 2006 pension law, influenced by framing research, reframed the choice. Now companies are given an incentive to enroll their employees automatically in the plan and to allow them to opt out (and to raise their take-home pay). The choice was preserved. But one study found that with the "opt out" framing, enrollments soared from 49% to 86% (Rosenberg, 2010).

The practical lesson of framing is illustrated by a young monk who was rebuffed when asking if he could smoke while he prayed. Ask a different question, advised a friend: Ask if you can pray while you smoke.

framing
The way a question or an issue is posed; framing can influence people's decisions and expressed opinions.

correlational research
The study of the naturally occurring relationships among variables.

experimental research
Studies that seek clues to cause–effect relationships by manipulating one or more factors (independent variables) while controlling others (holding them constant).

Correlational Research: Detecting Natural Associations

Social psychological research varies by method. Two of the most common types are **correlational** (asking whether two or more factors are naturally associated) and **experimental** (manipulating some factor to see its effect on another). If you want to be a critical reader of psychological research reported in the media, it helps to understand the difference between correlational and experimental research.

Some companies and institutions are seeking to "nudge" employees toward retirement savings by how they frame the options. By framing their choice as whether or not to *opt out* of an automatic savings plan, more people participate than when they must decide whether to *opt in.*
scyther5/iStock/Getty Images

Let's first consider correlational research, which has both a major advantage (examining important variables in natural settings) and a major disadvantage (difficulty determining cause and effect). In search of possible links between wealth and health, Douglas Carroll and his colleagues (1994) ventured into Glasgow, Scotland's old graveyards and noted the life spans of 843 individuals. As an indication of wealth, they measured the height of the grave pillars, reasoning that height reflected cost and therefore

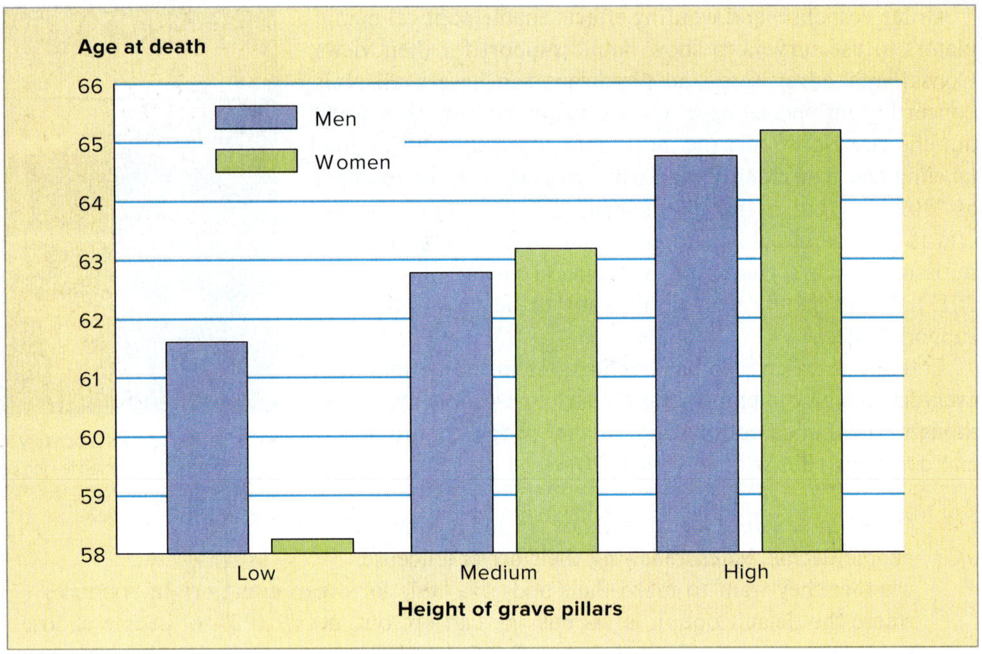

FIGURE 3

Correlating Wealth and Longevity

Tall grave pillars, indicating wealth, commemorated people who also tended to live longer.
Source: Carroll, D., Davey Smith, G., & Bennett, P. (1994).

affluence. As **Figure 3** shows, wealth (taller grave markers) predicted longer lives – a key indicator of health.

Data from other sources have confirmed the wealth – health correlation: Scottish postal-code regions with the highest incomes also have the longest average lifespans. In the United States, income correlates with longevity (poor and lower-status people are more likely to die sooner). Another study followed 17,350 British civil service workers over 10 years. Compared with high-status administrators, lower-status administrators were 1.6 times more likely to have died. Even lower-status clerical workers were 2.2 times more likely to have died, and laborers were 2.7 times more likely (Adler et al., 1993, 1994). Across times and places, the wealth–health correlation seems reliable.

But does that mean that more wealth causes a longer life? Maybe, but maybe not. The wealth–health question illustrates the most irresistible thinking error made by both amateur and professional social psychologists: When two factors such as wealth and health go together, it is tempting to conclude that one causes the other. Wealth, we might presume, somehow protects a person from health risks. But maybe it's the other way around: Perhaps healthy people are more likely to succeed economically, or people who live longer have more time to accumulate wealth. A third variable might also cause both health and wealth; for example, perhaps those of a certain race or religion are both healthier and more likely to become wealthy. In other words, correlations indicate a relationship, but that relationship could or could not be one of cause and effect. Correlational research allows us to roughly *predict* one variable from another, but it cannot tell us whether one variable (such as wealth) *causes* another (such as health). When two variables (let's call them X and Y) are correlated with each other, there are three possibilities: X causes Y, Y causes X, or a third variable (Z) causes both.

The correlation–causation confusion is behind much muddled thinking in popular psychology. Consider another very real correlation: between self-esteem and academic achievement. Children with high self-esteem tend also to have high academic achievement. (As with any correlation, we can also state this the other way around: High achievers tend to have high self-esteem.) Why do you suppose that is true (**Figure 4**)?

Some people believe self-esteem contributes to achievement. Thus, boosting a child's self-esteem may also boost school achievement. Believing so, 30 U.S. states have enacted more than 170 self-esteem–promoting statutes.

But other people, including psychologists Joachim Krueger (2022), William Damon (1995), Mark Leary (2012), Martin Seligman (1994, 2002), Roy Baumeister and Kathleen

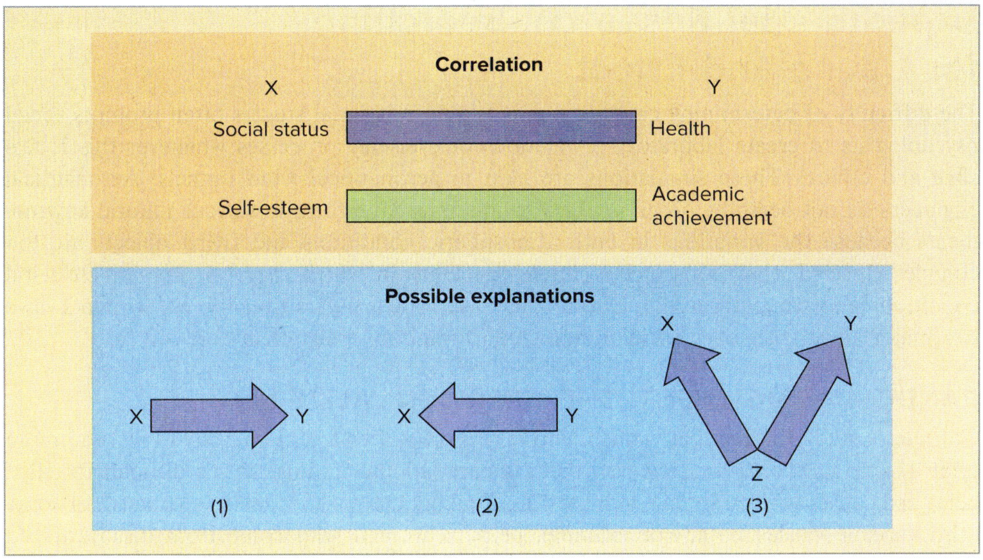

FIGURE 4

Correlation and Causations

When two variables correlate, any combination of three explanations is possible. Either one may cause the other, or both may be affected by an underlying "third factor."

Vohs (2003, 2018), and one of us (Twenge, 2013, 2014), doubt that self-esteem is really "the armor that protects kids" from underachievement (or drug abuse and delinquency). Perhaps it is the other way around: Perhaps doing well builds self-esteem. Some studies suggest that this is true: Children who do well and are praised for it develop high self-esteem (Skaalvik & Hagtvet, 1990).

It is also possible that self-esteem and achievement correlate because both are linked to underlying intelligence, family social status, or parental behavior. In studies of more than 2,000 people, the correlation between self-esteem and achievement evaporated when researchers mathematically removed the predictive power of intelligence and family status (Bachman & O'Malley, 1977; Maruyama et al., 1981). In one study, the correlation between self-esteem and delinquent behavior disappeared when factors such as drug use by parents were controlled (Boden et al., 2008). In other words, both low self-esteem and poor behavior are caused by the same thing: an unfortunate home environment. Both may be symptoms of a bad childhood rather than being caused by each other.

Using a coefficient known as *r,* correlations quantify the degree of relationship between two factors, from −1.0 (as one factor score goes up, the other goes down) to 0 (indicating no relationship) to +1.0 (as one factor goes up, the other also goes up). For example, self-reports of self-esteem and depression correlate negatively (about −.60). Identical twins' intelligence scores correlate positively (above +.80).

The great strength of correlational research is that it tends to occur in real-world settings where we can examine factors such as race, gender, and social status – factors that we cannot manipulate in the laboratory. Its great disadvantage lies in the ambiguity of the results. This point is so important that even if it fails to impress people the first 25 times they hear it, it is worth repeating a 26th time: Knowing that two variables change together (correlate) enables us to predict one when we know the other, but correlation does not specify cause and effect.

Advanced correlational techniques can, however, suggest cause-effect relationships. *Time-lagged* correlations reveal the *sequence* of events (for example, by indicating whether changed achievement more often precedes or follows changed self-esteem). Researchers can also use statistical techniques that extract the influence of third variables, as when the correlation between self-esteem *and* achievement evaporated after extracting intelligence and family status (this is known as adding a *control variable*). As another example, the Scottish research team wondered whether the status-longevity relationship would still exist after removing the influence of cigarette smoking, which was both more common among those of lower status and linked to dying earlier. The correlation remained, suggesting that other factors related to low status may account for poorer people's earlier demise.

Experimental Research: Searching for Cause and Effect

The difficulty of determining cause and effect in correlational studies often prompts social psychologists to create laboratory simulations of everyday processes whenever this is feasible and ethical. These simulations are akin to aeronautical wind tunnels. Aeronautical engineers do not begin by observing how flying objects perform in various natural environments because the variations in both atmospheric conditions and flying objects are too complex. Instead, they construct a simulated reality in which they can manipulate wind conditions and wing structures. Due to their use of a simulated reality, experiments have two major advantages over correlational studies: random assignment and control.

RANDOM ASSIGNMENT: THE GREAT EQUALIZER

Consider a study finding that women who take more selfies are more likely to feel sad more often (Lamp et al., 2019). However, that's a correlational finding, so it's difficult to tell if being sad causes women to take more selfies, if taking more selfies makes them sad, or some third variable causes both. For example, perhaps women who come from disadvantaged backgrounds are more likely to take more selfies and more likely to feel sad (see **Table 1** for more examples). A researcher might measure and statistically control for some possible third variables and see if the correlations survive. But researchers can never control for all the factors that might distinguish women who take more selfies from those who don't.

random assignment
The process of assigning participants to the conditions of an experiment such that all persons have the same chance of being in a given condition. (Note the distinction between random *assignment* in experiments and random *sampling* in surveys. Random assignment helps us infer cause and effect. Random sampling helps us generalize to a population.)

In one motion, **random assignment** eliminates all such extraneous factors. For example, a researcher might randomly assign women to take selfies (vs. taking pictures of objects) and then measure their mood. With random assignment, each person has an equal chance of taking selfies versus taking photos of objects. Thus, the people in both groups would, in every conceivable way – family background, intelligence, personality traits, education, hair color – average about the same. Because random assignment creates equivalent treatment and control groups, any later difference in mood between the two groups will almost surely have something to do with the only way they differ – whether or not they took selfies (**Figure 5**).

CONTROL: MANIPULATING VARIABLES

independent variable
The experimental factor that a researcher manipulates.

Social psychologists experiment by constructing social situations that simulate important features of our daily lives. By varying just one or two factors (called **independent variables**) at a time, the experimenter pinpoints their influence. As the wind tunnel helps the aeronautical engineer discover principles of aerodynamics, so the experiment enables the social psychologist to discover principles of social thinking, social influence, and social relations.

How exactly is this done? Let's continue with the example of selfies and negative mood.

TABLE 1 Recognizing Correlational and Experimental Research

	Can Participants Be Randomly Assigned to Condition?	Independent Variable	Dependent Variable
Are early-maturing children more confident?	No → Correlational		
Do students learn more in online or classroom courses?	Yes → Experimental	Take class online or in the classroom	Learning
Do school grades predict vocational success?	No → Correlational		
Do people cheer more loudly alone or when in a crowd?	Yes → Experimental	People are alone in a crowd	Decibel level of noise
Do people find comedy funnier when alone or with others?	(you answer)		
Do wealthier people live longer?	(you answer)		

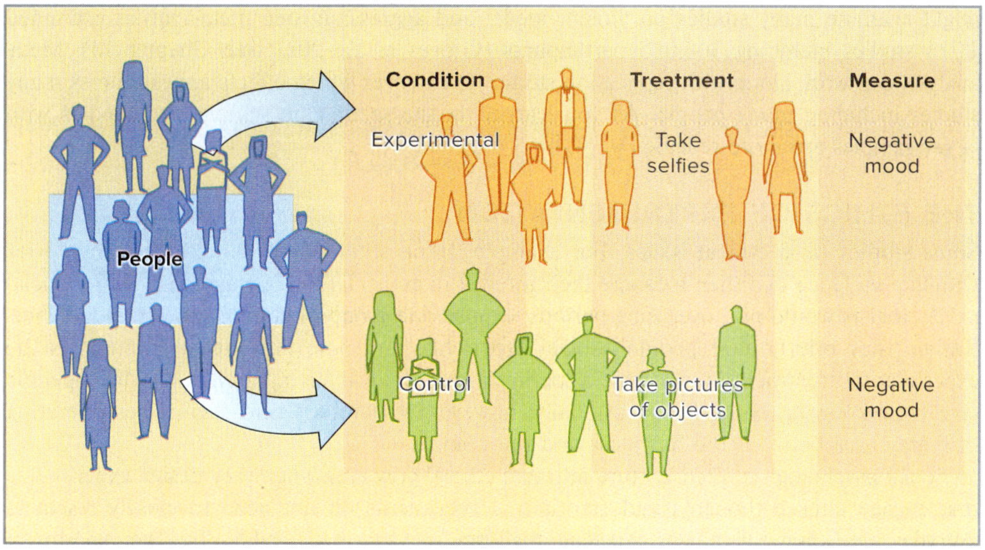

FIGURE 5

Random Assignment

Experiments randomly assign people either to a condition that receives the experimental treatment or to a control condition that does not. This gives the researcher confidence that any later difference is somehow caused by the treatment.

To study this question using an experimental method, Jesse Fox and colleagues asked some young women to take pictures of themselves (selfies) using a smartphone. The other group of young women were asked to take pictures of objects in the room (Fox et al., 2021). Thus, the researchers controlled the situation by having the groups take pictures of different things, an example of how researchers manipulate variables through control. Whether the women took pictures of themselves versus pictures of objects was the independent variable in this experiment.

After ten minutes taking photos, the women completed questionnaires including one measuring negative emotions (such as "upset" and "ashamed"). The women who took selfies reported more negative emotions than the women who took pictures of objects. Negative emotions was the **dependent variable** – the outcome being measured – in this study. Studies like this suggest that taking selfies isn't just correlated with negative mood – taking selfies can actually *cause* negative mood.

dependent variable
The variable being measured, so called because it may depend on manipulations of the independent variable.

replication
Repeating a research study, often with different participants in different settings, to determine whether a finding could be reproduced.

meta-analysis
A "study of studies" that statistically summarizes many studies on the same topic.

REPLICATION: ARE THE RESULTS REPRODUCIBLE?

The experiment on selfies and negative mood we just described was just one study. How do we know that its result was not just a fluke? If another researcher did the same experiment with different people, would they obtain the same results? Over the last decade, social psychologists have increasingly emphasized the importance of **replication** studies: those that run the same experiment again, sometimes multiple times by different people, to discover if the same results will still appear.

Teams of researchers have formed international collaborative efforts to replicate the results of published research papers. Across 307 attempts to replicate psychology studies, 64% found results similar to the original studies (Nosek et al., 2022). Two other recent initiatives replicated 54% and 67% of prior studies (Camerer et al., 2018; Klein et al., 2018). So most studies replicated, but not all.

Such replication forms an essential part of good science. Any single study provides some information; it's one estimate. Better is the aggregated data from multiple studies (Stanley & Spence, 2014). Replication = confirmation.

Having easy access to research materials and data aids in the process of replication and allows other scientists to verify results (Banks et al., 2019). Many psychologists now file their methods and their detailed data in public, online, "open science" archives (Brandt et al., 2014; Miguel et al., 2014), which may help increase trust in the results (Schneider et al., 2022).

Another useful method is **meta-analysis,** a "study of studies" that analyzes many studies on the same topic. Here, the emphasis is on summarizing the results across many different studies to discover the average effect. For example, a meta-analysis

Does taking selfies make women feel sad? A random-assignment experiment is a good way to find out.
Jimartinfotografo/Shutterstock

might examine many studies on violent media and aggression; one meta-analysis examined 1,723 studies including 360,045 participants (Groves et al., 2021; see Chapter 10). Meta-analysis can work along with replication studies to discover which effects appear across many studies including many people. As you learned in the section on sample size, studies with larger samples are more reliable.

THE ETHICS OF EXPERIMENTATION

Some studies raise ethical issues. For example, some studies have children watch movies with gun violence and then measure their interest in guns (Dillon & Bushman, 2017). Social psychologists would not, over long periods, expose one group of children to brutal violence. Rather, they briefly alter people's social experience and note the effects. Sometimes the experimental treatment is a harmless, perhaps even enjoyable, experience to which people give their knowing consent. Occasionally, however, researchers find themselves operating in a gray area between the harmless and the risky.

Social psychologists often venture into that ethical gray area when they design experiments that engage intense thoughts and emotions. Experiments do not need to closely resemble everyday life (known as having **mundane realism;** Aronson et al., 1985). But the experiment *should* have **experimental realism:** It should engage the participants. Experimenters do not want participants to be bored or just playing along; they want to engage in real psychological processes. For example, in one experimental procedure, an experimenter knocks over a cup of pencils and records whether the participant helps pick them up. A procedure like this functionally simulates real helping, much as a wind tunnel simulates atmospheric wind.

mundane realism
Degree to which an experiment is superficially similar to everyday situations.

experimental realism
Degree to which an experiment absorbs and involves its participants.

Achieving experimental realism sometimes requires deceiving people with a plausible *cover story.* The experimenter doesn't want the participant to know they knocked over the pencil cup on purpose so they could measure helping behavior. That would destroy the experimental realism. Thus, some social psychological studies use **deception,** in which participants did not know the study's true purpose.

deception
In research, a strategy by which participants are misinformed or misled about the study's methods and purposes.

Experimenters also seek to hide their predictions lest the participants, in their eagerness to be "good subjects," merely do what is expected (or, in an ornery mood, do the opposite). Small wonder, said Ukrainian professor Anatoly Koladny, that only 15% of Ukrainian survey respondents declared themselves "religious" while under Soviet communism in 1990 when religion was oppressed by the government, but 70% declared themselves "religious" in post-communist 1997 (Nielsen, 1998). In subtle ways, too, the experimenter's words, tone of voice, and gestures may call forth desired responses. Even search dogs trained to detect explosives and drugs are more likely to bark false alerts in places where their handlers have been misled into thinking such illegal items are located; the dogs must be picking up on the handlers' expectations (Lit et al., 2011). To minimize such **demand characteristics** – cues from experimenters that seem to "demand" certain behavior – experimenters typically standardize their instructions or even use a computer to present them.

demand characteristics
Cues in an experiment that tell the participant what behavior is expected.

Researchers often walk a tightrope in designing experiments that will be engaging yet ethical. It might be temporarily uncomfortable to believe that you are hurting someone or to be subjected to strong social pressure. Experiments using deception raise the age-old question of whether ends justify means. Do the risks exceed those we experience in everyday life (Fiske & Hauser, 2014)? Social psychologists' deceptions are usually brief and mild compared with many misrepresentations in real life and in some reality shows.

University ethics committees review social psychological research to ensure that it will treat people humanely and that the scientific merit justifies any temporary deception or distress. Ethical principles developed by the American Psychological Association (2017), the Canadian Psychological Association (2017), and the British Psychological Society (2018) mandate investigators to:

- Tell potential participants enough about the experiment to enable their **informed consent.**
- Be truthful. Use deception only if essential and justified by a significant purpose; do not deceive about aspects of the study that would influence participants' willingness to participate.

informed consent
An ethical principle requiring that research participants be told enough to enable them to choose whether they wish to participate.

- Protect participants (and bystanders, if any) from harm and significant discomfort.
- Keep information about individual participants confidential.
- **Debrief** participants. Fully explain the experiment afterward, including any deception. The only exception to this rule is when the feedback would be distressing, such as by making participants realize they have been stupid or cruel.

debriefing
In social psychology, the postexperimental explanation of a study to its participants. Debriefing usually discloses any deception and often queries participants regarding their understandings and feelings.

The experimenter should be informative *and* considerate enough that people leave feeling at least as good about themselves as when they came in. Better yet, the participants should be compensated by having learned something (Sharpe & Faye, 2009). When treated respectfully, few participants mind being deceived, and psychological after-effects are few (Boynton et al., 2013; Epley & Huff, 1998; Kimmel, 1998). Indeed, say social psychology's advocates, professors provoke far greater anxiety and distress by giving and returning course exams than researchers provoke in their experiments.

Generalizing from Laboratory to Life

Social psychology mixes everyday experience and laboratory analysis. Throughout this book, we do the same by drawing our data mostly from the laboratory and our examples mostly from life. Social psychology displays a healthy interplay between laboratory research and everyday life.

What people see in everyday life suggests correlational research, which then leads to the experimental research. Network and government policymakers, those with the power to make changes, are now aware of the results. In many areas, including studies of helping, leadership style, depression, and self-efficacy, effects found in the lab have been mirrored by effects in the field, especially when the laboratory effects have been large (Mitchell, 2012). "The psychology laboratory has generally produced psychological truths rather than trivialities," noted Craig Anderson and colleagues (1999).

We need to be cautious, however, in generalizing from laboratory to life. Although the laboratory uncovers the basic dynamics of human existence, it is still a simplified, controlled reality. It tells us what effect to expect of variable *X*, all other things being equal – which in real life they never are.

Sampling is also an issue. As we've discussed, most participants are from WEIRD (*W*estern, *E*ducated, *I*ndustrialized, *R*ich, and *D*emocratic) cultures that represent only 12% of humanity (Apicella et al., 2020; Henrich et al., 2010). The participants in many experiments are college students, hardly a random sample of all humanity (Henry, 2008; Pollet & Saxton, 2019). Would we get similar results with people of different ages, educational levels, and cultures? Sometimes results replicate across cultures and groups, and sometimes they do not.

Nevertheless, many psychological processes do appear across many cultures. Although our behaviors may differ, we are influenced by the same social forces. Beneath our surface diversity, we are more alike than different.

SUMMING UP: Research Methods: How Do We Do Social Psychology?

- Social psychologists organize their ideas and findings into *theories.* A good theory will distill an array of facts into a much shorter list of predictive principles. We can use those predictions to confirm or modify the theory, to generate new research, and to suggest practical applications.
- Researchers must decide whom to study – their sample of people. They also must make decisions about how to frame survey questions.
- Most social psychological research is either *correlational* or *experimental.* Correlational studies discern the relationship between variables, such as between the amount of education and the amount of income. Knowing two things are naturally related is valuable information, but it is not a reliable indicator of what is causing what – or whether a third variable is involved.

- When possible, social psychologists prefer to conduct experiments that explore cause and effect. By constructing a miniature reality that is under their control, experimenters can vary one thing and then another and discover how those things, separately or in combination, affect behavior. We *randomly assign* participants to an experimental condition, which receives the experimental treatment, or to a control condition, which does not. We can then attribute any resulting difference between the two conditions to the *independent variable* (**Figure 6**). By seeking to *replicate* findings, today's psychologists also assess their reproducibility.
- In creating experiments, social psychologists sometimes stage situations that engage people's emotions. In doing so, they are obliged to follow professional ethical guidelines, such as obtaining people's *informed consent*, protecting them from harm, and fully disclosing afterward any temporary deceptions. Laboratory experiments enable social psychologists to test ideas gleaned from life experience and then to apply the principles and findings to the real world.

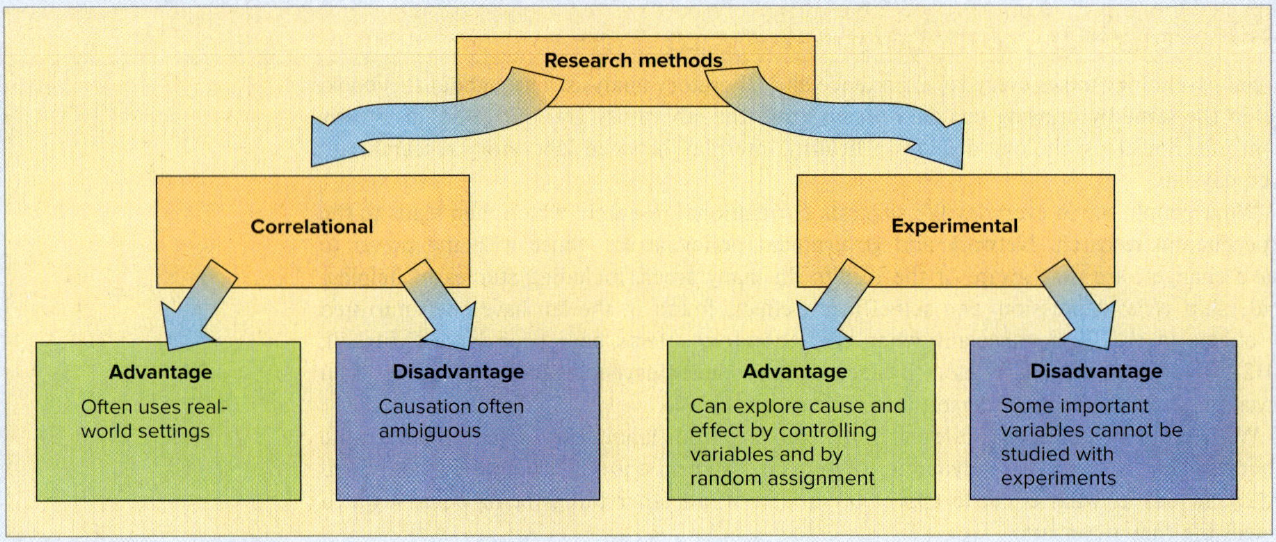

FIGURE 6
Two Methods of Doing Research: Correlational and Experimental

We conclude each chapter with a brief reflection on social psychology's human significance.

CONCLUDING THOUGHTS: Why We Wrote This Book . . . and a Preview of What's to Come

We write this text to offer social psychology's powerful, hard-wrought principles. They have, we believe, the power to expand your mind and enrich your life. If you finish this book with sharpened critical thinking skills and with a deeper understanding of how we view and affect one another – and why we sometimes like, love, and help one another and sometimes dislike, hate, and harm one another – then we will be satisfied authors and you, we trust, will be a rewarded reader.

We write knowing that many readers are in the process of defining their life goals, identities, values, and attitudes. Novelist Chaim Potok recalls being urged by his mother to forgo writing: "Be a brain surgeon. You'll keep a lot of people from dying; you'll make a lot more money." Potok's response: "Mama, I don't want to keep people from dying; I want to show them how to live" (quoted by Peterson, 1992, p. 47).

Many of us who teach and write about psychology are driven not only by a love for giving psychology away but also by wanting to help students live better lives – wiser, more fulfilling, more compassionate lives. In this, we are like teachers and writers in other fields.

"Why do we write?" asked theologian Robert McAfee Brown. "I submit that beyond all rewards . . . *we write because we want to change things.* We write because we have this [conviction that we] can make a difference. The 'difference' may be a new perception of beauty, a new insight into self-understanding, a new experience of joy, or a decision to join the revolution" (quoted by Marty, 1988). Indeed, we write hoping to do our part to restrain intuition with critical thinking, temper judgmentalism with compassion, and replace illusion with understanding.

This book unfolds around its definition of social psychology: the scientific study of how we *think about* (Part One), *influence* (Part Two), and *relate to* (Part Three) one another. Part Four offers additional, focused examples of how the research and the theories of social psychology are applied to real life.

Specifically, Part One examines the scientific study of how we think about one another (also called *social cognition*). Each chapter in this part confronts some overriding questions: How reasonable are our social attitudes, explanations, and beliefs? Are our impressions of ourselves and others generally accurate? How does our social thinking form? How is it prone to bias and error, and how might we bring it closer to reality?

The Self in a Social World

CHAPTER 2

Adam Lubroth/Getty Images

"There are three things extremely hard: steel, a diamond, and to know one's self."

—Benjamin Franklin, *Poor Richard's Almanack*, 1750

At the center of our worlds, more pivotal for us than anything else, is ourselves. As we navigate our daily lives, our sense of self continually engages the world.

Consider this: How is your online self different from your in-person self? Many social media users emphasize the positive, featuring the successes and not the failures, the beautiful vacation photos but not the mind-numbingly long road trip to get there. The way we present ourselves in person can also be carefully curated, from haircuts to clothes to not telling the whole truth when your friend asks, "What do you think of my new boyfriend?"

So which one of these is your "real" self: Your online self or your in-person self? Is there even such a thing as a "real" self, or are we just a composite of how we present ourselves to others? Even when we are alone, do we have a realistic view of our own characteristics and abilities? These are some of the questions we consider in this chapter.

SPOTLIGHTS AND ILLUSIONS: WHAT DO THEY TEACH US ABOUT OURSELVES?

Describe the spotlight effect and its relation to the illusion of transparency.

Rushing out the door one day, you forget to comb your hair. All morning, you are acutely self-conscious of your bad hair day. To your surprise, your friends in class don't say anything. You're not sure if they are secretly laughing to themselves or are too preoccupied to notice your uncombed hair.

Why do we often feel that others are paying more attention to us than they actually are? The **spotlight effect** means seeing ourselves at center stage, thus intuitively overestimating the extent to which others' attention is aimed at us.

spotlight effect
The belief that others are paying more attention to our appearance and behavior than they really are.

illusion of transparency
The illusion that our concealed emotions leak out and can be easily read by others.

Timothy Lawson (2010) explored the spotlight effect by having college students change into a sweatshirt emblazoned with "American Eagle" (the name of a clothing brand) before meeting a group of peers. Nearly 40% were sure the observers would remember what the shirt said, but only 10% actually did. Most observers did not even notice when the students changed sweatshirts after leaving the room for a few minutes. In another experiment, even embarrassing clothes, such as a T-shirt with singer Barry Manilow on it, provoked only 23% of observers to notice – many fewer than the 50% estimated by the students sporting the 1970s warbler on their chests (Gilovich et al., 2000).

Due to the spotlight effect, this new college student might think everyone is looking at her and feel embarrassed by her parents' attention – even though her peers don't really notice.
XiXinXing/Shutterstock

What's true of our dorky clothes and bad hair is also true of our emotions: our anxiety, irritation, disgust, deceit, or attraction to someone else (Gilovich et al., 1998). Fewer people notice than we presume. Keenly aware of our own emotions, we often suffer from an **illusion of transparency.** If we're happy and we know it, then our face will surely show it. And others, we presume, will notice. Actually, we can be more opaque than we realize. (See "Research Close-Up: On Being Nervous About Looking Nervous.")

In addition to thinking our emotions are transparent, we also overestimate the visibility of our social blunders and public mental slips. When we trigger the library alarm or accidentally insult someone, we may be mortified ("Everyone thinks I'm a jerk"). But research shows that what we agonize over, others may hardly notice and soon forget (Savitsky et al., 2001).

The spotlight effect and the related illusion of transparency are just two examples of the interplay between our sense of self and our social worlds. Here are a few more:

- *Social surroundings affect our self-awareness.* When we are the only member of our race, gender, or nationality in a group, we notice how we differ and how others are reacting to our difference – for example, Black students on a majority-White college campus (Osbourne et al., 2021). A White American friend once told me [DM] how self-consciously White he felt while living in a rural village in Nepal; an hour later, an African American friend told me

research CLOSE-UP

On Being Nervous About Looking Nervous

Have you ever felt self-conscious when approaching someone you felt attracted to, concerned that your nervousness was obvious? Or have you felt yourself trembling while speaking before an audience and presumed that everyone was noticing?

Kenneth Savitsky and Thomas Gilovich (2003) knew from their own and others' studies that people overestimate the extent to which their internal states "leak out." People asked to tell lies presume that others will detect their deceit, which feels so obvious. People asked to sample horrid-tasting drinks presume that others notice their disgust, which they can barely suppress.

Many people who give a presentation report not just feeling anxious, but anxious that others will notice their anxiety. And if they feel their knees shaking and hands trembling, their worry that others are noticing may compound and perpetuate their anxiety. This is similar to fretting about not falling asleep, which further impedes falling asleep, or feeling anxious about stuttering, which worsens the stuttering.

Savitsky and Gilovich wondered whether an illusion of transparency might surface among inexperienced public speakers — and whether it might disrupt their performance. To find out, they invited 40 Cornell University students to their laboratory in pairs. One person stood at the podium and spoke for 3 minutes (on a topic such as "The Best and Worst Things About Life Today") as the other sat and listened. Then the two switched positions, and the other person gave a different 3-minute impromptu talk. Afterward, each rated how nervous they thought they appeared while speaking (from 0, *not at all*, to 10, *very*) and how nervous the other person seemed.

The results? People rated themselves as appearing relatively nervous (6.65, on average). But to their partner, they appeared not so nervous (5.25), a difference great enough to be statistically significant (meaning that the difference is very unlikely to have been due to chance variation). Twenty-seven of the 40 participants (68%) believed that they appeared more nervous than did their partner.

To check on the reliability of their finding, Savitsky and Gilovich *replicated* (repeated) and extended the experiment by having people speak before an audience of people who weren't going to be giving speeches themselves, to rule out the possibility that this might explain the previous results. Again, speakers overestimated the transparency of their nervousness.

Savitsky and Gilovich next wondered whether informing speakers that their nervousness isn't so obvious might help them relax and perform better. They invited 77 more Cornell students to come to the lab and, after 5 minutes' preparation, give a 3-minute videotaped speech on race relations at their university. They divided the students into three groups. Those in one group — the *control condition* — were given no further instructions. Those in the second group — the *reassured condition* — were told that it was natural to feel anxious but that "You shouldn't worry much about what other people think. . . . With this in mind, you should just relax and try to do your best. Know that if you become nervous, you probably shouldn't worry about it." To the third group, those in the *informed condition*, they explained the illusion of transparency. After telling them it was natural to feel anxious, the experimenters added, "Research has found that audiences can't pick up on your anxiety as well as you might expect. . . . Those speaking feel that their nervousness is transparent, but in reality, their feelings are not so apparent. . . . With this in mind, you should just relax and try to do your best. Know that if you become nervous, you'll probably be the only one to know."

After the speeches, the speakers rated their speech quality and their perceived nervousness (this time using a 7-point scale) and were also rated by the observers. As **Table 1** shows, those informed about the illusion-of-transparency phenomenon felt better about their speeches and their appearance than did those in the control and reassurance conditions. What's more, the observers confirmed the speakers' self-assessments.

So, the next time you feel nervous about looking nervous, pause to remember the lesson of these experiments: Other people are noticing less than you might suppose.

TABLE 1 Average Ratings of Speeches by Speakers and Observers on a 1-to-7 Scale

Type of Rating	Control Condition	Reassured Condition	Informed Condition
Speakers' self-ratings			
Speech quality	3.04	2.83	3.50*
Relaxed appearance	3.35	2.69	4.20*
Observers' rating			
Speech quality	3.50	3.62	4.23*
Composed appearance	3.90	3.94	4.65*

*Each of these results differs by a statistically significant margin from those of the control and reassured conditions.

how self-consciously American she felt while in Africa. And when race comes up in a discussion, those in the minority feel an uncomfortable amount of attention directed their way (Crosby et al., 2014).

- *Self-interest colors our social judgment.* When problems arise in a close relationship, we usually blame our partners instead of ourselves. When things go *well* at home or work or play, we see ourselves as more responsible.
- *Self-concern motivates our social behavior.* In hopes of making a positive impression, we agonize about our appearance. We also monitor others' behavior and expectations and adjust our behavior accordingly.
- *Social relationships help define our sense of self.* "Selves don't emanate from some ineffable light within people," observes Brian Lowery (2023). "Selves are created in relationships." In our varied relationships, we have varying selves, noted Susan Andersen and Serena Chen (2002). We may be one self with a parent, another with friends, and another with teachers. How we think of ourselves is linked to the person we're with at the moment. And when relationships change, our self-concepts can change as well. College students who broke up with a romantic partner shifted their self-perceptions and felt less certain about who they were – one reason breakups can be so emotionally distressing (Slotter et al., 2010).

As these examples suggest, the traffic between ourselves and others runs both ways. Our sense of ourselves affects how we respond to others, and others help shape our sense of self.

No topic in psychology today is more heavily researched than the self. In 2022, the word "self" appeared in 27,279 book and article summaries in *PsycInfo* (the online archive of psychological research) – 16 times more than in 1970. Our sense of self organizes our thoughts, feelings, and actions and enables us to remember our past, assess our present, and project our future – and thus to behave adaptively.

"No topic is more interesting to people than people. For most people, moreover, the most interesting is the self."

—Roy F. Baumeister, *The Self in Social Psychology,* 1999

In later chapters, you will see that much of our behavior is not consciously controlled but, rather, automatic and unself-conscious. However, the self does enable long-term planning, goal setting, and restraint. It imagines alternatives, compares itself with others, and manages its reputation and relationships. Moreover, as Mark Leary (2004a) noted in his aptly titled *The Curse of the Self,* the self can sometimes be an impediment to a satisfying life. That's why religious or spiritual meditation practices seek to prune the self's egocentric preoccupations by quieting the ego, reducing its attractions to material pleasures, and redirecting it. "Mysticism," added psychologist Jonathan Haidt (2006), "everywhere and always, is about losing the self, transcending the self, and merging with something larger than the self."

In the remainder of this chapter, we examine our self-concept (how we come to know ourselves) and the self in action (how our sense of self drives our attitudes and actions).

SUMMING UP: Spotlights and Illusions: What Do They Teach Us About Ourselves?

- Concerned with the impression we make on others, we tend to believe that others are paying more attention to us than they are (the *spotlight effect*).
- We also tend to believe that our emotions are more obvious than they are (the *illusion of transparency*).

SELF-CONCEPT: WHO AM I?

Explain how, and how accurately, we know ourselves and what determines our self-concept.

Try this: Complete the sentence "I am _____" in five different ways. Your answers provide a glimpse of your **self-concept.**

self-concept
What we know and believe about ourselves.

At the Center of Our Worlds: Our Sense of Self

The most important aspect of yourself is your self. To discover where this sense of self arises, neuroscientists have explored the brain activity that underlies our constant sense of being oneself. Most studies suggest an important role for the right hemisphere (Choi et al., 2023; van Veluw & Chance, 2014). If your right hemisphere is put to sleep (with an anesthetic to your right carotid artery), you may have trouble recognizing your own face. One patient with right hemisphere damage failed to recognize that he owned and was controlling his left hand (Decety & Sommerville, 2003). The "medial prefrontal cortex," a neuron path located in the cleft between your brain hemispheres just behind your eyes, seemingly helps stitch together your sense of self. It becomes more active when you think about yourself (Farb et al., 2007; Heleven & Van Overwalle, 2019; Stendardi et al., 2021). Despite the many ways we adapt our behavior, most people believe that they have a true self that is unchangeable (Christy et al., 2019).

self-schema
Beliefs about self that organize and guide the processing of self-relevant information.

The elements of your self-concept, the specific beliefs by which you define yourself, are your **self-schemas** (Markus & Wurf, 1987). *Schemas* are mental templates by which we organize our worlds. Our *self-schemas* – our perceiving ourselves as athletic, overweight, smart, or anything else – powerfully affect how we perceive, remember, and evaluate other people and ourselves. If being an athlete is one of your self-schemas, then you will tend to notice others' bodies and skills, will quickly recall sports-related experiences, and will welcome information that is consistent with your self-schema as an athlete (Kihlstrom & Cantor, 1984). Because birthdays are within self-schemas, if your friend's birthday is close to yours, you'll be more likely to remember it (Kesebir & Oishi, 2010). People who are depressed often have negative self-schemas, leading them to remember negative information more easily (Branstrom et al., 2023). The self-schemas that make up our self-concepts help us organize and retrieve our experiences.

SOCIAL COMPARISONS

social comparison
Evaluating one's opinions and abilities by comparing oneself with others.

How do we decide if we are rich, smart, or short? One way is through **social comparisons** (Festinger, 1954; Gerber et al., 2018). Other people help define the standard by which we define ourselves as rich or poor, smart or dumb, tall or short: We compare ourselves with them and consider how we differ. Social comparison explains why high school students tend to think of themselves as better students if their peers are only average (Marsh et al., 2000; Wang, 2015). It also explains how self-concept can be threatened after graduation when a student who excelled in an average high school goes on to an academically selective university. The "big fish" is no longer in a small pond (Pekrun et al., 2019).

Much of life revolves around social comparisons. We feel handsome when others seem homely, smart when others seem dull, caring when others seem callous. More money doesn't always lead to more happiness, but having more money than those around you can (Solnick & Hemenway, 1998). When we witness a peer's performance, we cannot resist implicitly comparing ourselves (Gilbert et al., 1995). We may, therefore, privately take some pleasure in a peer's failure, especially when it happens to someone we envy and when we don't feel vulnerable to such misfortune ourselves (Boecker et al., 2022; Lockwood, 2002; Smith et al., 1996). You might have heard the German word for this: *Schadenfreude.*

Sometimes the social comparison is based on incomplete information. Have you ever been on Instagram and thought, "All of my friends are having a lot more fun than I am"? Of course, it can't be true that everyone is having more fun than everyone else; it's just that social media users feature the more exciting and positive aspects of their lives, leading people to compare themselves unfavorably with others (known as *upward social comparison*). One study found that young adults were significantly more likely to feel inferior to others while using social media than while engaged in other activities (Midgley et al., 2021). Social media users who socially compared themselves to others were more likely to be depressed – a phenomenon researchers called "seeing everyone else's highlight reels" (Sharma et al., 2022; Steers et al., 2014). This biased social comparison might be one reason young adults who used social media more often were more depressed, more lonely, and less satisfied with their lives (Huang, 2017; Lin et al., 2016; McComb et al., 2023; Primack et al., 2017). An

"Comparison is the thief of joy."
—Theodore Roosevelt

experiment found that college students randomly assigned to limit their social media use to 30 minutes a day were less depressed and less lonely than those who kept up their usual social media use (Hunt et al., 2018). Using that limited time solely to communicate with friends (by muting strangers on Instagram and eliminating TikTok use) also reduced depression (Hunt et al., 2023).

Even sexual activity is subject to social comparison. Adults who have sex more often are happier – you might have guessed that! But then social comparison kicks in: People who have a lot of sex are less happy if their peers are having more sex than they are (Wadsworth, 2014). Apparently, we judge not just how much fun we're having but how it measures up to the fun everyone else is having.

Social comparison. Because people tend to highlight only the best and most exciting parts of their lives on social media, social comparison online is often based on incomplete information.
Sam Edwards/Caiaimage/Getty Images

OTHER PEOPLE'S JUDGMENTS

When people think well of us, we think well of ourselves. Children whom others label as gifted, hardworking, or helpful tend to incorporate such ideas into their self-concepts and behavior. Children who are praised for "being a helper" (rather than "helping") later help more; it has become part of their identity (Bryan et al., 2014). If racial minority students feel threatened by negative stereotypes of their academic ability, or women feel threatened by low expectations for their math and science performance, they may "disidentify" with those realms. Rather than fight such prejudgments, they may shift their interests elsewhere (Steele, 2010).

The looking-glass self was how sociologist Charles H. Cooley (1902) described our use of how we think others perceive us as a mirror for perceiving ourselves. Fellow sociologist George Herbert Mead (1934) refined this concept, noting that what matters for our self-concepts is not how others actually see us but the way we *imagine* they see us. People generally feel freer to praise than to criticize; they voice their compliments and restrain their insults. We may, therefore, overestimate others' appraisal, inflating our self-images. For example, people tend to see themselves as more physically attractive than they actually are (Epley & Whitchurch, 2008).

Self and Culture

How did you complete the "I am _____" statement? Did you give information about your personal traits, such as "I am honest," "I am tall," or "I am outgoing"? Or did you also describe your social identity, such as "I am a Pisces," "I am a MacDonald," or "I am a Muslim"?

For some people, especially those in industrialized Western cultures, **individualism** prevails. Identity is self-contained. Becoming an adult means separating from parents, becoming self-reliant, and defining one's personal, **independent self.** One's identity – as a unique individual with particular abilities, traits, values, and dreams – remains fairly constant.

individualism
The concept of giving priority to one's own goals over group goals and defining one's identity in terms of personal attributes rather than group identifications.

independent self
Construing one's identity as an autonomous self.

Western culture assumes your life will be enriched by believing in your power of personal control. Western literature, from *The Iliad* to *Walden,* celebrates the self-reliant individual. Movie plots feature rugged heroes who buck the establishment. Songs state without irony that "I Am a God" or "I Believe the World Should Revolve Around Me," and Dr. Seuss tells children that "there is no one alive who is youer than you." Individualism flourishes when people experience affluence, mobility, urbanism, economic prosperity, and mass media, and when economies shift away from manufacturing and toward information and service industries (Bianchi, 2016; Grossmann & Varnum, 2015; Triandis, 1994).

Most cultures native to Asia, Africa, and Central and South America place a greater value on **collectivism,** by respecting and identifying with the group. In these cultures, people are more self-critical and focus less on self-esteem (Heine et al., 1999; Vaughan-Johnston & Jacobson, 2021). Malaysians, Indians, Koreans, Japanese, and traditional Kenyans such as the Maasai, for example, are much more likely than Australians, Americans, and the British to complete the "I am" statement with their group identities (Kanagawa et al., 2001;

collectivism
Giving priority to the goals of one's group (often one's extended family or work group) and defining one's identity accordingly.

Collectivistic cultures focus less on individual identity and more on group identity.
Xavier Arnau/E+/Getty Images

Ma & Schoeneman, 1997). When speaking, people using the languages of collectivist countries say "I" less often (Kashima & Kashima, 1998, 2003). Compared with U.S. church websites, Korean church websites place more emphasis on social connections and participation and less on personal spiritual growth and self-betterment (Sasaki & Kim, 2011).

Of course, pigeonholing cultures as solely individualistic or collectivistic oversimplifies because within any culture, individualism varies from person to person (Oyserman et al., 2002a, 2002b). There are individualistic Chinese and collectivistic Americans, and most people behave communally at some times and individualistically at others (Bandura, 2004). Individualism–collectivism also varies across other characteristics. Conservatives tend to be economic individualists ("don't tax or regulate me") and moral collectivists ("legislate against immorality"). Liberals tend to be economic collectivists ("let's pass universal health care") and moral individualists ("keep your laws off my body"). The rich are more individualistic than the poor, males more than females, Whites more than other races (Dabiriyan Tehrani & Yamini, 2022; Kraus et al., 2012). In China, people living in areas that grow rice (which requires more collective cooperation) are more collectivistic than those in areas that grow wheat (English & Geeraert, 2020; Talhelm et al., 2014). In the United States, Native Hawaiians and people living in the deep South are more collectivistic than are those in states in the West such as Oregon and Montana (Plaut et al., 2002; Vandello & Cohen, 1999).

GROWING INDIVIDUALISM WITHIN CULTURES

Cultures can also change over time, and many are growing more individualistic (Santos et al., 2017). One way to see this is using the Google Books Ngram Viewer, which shows the usage of words and phrases in the full text of 5 million books since the 1800s (try it yourself; it's online and free). In the 2000s and 2010s, compared to previous decades, books published in the United States used the word "get" more and "give" less (Greenfield, 2013), used "I" and "me" much more, and used "we" and "us" about the same amount (Twenge, 2023; Twenge et al., 2013; see **Figure 1**). This pattern of increasing individualism also appears in books in eight other languages worldwide (Yu et al., 2016).

In individualistic cultures, being different and standing out is seen as an asset. In collectivistic cultures, it is seen as a detriment.
Carlos Arguelles/Shutterstock

Popular song lyrics also became more likely to use "I" and "me" and less likely to use "we" and "us" between 1980 and 2007 (DeWall et al., 2011), with the norm shifting from the sappy love song of the 1980s ("Endless Love," 1981) to the self-celebration of the 2000s (Justin Timberlake singlehandedly bringing "Sexy Back," 2006). Another analysis of popular songs found a steady increase in expressions of anger, an emotion associated with individualism (Napier & Shamir, 2019).

Even your name might show the shift toward individualism: American parents are now less likely to give their children common names and more likely to help them stand out with an unusual name. Although nearly 20% of boys born in 1990 received one of the 10 most common names, only 7% received such a common name by 2021 (Twenge, 2023; Twenge et al., 2016). Today, you don't have to be the child of a celebrity to have a name as unique as Psalm, Dream, or Apple.

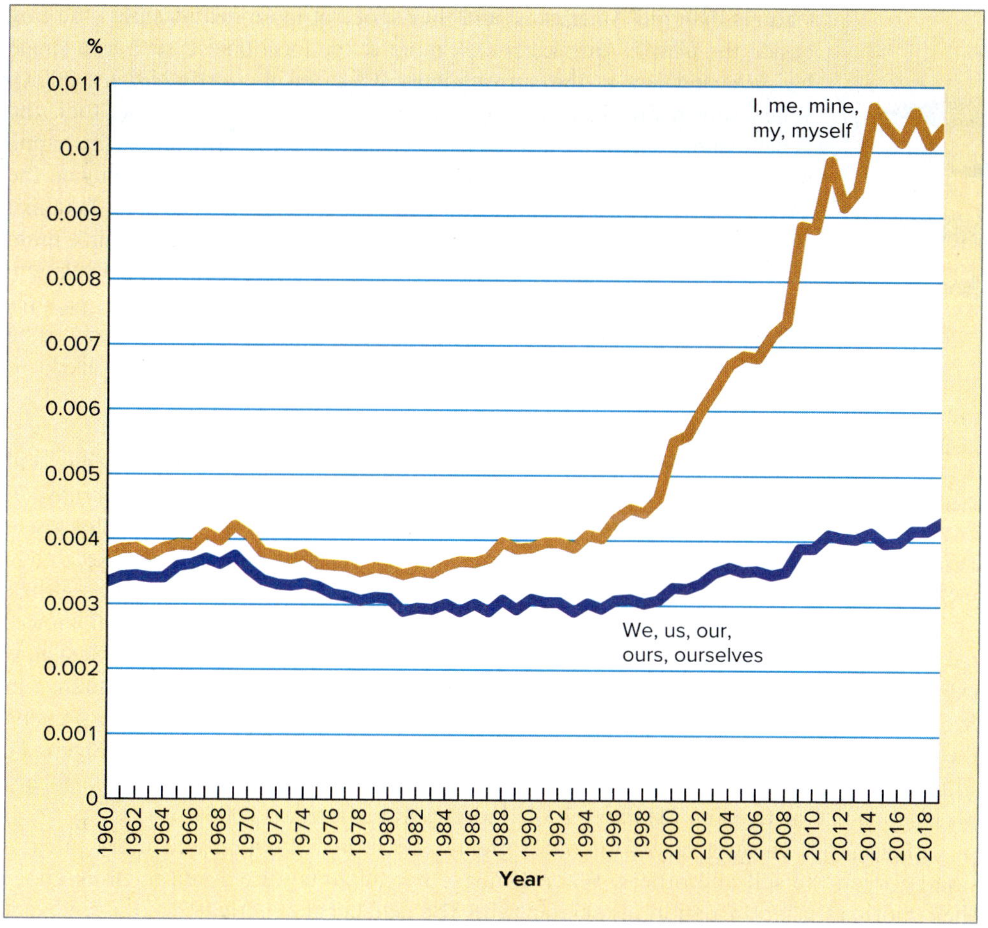

FIGURE 1

In the Google Books database, American books in the 2000s and 2010s (versus those from the 1960s and 1970s) used *I, me, my, mine*, and *myself* more often while the use of *we, us, our, ours, and ourselves* changed little.
Source: Twenge, 2023.

Americans and Australians, most of whom are descended from those who struck out on their own to emigrate, are more likely than Europeans to give their children uncommon names. Parents in the western United States and Canada, descended from independent pioneers, are also more likely than those in the more established east to give their children uncommon names (Varnum & Kitayama, 2011). The more individualistic the time or the place, the more children receive unique names.

These changes demonstrate a principle that goes deeper than a name: the interaction between individuals and society. Did the culture focus on uniqueness first and cause the parents' name choices, or did individual parents decide they wanted their children to be unique, thus creating the culture? A similar chicken-and-egg question applies to song lyrics: Did a more self-focused population listen to more self-focused songs, or did listening to more self-focused songs make people more self-focused? The answer, though not yet fully understood, is probably both (Ma et al., 2023; Markus & Kitayama, 2010).

CULTURE AND COGNITION

In his book *The Geography of Thought* (2003), social psychologist Richard Nisbett contended that collectivism also results in different ways of thinking. When shown an animated underwater scene (**Figure 2**), Japanese spontaneously recalled 60% more background

FIGURE 2

Asian and Western Thinking

When shown an underwater scene, Americans focus on the biggest fish. Asians are more likely to reference the background, such as the plants, bubbles, and rocks (Nisbett, 2003).

FIGURE 3

Which Pen Would You Choose?

When Heejung Kim and Hazel Markus (1999) invited people to choose one of these pens, 77% of Americans but only 31% of Asians chose the uncommon color (regardless of whether it was orange, as here, or green). This result illustrates differing cultural preferences for uniqueness and conformity, noted Kim and Markus.

features than did Americans, and they spoke of more relationships (the frog beside the plant). Americans look more at the focal object, such as a single big fish, and less at the surroundings (Chua et al., 2005; Nisbett, 2003). When shown drawings of groups of children, Japanese students took the facial expressions of all of the children into account when rating the happiness or anger of an individual child, whereas Americans focused only on the child they were asked to rate (Masuda et al., 2008). Nisbett and Takahiko Masuda (2003) concluded from such studies that East Asians think more holistically—perceiving and thinking about objects and people in relationship to one another and to their environment. Social media profile pictures show a similar cultural effect: U.S. students' selfies were more likely to be close-ups of their faces, whereas Taiwanese students were more likely to choose a picture with more background (Huang & Park, 2012).

If you grew up in a Western culture, you were probably told to "express yourself"—through writing, the choices you make, the products you buy, and perhaps through your tattoos or piercings. When asked about the purpose of language, American students were more likely to explain that it allows self-expression, whereas Korean students focused on how language allows communication with others. American students were also more likely to see their choices as expressions of themselves and to evaluate their personal choices more favorably (Kim & Sherman, 2007). The individualized latté—"decaf, single shot, skinny, extra hot"—that seems just right at a North American coffee shop would seem strange in Seoul, noted Kim and Hazel Markus (1999). In Korea, people place less value on expressing their uniqueness and more on tradition and shared practices (Choi & Choi, 2002; **Figure 3**). Korean advertisements tend to feature people together, whereas U.S. advertisements highlight personal choice or freedom (Markus, 2001; Morling & Lamoreaux, 2008).

Collectivistic cultures also promote a greater sense of belonging and more integration between the self and others. When Chinese participants were asked to think about their mothers, a brain region associated with the self became activated—an area that lit up for Western participants only when they thought about themselves (Zhu et al., 2007). As **Figure 4** and **Table 2** suggest, the interdependent self is embedded in social memberships. Conversation is less direct and more polite (Holtgraves, 1997), and people focus more on gaining social approval (Lalwani et al., 2006). Among Chinese students, half said they would stop dating someone if their parents disapproved, compared with less than one-third of U.S. students (Zhang & Kline, 2009). In a collectivistic culture, the goal of social life is to harmonize with and support one's communities, not—as it is in more individualistic societies—to enhance one's individual self and make independent choices. Perhaps as a result, people in collectivistic countries were more likely to follow mandates for mask-wearing and physical distancing during the COVID-19 pandemic (Lu et al., 2021).

FIGURE 4

Self-Construal as Independent or Interdependent

The independent self acknowledges relationships with others. But the interdependent self is more deeply embedded in others (Markus & Kitayama, 1991).

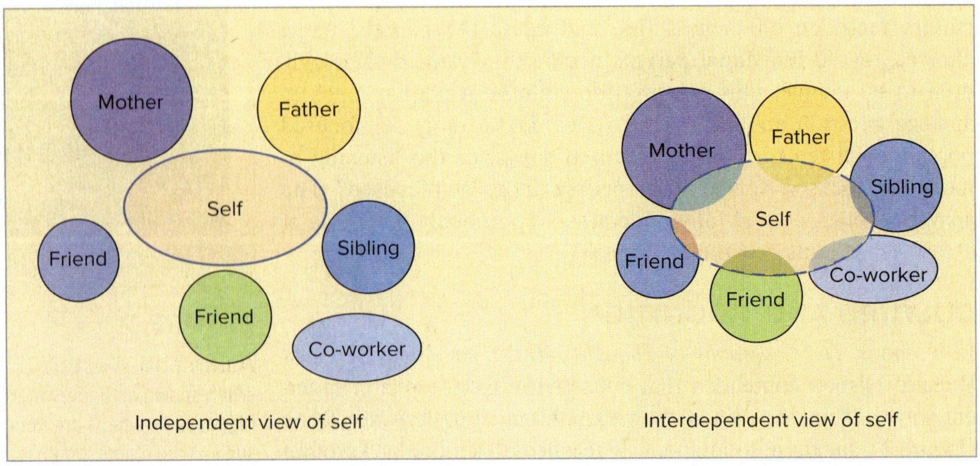

TABLE 2 Self-Concept: Independent or Interdependent

	Independent (Individualistic)	Interdependent (Collectivistic)
Identity is	Personal, defined by individual traits and goals	Social, defined by connections with others
What matters	Me – personal achievement and fulfillment; my rights and liberties	We – group goals and solidarity; our social responsibilities and relationships
Disapproves of	Conformity	Egotism
Illustrative motto	"To thine own self be true"	"No one is an island"
Cultures that support	Individualistic Western	Collectivistic Asian and developing countries

CULTURE AND SELF-ESTEEM

In collectivistic cultures, self-esteem tends to be malleable (context-specific) rather than stable (enduring across situations). In one study, only 1 in 3 Chinese and Japanese students agreed that they remained essentially the same person in different situations, compared with 4 in 5 Canadian students (Tafarodi et al., 2004). The idea of one "true self" is more common in individualistic cultures than in collectivistic ones (Rivera et al., 2019).

For those in individualistic cultures, self-esteem is more personal and less relational. If a Westerner's personal identity is threatened, they will feel angrier and sadder than when they collective identity is threatened (Gaertner et al., 1999). Unlike Japanese people, who persist more on tasks when they are failing, people in individualistic countries persist more when succeeding because success elevates self-esteem (Heine et al., 2001). Western individualists like to make comparisons with others that boost their self-esteem. Asian collectivists make comparisons (often upward, with those doing better) in ways that facilitate self-improvement (White & Lehman, 2005).

So when, do you suppose, are university students in collectivistic Japan and individualistic United States most likely to report positive emotions such as happiness and elation? For Japanese students, happiness comes with positive social engagement – with feeling close, friendly, and respectful. For U.S. students, it more often comes with disengaged emotions – with feeling effective, superior, and proud (Kitayama & Markus, 2000). Conflict in collectivistic cultures often takes place between groups; individualistic cultures breed more conflict (and crime and divorce) between individuals (Triandis, 2000).

"One needs to cultivate the spirits of sacrificing the *little me* to achieve the benefits of the *big me*."

—Chinese saying

When Shinobu Kitayama (1999), after 10 years of teaching and researching in the United States, visited his Japanese alma mater, Kyoto University, graduate students were "astounded" when he explained the Western idea of the individualistic self. "I persisted in explaining this Western notion of self-concept – one that my American students understood intuitively – and finally began to persuade them that, indeed, many Americans do have such a disconnected notion of self. Still, one of them, sighing deeply, said at the end, 'Could this *really* be true?'" (To read more about psychological differences between cultures, see "The Inside Story: Hazel Markus and Shinobu Kitayama on Cultural Psychology.")

When East meets West, does the self-concept become more individualized? What happens when Japanese people are exposed to Western advice to "believe in one's own possibilities" and to movies featuring the heroic individual police officer catching the crook *despite* others' interference? As Steven Heine and co-researchers reported (1999), they become more individualistic. Being an exchange student has a similar effect: Personal self-esteem increased among Japanese exchange students after spending 7 months at the University of British Columbia. In Canada, individual self-esteem is also higher among long-term Asian immigrants than among more recent immigrants (and higher than among those living in Asia). Culture can shape self-views even in short periods of time.

In collectivistic cultures, harmony comes from sameness and agreement.
Visage/Getty Images

THE inside STORY

Hazel Markus and Shinobu Kitayama on Cultural Psychology

We began our collaboration by wondering out loud. Japanese researcher Shinobu wondered why American life was so weird. American researcher Hazel countered with anecdotes about the strangeness of Japan. Cultural psychology is about making the strange familiar and the familiar strange. Our shared cultural encounters astonished us and convinced us that when it comes to psychological functioning, culture matters.

After weeks of lecturing in Japan to students with a good command of English, Hazel wondered why the students did not say anything — no questions, no comments. She assured students she was interested in ideas that were different from hers, so why was there no response? Where were the arguments, debates, and signs of critical thinking? Even if she asked a straightforward question, "Where is the best noodle shop?" the answer was invariably an audible intake of air followed by, "It depends." Didn't Japanese students have preferences, ideas, opinions, and attitudes? What is inside a head if it isn't these things? How could you know someone if she didn't tell you what she was thinking?

Shinobu was curious about why American students shouldn't just listen to a lecture and why they felt the need to be constantly interrupting each other and talking over each other and the professor. Why did the comments and questions reveal strong emotions and have a competitive edge? What was the point of this arguing? Why did intelligence seem to be associated with getting the best of another person, even within a class where people knew each other well?

Shinobu expressed his amazement at American hosts who bombard their guests with choices. Do you want wine or beer, or soft drinks or juice, or coffee or tea? Why burden the guest with trivial decisions? Surely the host knew what would be good refreshment on this occasion and could simply provide something appropriate.

Choice as a burden? Hazel wondered if this could be the key to one particularly humiliating experience in Japan. A group of eight — all native Japanese except for Hazel — was in a French restaurant, and everyone was following the universal restaurant script and studying the menu. The waiter approached and stood nearby. Hazel announced her choice of appetizer and entrée. Next was a tense conversation among the Japanese host and the Japanese guests. When the meal was served, it was not what she had ordered. Everyone at the table was served the same meal. This was deeply disturbing. If you can't choose your own dinner, how could it be enjoyable? What was the point of the menu if everybody is served the same meal?

Could a sense of sameness be a good or a desirable feeling in Japan? When Hazel walked around the grounds of a temple in Kyoto, there was a fork in the path and a sign that read: "ordinary path." Who would want to take the ordinary path? Where was the special, less-traveled path? Choosing the non-ordinary path may be an obvious course for Americans, but in this case, it led to the temple dump outside the temple grounds. The ordinary path did not denote the dull and unchallenging way, but meant the appropriate and the good way.

These exchanges inspired our experimental studies and remind us that there are ways of life beyond the ones that each of us knows best. So far, most of psychology has been produced by psychologists in middle-class White American settings studying middle-class White American respondents. In other sociocultural contexts, there can be different ideas and practices about how to be a person and how to live a meaningful life, and these differences have an influence on psychological functioning. This realization fuels our continuing interest in collaboration and in cultural psychology.

Hazel Rose Markus
Stanford University
Hazel Rose Markus

Shinobu Kitayama
University of Michigan
Courtesy of Shinobu Kitayama

Self-Knowledge

"Know thyself," admonished an ancient Greek oracle. We certainly try. We readily form beliefs about ourselves, and we in Western cultures don't hesitate to explain why we feel and act as we do. But how well do we actually know ourselves?

"There is one thing, and only one in the whole universe which we know more about than we could learn from external observation," noted C. S. Lewis (1952, pp. 18–19). "That one thing is [ourselves]. We have, so to speak, inside information; we are in the know." Indeed. Yet sometimes we *think* we know, but our inside information is wrong. That is the unavoidable conclusion of some fascinating research.

PREDICTING OUR BEHAVIOR

Consider three examples of how people's self-predictions can err:

- *Movie watching.* Netflix used to ask users to predict what films they later wanted to watch. Many predicted they would watch high-brow, intellectual films, but they actually watched low-brow, crowd-pleaser films. When Netflix stopped asking people what they wanted to watch and instead offered movies watched by similar customers, people watched more movies. What they thought they wanted and what they actually wanted were two different things (Stephens-Davidowitz, 2017).
- *Dating and romance future.* Inevitably, dating couples are optimistic about how long their relationship will last. Their friends and family often know better, reported Tara MacDonald and Michael Ross (1997). Among University of Waterloo students, their roommates were better predictors of whether their romances would survive than they were. So if you're in love and want to know whether it will last, don't listen to your heart—ask your roommate.
- *Performance.* Medical residents weren't very good at predicting whether they would do well on a surgical skills exam, but peers in the program predicted each other's performance with startling accuracy (Lutsky et al., 1993). Similarly, peers predicted psychology students' exam grades better than the students themselves—mostly because peers relied on past performance rather than the students' overly optimistic hopes for acing the test (Helzer & Dunning, 2012).

One of the most common errors in behavior prediction is underestimating how long it will take to complete a task (called the **planning fallacy**). A high-speed rail line between San Francisco and Los Angeles approved by California voters in 2008 was anticipated to take 12 years; it is now projected to be completed in 2033. The Sydney Opera House was supposed to be completed in 6 years; it took 16. Less than a third of couples engaged to be married completed their wedding planning as quickly as they expected, and only 4 out of 10 sweethearts bought a planned Valentine's Day gift by their self-imposed deadline (Min & Arkes, 2012). College students writing a senior thesis paper finished 3 weeks later than their "most realistic" estimate—and a week later than their "worst-case scenario" estimate (Buehler et al., 2002). However, friends and teachers were able to predict how late these papers would be. Just as you might ask your friends and family how long your relationship is likely to survive, if you want to know when you will finish your term paper, ask your roommate or your mom. You could also do what Microsoft does: Managers automatically add 30% onto a software developer's estimate of completion—and 50% if the project involves a new operating system (Dunning, 2006).

planning fallacy

The tendency to underestimate how long it will take to complete a task.

So, how can you improve your self-predictions? The best way is to be more realistic about how long tasks took in the past. Many people underestimate how long something will take because they misremember previous tasks as taking less time than they actually did (Roy et al., 2005). Another useful strategy: Estimate how long each step in the project will take. Engaged couples who described their wedding-planning steps in more detail more accurately predicted how long the process would take (Min & Arkes, 2012).

When will you finish your term paper? Your friends might have a more accurate answer than you do. Estimating each step separately might help you estimate more accurately.
Dean Drobot/Shutterstock

Are people equally bad at predicting how much money they will spend? Johanna Peetz and Roger Buehler (2009) found that the answer was yes. Canadian undergraduates predicted that they would spend $94 over the next week but actually spent $122. Considering that they had spent $126 in the week before the study, their guess should have been more accurate. When they came back a week later, they still predicted they would spend

"I was hoping you could tell me something mildly favorable – yet vague enough to be believable."

Predicting behavior, even one's own, is no easy matter, which may be why some people go to psychics and tarot card readers in hope of help.

only $85 in the coming week. U.S. homeowners renovating their kitchens planned to spend $18,658 but instead spent $38,769 (Kahneman, 2011, p. 250). So just as we think we will complete tasks quickly, we think we will save our money. The difficulty lies in actually doing so. If Chinese philosopher Lao-tzu was right – "He who knows others is learned. He who knows himself is enlightened" – then most people, it would seem, are more learned than enlightened.

PREDICTING OUR FEELINGS

Many of life's big decisions involve predicting our future feelings. Would marrying this person lead to lifelong contentment? Would entering this profession make for satisfying work? Would going on this vacation produce a happy experience? Or would the likelier results be divorce, job burnout, and holiday disappointment?

Sometimes we know how we will feel – if we fail that exam, win that big game, or soothe our tensions with a half-hour jog. We know what exhilarates us and what makes us anxious or bored. Other times we may mispredict our responses. Asked how they would feel if asked sexually harassing questions on a job interview, most women studied by Julie Woodzicka and Marianne LaFrance (2001) said they would feel angry. When actually asked such questions, however, women more often experienced fear.

Studies of "affective forecasting" reveal that people have the greatest difficulty predicting the *intensity* and the *duration* of their future emotions (Wilson & Gilbert, 2003). People mispredict how they would feel after a romantic breakup, receiving a gift, losing an election, winning or losing a game, or being insulted (Gilbert & Ebert, 2002; Kopp et al., 2017; Loewenstein & Schkade, 1999). Some examples:

"In sooth, I know not why I am so sad."

—William Shakespeare, *The Merchant of Venice, 1596*

- *Predicting one's hunger.* Hungry shoppers are more likely to impulse buy ("Those doughnuts would be delicious!") than shoppers who have just enjoyed a quarter-pound blueberry muffin (Gilbert & Wilson, 2000). When you are hungry, you mispredict how gross those deep-fried doughnuts will seem when you are sated. When stuffed, you may underestimate how yummy those doughnuts might be – a purchase whose appeal quickly fades after you've eaten one or two.
- *Predicting one's sadness or anger.* People asked how they would feel if they got COVID-19 predicted they would feel more upset and angry than those who had COVID actually did (Dillard & Meier, 2023). When natural disasters such as hurricanes occur, people predict that their sadness will be greater if more people are killed. But after Hurricane Katrina struck in 2005, students' sadness was similar when it was believed that 50 people had been killed to when they believed 1,000 had been killed (Dunn & Ashton-James, 2008). What *did* influence how sad people felt? Seeing pictures of victims. No wonder poignant images of disasters in the media have so much influence on us.
- *Predicting one's happiness.* People overestimate how much their well-being would be affected both by bad events (a romantic breakup, failing to reach an athletic goal, being physically injured [Dillard et al., 2021; Eastwick et al., 2007; van Dijk et al., 2008]) and good events (warmer winters, desired weight loss, more free time). Even extreme events, such as winning a state lottery or suffering a paralyzing accident, impact long-term happiness less than most people suppose.

"When a feeling was there, they felt as if it would never go; when it was gone, they felt as if it had never been; when it returned, they felt as if it had never gone."

—George MacDonald, *What's Mine's Mine*, 1886

Our intuitive theory seems to be: We want. We get. We are happy. If that were true, this chapter would have fewer words. In reality, noted Daniel Gilbert and Timothy Wilson (2000), we often "miswant." People who imagine an idyllic desert island holiday with sun, surf, and sand may be disappointed when they discover "how much they require daily structure, intellectual stimulation, or regular infusions of Pop Tarts." We think that if our candidate or team wins, we will be delighted for a long while. But study after study reveals our vulnerability to **impact bias** – overestimating the enduring impact of emotion-causing events. Faster than we expect, the emotional traces of such good tidings evaporate.

impact bias
Overestimating the enduring impact of emotion-causing events.

We are especially prone to impact bias after *negative* events. Let's make this personal. Gilbert and Wilson invite you to imagine how you might feel a year after losing your nondominant hand. Compared with today, how happy would you be?

You may have focused on what the calamity would mean: no clapping, no shoe tying, no competitive basketball, no speedy keyboarding. Although you likely would forever regret the loss, your general happiness some time after the event would be influenced by "two things: (a) the event, and (b) everything else" (Gilbert & Wilson, 2000). In focusing on the negative event, we discount the importance of everything else that contributes to happiness and thus overpredict our enduring misery. "Nothing that you focus on will make as much difference as you think," wrote researchers David Schkade and Daniel Kahneman (1998).

Moreover, said Wilson and Gilbert (2003), people neglect the speed and the power of their *coping mechanisms,* which include rationalizing, discounting, forgiving, and limiting emotional trauma. Because we are unaware of the speed and strength of our coping, we adapt to disabilities, romantic breakups, exam failures, layoffs, and personal and team defeats more readily than we would expect. Ironically, as Gilbert and colleagues reported (2004), major negative events (which activate our psychological defenses) can be less enduringly distressing than minor negative events (which don't activate our defenses). We are, under most circumstances, amazingly resilient.

"Weeping may tarry for the night, but joy comes with the morning."

—Psalm 30:5

THE WISDOM AND ILLUSIONS OF SELF-ANALYSIS

To a striking extent, then, our intuitions are often dead wrong about what has influenced us and what we will feel and do. But let's not overstate the case. When the causes of our behavior are conspicuous and the correct explanation fits our intuition, our self-perceptions will be accurate (Gavanski & Hoffman, 1987). When the causes of behavior are obvious to an observer, they are usually obvious to us as well. Overall, the correlation between predicted feelings and actual feelings was .28 – a significant but far from perfect link (Mathieu & Gosling, 2012).

We are unaware of much that goes on in our minds. Perception and memory studies show that we are more aware of the *results* of our thinking than of its process. Creative scientists and artists often cannot report the thought processes that produced their insights, although they have superb knowledge of the results.

Timothy Wilson (1985, 2002) offered a bold idea: Analyzing why we feel the way we do can actually make our judgments *less* accurate. In nine experiments, Wilson and colleagues (1989, 2008) found that the general feelings people expressed predicted their subsequent behavior reasonably well. Their reports became useless, however, if participants were first asked to *analyze* their feelings. For example, dating couples' level of happiness with their relationship accurately predicted whether they would still be dating several months later. But participants who first listed all the reasons why their relationship was good or bad before rating their happiness were misled: Their happiness ratings were useless in predicting the future of the relationship! Apparently, the process of dissecting the relationship drew attention to easily verbalized factors that were not as important as harder-to-verbalize happiness. We are often "strangers to ourselves," Wilson concluded (2002).

Such findings illustrate that we have a **dual attitude system,** said Wilson and colleagues (2000). Our automatic *implicit,* unconscious attitudes regarding someone or something often differ from our consciously controlled, *explicit* attitudes (Gawronski & Bodenhausen, 2006; Nosek, 2007). When someone says they make decisions by "trusting my gut," they're referring to their implicit attitudes (Kendrick & Olson, 2012). Although explicit attitudes may change with relative ease, noted Wilson, "implicit attitudes, like old habits, change more slowly." With repeated practice, however, new habitual attitudes can replace old ones.

dual attitude system

Differing implicit (automatic) and explicit (consciously controlled) attitudes toward the same object. Verbalized explicit attitudes may change with education and persuasion; implicit attitudes change slowly, with practice that forms new habits.

This research on the limits of our self-knowledge has two practical implications. The first is for psychological inquiry. *Self-reports are often untrustworthy.* Errors in self-understanding limit the scientific usefulness of subjective personal reports.

The second implication is for our everyday lives. Even if people report and interpret their experiences with complete honesty, that does not mean their reports are true. Personal testimonies are powerfully persuasive (as discussed in more detail in the chapter titled "Social Psychology in Court"). But they may also be wrong. Keeping this potential for error in mind can help us feel less intimidated by others and be less gullible.

SUMMING UP: Self-Concept: Who Am I?

- Our sense of self helps organize our thoughts and actions. When we process information with reference to ourselves, we remember it well (using our *self-schemas*). Self-schemas guide our processing of self-relevant information.
- Cultures shape the self, too. Many people in *individualistic* Western cultures assume an *independent self.* Others, often in *collectivistic* cultures, assume a more *interdependent self.* These contrasting ideas contribute to cultural differences in social behavior.
- Our self-knowledge is curiously flawed. We often do not know why we behave the way we do. When influences upon our behavior are not conspicuous enough for any observer to see, we, too, can miss them. The unconscious, implicit processes that control our behavior may differ from our conscious, explicit explanations of it.

WHAT IS THE NATURE AND MOTIVATING POWER OF SELF-ESTEEM?

Describe self-esteem and its implications for behavior and cognition.

self-esteem

A person's overall self-evaluation or sense of self-worth.

How do we decide how good we feel about ourselves – how much **self-esteem** we have?

One possibility: General self-esteem is the sum of all our self-views across various domains. This "bottom-up" theory of self-esteem says that if we see ourselves as attractive, athletic, smart, and moral, we will have high self-esteem. That is true – as long as we value those particular domains (Crocker & Wolfe, 2001). One person, for example, might have high self-esteem when they feel smart, while another will base their self-esteem on feeling moral.

But Jonathon Brown and Keith Dutton (1994) argued that self-esteem instead moves "top-down." People who value themselves in a general way – those with high self-esteem – are more likely to believe they are attractive, moral, and so on. Their general self-esteem impacts their domain-specific self-esteem. They are like new parents who, loving their infant, delight in the baby's fingers, toes, and hair: The parents do not first evaluate their infant's fingers or toes and then decide how much to value the whole baby.

Which one is right? A meta-analysis of 43 longitudinal studies suggests that self-esteem moves both "bottom-up" and "top-down" (Dapp et al., 2023). High self-esteem in particular domains leads to high general self-esteem, and high general self-esteem leads to confidence in particular domains (and, similarly, low self-esteem can move both ways).

Self-Esteem Motivation

Most people are extremely motivated to maintain their self-esteem. In fact, college students prefer a boost to their self-esteem to eating their favorite food, engaging in their favorite sexual activity, seeing a best friend, drinking alcohol, or receiving a paycheck (Bushman et al., 2011). So, somewhat incredibly, self-esteem was more important than pizza, sex, and beer!

What happens when your self-esteem is threatened – for example, by a failure or an unflattering comparison with someone else? When brothers have markedly different ability levels – for example, one is a great athlete and the other is not – they report not getting along well (Tesser et al., 1988). Dutch university students who experienced negative feedback felt more "Schadenfreude" (joy at another's misfortune) when they watched a young woman sing horribly out of tune in an audition for the Dutch version of "American Idol" (van Dijk et al., 2012). Misery loves to laugh at others' misery.

Self-esteem threats also occur among friends, whose success can be more threatening than that of strangers (Zuckerman & Jost, 2001). Whether someone has high or low self-esteem also makes a difference. People with high self-esteem usually react to a self-esteem threat by compensating for it (blaming someone else or trying harder next time). These reactions help them preserve their positive feelings about themselves. People with low self-esteem, however, are more likely to blame themselves or give up (VanDellen et al., 2011).

What underlies the motive to maintain or enhance self-esteem? Mark Leary (1998, 2004b, 2007) believed that self-esteem is similar to a fuel gauge. Relationships enable surviving and thriving, so the self-esteem gauge alerts us to threatened social rejection, motivating us to act with greater sensitivity to others' expectations. Studies confirm that social rejection lowers self-esteem and makes people more eager for approval. Spurned or jilted, we feel unattractive or inadequate. Like a blinking dashboard light, this pain can motivate action such as self-improvement or a search for acceptance and inclusion elsewhere. On the positive side, when people are satisfied with their social relationships, their self-esteem rises (de Moor et al., 2021). Self-esteem can also serve as a gauge of status with others, growing higher when we are respected as well as liked (Gebauer et al., 2015; Mahadevan et al., 2018).

Among sibling relationships, the threat to self-esteem is greatest for an older child with a highly capable younger brother or sister.
Hero/Corbis/Glow Images

However, actively pursuing self-esteem can backfire. Jennifer Crocker and colleagues found that students whose self-worth was contingent on external sources (such as grades or others' opinions) experienced more stress, anger, relationship problems, drug and alcohol use, and eating disorders than did those whose sense of self-worth was rooted more in internal sources, such as personal virtues (Crocker, 2002; Crocker & Luhtanen, 2003; Crocker & Park, 2004).

Ironically, noted Crocker and Lora Park (2004), those who pursue self-esteem, perhaps by seeking to become beautiful, rich, or popular, may lose sight of what really makes them feel good about themselves. University students who tried to impress their roommates by emphasizing their good qualities and hiding their bad ones found that their roommates actually liked them *less,* which then undermined their self-esteem (Canevello & Crocker, 2011). Pursuing self-esteem, Crocker explained, is like reaching into a small hole in a barrel to grasp a delicious apple – and then getting stuck because your hand's tight grip has made it too big for the hole (Crocker, 2011). When we focus on boosting our self-esteem, we may become less open to criticism, less likely to empathize with others, and more pressured to succeed at activities rather than enjoy them. So instead of reaching for the apple and failing, Crocker observed, it's better to emulate Johnny Appleseed, who altruistically planted seeds so others could eat apples – not so he could eat them himself. For example, college students who embraced compassionate goals toward their roommates ("I want to be supportive of my roommate") achieved better relationships with them and subsequently enjoyed higher self-esteem (Canevello & Crocker, 2011).

There are also benefits to being kind to oneself. Kristin Neff (2011, 2023) calls it self-compassion: leaving behind comparisons with others and instead treating ourselves with kindness. Self-compassion is linked to higher psychological well-being (Helminen et al., 2023; Reilly & Stuyvenberg, 2022). Self-compassion also has benefits for relationships with others. People who can accept their own flaws are more likely to accept others' flaws, a useful skill for relationships with humans who, inevitably, fall short of perfection (Zhang et al., 2019).

The Downsides of Low Self-Esteem

People low in self-esteem are more vulnerable to anxiety, loneliness, depression, drug abuse, eating disorders, and intentional self-harm such as cutting (Forrester et al., 2017; Krizan &

Herlache, 2017; Orth & Robins, 2013, 2022; Salmela-Aro & Nurmi, 2007). Feeling bad about yourself leads to bad things – or those bad things lead to feeling bad about yourself.

Several studies that followed people as they grew older (called a **longitudinal study**) found that people who had low self-esteem as teens were more likely to later be depressed, suggesting that low self-esteem causes depression instead of the other way around (Sowislo & Orth, 2013).

As you might remember from the chapter "Introducing Social Psychology," there's another possibility: A third variable. Childhood sexual abuse, poverty, or parental drug use might cause both low self-esteem and later depression. Sure enough, a study that controlled for these factors found that the link between self-esteem and negative outcomes disappeared (Boden et al., 2008). Low self-esteem was seemingly a symptom of an underlying disease – in this case, a tough childhood (Krauss et al., 2020). Still, low self-esteem may be a warning signal for problems down the road.

longitudinal study
Research in which the same people are studied over an extended period of time.

Across many longitudinal studies, high self-esteem predicted higher job satisfaction and more success at work later on, including better job performance and having a more prestigious job. However, self-esteem did not predict how much money people made at their job (Krauss & Orth, 2022). In general, high self-esteem is more strongly linked to self-reports of performance than objectively measured performance (Krueger et al., 2022).

People with high self-esteem tend to be more satisfied with their social relationships compared to those with low self-esteem (Harris & Orth, 2020). This may be due to several factors. When feeling bad or threatened, people with low self-esteem often take a negative view of everything. They notice and remember others' worst behaviors and think their partners don't love them (Murray et al., 2002; Vorauer & Quesnel, 2013). They may also sulk or complain when they seek support, a strategy that often leads relationship partners to react negatively (Don et al., 2019). Although people with low self-esteem do not choose less desirable partners, they are quicker to believe that their partners are criticizing or rejecting them.

Unfortunately, trying to boost low self-esteem through repeating positive phrases (such as "I'm a loveable person") backfires: It actually makes people low in self-esteem feel worse (Wood et al., 2009). Those low in self-esteem also don't want to hear positive things about negative experiences (such as "at least you learned something"). Instead, they prefer understanding responses, even if they are negative (such as "that really sucks" [Marigold et al., 2014]).

Narcissism: Self-Esteem's Conceited Sister

narcissism
An inflated sense of self.

Although high self-esteem has benefits, it can become problematic if it crosses over into **narcissism,** or having an inflated sense of self. Narcissism is not just high self-esteem; the two concepts have some fundamental differences (Rosenthal et al., 2020). For example, people high in self-esteem think they're worthy and good, but narcissists think they are better and smarter than others and seek the higher status that entails (Brummelman et al., 2016; Mahadevan & Jordan, 2022; Zajenkowski et al., 2020; Zeigler-Hill & Vrabel, 2023).

Most people with high self-esteem value both individual achievement and relationships with others. Narcissists usually have high self-esteem, but they are missing the piece about caring for others (Campbell et al., 2007; Grapsas et al., 2022; Hyatt et al., 2018; Jones & Brunell, 2014). Although narcissists can be outgoing and charming early on, their self-centeredness often leads to relationship problems in the long run because narcissists lack empathy (Campbell, 2005; Simard et al., 2023). The link between narcissism and problematic social relations led Delroy Paulhus and Kevin Williams (2002) to include narcissism in "The Dark Triad" of negative traits, along with Machiavellianism (manipulativeness) and antisocial psychopathy.

Narcissism is also linked to aggression. In a series of experiments conducted by Brad Bushman and Roy Baumeister (1998), undergraduate volunteers wrote essays and received

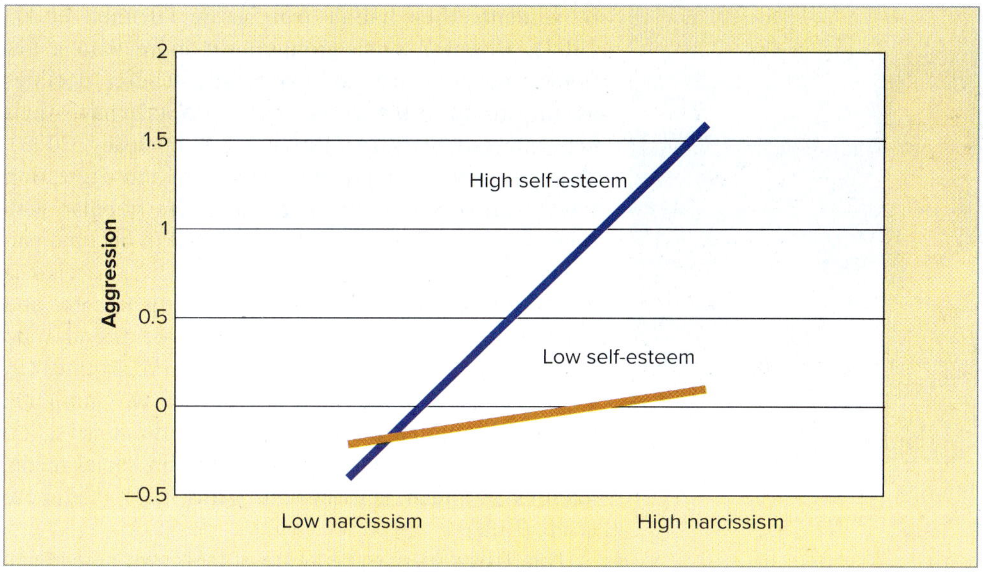

FIGURE 5

Narcissism, Self-Esteem, and Aggression

Narcissism and self-esteem interact to influence aggression. In an experiment by Brad Bushman and colleagues (2009), the recipe for retaliation against a critical classmate required both narcissism and high self-esteem.

rigged feedback that said, "This is one of the worst essays I've read!" Those who scored high on narcissism were much more likely to retaliate, blasting painful noise into the headphones of the student they believed had criticized them. Narcissists weren't aggressive toward someone who praised them ("great essay!"). It was the insult that set them off.

But what about self-esteem? Maybe only the "insecure" narcissists – those low in self-esteem – would lash out. But that's not what happened; instead, the students high in both self-esteem and narcissism were the most aggressive. In a classroom setting as well, those who were high in both self-esteem and narcissism were the most likely to retaliate against a classmate's criticism by giving them a bad grade (Bushman et al., 2009; **Figure 5**). Narcissists are especially likely to lash out when the insult is delivered publicly – and thus punctures their carefully constructed bubble of superiority. For that, someone must pay (Ferriday et al., 2011). In a meta-analysis of 437 studies, narcissism was consistently linked to higher levels of aggression and violence, especially after provocation (Kjaervik & Bushman, 2021). It's true that narcissists can be charming and entertaining. But as one commentator noted, "God help you if you cross them."

Perhaps narcissists act this way because they are actually insecure – maybe their overinflated egos are covering low self-esteem. In other words, do narcissistic people hate themselves "deep down inside"? Studies show that the answer is no. People who score high on measures of narcissistic personality traits also score high on measures of self-esteem. In case narcissists were claiming high self-esteem just for show, researchers also asked undergraduates to play a computer game in which they had to press a key as quickly as possible to match the word "me" with positive words such as "good," "wonderful," "great," and "right," and negative words such as "bad," "awful," "terrible," and "wrong." High scorers on the narcissism scale were faster than others to associate themselves with positive words and slower than others to pair themselves with negative words (Campbell et al., 2007). And narcissists were even faster to identify with words such as "outspoken," "dominant," and "assertive." Although it might be comforting to think that an arrogant classmate is just covering for their insecurity, chances are that deep down inside they think they're *awesome.*

That deep-seated feeling of superiority may originate in childhood. In a longitudinal study, when parents believed their children deserved special treatment, the children scored higher on narcissism 6 months later. In contrast, parents' feelings of love and kindness to their children were not linked to narcissism (Brummelman et al., 2015). This study suggests a straightforward piece of advice for parents: Instead of telling your children that they are special, tell them you love them.

Due to their self-confidence, narcissists are often initially popular with others. In one experiment, those higher in narcissism were more likely to emerge as the leader of a group

Narcissistic people are more active and more popular on social media sites, increasing their influence in these online communities. Narcissists also post more selfies (Koterba et al., 2021).
Maridav/Shutterstock

of students they hadn't met before (Brunell et al., 2008). However, once groups meet more than a few times, the popularity of narcissistic leaders declines as the group realizes the leader doesn't have their best interests at heart (Rosenthal & Pittinsky, 2006). As time passes, narcissists' antagonism and aggression toward others make them less and less popular with their peers (Leckelt et al., 2015). That can become particularly problematic on social media, where narcissists are both more active (posting more status updates and tweets) and more popular (having more friends and followers) (Gnambs & Appel, 2017; Liu & Baumeister, 2016; Marshall et al., 2020; McCain & Campbell, 2018). The above-average participation of narcissists on social media might be part of the reason social media features so much bullying and harassment (Bellmore et al., 2015).

Narcissists seem to be aware of their own narcissism. Simply asking people if they agree with the statement "I am a narcissist" predicts narcissistic behavior nearly as well as the standard 40-item measure (Konrath et al., 2014). Narcissists realize that they see themselves more positively than others see them and admit that they are arrogant and exaggerate their abilities (Carlson et al., 2011). They also recognize that they make good first impressions but are often actively disliked in the long run (Paulhus, 1998; Paulhus et al., 2013). But, to a narcissist, that's not their fault.

Self-Efficacy

self-efficacy
A sense that one is competent and effective, distinguished from self-esteem, which is one's sense of self-worth. A sharpshooter in the military might feel high self-efficacy and low self-esteem.

Stanford psychologist Albert Bandura (1997, 2000, 2008, 2018) captured the power of positive thinking in his research and theorizing about **self-efficacy** (how competent we feel on a task). Believing in our own competence and effectiveness pays dividends (Bandura et al., 1999; Maddux & Gosselin, 2003). Children and adults with strong feelings of self-efficacy are more persistent, less anxious, and less depressed. They also live healthier lives and are more academically successful (Stajkovic et al., 2018).

In everyday life, self-efficacy leads us to set challenging goals and to persist. More than 100 studies show that self-efficacy predicts worker productivity (Stajkovic & Luthans, 1998). The results of 241 studies show that performance self-efficacy is one of the strongest predictors of students' GPAs in college (Richardson et al., 2012). The causation goes both ways: Although good academic performance causes self-efficacy, self-efficacy also causes better academic performance (Talsma et al., 2018). When problems arise, a strong sense of self-efficacy leads people to stay calm and seek solutions rather than ruminate on their inadequacy. Competence plus persistence equals accomplishment. And with accomplishment, self-confidence grows.

Someone who thinks, "If I work hard, I can swim fast" has high self-efficacy. Someone who thinks, "I am a great swimmer" has high self-esteem.
Dean Drobot/Shutterstock

Self-efficacy and self-esteem sound similar but are different concepts. If you believe you can do something, that's self-efficacy. If you like yourself overall, that's self-esteem. When you were a child, your parents may have encouraged you by saying things such as, "You're special!" (intended to build self-esteem) or "I know you can do it!" (intended to build self-efficacy). One study showed that self-efficacy feedback ("You tried really hard") led to better performance than self-esteem feedback ("You're really smart"). Children told they were smart were afraid to try again; maybe they wouldn't look so smart next time.

Those praised for working hard, however, knew they could exert more effort again (Mueller & Dweck, 1998). If you want to encourage someone, focus on their self-efficacy, not their self-esteem.

SUMMING UP: What Is the Nature and Motivating Power of Self-Esteem?

- *Self-esteem* is the overall sense of self-worth we use to appraise our traits and abilities. Our self-concepts are determined by multiple influences, including the roles we play, the comparisons we make, our social identities, how we perceive others appraising us, and our experiences of success and failure.
- Self-esteem motivation influences our cognitive processes: Facing failure, people high in self-esteem sustain their self-worth by perceiving other people as failing, too, and by exaggerating their superiority over others.
- Although high self-esteem is generally more beneficial than low, researchers have found that people high in both self-esteem and *narcissism* are the most aggressive. Someone with a big ego who is threatened or deflated by social rejection is potentially aggressive.
- *Self-efficacy* is the belief that one is effective and competent and can do something. Unlike high self-esteem, high self-efficacy is consistently linked to success.

WHAT IS SELF-SERVING BIAS?

Explain self-serving bias and its adaptive and maladaptive aspects.

Most of us have a good reputation with ourselves. In a study including 53 nations, the average self-esteem score was above the midpoint in every country (Schmitt & Allik, 2005). One of social psychology's most provocative yet firmly established conclusions is the potency of **self-serving bias** – a tendency to perceive oneself favorably.

self-serving bias
The tendency to perceive oneself favorably.

Explaining Positive and Negative Events

Many dozens of experiments have found that people accept credit when told they have succeeded. They attribute success to their ability and effort, but they attribute failure to external factors, such as bad luck or the problem's inherent "impossibility" (Campbell & Sedikides, 1999; Wang et al., 2017). Similarly, in explaining their victories, athletes commonly credit themselves, but they attribute losses to something else: bad breaks, bad referee calls, or the other team's super effort or dirty play (Allen et al., 2020; Grove et al., 1991; Lalonde, 1992). And how much responsibility do you suppose car drivers tend to accept for their accidents? On insurance forms, drivers have described their accidents by writing, "An invisible car came out of nowhere, struck my car, and vanished"; "As I reached an intersection, a hedge sprang up, obscuring my vision, and I did not see the other car"; and "A pedestrian hit me and went under my car" (*Toronto News,* 1977).

"Victory finds a hundred fathers but defeat is an orphan."

—Count Galeazzo Ciano, *The Ciano Diaries,* 1938

Situations that combine skill and chance (games, exams, and job applications) are especially prone to the phenomenon. When you win at Scrabble, it's because of your verbal dexterity; when you lose, it's because "Who could get anywhere with a *Q* but no *U?*" Politicians similarly tend to attribute their wins to themselves (hard work, constituent service, reputation, and strategy) and their losses to factors beyond their control (their district's party makeup, their opponent's name, and political trends) (Kingdon, 1967). When corporate profits are up, the CEOs welcome big bonuses for their managerial skill. When profits turn to losses, well, what could you expect in a down economy? This phenomenon of **self-serving attributions** (attributing positive outcomes to oneself and negative outcomes to something else) is one of the most potent of human biases

self-serving attributions
A form of self-serving bias; the tendency to attribute positive outcomes to oneself and negative outcomes to other factors.

Self-serving bias at work. If a team loses a game, a player who received a critical penalty might blame the referee's call instead of their own lackluster play.
Steven Markham/Speed Media/Alamy Stock Photo

(Mezulis et al., 2004). That might be for a good reason: Making self-serving attributions activates brain areas associated with reward and pleasure (Seidel et al., 2010).

Self-serving attributions contribute to marital discord, worker dissatisfaction, and bargaining impasses (Kruger & Gilovich, 1999). Small wonder that divorced people usually blame their partner for the breakup (Gray & Silver, 1990), or that managers often blame poor performance on workers' lack of ability or effort, whereas workers blame external factors such as excessive workload or difficult co-workers (Imai, 1994; Rice, 1985). Small wonder, too, that people evaluate pay raises as fairer when they receive a bigger raise than most of their co-workers (Diekmann et al., 1997).

We help maintain our positive self-images by associating ourselves with success and distancing ourselves from failure. For example, "I got an A on my econ test" versus "The prof gave me a C on my history exam." Blaming failure or rejection on something external, even another's prejudice, is less depressing than seeing oneself as undeserving (Major et al., 2003). Journalists were more likely to write that "we" (people like them) had a positive outcome but "they" (those different from them) had a negative one (Sendén et al., 2014). Most people will, however, acknowledge their distant past failings – those by their "former" self, noted Anne Wilson and Michael Ross (2001). Describing their old precollege selves, their University of Waterloo students offered nearly as many negative as positive statements. When describing their present selves, they offered three times more positive statements. "I've learned and grown, and I'm a better person today," most people surmise. Chumps yesterday, champs today.

"I never blame myself when I'm not hitting. I just blame the bat and if it keeps up, I change bats."

—Baseball great Yogi Berra

Ironically, we are even biased against seeing our own bias. People claim they avoid self-serving bias themselves but readily acknowledge that others commit this bias (Pronin et al., 2002). This "bias blind spot" can have serious consequences during conflicts. If you're negotiating with your roommate over who does household chores and you believe your roommate has a biased view of the situation, you're much more likely to become angry (Pronin & Ross, 2006). Apparently, we see ourselves as objective and everyone else as biased. No wonder we fight: We're each convinced we're "right" and free from bias. As the T-shirt slogan says, "Everyone is entitled to my opinion."

Is self-serving bias universal, or are people in collectivistic cultures immune? Those in collectivistic cultures do associate themselves with positive words and valued traits (Gaertner et al., 2008; Yamaguchi et al., 2007). However, in some studies, collectivists are less likely to self-enhance by believing they are better than others (Church et al., 2014; Falk et al., 2009; Heine & Hamamura, 2007), particularly in individualistic domains such as leadership or individual achievement (Sedikides et al., 2003, 2005).

Can We All Be Better Than Average?

Self-serving bias also appears when people compare themselves with others. If the sixth-century BCE Chinese philosopher Lao-tzu was right that "at no time in the world will a man who is sane over-reach himself, over-spend himself, over-rate himself," then most of us are a little insane. On *subjective, socially desirable,* and *common dimensions,* most people see themselves as better than the average person – as more ethical, more competent at their job, friendlier, more intelligent, better looking, less prejudiced, healthier, and even more insightful and less biased in their self-assessments (Zell et al., 2020). Even men convicted of violent crimes rated themselves as more moral, kind, and trustworthy than most people (Taylor et al., 2021). (See "Focus On: Self-Serving Bias – How Do I Love Me? Let Me Count the Ways.")

focus ON Self-Serving Bias — How Do I Love Me? Let Me Count the Ways

"The one thing that unites all human beings, regardless of age, gender, religion, economic status, or ethnic background," noted columnist Dave Barry (1998), "is that deep down inside, we all believe that we are above average drivers." We also believe we are above average on most subjective and desirable traits. Among the many faces of self-serving bias are these:

- *Ethics.* Most people see themselves as more moral than others (Han & Kim, 2022). One national survey asked, "How would you rate your own morals and values on a scale from 1 to 100 (100 being perfect)?" Fifty percent of people rated themselves 90 or above; only 11% said 74 or less (Lovett, 1997).
- *Professional competence.* In Australia, 86% of people rated their job performance as above average and only 1% as below average (Headey & Wearing, 1987). Most surgeons believe *their* patients' mortality rate to be lower than average (Gawande, 2002).
- *Virtues.* Most people believe they are more likely than others to donate blood, give to charity, and give one's bus seat to a pregnant woman (Klein & Epley, 2017).
- *Preventing infection.* During the COVID-19 pandemic, the majority of people believed they were taking more precautions against infection than the average person (Kulesza et al., 2023; Mojzisch et al., 2022).
- *Concern for the environment.* Across the United States, the United Kingdom, and India, most people believe they are more pro-environmental than others — in both their attitudes and behaviors (Bergquist, 2020).
- *Voting.* When asked if they would vote in an upcoming election, 90% of students said they would but guessed that only 75% of their peers would vote. The actual result? Sixty-nine percent voted (Epley & Dunning, 2006). We are better at predicting others' socially desirable behaviors than our own.
- *Intelligence.* Most people perceive themselves as more intelligent, better looking, and much less prejudiced than their average peer (Watt & Larkin, 2010; Wylie, 1979).
- *Attractiveness.* Is it your experience, as it is mine [DM], that most photos of you seem not to do you justice? One experiment showed people a lineup of faces: one their own and the others being their face morphed into those of less and more attractive faces (Epley & Whitchurch, 2008). When asked which was their actual face, people tended to identify an attractively enhanced version of their face (Walker & Keller, 2019). People also judge themselves as thinner than those with their same body type. (Mazzurega et al., 2018).
- *Driving.* Most drivers — even most drivers who have been hospitalized for accidents — believe themselves to be safer and more skilled than the average driver (Koppel et al., 2023; Svenson, 1981). Dave Barry was right.

Every community, it seems, is like the fictional Lake Wobegon, where "all the women are strong, all the men are good-looking, and all the children are above average." Many people believe that they will become even more above average in the future – if I'm good now, I will be even better soon, they seem to think (Kanten & Teigen, 2008). The phenomenon lurks in Freud's joke about the husband who told his wife, "If one of us dies, I shall move to Paris."

The self-serving bias is also common in marriages. In a 2008 survey, 49% of married men said they did half to most of the child care. But only 31% of wives said their husbands did that much. In the same survey, 70% of women said they do most of the cooking, but 56% of the men said *they* do most of the cooking (Galinsky et al., 2009).

My wife and I [DM] used to pitch our laundry on the floor next to our bedroom clothes hamper. In the morning, one of us would put it in. When she suggested that I take more responsibility for this, I thought, "Huh? I already do it 75% of the time." So I asked her how often she thought she picked up the clothes. "Oh," she replied, "about 75% of the time."

The general rule: Group members' estimates of how much they contribute to a joint task typically sum to more than 100% (Savitsky et al., 2005). That's particularly true in large groups, a situation in which people are unaware of the contributions of many others (Schroeder et al., 2016).

Who's watching the kids? Dads think they do it half the time, but moms disagree.
Fabrice Lerouge/SuperStock

Self-serving bias is usually stronger for traits that are more subjective or difficult to measure. Seventy-five percent of college students in 2019 believed they were above average in "drive to achieve" (a more subjective attribute), but only 44% thought they were above average in the more quantifiable realm of math ability (Stolzenberg et al., 2020). In one College Entrance Examination Board survey of 829,000 high school seniors, *none* rated themselves below average in "ability to get along with others" (a subjective, desirable trait), 60% rated themselves in the top 10%, and 25% saw themselves among the top 1%! Subjective qualities give us leeway in constructing our own definition of success (Dunning et al., 1989, 1991). When I [JT] consider my athletic ability, I can focus on my swimming ability and choose to forget about the evenings I spent cowering in the softball outfield hoping no one would hit the ball my way.

Researchers have wondered: Do people really believe their above-average self-estimates? When Elanor Williams and Thomas Gilovich (2008) had people bet real money when estimating their relative performance on tests, they found that, yes, "people truly believe their self-enhancing self-assessments." Even when they put their money where their mouth is, self-serving bias endures.

Unrealistic Optimism

Optimism predisposes a positive approach to life. "The optimist," noted H. Jackson Brown (1990, p. 79), "goes to the window every morning and says, 'Good morning, God.' The pessimist goes to the window and says, 'Good God, morning.'"

Studies of more than 90,000 people across 22 cultures reveal that most humans are more disposed to optimism than pessimism (Fischer & Chalmers, 2008; Shepperd et al., 2013, 2015). Indeed, many of us have what researcher Neil Weinstein (1980, 1982) terms "an unrealistic optimism about future life events." Partly because of their relative pessimism about others' fates (Hoorens et al., 2008; Shepperd, 2003), students perceive themselves as far more likely than their classmates to get a good job, draw a good salary, and own a home. They also see themselves as far *less* likely to experience negative events, such as developing a drinking problem, having a heart attack before age 40, or being fired. In an international survey conducted in March 2020 during the coronavirus pandemic, 45% of participants believed that the average person might spread the virus if they traveled while infected – but only 25% thought that they themselves would spread the disease if they traveled (Kuper-Smith et al., 2020).

"Views of the future are so rosy that they would make Pollyanna blush."

—Shelley E. Taylor, *Positive Illusions*, 1989

Illusory optimism. Most couples marry feeling confident of long-term love. Actually, in individualistic cultures, about half of marriages fail.
Studio Zanello/Streetstock Images/Blend Images/Getty Images

Illusory optimism increases our vulnerability. Believing ourselves immune to misfortune, we do not take sensible precautions. People trying to quit smoking who believe they are above average in willpower are more likely to keep cigarettes around and stand near others who are smoking – behaviors likely to lead to a relapse into smoking (Nordgren et al., 2009). Elderly people who rated themselves as "above average" drivers were four times more likely than more modest drivers to flunk a driving test and be rated "unsafe" (Freund et al., 2005). Students who enter university with inflated assessments of their academic ability often suffer deflating self-esteem and well-being and are more likely to drop out (Robins & Beer, 2001).

They might initially believe they are so smart they don't need to study, but are quickly proven wrong.

On the other hand, optimism definitely beats pessimism in promoting self-efficacy, health, and well-being (Armor & Taylor, 1996; Segerstrom, 2001). As natural optimists, most people believe they will be happier with their lives in the future – a belief that surely helps create happiness in the present (Robinson & Ryff, 1999). Pessimists even die sooner – apparently because they are more likely to suffer unfortunate accidents as well as being more likely to have depression or heart disease (Peterson et al., 2001). Generally speaking, people who are unrealistically positive about themselves are usually happier, more satisfied with their lives, and less likely to be depressed (Dufner et al., 2019).

Yet a dash of realism – or what Julie Norem (2000) calls **defensive pessimism** – can sometimes save us from the perils of unrealistic optimism. Defensive pessimism anticipates problems and motivates effective coping. As a Chinese proverb says, "Be prepared for danger while staying in peace." Students who exhibit too much optimism do better at school when they acquire some self-doubt, motivating them to study (Prohaska, 1994; Sparrell & Shrauger, 1984). Students who are overconfident tend to underprepare, whereas their less confident peers study harder and get higher grades (Goodhart, 1986; Norem & Cantor, 1986; Showers & Ruben, 1987). In a longitudinal study of British adults, both those with overly pessimistic and those with overly optimistic expectations about their incomes later experienced declines in mental health (de Meza & Dawson, 2021). Neither being inevitably disappointed (as optimists are) and always expecting doom (as pessimists do) is conducive to happiness.

defensive pessimism
The adaptive value of anticipating problems and harnessing one's anxiety to motivate effective action.

It's also important to listen to criticism. "One gentle rule I often tell my students," wrote David Dunning (2006), "is that if two people independently give them the same piece of negative feedback, they should at least consider the possibility that it might be true." So, there is a power to balancing negative and positive thinking. The moral: Success in school and beyond requires enough optimism to sustain hope and enough pessimism to motivate concern.

"O God, give us grace to accept with serenity the things that cannot be changed, courage to change the things which should be changed, and the wisdom to distinguish the one from the other."

—Reinhold Niebuhr, "The Serenity Prayer," 1943

False Consensus and Uniqueness

We have a curious tendency to enhance our self-images by overestimating or underestimating how much others think and act as we do. On matters of *opinion,* we find support for our positions by overestimating how much others agree – a phenomenon called the **false consensus effect** (Krueger & Clement, 1994b; Marks & Miller, 1987; Welborn et al., 2017). In the summer before the 2020 U.S. presidential election, 83% of Democrats believed voters would elect their candidate, Joe Biden. Simultaneously, 84% of Republicans believed voters would reelect *their* candidate, Donald Trump (UMich, 2020). People who believe in conspiracy theories massively overestimate how common their beliefs are; in one study, the majority of people believed only 12% of the theories offered, but true believers thought they were in the majority 93% of the time (Pennycook et al., 2023). The sense we make of the world seems like common sense.

false consensus effect
The tendency to overestimate the commonality of one's opinions and one's undesirable or unsuccessful behaviors.

When we behave badly or fail in a task, we reassure ourselves by thinking that such lapses also are common. After one person lies to another, the liar begins to perceive the *other* person as dishonest (Sagarin et al., 1998). We guess that others think and act as we do: "I lie, but doesn't everyone?" If we cheat on our income taxes, smoke, or get plastic surgery, we are likely to overestimate the number of other people who do likewise, finds the research. When U.S. Representative George Santos admitted to lying about his education and job experience, he claimed that "we wouldn't have a single congressman in the House" if their backgrounds were also examined (Francis & Goodwin, 2022). "We don't see things as they are," says a proverb. "We see things as we are."

Robyn Dawes (1990) proposed that this false consensus may occur because we generalize from a limited sample, which prominently includes ourselves. Lacking other information, why not "project" ourselves; why not impute our own knowledge to others and use our responses as a clue to their likely responses? Also, we're more likely to spend time with

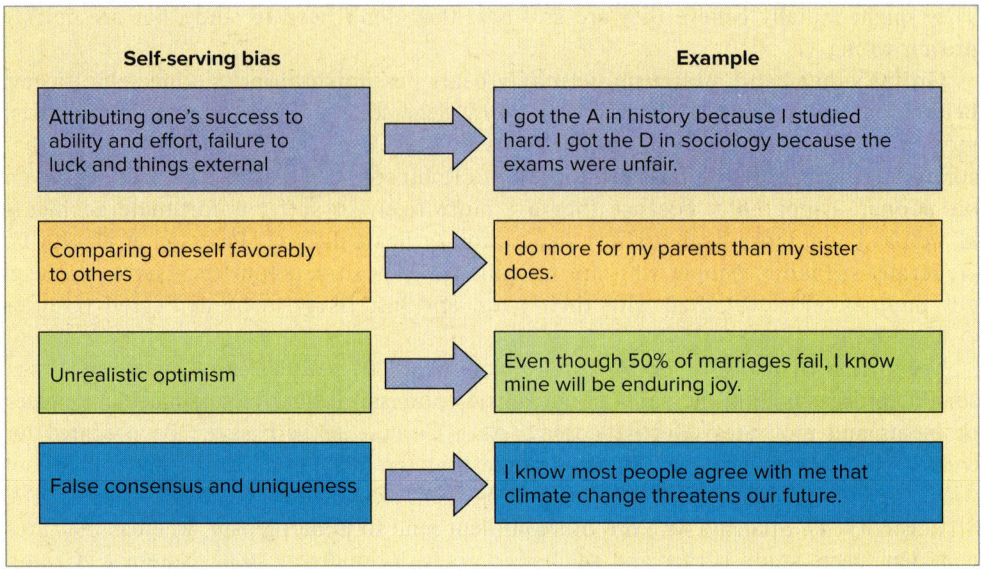

FIGURE 6
How Self-Serving Bias Works

people who share our attitudes and behaviors and, consequently, to judge the world from the people we know. Small wonder that Germans tend to think that the typical European looks rather German, whereas the Portuguese see Europeans as looking more Portuguese (Imhoff et al., 2011).

false uniqueness effect
The tendency to underestimate the commonality of one's abilities and one's desirable or successful behaviors.

On matters of *ability* or when we behave well or successfully, however, a **false uniqueness effect** more often occurs (Goethals et al., 1991). We serve our self-image by seeing our talents and moral behaviors as relatively unusual. Dutch college students preferred being part of a larger group in matters of opinion such as politics (false consensus) but wanted to be part of a smaller group in matters of taste such as musical preferences (false uniqueness; Spears et al., 2009). After all, a band isn't cool anymore if too many people like it. Female college students who chose a designated driver underestimated how many other women take the same precaution (Benton et al., 2008). Thus, we may see our failings as relatively normal and our virtues as relatively exceptional.

"Always remember that you are absolutely unique. Just like everyone else."

—Anonymous, sometimes attributed to Jim Wright

To sum up, self-serving bias appears as self-serving attributions, self-congratulatory comparisons, illusory optimism, and false consensus for one's failings (**Figure 6**).

Explaining Self-Serving Bias

Why do people perceive themselves in self-enhancing ways? Perhaps the self-serving bias occurs because of errors in how we process and remember information about ourselves. Comparing ourselves with others requires us to notice, assess, and recall their behavior and ours. This creates multiple opportunities for flaws in our information processing (Chambers & Windschitl, 2004). Recall that married people gave themselves credit for doing more housework than their spouses did. That might occur because we remember what we've done but not what our partner did (Kahneman & Deaton, 2010). I [DM] could easily picture myself picking up the laundry off the bedroom floor, but I was less aware of the times when I absentmindedly overlooked it.

"Other men's sins are before our eyes; our own are behind our back."

—Seneca, *De Ira*, AD 43

Are biased perceptions, then, simply a perceptual error, an emotion-free glitch in how we process information? Or are self-serving *motives* also involved? It's now clear from the research that we have multiple motives. Questing for self-knowledge, we're motivated to *assess our competence* (Dunning, 1995). Questing for self-confirmation, we're motivated to *verify our self-conceptions* (Sanitioso et al., 1990; Swann, 1996, 1997). Questing for self-affirmation, we're especially motivated to *enhance our self-image* (Sedikides, 1993). Trying to increase self-esteem, then, helps power our self-serving bias. As social psychologist Daniel Batson (2006) said, "The head is an extension of the heart."

SUMMING UP: What Is Self-Serving Bias?

- Contrary to the presumption that most people suffer from low self-esteem or feelings of inferiority, researchers consistently find that most people exhibit a *self-serving bias.* In experiments and everyday life, we often take credit for our successes while blaming failures on the situation.
- Most people rate themselves as better than average on subjective, desirable traits and abilities.
- We exhibit unrealistic optimism about our futures.
- We overestimate the commonality of our opinions and foibles (*false consensus*) while underestimating the commonality of our abilities and virtues (*false uniqueness*).
- Such perceptions arise partly from a motive to maintain and enhance self-esteem – a motive that protects people from depression but contributes to misjudgment and group conflict.
- Self-serving bias can be adaptive in that it allows us to savor the good things that happen in our lives. When bad things happen, however, self-serving bias can have the maladaptive effect of causing us to blame others or feel cheated out of something we "deserved."

HOW DO PEOPLE MANAGE THEIR SELF-PRESENTATION?

Define self-presentation and describe how impression management influences our behavior.

So far, we have seen that the self is at the center of our social worlds, that self-esteem and self-efficacy pay some dividends, and that self-serving bias influences self-evaluations. Perhaps you have wondered: Are self-enhancing expressions always sincere? Do people have the same feelings privately as they express publicly, or are they just putting on a positive face even while living with self-doubt?

Self-Handicapping

Sometimes people sabotage their chances for success by creating impediments that make success less likely – known as **self-handicapping.**

self-handicapping
Protecting one's self-image with behaviors that create a handy excuse for later failure.

Imagine yourself in the position of the Duke University participants of Steven Berglas and Edward Jones (1978). You guess answers to some difficult cognitive ability questions and are told, "Yours was one of the best scores seen to date!" Feeling incredibly lucky, you are then offered a choice of taking one of two drugs before answering more of these challenging questions. One drug will aid intellectual performance and the other will inhibit it. Which drug do you want? Most students wanted the drug that would supposedly disrupt their thinking, thus providing a handy excuse for doing badly.

"If you try to fail, and succeed, what have you done?"

—Anonymous

Researchers have documented other ways people self-handicap. Fearing failure, people will

- leave schoolwork to the last minute so they can use procrastination as an excuse for poor performance (Yu & McLellan, 2019);
- reduce their preparation for important athletic events (Finez et al., 2012; Rhodewalt et al., 1984);
- go out with friends the night before an important presentation instead of practicing (Shin & Park, 2021); and
- perform poorly at the beginning of a task to not create overly high expectations (Baumgardner & Brownlee, 1987).

"After losing to some younger rivals, tennis great Martina Navratilova confessed that she was 'afraid to play my best. . . . I was scared to find out if they could beat me when I'm playing my best because if they can, then I am finished.'"

—Frankel & Snyder (1987)

Far from being deliberately self-destructive, such behaviors typically have a self-protective aim (Arkin et al., 1986; Baumeister & Scher, 1988; Rhodewalt, 1987): "I'm really not a failure – I would have done well except for this problem." Unfortunately, this strategy

Group identity. In Asian countries, self-presentation is restrained. Children learn to identify themselves with their groups.
imtmphoto/Shutterstock

usually backfires: Students who self-handicap end up with lower GPAs (Schwinger et al., 2014).

Why would people handicap themselves with self-defeating behaviors? Recall that we eagerly protect our self-images by attributing failures to external factors. Thus, *fearing failure,* people might handicap themselves by partying half the night before a job interview or playing video games instead of studying before a big exam (Schwinger et al., 2022). When self-image is tied up with performance, it can be more self-deflating to try hard and fail than to procrastinate and have a ready excuse. If we fail while handicapped in some way, we can cling to a sense of competence; if we succeed under such conditions, it can only boost our self-image. Handicaps protect both self-esteem and public image by allowing us to attribute failures to something temporary or external ("I was feeling sick"; "I was out too late the night before") rather than to lack of talent or ability.

Impression Management

Self-serving bias, false modesty, and self-handicapping reveal the depth of our concern for self-image. To varying degrees, we are continually managing the impressions we create. Whether we wish to impress, intimidate, or seem helpless, we are social animals, playing to an audience (McFarland et al., 2023). So great is the human desire for social acceptance that it can lead people to risk harming themselves through smoking, binge eating, premature sex, or drug and alcohol abuse (Rawn & Vohs, 2011).

self-presentation
The act of expressing oneself and behaving in ways designed to create a favorable impression or an impression that corresponds to one's ideals.

Self-presentation refers to our wanting to present a desired image both to an external audience (other people) and to an internal audience (ourselves). We work at managing the impressions we create. We try to appear successful and agreeable to shore up our self-esteem and verify our self-images (Schlenker & Weigold, 1992). At the same time, we also must make sure not to brag too much and risk the disapproval of others (Anderson et al., 2006). Social interaction is a careful balance of seeming successful but not seeming *too* successful. That seems to be particularly true in collectivistic cultures, where modesty is a "default strategy" to avoid offending others. When there was no risk of offense, Japanese participants self-enhanced as much as Americans (Yamagishi et al., 2012).

One self-presentation strategy is the "humblebrag," an attempt to disguise bragging behind complaints or false humility ("I still can't believe I was the one who got the job out of 300 applicants!" "No makeup and I still get hit on!"). One study found that humblebragging usually backfires, failing to either convey humility or impress others (Sezer et al., 2018). Social media influencers who humblebrag damage the perception of brands they endorse—though celebrities can usually get away with it (Paramita et al., 2021).

In the age of the selfie, self-presentation can be a nearly constant concern.
Peter Bernik/mindof/123RF

In familiar situations, self-presentation happens without conscious effort. In unfamiliar situations, perhaps at a party with people we would like to impress or in conversation with a crush, we are acutely self-conscious of the impressions we are creating and we are therefore less modest than when among friends who know us well (Leary et al., 1994; Tice et al., 1995). Fortunately, most people make a better first impression than they think (Elsaadawy & Carlson, 2022). In addition, self-presentation can unexpectedly improve mood. People felt significantly better than they thought they would after doing their best to make a positive impression on their romantic partner. Elizabeth Dunn and colleagues (2008) concluded that "date nights" for long-term couples work because they encourage active self-presentation, which improves mood.

Social media sites such as Instagram provide a new and sometimes intense venue for self-presentation. They are, said communications professor Joseph Walther, "like impression management on steroids" (Rosenbloom, 2008). Users make careful decisions about which pictures, activities, and interests to highlight in their profiles. Especially for teen girls and young women, self-presentation on social media revolves around choosing the right pose and the right selfie (Veldhuis et al., 2020), a process that sometimes leads to anxiety (Mills et al., 2018; Zimmer-Gembeck et al., 2021).

"Hmmm...what shall I wear today...?"

Mike Marland

Given the concern for self-presentation, it's no wonder people will self-handicap when a failure might make them look bad. It's no wonder that people take health risks—tanning their skin with wrinkle- and cancer-causing radiation; having piercings or tattoos done without proper hygiene; becoming anorexic; or yielding to peer pressures to smoke, get drunk, and do drugs (Leary et al., 1994). It's no wonder that people express more modesty when their self-flattery is vulnerable to being debunked, perhaps by experts scrutinizing their self-descriptions (Arkin et al., 1980; Riess et al., 1981; Weary et al., 1982). Professor Smith will likely express more modesty about the significance of her work when presenting it to professional colleagues than when presenting it to students—her colleagues will have the ammunition to shoot her down.

For some people, conscious self-presentation is a way of life. They continually monitor their own behavior and note how others react, then adjust their social performance to gain a desired effect. Those who score high on a scale of **self-monitoring** (who, for example, agree that "I tend to be what people expect me to be") act like social chameleons: They use self-presentation to adjust their behavior in response to external situations (Gangestad & Snyder, 2000; Snyder, 1987; Tyler et al., 2015). As Mark Leary (2004b) observed, the self they know often differs from the self they show. As social chameleons, those who score high in self-monitoring are also less committed to their relationships and more likely to be dissatisfied in their marriages (Leone & Hawkins, 2006). On the other hand, high self-monitors may rack up more connections online. For example, they post more on social media and are more likely to seek and receive "likes" (Hall & Pennington, 2013; Wallace & Buil, 2023).

self-monitoring
Being attuned to the way one presents oneself in social situations and adjusting one's performance to create the desired impression.

Those low in self-monitoring care less about what others think. They are more internally guided and thus more likely to talk and act as they feel and believe (McCann & Hancock, 1983). For example, they are more likely to end a friendship if they feel they and their friend are no longer compatible (Leone & Yoho, 2022). As you might imagine, someone who is extremely low in self-monitoring could come across as an insensitive boor, whereas extremely high self-monitoring could result in dishonest behavior worthy of a con artist. Most of us fall somewhere between those two extremes.

"Public opinion is always more tyrannical towards those who obviously fear it than towards those who feel indifferent to it."

—Bertrand Russell, *The Conquest of Happiness*, 1930

SUMMING UP: How Do People Manage Their Self-Presentation?

- As social animals, we adjust our words and actions to suit our audiences. To varying degrees, we note our performance and adjust it to create the impressions we desire.
- Sometimes people *self-handicap* with self-defeating behaviors that protect self-esteem by providing excuses for failure.
- *Self-presentation* refers to our wanting to present a favorable image both to an external audience (other people) and to an internal audience (ourselves). With regard to an external audience, those who score high on a scale of *self-monitoring* adjust their behavior to each situation, whereas those low in self-monitoring may do so little social adjusting that they seem insensitive.

CONCLUDING THOUGHTS: Twin Truths — The Perils of Pride, the Powers of Positive Thinking

This chapter offered two memorable truths: the truth of self-efficacy and the truth of self-serving bias. The truth concerning self-efficacy encourages us not to resign ourselves to bad situations. We need to persist despite initial failures and to exert effort without being overly distracted by self-doubts. When we believe in our positive possibilities, we are less vulnerable to depression and we feel less insecure.

Thus, it's important to think positively and try hard but to not be so self-confident that our goals are illusory or we alienate others with our narcissism. Taking self-efficacy too far leads to blaming the victim: If positive thinking can accomplish anything, then we have only ourselves to blame if we are unhappily married, poor, or depressed. For shame! If only we had tried harder, been more disciplined, less stupid. This viewpoint fails to acknowledge that bad things can happen to good people. Life's greatest achievements, but also its greatest disappointments, are born of the highest expectations.

These twin truths – self-efficacy and self-serving bias – remind us of what Pascal taught 300 years ago: No single truth is ever sufficient because the world is complex. Any truth separated from its complementary truth is a half-truth.

Social Beliefs and Judgments

PeopleImages/DigitalVision/Getty Images

CHAPTER

3

There is curious power to partisanship. Consider U.S. politics:

- While 70% of Democrats said it was "very important" to find out what happened during the January 6, 2021 attack on the U.S. Capitol, only 21% of Republicans agreed. The majority of Republicans, 52%, said the investigation was "not important at all" (DePinto et al., 2022).
- In a 2020 poll, 82% of Democrats said the government (led by Republican president Donald Trump) was doing a poor job of handling the COVID-19 pandemic. In contrast, 80% of Republicans said it was doing a good job (Agiesta, 2020).
- When asked if protection of the environment should be given priority even at the risk of curbing economic growth, 78% of Democrats say yes, compared to 20% of Republicans (Jones, 2023).
- When a Democrat is president, Democrats say presidents can't do anything about high gas prices. Republicans say the same when a Republican is president. But when the president is from the other party, people in both parties believe presidents *can* affect gas prices (Vedantam, 2012).

"Motivated reasoning" — such as a gut-level liking or disliking of certain politicians — can powerfully influence how we interpret evidence and view reality. Partisanship predisposes perceptions — and perceptions predict partisanship. As an old a proverb says, "Two-thirds of what we see is behind our eyes."

The differing responses of those with different beliefs, findings replicated in political perceptions throughout the world, illustrate how we construct social perceptions and beliefs as we

- *judge* events, informed by implicit rules that guide our snap judgments, and by our moods;
- *perceive* and recall events through the filters of our own assumptions;
- *explain* events by sometimes attributing them to the situation, sometimes to the person; and
- *expect* certain events, thereby sometimes helping bring them about.

This chapter explores how we judge, perceive, and explain our social worlds and why our expectations matter.

HOW DO WE JUDGE OUR SOCIAL WORLDS, CONSCIOUSLY AND UNCONSCIOUSLY?

Describe how judgments are influenced by both unconscious and conscious systems.

System 1
The intuitive, automatic, unconscious, and fast way of thinking. Also known as automatic processing.

System 2
The deliberate, controlled, conscious, and slower way of thinking. Also known as controlled processing.

priming
Activating particular associations in memory.

We have two brain systems, noted Nobel Prize winner Daniel Kahneman in *Thinking, Fast and Slow* (2011). **System 1** functions automatically and out of our awareness (it's often called "intuition" or a "gut feeling"), whereas **System 2** requires our conscious attention and effort. System 1 influences more of our actions than we realize. For example, small reminders can influence our thinking without our knowing it, a process called priming. That's what we discuss next.

Priming

Things we don't even consciously notice can subtly influence how we interpret and recall events. Imagine wearing earphones and concentrating on ambiguous spoken sentences such as "We stood by the bank." When a related word (*river* or *money*) is simultaneously sent to your other ear, you don't consciously hear it. Yet the unheard word "primes" your interpretation of the sentence, much as reading this figure (below) from top-down or from left to right primes your interpretation of the central character (Baars & McGovern, 1994).

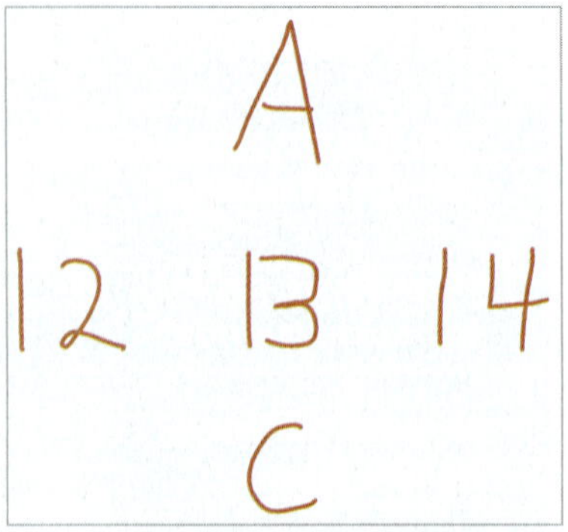

Try reading the above horizontally—what is the middle symbol? Now try reading it vertically and see if your perception changes.

Our memory system is a web of associations, and **priming** is the awakening or activating of certain associations. Experiments show that priming one thought, even without awareness, can influence another thought, or even an action (Herring et al., 2013). In a host of studies, priming effects occur even when the stimuli are presented subliminally — too briefly to be perceived consciously. What's out of sight may not be completely out of mind. If the word "bread" is flashed so briefly that it's just below your conscious awareness, you'll detect a related word like "butter" more quickly than an unrelated word like "bubble" (Epley et al., 1999; Merikle et al., 2001). Religious people subliminally exposed to words associated with religion are more likely to help others (Shariff et al., 2016). Students were more likely to wobble on a balance beam in a room with posters of beer and vodka as opposed to posters showing an apple or orange juice (Cox et al., 2014). In each case, an invisible or background image or word primes a response to a later task.

Unnoticed events can also subtly prime our thinking and behavior. Rob Holland and colleagues (2005) observed that Dutch students exposed to the scent of an all-purpose cleaner were quicker to identify cleaning-related words, recalled more cleaning-related activities when describing their day, and even kept their desk cleaner while eating a crumbly cookie. Another team of Dutch psychologists found that people exposed to the scent of a cleaning product were less likely to litter (de Lange et al., 2012). All these effects occurred without the participants' conscious awareness of the scent and its influence.

Priming experiments have their counterparts in everyday life, reported John Bargh (2006):

- Watching a scary movie alone at home can activate emotions that, without our realizing it, cause us to interpret furnace noises as a possible intruder. I [JT] experienced a version of this: Returning to my New Orleans hotel room after a "ghost tour," a shadow I hadn't noticed before looked ominous. Further inspection yielded not a ghost but an end table at a strange angle.
- Depressed moods tend to prime negative associations. But put people in a *good* mood and suddenly their past seems more wonderful, their future brighter.
- For many psychology students, reading about psychological disorders primes how they interpret their own anxieties and gloomy moods. Reading about disease symptoms similarly primes medical students to worry about their congestion, fever, or headache.

Studies of how implanted ideas and images can prime our interpretations and recall illustrate one of this book's take-home lessons: *Much of our social information processing is automatic.* It is unintentional, out of sight, and happens without our conscious awareness – relying on System 1.

Even physical sensations, thanks to our **embodied cognition,** prime our social judgments and vice versa:

embodied cognition
The mutual influence of bodily sensations on cognitive preferences and social judgments.

- After assessing a cold person, people judge the room as colder than those assessing a warm person (Szymkow et al., 2013; Zhong & Leonardelli, 2008). People who ate alone judged room temperature as colder than those who ate with others (Lee et al., 2014). Social exclusion literally feels cold.
- When holding a *hard* rather than *soft* ball, people judge the same face as more likely to be Republican than Democrat, and more likely to be a physicist than a historian (Slepian et al., 2012).
- People who feel hopeless perceive rooms to be darker – they don't have a "ray of hope" (Dong et al., 2015).
- When sitting in a wobbly chair (vs. a stable one), people rate other couples' relationships as more unstable (Kille et al., 2013).
- Embodied cognition can also be social. When two people synchronize their bodies, as when dancing, singing, or walking together, they may also synchronize their spirits. As two walkers attend to their environment and coordinate their steps, mutual rapport and empathy increase and conflicts may resolve (Webb et al., 2017).

The bottom line: Our social cognition is embodied. The brain systems that process our bodily sensations communicate with the brain systems responsible for our social thinking.

Walking together can lead to thinking and empathizing together.
McGraw Hill

Intuitive Judgments

What are our powers of intuition – of immediately knowing something without reasoning or analysis? Advocates of "intuitive management" believe we should tune into our hunches – to use System 1. When judging others, they say, we should plug in to the nonlogical smarts of our "right brain." When hiring, firing, and investing, we should listen to our premonitions. In making judgments, we should trust the force within.

Are the intuitionists right that important information is immediately available apart from our conscious analysis? Or are the skeptics correct in saying that intuition is "our knowing we are right, whether we are or not" and in finding that self-described "intuitive" people are actually no better than others at tasks that assess intuition (Leach & Weick, 2018)?

THE POWERS OF INTUITION

"The heart has its reasons which reason does not know," observed seventeenth-century philosopher-mathematician Blaise Pascal. Three centuries later, scientists have proved Pascal correct. We know more than we know we know. Studies of our unconscious information processing confirm our limited access to what's going on in our minds (Bargh et al., 2012; Banaji & Greenwald, 2013; Strack & Deutsch, 2004). Our thinking is partly **automatic** (impulsive, effortless, and without our awareness – System 1) and partly **controlled** (reflective, deliberate, and conscious – System 2). Automatic, intuitive thinking occurs not "onscreen" but offscreen, out of sight, where reason does not go. Consider these examples of automatic thinking:

automatic thinking
"Implicit" thinking that is effortless, habitual, and without awareness; roughly corresponds to "intuition." Also known as System 1.

controlled thinking
"Explicit" thinking that is deliberate, reflective, and conscious. Also known as System 2.

- *Schemas* are mental concepts or templates that intuitively guide our perceptions and interpretations. Whether we hear someone speaking of religious *sects* or *sex* depends on how we automatically interpret the sound.
- *Emotional reactions* are often nearly instantaneous, happening before there is time for deliberate thinking. A neural shortcut takes information from the eye or the ear to the brain's sensory switchboard (the thalamus) and to its threat detection center (the amygdala) before the thinking cortex has had any chance to intervene (LeDoux, 2002, 2014). Our ancestors who intuitively feared a sound in the bushes were usually fearing nothing. But when they were right and the sound was made by a dangerous predator, they became more likely to survive and pass their genes down to us.
- Given sufficient *expertise,* people may intuitively know the answer to a problem. Many skills, from piano playing to swinging a golf club, begin as a controlled, deliberate process and gradually become automatic and intuitive (Kruglanski & Gigerenzer, 2011). Master chess players intuitively recognize meaningful patterns that novices miss and often make their next move with only a glance at the board, as the situation cues information stored in their memory. Similarly, without knowing quite how, we recognize a friend's voice after the first spoken word of a phone conversation.
- Given but a very small exposure to someone – even just a quick glance at their photo – people's *snap judgments* do better than chance at guessing whether someone is outgoing or shy, straight or gay (Rule, 2014). Merely by seeing politicians' headshot photos, voters can guess with surprising accuracy who won the election and which politicians later went on to be corrupt (Casey, 2022).

We remember some things – facts, names, and past experiences – explicitly (consciously) using System 2. But we remember other things – skills and conditioned dispositions – *implicitly* with System 1, without consciously knowing or declaring that we know. This is seen most vividly in people with brain damage who cannot form new explicit memories. One such person never could learn to recognize her doctor, who would need to reintroduce himself each day. One day, the doctor affixed a tack to his hand, causing the patient to jump with pain when they shook hands. When the physician next returned, the patient still didn't explicitly recognize him. But, due to her implicit memory, she wouldn't shake his hand (LeDoux, 1996).

Equally dramatic are cases of *blindsight.* Someone who has lost a portion of their visual cortex to surgery or stroke may be functionally blind in part of their field of vision. Shown a series of sticks in the blind field, they report seeing nothing. After guessing whether the sticks are vertical or horizontal, the patients are astounded when told, "You got them all right." Like the patient who "remembered" the painful handshake, these people know more than they know they know.

Consider your own taken-for-granted capacity to recognize a face. As you look at it, your brain breaks the visual information into dimensions such as color, depth, movement, and form, and works on each aspect simultaneously before reassembling the components. Finally, using automatic processing, your brain compares the perceived image with previously stored images. Voilà! Instantly and effortlessly, you recognize your grandmother. If intuition is immediately knowing something without reasoned analysis, then visual perception is excellent intuition.

Thus, many routine cognitive functions occur automatically, unintentionally, without awareness. Picture your mind functioning like a large corporation. The CEO – your controlled consciousness – attends to many of the most important, complex, and novel issues, while subordinates deal with routine affairs and matters requiring instant action. Like a CEO, consciousness sets goals and priorities, often with little knowledge of operational activities in the underlying departments. This delegation of resources enables us to react to many situations quickly and efficiently. The bottom line: Our brain knows much more than it tells us.

THE LIMITS OF INTUITION

We have seen how automatic, intuitive thinking can "make us smart" (Gigerenzer, 2007, 2010). Elizabeth Loftus and Mark Klinger (1992), like other cognitive scientists, nevertheless had doubts about the brilliance of intuition. "The unconscious," they wrote, "may not be as smart as previously believed." For example, although subliminal stimuli can trigger a weak, fleeting response – enough to evoke a feeling if not conscious awareness – there is no evidence that (for example) subliminal audio recordings can "reprogram your unconscious mind" for success. In fact, a significant body of evidence indicates that they can't (Greenwald, 1992).

In addition, humans have an incredible capacity for illusion – for perceptual misinterpretations, fantasies, and constructed beliefs. Michael Gazzaniga (1992, 1998, 2008) reported that patients whose brain hemispheres have been surgically separated will instantly fabricate – and believe – explanations of their own puzzling behaviors. If the patient gets up and takes a few steps after the experimenter flashes the instruction "walk" to the patient's nonverbal right hemisphere, the verbal left hemisphere will instantly provide the patient with a plausible explanation ("I felt like getting a drink").

Illusory intuition also appears in how we take in, store, and retrieve social information. As perception researchers study visual illusions for what they reveal about our normal perceptual mechanisms, social psychologists study illusory thinking for what it reveals about normal information processing. These researchers want to give us a map of everyday social thinking, with the hazards clearly marked.

As we examine these efficient thinking patterns, remember this: Demonstrations of how people create false beliefs do not prove that all beliefs are false (although to recognize falsification, it helps to know how it's done).

Overconfidence

So far we have seen that our cognitive systems process a vast amount of information efficiently and automatically. But our efficiency has a trade-off; as we interpret our experiences and construct memories, our automatic System 1 intuitions are sometimes wrong. Usually, we don't realize our errors – in other words, we display **overconfidence.**

overconfidence phenomenon
The tendency to be more confident than correct – to overestimate the accuracy of one's beliefs.

Daniel Kahneman and Amos Tversky (1979) gave people factual statements and asked them to fill in the blanks, as in the following sentence: "I feel 98% certain that the air distance between New Delhi and Beijing is more than _____ miles but less than _____ miles."* Most people were overconfident: Approximately 30% of the time, the correct answers lay outside the range they felt 98% confident about (if they'd been accurate in their confidence, it should have been only 2%). Even when participants were offered lottery tickets for a correct answer,

*The air distance between New Delhi and Beijing is 2,500 miles.

Everyone knows a person like this — someone who thinks they have far more rizz than they actually do. In social psychology, that's an example of overconfidence.
G-Stock Faces/Getty Images

they were still too overconfident, identifying too narrow a range. "The consequence [of overconfidence] . . . is profound," note Albert Mannes and Don Moore (2013, p. 1196). "People frequently cut things too close – arriving late, missing planes, [or] bouncing checks." In thinking we know exactly how something will go, we too often miss the window.

That's exactly what happened when 18 infectious disease experts were polled early in the COVID-19 outbreak in the United States. On March 16–17, 2020, they were asked to estimate the number of COVID-19 cases the United States would have on March 29, 2020, and to give a range of 80% certainty from their lowest guess to their highest – very similar to Kahneman and Tversky's task (Boice, 2020). Were they right? Not really. Only three of the 18 gave a range that included the actual number of cases on March 29: 122,653. Their average estimate was 20,000, and the majority were so confident of their guesses that the top and bottom of their range differed by only a few thousand cases (Piper, 2020) – a classic example of overconfidence.

"Unlike the stomach, the brain does not alert you when empty."

—Kenyan proverb

Overconfidence is not limited to experts. Ironically, *incompetence feeds overconfidence.* It takes competence to recognize competence, noted Justin Kruger and David Dunning (1999). Students who score the lowest on tests of grammar, humor, and logic are the most prone to overestimating their abilities, known as the *Dunning-Kruger effect.* These "unskilled and unaware of it" participants, the authors concluded, suffered a "dual burden" – they knew so little they were not able to understand just how bad their performance was (Jansen et al., 2021). You don't know what you don't know. If incompetent people often don't recognize how incompetent they are, it explains a lot about the human tendency to make mistakes.

Ignorance of one's incompetence helps explain David Dunning's (2005) startling conclusion from employee assessment studies that "what others see in us . . . tends to be more highly correlated with objective outcomes than what we see in ourselves." If ignorance can beget false confidence, then – yikes! – where, we may ask, are you and I unknowingly deficient?

"What I'd dearly love would be to be able to see [myself] having a Dunning-Kruger moment. But according to my own theory, I'll never have it."

—David Dunning, NPR, 2016

In estimating their chances for success on a task, such as a major exam, people's confidence runs highest when the moment of truth is off in the future. By exam day, the possibility of failure looms larger and confidence typically drops (Gilovich et al., 1993; Shepperd et al., 2005). These students are not alone:

- *Stockbroker overconfidence.* Mutual fund portfolios selected by investment analysts perform about as well as randomly selected stocks (Malkiel, 2016). The analysts might think they can pick the best stocks, but everyone else does, too – stocks are a confidence game. Worse, people who are overconfident invest more and more even when things aren't going well, digging in their heels after publicly declaring their choices (Ronay et al., 2017).
- *Political overconfidence.* Overconfident decision-makers can wreak havoc. A confident Adolf Hitler waged war against the rest of Europe. A confident Lyndon Johnson invested U.S. weapons and soldiers in the effort to salvage democracy in South Vietnam in the 1960s. A confident President George W. Bush asserted that Iraq had weapons of mass destruction in 2003, but none were ever found.
- *Student overconfidence.* In one study, students memorizing psychology terms for a test predicted how much credit they expected to receive. The overconfident students – those who thought they were more accurate than they actually were – did worse on the test, mostly because they stopped studying (Dunlosky & Rawson, 2012). Overconfidence can lead to failure.

Regarding the atomic bomb: "That is the biggest fool thing we have ever done. The bomb will never go off, and I speak as an expert in explosives."

—Admiral William Leahy to President Truman, 1945

"When you know a thing, to hold that you know it; and when you do not know a thing, to allow that you do not know it; this is knowledge."

—Confucius, *The Analects of Confucius*

Why does overconfidence persist? Perhaps because we like those who are confident: In experiments, group members rewarded highly confident individuals with higher status – even when their confidence was not justified by actual ability. Overconfident individuals spoke first, talked longer, and used a more factual tone, making them appear more competent than they actually were (Anderson et al., 2012). Even when groups worked together repeatedly and learned that the overconfident individuals were not as accurate as they said, group members continued to accord them status (Kennedy et al., 2013). Overconfident people are seen as more desirable as romantic partners than the less confident (Murphy et al., 2015). If confidence, but not ability, helps people become leaders and attract mates, pervasive overconfidence seems less surprising – but perhaps more distressing.

CONFIRMATION BIAS

People also tend not to seek information that might disprove what they believe. We are eager to verify our beliefs but less inclined to seek evidence that might disprove them, a phenomenon called **confirmation bias.** When given the chance to read news articles on a topic, people in the United States, Germany, and Japan spent more time reading articles consistent with their beliefs than articles inconsistent with their beliefs (Knobloch-Westerwick et al., 2019). Sometimes people are willing to make sacrifices to not even hear arguments from the other side: In one study, opponents of same-sex marriage gave up the chance to win money to avoid hearing counter-arguments – and so did supporters of same-sex marriage (Frimer et al., 2017). While 80% of Democrats said they were paying a lot of attention to the January 6th committee hearings (an event associated with Republican President Trump), only 44% of Republicans said the same. The hearings did not change Republicans' views: Before the hearings, 10% said the attack was an insurrection and a threat to democracy; after the hearings, 12% said the same, which was not statistically different (Montanaro, 2022). Overall, even when people are exposed to information disconfirming their beliefs, most choose to stick with their original beliefs (Kappes et al., 2020; Stanley et al., 2020).

confirmation bias
A tendency to search for information that confirms one's preconceptions.

Similarly, people often choose their news sources to align with their beliefs, a phenomenon known as "ideological echo chambers" (Del Vicario et al., 2017). Even when a source is less reliable, people are more willing to believe it if it affirms their beliefs (Westerwick et al., 2017) – one reason why fake news can spread so widely, especially on social media (Mitchell et al., 2020). This goes beyond politics: People with a more pessimistic worldview are more likely to read negative news, a phenomenon researchers call "I knew it, the world is falling apart!" (van der Meer & Hameleers, 2022).[For how confirmation bias helps reinforce conspiracy theories, see Focus On: The psychology of conspiracy theories].

The same confirmation bias occurs with health information. Parents uncertain about vaccinating their children sought out more anti-vaccination information online, while those who favored vaccination sought out pro-vaccination information (Meppelink et al., 2019). When asked to interpret data on the efficacy of forearm tape for tennis elbow, anti-vax and pro-vax participants did not differ. But when the same numbers were presented as a test of COVID-19 vaccine efficacy, anti-vax participants were more likely to see them as proof the vaccine didn't work, while pro-vax participants were more likely to conclude they *did* work (Malthouse, 2023). These results explain why those who "did my own research" during the COVID-19 pandemic could come to such different conclusions.

Confirmation bias appears to be a System 1 snap judgment, where our default reaction is to look for information consistent with our presupposition (Gilead et al., 2019). Stopping and thinking a little – calling up System 2 – make us less likely to commit this error. For example, Ivan Hernandez and Jesse Lee Preston (2013) had college students read an article arguing for the death penalty. Those who read the article in a dark, standard font did not change their opinions. But when the words were in light gray and italics, more shifted their beliefs – probably because straining to read the words slowed down participants' thinking enough for them to consider both sides. Contemplation curtails confirmation.

Confirmation bias helps explain why our self-images are so remarkably stable. In experiments at the University of Texas at Austin, William Swann and his colleagues (1981; Swann et al., 1992a, 1992b, 2007) discovered that students seek, elicit, and recall feedback that confirms their beliefs about themselves. People seek as friends and spouses those who bolster their own self views – even if they think poorly of themselves (Swann et al., 1991, 2003).

REMEDIES FOR OVERCONFIDENCE

What lessons can we draw from research on overconfidence? One lesson is to be wary of other people's dogmatic statements. Even when people are sure they are right, they may be wrong. Confidence and competence do not always coincide.

Two techniques have successfully reduced the overconfidence bias. One is *prompt feedback* (Koriat et al., 1980). In everyday life, both weather forecasters and those who set the odds in horse racing receive clear, daily feedback. Perhaps as a result, experts in both groups do quite well at estimating their probable accuracy (Fischhoff, 1982).

focus ON The Psychology of Conspiracy Theories

"Walking into the darkened ballroom of the Crowne Plaza Hotel off the highway near the airport outside of Denver, the atmosphere was electric," report Philip Fernbach and Jonathan Bogard (2023). "A strobe light and pulsing music signaled the beginning of the opening act, a raucous musical performance by Flat Earth Man, a fixture of the Flat Earth community, whose popular YouTube videos feature catchy tunes, clever lyrics, and surprisingly high production value." They had entered the Flat Earth International Conference, a gathering of people who believe that the Earth is a flat disc covered by a dome containing projections of the sun, moon, and stars. What about the pictures of Earth taken from space, or the moon landing? All faked by the government, they believe.

Conspiracy theories are explanations for events or phenomena that involve powerful groups hiding the truth (Douglas et al., 2017). Although conspiracy theories have been shared for decades, they seem to have proliferated recently, with Flat Earthers just one example. The QAnon conspiracy theory contends that a group of Satan worshipers who run a child sex ring are trying to control the country, a false view embraced by 17% of Americans in a December 2020 poll (Roose, 2021). Others falsely contended that the COVID-19 pandemic was a hoax or that Bill Gates purposely created the virus to gain control of people via vaccines (Himelboim et al., 2023).

Conspiracy beliefs have real-world consequences. In 2016, a man fired a gun in a pizzeria in Washington, D.C., because he believed a child sex trafficking ring was being run in the back room (it was not; Fisher et al., 2016). Many in the mob who attacked the U.S. Capitol on January 6, 2021 were QAnon followers. People who believed in COVID-19 conspiracies were less likely to test for the virus, to violate public health guidelines, and were more likely to be prejudiced against people of Asian descent (van Mulukom et al., 2022; van Prooijen et al., 2023).

Why do people believe implausible conspiracy theories, and can those beliefs be changed? Conspiracy theories tend to gain ground when people feel under threat and thus feel they are losing control, one reason they became popular during the pandemic (Kim et al., 2022; Van Prooijen et al., 2015, 2019a). People who believe conspiracy theories tend to believe in paranormal phenomena (such as ghosts) as well (Bowes et al., 2023; Sebalo et al., 2023). They are more likely to rely on their intuitive System 1 processing and less likely to rely on analytical, System 2 processing (Newman et al., 2022; Van Prooijen, 2019b). Karen Douglas and her colleagues (2017, 2023) theorize that people adopt conspiracy theories to satisfy three major needs: The need to understand the world, the need to feel secure, and the need to feel good about one's group by blaming outsiders for negative events. Not surprisingly, people are more likely to believe conspiracy theories implicating the rival political party rather than their own.

Once entrenched, conspiracy theory adherents are difficult to budge. One reason is confirmation bias: Believers often trust only information from sources supporting the theory and do not revise their beliefs even in the face of contradictory evidence. Fernback and Bogard (2023) report that when Flat Earthers argued about 24-hour sunshine in the far north (a phenomenon inconsistent with a flat Earth), a Flat Earther flew to Scandinavia and reported back to the group that the sun did indeed shine for 24 hours a day there in late June. The group then made slight revisions to their theory, but kept their core belief that the Earth is flat. Another reason conspiracy theorists continue to believe is their reliance on intuition rather than logic, making it difficult to convince them with reasoned arguments. In addition, research has found that conspiracy theory posts gain more social approval ("likes") on social media than factual news, suggesting a substantial number of people are willing to share conspiracy theories even when they know they are not true (Ren et al., 2023).

Can people be convinced to stop believing in conspiracy theories? Research is just beginning to answer this question. One experiment trained people on the representativeness heuristic, teaching them that the probability of two or more events occurring is less than the probability of one (Stall & Petrocelli, 2022). Another intervention countered a conspiracy theory with objections based on scientific reasoning (Georgiou et al., 2023). A large meta-analysis of 25 studies determined that interventions teaching critical thinking skills were the most effective at changing conspiracy beliefs or keeping people from believing conspiracy theories in the first place. Arguing against the theory with facts produced only small changes, and mocking people for their beliefs didn't change beliefs at all (O'Mahony et al., 2023).

When people think about why an idea *might* be true, it begins to seem true (Koehler, 1991). Thus, a second way to reduce overconfidence is to get people to think of one good reason *why* their judgments *might be wrong;* that is, force them to consider disconfirming information (Koriat et al., 1980). Managers might foster more realistic judgments by insisting that all proposals and recommendations include reasons why they might *not* work.

Still, we should be careful not to undermine people's reasonable self-confidence or to destroy their decisiveness. In times when their wisdom is needed, those lacking self-confidence may shrink from speaking up or making tough decisions. Overconfidence can cost us, but realistic self-confidence is adaptive.

Heuristics: Mental Shortcuts

With precious little time to process so much information, our cognitive system is fast and frugal. It specializes in mental shortcuts. With remarkable ease, we form impressions, make judgments, and invent explanations. We do so by using **heuristics** – simple, efficient thinking strategies. Heuristics enable us to make routine decisions with minimal effort (Shah & Oppenheimer, 2008). In most situations, our System 1 snap generalizations – "That's dangerous!" – are adaptive. The speed of these intuitive guides promotes our survival. The biological purpose of thinking is not to make us right – it's to keep us alive. In some situations, however, haste makes errors.

heuristics
A thinking strategy that enables quick, efficient judgments.

THE REPRESENTATIVENESS HEURISTIC

University of Oregon students were told that a panel of psychologists interviewed 30 engineers and 70 lawyers and summarized their impressions in thumbnail descriptions. The following description, they were told, was drawn at random from the sample of 30 engineers and 70 lawyers:

> Twice divorced, James spends most of his free time hanging around the country club. His clubhouse bar conversations often center on his regrets at having tried to follow his esteemed father's footsteps. The long hours he had spent at academic drudgery would have been better invested in learning how to be less quarrelsome in his relations with other people.
>
> *Question:* What is the probability that James is a lawyer rather than an engineer?

Asked to guess James's occupation, more than 80% of the students surmised he was one of the lawyers (Fischhoff & Bar-Hillel, 1984). Fair enough – after all, lawyers were 70% of the sample. But how do you suppose those estimates changed when the sample description was given to another group of students, modified to say instead that 70% were engineers? Not in the slightest. The students took no account of the base rate of engineers (70%) and lawyers (30%); in their minds, James was more *representative* of lawyers, and that was all that seemed to matter. Or consider John, a 23-year-old White man who's an atheist and abuses drugs. What kind of music does he like? Most people guessed heavy metal, even though heavy metal fans are a very small minority of the population (Lonsdale & North, 2012).

To judge something by intuitively comparing it to our mental representation of a category is to use the **representativeness heuristic.** Representativeness (typicalness) usually reflects reality. But, as we saw with "James" above, it doesn't always. Consider Linda, who is 31, single, outspoken, and very bright. She majored in philosophy in college. As a student, she was deeply concerned with discrimination and other social issues, and she participated in antinuclear demonstrations. Based on that description, would you say it is more likely that

representativeness heuristic
The tendency to presume, sometimes despite contrary odds, that someone or something belongs to a particular group if resembling (representing) a typical member.

a. Linda is a bank teller.
b. Linda is a bank teller and active in the feminist movement.

Most people think *b* is more likely, partly because Linda better *represents* their image of feminists (Mellers et al., 2001). But ask yourself: Is there a better chance that Linda is *both* a bank teller *and* a feminist than that she's a bank teller (whether feminist or not)? As Amos Tversky and Daniel Kahneman (1983) reminded us, the conjunction of two events cannot be more likely than either one of the events alone.

TABLE 1 Fast and Frugal Heuristics

Heuristic	Definition	Example	But May Lead to
Representativeness	Snap judgments of whether someone or something fits a category	Deciding that Marie is a librarian rather than a trucker because she better represents one's image of librarians	Discounting other important information
Availability	Quick judgments of likelihood of events (how available in memory)	Estimating violent crime rates after school shootings	Overweighting vivid instances and thus, for example, fearing the wrong things

THE AVAILABILITY HEURISTIC

Consider the following: Do more people live in Ukraine or in Tanzania?

You probably answered according to how readily Ukrainians and Tanzanians come to mind. If examples are readily *available* in our memory – as Ukrainians tend to be – then we presume that other such examples are commonplace. Usually this is true, so we are often well served by this cognitive rule, called the **availability heuristic** (**Table 1**). Said simply, the more easily we recall something, the more likely it seems. *(Answer: Tanzania's 62 million people outnumber Ukraine's 41 million. Most people, having more vivid images of Ukrainians, guess wrong.)*

availability heuristic

A cognitive rule that judges the likelihood of things in terms of their availability in memory. If instances of something come readily to mind, we presume it to be commonplace.

Are you more likely to be killed by a shark or by a cow? Most people would guess a shark, but cows actually kill more people (about 22 a year in the United States, compared to 1 or less killed by sharks). People fear terrorist attacks, murders, and shark attacks, but should really fear the most common underlying causes of death: tobacco use, poor diet or inactivity, and alcohol use (Dale, 2015). That's partly because media coverage makes shark attacks, murders, and terrorist attacks cognitively available.

Try ordering these four cities according to their crime rates: Los Angeles, Memphis, New York, St. Louis. If, with available images from crime dramas in mind, you thought New York and Los Angeles were the most crime-ridden, guess again: They each have about one-third the violent crime rate of Memphis or St. Louis (FBI, 2020).

"Most people reason dramatically, not quantitatively."

—Jurist Oliver Wendell Holmes, Jr. (1841–1935)

Our use of the availability heuristic highlights a basic principle of social thinking: People are slow to understand specific examples from a general truth, but they are remarkably quick to infer general truth from a vivid example. No wonder that people who use neighborhood apps like Nextdoor that report local crime overestimate the crime rate in their neighborhood (Fetterman et al., 2023). No wonder that 74% of U.S. parents in 2019, after several high-profile school shootings, believed schools were more dangerous than in 1999 – even though crimes at schools dropped by half between 2001 and 2017 (Goldstein, 2019). And no wonder the breakfast server at a hotel for stranded airline passengers told me [DM] that, after hearing so many vivid stories of flights delayed by weather and mechanical problems, she would *never* fly.

Dave Coverly/Speedbump.com

Powerful anecdotes can be more compelling than statistical information. We fret over extremely rare child abduction, even if we don't buckle children in their car seats every time. We dread terrorism but are indifferent to global climate change – "Armageddon in slow motion." In short, we worry about remote possibilities while ignoring higher probabilities, a phenomenon that social scientists call our "probability neglect."

Because news footage of airplane crashes is a readily available memory for most of us, we often suppose we are more at risk traveling in commercial airplanes than in cars. But in 2021, only two people died on a U.S. commercial airplane, compared to the 26,325 killed in car accidents that year (National Safety Council, 2023). For most air travelers, the most dangerous part of the journey is the drive to the airport.

Soon after 9/11, as many people abandoned air travel and took to the roads, I [DM] estimated that if Americans flew 20% less and instead drove half those unflown miles, we could expect an additional 800 traffic deaths in the ensuing year (Myers, 2001). A curious German researcher checked that prediction against accident data, which confirmed an excess of some 1595 traffic deaths in the ensuing year (Gigerenzer, 2004). The 9/11 terrorists appear to have killed well over a thousand more people on America's roads, mostly unnoticed, than they did with the 265 fatalities on those four planes.

Vivid, memorable — and therefore cognitively available — events influence our perception of the social world. The resulting *probability neglect* often leads people to fear the wrong things, such as fearing flying or terrorism more than smoking, driving, or climate change. If two large jets filled with children crashed every day — approximating the number of childhood diarrhea deaths resulting from the rotavirus — something would have been done about it.

The availability heuristic may also make us more sensitive to unfairness, as our struggles are more memorable than our advantages. Democrats and Republicans both believe that the U.S. electoral map works against their party. Students think that their parents were harder on them than on their siblings. And academics believe that they have had a more difficult time with journal-article reviewers than average (Davidai & Gilovich, 2016).

By now it is clear that our naive statistical intuitions, and our resulting fears, are driven not by calculation and reason but by emotions attuned to the availability heuristic. After this book is published, there likely will be another dramatic shooting or terrorist event which will again propel our fears, vigilance, and resources in a new direction. Terrorists and mass shooters, aided by the media, may again achieve their objective of capturing our attention, draining our resources, and distracting us from the mundane, undramatic, insidious risks that, over time, devastate lives, such as the rotavirus (an intestinal infection) that each day claims the equivalent of two large jets filled with children (WHO, 2016).

But then again, dramatic events can also serve to awaken us to real risks. That, say some scientists, is what happens when extreme weather events remind us that global climate change, by raising sea levels and spawning extreme weather, is destined to become nature's own weapon of mass destruction (AP, 2019). For Australians and Americans, a hot day can prime people to believe more in global warming (Li et al., 2011). Even feeling hot in an *indoor* room increases people's belief in global warming (Risen & Critcher, 2011).

"Testimonials may be more compelling than mountains of facts and figures (as mountains of facts and figures in social psychology so compellingly demonstrate)."

—Mark Snyder (1988)

Counterfactual Thinking

Easily imagined, cognitively available events also influence our experiences of guilt, regret, frustration, and relief. If our team loses (or wins) a big game by one point, we can easily imagine the other outcome, and thus we feel regret (or relief). Imagining worse alternatives helps us feel better. When skier Lindsay Vonn lost a World Cup slalom event by just 0.03 seconds, she was happy for her competitor but noted that "I'd rather she beat me by a second" (AP, 2012). Imagining better alternatives, and pondering what we might do differently next time, helps us prepare to do better in the future (Epstude & Roese, 2008; Scholl & Sassenberg, 2014).

In Olympic competition, athletes' emotions after an event reflect mostly how they did relative to expectations, but also their **counterfactual thinking** – their *mentally simulating what might have been* (McGraw et al., 2005; Parikh et al., 2018). Bronze medalists (for whom an easily imagined alternative was finishing fourth – without a medal) exhibit more joy than silver medalists, who express regret at not having won the gold (Allen et al., 2019; Hedgecock et al., 2021). On the medal stand, happiness is as simple as 1-3-2. Similarly, the higher a student's score within a grade category (such as B+), the *worse* they feel (Medvec & Savitsky, 1997). The B+ student who misses an A– by a point feels worse than the B+ student who actually did worse and just made a B+ by a point.

counterfactual thinking
Imagining alternative scenarios and outcomes that might have happened, but didn't.

Counterfactual thinking. When *The Price is Right* contestants give the wrong answer and lose out on a prize, they likely experience counterfactual thinking — imagining what might have been.
Monty Brinton/CBS/Getty Images

Such counterfactual thinking — imagining what could have been — occurs when we can easily picture an alternative outcome (Kahneman & Miller, 1986; Maitner & Summerville, 2022; Petrocelli et al., 2011):

- If we barely miss a plane or a bus, we imagine making it *if only* we had left at our usual time, taken our usual route, or not paused to talk. If we miss our connection by a half-hour or after taking our usual route, it's harder to simulate a different outcome, so we feel less frustration.
- If we change an exam answer, then get it wrong, we will inevitably think "If only . . ." and will vow next time to trust our immediate intuition — although, contrary to student lore, answer changes are more often from incorrect to correct (Kruger et al., 2005).
- If you book your trip and later find out the airline cut fares, you can easily imagine having waited another day or two and gotten the cheaper ticket (Park & Jang, 2018).
- People trying to manage their weight who didn't resist that second dessert imagine how they could have avoided overindulging (Wang et al., 2021).

Counterfactual thinking underlies our feelings of luck. When we have barely escaped a bad event — avoiding defeat with a last-minute goal or standing near a falling icicle — we easily imagine a negative counterfactual (losing, being hit) and therefore feel "good luck" (Teigen et al., 1999). "*Bad* luck" refers to bad events that did happen but easily might not have.

The more significant and unlikely the event, the more intense the counterfactual thinking (Roese & Hur, 1997). Bereaved people who have lost a spouse or a child in a vehicle accident, or a child to sudden infant death syndrome, commonly report replaying and undoing the event (Davis et al., 1995, 1996; Neimeyer et al., 2020). One friend of mine [DM] survived a head-on collision with a drunk driver that killed his wife, daughter, and mother. "For months," he recalled, "I turned the events of that day over and over in my mind. I kept reliving the day, changing the order of events so that the accident wouldn't occur" (Sittser, 1994).

Most people, however, live with more regret over things they *didn't* do than what they did, such as, "I should have told my father I loved him before he died" or "I wish I had been more serious in college" (Gilovich & Medvec, 1994; Rajagopal et al., 2006). In one survey of adults, the most common regret was not taking their education more seriously (Kinnier & Metha, 1989). Would we live with less regret if we dared more often to reach beyond our comfort zone — to venture out, risking failure, but at least having tried?

Illusory Thinking

illusory correlation
Perception of a relationship where none exists, or perception of a stronger relationship than actually exists.

It is easy to see a correlation where none exists. When we expect to find significant relationships, we easily associate random events, perceiving an **illusory correlation.** William Ward and Herbert Jenkins (1965) showed people the results of a hypothetical 50-day cloud-seeding experiment. They told participants which of the 50 days the clouds had been seeded and which days it rained. The information was nothing more than a random mix of results: Sometimes it rained after seeding; sometimes it didn't. Participants nevertheless became convinced — in conformity with their opinion about the efficacy of cloud seeding — that they really had observed a relationship between cloud seeding and rain.

Other experiments confirm this illusory correlation phenomenon: *People easily misperceive random events as confirming their beliefs* (Crocker, 1981; Ratliff & Nosek, 2010; Trolier & Hamilton, 1986). If we believe a correlation exists, we are more likely to notice and recall confirming instances. If we believe that premonitions correlate with events, we notice and remember any joint occurrence of the premonition and the event's later occurrence. If we believe that overweight people are less happy, we perceive that we have witnessed such a correlation even when we have not (Viken et al., 2005). We ignore or forget all the times unusual events do not coincide. If, after we think about a friend, the friend calls us, we notice and remember that coincidence. We don't notice all the times we think of a friend without any ensuing call, or receive a call from a friend we haven't been thinking about.

Regression to the average. When we are at an extremely low point, anything we try will often seem effective: "Maybe a yoga class will improve my life." Events seldom continue at an abnormal low.
wavebreakmedia/Shutterstock

Tversky and Kahneman (1974) also noted ways in which an *illusion of control* may arise: We fail to recognize the statistical phenomenon of **regression toward the average.** Because exam scores fluctuate partly by chance, most students who get extremely high scores on an exam will get lower scores on the next exam. If their first score is at the ceiling, their second score is more likely to fall back ("regress") toward their own average than to push the ceiling even higher. That is why a student who does consistently good work, even if never the best, will sometimes end a course at the top of the class. Conversely, students who earn low scores on the first exam are likely to improve. If those who scored lowest go for tutoring after the first exam, the tutors are likely to feel effective when the student improves, even if the tutoring had no effect.

regression toward the average
The statistical tendency for extreme scores or extreme behavior to return toward their average.

Indeed, when things reach a low point, we will try anything, and whatever we try – going to a psychotherapist, starting a new diet-exercise plan, reading a self-help book – is more likely to be followed by improvement than by further deterioration. Sometimes we recognize that events are not likely to continue at an unusually good or bad extreme. Experience has taught us that when everything is going great, something will go wrong, and that when life is dealing us terrible blows, we can usually look forward to things getting better. Often, though, we fail to recognize this regression effect. We puzzle at why baseball's rookie of the year often has a more ordinary second year – did he become overconfident? Self-conscious? We forget that exceptional performance tends to regress toward normality.

By simulating the consequences of using praise and punishment, Paul Schaffner (1985) showed how the illusion of control might infiltrate human relations. He invited Bowdoin College students to train an imaginary fourth-grade boy, "Harold," to come to school by 8:30 each morning. For each school day during a 3-week period, a computer displayed Harold's arrival time, which was always between 8:20 and 8:40. The students would then select a response to Harold, ranging from strong praise to strong reprimand. As you might expect, they usually praised Harold when he arrived before 8:30 and reprimanded him when he arrived after 8:30. Because Schaffner had programmed the computer to display a random sequence of arrival times, Harold's arrival time tended to improve (to regress toward 8:30) after he was reprimanded. For example, if Harold arrived at 8:39, he was almost sure to be reprimanded, and his randomly selected next-day arrival time was likely to be earlier than 8:39. Thus, *even though their reprimands were having no effect,* most students ended the experiment believing that their reprimands had been effective.

This experiment demonstrates Tversky and Kahneman's provocative conclusion: *Nature operates in such a way that we often feel punished for rewarding others and rewarded for punishing them.* In actuality, as you probably learned in introductory psychology, positive reinforcement for doing things right is usually more effective than punishment.

Moods and Judgments

Social judgment involves efficient information processing. It also involves our feelings: Our moods infuse our judgments. Unhappy people – especially the bereaved or depressed – tend to be more self-focused and brooding (Myers, 1993; 2000b). But there is also a bright side to sadness (Forgas, 2013). A depressed mood motivates intense thinking – a search for information that makes one's environment more memorable, understandable, and controllable.

Happy people, by contrast, are more trusting, more loving, more responsive. If people are made temporarily happy by receiving a small gift while shopping, they will report, a few moments later on an unrelated survey, that their cars and phones are working beautifully – better, if you took their word for it, than those belonging to folks who replied after not receiving gifts. When

FIGURE 1

Mood and Perceptions of Behavior

A temporary good or bad mood strongly influenced people's ratings of their videotaped behavior. Those in a bad mood detected far fewer positive behaviors.

Source: Forgas et al., 1984.

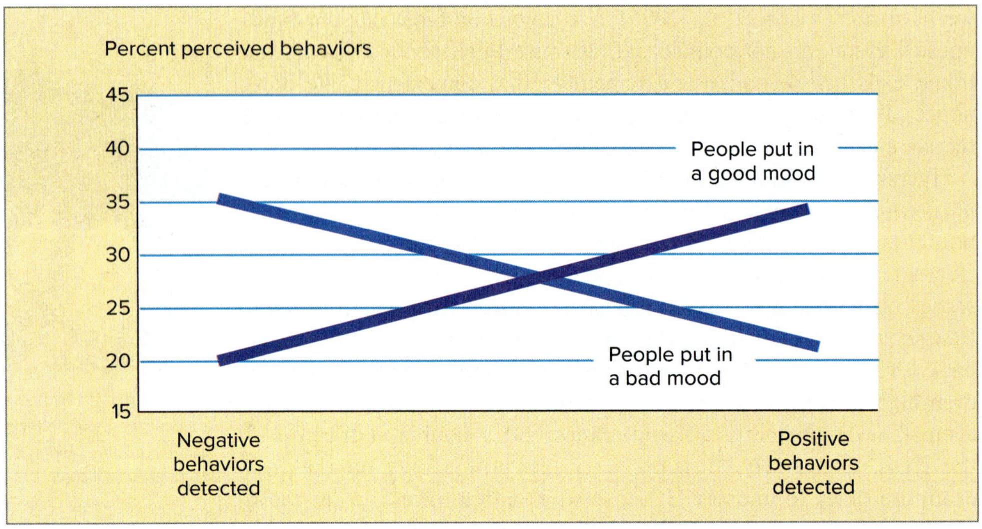

we are in a happy mood, the world seems friendlier, decisions are easier, and good news more readily comes to mind (DeSteno et al., 2000; Isen & Means, 1983; Stone & Glass, 1986).

Let a mood turn gloomy, however, and thoughts switch onto a different track. Off come the rose-colored glasses; on come the dark glasses. Now the bad mood primes our recollections of negative events and leads us to think more bad things will happen in the future (Booth et al., 2023; Johnson & Magaro, 1987). Our relationships seem to sour. Our self-images take a dive. Our hopes for the future dim. And other people's faces and behaviors seem more sinister (Brown & Taylor, 1986; Suslow et al., 2019).

Joseph Forgas (2008, 2010, 2011, 2022) had often been struck by how people's "memories and judgments change with the color of their mood." Say you're put in a good or a bad mood and then watch a recording (made the day before) of you talking with someone. If made to feel happy, you feel pleased with what you see, and you are able to detect many instances of your poise, interest, and social skill. If you've been put in a bad mood, viewing the same recording seems to reveal a quite different you – one who is stiff, nervous, and inarticulate (Forgas et al., 1984; **Figure 1**). Given how your mood colors your judgments, you feel relieved at how things brighten when the experimenter switches you to a happy

THE inside STORY

Joseph P. Forgas: Can Bad Weather Improve Your Memory?

I noticed some time ago that I not only get into a worse mood on cold, rainy days, but surprisingly, I also seem to remember more clearly the details of what happens on such days. Could it be that negative mood also influences how well we monitor our environment? Perhaps a negative mood works like a mild alarm signal, alerting us to pay better attention to what is around us? I decided to examine this possibility in a natural experiment. We placed a number of small unusual trinkets around a Sydney suburban news agency, and then checked how well departing customers could remember these objects when they left the shop on cold, rainy days, or warm sunny days (Forgas et al., 2009).

My hunch was confirmed: Memory for objects in the shop was significantly better when customers were in a bad mood (on unpleasant days) than on pleasant sunny days. It seems that moods subconsciously influence how closely we observe the outside around us, with negative mood-improving attention and memory. The take-home message from our research is that all our moods, including the negative ones, serve a useful evolutionary purpose and we should learn to accept temporary states of a bad mood as a normal, and even useful part of life.

Joseph P. Forgas
The University of New South Wales, Australia

Joseph P. Forgas

mood before leaving the experiment. Curiously, noted Michael Ross and Garth Fletcher (1985), we don't attribute our changing perceptions to our mood shifts. Rather, the world really seems different. (To read more about moods and memory, see "The Inside Story: Joseph P. Forgas: Can Bad Weather Improve Your Memory?")

Our moods color how we judge our worlds partly by bringing to mind past experiences associated with the mood. When we are in a bad mood, we have more depressing thoughts. Mood-related thoughts may distract us from complex thinking about something else. Thus, when emotionally aroused – when either angry or in a very good mood – we become more likely to make System 1 snap judgments and evaluate others based on stereotypes (Bodenhausen et al., 1994; Paulhus & Lim, 1994).

SUMMING UP: How Do We Judge Our Social Worlds?

- We have an enormous capacity for automatic, efficient, intuitive thinking *(System 1)*. Our cognitive efficiency, although generally adaptive, comes at the price of occasional error. Because we are generally unaware of those errors entering our thinking, it is useful to identify ways in which we form and sustain false beliefs.
- Our preconceptions strongly influence how we interpret and remember events. In a phenomenon called *priming,* people's prejudgments have striking effects on how they perceive and interpret information.
- We often overestimate our judgments. This *overconfidence phenomenon* stems partly from the much greater ease with which we can imagine why we might be right than why we might be wrong. Moreover, people are much more likely to search for information that can confirm their beliefs than for information that can disconfirm them.
- When given compelling anecdotes or even useless information, we often ignore useful base-rate information. This is partly due to the later ease of recall of vivid information (the *availability heuristic*).
- We are often swayed by illusions of correlation and personal control. It is tempting to perceive correlations where none exist *(illusory correlation)* and to think we can predict or control chance events (an *illusion of control*).
- Moods infuse judgments. Good and bad moods trigger memories of experiences associated with those moods. Moods color our interpretations of current experiences. And by distracting us, moods can also influence how deeply or superficially we think when making judgments.

HOW DO WE PERCEIVE OUR SOCIAL WORLDS?

Explain how our assumptions and prejudgments guide our perceptions, interpretations, and recall.

Our preconceptions guide how we perceive and interpret information. We construe the world through belief-tinted glasses. "Sure, preconceptions matter," people agree; yet they fail to fully appreciate the impact of their own predispositions.

Let's consider some provocative experiments. The first group examines how predispositions and prejudgments affect how we perceive and interpret information. The second group plants a judgment in people's minds *after* they have been given information to see how after-the-fact ideas bias recall. The overarching point: *We respond not to reality as it is but to reality as we construe it.*

Perceiving and Interpreting Events

Despite some startling biases and logical flaws in how we perceive and understand one another, we're mostly accurate (Jussim, 2012; Tissera et al., 2023). Our first impressions of one another are more often right than wrong. Moreover, the better we know people, the more accurately we can read their minds and feelings.

FIGURE 2

Perceptions of Media Bias Depend on Point of View

Pro-Israeli and pro-Arab U.S. students who viewed network news descriptions of the "Beirut massacre" believed the coverage was biased against their point of view.

Source: Data from Vallone et al., 1985.

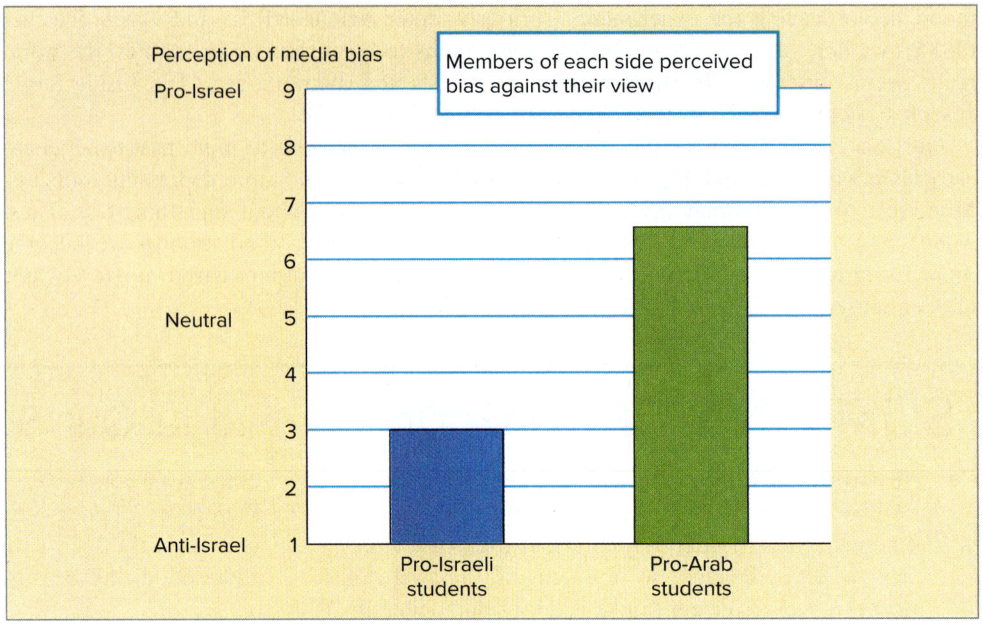

But on occasion, our prejudgments err. The effects of prejudgments and expectations are standard fare for psychology's introductory course. Consider this phrase:

A
BIRD
IN THE
THE HAND

Did you notice anything wrong with it? There is more to perception than meets the eye.*

"Once you have a belief, it influences how you perceive all other relevant information. Once you see a country as hostile, you are likely to interpret ambiguous actions on their part as signifying their hostility."

—Political Scientist Robert Jervis (1985)

POLITICAL PERCEPTIONS

The same is true of political perception. Because political perceptions are very much in the eye of the beholder, even a simple stimulus may strike two people quite differently. An experiment by Robert Vallone, Lee Ross, and Mark Lepper (1985) revealed just how powerful preconceptions can be. They showed pro-Israeli and pro-Arab U.S. students six network news segments describing the killing of civilian refugees at two camps in Beirut, Lebanon. As **Figure 2** illustrates, each group perceived the networks as hostile to its side.

The phenomenon is commonplace. Political candidates and their supporters nearly always view the news media as unsympathetic to their cause and news articles as biased against their party (Lee et al., 2018; Richardson et al., 2008). In the runup to the 2020 election, Republicans believed Facebook was biased against Republican President Trump, while Democrats believed Facebook was slightly pro-Trump (Yair, 2021). Democrats and Republicans both expected that their party would be more targeted by fake news attacks in the 2020 election (Gramlich, 2020). The biased perception of bias happens in sports, too: Sports fans perceive referees as partial to the other side.

"There is no subject about which people are less objective than objectivity," noted one media commentator (Poniewozik, 2003). Indeed, people's perceptions of bias can be used to assess their attitudes on a topic (Saucier & Miller, 2003). Say where you see bias, and you will signal your attitudes.

Alex Gregory

Some circumstances make it difficult to be unbiased.

*The word "the" appears twice.

Perhaps this is why ambiguous information often fuels conflict in politics, religion, and science. Presidential debates in the United States have mostly reinforced pre-debate opinions. By nearly a 10-to-1 margin, those who already favored one candidate or the other perceived their candidate as having won (Kinder & Sears, 1985; Richardson et al., 2008). Thus, Geoffrey Munro and colleagues (1997) reported that people on both sides may become even more supportive of their respective candidates after viewing a presidential debate.

The bottom line: We view our social worlds through the spectacles of our beliefs, attitudes, and values. That is one reason our beliefs are so important; they shape our interpretation of everything else.

Partisan perceptions. Supporters of candidates usually believe their candidate won the debate.
Christos S/Shutterstock

Belief Perseverance

Imagine a babysitter who decides, during an evening with a crying infant, that bottle-feeding produces colicky babies: "Come to think of it, cow's milk obviously suits calves better than babies." If the infant turns out to be suffering a high fever, will the sitter nevertheless persist in believing that bottle-feeding causes colic (Ross & Anderson, 1982)? To find out, Lee Ross, Craig Anderson, and colleagues planted a falsehood in people's minds and then tried to discredit it.

Their research reveals that it is surprisingly difficult to demolish a falsehood after the person conjures up a rationale for it. Each experiment first *implanted a belief,* either by proclaiming it to be true or by showing the participants some anecdotal evidence. Then the participants were asked to *explain why* it was true. Finally, the researchers totally *discredited* the initial information by telling the participants the truth: The information was manufactured for the experiment, and half the participants in the experiment had received the opposite information. Nevertheless, the false belief survived approximately 75% intact, presumably because the participants still retained their invented explanations for the belief. Even though the belief was false, the participants still held it tight. This phenomenon, called **belief perseverance,** shows that beliefs can grow their own legs and survive discrediting, especially if there's any uncertainty or debate about what's true and what's not (Anglin, 2019). In a time when "fake news" (false stories often designed to attract clicks and thus advertising profits) spreads on social media (Figl et al., 2023), it's especially important to understand why people continue to believe false information.

belief perseverance
Persistence of one's initial conceptions, such as when the basis for one's belief is discredited but an explanation of why the belief might be true survives.

In addition, what we continue to believe can be influenced by our attitudes and affiliations. Dustin Calvillo, Justin Harris, and Whitney Hawkins (2023) presented people with 12 stories about events related to the January 6, 2021 attack on the U.S. Capitol – 6 that were true and 6 that were false. Democrats were more likely to remember stories that favored Democrats and less likely to remember those that favored Republicans, and Republicans remembered the opposite (see **Figure 3** for the results for false stories). Although people were more likely to recall true events than false ones, their beliefs colored what they remembered.

The evidence is compelling: Our beliefs and expectations powerfully affect how we mentally construct events. Usually, we benefit from our preconceptions, just as scientists benefit from creating theories that guide them in noticing and interpreting events. But the benefits sometimes entail a cost: We become prisoners of our own thought patterns.

"We hear and apprehend only what we already half know."

—Henry David Thoreau, In *The Heart of Thoreau's Journals,* 1961

Constructing Memories of Ourselves and Our Worlds

Do you agree or disagree with this statement?

> Memory can be likened to a storage chest in the brain into which we deposit material and from which we can withdraw it later if needed. Occasionally, something is lost from the "chest," and then we say we have forgotten.

FIGURE 3

Memories for Pro-Democrat and Pro-Republican False News Stories, by Political Affiliation

Whether we believe and remember particular fake news stories is influenced by our political beliefs.

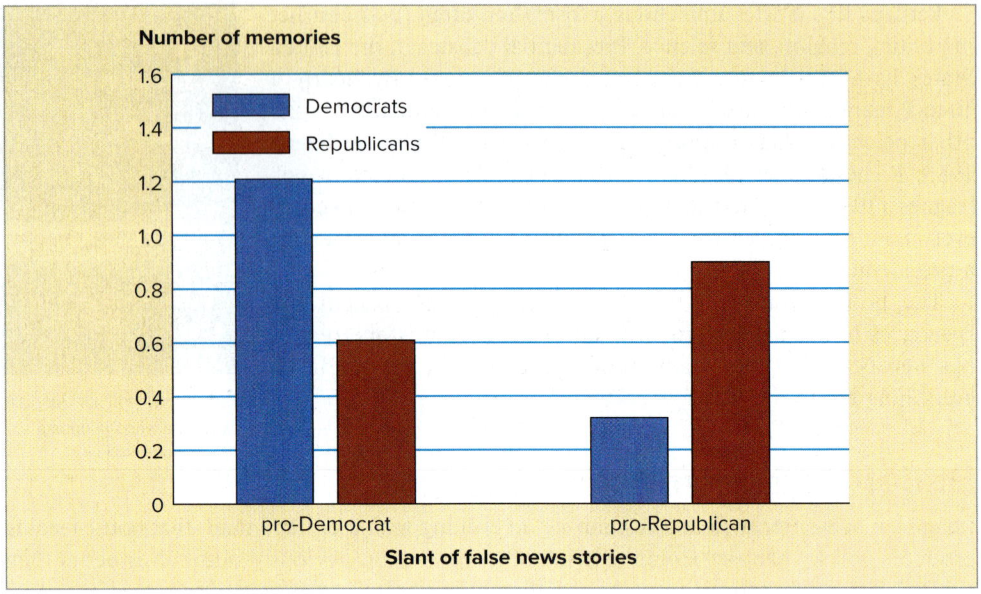

In one survey, 85% of college students agreed (Lamal, 1979). As one magazine ad put it, "Science has proven the accumulated experience of a lifetime is preserved perfectly in your mind."

Actually, psychological research has proved the opposite. Our memories are not exact copies of experiences that remain on deposit in a memory bank. Rather, we construct memories at the time of withdrawal. Like a paleontologist inferring the appearance of a dinosaur from bone fragments, we reconstruct our distant past by using our current feelings and expectations to combine information fragments. Thus, we can easily (although unconsciously) revise our memories to suit our current knowledge. When one of my [DM] sons complained, "The June issue of *Cricket* never came," and was then shown where it was, he delightedly responded, "Oh good, I knew I'd gotten it."

"Memory isn't like reading a book: It's more like writing a book from fragmentary notes."

—John F. Kihlstrom (1994)

When an experimenter or a therapist manipulates people's presumptions about their past, many people will construct false memories. Asked to imagine that, as a child, they knocked over a punch bowl at a wedding, about one-fourth will later recall the fictitious event as something that actually happened (Loftus & Bernstein, 2005). In its search for truth, the mind sometimes constructs a falsehood (Muschalla & Schönborn, 2021).

In experiments involving more than 20,000 people, Elizabeth Loftus (2003, 2007, 2011a) and collaborators have explored the mind's tendency to construct memories. In the typical experiment, people witness an event, receive misleading information about it (or not), and then take a memory test. The results find a **misinformation effect** in which people incorporate the misinformation into their memories (Loftus & Klemfuss, 2023; Scoboria et al., 2017). They recall a yield sign as a stop sign, hammers as screwdrivers, *Vogue* magazine as *Mademoiselle,* Dr. Henderson as "Dr. Davidson," breakfast cereal as eggs, and a clean-shaven man as a guy with a mustache. Suggested misinformation may even produce false memories of supposed child sexual abuse, argues Loftus.

misinformation effect

Incorporating "misinformation" into one's memory of the event after witnessing an event and receiving misleading information about it.

This process affects our recall of social as well as physical events. Jack Croxton and colleagues (1984) had students spend 15 minutes talking with someone. Those who were later informed that this person liked them recalled the person's behavior as relaxed, comfortable, and happy. Those who heard the person disliked them recalled the person as nervous, uncomfortable, and not so happy.

RECONSTRUCTING OUR PAST ATTITUDES

Five years ago, how did you feel about immigration? About your country's president or prime minister? About your parents? If your attitudes have changed, how much have they changed?

"A man should never be ashamed to own that he has been in the wrong, which is but saying in other words, that he is wiser today than he was yesterday."

—Jonathan Swift, *Thoughts on Various Subjects,* 1711

Experimenters have explored such questions, and the results have been unnerving. People whose beliefs or attitudes have changed often insist that they have always felt much as they now feel (Wolfe & Williams, 2018). Carnegie Mellon University students answered a long survey that included a question about student control over the university curriculum. A week later, they agreed to write an essay opposing student control. After doing so, their attitudes shifted toward greater opposition to student control. When asked to recall how they had answered the question before writing the essay, the students "remembered" holding the opinion that they *now* held and denied that the experiment had affected them (Bem & McConnell, 1970).

Fight now, and you might falsely recall that your relationship was never that happy.
Prostock-studio/Alamy Stock Photo

After observing students similarly denying their former attitudes, researchers D. R. Wixon and James Laird (1976) commented, "The speed, magnitude, and certainty" with which the students revised their own histories "was striking." As George Vaillant (1977) noted after following adults as they matured, "It is all too common for caterpillars to become butterflies and then to maintain that in their youth they had been little butterflies. Maturation makes liars of us all."

The construction of positive memories brightens our recollections. Terence Mitchell, Leigh Thompson, and colleagues (1994, 1997) reported that people often exhibit *rosy retrospection* – they recall mildly pleasant events more favorably than they experienced them. College students on a 3-week bike trip, older adults on a guided tour of Austria, and undergraduates on vacation all reported enjoying their experiences as they were having them. But they later recalled such experiences even more fondly, minimizing the unpleasant or boring aspects and remembering the high points. Even more negative experiences can grow more positive in recollection: High school students remembered their middle school years with more positive emotions than they actually felt at the time (Zurbriggen et al., 2021).

"Travel is glamorous only in retrospect."

—Paul Theroux, *The Washington Post,* 1979

Cathy McFarland and Michael Ross (1985) found that as our relationships change, we also revise our recollections of other people. They had university students rate their steady dating partners. Two months later, they rated them again. Students who were still in love had a tendency to overestimate their first impressions – it was "love at first sight." Those who had broken up were more likely to *underestimate* their earlier liking – recalling their ex as somewhat selfish and bad-tempered.

Diane Holmberg and John Holmes (1994) discovered the phenomenon also operating among 373 newlywed couples, most of whom reported being very happy. When resurveyed 2 years later, those whose marriages had soured recalled that things had always been bad. The results are "frightening," said Holmberg and Holmes: "Such biases can lead to a dangerous downward spiral. The worse your current view of your partner is, the worse your memories are, which only further confirms your negative attitudes."

It's not that we are totally unaware of how we used to feel, but when memories are hazy, current feelings guide our recall. When widows and widowers try to recall the grief they felt on their spouse's death five years ago, their current emotional state colors their memories (Safer et al., 2001). When patients recall their previous day's headache pain, their current feelings sway their recollections (Eich et al., 1985).

RECONSTRUCTING OUR PAST BEHAVIOR

Memory construction enables us to revise our own histories. In one study, University of Waterloo students read a message about the benefits of toothbrushing. Later, in a supposedly different experiment, these students recalled brushing their teeth more often during the preceding 2 weeks than students who had not heard the message (Ross, 1981). Likewise, people recall casting more votes than were actually recorded (Bureau of the Census, 2020).

Social psychologist Anthony Greenwald (1980) noted the similarity of such findings in George Orwell's novel *1984* – in which it was "necessary to remember that events happened in the desired manner." Indeed, argued Greenwald, we all have "totalitarian egos" that revise the past to suit our present views. Thus, we underreport bad behavior and overreport good behavior.

"Vanity plays lurid tricks with our memory."

—Joseph Conrad, *Lord Jim,* 1900

If people believe that their lives have improved, they may misrecall their past as worse than it actually was. This might explain why people who participate in programs for weight control, smoking cessation, and exercise show only modest improvements on average but often claim they have benefited enormously. Having expended so much time, effort, and money on self-improvement, people may think, "I may not be perfect now, but I was worse before; this did me a lot of good" (Conway & Ross, 1986).

Our social judgments are a mix of observation and expectation, reason, and passion.

SUMMING UP: How Do We Perceive Our Social Worlds?

- Experiments have planted judgments or false ideas in people's minds *after* they have been given information. These experiments reveal that as before-the-fact judgments bias our perceptions and interpretations, so after-the-fact judgments bias our recall.
- *Belief perseverance* is the phenomenon in which people cling to their initial beliefs and the reasons why a belief might be true, even when the basis for the belief is discredited.
- Far from being a repository for facts about the past, our memories are actually formed when we retrieve them, and they are subject to strong influence by the attitudes and feelings we hold at the time of retrieval, sometimes leading to the *misinformation effect.*

HOW DO WE EXPLAIN OUR SOCIAL WORLDS?

Recognize how — and how accurately — we explain others' behavior.

People make it their business to explain other people, and social psychologists make it their business to explain people's explanations.

Our judgments of people depend on how we explain their behavior. Depending on our explanation, we may judge killing as murder, manslaughter, self-defense, or heroism. Depending on our explanation, we may view a homeless person as lacking initiative or as victimized by job and welfare cutbacks. Depending on our explanation, we may interpret someone's friendly behavior as genuine warmth or as ingratiation. Attribution theory helps us make sense of how such explanations work.

Attributing Causality: To the Person or the Situation

We endlessly analyze and discuss why things happen as they do, especially when we experience something negative or unexpected (Weiner, 1985, 2008, 2010). If worker productivity declines, do we assume the workers are getting lazier – or has their workplace become less efficient? Does a young boy who hits his classmates have a hostile personality – or is he responding to relentless teasing?

Attribution theory analyzes how we explain people's behavior and what we infer from it (Gilbert & Malone, 1995; Heider, 1958). We sometimes attribute people's behavior to *internal* causes (for example, someone's disposition or mental state) and sometimes to *external* causes (for example, something about the situation). A teacher may wonder whether a child's underachievement is due to a lack of motivation and ability (an internal cause or a **dispositional attribution**) or to physical and social circumstances (an external cause or **situational attribution**). Also, some people are more inclined to attribute behavior to stable personality, whereas others are more likely to attribute behavior to situations (Bastian & Haslam, 2006; Robins et al., 2004).

attribution theory
The theory of how people explain others' behavior—for example, by attributing it either to internal dispositions (enduring traits, motives, and attitudes) or to external situations.

dispositional attribution
Attributing behavior to the person's disposition and traits.

situational attribution
Attributing behavior to the environment.

Researchers found that married people often analyze their partners' behaviors, especially their negative behaviors. Cold hostility, more than a warm hug, is likely to leave the partner wondering "Why?" (Holtzworth & Jacobson, 1988). Spouses' answers correlate with marital satisfaction. Unhappy couples usually offer internal explanations for negative acts ("She was late because she doesn't care about me."). Happy couples more often externalize ("She was late because of heavy traffic."). Explanations for positive acts similarly work either to maintain distress ("He brought me flowers because he wants sex.") or to enhance the relationship ("He brought me flowers to show he loves me.") (Hewstone & Fincham, 1996; McNulty et al., 2008; Weiner, 1995).

A misattribution? Sexual harassment sometimes begins with a man's misreading a woman's warmth as a sexual come-on.
PeopleImages/Getty Images

Antonia Abbey (1987, 1991, 2011) have repeatedly found that straight men are more likely than women to attribute a woman's friendliness to sexual interest. Men's misreading of women's warmth as a sexual come-on – an example of **misattribution** – can contribute to sexual harassment or even sexual assault (Farris et al., 2008; Kolivas & Gross, 2007; Pryor et al., 1997). Many men believe women are flattered by repeated requests for dates, which women more often view as harassment (Rotundo et al., 2001).

misattribution
Mistakenly attributing a behavior to the wrong source.

Misattribution is particularly likely when men are in positions of power. A manager may misinterpret a subordinate woman's submissive or friendly behavior and, full of himself, see her in sexual terms (Bargh & Raymond, 1995). Men think about sex more often than do women. Men also are more likely than women to assume that others share their feelings (Lee et al., 2020). Thus, a man with sex on his mind may greatly overestimate the sexual significance of a woman's courtesy smile (Levesque et al., 2006; Nelson & LeBoeuf, 2002).

INFERRING TRAITS

We often assume or infer that other people's actions are indicative of their intentions and dispositions (Jones & Davis, 1965). If we observe Mason making a sarcastic comment to Kiara, we decide that Mason is a hostile person. When are people more likely to infer that others' behavior is caused by traits? For one thing, behavior that's normal for a particular situation tells us less about the person than does behavior unusual for that situation. If Imani is sarcastic in a job interview, a situation in which sarcasm is rare, that tells us more about Imani than if she is sarcastic with her siblings.

The ease with which we infer traits – a phenomenon called **spontaneous trait inference** – is remarkable (Hupbach et al., 2022). In experiments at New York University, James Uleman (1989; Uleman et al., 2008) gave students statements to remember, such as "The librarian carries the old woman's groceries across the street." The students would instantly, unintentionally, and unconsciously infer a trait. When later they were helped to recall the sentence, the most valuable clue word was not "books" (to cue librarian) or "bags" (to cue groceries) but "helpful" – the inferred trait that we suspect you, too, spontaneously attributed to the librarian. And just 1/10th of a second exposure to someone's face leads people to spontaneously infer some personality traits (Willis & Todorov, 2006).

spontaneous trait inference
An effortless, automatic inference of a trait after exposure to someone's behavior.

The Fundamental Attribution Error

Social psychology's most important lesson concerns the influence of our social environment. At any moment, our internal state, and therefore, what we say and do, depends on the situation as well as on what we bring to the situation. In experiments, a slight difference between two situations sometimes greatly affects how people respond. As a professor, I [DM] have seen this when teaching the same class at both 8:30 A.M. and 7:00 P.M. Silent stares would greet me in the morning; in the evening, I had to break up a party. In each situation, some individuals were more talkative than others, but the difference between the two situations exceeded the individual differences.

To what should we attribute a student's sleepiness? To lack of sleep? To boredom? Whether we make internal or external attributions depends on whether we notice her consistently sleeping in this and other classes, and on whether other students react as she does to this particular class.
wavebreakmedia/Shutterstock

Attribution researchers have found a common problem with our attributions. When explaining someone's behavior, we often underestimate the impact of the situation and overestimate the extent to which it reflects the individual's traits and attitudes. Thus, even knowing the effect of the time of day on classroom conversation, I found it terribly tempting to assume that the people in the evening class were more extraverted than the "silent types" who came in the morning. Likewise, we may infer that people fall because they're clumsy rather than because they were tripped; that people smile because they're happy rather than faking friendliness; and that people speed past us on the highway because they're aggressive rather than late for an important meeting.

This discounting of the situation, called the **fundamental attribution error** (Ross, 1977, 2018), appears in many experiments. In the first such study, Edward Jones and Victor Harris (1967) had Duke University students read debaters' speeches supporting or attacking communist Cuba's leader at the time, Fidel Castro. When told that the debater chose which position to take, the students logically assumed it reflected the person's own attitude. But what happened when the students were told that the debate coach had assigned the position? Students still inferred that the debater had the assigned leanings (**Figure 4**). People seemed to think, "I know he was assigned that position, but I think he really believes it."

fundamental attribution error
The tendency for observers to underestimate situational influences and overestimate dispositional influences upon others' behavior.

Even when people know they are *causing* someone else's behavior, they still underestimate external influences. If individuals dictate an opinion that someone else must then express, they still tend to see the person as actually holding that opinion (Gilbert & Jones, 1986). If people are asked to be either self-enhancing or self-deprecating during an interview, they are very aware of why they are acting so. But they are *un*aware of their effect on another person. If Juan acts modestly, his conversation partner Ethan is likely to exhibit modesty as well. Juan will easily understand his own behavior, but he will think that poor

FIGURE 4
The Fundamental Attribution Error
When people read a debate speech supporting or attacking Fidel Castro, they attributed corresponding attitudes to the speechwriter, even when the debate coach assigned the writer's position.
Source: Data from Jones and Harris (1967)

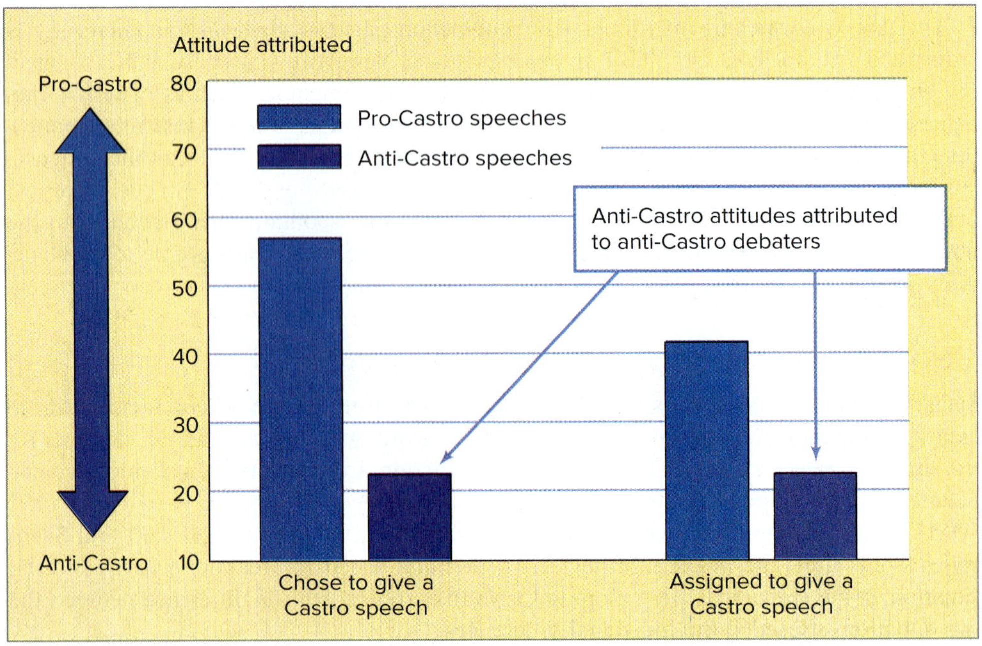

Ethan suffers from low self-esteem. In short, we tend to presume that others are the way they act—even when we don't make the same presumption about ourselves. Observing Cinderella cowering in her oppressive home, people (ignoring the situation) infer that she is meek; dancing with her at the ball, the prince sees a suave and glamorous person. Cinderella knows she is the same person in both situations.

Lee Ross, one of the first to research the fundamental attribution error, had firsthand experience with the phenomenon when he went from being a graduate student to a professor. His doctoral oral exam had proved a humbling experience as his apparently brilliant professors quizzed him on topics they specialized in. Six months later, *Dr.* Ross was himself an examiner, now able to ask penetrating questions on *his* favorite topics. Ross's hapless student later confessed to feeling exactly as Ross had a half-year before—dissatisfied with his ignorance and impressed with the apparent brilliance of the examiners (Ross, 2018).

When viewing an actor playing a "hero" or "villain" role, we find it difficult to escape the illusion that the scripted behavior reflects their real-life inner disposition (Tukachinsky, 2020). Thus, we might see actor Lena Headey as scheming and manipulative, similar to the character she plays in the show *Game of Thrones*.
HBO/BSkyB/Kobal/Shutterstock

In an experiment mimicking his student-to-professor experience, Ross set up a simulated quiz game. He randomly assigned some Stanford University students to play the role of questioner, some to play the role of a contestant, and others to observe. The researchers invited the questioners to make up difficult questions that would demonstrate their wealth of knowledge. Any one of us can imagine such questions using one's own domain of competence: "Where is Bainbridge Island?" "How did Mary, Queen of Scots, die?" "Which has the longer coastline, Europe or Africa?" If even those few questions have you feeling a little uninformed, then you will appreciate the results of this experiment (Ross et al., 1977).*

Everyone had to know that the questioners would have the advantage. Yet both contestants and observers came to the erroneous conclusion that the questioners *really were* more knowledgeable overall than the contestants (**Figure 5**). Follow-up research shows

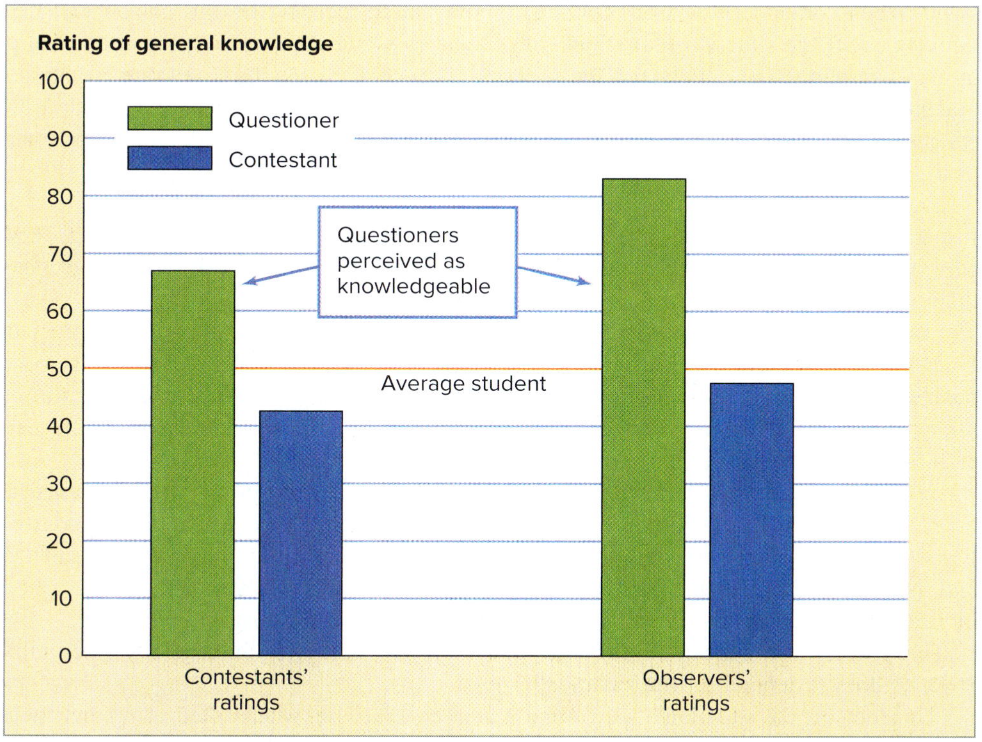

FIGURE 5

Those Asking the Questions are Seen As More Knowledgable

Both contestants and observers of a simulated quiz game assumed that a person who had been randomly assigned the role of questioner was far more knowledgeable than the contestant. Actually, the assigned roles of questioner and contestant simply made the questioner seem more knowledgeable. The failure to appreciate this illustrates the fundamental attribution error.
Source: Data from Vallone et al., 1985.

*Bainbridge Island is across Puget Sound from Seattle. Mary was ordered beheaded by her cousin Queen Elizabeth I. Although the African continent is more than double the area of Europe, Europe's coastline is longer. (It is more convoluted, with many harbors and inlets, a geographical fact that contributed to its role in the history of maritime trade.)

People often attribute keen intelligence to those, such as teachers and quiz show hosts, who test others' knowledge.
Barry King/Alamy Stock Photo

that these misimpressions are not a reflection of low social intelligence. If anything, college students and other intelligent and socially competent people are *more* likely to make the attribution error (Bauman & Skitka, 2010; Block & Funder, 1986).

In real life, those with social power usually initiate and control conversations, which often leads underlings to overestimate their knowledge and intelligence (Jouffre & Croizet, 2016). Medical doctors, for example, are often presumed to be experts on all sorts of questions unrelated to medicine. Similarly, students often overestimate the brilliance of their teachers. (As in the experiment, teachers are the questioners on subjects of their special expertise.) When some of these students later become teachers, they are often amazed to discover that teachers are not so brilliant after all.

WHY DO WE MAKE THE ATTRIBUTION ERROR?

So far, we have seen a bias in the way we explain other people's behavior: We often ignore powerful situational determinants. Why do we tend to underestimate the situational determinants of others' behavior but not of our own?

PERSPECTIVE AND SITUATIONAL AWARENESS Attribution theorists have pointed out that we observe others from a different perspective than we observe ourselves (Jones, 1976; Jones & Nisbett, 1971; Malle, 2006). When we act, the *environment* commands our attention. When we watch another *person* act, that *person* occupies the center of our attention and the environment becomes relatively invisible. If I'm mad, it's the situation that's making me angry. But someone else getting mad may seem like an ill-tempered person.

Nearly everyone has had the experience of feeling annoyed when someone else looks at their phone during a conversation – yet nearly everyone has also done this themselves. Why? When someone else takes out their phone, we're focusing on the person and not thinking about the situation that might cause them to be on their phone. But when we are on our own phone, we understand the situation – checking to see if a loved one got home, looking up a quick fact – that caused us to look. Across four experiments, people said others' phone use made the conversation less enjoyable, but underestimated the impact of their own phone use on others' enjoyment (Barrick et al., 2022).

Even when observing others, perspective matters. When people viewed a videotape of a suspect confessing during a police interview with a camera focused on the suspect, they perceived the confession as genuine. If the camera was instead focused on the detective, they perceived it as more coerced (Lassiter et al., 2005, 2007; Lassiter & Irvine, 1986). The camera perspective influenced people's guilt judgments even when the judge instructed them not to allow the camera angle to influence them (Lassiter et al., 2002). Likewise, people who view an incident from a police officer's body-cam are more sympathetic to the officer than those who view the scene from a dash-cam, which has a broader angle (Turner et al., 2019).

In courtrooms, most confession videotapes focus on the confessor. As we might expect, noted Daniel Lassiter and Kimberly Dudley (1991), such tapes yield a nearly 100% conviction rate when played by prosecutors. Aware of Lassiter's research on the *camera perspective bias*, New Zealand and some parts of Canada and the United States now require that police interrogations be filmed with equal focus on the officer and the suspect.

This process also appears in day-to-day life. Consider this: Are you generally quiet, talkative, or does it depend on the situation?

"Depends on the situation" is a common answer. Likewise, when asked to predict their feelings 2 weeks after receiving grades or learning the outcome of their country's national election, people expect the situation to rule their emotions; they underestimate the importance of their own sunny or dour dispositions (Quoidbach & Dunn, 2010). But when asked to describe a friend – or to describe what they were like 5 years ago – people more often ascribe trait descriptions. *When recalling our past, we become like observers of someone else* (Pronin & Ross, 2006). For most of us, the "old you" is someone other than today's "real you." We regard our distant past selves (and our distant future selves) almost as if they were other people occupying our body.

The fundamental attribution error can cause observers to underestimate the effects of the situation. Driving into a gas station, we may think the person parked at the second pump (blocking easy access to the first) is inconsiderate. That person, having arrived when the first pump was in use, attributes their behavior to the situation.
FotograFFF/Shutterstock

All these experiments point to a reason for the attribution error: *We find causes where we look for them.* To see this in your own experience, consider this: Would you say your social psychology instructor is a quiet or a talkative person?

You may have guessed that they are fairly outgoing. But consider: Your attention focuses on your instructor while they behave in a public context that demands speaking. The instructor also observes their own behavior in many situations – in the classroom, in meetings, at home. "Me, talkative?" your instructor might say. "Well, it all depends on the situation. When I'm in class or with good friends, I'm rather outgoing. But at conferences and in unfamiliar situations I'm rather shy." Because we are acutely aware of how our behavior varies with the situation, we see ourselves as more variable than do other people (Baxter & Goldberg, 1987; Kammer, 1982; Sande et al., 1988). We think, "Nigel is uptight, but Fiona is relaxed. With me it varies."

"And in imagination he began to recall the best moments of his pleasant life. . . . But the child who had experienced that happiness existed no longer, it was like a reminiscence of somebody else."

—Leo Tolstoy, *The Death of Ivan Ilyich*, 1886

CULTURAL DIFFERENCES Cultures also influence attribution error (Ma-Kellams 2020; Watson, 1982). An individualistic Western worldview predisposes people to assume that people, not situations, cause events. Internal explanations are more socially approved (Jellison & Green, 1981). "You can do it!" we are assured by the pop psychology of positive-thinking Western culture. You get what you deserve and deserve what you get.

As Western children grow up, they learn to explain other people's behavior in terms of their personal characteristics (Rholes et al., 1990; Ross, 1981). As a first-grader, one of my [DM] sons unscrambled the words "gate the sleeve caught Tom on his" into "The gate caught Tom on his sleeve." His teacher, applying Western cultural assumptions, marked that wrong. The "right" answer located the cause within Tom: "Tom caught his sleeve on the gate."

The fundamental attribution error occurs across varied cultures (Krull et al., 1999). Yet people in Eastern Asian cultures are somewhat more sensitive than Westerners to the importance of situations (Di et al., 2021). Thus, when aware of the social context, they are less inclined to assume that others' behavior corresponds to their traits (Choi et al., 1999; Farwell & Weiner, 2000; Masuda & Kitayama, 2004).

Some languages promote external attributions. Instead of "I was late," Spanish idiom allows one to say, "The clock caused me to be late." In collectivistic cultures, people less often perceive others in terms of personal dispositions (Lee et al., 1996; Zebrowitz-McArthur, 1988). They are less likely to spontaneously interpret a behavior as reflecting an inner trait (Newman, 1993). When told of someone's actions, Indians are less likely than Americans to offer dispositional explanations ("She is kind") and more likely to offer situational explanations ("Her friends were with her") (Miller, 1984).

The fundamental attribution error is *fundamental* because it colors our explanations in basic and important ways. Researchers in Britain, India, Australia, and the United States have found that people's attributions predict their attitudes toward those in poverty and the unemployed (Bridger et al., 2022; Pandey et al., 1982; Skitka, 1999; Weiner et al., 2011). Those who attribute poverty and unemployment to personal dispositions ("They're just lazy and undeserving") tend to adopt political positions unsympathetic to such people (**Figure 6**). This *dispositional attribution* ascribes behavior to the person's disposition and traits. Those who make *situational*

Focusing on the person. Would you infer that your professor is naturally outgoing?
LightField Studios/Shutterstock

FIGURE 6

Attributions and Reactions

How we explain someone's negative behavior determines how we feel about it.

(Photo): skynesher/Getty Images

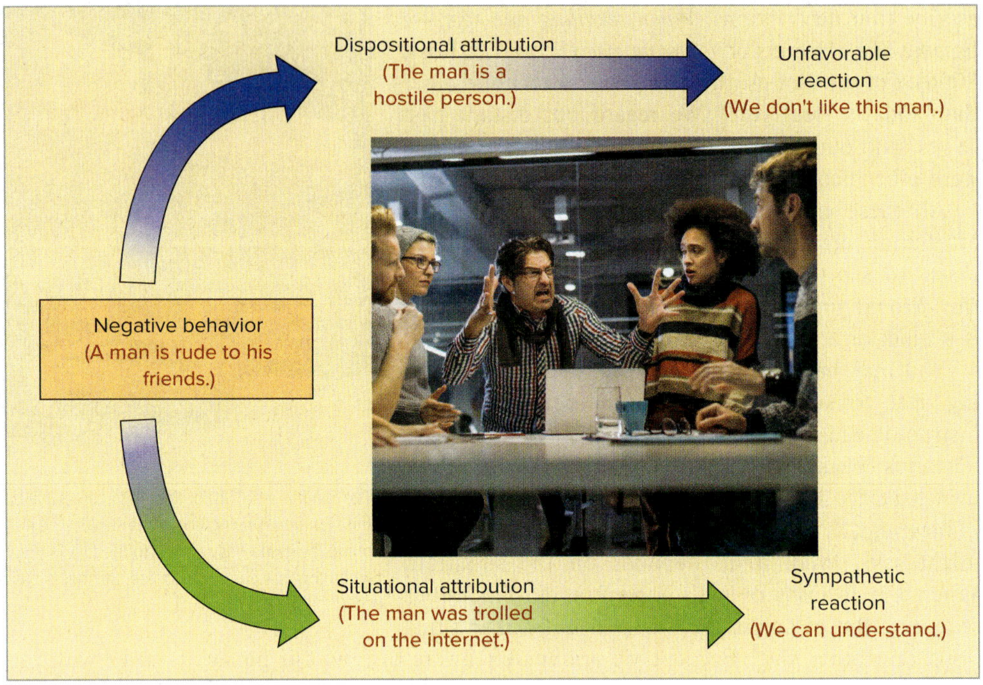

"Most poor people are not lazy. . . . They catch the early bus. They raise other people's children. They clean the streets. No, no, they're not lazy."

—The Reverend Jesse Jackson, Address to the Democratic National Convention, July, 1988

attributions ("If you or I were to live with the same overcrowding and poor education, would we be any better off?") tend to adopt political positions that offer more direct support to the poor. Tell us your attributions for poverty and we will guess your politics.

Can we benefit from being aware of the attribution error? I [DM] once assisted with some interviews for a faculty position. One candidate was interviewed by six of us at once; each of us had the opportunity to ask two or three questions. I came away thinking, "What a stiff, awkward person he is." The second candidate I met privately over coffee, and we immediately discovered we had a close, mutual friend. As we talked, I became increasingly impressed by what a "warm, engaging, stimulating person she is." Only later did I remember the fundamental attribution error and reassess my analysis. I had attributed his stiffness and her warmth to their dispositions; in fact, I later realized, such behavior resulted partly from the difference in their interview situations.

WHY WE STUDY ATTRIBUTION ERRORS

This chapter, like the one before it, explains some foibles and fallacies in our social thinking. Reading about these may make it seem, as one of my [DM] students put it, that "social psychologists get their kicks out of playing tricks on people." Actually, the experiments, though sometimes amusing, are not designed to demonstrate "what fools these mortals be." Their serious purpose is to reveal how we think about ourselves and others.

If our capacity for illusion and self-deception is shocking, remember that our modes of thought are generally adaptive. Illusory thinking is a by-product of our mind's strategies for simplifying complex information. It parallels our perceptual mechanisms, which generally give us useful images of the world but sometimes lead us astray.

A second reason for focusing on thinking biases such as the fundamental attribution error is humanitarian. One of social psychology's "great humanizing messages," noted Thomas Gilovich and Richard Eibach (2001), is that people should not always be blamed for their problems: "More often than people are willing to acknowledge, failure, disability, and misfortune are . . . the product of real environmental causes."

A third reason for focusing on biases is that we are mostly unaware of them and can benefit from greater awareness. As with other biases, such as the self-serving bias, people see themselves as less susceptible than others to attribution errors (Pronin, 2008). You will probably find more surprises, more challenges, and more benefit in an analysis of errors and biases than you would in a string of testimonies to the human capacity for logic and intellectual achievement. That is also why world literature so often portrays pride and other human failings. Social psychology aims to expose us to fallacies in our thinking in the hope that we will become more rational, more in touch with reality, and more receptive to critical thinking.

SUMMING UP: How Do We Explain Our Social Worlds?

- *Attribution theory* involves how we explain people's behavior. *Misattribution* – attributing a behavior to the wrong source – is a major factor in sexual harassment, as a person in power (typically male) interprets friendliness as a sexual come-on.
- Although we usually make reasonable attributions, we often commit the *fundamental attribution error* when explaining other people's behavior. We attribute their behavior so much to their inner traits and attitudes that we discount situational constraints, even when those are obvious. We make this attribution error partly because when we watch someone act, that *person* is the focus of our attention and the situation is relatively invisible. When *we* act, our attention is usually on what we are reacting to – the situation is more visible.

HOW DO OUR SOCIAL BELIEFS MATTER?

Describe how our expectations of our social worlds matter.

Having considered how we explain and judge others – efficiently, adaptively, but sometimes erroneously – we conclude this chapter by pondering the effects of our social judgments. Do our social beliefs matter? Can they change reality?

Our social beliefs and judgments do matter. They influence how we feel and act, and by so doing may help generate their own reality. When our ideas lead us to act in ways that produce their apparent confirmation, they have become what sociologist Robert Merton (1948) termed **self-fulfilling prophecies** – beliefs that lead to their own fulfillment. If, led to believe that their bank is about to crash, its customers race to withdraw their money, their false perceptions may create reality, noted Merton. If people are led to believe that stocks are about to soar, they will indeed. (See "Focus On: The Self-Fulfilling Psychology of the Stock Market.")

self-fulfilling prophecy
A belief that leads to its own fulfillment.

In his well-known studies of *experimenter bias,* Robert Rosenthal (1985, 2006) found that research participants sometimes live up to what they believe experimenters expect of them. In one study, experimenters asked individuals to judge the success of people in various photographs. The experimenters read the same instructions to all their participants and showed them the same photos. Nevertheless, experimenters who expected their participants to see the photographed people as successful obtained higher ratings than did those who expected their participants to see the people as failures. Even more startling – and controversial – are reports that teachers' beliefs about their students similarly serve as self-fulfilling prophecies. If a teacher believes a student is good at math, will the student do well in the class? Let's examine this.

Teacher Expectations and Student Performance

Teachers do have higher expectations for some students than for others. Perhaps you have detected this after having a brother or sister precede you in school, after receiving a label such as "gifted" or after taking "honors" classes. It's not just vague reputations that influence

focus ON: The Self-Fulfilling Psychology of the Stock Market

On the evening of January 6, 1981, Joseph Granville, a popular Florida investment adviser, wired his clients: "Stock prices will nosedive; sell tomorrow." Word of Granville's advice soon spread, and January 7 became the heaviest day of trading in the previous history of the New York Stock Exchange. All told, stock values lost $40 billion.

Nearly a half-century ago, John Maynard Keynes likened such stock market psychology to the popular beauty contests then conducted by London newspapers. To win, one had to pick the six faces out of a hundred that were, in turn, chosen most frequently by the other newspaper contestants. Thus, as Keynes (1936) wrote, "Each competitor has to pick not those faces which he himself finds prettiest, but those which he thinks likeliest to catch the fancy of the other competitors."

Investors likewise try to pick not the stocks that touch their fancy but the stocks that other investors will favor. The name of the game is predicting others' behavior. As one Wall Street fund manager explained, "You may or may not agree with Granville's view — but that's usually beside the point." If you think his advice will cause others to sell, you want to sell quickly, before prices drop more. If you expect others to buy, you buy now to beat the rush.

The self-fulfilling psychology of the stock market worked to an extreme on Monday, October 19, 1987, when the Dow Jones Industrial Average lost 20%. Part of what happens during such crashes is that the media and the rumor mill focus on whatever bad news is available to explain them. Once reported, the explanatory news stories further diminish people's expectations, causing declining prices to fall still lower. The process also works in reverse by amplifying good news when stock prices are rising.

In April of 2000, the volatile technology market again demonstrated a self-fulfilling psychology, now called "momentum investing." After 2 years of eagerly buying stocks (because prices were rising), people started frantically selling them (because prices were falling). Such wild market swings — "irrational exuberance" followed by a crash — are mainly self-generated, noted economist Robert Shiller (2005). In 2008 and 2009, the market psychology headed south again as another bubble burst.

these judgments, however; teachers accurately perceive their students' abilities and achievements and expect more of students who have performed well in the past (Jussim, 2017; Jussim et al., 2009). Thus, better past performance leads to higher expectations.

But could teachers' expectations also *cause* better student performance? One correlational study of 4,300 British schoolchildren suggested yes; students whose teachers expected them to perform well indeed performed well (Crano & Mellon, 1978). In several later studies, teachers' judgments predicted students' later performance even beyond their actual ability (Bergold & Steinmayr, 2023; Sorhagen, 2013; Timmermans et al., 2022).

How much can a teacher's expectations influence a student's performance?
Shutterstock

Could we test this "teacher-expectations effect" experimentally? Imagine we gave a teacher the impression that four randomly selected students are unusually capable. Will the teacher give special treatment to these four and elicit superior performance from them? In a now-famous experiment, Rosenthal and Lenore Jacobson (1968) reported precisely that. Randomly selected children in a San Francisco elementary school who were said (on the basis of a fictitious test) to be on the verge of a dramatic intellectual spurt did then spurt ahead in IQ score.

That dramatic result seemed to suggest that the academic issues of "disadvantaged" children might reflect their teachers' low expectations. The findings were soon publicized in the national media as well as in many college textbooks. However, further analysis — which was not as highly publicized — revealed the teacher-expectations effect to be not as powerful and reliable as this initial study had led many people to believe (Jussim et al., 2009; Spitz, 1999). By Rosenthal's own count, only about 40% of the nearly 500 published experiments showed expectations significantly affecting performance (Rosenthal, 1991, 2002). Low expectations do not doom a capable child, nor do high expectations magically transform a slow learner into a valedictorian. Human nature is not so pliable.

How are such expectations transmitted? Rosenthal and other investigators report that teachers look, smile, and nod more at "high-potential students." Teachers also may teach more to their "gifted" students, set higher goals for them, call on them more, and give them more time to answer (Cooper, 1983; Harris & Rosenthal, 1985, 1986; Jussim, 1986).

In one study, teachers were videotaped talking to, or about, unseen students for whom they held high or low expectations. A random 10-second clip of either the teacher's voice or the teacher's face was enough to tell viewers – both children and adults – whether this was a good or a poor student and how much the teacher liked the student. (You read that right: 10 seconds.) Although teachers may think they can conceal their feelings and behave impartially toward the class, students are acutely sensitive to teachers' facial expressions and body movements (Babad et al., 1991).

What about the effect of *students'* expectations upon their teachers? You no doubt begin many of your courses having heard "This professor is interesting" and "That professor is a bore." Robert Feldman and Thomas Prohaska (1979; Feldman & Theiss, 1982) found that such expectations can affect both student and teacher. Students who expected to be taught by an excellent teacher perceived their teacher (who was unaware of their expectations) as more competent and interesting than did students with low expectations. Furthermore, the students actually learned more. In a later experiment, women who were falsely told that their male instructor was sexist had a less positive experience with him, performed worse, and rated him as less competent than did women not given the expectation of sexism (Adams et al., 2006).

Were these results due entirely to the students' perceptions or also to a self-fulfilling prophecy that affected the teacher? In a follow-up experiment, Feldman and Prohaska (1979) videotaped teachers and had observers rate their performances. Teachers were judged most capable when assigned a student who nonverbally conveyed positive expectations.

To see whether such effects might also occur in actual classrooms, a research team led by David Jamieson (Jamieson et al., 1987) experimented with four Ontario high school classes taught by a newly transferred teacher. During individual interviews, they told students in two of the classes that both other students and the research team rated the teacher very highly. Compared with the control classes, students who were given positive expectations paid better attention during class. At the end of the teaching unit, they also got better grades and rated the teacher as clearer in their teaching. The attitudes that a class has toward its teacher are as important, it seems, as the teacher's attitude toward the students.

Getting from Others What We Expect

So the expectations of experimenters and teachers, although usually reasonably accurate, occasionally act as self-fulfilling prophecies. Self-fulfilling prophecies can operate in work settings (with managers who have high or low expectations), in courtrooms (as judges instruct juries), and in simulated police contexts (as interrogators with expectations of guilt or innocence interrogate and pressure suspects) (Kassin et al., 2003; Rosenthal, 2003, 2006). Self-fulfilling prophecies can operate at home, too: Teens whose parents thought they'd tried marijuana – even though they hadn't – were more likely to subsequently try it (Lamb & Crano, 2014).

Do self-fulfilling prophecies color our personal relationships? Sometimes, negative expectations of someone lead us to be extra nice to that person, which induces them to be nice in return – thus *dis*confirming our expectations. But a more common finding in studies of social interaction is that, yes, we do to some extent get what we expect (Olson et al., 1996).

In laboratory games, hostility nearly always begets hostility: If someone believes an opponent will be noncooperative, the opponent often responds by becoming noncooperative

According to Sandra Murray's research, viewing your partner through rose-colored glasses has benefits.
wavebreakmedia/Shutterstock

(Kelley & Stahelski, 1970). Each party's perception of the other as aggressive, resentful, and vindictive induces the other to display those behaviors in self-defense, thus creating a vicious, self-perpetuating circle. In another experiment, people anticipated interacting with another person of a different race. When led to expect that this person disliked interacting with someone of their race, they felt more anger and displayed more hostility toward the person (Butz & Plant, 2006). Likewise, whether someone expects their partner to be in a bad mood or in a loving mood may affect how they relate to them, thereby inducing the partner to confirm their belief.

So, do intimate relationships prosper when partners idealize each other? Are positive illusions of the other's virtues self-fulfilling? Or are they more often self-defeating, by creating high expectations that can't be met? Among University of Waterloo dating couples followed by Sandra Murray and associates (1996a, 1996b, 2000), positive ideals of one's partner were good omens. Idealization helped buffer conflict, bolster satisfaction, and turn self-perceived frogs into princes or princesses. When someone loves and admires us, it helps us become more the person they imagine us to be.

behavioral confirmation
A type of self-fulfilling prophecy whereby people's social expectations lead them to behave in ways that cause others to confirm their expectations.

"The more he treated her as though she were really very nice, the more Lotty expanded and became really very nice, and the more he, affected in his turn, became really very nice himself; so that they went round and round, not in a vicious but in a highly virtuous circle."

—Elizabeth Von Arnim, *The Enchanted April*, 1922

When dating couples deal with conflicts, hopeful optimists and their partners tend to perceive each other as engaging constructively. Compared to those with more pessimistic expectations, they then feel more supported and more satisfied with the outcome (Srivastava et al., 2006). Among married couples, too, those who worry that their partner doesn't love and accept them interpret slight hurts as rejections, which motivates them to devalue the partner and distance themselves. Those who presume their partner's love and acceptance respond less defensively, read less into stressful events, and treat the partner better (Murray et al., 2003). Love helps create its presumed reality.

Several experiments conducted by Mark Snyder (1984) at the University of Minnesota show how, once formed, erroneous beliefs about the social world can induce others to confirm those beliefs, a phenomenon called **behavioral confirmation.** For example, straight male students talked on the telephone with women they thought (from having been shown a picture) were either attractive or unattractive. The supposedly attractive women spoke more warmly than the supposedly unattractive women. The men's erroneous beliefs had become a self-fulfilling prophecy by leading them to act in a way that influenced the women to fulfill the men's stereotype that beautiful people are desirable people (Snyder et al., 1977).

Imagine yourself as one of the 60 young straight men or 60 young straight women in an experiment by Robert Ridge and Jeffrey Reber (2002). Each man is to interview one of the women for a teaching assistant position. Before doing so, he is told either that she feels attracted to him (based on his answers to a biographical questionnaire) or not attracted. (Imagine being told that someone you were about to meet reported considerable interest in dating you, or had no interest whatsoever.) The result was behavioral confirmation: Applicants believed to feel an attraction were more flirtatious (without being aware of doing so). Ridge and Reber believe that this process, like the misattribution phenomenon discussed previously, may be one of the roots of sexual harassment. If a woman's behavior seems to confirm a man's beliefs, he may then escalate his overtures until they become sufficiently overt for the woman to recognize and interpret them as inappropriate or harassing.

Behavioral confirmation. If each of these people feels attracted to the other, but presumes that feeling isn't reciprocated, they may each act cool to avoid feeling rejected — and decide that the other's coolness confirms the presumption. Danu Stinson and colleagues (2009) note that such "self-protective inhibition of warmth" dooms some would-be relationships.
Fabrice LEROUGE/Getty Images

Expectations influence children's behavior, too. After observing the amount of littering in three classrooms, Richard Miller and colleagues (1975) had the teacher and others repeatedly tell one class that they should be neat and tidy.

This persuasion increased the amount of trash placed in wastebaskets from 15% to 45%, but only temporarily. Another class, which also had been placing only 15% of its trash in wastebaskets, was repeatedly congratulated for being so neat and tidy. After 8 days of hearing this, and still 2 weeks later, these children were fulfilling the expectation by putting more than 80% of their litter in wastebaskets. Tell children they are hardworking and kind (rather than lazy and mean), and they may live up to their labels.

Overall, these experiments help us understand how social beliefs, such as stereotypes about people with disabilities or about people of a particular race or sex, may be self-confirming. How others treat us reflects how we and others have treated them.

SUMMING UP: How Do Our Social Beliefs Matter?

- Our beliefs sometimes take on lives of their own. Usually, our beliefs about others have a basis in reality. But studies of experimenter bias and teacher expectations show that an erroneous belief that certain people are unusually capable (or incapable) can lead teachers and researchers to treat those people differently. This may elicit superior (or inferior) performance and, therefore, seem to confirm an assumption that is actually false – a *self-fulfilling prophecy*.
- Similarly, in everyday life we often get *behavioral confirmation* of what we expect. Told that someone we are about to meet is intelligent and attractive, we may come away impressed with just how intelligent and attractive they are.

CONCLUDING THOUGHTS: Reflecting on Illusory Thinking

Is research on cognitive errors too humbling? Surely we can acknowledge the hard truth of our human limits and still sympathize with the deeper message that people are more than machines. Our subjective experiences are the stuff of our humanity – our art and our music, our enjoyment of friendship and love, our mystical and religious experiences.

The cognitive and social psychologists who explore illusory thinking are not out to remake us into unfeeling logical machines. They know that emotions enrich human experience and that intuitions are an important source of creative ideas. They add, however, the reminder that our susceptibility to error also makes clear the need for disciplined training of the mind. The American writer Norman Cousins (1978) called this "the biggest truth of all about learning: that its purpose is to unlock the human mind and to develop it into an organ capable of thought – conceptual thought, analytical thought, sequential thought."

"Rob the average man of his life-illusion, and you rob him also of his happiness."

—Henrik Ibsen, *The Wild Duck*, 1884

Research on error and illusion in social judgment reminds us to "judge not" – to remember, with a dash of humility, our potential for misjudgment. It also encourages us not to feel intimidated by the arrogance of those who cannot see their own potential for bias and error. We humans are wonderfully intelligent yet fallible creatures. We have dignity but not deity.

Such humility and distrust of human authority are at the heart of both religion and science. No wonder many of the founders of modern science were religious people whose convictions predisposed them to be humble before nature and skeptical of human authority (Hooykaas, 1972; Merton, 1938). Science always involves an interplay between intuition and rigorous test, between creative hunch and skepticism. To sift reality from illusion requires both open-minded curiosity and hard-headed rigor. This perspective could prove to be a good attitude for approaching all of life: to be critical but not cynical, curious but not gullible, open but not exploitable.

"The more powerful you are . . . the more responsible you are to act humbly. If you don't, your power will ruin you, and you will ruin the other."

—Pope Francis, TED talk, 2017

Behavior and Attitudes

CHAPTER

4

AntonioGuillem/Getty Images

How well do our attitudes predict our behavior?

When does our behavior affect our attitudes?

Why does our behavior affect our attitudes?

Concluding Thoughts: Changing ourselves through action

"The ancestor of every action is a thought."

—Ralph Waldo Emerson, *Essays, First Series,* 1841

On a rainy October morning in 2018, congregants gathered for Saturday services at the Tree of Life synagogue in Pittsburgh. Within a half hour, 11 were dead, shot by a man armed with an assault rifle and three handguns. Before it was over, the gunman had also wounded six others, including four police officers attempting to stop him.

The shooter was Robert Bowers, a trucker who lived in suburban Pittsburgh. In the months leading up to the shooting, Bowers freely expressed his hatred of Jewish people, primarily by posting anti-Semitic statements online (Katz, 2018).

Bowers's hateful and extreme attitudes seemed to spur his hateful and extreme behavior. This is what we usually expect: Private beliefs and feelings determine our public behavior. Thus, the thinking goes, if we want to change behavior, we must first change hearts and minds.

But, in general, how much does what we *are* (on the inside) predict what we *do* (on the outside)? Not as much as you might think. This chapter explores the interplay of attitudes (our inside beliefs) and behavior (our outside actions).

In social psychology, **attitudes** are defined as beliefs and feelings related to a person or an event (Eagly & Chaiken, 2005). Thus, a person may have a negative attitude toward coffee, a neutral attitude toward baseball, and a positive attitude toward their next-door neighbor.

attitude

Feelings, often influenced by our beliefs, that predispose us to respond favorably or unfavorably to objects, people, and events.

Attitudes efficiently size up the world. When we have to respond quickly to something, the way we feel about it can guide how we react. For example, a person who *believes* a particular ethnic group is lazy and aggressive may *feel* dislike for such people and therefore intend to act in a discriminatory manner. You can remember these three dimensions as the ABCs of attitudes: *A*ffect (feelings), *B*ehavior tendency, and *C*ognition (thoughts) (**Figure 1**).

"All that we are is the result of what we have thought."

—Buddha, *Dhamma-Pada,* BC 563–483

The study of attitudes is central to social psychology and was one of its first concerns. For much of the last century, researchers have examined how much our attitudes affect our actions.

"Thought is the child of action."

—Benjamin Disraeli, *Vivian Gray,* 1926

HOW WELL DO OUR ATTITUDES PREDICT OUR BEHAVIOR?

State the extent to which, and under what conditions, our inner attitudes drive our outward actions.

A blow to the supposed power of attitudes came when social psychologist Allan Wicker (1969) reviewed several dozen research studies covering a variety of people, attitudes, and behaviors. Wicker offered a shocking conclusion: People's expressed attitudes hardly predicted their varying behaviors. More recent research has verified those conclusions.

- Student attitudes toward cheating bore little relation to the likelihood of their actually cheating.
- Attitudes toward organized religion were only modestly linked with weekly worship attendance.
- Pro-environment attitudes did not predict how much car owners drove (Kwan & Hung, 2023).
- Self-described racial attitudes provided little clue to behaviors in actual situations. Many people *say* they are upset when someone makes racist remarks; yet when they hear racist language, many respond with indifference (Kawakami et al., 2009).

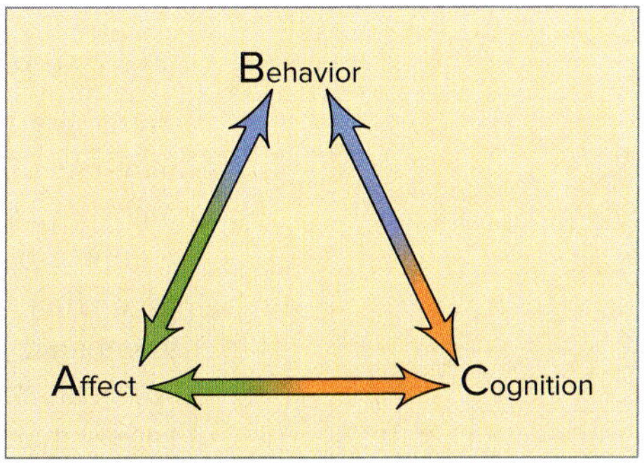

FIGURE 1
The ABCs of Attitudes

The disjuncture between attitudes and actions is what Daniel Batson and his colleagues (1997, 2001, 2002; Valdesolo & DeSteno, 2007, 2008) call "moral hypocrisy" (appearing moral while avoiding the costs of being so). Their studies presented people with an appealing task with a possible $30 prize and a dull task with no rewards. The participants had to do one of the tasks and assign a supposed second participant to the other. Only 1 in 20 believed that assigning the appealing task with the reward to themselves was the more moral thing to do, yet 80% did so. Even when told to randomly assign tasks with a coin flip, more than 85% still gave themselves the better-paying assignment – meaning a good number were

Behaviors and attitudes don't always match: Arizona Governor Doug Ducey (shown above) went maskless at the Republican National Convention in 2020 weeks after rolling out a "Mask Up, Arizona" advertising campaign encouraging citizens to wear masks when around others. Similarly, California Governor Gavin Newsom attended a large gathering at a restaurant in November 2020 after advising others not to gather in large groups.
SAUL LOEB/AFP/Getty Images

fibbing about the coin flip's outcome. When morality and greed were put on a collision course, greed usually won. Overall, people who perceive themselves as moral nevertheless often judge others more harshly than they judge themselves (Dong et al., 2023).

U.S. Representative Tim Murphy of Pennsylvania provided a shocking example of the disconnect between stated attitudes and actual behavior. Stridently antiabortion from the beginning of his political career, his behavior was different when the woman he was having an extramarital affair with believed she was pregnant, he asked her to get an abortion (Doubeck & Taylor, 2017). When his hypocrisy became public, Murphy resigned. "Pro-life in the streets, pro-choice in the sheets," quipped one pundit (Weiner, 2017).

If people don't walk the same line that they talk, it's little wonder that attempts to change behavior by changing attitudes often fail. Warnings about the dangers of smoking barely affect people who already smoke. Sex education programs have often influenced *attitudes* toward abstinence and condom use without affecting long-term abstinence and condom use *behaviors*. Australians consume about the same energy, water, and housing space whether they are committed to environmental awareness or skeptical of it (Newton & Meyer, 2013). Well-ingrained habits and practices override attitudes. We are, it seems, a horde of hypocrites.

"I have found . . . that when something is in your personal best interests, the ability of the mind to rationalize that that's the right thing is really quite extraordinary."

—U.S. Senator Mitt Romney, before casting the lone Republican vote to remove President Donald Trump from office during his first impeachment trial in February 2020

This surprising finding that what people *say* often differs from what they *do* sent social psychologists scurrying to find out why. Surely, we reasoned, convictions and feelings *sometimes* make a difference.

When Attitudes Predict Behavior

The reason why our behavior and our expressed attitudes differ is that both are subject to other influences – many other influences. One social psychologist counted 40 factors that complicate the relationship between attitudes and behavior (Triandis, 1982; see also Kraus, 1995). For an attitude to lead to a behavior, liking must become wanting, a goal must be set, the goal must be important enough to overwhelm other demands, and a specific behavior must be chosen (Kruglanski et al., 2015). Our attitudes do predict our behavior when *behavior is aggregated,* when *the attitude is specific to the behavior,* and when the *attitude is potent.*

WHEN BEHAVIOR IS AGGREGATED

Predicting people's behavior is like predicting a baseball or cricket player's hitting. The outcome of any particular turn at bat is nearly impossible to predict. But when we aggregate many times at bat, we can compare their approximate batting *averages.*

For example, people's general attitude toward religion doesn't do a very good job at predicting whether they will go to religious services during the coming week, because attendance is also influenced by the weather, the religious leader, how one is feeling, and so forth. But religious attitudes predict the *total* quantity of religious behaviors over time across many situations (Fishbein & Ajzen, 1974; Kahle & Berman, 1979). The findings define a *principle of aggregation:* The effects of an attitude become more apparent when we look at a person's aggregate or average behavior.

WHEN ATTITUDES ARE SPECIFIC TO THE BEHAVIOR

Other conditions further improve the predictive accuracy of attitudes. As Icek Ajzen and Martin Fishbein (1977, 2005) pointed out, when the measured attitude is a general one and the behavior is very specific we should not expect a close correspondence between words and actions. Indeed, reported Fishbein and Ajzen, attitudes did not predict behavior in most studies. But attitudes *did* predict behavior in all 26 studies in which the measured attitude was specific to the situation. Thus, attitudes toward the general concept of "health fitness" poorly predict specific exercise and dietary practices. But someone's attitudes about the costs and benefits of *jogging* are a fairly strong predictor of whether they *jog* regularly.

Further studies – more than 700 studies with 276,000 participants – confirmed that specific, relevant attitudes do predict intended and actual behavior (Armitage & Conner, 2001; Six & Eckes, 1996; Wallace et al., 2005). For example, attitudes toward traffic safety predict traffic tickets and car accidents (Lucidi et al., 2019). Attitudes toward recycling (but not general attitudes toward environmental issues) predict intention to recycle, which predicts actual recycling (Nigbur et al., 2010; Oskamp, 1991). A practical lesson: To change habits through persuasion, we must alter people's attitudes toward *specific* practices.

Better yet for predicting behavior, says Ajzen and Fishbein's "theory of planned behavior," is knowing people's *intended* behaviors and their perceived self-efficacy and control (**Figure 2**). When, for example, someone's general attitude toward exercise is combined with social norms and perceived control (similar to self-efficacy), it can become a more specific intention to exercise. That specific intention predicts behavior better than a general attitude (Hagger et al., 2022).

Even asking people about their intentions to engage in a behavior often increases its likelihood (Levav & Fitzsimons, 2006; Wood et al., 2016). Ask people if they intend to floss their teeth in the next two weeks, and they will become more likely to do so. Ask people if they intend to vote in an upcoming election, and most will answer yes and become more likely to do so.

WHEN ATTITUDES ARE POTENT

Much of our behavior is automatic. We act out familiar scripts without reflecting on what we're doing. We respond to people we meet in the hall with an automatic "Hi." We answer the restaurant cashier's question "How was your meal?" by saying, "Fine," even if we found it only so-so.

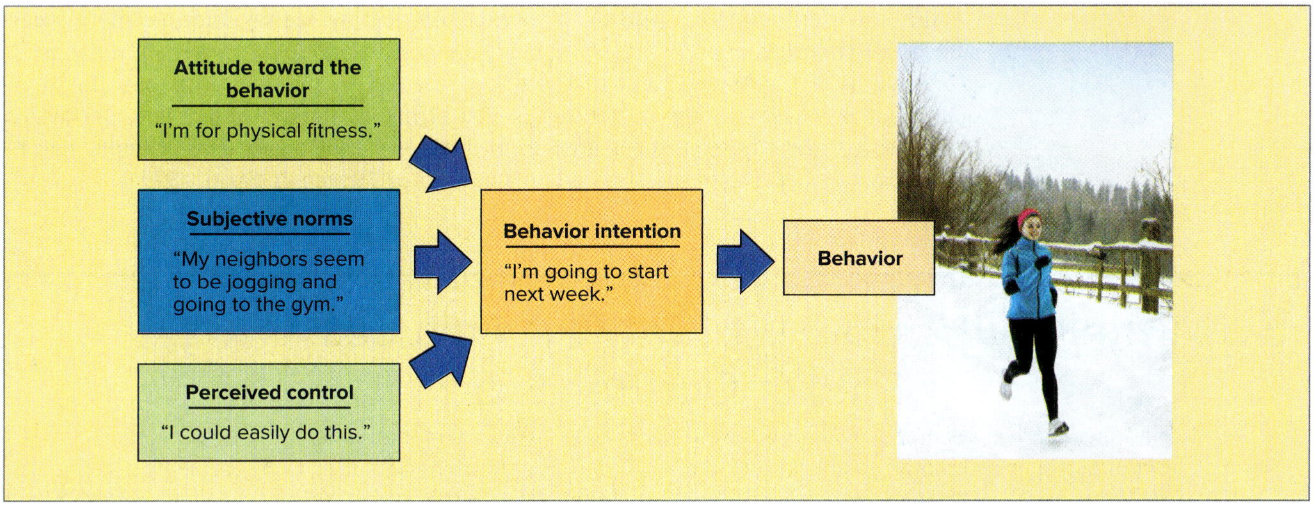

FIGURE 2

The Theory of Planned Behavior

Icek Ajzen, working with Martin Fishbein, has shown that one's (a) attitudes, (b) perceived social norms, and (c) feelings of control together determine one's intentions, which guide behavior. Compared with their general attitudes toward a healthy lifestyle, people's specific attitudes regarding jogging predict their jogging behavior much better.

(photo): Jozef Polc/halfpoint/123RF

"Thinking is easy, acting difficult, and to put one's thoughts into action, the most difficult thing in the world."

—Johann Wolfgang von Goethe (1749–1832)

"Without doubt it is a delightful harmony when doing and saying go together."

—Michel de Montaigne, *Essays*, 1588

"It is easier to preach virtue than to practice it."

—Francois La Rochefoucauld, *Maxims*, 1665

Such mindlessness is adaptive. It frees our minds to work on other things. For habitual behaviors – seat belt use, coffee consumption, class attendance – conscious intentions are hardly activated (Wood, 2017).

If we were prompted to think about our attitudes before acting, would we be truer to ourselves? Some research suggests yes. If people are reminded of their attitudes before they act, they are more likely to behave in a way consistent with them (Snyder & Swann, 1976).

That suggests another way to induce people to focus on their inner convictions: *Make them self-aware,* perhaps by having them act in front of a mirror (Carver & Scheier, 1981). Maybe you, too, can recall suddenly being acutely aware of yourself upon entering a room with a large mirror. Making people self-aware in this way promotes consistency between words and deeds (Froming et al., 1982; Gibbons, 1978).

Edward Diener and Mark Wallbom (1976) noted that nearly all college students say that cheating is morally wrong. But will they follow the advice of Shakespeare's Polonius, "To thine own self be true"? Diener and Wallbom had University of Washington students work on an IQ test and told them to stop when a bell in the room sounded. Left alone, 71% cheated by working past the bell. Among students made self-aware – by working in front of a mirror while hearing their own tape-recorded voices – only 7% cheated. Trick-or-treating children asked to take only one candy from a bowl were more likely to do so when the bowl was in front of a mirror (Beaman et al., 1979). It makes one wonder: Would eye-level mirrors in stores make people more self-conscious of their attitudes about shoplifting?

Remember Batson's studies of moral hypocrisy? In a later experiment, Batson and his colleagues (2002) found that mirrors did bring behavior into line with espoused moral attitudes. When people flipped a coin while facing a mirror, the coin flipper became scrupulously fair. Exactly half of the self-conscious participants assigned the other person to the appealing task.

The attitudes that best predict behavior are accessible (easily brought to mind) as well as stable (Glasman & Albarracin, 2006). If you can quickly say you are against the death penalty and have always felt that way, you might be more likely to sign a petition to end it. Attitudes rooted in emotion (vs. logic) are especially likely to stay the same over time, and thus especially likely to consistently predict behavior. For example, people who felt stronger emotions toward certain stores or brands were more likely to have the same attitude toward them a month later (Rocklage & Luttrell, 2021).

And when attitudes are forged by experience, not just by hearsay, they are more accessible, more enduring, and more likely to guide actions. In one study, university students all expressed negative attitudes about their school's response to a housing shortage. But given opportunities to act – to sign a petition, solicit signatures, join a committee, or write a letter – only those whose attitudes grew from direct experience (who, for example, had to live off-campus because of the shortage) actually acted (Regan & Fazio, 1977).

SUMMING UP: How Well Do Our Attitudes Predict Our Behavior?

- How do our inner *attitudes* (evaluative reactions toward some object or person, often rooted in beliefs) relate to our external behavior? Although popular wisdom stresses the impact of attitudes on behavior, in fact, attitudes are often poor predictors of behaviors. Moreover, changing people's attitudes typically fails to produce much change in their behavior. These findings inspired social psychologists to find out why we so often fail to walk the walk we talk.
- The answer: Our expressions of attitudes and our behaviors are each subject to many influences. Our attitudes will predict our behavior (1) if behavior is aggregated, (2) if the attitude is more specific to the predicted behavior, and (3) if the attitude is potent (because something reminds us of it, such as becoming self-conscious, or because we acquired it by direct experience). Under these conditions, what we think and feel predict what we do.

WHEN DOES OUR BEHAVIOR AFFECT OUR ATTITUDES?

Summarize evidence that we can act ourselves into a way of thinking.

So, to some extent, our attitudes matter. We can think ourselves into a way of acting. Now we turn to a more startling idea: that *behavior determines attitudes.* It's true that we sometimes stand up for what we believe. But it's also true that we come to believe in what we stand up for.

Consider the following incidents:

- Shonda is hypnotized and told to take off her shoes when she hears a book drop to the floor. Fifteen minutes later, a book drops, and Shonda quietly slips out of her loafers. "Shonda," asks the hypnotist, "why did you take off your shoes?" "Well . . . my feet are hot and tired," Shonda replies. "It has been a long day." The act produces the idea.
- George has electrodes temporarily implanted in the brain region that controls his head movements. When neurosurgeon José Delgado (1973) stimulates the electrodes by remote control, George always turns his head. Unaware of the remote stimulation, he offers a reasonable explanation for his head turning: "I'm looking for my slipper." "I heard a noise." "I'm restless." "I was looking under the bed."
- Carol's severe seizures were relieved by surgically separating her two brain hemispheres. Now, in an experiment, psychologist Michael Gazzaniga (1985) flashes a picture of a nude woman to the left half of Carol's field of vision, which projects to her nonverbal right brain hemisphere. A sheepish smile spreads over her face, and she begins chuckling. Asked why, she invents – and apparently believes – a plausible explanation: "Oh – that funny machine." Frank, another split-brain patient, has the word "smile" flashed to his nonverbal right hemisphere. He obliges and forces a smile. Asked why, he explains, "This experiment is very funny."

The mental aftereffects of our behavior also appear in many social-psychological examples of self-persuasion. As we will see over and over, attitudes follow behavior.

Role Playing

The word **role** is borrowed from the theater and, as in the theater, refers to actions expected of those who occupy a particular social position. When enacting new social roles, we may at first feel phony. But our unease seldom lasts.

role
A set of norms that defines how people in a given social position ought to behave.

Think of a time when you stepped into some new role – perhaps your first days on a job or at college. That first week on campus, for example, you may have been hypersensitive to your new social situation and tried valiantly to act mature and to suppress your high school behavior. At such times, you may have felt self-conscious. You observed your new speech and actions because they weren't natural to you. Then something amazing happened: Your pseudo-intellectual talk no longer felt forced. The role began to fit as comfortably as your old jeans and T-shirt.

University of California Riverside psychologists Seth Margolis and Sonja Lyubomirsky asked college students to be as talkative, outgoing, and assertive (extraverted) as they possibly could for a week – or as quiet, shy, and reserved (introverted) as they could. The students then switched, trying out the opposite way of behaving for another week. After the introversion week, students felt less connected and less happy, but after the extraversion week, they felt more connected and happier (Margolis & Lyubomirsky, 2020). They faked it until they made it.

When 4- to 7-year-old girls were given the opportunity to pretend to be a scientist, they spent longer on a challenging science activity than girls who did not pretend to be a scientist. Playing the role of a scientist, even in a young girl's pretend play, had an impact on their behavior (Shachnai et al., 2022).

What is unreal (an artificial role) can subtly morph into what is real. In a new career – as teacher, soldier, or businessperson, for example – we often begin by playacting the new role but then find that it shapes our attitudes. In one study, military training toughened German males' personalities. Compared to a control group, they were more assertive and antagonistic, even 5 years after leaving the military (Jackson et al., 2012). And in one national study of U.S. adolescents, playing "risk-glorifying" video games was followed by increased risky and deviant real-life behaviors (Hull et al., 2014). The moral: When we act out a role, we slightly change our former selves into being more like the role.

This type of transformation can be particularly severe if it persists for months or years, as was often the case during the time of slavery in the United States. Abolitionist, orator, and writer Frederick Douglass, who was once an enslaved person, recalled the transformation over time in the disposition of the woman he had been sold to:

> My new mistress proved to be all she appeared when I first met her at the door – a woman of the kindest heart and finest feelings. . . . I was utterly astonished at her goodness. I scarcely knew how to behave towards her. She was entirely unlike any other white woman I had ever seen. . . . The meanest slave was put fully at ease in her presence, and none left without feeling better for having seen her. Her face was made of heavenly smiles, and her voice of tranquil music. But, alas! this kind heart had but a short time to remain such. The fatal poison of irresponsible power was already in her hands, and soon commenced its infernal work. That cheerful eye, under the influence of slavery, soon became red with rage; that voice, made all of sweet accord, changed to one of harsh and horrid discord; and that angelic face gave place to that of a demon. (Douglass, 1845, pp. 57–58)

"Our self-definitions are not constructed in our heads; they are forged by our deeds."

—Robert McAfee Brown, *Creative Dislocation: The Movement of Grace,* 1980

Saying Becomes Believing

People often adapt what they say to please their listeners. They are quicker to tell people good news than bad, and they adjust their message toward their listener's views (Manis et al., 1974; Tesser et al., 1972; Tetlock, 1983). When induced to give spoken or written support to something they doubt, people will often feel bad about their deceit. Nevertheless, they begin to believe what they are saying (assuming they weren't bribed or coerced into doing so). When there is no compelling external explanation for one's words, saying becomes believing (Klaas, 1978).

Tory Higgins and his colleagues (Hausmann et al., 2008; Higgins & McCann, 1984; Higgins & Rholes, 1978) illustrated how saying becomes believing. They had university students read a personality description of someone (let's call her Emily) and then summarize it for someone else (Isabella), whom they believed either liked or disliked Emily. The students wrote a more positive description when Isabella liked Emily. Having said positive things about her, they also then liked Emily more themselves. Asked to recall what they had read, they remembered the description as more positive than it was. In short, people tend to adjust their messages to their listeners and, having done so, to believe the altered message.

"Good God! He's giving the white-collar voter's speech to the blue collars. . ."

Joseph Farris

Saying becomes believing: In expressing our thoughts to others, we sometimes tailor our words to what we think the others will want to hear and then come to believe our own words.

Evil and Moral Acts

The attitudes-follow-behavior principle also occurs for immoral acts. Evil sometimes results from gradually escalating commitments. A trifling evil act erodes one's moral sensitivity, making it easier to perform a worse act. To paraphrase La Rochefoucauld's 1665 book of *Maxims,* it is not as difficult to find a person who has never succumbed to a given temptation as to find a person who has succumbed only once. After telling a "white lie" and thinking, "Well, that wasn't so bad," the person may go on to tell a bigger lie.

Harmful acts change us in other ways, too. We tend not only to hurt those we dislike but also to dislike those we hurt. Harming an innocent victim – by uttering hurtful comments or delivering supposed electric shocks – typically leads aggressors to disparage their victims, thus helping them justify their cruel behavior (Berscheid et al., 1968; Davis & Jones, 1960; Glass, 1964). This is especially so when we are coaxed rather than coerced and thus feel responsible for our act.

Cruel acts, such as the 1994 Rwandan genocide, tend to breed even crueler and more hate-filled attitudes. "At first, killing was obligatory," explained one participant in the Rwandan genocide. "Afterward, we got used to it. We became naturally cruel. We no longer needed encouragement or fines to kill, or even orders or advice" (quoted by Hatzfeld, 2005, p. 71).
Sylvia Buchholz/REUTERS/Alamy Stock Photo

The attitudes-follow-behavior phenomenon appears in wartime. Prisoner-of-war camp guards would sometimes display good manners to captives in their first days on the job. Soldiers ordered to kill may initially react with revulsion to the point of sickness over their act. But not for long, as they became desensitized and dehumanized their victims (Waller, 2002). Seeing another group as less than human is one of the most pervasive and pernicious ways prejudice, mistreatment and violence are wrongly justified (Fourie et al., 2022; Kteily & Bruneau, 2017). When Russian soldiers executed Ukrainians during the war beginning in 2022, they made them lie on their stomachs – probably so the soldiers could not see their victims' faces (Gerson, 2022).

Attitudes also follow behavior in peacetime. A group that holds another in slavery will likely come to perceive the enslaved people as having traits that justify their oppression. Prison staff who participate in executions experience "moral disengagement" by coming to believe (more strongly than other prison staff) that their victims deserve their fate (Osofsky et al., 2005). Actions and attitudes feed each other, sometimes to the point of moral numbness. The more one harms another and adjusts one's attitudes, the easier it becomes to do harm. Conscience is corroded.

To simulate the "killing begets killing" process, Andy Martens and his collaborators (2007, 2010, 2012) asked University of Arizona students to kill some bugs. They wondered: Would killing a few bugs in a "practice" trial increase students' willingness to kill more bugs later? To find out, they asked some students to look at one small bug in a container, then to dump it into the coffee grinding machine shown in **Figure 3,** and then to press the "on" button for 3 seconds. (No bugs were actually killed. An unseen stopper at the base of the insert tube prevented the bug from actually entering the killing machine, which tore bits of paper to simulate the sound of a killing.) Those who believed they killed five bugs went on to "kill" significantly more bugs during an ensuing 20-second period.

FIGURE 3

Killing Begets Killing

Students who believed they killed several bugs by dropping them in this apparent killing machine later killed more bugs during a self-paced killing period. (In reality, no bugs were harmed.)
Courtesy of Andy Martens, University of Canterbury

Harmful acts shape the self, but so, thankfully, do moral acts. Our character is reflected in what we do when we think no one is looking. Researchers have tested character by giving children temptations when it seems no one is watching. Consider what happens when children resist the temptation. In a dramatic experiment, Jonathan Freedman (1965) introduced elementary school children to an enticing battery-controlled robot, instructing them not to play with it while he was out of the room. Freedman used a severe threat with half the children and a mild threat with the others. Both were sufficient to deter the children.

Several weeks later, a different researcher, with no apparent relation to the earlier events, left each child to play in the same room with the same toys. Three-fourths of those who had heard the severe threat now freely played with the robot; of those given the mild threat, only a third played with it. Apparently, the mild threat was strong enough to elicit the desired behavior yet mild enough to leave them with a sense of choice. Having earlier chosen consciously *not* to play with the toy, the children who only heard the mild threat internalized their decisions. Moral action, especially when chosen rather than coerced, affects moral thinking.

Moreover, positive behavior fosters a liking for the person. Doing a favor for an experimenter or another participant, or tutoring a student, usually increases the liking of the person helped (Blanchard & Cook, 1976). People who pray for a romantic partner (even in controlled experiments) thereafter exhibit greater commitment and fidelity to the partner (Fincham et al., 2010). It is a lesson worth remembering: If you wish to love someone more, act as if you do.

"We do not love people so much for the good they have done us, as for the good we have done them."

—Leo Tolstoy, *War and Peace*, 1867–1869

Now let us ask you, before reading further, to play theorist. Ask yourself: Why in these studies and real-life examples did attitudes follow behavior? Why might playing a role or making a speech influence your attitude?

SUMMING UP: When Does Our Behavior Affect Our Attitudes?

- The attitude–action relation also works in the reverse direction: We are likely not only to think ourselves into action but also to act ourselves into a way of thinking. When we act, we amplify the idea underlying what we have done, especially when we feel responsible for it. Many streams of evidence converge on this principle.
- Similarly, what we say or write can strongly influence attitudes that we subsequently hold.
- Actions also affect our moral attitudes: That which we have done, even if it is evil, we tend to justify as right.

WHY DOES OUR BEHAVIOR AFFECT OUR ATTITUDES?

Summarize the theories that help explain the attitudes-follow-behavior phenomenon and how these competing theories illustrate the scientific process.

We have seen that several streams of evidence merge to form a river: Our behaviors influence our attitudes. Do these observations offer clues to *why* behavior affects attitude? Social psychology's detectives suspect three possible sources:

- *Self-presentation theory* assumes that for strategic reasons, we express attitudes that make us appear consistent.
- *Cognitive dissonance theory* assumes that to reduce discomfort, we justify our actions to ourselves.
- *Self-perception theory* assumes that our actions are self-revealing: When uncertain about our feelings or beliefs, we look to our behavior, much as anyone else would.

Self-Presentation: Impression Management

The first explanation begins as a simple idea: We all care about what other people think of us. People spend billions on clothes, diets, cosmetics, and plastic surgery—all because of their fretting over what others think. We see making a good impression as a way to gain social and material rewards, to feel better about ourselves, even to become more secure in our social identities (Leary, 1994, 2010, 2012).

No one wants to look foolishly inconsistent. To avoid seeming so, we express attitudes that match our actions. To appear consistent to others, we may automatically pretend we hold attitudes consistent with our behaviors (Leary et al., 2015; Tyler, 2012). Even a little insincerity or hypocrisy can pay off in managing the impression we are making—or so self-presentation theory suggests.

Does our feigning consistency explain why expressed attitudes shift toward consistency with behavior? To some extent, yes; people exhibit a much smaller attitude change when a fake lie detector discourages them from trying to make a good impression (Paulhus, 1982; Tedeschi et al., 1987).

But there is more to attitudes than self-presentation, for people express their changed attitudes even to someone who has no knowledge of their earlier behavior. Two other theories explain why people sometimes internalize their self-presentations as genuine attitude changes.

"I see he finally got rid of the idiotic comb-over."

Self-Justification: Cognitive Dissonance

One theory is that our attitudes change because we are motivated to maintain consistency among our thoughts (known as cognitions). That is the implication of Leon Festinger's (1957) famous **cognitive dissonance** theory. The theory is simple, but its range of application is enormous, making "cognitive dissonance" part of the vocabulary of today's educated people. It assumes that we feel tension, or "dissonance," when two of our thoughts or beliefs ("cognitions") are inconsistent. Festinger argued that to reduce this unpleasant arousal caused by inconsistency, we often adjust our thinking. This simple idea, and some surprising predictions derived from it, have spawned thousands of studies (Cooper, 1999).

cognitive dissonance
Tension that arises when one is simultaneously aware of two inconsistent cognitions. For example, dissonance may occur when we realize that we have, with little justification, acted contrary to our attitudes or made a decision favoring one alternative despite reasons favoring another.

One inspiration for the theory was a participant-observation study by Festinger and his colleagues (1956) – a study that an Association for Psychological Science president declared as his all-time favorite psychological study (Medin, 2011). Festinger and his collaborators read a news report of a UFO cult expecting to be rescued by flying saucers from a cataclysmic flood anticipated on December 21, 1954. The researchers' response? They joined the cult and observed what happened next.

As December 21 approached, the most devoted followers quit their jobs and disposed of their possessions, with some even leaving their spouses. So what happened "when prophecy fails"? When December 21 passed uneventfully, the group coped with its massive dissonance not by abandoning their beliefs but with increased fervor for them. Their faithfulness had, they decided, persuaded God to spare the world – a message they now proclaimed boldly. In modern experiments, too, people whose confident beliefs are shaken will often respond by seeking to persuade others. "When in doubt, shout!" concluded researchers (Gal & Rucker, 2010).

selective exposure
The tendency to seek information and media that agree with one's views and to avoid dissonant information.

Another way people minimize dissonance, Festinger believed, is through **selective exposure** to agreeable information. Studies have asked people about their views on various topics and then invited them to choose whether they wanted to view information supporting or opposing their viewpoint. Twice as many preferred supporting rather than challenging information (Fischer & Greitemeyer, 2010; Hart et al., 2009; Sweeny et al., 2010). We prefer news that affirms us over news that informs us, likely because we (often naively) believe it is objectively correct (Minson & Dorison, 2022). Today's media environment of left- and right-leaning news outlets and social media feeds makes this easier than ever (Bump, 2023; Westermann & Coscia, 2022).

Selective exposure: Many people choose to read news and opinion articles from sources that favor their political viewpoint, while avoiding sources that oppose it.
damircudic/Getty Images

Conspiracy beliefs are also often the product of selective exposure. For example, adherents of the QAnon conspiracy theory relied on alternative social media platforms and discounted information from other sources. When the prophesied "Great Awakening" of Donald Trump staying in power failed to occur on President Biden's inauguration day in January 2021, some doubled down while others moved on to other extreme beliefs (Wong, 2021).

People are especially keen on reading information that supports their political, religious, and ethical views – a phenomenon that most of us can recognize from our own favorite news sources. Moreover, people who have strong views on some topic – for instance, gun control, climate change, or economic policy – are prone to "identity-protective cognition" (Kahan et al., 2011, 2014; Landrum et al., 2017). To minimize dissonance, their beliefs steer their reasoning and their evaluation of data. Shown the same data about COVID-19 vaccines, people will read it differently depending on their preexisting views (Hornsey et al., 2021). On more practical and less values-relevant topics, "accuracy motives" drive us. Thus, we welcome a home inspection before buying or a second opinion before surgery.

Sometimes, we simply choose to ignore or not focus on uncomfortable information. For example, many people who eat meat dislike the harm to animals it involves. To resolve this, many try to disassociate meat from its animal origins (Benningstad & Kunst, 2020; Rothgerber, 2020). This might explain the popularity of hamburgers, chicken nuggets, and other meat-based foods that don't explicitly resemble the animals they came from. People can also change their behaviors to align with their attitudes. Meat-eaters prompted to think about animal welfare (creating dissonance between their behaviors and attitudes) are more likely to say they will choose more vegetarian meals in the future (Bouwman et al., 2022).

Dissonance theory pertains mostly to discrepancies between behavior and attitudes. We are aware of both. Thus, if we sense an inconsistency, perhaps some hypocrisy, we feel pressure for change. That helps explain why people who vape are less likely to believe that e-cigarettes are harmful than those who don't vape, just as cigarette smokers are much more likely than nonsmokers to doubt that smoking is dangerous (Eiser et al., 1979; McLeish et al., 2022). They find it difficult to change their behavior (vaping), so they instead cling to their attitude (vaping isn't dangerous). Similarly, men who cheat on their wives may continue to be unfaithful (behavior), but change their attitudes toward infidelity by telling themselves things like "Being unfaithful never hurt anyone" or "I feel energized" (Alexopoulos, 2021).

This can also be flipped around: Get someone to change their attitude by making a public statement, and they may change their behavior. Someone asked to make a video advocating exercise (attitude) will be more likely to exercise (behavior) (Priolo et al., 2019). Someone who writes about why people should follow COVID-19 safety measures (attitude) is more likely follow those measures (behavior) (Pearce & Cooper, 2021).

Cognitive dissonance theory also offers several surprising predictions. See if you can anticipate them.

INSUFFICIENT JUSTIFICATION

Imagine you are a participant in a famous experiment staged by the creative Festinger and his student J. Merrill Carlsmith (1959). For an hour, you are required to perform dull tasks, such as turning wooden knobs again and again. After you finish, the experimenter (Carlsmith) explains that the study concerns how expectations affect performance. The next participant, waiting outside, must be led to expect an *interesting* experiment. The seemingly upset experimenter, whom Festinger had spent hours coaching until he became extremely convincing, explains that the assistant who usually creates this expectation couldn't make this session. Wringing his hands, he pleads, "Could you fill in and do this?"

It's for science and you are being paid, so you agree to tell the next participant (who is actually the experimenter's accomplice) what a delightful experience you have just had. "Really?" responds the supposed participant. "A friend of mine was in this experiment a week ago, and she said it was boring." "Oh, no," you respond, "it's really very interesting. You get good exercise while turning some knobs. I'm sure you'll enjoy it." Finally, you complete a questionnaire that asks how much you actually enjoyed your knob-turning experience.

Now for the prediction: Under which condition are you most likely to believe your little lie and say that the dull experiment was indeed interesting? When paid $1 (about $10 today) for fibbing, as some of the participants were? Or when paid a lavish $20 (about $200 today), as others were? Contrary to the common notion that big rewards produce big effects, Festinger

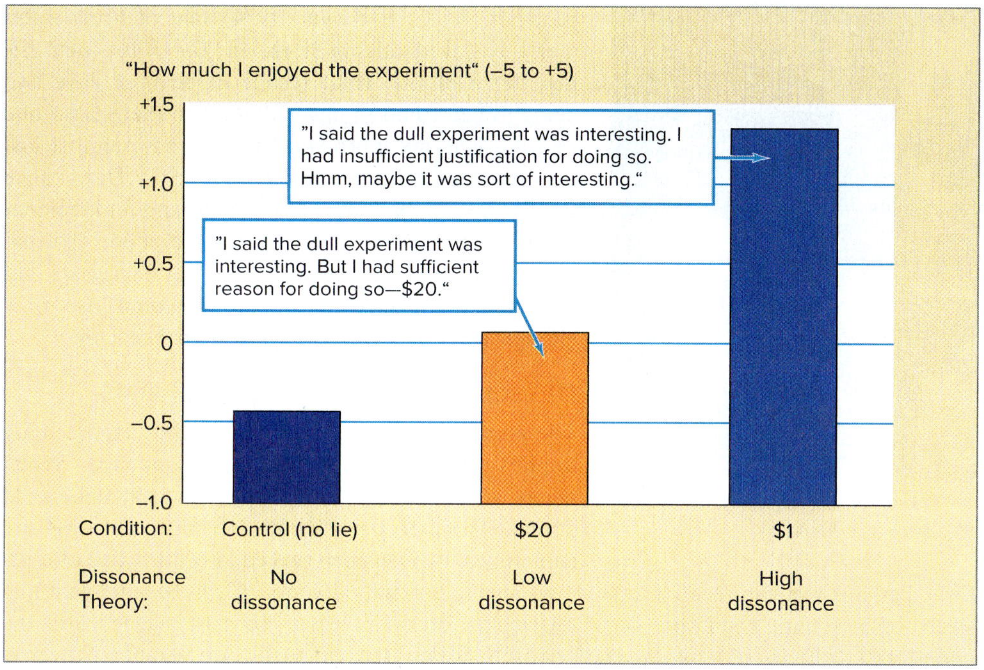

FIGURE 4

Insufficient Justification

Dissonance theory predicts that when our actions are not fully explained by external rewards or coercion, we will experience dissonance, which we can reduce by believing in what we have done.

Source: Data from Festinger & Carlsmith, 1959.

and Carlsmith made an outrageous prediction: Those paid just $1 (hardly sufficient justification for a lie) would be most likely to adjust their attitudes to their actions. Having **insufficient justification** for their actions, they would experience more discomfort (dissonance) and thus be more motivated to believe in what they had done. Those paid $20 had sufficient justification for what they had done (so much money!) and hence should have experienced less dissonance. As **Figure 4** shows, the results confirmed this intriguing prediction — as have replication experiments across several age groups (Cooper & Feldman, 2019).*

insufficient justification
Reduction of dissonance by internally justifying one's behavior when external justification is "insufficient."

In dozens of later experiments, this attitudes-follow-behavior effect was strongest when people felt some choice and when their actions had foreseeable consequences. One experiment had people read disparaging lawyer jokes into a recorder (for example, "How can you tell when a lawyer is lying? Their lips are moving."). The reading produced more negative attitudes toward lawyers when it was a chosen rather than a coerced activity (Hobden & Olson, 1994). Other experiments have engaged people to write essays for a measly $1.50 or so. When the essay argues something they don't believe in — for instance, support for a tuition increase — the underpaid writers begin to feel somewhat greater sympathy with the policy. Pretense becomes reality.

The insufficient justification principle also works with punishments. Children were more likely to internalize a request not to play with an attractive toy if they were given a mild threat that insufficiently justified their compliance. When a parent says, "Clean up your room, Joshua, or I'll take all of your toys away," Joshua won't need to internally justify cleaning his room. The severe threat is justification enough.

But if a milder threat is used, that might lead Joshua to think, "I am cleaning up my room because I want a clean room," rather than, "I am cleaning up my room because my parents will take away all my toys if I don't." The principle is this: *Attitudes follow behaviors for which we feel some responsibility.*

Authoritarian management will be effective, the theory predicts, only when the authority is present — because people are unlikely to internalize forced

Cognitive dissonance theory focuses on what induces a desired action. Research suggests that parents use "only enough" incentive to elicit desired behavior.
Prostock-studio/Shutterstock

*There is a seldom-reported final aspect of this 1950s experiment. Imagine yourself finally back with the experimenter, who is truthfully explaining the whole study. Not only do you learn that you've been duped, but also the experimenter asks for the $20 back. Do you comply? Festinger and Carlsmith note that all their student participants willingly reached into their pockets and gave back the money. This is a foretaste of some quite amazing observations on compliance and conformity. As we will see, when the social situation makes clear demands, people usually respond accordingly.

Big decisions can produce big dissonance when one later ponders the negative aspects of what is chosen and the positive aspects of what was not chosen.
Thinkstock/Stockbyte/Getty Images

behavior. As C. S. Lewis (1974) said of Bree, a formerly enslaved talking horse in *The Horse and His Boy,* "One of the worst results of being a slave and being forced to do things is that when there is no one to force you any more you find you have almost lost the power of forcing yourself" (p. 193). Dissonance theory insists that encouragement and inducement should be enough to elicit the desired action (so that attitudes may follow the behavior). But it suggests that managers, teachers, and parents should use only enough incentive to elicit the desired behavior.

DISSONANCE AFTER DECISIONS

The emphasis on perceived choice and responsibility implies that decisions produce dissonance. When faced with an important decision – what college to attend, whom to date, which job to accept – we are sometimes torn between two equally attractive alternatives. Perhaps you can recall a time when, having committed yourself, you became painfully aware of dissonant cognitions – the desirable features of what you had rejected and the undesirable features of what you had chosen. If you decided to live on campus, you may have realized you were giving up the spaciousness and freedom of an apartment in favor of cramped, noisy dorm quarters. If you elected to live off campus, you may have realized that your decision meant physical separation from campus and friends, and having to cook and clean for yourself.

After making important decisions, you can reduce dissonance by upgrading the chosen alternative and downgrading the unchosen option. In the first published dissonance experiment (1956), Jack Brehm brought some of his wedding gifts to his University of Minnesota lab and had women rate eight products, such as a toaster, a radio, and a hairdryer. Brehm then showed the women two objects they had rated similarly and told them they could have whichever they chose. Later, when rerating the eight objects, the women increased their evaluations of the item they had chosen and decreased their evaluations of the rejected item. It seems that after we have made our choices, the grass does not then grow greener on the other side of the fence. (Afterward, Brehm confessed he couldn't afford to let them keep what they chose.) A later meta-analysis of 43 studies confirmed the effect: Choosing something really does make it more attractive (Enisman et al., 2021).

With simple decisions, this deciding-becomes-believing effect can breed overconfidence (Blanton et al., 2001): "What I've decided must be right." The effect can occur very quickly. Robert Knox and James Inkster (1968) found that racetrack bettors who had just put down their money felt more optimistic about their bets than did those who were about to bet. In the few moments that intervened between standing in line and walking away from the betting window, nothing had changed – except the decisive action and the person's feelings about it.

Our preferences influence our decisions, which then sharpen our preferences. This choices-influence-preferences effect occurs even after people press a button to choose what they think was a subliminally presented vacation alternative (nothing was actually shown them). They later tended to prefer the holiday that they believed they had chosen (Sharot et al., 2010, 2012). Moreover, once people chose a holiday destination, they preferred it up to three years later.

"Every time you make a choice you are turning the central part of you, the part of you that chooses, into something a little different from what it was before."

—C. S. Lewis, *Mere Christianity,* 1942

Decisions, once made, grow their own self-justifying legs of support. Often, these new legs are strong enough that when one leg is pulled away the decision does not collapse. Rosalia decides to take a trip home if it can be done for an airfare under $500. It can, and she begins to think of additional reasons why she will be glad to see her family. When she goes to buy the tickets, however, she learns there has been a fare increase to $575. No matter; she is now determined to go. It rarely occurs to people, reported Robert Cialdini (1984, p. 103), "that those additional reasons might never have existed had the choice not been made in the first place."

Self-Perception

Although dissonance theory has inspired much research, an even simpler theory also explains its phenomena. Consider how we make inferences about other people's attitudes. We see how a person acts in a particular situation, and then we attribute the behavior either to the person's traits and attitudes or to environmental forces. If we see parents coercing 10-year-old Jaden into saying, "I'm sorry," we attribute Jaden's apology to the situation, not to his personal regret. If we see Jaden apologizing with no coercion, we attribute the apology to Jaden himself (**Figure 5**).

Self-perception theory (proposed by Daryl Bem, 1972) assumes that we make similar inferences when we observe our own behavior. When our attitudes are weak or ambiguous, it's similar to someone observing us from the outside. Hearing myself talk informs me of my attitudes; seeing my actions provides clues to how strong my beliefs are. If we observe ourselves acting as a leader, we begin to think of ourselves as leaders (Miscenko et al., 2017). When we buy organic food, we begin to think of ourselves as people who believe organic food is healthy (Koklic et al., 2019). When we post selfies on social media, we begin to think of ourselves as someone who needs to lose weight (Niu et al., 2020). This is especially so when we can't easily attribute our behavior to external constraints. The acts we freely commit are self-revealing.

self-perception theory
The theory that when we are unsure of our attitudes, we infer them much as would someone observing us — by looking at our behavior and the circumstances under which it occurs.

How much our behavior guides our self-perceptions was cleverly demonstrated by researchers at Sweden's Lund University (Lind et al., 2014). They wondered: What would we experience if we said one thing but heard ourselves saying something else? Would we believe our ears? Through a headset, people heard themselves name various font colors such as "gray" when shown the word "green" in a gray color. But sometimes, the prankster researchers substituted the participant's own voice saying a previously recorded word, such as "green." Remarkably, two-thirds of the word switches went undetected. People experienced the inserted word as self-produced!

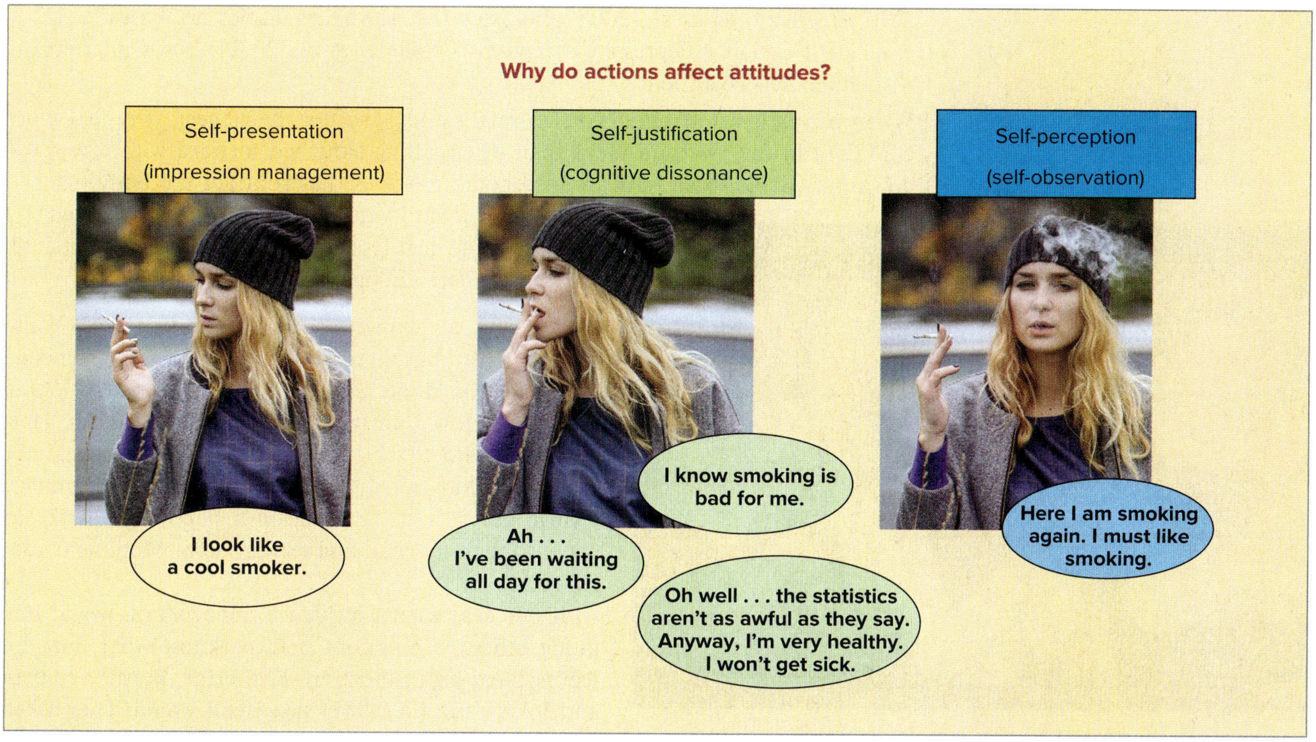

FIGURE 5

Three Theories Explain Why Attitudes Follow Behavior
ANTON DOTSENKO/123RF

Behavior also guides self-perceptions of our emotions: Are we anxious because we tremble, or do we tremble because we are anxious? One friend of mine [DM] was shaking while standing offstage waiting to give a lecture and inferred he was really nervous. When he discovered the floor over the air-handling system was vibrating, his self-perceived nervousness vanished.

"I can watch myself and my actions, just like an outsider."

—Anne Frank, *The Diary of a Young Girl*, 1947

EXPRESSIONS AND ATTITUDE

You may be skeptical of the self-perception effect, as many initially are. Experiments on the effects of facial expressions suggest a way for you to experience it. When James Laird (1974, 1984) induced college students to frown while attaching electrodes to their faces – "contract these muscles," "pull your brows together" – they reported feeling angry. It's more fun to try Laird's other finding: Those induced to make a smiling face felt happier and found cartoons more humorous. Across nearly 4,000 participants in 19 countries, people asked to mimic the facial expressions of smiling people reported feeling happier than those asked to mimic more neutral expressions (Coles et al., 2022). Even when people believed that their facial expressions did not influence emotions, they still reported more happiness when posing with a smiling expression (Coles et al., 2023).

Or try this: Put a pen in your mouth and hold it with your teeth; your mouth will automatically form a smile. Then try holding it with your lips, which actually prevents you from smiling. Participants who held a pen with their teeth found a set of cartoons funnier than those who held it with their lips – as long as they weren't being videoed (Coles et al., 2019; Marsh et al., 2019; Noah et al., 2018; Strack et al., 1988). Even a forced smile created mirth.

facial feedback effect
The tendency of facial expressions to trigger corresponding feelings such as fear, anger, or happiness.

Clever follow-up studies have found more examples of this **facial** (and body) **feedback effect:**

- Botox smooths emotional wrinkles. If it's hard for us to know what the frozen-faced Botoxed are feeling, it's also hard for them to know themselves. Paralyzing the frowning muscles with Botox slows activity in people's emotion-related brain circuits and slows their reading of sadness- or anger-related sentences (Havas et al., 2010; Hennenlotter et al., 2008). Botoxing the frowning muscles decreases psychiatric patients' depressive symptoms (Wollmer et al., 2012). Botox interferes with embodied cognition.
- When people are instructed to sit straight and push out their chest, they feel more confident in their written ideas than when sitting slouched forward with eyes downcast (Briñol et al., 2009). In general, postures that contract the body (such as leaning forward with your arms around yourself) lead people to feel less powerful and happy compared to neutral poses (Elkjaer et al., 2022).

Air Nippon Airways employees, biting wooden chopsticks, beam during a smile training session. Researchers report that people who use chopsticks to activate smiling muscles recover more quickly from stressful experiences (Kraft & Pressman, 2012).
Kyodo News International, Inc.

We have all experienced this phenomenon. We're feeling crabby, but then we get a phone call or someone comes to the door and elicits from us warm, polite behavior. "How's everything?" "Just fine, thanks. How are things with you?" "Oh, not bad. . . ." As long as our crabbiness was not intense, our chipper behavior may change our attitude. Putting on a happy face perks us up. It's tough to smile and feel grouchy. Motions trigger emotions.

If our expressions influence our feelings, would imitating others' expressions help us know what they are feeling? An experiment by Katherine Burns Vaughan and John Lanzetta (1981) suggests it would. They asked Dartmouth College students to observe someone receiving a supposed electric shock. They told some of the observers to make a pained expression whenever the shock came on. If, as Freud and others supposed, expressing an emotion allows us to discharge it, then the pained expression should be inwardly calming (Cacioppo et al., 1991). However, compared with other students who did not act out the expressions, these grimacing students perspired more and had faster heart rates whenever they saw the shock being delivered. Acting out the person's emotion enabled the observers to feel more empathy. So, to sense how other people are feeling, let your own face and body mirror their expressions.

Actually, you hardly need to try. Observing others' faces, postures, writing styles, and voices, we naturally and unconsciously mimic them (Hatfield et al., 1992; Ireland & Pennebaker, 2010). We synchronize our movements, postures, and tones of voice with theirs. Doing so helps us tune in to what they're feeling (Wróbel & Imbir, 2019). It also makes for "emotional contagion," which helps explain why it's fun to be around happy people and depressing to be around depressed people – whether in-person or online (Rosenbusch et al., 2019).

Our nonverbal behaviors also influence our attitudes. In a clever experiment, Gary Wells and Richard Petty (1980) had University of Alberta students "test headphone sets" by making either vertical or horizontal head movements while listening to a radio opinion piece. The students who made vertical head movements – who were nodding (a nonverbal signal of agreement) – were most likely to later say they agreed with the opinion piece. Try it yourself when listening to someone: Do you feel more agreeable when nodding (nonverbally saying "yes") rather than shaking your head (nonverbally saying "no")? Even being seated in a left- rather than right-leaning chair has led people to lean more left in their expressed political attitudes (Oppenheimer & Trail, 2010)!

"I don't sing because I am happy. I am happy because I sing."

Self-perception at work.

"The free expression by outward signs of emotion intensifies it. On the other hand, the repression, as far as possible, of all outward signs softens our emotions."

—Charles Darwin, *The Expression of the Emotions in Man and Animals*, 1897

OVERJUSTIFICATION AND INTRINSIC MOTIVATIONS

Imagine being a parent who wants your child to enjoy reading. What if you paid $10 for every book your child read? Would they then learn to love reading?

Maybe not. The incentive might get the child to read more, but it may also lead them to think they are reading only to get the money and not because they enjoy the activity. Rewarding people for doing what they already enjoy may lead them to attribute their action to the reward. If so, this would undermine their self-perception that they do it because they like it. Thus, the *extrinsic* (or external) motivation of the reward can interfere with the *intrinsic* (or internal) motivation of true enjoyment in the activity. Experiments have confirmed this **overjustification effect** (Deci & Ryan, 1991, 2012; Lepper & Greene, 1979). Pay people for playing with puzzles, and they will later play with the puzzles less than those who played for no pay. Promise children a reward for doing what they intrinsically enjoy (for example, playing with markers), and you will turn their play into work (**Figure 6**).

overjustification effect
The result of bribing people to do what they already like doing; they may then see their actions as externally controlled rather than intrinsically appealing.

Situations outside the lab show the overjustification effect as well. My [DM's] younger son eagerly consumed six or eight library books a week – until our library started a reading club that promised a party to those who read 10 books in 3 months. He then began checking out only one or two books during our weekly visits. Why? "Because you only need to read 10 books, you know." College athletes who received scholarships, compared with those who didn't, were less likely to say they still enjoyed the sport they played in college, even decades later (Moller & Sheldon, 2020).

However, rewards and praise that inform people of their achievements – that make them feel, "I'm very good at this" – boost intrinsic motivation. In addition, an *unanticipated* reward does not diminish intrinsic interest because people can still attribute their actions to their own motivation (Bradley & Mannell, 1984; Tang & Hall, 1995).

Many life tasks combine intrinsic and extrinsic rewards. A nurse takes satisfaction in caring for patients and gets paid. A student learns and gets a good grade. Ironically, Amy Wrzesniewski, Barry Schwartz, and their colleagues (2014a, b) report that helping people

FIGURE 6

Intrinsic and Extrinsic Motivation

When people do something they enjoy, without reward or coercion, they attribute their behavior to their love of the activity. External rewards undermine intrinsic motivation by leading people to attribute their behavior to the incentive.

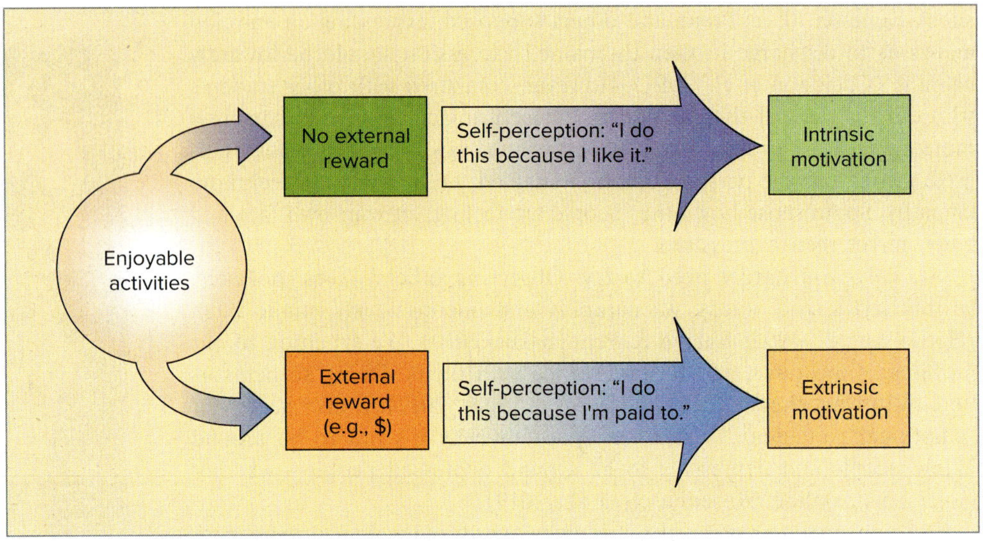

focus on the intrinsic meaning of their work boosts both their work quality and their vocational and financial success – both extrinsic outcomes.

However, not all tasks are initially appealing and thus might need some extrinsic incentives, at least at first. Maria may find her first piano lessons frustrating. Toshi may not have an intrinsic love of ninth-grade science. DeShawn may not look forward to making his first sales calls. In such cases, the parent, the teacher, or the manager should probably use some small extrinsic incentives to coax the desired behavior (Boggiano & Ruble, 1985; Cooke et al., 2011; Workman & Williams, 1980). After the person complies, give them an intrinsic reason for continuing their work: "I'm not surprised that sales call went well because you are so good at making a first impression."

If we provide students with just enough justification to perform a learning task and use rewards and labels to help them feel competent, we may enhance their enjoyment and their eagerness to pursue the subject on their own. When there is too much justification – as happens in classrooms where teachers dictate behavior and use rewards to control the children – student-driven learning may diminish (Deci & Ryan, 1985, 1991, 2008).

Comparing the Theories

We have seen one explanation of why our actions might only *seem* to affect our attitudes (*self-presentation* theory). And we have seen two explanations of why our actions genuinely affect our attitudes: (1) the *dissonance*-theory assumption that we justify our behavior to reduce our internal discomfort, and (2) the *self-perception*-theory assumption that we observe our behavior and make reasonable inferences about our attitudes, much as we observe other people and infer *their* attitudes.

These two explanations seem to contradict each other. Which is right? It's difficult to find a definitive test. In most instances, they make the same predictions, and we can bend each theory to accommodate most of the findings we have considered (Greenwald, 1975). Self-perception theorist Daryl Bem (1972) even suggested it boils down to personal loyalties and preferences. This illustrates the human element in scientific theorizing. Neither dissonance theory nor self-perception theory has been handed to us by nature. Both are products of human imagination – creative attempts to simplify and explain what we've observed.

It is not unusual in science to find that a principle, such as "attitudes follow behavior," is predictable from more than one theory. Physicist Richard Feynman (1967) marveled that "one of the amazing characteristics of nature" is the "wide range of beautiful ways" we can describe it: "I do not understand the reason why it is that the correct laws of physics seem to be expressible in such a tremendous variety of ways" (pp. 53–55). Like different roads leading to the same place, different sets of assumptions can lead to the same principle. If anything, this strengthens our confidence in the principle. It becomes credible not only because of the data supporting it but also because it rests on more than one theoretical pillar.

After doing something undesirable or embarrassing, people can reaffirm their self-image by doing a good deed.
Ariel Skelley/Blend Images

DISSONANCE AS AROUSAL

Can we say that one of the theories is better? Dissonance theory wins out on one count: having attitudes and behavior disagree does seem to produce arousal – especially if the behavior has unwanted consequences for which the person feels responsible (Cooper, 1999; Elliot & Devine, 1994). If, in the privacy of your room, you say something you don't believe, your dissonance will be minimal. It will be much greater if there are unpleasant results: if someone hears and believes you, if the statement causes harm and the negative effects are irrevocable, and if the person harmed is someone you like. If, moreover, you feel responsible for those consequences – if you can't easily excuse your act because you freely agreed to it and if you were able to foresee its consequences – then uncomfortable dissonance will be aroused. Such dissonance-related arousal is detectable as increased perspiration and heart rate (Cacioppo & Petty, 1986; Croyle & Cooper, 1983; Losch & Cacioppo, 1990).

Why is "volunteering" to say or do undesirable things so arousing? Because, as the **self-affirmation theory** suggests, such acts are embarrassing (Steele, 1988). They make us feel foolish. They threaten our sense of personal competence and goodness. Justifying our actions and decisions is therefore *self-affirming;* it protects and supports our sense of integrity and self-worth. When people engage in dissonance-generating actions, their thinking left frontal lobes buzz with extra arousal (Harmon-Jones et al., 2008). This is the grinding gears of belief change at work.

self-affirmation theory
A theory that (a) people often experience a self-image threat after engaging in an undesirable behavior; and (b) they can compensate by affirming another aspect of the self. Threaten people's self-concept in one domain, and they will compensate either by refocusing or by doing good deeds in some other domain.

What do you suppose happens, then, if we offer people who have committed self-contradictory acts a way to reaffirm their self-worth, such as doing good deeds? In several experiments, people whose self-concepts were restored felt much less need to justify their acts (Steele et al., 1993). Similarly, people who affirmed their personal values were less likely to cheat under pressure (Spoelma, 2022).

So, dissonance conditions do indeed arouse tension, especially when they threaten positive feelings of self-worth. But is this arousal necessary for the attitudes-follow-behavior effect? Steele and his colleagues (1981) believed the answer is yes. In one of their experiments, they induced University of Washington students to write essays favoring a big tuition increase. The students reduced their resulting dissonance by softening their antituition attitudes – *unless* after writing the unpleasant essays they drank alcohol. Apparently, drinking relaxed them enough to eliminate the arousal of dissonance.

SELF-PERCEIVING WHEN NOT SELF-CONTRADICTING

Dissonance is uncomfortably arousing. That leads to self-persuasion after acting contrary to one's attitudes. But dissonance theory cannot explain the attitude changes that occur without dissonance. When people argue a position that is in line with their opinion, although a step or two beyond it, they don't experience dissonance arousal yet still adjust their attitudes toward what they've expressed (Fazio et al., 1977, 1979). Dissonance theory also does not explain the overjustification effect because being paid to do what you like to do should not arouse great tension. And what about situations in which the action does not contradict any attitude – when, for example, people are induced to smile or grimace? Here, too, there should be no dissonance. For these cases, self-perception theory has a ready explanation.

In short, dissonance theory successfully explains what happens when we act contrary to clearly defined attitudes: We feel tension, so we adjust our attitudes to reduce it. Dissonance theory, then, explains attitude *change.* In situations in which our attitudes are not well formed, self-perception theory explains attitude *formation.* As we act and reflect, we develop more readily accessible attitudes to guide our future behavior (Fazio, 1987; Roese & Olson, 1994).

"Rather amazingly, 40 years after its publication, the theory of cognitive dissonance looks as strong and as interesting as ever."

—Social psychologist Jack W. Brehm (1999)

SUMMING UP: Why Does Our Behavior Affect Our Attitudes?

Three different theories explain why our actions affect our attitude reports.

- *Self-presentation theory* assumes that people, especially those who self-monitor their behavior hoping to create good impressions, will adapt their attitude reports to appear consistent with their actions. The available evidence confirms that people do adjust their attitude statements out of concern for what other people will think. But it also shows that some genuine attitude change occurs.

Two of these theories propose that our actions trigger genuine attitude change.

- *Dissonance theory* explains this attitude change by assuming that we feel tension after acting contrary to our attitudes or making difficult decisions. To reduce that arousal, we internally justify our behavior. Dissonance theory further proposes that the less external justification we have for our undesirable actions, the more we feel responsible for them, and thus the more dissonance arises and the more attitudes change to come into line with our actions.
- *Self-perception theory* assumes that when our attitudes are weak, we simply observe our behavior and its circumstances, then infer our attitudes. One interesting implication of self-perception theory is the "overjustification effect": Rewarding people to do what they like doing anyway can turn their pleasure into drudgery (if the reward leads them to attribute their behavior to the reward).
- Evidence supports predictions from both theories, suggesting that each describes what happens under certain conditions.

CONCLUDING THOUGHTS: Changing Ourselves Through Action

To make anything a habit, do it.

To not make it a habit, do not do it.

To unmake a habit, do something else in place of it.

—Greek Stoic philosopher Epictetus

This chapter's attitudes-follow-behavior principle offers a powerful lesson for life: If we want to change ourselves in some important way, it's best not to wait for insight or inspiration. Sometimes we need to act – to begin to write that paper, to make those phone calls, to see that person – even if we don't feel like acting. Jacques Barzun (1975) recognized the energizing power of action when he advised aspiring writers to engage in the act of writing even if contemplation had left them feeling uncertain about their ideas:

> If you are too modest about yourself or too plain indifferent about the possible reader and yet are required to write, then you have to pretend. Make believe that you want to bring somebody around to your opinion; in other words, adopt a thesis and start expounding it. . . . With a slight effort of the kind at the start – a challenge to utterance – you will find your pretense disappearing and a real concern creeping in. The subject will have taken hold of you as it does in the work of all habitual writers. (pp. 173–174)

"If we wish to conquer undesirable emotional tendencies in ourselves we must . . . cold-bloodedly go through the outward motions of those contrary dispositions we prefer to cultivate."

—William James, "What Is an Emotion?" 1884

This attitudes-follow-behavior phenomenon is not irrational or magical. That which prompts us to act may also prompt us to think. Writing an essay or role-playing an opposing view forces us to consider arguments we otherwise might have ignored. Also, we remember the information best after explaining it in our own terms. As one student wrote me [DM], "It wasn't until I tried to verbalize my beliefs that I really understood them." As a teacher and a writer, I must therefore remind myself to not always lay out finished results. It is better to stimulate students to think through the implications of a theory, to make them active listeners, readers, and writers. Even taking notes deepens the impression. William James (1899) made the point a century ago: "No reception without reaction, no impression without correlative expression – this is the great maxim which the teacher ought never to forget."

PART TWO **Social Influence**

Genes, Culture, and Gender

hadynyah/E+/Getty Images

CHAPTER

5

How are we influenced by biology?

How are we influenced by culture?

How are females and males alike and different?

What can we conclude about genes, culture, and gender?

Concluding Thoughts: Should we view ourselves as products of our biology or our culture?

"By birth, the same; by custom, different."

—Confucius, *The Analects of Confucius*

The preceding chapters were about how we *think about* one another. The next chapters are about how we *influence and relate to* one another. We will probe social psychology's central concern: the powers of social influence. What are these unseen social forces that push and pull us? How powerful are they? Research on social influence helps illuminate the invisible strings by which our social worlds move us about. In this chapter, we consider three related topics: biological influences, cultural influences, and gender differences.

For most of human history, fighting wars was the sole province of men. Even today, more men than women serve in militaries, and most countries do not draft women to serve (DeSilver, 2019). Women's roles in the military today differ significantly depending on culture. In some countries, such as Pakistan, women are not allowed to serve in military combat roles; in contrast, women in Israel have done so since the 1970s (Army Technology, 2018; Neuman, 2013). In the United States, women first served in military combat roles in 2015, and in 2020 a bipartisan commission recommended that women be required to register for a military draft (Welna, 2020). In 2021, the U.S. military changed its policy to allow transgender people to serve openly (Suits, 2021).

Thinking about the role of gender in the military around the world prompts us to consider the questions we explore in this chapter: How much does biology shape who we are? How are we influenced by culture? And how do the influences of biology and culture combine to create similarities and differences among men and women?

HOW ARE WE INFLUENCED BY BIOLOGY?

Describe how the biological perspective explains human behavior, including gender differences.

In many important ways, people from different cultures and of different genders are more alike than different. As members of one great family with common ancestors, we share not only a common biology but also common behavioral tendencies. Everyone sleeps and wakes, feels hunger and thirst, and develops language through identical mechanisms. Everywhere, humans prefer sweet tastes to sour and fear snakes more than sparrows. People across the globe all understand each other's frowns and smiles.

Humans are intensely social. We join groups, conform, and recognize distinctions of social status. We return favors, punish offenses, and grieve a loved one's death. As children, beginning at about 8 months of age, we displayed fear of strangers, and as adults, we favor members of our own groups. Confronted by those with dissimilar attitudes or attributes, we react warily or negatively. Anthropologist Donald Brown (1991, 2000) identified several hundred universal behavior and language patterns. To sample among just those beginning with "v," all human societies have verbs, violence, visiting, and vowels.

Even much of our morality is common across cultures and eras. Before they can walk, babies will display a moral sense by disapproving of what's wrong or naughty (Bloom, 2010). People old and young, female and male, whether living in Tokyo, Tehran, or Toledo, all say "no" when asked, "If a lethal gas is leaking into a vent and is headed toward a room with seven people, is it okay to push someone into the vent – preventing the gas from reaching the seven but killing the one?" And they are more likely to say "yes" when asked if it's okay to allow someone to fall into the vent, voluntarily sacrificing one life but saving seven (Hauser, 2006, 2009).

You could drop in anywhere and find humans conversing and arguing, laughing and crying, feasting and dancing, singing and worshiping. Everywhere, humans prefer living with others – in families and communal groups – to living alone. Everywhere, the family dramas that entertain us – from Greek tragedies to Chinese fiction to Mexican soap operas – portray similar plots (Dutton, 2006). Similar, too, are adventure stories in which strong and courageous people, supported by wise old people, overcome evil to the delight of the community.

Such commonalities define our shared human nature. Although differences draw our attention, we're more alike than different. We're all kin beneath the skin.

Genes, Evolution, and Behavior

The universal behaviors that define human nature arise from our biological similarity. Someone may say, "My ancestors came from Ireland" or "My roots are in China" or "I'm

Brazilian," but if we trace our ancestors back 100,000 or more years, we are all Africans (Shipman, 2003). In response to climate change and the availability of food, early hominids migrated across Africa into Asia, Europe, the Australian subcontinent and, eventually, the Americas. As they adapted to their new environments, early humans developed differences that, measured on anthropological scales, are recent and superficial. Those who stayed in Africa had darker skin pigment – what Harvard psychologist Steven Pinker (2002) called "sunscreen for the tropics" – and those who went far north of the equator evolved lighter skins capable of synthesizing vitamin D in less direct sunlight.

We were all Africans recently enough that "there has not been much time to accumulate many new versions of the genes," noted Pinker (2002, p. 143). Indeed, biologists who study our genes have found that we humans – even humans from very different cultures – are strikingly similar, like members of one tribe.

To explain the traits of our species, and all species, the British naturalist Charles Darwin (1859) proposed an evolutionary process. Follow the genes, he advised. Darwin's idea, to which philosopher Daniel Dennett (2005) would give "the gold medal for the best idea anybody ever had," was that **natural selection** enables evolution.

natural selection
The evolutionary process by which heritable traits that best enable organisms to survive and reproduce in particular environments are passed to ensuing generations.

The idea, simplified, is this:

- Organisms have many and varied offspring.
- Those offspring compete for survival in their environment.
- Certain biological and behavioral variations increase their chances of survival and reproduction in that environment.
- Those offspring that do survive and reproduce are more likely to pass their genes to ensuing generations.
- Thus, over time, population characteristics may change.

Natural selection implies that certain genes – those producing traits that increased the odds of surviving long enough to reproduce and nurture descendants – became more abundant. In the snowy Arctic environment, for example, genes programming a thick coat of camouflaging white fur have won the genetic competition among bears. Where thick, dark forest is instead the norm, brown and black bears have instead won out.

Natural selection, long an organizing principle of biology, is an important principle for psychology as well. **Evolutionary psychology** studies how natural selection also predisposes psychological traits and social behaviors that enhance the preservation and spread of one's genes (Buss & Schmitt, 2019). Humans are the way we are, say evolutionary psychologists, because nature selected those who had advantageous traits – those who, for example, preferred the sweet taste of nutritious, energy-providing foods and who disliked the bitter or sour flavors of toxic foods. Those lacking such preferences were less likely to survive to contribute their genes to posterity.

evolutionary psychology
The study of the evolution of cognition and behavior using principles of natural selection.

As mobile gene machines, we carry not only the physical legacy but also the psychological legacy of our ancestors' adaptive preferences. We desire whatever helped our ancestors survive, reproduce, and nurture their offspring to survive and reproduce. Even negative emotions – anxiety, loneliness, depression, anger – are nature's way of motivating us to cope with survival challenges. "The purpose of the heart is to pump blood," noted evolutionary psychologist David Barash (2003). "The brain's purpose," he continued, is to direct our organs and our behavior "in a way that maximizes our evolutionary success. That's it."

The evolutionary perspective highlights our universal human nature. We not only share certain food preferences, but we also share answers to social questions, such as, Whom should I trust? Whom should I help? When, and with whom, should I mate? Who has status, and who doesn't? Evolutionary psychologists contend that our emotional and behavioral answers to those questions are the same answers that worked for our ancestors.

"Eating is dangerous," notes a review of research on taste and smell (Reed & Knaapila, 2010). Kids often dislike bitter foods even when the food is otherwise healthy, perhaps due to an evolutionary past when some bitter foods were poisonous.
Aycan/Getty Images

"Psychology will be based on a new foundation."

—Charles Darwin, *On the Origin of Species*, 1859

And what should we fear? Mostly, we fear dangers faced by our distant ancestors. We fear foes, unfamiliar faces, and heights – and thus, nations we consider hostile, those who are ethnically different, and skydiving. We fear what's immediate and sudden more than greater, gradual harms from historically newer threats, such as smoking or climate change.

Because our social tasks are common to people everywhere, humans everywhere tend to agree on the answers. For example, all humans rank others by authority and status. And all have ideas about economic justice (Fiske, 1992). Evolutionary psychologists highlight these universal characteristics that have evolved through natural selection. Cultures, however, provide the specific rules for working out these elements of social life.

Biology and Gender

Visit an elementary school playground at recess and take note of how the boys and girls behave. More of the boys will be running or jumping and might even physically fight with each other when the playground monitor isn't looking. More of the girls will be playing in small groups and talking to each other.

Here's what you might wonder: Are these differences due to biology (and thus tied to our evolutionary past) or instead a product of upbringing and culture (and thus something that varies by region and era)? The study of gender is one of the most researched and contentious areas of psychology, so we will use it as our primary example to illustrate how biology and culture interact to make us who we are. We'll begin by discussing biology as it relates to gender differences.

TERMS FOR STUDYING SEX AND GENDER

sex
The two biological categories of male and female.

gender
In psychology, the characteristics, whether biological or socially influenced, that we associate with males and females.

First, let's define some terms. Many people use the terms "sex" and "gender" interchangeably, but in psychology, they refer to different things. **Sex** refers to males and females as two biological categories based on chromosomes, genitals, and secondary sex characteristics such as greater muscle mass in males and breasts in females.

Gender instead refers to the characteristics people *associate* with males and females that can be rooted in biology, culture, or both, such as wearing dresses, liking sports, having long hair, wanting more sexual partners, being more physically aggressive, or liking to shop. The differences in behavior on the preschool playground are gendered behaviors; whether each child is biologically male or female is their sex.

Not that long ago, gender and sex were seen as fairly rigid: There were only two sexes, and if someone was born female, she stayed female and usually enacted female gender roles. All of these ideas are now being challenged in one way or another. Until very recently, most cultures delivered a strong message: Everyone *must* be assigned a sex, and there were only two choices. When an intersex child was born with a combination of male and female sex organs (known as ambiguous genitalia), physicians and the family felt compelled to assign the child a sex by diminishing the ambiguity surgically. Between day and night, there is dusk. Between hot and cold, there is warm. But between male and female there was, socially speaking, essentially nothing (Sanz, 2017).

That is not as true now. Many doctors now advise that surgery for ambiguous genitalia be postponed until the child expresses whether they identify as a boy or a girl. No matter what their physical characteristics, some people identify as *gender fluid* or as *nonbinary*, wishing to be identified as neither male or female (Broussard et al., 2018). The concept has a longer history than you might think: Throughout the centuries, many cultures have recognized third genders (Scobey-Thal, 2014).

Defining who is male and who is female is also not as clear-cut as it sounds: Do we use chromosomes? Gametes? Body appearance? Hormone levels? Sometimes these disagree in the same person. Olympic runner Caster Semenya was assigned female at birth but has a more male-typical level of testosterone due to a genetic condition in which a XY chromosome individual has female genitalia during childhood and a masculinized body later on. Some have argued that Semenya's higher testosterone levels gave her an unfair advantage in competing against other women. This is one of many controversial cases centering around how to define sex categories in women's sports (Burns, 2019; Ewing, 2023).

In addition, some people – about 8 in 1,000 American adults overall and 23 in 1,000 American young adults – are **transgender,** those whose sense of being male or female differs from their sex assigned at birth (APA, 2023; Twenge, 2023). A trans person may feel like a woman in a man's body or a man in a woman's body. Being transgender is not the same as enacting atypical gender roles; for example, some women have short hair, don't like to shop, and like sports, but still have a fundamental belief that their sex is female. (Thus, they are **cisgender:** Their gender identity is the same as their birth sex.) A transgender person who was born female might show any constellation of gender roles but has a fundamental sense of actually being male. When he is ready to transition, he may start living as a man. Some transgender people choose to have surgery to change their sex to fit their identity. Others do not change their bodies but instead present socially as their chosen sex (Testa et al., 2017). For example, Thomas Beatie was born female, lived as a man as an adult, and kept his female reproductive organs, giving birth to three children (Abbey, 2012).

In this section, we'll explore evolutionary and biological explanations for gender differences in mating preferences, sex, and hormones. We'll detail the research on gender differences in other areas later in the chapter. For now, consider this well-researched difference: Males think about sex more, masturbate more, and desire a greater number of sexual partners (Baumeister et al., 2001; Petersen & Hyde, 2011). The question is: Why?

Runner Caster Semenya has a genetic condition known as 5-alpha reductase 2 deficiency, which results in a more female body appearance in childhood and a more male body appearance after puberty.
Sport In Pictures/Alamy Stock Photo

GENDER AND MATING PREFERENCES

Evolutionary psychology posits a fairly straightforward answer to this question: Males have stronger sex drives because sex is a cheap investment for men and a big commitment for women. Males and females, note evolutionary psychologists, faced different adaptive challenges when it came to sex and reproduction (Buss, 1995b, 2009). (These ideas are not without controversy; later in this section, we'll explore challenges to this point of view.)

transgender
Someone whose psychological sense of being male or female differs from their birth sex.

cisgender
Someone whose gender identity is the same as their sex assigned at birth.

Thus, say evolutionary psychologists, females invest their reproductive opportunities carefully, by looking for signs of resources and commitment. Males compete with other males for chances to win the genetic sweepstakes by sending their genes into the future and thus look for healthy, fertile soil in which to plant their seed. Women want to find men who will help them tend the garden – resourceful and monogamous dads rather than wandering cads. Women seek to reproduce wisely, men widely. Or so the theory goes.

Evolutionary psychology also suggests that those elementary school boys fighting with each other on the playground might be in a dress rehearsal for a more serious game. Over much of human history, physically dominant males excelled in gaining access to females. Over generations, this enhanced male aggression as the less-aggressive males had fewer chances to reproduce. The genes that may have helped Montezuma II to become Aztec king were also given to his offspring, with the help of the 4,000 women in his harem (Wright, 1998). Genghis Khan, who led invasions that brought much of Asia under his empire, is an ancestor of approximately 1 in 200 men worldwide (Zerjal, 2003). Even today, men are more aggressive toward other men when they are thinking about dating and mating (Ainsworth & Maner, 2012, 2014). Underlying all these presumptions is a principle: *Nature selects traits that help send one's genes into the future.*

What attracts you to someone? Both men and women value kindness, but gender differences appear in valuing physical appearance and status.
Sam Edwards/OJO Images/age fotostock

Little of this process is conscious. Few people in the throes of passion stop to think, "I want to give my genes to posterity." Rather, say evolutionary psychologists, our natural desires are our genes' way of making more genes. Emotions execute evolution's dispositions, much as hunger executes the body's need for nutrients.

"Every living human is a descendant of a long line of successful maters," says evolutionary psychologist David Buss (Kluger, 2020).

"A hen is only an egg's way of making another egg."

—Samuel Butler, *Life and Habit*, 1878

"We've adapted to pick certain types of mates and to fulfill the desires of the opposite sex." And that, evolutionary psychologists believe, helps explain not only male aggression but also the differing sexual attitudes and behaviors of females and males.

Evolutionary psychology also predicts that women will prefer men with the resources to help with the labor-intensive and expensive process of raising a child to full adulthood. Thus, men will strive to offer what women will desire—external resources and physical protection. Male peacocks strut their feathers; male humans, their abs, Audis, and assets (Sundie et al., 2011). In one experiment, teen males rated "having lots of money" as more important after they were put alone in a room with a teen female (Roney, 2003). In one Cardiff, Wales, study, men rated a woman as equally attractive whether she was at the wheel of a humble Ford Fiesta or a swanky Bentley; women found the man more attractive if he was in the luxury car (Dunn & Searle, 2010). "Male achievement is ultimately a courtship display," said Glenn Wilson (1994).

And what do men want? Evolutionary psychologists posit that men favor fertility in women, generally signaled by a youthful and healthy appearance. Men with these preferences, they note, were the most likely to have many offspring. That may not be the conscious desire of most men today, but their evolutionary history unconsciously pulls them to prefer these characteristics and to see physically attractive women as high in status (Buss et al., 2020). Evolutionary psychology studies note that gender differences in mate preferences are very large compared to most other psychological sex differences (Conroy-Beam et al., 2015). They are also fairly universal across cultures:

- Studies in 45 cultures, from Australia to Zambia, reveal that straight men around the world feel attracted to women whose physical features, such as youthful faces and forms, suggest fertility. Straight women feel attracted to men whose wealth, power, and ambition promise resources for protecting and nurturing offspring (Walter et al., 2020). But there are gender similarities, too: Whether residing on an Indonesian island or in urban São Paulo, both women and men desire kindness, love, and mutual attraction in their partners.
- Straight men around the world tend to be most attracted to women whose age and features suggest peak fertility. For teen boys, this is a woman several years older than themselves. For men in their mid-20s, it's women their own age. For older men, it's younger women; the older the man, the greater the age difference he prefers when selecting a mate (Kenrick et al., 2009). This pattern appears worldwide, in European singles ads, Indian marital ads, online dating, and marriage records from the Americas, Africa, and the Philippines, especially among men who want to have children (Kramer & Jones, 2023; Singh, 1993; Singh & Randall, 2007). It also appears, though to a somewhat lesser extent, among gays and lesbians, with many gay men preferring younger partners and lesbian women preferring older partners (Conway et al., 2015). Men married to physically attractive wives reported higher martial satisfaction, whereas husbands' physical attractiveness had little impact on wives' satisfaction (Meltzer et al., 2014). Again, say the evolutionary psychologists, we see that natural selection predisposes men to feel attracted to female features associated with fertility.
- Monthly fertility also matters. Women's behaviors, scents, and voices provide subtle clues to their ovulation, which men can unconsciously detect (Haselton & Gildersleeve, 2011). When at peak fertility, women express greater apprehensiveness of potentially threatening men and greater ability to detect men's sexual orientation (Gildersleeve et al., 2014). They also behave more flirtatiously with men who are confident and socially dominant (Cantu et al., 2014).

Al Pacino is more than 50 years older than his girlfriend, film producer Noor Alfallah.
Imago/Alamy Stock Photo

Reflecting on the mate preference findings, Buss (1999) reported feeling somewhat astonished "that men and women across the world differ in their mate preferences in precisely the ways predicted by the evolutionists. Just as our fears of snakes, heights, and spiders provide a window for viewing the survival hazards of our evolutionary ancestors, our mating desires provide a window for viewing the resources our ancestors needed for reproduction. We all carry with us today the desires of our successful forebears." Our ancestral past lives on, in us.

Gender and Hormones

The sex difference in risk-taking is at least partially fueled by testosterone.
Drpixel/Shutterstock

Evolutionary psychology may explain why sex differences are rooted in biological processes, but it doesn't explain *how*. One way that biology influences sex differences is through hormones, chemicals in our bodies that can influence behavior and mood. For example, men on average have a higher level of **testosterone,** a hormone linked to dominance and aggression.

Hormones are important because genes by themselves cannot be the source of gender differences: Genetically, males and females differ on only a single chromosome out of 46, and the Y (male) chromosome is distinguished primarily by one gene. That gene directs the formation of the testicles, which begin to secrete testosterone. Girls exposed to excess testosterone during fetal development are more interested in rough-and-tumble play than other girls (Berenbaum et al., 2018) and resemble males in their career preferences, with a greater interest in things than people (Beltz et al., 2011). Overall, children exposed to more testosterone in the womb exhibit the psychological pattern more typical of males, including less eye contact, lower language skill, and less empathy (Auyeung et al., 2013). The converse is true as well. When asked to rotate objects, people who have XY (male) chromosomes but a genetic condition that leaves them unable to process testosterone show brain activity more typical of females (Van Hemmen et al., 2016). Similarly, men with an endocrine disorder resulting in low testosterone exposure in childhood were more likely to report favoring toys and activities more associated with girls (Shirazi et al., 2022).

testosterone
A hormone more prevalent in males than females that is linked to dominance and aggression.

The gender gap in aggression also seems influenced by testosterone. In various animals, administering testosterone heightens aggressiveness. In humans, violent male criminals, on average, have higher than normal testosterone levels; so do National Football League players, boisterous fraternity members, and college men involved in a sport (Dabbs, 2000; Reed & Meggs, 2017). Moreover, for both humans and monkeys, the gender difference in aggression appears early in life (before culture has much effect) and wanes as testosterone levels decline during adulthood. However, testosterone levels also fluctuate depending on the situation: Acting aggressively can increase testosterone in men (Geniole et al., 2020), and acting compassionately (such as while taking care of a baby) can decrease it (Gettler et al., 2011). "The finest people marry the two sexes in their own person."

"The finest people marry the two sexes in their own person."

—Ralph Waldo Emerson, *Journals*, 1843

As people mature to middle age and beyond, a curious thing happens. Women become more assertive and self-confident, and men become more empathic and less domineering (Kasen et al., 2006; Pratt et al., 1990). The decline in testosterone with age among men is one possible explanation for the shrinking gender differences. Role demands are another. Some speculate that during courtship and early parenthood, social expectations lead both sexes to emphasize gender-stereotypical traits that enhance their roles. While courting, providing, and protecting, men play up their macho sides and focus less on nurturing. While dating or rearing young children, young women may restrain their impulses to be assertive and independent (Zhu & Chang, 2019). As men and women graduate from these early adult roles, they supposedly express more of their restrained tendencies. Each becomes more **androgynous** – capable of both assertiveness and nurturance.

androgynous
From *andro* (man) + *gyn* (woman) — thus mixing both masculine and feminine characteristics.

Reflections on Evolutionary Psychology

Without disputing natural selection – nature's process of selecting physical and behavioral traits that enhance gene survival – critics see a problem with evolutionary explanations. Evolutionary psychologists sometimes start with a finding (such as the male-female difference in sexual initiative) and then work backward to construct an explanation for it. As biologists Paul Ehrlich and Marcus Feldman (2003) have pointed out, the evolutionary theorist can hardly lose when employing hindsight. Today's evolutionary psychology is like yesterday's Freudian psychology, say such critics: Either theory can be retrofitted to whatever happens.

The way to overcome the hindsight bias is to imagine things turning out otherwise. Let's try it. Imagine that women were stronger and more physically aggressive than men. "But of course!" someone might say, "all the better for protecting their young." And if human males were never known to have extramarital affairs, might we not see the evolutionary wisdom behind their fidelity? There is more to bringing offspring to maturity than merely depositing sperm, so men and women both gain by investing jointly in their children. Males who are loyal to their mates and offspring are more likely to see their young survive to perpetuate their genes. Monogamy also increases men's certainty of paternity. (These are, in fact, evolutionary explanations – again based on hindsight – for why humans, and certain other species whose young require a heavy parental investment, tend to pair off and be monogamous).

focus ON Evolutionary Science and Religion

A century and a half after Charles Darwin wrote *On the Origin of Species,* controversy continues over his big idea: that natural selection resulted in humans evolving from other animals. The controversy rages most intensely in the United States, where a Gallup survey reveals that half of adults do not believe that evolution accounts for "how human beings came to exist on Earth" and that 38% believe humans were created "within the past 10,000 years or so" (Swift, 2017). This skepticism of evolution persists despite the evidence, including research showing species' genetic relatedness, which long ago persuaded 95% of scientists that "human beings have developed over millions of years" (Gallup, 1996).

For most scientists, mutation and natural selection explain the emergence of life, including its ingenious designs. For example, the human eye, an engineering marvel that encodes and transmits a rich stream of information, has its building blocks "dotted around the animal kingdom," enabling nature to select mutations that over time improved the design (Dennett, 2005). Indeed, many scientists are fond of quoting the famous dictum of geneticist (and Russian Orthodox Church member) Theodosius Dobzhansky (1973), "Nothing makes sense in biology except in the light of evolution."

Alan Leshner (2005), the American Association for the Advancement of Science's former executive director, lamented the polarization caused by zealots at both the antiscience and the antireligion extremes. To resolve the growing science-religion tension, he believes scientists should communicate to the public that science and religion can co-exist, with each providing benefits to society.

Many scientists concur with Leshner, believing that science offers answers to questions such as "when?" and "how?" and that religion offers answers to "who?" and "why?" In the fifth century, St. Augustine anticipated today's science-affirming people of faith: "The universe was brought into being in a less than fully formed state, but was gifted with the capacity to transform itself from unformed matter into a truly marvelous array of structures and forms" (Wilford, 1999).

And the universe truly is marvelous, say cosmologists. Had gravity been a tiny bit stronger or weaker, or had the carbon proton weighed ever so slightly more or less, our universe — which is so extraordinarily right for producing life — would never have produced us. Although there are questions beyond science (why is there something rather than nothing?), this much appears true, concludes cosmologist Paul Davies (2004, 2007): Nature seems ingeniously devised to produce self-replicating, information-processing systems (us). Although we appear to have been created over eons of time, the end result is our wonderfully complex, meaningful, and hope-filled existence.

Critics also worry that evolutionary explanations for gang violence, homicidal jealousy, and sexual assault might reinforce and justify male aggression as natural behaviors — and do the same for men who cheat on their wives with younger women. But remember, reply the evolutionary psychologists, evolutionary wisdom is wisdom from the past. It tells us what behaviors worked in our early history as a species. Whether such tendencies are still adaptive today or much less socially acceptable is an entirely different question.

Evolutionary psychology's critics acknowledge that evolution helps explain both our commonalities and our differences (a certain amount of diversity aids survival). But they contend that our common evolutionary heritage does not, by itself, predict the enormous cultural variation in human marriage patterns (from one spouse to a succession of spouses to multiple wives to multiple husbands to spouse swapping). Nor does it explain cultural changes in behavior patterns over mere decades of time. The most significant trait that nature has endowed us with, it seems, is the capacity to adapt — to learn and to change. Evolution is *not* genetic determinism, say its defenders, because evolution has prepared us to adapt to varied environments (Confer et al., 2010). As everyone agrees, cultures vary and cultures change — and that's where we turn next.

Evolutionary psychologists argue that hindsight plays no less a role in cultural explanations: Why do women and men differ? Because their culture *socializes* their behavior! When people's roles vary across time and place, "culture" *describes* those roles better than it explains them. And far from being mere hindsight conjecture, say evolutionary psychologists, their field is an empirical science that tests evolutionary predictions with data from animal behavior, cross-cultural observations, and hormonal and genetic studies. As in many scientific fields, observations inspire a theory that generates new, testable predictions. The predictions alert us to unnoticed phenomena and allow us to confirm, refute, or revise the theory. (Outside of mainstream science, other critics challenge the teaching of evolution; see "Focus On: Evolutionary Science and Religion").

SUMMING UP: How Are We Influenced by Biology?

- How are we humans alike, how do we differ – and why? *Evolutionary psychologists* study how *natural selection* favors behavioral traits that promote the perpetuation of one's genes. Although part of evolution's legacy is our human capacity to learn and adapt (and therefore to differ from one another), the evolutionary perspective highlights the kinship that results from our shared human nature.
- Evolutionary psychologists theorize how evolution might have predisposed gender differences in behaviors such as aggression and sexual initiative. Nature's mating game favors males who take sexual initiative toward females – especially those with physical features suggesting fertility – and who seek aggressive dominance in competing with other males. Females, who have fewer reproductive chances, place a greater priority on selecting mates offering the resources to protect and nurture their young.
- Hormonal influences on behavior may be one mechanism by which sex differences are influenced by biology.
- Critics say that evolutionary explanations are sometimes after-the-fact conjectures that fail to account for the reality of cultural diversity; they also question whether enough empirical evidence exists to support evolutionary psychology's theories and are concerned that these theories will reinforce problematic stereotypes.

HOW ARE WE INFLUENCED BY CULTURE?

Explain how culture shapes behavior and gender roles.

Imagine getting on a plane tonight, settling down to sleep, and waking up tomorrow in another country. You immediately notice that people are speaking a different language, greeting each other in different ways, and wearing different clothing than in the country you inhabited just the day before. For all of our similarities as humans, we also exhibit a breathtaking diversity in the way we live our lives around the world.

We'll begin by discussing cultural influences in general and then, as we did in the previous section on biology, will use gender as a vehicle to explore cultural influences on behavior.

Culture and Behavior

We humans have been selected not only for big brains and biceps but also for culture. We come prepared to learn language and to bond and cooperate with others in securing food, caring for the young, and protecting ourselves. Perhaps our most important similarity, the

"Stand tall, Bipedal Ape. The shark may outswim you, the cheetah outrun you, the swift outfly you, the redwood outlast you. But you have the biggest gifts of all."

—Richard Dawkins, *The Devil's Chaplain*, 2003

culture
The enduring behaviors, ideas, attitudes, and traditions shared by a large group of people and transmitted from one generation to the next.

epigenetics
The study of environmental influences on gene expression that occur without DNA change.

hallmark of our species, is our capacity to learn and adapt. Our genes enable an adaptive human brain – a cerebral hard drive that receives the culture's software. Evolution has prepared us to live creatively in a changing world and to thrive in environments from equatorial jungles to Arctic ice fields. Compared with bees, birds, and bulldogs, nature has humans on a looser genetic leash. Ironically, our shared human biology enables our cultural diversity. It enables those in one **culture** to value promptness, welcome frankness, or accept premarital sex, whereas those in another culture do not. As social psychologist Roy Baumeister (2005, p. 29) observed, "Evolution made us for culture." (See "Focus On: The Cultural Animal.")

It's important to understand that biology and culture are not two completely separate influences. More often than not, they interact to produce the diversity of behavior you see around you. Genes are not fixed blueprints; their expression depends on the environment, much as the taste of tea is not "expressed" until meeting a hot water environment. One study of New Zealand young adults revealed a gene variation that put people at risk for depression, but only if they had also experienced major life stresses such as their parents' divorce (Caspi et al., 2003). Neither the stress nor the gene alone produced depression, but the two interacting did. Such findings have spawned the science of **epigenetics,** which considers how environments modify gene expression. For example, adverse life experiences, including mental health issues, can modify epigenetic markers of cell aging (Yusupov et al., 2023). In some cases, epigenetic changes caused by adverse experiences can even be passed down from mothers to children (Scorza et al., 2023). This research documents how the psychological – often shaped by culture – can become the physical.

Nature predisposes us to learn whatever culture we are born into. The cultural perspective highlights human adaptability. People's "natures are alike," said Confucius; "it is their habits that carry them far apart." And we are still far apart, noted world culture researchers Ronald

focus ON The Cultural Animal

We are, said Aristotle, the social animal. We humans have at least one thing in common with wolves and bees: We flourish by organizing ourselves into groups and working together.

But more than that, noted Roy Baumeister, we are — as he labeled us in the title of his 2005 book — *The Cultural Animal*. Humans more than other animals harness the power of culture to make life better. "Culture is a better way of being social," he wrote. We have culture to thank for our communication through language, our driving safely on one side of the road, our eating fruit in winter, and our use of money to pay for our cars and fruit. Culture facilitates our survival and reproduction, and nature has blessed us with a brain that, like no other, enables culture.

Other animals show the rudiments of culture and language. Monkeys who learn new food-washing techniques then pass them to future generations. And chimps exhibit a modest capacity for language. But no species can accumulate progress across generations as smartly as humans. Your nineteenth-century ancestors had no cars, no indoor plumbing, no electricity, no air conditioning, no internet, no smartphones, and no social media — all things for which you can thank culture. Intelligence enables innovation, and culture enables dissemination — the transmission of information and innovation across time and place.

The division of labor is "another huge and powerful advantage of culture," noted Baumeister. Few of us grow food or build shelter, yet nearly everyone reading this book enjoys food and shelter. Indeed, books themselves are a tribute to the division of labor enabled by culture. Although only two lucky people's names go on this book's cover, the product is actually the work of a coordinated team of researchers, reviewers, assistants, and editors. Books and other media disseminate knowledge, providing the engine of progress.

"Culture is what is special about human beings," concluded Baumeister. "Culture helps us to become something much more than the sum of our talents, efforts, and other individual blessings. In that sense, culture is the greatest blessing of all. . . . Alone we would be but cunning brutes, at the mercy of our surroundings. Together, we can sustain a system that enables us to make life progressively better for ourselves, our children, and those who come after."

Inglehart and Christian Welzel (2005). Despite increasing education, "we are not moving toward a uniform global culture: cultural convergence is not taking place. A society's cultural heritage is remarkably enduring" (p. 46).

CULTURAL DIVERSITY

The diversity of our languages, customs, and expressive behaviors confirms that much of our behavior is socially programmed, not hardwired. The genetic leash is long. As sociologist Ian Robertson (1987) has noted:

> Americans eat oysters but not snails. The French eat snails but not locusts. The Zulus eat locusts but not fish. The Jews eat fish but not pork. The Hindus eat pork but not beef. The Russians eat beef but not snakes. The Chinese eat snakes but not people. The Jalé of New Guinea find people delicious. (p. 67)

If we all lived as homogeneous ethnic groups in separate regions of the world, as some people still do, cultural diversity would be less relevant to our daily living. In Japan, where 98.5% of people are Japanese (CIA, 2017), internal cultural differences are minimal. In contrast, cultural differences abound in New York City, where more than one-third of the 8 million residents are foreign born.

Increasingly, cultural diversity surrounds us. More and more, we live in a global village, connected to our fellow villagers by electronic social networks, jumbo jets, and international trade. The mingling of cultures is nothing new. "American" jeans were invented in 1872 by German immigrant Levi Strauss by combining "Genes," the trouser style of Genoese sailors, with denim cloth from a French town (Legrain, 2003).

Women kiss women good night. Men kiss women good night. But men do not kiss men good night — especially in Armonk."

J. B. Handelsman

Although some norms are universal, every era and culture has its own norms — rules for accepted and expected social behavior.

Confronting another culture is sometimes a startling experience. U.S. males may feel uncomfortable when Middle Eastern heads of state greet the U.S. president with a kiss on the cheek. A German student, accustomed to speaking to "Herr Professor" only on rare occasions, considers it strange that at my [DM's] institution, most faculty office doors are open and students stop by freely. An Iranian student on her first visit to an American McDonald's restaurant fumbles around in her paper bag looking for the eating utensils until she sees the other customers eating their french fries with, of all things, their hands. In many areas of the globe, your best manners and mine are serious breaches of etiquette. Foreigners visiting Japan often struggle to master the rules of the social game — when to take off their shoes, how to pour the tea, when to give and open gifts, how to act toward someone higher or lower in the social hierarchy.

Migration and refugee evacuations are mixing cultures more than ever. Today, East and West, and North and South, meet all the time. Italy is home to many Albanians, Germany to Turks, England — where Mohammed in its various spellings is now the most common boy's name (Cohen, 2011) — to Pakistanis. The result is both friendship and conflict. One in 5 Canadians and 1 in 8 Americans are immigrants. As we work, play, and live with people from diverse cultural backgrounds, it helps to understand how our cultures influence us and how our cultures differ. In a conflict-laden world, achieving peace requires appreciation for both our genuine differences and our deep similarities.

Cultures mixing. As this family (with an Asian American mother and White American father) illustrates, immigration and globalization are bringing once-distant cultures together.
Maximoff/Shutterstock

NORMS: EXPECTED BEHAVIOR

As etiquette rules illustrate, all cultures have their accepted ideas about appropriate behavior. We often view these social expectations, or **norms,** as a negative force that imprisons people in a blind effort to perpetuate tradition. Norms do restrain and control us — so successfully and so subtly that we hardly sense their existence. Social norms don't just influence our behavior but restrict the behaviors we would even consider. When considering how to behave in the lobby of a bank, few would even think about singing aloud, taking off their shoes, or stretching out on a couch for a nap — even though these are behaviors accepted in other contexts. Social norms give us a crib sheet on how to behave (Kalkstein et al., 2023).

norms
Standards for accepted and expected behavior. Norms prescribe "proper" behavior. (In a different sense of the word, norms also describe what most others do — what is *normal.*)

In some cultures and regions, hugging and even hand-holding by male friends is the norm, but in others, such physical closeness between male friends would be seen as odd.
vystekimages/Shutterstock

Yet those norms often differ across cultures, even if we don't consciously realize the norms of our own culture. Like fish in the ocean, we are all so immersed in our cultures that we must leap out of them to understand their influence. "When we see other Dutch people behaving in what foreigners would call a Dutch way," noted Dutch psychologists Willem Koomen and Anton Dijker (1997), "we often do not realize that the behavior is typically Dutch."

There is no better way to learn the norms of our native culture than to visit another culture and see that its members do things *that* way, whereas we do them *this* way. When living in Scotland, I [DM] acknowledged to my children that, yes, Europeans eat meat with the fork facing down in the left hand. "But we Americans consider it good manners to cut the meat and then transfer the fork to the right hand. I admit it's inefficient. But it's the way *we* do it."

To those who don't accept them, such norms may seem arbitrary and confining. To most in the Western world, the Muslim woman's head covering (known as the hijab) seems arbitrary and confining, but not to most in Muslim cultures. The Muslim women in my [JT's] classes believe the hijab encourages men to see them as people rather than as sexual objects. Just as a stage play moves smoothly when the actors know their lines, so social behavior occurs smoothly when people know what to expect. Norms grease the social machinery. In unfamiliar situations, when the norms may be unclear, we monitor others' behavior and adjust our own accordingly.

Cultures vary in their norms for expressiveness, punctuality, rule breaking, and personal space. Consider the following:

INDIVIDUAL CHOICES Cultures vary in how much they emphasize the individual self (individualistic cultures) versus others and the society (collectivistic cultures; Kitayama et al., 2022). As a result, Western (usually individualistic) countries allow people more latitude in making their own decisions. When I [JT] was in college, my Pakistani-American friend wanted to go to graduate school to study Latin. Her parents insisted she go to medical school, saying they would cut off their financial support if she did not. Having grown up in the United States, I was shocked that her parents would tell her what profession to pursue, but in collectivistic cultures, this type of obedience to one's parents is more widely accepted (Lum et al., 2016).

Differences rooted in individualism and collectivism also appear on social media sites. People in collectivistic countries are more likely to use social media to promote group belonging, such as by commenting on others' posts. Those in individualistic countries, however, are more likely to use social media for self-expression, such as posting about their thoughts and activities (Hong & Na, 2018).

EXPRESSIVENESS AND PUNCTUALITY To someone from a relatively formal northern European culture, a person whose roots are in an expressive Latin American culture may seem "warm, charming, inefficient, and time-wasting." Latin American business executives who arrive late for a dinner engagement may be mystified by the irritation of their time-obsessed North American counterparts. To the Latin American person, the northern European may seem "efficient, cold, and overconcerned with time" (Beaulieu, 2004; Triandis, 1981). And they might be right: Northern Europeans walk faster on public streets than those in Latin America, and northern European bank clocks are more accurate (Levine & Norenzayan, 1999). North American tourists in Japan may wonder about the lack of eye contact from passing pedestrians. (See "Research Close-Up: Passing Encounters, East and West.")

RULE-FOLLOWING Norms and rule-following are especially important in traditional, collectivistic cultures, where violating norms is punished most harshly when others are harmed (Feinberg et al., 2019). However, rules can go beyond harm protection to promoting group sameness and harmony. In one study, South Koreans (compared to Americans) were more likely to avoid co-workers who were vegetarians, perhaps because this is a nonnormative choice. To most Americans, being a vegetarian is a personal preference; to a Korean, it signals standing out from the group and is thus undesirable (Kinias et al., 2014). Many collectivistic

research CLOSE-UP

Passing Encounters, East and West

On my [DM's] Midwestern American campus and in my town, sidewalk passersby routinely glance and smile at one another. In Britain and China, where I have spent time, I have rarely observed such microinteractions. To a European, our greeting passing strangers might seem a bit silly and disrespectful of privacy; to a Midwesterner, avoiding eye contact — what sociologists have called "civil inattention" — might seem aloof.

To quantify the culture difference in pedestrian interactions, an international team led by Miles Patterson and Yuichi Iizuka (2007) conducted a simple field experiment both in the United States and in Japan with the unwitting participation of more than 1,000 pedestrians. Their procedure illustrates how social psychologists sometimes conduct unobtrusive research in natural settings (Patterson, 2008). As **Figure 1** depicts, an accomplice of the experimenter would initiate one of three behaviors when within about 12 feet of an approaching pedestrian on an uncrowded sidewalk: (1) *avoidance* (looking straight ahead), (2) *glancing* at the person for less than a second, and (3) *looking* at the person and *smiling*. A trailing observer would then record the pedestrian's reaction. Did the pedestrian glance at the accomplice? Smile? Nod? Verbally greet the accomplice? (The order of the three conditions was randomized and unknown to the trailing observer, ensuring that the person recording the data was "blind" to the experimental condition.)

As you might expect, the pedestrians were more likely to look at someone who looked at them and to smile at, nod to, or greet someone who also smiled at them. This was especially so when that someone was female rather than male. But as **Figure 2** shows, the culture differences were nevertheless striking. As the research team expected, in view of Japan's greater respect for privacy and cultural reserve when interacting with outgroups, Americans were much more likely to smile at, nod to, or greet the accomplice.

In Japan, they conclude, "there is little pressure to reciprocate the smile of the accomplice because there is no relationship with the accomplice and no obligation to respond."

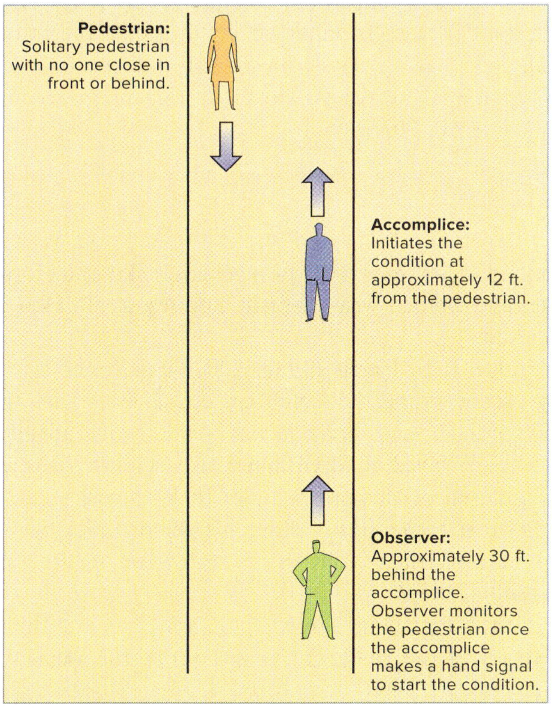

FIGURE 1

Illustration of a Passing Encounter

Source: Patterson et al., (2007).

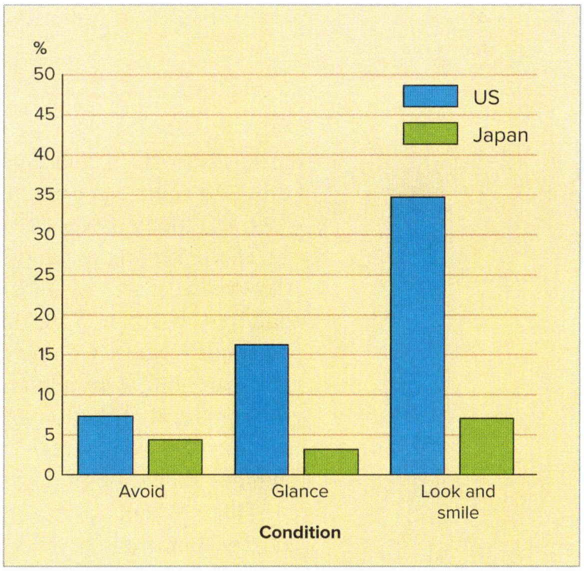

FIGURE 2

American and Japanese Pedestrian Responses, by Condition

Source: Adapted from Patterson et al., (2007).

Norms — rules for accepted and expected behavior — vary by culture. Collectivistic countries such as Japan often have stronger norms.
georgeclerk/E+/Getty Images

cultures promote the belief that human suffering – such as contracting a disease – is caused by violating social norms (Sullivan et al., 2012). Collectivistic cultures are more likely to stigmatize people seen as different, whether through identity (gays and lesbians, immigrants) or behavior (those with substance use issues [Shin et al., 2013]).

Collectivistic or "tight" cultures may have developed strong norms because they were historically more likely to experience threats such as wars or famines (Gelfand et al., 2011). Collectivistic cultures are also more likely than individualistic cultures to have experienced frequent outbreaks of infectious diseases that necessitate specific rules such as physical distancing, hand washing, and wearing masks in public (Grossmann & Varnum, 2015; Morand & Walther, 2018). This might be one reason why the citizens of individualistic countries such as the United States found it difficult to adapt to the restrictions imposed during the COVID-19 pandemic: Americans were not used to being told what to do. In an analysis of location data from millions of smartphones during 2020, people in individualistic countries were less likely to follow pandemic lockdown rules, visiting more places than those in collectivistic cultures during the same period (Feng et al., 2023).

personal space
The buffer zone we like to maintain around our bodies. Its size depends on our culture and our familiarity with whoever is near us.

PERSONAL SPACE **Personal space** is a sort of portable bubble or buffer zone that we like to maintain between ourselves and others. As the situation changes, the bubble varies in size. With strangers, most Americans maintain a fairly large personal space, keeping 4 feet or more between us. On uncrowded buses or in restrooms or libraries, we protect our space and respect others' space. We let friends come closer (Novelli et al., 2010).

Individuals differ: Some people prefer more personal space than others (Perry et al., 2013). Groups differ, too: Adults maintain more distance than do children. Men keep more distance from one another than women do. For reasons unknown, cultures near the equator prefer less distance and more touching and hugging. Thus, the British and the Scandinavians prefer more distance than the French and the Arabs; North Americans prefer more space than Latin Americans (Sorokowska et al., 2017).

Peer-Transmitted Culture

Cultures, like ice cream, come in many flavors. In the United States, women – but very few men – wear skirts and dresses. In Scotland, many *men* wear pleated skirts (kilts) as formal dress. In some equatorial cultures, men and women wear virtually nothing at all. How are such traditions preserved across generations?

The prevailing assumption is what Judith Rich Harris (1998, 2007) called *The Nurture Assumption:* Parental nurture, the way parents bring their children up, governs who their children become. On that much, Freudians and behaviorists – and your next-door neighbor – agree. Comparing the extremes of loved children and abused children suggests that parenting *does* matter. Moreover, children do acquire many of their values, including their political affiliation and religious faith, at home. But if children's personalities likewise are molded by parental example and nurture, then children who grow up in the same families should be noticeably alike, shouldn't they?

That presumption is refuted by the most astonishing, agreed-upon, and dramatic finding of developmental psychology: Growing up in the same family has very little impact on personality traits and many behaviors.

So what accounts for why humans differ in personality traits and behaviors? Genetic influences explain about half of the variation (Vukasović & Bratko, 2015). Some of the rest is due to *peer influence,* Harris argued. What children and teens care about most is not what their parents think but what their friends think. Children and youths learn their culture – their games, their musical tastes, their accents, even their dirty words – mostly from peers. Most teens therefore talk, act, and dress more like their peers than their parents. Across 233 longitudinal studies, adolescents whose peers used drugs, broke school rules, or experienced depression were more likely to do those things themselves (Giletta et al., 2021).

In hindsight, that makes sense. It's their peers with whom they play and eventually will work and mate. Consider:

- Preschoolers will often refuse to try a certain food despite parents' urgings – until they are put at a table with a group of children who like it.
- Having friends who text while driving triples the odds of your doing so (Trivedi et al., 2017).
- Girls whose peers believed that boys are innately better at math performed more poorly in math classes (Wu & Cai, 2023).
- Young immigrant children whose families are transplanted into foreign cultures usually grow up preferring the language and norms of their new peer culture. A young child who moves with their family from China to the United States will speak English with an American accent – even if their parents never learn English or have heavy accents. Youth may "code-switch" when they step back into their homes, but their hearts and minds are with their peer groups. Likewise, deaf children of hearing parents who attend schools for the deaf usually leave their parents' culture and assimilate into deaf culture.

Children learn many of their attitudes from their peers.
wavebreakmedia/Shutterstock

Therefore, if we left a group of children with their same schools, neighborhoods, and peers but switched the parents around, said Harris (1996) in taking her argument to its limits, they "would develop into the same sort of adults." Parents have an important influence, but it's substantially indirect; parents help define the schools, neighborhoods, and peers that directly influence whether their children become delinquent, use drugs, or get pregnant. Moreover, children often take their cues from slightly older children, who get their cues from older youth, who take theirs from young adults in the parents' generation.

The links of influence from parental group to child group are loose enough that the cultural transmission is never perfect. And in both human and primate cultures, change comes from the young. When one monkey discovers a better way of washing food or when people develop a new idea about fashion or gender roles, the innovation usually comes from the young and is more readily embraced by younger adults. Thus, cultural traditions continue; yet cultures change.

Cultural Similarity

Thanks to human adaptability, cultures differ. Yet beneath the veneer of cultural differences, cross-cultural psychologists see "an essential universality" (Lonner, 1980). How much we are similar is usually larger than how much we differ (Hanel et al., 2019). As members of one species, the processes that underlie our differing behaviors are much the same everywhere (**Figure 3**).

People everywhere have some common norms for friendship. From studies conducted in Britain, Italy, Hong Kong, and Japan, Michael Argyle and Monika Henderson (1985) noted several cultural variations in the norms that define the role of friend. For example, in Japan it's especially important not to embarrass a friend with public criticism. But there are also some apparently universal norms: Respect the friend's privacy; make eye contact while talking; don't divulge things said in confidence. Across 75 nations, the most valued traits were honesty, fairness, kindness, good judgment, and curiosity – nearly all crucial virtues for friendships and relationships (McGrath, 2015).

Around the world, people describe others with between two and five universal personality dimensions (McCrae & Costa, 2008; Saucier et al., 2014). Evaluating others as good or bad appears across almost all cultures and languages. All cultures have norms, so all cultures evaluate how well others follow those norms (Saucier et al., 2014).

"Whatever the conditions of people's lives, wherever they live, however they live, we all share the same dreams."
—Melinda Gates (2020)

Likewise, there are six universal dimensions of moral beliefs – care, equality, proportionality, loyalty, authority, and purity – that shape a culture's judgments of behaviors (Atari et al., 2023;

FIGURE 3

Words Used to Express Positive Emotion in (a) India and (b) The United States

In a study of the language of Facebook users, positive emotion was expressed in similar ways in India (top) and the United States (bottom), with a few cultural differences (such as the greater use of "thanks" in India).

(a-b) *Source*: Kern, M. L., & Sap, M. (2015).

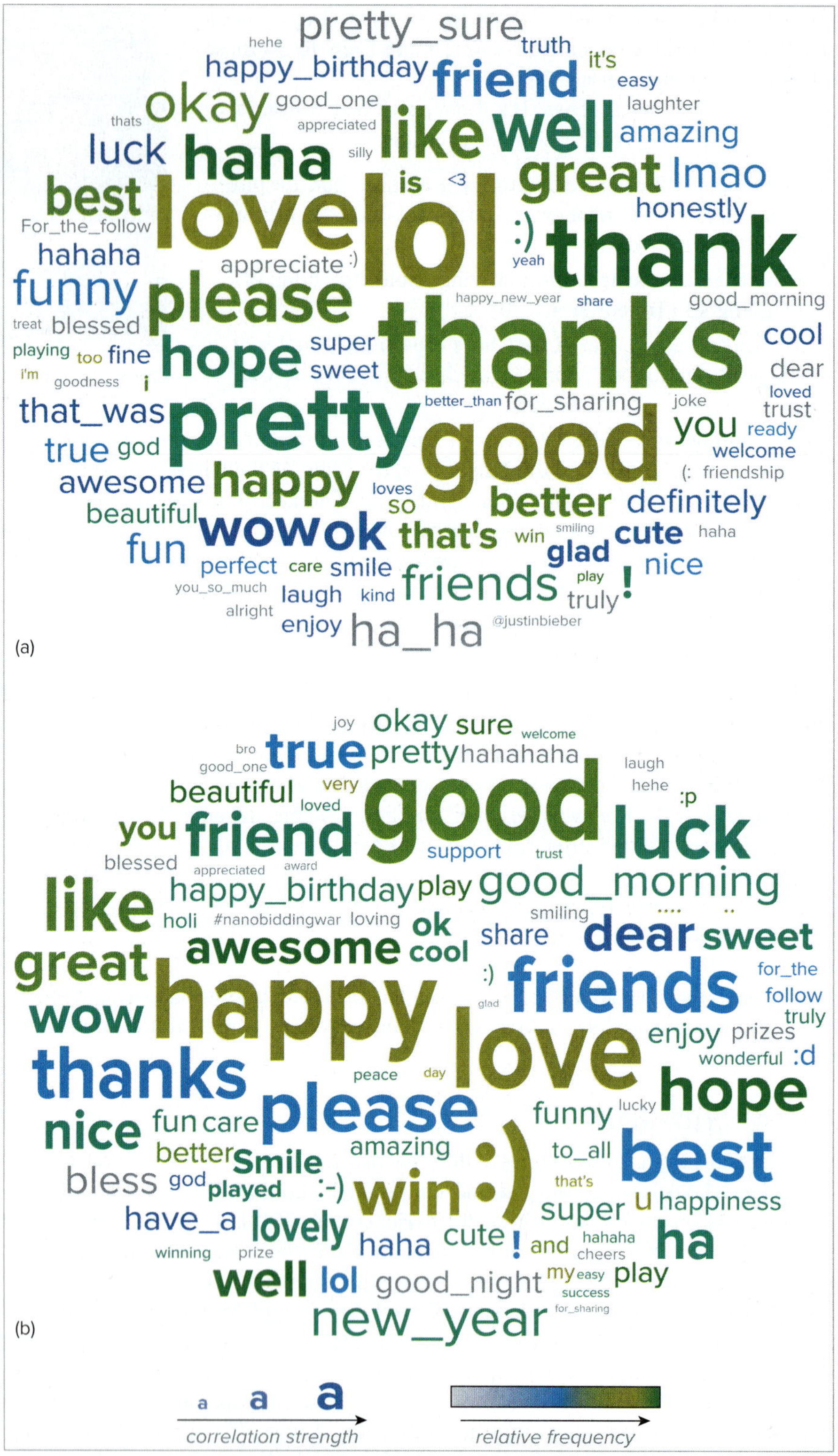

see **Figure 4**). These moral values influence a culture's social norms and laws and may also explain subcultural differences within a country. For example, U.S. conservatives tend to value loyalty, authority, and purity more than U.S. liberals, and liberals tend to value care and equality more (Kivikangas et al., 2021).

Wherever people form status hierarchies, they also talk to higher-status people in the respectful way they often talk to strangers. And they talk to lower-status people in the more familiar, first-name way they speak to friends (Brown, 1965, 1987; Kroger & Wood, 1992).

6 Dimensions of Moral Judgments.	Sample Claims
Care	"I am empathetic toward those people who have suffered in their lives"
Equality	"The world would be a better place if everyone made the same amount of money."
Proportionality	"I think people who are more hardworking should end up with more money"
Loyalty	"I think children should be taught to be loyal to their country"
Authority	"I think it is important for societies to cherish their traditional values"
Purity	"I admire people who keep their virginity until marriage."

FIGURE 4
Moral Concerns Across Cultures

Patients call their physician "Dr. So and So"; the physician may reply using the patients' first names. Students and professors typically address one another in a similarly nonmutual way.

Most languages have two forms of the English pronoun "you": a respectful form and a familiar form (for example, *Sie* and *du* in German, *vous* and *tu* in French, *usted* and *tu* in Spanish). People typically use the familiar form with intimates and subordinates, with close friends and family members, but also in speaking to children and pets. A German adolescent receives a boost when strangers begin addressing them as "Sie" instead of "du."

Culture and Gender

In the first part of this chapter, we considered biological and evolutionary explanations for why men and women differ. Yet biology is not the entire story: What it means to be a man or woman, boy or girl, differs from one culture to another.

We can see the shaping power of culture in ideas about how men and women should behave. And we can see culture in the disapproval men and women endure when they violate those expectations (Kite, 2001). In countries everywhere, girls spend more time helping with housework and child care, and boys spend more time in unsupervised physical play (Gracia et al., 2022; Kalenkoski et al., 2009; Prochnow et al., 2021). Even in contemporary, dual-career, North American marriages, men do most of the household repairs, and women arrange the child care (BLS, 2017; Fisher et al., 2007; Fry et al., 2023). Such behavior expectations for males and females – of who should cook, wash dishes, hunt game, and lead companies and countries – define **gender roles.**

"At the United Nations, we have always understood that our work for development depends on building a successful partnership with the African farmer and her husband."

—Former Secretary-General Kofi Annan (2002)

gender role
A set of behavior expectations (norms) for males and females.

Does culture construct these gender roles? Or do gender roles merely reflect men's and women's natural behavior tendencies? The variety of gender roles across cultures and over time shows that culture indeed helps construct our gender roles.

Gender Roles Vary with Culture

Despite gender role inequalities, the majority of the world's people would ideally like to see more parallel male and female roles. A 2010 Pew Global Attitudes survey asked 25,000 people whether life was more satisfying when both spouses work and share child care or when women stay home and care for the children while the husband provides. In 21 of 22 countries, most chose both spouses working.

However, large country-to-country differences exist. Pakistanis disagreed with the world majority opinion by 4 to 1, whereas the Spanish agreed by 13 to 1. When jobs are scarce, should men have more right to a job? Yes, concurred about 1 in 8 people in Britain, Spain, and the United States – and 4 in 5 people in Indonesia, Pakistan, and Nigeria (Pew, 2010).

Overall, observed Wendy Wood and Alice Eagly (2000, 2002), culture often reinforces gender roles that may have originated with biological demands. Women gathered food because they needed to stay close to home; men hunted because they didn't. Cultural

In Western countries, gender roles are becoming more flexible. No longer is piloting necessarily men's work or preschool teaching necessarily women's work.
(Left): U.S. Air Force photo by Master Sgt. Alfred A. Gerloff Jr.; (Right): DGLimages/Shutterstock

differences may also begin with one difference between men and women influencing many others. Men's greater physical strength may have also led to patriarchy being the most common system. Virtually all societies have men in positions of social power and assign different roles to men and women. As a consequence, similarities across cultures might represent male social power rather than evolved differences.

Gender Roles Vary over Time

In the past half century – a thin slice of our long history – gender roles have changed dramatically. In 1938, just 1 in 5 Americans approved "of a married woman earning money in business or industry if she has a husband capable of supporting her." By 1996, 4 in 5 approved (Niemi et al., 1989; NORC, 1996). Among U.S. 12th graders in the late 1970s, 59% agreed that "A preschooler is likely to suffer if the mother works," but by 2017 only 16% agreed (Donnelly et al., 2015; Meich et al., 2018). While the majority of Americans in the 1950s saw men as more competent than women, a sizable majority now view women as more competent (Eagly et al., 2020).

Behavioral changes have accompanied this attitude shift. In 1965, the Harvard Business School had never granted a degree to a woman. In its 2024 class, 46% of students were women (Harvard Business School, 2022). From 1960 to 2021, women rose from 6% to 51% of U.S. medical students and from 3% to 55% of law students (AAMC, 2023; ABA, 2023). Thus, the majority of those studying to be doctors and lawyers are now women. Role models may be a crucial catalyst for such shifts. When a law in India reserved leadership positions in some villages for women, girls became more likely to aspire to higher education and careers compared to the villages without female role models (Beaman et al., 2012).

Things have changed at home, too. In the mid-1960s, American married women devoted *seven times* as many hours to housework as did their husbands (Bianchi et al., 2000). By 2022, the gender gap had shrunk yet persisted: 22% of men and 47% of women did housework in an average day, with women averaging 2.7 hours and men 2.2 hours. The time fathers spent caring for children has tripled since 1965, though mothers in 2022 still spent twice as much time caring for young children as fathers (BLS, 2023). The number of stay-at-home dads has doubled since 1989, and just as many dads as moms in 2015 said that parenting was extremely important to their identity (Livingston & Parker, 2019).

The trends toward more gender equality appear across many cultures; for example, women are increasingly represented in the legislative bodies of most nations (IPU, 2023). In 45% of U.S. marriages, wives make the same or more than their husbands, up from 15% of marriages in 1972 (Fry et al., 2023). Such changes, across cultures and over a remarkably short time, signal that evolution and biology do not render gender roles unchangeable: Time also bends the genders. Progressive gender roles may also bend cultures toward peace:

Societies with more gender equality are less likely to engage in war and are less violent (Caprioli & Boyer, 2001; Melander et al., 2005).

Overall, gender roles have shifted considerably over the decades, yet many gender differences still persist. The interplay of biology and culture will continue, and in the decades to come, gender roles may continue to evolve.

SUMMING UP: How Are We Influenced by Culture?

- The cultural perspective highlights human diversity—the behaviors and ideas that define a group and that are transmitted across generations. The differences in attitudes and behaviors from one *culture* to another indicate the extent to which we are the products of cultural *norms* and roles. Yet cross-cultural psychologists also examine the "essential universality" of all people. For example, despite their differences, cultures have a number of norms in common.
- Much of culture's influence is transmitted to children by their peers.
- The most heavily researched of roles—*gender roles*—reflect biological influence but also illustrate culture's strong impact. The universal tendency has been for males, more than females, to occupy socially dominant roles.
- Gender roles show significant variation from culture to culture and from one era to another.

HOW ARE FEMALES AND MALES ALIKE AND DIFFERENT?

Describe how males and females are alike and how they differ.

As we've seen, nowhere is the interplay of biology and culture more evident than in the differences between men and women. So, what are those differences—not the popular conceptions or stereotypes, but the actual average differences found in research?

First, let's consider how men and women are similar. "Of the 46 chromosomes in the human genome, 45 are unisex," noted Judith Rich Harris (1998). Females and males are therefore similar in many physical traits and developmental milestones during infancy, such as the age of sitting up, teething, and walking. They also are alike in many psychological traits, such as overall vocabulary, creativity, intelligence, extraversion, and happiness. Women and men feel the same emotions and longings, both dote on their children, and they have similar-appearing brains. Indeed, noted Ethan Zell and his colleagues (2015) in their review of 106 meta-analyses (each a statistical digest of dozens of studies), the common result for most variables studied is *gender similarity* (Hyde, 2018). On most psychological attributes, the overlap between the sexes is larger than the difference (Carothers & Reis, 2013; Hyde, 2005). Your "opposite sex" is actually your similar sex.

Yet of course there are also pronounced gender differences, including in psychological traits and behaviors (Eagly & Revelle, 2022). Compared to males, the average female

- has 70% more fat, has 40% less muscle, is 5 inches shorter, and weighs 40 pounds less;
- is more sensitive to smells and sounds; and
- is twice as likely to experience anxiety disorders or depression (Salk et al., 2017).

Compared to females, the average male is

- slower to enter puberty (by about 2 years) but quicker to die (by 5 years, worldwide);
- three times more likely to be diagnosed with ADHD (attention-deficit/hyperactivity disorder), four times more likely to commit suicide, and five times more likely to be killed by lightning; and
- more likely to do repair work around the house or watch sports on television (Eagly & Revelle, 2022).

During the 1970s, many scholars worried that studies of such gender differences might reinforce stereotypes. Would gender differences be construed as women's deficits? Although the findings confirm some stereotypes of women – as less physically aggressive, more nurturing, and more socially sensitive – those traits are actually preferred by most people, whether male or female (Folberg et al., 2022; Prentice & Carranza, 2002; Swim, 1994). Small wonder, then, that most people rate their beliefs and feelings regarding women as more *favorable* than their feelings regarding men – a phenomenon some have labeled the "women are wonderful" effect (Eagly, 1994; Haddock & Zanna, 1994; Krys et al., 2018). Still, women in individualistic cultures often find themselves caught between the cultural standard that they be assertive and autonomous and the gender standard that they be caring and interdependent (Proudfoot & Kay, 2023).

"There should be no qualms about the forthright study of racial and gender differences; science is in desperate need of good studies that . . . inform us of what we need to do to help underrepresented people to succeed in this society. Unlike the ostrich, we cannot afford to hide our heads for fear of socially uncomfortable discoveries."

—Developmental psychologist Sandra Scarr (1988)

As we discuss the gender differences found in research, keep in mind they are differences based on averages; *they do not apply to every member of the group*. Many of these differences may resonate with your own experiences. Others might not, but that doesn't necessarily mean they are incorrect. For example, despite being female, I [JT] am not particularly interested in shopping. So if a study found that women are more interested in shopping, I would be the exception. When I was younger, I didn't like reading about gender differences (such as in shopping) that made women look frivolous. Slowly, I started to realize that just because something was true of the average woman didn't mean it had to be true of *me*. For men, the equivalent might be reading about gender differences in undesirable acts such as aggression and violence; even if it's true on average, it doesn't have to be true of *you*. Keep that in mind as you read.

Independence versus Connectedness

Individual men display outlooks and behavior that vary from fierce competitiveness to caring nurturance. So do individual women. Without denying that, several late-twentieth-century feminist psychologists contended that women more than men give priority to close, intimate relationships (Chodorow, 1978, 1989; Gilligan, 1982; Gilligan et al., 1990; Miller, 1986). In short, men are more independent on average, and women are more communal on average (Hsu et al., 2021). Consider the evidence:

PLAY Compared to boys, girls talk more intimately and play less aggressively, noted Eleanor Maccoby (2002) from her decades of research on gender development. They also play in smaller groups, often talking with one friend. Boys more often engage in larger group activities (Rose & Rudolph, 2006). Even today, boys and girls strongly prefer to play with toys associated with their gender (Davis & Hines, 2020). And as boys play with boys and girls play with girls, sex differences grow larger. These sex differences in play among youngsters appear in nonhuman primates such as monkeys as well, suggesting fairly universal and perhaps biological roots (Lonsdorf, 2017).

Girls' play is often in small groups and imitates relationships. Boys' play is more often competitive or aggressive.
(Girls): FatCamera/iStock/Getty Images; (Boys): Fuse/Corbis/Getty Images

FRIENDSHIP AND PEER RELATIONSHIPS As adults, women – at least in individualistic cultures like the United States – are more likely than men to describe themselves in relational terms, experience relationship-linked emotions, value social goals, and be attuned to others' relationships (Gabriel & Gardner, 1999; Tamres et al., 2002; Vilar et al., 2020; Watkins et al., 1998, 2003; Yang & Girgus, 2019). On social media, women use more words about relationships ("friends," "family," "sister"), while men use more words about specific activities and ideas ("political," "football," "battle"); overall, women's language online is warmer, more compassionate, and more polite, while men's is colder, more hostile, and more impersonal (Park et al., 2016; Statista, 2019; Tifferet, 2020). On average, women are more aware of how their actions affect other people (You et al., 2011) and feel a closer attachment to their friends (Gorrese & Ruggieri, 2012). "Perhaps because of their greater desire for intimacy," reported Joyce Benenson and colleagues (2009), during their first year of college, women are twice as likely as men to change roommates.

Women's phone conversations last longer, and girls send more than twice as many text messages as do boys (Friebel & Seabright, 2011; Lenhart, 2010; Smoreda & Licoppe, 2000). Women talk for longer when the goal is affiliation with others – though men actually talk more overall, especially in work contexts and when expressing opinions (Leaper & Ayres, 2007). Women spend more time sending emails in which they express more emotion (Crabtree, 2002; Thomson & Murachver, 2001). Women and girls spend more time on social networking sites such as Instagram, while boys and men spend more time on electronic gaming (Twenge & Martin, 2020).

When in groups, women share more of their lives and offer more support, and are generally more focused on maintaining positive social relationships (Dindia & Allen, 1992; Eagly, 1987; Yang & Girgus, 2019). When facing stress, men tend to respond with "fight or flight"; often, their response to a threat is combat. In nearly all studies, noted Shelley Taylor (2002), women who are under stress more often "tend and befriend"; they turn to friends and family for support. Among first-year college students, 72% of men, but 83% of women, say it is *very* important to "help others who are in difficulty" (Stolzenberg et al., 2019). The sex difference in independence versus connectedness can readily be seen in a study of language use on Facebook (Schwartz et al., 2013; **Figure 5**).

"In the different voice of women lies the truth of an ethic of care."

—Carol Gilligan,
In a Different Voice, 1982

In writing, women tend to use more communal prepositions ("with"), fewer quantitative words, and more present tense. Men use more complex language and women use more social words and pronouns (Newman et al., 2008). The Twitter accounts of female city mayors have been more informal and mentioned danger and doubts more often than the accounts of male mayors (Stone & Can, 2021). One computer program, which taught itself to recognize gender differences in word usage and sentence structure, successfully identified the author's gender in 80% of 920 British fiction and nonfiction works (Koppel et al., 2002).

In conversation, men's style reflects their concern for independence, women's for connectedness. Men are more likely to act as powerful people often do: talking assertively, interrupting intrusively, touching with the hand, staring more, smiling less (Leaper & Robnett, 2011). At academic conferences, men ask more questions than women do (Jarvis et al., 2022). On the U.S. Supreme Court and in the U.S. Congress, women are disproportionately interrupted by their male colleagues (Jacobi & Schweers, 2017; Miller & Sutherland, 2023). Women's influence style tends to be more indirect: less interruptive, more sensitive, more polite, less cocky, and more qualified and hedged.

With women more interested in jobs focusing on people, medicine may eventually become a female-dominated profession.
Rocketclips, Inc./Shutterstock

VOCATIONS In general, women are more interested in jobs dealing with people (teacher, doctor) and men in jobs with things (truck driver, engineer) (Diekman et al., 2010; Eagly, 2009, 2017; Lippa, 2010; Lordan & Pischke, 2022; Su et al., 2009). Females are less interested in math-intensive careers than are males, even among those with a talent for math (Lubinski & Benbow, 2006; Watt et al., 2017), and even though more girls than boys around the world appear capable of college-level math and science work (Stoet & Geary, 2018). Another distinction:

FIGURE 5

Words and Phrases with the Largest Gender Differences Among More than 70,000 English-Speaking Facebook Users

The gender difference in independence versus connectedness is readily apparent in this natural language study, as are other differences such as men's greater propensity to swear and women's greater focus on shopping. The red clusters show the specific topics with the largest gender differences.

Source: Schwartz et al., (2013).

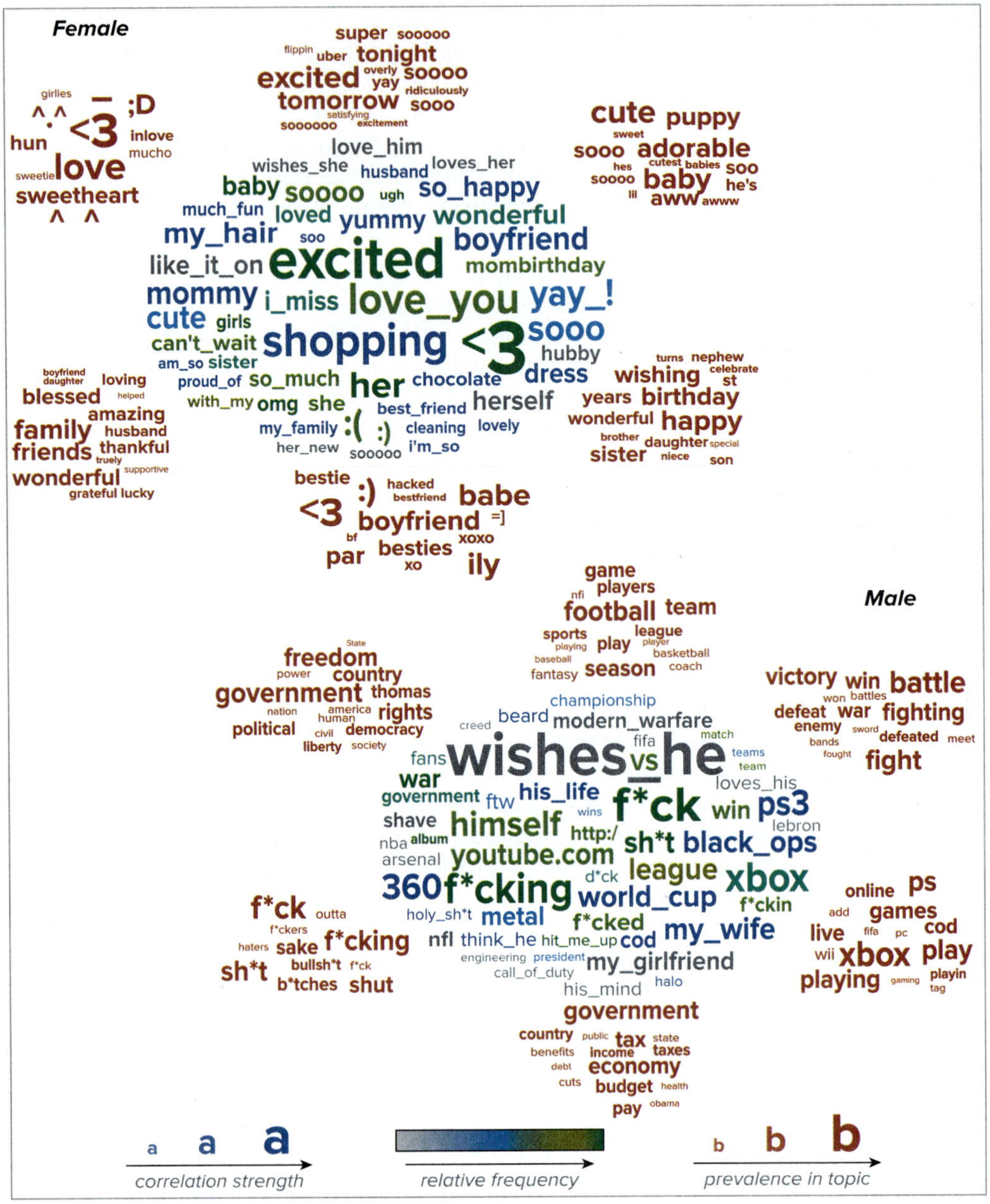

Men gravitate disproportionately to jobs that enhance inequalities (prosecuting attorney, corporate advertising); women gravitate to jobs that reduce inequalities (public defender, advertising work for a charity [Pratto et al., 1997]). Studies of 640,000 people's job preferences reveal that men more than women value earnings, promotion, leadership, challenge, and power; women more than men value good hours, personal relationships, and opportunities to help others (Konrad et al., 2000; Pinker, 2008; Sheppard, 2018). Indeed, in most of the North American caregiving professions, such as social worker, teacher, and nurse, women outnumber men. Recent decades have seen a few changes: Among Israeli young adults, men and women did not differ in their preferences for management careers in 2010 (versus 1990, when men preferred these careers), but men still preferred technical careers more than women did (Gati & Perez, 2014).

FAMILY RELATIONS Women's connections as mothers, daughters, sisters, and grandmothers often bind families (Rossi & Rossi, 1990). Following their child's birth, parents (women especially) become more traditional in their gender-related attitudes and behaviors (Ferriman et al., 2009; Katz-Wise et al., 2010). Among 500 randomly selected Facebook pages around the world, women displayed more family photos and expressed more emotion, and men were more likely to display status or risk taking (Tiffert & Vilnai-Yavetz, 2014).

SMILING Smiling, of course, varies with situations. Yet across more than 400 studies, women's greater connectedness has been expressed in their generally higher rate of smiling (Fischer & LaFrance, 2015; LaFrance et al., 2003). For example, when Marianne LaFrance (1985) analyzed 9,000 U.S. college yearbook photos, she found females more often smiling. So did Amy Halberstadt and Martha Saitta (1987) in 1,100 magazine and newspaper photos and 1,300 people in shopping malls, parks, and streets. Apparently, boys learn not to smile as much by age 11: U.S. boys and girls smile just as often in their elementary school pictures, but by sixth grade, girls smile significantly more than boys (Wondergem & Friedmeier, 2012). This does not appear to be due to gender differences in happiness: Around the world, men and women are equally satisfied with their lives (Batz-Barbarich et al., 2018).

EMPATHY When surveyed, women are far more likely to describe themselves as having **empathy,** or being able to feel what another feels – to rejoice with those who rejoice and weep with those who weep (Chopik et al., 2017; O'Brien et al., 2013). To a lesser extent, the empathy difference extends to laboratory studies:

empathy
The vicarious experience of another's feelings; putting oneself in another's shoes.

- Shown pictures or told stories, girls react with more empathy (Hunt, 1990).
- Women more than men express empathy for others enduring similar upsetting experiences (Batson et al., 1996).
- Asked to discern the emotion someone is feeling from just an image of their eyes, women - among more than 300,000 people across 57 countries – performed slightly better than men (Greenberg et al., 2023).
- Observing someone receiving supposed painful shocks, women's empathy-related brain circuits display elevated activity when men's do not (Singer et al., 2006).

All these differences help to explain why, compared with male friendships, both men and women report friendships with women to be more intimate, enjoyable, and nurturing (Rubin, 1985; Sapadin, 1988; Williams et al., 2021). When you want empathy and understanding, someone to whom you can disclose your joys and hurts, to whom do you turn? Most men and women usually turn to women.

One explanation for this male-female empathy difference is that women tend to outperform men at reading others' emotions. In her analysis of 125 studies of men's and women's sensitivity to nonverbal cues, Judith Hall (1984, 2006) discerned that women are generally superior at decoding others' emotional messages. For example, shown a 2-second silent film clip of the face of an upset woman, women guess more accurately whether she is criticizing someone or discussing her divorce. Women also are more often strikingly better than men at recalling others' appearance (Mast & Hall, 2006).

Finally, women are more skilled at *expressing* emotions nonverbally, said Hall. This is especially so for positive emotion, reported Erick Coats and Robert Feldman (1996). They had people talk about times they had been happy, sad, and angry. When shown 5-second silent video clips of happy reports, observers could much more accurately discern women's emotions than men's. Men, however, were slightly more successful in conveying anger.

Social Dominance

Imagine two people: One is "adventurous, autocratic, coarse, dominant, forceful, independent, and strong." The other is "affectionate, dependent, dreamy, emotional, submissive, and weak." If the first person sounds more to you like a man and the second like a woman, you are not alone, reported John Williams and Deborah Best (1990, p. 15). From Asia to Africa and Europe to Australia, people rate men as more dominant, driven, and aggressive. Moreover, studies of nearly 80,000 people across 70 countries show that men more than women rate power as important (Schwartz & Rubel, 2005).

These perceptions and expectations correlate with reality. In essentially every society, men are more socially dominant (Pratto, 1996). As Peter Hegarty and his colleagues (2010) have observed, across time, men's titles and names have come first: "King and Queen," "his and hers," "husband and wife," "Mr. and Mrs." Shakespeare never wrote plays with titles such as *Juliet and Romeo* or *Cleopatra and Antony.*

As we will see, gender differences vary greatly by culture, and gender differences are shrinking in many industrialized societies as women assume more managerial and leadership positions (Desilver, 2018; Koenig et al., 2011). However:

- In 2022, women were only 26% of the world's legislators (IPU, 2023).
- In the United States, men are half of all jurors but the vast majority of elected jury leaders; men are also the leaders of most ad hoc laboratory groups (Colarelli et al., 2006).
- In Britain, men hold 60% of top-100 corporate board positions, down from 88% in 2011 (Reuters, 2023).
- Women in most countries earn an average of 78% to 84% of men's wages. Less than one-tenth of this wage gap is attributable to gender differences in education, work experience, or job characteristics (Hoon, 2023; World Bank, 2019).

Across many studies, people *perceive* leaders as having more culturally masculine traits – as being more confident, forceful, independent, and outspoken (Koenig et al., 2011). When writing letters of recommendation, people more often use such "agentic" adjectives when describing male candidates, and more "communal" adjectives (helpful, kind, sympathetic, nurturing, tactful) when describing women candidates (Madera et al., 2009). The net effect may be to disadvantage women applying for leadership roles. And when women do act in dominant ways, they are often seen as less likable (Williams & Tiedens, 2016), creating another barrier. When a man speaks assertively, he is more likely to be seen as a leader, but not so for women (McClean et al., 2018).

Men's style of communicating undergirds their social power. In leadership roles, men tend to excel as directive, task-focused leaders; women excel more often in the "transformational" or "relational" leadership that is favored by more and more organizations, with inspirational and social skills that build team spirit (Pfaff et al., 2013). Men more than women place priority on winning, getting ahead, and dominating others (Sidanius et al., 1994). This may explain why people's preference for a male leader is greater for competitions between groups, such as when countries are at war, than when conflicts occur within a group (Van Vugt & Spisak, 2008).

Men's greater social power is not entirely positive, as they may fear losing it – a phenomenon known as *precarious manhood* (Kroeper et al., 2014; Vandello & Bosson, 2013). Across many cultures, masculinity is seen as something that must be earned and defended (Bosson et al., 2021). As Joseph Vandello and Jennifer Bosson point out, "We implore [men] to 'man up' in the face of difficulties and we question whether someone is 'man enough' for the job. . . . In contrast, one rarely if ever encounters questions about whether a woman is a 'real woman' or 'woman enough'" (Vandello & Bosson, 2013, p. 101). Men are much more concerned about being identified as feminine than women are at being identified as masculine (Bosson & Michniewicz, 2013) – perhaps one reason why men, particularly those focused on masculinity, are more likely than women to be prejudiced against gay men and transgender people (Carnaghi et al., 2011; Ching, 2022; Glick et al., 2007). Men may also defend their masculinity when they have a female boss, acting more assertively than they do toward a male boss (Netchaeva et al., 2015).

Males are more likely than females to take risks — both physical and financial.
Paul Cowan/Shutterstock

Men act more impulsively and take more risks (Byrnes et al., 1999; Cross et al., 2011; Petraitis et al., 2014), perhaps because they are trying to prove their masculinity (Parent et al., 2017). One study of data from 35,000 stockbroker accounts found that "men are more overconfident than women" and therefore made 45% more stock trades (Barber & Odean, 2001a). Because trading costs money and because men's trades proved no more successful, their results underperformed the stock market by 2.65%, compared with women's 1.72% underperformance. The men's trades were riskier – and the men were the poorer for it. Even in Finland, a country with high gender equality, men take more risks in their stock market holdings (Halko et al., 2012). Men and women do not differ, however, in taking social risks, such as expressing an unpopular opinion (Harris et al., 2006).

Aggression

By **aggression,** psychologists mean behavior intended to hurt. Throughout the world, hunting, fighting, and warring are primarily male activities (Wood & Eagly, 2007). In surveys, men admit to more aggression than women do. In laboratory experiments, men indeed exhibit more physical aggression, for example, by administering what they believe are hurtful electric shocks (Knight et al., 2002). Worldwide, about 9 out of 10 murders are committed by men (United Nations, 2019). In the United states, women age 50 and older commit fewer than 100 gun homicides a year, while men 49 and younger kill 7,000 with guns and more than 500 with fists and feet. Thus, firearms in the hands of older women kill fewer people than the bare hands of younger men (Kristof, 2023).

aggression
Physical or verbal behavior intended to hurt someone. In laboratory experiments, this might mean delivering supposed electric shocks or saying something likely to hurt another's feelings.

But again, the gender difference fluctuates with the context. When people are provoked, the gender gap shrinks (Bettencourt & Kernahan, 1997; Richardson, 2005). And within less assaultive forms of aggression – for instance, slapping a family member, throwing something, or verbally attacking someone – women are no less aggressive than men and may even be more aggressive (Archer, 2000; Björkqvist, 1994; White & Kowalski, 1994). Women are also slightly more likely to commit indirect aggressive acts, such as spreading malicious gossip (Archer, 2009). But all across the world and at all ages, men much more often injure others with physical aggression.

Sexuality

In their physiological and subjective responses to sexual stimuli, women and men are "more similar than different" (Griffitt, 1987). The differences lie in what happens beforehand. Consider the following:

- Imagine you are walking on campus one day when an attractive member of the other sex approaches you. "Hi, I've been noticing you around campus lately, and I find you very attractive. Would you have sex with me tonight?" he or she asks. What would you do? In one study, not a single woman said yes, and 3 out of 4 of the men said yes (Clark & Hatfield, 1989). When asked instead if they would go on a date, about half of both men and women said yes (Clark, 1990; Clark & Hatfield, 1989). A later study found similar results; when the request was made on campus, no women and 14% of men consented to sex, and when the request was made at a party, 4% of women and half of men said yes (Baranowski & Hecht, 2015).
- "I can imagine myself being comfortable and enjoying 'casual' sex with different partners," agreed 48% of men and 12% of women in an Australian survey (Bailey et al., 2000). One 48-nation study showed country-by-country variation in acceptance of unrestricted sexuality, ranging from relatively promiscuous Finland to relatively monogamous Taiwan (Schmitt, 2005). But in every country studied, men expressed more desire for unrestricted sex. More recent data suggest the difference has persisted, with men more approving of casual sex (Sprecher et al., 2013) and more likely to favor hookups without obligations (Weitbrecht & Whitton, 2020). These sex differences appear among gay men and lesbian women as well (Howard & Periloux, 2017).
- In a survey of 3,400 U.S. adults, half as many men (25%) as women (48%) cited affection for the partner as a reason for losing their virginity. Among 18- to 25-year-old college students, the average man thought about sex about once per hour, the average woman about once every 2 hours – though there was lots of individual variation (Fisher et al., 2011). Men also thought about food and sleep more than women, suggesting they might just think about all needs more (Fisher et al., 2012).

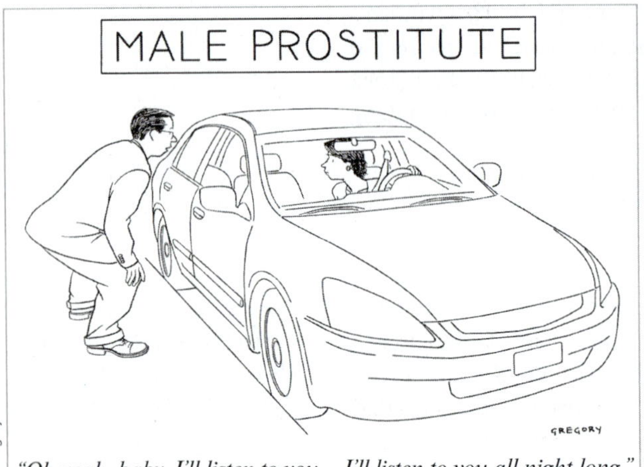

"Oh yeah, baby, I'll listen to you—I'll listen to you all night long."
Alex Gregory

The gender difference in sexual attitudes carries over to behavior (Frankenbach et al., 2023). "With few exceptions anywhere in the world," reported cross-cultural psychologist Marshall Segall and his colleagues (1990, p. 244), "males are more likely than females to initiate sexual activity."

Compared with lesbians, gay men also report more interest in uncommitted sex, more frequent sex, more interest in pornography, more responsiveness to visual stimuli, and more concern with partner attractiveness (Peplau & Fingerhut, 2007; Rupp & Wallen, 2008; Schmitt, 2007). In Finland, 69% of same-sex marriages are two women, 31% two men; in the United States, it's 55% women vs. 45% men (Bui, 2016; DeSilver, 2023). "It's not that gay men are oversexed," observed Steven Pinker (1997). "They are simply men whose male desires bounce off other male desires rather than off female desires."

Indeed, not only do men fantasize more about sex, have more permissive attitudes, and seek more partners, they also are more quickly aroused, desire sex more often, masturbate more frequently, use more pornography, are less successful at celibacy, refuse sex less often, take more risks, expend more resources to gain sex, and prefer more sexual variety (Baumeister et al., 2001; Frankenbach et al., 2023; Petersen & Hyde, 2011). **Figure 6** displays the large gender difference in pornography use in one national survey (Carroll et al., 2017).

On many college campuses, sex is often pursued via hookups rather than committed relationships, a system that research suggests may be especially attractive for men.
Ingram Publishing/Getty Images

Another survey asked 16,288 people from 52 nations how many sexual partners they desired in the next month. Among the unattached, 29% of men and 6% of women wanted more than one partner (Schmitt, 2003, 2005). These results were identical for straight and gay people (29% of gay men and 6% of lesbians desired more than one partner).

"Everywhere sex is understood to be something females have that males want," offered anthropologist Donald Symons (1979, p. 253). Small wonder, said Roy Baumeister and Kathleen Vohs, that cultures everywhere attribute greater value to female than male sexuality, as indicated in gender asymmetries in

FIGURE 6

The Pornography Gap

A large national survey of heterosexual couples found a substantial gender gap in pornography consumption.
Source: Carroll et al., (2017).

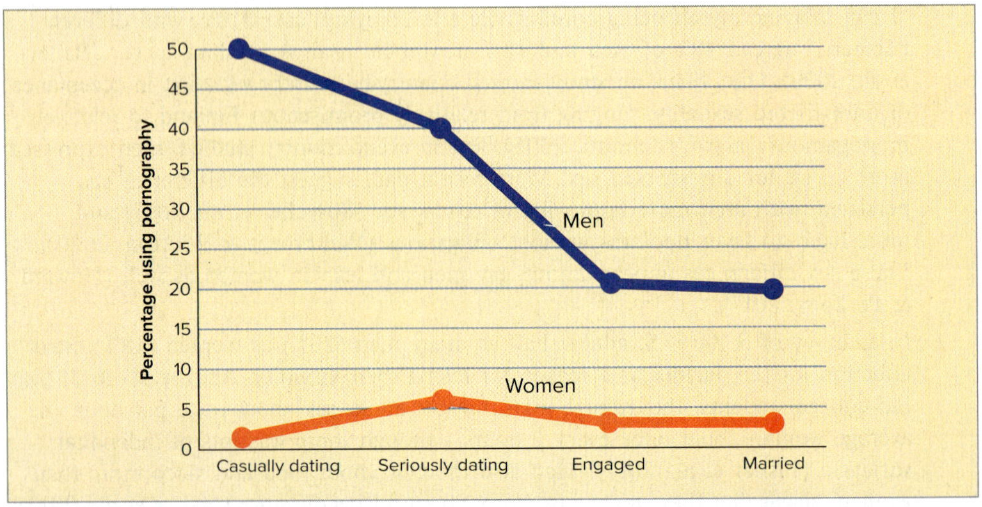

prostitution and courtship, where men generally offer money, gifts, praise, or commitment in implicit exchange for a woman's sexual engagement. In human sexual economics, they noted, women rarely pay for sex. Like labor unions opposing "scab labor" as undermining the value of their own work, most women oppose other women offering "cheap sex," which reduces the value of their own sexuality. Across 185 countries, the fewer the available men, the *higher* is the teen pregnancy rate – because when men are scarce, "women compete against each other by offering sex at a lower price in terms of commitment" (Barber, 2000; Baumeister & Vohs, 2004; Moss & Maner, 2016). Men are scarce on many college campuses these days (where they are only 43% of students); perhaps that's why more campuses now have social norms favoring uncommitted hookups (Olmstead, 2020; Wade, 2017). In contrast, where women are scarce, as is increasingly the case in China and India, the market value of their sexuality rises, and they are able to command greater commitment.

Sexual fantasies, too, differ between men and women (Ellis & Symons, 1990). In male-oriented erotica, women are unattached and lust driven. In romance novels, primarily read by women, a strong male is emotionally consumed by his devoted passion for the heroine. Social scientists aren't the only ones to have noticed. "Women can be fascinated by a four-hour movie with subtitles wherein the entire plot consists of a man and a woman yearning to have, but never actually having a relationship," observed humorist Dave Barry (1995). "Men HATE that. Men can take maybe 45 seconds of yearning, and they want everybody to get naked. Followed by a car chase. A movie called 'Naked People in Car Chases' would do really well among men."

Just as police detectives are more intrigued by crime than virtue, so psychological detectives are more intrigued by differences than similarities. Let us therefore remind ourselves: *Individual* differences far exceed gender differences. Females and males are hardly "opposite" sexes. Rather, they differ like two folded hands – similar but not the same, fitting together yet differing as they grasp each other.

"[We live in] a culture that sends very confusing messages to women about sex. There's the only-sexy-women-are-valuable message, which seems to contradict the equally prevalent women-who-are-sexually-aggressive-are-scary message, which also contradicts the women-who-don't-put-out-are-uptight-control-freaks message."

—U.S. journalist Belinda Luscombe (2020)

SUMMING UP: How Are Males and Females Alike and Different?

- Boys and girls, and men and women, are in many ways alike. Yet their differences attract more attention than their similarities.
- Social psychologists have explored gender differences in independence versus connectedness. Women typically do more caring, express more *empathy* and emotion, and define themselves more in terms of relationships than men.
- Men and women also tend to exhibit differing social dominance and *aggression*. In every known culture on earth, men tend to have more social power and are more likely than women to engage in physical aggression.
- Sexuality is another area of marked gender differences. Men more often think about and initiate sex, whereas women's sexuality tends to be inspired by emotional passion.

WHAT CAN WE CONCLUDE ABOUT GENES, CULTURE, AND GENDER?

Explain how biology and culture interact.

We needn't think of biology and culture as competitors. Cultural norms subtly yet powerfully affect our attitudes and behavior. But they don't do so independent of biology. Everything social and psychological is ultimately biological. If others' expectations influence us, that is part of our biological programming. Moreover, what our biological heritage initiates, culture may accentuate. Genes and hormones predispose males to be more physically aggressive than females. But culture amplifies that difference through norms that

Genes and environment interact. When families are calm and happy, genetic variation in anxiety has more influence than it does in more difficult environments.
BJI/Blue Jean Images/Getty Images

expect males to be tough and females to be the kinder, gentler sex. (When explaining gender differences, women more than men point to such social influences [Pew Research Center, 2017].)

Biology and culture may also **interact.** Advances in genetic science indicate how experience uses genes to change the brain (Carlson et al., 2015; Quartz & Sejnowski, 2002). Environmental stimuli can activate genes that produce new brain cell-branching receptors. Visual experience activates genes that develop the brain's visual area. Parental touch activates genes that help offspring cope with future stressful events. Genes are not set in stone; they respond adaptively to our experiences.

interaction
A relationship in which the effect of one factor (such as biology) depends on another factor (such as environment).

As we mentioned earlier in the chapter, the field of *epigenetics* (meaning "in addition to" genetics) explores the mechanisms by which environments trigger genetic expression. Diet, drugs, and stress, including child abuse, can all regulate gene expression (Champagne & Mashoodh, 2009; McGowan et al., 2010; Yang et al., 2013). Animal studies suggest that epigenetic changes can be passed down through several generations. When pregnant females are exposed to toxins or unhealthy diets, for example, the effects are seen not just in their babies but in their offspring as well (the "grandchildren") (de Assis et al., 2012). Thus far, studies on humans have focused more on how the environment changes genetic tendencies. For example, in families who fight frequently, the genetic prediction of anxiety is reduced because everyone is anxious. But when families are fairly calm, only those more genetically prone to anxiety are anxious, so genetics have more influence (Jang et al., 2005). Overall, the science of epigenetics suggests that environmental factors shape lifelong biological changes, showing that nature and nurture work together – not independently.

Biology and experience also interact when biological traits influence how the environment reacts. Men, being 8% taller and averaging almost double the proportion of muscle mass, are bound to experience life differently from women. Or consider this: A strong cultural norm dictates that males should be taller than their female mates, and thus the man is taller than the woman in more couples than would be expected by chance (Stulp et al., 2013). With hindsight, we can speculate a psychological explanation: Perhaps being taller helps men perpetuate their social power over women. But we can also speculate evolutionary wisdom that might underlie the cultural norm: If people preferred partners of their own height, tall men and short women would often be without partners. As it is, evolution dictates that men tend to be taller than women, and culture dictates the same for straight couples. So the height norm might well be a result of biology *and* culture.

It is still unusual to see a couple where the woman is taller than the man. That might be due to biology, culture, or most likely, both.
Jasper Cole/Blend Images/Getty Images

Alice Eagly (2009, 2017) and Wendy Wood (Eagly & Wood, 2013; Wood & Eagly, 2007) theorize how biology and culture interact (**Figure 7**). They believe that a variety of factors, including biological influences and childhood socialization, predispose a sexual division of labor. In adult life, the immediate causes of gender differences in social behavior are the *roles* that reflect this sexual division of labor. Men, because of their biologically endowed strength and speed, tend to be found in roles demanding physical power. Women's capacity for childbearing and breastfeeding inclines them to more nurturant roles. Each sex then tends to exhibit the behaviors expected of those who fill such roles and to have their skills and beliefs shaped accordingly. Nature and nurture are a "tangled web." As role assignments become more equal, Eagly predicts that gender differences "will gradually lessen."

Indeed, note Eagly and Wood, in cultures with greater equality of gender roles, the gender difference in mate preferences (men seeking youth and domestic skill, women seeking status and earning potential) is less. Likewise, as women's employment in formerly male occupations has increased, the gender difference in self-reported

THE inside STORY

Alice Eagly on Gender Similarities and Differences

I began my research on gender in the early 1970s. Like many feminist psychologists of the day, I initially assumed that, despite cultural gender stereotypes, women and men are generally equivalent in their psychology and social behavior. Over the years, my views have evolved considerably. I have found that some social behaviors do differ between women and men, especially in situations in which gender norms become salient. Also, women and men differ substantially when scientists step back from the specifics of narrowly defined psychological variables and instead examine general themes in the psychology of women and men. In particular, women tend to manifest more communion than men do — that is, warmth and concern for others; men tend to manifest more agency than women do — that is, dominance and competitiveness.

People should not assume that these thematic differences reflect unfavorably on women. Instead, these tendencies to be more attuned to others' concerns are generally admired and can be assets in many situations and roles. In fact, the female stereotype is in general more positive than the male stereotype. However, the qualities of niceness and nurturance that are important in expectations about women can decrease their power and effectiveness in situations that call for assertive and competitive behavior. Women's awareness of this pitfall can foster innovative approaches to exerting influence without necessarily enacting typically masculine behaviors.

Alice Eagly
Northwestern University
Courtesy of Alice Eagly

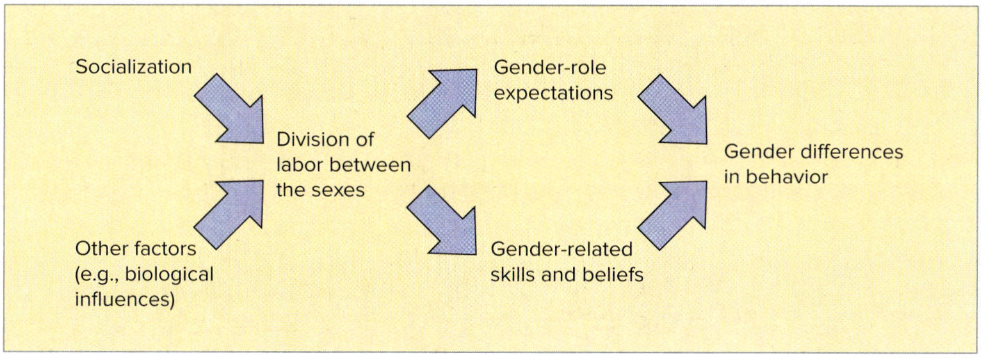

FIGURE 7

A Social-Role Theory of Gender Differences in Social Behavior

Various influences, including childhood experiences and factors, bend males and females toward differing roles. It is the expectations and the skills and beliefs associated with these differing roles that affect men's and women's behavior.
Source: Adapted from Eagly, A. (1987).

assertiveness has decreased (Donnelly & Twenge, 2017; Twenge, 1997). As men and women enact more similar roles, some psychological differences shrink – though they may not disappear (see "The Inside Story: Alice Eagly on Gender Similarities and Differences").

But not all gender differences have shrunk, report David Schmitt and his international colleagues (2008, 2016). Across 55 nations, women report more extraversion, agreeableness, and conscientiousness. These gender differences are greatest in (surprise!) prosperous, educated, egalitarian countries. In less fortunate economic and social contexts, suggests Schmitt, "the development of one's inherent personality traits is more restrained."

Although biology predisposes men to strength tasks and women to infant care, Wood and Eagly (2002) concluded that "the behavior of women and men is sufficiently malleable that individuals of both sexes are fully capable of effectively carrying out organizational roles at all levels." For today's high-status and often high-tech work roles, male size and aggressiveness matter little. Moreover, lower birthrates mean that women are less constrained by pregnancy and nursing. The end result, when combined with competitive pressures for employers to hire the best talent regardless of gender, is greater gender equality.

SUMMING UP: What Can We Conclude about Genes, Culture, and Gender?

- Biological and cultural explanations need not be contradictory. Indeed, they *interact*. Biological factors operate within a cultural context, and culture builds on a biological foundation. Emerging research in the field of *epigenetics* shows that genes are expressed in some environments and not others.

CONCLUDING THOUGHTS: Should We View Ourselves as Products of Our Biology or Our Culture?

In considering whether biology or culture has the strongest influence on us, we might be asking the wrong question. Instead, we can consider how biology and culture work together to create who we are. Especially with the new science of epigenetics, the question is increasingly not nature *versus* nurture as if they were two teams playing against each other, but nature and nurture as one team working together to shape us.

That is particularly true for differences between men and women. Sex differences may begin in the biological demands of being male or female, but they do not end there. Culture takes biological sex differences and molds them into both culturally universal and culturally distinct gender roles and expectations. Even in an era of more gender equality and an increasing focus on gender fluidity, gender – like biology and culture – still influences us.

Conformity and Obedience

AF archive/Alamy Stock Photo

CHAPTER 6

"Whatever crushes individuality is despotism, by whatever name it may be called."

—John Stuart Mill, *On Liberty*, 1859

"The social pressures community brings to bear are a mainstay of our moral values."

—Amitai Etzioni, *The Spirit of Community*, 1993

As a music concert finishes, the adoring fans near the front leap to their feet, applauding. Those just behind them follow their example and join the standing ovation. Now the wave of people standing reaches people who, unprompted, would merely be giving polite applause from their comfortable seats. Seated among them, part of you wants to stay seated ("the concert was only okay"). But as the wave of standing people sweeps by, will you alone stay seated? It's not easy being a minority of one. So you'll likely rise to your feet, at least briefly.

Trends that go viral are similar. A lot of people who did Tik Tok dance challenges, bought a fidget spinner, or posted popular memes did so because everyone else was — not because they had a unique urge to spend hours learning a dance, have a toy taken away from them in class, or constantly think about "how it started" vs. "how it's going." People rarely want to be the only one left out.

Such scenes of conformity raise this chapter's questions:

- Why, given our diversity, do we so often behave as social clones?
- Under what circumstances are we most likely to conform?
- Are certain people more likely than others to conform?
- Who resists the pressure to conform?
- Is conformity bad, or should we instead refer to it as "group solidarity" and "social sensitivity"?

WHAT IS CONFORMITY?

Define conformity, and compare compliance, obedience, and acceptance.

Is conformity good or bad? That question has no scientific answer. Conformity is sometimes bad (when it leads someone to drive drunk or to join in racist behavior), sometimes good (when it keeps people from cutting in line or encourages everyone to wash their hands), and sometimes inconsequential (when it directs tennis players to wear white).

In Western individualistic cultures, where submitting to peer pressure is discouraged, the word "conformity" carries a negative connotation. How would you feel if you overheard someone describing you as a "real conformist"? We suspect you would feel hurt. North American and European social psychologists, reflecting their individualistic cultures, give social influence negative labels (conformity, submission, compliance) rather than positive ones (communal sensitivity, responsiveness, cooperative team play). In Japan, going along with others is a sign not of weakness but of tolerance, self-control, and maturity (Markus & Kitayama, 1994).

Conformity is the overall term for acting differently due to the influence of others. Conformity is not just acting as other people act; it is also being *affected* by how they act. It is acting or thinking differently from the way you would act and think if you were alone. Thus, **conformity** is a change in behavior or belief to accord with others. If you rise to cheer a game-winning goal, drink coffee, or wear your hair in a certain style because you want to, and not due to the influence of others, that is not conformity. But if you do those things because other people do them, that is conformity.

conformity
A change in behavior or belief as the result of real or imagined group pressure.

acceptance
Conformity that involves both acting and believing in accord with social pressure.

compliance
Conformity that involves publicly acting in accord with an implied or explicit request while privately disagreeing.

obedience
A type of compliance involving acting in accord with a direct order or command.

Dave Coverly, The Comic Strips

Acceptance and compliance are two varieties of conformity (Nail et al., 2000). **Acceptance** occurs when you genuinely believe in what the group has persuaded you to do; you inwardly and sincerely believe that the group's actions are right. For example, you might exercise because you accept that exercise is healthy. You stop at red lights because you accept that not doing so is dangerous. You get a flu shot because you believe that it will help prevent you from getting sick. You wore a face mask because you believed it would help slow the spread of COVID-19.

In contrast, **compliance** is conforming to an expectation or a request without really believing in what you are doing. You put on the necktie or the dress, although you dislike doing so. You say you like your friend's favorite band even though you don't. These acts of compliance are often to reap a reward or avoid a punishment; for example, you might have followed your high school's dress code, even though you thought it was dumb, because that was better than detention. In other words, compliance is an insincere, outward conformity.

Obedience, or compliance in response to a command, is a type of compliance. If your father tells you to clean up your room and you do – even if you don't want to – that's obedience (**Figure 1**). Obedience means doing something you wouldn't do otherwise because someone else says you need to or because rules or laws require it (Gibson, 2019). If you get a flu shot because your mom tells you to or because it's required for your job – rather than because *you* think it will help – that's obedience.

Compliance and acceptance even differ in the brain: The shorter-lived memories that underlie public compliance have a different neural basis than the memories that underlie longer-term private acceptance (Edelson et al., 2011; Zaki et al., 2011). Enhanced brain activity after obedience captures its nonvoluntary nature, leading to the most cognitive arousal (Xie et al., 2016).

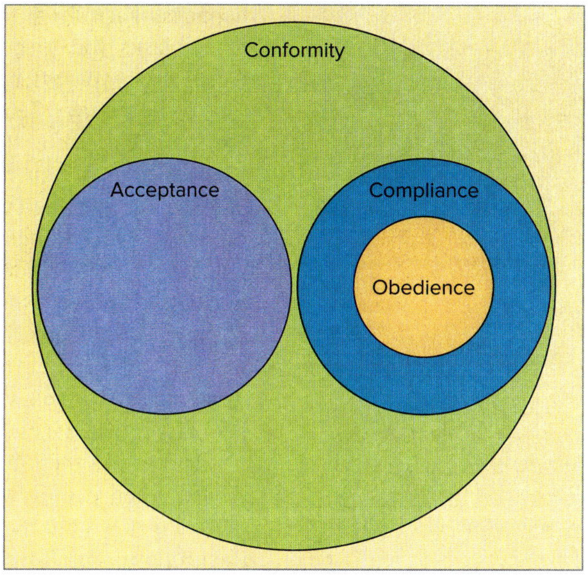

FIGURE 1
Types of Conformity

SUMMING UP: What Is Conformity?

Conformity – changing one's behavior or belief as a result of group pressure – comes in two forms. *Acceptance* is believing in as well as acting in accord with social pressure. *Compliance* is outwardly going along with the group while inwardly disagreeing; a subset of compliance is *obedience,* compliance with a direct command or requirement, whether you agree with it or not.

WHAT ARE THE CLASSIC CONFORMITY AND OBEDIENCE STUDIES?

Explain what social psychology studies reveal about the potency of social forces and the nature of evil.

Researchers who study conformity and obedience construct miniature social worlds – laboratory microcultures that simplify and simulate important features of everyday social influence. Some of these studies revealed such startling findings that they have been widely discussed and replicated, making them "classic" experiments. We will consider three, each of which provides a method for studying conformity – and plenty of food for thought.

Studies of Norm Formation

Muzafer Sherif (1935, 1937) wondered whether it was possible to observe the emergence of a social norm in the laboratory. Like biologists seeking to isolate a virus so they can experiment with it, Sherif wanted to isolate and then experiment with norm formation – to figure out how people come to agree on something.

Imagine you are a participant in one of Sherif's experiments. You find yourself seated in a dark room. Fifteen feet in front of you, a pinpoint of light appears. At first, nothing happens. Then for a few seconds, it moves erratically and finally disappears. The experimenter asks you to guess how far it moved. The dark room gives you no way to judge distance, so you offer an uncertain "6 inches." The experimenter repeats the procedure. This time you say, "Ten inches." With further repetitions, your estimates continue to average about 8 inches.

The next day you return to the darkened room, joined by two other participants who had the same experience the day before. When the light goes off for the first time, the other two people offer their best guesses from the day before. "One inch," says one. "Two inches," says the other. A bit taken aback, you nevertheless say, "Six inches." With repetitions of this group experience, both on this day and for the next 2 days, will your responses change? The results suggest they will: Sherif's male student participants changed their estimates markedly. All participants' answers eventually converged. As **Figure 2** illustrates, a group norm typically emerged. (The norm was false. Why? The light never moved! Sherif had taken advantage of an optical illusion called the **autokinetic phenomenon.**)

autokinetic phenomenon
Self *(auto)* motion *(kinetic)*. The apparent movement of a stationary point of light in the dark.

Sherif and others have used this technique to answer questions about people's suggestibility. When people were retested alone a year later, would their estimates again diverge or would they continue to follow the group norm? Remarkably, they continued to support the group norm (Rohrer et al., 1954). (Does that suggest acceptance or compliance?)

Struck by culture's seeming power to perpetuate false beliefs, Robert Jacobs and Donald Campbell (1961) studied the transmission of false beliefs in their Northwestern University laboratory. Using the autokinetic phenomenon, they had an accomplice give an inflated estimate of how far the light had moved. The accomplice then left the experiment and was replaced by another real participant, who was in turn replaced by a still newer member. The inflated illusion persisted (although diminishing) for five generations of participants. These people had become "unwitting conspirators in perpetuating a cultural fraud." The lesson of these experiments: Our views of reality are not ours alone. If you've ever accepted a story on social media that later turned out to be "fake news," you've experienced this firsthand.

In everyday life, the results of suggestibility are sometimes amusing. One person coughs, laughs, or yawns, and others are soon doing the same. (See "Research Close-Up: Contagious Yawning.") One person checks her cell phone, and then others check theirs.

"Why doth one man's yawning make another yawn?"

—Robert Burton, *Anatomy of Melancholy*, 1621

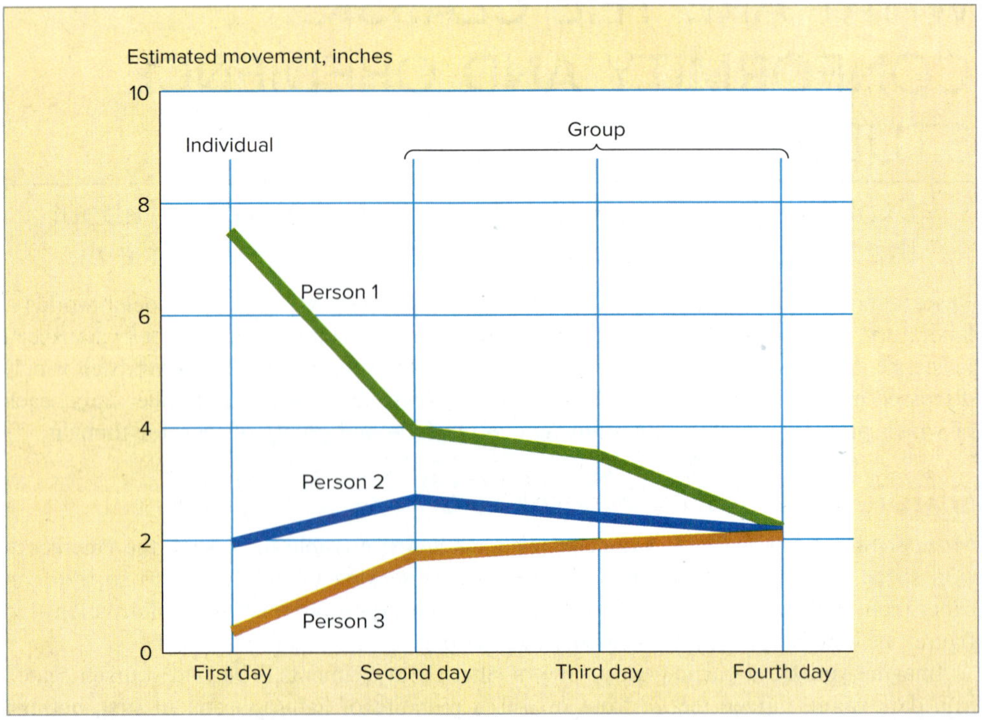

FIGURE 2

A Sample Group from Sherif's Study of Norm Formation

Three individuals converge as they give repeated estimates of the apparent movement of a point of light.

Source: Data from Sherif, M., & Sherif, C. W. (1969).

research CLOSE-UP

Contagious Yawning

Yawning is a behavior that we share with most vertebrates. Primates do it. So do cats and crocodiles and birds and turtles and even fish. But why, and when?

Sometimes, noted University of Maryland, Baltimore County, psychologist Robert Provine (2005), scientific research neglects commonplace behavior — including the behaviors he loves to study, such as laughing and yawning. To study yawning by the method of naturalistic observation, noted Provine, one needs only a stopwatch, a notepad, and a pencil. Yawning, he reported, is a "fixed action pattern" that lasts about 6 seconds, with a long inward breath and shorter climactic (and pleasurable) exhalation. It often comes in bouts, with just over a minute between yawns. And it is equally common among men and women. Even patients who are totally paralyzed and unable to move their body voluntarily may yawn normally, indicating that this is automatic behavior.

When do we yawn?

We yawn when we are bored or tense. When Provine asked participants to watch a TV test pattern for 30 minutes, they yawned 70% more often than others in a control group who watched less-boring music videos. But tension can also elicit yawning, which is commonly observed among paratroopers before their first jump, Olympic athletes before their event, and musicians waiting to go onstage. A friend of mine [DM] says she has often been embarrassed when learning something new at work because her anxiety about getting it right invariably causes her to have a "yawning fit."

We yawn when we are sleepy. No surprise here, except perhaps that people who kept a yawning diary for Provine recorded even more yawns in the hour after waking than in the yawn-prone hour before sleeping. Often, we awaken and yawn-stretch. And so do our dogs and cats when they rouse from slumber.

We yawn when others yawn. To test whether yawning, like laughter, is contagious, Provine exposed people to a 5-minute video of a man yawning repeatedly. Sure enough, 55% of viewers yawned, as did only 21% of those viewing a video of smiles. A yawning face acts as a stimulus that activates a yawn's fixed-action pattern, even if the yawn is presented in black and white, upside down, or as a mid-yawn still image. The discovery of brain "mirror neurons" — neurons that rehearse or mimic witnessed actions — suggests a biological mechanism that explains why our yawns so often mirror others' yawns — and why even some dogs often yawn after observing a human yawn (Joly-Mascheroni et al., 2008; Silva et al., 2012).

To see what parts of the yawning face are most potent, Provine had viewers watch a whole face, a face with the mouth masked, a mouth with the rest of face masked, or (as a control condition) a nonyawning smiling face. As **Figure 3** shows, the yawning faces triggered yawns even with the mouth masked. Thus, covering your mouth when yawning likely won't suppress yawn contagion.

Just thinking about yawning usually produces yawns, reported Provine — a phenomenon you may have noticed while reading this box. While reading Provine's research on contagious yawning, I [DM] yawned four times (and felt a little silly).

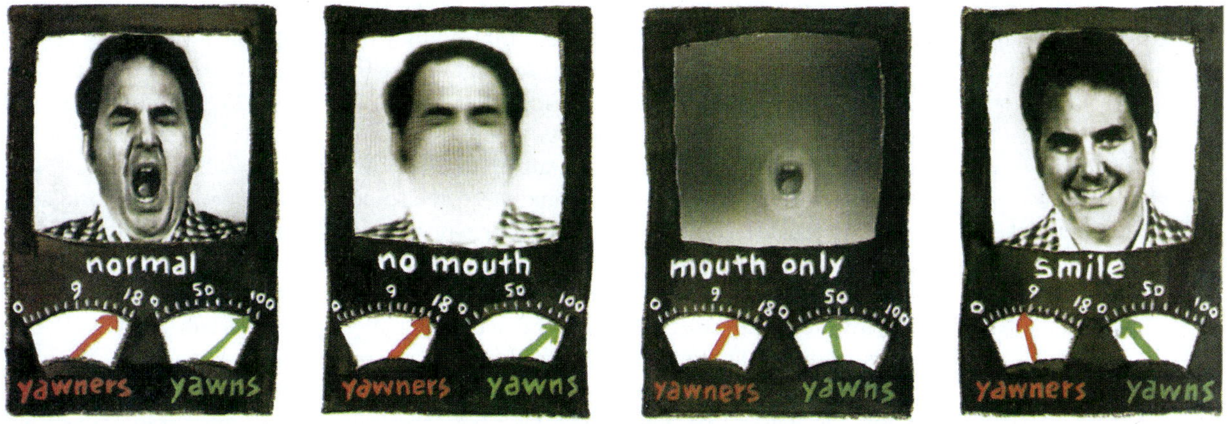

FIGURE 3

What Facial Features Trigger Contagious Yawns?

Robert Provine (2005) invited four groups of 30 people each to watch 5-minute videotapes of a smiling adult or a yawning adult, parts of whose face were masked for two of the groups. A yawning mouth triggered some yawns, but yawning eyes and head motion triggered even more.

From Provine (2005). Image courtesy, Dr. Robert R. Provine, Department of Psychology, University of Maryland.

"I don't know why. I just suddenly felt like calling."

Mick Stevens

Comedy-show laugh tracks capitalize on our suggestibility. Laugh tracks work especially well when we presume that the laughing audience is made up of people similar to us – "recorded here at La Trobe University" in one study by Michael Platow and colleagues (2004) – rather than a group that's unlike us. Just being around happy people can help us feel happier, a phenomenon that Peter Totterdell and his colleagues (1998) called "mood linkage." In their studies of British nurses and accountants, people within the same workgroups tended to share positive and negative moods. People within a social network also move toward sharing similar obesity, sleep loss, loneliness, happiness, alcohol use, and drug use (Christakis & Fowler, 2009; Kim et al., 2015; Russell et al., 2023). An ethically controversial experiment manipulated 700,000 people's Facebook accounts, finding that when news feeds included less positive emotion, users produced fewer positive posts and more negative posts – although the effects were very small (Kramer et al., 2014). Nevertheless, this study and others show that friends function as a social system, swimming in the same emotional sea.

"When people are free to do as they please, they usually imitate each other."

—Eric Hoffer, *The Passionate State of Mind*, 1955

Another form of social contagion is what Tanya Chartrand and John Bargh (1999) called "the chameleon effect" – or mimicking someone else's behavior. Picture yourself in one of their experiments, working alongside an accomplice who occasionally either rubbed their face or shook their foot. Would you – like their participants – be more likely to rub your face when around the face-rubber or shake your foot when around the foot-shaker? If so, it would quite likely be an automatic behavior, done without any conscious intention to conform; this social mimicry apparently develops in early childhood (Cracco et al., 2018; van Schaik & Hunnius, 2016). Brain scans confirm the automatic nature of mimicry: When women viewed avatars with happy, sad, or angry facial expressions, they unconsciously made the same expressions, and the brain regions responsible for these emotional expressions were activated (Likowski et al., 2012). Behavior synchronizing includes speaking; people tend to mirror the grammar that they read and hear (Ireland & Pennebaker, 2010). And, because our behavior influences our attitudes and emotions, our natural mimicry inclines us to feel what the other feels (Neumann & Strack, 2000).

An experiment in the Netherlands by Rick van Baaren and his colleagues (2004) found that people were more likely to help someone whose behavior mimicked their own. In a follow-up experiment, an interviewer invited students to try a new sports drink while subtly mirroring the student's postures and movements, or not. By the experiment's end, the mimicked students became more likely to consume the new drink and say they would buy it (Tanner et al., 2008). As a general rule, we mimic people we like, and we like them more when they mimic us – even if they otherwise differ from ourselves (Bretter et al., 2023; Hess, 2021; Kampf et al., 2018). Thus, one way to reduce dislike across groups – or among individuals in conflict – might be to synchronize their movements by walking together (Webb et al., 2017).

mass hysteria

Suggestibility to problems that spreads throughout a large group of people.

Mimicry – also known as suggestibility – can also occur on a large scale, known as **mass hysteria.** In August 2009, a Lexus with four passengers suddenly accelerated past 100 miles per hour on a San Diego freeway. The driver called 911 but was unable to stop the car's acceleration. The car crashed and burst into flames, killing all four passengers. The accident received widespread news coverage, and suddenly many people started reporting that their vehicles were accelerating out of control. However, an investigation later determined that the car that crashed, a loaner from a repair shop, had a floor mat from a larger vehicle that was too big and became lodged over the accelerator pedal. There was nothing wrong with Lexuses, no issue with the car's original floor mats, and no "demons" making the cars accelerate, as some speculated. There were no runaway cars – just runaway news coverage that led to "unintended acceleration" as a convenient explanation for any driving mishap. It was all mass hysteria (Fumento, 2014).

Another disturbing case began with a mystery. One day in 2011, high school student Katie Krautwurst woke up from a nap twitching uncontrollably, her arms flailing and head thrashing, and continued to twitch every few seconds. A few weeks later her best friend started twitching, too, and then more and more girls, until 18 girls at the school were affected. Parents became concerned that some contaminant at the school was causing the disorder, and two of the girls and their mothers told the *Today Show* they were desperately seeking a cure. The next day, a neurologist who had treated several of the girls offered his diagnosis: *conversion disorder,* or a form of mass hysteria caused when psychological stress is unconsciously expressed in physical symptoms (Dominus, 2012). It then spread as a social contagion. The case fit the usual profile for mass hysteria, which is more common among young women. The same was true for the mass spread of what became known as "Tik Tok tics," where teens, mostly girls, suddenly developed severe, involuntary tics after watching videos of people claiming to have Tourette's Syndrome. When examined, however, the teens' tics were not typical for Tourette's – but they all resembled the tics in the videos (Giedinghagen, 2023; Olvera et al., 2021).

Suicide and gun violence can also be socially contagious. When Marilyn Monroe took her own life in August 1962, 303 more people than average took their lives that month (Stack, 2000). After Robin Williams took his own life in 2014, calls to the National Suicide Prevention Lifeline increased (Carroll, 2014). One study found that copycat suicides were 14 times more likely when the victim was a celebrity and 87% more common when the coverage was on television rather than in a newspaper (Stack, 2003). After the popular Netflix series *13 Reasons Why*, which portrayed a teen girl's suicide, was released in late March 2017, Google searches for "how to commit suicide" jumped 26% (Ayers et al., 2017). More recently, social media "challenges" encouraging dangerous or self-harming behaviors have been linked to suicides (Upadhyaya & Kozman, 2022).

In a study of mass shootings between 1997 and 2013, Sherry Towers and her colleagues (2015, 2018) found that such incidents were contagious: Shootings causing at least four deaths led to a 2-week period of increased gun violence. In light of such contagions, some psychologists have called for media outlets to stop identifying the perpetrators of mass shootings. If the shooters don't get media attention, the thinking goes, fewer people will be tempted to repeat their violent acts (Perrin, 2016).

Asch's Studies of Group Pressure

Participants in Sherif's darkened-room autokinetic experiments, like those interpreting their own mysterious symptoms, faced an ambiguous reality. Consider a less ambiguous perceptual problem faced by a young boy named Solomon Asch (1907–1996). While attending the traditional Jewish Seder at Passover, Asch recalled,

> I asked my uncle, who was sitting next to me, why the door was being opened. He replied, "The prophet Elijah visits this evening every Jewish home and takes a sip of wine from the cup reserved for him."
>
> I was amazed at this news and repeated, "Does he really come? Does he really take a sip?"
>
> My uncle said, "If you watch very closely, when the door is opened you will see – you watch the cup – you will see that the wine will go down a little."
>
> And that's what happened. My eyes were riveted upon the cup of wine. I was determined to see whether there would be a change. And to me it seemed . . . that indeed something was happening at the rim of the cup, and the wine did go down a little. (Aron & Aron, 1989, p. 27)

Years later, social psychologist Asch re-created his boyhood experience in his laboratory. Imagine yourself as one of Asch's volunteer subjects. You are seated sixth in a row of seven people. The experimenter explains that you will be in a study of perceptual judgments and then asks you to say which of the three lines in **Figure 4** matches the standard line. You can easily see that it's line 2. So it's no surprise when the five people responding before you all say, "Line 2."

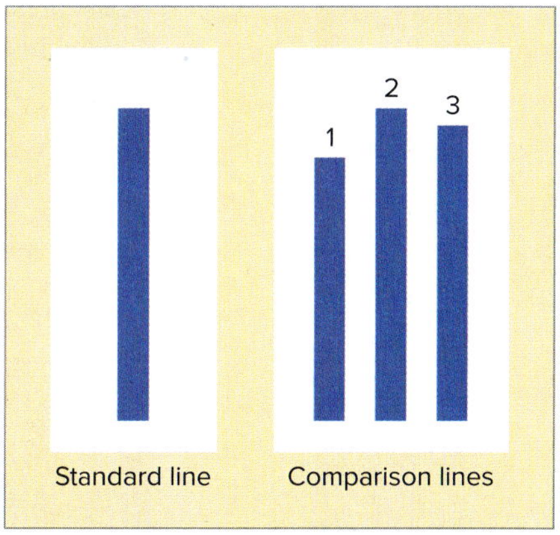

FIGURE 4

Sample Comparison from Solomon Asch's Conformity Procedure

The participants judged which of three comparison lines matched the standard.

The next comparison proves as easy, and you settle in for what seems like a simple test. But the third trial startles you. Although the correct answer seems just as clear-cut, the first person gives a wrong answer: "Line 1." When the second person gives the same wrong answer, you sit up in your chair and stare at the cards. The third person agrees with the first two. Your jaw drops; you start to perspire. "What is this?" you ask yourself. "Are they blind? Or am I?" The fourth and fifth people agree with the others. Then the experimenter looks at you. Now you are experiencing an epistemological dilemma: "What is true? Is it what my peers tell me or what my eyes tell me?"

Dozens of college students experienced that conflict in Asch's experiments. Those in a control condition who answered alone were correct more than 99% of the time. Asch wondered: If accomplices coached by the experimenter gave identical wrong answers, would people declare what they would otherwise have denied? Although some people never conformed by giving the wrong answer, 75% did so at least once. All told, 37% of the responses were conforming (or, from another perspective, "*trusting* of others").

Of course, that means 63% of the time people did *not* conform (Griggs, 2015). The experiments show that most people "tell the truth even when others do not," noted Bert Hodges and Anne Geyer (2006). Despite the independence shown by many of his participants, Asch's (1955) feelings about the conformity were as clear as the correct answers to his questions: "That reasonably intelligent and well-meaning young people are willing to call white black is a matter of concern. It raises questions about our ways of education and about the values that guide our conduct."

"He who sees the truth, let him proclaim it, without asking who is for it or who is against it."

—Henry George, *The Irish Land Question*, 1881

Asch's experiment was conducted in the 1950s, often considered a time of high conformity in U.S. culture. Sure enough, fewer students in the more individualistic times of the 1970s and 1980s were willing to conform to the group judgment in experiments similar to Asch's. In addition, people in collectivistic countries were more willing to conform than those in individualistic countries, those in more recently settled frontier states less than those in nonfrontier states, and women more than men (Bond & Smith, 1996; Ušto et al., 2019; Varnum, 2012). These are precisely the results you'd expect if culture and gender shaped conformity, with recent, individualistic cultures and maleness promoting the autonomy of the self and established, collectivistic cultures and femaleness encouraging fitting in with the group. Nevertheless, even modern internet-savvy citizens are not immune to conformity. Michael Rosander and Oskar Eriksson (2012) showed internet users questions such as "In what city can you find Hollywood?" along with a graph showing most users thought it was San Francisco (it's Los Angeles). Fifty-three percent conformed to the incorrect "majority" answer on at least one question – less than the 75% who conformed at least once in Asch's line experiment in the 1950s, but still the majority.

Asch's experiment and others like it lacked the "mundane realism" of everyday conformity, but they did have "experimental realism," with people becoming emotionally involved in the experience. The Sherif and Asch results are startling because they involved no obvious pressure to conform – there were no rewards for "team play," no punishments for individuality – just the increased arousal of knowing you're standing out (Hatcher et al., 2017). Other experiments have explored conformity in everyday situations, such as these:

- *Dental flossing.* Sarah Schmiege and her cohorts (2010) told students either that "Our studies show that [fellow] University of Colorado students your age floss approximately [X] times per week," where X was either the participant's own flossing rate, as reported in prior questioning, or five greater than that number. Those given the inflated estimate flossed more often over the ensuing 3 months.
- *Cancer screening.* Monika Sieverding and her colleagues (2010) approached middle-aged German men on the street and invited them to sign up to receive information about cancer screening. If led to believe few ("only 18%!") of other men in Germany had undergone the screening, a similar 18% signed up. But 39% signed up after being told that most other men ("indeed 65%!") had been screened. Health education campaigns had best not publicize low participation rates, surmised the researchers.
- *Soccer referee decisions.* In many sports, from figure skating to soccer football, referees make instantaneous decisions amid noise from the crowd, which often erupts when the opposing team (but not the home team) commits a foul. Christian Unkelbach and Daniel Memmert (2010) examined 1,530 soccer matches across

five seasons in Germany's premier league. On average, home teams received 1.89 penalty cards and opposing teams, 2.35. Moreover, the difference was greater in louder soccer stadiums. And in laboratory experiments, professional referees who judged filmed scenes of fouls awarded more penalty cards when a scene was accompanied by high-volume noise.

- *Eating.* Across 38 studies, people ate more when sitting with someone else who ate more and ate less when their companion ate less (Vartanian et al., 2015). Shovel in the food, and the other people at your table might follow suit; eat little, and others are more likely to pick at their plates. Conforming to gender norms also comes into play with eating. Women trying to conform to feminine norms ate less food overall, and men trying to conform to masculine norms preferred to eat more meat (Le, 2019; Timeo & Suitner, 2018).

Away teams receive more penalty cards, apparently due to referees being influenced by the noise of the home crowd expressing their opinions.
David Madison/Getty Images

If people are that conforming in response to such minimal pressure, how compliant will they be if they are directly coerced? Could the average North American or European be talked into committing cruel acts? We would have guessed not: Their humane, democratic, individualistic values would make them resist such pressure. Besides, the easy verbal pronouncements of those experiments are a giant step away from actually harming someone; we would never yield to coercion to hurt another. Or would we? Social psychologist Stanley Milgram wondered.

Milgram's Obedience Studies

Milgram's (1965, 1974) studies – "the most famous, or infamous, stud[ies] in the annals of scientific psychology" (Benjamin & Simpson, 2009) – tested what happens when the demands of authority clash with the demands of conscience. "Perhaps more than any other empirical contributions in the history of social science," noted Lee Ross (1988), Milgram's obedience studies "have become part of our society's shared intellectual legacy – that small body of historical incidents, biblical parables, and classic literature that serious thinkers feel free to draw on when they debate about human nature or contemplate human history."

Let's go backstage and examine the studies in depth. Here is the scene staged by Milgram, a creative artist who – in addition to being a social psychologist – wrote stories and stage plays and who used trial-and-error pilot testing to hone this drama for maximum impact (Russell, 2011): Two men come to Yale University's psychology laboratory to participate in a study of learning and memory. A stern experimenter in a lab coat explains that this is a pioneering study of the effect of punishment on learning. The experiment requires one of them to teach a list of word pairs to the other and to punish errors by delivering shocks of increasing intensity. To assign the roles, they draw slips out of a hat. One of the men (a cheerful 47-year-old accountant who is actually the experimenter's accomplice) says that his slip says "learner." The other man (a volunteer who has come in response to a newspaper ad) is assigned to the role of "teacher." He takes a mild sample shock and then looks on as the experimenter straps the learner into a chair and attaches an electrode to his wrist.

Teacher and experimenter go to the main room, where the teacher takes his place before a "shock generator" with switches ranging from 15 to 450 volts in 15-volt increments. The switches are labeled "Slight Shock," "Very Strong Shock," "Danger: Severe Shock," and so forth. Under the 435- and 450-volt switches appears "XXX." The experimenter tells the teacher to "move one level higher on the shock generator" each time the learner gives a wrong answer. With each flick of a switch, lights flash, relay switches click, and an electric buzzer sounds.

If the participant complies with the experimenter's requests, he hears the learner grunt at 75, 90, and 105 volts. At 120 volts, the learner shouts that the shocks are painful. And at 150 volts, he cries out, "Experimenter, get me out of here! I won't be in the experiment anymore! I refuse to go on!" By 270 volts, his protests have become screams of agony, and his pleas to be let out continue. At 300 and 315 volts, he screams his refusal to answer. After 330 volts, he falls silent. In answer to the teacher's inquiries and pleas to end the experiment, the experimenter states that the nonresponses should be treated as wrong answers. To keep the participant going, he drew on four verbal prods along with his own improvised pressuring:

Prod 1: Please continue (or Please go on).

Prod 2: The experiment requires that you continue.

Prod 3: It is absolutely essential that you continue.

Prod 4: You have no other choice; you must go on.

How far would you go? Milgram described the study to 110 psychiatrists, college students, and middle-class adults. People in all three groups guessed that they would disobey by about 135 volts; none expected to go beyond 300 volts. Recognizing that self-estimates may reflect self-serving bias, Milgram asked them how far they thought *other* people would go. Virtually no one expected anyone to proceed to XXX on the shock panel. (The psychiatrists guessed that only about 1 in 1,000 would.)

But when Milgram conducted the study with 40 men – 20- to 50-year-olds with varying jobs – 26 of them (65%) progressed all the way to 450 volts. In other words, they followed orders to hurt someone – just as Nazi soldiers did (see "The Inside Story: Stanley Milgram on Obedience"). Those who stopped usually did so at the 150-volt point, when the learner's protestations became more compelling (Packer, 2008).

THE inside STORY

Stanley Milgram on Obedience

While working for Solomon E. Asch, I wondered whether his conformity experiments could be made more humanly significant. First, I imagined an experiment similar to Asch's, except that the group induced the person to deliver shocks to a protesting victim. But a control was needed to see how much shock a person would give in the absence of group pressure. Someone, presumably the experimenter, would have to instruct the subject to give the shocks. But now a new question arose: Just how far would a person go when ordered to administer such shocks? In my mind, the issue had shifted to the willingness of people to comply with destructive orders. It was an exciting moment for me. I realized that this simple question was both humanly important and capable of being precisely answered.

The laboratory procedure gave scientific expression to a more general concern about authority, a concern forced upon members of my generation, in particular upon Jews such as myself, by the atrocities of World War II. The impact of the Holocaust on my own psyche energized my interest in obedience and shaped the particular form in which it was examined.

Abridged from the original for this book and from Milgram, 1977, with permission of Alexandra Milgram.

Stanley Milgram (1933–1984)

Courtesy of Alexandra Milgram

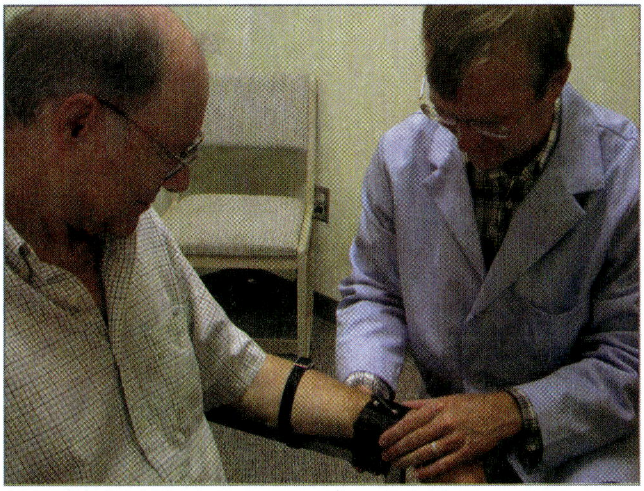

Recent replications of Milgram's obedience study have shown levels of obedience somewhat lower than in the 1960s, but two-thirds of men still administer high levels of shock.
Jerry Burger

Wondering if 21st-century citizens would similarly obey, Jerry Burger (2009) replicated Milgram's study – though only to the 150-volt point. Burger found at that point, 70% of 2,000 participants were still obeying, less than Milgram's result of 84%. (In Milgram's study, most who were obedient to this point continued to the end.) However, nearly twice as many men in Burger's study (33%) disobeyed as had in 1962 (18%). Cultural change toward more individualism might have reduced obedience, but far from eliminated it. Even 54 years later, Milgram's obedience paradigm was powerful – just a little less so (Twenge, 2009).

Having expected a low rate of obedience, Milgram was disturbed (Milgram, 2000). He decided to make the learner's protests even more compelling in later experiments. As the learner was strapped into the chair, the teacher heard him mention his "slight heart condition" and heard the experimenter's reassurance that "although the shocks may be painful, they cause no permanent tissue damage." The learner's anguished protests did little good; of 40 men in this new study, 25 (63%) fully complied with the experimenter's demands (**Figure 5**). Many participants who obeyed later said they did not believe the shocks were dangerous to the learner, or they didn't believe the learner was actually being shocked (Hollander & Turowetz, 2017).

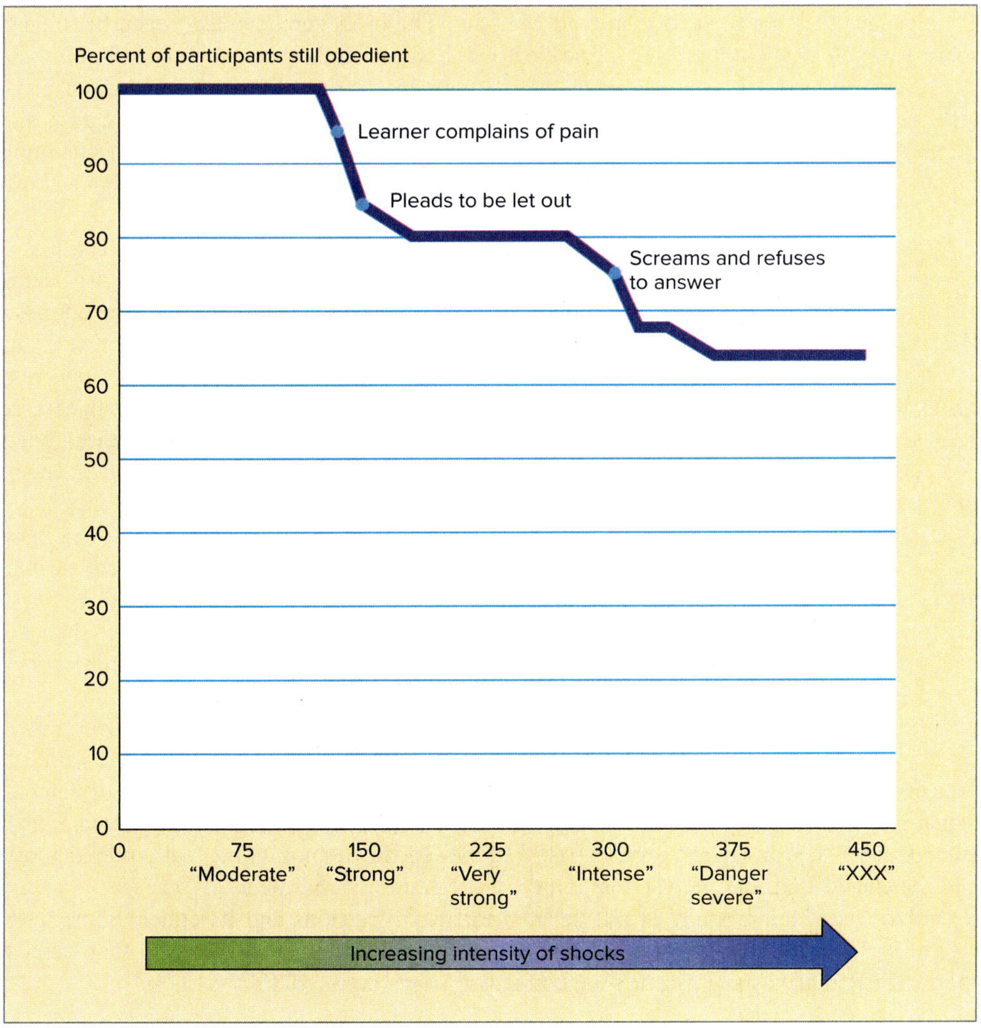

FIGURE 5

The Milgram Obedience Study

Percentage of participants complying despite the learner's cries of protest and failure to respond.
Source: From Milgram, S. (1965).

It's important to note that Milgram's participants did not automatically obey the experimenter; nearly all stopped and expressed concern for the learner, at which point the experimenter prompted them to continue ("You have no other choice; you must go on."). Many argued back and forth with the experimenter over several rounds of increasing tension (Kaposi, 2022). Some psychologists have maintained that Milgram's study shows something more wide-ranging than mere obedience (obeying a direct order): It challenges participants' feelings of control. In fact, many participants stopped after they argued that they *did* have a choice about whether to continue (Gibson, 2013). In a recent virtual reality replication of the Milgram paradigm, many participants sought to reassert some control by reading the correct answer more loudly, presumably in an attempt to prevent the learner from receiving a shock (Gonzalez-Franco et al., 2018).

Further, notes Burger (2014), Milgram's results were not as surprising as they first seem. Four features of Milgram's study design, he argues, mirror well-documented psychological effects:

- the "slippery slope" of small requests that escalate into large ones;
- the framing of shock-giving as the social norm for the situation;
- the opportunity to deny responsibility, and
- the limited time to reflect on the decision.

All of these, in Milgram's studies and in other research, increase compliance and obedience.

THE ETHICS OF MILGRAM'S STUDIES

The obedience of his subjects disturbed Milgram. The procedures he used disturbed many social psychologists (Miller, 1986). The "learner" in these studies actually received no shock (he disengaged himself from the chair where the shocks were delivered and turned on a tape recorder that delivered the protests). Nevertheless, some critics said that Milgram did to his participants, most of whom were not told they had not actually shocked anyone until months later, what they assumed they were doing to their victims: He stressed them against their will (Perry, 2013).

Indeed, like Nazi executioners in the early days of the Holocaust (Brooks, 2011), many of the "teachers" did experience agony. Some of the teachers doubted the learner was actually being shocked (and these doubters, critics note, were the most willing to comply; Hollander & Turowetz, 2017). Other teachers sweated, trembled, stuttered, bit their lips, groaned, or even broke into uncontrollable nervous laughter. A *New York Times* reviewer complained that the cruelty inflicted by the studies "upon their unwitting subjects is surpassed only by the cruelty that they elicit from them" (Marcus, 1974). Others have argued that Milgram's studies were unethical because the participants were deceived about their purpose and thus could not give truly informed consent (Baumrind, 1964, 2015).

Critics also argued that the participants' self-concepts may have been altered. One participant's wife told him, "You can call yourself Eichmann" (referring to Nazi death camp administrator Adolf Eichmann). Some scholars, after delving into Milgram's archives, report that his debriefing was less extensive and his participants' distress greater than he had suggested. For example, most participants did not learn they had not actually shocked the learner until 9 months later (Nicholson, 2011; Perry, 2013).

In his own defense, Milgram pointed to the important lessons taught by his nearly two-dozen studies with more than 1,000 participants. He also reminded critics of the support he received from the participants after the deception was revealed and the study explained. When surveyed afterward, 84% said they were glad to have participated; only 1% regretted volunteering. A year later, a psychiatrist interviewed 40 of those who had suffered most and concluded that, despite the temporary stress, none was harmed.

Today, the Milgram study is still debated for its conclusions and its ethics. Some have argued it should be taught not as fact but as a "contentious classic" – a study that shaped the field but that has significant shortcomings (Griggs et al., 2020).

WHAT BREEDS OBEDIENCE?

Milgram did more than reveal that people will obey an authority; he also examined the conditions that breed obedience. When he varied the social conditions, compliance ranged from 0 to 93% fully obedient. Four factors determined obedience: the victim's emotional distance, the authority's closeness and legitimacy, whether the authority was part of a respected institution, and the liberating effects of a disobedient fellow participant.

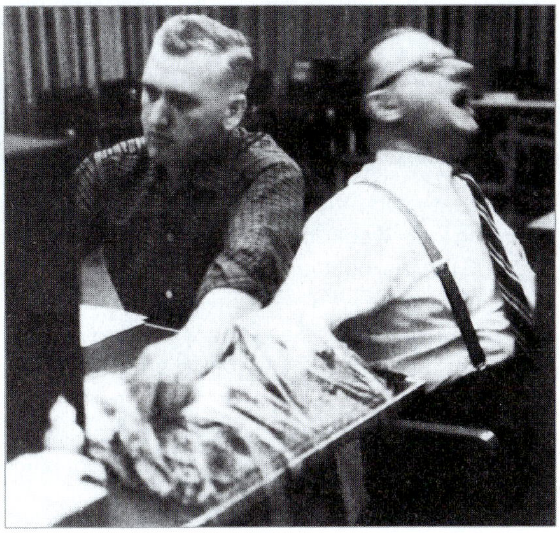

An obedient participant in Milgram's "touch" condition forces the victim's hand onto the shock plate. Usually, however, "teachers" were more merciful to victims who were this close to them.
Stanley Milgram, 1965, from the film *Obedience*, distributed by Alexandra Street Press

THE VICTIM'S DISTANCE Milgram's participants acted with the greatest obedience and least compassion when the "learners" could not be seen and could not see the "teachers." When the victim was remote and the "teachers" heard no complaints, nearly all obeyed calmly to the end. But when the learner was in the same room, "only" 40% obeyed to 450 volts. Full compliance dropped to a still-astonishing 30% when teachers were required to force the learner's hand into contact with a shock plate. Similarly, teachers who were skeptical they were actually inflicting pain used higher levels of shock (Perry et al., 2020). In a reenacted Milgram study – with videotaped actors who were either hidden or seen appearing in pain on a computer screen – participants were, again, much less obedient when the victim was visible (Dambrun & Vatiné, 2010). Close relationships mattered, too: In a study Milgram conducted but never published, only 15% of participants asked to shock a relative, friend, or neighbor complied (Perry, 2013). Teachers were also less willing to shock learners they saw as similar to themselves (Grzyb & Dolinski, 2023). Known and seen victims are more difficult to hurt than unknown and unseen victims.

In everyday life, too, it is easiest to abuse someone who is distant or depersonalized. People who might never be cruel to someone face-to-face may be nasty when posting comments about that same person online or on social media. Throughout history, executioners have often depersonalized those being executed by placing hoods over their heads. The ethics of war allow soldiers to bomb a helpless village from 40,000 feet but not to shoot an equally helpless villager. In combat with an enemy they can see, many soldiers either do not fire or do not aim. Such disobedience is rare among those given orders to kill with the more distant artillery or aircraft weapons (Padgett, 1989). It may even be true for nuclear war (see "Focus On: Personalizing the Victims").

In recent years, distance from victims has further lengthened with the use of unmanned flying drones that can drop bombs, with the controller sitting at a console many miles away from the destruction and death on the ground. Yet when the drone transmits clear video of a potential victim asking to surrender, as happened when in 2023 a Russian soldier put down his weapon and gestured toward a Ukrainian drone, it becomes harder to kill. The Ukrainian drone pilot decided not to kill the Russian soldier and instead instructed him how to surrender. "Despite that he is an enemy . . . I still felt sorry for him," said the pilot (McCluskey et al., 2023).

"Distance negates responsibility."

—Guy Davenport, "The Master Builder," 1966

CLOSENESS AND LEGITIMACY OF THE AUTHORITY The physical presence of the experimenter in the Milgram experiments also affected obedience. When Milgram's experimenter gave the commands by telephone, full obedience dropped to 21% (although many lied and said they were obeying). Other studies confirm that when the one making the command is physically close, compliance increases. Given a light touch on the arm, people are more likely to lend a dime, sign a petition, or sample a new kind of pizza (Kleinke, 1977; Smith et al., 1982; Willis & Hamm, 1980).

The authority, however, must be perceived as legitimate. In another twist on the basic Milgram study, the researcher received a rigged telephone call that required him to leave the laboratory. He said that since the equipment recorded data automatically, the "teacher"

focus ON Personalizing the Victims

Innocent victims trigger more compassion if personalized. During one week in 1981, an earthquake in Iran killed 3,000 people, but the media and the world quickly moved on. In the same week, one small boy in Italy died, trapped in a well shaft, and the whole world grieved. Concerned that the projected death statistics of a nuclear war are impersonal to the point of being incomprehensible, international law professor Roger Fisher proposed a way to personalize the victims for U.S. government officials:

> It so happens that a young man, usually a navy officer, accompanies the president wherever he goes. This young man has a black attachè case which contains the codes that are needed to fire nuclear weapons.
>
> I can see the president at a staff meeting considering nuclear war as an abstract question. He might conclude, "On SIOP Plan One, the decision is affirmative. Communicate the Alpha line XYZ." Such jargon keeps what is involved at a distance.
>
> My suggestion, then, is quite simple. Put that needed code number in a little capsule and implant that capsule right next to the heart of a volunteer. The volunteer will carry with him a big, heavy butcher knife as he accompanies the president. If ever the president wants to fire nuclear weapons, the only way he can do so is by first, with his own hands, killing one human being.
>
> "George," the president would say, "I'm sorry, but tens of millions must die." The president then would have to look at someone and realize what death is — what an *innocent* death is. Blood on the White House carpet: it's reality brought home.
>
> When I suggested this to friends in the Pentagon, they said, "My God, that's terrible. Having to kill someone would distort the president's judgment. He might never push the button."

Source: Adapted from Fisher (1981).

should just go ahead. After the researcher left, an assistant (actually a second accomplice) assumed command. The assistant "decided" that the shock should be increased even more for each wrong answer and instructed the teacher accordingly. Now 80% of the teachers refused to comply fully. The assistant, feigning disgust at this defiance, sat down in front of the shock generator and tried to take over the teacher's role. At that point, most of the defiant participants protested. Some tried to unplug the generator. One large man lifted the zealous assistant from his chair and threw him across the room. This rebellion against an illegitimate authority contrasted sharply with the deferential politeness usually shown the experimenter (da Costa et al., 2021). In a later reanalysis of the Milgram studies, Stephen Reicher and his colleagues (2012; Haslam et al., 2015) found that participants were significantly more obedient when they identified with the researcher or the scientific community he represented. They obeyed orders because they believed they were making a contribution to science and were thus doing something worthy and noble. "Followers do not lose their moral compass so much as choose particular authorities to guide them through the dilemmas of everyday life," they noted (Reicher & Haslam, 2011, p. 61).

In another study, hospital nurses were called by an unknown physician and ordered to administer an obvious drug overdose (Hofling et al., 1966). When told about the experiment, everyone in a group of nurses said they would not have followed the order. Nevertheless, when 22 other nurses were actually given the phoned-in overdose order, all but one obeyed without delay (until being intercepted on their way to the patient). Although not all nurses are so compliant (Krackow & Blass, 1995; Rank & Jacobson, 1977), these nurses were following a familiar script: Doctor (a legitimate authority) orders; nurse obeys.

Compliance with legitimate authority was also apparent in the strange case of the "rectal ear ache" (Cohen & Davis, 1981). A doctor ordered eardrops for a patient suffering an infection in the right ear. On the prescription, the doctor abbreviated "place in right ear" as "place in R ear." Reading the order, the compliant nurse put the required drops in the compliant patient's rectum.

INSTITUTIONAL AUTHORITY If the prestige of the authority is that important, then perhaps the institutional prestige of Yale University legitimized the Milgram experiment commands. In post-experimental interviews, many participants said that had it not been for Yale's reputation, they would not have obeyed. To see whether that was true, Milgram moved the study to less prestigious Bridgeport, Connecticut. He set himself up in a modest commercial building as the "Research Associates of Bridgeport." When the "learner-has-a-heart-condition" study was run with the same personnel, what percentage of the men do you suppose fully obeyed? Although the obedience rate (48%) was still remarkably high, it was lower than the 65% rate at Yale.

Given orders, most soldiers will drop bombs that kill large numbers of people — a behavior that in other contexts they would consider immoral.
Fly_and_Dive/Shutterstock

In everyday life, too, authorities backed by institutions wield social power. Robert Ornstein (1991) told of a psychiatrist friend who was called to the edge of a cliff above San Mateo, California, where one of his patients, Alfred, was threatening to jump. When the psychiatrist's reasoned reassurance failed to persuade Alfred to come down, the psychiatrist could only hope that a police crisis expert would soon arrive.

Although no expert came, another police officer, unaware of the drama, happened onto the scene, took out his bullhorn, and yelled at the assembled cliffside group: "Who's the ass who left that Pontiac station wagon double-parked out there in the middle of the road? I almost hit it. Move it *now,* whoever you are." Hearing this command, Alfred obediently got down at once, moved his car, and then without a word got into the police cruiser for a trip to a nearby hospital.

THE LIBERATING EFFECTS OF GROUP INFLUENCE The classic experiments of Sherif, Asch, and Milgram give us a negative view of conformity. However, conformity can also be constructive. The heroic firefighters who rushed into the flaming World Trade Center towers on 9/11 were "incredibly brave," noted social psychologist Susan Fiske and her colleagues (2004), but they were also "partly obeying their superiors, partly conforming to extraordinary group loyalty." Consider, too, the occasional liberating effect of conformity. Perhaps you can recall a time you felt justifiably angry at an unfair teacher but you hesitated to object. Then one or two other students spoke up about the unfair practices, and you followed their example, which had a liberating effect. Milgram captured this liberating effect of conformity by placing the teacher with two accomplices who were to help conduct the procedure. During the study, both accomplices defied the experimenter, who then ordered the real participant to continue alone. Did he? No. Ninety percent liberated themselves by conforming to the defiant accomplices.

Reflections on the Classic Studies

The common response to Milgram's results is to note their counterparts in the "I was only following orders" defenses of Adolf Eichmann in Nazi Germany; of U.S. Lieutenant William Calley, who in 1968 directed the unprovoked slaughter of hundreds of Vietnamese in the village of My Lai; and of the "ethnic cleansings" that occurred in Iraq, Rwanda, Bosnia, and Kosovo.

Soldiers are trained to obey superiors. Thus, one participant in the My Lai massacre recalled:

> [Lieutenant Calley] told me to start shooting. So I started shooting, I poured about four clips into the group. . . . They were begging and saying, "No, no." And the mothers were hugging their children and. . . . Well, we kept right on firing. They was waving their arms and begging. (Wallace, 1969)

The "safe" scientific contexts of the obedience experiments differ from the wartime contexts. Moreover, much of the brutality of war and genocide goes beyond obedience (Miller, 2004). George Mastroianni (2015) and Allan Fenigstein (2015) both argue that most German soldiers killed willingly – not because they were obeying orders or because they were inherently evil, but because they had been indoctrinated to the Nazi view so thoroughly that they no longer saw Jews as human and thus deserving of empathy. The Holocaust, Mastroianni believes, is better explained by theories of socialization and interpersonal influence – conformity of attitudes – than by simple behavioral obedience. "The idea that any of us could be transformed into genocidaires [people who propagate genocide] in a few hours in a social psychology laboratory is wrong," he maintains. In contrast, "growing up a certain way, in a particular culture, steeped in destructive ideologies can produce people who will commit terrible acts of destruction."

The Milgram obedience studies also differ from other conformity studies in the strength of the social pressure: Obedience is explicitly commanded. Yet the Asch and the Milgram studies share four similarities:

- They show how compliance can take precedence over moral sense.
- They succeed in pressuring people to go against their own consciences.
- They sensitize us to moral conflicts in our own lives.
- They affirm two familiar social psychological principles: the link between *behavior and attitudes* and the *power of the situation.*

BEHAVIOR AND ATTITUDES

When external influences override inner convictions, attitudes fail to determine behavior. These experiments vividly illustrate that principle. When responding alone, Asch's participants nearly always gave the correct answer. It was another matter when they stood alone against a group.

In the obedience experiments, a powerful social pressure (the experimenter's commands) overcame a weaker one (the remote victim's pleas). Torn between the pleas of the victim and the orders of the experimenter, between the desire to avoid doing harm and the desire to be a good participant, a surprising number of people chose to obey.

Compliance breeds acceptance. Ex-torturer Jeffrey Benzien demonstrates the "wet bag" technique of almost asphyxiating someone to South Africa's Truth and Reconciliation Commission. "I did terrible things," Benzien admitted with apologies to his victims, though he claimed only to be following orders.
Benny Gool/Capetown Independent Newspaper

Why were the participants unable to disengage themselves? Imagine yourself as the teacher in a hypothetical version of Milgram's experiment. Assume that when the learner gives the first wrong answer, the experimenter asks you to zap him with 330 volts. After flicking the switch, you hear the learner scream, complain of a heart disturbance, and plead for mercy. Do you continue?

Perhaps not. In Milgram's real experiment, the first commitment was mild – 15 volts – and elicited no protest. By the time participants delivered 75 volts and heard the learner's first groan, they already had complied five times, and the next request was to deliver only slightly more. By the time they delivered 330 volts, the participants had complied 22 times and reduced some of their dissonance. They were therefore in a different psychological state from that of someone beginning the experiment at that point; it was a "slippery slope" of obedience, and once they started down, it was difficult to stop. One experiment on cheating captured the effects of the slippery slope. Some participants received 25 cents for a correct answer in the first round, $1 in the second, and $2.50 in the third, while others were paid $2.50 for each correct answer from the beginning. Those with the progressive incentives were more likely to cheat and say they got more answers correct, possibly because their infraction started out small – what's 25 cents? – and then grew (Welch et al., 2015). However, this principle doesn't work perfectly: When asked to administer a painful but not extreme amount of shock (150 volts), nearly all participants complied – more than those who worked up to that level through 10 trials (Dolinski & Grzyb, 2016). They had not yet heard the learner protest, so at this point, one request might have been easier to follow than 10.

External behavior and internal disposition can also feed each other, sometimes in an escalating spiral. Thus, reported Milgram (1974, p. 10):

> Many subjects harshly devalue the victim as a consequence of acting against him. Such comments as, "He was so stupid and stubborn he deserved to get shocked," were common. Once having acted against the victim, these subjects found it necessary to view him as an unworthy individual, whose punishment was made inevitable by his own deficiencies of intellect and character.

During the early 1970s, Greece's military junta used this "blame-the-victim" process to train torturers (Haritos-Fatouros, 1988, 2002; Staub, 1989, 2003). There, as in the earlier training of SS officers in Nazi Germany, the military selected candidates based on their respect for and submission to authority. But such tendencies alone do not a torturer make. Thus, they would first assign the trainee to guard prisoners, then to participate in arrest squads, then to hit prisoners, then to observe torture, and only then to practice it. Step by step, an obedient but otherwise decent person evolved into an agent of cruelty. Compliance bred acceptance. If we focus on the endpoint — 450 volts of torture administered — we are aghast at the evil conduct. If we consider how one gets there — in tiny steps — we can understand.

"The social psychology of this century reveals a major lesson: Often it is not so much the kind of person a man is as the kind of situation in which he finds himself that determines how he will act."

—Stanley Milgram, *Obedience to Authority*, 1974

As a Holocaust survivor, University of Massachusetts social psychologist Ervin Staub knows too well the forces that can transform citizens into agents of death. From his study of human genocide across the world, Staub (2003) showed where gradually increasing aggression can lead. Too often, criticism produces contempt, which licenses cruelty, which, when justified, leads to brutality, then killing, then systematic killing. Evolving attitudes both follow and justify actions. Staub's disturbing conclusion: "Human beings have the capacity to come to experience killing other people as nothing extraordinary" (1989, p. 13).

But humans also have a capacity for heroism. During the Nazi Holocaust, the French village of Le Chambon sheltered 5,000 Jews and other refugees destined for deportation to Germany. The villagers were mostly Protestants whose own authorities, their pastors, had taught them to "resist whenever our adversaries will demand of us obedience contrary to the orders of the Gospel" (Rochat, 1993; Rochat & Modigliani, 1995). Ordered to divulge the locations of sheltered Jews, the head pastor modeled disobedience: "I don't know of Jews, I only know of human beings." Without knowing how terrible the war would be, the resisters, beginning in 1940, made an initial commitment and then — supported by their beliefs, by their own authorities, and by one another — remained defiant until the village's liberation in 1944. Here and elsewhere, the ultimate response to Nazi occupation came early. Their initial helping heightened commitment, leading to more helping.

Even in an individualistic culture, few of us desire to challenge our culture's clearest social norms, as did Stephen Gough while walking the length of Britain naked (apart from hat, socks, boots, and a rucksack). Starting in June 2003, he made it the length of Britain, from Lands' End in England's southwest to John o'Groats, in Scotland's northeast. During his 7-month, 847-mile trek, he was arrested 15 times and spent about 5 months behind bars. "My naked activism is firstly and most importantly about me standing up for myself, a declaration of myself as a beautiful human being," Gough (2003) declared from his website.

Tom Pilston/The Independent/Shutterstock

THE POWER OF SOCIAL NORMS

Imagine violating some minor norms: standing up in the middle of a class; singing out loud in a restaurant; playing golf in a suit. In trying to break with social constraints, we suddenly realize how strong they are.

The students in one Pennsylvania State University experiment led by Janet Swim and Lauri Hyers (1999) found it surprisingly difficult to violate the social norm of being "nice" rather than confrontational — even when they were thoroughly provoked. Participants imagined themselves discussing with three others whom to select for survival on a desert island. They were asked to imagine one of the others, a man, injecting three sexist comments, such as, "I think we need more women on the island to keep the men satisfied." How would they react to such sexist remarks? Only 5% predicted they would ignore the comments or wait to see how others reacted. But when other students were actually in the situation and heard a male accomplice make these comments, 55% (not 5%) said nothing. Likewise, although people predicted they would be upset by witnessing a person making a racial slur and would reject that person, those who actually experienced such an event typically exhibited indifference (Kawakami et al., 2009). These experiments demonstrate the power of social norms and show how hard it is to predict behavior, even our own behavior.

How ironic that in 2011, the human struggle with confrontation should play out at Swim and Hyers' university – Penn State – in a public debate about how its revered football coach and other university officials should have responded to learning that a fellow coach had sexually abused young boys. (The coaches reportedly did pass on the reports to superiors but allowed the alleged abuser to continue using university facilities.) Commentators were outraged; they presumed that *they* themselves would have acted more strongly. These experiments remind us that *saying* what we would do in a hypothetical situation is often easier than *doing* it in a real situation.

Milgram's studies also offer a lesson about evil. In horror movies and suspense novels, evil results from a few bad apples, a few depraved killers. In real life we think of Hitler's extermination of Jews or of Osama bin Laden's terrorist plot. But evil also results from social forces – from the powerful situations that help make a whole barrel of apples go bad. The U.S. military police, whose abuse of Iraqi prisoners at Abu Ghraib prison horrified the world, were under stress, taunted by many they had come to save, angered by comrades' deaths, overdue to return home, and under lax supervision – an evil situation that produced evil behavior (Fiske, 2004; Lankford, 2009). Situations and strong beliefs can induce ordinary people to capitulate to cruelty.

This is especially true when, as happens often in large societies, the most terrible evil evolves from a sequence of small evils. German civil servants surprised Nazi leaders with their willingness to handle the paperwork of the Holocaust. They were not killing Jews, of course; they were merely pushing paper (Silver & Geller, 1978). When fragmented, evil becomes easier. Milgram studied this compartmentalization of evil by involving yet another 40 men more indirectly. With someone else triggering the shock, they had only to administer the learning test. Now, 37 of the 40 fully complied.

So it is in our everyday lives: The drift toward evil usually comes in small increments, without any conscious intent to do evil. Procrastination involves a similar unintended drift toward self-harm (Sabini & Silver, 1982). A student knows the deadline for a term paper weeks ahead. Each diversion from work on the paper – a video game here, a social media scroll there – seems harmless enough. Yet gradually the student veers toward putting off writing the paper without ever consciously deciding to.

Under the sway of evil forces, even nice people are sometimes corrupted as they construct moral rationalizations for immoral behavior (Tsang, 2002). So it is that ordinary soldiers may, in the end, follow orders to shoot defenseless civilians; admired political leaders may lead their citizens into ill-fated wars; ordinary employees may follow instructions to produce and distribute harmful, degrading products; and ordinary group members may heed commands to brutally haze initiates.

So, does a situational analysis of harm-doing exonerate harm-doers? Does it absolve them of responsibility? In laypeople's minds, the answer is, to some extent, yes, noted Arthur Miller (2006). But the psychologists who study the roots of evil insist otherwise. To explain is not to excuse. To understand is not to forgive. You can forgive someone whose behavior you don't understand, and you can understand someone whom you do not forgive. Moreover, added James Waller (2002), "When we understand the ordinariness of extraordinary evil, we will be less surprised by evil, less likely to be unwitting contributors to evil, and perhaps better equipped to forestall evil." Jerry Burger's (2009) replication of the famous Milgram study excluded those familiar with it. Had such people – with the knowledge you now have – been included, might the obedience rate have been much lower (Elms, 2009)?

Finally, a comment on the experimental method used in conformity research: Conformity and obedience situations in the laboratory differ from those in everyday life. How often are we asked to judge line lengths or administer shock? But just as a match and a forest fire both burn, we assume that psychological processes in the laboratory and in everyday life are similar (Milgram, 1974). We must be careful in generalizing from the simplicity of a burning match to the complexity of a forest fire. Yet controlled experiments

TABLE 1 Summary of Classic Obedience Studies

Topic	Researcher	Method	Real-Life Example
Norm formation	Sherif	Assessing suggestibility regarding seeming movement of light	Interpreting events differently after hearing from others; appreciating a food that others love
Conformity	Asch	Agreement with others' obviously wrong perceptual judgments	Doing as others do; dangerous social media "challenges"
Obedience	Milgram	Complying with commands to shock another	Soldiers or employees following questionable orders

on burning matches can give us insights into combustion that we cannot gain by observing forest fires. So, too, the social-psychological experiment offers insights into behavior not readily revealed in everyday life. The experimental situation is unique, but so is every social situation. By testing with a variety of unique tasks and by repeating experiments at different times and places, researchers probe for the common principles that lie beneath the surface diversity. For a summary of these classic obedience studies, review **Table 1**.

The classic conformity experiments answered some questions but raised others: Sometimes people conform; sometimes they do not. Given that, we can ask: (1) *When* do they conform? (2) *Why* do people conform? Why don't they ignore the group and "to their own selves be true"? (3) Is there a type of *person* who is likely to conform? In the next sections, we will take these questions one at a time.

SUMMING UP: What Are the Classic Conformity and Obedience Studies?

Three classic sets of experiments illustrate how researchers have studied conformity.

- Muzafer Sherif observed that others' judgments influenced people's estimates of the movement of a point of light that actually did not move. Norms for "proper" answers emerged and survived both over long periods of time and through succeeding generations of research participants.
- Solomon Asch had people listen to others' judgments of which of three comparison lines was equal to a standard line and then make the same judgment themselves. When the others unanimously gave a wrong answer, the participants conformed 37% of the time.
- Stanley Milgram's studies of obedience elicited an extreme form of compliance. Under optimum conditions – a legitimate, close-at-hand commander, a remote victim, and no one else to exemplify disobedience – 65% of his adult male participants fully obeyed instructions to deliver what were supposedly traumatizing electric shocks to a screaming, innocent victim in an adjacent room.
- Behavior and attitudes are mutually reinforcing, enabling a small act of evil to foster the attitude that leads to a bigger evil act.

WHAT PREDICTS CONFORMITY?

Identify situations that trigger much — and little — conformity.

Social psychologists wondered: If even Asch's noncoercive, unambiguous situation could elicit a 37% conformity rate, would other settings produce even more? Researchers soon discovered that conformity did grow if the judgments were difficult or if the participants felt incompetent. The more insecure we are about our judgments, the more influenced we are by others.

Group attributes also matter. Conformity is highest when the group has three or more people and is unanimous, cohesive, and high in status. Conformity is also highest when the response is public and made without prior commitment. Let's look at each of these conditions.

Group Size

Asch and other researchers found that three to five people will elicit much more conformity than just one or two. Increasing the number of people beyond five yields diminishing returns (Gerard et al., 1968; Rosenberg, 1961); a small group can have a big effect. In a field experiment, Milgram and his colleagues (1969) had 1, 2, 3, 5, 10, or 15 people pause on a busy New York City sidewalk and look up. As **Figure 6** shows, the percentage of passersby who also looked up increased as the number looking up increased from one to five persons. Try this on your campus: Get a few friends to stand with you looking up at the sky, and you'll find that almost everyone who walks by does the same. I [JT] did this with my students when I was a teaching assistant at the University of Michigan. When only one or two volunteers stood outside the classroom building, a few people glanced at them but no one looked up. But when four or five students stood outside the door, staring up at the sky, nearly every student stepping out of the building instantly lifted their head skyward. My students and I laughed so hard we embarrassed ourselves.

The same is true online: Several people are more convincing than one. When reading a false news headline on social media, people were less likely to believe it if several others commented that it was untrue ("Fake story!"). Seeing comments like these from at least three other people was actually more effective in debunking the information than seeing a warning that the story was disputed by the Associated Press (Colliander, 2019). People are more likely to believe misinformation on social media when it has a higher number of "likes" from others (Butler et al., 2023). Similarly, people were twice as likely to "like" content on Facebook if they saw that three people (versus one) had liked the content (Egebark & Ekstrom, 2018).

The way the group is "packaged" also makes a difference. Rutgers University researcher David Wilder (1977) gave students a jury case. Before giving their own judgments, the

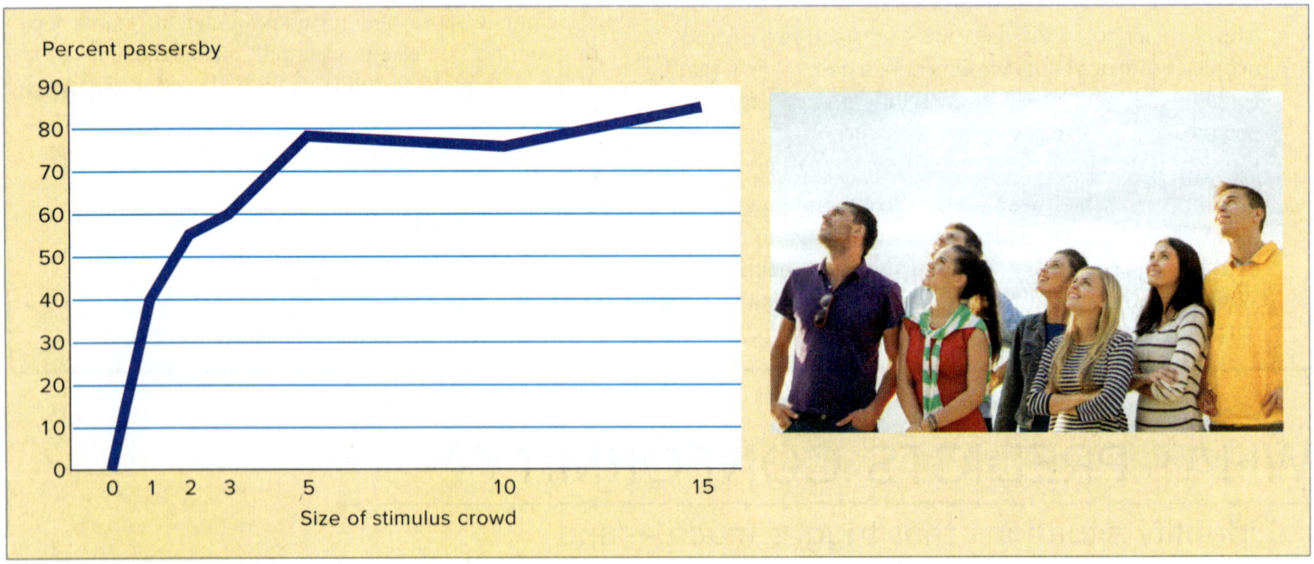

FIGURE 6

Group Size and Conformity

The percentage of passersby who imitated a group looking upward increased as group size increased to five persons.

Source: Data from Milgram, S., Bickman, L., & Berkowitz, L. (1969). Lev Dolgatsjov/dolgachov/123RF students watched videotapes of four accomplices giving their judgments. When the accomplices were presented as two independent groups of two people, the participants conformed more than when the four accomplices presented their judgments as a single group. Similarly, two groups of three people elicited more conformity than one group of six, and three groups of two people elicited even more. The agreement of independent small groups makes a position more credible.

Unanimity

Imagine yourself in a conformity experiment in which all but one of the people responding before you give the same wrong answer. Would the example of this one nonconforming accomplice be as liberating as it was for the individuals in Milgram's obedience study? Several experiments reveal that someone who punctures a group's unanimity deflates its social power (Allen & Levine, 1969; Asch, 1955; Morris & Miller, 1975). As **Figure 7** illustrates, people will usually voice their own convictions if just one other person has also differed from the majority. The participants in such experiments often later say they felt warm toward and close to their nonconforming ally. Yet they deny that the ally influenced them: "I would have answered just the same if he weren't there."

It's difficult to be a minority of one; few juries are hung because of one dissenting juror. Only one in 10 U.S. Supreme Court decisions during the late-20th century had a lone dissenter; most were unanimous or a 5–4 split (Granberg & Bartels, 2005). Lindsey Levitan and Brad Verhulst (2016) asked college students to privately state their views on issues such as gun control, the death penalty, and abortion. When they later restated their views before others who thought differently, they were less likely to change their position if they had even one ally.

Conformity experiments teach the practical lesson that it is easier to stand up for something if you can find someone else to stand up with you. Many religious groups recognize this. Following the example of Jesus, who sent his disciples out in pairs, the Mormons send two missionaries into a neighborhood together. The support of the one comrade greatly increases a person's social courage.

"My opinion, my conviction, gains infinitely in strength and success, the moment a second mind has adopted it."

—Novalis, Fragment

Observing someone else's dissent – even when it is wrong – can increase our own independence. Charlan Nemeth and Cynthia Chiles (1988) discovered this after having people observe a lone individual in a group of four misjudge blue stimuli as green. Although the dissenter was wrong, after they had observed him, the observers were more likely to exhibit their own form of independence: 76% of the time they correctly labeled red slides "red" even when everyone else was incorrectly calling them "orange." Participants who had no opportunity to observe the "green" dissenter gave the correct answer only 30% of the time (and thus conformed 70% of the time).

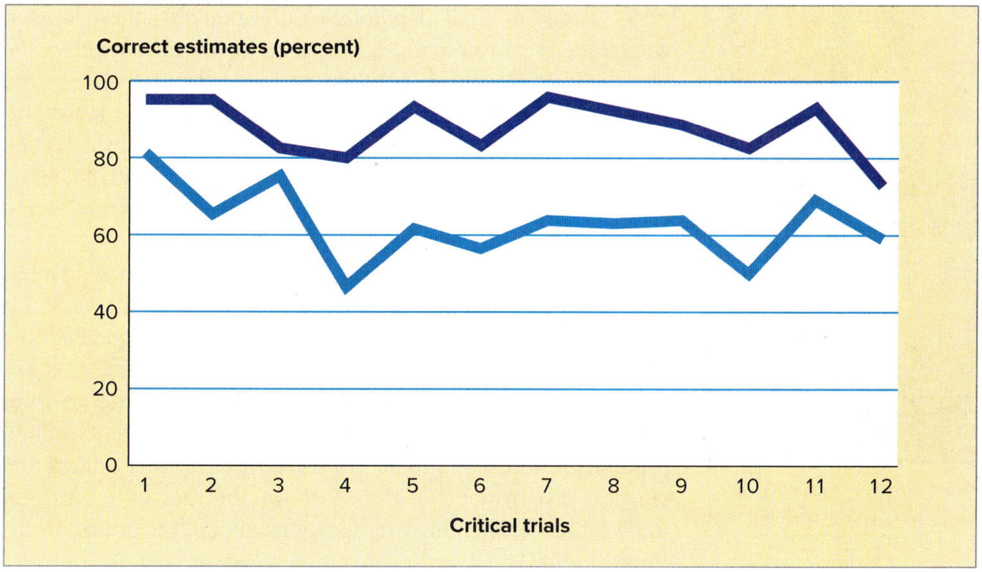

FIGURE 7

The Effect of Unanimity on Conformity

When someone giving correct answers punctures the group's unanimity, individuals conform only one-fourth as often.

Source: Data from Asch (1955).

Cohesion

A minority opinion from someone outside the groups we identify with – from someone at another college or of a different religion – sways us less than the same minority opinion from someone within our group (Clark & Maass, 1988). Facebook likes from friends are four times more likely to prompt us to also "like" something than a Facebook like from a stranger (Egebark & Ekström, 2018). People even comply more readily with requests from those said to share their birthday, their first name, or features of their fingerprint (Burger et al., 2004; Silvia, 2005).

cohesiveness
A "we feeling"; the extent to which members of a group are bound together, such as by attraction to one another.

The more **cohesive** a group is, the more power it gains over its members. In other words, a group of your closest friends would influence you more than a group of acquaintances you don't feel very close to. In college sororities, for example, friends tend to share binge-eating tendencies, especially as they grow closer (Crandall, 1988). High school, often a time of cohesive groups, often leads students to drink as much alcohol as their peers in order to become (or stay) popular (Balsa et al., 2010). People within an ethnic group may feel a similar "own-group conformity pressure" – to talk, act, and dress just as everyone else does in their own group. In fact, Black people who "act White" or White people who "act Black" may be mocked by their peers for not conforming to their own ethnic group (Contrada et al., 2000; Durkee et al., 2022).

Our inclination to go with our group – to think what it thinks and do what it does – surfaced in one experiment as people reported greater liking for a piece of music that was said to be liked by people akin to themselves (but *dis*liked the music more when it was liked by someone *un*like themselves [Hilmert et al., 2006]). Similarly, when university students compare themselves with alcohol drinkers who are different from themselves, they become *less* likely to drink alcohol (Lane et al., 2011). And after observing cheating by someone wearing a T-shirt from their own university, participants in another experiment became more likely to cheat. But if the cheater wore a T-shirt from a competing university, it had the opposite effect: The participants became more honest (Gino et al., 2009).

Status

As you might suspect, higher-status people tend to have more impact (Driskell & Mullen, 1990). Among university friend groups, higher status members had more influence on group members' alcohol consumption than lower status members (Dumas et al., 2018). Chinese consumers who felt more powerful were less likely to conform by choosing popular products and came up with more unique (and thus less conformist) advertising slogans than those who did not feel powerful (Zou et al., 2014). Jeff Galak and his colleagues (2016) found a creative way to test status and conformity, examining 16,000 purchases of women's shoes. Women who recently moved to a neighborhood higher in status than the one they left were more likely to buy the type of shoes favored in the new neighborhood, but those who moved to a lower-status neighborhood were more likely to ignore the local norms. Even chimps are more likely to imitate the behaviors of high-ranking group members (Horner et al., 2010). Among both humans and other primates, prestige predicts influence.

People are more likely to jaywalk when someone else does and not jaywalk when someone else doesn't, especially when the other person is well-dressed and thus appears to be high in status (Mullen et al., 1990).
Daniel Thistlewaite/Image Source

Milgram (1974) reported that in his obedience studies, people of lower status accepted the experimenter's commands more readily than people of higher status. After delivering 450 volts, a 37-year-old welder turned to the higher-status experimenter and deferentially asked, "Where do we go from here, Professor?" (p. 46). Another participant, a divinity school professor who disobeyed at 150 volts, said, "I don't understand why the experiment is placed above this person's life" and plied the experimenter with questions about "the ethics of this thing" (p. 48).

Public Response

One of the conformity researchers' first questions was this: Would people conform more in their public responses than in their private opinions? Or would they wobble more in their private opinions but be unwilling to conform publicly, lest they appear wishy-washy?

The answer is now clear: In experiments, people conform more when they must respond in front of others rather than writing their answers privately. Asch's participants, after hearing others respond, were less influenced by group pressure if they could write answers that only the experimenter would see. As shown in a study in China, adolescents are more likely than children to change their answers when they are displayed publicly to their peers, suggesting adolescents feel more group pressure to conform (Zhang et al., 2017). Thus, when college instructors ask controversial questions, students express more diverse opinions when answering anonymously, with clickers, than when raising hands (Stowell et al., 2010). It is much easier to stand up for what we believe in the privacy of the voting booth than before a group.

Prior Commitment

In 1980, Genuine Risk became the second filly ever to win the Kentucky Derby. In her next race, the Preakness, she came off the last turn gaining on the leader, Codex, a colt. As they came out of the turn neck and neck, Codex moved sideways toward Genuine Risk, causing her to hesitate and giving him a narrow victory. Had Codex brushed Genuine Risk? Had his jockey even whipped Genuine Risk in the face? The race referees huddled. After a brief deliberation, they judged that no foul had occurred and confirmed Codex as the winner. The decision caused an uproar. Televised instant replays showed that Codex had indeed brushed Genuine Risk, the sentimental favorite. A protest was filed. The officials reconsidered their decision, but they did not change it.

Did their declared judgment immediately after the race affect officials' openness toward reaching a different decision later? We will never know for sure. We can, however, put people through a laboratory version of this event – with and without the immediate public commitment – and observe whether the commitment makes a difference. Again, imagine yourself in an Asch-type experiment. The experimenter displays the lines and asks you to respond first. After you give your judgment and then hear everyone else disagree, the experimenter offers you an opportunity to reconsider. In the face of group pressure, do you now back down?

"Those who never retract their opinions love themselves more than they love truth."

—J. Joubert, *Pensées*, 1877

People almost never do (Deutsch & Gerard, 1955). After having made a public commitment, they stick to it (Bradford et al., 2017). We may therefore expect that judges of diving or gymnastic competitions, for example, will seldom change their ratings after seeing the other judges' ratings. When people apologize and admit they are wrong, they often feel less in control (Okimoto et al., 2013).

Prior commitments restrain persuasion, too. When simulated juries make decisions, hung verdicts are more likely in cases when jurors are polled by a show of hands rather than by secret ballot (Kerr & MacCoun, 1985). Making a public commitment makes people hesitant to back down.

Smart persuaders know this. Salespeople and service workers ask questions that prompt us to make statements for, rather than against, what they are marketing or providing. For example, waiters who ask "How is everything so far?" know it is difficult for

Prior commitment: Once they commit themselves to a position, people seldom yield to social pressure. Did Codex, the front horse closest to the inside, brush against Genuine Risk? After race referees publicly announced their decision, no amount of evidence from replays of the race could budge them.
Ira Schwarz/AP Images

you to answer "only okay." They hope your answer of "great" may improve your impression of the meal – and they might be right. Environmentalists ask people to verbally declare their commitment to recycling, energy conservation, or bus riding. That's because behavior changes more when people declare their commitment to environmental sustainability than when they merely hear an appeal for it (Katzev & Wang, 1994). This principle works for health behaviors as well: Compared to those who merely received education about alcohol and drugs, Spanish teens who publicly pledged not to drink alcohol or do drugs were less likely to do so (Hernández-Serrano et al., 2013). People who publicly pledged to lose weight were not only more motivated to lose weight but actually did drop more pounds (Nyer & Dellande, 2010).

SUMMING UP: What Predicts Conformity?

- Certain situations appear to be especially powerful for eliciting conformity. For example, people conform most when three or more people model the behavior or belief.
- Conformity is reduced if the modeled behavior or belief is not unanimous – if one or more people dissent.
- Conformity is enhanced by group *cohesion.*
- The higher the status of those modeling the behavior or belief, the greater likelihood of conformity.
- People also conform most when their responses are public (in the presence of a group).
- A prior commitment to a certain behavior or belief increases the likelihood that a person will stick with that commitment.

WHY CONFORM?

Summarize the two forms of social influence that explain why people will conform to others.

There I [DM] was, an American attending my first lecture during an extended visit at a German university. As the lecturer finished, I lifted my hands to join in the clapping. But rather than clap, the other people began rapping the tables with their knuckles. What did this mean? Did they disapprove of the speech? Surely, not everyone would be so openly rude to a visiting dignitary. Nor did their faces express displeasure. No, I realized, this must be a German ovation. So I added my knuckles to the chorus.

What prompted this conformity? Why had I not clapped even while the others rapped? There are two possibilities: A person may accede to the group (a) to be accepted by others or (b) to obtain important information. Morton Deutsch and Harold Gerard (1955) named these two possibilities **normative influence** and **informational influence.** The first springs from our desire to be *liked,* and the second from our desire to be *right.*

normative influence
Conformity based on a person's desire to fulfill others' expectations, often to gain acceptance.

informational influence
Conformity occurring when people accept evidence about reality provided by other people.

Normative influence is "going along with the crowd" to avoid rejection, to stay in people's good graces, or to gain their approval by following social norms. Informational influence captures how beliefs spread. Just as people look up when they see others looking up, they use the same fork others are using at a fancy dinner party.

In the laboratory and in everyday life, groups often reject consistent nonconformers (Miller & Anderson, 1979; Schachter, 1951). That's a lesson learned by a media studies professor who became an outcast while playing the online game "City of Heroes" (Vargas, 2009). The professor, with whom I [DM] empathize because we share the same name – David Myers – played by the rules but did not conform to the customs. Myers was derided with instant messages: "I hope your mother gets cancer." "EVERYONE HATES YOU." "If you kill me one more time I will come and kill you for real and I am not kidding."

"A lot of our thinking is for bonding, not truth-seeking, so most of us are quite willing to think or say anything that will help us be liked by our group."
—David Brooks, "The Art of Thinking Well," 2017

In the years since, the rise of cancel culture and online outrage has continued to show harsh consequences for perceived nonconformity. Online "firestorms" often occur when a person or group says or does something others find objectionable, whether it was intended that way or not. One study found that online firestorms encourage other users to comply with the opinions and emotions expressed by the initial outraged commenters – thus encouraging conformity among the participants in the firestorm as well as pushing its original target to conform (Johnen et al., 2018).

As most of us know, social rejection is painful; when we deviate from group norms, we often pay an emotional price. Gerard (1999) recalls that in one of his conformity experiments, an initially friendly participant became upset, asked to leave the room, and returned looking

> sick and visibly shaken. I became worried and suggested that we discontinue the session. He absolutely refused to stop and continued through all 36 trials, not yielding to the others on a single trial. After the experiment was over and I explained the subterfuge to him, his entire body relaxed and he sighed with relief. Color returned to his face. I asked him why he had left the room. "To vomit," he said. He did not yield, but at what a price! He wanted so much to be accepted and liked by the others and was afraid he would not be because he had stood his ground against them. There you have normative pressure operating with a vengeance.

Sometimes the high price of deviation compels people to support what they do not believe in or at least to suppress their disagreement. In one experiment, participants who were ostracized by others were more likely to obey an experimenter's command to go outside in freezing weather to take 39 photographs (Riva et al., 2014). When we experience or even fear rejection, we're more likely to follow along. "I was afraid that Leideritz and others would think I was a coward," reported one Nazi officer, explaining his reluctance to dissent from mass executions (Waller, 2002). Normative influence leads to compliance, especially for people who have recently seen others ridiculed or who are seeking to climb a status ladder (Hollander, 1958; Janes & Olson, 2000). As John F. Kennedy (1956) recalled, "'The way to get along,' I was told when I entered Congress, 'is to go along'" (p. 4).

Normative influence – knowing how most other people behave – often sways us without our awareness. Administrators at Northern Illinois University wanted to reduce students' dangerous binge drinking at parties. At first, they tried warning students about the consequences of binge drinking, but binge-drinking rates stayed about the same. Then they spread information about the norm, telling them that "most students drink moderately." That technique was more successful: Binge drinking was cut in half over 10 years (Haines, 1996). Similarly, high school students are much more likely to smoke when their friends smoke and thus they see smoking as the norm (Liu et al., 2017). People follow others' lead when deciding what to eat, too. In one study, customers at a bakery ate significantly more chocolates when 20 candy wrappers were left next to the bowl (Prinsen et al., 2013).

Informational influence, on the other hand, leads people to privately accept others' influence as a source of information. When reality is ambiguous, as it was for participants in Sherif's autokinetic situation, other people can be a valuable source of information. The individual may reason, "I can't tell how far the light is moving. But this guy seems to know." The same is true while you're reading the restaurant reviews on Yelp or the hotel reviews on TripAdvisor: If you haven't been there before, other people's experiences can provide important information. These types of reviews are good examples of informational influence (Chen et al., 2016).

Your friends have extra influence on you for informational as well as normative reasons (Denrell, 2008; Denrell & Le Mens, 2007). If your friend buys a particular car or takes you to a particular restaurant, you will gain information that may lead you to like what your friend likes – even if you don't care what your friend likes. Our friends influence the experiences that inform our attitudes. However, that influence doesn't last forever: In one study, conformity to others' opinions lasted no more than 3 days (Huang et al., 2014).

To discover what the brain is doing when people experience an Asch-type conformity experiment, an Emory University neuroscience team put participants in a functional magnetic resonance imaging (fMRI) brain scanner while having them answer questions after hearing others' responses (Berns et al., 2005). When the participants conformed to a wrong answer, the brain regions dedicated to perception became active. And when they went *against* the group, brain regions associated with emotion became active. These results suggest that conformity may genuinely shape perceptions: People may conform because they

When you're deciding where to go next, online reviews can provide informational influence. So can your friend who has been there before.
fizkes/123rf

are afraid of being wrong. Follow-up fMRI studies found that a brain area associated with social rejection was activated during normative influence and an area associated with judgment was activated during informational influence (Zaki et al., 2011).

So, concern for *social image* produces *normative influence.* The desire to be *correct* produces *informational influence.* In day-to-day life, normative and informational influence often occur together. I [DM] was not about to be the only person in that German lecture hall clapping (normative influence). Yet the others' behavior also showed me the appropriate way to express my appreciation (informational influence).

Conformity experiments have sometimes isolated either normative or informational influence. Conformity is greater when people respond publicly before a group; this surely reflects normative influence (because people receive the same information whether they respond publicly or privately). On the other hand, conformity is greater when participants feel incompetent, when the task is difficult, and when the individuals care about being right – all signs of informational influence.

SUMMING UP: Why Conform?

- Experiments reveal two reasons people conform. *Normative influence* results from our desire for acceptance: We want to be liked. The tendency to conform more when responding publicly reflects normative influence.
- *Informational influence* results from others' providing evidence about reality. The tendency to conform more on difficult decision-making tasks reflects informational influence: We want to be right.

WHO CONFORMS?

Describe how conformity varies not only with situations but also with persons.

Are some people generally more swayed by social influence? Among your friends, can you identify some who are "conformists" and others who are "independent"? In their search for the conformer, researchers have focused on three predictors: personality, culture, and social roles.

Personality

In Milgram's time, the personality factors predicting greater conformity were unknown. As Milgram (1974) concluded: "I am certain that there is a complex personality basis to obedience and disobedience. But I know we have not found it" (p. 205). Yet individual differences clearly existed: Recall that not all of Milgram's participants obeyed the experimenter to the end. We now know more about which personality factors predict conformity. In general, people higher in agreeableness (who value getting along with others) and conscientiousness (who follow social norms for neatness and punctuality) are more likely to conform (Begue et al., 2015; Fürst et al., 2014; Haas et al., 2023). People who want to please others eat more candy when a peer eats some and then hands them the bowl, apparently conforming to help the other person feel more comfortable (Exline et al., 2012). In other words, "hold the extra burgers and fries when people pleasers arrive" (Griffith, 2012).

In contrast, people high in openness to experience – a personality trait connected to creativity and socially progressive thinking – are less likely to conform (Eck & Gebauer, 2022; Jugert et al., 2009). Novelty seekers, who leap into experiences seeking stimulation, are also less likely to conform (Athota & O'Connor, 2014). Students with a strong belief in their own free will were less likely to conform to the group (Alquist et al., 2013; Fennis & Aarts, 2012), as were those with more liberal political beliefs (Begue et al., 2015). So if you favor smooth social experiences over disagreements, follow the rules, have traditional beliefs, and doubt the existence of a free will, you may be more likely to conform.

Personality effects loom larger when we note people's differing reactions to the same situation, as when one person reacts with terror and another with delight to a roller coaster ride.
Jacob Lund/Shutterstock

These individual variations help explain instances when people chose not to conform to the group. An Army report on the Abu Ghraib prison scandal (which involved U.S. soldiers abusing Iraqi prisoners) praised three men who, despite threats of ridicule and court-martial, stood apart from their comrades (O'Connor, 2004). Specialist Joseph Darby blew the whistle, giving military police the evidence that raised the alarm. Darby, called a "rat" by some, received death threats for his dissent and was given military protection. But back home, his mother joined others in applauding: "Honey, I'm so proud of you because you did the good thing and good always triumphs over evil, and the truth will always set you free" (ABC News, 2004). In the end, both personality and the situation shape behavior.

Culture

When researchers in Australia, Austria, Germany, Italy, Jordan, South Africa, Spain, and the United States repeated the obedience experiments, how do you think the results compared with those with U.S. participants? The obedience rates were similar or even higher – 85% in Munich and 90% in Poland (Blass, 2000; Dolinski et al., 2017). As a general rule, conformity rates are higher in collectivistic countries and more conformist times such as the 1950s (Bond & Smith, 1996).

In collectivistic Japan, Western observers were struck by the absence of looting and lawlessness following the 2011 earthquake and tsunami; respect for social norms prevailed (Cafferty, 2011). Many Japanese schools have strict dress codes that mandate not just school uniforms but forbid makeup and jewelry. In one extreme case, a student with naturally brown hair was told to dye her hair black so it looked like everyone else's (McCurry, 2017). In individualistic countries, university students were instead more interested in standing out and believed they were more unique than their peers in their preferences and views (Pronin et al., 2007). U.S. adults believed that children who conformed were less intelligent, whereas Pacific Islanders thought conforming children were more intelligent (Clegg et al., 2017).

There may be some biological wisdom to cultural differences in conformity. Although nonconformity supports creative problem solving, groups thrive when coordinating their responses to threats. For example, countries that have historically high rates of infectious diseases such as malaria, typhus, and tuberculosis are more conforming, and those with lower disease risk promote less conformity and encourage more innovation and new ideas in science, technology, and business (Murray, 2014). Similarly, people living in U.S. states with higher rates of infectious disease are less likely to vote for third-party candidates – a nonconformist action (Varnum, 2013). Why the connection? Conformity supports social norms regarding hygiene, public health, and contact with unknown people – all useful behaviors during disease outbreaks (Grossmann & Varnum, 2015). Thinking of pathogens

Social class as cultural influence: People from working-class backgrounds are more likely to prefer to fit in, while those from middle-class backgrounds are more likely to want to stand out.
Dwight Smith/Shutterstock

(such as viruses and bacteria) can actually cause conformity: Students randomly assigned to see pathogen-related pictures or to talk about feeling vulnerable to germs were more likely to conform than those who instead saw pictures of accidents (Murray & Schaller, 2012; Wu & Chang, 2012). When we think about getting sick, we embrace the perceived safety of fitting in with the group.

The COVID-19 pandemic was a natural experiment in pathogens and conformity, with vaccines, face masks, and staying at home as new social norms intended to prevent the spread of the disease. Conformity to these norms may have saved lives: Collectivistic countries, which encourage more conformity, had fewer deaths from COVID on average (Chen & Biswas, 2022; Guss & Tuason, 2021; Kumar, 2021). As we have seen throughout this chapter, conformity is not always negative; during a disease outbreak, following social norms has public health benefits.

Cultural differences also exist within social classes. For example, in five studies, Nicole Stephens and her co-researchers (2007) found that working-class people tended to prefer similarity to others, whereas middle-class people more strongly preferred to see themselves as unique. In one of her experiments, people chose a pen from among five green and orange pens (with three or four of one color). Of university students from working-class backgrounds, 72% picked one from the majority color, compared to only 44% of those from middle-class backgrounds. Those from working-class backgrounds also were more likely to prefer visual images that they knew others had chosen and responded more positively to a friend buying the same car as theirs. Subsequent studies confirmed that college students from working-class backgrounds are more likely to have a more collectivistic or interdependent view of themselves, and those from middle-class backgrounds a more individualistic and independent one (Fiske & Markus, 2012; Phillips et al., 2020).

Social Roles

"All the world's a stage, And all the men and women merely players: They have their exits and their entrances; And one man in his time plays many parts."

—William Shakespeare, *As You Like It,* 1623

Role theorists have assumed, as did William Shakespeare's character Jaques in *As You Like It,* that social life is like acting on a theatrical stage, with all its scenes, masks, and scripts. And those roles have much to do with conformity. Social roles allow some freedom of interpretation to those who act them out, but some aspects of any role *must* be performed. A student must at least show up for exams, turn in papers, and maintain some minimum grade point average.

When only a few norms are associated with a social category (for example, riders on an escalator should stand to the right and walk to the left), we do not regard the position as a social role. It takes a whole cluster of norms to define a role. My [DM's] roles as a professor or as a father compel me to honor a whole set of norms. Although I may acquire my particular image by violating the least important norms (valuing efficiency, I rarely arrive early for anything), violating my role's most important norms (not showing up for class, abusing my children) could lead to my being fired or having my children removed from my care.

Roles have powerful effects. On a first date or on a new job, you may act the role self-consciously. As you internalize the role, self-consciousness subsides. What felt awkward now feels genuine.

That is the experience of many immigrants, Peace Corps workers, international students, and executives. After arriving in a new country, it takes time to learn how to talk and act appropriately in the new context – to conform, as I [DM] did with the Germans who rapped their knuckles on their desks. And the almost universal experience of those who repatriate back to their home country is reentry distress (Sussman, 2000). In ways one may not have been aware of, the process of conforming will have shifted one's behavior, values, and identity to accommodate a different place. One must "re-conform" to one's former roles before being back in sync.

Moving from one culture to another — for example, from a rural location to an urban one — shows how the social roles we conform to depend on the culture around us.
Diego Cervo/Shutterstock

As we saw earlier in this chapter, our actions depend not only on the power of the situation but also on our personalities. Not everyone responds in the same way to pressure to conform. Nevertheless, we have seen that social situations can move most "normal" people to behave in "abnormal" ways. This is clear from those experiments that put well-intentioned people in bad situations to see whether good or evil prevails. To a dismaying extent, evil wins. Nice guys often don't finish nice.

Role playing can also be a positive force. By intentionally playing a new role and conforming to its expectations, people sometimes change themselves or empathize with people whose roles differ from their own.

"Great Spirit, grant that I may not criticize my neighbor until I have walked for a moon in his moccasins."

—Native American prayer

Roles often come in pairs defined by relationships: parent and child, teacher and student, doctor and patient, and employer and employee. Role reversals can help each understand the other. A negotiator or a group leader can therefore create better communication by having the two sides reverse roles, with each arguing the other's position. Or each side can be asked to restate the other party's point (to the other's satisfaction) before replying. The next time you get into a difficult argument with a friend or parent, try to restate the other person's perceptions and feelings before going on with your own. This intentional, temporary conformity may repair your relationship.

So far in this chapter, we have discussed classic studies of conformity and obedience, identified the factors that predict conformity, and considered who conforms and why. Remember that our primary quest in social psychology is not to catalog differences but to identify universal principles of behavior.

Social roles will always vary with culture, but the processes by which those roles influence behavior vary much less. People in Nigeria and Japan define social roles differently from people in Europe and North America, but in all cultures, role expectations guide the conformity found in social relations.

SUMMING UP: Who Conforms?

- People who seek to please others and are comfortable following social rules (those high in agreeableness and conscientiousness) are the most likely to conform.
- Although conformity and obedience are universal, different cultures socialize people to be more or less socially responsive.
- Social roles involve a certain degree of conformity, and conforming to expectations is an important task when stepping into a new social role.

DO WE EVER WANT TO BE DIFFERENT?

Explain what can motivate people to actively resist social pressure — by doing Z when pressured to do A.

This chapter emphasizes the power of social forces. It is therefore fitting that we conclude by again reminding ourselves of the power of the person. We are not just billiard balls moving where pushed. We may act according to our own values, independently of the forces that push upon us. Knowing that someone is trying to coerce us may even prompt us to react in the *opposite* direction.

"To do just the opposite is also a form of imitation."
—Lichtenberg, *Aphorismen*, 1764–1799

Reactance

Individuals value their sense of freedom and self-efficacy. When blatant social pressure threatens their sense of freedom, they often rebel. The dating partner your parents reject may seem even more alluring. Told not to go out or to wear masks during the COVID-19 pandemic, some people refused (usually with some version of "You can't tell me what to do;" Diaz & Cova, 2022). Or think of children asserting their freedom and independence by doing the opposite of what their parents ask. Savvy parents, therefore, offer their children limited choices instead of commands: "It's time to get clean: Do you want a bath or a shower?"

reactance
A motive to protect or restore one's sense of freedom. Reactance arises when someone threatens our freedom of action.

The theory of psychological **reactance** – that people act to protect their sense of freedom – is supported by experiments showing that attempts to restrict a person's freedom often produce an anticonformity "boomerang effect" (Brehm & Brehm, 1981; Nail et al., 2000; Rains, 2013; Rosenberg & Siegel, 2018). People who read an aggressive and emotional appeal to stop eating meat (vs. a more neutral message) were more frustrated and annoyed. They also found more words related to meat in a word search task, suggesting the appeal had backfired and caused them to think about eating meat even more (Sprengholz et al., 2023).

Reactance might also explain why most people find it so difficult to eat right and exercise. For example, 78% of the population does not exercise regularly. As Seppo Iso-Ahola (2013) explains, "Exercise has become a 'must' or 'should' activity that sets up a confrontation between fitness activity and freedom" (p. 100). The same is often true for healthy eating. If your partner tries to tell you to eat healthier food, it's tempting to reject the advice to save face (Dorrance-Hall et al., 2021). When teens were told that others believed eating fruit was healthy, they said they intended to eat less fruit. But when they heard that most other teens made an effort to eat sufficient fruit, they ate more fruit over the next 2 days (Stok et al., 2014). Because we know we should do something that's healthy, it becomes difficult to actually do it without feeling our freedom is compromised. If we know others are doing it (normative influence again), we're more likely to do it too, due to the principles of conformity. The lesson seems to be: Do what I do, not what I say is right.

We're more likely to eat healthy when others do (normative influence) — but not when we're lectured about how healthy it is (reactance).
HONGQI ZHANG/michaeljung/123RF

Asserting Uniqueness

Imagine a world of complete conformity, where there were no differences among people. Would such a world be a happy place? If nonconformity can create discomfort, can sameness create comfort?

People feel uncomfortable when they appear too different from others. But, especially in individualistic Western cultures, they also feel uncomfortable when they appear exactly like everyone else. That might be because nonconformity has become associated with high status. In a series of experiments, Silvia Bellezza and colleagues (2014) found that people wearing nonconformist clothing were perceived by others as higher in status.

Asserting our uniqueness: Although not wishing to be greatly deviant, most of us express our distinctiveness through our personal styles and dress.
Igor Emmerich/Image Source

Overall, people feel better when they see themselves as moderately unique and act in ways that will assert their individuality. For example, students in one study believed that their first names were less common than their peers did. Apparently, people with common names wanted to believe their names—and thus, they—were more unique. In addition, students who thought about changing their names usually chose more unique names (Kulig, 2012). In an experiment, Charles Snyder (1980) led Purdue University students to believe that their "10 most important attitudes" were either distinct from or nearly identical to the attitudes of 10,000 other students. When they next participated in a conformity experiment, those deprived of their feeling of uniqueness were the ones most likely to assert their individuality via nonconformity. Overall, individuals who have the highest "need for uniqueness" tend to conform the least (Imhoff & Erb, 2009). In some cases, they make their nonconformity visible: People high in need for uniqueness are more likely to have tattoos, body piercings, and other body modifications (Weiler et al., 2021).

"When I'm in America, I have no doubt I'm a Jew, but I have strong doubts about whether I'm really an American. And when I get to Israel, I know I'm an American, but I have strong doubts about whether I'm a Jew."

—Leslie Fiedler,
Fiedler on the Roof, 1991

Both social influence and the desire for uniqueness appear in popular baby names. People seeking less commonplace names often hit upon the same ones at the same time. Those who, in the 1960s, broke out of the pack by naming their baby Rebecca soon discovered their choice was part of a new pack, noted Peggy Orenstein (2003). Hillary, a popular name in the late 1980s and early 1990s, became less original-seeming and less frequent (even among her admirers) after Hillary Clinton became well-known. In 2022, among the top 10 U.S. baby names for girls were Olivia (#1), Amelia (#4), and Luna (#10). Although the popularity of such names then fades, observed Orenstein, it may resurface with a future generation. Max, Rose, and Sophie sound like the roster of a retirement home—or an elementary school. These trends seem to be driven by a nonconformist urge. In one large study of names in the United States and France, when names become popular quickly, they also faded from popularity more quickly—perhaps because they were seen as fads (Berger & Le Mens, 2009).

Seeing oneself as unique also appears in people's "spontaneous self-concepts." William McGuire and his Yale University colleagues (McGuire et al., 1979; McGuire & Padawer-Singer, 1978) invited children to "tell us about yourself." In reply, the children mostly mentioned their most distinctive attributes. Foreign-born children were more likely than others to mention their birthplace. Redheads were more likely than black- and brown-haired children to volunteer their hair color. Thin and overweight children were the most likely to refer to their body weight. Minority children were the most likely to mention their race.

Likewise, we become more keenly aware of our gender when we are with people of the other gender (Cota & Dion, 1986). When I [DM] attended an American Psychological Association meeting with 10 others—all women, as it happened—I immediately was aware of my gender. As we took a break at the end of the second day, I joked that the line would be short at my bathroom, triggering the woman sitting next to me to notice what hadn't crossed her mind—the group's gender makeup.

The principle, said McGuire, is that "one is conscious of oneself insofar as, and in the ways that, one is different." Thus, "If I am a Black woman in a group of White women, I tend to think of myself as a Black; if I move to a group of Black men, my blackness loses salience and I become more conscious of being a woman" (McGuire et al., 1978). This insight helps us understand why White people who grow up in racially diverse communities tend to have a strong White identity, why gay people may be more conscious of their sexual identity than straight people, and why any ethnic minority group tends to be conscious of

"Self-consciousness, the recognition of a creature by itself as a 'self,' [cannot] exist except in contrast with an 'other,' a something which is not the self."

—C. S. Lewis,
The Problem of Pain, 1940

its distinctiveness and how the surrounding culture relates to it (Knowles & Peng, 2005). Asian Americans are less conscious of their ethnic identity when living in Hawaii, where they are the majority, and more conscious of it in other U.S. states (Xu et al., 2015). The majority group, being less conscious of race, may see the minority group as hypersensitive. When traveling in Australia, where my [JT's] American accent marks me as a foreigner, I become conscious of my national identity and sensitive to how others react to it.

When the people of two cultures are nearly identical, they will still notice their differences, however small. The differences between Sunni and Shia Muslims, which seem small to many non-Muslims, have been a source of war. Even trivial distinctions may provoke scorn and conflict. As a child in Minnesota, I [JT] remember Minnesotans joking that nearby Iowa stood for "Idiots out walking around." As a teen in Dallas, Texas, I heard football fans deride those who supported a rival team from Oklahoma, less than 200 miles away. Rivalry is often most intense when the other group closely resembles you. So, although we do not like being greatly deviant, we are, ironically, all alike in wanting to feel distinctive and in noticing how we are distinctive. (In thinking you are different, you are like everyone else.) But as research on the self-serving bias makes clear, it is not just any kind of distinctiveness we seek but distinctiveness in the right direction. Our quest is not merely to be different from the average but *better* than average.

SUMMING UP: Do We Ever Want to Be Different?

- Social psychology's emphasis on the power of social pressure must be joined by a complementary emphasis on the power of the person. We are not puppets. When social coercion becomes blatant, people often experience *reactance* – a motivation to defy the coercion in order to maintain their sense of freedom.
- We are not comfortable being greatly different from a group, but neither do we want to appear the same as everyone else. Thus, we act in ways that preserve our sense of uniqueness and individuality. In a group, we are most conscious of how we differ from the others.

CONCLUDING THOUGHTS: On Being an Individual within a Community

Do your own thing. Question authority. If it feels good, do it. Follow your bliss. Don't conform. Think for yourself. Be true to yourself. You owe it to yourself.

We hear phrases like those over and again *if* we live in an individualistic Western nation, such as those of Western Europe, Australia, New Zealand, Canada, or, especially, the United States. Our mythical cultural heroes – from Wonder Woman to Black Panther – often stand up against institutional rules. Individualists assume the preeminence of individual rights and celebrate the one who stands against the group.

In 1831 the French writer Alexis de Tocqueville coined the term "individualism" after traveling in America. Individualists, he noted, owe no one "anything and hardly expect anything from anybody. They form the habit of thinking of themselves in isolation and imagine that their whole destiny is in their hands." Psychologist Carl Rogers (1985) agreed: "The only question which matters is, 'Am I living in a way which is deeply satisfying to me, and which truly expresses me?'"

That is hardly the only question that matters to people in many other cultures, including those of Asia, South America, and most of Africa. Where *community* is prized, conformity is accepted. Schoolchildren often display their solidarity by wearing uniforms; many workers do the same. To maintain harmony, confrontation and dissent are muted. "The nail that stands out gets pounded down," say the Japanese. South Africans have a word that expresses human connection. *Ubuntu,* explained Desmond Tutu (1999), conveys the idea that "my humanity is caught up by, is inextricably bound up in, yours." *Umuntu ngumuntu ngabantu,* says a Zulu maxim: "A person is a person through other persons."

Amitai Etzioni (1993), a past president of the American Sociological Association, urges us toward a "communitarian" individualism that balances our nonconformist individualism with a spirit of community. Fellow sociologist Robert Bellah (1995/1996) concurs. "Communitarianism is based on the value of the sacredness of the individual," he explained. But it also "affirms the central value of solidarity . . . that we become who we are through our relationships."

As Westerners in various nations, most readers of this book enjoy the benefits of nonconformist individualism. Communitarians remind us that we also are social creatures having a basic need to belong and to take actions that help the group. Conformity is neither all bad nor all good. We, therefore, do well to balance our "me" and our "we," our needs for independence and for attachment, our individuality, and our social identity.

Persuasion

CHAPTER

7

Heidi Besen/Shutterstock

"To swallow and follow, whether old doctrine or new propaganda, is a weakness still dominating the human mind."

—Charlotte Perkins Gilman, *Human Work,* 1904

What paths lead to persuasion?

What are the elements of persuasion?

How can persuasion be resisted?

Concluding Thoughts: Being open but not naïve

Many of life's powers can either harm or help us. Nuclear power can light up homes or wipe out cities. Sexual power helps us express committed love or seek selfish gratification. Similarly, **persuasion**'s power enables us to promote health or to sell addiction, to advance peace or stir up hate, to enlighten or deceive. And such powers are great. Consider the following:

- *The spread of false beliefs:* About 1 in 4 Americans and 1 in 3 Europeans think the sun revolves around the earth (Grossman, 2014). Others deny that the moon landing or the Holocaust occurred, or contend the Earth is flat (Hamilton, 2022).
- *Attitudes around equality:* In the space of 50 years, the United States went from a country that asked its Black citizens to sit in the back of the bus to one that elected an African American president — twice. In less than 30 years, it went from 12% of adults believing that two people of the same sex should

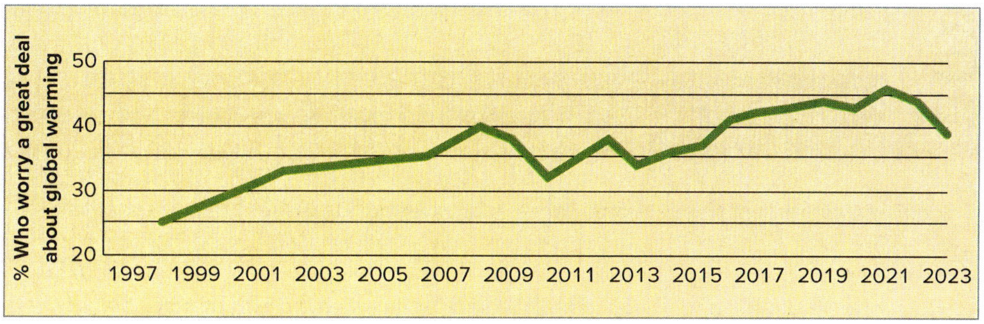

FIGURE 1

Percentage of American Adults Who Worry About Global Warming, 1997 to 2023.
Source: Gallup, 2023

persuasion
The process by which a message induces change in beliefs, attitudes, or behaviors.

be able to get married to 71% supporting same-sex marriage (McCarthy, 2023; Twenge & Blake, 2020). Civil rights campaigns, news stories, and positive media portrayals of people of color and LGBT individuals have been powerful persuaders.

- *Climate change skepticism:* The scientific community, represented by various national academies of science and the Intergovernmental Panel on Climate Change, is in a virtual consensus that climate change will cause sea levels to rise and weather to become more extreme. Yet 23% of Americans still believe there is a lot of disagreement among scientists on this point (Marlon et al., 2022). Still, concern about global warming has increased, suggesting scientists' messages are getting through (see **Figure 1**).

"Speech has power. Words do not fade. What starts out as a sound ends in a deed."
—Rabbi Abraham Heschel (1907–1972)

As these examples show, efforts to persuade are sometimes diabolical, sometimes controversial, and sometimes beneficial. Persuasion is neither inherently good nor bad. Instead, a message's purpose and content elicit judgments of good or bad. The bad we call "propaganda." The good we call "education." Education is more factually based and less coercive than propaganda. Yet generally we call it "education" when we believe it, "propaganda" when we don't (Lumsden et al., 1980).

Persuasion is at the heart of politics, marketing, dating, parenting, negotiation, religion, and courtroom decision making — and played a key role in shaping behavior during the early months of the COVID-19 pandemic (see "The Inside Story: Stephen Reicher on Human Behavior during the Pandemic: A Social Psychologist Advises His Country."). Social psychologists, therefore, seek to understand what leads to effective, long-lasting attitude change. What factors affect persuasion? As persuaders, how can we most effectively "educate" others?

Persuasion is everywhere. When we approve of it, we may call it "education."
Mick Sinclair/Alamy Stock Photo

Imagine that you are a marketing or advertising executive. Or imagine that you are a preacher, trying

THE inside STORY

Stephen Reicher on Human Behavior during the Pandemic: A Social Psychologist Advises His Country in 2020

I began advising the UK and Scottish Governments on COVID-19 through my work with John Drury on how crowds behave in emergencies. I had long been skeptical of considering people in groups to be irrational and fragile — all rushing for the exits, blocking them, and thereby turning a crisis into a tragedy. Studies of disasters show the opposite: People generally help each other in a crisis. When people face the same dangers together, they develop a shared identity, which leads to empathy, mutual support, and collective resilience.

Through this work, John and I had been involved in various government groups looking at public behavior after a terrorist attack and were then invited to join the UK and Scotland's behavioral science advisory groups on COVID-19. We advised our governments on how to build and maintain collective resilience. We also provided psychological insights into human behavior under the pandemic: the importance of social norms, the ways to achieve social influence, the nature of leadership, how to build trust, and what leads to compliance with regulations, rules, and laws. For instance, we have stressed the importance of delivering messages from respected in-group sources. We have also discussed how to frame them so as to draw on group norms (for example, "We are Scotland. We stick at things and see them through.").

It has been exhausting. I am used to writing papers in weeks or even months. Government ministers generally want them in days (or even hours). But it has also been rewarding. I used to say that until we get a vaccine, changing behavior will be at the very heart of the pandemic response. Then it became clear that, even with a vaccine, understanding behavior is critical — for one thing, to convince people to be vaccinated. Never, in my 40 years as an academic, have I seen psychological research and psychological ideas so central to public discourse and to government policy.

Stephen Reicher
University of St. Andrews

Stephen Reicher

to increase love and charity among your parishioners. Or imagine that you want to reduce climate change, encourage breastfeeding, or campaign for a political candidate. What can you do to make yourself and your message persuasive? And if you are wary of being influenced, to what tactics should you be alert?

WHAT PATHS LEAD TO PERSUASION?

Describe the cognitive processing involved in the two paths to persuasion and the effects of that processing.

"A fanatic is one who can't change his mind and won't change the subject."
—Attributed to Winston Churchill (1874–1965)

Persuasion entails clearing several hurdles (see **Figure 2**). Any factors that help people clear the persuasion hurdles will increase persuasion. For example, if an attractive source increases your attention to a message, the message will have a better chance of persuading you.

The Central Route

central route to persuasion Occurs when interested people focus on the arguments and respond with favorable thoughts.

Richard Petty and John Cacioppo (Cass-ee-OH-poh) (1986; Petty et al., 2009) and Alice Eagly and Shelly Chaiken (1993, 1998) took the idea of persuasion routes one step further in their Elaboration Likelihood Model. They theorized that persuasion is likely to occur via one of two routes. When people are motivated and able to think about an issue, they are likely to take the **central route to persuasion** – focusing on the arguments. If those arguments

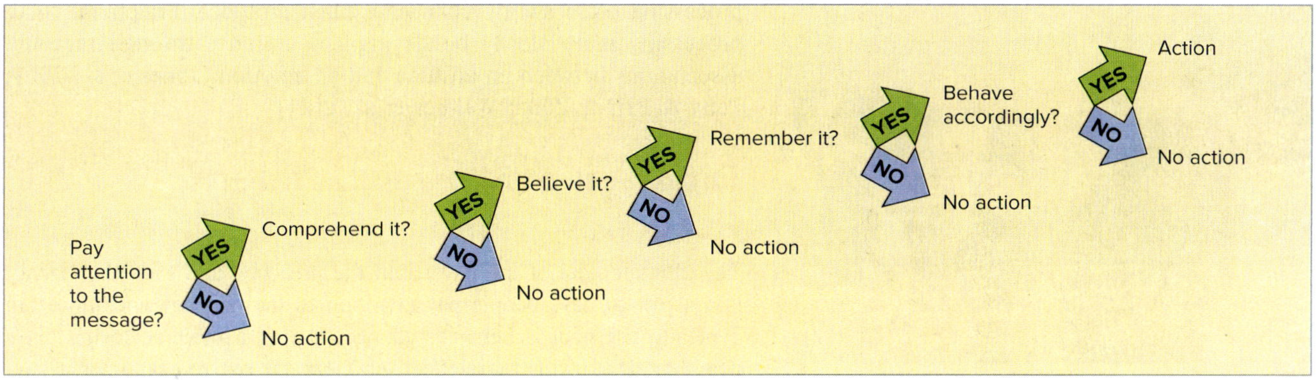

FIGURE 2

The Hurdles of the Persuasion Process

To elicit action, a persuasive message must clear several hurdles. Remembering the message itself is not as important as remembering one's own thoughts in response.

Source: Adapted from McGuire (1978).

are strong and compelling, persuasion is likely. If the message offers only weak arguments, thoughtful people will notice that the arguments aren't very compelling and will counterargue against them.

"All effective propaganda must be limited to a very few points and must harp on these in slogans until the last member of the public understands."

—Adolf Hitler, *Mein Kampf,* 1926

The Peripheral Route

However, when we're not motivated or able to think carefully, the strength of the arguments might not matter. If we're distracted, uninvolved, or just plain busy, we may not take the time to reflect on the message's content. Rather than analyzing whether the arguments are compelling, we might follow the **peripheral route to persuasion** – focusing on cues that trigger automatic acceptance without much thinking. In these situations, easily understood, familiar statements are more persuasive than novel statements with the same meaning. Thus, for uninvolved or distracted people, "Don't put all your eggs in one basket" has more impact than "Don't risk everything on a single venture" (Howard, 1997).

peripheral route to persuasion

Occurs when people are influenced by incidental cues, such as a speaker's attractiveness.

Smart advertisers adapt ads to their consumers' thinking. They do so for good reason. Many consumer decisions – such as a spontaneous decision to buy ice cream of a particular brand – are made without thinking (Dijksterhuis et al., 2005). Hearing German music in a store may lead customers to buy German wine, and those hearing French music may reach for French wine (North et al., 1997). Billboards and television commercials – media that consumers are able to take in for only brief amounts of time – often use the peripheral route, with visual images as peripheral cues. Instead of providing arguments in favor of smoking, cigarette ads associate the product with images of beauty and pleasure. So do soft-drink ads that show happy people and fun outdoor activities. Although this model of central versus peripheral routes was developed before the internet existed, similar dynamics occur in online contexts, with many ads using eye-catching images (Cyr et al., 2018).

The peripheral route can also subtly push people toward certain behaviors. Putting an image of a fly at the center of the urinals at the Amsterdam airport led more men to aim, reducing mess even though most didn't consciously recall the image. Putting fruits and vegetables at eye level in a grocery store or cafeteria led more people to choose these healthier foods (Thaler & Sunstein, 2021). A meta-analysis of more than 200 studies found that these types of "nudges" produced significant changes in behaviors (Mertens et al., 2022).

Peripheral route processing. "Product placements" on TV and in movies aim to influence implicit attitudes.
s_bukley/Shutterstock

These two routes to persuasion – one explicit and reflective, the other more implicit and automatic – were a forerunner to today's "dual processing" models of the human mind. Central route

Decisions in the voting booth: When careful central route processing takes too much time and effort, we may rely on peripheral route processing to make a quick judgment.
LPETTET/Getty Images

processing often swiftly changes explicit attitudes. Peripheral route processing more slowly builds implicit attitudes through repeated associations between an attitude and an emotion (Jones et al., 2009; Petty & Briñol, 2008; Walther et al., 2011).

Different Paths for Different Purposes

The ultimate goal of the advertiser, the preacher, and even the teacher is not just to have people pay attention to the message and move on. Typically, the goal is behavior change (buying a product, loving one's neighbor, or studying more effectively). Are the two routes to persuasion equally likely to fulfill that goal? Petty and colleagues (1995, 2009) noted that central route processing can lead to more enduring change than the peripheral route. When people are thinking carefully, they rely not only on the strength of persuasive appeals but on their own thoughts in response. It's not so much the arguments that are persuasive as the way they get people thinking. And when people think deeply rather than superficially, any changed attitude will more likely persist, resist attack, and influence behavior (Petty et al., 1995, 2009; Verplanken, 1991).

Deep thinking often involves moral beliefs, as many political beliefs do. In such cases, using arguments based on your audience's moral convictions is one of the best ways to persuade (Luttrell et al., 2019). Yet those on opposite sides of the political spectrum often find it difficult, if not impossible, to view things from the other side's moral perspective. When asked to convince conservatives to support same-sex marriage, for example, only 9% of liberals were able to frame their arguments using conservative moral principles such as loyalty and purity – even though these were the arguments that best convinced conservatives (Feinberg & Willer, 2015, 2019).

None of us has the time to thoughtfully analyze all issues. We often take the peripheral route by using simple rule-of-thumb heuristics, such as "trust the experts" or "long messages are credible" (Chaiken & Maheswaran, 1994). Residents of my [DM's] community once voted on a complicated issue involving the legal ownership of our local hospital. I didn't have the time or the interest to study that question myself (I had this book to write). But I noted that referendum supporters were all people I either liked or regarded as experts. So I used a simple heuristic – friends and experts can be trusted – and voted accordingly. We all make snap judgments using such heuristics: If a speaker is articulate and appealing, has apparently good motives, and has several arguments (or better, if the different arguments come from different sources), we usually take the easy peripheral route and accept the message without much thought.

Central route appeals seem to have dwindled in the last decade, most likely because advertisers have found that peripheral, emotion-based appeals are more effective across a variety of products. In one study, researchers recorded viewers' facial expressions while they watched recent TV commercials. These facial expressions – particularly those indicating happiness – were better predictors of product sales than viewers' survey responses about how persuasive they found the ad, how closely the ad was linked to the brand, or how the ad conveyed the brand's key message (Wood, 2012). Emotion, not reason, sold the goods.

SUMMING UP: What Paths Lead to Persuasion?

- Sometimes *persuasion* occurs as people focus on arguments and respond with favorable thoughts. Such systematic, or *central route,* persuasion occurs when people are naturally analytical or involved in the issue.
- When issues don't engage systematic thinking, persuasion may occur through a faster, *peripheral route* as people use heuristics or incidental cues to make snap judgments.
- Central route persuasion, being more thoughtful and less superficial, is more durable and more likely to influence behavior.

WHAT ARE THE ELEMENTS OF PERSUASION?

Explain the elements that influence whether we will take the central or the peripheral route to persuasion.

Among the elements of persuasion explored by social psychologists are these four: (1) the communicator, (2) the message, (3) how the message is communicated, and (4) the audience. In other words, *who* says *what*, by what *method*, to *whom*?

Who Says? The Communicator

It's about a month before an election, and you're trying to decide how to vote on a proposed tax on carbon emissions, a policy designed to combat climate change. You've seen ads both for and against the measure, and you're not sure how to vote. Then you see a statement of support from someone from your political party—or someone from the other party. How will you vote?

This was the choice presented to Democrats and Republicans in an experiment based on a real 2016 ballot measure in Washington state. Regardless of the specifics of the measure, Democrats approved of policies supported by other Democrats, and Republicans approved of policies supported by other Republicans. Even though climate policies are often associated with Democrats, Republicans supported them when they were endorsed by other Republicans—but not when they were touted by Democrats. As former Republican congressman Bob Inglis put it about his time in Congress, "All I knew was that Al Gore [a Democrat] was for it, and therefore I was against it" (Van Boven et al., 2018).

Similar examples abound. In one experiment, when participants heard Socialist and Liberal leaders in the Dutch parliament argue identical positions using the same words, each was most effective at convincing members of his own party (Wiegman, 1985). After the New Zealand Prime Minister championed changing the country's flag in 2016, voters in his party became more supportive of the change, while those in the other party became less supportive: In other words, "if they say 'yes,' we say 'no'" (Satherley et al., 2018). When a politician of the opposing political party offered fact-checking corrections of misinformation, they were 52% less likely to be believed, leaving beliefs in misinformation even more entrenched (Reinero et al., 2024).

Wearing masks to help prevent the spread of COVID-19 was at first blandly apolitical, but after some politicians spoke out for or against masks, they became politicized (Aratini, 2020; Gelfand et al., 2022). For example, after liberal Canadian Prime Minister Justin Trudeau publicly stated he would wear a mask, liberals became more positive about masks than conservatives (Courtice et al., 2023).

In other words, it's not just the message that matters, but also who says it. So, what makes one communicator more persuasive than another?

credibility
Believability. A credible communicator is perceived as both expert and trustworthy.

sleeper effect
A delayed impact of a message that occurs when an initially discounted message becomes effective, such as we remember the message but forget the reason for discounting it.

CREDIBILITY

Any of us would find a statement about the benefits of exercise more believable if it came from the Royal Society or National Academy of Sciences rather than from a tabloid newspaper. But the effects of source **credibility** (perceived expertise and trustworthiness) diminish after a month or so. If a credible person's message is persuasive, its impact may fade as its source is forgotten or dissociated from the message. And the impact of a noncredible person may correspondingly increase over time if people remember the message better than the reason for discounting it (Kumkale & Albarracin, 2004; Pratkanis et al., 1988). This delayed persuasion, after people forget the source or its connection with the message, is called the **sleeper effect.**

Is this politician liberal or conservative? That and your own party affiliation might heavily influence whether you believe her.
Pressmaster/Shutterstock

PERCEIVED EXPERTISE How do you become an authoritative "expert"? One way is to be seen as *knowledgeable* on the topic. A message about toothbrushing from "Dr. James Rundle of the Canadian Dental Association" is more convincing than the same message from "Jim Rundle, a local high school student who did a project with some of his classmates on dental hygiene" (Olson & Cal, 1984). Celebrity communicators are more persuasive when they are perceived as expert users of the product; when they are not, these appeals are ineffective (Rossiter & Smidts, 2012).

Some television ads are obviously constructed to make the communicator appear expert. A drug company may peddle its pain reliever using a speaker in a white lab coat who declares confidently that most doctors recommend the product's key ingredient (which is merely aspirin). Some makeup brands have their store employees wear lab coats, perhaps to imply that their product is uniquely scientific. Given such peripheral cues, people may automatically infer that the product is special.

Imagine being in charge of patient safety at a large hospital. You've put hand sanitizing stations in the lobby, but very few visitors use them. How can you change their behavior? When Susanne Gaube and her Regensburg University (Germany) colleagues designed seven signs encouraging hand-sanitizing, the most effective sign emphasized expertise: It was a picture of the hospital's medical director, looking somewhat stern, with a message saying "Hand hygiene is of great concern to me" (Gaube et al., 2020).

Expertise can also be simulated through agreement. A speaker who says things the audience agrees with comes across as smart. The scientific consensus about climate change may fail to persuade climate-change deniers because they see the small number of dissenting scientists as more expert. Researchers have observed this "similar views seem more expert" phenomenon on topics ranging from climate change to nuclear waste to gun laws (Kahan et al., 2011).

"Believe an expert."

—Virgil,
Aeneid, BC 19

SPEAKING STYLE Another way to appear credible is to *speak confidently and fluently.* Whether pitching a business plan or giving advice, a charismatic, energetic, confident-seeming person who speaks fluently (without saying "you know" or "uh") is often more convincing (Moore & Swift, 2011; Pentland, 2010). Speakers who stumble over their words are perceived as less credible, which then leads people to question their message, which then makes them less likely to accept what the speaker is saying (Carpenter, 2012). Speakers who answer questions immediately, as opposed to pausing for longer, are also seen as more likely to be truthful – many people assume that people who pause are fabricating an answer (Ziano & Wang, 2021).

Bonnie Erickson and collaborators (1978) had University of North Carolina students evaluate courtroom testimony given in a straightforward manner or in a more hesitant, disfluent way. For example:

Question: Approximately how long did you stay there before the ambulance arrived?
Answer: *[Straightforward]* Twenty minutes. Long enough to help get Mrs. David straightened out.
[Hesitating] Oh, it seems like it was about uh, 20 minutes. Just long enough to help my friend Mrs. David, you know, get straightened out.

The students found the straightforward, fluent witnesses much more competent and credible, suggesting that juries can be swayed by how a witness speaks and not just by what the witness says (Kaminski & Sporer, 2018).

Think of an ad you liked and found persuasive. Did the speaker use a monotone or speak glumly? Probably not. More than likely, they varied their tone and spoke enthusiastically. People who speak this way are more persuasive, partially because they come across as more confident and sincere (Van Zant & Berger, 2020).

In one-on-one communication, though, it's not good to speak too much and not listen. Telemarketers who take this approach are less successful. The best approach? A balance between talking and listening (Grant, 2013).

Charles Barsotti

Effective persuaders know how to convey a message effectively.

PERCEIVED TRUSTWORTHINESS We are more willing to listen to a communicator we trust. An experiment by the Media Insight Project (2017) found that Facebook users were more willing to believe an article shared by a trusted friend compared to one shared by someone they didn't trust. Surprisingly, who shared the article made a bigger difference than whether the news source was the established, well-respected Associated Press or the made-up "DailyNewsReview.com." This might explain why "fake news" spreads so quickly on social media sites. Using a trusted communicator can also lead to positive results. An October 2021 YouTube ad featuring news footage of Donald Trump encouraging people to get vaccinated against COVID-19 resulted in 100,000 more vaccinations above the baseline in places where people saw the ad – likely because Trump was a trusted communicator for many who had yet to be vaccinated (Larsen et al., 2022).

When you read a news article online, how do you decide whether to believe it? It might depend on whether it was shared on social media by a trusted friend.
Yuttana Jaowattana/Shutterstock

The same is true for evaluating products. People preferred a product more if the same description came from a consumer protection board rather than a company promoting its product after a recall (Smith et al., 2013). Social media influencers are the most successful when their product promotions are tied to their lifestyle and personal brand. In a set of studies, only influencers perceived as honest and sincere influenced people's decisions to buy a product (Filieri et al., 2023).

Online reviews of products are seen as more trustworthy if they are negative – at least for practical products such as cameras (Hong & Park, 2012; Sen & Lerman, 2007). Apparently, we're more willing to believe that negative comments are more honest than positive comments.

Trustworthiness is also higher if the audience believes the *communicator is not trying to persuade them*. Researchers showed British adults fake newspaper articles suggesting either that most scientists just want to inform the public about climate change, or that most scientists aim to persuade people to take action to stop climate change. Those who heard scientists aim only to inform were more likely to report more trust in climate scientists and say they would reduce water use or join in community environmental activities (Rabinovich et al., 2012). If you want to persuade someone, start with information, not arguments.

attractiveness
Having qualities that appeal to an audience. An appealing communicator (often someone similar to the audience) is most persuasive on matters of subjective preference.

Another effective strategy is to have someone else convey your expertise. In one study, customers calling a real estate agency were told, truthfully, "I'm going to put you through to Peter. He is our head of sales and has 20 years of experience selling properties in this area." Compared to a simple call transfer, 20% more customers came in for in-person meetings and 15% more decided to use the agency (Martin et al., 2014).

Is there any way to overcome people's resistance to communicators they don't trust? Humor can work. One study told students a supermarket manager who cared only about making money was planning to target them with emails and texts. Not surprisingly, students were resistant to hearing anything from such a distrusted source. But if they then received 15 humorous texts (for example, "There are 10 types of people that understand binary. Those that do and those that don't"), their negative views of the distrusted brand disappeared (Strick et al., 2012).

Attractive communicators, such as Zendaya endorsing Lancome, often trigger peripheral route persuasion. We associate their message or product with our good feelings toward the communicators.
Steven Bergman/AFF-USA/Alamy Stock Photo

ATTRACTIVENESS AND LIKING

Ads featuring star athletes and entertainers abound. Such ads are based on another characteristic of an effective communicator: **attractiveness.** When George Clooney starred in ads for Nespresso coffee, the coffee was suddenly seen not just as more desirable to drink, but also more sophisticated and seductive. Clooney made Nespresso coffee seem sexy (Unkelbach & Högden, 2019).

We may think we are not influenced by attractiveness or likability, but researchers have found otherwise. We're more likely to respond to those we like, a phenomenon well known to those organizing charitable solicitations and candy sales. Sure, Girl Scout cookies are tasty, but a lot fewer people would buy them if they were sold by unattractive middle-aged men instead of cute little girls. Even a fleeting conversation with someone is enough to increase our liking for that person and our responsiveness to their influence (Burger et al., 2001). Our liking may open us up to the communicator's arguments (central route persuasion), or it may trigger positive associations when we see the product later (peripheral route persuasion). As with credibility, the liking-begets-persuasion principle suggests applications (**Table 1**).

Attractiveness comes in several forms. *Physical attractiveness* is one. Arguments, especially emotional ones, are often more influential when they come from people we consider beautiful (Chaiken, 1979; Dion & Stein, 1978; Pallak et al., 1983). Attractiveness and fame often matter most when people are making superficial judgments. Young adults were more persuaded by ads on Instagram for e-cigarettes when the products were endorsed by celebrities compared to noncelebrities (Phua et al., 2018).

Similarity also makes for attractiveness. We tend to like people who are like us. That's one reason consumer-generated ads – those generated by regular people instead of ad companies – can be persuasive. One experiment found that consumer-generated ads were more effective when the ad creator was seen as similar to the participant (Thompson & Malaviya, 2013). Some of the most effective ads discouraging teens from smoking and drug use were created by teens themselves (Peña-Alves et al., 2019). Overall, we are more persuaded by messages that match our personalities and values (Joyal-Desmarais et al., 2022).

People who *act* as we do, subtly mimicking our postures, are also more influential. Thus, salespeople are sometimes taught to "mimic and mirror": If the customer's arms or legs are crossed, cross yours; if they smile, smile back.

TABLE 1 Seven Persuasion Principles

In his book *Influence: Science and Practice,* persuasion researcher Robert Cialdini (2021) illustrated seven principles that underlie human relationships and human influence. (This chapter describes the first two.)

Principle	Application
Authority: People defer to credible experts.	Establish your expertise; identify problems you have solved and people you have served.
Liking: People respond more affirmatively to those they like.	Win friends and influence people. Create bonds based on similar interest; praise freely.
Social proof: People allow the example of others to validate how to think, feel, and act.	Use "peer power": Have respected others lead the way.
Reciprocity: People feel obliged to repay in kind what they've received.	Be generous with your time and resources. What goes around, comes around.
Consistency: People tend to honor their public commitments.	Instead of telling restaurant reservation callers "Please call if you change your plans," ask, "Will you call if you change your plans?" and the number of no-shows will drop.
Scarcity: People prize what's scarce.	Highlight genuinely exclusive information or opportunities.
Unity: People often say yes to someone they see as one of them.	Mention one's shared identity–perhaps common roots or kindred group membership.

What Is Said? The Message Content

It matters not only who says something but also *what* that person says. If you were to help organize an appeal to get people to vote for school taxes or to stop smoking or to give money to world hunger relief, you might wonder how best to persuade.

- Is a logical message more persuasive – or one that arouses emotion?
- How should you present your message?
- Should the message express your side only, or should it acknowledge and refute the opposing views?
- If people are to present both sides – say, in successive talks at a community meeting or in a political debate – is there an advantage to going first or last?
- How much information should you include?

Let's take these questions one at a time.

REASON VERSUS EMOTION

Suppose you were campaigning in support of world hunger relief. Would you best itemize your arguments and cite an array of impressive statistics? Or would you be more effective presenting an emotional approach – perhaps the compelling story of one starving child? Of course, an argument can be both reasonable and emotional. You can marry passion and logic. Still, which is *more* influential: reason or emotion?

"The truth is always the strongest argument."

—Sophocles, *Phaedra*, BC 496–406

"Opinion is ultimately determined by the feelings and not the intellect."

—Herbert Spencer, *Social Statics*, 1851

The answer: It depends on the audience. Well-educated or analytical people are responsive to rational appeals (Cacioppo et al., 1983, 1996; Hovland et al., 1949). So are audiences that have the time and motivation to think through an issue (Petty & Briñol, 2015). Thus, thoughtful, involved audiences often travel the central route to persuasion; they are more responsive to reasoned arguments. Uninterested audiences more often travel the peripheral route; they are more affected by their liking of the communicator (Chaiken, 1980; Petty et al., 1981).

In general, however, messages that tell a story – that contain a narrative about people – are more persuasive than those that don't, possibly because they are less direct and thus harder to counter (Ratcliff & Sun, 2020). The citizens of West African villages who listened to a radio program dramatizing the effects of violence on a community were later less likely to support extremist violence compared to those in control villages who did not hear the program (Bilali, 2022).

It also matters how people's attitudes were formed. When people's initial attitudes are formed primarily through the peripheral route, they are more persuaded by later peripheral, emotional appeals; when their initial attitudes are formed primarily through the central route, they are more persuaded by later information-based, central route arguments (Edwards, 1990; Fabrigar & Petty, 1999). For example, many people who distrust vaccines developed their attitudes through the emotion-laden idea that their children might be harmed. Informing them that this attitude was wrong – that vaccines do not harm children – did little to change attitudes. But when they read a mother's emotional story about her unvaccinated child contracting measles and saw pictures of children with the disease, their attitudes toward vaccines became markedly more positive (Horne et al., 2015). New emotions may sway an emotion-based attitude. But to change an information-based attitude, more information may be needed.

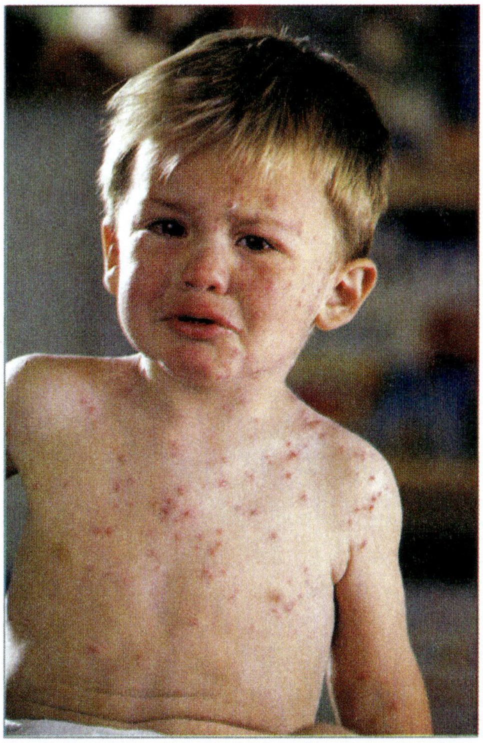

Attitude matching: To convince parents worried about vaccines to vaccinate their children, an effective strategy is to provide vivid examples (such as the picture, above) of unvaccinated children who got sick, using the same peripheral route that formed their initially distrustful attitude.
SW Productions/Brand X Pictures/Getty Images

THE EFFECT OF GOOD FEELINGS Messages also become more persuasive through association with good feelings, such as what often accompanies munching food or hearing pleasant music. Receiving money or free samples often induces people to donate money or buy something (Cialdini, 2021). That might be why so many charities include address labels, stickers, and even coins in their mailings.

"If the jury had been sequestered in a nicer hotel, this would probably never have happened."

Frank Cotham

Good feelings help create positive attitudes.

Good feelings often enhance persuasion, partly by enhancing positive thinking and partly by linking good feelings with the message (Petty et al., 1993). People who are in a good mood view the world through rose-colored glasses. But happy people also make faster, more impulsive decisions; they rely more on peripheral cues (Bodenhausen, 1993; Braverman, 2005; Moons & Mackie, 2007). Unhappy people ruminate more before reacting, so they are less easily swayed by weak arguments. (They also *produce* more cogent persuasive messages [Forgas, 2007].) Thus, if you can't make a strong case, you might want to put your audience in a good mood and hope they'll feel good about your message without thinking too much about it (Sar & Rodriguez, 2019).

Knowing that humor can put people in a good mood, a Dutch research team led by Madelijn Strick (Strick et al., 2009) invited people to view ads in the vicinity of either funny cartoons or the same cartoons altered to be unfunny. Their finding: Products associated with humor were liked more and chosen more often. Similarly, attitudes about political topics and health behaviors are more likely to change after people view a satirical news show featuring humor (such as *The Daily Show*) compared to a straight news segment (Feldman & Chattoo, 2019; Moyer-Gusé et al., 2018).

THE EFFECT OF AROUSING FEAR Messages can also be effective by evoking negative emotions. When persuading people to cut down on smoking, get a tetanus shot, or drive carefully, a fear-arousing message can be potent (de Hoog et al., 2007; Muller & Johnson, 1990). Young adults who saw warning labels with graphic images of blackened lungs and stained teeth (versus text-only warnings) were more likely to correctly remember the messages (Strasser et al., 2012), experienced more fear, and were less inclined to smoke (Cameron et al., 2015). Most important, 50% more of those who saw the graphic images (versus text-only) quit smoking within a month (Brewer et al., 2016). When Australia added graphic images of sick and dying smokers to cigarette packages in 2012, smoking rates fell nearly 5% (Innis, 2014). Dozens of countries around the world, including Canada, Egypt, and Bangladesh, have added graphic, fear-inducing images to cigarette packaging (Cohen, 2016). In 2022, a federal court blocked the graphic warnings from being placed on cigarette packs in the United States (Pierson, 2022), and as of 2023, U.S. cigarette packs only carry text warnings – though the legal case is ongoing.

But how much fear should you arouse? Should you evoke just a little fear, lest people become so frightened that they tune out your painful message? Or should you try to scare the daylights out of them? Experiments show that, often, the more frightened and vulnerable people feel, the more they respond (de Hoog et al., 2007; Robberson & Rogers, 1988). In a meta-analysis of 127 articles including 27,372 people, Melanie Tannenbaum and her colleagues (2015) concluded that "fear appeals are effective . . . there are no identified circumstances under which they backfire and lead to undesirable outcomes."

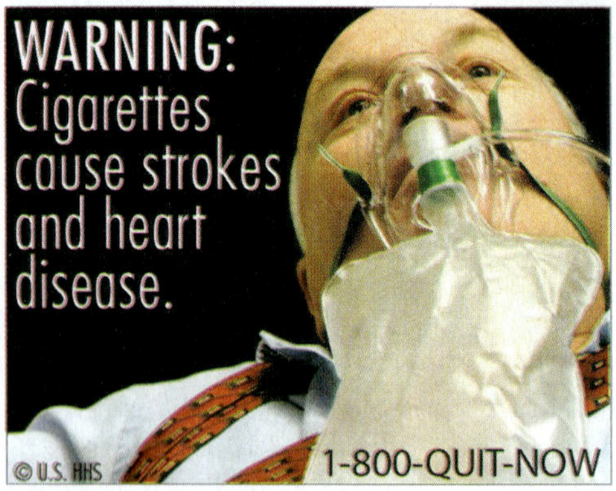

A proposed U.S. cigarette warning, shown here, uses fear arousal. In 2012, a federal court blocked the requirement for such warnings.
UPI/FDA/Alamy Stock Photo

The effectiveness of fear-arousing communications has been applied in ads discouraging not only smoking but also risky sexual behaviors and drinking and driving. When Claude Levy-Leboyer (1988) found that French youth drank less alcohol after seeing fear-arousing pictures, the French government incorporated such pictures into its TV spots.

Fear-arousing communications have also been used to increase breast cancer detection behaviors, such as getting mammograms or doing breast self-exams. Sara Banks, Peter Salovey, and colleagues (1995) had women aged 40 to 66 years who had not obtained mammograms view an educational video on mammography. Of those who received a positively framed message (emphasizing that getting a mammogram can save your life through early detection), only half got a mammogram within 12 months. Of those who received a fear-framed message (emphasizing that not getting a mammogram can cost you your life), two-thirds got a mammogram within 12 months. People who see ultraviolet photographs of sun-damaged faces – showing all of the freckles and spots destined to appear as they age – are significantly more likely to use sunscreen. In this case, the intervention focuses not just on the fear of getting cancer but also on the fear of looking unattractive (Williams et al., 2013).

People who see ultraviolet filtered photographs showing skin damage caused by the sun are more likely to use sunscreen.
SCIENCE PHOTO LIBRARY/Newscom

Playing on fear works best if a message leads people not only to fear but also to perceive a solution and feel capable of implementing it (Devos-Comby & Salovey, 2002; Maddux & Rogers, 1983; Ruiter et al., 2001). Many ads designed to reduce sexual risks will aim to both arouse fear – "AIDS kills" – and to offer a protective strategy: Abstain, wear a condom, or save sex for a committed relationship. These types of appeals tell people not just to be scared, but to do something about it, increasing their sense of efficacy (Ruiter et al., 2014; Salomon et al., 2017). A global climate change article that ends by discussing possible solutions is more persuasive than one describing future catastrophic consequences (Feinberg & Willer, 2011).

MESSAGE CONTEXT

The context of your message – especially what immediately precedes it – can make a big difference in how persuasive it is. In one study, an accomplice approached a passerby at a Polish train station and said, "Excuse me . . . Haven't you lost your wallet?" Everyone immediately checked their pockets or bags to find, to their relief, that their wallet was still in place. The accomplice then explained she was selling Christmas cards for a charity. Nearly 40% bought the cards, compared to only 10% who heard the appeal but had not felt the relief of still having their wallets. The researchers named this highly effective approach fear-then-relief (Dolinski & Szczucka, 2012).

foot-in-the-door phenomenon
The tendency for people who have first agreed to a small request to comply later with a larger request.

Other persuasion techniques rely on the size of the request being made. Experiments suggest that if you want people to do a big favor for you, you should get them to do a small favor first. In the best-known demonstration of this **foot-in-the-door phenomenon,** researchers posing as volunteers asked Californians to permit the installation of huge, poorly lettered "Drive Carefully" signs in their front yards. Only 17% consented. Others were first approached with a small request: Would they display 3-inch-high "Be a safe driver" window signs? Nearly all readily agreed. When approached 2 weeks later to allow the large, ugly signs in their front yards, 76% consented (Freedman & Fraser, 1966).

In this and many of the 100+ other foot-in-the-door experiments, the initial compliance – wearing a lapel pin, giving directions, signing a petition – was voluntary (Burger & Guadagno, 2003). When people commit themselves to public behaviors and perceive those acts to be their own doing, they come to believe more strongly in what they have done. One study found this was true even when the request came from a robot instead of a person (Lee & Laing, 2019). Apparently, foot-in-the-door works for birds, too: Lab pigeons were more likely to respond to a large request (to peck a square many times for a reward) if it was preceded by a smaller request (pecking the square fewer times), an effect the researchers dubbed "claw-in-the-door" (Bartonicek & Colombo, 2020).

Would you allow a campaign worker to put this large sign in your yard? Research suggests you'd be more likely to do so if you had first been asked to display a small sign or window sticker.
Aaron Roeth Photography

If a customer has already publicly committed by filling out the sales paperwork, they are more likely to agree to a higher price, an example of the lowball technique.
Freeograph/Shutterstock

Social psychologist Robert Cialdini is a self-described "patsy": "For as long as I can recall, I've been an easy mark for the pitches of peddlers, fund-raisers, and operators of one sort or another." To better understand why one person says yes to another, he spent 3 years as a trainee in sales, fund-raising, and advertising organizations, discovering how they exploit "the weapons of influence." He also put those weapons to the test in simple experiments. In one, Cialdini and his collaborators (1978) explored a variation of the foot-in-the-door phenomenon by experimenting with the **lowball technique** (Pascual et al., 2016). After the customer agrees to buy a new car with a bargain price and begins completing the sales forms, the salesperson removes the price advantage by charging for options or by checking with a boss who disallows the deal. Folklore has it that more lowballed customers now stick with the higher-priced purchase than would have agreed to it at the outset. Airlines and hotels use the tactic by attracting inquiries with great deals available on only a few seats or rooms; then, when those aren't available, they hope the customer will agree to a higher-priced option. Later experiments found that this works only if people verbally commit to their choice (Burger & Cornelius, 2003).

lowball technique
A tactic for getting people to agree to something. People who agree to an initial request will often still comply when the requester ups the ante. People who receive only the costly request are less likely to comply with it.

Marketing researchers and salespeople have found that the lowball technique works even when we are aware of a profit motive (Cialdini, 1988). A harmless initial commitment – returning a postcard for more information and a "free gift," agreeing to listen to an investment possibility – often moves us toward a larger commitment. Because salespeople sometimes exploited the power of those small commitments by trying to hold people to purchase agreements, many states now have laws that allow customers a few days to think over their purchases and cancel. To counter the effect of these laws, many companies use what the sales-training program of one company calls "a very important psychological aid in preventing customers from backing out of their contracts" (Cialdini, 1988, p. 78). They simply have the customer, rather than the salesperson, fill out the agreement. Having written it themselves, people usually live up to their commitment.

The foot-in-the-door phenomenon is a lesson worth remembering. Someone trying to seduce us – financially, politically, or sexually – will often sneak their foot in the door to create a momentum of compliance. The practical lesson: Before agreeing to a small request, think about what may follow.

And think, too, about what you might do next if you refuse a large request, known as the **door-in-the-face technique.** When Cialdini and his colleagues (1975) asked some of their Arizona State University students to chaperone delinquent children on a zoo trip, only 32% agreed to do so. With other students, though, the questioner asked if the students would commit 2 years as volunteer counselors to delinquent children. All refused (the equivalent of shutting a door in a salesperson's face). The questioner then counteroffered by asking if they would take the children on the zoo trip, saying, in effect, "OK, if you won't do that, would you do just this much?" With this technique, nearly twice as many – 56% – agreed to help. Forty-five years later in Germany, a group of researchers replicated the study and found the same result (Genschow et al., 2021).

door-in-the-face technique
A strategy for gaining a concession. After someone first turns down a large request (the door-in-the-face), the same requester counteroffers with a more reasonable request.

ONE-SIDED VERSUS TWO-SIDED APPEALS

Supporters of my [DM's] community's gay rights initiative faced a strategic question: Should they acknowledge and seek to refute each of the opposition's arguments? Or would that likely backfire, by planting ideas that people would remember long after forgetting the discounting? Again, common sense offers no clear answer. Acknowledging the opposing arguments might confuse the audience and weaken the case. On the other hand, a message might seem fairer and be more disarming if it recognizes the opposition's arguments.

Carol Werner and colleagues (2002) showed the disarming power of a simple two-sided message in an experiment on aluminum-can recycling. Signs added to wastebaskets in a University of Utah classroom building said, for example, "No Aluminum Cans Please!!!!! Use the Recycler Located on the First Floor, Near the Entrance." When a final persuasive message acknowledged and responded to the main counterargument – "It May Be Inconvenient. But It Is Important!!!!!!!!!!" – recycling reached 80%.

In simulated court trials, a defense case becomes more credible when the defense brings up damaging evidence before the prosecution does (Williams et al., 1993). Thus, a political candidate speaking to a politically informed group, or a community group advocating for or against gay rights, would indeed be wise to respectfully acknowledge the opposing viewpoint (Xu & Petty, 2022). So, *if your audience will be exposed to opposing views, offer a two-sided appeal.*

Two-sided appeals have another advantage: They can make the communicator seem more honest. When a salesperson mentioned a negative attribute of a product that was unimportant to the customer, the customer trusted the salesperson more and became more likely to buy the product (Pizzutti et al., 2016).

PRIMACY VERSUS RECENCY

Imagine you are participating in a debate. Are you more likely to win if you speak first or last?

Most of the time, you'll want to go first, as there is a **primacy effect:** Information presented early is most persuasive. First impressions are important. For example, can you sense a difference between these two descriptions?

primacy effect
Other things being equal, information presented first usually has the most influence.

- John is intelligent, industrious, impulsive, critical, stubborn, and envious.
- John is envious, stubborn, critical, impulsive, industrious, and intelligent.

When Solomon Asch (1946) gave these sentences to college students in New York City, those who read the adjectives in the intelligent-to-envious order rated the person more positively than did those given the envious-to-intelligent order. The earlier information seemed to color their interpretation of the later information, producing the primacy effect.

Some other primacy effect examples:

- Students who read positive TripAdvisor.com reviews of a hotel before the negative reviews liked the hotel more than those who read the negative reviews first (Coker, 2012).
- In political polls and in primary election voting, candidates benefit from being listed first on the ballot (Moore, 2004). Especially in "down ballot" races such as for judges and the school board, being first on the ballot can result in up to a 20 percentage point difference in votes – though usually the difference is between 2 and 8 percentage points, still more than enough to sway a close race (Grant, 2017, 2020).
- Super Bowl viewers were more likely to remember brands when commercials advertising them were first in the block of commercials (Li, 2010).
- Norman Miller and Donald Campbell (1959) found that students who read a trial transcript with the plaintiff's case presented first favored the plaintiff and those who read the defendant's case first favored the defendant.

recency effect
Information presented last sometimes has the most influence. Recency effects are less common than primacy effects.

What about the opposite possibility? Would our better memory of recent information ever create a **recency effect?** We have all experienced what the book of Proverbs observed: "The one who first states a case seems right, until the other comes and cross-examines." We know from our experience (as well as from memory experiments) that today's events can temporarily outweigh significant past events. Today's blizzard makes long-term global warming seem less a threat, just as today's sweltering heat makes it seem more a threat.

Would you stay in this hotel? Your decision might depend on whether you read the positive or negative online reviews first.
Ivanastar/Getty Images

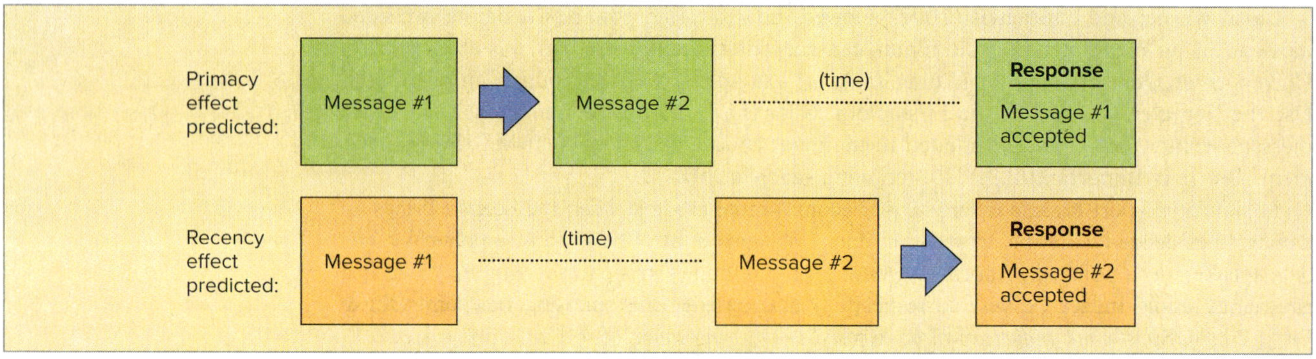

FIGURE 3

Primacy Effect versus Recency Effect

When two persuasive messages are back-to-back and the audience then responds at some later time, the first message has the advantage (primacy effect). When the two messages are separated in time and the audience responds soon after the second message, the second message has the advantage (recency effect).

To test for a possible recency effect, Miller and Campbell gave another group of students either the plaintiff's case or the defendant's case to read. A week later, the researchers had them read the other side's case and then immediately state their opinions. The results were the reverse of the other experiment – a recency effect. Apparently, the first section of arguments had largely faded from memory in the ensuing week, a result replicated in more recent studies using court cases (Engel et al., 2020).

Forgetting creates the recency effect (1) when enough time separates the two messages *and* (2) when the audience commits itself soon after the second message. When the two messages are back-to-back, followed by a time gap, the primacy effect usually occurs (**Figure 3**). This is especially so when the first message stimulates thinking (Haugtvedt & Wegener, 1994).

Dana Carney and Mahzarin Banaji (2008) discovered that order can also affect simple preferences. When encountering two people or products, people tend to prefer the first presented option. For example, when offered two similar-looking pieces of bubble gum, one placed after the other on a white clipboard, 62%, when asked to make a snap judgment, chose the first-presented piece. Across four experiments, the findings were consistent: "First is best."

In answer to the list of questions at the beginning of this section, the best advice for persuasion is the following:

- Use logic or emotion, depending on the audience and the message.
- Ask a small favor before making a big request.
- Offer two-sided messages that challenge arguments against your message.
- Go first or last – not in the middle – for best results.

In 2024, the U.S. Republican Party convention was followed by the Democratic Party convention a month later, after which there was a 3-month time gap before the election. Given experiments on primacy and recency, which party would benefit most from this timing?

(Left): ELIJAH NOUVELAGE/AFP/Getty Images; (Right): Ian Maule/Bloomberg/Getty Images

How Is It Said? The Channel of Communication

For persuasion, there must be communication. And for communication, there must be a **channel:** a face-to-face appeal, a written sign or document, a media advertisement.

channel of communication
The way the message is delivered — whether face-to-face, in writing, via video, or in some other way.

Commonsense psychology places faith in the power of written words. How do we try to get people to attend a campus event? We post notices. How do we get drivers to slow down and keep their eyes on the road? We put "Drive Carefully" messages on billboards. How do we discourage students from dropping trash on campus? We post antilitter messages on campus bulletin boards.

ACTIVE EXPERIENCE OR PASSIVE RECEPTION?

Are spoken appeals more persuasive? Not necessarily. Those of us who speak publicly, as teachers or persuaders, often become so enamored of our spoken words that we overestimate their power. Ask college students what aspect of their college experience has been most valuable or what they remember from their first year, and few, we are sad to say, recall the brilliant lectures that we faculty remember giving.

Written and visual appeals are both passive and thus have similar hurdles to overcome. Many are relatively ineffective. For example, only 1 out of 1,000 online ads results in someone clicking on the link. Yet the ads do have an effect: When a website was advertised, traffic increased 65% over the week (Fulgoni & Mörn, 2009).

With such power, can the media help a wealthy political candidate buy an election? In the United States, the candidate with more money wins about 90% of the time, especially in House races (Open Secrets, 2023). Winning candidates for Congress outspent their opponents 2 to 1: $2.3 million compared to $1.1 million (Lowery, 2014). Advertising exposure helps make an unfamiliar candidate into a familiar one. Mere exposure to unfamiliar stimuli breeds liking.

Mere repetition can also make statements believable (Dechêne et al., 2010; De Keersmaecker et al., 2020). Both adults and children are more likely to believe a statement they have heard twice instead of once (Fazio & Sherry, 2020; Unkelbach & Speckmann, 2021). The more familiar and recognizable a statement is, the more likely people will come to believe it's true even if it is not (Unkelbach et al., 2019). If people hear something enough, they often come to believe it — a principle used by advertisers and politicians alike.

"If they just repeat attacks enough, and outright lies over and over again . . . people start believing it."

—Barack Obama, speaking at the University of Michigan, July 2016

Researcher Hal Arkes (1990) called such findings "scary." As political manipulators know, believable lies can displace hard truths. Repeated clichés can conceal complex realities. In the political realm, even correct information may fail to discount implanted misinformation (Bullock, 2006; Nyhan & Reifler, 2008). Such politically biased information processing is bipartisan, report Peter Ditto and his colleagues (2019). They found "clear evidence of partisan bias in both liberals and conservatives, and at virtually identical levels." When evidence supports our views, we find it cogent; when the same evidence contradicts our views, we fault it.

Overall, retractions of previously provided information rarely work; people tend to remember the original story, not the retraction (Ecker et al., 2011; Lewandowsky et al., 2012). In the romantic comedy *When Harry Met Sally*, Harry says he'll take back a statement that offended Sally. "You can't take it back — it's already out there," Sally replies. Courtroom lawyers understand this, which is why they will take the risk of saying something that might be retracted, knowing the jury will remember it anyway. If you're trying to counteract a falsehood, research suggests you should provide an alternative story that's simple — and repeat it several times (Ecker et al., 2011; Schwarz et al., 2007).

Mere repetition of a statement also serves to increase its fluency — the ease with which it spills off our tongue — which increases believability (McGlone & Tofighbakhsh, 2000). Other factors, such as rhyming, further increase fluency and believability. "Haste makes waste" may say essentially the same thing as "rushing causes mistakes," but it seems more true. Whatever makes for fluency (familiarity, rhyming) also makes for credibility.

Because passively received appeals are sometimes effective and sometimes not, can we specify in advance the issues most amenable to persuasion? There is a simple rule: The more familiar people are with an issue, the less persuadable they are. On minor issues, such as which brand of aspirin to buy, it's easy to demonstrate the media's power. On more familiar and important issues, such as attitudes about a lengthy and controversial war, persuading people is like trying to push a piano uphill. It is not impossible, but one shove won't do it.

Active experience also strengthens attitudes. When we act, we amplify the idea behind what we've done, especially when we feel responsible. In addition, attitudes more often endure and influence our behavior when rooted in our own experience. Compared with attitudes formed passively, experience-based attitudes are more confident, more stable, and less vulnerable to attack. That's one reason why so many companies now aim to advertise through consumer-generated ads, viral videos, Instagram pages, Twitter/X feeds, and online games: Consumers who have interactive experiences with brands and products are more engaged than those who merely see or hear advertisements (Huang et al., 2013). Someone who shares a viral video with others will remember the experience much longer than someone who saw the same video as a TV commercial. Interactive websites also seem to be more effective. In one study, Dutch students viewed one of two websites for the fictional company HappyBev: one that simply displayed its corporate message and another that allowed users to comment on the message and then displayed those comments. Those who appreciated the interactivity of the comment-enabled site saw the company as more credible and identified with it more (Eberle et al., 2013).

PERSONAL VERSUS MEDIA INFLUENCE

Persuasion studies demonstrate that the major influence on us is not the media but our contact with people. Modern selling strategies seek to harness the power of word-of-mouth personal influence through "viral marketing," "creating a buzz," and "seeding" sales (Walker, 2004). The *Harry Potter* series was not expected to be a bestseller (the first book in the series had a first printing of 500 copies). It was kids talking to other kids that made it so.

"You do realize, you will never make a fortune out of writing children's books?"

—J. K. Rowling's literary agent before the release of *Harry Potter and the Sorcerer's Stone*, 1998

During the 2010 midterm elections, people who saw photos of their friends voting on Facebook were more likely to vote (Bond et al., 2012). In the 2012 election, campaign contacts such as knocking on doors and calling voters increased turnout by 7 to 8 percentage points in heavily targeted areas (Enos & Fowler, 2016). These strategies work in public health arenas as well. In Kenya, untreated tap water causes disease and death, especially among children. Yet few families treated their water until a nonprofit organization enlisted one person in each community to refill the communal chlorine tank and teach everyone about the importance of treating their water (Coster, 2014). Personal contact persuades.

In a field experiment, researchers tried to reduce the frequency of heart disease among middle-aged adults in three small California cities. To check the relative effectiveness of personal and media influence, they examined 1,200 participants before the project began and at the end of each of the following 3 years. Residents of Tracy, California, received no persuasive appeals other than those occurring in their regular media. In Gilroy, California, a 2-year multimedia campaign used TV, radio, newspapers, and direct mail to teach people about coronary risk and what they could do to reduce it. In Watsonville, California, this media campaign was supplemented by personal contacts with two-thirds of those participants whose blood pressure, weight, and age put them in a high-risk group. Using behavior-modification principles, the researchers helped the Watsonville participants set specific goals and reinforced their successes (Farquhar et al., 1977; Maccoby, 1980; Maccoby & Alexander, 1980).

Personal contact can increase voter turnout.
Ariel Skelley/Blend Images LLC

As **Figure 4** shows, after 1, 2, and 3 years, the high-risk participants in Tracy (the control town) were at about as much at risk as before. High-risk participants in Gilroy, who were deluged with

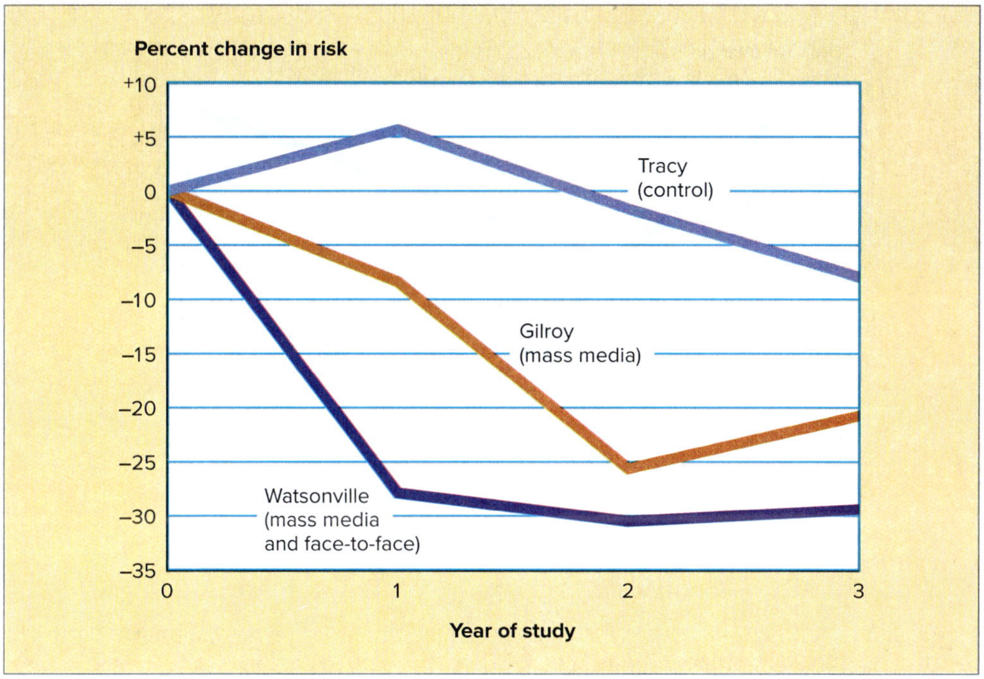

FIGURE 4

Percentage Change from Baseline (0) in Coronary Risk After 1, 2, or 3 Years of Health Education

Source: Data from Maccoby, 1980.

media appeals, improved their health habits and decreased their risk. Those in Watsonville, who received personal contacts as well as the media campaign, changed the most. Given these results, what techniques might be effective for the important public health messages of the current time?

MEDIA INFLUENCE: THE TWO-STEP FLOW Although face-to-face influence is usually greater than media influence, we should not underestimate the media's power. Those who personally influence our opinions must get their ideas from some source, and often their sources are the media. Elihu Katz (1957) observed that many of the media's effects operate in a **two-step flow of communication:** from media to opinion leaders to everyone else. In any large group, it is these *opinion leaders* and trendsetters – "the influentials" – that marketers and politicians seek to woo (Keller & Berry, 2003). Opinion leaders are individuals perceived as experts. They may include talk show hosts and editorial columnists; doctors, teachers, and scientists; and people in all walks of life who have made it their business to absorb information and to inform their friends and family. If I [DM] want to evaluate computer equipment, I defer to the opinions of my sons, who get many of their ideas from what they read online. Sell them and you will sell me.

two-step flow of communication

The process by which media influence often occurs through opinion leaders, who in turn influence others.

The two-step flow of information influences the drugs your doctor describes, reported a Stanford School of Business research team (Nair et al., 2008). Doctors look to opinion leaders within their social network – often a university hospital-based specialist – when deciding what drugs to favor. For more than 9 in 10 doctors, this influence comes through personal contact. The largest drug companies know that opinion leaders drive sales, and therefore, they target about one-third of their marketing dollars on these influential people.

The two-step flow model reminds us that media influences penetrate the culture in subtle ways. Even if the media had little direct effect on people's attitudes, they could still have a major indirect effect. Those rare children who grow up without watching television do not grow up beyond television's influence. Unless they live as hermits, they will join in TV-imitative play on the schoolground. They will ask their parents for the TV-related toys their friends have. They will beg or demand to watch their friends' favorite programs, and they will do so when visiting friends' homes. Parents can just say no, but they cannot switch off television's influence.

COMPARING MEDIA Lumping together all media, from mass mailings to television to social media, oversimplifies. Studies comparing different media find that the more lifelike

FIGURE 5

Opinion Change Based on Message Difficulty and By Medium

Easy-to-understand messages are most persuasive when videotaped. Difficult messages are most persuasive when written. Thus, the difficulty of the message interacts with the medium to determine persuasiveness.
Source: Chaiken & Eagly (1976).

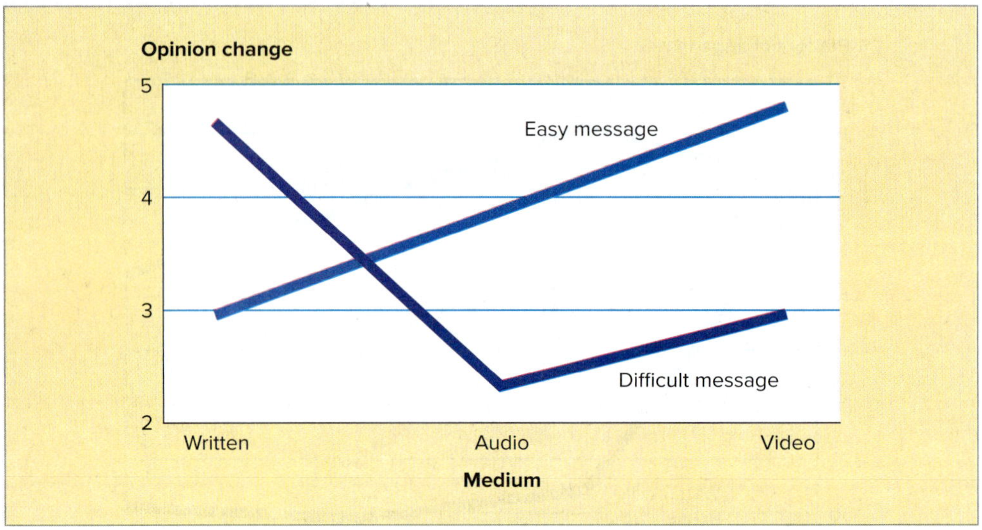

the medium, the more persuasive its message. Thus, the order of persuasiveness seems to be: live (face-to-face), video, audio, and written. If you want to persuade someone who disagrees with you, it's better to speak than to write to them. Your voice humanizes you (Schroeder et al., 2017). In this case, choose FaceTime, not texting.

However, messages are best *comprehended* and *recalled* when written. Comprehension is one of the first steps in the persuasion process (recall Figure 2). Shelly Chaiken and Alice Eagly (1976) reasoned that if a message is difficult to comprehend, persuasion should be greatest when the message is written because readers will be able to work through the message at their own pace. They gave University of Massachusetts students easy or difficult messages in writing, as audio, or as video. **Figure 5** displays their results: Difficult messages were indeed most persuasive when written; easy messages, when videoed. The TV medium takes control of the pacing of the message away from the recipients. By drawing attention to the communicator and away from the message itself, TV also encourages people to focus on peripheral cues, such as the communicator's attractiveness (Chaiken & Eagly, 1983).

THE INFLUENCE OF ADULTS ON CHILDREN Communication flows from adults to children – although as most parents and teachers can tell you, getting them to listen is not always easy. Your parents likely taught you which foods are healthy and which aren't. But how effective were their appeals? In one experiment, children read one of three versions of a story about a girl who ate wheat crackers: one in which she "felt strong and healthy," another in which she "thought the crackers were yummy, and she was happy," and a third with no additional description. The children then had the opportunity to eat some of the crackers. Guess who ate the most? Surprisingly, it was the children who read that the girl ate them – and nothing else. Those who heard they were yummy ate fewer, and those who heard they were healthy ate less than half as many. The same was true for younger children given messages about carrots (Maimaran & Fishbach, 2014). The lesson: When you're trying to get children to eat healthy food, just give it to them, and forget about saying anything else. If you have to say something, say it's yummy, not healthy.

To Whom Is It Said? The Audience

Persuasion varies with who . . . says what . . . by what medium . . . to whom. Let's consider two audience characteristics: age and thoughtfulness.

HOW OLD ARE THEY?

As was evident during the 2016 and 2020 U.S. presidential campaigns – with Donald Trump the decided favorite of older voters and Bernie Sanders of younger voters – people's social and political attitudes correlated with their age. Social psychologists offer two possible explanations for age differences:

- A *life cycle explanation:* Attitudes change (for example, become more conservative) as people grow older.
- A *generational explanation:* Attitudes do *not* change; older people largely hold onto the attitudes they adopted when they were young. Because these attitudes are different from those being adopted by young people today, a generation gap develops. (**Figure 6** offers one example of a larger generation gap.)

The evidence mostly supports the generational explanation. In surveys and resurveys of groups of younger and older people over several years, the attitudes of older people usually show less change than do those of young people. As David Sears (1979, 1986) put it, researchers have "almost invariably found generational rather than life cycle effects."

The teens and early twenties are important formative years (Koenig et al., 2008; Krosnick & Alwin, 1989). Attitudes are changeable during young adulthood, and the attitudes formed tend to stabilize through middle adulthood. Polling data on more than 300,000 people shows that political attitudes formed at age 18 – Republican-favoring during the Reagan era and Democratic-favoring during the Obama era – tend to last into later adulthood (Ghitza et al., 2019). Young adulthood is also the time when people are more susceptible to joining cults or terrorist organizations – entities also influenced by several other elements of persuasion, including personal communications, group influences, and emotional appeals (Bloom, 2017; Jasko et al., 2020).

Adolescent and early adult experiences are formative partly because they make deep and lasting impressions. When Howard Schuman and Jacqueline Scott (1989) asked people to name the one or two most important national or world events of the previous half-century, most recalled events from their teens or early twenties – perhaps partially because these events impacted the course of their lives (Gluck et al., 2019). While few people are likely to forget the COVID-19 pandemic and its associated disruptions, these events had a larger impact on the attitudes and livelihood of teens and younger adults.

That is not to say that older adults are inflexible. People born in the 1930s, often known as the Silent Generation for their conservative outlook, increased their approval of modern cultural ideas such as premarital sex and working mothers as they aged from their 40s to their 70s (Donnelly et al., 2015; Twenge et al., 2015). They also became more supportive

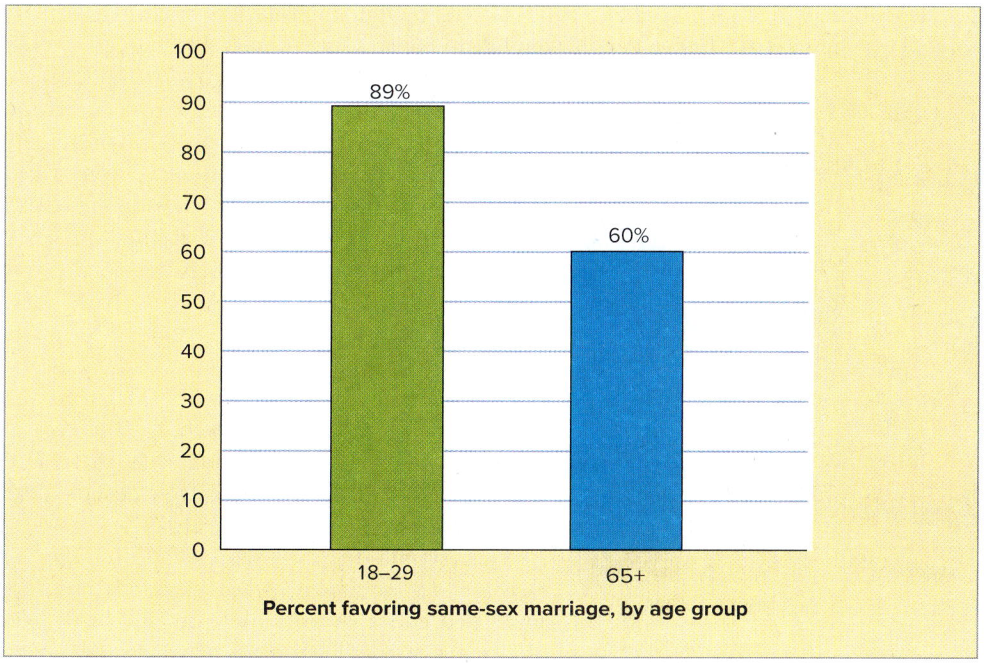

FIGURE 6

The Generation Gap in U.S. Attitudes toward Same-Sex Marriage, 2023.

A "life cycle" explanation of generational differences in attitudes suggests that people become more conservative with age. A "generational explanation" suggests that each generation holds on to attitudes formed during the adolescent and early adult years.
Source: Gallup polls

of same-sex marriage (Twenge & Blake, 2020). They had apparently changed with the times. Few of us are utterly uninfluenced by changing cultural norms.

WHAT ARE THEY THINKING?

The crucial aspect of central route persuasion is not the message but the responses it evokes in a person's mind. Our minds are not sponges that soak up whatever pours over them. If a message summons favorable thoughts, it persuades us. If it provokes us to think of contrary arguments, we remain unpersuaded.

FOREWARNED IS FOREARMED – IF YOU CARE ENOUGH TO COUNTERARGUE What circumstances breed **counterargument** – being able to come up with arguments against something? First, knowing someone is going to try to persuade you allows you to think of counterarguments. If you had to tell your family that you wanted to drop out of school, you would likely anticipate their pleading with you to stay. So you might develop a list of arguments to counter every conceivable reason they might give – and you'd then be less likely to be persuaded by them (Freedman & Sears, 1965). In courtrooms, too, defense attorneys sometimes forewarn juries about prosecution evidence to come. With mock juries, such "stealing thunder" neutralizes its impact (Dolnik et al., 2003).

counterargument
Thinking of reasons why a persuasive message might be wrong.

"To be forewarned and therefore forearmed . . . is eminently rational if our belief is true; but if our belief is a delusion, this same forewarning and forearming would obviously be the method whereby the delusion rendered itself incurable."

—C. S. Lewis, *Screwtape Proposes a Toast*, 1965

DISTRACTION DISARMS COUNTERARGUING Persuasion is also enhanced by a distraction that keeps people from thinking about counterarguments (Festinger & Maccoby, 1964; Keating & Brock, 1974; Osterhouse & Brock, 1970). Participants who read a message while also watching a video (and thus "multitasking") were less likely to counterargue (Jeong & Hwang, 2012). Political ads often use this technique. The words promote the candidate, and the visual images keep us occupied so we don't analyze the words. Distraction is especially effective when the message is simple (Harkins & Petty, 1982; Regan & Cheng, 1973). Sometimes, though, distraction keeps us from processing an ad. That helps explain why ads viewed during violent or sexual shows are so often forgotten and ineffective (Bushman, 2005, 2007).

UNINVOLVED AUDIENCES USE PERIPHERAL CUES Recall the two routes to persuasion: the central route of systematic thinking and the peripheral route of heuristic cues. Like a road that winds through a small town, the central route has starts and stops as the mind analyzes arguments and formulates responses. Like the freeway that bypasses the town, the peripheral route speeds people to their destination. Analytical people – those with a high **need for cognition** – enjoy thinking carefully and prefer central routes (Cacioppo et al., 1996). People who like to conserve their mental resources – those with a low need for cognition – are quicker to respond to such peripheral cues as the communicator's attractiveness and the pleasantness of the surroundings. In one study, students were asked to imagine they were planning a spring break trip and were trying to decide on a destination. They then looked at the tourism websites of the five most-visited U.S. cities (Los Angeles, New York, San Francisco, Orlando, and Miami). Students who were more interested in a particular destination were more persuaded by the focus on the information provided on the website (the central route), while those who were less interested focused more on the website's design (the peripheral route) (Tang et al., 2012).

need for cognition
The motivation to think and analyze. Assessed by agreement with items such as "The notion of thinking abstractly is appealing to me" and disagreement with items such as "I only think as hard as I have to."

Are you more focused on the information on this website or its design? Your answer might depend on how interested you are in visiting New York.
NetPhotos/Alamy Stock Photo

This simple theory – that *what we think in response to a message is crucial,* especially if we are motivated and able to think about it – has generated many predictions, most of which have been confirmed (Axsom et al., 1987; Haddock et al., 2008; Harkins & Petty, 1987). Many experiments have explored ways to stimulate people's thinking,

- by using *rhetorical questions;*
- by presenting *multiple speakers* (for example, having each of three speakers give one argument instead of one speaker giving three);
- by making people *feel responsible* for evaluating or passing along the message;
- by *repeating* the message; or
- by getting people's *undistracted attention.*

The consistent finding with each of these techniques: *Stimulating thinking makes strong messages more persuasive and weak messages less persuasive (because of counterarguing).*

The theory also has practical implications. Effective communicators care not only about their images and their messages but also about how their audience is likely to react. In one series of experiments, liberals were more supportive of future-oriented messages, such as on gun control: "I would prefer to make a change, so that in the future people may own hunting rifles and pistols, but no one will have assault rifles." Conservatives responded more favorably when the same message appealed to nostalgia: "I would like to go back to the good old days, when people may have owned hunting rifles and pistols, but no one had assault rifles" (Lammers & Baldwin, 2018).

The best instructors get students to think actively. They ask rhetorical questions, provide intriguing examples, and challenge students with difficult problems. Such techniques foster the central route to persuasion. In classes in which the instruction is less engaging, you can still provide your own central processing. If you think about the material and elaborate on the arguments, you are likely to do better in the course.

SUMMING UP: What Are the Elements of Persuasion?

- What makes persuasion effective? Researchers have explored four factors: the communicator (who says it), the message (what is said), the *channel* (how it is said), and the audience (to whom it is said).
- *Credible* communicators tend to be persuasive. People who speak unhesitatingly and who talk fast seem more credible. So do people who argue against their own self-interest. An *attractive* communicator is especially effective when the peripheral route is used, such as in matters of taste and personal values.
- Associating a message with good feelings makes it more convincing. People often make quicker, less reflective judgments while in good moods. Fear-arousing messages can also be effective, especially if the recipients feel vulnerable but can take protective action.
- People are more likely to do a small favor if they are asked to do a big favor first (the *door-in-the-face technique*) and are more likely to agree to a big favor if they agree to a small favor first (the *foot-in-the-door phenomenon*). A variation on the foot-in-the-door phenomenon is the *lowball technique,* in which a salesperson offers a low price, elicits a commitment from the buyer, and then increases the price.
- How discrepant a message should be from an audience's existing opinions depends on the communicator's credibility. And whether a one- or two-sided message is more persuasive depends on whether the audience already agrees with the message, is unaware of opposing arguments, and is unlikely later to consider the opposition.
- When two sides of an issue are presented separately, the *primacy effect* often makes the first message more persuasive. If a time gap separates the presentations, the more likely result will be a *recency effect* in which the second message prevails.
- Another important consideration is how the message is communicated. Usually, face-to-face appeals work best. Print media can be effective for complex messages. The mass media can be effective when the issue is minor or unfamiliar and when the media reach opinion leaders.
- Finally, it matters who receives the message. The age of the audience makes a difference; young people's attitudes are more subject to change. What does the audience think while receiving a message? Do they think favorable thoughts? Do they counterargue? Were they forewarned?

HOW CAN PERSUASION BE RESISTED?

Explain some tactics to resist unwanted persuasion attempts.

Martial arts trainers devote just as much time teaching defensive blocks, deflections, and parries as they do teaching attack. Yet when it comes to social influence and persuasion, researchers have focused more on persuasive attack than on defense (Sagarin, 2002). Being persuaded comes naturally, Daniel Gilbert and colleagues (1990, 1993) reported. It is easier to accept persuasive messages than to doubt them. To *understand* an assertion (say, that lead pencils are a health hazard) is to *believe* it – at least temporarily, until one actively undoes the initial, automatic acceptance. If a distracting event prevents the undoing, the acceptance lingers.

Still, blessed with logic, information, and motivation, we do resist falsehoods. If the repair person's uniform and the doctor's title have intimidated us into unthinking agreement, we can rethink our habitual responses to authority. We can seek more information before committing time or money. We can question what we don't understand.

Attitude Inoculation

William McGuire wondered: Could we inoculate people against persuasion much as we inoculate them against a virus by giving them a vaccine with a milder form of the virus? Is there such a thing as **attitude inoculation?** He found there was: When participants were "immunized" by writing an essay refuting a mild attack on a belief, they were better able to resist a more powerful attack later (McGuire, 1964). With the spread of misinformation online, attitude inoculation can be likened to vaccinating against the virus of fake news.

attitude inoculation
Exposing people to weak attacks upon their attitudes so that when stronger attacks come, they will have refutations available.

DEVELOPING COUNTERARGUMENTS

One way inoculation can occur is by leading people to consider counterarguments – reasons why a persuasive message is wrong. Robert Cialdini and colleagues (2003) wondered how to bring counterarguments to mind in response to an opponent's ads. The answer, they suggested, is a "poison parasite" defense – one that combines a poison (strong counterarguments) with a parasite (similarities to an opponent's ads). In their studies, participants who viewed a familiar political ad were least persuaded by it when they had earlier seen counterarguments overlaid on a replica of the ad. Seeing the ad again thus also brought to mind the puncturing counterarguments. Antismoking ads have effectively done this, for example, by re-creating a "Marlboro Man" ad set in the rugged outdoors but instead showing a cowboy saying he "misses" his lung. These ads use images similar to the real ones but feature the powerful counterargument that smoking harms health.

Cialdini and his colleagues (2021) found the same was true for political ads. Poison parasite ads that combined a candidate's original ad with the counterargument were more persuasive than those only containing the counterargument. For example, a poison parasite

A "poison parasite" ad.
Retro AdArchives/Alamy Stock Photo

ad might reprint the candidate's original statement that he "helped create more than 5,000 jobs" but then note "all of the jobs [he] created were TEMPORARY and OUT-OF-STATE." That was more effective than the statement about temporary and out-of-state jobs alone.

Counterarguments also came into play when psychologist Christopher Bryan and his colleagues (2016) wondered how teens could be persuaded to choose healthier snacks. In a Texas middle school, one group of eighth-graders received the usual health-class appeal for healthier eating. But another group learned that the food industry used manipulative and deceptive strategies to sell junk food to young people, describing industry executives as "controlling, hypocritical adults." When later given the chance to choose snacks for a class party, teens who had learned the counterargument that junk food was a profit-grab by older people were more likely to favor carrots and water over cookies and soda. The lesson? Teens might be more likely to eat healthy food if it's framed as a rebellion.

Could attitude inoculation help counter the growing problem of "fake news" (false online news stories often shared via social media) and misinformation? Sander van der Linden and his colleagues (2017) exposed participants to a fake news story claiming that scientists have yet to reach a consensus about whether global warming is caused by humans (a false claim; 97% of climate scientists agree it is). Those who saw the false claim were later more likely to believe no consensus had been reached. But if readers were warned that "politically motivated groups" use "misleading tactics" to claim that there is no consensus – helping them develop a counterargument – they were less likely to believe the false claim. For more on countering misinformation, see "Focus On: Misinformation: Can Inoculation and Debunking Help?"

focus ON Misinformation: Can Inoculation and debunking Help?

When you open your social media feed, you see numerous news stories, some of them sensational. How do you know if they are true?

That is a challenge many people face in the age of instant information and artificial intelligence, including "deep fakes" that can manipulate images and videos (Duffy, 2023). With most people getting their news online, the spread of misinformation has become an enormous challenge for societies. Misinformation has led to real-life violence as well as negative public health outcomes such as lower vaccination rates (Pilditch et al., 2022).

Why do people believe fake news? Online platforms can make money by posting fake stories. In an analysis of 126,000 stories shared by 3 million people, fake news stories — especially about politics — spread faster and further than true stories (Vosoughi et al., 2018). Similarly, health news stories from lower-quality sources were discussed more on social media than those from higher-quality sources (Zhong, 2023).

Because it's shared more, fake news is often repeated more frequently, making it seem more believable (Effron & Raj, 2020; Fazio & Sherry, 2020). Even highly implausible statements, like "The Earth is a perfect square" or "Benjamin Franklin lived 150 years," are believed more often if they are repeated (Fazio et al. 2019; Lacassagne et al., 2022).

Misinformation also plays into people's tendency to want to feel good about their own group and denigrate the opposing group. Across three experiments, Democrats were more likely to believe positive news stories about Democrats and negative stories about Republicans; Republicans had the opposite beliefs. Adherents of both parties were more likely to share the information they believed, whether it was true or false. "It is an irony of our modern world that when so much of human knowledge is readily accessible in most people's pockets, misinformation remains such a critical issue," write Andrea Pereira, Elizabeth Harris, and Jay Van Bavel (2023). "Partisans who filter information through the lens of their identity are likely to come to different conclusions."

Social psychology researchers have begun to explore whether people can be inoculated against misinformation. One technique is a game called "Bad News" in which people are exposed to weakened "doses" of misinformation strategies (such as using emotional language or group polarization) and learn how to produce fake information themselves. This inoculation improves people's ability to spot misinformation (Basol, 2020; Pilditch et al., 2022). Similarly, people who tried their hand at writing fake news articles — and thus learned the techniques fake news uses to trick people — were later less likely to believe misinformation themselves (Maertens et al., 2021).

In a meta-analysis of 52 studies, researchers found that people who learned detailed counterarguments (rather than simply hearing the information was wrong) were less likely to believe false claims (Chan et al., 2017). So if your social media friend spreads a fake news story, don't just post that it's wrong; instead, link to a story from a reliable source that debunks it with counterarguments (van der Meer & Jin, 2020).

Another intervention, called "Project Real," trains teens with strategies to recognize fake news, such as reading beyond the headline and checking with other online sources (Skipper et al., 2023). This type of *prebunking* seems to work better than trying to debunk fake news stories after exposure when they are already encoded in memory (van der Linden, 2023). Whether through inoculation before exposure or debunking through reliable sources afterward, the fight against misinformation continues to be one of the major challenges of our time.

INOCULATING CHILDREN AGAINST PEER PRESSURE TO SMOKE

Consider how laboratory research findings can lead to practical applications. One research team had high school students "inoculate" seventh-graders against peer pressures to smoke cigarettes (McAlister et al., 1980). The seventh-graders were taught to respond to advertisements with counterarguments. They also acted in role plays in which, after being called "chicken" for not taking a cigarette, they answered with statements such as "I'd be a real chicken if I smoked just to impress you." After several of these sessions during the seventh and eighth grades, the inoculated students were half as likely to begin smoking as were uninoculated students at another middle school – one that had an identical parental smoking rate (**Figure 7**).

Other research teams have confirmed that inoculation procedures reduce teen smoking (Botvin et al., 1995, 2008; Evans et al., 1984; Flay et al., 1985). Most newer efforts emphasize strategies for resisting social pressure. One study exposed sixth- to eighth-graders to antismoking films or to information about smoking, together with role plays of student-generated ways of refusing a cigarette (Hirschman & Leventhal, 1989). A year and a half later, 31% of those who watched the antismoking films had taken up smoking. Among those who role-played refusing, only 19% had begun smoking.

Antismoking and drug education programs apply other persuasion principles, too. They use attractive peers to communicate information. They trigger the students' own cognitive processing ("Here's something you might want to think about"). They get the students to make a public commitment (by making a rational decision about smoking and then

FIGURE 7

Percent of Teens Smoking by Experimental Condition

The percentage of cigarette smokers at an "inoculated" middle school was much less than at a matched control school using a more typical smoking education program.
Source: Data from McAlister et al., 1980; Telch et al., 1981.

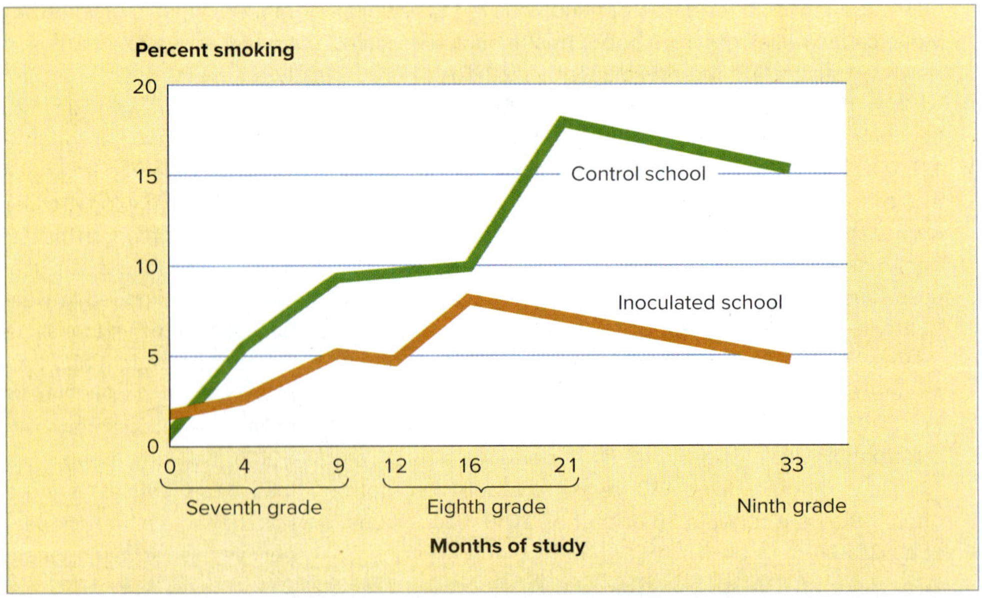

announcing it, along with their reasoning, to their classmates). These appeals and others seem to have worked: Only 6% of twelfth-graders in the United States smoked tobacco cigarettes in the last month in 2019, down from 38% in 1976.

The new concern is e-cigarettes, which 21% of twelfth-graders in 2022 used to vape nicotine in the last month (Miech et al., 2022). Just as with cigarettes, e-cigarette advertisements appear to increase teen vaping (Hansen et al., 2020; Loukas et al., 2019; Padon et al., 2018). Programs teaching teens to counter-argue vaping ads should be effective; those who were aware of how e-cigarette brands advertise their products were less likely to vape (Dai et al., 2022).

Children are the advertiser's dream. Researchers have therefore studied ways to inoculate children against the more than 10,000 ads they see each year, many as they are glued to a TV set, tablet, or phone.
JGI/Jamie Grill/Getty Images

INOCULATING CHILDREN AGAINST THE INFLUENCE OF ADVERTISING

In 2022, the European Union passed a law banning targeted advertising aimed at children online (Gill, 2022). The effort is only the latest aimed at protecting children from advertising's influence.

"In general, my children refuse to eat anything that hasn't danced on television."
—Erma Bombeck

Past research found that children, especially those under 8 years old, (1) had trouble distinguishing commercials from programs and fail to grasp their persuasive intent, (2) trust advertising rather indiscriminately, and (3) badger their parents for advertised products (Adler et al., 1980; Feshbach, 1980; Palmer & Dorr, 1980). In a more recent study, preschool children implicitly trusted ads on YouTube (Vanwesenbeeck et al., 2020) – which is important, as YouTube is now the primary source of video for young children. Children, it seems, are an advertiser's dream: gullible, vulnerable, and an easy sell.

Armed with these findings, citizens' groups have given the advertisers of such products a chewing out. A "Mothers' Statement to Advertisers" (Motherhood Project, 2001) noted:

> For us, our children are priceless gifts. For you, our children are customers, and childhood is a "market segment" to be exploited. . . . The line between meeting and creating consumer needs and desire is increasingly being crossed, as your battery of highly trained and creative experts study, analyze, persuade, and manipulate our children. . . . The driving messages are "You deserve a break today," "Have it your way," "Follow your instincts. Obey your thirst," "Just Do It," "No Boundaries," "Got the Urge?" These [exemplify] the dominant message of advertising and marketing: that life is about selfishness, instant gratification, and materialism.

With much advertising moving online, new concerns arise. For example, young children may not recognize that online games they play (such as "Snack! in the Face" for Kentucky Fried Chicken) are actually advertising – often for unhealthy food (An & Kang, 2013). In one experiment, 7- and 8-year-old children who played these "advergames" were more likely to choose foods higher in sugar and fat than those who did not play the games (Mallinckrodt & Mizerski, 2007). Children were more likely to want to buy products featured in advergames than in ads placed in games not focused on the product (Ghosh & Dwivedi, 2022).

Children may not realize that online games are actually advertisements — or that cereal with the word "fruit" in its name doesn't actually contain any fruit.

On the other side are the commercial interests. They claim that ads allow parents to teach their children consumer skills and, more important, finance children's shows and videos. In the United States, the Federal Trade Commission has been in the middle, pushed by research findings and political pressures while trying to decide whether to place new constraints on ads for unhealthy foods and for R-rated movies aimed at underage youth.

As we saw previously, children can receive media literacy training to inoculate them – to an extent. Consumer advocates worry that inoculation may be insufficient. Better to clean the air than to wear gas masks, they argue.

Implications of Attitude Inoculation

The best way to build resistance to brainwashing probably is not just stronger indoctrination into one's current beliefs. If parents are worried that their children might start vaping, they might better teach their children how to counter persuasive appeals about vaping.

For the same reason, educators should be wary of creating a "germ-free ideological environment" in their churches and schools. People who live amid diverse views become more discerning and more likely to modify their views only in response to credible arguments (Levitan & Visser, 2008). Also, a challenge to one's views, if refuted, is more likely to solidify one's position than to undermine it, particularly if the threatening material can be examined with like-minded others (Visser & Mirabile, 2004). Cults apply this principle by forewarning members of how families and friends will attack the cult's beliefs. When the expected challenge comes, the member is armed with counterarguments.

SUMMING UP: How Can Persuasion Be Resisted?

- How do people resist persuasion? Developing *counter-arguments* can help.
- A mild attack can also serve as an *inoculation,* stimulating one to develop counterarguments that will then be available if and when a strong attack comes.
- This implies, paradoxically, that one way to strengthen existing attitudes is to challenge them, although the challenge must not be so strong as to overwhelm them.

CONCLUDING THOUGHTS: Being Open but Not Naïve

As recipients of persuasion, our human task is to live in the land between gullibility and cynicism. Some people say that being persuadable is a weakness. "Think for yourself," we are urged. But is being closed to informational influence a virtue, or is it the mark of a fanatic? How can we live with humility and openness to others and yet be critical consumers of persuasive appeals?

To be open, we can assume that every person we meet is, in some ways, our superior. Each person we encounter has some expertise that exceeds our own and thus has something to teach us. As we connect, we can hope to think critically, yet also to learn from this person and to reciprocate by sharing our knowledge.

Group Influence

CHAPTER

8

Peter Muller/Image Source

"Never doubt that a small group of thoughtful, committed citizens can change the world."

—Attributed to anthropologist Margaret Mead

We live in groups. Our world contains not only nearly 8 billion individuals but also 195 countries and hundreds of millions of other formal and informal groups — couples having dinner, roommates hanging out, business teams plotting strategy. How do such groups influence us? And how do individuals influence groups?

And what sets groups apart or drives groups to extremes? Researchers are looking more closely at this question in the age of social media. Imagine seeing a post from a politician in your favored political party. Do you share or retweet it? According to a study from New York University, you're more likely to share the post if it uses emotional or moral words such as "sad," "justice," or "shame" (Brady et al., 2019). Thus, the messages that spread the most widely online are those that pack the biggest emotional punch. With more angry posts circulating online, one side will feel morally justified in their position, while the other side reacts with distaste, further entrenching each side's views (Bail et al., 2018). When the views of individuals swirl within polarized groups, what comes out is different from what went in.

In this chapter, we will examine several intriguing phenomena of group influence. But first things first: What is a group and why do groups exist?

WHAT IS A GROUP?

Define *group*.

The answer to "What is a group?" seems self-evident – until several people compare their definitions. Are jogging partners a group? Are airplane passengers a group? Is a group those who identify with one another, who sense they belong together? Is a group those who share common goals and rely on one another? Does a group form when individuals become organized? When their relationships with one another continue over time? These are among the social-psychological definitions of a group (McGrath, 1984).

group
Two or more people who, for longer than a few moments, interact with and influence one another and perceive one another as "us."

Group dynamics expert Marvin Shaw (1981) argued that all groups have one thing in common: Their members interact. Therefore, he defines a **group** as two or more people who interact and who influence one another. A pair of jogging companions, then, would indeed constitute a group.

Different groups help us meet different human needs – to *affiliate* (to belong to and connect with others), to *achieve,* and to gain a social *identity* (Johnson et al., 2006). Unlike the great apes, we humans are "the cooperative animal" – "the ultra-social animal" (Tomasello, 2014). From our early ancestors to the present, we have intentionally collaborated to forage and hunt.

Given what you've just learned, do you think this is a group? What questions could you ask to find out?
Hill Street Studios/Tobin Rogers/Blend Images LLC

By Shaw's definition, students working individually in a computer lab would not be a group. Although physically together, they are more a collection of individuals than an interacting group. The distinction between unrelated individuals in a computer lab and interacting individuals sometimes blurs. People who are merely in one another's presence do sometimes, as we will see, influence one another. And at a football game, we may perceive ourselves as "us" fans in contrast with "them" – the opposing fans.

In this chapter, we consider three effects of others' mere presence: *social facilitation, social loafing,* and *deindividuation.* These three phenomena can occur with minimal interaction (in "minimal group situations"). Then we consider three examples of social influence in interacting groups: *group polarization, groupthink,* and *minority influence.*

SUMMING UP: What Is a Group?

A *group* exists when two or more people interact for more than a few moments, affect one another in some way, and think of themselves as "us."

SOCIAL FACILITATION: HOW ARE WE AFFECTED BY THE PRESENCE OF OTHERS?

Describe how we are affected by the mere presence of another person — by people who are merely present as a passive audience or as co-actors.

Have you ever sung to yourself in the shower and then tried to sing the same song with other people around? These are very different experiences. As social animals, we are primed to be ever-conscious of others. In this chapter, we'll explore how the presence of others affects us.

The Presence of Others and Dominant Responses

More than a century ago, Norman Triplett (1898), a psychologist interested in bicycle racing, noticed that cyclists' times were faster when they raced together than when each raced alone against the clock. Before he peddled his hunch (that others' presence boosts performance), Triplett conducted one of social psychology's first laboratory experiments. Children told to wind string on a fishing reel as rapidly as possible wound faster when they worked with competing co-actors than when they worked alone. "The bodily presence of another contestant . . . serves to liberate latent energy," concluded Triplett.

Later experiments found that others' presence led people to do simple multiplication problems and cross out designated letters faster. It also improves accuracy on simple motor tasks, such as keeping a metal stick in contact with a dime-sized disk on a moving turntable (Allport, 1920; Dashiell, 1930; Travis, 1925). People also – have you noticed? – eat more in the presence of others (Herman, 2015, 2017; Ruddock et al., 2019, 2021).

This **social facilitation** effect also occurs with animals. In the presence of others of their species, ants excavate more sand, chickens eat more grain, bats find food more quickly, and sexually active rat pairs mate more often (Bayer, 1929; Chen, 1937; Larsson, 1956; Wright et al., 2020).

social facilitation

(1) Original meaning: the tendency of people to perform simple or well-learned tasks better when others are present. (2) Current meaning: the strengthening of dominant (prevalent, likely) responses in the presence of others.

But wait: On other tasks, the presence of others instead *hinders* performance. Cockroaches, parakeets, and green finches learn mazes more slowly when in the presence of others of their species (Allee & Masure, 1936; Gates & Allee, 1933; Halfmann et al., 2020; Klopfer, 1958). This disruptive effect also occurs with people. Others' presence diminishes efficiency at learning nonsense syllables, completing a maze, and performing complex multiplication problems (Dashiell, 1930; Pessin, 1933; Pessin & Husband, 1933). In other words, people sometimes choke under pressure when they perform in front of others.

Social facilitation: Do you ride faster when cycling with others?
vm/Getty Images

Saying that others' presence sometimes facilitates performance and sometimes hinders it is about as satisfying as the typical Scottish weather forecast – predicting that it might be sunny but then again it might rain. By 1940, social facilitation research ground to a halt, and it lay dormant for 25 years until awakened by the touch of a new idea.

Social psychologist Robert Zajonc (1923–2008, pronounced *Zy-ence,* rhymes with *science*) wondered whether these seemingly contradictory findings could be reconciled. As often happens at creative moments in science, Zajonc (1965) used one field of

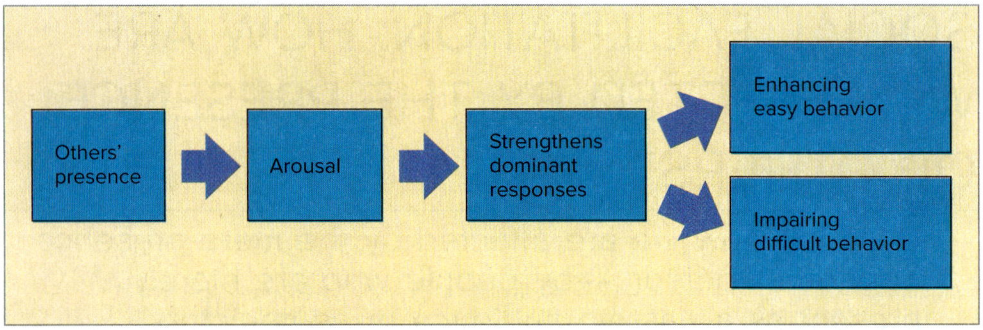

FIGURE 1

The Effects of Social Arousal

Robert Zajonc reconciled apparently conflicting findings by proposing that arousal from others' presence strengthens dominant responses (the correct responses only on easy or well-learned tasks).

research to illuminate another. The illumination came from a well-established experimental psychology principle: Arousal enhances whatever response tendency is dominant. Increased arousal enhances performance on easy tasks for which the most likely – "dominant" – response is correct. People solve easy anagrams, such as *akec,* fastest when aroused. On complex tasks, for which the correct answer is not dominant, increased arousal promotes *incorrect* responding. On more difficult anagrams, such as *theloacco,* people do worse when aroused.

Could this principle solve the mystery of social facilitation? It seemed reasonable to assume that others' presence will arouse or energize people (Mullen et al., 1997); most of us can recall feeling tense or excited in front of an audience. If social arousal facilitates dominant responses, it should *boost performance on easy tasks* and *hurt performance on difficult tasks.*

With that explanation, the confusing results made sense. Winding fishing reels, doing simple multiplication problems, and eating were all easy tasks, with well-learned or naturally dominant responses. Sure enough, having others around boosted performance.

Learning new material, doing a maze, and solving complex math problems were more difficult tasks with initially less probable correct responses. In these cases, the presence of others increased the number of *incorrect* responses on these tasks.

So, the same general rule – *arousal facilitates dominant responses* – worked in both cases (**Figure 1**). Suddenly, what had looked like contradictory results no longer seemed contradictory.

> "Discovery consists of seeing what everybody has seen and thinking what nobody had thought."
>
> —Albert von Szent-Györgyi, *The Scientist Speculates,* 1962

Zajonc's solution, so simple and elegant, left other social psychologists thinking what Thomas H. Huxley thought after first reading Darwin's *On the Origin of Species:* "How extremely stupid not to have thought of that!" It seemed obvious – once Zajonc had pointed it out. Perhaps, however, the pieces fit so neatly only through the spectacles of hindsight. Would the solution survive direct experimental tests?

After almost 300 studies of more than 25,000 people, the solution has survived (Bond & Titus, 1983; Guerin, 1993, 1999; van Meurs et al., 2022). Social arousal facilitates dominant, well-learned responses. For example, Peter Hunt and Joseph Hillery (1973) found that in others' presence, students took less time to learn a simple maze and more time to learn a complex one. And James Michaels and collaborators (1982) found that good pool players in a student union (who had made 71% of their shots while being unobtrusively observed) did even better when they knew they were being observed (80% when four observers came up to watch them play). Poor shooters (who had previously averaged 36%) did even worse (25%) when closely observed.

Athletes, actors, and musicians perform well-practiced skills, which helps explain why they often perform best when energized by the responses of a supportive audience. Studies of more than a quarter million college and professional athletic events worldwide reveal that home teams win approximately 6 in 10 games, with the home advantage larger for teamwork-focused sports (Jones, 2015; **Table 1**). The home advantage is amazingly constant over time and across sports. NBA basketball teams, NHL hockey teams, and international soccer football league teams have won more home games every year, without exception (Moskowitz & Wertheim, 2011).

TABLE 1 Home Advantage in Major Team Sports

Sport	Games Studied	Percentage of Home Games Won
Baseball	120,576	55.6
American football	11,708	57.3
Ice hockey	50,739	56.5
Basketball	30,174	63.7
Soccer	40,380	67.4

Source: Jeremy Jamieson (2010).

During the COVID-19 pandemic in 2020, when Germany's professional soccer league played games in empty stadiums – and thus without the energizing effect of a crowd – the home advantage disappeared (Smith, 2020). For elite athletes, in contrast to novices, *not* having a crowd can be anxiety-provoking. The empty stands at the 2020 summer Olympics (held in 2021) may have played a role in the performance of gymnast Simone Biles, who said the Games had been "really stressful" partially due to "not having an audience." She later withdrew from the individual all-around event (Bender, 2021).

Crowds: The Presence of Many Others

The effect of others' presence increases with their number (Jackson & Latané, 1981; Knowles, 1983). Sometimes the arousal and self-conscious attention created by a large audience interferes even with well-learned, automatic behaviors, such as speaking. Given *extreme* pressure and large crowds, we're vulnerable to "choking" (Böheim et al., 2019). Stutterers tend to stutter more in front of larger audiences than when speaking to just one or two people (Mullen, 1986b). Over 28 years of major tournaments, professional golfers' scores are worse in the final day's round than on the previous day – especially when they are in the lead and thus under more pressure (Wells & Skowronski, 2012).

Being *in* a crowd also intensifies positive or negative reactions. When they sit close together, friendly people are liked even more, and *un*friendly people are *dis*liked even more (Schiffenbauer & Schiavo, 1976; Storms & Thomas, 1977). In experiments with Columbia University students and with Ontario Science Center visitors, Jonathan Freedman and co-workers (1979, 1980) had people listen to a humorous tape or watch a movie with other participants. When they all sat close together, an accomplice could more readily induce the individuals to laugh and clap. As theater directors and sports fans know, and as researchers have confirmed, a "good house" is a full house (Aiello et al., 1983; Worchel & Brown, 1984). As recent experiments confirm, fun shared with others is more energizing – and fun (Reis et al., 2017). Being with others can also make negative experiences less negative: University rowing team members, perhaps aided by an endorphin boost from the communal activity, tolerate twice as much pain after rowing together than when rowing solo (Cohen et al., 2009).

Perhaps you've noticed that a class of 35 students feels more warm and lively in a room that seats just 35 than when spread around a room that seats 100. When others are close by, we are more likely to notice and join in their laughter or clapping. But crowding also enhances arousal, as Gary Evans (1979) found. He tested 10-person groups of University of Massachusetts students, either in a room 20 by 30 feet or in one 8 by 12 feet. Compared with those in the large room, those densely packed had higher pulse rates and blood pressure (indicating arousal). On difficult tasks, they made more errors, an effect of crowding replicated with university students in India (Nagar & Pandey, 1987). Crowding, then, has a similar effect to being observed by a crowd: it enhances arousal, which facilitates dominant responses.

Performing for a large, engaged audience can be highly arousing—energizing well-learned behaviors but sometimes creating self-conscious "choking."
Lynne Powe

Why Are We Aroused in the Presence of Others?

For something you do well, you will be energized to do best in front of others (unless you become hyperaroused and self-conscious and "choke"). For something you find difficult, good performance may seem impossible in the same circumstances. What is it about other people that creates arousal? Evidence supports three possible factors (Aiello & Douthitt, 2001; Feinberg & Aiello, 2006; Roberts et al., 2019): *evaluation apprehension, distraction,* and *mere presence.*

EVALUATION APPREHENSION

evaluation apprehension

Concern for how others are evaluating us.

Nickolas Cottrell surmised that observers make us apprehensive because we wonder how they are evaluating us. To test whether **evaluation apprehension** exists, Cottrell and associates (1968) blindfolded observers, supposedly in preparation for a perception experiment. In contrast to the effect of a watching audience, the mere presence of these blindfolded people did *not* boost a performer's well-practiced responses.

Other experiments confirmed that the enhancement of dominant responses is strongest when people think they are being evaluated. In one experiment, individuals running on a jogging path sped up as they came upon a woman seated on the grass—*if* she was facing them rather than sitting with her back turned (Worringham & Messick, 1983). However, for newer and more difficult tasks, performance can be hindered by being evaluated. Students who were just learning how to swing a golf club performed worse when told that a "golf expert" would critically evaluate their performance and give them a grade (Daou et al., 2019).

The self-consciousness we feel when being evaluated can also interfere with behaviors that we perform best automatically (Mullen & Baumeister, 1987). If self-conscious basketball players analyze their body movements while shooting critical free throws, they are more likely to miss. We perform some well-learned behaviors best without overthinking them.

DRIVEN BY DISTRACTION

Glenn Sanders, Robert Baron, and Danny Moore (1978; Baron, 1986) carried evaluation apprehension a step further. They theorized that when we wonder how co-actors are doing or how an audience is reacting, we become distracted. This *conflict* between paying attention to others and paying attention to the task overloads our cognitive system, causing arousal. We are "driven by distraction." This arousal comes not just from the presence of another person but also from other distractions, such as bursts of light (Sanders, 1981a, b).

In the open-office plan, people work in the presence of others. Office environments increasingly provide their workers with collaborative spaces (Arieff, 2011).
Cathy Yeulet/123RF

The presence of others is distracting because it diverts our attention from what we are doing. If you're thinking about others' reactions, you have less cognitive capacity for focusing on a difficult task. This is often what happens when athletes or performers "choke" under pressure during the big game or the opening night performance, even when they performed well during practice or during the dress rehearsal (Belletier et al., 2019).

Many new office buildings have replaced private offices with large, open areas. If the presence of others is distracting, open-office plans should disrupt performance on complex tasks. Due to social facilitation, however, performance on well-learned tasks might be better with an open office plan. Can you think of other examples of situations that might be distracting and thus affect performance?

SUMMING UP: Social Facilitation: How Are We Affected by the Presence of Others?

- Social psychology's most elementary issue concerns the mere presence of others. Some early experiments on this question found that performance improved with observers or co-actors present. Others found that the presence of others can hurt performance. Robert Zajonc reconciled those findings by applying a well-known principle from experimental psychology: Arousal facilitates dominant responses. Because the presence of others is arousing, the presence of observers or co-actors boosts performance on easy tasks (for which the correct response is dominant) and hinders performance on difficult tasks (for which incorrect responses are dominant) known as *social facilitation*.
- Being in a crowd, or in crowded conditions, is similarly arousing and facilitates dominant responses. That helps explain the home-field advantage in sports.
- But why are we aroused by others' presence? Experiments suggest that the arousal stems partly from *evaluation apprehension* and partly from distraction – a conflict between paying attention to others and concentrating on the task.

SOCIAL LOAFING: DO INDIVIDUALS EXERT LESS EFFORT IN A GROUP?

Assess the level of individual effort we can expect from members of workgroups.

Social facilitation usually occurs when people work toward individual goals and when their efforts, whether winding fishing reels or solving math problems, can be individually evaluated. These situations parallel some everyday work situations. But what happens when people pool their efforts toward a *common* goal and individuals are *not* accountable for their efforts? A team tug-of-war provides one such example. Organizational fundraising – using candy sale proceeds to pay for the class trip – provides another. So does a class group project on which all students get the same grade. On such "additive tasks" – tasks where the group's achievement depends on the sum of the individual efforts – will team spirit boost productivity? Will bricklayers lay bricks faster when working as a team than when working alone? Laboratory simulations provide answers.

Many Hands Make Light Work

Nearly a century ago, French engineer Max Ringelmann (reported by Kravitz & Martin, 1986) found that the collective effort of tug-of-war teams was but half the sum of the individual efforts. Contrary to the presumption that "in unity there is strength," this suggested that group members may actually be *less* motivated when performing additive tasks. Maybe, though, poor performance stemmed from poor coordination: people pulling a rope in slightly different directions at slightly different times. A group of Massachusetts researchers led by Alan Ingham (1974) cleverly eliminated that problem by making individuals think others were pulling with them, when, actually, they were pulling alone. Blindfolded participants were assigned the first position in the apparatus shown in **Figure 2** and told, "Pull as hard as you can."

FIGURE 2

The Rope-Pulling Apparatus

People in the first position pulled less hard when they thought people behind them were also pulling.

Alan G. Ingham

Due to social loafing, people make less noise clapping and shouting when in a crowd than when alone.
ferrantraite/Getty Images

They pulled 18% harder when they knew they were pulling alone than when they believed people behind them were also pulling.

Researchers Bibb Latané, Kipling Williams, and Stephen Harkins (1979; Harkins et al., 1980) kept their ears open for other ways to investigate this diminished effort, which they labeled **social loafing.** They observed that the noise produced by six people shouting or clapping "as loud as you can" was less than 3 times that produced by one person alone. Like the tug-of-war task, however, noisemaking is vulnerable to group inefficiency. So Latané and associates followed Ingham's example by leading their Ohio State University participants to believe others were shouting or clapping with them, when in fact they were doing so alone.

Their clever method was to blindfold six people, seat them in a semicircle, and have them put on headphones, over which they were blasted with noise. People could not hear their own shouting or clapping, much less than that of others in the semicircle. On various trials they were instructed to shout or clap either alone or along with the group. People who were told about this experiment guessed the participants would shout louder when with others because they would be less inhibited (Harkins & Petty, 1982). The actual result? Social loafing: When the participants believed five others were also either shouting or clapping, they produced one-third *less* noise than when they thought themselves alone. Social loafing occurred even when the participants were high school cheerleaders who believed themselves to be cheering together rather than alone (Hardy & Latané, 1986).

social loafing
The tendency for people to exert less effort when they pool their efforts toward a common goal than when they are individually accountable.

free riders
People who benefit from the group but give little in return.

Curiously, those who clapped both alone and in groups did not view themselves as loafing; they perceived themselves as clapping equally in both situations. This parallels what happens when students work on group projects for a shared grade. Williams reported that all agree loafing occurs – but no one admits to doing the loafing.

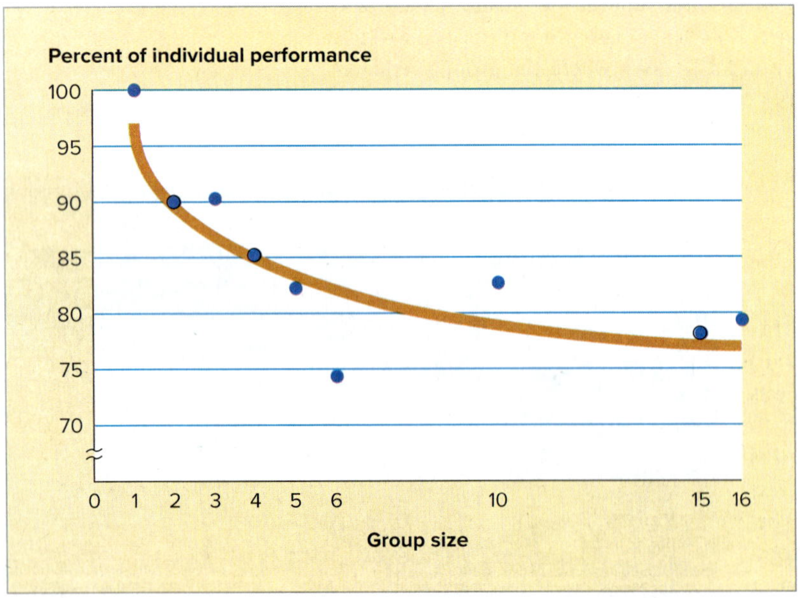

FIGURE 3

Effort Decreases as Group Size Increases

A statistical digest of 49 studies, involving more than 4,000 participants, revealed that effort decreases (loafing increases) as the size of the group increases. Each dot represents the aggregate data from one of these studies.
Source: Williams et al., (1992).

Political scientist John Sweeney (1973) observed social loafing in a cycling experiment. University of Texas students pumped exercise bicycles more energetically (as measured by electrical output) when they knew they were being individually monitored than when they thought their output was being pooled with that of other riders. In the group condition, people were tempted to **free-ride** on the group effort.

In this and 160 other studies (Karau & Williams, 1993; **Figure 3**), we see a twist on one of the psychological forces that makes for social facilitation: evaluation apprehension. In the social loafing experiments, individuals believed they were evaluated only when they acted alone. The group situation (rope pulling, shouting, and so forth) *decreased* evaluation apprehension. When people are not accountable and cannot evaluate their own efforts, responsibility is diffused across all group members (Harkins & Jackson, 1985;

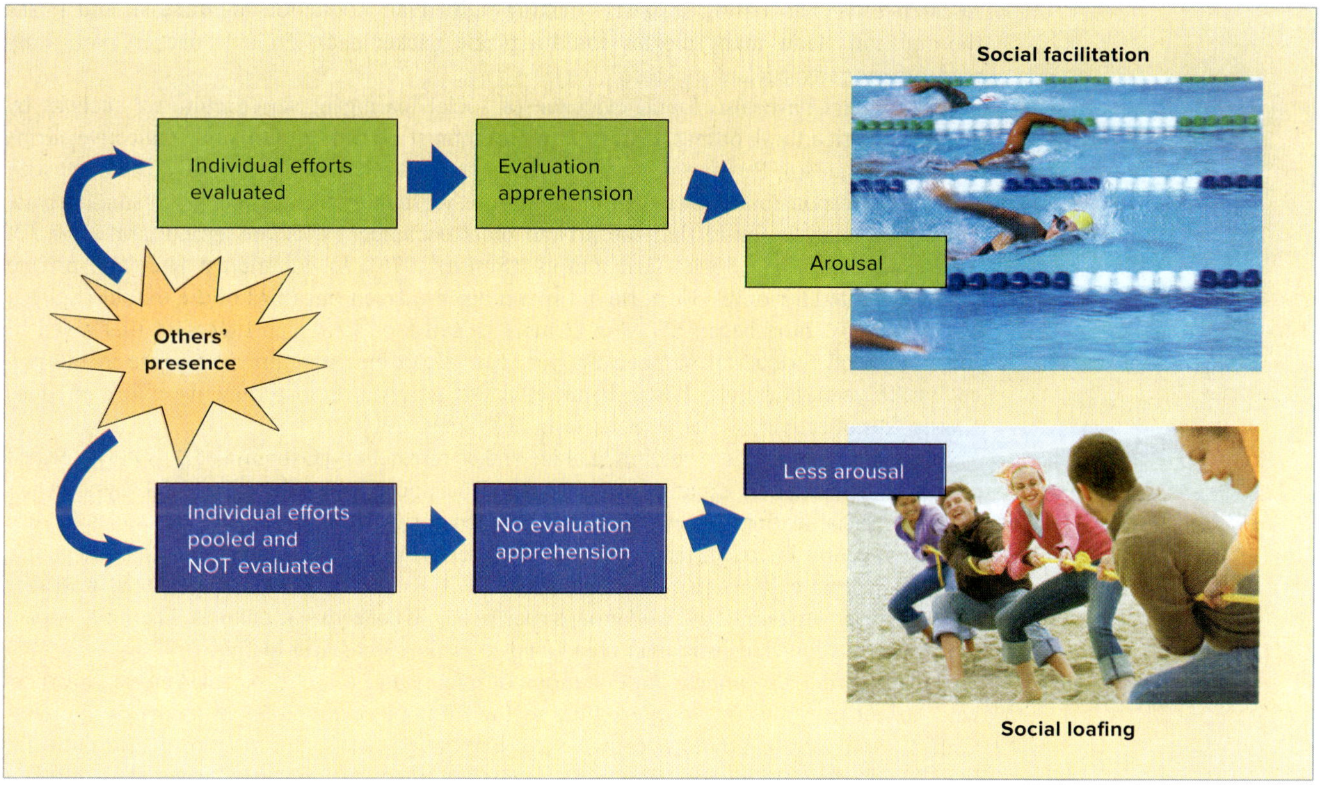

FIGURE 4

Social Facilitation or Social Loafing?

When individuals cannot be evaluated or held accountable, loafing becomes more likely. An individual swimmer is evaluated on her ability to win the race. In tug-of-war, no single person on the team is held accountable, so any one member might relax or loaf.

(Swimmers): imagenavi/Getty Images; *(Tug-of-war):* Thinkstock Images/Getty Images

Kerr & Bruun, 1981). By contrast, the social facilitation experiments *increased* exposure to evaluation. When made the center of attention, people self-consciously monitor their behavior (Mullen & Baumeister, 1987). So, when being observed *increases* evaluation concerns, social facilitation occurs; when being lost in a crowd *decreases* evaluation concerns, social loafing occurs (**Figure 4**).

To motivate group members, one strategy is to make individual performance identifiable. Some football coaches do this by filming and evaluating each player individually. Whether in a group or not, people exert more effort when their outputs are individually identifiable: University swim team members swim faster in intrasquad relay races when someone monitors and announces their individual times (Williams et al., 1989).

Social Loafing in Everyday Life

How widespread is social loafing? In the laboratory, the phenomenon occurs not only among people who are pulling ropes, cycling, shouting, and clapping but also among those who are pumping water or air, evaluating poems or editorials, producing ideas, typing, and detecting signals. Do these consistent results generalize to everyday worker productivity?

In workplace group experiments, employees have produced more when their individual performance was posted (Lount & Wilk, 2014). In one such experiment, assembly-line workers produced 16% more product when their individual output was identified, even though they knew their pay would be unaffected (Faulkner & Williams, 1996). Consider the example of workers in a pickle factory who were supposed to put only the big pickles into jars. But because the jars were then merged (and their individual work unchecked), the workers just stuffed in any size pickle. Williams, Harkins, and Latané (1981) noted that research on social loafing suggests "making individual production identifiable, and raises the question: 'How many pickles could a pickle packer pack if pickle packers were only paid for properly packed pickles?'"

Researchers have also found evidence of social loafing in varied cultures, such as by assessing agricultural output in formerly communist countries. On their collective farms under communism, Russian peasants worked one field one day, another field the next, with little direct responsibility for any given plot. For their own use, they were given small private plots. One analysis found that the private plots occupied 1% of the agricultural land, yet produced 27% of the Soviet farm output (Smith, 1976). In communist Hungary, private plots accounted for only 13% of the farmland but produced one-third of the output (Spivak, 1979). When China began allowing farmers to sell food grown in excess of that owed to the state, food production jumped 8% per year – 2.5 times the annual increase in the preceding 26 years (Church, 1986). In an effort to tie rewards to productive effort, modern Russia "decollectivized" many of its farms (Kramer, 2008).

What about collectivistic cultures? Latané and co-researchers (Gabrenya et al., 1985) repeated their sound-production experiments in Japan, Thailand, Taiwan, India, and Malaysia. Their findings? Social loafing was evident in all those countries, too. Seventeen later studies in Asia reveal that people in collectivistic cultures do, however, exhibit less social loafing than do people in individualistic cultures (Karau & Williams, 1993; Kugihara, 1999). As we noted in earlier chapters, loyalty to family and workgroups runs strong in collectivistic cultures. Likewise, women tend to be less individualistic than men – and to exhibit less social loafing.

Social loafing also appears in donations of money and time. In North America, workers who do not pay dues or volunteer time to their unions or professional associations nevertheless are usually happy to accept the associations' benefits. So, too, are public radio listeners and television viewers who don't respond to their station's fund drives. This hints at another possible explanation of social loafing: When rewards are divided equally, regardless of how much one contributes to the group, any individual gets more reward per unit of effort by free-riding on the group. Thus, people may slack off when their efforts are not individually monitored and rewarded – which may also enable them to overestimate their own relative contribution (Schroeder et al., 2016). Situations that welcome free riders can therefore be, in the words of one commune member, a "paradise for parasites." Humans are highly attuned to so-called free riders who mooch off group efforts: Children as young as 4 dislike people who are not contributing their share of work (Yang et al., 2018).

But surely collective effort does not always lead to slacking off. Sometimes the goal is so compelling and maximum output from everyone is so essential that team spirit maintains or intensifies effort. In an Olympic crew race, will the individual rowers in an eight-person crew pull their oars with less effort than those in a one- or two-person crew?

The evidence assures us they will not. People in groups loaf less when the task is *challenging, appealing,* or *involving* (Karau & Williams, 1993; Tan & Tan, 2008). On challenging tasks, people may perceive their efforts as indispensable (Harkins & Petty, 1982; Kerr, 1983; Kerr et al., 2007). When swimming the last leg of a relay race with a medal at stake, swimmers tend to swim even faster than in individual competition (Hüffmeier et al., 2012).

Teamwork at the Charles River regatta in Boston. Social loafing occurs when people work in groups but without individual accountability – unless the task is challenging, appealing, or involving, and the group members are friends.
leezsnow/E+/Getty Images

Groups also loaf less when their members are *friends* or they feel identified with or indispensable to their group (Gockel et al., 2008; Hou & Zhang, 2021; Karau & Williams, 1997; Worchel et al., 1998). On websites where people post informative tips about travel destinations, some people socially loaf by just reading others' contributions, while others contribute tips. Among Chinese citizens using these websites, those who more strongly identified with the travel site as a community were more likely to post tips; their identification with the group made them less likely to loaf (Chang et al., 2020). Perhaps because they have experience identifying with a group, people who have played team sports less often loaf (Czyz et al., 2016).

Even just expecting to interact with someone again serves to increase effort on team projects (Groenenboom et al., 2001). Collaborate on a class project with others you'll see often and you will feel more motivated than if you never expect to see them again. Cohesiveness intensifies effort.

These findings parallel those from studies of everyday workgroups. When groups are given challenging objectives, when they are rewarded for group success, and when there is a spirit of commitment to the "team," group members work hard (Hackman, 1986). Keeping workgroups small can also help members believe their contributions are indispensable (Comer, 1995).

SUMMING UP: Social Loafing: Do Individuals Exert Less Effort in a Group?

- Researchers study people's performance on tasks on which they can be evaluated individually. However, in many work situations, people pool their efforts and work toward a common goal without individual accountability.
- Group members often work less hard when performing such "additive tasks." This finding parallels everyday situations in which diffused responsibility tempts individual group members to *free-ride* on the group's effort, known as *social loafing*.
- People may, however, put forth even more effort in a group when the goal is important, rewards are significant, and team spirit exists.

DEINDIVIDUATION: WHEN DO PEOPLE LOSE THEIR SENSE OF SELF IN GROUPS?

Define "deindividuation" and identify the circumstances that trigger it.

In May 2020, George Floyd was brutally killed by police in Minneapolis, Minnesota. A bystander filmed the murder, capturing the agonizing moments when Floyd called out for his mother as he struggled to breathe and then died. Almost immediately after the video circulated, protests began, first in Minnesota and then in other cities. During the day, these protests were overwhelmingly peaceful, with people marching, chanting, and holding signs.

After dark, however, some people acted differently: They broke windows, stole merchandise, and set fires that burned down stores and vehicles. George Floyd's family condemned the violence in a statement, saying, "we cannot endanger each other as we respond to the necessary urge to raise our voices in unison and in outrage. Looting and violence distract from the strength of our collective voice" (Faircloth, 2020; Goldbaum, 2020; KSTP, 2020).

Six months later in January 2021, a mob wishing to disrupt the counting of the electoral votes for the U.S. presidential election stormed the Capitol building, breaking windows and doors, vandalizing offices, and beating police officers with flagpoles, fire extinguishers, and fists. At one point, a huge crowd of rioters rocked back and forth yelling "Heave, ho!" in an attempt to break through a line of police officers, crushing a police officer's arm in a door. When the riot was over, 5 people had been killed and more than 100 others were injured. Within days of the riot, two additional police officers took their own lives (Cameron, 2022; Jackman, 2021).

Many of the spring 2020 rioters later wondered what had possessed them. One man arrested for looting in North Carolina in May 2020 later said, "I'm kind of ashamed of myself, because I knew better" (Lamb, 2020). Similarly, some participants in the January 2021 Capitol riot expressed remorse. "I got caught up in the moment," lamented one. "I realize now that my actions were inappropriate and I beg for forgiveness" (Colt, 2021).

Deindividuation: During the insurrection at the U.S. Capitol on January 6, 2021, rioters were disinhibited by social arousal and the anonymity provided by the size of the crowd.
lev radin/Shutterstock

Doing Together What We Would Not Do Alone

Why did these individuals act this way? They were so caught up in the behavior of the group that they disregarded rules they would usually follow. As we saw earlier, being in a group can lead to arousal and to a diffusion of responsibility. When arousal and diffused responsibility combine and normal inhibitions diminish, the results may be startling. People may commit acts that range from a mild lessening of restraint (throwing food in the dining hall, snarling at a referee, screaming during a rock concert, insulting others online) to impulsive self-gratification (group vandalism, orgies, thefts) to destructive social explosions (police brutality, riots, lynchings). As West Virginia State representative Derrick Evans said on January 6, 2021 at the Capitol, "I don't know where we're going, but I'm following the crowd" (Duffy, 2021). Evans was later sentenced to three months in prison for his involvement in the riot (Millman, 2022).

These unrestrained behaviors have something in common: They are provoked by the power of being in a group. Groups can generate a sense of excitement, of being caught up in something bigger than one's self. It is hard to imagine a single rock fan screaming deliriously at a private rock concert or a single rioter setting a car on fire. In group situations, people are more likely to abandon normal restraints, to forget their individual identity, to become responsive to group or crowd norms – in a word, to become what Leon Festinger, Albert Pepitone, and Theodore Newcomb (1952) labeled **deindividuated.** When deindividuation occurs, individuals lose their self-awareness and go along with the group. What circumstances elicit this psychological state?

deindividuation
Loss of self-awareness and evaluation apprehension; occurs in group situations that foster responsiveness to group norms, good or bad.

GROUP SIZE

A group has the power not only to arouse its members but also to render them unidentifiable. The snarling crowd hides the snarling basketball fan. A lynch mob enables its members to believe they will not be prosecuted; they perceive the action as the *group's.* Looters, made faceless by the mob, are freed to loot. One researcher analyzed 21 instances in which crowds were present as someone threatened to jump from a building or a bridge (Mann, 1981). When the crowd was small and exposed by daylight, people usually did not try to bait the person with cries of "Jump!" But when a large crowd or the cover of night gave people anonymity and many people were frustrated by road blockages due to the incident, the crowd usually did bait and jeer (Smith et al., 2019).

Lynch mobs produced a similar effect: The bigger the mob, the more its members lost self-awareness and became willing to commit atrocities, such as burning, lacerating, or dismembering the victim (Leader et al., 2007; Mullen, 1986a; Ritchey & Ruback, 2018).

In each of these examples, from sports crowds to lynch mobs, evaluation apprehension plummets. People's attention is focused on the situation, not on themselves. And because "everyone is doing it," all can attribute their behavior to the situation rather than to their own choices.

ANONYMITY

How can we be sure that crowds offer anonymity? We can't. But we can experiment with anonymity to see if it actually lessens inhibitions. Philip Zimbardo (1970, 2002) got the idea for such an experiment from his undergraduate students, who questioned how good boys in William Golding's *Lord of the Flies* could so suddenly become monsters after painting their faces. To experiment with such anonymity, he dressed New York University women in identical white coats and hoods, rather like Ku Klux Klan members (**Figure 5**). Asked to deliver electric shocks to a woman, they pressed the shock button twice as long as did women who were unconcealed and wearing large name tags.

FIGURE 5

Costumes Used in Deindividuation Experiment

In Philip Zimbardo's deindividuation research, women who had their identities concealed with white coats and hoods — who were effectively anonymous — delivered more shock to helpless victims than did women whose faces and identities were clearly visible and known.
Philip Zimbardo

In Northern Ireland, 206 of 500 violent attacks studied by Andrew Silke (2003) were conducted by attackers who wore masks, hoods, or other face disguises. Compared with undisguised attackers, these anonymous attackers inflicted more serious injuries, attacked more people, and committed more vandalism.

Testing deindividuation on the streets, Patricia Ellison, John Govern, and their colleagues (1995) had a driver stop at a red light and wait for 12 seconds whenever she was followed by a convertible or a 4 × 4 vehicle. During the wait, she recorded horn-honking (a mild aggressive act) by the car behind. Compared with drivers of convertibles and 4 × 4s with the car tops down, those who were relatively anonymous (with the tops up) honked one-third sooner, twice as often, and for nearly twice as long. Anonymity feeds incivility. Even dimmed lighting or wearing sunglasses increases people's perceived anonymity and thus their willingness to cheat or behave selfishly (Zhong et al., 2010).

A research team led by Ed Diener (1976) cleverly demonstrated the effect both of being in a group and of being physically anonymous. At Halloween, they observed 1,352 Seattle children trick-or-treating. As the children, either alone or in groups, approached 1 of 27 homes scattered throughout the city, an experimenter greeted them warmly, invited them to "take *one* of the candies," and then left the candy unattended. Hidden observers noted that children in groups were more than twice as likely to take extra candy than were solo children. Also, children who had been asked their names and where they lived were less than half as likely to transgress as those who were left anonymous. As **Figure 6** shows, when they were deindividuated both by group immersion and by anonymity, most children stole extra candy.

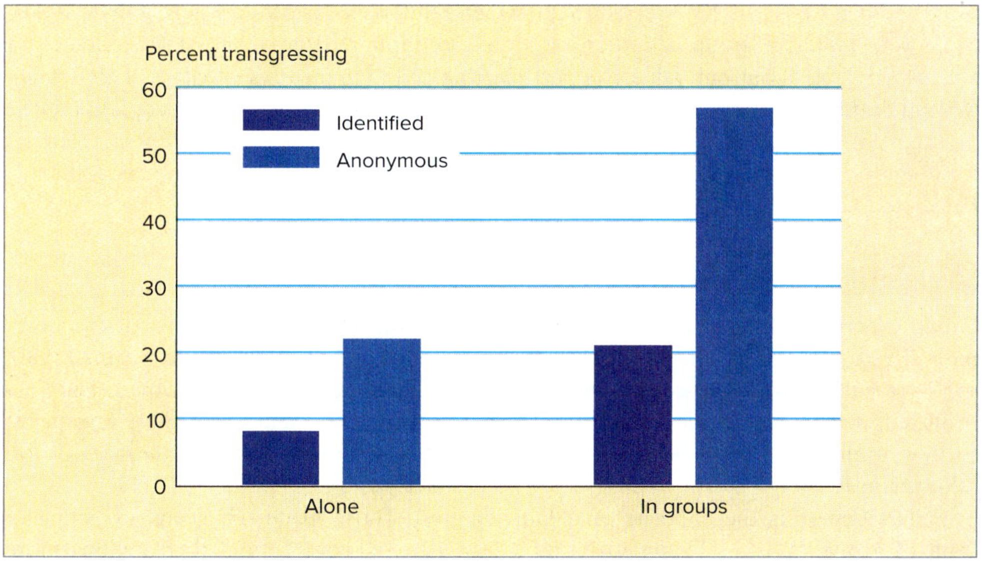

FIGURE 6

Percent Taking Extra Candy

Children were more likely to transgress by taking extra Halloween candy when in a group, when anonymous, and, especially, when deindividuated by the combination of group immersion and anonymity.
Source: Data from Diener et al., (1976).

The internet also offers anonymity. News story comment sections and social media sites that do not require real names (such as Twitter/X) often descend into insults and name-calling. Even with their names displayed, users are not physically facing the people they attack and may feel anonymous as they type into their phone or sit at their computer (Perfumi et al., 2019). People say things online they would never say to someone's face. Demands also grow more extreme when more people participate; one person's condemnation of someone's speech or behavior can become calls for getting them fired once more people pile on – an online mob mentality some call "cancel culture" (McArdle, 2020).

Similar deindividuated behaviors occur in online games, where some players engage in toxic behaviors such as insulting others. Players of the online game *World of Tanks,* for example, were more likely to insult other players when their teammates did the same, suggesting that toxicity spreads within groups (Shen et al., 2020). The combination of feeling part of a group while also being anonymous is the perfect setup for toxic behavior.

On several occasions, anonymous internet users have egged on or otherwise encouraged people threatening suicide or self-harm (Cupp, 2018). This is the online equivalent of a crowd gathering around someone who is threatening to jump off a building and chanting, "Jump! Jump!" Online, people may feel anonymous enough to indulge the cruel impulse to encourage another's suicide. "The anonymous nature of these communities only emboldens the meanness or callousness of the people on these sites," noted one analyst of technology's social effects (quoted by Stelter, 2008).

Does becoming physically anonymous *always* unleash our worst impulses? Fortunately, no. In all these situations, people were responding to clear antisocial cues. Robert Johnson and Leslie Downing (1979) pointed out that the Klan-like outfits worn by Zimbardo's participants may have been stimulus cues for hostility. In an experiment at the University of Georgia, women put on nurses' uniforms before deciding how much shock someone should receive. When those wearing the nurses' uniforms were made anonymous, they became *less* aggressive in administering shocks. From their analysis of 60 deindividuation studies, Tom Postmes and Russell Spears (1998; Reicher et al., 1995) concluded that being anonymous makes one less self-conscious, more group-conscious, and *more responsive to situational cues,* whether negative (Klan outfits) or positive (nurses' uniforms).

AROUSING AND DISTRACTING ACTIVITIES

Aggressive outbursts by large groups are often preceded by minor actions that arouse and divert people's attention. Group shouting, chanting, clapping, or dancing serve both to hype people up and to reduce self-consciousness.

Experiments have shown that activities such as throwing rocks and group singing can set the stage for more disinhibited behavior (Diener, 1976, 1979). There is a self-reinforcing pleasure in acting impulsively while seeing others do likewise. When we see others act as we are acting, we think they feel as we do, which reinforces our own feelings (Orive, 1984). Moreover, impulsive group action absorbs our attention. When we yell at the referee, we are not thinking about our values; we are reacting to the immediate situation. Later, when we stop to think about what we have done or said, we sometimes feel chagrined. Sometimes. At other times, we *seek* deindividuating group experiences – dances, worship experiences, team sports – where we enjoy intense positive feelings and closeness to others (Rime & Paez, 2023).

"Attending a service in the Gothic cathedral, we have the sensation of being enclosed and steeped in an integral universe, and of losing a prickly sense of self in the community of worshipers."

—Yi-Fu Tuan, *Segmented Worlds and Self,* 1982

Diminished Self-Awareness

Group experiences that diminish self-consciousness tend to disconnect behavior from attitudes. Research by Ed Diener (1980) and Steven Prentice-Dunn and Ronald Rogers (1980, 1989) revealed that unself-conscious, deindividuated people are less restrained, less self-regulated, more likely to act without thinking about their own values, and more responsive to the situation. These findings complement and reinforce the experiments on **self-awareness.**

self-awareness
A self-conscious state in which attention focuses on oneself. It makes people more sensitive to their own attitudes and dispositions.

Self-awareness is the opposite of deindividuation. Those made self-aware, by acting in front of a mirror or a TV camera, exhibit *increased* self-control, and their actions more clearly reflect their attitudes. In front of a mirror, people taste-testing cream cheese varieties ate less of the high-fat variety (Sentyrz & Bushman, 1998).

People made self-aware are also less likely to cheat (Beaman et al., 1979; Diener & Wallbom, 1976). The principle: People who are self-conscious, or who are temporarily made so, exhibit greater consistency between their words outside a situation and their deeds in it. In Japan, where people more often imagine how their actions appear to others, the presence of a mirror had no effect on cheating (Heine et al., 2008).

Looking in a mirror or being on camera increases self-awareness, making us think about our individual actions more carefully.
Syda Productions/Shutterstock

We can apply those findings to many situations in everyday life. Circumstances that decrease self-awareness, as alcohol consumption does, *increase* deindividuation (Hull et al., 1983). So does being part of a large crowd, like occurred at the 2021 Capitol riot (Paulus & Kenworthy, 2022). Deindividuation *decreases* in circumstances that increase self-awareness: mirrors and cameras, small towns, bright lights, large name tags, undistracted quiet, individual clothes, and houses (Ickes et al., 1978). When a teenager leaves for a party, a parent's parting advice could well be "Have fun, and remember who you are." In other words, enjoy being with the group, but be self-aware; maintain your personal identity; be wary of deindividuation.

SUMMING UP: Deindividuation: When Do People Lose Their Sense of Self in Groups?

- When high levels of social arousal combine with diffused responsibility, people may abandon their normal restraints and lose their sense of individuality.
- Such *deindividuation* is especially likely when people are in a large group, are physically anonymous, and are aroused and distracted.
- The resulting diminished *self-awareness* and self-restraint tend to increase people's responsiveness to the immediate situation, be it negative or positive. Deindividuation is less likely when self-awareness is high.

GROUP POLARIZATION: DO GROUPS INTENSIFY OUR OPINIONS?

Describe and explain how interaction with like-minded people tends to amplify preexisting attitudes.

Do group interactions more often have good or bad outcomes? Police brutality and mob violence demonstrate the destructive potential of groups. Yet support-group leaders, work-group consultants, and educational theorists proclaim the beneficial effects of group interaction. And self-help group members and religious adherents strengthen their identities by fellowship with like-minded others.

Studies of small groups have produced a principle that helps explain both bad and good outcomes: Group discussion often strengthens members' initial inclinations. The unfolding of this research on group polarization illustrates the process of inquiry – how an interesting discovery often leads researchers to hasty and erroneous conclusions, which get replaced with more accurate conclusions. This is a scientific mystery I [DM] can discuss firsthand, having been one of the detectives.

The Case of the "Risky Shift"

More than 300 studies began with a surprising finding by James Stoner (1961), then an MIT graduate student. For his master's thesis in management, Stoner tested the commonly held belief that groups are more cautious than individuals. He posed decision dilemmas in which the participant's task was to advise imagined characters how much risk to take. Put yourself in the participant's shoes: What advice would you give the character in this situation?[1]

> Helen is a writer who is said to have considerable creative talent but who so far has been earning a comfortable living by writing cheap westerns. Recently she has come up with an idea for a potentially significant novel. If it could be written and accepted, it might have considerable literary impact and be a big boost to her career. On the other hand, if she cannot work out her idea or if the novel is a flop, she will have expended considerable time and energy without remuneration.
>
> Imagine that you are advising Helen. Please check the *lowest* probability that you would consider acceptable for Helen to attempt to write the novel.
>
> Helen should attempt to write the novel if the chances that the novel will be a success are at least
>
> _____ 1 in 10
> _____ 2 in 10
> _____ 3 in 10
> _____ 4 in 10
> _____ 5 in 10
> _____ 6 in 10
> _____ 7 in 10
> _____ 8 in 10
> _____ 9 in 10
> _____ 10 in 10 (Place a check here if you think Helen should attempt the novel only if it is certain that the novel will be a success.)

After making your decision, guess what this book's average reader would advise.

Having marked their advice on a dozen items, five or so individuals would then discuss and reach an agreement on each item. How do you think the group decisions compared with the average decision before the discussions? Would the groups be likely to take greater risks, be more cautious, or stay the same?

To everyone's amazement, the group decisions were usually riskier. This "risky shift phenomenon" set off a wave of group risk-taking studies. These revealed that risky shift occurs not only when a group decides by consensus; after a brief discussion, individuals, too, will alter their decisions. What is more, researchers successfully repeated Stoner's finding with people of varying ages and occupations in a dozen nations.

During discussion, opinions converged. Curiously, however, the point toward which they converged was usually a lower (riskier) number than their initial average. Here was an intriguing puzzle. The small risky shift effect was reliable, unexpected, and without any immediately obvious explanation. What group influences produce such an effect? And how widespread is it? Do discussions in juries, business committees, and military organizations also promote risk taking? Does this explain why teenage reckless driving, as measured by death rates, nearly doubles when a 16- or 17-year-old driver has two teenage passengers rather than none (Chen et al., 2000)? Does it explain stock bubbles, as people discuss why stocks are rising, thus creating an informational cascade that drives stocks even higher (Sunstein, 2009)?

The risky shift: Groups of people, like these teens in a car together, may make more risky decisions than individuals alone.
View Stock/Getty Images

After several years of study, my [DM's] colleagues and I discovered that the risky shift was not universal. We could write decision dilemmas on which people became more *cautious* after discussion. One of these featured "Roger," a young married man

[1]This item, constructed for my [DM's] own research, illustrates the sort of decision dilemma posed by Stoner.

with two school-age children and a secure but low-paying job. Roger can afford life's necessities but few of its luxuries. He hears that the stock of a relatively unknown company may soon triple in value if its new product is favorably received or decline considerably if it does not sell. Roger has no savings. To invest in the company, he is considering selling his life insurance policy.

Can you see a general principle that predicts both the tendency to give riskier advice after discussing Helen's situation and more cautious advice after discussing Roger's? If you are like most people, you would advise Helen to take a greater risk than Roger, even before talking with others. It turns out there is a strong tendency for discussion to accentuate these initial leanings. Thus, groups discussing the "Roger" dilemma became more risk-averse than they were before discussion (Myers, 2010).

Do Groups Intensify Opinions?

Realizing that this group phenomenon was not a consistent shift toward increased risk, we reconceived the phenomenon as a tendency for group discussion to *enhance* group members' initial leanings. Similar minds polarize. This idea led investigators to propose what French researchers Serge Moscovici and Marisa Zavalloni (1969) called group polarization: *Discussion typically strengthens the average inclination of group members.*

GROUP POLARIZATION EXPERIMENTS

This new view of the group-induced changes prompted experimenters to have people discuss attitude statements that most of them favored or that most of them opposed. Would talking in groups enhance their shared initial inclinations? In groups, would risk takers take bigger risks, bigots become more hostile, and givers become more generous? That's what the group polarization hypothesis predicts (**Figure 7**).

Dozens of studies confirm group polarization. Some examples:

- When voters who opposed Donald Trump in 2016 discussed their views as a group, their opinions on issues such as immigration became even more anti-Trump after talking with other like-minded people (Bekafigo et al., 2019).
- When online groups share moral concerns involving emotions such as anger and disgust, they become more radical and more willing to fight and die for the group (Atari et al., 2022).
- Japanese university students gave more pronounced judgments of "guilty" after discussing a traffic case as a group (Isozaki, 1984). When jury members decide to award money to the wronged party in a civil trial, the group award tends to exceed that preferred by the median jury member (Sunstein, 2007).
- When people believed they were watching an online video of a political speech at the same time as many other viewers (versus with no other viewers), their judgments of the speech were more extreme (Shteynberg et al., 2016).
- French students were more adamant in their dislike of someone after discussing their shared negative impressions with others (Brauer et al., 2001). If some individuals dislike you, together they may dislike you more.

Another research strategy has been to pick issues on which opinions are divided and then isolate people who hold the same view. George Bishop and I [DM] wondered: Does discussion with like-minded people strengthen shared views? Does it magnify the attitude gap that separates the two sides?

So we set up groups of relatively prejudiced and unprejudiced high school students and asked them to respond – before and after discussion – to issues involving racial attitudes (Myers & Bishop, 1970). For example, they responded to a case involving the property right to rent only to one's race versus the civil right to not face discrimination. We found that the discussions among like-minded students did indeed increase the initial gap between

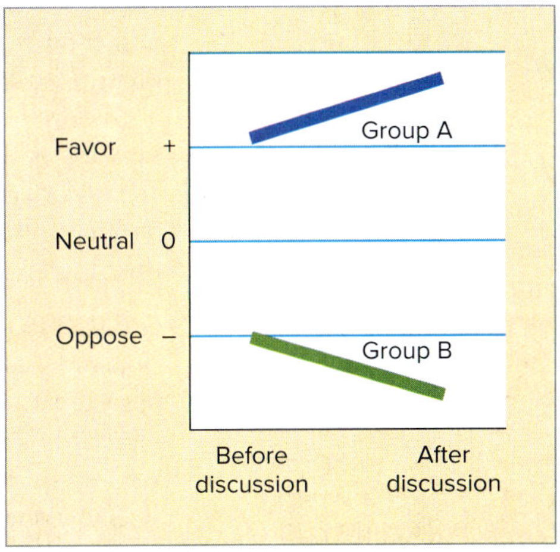

FIGURE 7

Group Polarization

The group polarization hypothesis predicts that discussion will strengthen an attitude shared by group members.

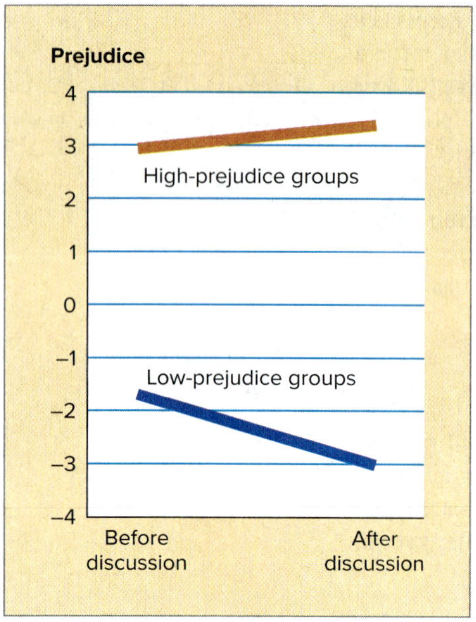

FIGURE 8

Level of Prejudice Before and After Discussion

Discussion increased polarization between homogeneous groups of high- and low-prejudice high school students. Talking over racial issues increased prejudice in a high-prejudice group and decreased it in a low-prejudice group.
Source: Data from Myers & Bishop, (1970).

the two groups (**Figure 8**). Moreover, Jessica Keating and her collaborators (2016) report that people are unaware of the phenomenon in their own lives. When small groups of like-minded people discussed whether Barack Obama or George W. Bush was the better president, participants underestimated how much the discussion polarized their attitudes, misremembering their earlier attitudes as less extreme than they actually were.

Studies in Britain, the Netherlands, and Australia confirm that group discussion can magnify both negative and positive tendencies. When people share negative impressions of a group, such as an immigrant group, discussion with others supports their negative views and increases their willingness to discriminate (Koudenberg et al., 2019; Smith & Postmes, 2011). And when people share concern about an injustice, discussion amplifies their moral concern (Thomas & McGarty, 2009). An example was the U.S. Capitol riot on January 6, 2021, where beliefs were amplified to extremes in online groups, resulting in a day of violence (Hinsz & Jackson, 2022). Like hot coals together, like minds strengthen one another.

GROUP POLARIZATION IN EVERYDAY LIFE

In everyday life, people associate mostly with others whose attitudes are similar to their own. (See the "Attraction" chapter or just look at your own circle of friends.) So, outside the laboratory, do everyday group interactions with like-minded friends intensify shared attitudes? Do the nerds become nerdier, the jocks jockier, and the rebels more rebellious?

It happens. The self-segregation of boys into all-male groups and of girls into all-female groups increases their initially modest gender differences, noted Eleanor Maccoby (2002). Boys with boys become gradually more competitive and action oriented in their play and fictional fare. Girls with girls become more relationally oriented.

On U.S. federal appellate court cases, judges appointed by Republican presidents tend to vote like Republicans and judges appointed by Democratic presidents tend to vote like Democrats. No surprise there. But such tendencies are accentuated when among like-minded judges, reported David Schkade and Cass Sunstein (2003): "A Republican appointee sitting with two other Republicans votes far more conservatively than when the same judge sits with at least one Democratic appointee. A Democratic appointee, meanwhile, shows the same tendency in the opposite ideological direction."

GROUP POLARIZATION IN SCHOOLS Another real-life parallel to the laboratory phenomenon is what education researchers have called the *accentuation effect*: Over time, initial differences among groups of college students become accentuated. If the first-year students at Big Brain College are initially more intellectual than the students at Party School College, that gap is likely to increase by the time they graduate. Likewise, compared with fraternity and sorority members, nonmembers have tended to have more liberal political attitudes, a difference that grows with time in college (Pascarella & Terenzini, 1991). Researchers believe this results partly from group members reinforcing shared inclinations.

GROUP POLARIZATION IN COMMUNITIES Polarization also occurs in communities, as people self-segregate. "Crunchy places . . . attract crunchy types and become crunchier," observed David Brooks (2005). "Conservative places . . . attract conservatives and become more so." Neighborhoods can become echo chambers, with opinions ricocheting off kindred-spirited friends.

Show social psychologists a like-minded group that interacts mostly among themselves and they will show you a group that may become more extreme. While diversity moderates us, like minds polarize.

One experiment assembled small groups of Coloradoans in liberal Boulder and conservative Colorado Springs. The discussions increased agreement within small groups about global warming, affirmative action, and same-sex unions. Nevertheless, those in Boulder generally converged further left and those in Colorado Springs further right (Schkade et al., 2007).

"What explains the rise of fascism in the 1930s? The emergence of student radicalism in the 1960s? The growth of Islamic terrorism in the 1990s? . . . The unifying theme is simple: *When people find themselves in groups of like-minded types, they are especially likely to move to extremes.* [This] is the phenomenon of *group polarization.*"

—Cass Sunstein, *Going to Extremes*, 2009

Groups often exceed individuals. A gang is more dangerous than the sum of its parts, much as "the pack is greater than the wolf."
Raimund Linke/Radius Images/Getty Images

In laboratory studies, the competitive relationships and mistrust that individuals often display when playing games with one another often worsen when the players are groups (Winquist & Larson, 2004). During actual community conflicts, like-minded people associate increasingly with one another, amplifying their shared tendencies. Gang delinquency emerges from a process of mutual reinforcement within neighborhood gangs, whose members share attributes and hostilities (Cartwright, 1975). If "a second out-of-control 15-year-old moves in [on your block]," surmised David Lykken (1997), "the mischief they get into as a team is likely to be more than merely double what the first would do on his own. . . . A gang is more dangerous than the sum of its individual parts." (Or, as one friend of mine [JT] put it when we were in college and had witnessed a few too many drunken antics, "Boys do dumb things when they get together in groups.") Indeed, "unsupervised peer groups" are "the strongest predictor" of a neighborhood's crime victimization rate, reported Bonita Veysey and Steven Messner (1999). Moreover, experimental interventions that take delinquent adolescents and group them with other delinquents – no surprise to any group polarization researcher – increase the rate of problem behavior (Dishion et al., 1999).

GROUP POLARIZATION IN POLITICS With like-minded communities and online groups serving as political echo chambers, the United States offers a case example of an urgent social problem: political polarization. As more and more people view their party as morally superior and the opposition as corrupt, cooperation and shared goals get replaced by gridlock (Cole et al., 2023; Finkel et al., 2020). Consider:

- *Like-minded counties.* The percentage of Americans living in "landslide counties" – those in which 60% or more voted for the same presidential candidate – rose from 38% in 1992 to 58% in 2020 (Aisch et al., 2016; Bishop, 2020).
- *Minimized middle ground.* The percentage of entering college students declaring themselves as politically "middle of the road" dropped from 60% in 1983 to 44% in 2019, and those identifying as "far left" or "far right" increased (Stolzenberg et al., 2020; Twenge et al., 2016).
- *Increasing partisan divide.* The gap between Republicans and Democrats, as expressed in congressional speeches and in citizens' beliefs and attitudes, has never been greater (DeSilver, 2022; Dunn, 2020; Pew, 2019; **Figure 9**). Eight in 10 Republicans believe that the Democratic party has been taken over by socialists, and 8 in 10 Democrats believe that the Republican party has been taken over by racists (PPRI, 2019).
- *Antagonism.* In 2016, for the first time, the majority of Republicans and Democrats acknowledged having "*very* unfavorable" views of the other party (Doherty & Kiley, 2016). By 2022, 62% of Republicans had a very unfavorable view of Democrats, and 54% of Democrats had a very unfavorable view of Republicans (Pew, 2022).

This worsening divide is increasingly apparent to all, with 85% of Americans saying the nation is greatly divided over its most important values (PBS, 2020).

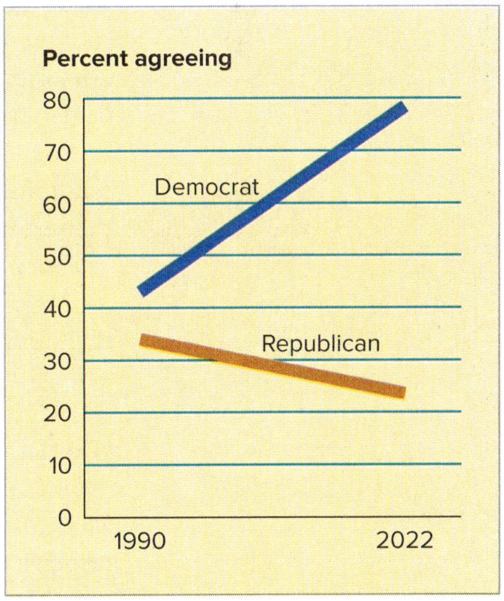

FIGURE 9

Views of discrimination

White Democrats have increasingly agreed that "Discrimination is the main reason why Black people have worse jobs, income, and housing." White Republicans have become less likely to agree (Twenge, 2023). Data from the General Social Survey.

In 2023, 56% of Republicans and 20% of Democrats said the United States is in danger of failing as a nation (Igielnik, 2023).

GROUP POLARIZATION ONLINE From the long-ago invention of the printing press to today's internet, the amount of available information has mushroomed. Where once people shared the same information from a few networks and national news magazines, today we choose from a myriad of sources. With so many choices, we naturally "selectively expose" ourselves to like-minded media (Dylko et al., 2017). We embrace media feeds that support our views and slam those we despise. (Tell us which media you consume, and we'll guess your political ideology.)

Do people tend to click on content they agree with and block what they disagree with? Do the internet's segregated communities, with news feeds catering to their interests, amplify social fragmentation and political polarization?

The internet's countless virtual groups enable peacemakers and neo-Nazis, sports fans and *Star Trek* fans, conspiracy schemers and cancer survivors to isolate themselves with like-minded others and find support for their shared concerns, interests, and suspicions (Gerstenfeld et al., 2003; McKenna & Bargh, 1998, 2000; Sunstein, 2009, 2016). Communicating with people who share your interests has many benefits, yet when people isolate themselves from other opinions, the internet can become an echo chamber (B. Johnson et al., 2020; S. Johnson et al., 2020). Thus, disagreements can become demonizations and suspicions can escalate to paranoia. The internet, writes columnist Frank Bruni, was once "a glittering dream of expanded knowledge and enhanced connection" but has morphed into "a nightmare of manipulated biases and metastasized hate" (Bruni, 2018).

With retweets, customized news feeds, and self-selections from the news buffet, like minds can also feed one another toxic misinformation: untruths that, after many retellings, get accepted as fact (Barberá et al., 2015; Humprecht, 2019). This is exactly what happened during the COVID-19 pandemic, as misinformation and conspiracy theories spread like wildfire through the dry brush of the internet (Knowles, 2020).

"We thought internet would give us access to ppl w different points of view. Instead it gives us access to many ppl w the same point of view."

—Comedian Kumail Nanjiani, 2016 tweet

Research confirms that most of us read online sources that reinforce rather than challenge our views, and those sources link mostly to like-minded sources – connecting liberals with liberals, conservatives with conservatives – like having conversations with the bathroom mirror (Lazer et al., 2009). Online, we can decide what information we expose ourselves to (Sude et al., 2019). With angry, morally charged, and extreme posts more likely to be shared on social media, polarization grows (Van Bavel et al., 2021).

Social media posts may play a role in seemingly apolitical choices becoming political as opinions become amplified within groups. In March 2022, 48% of parents who described themselves as very liberal said COVID-19 was a great risk to children, compared to 27% of the very conservative (Leonhardt, 2022).

The bottom line: On our list of the future's great challenges, somewhere not far below restraining climate change, is learning how to harness the great benefits of the digital future and its more connected world but without exacerbating group polarization.

GROUP POLARIZATION IN TERRORIST ORGANIZATIONS From their analysis of terrorist organizations throughout the world, Clark McCauley and his colleagues (2002; McCauley & Moskalenko, 2017) note that terrorism does not erupt suddenly: "Lone-wolf terrorists are rare." Rather, it arises among people whose shared grievances bring them together and fan their fire. As they interact in isolation from moderating influences, they become progressively more extreme. The social amplifier brings the signal in more strongly. The result is violent acts that the individuals, apart from the group, would never have committed.

For example, the September 11, 2001, terrorists were bred by a long process that engaged the polarizing effect of interaction among the like-minded. The process of becoming a terrorist, noted a National Research Council panel, isolates individuals from other belief systems, dehumanizes potential targets, and tolerates no dissent (Smelser & Mitchell, 2002). Group members come to categorize the world as "us" and "them" (Moghaddam, 2005;

Qirko, 2004). Ariel Merari (2002), an investigator of Middle Eastern and Sri Lankan suicide terrorism, believed the key to creating a terrorist suicide is the group process. "To the best of my knowledge, there has not been a single case of suicide terrorism which was done on a personal whim."

According to one analysis of terrorists who were members of the Salafi Jihad – an Islamic fundamentalist movement, including al Qaeda – 70% joined while living as expatriates. After moving to foreign places in search of jobs or education, they became keenly mindful of their Muslim identity. They often gravitated to mosques and moved in with other expatriate Muslims, who sometimes recruited them into cell groups that provided "mutual emotional and social support" and "development of a common identity" (Reicher & Haslam, 2016; Sageman, 2004). One of the senior militants in the Islamic State (IS) reported that his movement was born inside an American prison in Iraq: "If there was no American prison in Iraq, there would be no IS now. [The prison] was a factory. It made us all. It built our ideology. . . . We had so much time to sit and plan. It was the perfect environment" (quoted by Chulov, 2014).

Massacres, similarly, are group phenomena. The violence is enabled and escalated by the killers egging one another on, noted Robert Zajonc (2000), who knew violence as a survivor of a World War II Warsaw air raid that killed both his parents (Burnstein, 2009). It is difficult to influence someone once "in the pressure cooker of the terrorist group," noted Jerrold Post (2005) after interviewing many accused terrorists. "In the long run, the most effective antiterrorist policy is one that inhibits potential recruits from joining in the first place."

Explaining Group Polarization

Why do groups adopt stances that are more exaggerated than that of their average individual member? Researchers hoped that solving the mystery of group polarization might provide some insights into group influence. Solving small puzzles sometimes provides clues for solving larger ones.

Among several proposed theories of group polarization, two have survived scientific scrutiny. One deals with the *arguments* presented during a discussion and is an example of *informational influence* (influence that results from accepting evidence about reality). The other concerns how members of a group view themselves vis-à-vis the other members, an example of *normative influence* (influence based on a person's desire to be accepted or admired by others).

INFORMATIONAL INFLUENCE

According to the best-supported explanation, group discussion elicits a pooling of ideas, most of which favor the dominant viewpoint. Some discussed ideas are common knowledge to group members (Gigone & Hastie, 1993; Larson et al., 1994; Stasser, 1991). Other ideas may include persuasive arguments that some group members had not previously considered. When discussing Helen the writer, someone may say, "Helen should go for it because she has little to lose. If her novel flops, she can always go back to writing cheap westerns." Such statements often entangle information about the person's *arguments* with cues concerning the person's *position* on the issue. But when people hear relevant arguments without learning the specific stands other people assume, they still shift their positions (Burnstein & Vinokur, 1977; Hinsz et al., 1997). *Arguments,* in and of themselves, matter.

"If you have an apple and I have an apple and we exchange apples, then you and I will still each have one apple. But if you have an idea and I have an idea and we exchange these ideas, then each of us will have two ideas."

—Charles F. Brannan, Secretary of Agriculture, NBC broadcast, April 3, 1949

But there's more to attitude change than merely hearing someone else's arguments. *Active participation* in discussion produces more attitude change than does passive listening. Participants and observers hear the same ideas. But when participants express them in their own words, the verbal commitment magnifies the impact. The more group members repeat one another's ideas, the more they rehearse and validate them (Brauer et al., 1995).

People's minds are not just blank tablets for persuaders to write upon. With central route persuasion, what people think in response to a message is crucial. Indeed, just thinking about an issue for a couple of minutes can strengthen opinions (Tesser et al., 1995). (Perhaps you can recall your feelings becoming polarized as you merely ruminated about someone you disliked or liked.)

Reprinted by permission of Kevin Kal Kallaugher, The Economist, Kaltoons.com

An *Economist* cover about a stock market crash.

NORMATIVE INFLUENCE

A second explanation of polarization involves comparison with others. As Leon Festinger (1954) argued in his influential theory of **social comparison,** we humans want to evaluate our opinions and abilities by comparing our views with others'. We are most persuaded by people in our "reference groups" – groups we identify with (Abrams et al., 1990; Hogg et al., 1990). Moreover, we want people to like us, so we may express stronger opinions after discovering that others share our views.

When we ask people (as we asked you earlier) to predict how others would respond to items such as the "Helen" dilemma, they typically exhibit **pluralistic ignorance:** They don't realize how strongly others support the socially preferred tendency (in this case, writing the novel). A typical person will advise writing the novel even if its chance of success is only 4 in 10 but will estimate that most other people would require 5 or 6 in 10. (This finding is reminiscent of the self-serving bias: People tend to view themselves as better-than-average embodiments of socially desirable traits and attitudes.) When the discussion begins, most people discover they are not outshining the others as they had supposed. In fact, others are ahead of them, having taken an even stronger position in favor of writing the novel. No longer restrained by a misperceived group norm, they are liberated to voice their preferences more strongly.

social comparison
Evaluating one's opinions and abilities by comparing oneself with others.

pluralistic ignorance
A false impression of what most other people are thinking or feeling, or how they are responding.

Perhaps you can recall a time when you and someone else wanted to date each other but each of you feared to make the first move, presuming the other was not interested. Such pluralistic ignorance impedes the start-up of relationships (Vorauer & Ratner, 1996).

Or perhaps you can recall when you and others were guarded and reserved in a group until someone broke the ice and said, "Well, to be perfectly honest, I think. . . ." Soon you were all surprised to discover strong support for your shared views. Sometimes when a professor asks if anyone has any questions, no one will respond, leading each student to infer that they are the only one who is confused. All presume that fear of embarrassment explains their own silence but that everyone else's silence means they understand the material.

Social comparison theory prompted experiments that exposed people to others' positions but not to their arguments. This is roughly the experience we have when reading the results of an opinion poll or of exit polling on election day. When people learn others' positions – without prior commitment and without discussion or sharing of arguments – will they adjust their responses to maintain a socially favorable position? As **Figure 10** illustrates, they will. This comparison-based polarization is usually less than that produced by a lively discussion. Still, it's surprising that instead of simply conforming to the group average, people often go it one better.

Merely learning others' choices also contributes to the bandwagon effect that creates blockbuster songs, books, and movies. One experiment engaged 14,341 internet participants in listening to and, if they wished, downloading previously unknown songs (Salganik et al., 2006). The researchers randomly assigned some participants to a condition that disclosed previous participants' download choices. Among those given that information, popular songs became more popular and unpopular songs became less popular.

Pluralistic ignorance: Sometimes a false presumption of another's disinterest may prevent two people with a mutual romantic interest from connecting.
visualspace/E+/Getty Images

Group polarization research illustrates the complexity of social-psychological inquiry. Much as we like our explanations of a phenomenon to be simple, one explanation seldom accounts for all the data. Because people are complex, more than one factor frequently influences an outcome. In group discussions, persuasive arguments predominate on issues that have a factual element ("Is she guilty of the crime?"). Social comparison sways responses on value-laden judgments ("How long a sentence should she serve?")

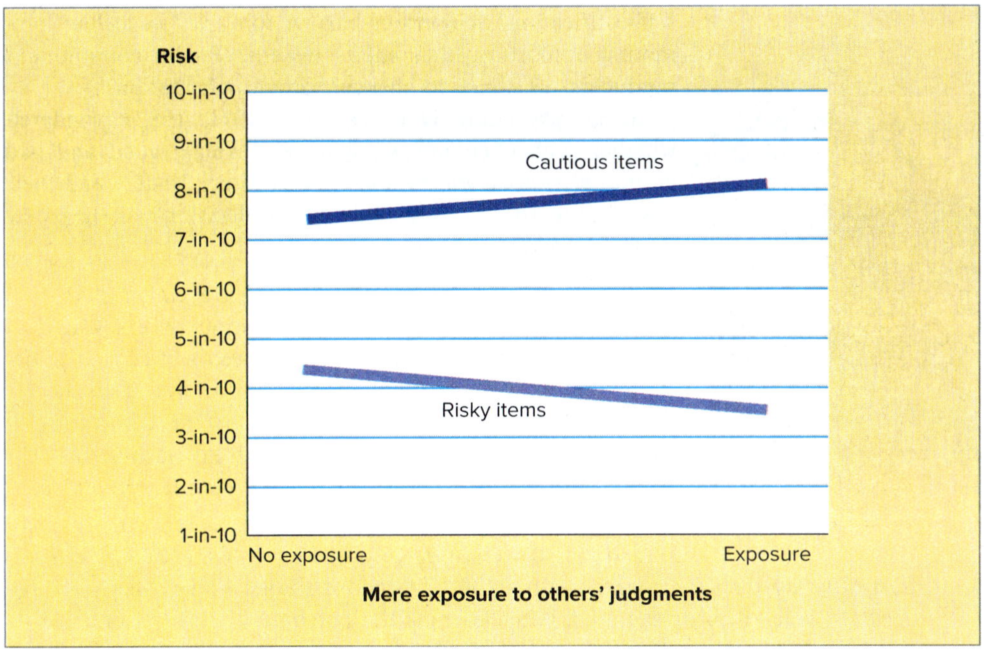

FIGURE 10

Willingness to Take Risks

On "risky" dilemma items (such as the case of Helen), mere exposure to others' judgments enhanced individuals' risk-prone tendencies. On "cautious" dilemma items (such as the case of Roger), exposure to others' judgments enhanced their cautiousness.

Source: Data from Myers, (1978).

(Kaplan, 1989). On the many issues that have both factual and value-laden aspects, the two factors work together. Discovering that others share one's feelings (social comparison) unleashes arguments (informational influence) supporting what everyone secretly favors.

SUMMING UP: Group Polarization: Do Groups Intensify Our Opinions?

- Potentially positive and negative results arise from group discussion. While trying to understand the curious finding that discussion increased risk taking, investigators discovered that discussion actually tends to strengthen whatever is the initially dominant point of view, whether risky or cautious.
- In everyday situations, too, group interaction tends to intensify opinions. This *group polarization* phenomenon provided a window through which researchers could observe group influence.
- Experiments confirmed two group influences: informational and normative. The information gleaned from a discussion mostly favors the initially preferred alternative, thus reinforcing support for it.

GROUP DECISION-MAKING: DO GROUPS HELP OR HINDER GOOD DECISIONS?

Describe when and how groups can help or hinder good decisions and how we can optimize group decision-making.

Do the social psychological phenomena we have been considering occur in sophisticated groups such as corporate boards or a president's cabinet? Is there likely to be

The USS *Arizona* burning after the Japanese attack on Pearl Harbor.
National Archives and Records Administration (NLR-PHOCO-A-8150(29))

self-justification? Self-serving bias? A cohesive "we feeling" promoting conformity that stifles dissent? Public commitment producing resistance to change? Group polarization?

Social psychologist Irving Janis (1971, 1982) wondered whether such phenomena might help explain good and bad group decisions made by some 20th-century leaders and their advisers. To find out, he analyzed the decision-making procedures behind several major fiascos:

- *Pearl Harbor.* In the weeks before the December 1941 attack that brought the United States into World War II, military commanders in Hawaii received a stream of information about Japan's preparations for an attack on the United States somewhere in the Pacific. But complacent commanders took no action, and with no warning of the Japanese air attack, more than 2,400 people were killed.
- *The Bay of Pigs Invasion.* In 1961, President John Kennedy and his advisers tried to overthrow Cuban leader Fidel Castro by invading the country with 1,400 CIA-trained Cuban exiles. Nearly all the invaders were killed or captured. After learning the outcome, Kennedy wondered aloud, "How could we have been so stupid?"
- *The Vietnam War.* From 1964 to 1967, President Lyndon Johnson escalated the war in Vietnam despite warnings from others that the war was unwinnable. The resulting disaster cost more than 58,000 American and 1 million Vietnamese lives.

groupthink
"The mode of thinking that persons engage in when concurrence-seeking becomes so dominant in a cohesive in-group that it tends to override realistic appraisal of alternative courses of action." —Irving Janis, "*Groupthink,*" 1971

Janis believed those blunders were bred by the tendency of decision-making groups to suppress opposing views in the interest of group harmony, a phenomenon he called **groupthink.** (See "The Inside Story: Irving Janis on Groupthink.") Although team spirit can increase motivation (Haslam et al., 2014), decision-making can be hampered when groups are too close-knit. Janis believed that the soil from which groupthink sprouts includes

- an amiable, *cohesive* group;
- relative *isolation* of the group from dissenting viewpoints; and
- a *directive leader* who signals what decision they favor.

THE inside STORY

Irving Janis on Groupthink

The idea of *groupthink* hit me while reading Arthur Schlesinger's account of how the Kennedy administration decided to invade the Bay of Pigs. At first, I was puzzled: How could bright, shrewd people like John F. Kennedy and his advisers be taken in by the CIA's stupid, patchwork plan? I began to wonder whether some kind of psychological contagion had interfered, such as social conformity or the concurrence-seeking that I had observed in cohesive small groups. Further study (initially aided by my daughter Charlotte's work on a high school term paper) convinced me that subtle group processes had hampered their carefully appraising the risks and debating the issues. When I then analyzed other U.S. foreign policy fiascos and the Watergate cover-up, I found the same detrimental group processes at work.

Irving Janis (1918–1990)
Courtesy of Irving Janis

When planning the ill-fated Bay of Pigs invasion, for example, the newly elected President Kennedy and his advisers enjoyed a strong group morale. Arguments critical of the plan were suppressed or excluded, and the president soon endorsed the invasion.

Henry Martin

Self-censorship contributes to an illusion of unanimity.

Symptoms of Groupthink

From historical records and the memoirs of participants and observers, Janis identified eight groupthink symptoms. Later research found these symptoms are most likely to occur when group members try to maintain their positive group feeling while facing a threat (Turner & Pratkanis, 1994; Turner et al., 1992).

The first two groupthink symptoms lead group members to *overestimate their group's might and right.*

- *An illusion of invulnerability.* The groups Janis studied all developed an excessive optimism that blinded them to warnings of danger. The chief naval officer at Pearl Harbor laughed off the possibility that the Japanese might be close to Honolulu.
- *Unquestioned belief in the group's morality.* Group members assume the inherent morality of their group and ignore ethical and moral issues. The Kennedy group knew that two of its members had moral reservations about invading Cuba, but the group never discussed those moral qualms.

Group members also become *closed-minded.*

- *Rationalization.* The groups discount challenges by collectively justifying their decisions. President Johnson's advisers spent far more time explaining their decisions than reconsidering them.
- *Stereotyped view of opponent.* Groupthinkers consider their enemies too evil to negotiate with or too weak and unintelligent to defend themselves against the planned initiative. The Kennedy group convinced itself that Castro's military was so weak and his popular support so shallow that a single brigade could easily overturn his regime.

Finally, the group suffers from pressures toward *uniformity.*

- *Conformity pressure.* Group members rebuffed those who raised doubts about the group's assumptions and plans, at times by personal sarcasm. Once, when President Johnson's assistant arrived at a meeting, the president said, "Well, here comes Mr. Stop-the-Bombing." Faced with such ridicule, most people fall into line. As with social loafing and deindividuation, groupthink debilitates performance when the individual self is submerged to a group (Baumeister et al., 2016).
- *Self-censorship.* To avoid uncomfortable disagreements, members withheld or discounted their misgivings. In the months following the Bay of Pigs invasion, Kennedy advisor Arthur Schlesinger (1965, p. 255) reproached himself "for having kept so silent during those crucial discussions in the Cabinet Room, though [objecting] would have accomplished little save to gain me a name as a nuisance." It's not just politicians. Both online and in person, people are less willing to share their view when they think others disagree (Hampton et al., 2014).
- *Illusion of unanimity.* Self-censorship and pressure not to puncture the consensus create an illusion of unanimity. What is more, the apparent consensus confirms the group's decision. This appearance of consensus was evident in the Pearl Harbor, Bay of Pigs, and Vietnam fiascos and in other fiascos before and since.

"People 'are never so likely to settle a question rightly as when they discuss it freely.'"

—John Stuart Mill, *On Liberty,* 1859

Albert Speer (1971), an adviser to Adolf Hitler, described the atmosphere around Hitler as one where pressure to conform suppressed all deviation. The absence of dissent created an illusion of unanimity:

> In normal circumstances people who turn their backs on reality are soon set straight by the mockery and criticism of those around them, which makes them aware they have lost credibility. In the Third Reich there were no such correctives. . . . No external factors disturbed the uniformity of hundreds of unchanging faces, all mine. (p. 379)

- *Mindguards.* Some members protect the group from information that would call into question the effectiveness or morality of its decisions. Before the Bay of Pigs invasion, Attorney General Robert Kennedy took Schlesinger aside and told him, "Don't push it any further." Secretary of State Dean Rusk withheld diplomatic and intelligence experts' warnings against the invasion. Robert Kennedy and Dean Rusk thus served as the president's "mindguards," protecting him from disagreeable facts rather than physical harm.

Groupthink symptoms can produce a failure to seek and discuss contrary information and alternative possibilities (**Figure 11**). When a leader promotes an idea and when a group insulates itself from dissenting views, groupthink may produce defective decisions (McCauley, 1989).

Experimental Evidence for Groupthink

Follow-up experiments have supported aspects of groupthink theory:

- Directive leadership is associated with poorer decisions because subordinates sometimes feel too weak or insecure to speak up (Granstrom & Stiwne, 1998; McCauley, 1998).
- Groups do prefer supporting over challenging information (Schulz-Hardt et al., 2000).
- When members look to a group for acceptance, approval, and social identity, they may suppress disagreeable thoughts (Hogg & Hains, 1998; Turner & Pratkanis, 1997).
- Groups that make smart decisions have widely distributed conversations, with socially attuned members who take turns speaking (Woolley et al., 2010).
- Groups with diverse perspectives outperform groups of like-minded experts (Mellers & Tetlock, 2019; Nemeth & Ormiston, 2007; Page, 2007). Talking with people who think differently from you can make you feel uncomfortable. But compared with comfortably homogeneous groups, diverse groups tend to produce more ideas and greater creativity.
- Group success depends both on what group members know and how effectively they can share that information (Bonner & Baumann, 2012). In discussion, unshared information often gets suppressed as discussion focuses on what group members all know already (Sunstein & Hastie, 2008).

Groupthink on a Titanic scale. Despite four messages of possible icebergs ahead, Captain Edward Smith — a directive and respected leader — kept his ship sailing at full speed into the night. There was an illusion of invulnerability (many believed the ship to be unsinkable). There was conformity pressure (crew mates chided the lookout for not being able to use his naked eye and dismissed his misgivings). And there was mindguarding (a *Titanic* telegraph operator failed to pass the last and most complete iceberg warning to Captain Smith).
Everett Historical/Shutterstock

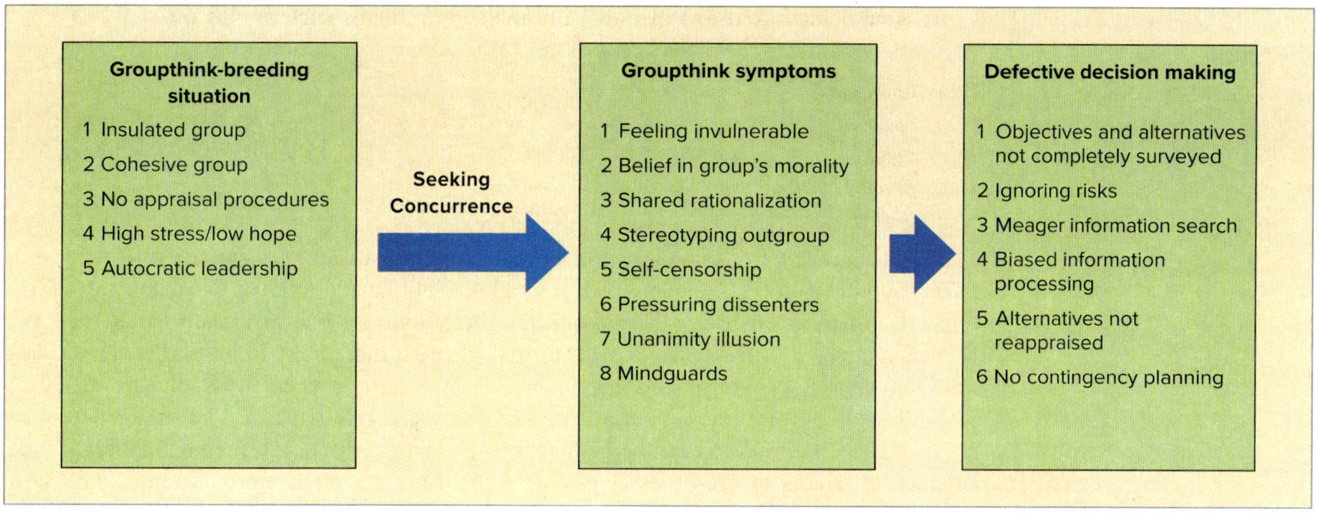

FIGURE 11

Theoretical Analysis of Groupthink

Source: Adapted from Janis & Mann, (1977, p. 132).

Preventing Groupthink

Flawed group dynamics help explain many failed decisions; sometimes too many cooks spoil the broth. However, given open leadership, a cohesive team spirit can improve decisions. Sometimes two or more heads are better than one.

In search of conditions that breed good decisions, Janis also analyzed two successful ventures: the Truman administration's formulation of the Marshall Plan for getting Europe back on its feet after World War II and the Kennedy administration's successful challenge of the Soviet Union's 1962 attempt to install missile bases in Cuba by using a naval blockade. Janis's (1982) recommendations for preventing groupthink incorporate many of the effective group procedures used in both cases:

- *Be impartial*; do not endorse any position. Don't start group discussions by having people state their positions; doing so suppresses information sharing and degrades the quality of decisions (Mojzisch & Schulz-Hardt, 2010). Accept the discussion of unpopular ideas and a diversity of thinking within the group (Lilienfeld, 2020).
- *Encourage critical evaluation;* assign a "devil's advocate." Better yet, welcome the input of a genuine dissenter, which does even more to stimulate original thinking and to open a group to opposing views (Nemeth et al., 2001a, b).
- *Occasionally subdivide the group into smaller groups,* then reunite to air differences. In a study of 65 million scientific papers, smaller groups of authors were more likely to produce creative findings than larger groups (Wu et al., 2019).
- *Welcome critiques* from outside experts and associates.
- Before implementing, *call a "second-chance" meeting* to air any lingering doubts.

"One of the dangers in the White House, based on my reading of history, is that you get wrapped up in groupthink and everybody agrees with everything and there's no discussion and there are no dissenting views. So I'm going to be welcoming a vigorous debate inside the White House."

—President Barack Obama, at a December 1, 2008, press conference

When such steps are taken, group decisions may take longer to make, yet ultimately prove less defective and more effective.

When Groups Perform Better

Not every group decision is flawed by groupthink. When groups make sure to incorporate diverse perspectives, groups can perform better than individuals. In these cases, the combination of several people's skills and knowledge adds up to more than the skills and knowledge of one individual, improving decisions (Mesmer-Magnus & DeChurch, 2009).

Should some ideas not be heard? Groupthink suggests that groups come to better decisions when disagreement is encouraged rather than discouraged — something to keep in mind when discussing issues on campus or deciding whether speakers invited to campus should be heard (Ceci & Williams, 2018).
MB Images/Shutterstock

Imagine being asked to solve difficult analogy problems such as this one: *Assertion* is to *disproved* as *action* is to

a. *hindered*
b. *opposed*
c. *illegal*
d. *precipitate*
e. *thwarted*

Most college students miss this question when answering alone, but answer correctly *(thwarted)* after group discussion (Laughlin & Adamopoulos, 1980; Laughlin, 1996; Laughlin et al., 2003). Similarly, when given tricky logic problems, three, four, or five heads are better than two (Laughlin et al., 2006). Groups of medical students were more likely to hit on the correct diagnosis for emergency room patients than individuals working independently (Kämmer et al., 2017).

Studies of the accuracy of eyewitness reports of a videotaped crime or job interview confirm that several heads can be better than one (Hinsz, 1990; Warnick & Sanders, 1980). Interacting groups of eyewitnesses give accounts that are much more accurate than those provided by the average isolated individual. Weather forecasts made by two people are more accurate than those made by one person (Myers, 1997). When unsure of what they've seen, sports referees are smart to confer before making their call.

"Iron sharpens iron, and one person sharpens the wits of another."

—Proverbs 27:17

Several heads critiquing one another can also allow the group to avoid some forms of cognitive bias and produce higher quality ideas (McGlynn et al., 1995; Wright et al., 1990). Out of the arguments of the Wright brothers came the first airplane. Out of the incessant debates between Steve Jobs and Steve Wozniak came the first Apple computer (Grant, 2017). Teams also have surpassed individuals in predicting world political events (Mellers et al., 2014, 2015).

As James Watson and Francis Crick demonstrated in discovering DNA, challenging two-person conversations can effectively engage creative thinking. Watson later recalled that he and Crick benefited from *not* being the most brilliant people seeking to crack the genetic code. The most brilliant researcher "was so intelligent that she rarely sought advice" (quoted by Cialdini, 2005). Like Watson and Crick, psychologists Daniel Kahneman and the late Amos Tversky similarly collaborated in their exploration of intuition and its influence on economic decision making. (See "The Inside Story: Behind a Nobel Prize.")

"If you want to go quickly, go alone. If you want to go far, go together."

—African Proverb

THE inside STORY

Behind a Nobel Prize: Two Minds Are Better Than One

In the spring of 1969, Amos Tversky, my younger colleague at the Hebrew University of Jerusalem, and I met over lunch and shared our own recurrent errors of judgment. From there were born our studies of human intuition.

I had enjoyed collaboration before, but this was magical. Amos was very smart, and also very funny. We could spend hours of solid work in continuous mirth. His work was always characterized by confidence and by a crisp elegance, and it was a joy to find those characteristics now attached to my ideas as well. As we were writing our first paper, I was conscious of how much better it was than the more hesitant piece I would have written by myself.

All our ideas were jointly owned. We did almost all the work on our joint projects while physically together, including the drafting of questionnaires and papers. Our principle was to discuss every disagreement until it had been resolved to our mutual satisfaction.

Some of the greatest joys of our collaboration — and probably much of its success — came from our ability to elaborate on each other's nascent thoughts: If I expressed a half-formed idea, I knew that Amos would be there to understand it, probably more clearly than I did, and that if it had merit, he would see it.

Amos and I shared the wonder of together owning a goose that could lay golden eggs — a joint mind that was better than our separate minds. We were a team, and we remained in that mode for well over a decade. The Nobel Prize was awarded for work that we produced during that period of intense collaboration.

Daniel Kahneman
Princeton University
Nobel Laureate, 2002
Courtesy of Daniel Kahneman

However, there are limits to group performance, especially for creative tasks. Generally, people working alone generate more creative ideas than those brainstorming in groups (Paulus et al., 1995, 2000, 2011; Rietzschel et al., 2006; Stroebe & Diehl, 1994). Large brainstorming groups are especially inefficient. In accord with social loafing theory, large groups cause some individuals to free-ride on others' efforts, to feel apprehensive about voicing oddball ideas, and to lose their ideas while awaiting a turn to speak (Nijstad & Stroebe, 2006).

When people work together in creative teams, one solution is to alternate group and individual brainstorming (Brown & Paulus, 2002; Paulus & Coskun, 2012; Paulus & Korde, 2014). Team members can also generate ideas individually but then post them to an online group document, which helps keep ideas flowing without having to wait for a turn to speak (Ivanov & Zelchenko, 2020).

Contrary to popular belief, brainstorming sessions with groups do not generate better or more creative ideas.
Wavebreakmedia/Shutterstock

Overall, when group members freely combine their creative ideas and varied insights, the frequent result is not groupthink but group problem-solving. Thus, we can conclude that when information from many, diverse people is combined, all of us together can become smarter than almost any of us alone – assuming we can avoid the pitfalls of groupthink. We're in some ways like a flock of geese, no one of which has a perfect navigational sense. Nevertheless, by staying close to one another, a group of geese can navigate accurately. The flock is smarter than the bird.

SUMMING UP: Group Decision-Making: Do Groups Help or Hinder Good Decisions?

- Analysis of several international fiascos indicates that group cohesion can override realistic appraisal of a situation. This is especially true when group members strongly desire unity, when they are isolated from opposing ideas, and when the leader signals what they want from the group.
- Symptomatic of this overriding concern for harmony, labeled *groupthink*, are (1) an illusion of invulnerability, (2) rationalization, (3) unquestioned belief in the group's morality, (4) stereotyped views of the opposition, (5) pressure to conform, (6) self-censorship of misgivings, (7) an illusion of unanimity, and (8) "mindguards" who protect the group from unpleasant information.
- However, groups sometimes decide wisely. These cases suggest ways to prevent groupthink: upholding impartiality, encouraging "devil's advocate" positions, subdividing and then reuniting to discuss a decision, seeking outside input, and having a "second-chance" meeting before implementing a decision.
- Research on group problem solving suggests that groups can be more accurate than individuals in many realms. For generating creative ideas, a combination of individual and group contributions works best.

THE INFLUENCE OF THE MINORITY: HOW DO INDIVIDUALS INFLUENCE THE GROUP?

Explain when — and how — individuals influence their groups, either as group members or leaders.

Each chapter in this social influence unit concludes with a reminder of our power as individuals. We have seen that

- cultural situations mold us, but we also help create and choose these situations.
- pressures to conform sometimes overwhelm our better judgment, but blatant pressure motivates reactance as we assert our individuality and freedom.
- persuasive forces are powerful, but we can resist persuasion by making public commitments and by anticipating persuasive appeals.

When 15-year-old Greta Thunberg went on a school strike outside the Swedish Parliament to raise awareness of climate change in August 2018, she was alone. A little more than a year later, in September 2019, an estimated quarter of a million people joined her at the Global Strike for Climate Change in New York City — showing the power of the individual in influencing groups.

(Left): Michael Campanella/Getty Images; (Right): PETER FOLEY/EPA-EFE/Shutterstock

This chapter has emphasized group influences on the individual, so we conclude by seeing how individuals can influence their groups. We do this in two ways: considering how individual group members can sway a group and how individual leaders can influence groups and societies. We will first consider how group members who have a different view than the rest of the group – often called a *minority opinion* or a *minority* – can sometimes change the rest of the group's views. (In this case, a minority refers to individuals with views in the minority and not to ethnic minorities.)

The Influence of Individual Group Members

In the classic film *12 Angry Men,* a lone juror eventually wins over 11 others. In a jury room, that's a rare occurrence. Yet in most social movements, a small minority opinion will sway, and then eventually become, the majority opinion. "All history," wrote Ralph Waldo Emerson (1863/2001, p. 315), "is a record of the power of minorities, and of minorities of one." Think of Copernicus and Galileo, of Martin Luther King, Jr., of Susan B. Anthony, of Nelson Mandela. The American civil rights movement was ignited by the refusal of one African American woman, Rosa Parks, to relinquish her seat on a Montgomery, Alabama, bus. Technological history has also been made by innovative individuals defying the group norm. As Robert Fulton developed his steamboat, "Fulton's Folly," he endured constant derision: "Never did a single encouraging remark, a bright hope, a warm wish, cross my path" (Cantril & Bumstead, 1960). Despite these barriers, these individuals in the minority persisted and eventually won others to their point of view. Think about it: If minority viewpoints never prevail, history would be static and nothing would ever change (Jung et al., 2018).

What makes a minority within a group persuasive? What might Arthur Schlesinger have done to get the Kennedy group to consider his doubts about the Bay of Pigs invasion? Experiments initiated by Serge Moscovici in Paris identified several determinants of minority influence: *consistency, self-confidence,* and *defection.*

CONSISTENCY

More influential than a minority that wavers is a minority that sticks to its position. Moscovici and associates (1969; Moscovici, 1985) found that if a minority of participants consistently judges blue slides as green, members of the majority will occasionally agree. But if the minority wavers, saying "blue" to one-third of the blue slides and "green" to the rest, virtually no one in the majority will ever agree with "green."

Experiments show – and experience confirms – that nonconformity, especially persistent nonconformity, is often painful and that being a minority in a group can be unpleasant

(Levine, 1989; Lücken & Simon, 2005). That helps explain a *minority slowness effect*: a tendency for people with minority views to express those views less quickly than do people in the majority (Bassili, 2003). If you set out to be a minority of one, prepare yourself for ridicule – especially when you argue an issue that's personally relevant to the majority and when the group wants to settle an issue by reaching consensus (Kameda & Sugimori, 1993; Kruglanski & Webster, 1991; Trost et al., 1992).

Even when people in the majority know that the disagreeing person is factually or morally right, they may still, if refusing to change, dislike the person (Chan et al., 2010). When Charlan Nemeth (1979, 2011) planted a minority of two within a simulated jury and had them oppose the majority's opinions, the duo was inevitably disliked. Nevertheless, the majority acknowledged that the persistence of the two made them rethink their positions. Compared to majority influence that often triggers unthinking agreement, minority influence stimulates a deeper processing of arguments, often with increased creativity (Kenworthy et al., 2008; Martin et al., 2007, 2008). Minority views may get you disliked, especially if you are on the fringe of a group, but they can also increase creative innovation (Rijnbout & McKimmie, 2012).

Some successful companies have recognized that minority perspectives can feed creativity and innovation. 3M, which has been famed for valuing "respect for individual initiative," has welcomed employees spending time on wild ideas. The Post-it note's adhesive came from an earlier failed attempt by Spencer Silver to develop a super-strong glue. Art Fry, after having trouble bookmarking his church choir hymnal with pieces of paper, thought, "What I need is a bookmark with Spence's adhesive along the edge." His was a minority view that eventually won over a skeptical marketing department (Nemeth, 1997).

SELF-CONFIDENCE

Consistency and persistence convey self-confidence. Furthermore, Charlan Nemeth and Joel Wachtler (1974) reported that any behavior by a minority that conveys self-confidence – for example, taking the head seat at the table – tends to raise self-doubts among the majority. By being firm and forceful, the minority's apparent self-assurance may prompt the majority to reconsider its position. This is especially so on matters of opinion ("from which country should Italy import most of its raw oil?"), rather than fact ("from which country does Italy import most of its raw oil?") (Maass et al., 1996).

DEFECTIONS FROM THE MAJORITY

A persistent minority punctures any illusion of unanimity. When a minority consistently doubts the majority's wisdom, majority members become freer to express their own doubts and may even switch to the minority position. But what about a lone defector, someone who initially agreed with the majority but then reconsidered and dissented? In research with University of Pittsburgh students, John Levine (1989) found that a person who had defected from the majority was even more persuasive than a consistent minority voice. Nemeth's jury-simulation experiments found that – not unlike the *12 Angry Men* scenario – once defections begin, others soon follow, initiating a snowball effect.

There is a delightful irony in this new emphasis on how individuals can influence the group. Until recently, the idea that the minority could sway the majority was itself a minority view in social psychology. Nevertheless, by arguing consistently and forcefully, Moscovici, Nemeth, Maass, and others convinced the majority of group influence researchers that minority influence is a phenomenon worthy of study. And the way that several of these minority influence researchers came by their interests should, perhaps, not surprise us. Anne Maass (1998) became interested in how minorities could effect social change after growing up in postwar Germany and hearing her grandmother's personal accounts of fascism. Charlan Nemeth (1999) developed her interest while she was a visiting professor in Europe "working with Henri Tajfel and Serge Moscovici," she said. "The three of us were 'outsiders' – I an American Roman Catholic female in Europe, they having survived World War II as Eastern European Jews. Sensitivity to the value and the struggles of the minority perspective came to dominate our work."

leadership
The process by which certain group members motivate and guide the group.

task leadership
Leadership that organizes work, sets standards, and focuses on goals.

social leadership
Leadership that builds teamwork, mediates conflict, and offers support.

The Influence of Leaders

In 1910, the Norwegians and the English engaged in an epic race to the South Pole. The Norwegians, effectively led by Roald Amundsen, made it. The English, ineptly led by Robert Falcon Scott, did not; Scott and three team members died. Amundsen illustrated the power of **leadership,** the process by which individuals mobilize and guide groups.

Some leaders are formally appointed or elected; others emerge informally as the group interacts. What makes for good leadership often depends on the situation. The best person to lead the engineering team may not make the best leader of the sales force. Some people excel at **task leadership** – at organizing work, setting standards, and focusing on goal attainment. Others excel at **social leadership** – at building teamwork, mediating conflicts, and being supportive (see "Focus On: Transformational Community Leadership").

focus ON Transformational Community Leadership

As a striking example of transformational (consistent, self-confident, inspirational) leadership, consider Walt and Mildred Woodward. During World War II and in the two decades after, they owned and edited the Bainbridge Island, Washington, newspaper. It was from Bainbridge that, on March 30, 1942, the first of nearly 120,000 West Coast people of Japanese descent were relocated to internment camps. With 6 days' notice and under armed guard, they boarded a ferry and were sent away, leaving behind on the dock tearful friends and neighbors (one of whom was their insurance agent, my [DM's] father). "Where, in the face of their fine record since December 7 [Pearl Harbor Day], in the face of their rights of citizenship, in the face of their own relatives being drafted and enlisting in our Army, in the face of American decency, is there any excuse for this high-handed, much-too-short evacuation order?" editorialized the Woodwards (1942) in their *Bainbridge Review.* Throughout the war, the Woodwards, alone among West Coast newspaper editors, continued to voice opposition to the internment. They also recruited their former part-time employee, Paul Ohtaki, to write a weekly column bringing news of the incarcerated islanders. Stories by Ohtaki and others of "Pneumonia Hits 'Grandpa Koura'" and "First Island Baby at Manzanar Born" reminded those back home of their absent neighbors and prepared the way for their eventual welcome home — a contrast to the prejudice that greeted their return to other West Coast communities where newspapers supported the internment and fostered hostility toward the Japanese.

In March 1942, 274 Bainbridge Islanders became the first of some 120,000 Japanese Americans and Japanese immigrants interned during World War II. Sixty-two years later, ground was broken for a national memorial (*Nidoto Nai Yoni* — Let It Not Happen Again), remembering the internees and the transformational leaders who supported them and prepared for their welcome home.
Library of Congress/Corbis Historical/Getty Images

After enduring some vitriolic opposition, the Woodwards lived to be honored for their courage, which was dramatized in the book and movie *Snow Falling on Cedars.* At the March 30, 2004, groundbreaking for a national memorial on the ferry departure site, former internee and Bainbridge Island Japanese American Community president Frank Kitamoto declared that "this memorial is also for Walt and Millie Woodward, for Ken

Myers, for Genevive Williams . . . and the many others who supported us," and who challenged the forced removal at the risk of being called unpatriotic. "Walt Woodward said if we can suspend the Bill of Rights for Japanese Americans it can be suspended for fat Americans or blue-eyed Americans." Reflecting on the Woodwards' transformational leadership, cub reporter Ohtaki (1999) observed that "on Bainbridge Island there was none of the hostility to the returning Japanese that you saw in other places, and I think that's in large part because of the Woodwards." When, later, he asked the Woodwards, "Why did you do this, when you could have dropped it and not suffered the anger of some of your readers?" they would always answer, "It was the right thing to do."

Task leaders generally have a directive style – one that can work well if the leader is bright enough to give good orders (Fiedler, 1987). Being goal oriented, such leaders also keep the group's attention and effort focused on its mission. Experiments show that the combination of specific, challenging goals and periodic progress reports helps motivate high achievement (Locke & Latham, 1990, 2002, 2009). Men who have the traits associated with traditional male leadership – fitness, height, masculine (wide) faces – tend to be perceived as dominant leaders and to succeed as CEOs (Blaker et al., 2013; Wong et al., 2011).

Social leaders generally have a democratic style – one that delegates authority, welcomes input from team members, and, as we have seen, helps prevent groupthink. Data amassed from 118 studies reveal that women are much more egalitarian than men (Lee et al., 2011) and are thus more likely to have a social leadership style. This type of leadership style is especially effective during uncertain times. At the beginning of the COVID-19 pandemic in 2020, female state governors in the United States expressed more empathy and confidence than male governors during their briefings, and their states had fewer deaths from COVID-19 than states with male governors (Sergent & Stajkovic, 2020).

Many experiments reveal that social leadership is good for morale. Group members usually feel more satisfied when they participate in making decisions (Spector, 1986; Vanderslice et al., 1987). Given control over their tasks, workers also become more motivated to achieve (Burger, 1987).

The once-popular "great person" theory of leadership – that all great leaders share certain traits – has fallen out of favor. Effective leadership styles, we now know, are less about the big "I" than the big "we." Effective leaders represent, enhance, and champion a group's identity (Haslam et al., 2010). Effective leadership also varies with the situation. Subordinates who know what they are doing may resent working under task leadership, whereas those who don't may welcome it. However, social psychologists have again wondered if there might be qualities that mark a good leader in many situations (Hogan et al., 1994). British social psychologists Peter Smith and Monir Tayeb (1989) reported that studies done in India, Taiwan, and Iran have found that the most effective supervisors in coal mines, banks, and government offices scored high on tests of *both* task and social leadership. They are actively concerned with how work is progressing *and* sensitive to the needs of their subordinates.

Studies also reveal that many effective leaders of laboratory groups, work teams, and large corporations not only avoid groupthink by welcoming diverse views, they also exhibit the behaviors that help make a minority view persuasive. Such leaders engender trust by *consistently* sticking to their goals. And they often exude a *self-confident* charisma that kindles the allegiance of their followers (Bennis, 1984; House & Singh, 1987). Effective leaders typically have a compelling *vision* of some desired state of affairs, especially during times of collective stress

Participative management, requires democratic rather than autocratic leaders.
Morsa Images/E+/Getty Images

Transformational leadership: Charismatic, energetic, self-confident people will sometimes change organizations or societies by inspiring others to embrace their vision. Martin Luther King, Jr., was this type of leader.
Lei Yixin/U.S. National Park Service

(Halevy et al., 2011). They also have an ability to *communicate* that vision to others in clear and simple language, and enough optimism and faith in their group to *inspire* others to follow.

In one analysis of 50 Dutch companies, the highest morale was at firms with chief executives who most inspired their colleagues "to transcend their own self-interests for the sake of the collective" (de Hoogh et al., 2004). Leadership of this kind – **transformational leadership** – motivates others to identify with and commit themselves to the group's mission (Groves, 2020). Transformational leaders – many of whom are charismatic, energetic, self-confident extraverts – articulate high standards, inspire people to share their vision, and offer personal attention (Bono & Judge, 2004). In organizations, the frequent result of such leadership is a more engaged, trusting, and effective workforce (Ng, 2017; Turner et al., 2002).

transformational leadership
Leadership that, enabled by a leader's vision and inspiration, exerts significant influence.

To be sure, groups also influence their leaders. Sometimes those at the front of the herd have simply sensed where it is already heading. Political candidates know how to read the opinion polls. Someone who typifies the group's views is more likely to be selected as a leader; a leader who deviates too radically from the group's standards may be rejected (Hogg et al., 1998). Smart leaders usually remain with the majority and spend their influence prudently. In rare circumstances, the right traits matched with the right situation yield history-making greatness, notes Dean Keith Simonton (1994). To have a Winston Churchill or a Nelson Mandela, an Abraham Lincoln or a Martin Luther King, Jr., takes the right person in the right place at the right time. When an apt combination of intelligence, skill, determination, self-confidence, and social charisma meets a rare opportunity, the result is sometimes a championship, a Nobel Prize, or a social revolution.

SUMMING UP: The Influence of the Minority: How Do Individuals Influence the Group?

- Although a majority opinion often prevails, sometimes individuals with a minority opinion can influence and even overturn a majority position. Even if the majority does not adopt the minority's views, the minority's speaking up can increase the majority's self-doubts and prompt it to consider other alternatives, often leading to better, more creative decisions.
- In experiments, a minority is most influential when it is consistent and persistent in its views, when its actions convey self-confidence, and after it begins to elicit some defections from the majority. Such minority influence can enable creative motivation.
- Through their *task* and *social leadership,* formal and informal group leaders exert disproportionate influence. Those who consistently press toward their goals and exude a self-confident charisma often engender trust and inspire others to follow.

CONCLUDING THOUGHTS: Are Groups Bad for Us?

A selective reading of this chapter could, we must admit, leave readers with the impression that, on balance, groups are bad. In groups, we become more aroused, more stressed, more tense, more error-prone on complex tasks. Submerged in a group that gives us anonymity, we have a tendency to loaf or have our worst impulses unleashed by deindividuation. Police brutality, lynchings, gang destruction, and terrorism are all group phenomena. Discussion in groups often polarizes our views, enhancing mutual racism or hostility. It may also suppress dissent, creating a homogenized groupthink that produces disastrous decisions. No wonder we celebrate those individuals – minorities of one – who, alone against a group, have stood up for truth and justice. Groups, it seems, are ba-a-a-d. One can understand statistician-writer Nate Silver's (2023) statement: "I'm generally an optimist about how humans behave as individuals and a pessimist about how they behave in groups."

All that is true, but it's only half the truth. The other half is that, as social animals, we are group-dwelling creatures. Like our distant ancestors, we depend on one another for sustenance, support, and security. Moreover, when our individual tendencies are positive, group interaction accentuates our best. In groups, runners run faster, audiences laugh louder, and givers become more generous. In support groups, people strengthen their resolve to stop drinking, lose weight, and study harder. In kindred-spirited groups, people expand their spiritual consciousness. "A devout communing on spiritual things sometimes greatly helps the health of the soul," observed fifteenth-century cleric Thomas à Kempis, especially when people of faith "meet and speak and commune together."

Depending on which tendency a group is magnifying or disinhibiting, groups can be very, very bad or very, very good. So we had best choose our groups wisely and intentionally.

PART THREE

Social Relations

Prejudice

CHAPTER 9

Ira L. Black/Corbis/Getty Images

What is the nature and power of prejudice?

What are the social sources of prejudice?

What are the motivational sources of prejudice?

What are the cognitive sources of prejudice?

What are the consequences of prejudice?

Concluding Thoughts: Can we reduce prejudice?

We have now explored how we *think about* (Part One) and how we *influence* one another (Part Two). In these next chapters, we consider how we *relate* to one another (Part Three). Why do we sometimes dislike, even despise, one another? Why and when do we hurt one another? Why do we like or love particular people? When will we offer help to friends or strangers? How do social conflicts develop, and how they can be justly and amicably resolved?

Prejudice comes in many forms — for our own group and against some other group. Researchers, as we will see, have explored race, gender, and sexual orientation prejudice but also prejudices involving:

- *Religion.* Antisemitic incidents reached all-time highs in the United States in 2022, rising 36% in just one year, with organized white supremacist groups behind much of the increase. Hate crimes against Jewish people also increased in Germany (Graham & Stack, 2021; Grieshaber, 2023; Romo, 2023).
- *Obesity.* An analysis of 2.2 million social media posts containing "obese" or "fat" revealed a stream of insults, criticisms, and derogatory jokes (Chou et al., 2014). When seeking love and employment, people who are overweight — especially

White women — face diminished prospects. People who are overweight marry less often, have less desirable jobs, and make less money (Swami et al., 2008). Bias against people who are overweight is the one type of prejudice that has *not* declined since 2007 (Charlesworth & Banaji, 2019). Weight discrimination, in fact, exceeds racial or gender discrimination and occurs at every employment stage: hiring, placement, promotion, compensation, discipline, and discharge (Roehling, 2000). It also is at the root of much child bullying (Brody, 2017; Reece, 2017).

- *Age.* People's perceptions of the elderly — as kind but frail, incompetent, and unproductive — predispose patronizing behavior. Speaking to them using baby-talk, for example, leads elderly people to feel less competent and to act less capably (Bugental & Hehman, 2007).
- *Immigrants.* Research documents anti-immigrant prejudice among Germans toward Turks, the French toward North Africans, the British toward West Indians and Pakistanis, and Americans toward Latin Americans and Muslims (Crocetti et al., 2021; Murray & Marx, 2013; Pettigrew, 2006). In 2018, 3 out of 4 people in Hungary and Greece believed that immigrants were a burden on their country (Gonzalez-Barrera & Connor, 2019).
- *Politics.* Liberals and conservatives dislike, and sometimes detest, one another — and to roughly equal degrees (Crawford et al., 2017). They also display "virtually identical" amounts of bias toward their side (Ditto et al., 2019). In 2022, 72% of Republicans said they thought Democrats were "more immoral" than other Americans — and 63% of Democrats thought the same about Republicans (Pew, 2022).

WHAT IS THE NATURE AND POWER OF PREJUDICE?

Explain the nature of prejudice and the differences between prejudice, stereotypes, and discrimination.

Prejudice, stereotyping, discrimination, racism, sexism – the terms often overlap. Let's clarify them.

Defining Prejudice

Each of the situations described in the introduction involved a negative evaluation of some group. And that is the essence of **prejudice:** *a preconceived negative judgment of a group and its individual members.* (Some prejudice definitions include *positive* judgments, but nearly all uses of "prejudice" refer to *negative* ones.)

prejudice
A preconceived negative judgment of a group and its individual members.

Prejudice is an attitude – a combination of feelings, inclinations to act, and beliefs. It can be remembered as the ABCs of attitudes: *a*ffect (feelings), *b*ehavior tendency (inclination to act), and *c*ognition (beliefs). A prejudiced person may *feel dislike* toward those different from themselves and *behave* toward them in a discriminatory manner, *believing* them ignorant and dangerous.

Robin Bergh and Mark J. Brandt (2022) concluded that the targets of prejudice in the United States cluster into three categories: marginalized groups (Blacks, Asians, homeless people, immigrants, Muslims, people in poverty), unconventional groups (gays, lesbians,

What stereotypes might each of these people hold about the others? Even if stereotypes are somewhat accurate of a group as a whole, they are often not accurate for a particular individual.
Adam Hester/Blend Images

transgender people, atheists, liberals), and privileged or conservative groups (Christians, conservatives, athletes, Whites, wealthy people). This breakdown suggests people may be prejudiced against a wide variety of groups – usually those different from themselves.

The negative evaluations that mark prejudice are often supported by social beliefs about groups of people, called **stereotypes**. To stereotype is to generalize. To simplify the world, we generalize: The British are reserved; Americans are outgoing. Women love children; men love sports. Professors are absentminded. The elderly are frail.

stereotype
A belief about the personal attributes of a group of people. Stereotypes are sometimes overgeneralized, inaccurate, and resistant to new information (and sometimes accurate).

Such generalizations can be more or less true (and are not always negative). The elderly *are* generally more frail than younger people, for example. So stereotypes of groups are sometimes accurate – at least in terms of the group average. People perceive Australians as having a more free-wheeling culture than Britons – and they do use more profanity in their millions of Facebook posts (Kramer & Chung, 2011). "It's a stereotype that Texans like barbecue," observed Texas Senator Ted Cruz (2018). "It also happens that pretty much all Texans like barbecue."

The problem with stereotypes arises when they are inaccurate or *overgeneralized*. Inaccuracy occurs when perceptions of groups are incorrect, as when liberals and conservatives overestimate how extreme the others' views are or when people believe Black men are taller, more muscular, and thus potentially more threatening than same-sized White men (Graham et al., 2012; Wilson et al., 2017). To presume that most American welfare clients are Black is inaccurate because it just isn't so (most are White). To presume that single people are less conscientious and more neurotic than partnered people, as did people in one German study, was wrong because it just isn't so (Greitemeyer, 2009c). To presume that people with disabilities are incompetent and asexual, as did Oregonians in another study, misrepresents reality (Nario-Redmond, 2010). To stigmatize people who are obese as slow, lazy, and undisciplined is inaccurate (Puhl & Heuer, 2009, 2010). Overgeneralizing from vivid examples to an entire group is also a road to inaccuracy. To presume that Muslims are terrorists, priests are pedophiles, and evangelicals hate people who are gay overgeneralizes from the worst examples of each. Stereotypes are important because when stereotypes are negative, prejudice often follows (Phills et al., 2020).

Defining Discrimination

discrimination
Unjustified negative behavior toward a group or its members.

Prejudice is a negative *attitude;* **discrimination** is negative *behavior.* Merely feeling a prejudice isn't enough: Someone has to act on their attitude for it to qualify as discrimination. Consider what happened when researchers sent people to try to board a public bus in Brisbane, Australia, without any money to pay for the ride. Bus drivers allowed Whites to ride for free 72% of the time – twice as often as they let Black people ride for free (36%) (Mujcic & Frijters, 2020). Since letting someone ride for free is a behavior, not just an attitude, this study shows evidence of discrimination based on race.

In another study, researchers analyzed the responses to 1,115 identically worded emails sent to Los Angeles area landlords regarding vacant apartments. Encouraging replies came back to 89% of notes signed "Patrick McDougall," to 66% from "Said Al-Rahman," and to 56% from "Tyrell Jackson" – names associated with White, Muslim, and Black men, respectively (Carpusor & Loges, 2006). Similarly, when 4,859 U.S. state legislators received emails shortly before the 2008 election asking how to register to vote, "Jake Mueller" received more replies than "DeShawn Jackson," another demonstration of anti-Black discrimination (Butler & Broockman, 2011). Likewise, Jewish Israeli students were less likely to alert the sender to a misaddressed email that came from an Arab name and town ("Muhammed of Um-El Fachem") than from one of their own group ("Yoav Marom of Tel Aviv") (Tykocinski & Bareket-Bojmel, 2009). Black inmates with more stereotypically Black names (such as "Jamal") had received longer prison sentences than those with more stereotypically White names (such as "James") (Kenthirarajah et al., 2023). All of these studies involve behaviors and thus show discrimination.

The good news: Only a minority of people discriminate. Mitchell Campbell and Markus Brauer (2021) had research assistants interact with fellow students at the University of Wisconsin Madison – they asked for directions, dropped items, and rode buses to see whether their fellow students treated them differently depending on their race (Black or White), religion (wearing a hijab), or sexual orientation (wearing a t-shirt reading "Legalize Gay!"). Between 5% and 20% of students treated the research assistants more negatively when they belonged to a marginalized group. Thus, more than 4 out of 5 students did not discriminate. If only a minority of people are responsible for most discrimination, Campbell and Brauer argue, then instituting bias training for all students or employees might not be the best approach.

In addition, attitudes and behavior don't always predict one another. Prejudiced attitudes need not breed hostile acts, nor does all discrimination spring from prejudice. Consider: If word-of-mouth hiring practices in an all-white business have the effect of excluding potential non-White employees, the end result is discrimination – even if it was not intended (and thus was not rooted in prejudice per se). Much discrimination reflects no intended harm; it's simply favoritism toward people like oneself (Greenwald & Pettigrew, 2014). Most movie-studio heads are male, which may explain why only 4% of the directors of the top 100 films from 2007 to 2016 were female (Smith et al., 2017).

And consider this: Job ads for male-dominated vocations feature words associated with male stereotypes ("We are a dominant engineering firm seeking individuals who can perform in a competitive environment"), and job ads for female-dominated vocations feature the opposite ("We seek people who will be sensitive to clients' needs and can develop warm client relationships"). The result of such ads may be institutional sexism. Without intending any prejudice, the gendered wording helps sustain gender inequality (Gaucher et al., 2011).

Implicit Prejudice

Prejudice illustrates our *dual attitude* system. Some attitudes are explicit (conscious) and others are implicit (automatic) (Greenwald & Banaji, 2017). For example, the Implicit Association Test (IAT) assesses "implicit cognition" – our often unacknowledged inner beliefs that may or may not correspond to our explicit (conscious) attitudes. The IAT does this by measuring people's speed of associations. Much as we more quickly associate a hammer with a nail than with a bucket, the test can measure how speedily we associate white faces with "good" compared to Black faces with "good." Thus, people may have a spontaneous emotional reaction toward different groups (Hahn & Gawronski, 2019).

"Although our [conscious] minds are in the right places, and we may truly believe we are not prejudiced, our hearts aren't quite there yet."

—Social psychologist John Dovidio, *Time*, 2009

One can, for example, measure implicit racial attitudes by assessing whether White people take longer to associate positive words with Black faces than with White faces. Implicit attitude researchers have offered various IAT assessments online (projectimplicit.net), from the serious (do you implicitly associate men with careers and women with home?) to the trivial (do you prefer *Harry Potter* or *Lord of the Rings?*). Although explicit attitudes may change dramatically with education, implicit attitudes may linger, changing only as we form new habits through practice (Kawakami et al., 2000).

Critics contend that the IAT does not predict behavior well enough to assess or label individuals. Someone who is implicitly biased according to the IAT will not necessarily behave in a discriminatory way (Blanton et al., 2006, 2009, 2015; Oswald et al., 2013, 2015; Schimmack, 2021).

The test performs better in research on the average responses of large groups. For example, metro areas with higher implicit bias scores also have larger racial disparities in police shootings and traffic stops (Ekstrom et al., 2022; Hehman et al., 2018). Barack Obama's election to the U.S. presidency in 2008 led to an average reduction in implicit prejudice toward Black Americans (Bernstein et al., 2010; Columb & Plant, 2016; Goldman, 2012). Implicit prejudice against Black people in the United States declined between 2013 and 2016 when the Black Lives Matter movement brought attention to anti-Black prejudice (Sawyer & Gampa, 2018).

As U.S. states one by one passed legislation legalizing same-sex marriage, implicit prejudice against gays and lesbians declined in those states; nationwide, implicit prejudice based on sexual orientation declined 65% between 2007 and 2020 (Charlesworth & Banaji, 2022; Ofosu et al., 2019). Even a small change in implicit prejudice may, over time and across people, accumulate to a large societal effect (Greenwald et al., 2015; Jost, 2019). Thus, while the IAT, like most psychological measures, only modestly predicts individual acts, it better predicts average outcomes (Vuletich & Payne, 2019).

"No one is born hating another person because of the color of his skin, or his background, or his religion. People must learn to hate, and if they can learn to hate, they can be taught to love, for love comes more naturally to the human heart than its opposite."

—Nelson Mandela, *Long Walk to Freedom*, 1994

Keeping in mind the distinction between conscious, explicit prejudice and unconscious, implicit prejudice, let's examine three common forms of prejudice: racial prejudice, gender prejudice, and LGBTQ+ prejudice. In each case, we will look first at explicit prejudice, which is the greater (though not the only) predictor of discriminatory acts.

Racial Prejudice

In the context of the world, every race is a minority. Non-Hispanic Whites, for example, are one-fifth of the world's people and will be one-eighth within another half-century. Thanks to mobility and migration over the past two centuries, the world's races now intermingle, in relations that are sometimes amiable, sometimes hostile.

To a molecular biologist, skin color is a trivial human characteristic, one controlled by a minuscule genetic difference. Moreover, nature doesn't cluster races in neatly defined categories. It is people, not nature, who label Barack Obama (the son of a White woman and Black man) and Meghan Markle, the Duchess of Sussex (the daughter of a Black woman and White man) as "Black."

IS RACIAL PREJUDICE DISAPPEARING?

Explicitly prejudicial attitudes can change very quickly.

- In 1942, fewer than a third of all U.S. Whites (and only 1 in 50 in the South) supported school integration by race; by 1980, support for White and Black children going to school together was 90%.
- Among U.S. adults, approval of Black people and White people marrying each other went from 4% in 1958 to 94% in 2021 (McCarthy, 2021).
- Scores on both explicit and implicit tests of racial prejudice declined between 2007 and 2020 (Charlesworth & Banaji, 2019, 2022).

Although prejudice dies last in socially intimate contacts, interracial marriage has increased in most countries, and 94% of Americans now approve of "marriage between Blacks and Whites" — a sharp increase from the 4% who approved in 1958 (McCarthy, 2021).
Darren Greenwood/Design Pics

Considering the thin slice of history covered by the years of these surveys, these changes are dramatic. Overt racial prejudice has also declined in Britain; for example, 89% say they would be happy for their child to marry someone from another ethnic group, up from 75% in 2009 (Kaur-Ballagan, 2020). In 2019, 76% of U.S. adults said it's a good thing that the U.S. population is made up of people of many different races and ethnicities (Horowitz, 2019).

African Americans' attitudes also have changed since the 1940s, when Kenneth Clark and Mamie Clark (1947) demonstrated that many African Americans held anti-Black prejudices. In making its historic 1954 decision declaring segregated schools unconstitutional, the Supreme Court found it noteworthy that when the Clarks gave African American children a choice between Black dolls and White dolls, most chose the White. By the 1970s, however, Black children were increasingly likely to prefer Black dolls, and adult Blacks came to view Blacks and Whites as similar in such traits as intelligence, laziness, and dependability (Jackman & Senter, 1981; Smedley & Bayton, 1978).

Shall we conclude, then, that racial prejudice is nearing extinction in countries such as the United States, Britain, and Canada? Not if we consider the recent increase in reported hate crime incidents in the United States – up 11% between 2001 and 2021 (Nakamura, 2023). Not if we consider the 29% of White Americans who agree that the country needs to "protect and preserve its White European heritage" (Kahn, 2019). And not if we consider that people tend to underreport their negative stereotypes and feelings (Bergsieker et al., 2012).

So, how great is the progress toward racial equality? In the United States, White people have tended to contrast the present with the oppressive past, perceiving swift and radical progress. Black people have tended to contrast the present with an equally fair world, which has not yet been realized, and perceive somewhat less progress (Eibach & Ehrlinger, 2006). For example, Americans misperceive the considerable Black-White race gap in wealth and income, underestimating it by 80 percentage points. Americans also underestimate the chances that a lower-income Black American will move up the economic ladder (Davidai & Walker, 2022; Kraus et al., 2019).

In 1962, riots erupted when African-American James Meredith attended the University of Mississippi after winning a court ruling. He became the school's first Black graduate in August 1963.
Library of Congress Prints and Photographs Division LC-DIG-ppmsca-04292

DISPLAYS OF RACIAL PREJUDICE AND DISCRIMINATION

In addition to overt discrimination, more subtle prejudice also persists. Most people support racial equality and deplore discrimination. Yet 3 in 4 people who take the Implicit Association Test display an automatic, unconscious tendency to associate White, more than Black, with favorable words (Banaji & Greenwald, 2013). When both college student or police officer participants were subliminally exposed to photos of Black men, they were faster to identify pictures of weapons than participants who had instead seen photos of White men (Eberhardt et al., 2004).

Racial prejudice can also appear indirectly; for example, all American adults judged spaces (such as neighborhoods and schools) associated with Black Americans as impoverished, crime-ridden, and dirty (Bonam et al., 2016). Modern prejudice also appears subtly, in our preferences for what is familiar, similar, and comfortable (Dovidio et al., 1992; Esses et al., 1993a; Gaertner & Dovidio, 2005).

We can also detect bias in *behaviors* and thus discrimination:

- *Employment discrimination.* MIT researchers sent 5,000 résumés out in response to 1,300 varied employment ads (Bertrand & Mullainathan, 2004). Applicants who were randomly assigned White names (Emily, Greg) received one callback for every 10 résumés sent. Those given Black names (Lakisha, Jamal) received one callback for every 15 résumés sent. In meta-analyses of 90 studies across 6 countries, this bias was just as strong in 2017 as it had been in 1969 (Quillian & Lee, 2023; Quillian et al., 2017). As if aware of the result, Barack Obama (2015) reminded Americans to guard "against the subtle impulse to call Johnny back for a job interview but not Jamal." Racial biases may also influence the starting salary offered to Black job seekers (Hernandez et al., 2019).
- *Favoritism galore.* Similar experiments have found
  - Airbnb hosts less likely to accept applications from would-be guests with African American names (Edelman et al., 2017), and
  - longer Uber and Lyft wait times and more cancellations for passengers with African American names (Ge et al., 2016).
- *Interactions with police.* Even after controlling for neighborhood crime rates and other factors, African Americans were more likely than Whites to be stopped,

"If we can't help our latent biases, we can help our behavior in response to those instinctive reactions, which is why we work to design systems and processes that overcome that very human part of us all."

—FBI Director James B. Comey, *Hard Truths: Law Enforcement and Race*, 2015

searched, handcuffed, and arrested by police (Hetey & Eberhardt, 2018; Stelter et al., 2022). African Americans were more likely than Whites to be physically grabbed or pushed to the ground during encounters with the police (Fryer, 2016). In an analysis of body camera footage of 918 Oakland Police traffic stops, officers of all races showed less respect for Black than for White drivers (Voigt et al., 2017). In the U.K., 38% of ethnic minorities said they had been wrongly accused of shoplifting in the past 5 years, compared to only 14% of Whites (Booth & Mohdin, 2018).

- *Patronizing behavior.* Modern prejudice can also appear as a race sensitivity that leads to exaggerated reactions to isolated ethnic minority persons – overpraising their accomplishments and failing to warn Black students, as they would White students, about potential academic difficulty (Crosby & Monin, 2007; Fiske, 1989; Hart & Morry, 1997; Hass et al., 1991). At Stanford University, Kent Harber (1998) gave White students a poorly written essay to evaluate. When the students thought the writer was Black, they rated it *higher* than when they thought the author was White, and they rarely offered harsh criticisms. The evaluators, perhaps wanting to avoid the appearance of bias, patronized the Black essayists with lower standards. Such "inflated praise and insufficient criticism" may hinder ethnic minority student achievement, Harber noted. In follow-up research, Harber and his colleagues (2010) found that Whites concerned about appearing biased not only rated and commented more favorably on weak essays attributed to Black students, they also recommended less time for skill development. To appear unprejudiced, they bent over backward to give positive and unchallenging feedback.

"I cannot totally grasp all that I am. . . . For that darkness is lamentable in which the possibilities in me are hidden from myself."

—St. Augustine, *Confessions*, AD 398

"Prejudice is a burden that confuses the past, threatens the future and renders the present inaccessible. . . . We may encounter many defeats but we must not be defeated."

—Maya Angelou

THE IMPACT OF RACIAL PREJUDICE

In some situations, automatic, implicit prejudice can have life or death consequences. In separate experiments, Joshua Correll and his co-workers (2002, 2007, 2015; Sadler et al., 2012) and Anthony Greenwald and his co-workers (2003) invited people to press buttons quickly to "shoot" or "not shoot" men who suddenly appeared onscreen holding either a gun or a harmless object such as a flashlight or a bottle. The participants more often misperceived the object and mistakenly shot harmless targets who were Black. (Follow-up computerized simulations revealed that it's Black *male* suspects – not females, whether Black or White – that are more likely to be associated with threat and to be shot [Plant et al., 2011].)

Other studies have found that when primed with a Black rather than a White face, people think guns: They more quickly recognize a gun, and they more often mistake a tool, such as a wrench, for a gun (Eberhardt et al., 2004; Judd et al., 2004; Payne, 2001, 2006; Todd et al., 2021). In one study, Whites who had seen Black male faces (vs. White male faces) reacted faster to threatening images, suggesting they automatically associated Black males with physical threat (March et al., 2021).

Automatic prejudice. When Joshua Correll and his colleagues invited people to react quickly to people holding either a gun or a harmless object such as a phone, race influenced perceptions and reactions.
Pawel Radomski/Shutterstock

When people are fatigued or feeling threatened by a dangerous world, they become even more likely to mistakenly shoot a minority person (Ma et al., 2013; Miller et al., 2012). Brain activity in the amygdala, a region that underlies fear and aggression, facilitates such automatic responding (Eberhardt, 2005; Harris & Fiske, 2006). When under threat, people act more impulsively after they see Black faces compared to White faces (Rubien-Thomas et al., 2023). Although implicit bias training programs have been implemented in many police departments, results so far show they do not lead to meaningful changes in officers' behaviors (Worden et al., 2020).

Police killings of unarmed Black citizens also have ripple effects across the entire society, especially among Black Americans. In the 3 months following a publicized shooting of an unarmed Black person, Black Americans living in the same state experienced more days with poor mental health than before the incident (Bor et al., 2018).

Gender Prejudice

How pervasive is prejudice against women? In another chapter, we examined gender-role norms – people's ideas about how women and men *ought* to behave. Here we consider gender *stereotypes* – people's beliefs about how women and men *do* behave. Norms are *pre*scriptive; stereotypes are *de*scriptive.

GENDER STEREOTYPES

From research on stereotypes, two conclusions are indisputable: Strong gender stereotypes exist, and, as often happens, members of the stereotyped group accept them. Men and women agree that you *can* judge the book by its gendered cover. In a 2017 Pew survey, 87% of Americans agreed that men and women are "basically different" in "how they express their feelings" (Parker et al., 2017).

Remember that stereotypes are generalizations about a group of people and may be true, false, or overgeneralized from a kernel of truth. In another chapter, we noted that the average man and woman do differ somewhat in social connectedness, empathy, social power, aggressiveness, and sexual initiative (though not in intelligence). Do we then conclude that gender stereotypes are accurate? Sometimes stereotypes exaggerate differences. But not always, observed Janet Swim (1994). She found that Pennsylvania State University students' stereotypes of men's and women's restlessness, nonverbal sensitivity, aggressiveness, and so forth were reasonable approximations of actual gender differences.

Gender stereotypes have persisted across time and culture. Over decades, even as Americans have become more supportive of equal work roles for women and men, their beliefs about gender differences have endured (Donnelly et al., 2016; Haines et al., 2016). Averaging data from 27 countries, John Williams and his colleagues (1999, 2000) found that people everywhere perceive women as more agreeable and men as more outgoing. In 16 polls between 1946 and 2018, Americans became more likely to view men and women as equal in competence and intelligence but also became even more likely to see women as more agreeable and caring than men (Eagly et al., 2020). Sarah Ariel Lamer and her colleagues (2022) found that characters in popular children's TV shows were treated more positively for gender-stereotypical behavior. Girls who watched clips displaying this bias later reported more pressure to behave in stereotypically feminine ways.

"We may not realize it, but we are all affected by unconscious bias."

—Facebook Chief Operating Officer Sheryl Sandberg, Facebook post, June 16, 2017

Stereotypes (beliefs) are not prejudices (attitudes). Stereotypes may support prejudice. Yet one might believe, without prejudice, that men and women are "different yet equal." Let us, therefore, see how researchers probe for gender prejudice.

SEXISM: BENEVOLENT AND HOSTILE

Judging from what people tell survey researchers, attitudes toward women have changed as rapidly as racial attitudes. As **Figure 1** shows, the percentage of Americans willing to vote for a female presidential candidate increased sharply. In 1967, 67% of first-year American college students agreed that "the activities of married women are best confined to the home and family"; by 2002, only 22% agreed (Sax et al., 2002). After that, the home-family question no longer seemed worth asking.

Alice Eagly and her associates (1991) and Geoffrey Haddock and Mark Zanna (1994) also reported that people don't respond to women with gut-level negative emotions as they do to certain other groups. Most people *like* women more than men. They perceive women as more understanding, kind, and helpful. Eagly (1994) dubbed this *favorable* stereotype the *women-are-wonderful effect,* and it appears in countries around the world (Krys et al., 2018).

"Women are wonderful primarily because they are [perceived as] so nice. [Men are] perceived as superior to women in agentic [competitive, dominant] attributes that are viewed as equipping people for success in paid work, especially in male-dominated occupations."

—Alice Eagly, *Are People Prejudiced Against Women?,* 1994

But gender attitudes often are ambivalent, reported Peter Glick, Susan Fiske, and their colleagues (1996, 2007, 2011) from their surveys of 15,000 people in 19 nations. Gender attitudes frequently mix a *benevolent sexism* ("Women have a superior moral sensibility") with *hostile sexism* ("Women shouldn't be construction workers.") Benevolent sexism, though sounding positive ("women deserve protection"), may still impede gender equity by

FIGURE 1

Changing Gender Attitudes from 1940 to 2020

Source: Gallup, 2021.

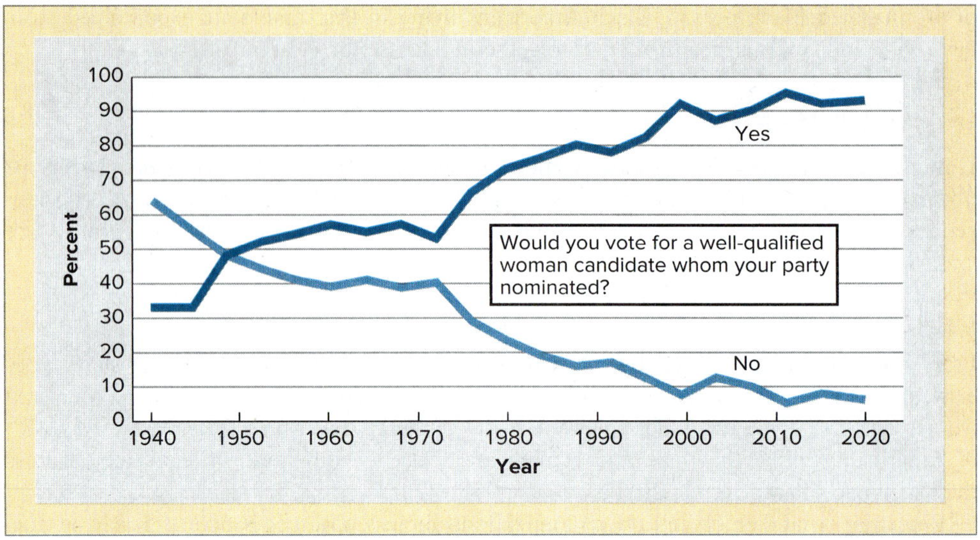

discouraging the hiring of women in traditionally male-dominated occupations (Barreto & Doyle, 2023; Hideg & Ferris, 2016). Both hostile sexism and benevolent sexism declined among New Zealand adults between 2009 and 2016 (Huang et al., 2019).

GENDER DISCRIMINATION

Summarizing other studies of people's evaluations of women and men as leaders, professors, and so forth, Alice Eagly (1994) concluded, "Experiments have *not* demonstrated any *overall* tendency to devalue women's work." An extensive analysis showed that female applicants for university faculty positions were actually more likely to be hired than male applicants. However, the analysis also found evidence of bias against women in salaries (women made less) and teaching evaluations (students judged female faculty more harshly; Ceci et al., 2023). Even after controlling for actual performance, women's performance in group discussions were valued less than men's (Dorrough et al., 2022).

Another area of concern is sexual assault and sexual harassment. Movie producer Harvey Weinstein, for example, was eventually convicted for multiple rapes (Tsioulcas, 2023). Yet when women initially reported Weinstein's actions, they were ignored or fired (Farrow, 2019). These incidents are just the most high-profile examples of a broader problem. A 2018 poll found that 81% of U.S. women had experienced some form of sexual harassment in their lifetime (as did 43% of men [Kearl, 2018]). Nearly a third of U.S. women said they had experienced unwanted sexual advances at work, in most cases from someone who had influence over their work (Gibson & Guskin, 2017). The World Health Organization estimates that 1 in 3 women worldwide have experienced sexual assault or partner violence (Devries et al., 2013; WHO, 2016).

In the non-Western world, gender discrimination is prominent. Although 86% of Europeans say it "is *very* important that women have the same rights as men," only 48% of Middle Easterners agree (Zainulbhai, 2016). Women are two-thirds of the world's illiterate (UN, 2015).

But the biggest violence against women may occur prenatally. Around the world, people tend to prefer having baby boys. In 1941, 38% of expectant parents in the United States said they preferred a boy if they could have only one child. In 2018, the answers were virtually unchanged, with 36% still preferring a boy (28% said they would prefer a girl, and 36% said it didn't matter [Newport, 2018a]).

With the widespread use of ultrasound to determine the sex of a fetus, these preferences are affecting the number of boys and girls born in several countries. In 2017 in China, there were 115 boy births for every 100 girl births (see **Figure 2**); by 2021 there were still 112 boy births for every 100 girls (Silver & Huang, 2022). The 32 million missing women in China

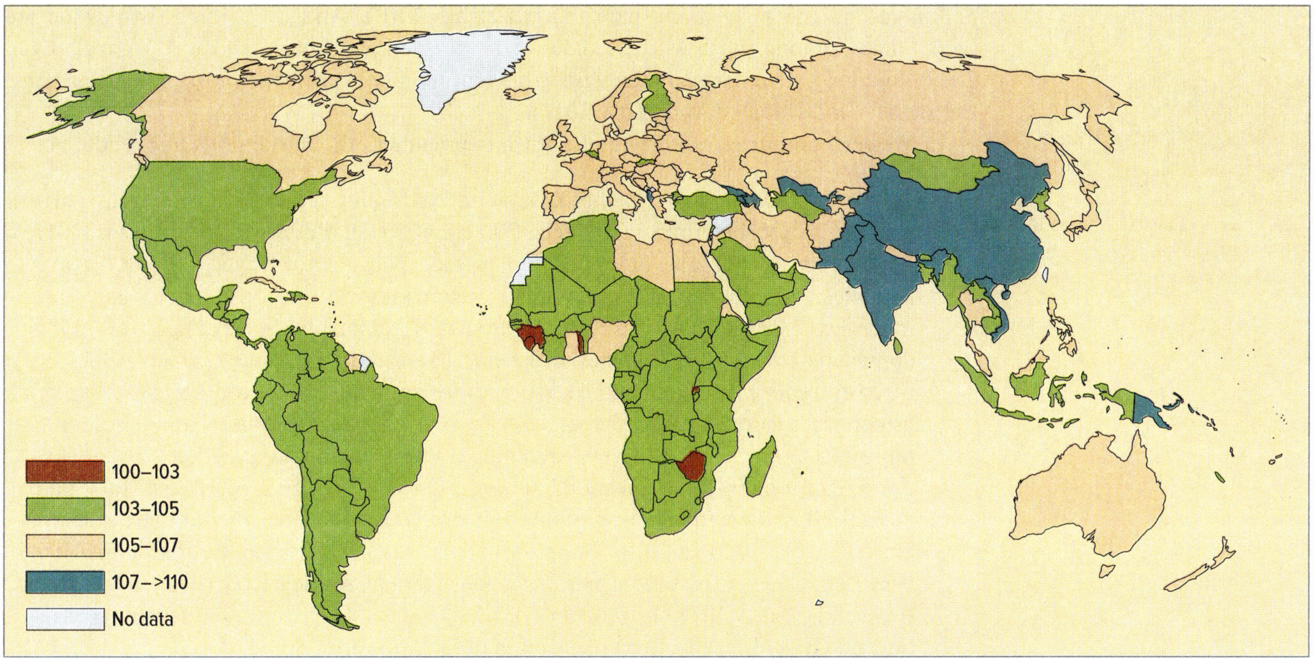

FIGURE 2

Sex Ratio at Birth, 2017

Higher numbers indicate more boys born (vs. girls). Countries in blue indicate an unusually high number of boy versus girl births.
Source: OurWorldinData.org, 2019.

have created an excess of 32 million young adult males. These are tomorrow's "bare branches": bachelors who will have trouble finding mates (Denyer & Gowen, 2018; Zhu et al., 2009). This female shortage also contributes to increased violence, crime, prostitution, and trafficking of women (Brooks, 2012). In response, China made sex-selective abortions a criminal offense. India's "save the girl child" campaign brought the sex ratio down to 108 from 111 (Tong, 2022). And in South Korea, which also for many years had experienced a deficit of girl births, the child sex ratio has returned to normal (Gupta, 2017).

Aggregate data from Google searches reveal parents' hopes for their children are also not gender-neutral (Stephens-Davidowitz, 2014). Many parents seem eager to have smart sons and slender, beautiful daughters – and often perceive their fathers and sons as smarter than their mothers and daughters (Furnham, 2016). You can see the search data for yourself. Google these phrases (with quotation marks) and note the number of results:

- "Is my daughter smart?"
- "Is my son smart?"
- "Is my son overweight?"
- "Is my daughter overweight?"

Although rapidly diminishing, antigay prejudice endures – in some cultures much more than others.
phototravelua/Shutterstock

LGBTQ+ Prejudice

Most of the world's gay and lesbian people cannot comfortably disclose who they are and whom they love (UN News, 2019). In many countries, same-sex relationships are a criminal offense (BBC, 2023). But cultures vary – from the 94% in Sweden who say homosexuality should be accepted by society to the 9% who agree in Indonesia (Poushter & Kent, 2020). In surveys across 23 countries, support of transgender rights was the lowest in Russia and the highest in Spain (Flores et al., 2016). Antigay attitudes worldwide are the strongest among those who are older, less educated, and male (Jäckle & Wenzelburger, 2015). Similarly, heterosexual men who value masculinity express the most prejudice against transgender individuals (Anderson, 2017).

In Western countries, antigay and antitrans prejudice, though diminishing, endures:

- *Job discrimination.* Experiments have submitted many hundreds of fictitious pairs of résumés to job openings (Drydakis, 2009; LeCroy & Rodefer, 2019; Tilcsik, 2011). By random assignment, one applicant in each pair acknowledged, among other activities, volunteering in a gay-lesbian organization. In response, callbacks were much less likely to come to the gay-associated applicants. For example, 7.2% of applicants whose activities included being "Treasurer, Gay and Lesbian Alliance" received replies, compared to 11.5% of those associated with a different left-seeming group ("Treasurer, Progressive and Socialist Alliance"). Job discrimination is even more pronounced for transgender people, half of whom say they have been asked unnecessary or invasive questions at work. One in five trans adults said they had been fired or denied a job or promotion due to their gender identity (Kirzinger et al., 2023). In 2020, the U.S. Supreme Court ruled that workplace discrimination based on sexual orientation or transgender status was illegal (Barnes, 2020). Before this ruling, an LGBTQ+ individual in the United States could get legally married on Sunday and legally fired on Monday. But no more.
- *Support for same-sex relationships is now very high.* In Western countries, support for same-sex marriage has soared over the past 2 decades: in the United States, for example, from 27% in 1996 to 71% in 2023 (McCarthy, 2023). In the U.K., less than 10% approved of same-sex relationships in 1987 – compared to 78% in 2023 (Smith, 2023).
- *Harassment hurts.* In a National School Climate Survey, 3 out of 4 LGBTQ+ students said they were verbally harassed (called names or threatened) at school. Nearly a third were physically harassed, such as being pushed or shoved (GLSEN, 2022).
- *Rejection hurts.* One in three U.S. transgender adults say their families are unsupportive of their gender identity (Kirzinger et al., 2023). One out of 4 gay and lesbian adults and 81% of bisexual adults in the U.S. are not "out" to most of the important people in their lives (Brown, 2019).

But do disparaging attitudes and discriminatory practices against gay, lesbian, and transgender people cause actual harm? Do they increase LGBTQ+ people's risk of poor mental or physical health? Consider (from U.S. research summarized by Hatzenbuehler, 2014):

- *State policies predict gay folks' health and well-being.* In U.S. states without gay-lesbian hate crime and nondiscrimination protection, LGBTQ+ people experience substantially higher mood disorder rates, even after controlling for state differences in education and income. When states implement non-discrimination policies, LGBTQ+ youth suicide decreases afterward (McDowell et al., 2020).
- *Community attitudes also predict LGBTQ+ health.* Communities where antigay prejudice is commonplace are communities with high rates of gay-lesbian suicide and cardiovascular death. Moreover, gay and lesbian individuals who experience discrimination are at increased risk of depression and anxiety (Schmitt et al., 2014). Overall, the suicide rate among gay and lesbian teens – who often experience bullying – is at least 3 times higher than the general rate for teens in the United States (Raifman et al., 2020). Half of U.S. transgender teens and young adults report having attempted suicide (Trevor Project, 2023), although they were less likely to do so if their families supported them (Klein & Golub, 2016).

As the public's support for same-sex marriage has increased, more countries have legalized marriages between two men or two women.
Lisa F. Young/Shutterstock

- *Three quasi-experiments confirm the toxicity of gay stigma and the benefits of its removal.* Between 2001 and 2005, 16 U.S. states banned same-sex marriage. In those states, gays and lesbians (but not heterosexuals) experienced a 37% increase in mood disorders, a 42% increase in alcohol use disorders, and a 248% increase in general anxiety disorders (Hatzenbuehler, 2014). In states without a same-sex marriage ban, gays and lesbians experienced no such increases in psychiatric disorders. And when the tide turned and some states legalized same-sex marriage between 2004 and 2015, fewer teens in those states attempted suicide in the years afterward (Raifman et al., 2017). Over the period when Denmark and Sweden legalized same-sex marriage, suicide rates among partnered LGBT individuals declined sharply (Erlangsen et al., 2020).

SUMMING UP: What Is the Nature and Power of Prejudice?

- *Prejudice* is a preconceived negative attitude. *Stereotypes* are beliefs about another group – beliefs that may be accurate, inaccurate, or overgeneralized but based on a kernel of truth. *Discrimination* is unjustified negative behavior. Racism and sexism may refer to individuals' prejudicial attitudes or discriminatory behavior, or to oppressive institutional practices (even if not intentionally prejudicial).
- Prejudice exists in subtle and unconscious guises as well as overt, conscious forms. Researchers have devised subtle survey questions and indirect methods for assessing people's attitudes and behavior to detect unconscious prejudice.
- Racial prejudice against Blacks in the United States was widely accepted until the 1960s; since that time, it has become far less prevalent, but it still exists.
- Similarly, prejudice against women, gays and lesbians, and transgender people has lessened in recent decades. Nevertheless, strong gender stereotypes and a fair amount of gender, sexual orientation, and transgender bias are still found in the United States and, to a greater degree, elsewhere around the world.

WHAT ARE THE SOCIAL SOURCES OF PREJUDICE?

Explain the influences that give rise to and maintain prejudice.

Where does prejudice come from? It may arise from people differing in social status and in their desire to justify and maintain those differences. It may also be learned from our parents as they socialize us about what differences they believe matter between people. Our social institutions, too, may maintain and support prejudice. Consider first how prejudice can function to defend one's social position.

Social Inequalities: Unequal Status and Prejudice

A principle to remember: *Unequal status breeds prejudice.* Owners of enslaved people viewed them as lazy, irresponsible, lacking ambition – as having exactly those traits that justified the slavery. Historians debate the forces that create unequal status. But after those inequalities exist, prejudice helps justify the economic and social superiority of those who have wealth and power. Tell us the economic relationship between the two groups, and we'll predict the intergroup attitudes. Upper-class individuals are more likely than those in poverty to see people's fortunes as the outcomes they have earned – thanks to skill and effort, and not as the result of connections, money, and luck (Costa-Lopes et al., 2013; Kraus & Keltner, 2013).

As the #MeToo movement has shown, women are often confronted with discriminatory and predatory behavior that endangers their lives and their livelihoods. For years, Harvey Weinstein abused his power in Hollywood to harass and sexually assault dozens of women until he was arrested in 2018 and then convicted in 2020.
Steven Ferdman/Getty Images

Historical examples abound. Where slavery was practiced, prejudice ran strong. Nineteenth-century politicians justified imperial expansion by describing exploited colonized people as "inferior," "requiring protection," and a "burden" to be borne (Allport, 1958, pp. 204–205). Sociologist Helen Mayer Hacker (1951) noted how stereotypes of Black people and women helped rationalize the inferior status of each: Many people thought both groups were mentally slow, emotional and primitive, and "contented" with their subordinate role. Black people were "inferior"; women were "weak." Black people were fine if they kept their place; women's place was in the home.

Theresa Vescio and her colleagues (2005) tested that reasoning. They found that powerful men who stereotyped their female subordinates also gave them plenty of praise but fewer resources, thus undermining their performance and allowing the men to maintain their power. In the laboratory, too, patronizing benevolent sexism (statements implying that women, as the weaker sex, need support) has undermined women's cognitive performance by planting intrusive thoughts – self-doubts, preoccupations, and decreased self-esteem (Dardenne et al., 2007).

Peter Glick and Susan Fiske's distinction between "hostile" and "benevolent" sexism extends to other prejudices. We see other groups as *competent* or as *likable* but often not as both. These two culturally universal dimensions of social perception – competence and likability (warmth) – were illustrated by one European's comment that "Germans love Italians, but don't admire them. Italians admire Germans, but don't love them" (Cuddy et al., 2009). We typically *respect* the competence of those high in status and *like* those who agreeably accept a lower status. Depending on the situation, we may seek to impress people with either our competence or warmth. When wanting to appear competent, people will often downplay their warmth. And when wanting to appear warm and likable, people will downplay their competence (Holoien & Fiske, 2013).

social dominance orientation
A motivation to have one's group dominate other social groups.

Some people, more than others, notice and justify status differences. Those high in **social dominance orientation** tend to view people in terms of hierarchies. They like their own social groups to be high status; they prefer being on the top. Being in a dominant, high-status position also tends to promote this orientation (Guimond et al., 2003). Jim Sidanius, Felicia Pratto, and their colleagues (Bratt et al., 2016; Ho et al., 2015; Pratto et al., 1994) argue that this desire to be on top leads people high in social dominance to embrace prejudice and to support political positions that justify prejudice.

Indeed, people high in social dominance orientation often support policies that maintain hierarchies, such as tax cuts for the well-off. They tend to prefer professions, such as politics and business, that increase their status and maintain hierarchies. They typically avoid jobs, such as social work, that, by virtue of their aid to disadvantaged groups, undermine hierarchies. And they frequently express more negative attitudes toward minority persons, especially those who exhibit strong racial identities (Kaiser & Pratt-Hyatt, 2009; Meeusen et al., 2017). Status breeds prejudice, especially for people high in social dominance orientation.

Socialization

Prejudice springs from unequal status and from other social sources, including our acquired values and attitudes. The influence of family socialization appears in children's prejudices, which often mirror those perceived in their mothers (Castelli et al., 2007). For example, Swedish teens display increasing anti-immigrant prejudice over time if their parents voice such prejudice (Miklikowska, 2017). Even children's implicit racial attitudes reflect their parents' explicit prejudice (Sinclair et al., 2004). Our families and cultures pass on all kinds of information: how to find mates, drive cars, and divide the household chores, and whom to distrust and dislike. Parental attitudes assessed shortly after their babies are born predict their children's attitudes 17 years later (Fraley et al., 2012).

THE AUTHORITARIAN PERSONALITY

In the 1940s, University of California, Berkeley, researchers – two of whom had fled Nazi Germany – set out on an urgent research mission: to uncover the psychological roots of the poisonous anti-Semitism that caused the slaughter of millions of Jewish people. In studies of American adults, Theodor Adorno and his colleagues (1950) discovered that hostility toward Jewish people often coexisted with hostility toward other minorities; prejudice against one group extended to prejudice against other marginalized groups. Adorno and his colleagues (1950) surmised that these tendencies defined a prejudice-prone **authoritarian personality**. This personality type, they found, has an intolerance for weakness, a punitive attitude, and a submissive respect for their group's authorities. For example, they were more likely to agree with statements such as "Obedience and respect for authority are the most important virtues children should learn."

authoritarian personality
A personality that is disposed to favor obedience to authority and intolerance of outgroups and those lower in status.

Even today, this personality type co-occurs with prejudiced attitudes. For example, those with authoritarian personalities react negatively to ethnic diversity and are more likely to express prejudice against transgender individuals (Hatch et al., 2023; Van Assche et al., 2019). And prejudices still co-occur: Antigay, anti-immigrant, anti-Black, anti-Muslim, and anti-women sentiments often live inside the same skin (Akrami et al., 2011; Zick et al., 2008). People intuitively know this. Thus, White women often feel threatened by someone who displays racism, and men of color by sexism (Sanchez et al., 2017).

Although authoritarianism is often associated with right-leaning political beliefs, it can occur on the left as well (Conway et al., 2021; van Prooijen & Krouwel, 2019). Left-wing authoritarianism can include anti-democratic beliefs such as justifying violence against those in power, rejecting people with conservative beliefs as inherently amoral, and favoring the use of governmental or institutional authority to bar speech they deem offensive (Costello et al., 2022). For example, a left-wing authoritarian might agree that "The rich should be stripped of their belongings and status," "Deep down, just about all conservatives are racist, sexist, and homophobic," and "Classroom discussions should be safe places that protect students from disturbing ideas"(Costello & Patrick, 2023).

Extremism, on both the political left and the right, shares some common themes, such as catastrophizing, desiring vengeance, dehumanizing the enemy, and seeking a sense of control (Kay & Eibach, 2013; Saucier et al., 2009). Moreover, people on both the left and right express similar intolerance of groups with values and beliefs unlike their own (Brandt & Van Tongeren, 2017; van Prooijen et al., 2015). In general, authoritarian beliefs tend to increase when people feel the world is a more dangerous and unstable place, which leads them to favor social control to maintain order (Osborne et al., 2023).

CONFORMITY

Once established, prejudice is maintained largely by inertia. If prejudice is socially accepted, many people will follow the path of least resistance and conform to the fashion. They will follow social norms not out of a need to hate but out of a need to be liked and accepted. During the 1950s, Thomas Pettigrew (1958) studied Whites in South Africa and the American South. His discovery: Those who conformed most to other social norms were also most prejudiced; those who were less conforming mirrored less of the surrounding prejudice.

Thus, people become more likely to favor (or oppose) discrimination after hearing someone else do so, and they are less supportive of women after hearing sexist humor (Ford et al., 2008; Zitek & Hebl, 2007). Similarly, White U.S. college students who learned that their fellow students embraced diversity and inclusion reported more positive feelings toward minority students. Establishing a prodiversity social norm seemed to have behavioral effects as well, as students of color reported being treated more inclusively. Thus, Sohad Murrar and colleagues suggest publicizing inclusion as a social norm may have a bigger impact than informing people that implicit bias is common (Murrar et al., 2020; see "The Inside Story: Sohad Murrar on Prodiversity Social Norms").

Conformity also maintains gender prejudice. If young people continually see technology firms and science labs overwhelmingly populated by men, it becomes expected that men

THE inside STORY

Sohad Murrar on Pro-Diversity Social Norms

As a PhD student at the University of Wisconsin-Madison, I often engaged in conversations with my advisor, Markus Brauer, about reducing prejudice and promoting inclusion. At the time, diversity interventions often communicated the idea that most people are biased. However, this went against what we knew about communicating social norms. Usually, it works best to tell people that most of their peers behave in a certain way — to set a social norm. People then see this way of behaving as common and are more likely to behave that way themselves. This social norms approach had previously been used successfully to increase helping behaviors.

We wondered whether telling people that most of their peers are pro-diversity — and thus setting pro-diversity as the social norm — would encourage more pro-diversity behaviors. Through a poster and a 5-minute video, we communicated the message that most students on campus embraced diversity and behaved in welcoming ways towards people from all backgrounds. Along with Dr. Brauer and my co-author Mitchell Campbell, we found that communicating a pro-diversity norm improved students' pro-diversity attitudes and behaviors up to 12 weeks later. Minority students' well-being and grades also improved over this time. With educational institutions, corporations, hospitals, governments, and social service organizations motivated to address discrimination, this work tells us we should be promoting the idea that most people are inclusive — not that most people are biased.

Sohad Murrar
University of Illinois, Chicago
Courtesy of Sohad Murrar

Advertising can communicate social norms around skin tone. This skin-lightening product, advertised here in India, seems to imply that to be lovely, one must be "fair" (meaning a lighter skin tone).
Jenny Matthews/Alamy Stock Photo

will dominate these fields and women need not apply. In contrast, female students exposed to female science, technology, engineering, and mathematics (STEM) experts express more positive implicit attitudes toward STEM studies and display more effort on STEM tests (Stout et al., 2011). Conversely, if the CEO of a company expressed prejudice against women in a simulated scenario, people were less willing to hire a woman for a leadership position even if they were not prejudiced themselves (Vial et al., 2019).

Or consider the media phenomena of "fat-shaming," when celebrities — almost always women — are publicly criticized for their weight. In a large sample of U.S. women, implicit antifat attitudes were higher in the weeks following widely publicized fat-shaming incidents. Thus, when the culture at large was focusing on women's weight, women on average showed more antifat prejudice, at least implicitly. Celebrity fat-shaming in the media, write Amanda Ravary and her colleagues (2019), "increases women's gut-level association that *fat is bad*."

In all this, there is a message of hope. If prejudice is not deeply ingrained, then as fashions change and new norms evolve, prejudice can diminish. And so it has. After U.S. Supreme Court decisions affirmed same-sex marriage in 2015, Americans believed that the social norm had shifted toward support of same-sex marriage even if their own beliefs did not change (Tankard & Paluck, 2017). And then average beliefs did change, with support of same-sex marriage continuing to increase after the social norm switched in that direction.

Systemic Supports

Social institutions (schools, government, media, families) may bolster prejudice through overt policies such as segregation or by passively reinforcing the status quo. Until the 1970s, many banks routinely denied mortgages to unmarried women and to ethnic minority applicants, with the result that most homeowners were White married couples. In more recent years, lenders have charged Black and Latino homebuyers slightly higher interest rates than Whites and have been more likely to reject their mortgage applications (Bartlett et al., 2019; Quillian et al., 2020).

Media may also strengthen stereotypes. In several studies, exposure to news portrayals of Muslims as terrorists was associated with increased perceptions of Muslims as aggressive and increased support for military action in Muslim territories (Saleem et al., 2017). Even language can influence prejudice: In countries where people speak languages that emphasize gender (such as the masculine *el* and feminine *la* in Spanish, as in *el sol* and *la luna*), women were described in more negative terms than men on webpages such as Wikipedia (Defranza et al., 2020).

Institutional supports for prejudice are often unintended and unnoticed. By examining 1,750 photographs of people in magazines and newspapers, Dane Archer and his associates (1983) discovered that about two-thirds of the average male photo but less than half of the average female photo was devoted to the face. That's important because people in photos showing more of the face (and thus less of the body) are rated as more ambitious and intelligent. As Archer widened his search, he discovered that such "face-ism" is common. He found it in the periodicals of 11 other countries, in 920 portraits gathered from the artwork of six centuries, and in the amateur drawings of students at the University of California, Santa Cruz. Follow-up studies have confirmed the face-ism phenomenon in magazines (including in the feminist *Ms.* magazine) and in website photos of male and female politicians even in countries with relative gender equality (Konrath et al., 2012; Nigro et al., 1988; Sczesny & Kaufmann, 2018). The researchers suspect that the visual prominence given men's faces and women's bodies both reflects and perpetuates gender bias.

SUMMING UP: What Are the Social Sources of Prejudice?

- The social situation breeds and maintains prejudice in several ways. A group that enjoys social and economic superiority will often use prejudicial beliefs to justify its privileged position, particularly if they are high in *social dominance orientation*.
- Children are also brought up in ways that foster or reduce prejudice. Those with *authoritarian personalities* are said to be socialized into obedience and intolerance. The family, religious communities, and the broader society can sustain or reduce prejudices.
- Social institutions (government, schools, media) also support prejudice, sometimes through overt policies and sometimes through unintentional inertia.

WHAT ARE THE MOTIVATIONAL SOURCES OF PREJUDICE?

Identify and examine the motivational sources of prejudice.

Various motivations underlie prejudice. But motivations can also lead people to avoid prejudice.

Frustration and Aggression: The Scapegoat Theory

Frustration (from the blocking of a goal) feeds hostility. When the cause of our frustration is intimidating or unknown, we often redirect our hostility. This phenomenon of "displaced aggression" (scapegoating) contributed to the lynchings of African Americans in the South after the Civil War. Between 1882 and 1930, more lynchings occurred in years when cotton prices were low and economic frustration was therefore presumably high (Hepworth & West, 1988; Hovland & Sears, 1940). The same was true of prejudiced attitudes in more recent times: Between 1964 and 2012, White Americans' prejudice toward Black Americans was more pronounced during economic recessions (Bianchi et al., 2018). Ethnic peace is easier to maintain during prosperous times.

Targets for displaced aggression vary. Following their defeat in World War I and their country's subsequent economic chaos, many Germans saw Jewish people as villains. Long before Hitler came to power, one German leader explained: "The Jew is just convenient. . . . If there were no Jews, the anti-Semites would have to invent them" (quoted by Allport, 1958, p. 325).

More recently, Americans who reacted to the 9/11 attack with more anger than fear expressed greater intolerance toward immigrants and Middle Easterners (Skitka et al., 2004). As Greece sank into economic misery after 2009, rage against foreign immigrants increased (Becatoros, 2012). Passions provoke prejudice.

By contrast, individuals who experience no negative emotional response to social threats – namely, children with the genetic disorder called Williams syndrome – display a notable lack of racial stereotypes and prejudice (Santos et al., 2010). No passion, no prejudice.

Competition is an important source of frustration that can fuel prejudice. When two groups compete for jobs, housing, or social prestige, one group's goal fulfillment can become the other group's frustration. Thus, the **realistic group conflict theory** suggests that prejudice arises when groups compete for scarce resources (Maddux et al., 2008; Pereira et al., 2010; Sassenberg et al., 2007). In evolutionary biology, Gause's law states the idea: Species with identical needs will experience maximum competition. In the modern world, competition often involves economic resources, which are closely linked to an individual's sense of significance and status. Aggression generally increases as people lose resources tied to their feelings of significance (Kruglanski et al., 2023). That suggests an association between economic prospects and prejudice.

realistic group conflict theory
The theory that prejudice arises from competition between groups for scarce resources.

Consider how this has played out across the world:

- In Western Europe, economically frustrated people express relatively high levels of blatant prejudice toward ethnic minorities (Pettigrew et al., 2008, 2010).
- In Canada, opposition to immigration since 1975 went up and down with the unemployment rate (Palmer, 1996).
- Around the world, concerns about immigrants taking jobs away from current residents are largest among those with the lowest incomes, polls show (Gonzalez-Barrera & Connor, 2019).
- Countries with more economic inequality and more globalization (via immigration and tourism) have the highest levels of prejudice (Caluori et al., 2021).

- In South Africa, dozens of African immigrants were killed by mobs and 35,000 people were hounded from squatter camps by lower-income South Africans who resented the economic competition. "These foreigners have no IDs, no papers, and yet they get the jobs," said one unemployed South African, noting that "They are willing to work for 15 rand [about $2] a day" (Bearak, 2010). When economic interests clash, prejudice often results.

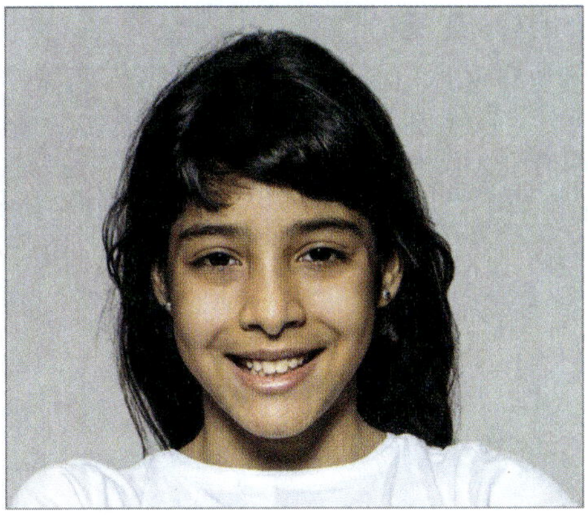

What group does she belong to? Social identity theory suggests that people automatically seek to categorize others, partially to determine whether they belong to the same group as themselves (the ingroup) or not (the outgroup).
Juanmonino/iStock/Getty Images Plus/Getty Images

Social Identity Theory: Feeling Superior to Others

Humans are a social species. Our ancestral history prepares us to feed and protect ourselves in groups. Humans cheer for their groups, kill for their groups, die for their groups. Evolution prepares us, when encountering strangers, to make a quick judgment: friend or foe? We instantly tend to like those from our group, those who look like us, even those who *sound* like us, with accents like our own (Gluszek & Dovidio, 2010; Kinzler et al., 2009; Roessel et al., 2018).

Not surprisingly, as noted by social psychologists John Turner (1981, 2000), Michael Hogg (1992, 2010, 2014), and their colleagues, we also *define* ourselves by our groups. Self-concept – our sense of who we are – contains not just a *personal identity* (our sense of our personal attributes and attitudes) but also a **social identity** (Chen et al., 2006; Haslam, 2014). Fiona identifies herself as a woman, an Aussie, a Labourite, a University of New South Wales student, a MacDonald family member.

social identity
The "we" aspect of our self-concept; the part of our answer to "Who am I?" that comes from our group memberships.

Working with British social psychologist Henri Tajfel, a Jewish Polish native who lost family and friends in the Holocaust and then devoted much of his career to studying ethnic hatred, Turner (1947–2011) proposed *social identity theory.* Tajfel and his colleagues (1979) observed that:

- *We categorize:* We find it useful to put people, ourselves included, into categories. To label someone as a Hindu, a Scot, or a bus driver is a shorthand way of saying some other things about the person.
- *We identify:* We associate ourselves with certain groups (our **ingroups**) and gain self-esteem by doing so.
- *We compare:* We contrast our groups with other groups (**outgroups**), with a favorable bias toward our own group.

ingroup
"Us": a group of people who share a sense of belonging, a feeling of common identity.

outgroup
"Them": a group that people perceive as distinctively different from or apart from their ingroup.

Beginning in our preschool years, we humans naturally divide others into those inside and those outside our group (Buttelmann & Böhm, 2014; Dunham et al., 2013). We also evaluate ourselves partly by our group memberships. Having a sense of "we-ness" strengthens our self-concepts. It *feels* good. We seek not only *respect* for ourselves but also *pride* in our groups (Greenaway et al., 2016; Sani et al., 2012). Moreover, seeing our groups as superior helps us feel even better. It's as if we all think, "I am an X [name your group]. X is good. Therefore, I am good."

Lacking a positive personal identity, people often seek self-esteem by identifying with a group. Thus, many disadvantaged youths find pride, power, security, and identity in gang affiliations. Much as dissonance motivates its reduction and insecurity feeds authoritarianism, so also uncertainty motivates people's seeking social identity. Their uncertainty subsides as they perceive who "we" and "they" are. Especially in a chaotic or an uncertain world, being part of a zealous, tightly knit group feels good; it validates who one is (Hogg, 2021). And that explains the appeal of extreme, radical groups in today's world.

"Whoever is dissatisfied with himself is continually ready for revenge."

—Friedrich Nietzsche, *The Gay Science*, 1882

When people's personal and social identities become *fused* – when the boundary between self and group blurs – they become more willing to fight or die for their group (Gómez et al., 2011; Swann et al., 2012, 2014a,b). Many patriotic individuals, for example, define themselves by their national identities (Staub, 1997, 2005a). And many people at loose ends find identity in their associations with new religious movements, self-help groups, or fraternal clubs **(Figure 3)**.

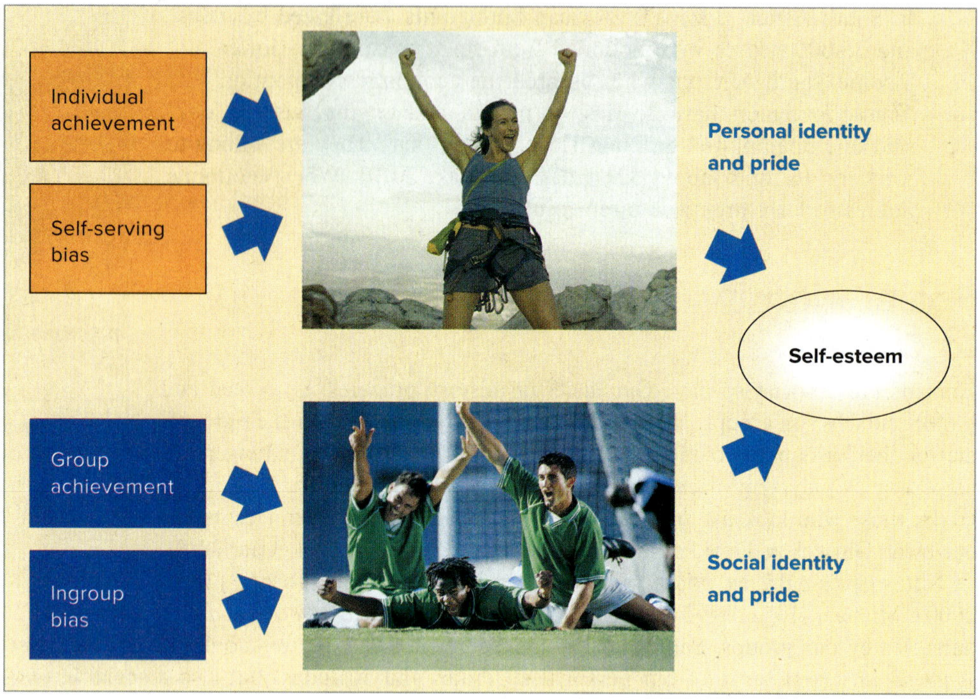

FIGURE 3

The Origins of Self-esteem

Personal identity and social identity together feed self-esteem.

(photo, top): Sam Edwards/OJO Images/age fotostock; (photo, bottom): Digital Vision/Getty Images

Because of our social identifications, we conform to our group norms. We sacrifice ourselves for team, family, and nation. The more important our social identity, the more we react prejudicially to threats from another group (Crocker & Luhtanen, 1990; Hinkle et al., 1992).

Take, for example, members of the online group Nextdoor, which allows neighbors to communicate with each other online. Perhaps due to a misplaced desire to defend their neighborhood from outsiders, members sometimes posted on Nextdoor about seeing a suspicious Black person in a primarily White neighborhood, even when no criminal behavior was occurring. Social psychologist Jennifer Eberhardt, who studies unconscious bias, worked with Nextdoor to develop a new protocol in which users must identify the specific behavior that made the person suspicious. This addition reduced racial profiling by 75%. Thus, to overwhelm unconscious bias, it might be necessary to change the advice from "If you see something, say something" to "If you see something suspicious, say something specific" (Eberhardt, 2019; Frueh, 2019).

INGROUP BIAS

The group definition of who you are—your gender, race, religion, marital status, academic major—implies a definition of who you are not. The circle that includes "us" (the ingroup) excludes "them" (the outgroup). The more that ethnic Turks in the Netherlands see themselves as Turks or as Muslims, the less they see themselves as Dutch (Verkuyten & Yildiz, 2007).

Beginning in early childhood, the mere experience of being formed into groups may promote **ingroup bias** (Wynn et al., 2018). Ask children, "Which are better, the children in your school or the children at [another school nearby]?" Virtually all will say their own school has the better children.

ingroup bias
The tendency to favor one's own group.

"There is a tendency to define one's own group positively in order to evaluate oneself positively."

—John C. Turner, "Social Identity," 1984

INGROUP BIAS SUPPORTS A POSITIVE SELF-CONCEPT Ingroup bias is one more example of the human quest for a positive self-concept. When our group has been successful, we can make ourselves feel better by identifying more strongly with it. College students whose team has just been victorious frequently report, "*We* won." After their team's defeat, students are more likely to say, "*They* lost." Basking in the reflected glory of a successful ingroup is strongest among those who have just experienced an ego blow, such as learning they did poorly on a "creativity test" (Cialdini et al., 1976). We can also bask in the reflected glory of a friend's achievement—except when the friend outperforms us on something pertinent to our identity (Tesser et al., 1988). If you think of yourself as an outstanding psychology student, you will likely take more pleasure in a friend's excellence in mathematics.

Basking in reflected glory. After Jamaican-Canadian sprinter Ben Johnson won the Olympic 100-meter race, Canadian media described his victory as that of a "Canadian." After Johnson's gold medal was taken away because of steroid use, Canadian media then emphasized his "Jamaican" identity (Stelzl et al., 2008).
ROMEO GACAD/AFP/Getty Images

INGROUP BIAS FEEDS FAVORITISM We are so group conscious that, given any excuse to think of ourselves as a group, we will do so—and we will then exhibit ingroup bias. Even forming groups on no logical basis—for instance, merely by composing groups X and Y with the flip of a coin—will produce some ingroup bias (Billig & Tajfel, 1973; Brewer & Silver, 1978; Locksley et al., 1980). People put in an arbitrarily assigned group will favor it and then, after being arbitrarily assigned to another group, favor the new group a few moments later (Xiao & Van Bavel, 2019). The self-serving bias rides again, enabling people to achieve a more positive social identity: "We" are better than "they," even when "we" and "they" are defined randomly!

In experiments, Tajfel and Michael Billig (1974; Tajfel, 1970, 1981, 1982) further explored how little it takes to provoke favoritism toward *us* and unfairness toward *them.* In one study, Tajfel and Billig had individual British teenagers evaluate modern abstract paintings and then told them that they and some other teens had favored the art of Paul Klee over that of Wassily Kandinsky, while others favored Kandinsky. Finally, without ever meeting the other members of their Klee-favoring group, each teen divided some money among members of the Klee- and Kandinsky-favoring groups. In this and other experiments, defining groups even in this trivial way produced ingroup favoritism. David Wilder (1981) summarized the typical result: "When given the opportunity to divide 15 points, subjects generally award 9 or 10 points to their own group and 5 or 6 points to the other group."

We are more prone to ingroup bias when our group is small and differs in status relative to the outgroup (Ellemers et al., 1997; Moscatelli et al., 2014). When we're part of a small group surrounded by a larger group, we are more conscious of our group membership. When our ingroup is the majority, we think less about it. To be a foreign student, to be gay or lesbian, or to be of a marginalized race or gender is to feel one's social identity more keenly and to react accordingly.

MUST INGROUP LIKING FOSTER OUTGROUP DISLIKING? Does ingroup bias reflect liking for one's ingroup, dislike for the outgroup, or both? Does ethnic pride cause prejudice? Does a strong feminist identity lead feminists to dislike nonfeminists? Does loyalty to a particular fraternity or sorority lead its members to deprecate independents and members of other fraternities and sororities? Or do people merely favor their own group without any animosity toward others?

"Father, Mother, and Me / Sister and Auntie say / All the people like us are We / And every one else is They. / And They live over the sea, / While We live over the way, / But - would you believe it? - They look upon We / As only a sort of They!"

—Rudyard Kipling, "We and They," in *Debits and Credits*, 1926

Experiments reveal both ingroup liking and outgroup disliking. Sometimes, love and hate are opposite sides of the same coin. If you love the Boston Red Sox, you may hate the New York Yankees. A patriot's love of country motivates dying to defend it against enemies. To the extent that we see virtue in *us,* we likely see evil in *them.* Moreover, outgroup stereotypes prosper when people feel their ingroup identity most keenly (Wilder & Shapiro, 1991).

We also ascribe uniquely human emotions (love, hope, contempt, resentment) to ingroup members and are more reluctant to see such human emotions in outgroup members (Demoulin et al., 2008; Kteily et al., 2016; Leyens et al., 2003, 2007). There is a long history of denying human attributes to outgroups—a process called *dehumanization* (Landry et al., 2023; Mendez, 2023). European explorers pictured many of the peoples they encountered as savages ruled by animal instinct. "Africans have been likened to apes, Jews to vermin, and immigrants to parasites," noted Australian social psychologists Stephen Loughman and Nick Haslam (2007). We humanize pets and dehumanize outgroups.

Yet ingroup bias and discrimination result less from outgroup hostility than from ingroup favoritism (Balliet et al., 2014; Greenwald & Pettigrew, 2014). Bias is less a matter of dislike toward those who are different than of networking and mutual support among those in one's group (Grigoryan et al., 2023). Even when there is no "them" (imagine yourself bonding with a handful of fellow survivors on a deserted island), one can come to love "us" (Gaertner et al., 2006). Thus, positive feelings for our own groups need not be mirrored by equally strong negative feelings for outgroups.

NEED FOR STATUS, SELF-REGARD, AND BELONGING

Status is relative: To perceive ourselves as having status, we need people below us. Consider a high school status hierarchy: The popular kids have status and (often) a feeling of superiority because they are more popular than others. But what happens when a popular kid senses their status is slipping? They might feel the need to defend their status and feelings of superiority.

In the larger world, defending your own status and superiority can translate into prejudice: Putting down someone else may lead to feeling better about your own status. Thus, someone who is insecure about their own status may try to gain back feelings of superiority by denigrating others.

Prejudice is often greater among those who are low or slipping on the socioeconomic ladder and among those whose positive self-image is threatened (Lemyre & Smith, 1985; Pettigrew et al., 1998; Thompson & Crocker, 1985). For example, members of lower-status sororities were more disparaging of competing sororities than were members of higher-status sororities (Crocker et al., 1987). People who fear failing economically are more likely to oppose immigration (Jetten et al., 2021). If our status is secure, we have less need to feel superior, and we express less prejudice (Ashton-James & Tracy, 2012).

The need for status and security suggests that a man who doubts his own strength and independence might, by proclaiming women to be weak and dependent, boost his masculine image. Indeed, when Washington State University men viewed young women's videotaped job interviews, men with low self-acceptance disliked assertive women. Men with high self-acceptance preferred them (Grube et al., 1982). Experiments confirm the connection between self-image and prejudice: Affirm people and they will evaluate an outgroup more positively; threaten their self-esteem and they will restore it by denigrating an outgroup (Fein & Spencer, 1997; Spencer et al., 1998).

"Strong men, men who are truly role models, don't need to put down women to make themselves feel powerful."

—Former First Lady Michelle Obama, 2016

Despising outgroups strengthens the ingroup. School spirit is seldom so strong as when the game is with the arch rival. The sense of comradeship among workers is often highest when they all feel a common antagonism toward management.

When the need to belong is met, people become more accepting of outgroups, reported Mario Mikulincer and Phillip Shaver (2001). They subliminally primed some Israeli students with words that fostered a sense of belonging *(love, support, hug)* and primed others with neutral words. The students then read an essay that was supposedly written by a fellow Jewish student and another by an Arab student. When primed with neutral words, the Israeli students evaluated the supposed Israeli student's essay as superior to the supposed Arab student's essay. When the participants were primed with a sense of belonging, that bias disappeared.

Motivation to Avoid Prejudice

Motivations lead people not only to be prejudiced but also to avoid prejudice. But try as we might to suppress unwanted thoughts – thoughts about food, thoughts about romance with a friend's partner, judgmental thoughts about another group – they sometimes refuse to go away (Macrae et al., 1994; Wegner & Erber, 1992). This is especially so for older adults as well as for people under alcohol's influence who lose some of their ability to inhibit unwanted thoughts and therefore to suppress old stereotypes (Bartholow et al., 2006; von Hippel et al., 2000). Patricia Devine and her colleagues (1989, 2012; Forscher et al., 2015) reported that people low and high in prejudice sometimes have similar automatic (unintentional) prejudicial responses. The result: Unwanted (dissonant) thoughts and feelings often persist. Breaking the prejudice habit is not easy.

In real life, a White person's encountering someone from a marginalized group may trigger a knee-jerk stereotype. Encountering an unfamiliar Black male, people – even those who pride themselves on not being prejudiced – may respond warily. Seeking not to appear prejudiced, they may divert their attention away from the person (Richeson & Trawalter, 2008).

Researchers who study stereotyping contend, however, that prejudicial reactions are not inevitable (Crandall & Eshleman, 2003; Kunda & Spencer, 2003). The motivation to avoid prejudice can lead people to modify their thoughts and actions (Mattan et al., 2018). Aware of the gap between how they *should* feel and how they *do* feel, self-conscious people will feel guilt and try to inhibit their prejudicial response (Bodenhausen & Macrae, 1998; Dasgupta & Rivera, 2006; Zuwerink et al., 1996). Even automatic prejudices subside, noted Devine and her colleagues (2005), when people's motivation to avoid prejudice is internal (because they believe prejudice is wrong) rather than external (because they don't want others to think badly of them).

The moral: Overcoming what Devine calls "the prejudice habit" isn't easy. But it can be done. One team of 24 researchers held a "research contest" that compared 17 interventions for reducing unintended prejudice among more than 17,000 individuals (Lai et al., 2014). Eight of the interventions proved effective, especially giving people experiences with vivid, positive examples of Black people who countered stereotypes. A similar technique, with people going door to door and having 10-minute nonjudgmental conversations, also worked to reduce prejudice against transgender individuals, as did a similar intervention using online interactions (Boccanfuso et al., 2021; Broockman & Kalla, 2016). However, interventions that threatened someone's identity or focused on improving mood were not as effective (Forscher et al., 2019).

In another study, Devine and her colleagues (2012) trained willing volunteers to replace biased knee-jerk responses with unbiased ones. Throughout the 2-year study follow-up period, participants in the experimental intervention condition displayed reduced implicit prejudice. If you find yourself reacting with knee-jerk presumptions or feelings, don't despair; that's not unusual. It's what you do with that awareness that matters. Do you let those feelings hijack your behavior? Or do you compensate by monitoring and correcting your behavior in future situations?

SUMMING UP: What Are the Motivational Sources of Prejudice?

- People's motivations affect prejudice. Frustration breeds hostility, which people sometimes vent on scapegoats and sometimes express more directly against competing groups.
- People also are motivated to view themselves and their groups *(ingroups)* as superior to other groups *(outgroups)*. Even trivial group memberships lead people to favor their group over others. A threat to self-image heightens such *ingroup bias,* as does the need to belong.
- On a more positive note, if people are motivated to avoid prejudice, they can break the prejudice habit.

WHAT ARE THE COGNITIVE SOURCES OF PREJUDICE?

Describe the different cognitive sources of prejudice.

How does the way we think about the world influence our stereotypes? And how do our stereotypes affect our everyday judgments? Stereotyped beliefs and prejudiced attitudes exist not only because of socialization and because they displace hostilities but also as by-products of normal thinking processes. Stereotypes spring less from malice of the heart than from the machinery of the mind. Like perceptual illusions, which are by-products of our knack for interpreting the world, stereotypes can be by-products of how we simplify our complex worlds.

Categorization: Classifying People into Groups

One way we simplify our environment is to *categorize:* to organize the world by clustering objects into groups (Macrae & Bodenhausen, 2000, 2001). A biologist classifies plants and animals. A human classifies people. Having done so, we think about them more easily (Liberman et al., 2017). If persons in a group share some similarities – if most National Honor Society members are smart, and most basketball players are tall – knowing their group memberships can provide useful information with minimal effort (Macrae et al., 1994). Stereotypes sometimes offer "a beneficial ratio of information gained to effort expended" (Sherman et al., 1998). Stereotypes represent cognitive efficiency. They are energy-saving schemes for making speedy judgments and predicting how others will think and act. We judge people in outgroups quickly; when assessing ingroup individuals, we take longer to form impressions (Vala et al., 2012). Thus, stereotypes and outgroup bias may have served evolutionary functions by enabling our ancestors to cope and survive (Navarrete et al., 2010).

SPONTANEOUS CATEGORIZATION

We find it especially easy and efficient to rely on stereotypes when we are

- pressed for time (Kaplan et al., 1993; Rivers et al., 2020);
- preoccupied (Gilbert & Hixon, 1991);
- tired (Bodenhausen, 1990; Ghumman & Barnes, 2013); or
- emotionally aroused (Esses et al., 1993b; Stroessner & Mackie, 1993).

Ethnicity and sex are powerful ways of categorizing people. Imagine Julius, a 45-year-old African American real-estate agent in Atlanta. We suspect that your image of "Black male" predominates over the categories "middle-aged," "businessperson," and "American southerner."

Experiments expose our quick, spontaneous categorization of people by race. Much as we organize what is actually a color continuum into what we perceive as distinct colors, such as red, blue, and green, so our "discontinuous minds" (Dawkins, 1993) cannot resist categorizing people into groups. We label people of widely varying ancestry as simply "Black" or "White," as if such categories were black and white. By itself, such categorization is not prejudice, but it does provide a foundation for prejudice.

PERCEIVED SIMILARITIES AND DIFFERENCES

Picture the following objects: apples, chairs, pencils.

There is a strong tendency to see objects within a group as being more uniform than they really are. Were your apples all red? Your chairs all straight-backed? Your pencils all yellow? Once we classify two days as in the same month, they seem more alike, temperature-wise, than the same interval across months. For example, people guess the 8-day average temperature difference between, for instance, November 15 and 23 to be less than the 8-day difference between November 30 and December 8 (Krueger & Clement, 1994a).

It's the same with categorizing people. When we assign people to groups – athletes, drama majors, math professors – we are likely to exaggerate the similarities within the groups and the differences between them (Taylor, 1981; Wilder, 1978). We assume that other groups are more homogenous than our own. Mere division into groups can create an **outgroup homogeneity effect:** a sense that *they* are "all alike" and different from "us" and "our" group (Ostrom & Sedikides, 1992). Consider:

outgroup homogeneity effect

Perception of outgroup members as more similar to one another than are ingroup members. Thus "they are alike; we are diverse."

- Many non-Europeans see the Swiss as a fairly homogenous people. But to the people of Switzerland, the Swiss are diverse, encompassing French-, German-, Italian-, and Romansh-speaking groups.
- Many non-Latino Americans lump "Latinos" together. However, Mexican Americans, Cuban Americans, and Puerto Ricans – among others – see important differences (Huddy & Virtanen, 1995).
- Sorority sisters perceive the members of any other sorority as less diverse than the members of their own (Park & Rothbart, 1982).

In general, the greater our familiarity with a social group, the more we see its diversity (Brown & Wootton-Millward, 1993; Linville et al., 1989). The less our familiarity, the more we stereotype.

Perhaps you have noticed: *They* – the members of any racial group other than your own – even *look* alike. Many people can recall embarrassing themselves by confusing two people of another racial group, prompting the person they've misnamed to say, "You think we all look alike." Experiments in the United States, Scotland, and Germany reveal that people

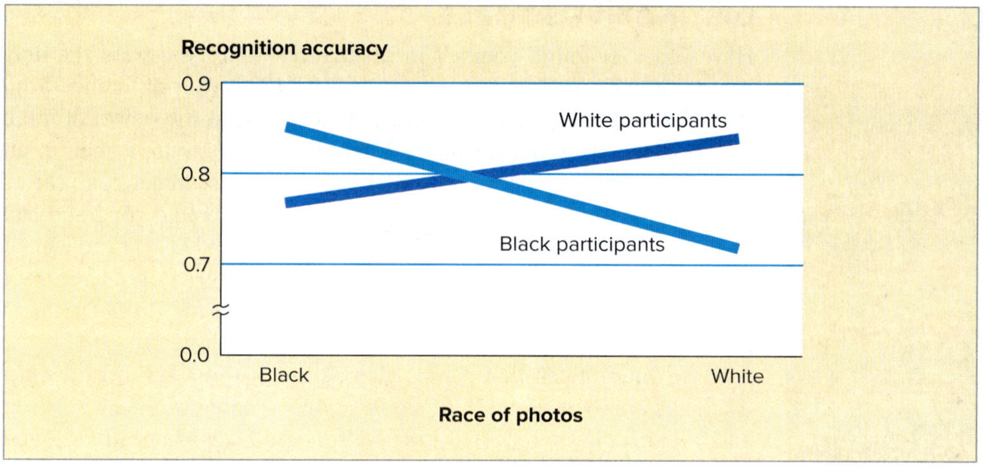

FIGURE 4

The Own-Race Bias

White participants more accurately recognize the faces of Whites than of Blacks; Black participants more accurately recognize the faces of Blacks than of Whites.

Source: Devine & Malpass, 1985.

of other races do in fact *seem* to look more alike than do people of one's own race (Lee & Penrod, 2022; Meissner & Brigham, 2001; Stelter & Schweinberger, 2023). When White students are shown faces of a few White and a few Black individuals and then asked to pick those individuals out of a photographic lineup, they show an **own-race bias:** They more accurately recognize the White faces than the Black ones, and they often falsely recognize Black faces never before seen.

own-race bias

The tendency for people to more accurately recognize faces of their own race. (Also called the *cross-race effect* or *other-race effect.*)

As **Figure 4** illustrates, Black people more easily recognize another Black person than they do a White person (Bothwell et al., 1989). Hispanics, Blacks, and Asians all recognize faces from their own races better than those from one another (Gross, 2009). Likewise, British South Asians are quicker than White Brits to recognize South Asian faces (Walker & Hewstone, 2008). And 10- to 15-year-old Turkish children are quicker than Austrian children to recognize Turkish faces (Sporer et al., 2007). Even infants as young as 9 months display better own-race recognition of faces (Kelly et al., 2005, 2007; Sugden & Marquis, 2017). Studies using brain scans show that this own-race recognition effect occurs at the earliest stages of perception (Hughes et al., 2019).

Difficulty recognizing the faces of other-race individuals has practical consequences. Elinor McCone and her colleagues (2023) found that East Asian students at an Australian university who had the most difficulty telling White people apart also reported having the most difficulty socializing with them. White people's difficulty in recognizing Asian faces was also a significant barrier to socializing. McCone recalls experiencing this herself: She could recognize her other-race professor only by the coat he wore.

It's not that we cannot perceive differences among faces of another group. Rather, when looking at a face from another racial group, people often attend, first, to group ("that man is Asian") rather than to individual features. When viewing someone of our own group, we are less attentive to the race category and more attentive to individual details such as the eyes (Herzmann et al., 2022; Kawakami et al., 2021; Shriver et al., 2008; Van Bavel & Cunningham, 2012; Young et al., 2010).

Our attending to someone's being in a different social category also contributes to a parallel *own-age bias:* the tendency for both children and older adults to more accurately identify faces from their own age groups (He et al., 2011; Rhodes & Anastasi, 2012; Wright & Stroud, 2002). (Perhaps you have noticed that senior citizens look more alike than do your fellow students?)

Dave Coverly. Speedbump.com

To a human cartoonist, all penguins look alike. To a penguin, they differ.

Distinctiveness: Perceiving People Who Stand Out

In other ways, too, our normal social perceptions breed stereotypes. Distinctive people and vivid or extreme occurrences often capture attention and distort judgments.

Distinctive people, such as former Houston Rockets 7′6″ player Yao Ming, draw attention.
Eugene Hoshiko/AP Images

DISTINCTIVE PEOPLE

Have you ever found yourself in a situation where you were the only person of your gender, race, or nationality? If so, your difference from the others probably made you more noticeable and the object of more attention. A Black person in an otherwise White group, a man in an otherwise female group, or a woman in an otherwise male group seems more prominent and influential and to have exaggerated good and bad qualities (Crocker & McGraw, 1984; Taylor et al., 1979). In the United States, 74% of Blacks (who are in the racial minority) see their race as "being extremely or very important to how they think of themselves," compared to only 15% of Whites (Horowitz et al., 2019).

Have you noticed that people also define you by your most distinctive traits and behaviors? Tell people about someone who is a skydiver and a tennis player, reported Lori Nelson and Dale Miller (1995), and they will think of the person as a skydiver. Asked to choose a gift book for the person, they will pick a skydiving book over a tennis book. A person who has both a pet snake and a pet dog is seen more as a snake owner than a dog owner.

Ellen Langer and Lois Imber (1980) cleverly demonstrated the attention paid to distinctive people. They asked Harvard University students to watch a video of a man reading. The students paid closer attention when they were told the man belonged to a distinctive group – a cancer patient, a gay person, or a millionaire. They noticed characteristics that other viewers ignored, and their evaluation of him was more extreme. Those who thought the man was a cancer patient noticed distinctive facial characteristics and bodily movements and thus perceived him to be much more "different from most people" than did the other viewers. The extra attention we pay to distinctive people creates an illusion that they differ from others more than they really do. If people thought you had the IQ of a genius, they would probably notice things about you that otherwise would pass unnoticed.

DISTINCTIVENESS FEEDS SELF-CONSCIOUSNESS When surrounded by White people, Black people sometimes detect Whites reacting to their distinctiveness. Many have reported being stared or glared at, being subject to insensitive comments, and receiving bad service (Swim et al., 1998). Recent years have seen a proliferation in reports of Black Americans being harassed or worse for driving or walking in their own neighborhoods, especially if those neighborhoods are mostly White (McNamarah, 2019; Steinbuch, 2020).

Sometimes, however, we misperceive others as reacting to our distinctiveness. Researchers Robert Kleck and Angelo Strenta (1980) discovered this when they led Dartmouth College women to feel disfigured. The women thought the purpose of the experiment was to assess how someone would react to a facial scar created with theatrical makeup; the scar ran down their face from the ear to the mouth. Actually, the purpose was to see how the women themselves, when made to feel distinctive, would perceive others' behavior toward them. After applying the makeup, the experimenter gave each woman a small hand mirror so she could see the authentic-looking scar. When she put the mirror down, he then applied some "moisturizer" to "keep the makeup from cracking." What the "moisturizer" really did was remove the scar.

The scene that followed was poignant. A young woman, feeling terribly self-conscious about her supposedly disfigured face, talked with another woman who saw no such disfigurement and knew nothing of what had gone on before. If you have ever felt similarly self-conscious – perhaps about a physical handicap, acne, even just a bad hair day – then perhaps you can sympathize with the self-conscious woman. Compared with women who were led to believe their conversational partners merely thought they had an allergy, the "disfigured" women became acutely sensitive to how their partners were looking at them. They rated their partners as more tense, distant, and patronizing. Observers who later analyzed videotapes of how the partners treated "disfigured" persons could find no such differences in treatment. Self-conscious about being different, the "disfigured" women had misinterpreted mannerisms and comments they would otherwise not have noticed.

Self-conscious interactions between a majority and a minority person can therefore feel tense even when both are well intentioned (Devine et al., 1996). Malik, who identifies as gay, meets tolerant Will, who is straight and wants to respond without prejudice. But feeling unsure of himself, Will holds back a bit. Malik, expecting negative attitudes from most people, misreads Will's hesitancy as hostility and responds accordingly.

Anyone can experience this phenomenon. Majority group members (in one study, White residents of Manitoba) often have beliefs – "meta-stereotypes" – about how other groups stereotype them (Vorauer et al., 1998). Even relatively unprejudiced Canadian Whites, Israeli Jews, or American Christians may sense that outgroup minorities stereotype them as prejudiced, arrogant, or patronizing. If George worries that Gamal perceives him as "your typical educated racist," he may be self-consciously on guard when talking with Gamal.

VIVID CASES Our minds also use distinctive cases as a shortcut to judging groups. Are the Japanese good baseball players? "Well, there's Ichiro Suzuki and Shohei Ohtani and Yu Darvish. Yeah, I'd say so." Note the thought processes at work here: Given limited experience with a particular social group, we recall examples of it and generalize from those (Sherman, 1996). Moreover, encountering an example of a negative stereotype (for instance, a hostile Black person) can prime the stereotype, leading some people to minimize contact with the group (Henderson-King & Nisbett, 1996).

Such generalizing from a single case can cause problems. Vivid instances, though more available in memory, seldom represent the larger group. Exceptional athletes, though distinctive and memorable, are not the best basis for judging the distribution of athletic talent among an entire group.

Those in a numerical minority, being more distinctive, also may be numerically overestimated by the majority. What proportion of your country's population would you say is Muslim? People in non-Muslim countries often overestimate this proportion.

Or consider a 2017 Gallup survey in which the average American guessed that 25% of people are gay or lesbian (McCarthy, 2019). Most surveys suggest the number is closer to 6% of U.S. adults (Twenge et al., 2023).

Myron Rothbart and his colleagues (1978) showed how distinctive cases also fuel stereotypes. They had University of Oregon students read descriptions of the actions of 50 men, 10 of whom had committed either nonviolent crimes, such as forgery, or violent crimes, such as rape. Of those shown the list with the violent crimes, most overestimated the total number of criminal acts. Vivid cases distort judgments and create stereotypes.

DISTINCTIVE EVENTS FOSTER ILLUSORY CORRELATIONS

Stereotypes assume a correlation between group membership and individuals' presumed characteristics ("Italians are emotional," "Jews are shrewd," "Accountants are perfectionists"). Often, people's stereotypes are accurate (Jussim et al., 2018). But sometimes our attentiveness to unusual occurrences creates illusory correlations. Because we are sensitive to distinctive events, the co-occurrence of two such events is especially noticeable – more noticeable than each of the times the unusual events do *not* occur together.

In a classic experiment, David Hamilton and Robert Gifford (1976) demonstrated illusory correlation. They showed students slides in which various people, members of "Group A" or "Group B," were said to have done something desirable or undesirable. For example, "John, a member of Group A, visited

What percentage of the U.S. population would you guess is Muslim? Americans guess 15%, but actually only barely more than 1% of the U.S. population is Muslim.
Rawpixel.com/Shutterstock

a sick friend in the hospital." Twice as many statements described members of Group A as Group B. But both groups performed nine desirable acts for every four undesirable behaviors. Since both Group B and the undesirable acts were less frequent, their co-occurrence – for example, "Allen, a member of Group B, dented the fender of a parked car and didn't leave his name" – was an unusual combination that caught people's attention. The students therefore overestimated the frequency with which the "minority" group (B) acted undesirably, and they judged Group B more harshly.

Remember, Group A members outnumbered Group B members 2 to 1, and Group B members committed undesirable acts in the same *proportion* as Group A members. Moreover, the students had no preexisting biases for or against Group B, and they received the information more systematically than daily experience ever offers it. Although researchers debate why it happens, they agree that illusory correlation occurs and provides yet another source for the formation of racial stereotypes (Berndsen et al., 2002). Thus, the features that most distinguish a minority from a majority are those that become associated with it (Sherman et al., 2009). Your ethnic or social group may in most ways be like other groups, but people will notice how it differs.

In experiments, even single co-occurrences of an unusual characteristic by someone in an atypical group – "Ben, a Jehovah's Witness, owns a pet sloth" – can embed illusory correlations in people's minds (Risen et al., 2007). This enables the mass media to feed illusory correlations. When a self-described gay person murders or sexually abuses someone, homosexuality is often mentioned. When a straight person does the same, the person's sexual orientation is seldom mentioned.

Unlike the students who judged Groups A and B, we often have preexisting biases. David Hamilton's further research with Terrence Rose (1980) revealed that our preexisting stereotypes can lead us to "see" correlations that aren't there. The researchers had University of California at Santa Barbara students read sentences in which various adjectives described the members of different occupational groups ("Juan, an accountant, is timid and thoughtful"). In actuality, each occupation was described equally often by each adjective; accountants, doctors, and salespeople were equally often timid, wealthy, and talkative. The students, however, *thought* they had more often read descriptions of timid accountants, wealthy doctors, and talkative salespeople. Their stereotyping led them to perceive correlations that weren't there, thus helping to perpetuate the stereotypes.

Likewise, guess what happened when Vaughn Becker and his colleagues (2010) invited university students to view a White and a Black face – one angry, one not – for one-tenth of a second (as in **Figure 5**). The participants' subsequent recollections of what they had viewed revealed racial bias. "White anger flowed to neutral Black faces (34% likelihood) more readily than Black anger flowed to neutral White faces (19% likelihood)," the researchers reported. A later study found that teachers were more likely to misperceive anger in the expressions of Black children compared to White children (Halberstadt et al., 2022).

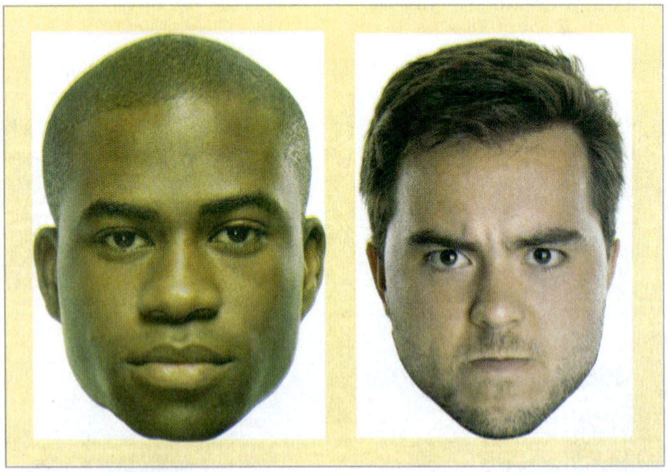

FIGURE 5

Race and Perceptions of Emotion

Ingroup biases influence perceptions. When briefly shown two faces, one neutral, one angry, people more often misrecalled the Black rather than the white face as angry (Becker et al., 2010).

(left): Paul Burns/Blend Image/Getty Images; (right): Rommel Canlas/Shutterstock

Attribution: Is It a Just World?

In explaining others' actions, we frequently commit the fundamental attribution error: We attribute others' behavior so much to their inner dispositions that we discount important situational forces. The error occurs partly because our attention focuses on the person, not on the situation. A person's race or sex is vivid and gets attention; the situational forces working upon that person are usually less visible. Slavery was often overlooked as an explanation for enslaved people's behavior; the behavior was instead attributed to the enslaved person's own nature.

The same was once true of how we explained the perceived differences between women and men (and may still sometimes be true). Because gender-role constraints are hard to see, we attributed men's and women's behavior solely to their presumed innate dispositions. The more people assume that human traits are fixed dispositions, the stronger are their stereotypes and the greater their acceptance of racial inequities (Levy et al., 1998; Williams & Eberhardt, 2008).

GROUP-SERVING BIAS

Thomas Pettigrew (1979, 1980) showed how attribution errors can bias people's explanations of group members' behaviors. We grant members of our own group the benefit of the doubt: "He refused because he's using every penny to help support his mother." When explaining acts by members of other groups, we more often assume the worst: "He refused because he's selfish." In one classic study, the light shove that Whites perceived as mere "horsing around" when done by another White person became a "violent gesture" when done by a Black person (Duncan, 1976).

Positive behavior by outgroup members is more often dismissed. It may be seen as a "special case" ("He is certainly bright and hardworking – not like other . . ."), as owing to luck or some special advantage ("She probably got admitted just because the physics department had to fill its quota for women applicants"), as demanded by the situation ("Under the circumstances, what could the cheap Scot do but pay the whole check?"), or as attributable to extra effort ("Asian students get better grades because they're so compulsive").

Disadvantaged groups and groups that stress modesty (such as the Chinese) exhibit less of this **group-serving bias** (Fletcher & Ward, 1989; Heine & Lehman, 1997; Jackson et al., 1993). By contrast, egotistical groups that are invested in their own greatness react to threats with group-serving bias and hostility (de Zavala et al., 2013). Social psychologists Jacquie Vorauer and Stacey Sasaki (2010, 2011) note that multiculturalism's focus on differences, which can be positive in the absence of conflict (making intergroup exchanges seem interesting and stimulating), sometimes comes at a cost. When there is conflict or threat, a focus on differences can foster group-level attributions and increased hostility.

group-serving bias
Explaining away outgroup members' positive behaviors; also attributing negative behaviors to their dispositions (while excusing such behavior by one's own group).

The group-serving bias can subtly color our language. A team of University of Padua (Italy) researchers led by Anne Maass (Maass, 1999; Maass et al., 1995) has found that positive behaviors by another ingroup member are often described as general dispositions (for example, "Abby is helpful"). When performed by an outgroup member, the same behavior is often described as a specific, isolated act ("Carmen opened the door for the man with the cane"). With negative behavior, the specificity reverses: "Eric shoved her" (an isolated act by an ingroup member) but "Enrique was aggressive" (an outgroup member's general disposition).

"For if [people were] to choose out of all the customs in the world such as seemed to them the best, they would examine the whole number, and end by preferring their own."

—Greek historian Herodotus, *The Histories*, Book III, BC 440

Earlier we noted that blaming the victim can justify the blamer's own superior status (see **Table 1**). Blaming occurs as people attribute an outgroup's failures to its members' flawed dispositions, noted Miles Hewstone (1990): "They fail because they're stupid; we fail because we didn't try." If women, Black people, or Jewish people have been abused, they must somehow have brought it on themselves. When the British made a group of German civilians walk through the Bergen-Belsen concentration camp at the close of World War II, one German responded: "What terrible criminals these prisoners must have been to receive such treatment." (Such group-serving bias illustrates the motivations that underlie prejudice, as well as the cognition. Motivation and cognition, emotion and thinking, are inseparable.)

TABLE 1 How Self-Enhancing Social Identities Support Stereotypes

	Ingroup	Outgroup
Attitude	Favoritism	Denigration
Perceptions	Heterogeneity (we differ)	Homogeneity (they're alike)
Attributions for negative behavior	To situations	To dispositions

THE JUST-WORLD PHENOMENON

In a famous series of experiments, Melvin Lerner and his colleagues (Lerner, 1980; Lerner & Miller, 1978) discovered that merely *observing* another innocent person being victimized is enough to make the victim seem less worthy.

Lerner (1980) noted that such disparaging of hapless victims results from the need to believe that "I am a just person living in a just world, a world where people get what they deserve." From early childhood, he argues, we are taught that good is rewarded and evil punished. Hard work and virtue pay dividends; laziness and immorality do not. From this, it is but a short leap to assuming that those who flourish must be good and those who suffer must deserve their fate.

just-world phenomenon
The tendency of people to believe that the world is just and that people therefore get what they deserve and deserve what they get.

Numerous studies have confirmed this **just-world phenomenon** (Hafer & Rubel, 2015). Imagine that you, along with some others, are participating in one of Lerner's studies—supposedly on the perception of emotional cues (Lerner & Simmons, 1966). One of the participants, an accomplice, is selected by lottery to perform a memory task. This person receives supposed painful shocks whenever they give a wrong answer. You and the others note their emotional responses.

After watching the victim receive these apparently painful shocks, the experimenter asks you to evaluate them. How would you respond? With compassionate sympathy? Most did not. When observers were powerless to alter the victim's fate, they often rejected and devalued the victim. The more ongoing the suffering, as with Jewish people even after the Holocaust, the greater the dislike of the victims (Imhoff & Banse, 2009).

Linda Carli and her colleagues (1989, 1999) reported that the just-world phenomenon colors our impressions of rape victims. Carli had people read detailed descriptions of interactions between a man and a woman. In one scenario, a woman and her boss meet for dinner, go to his home, and each has a glass of wine. Some read this scenario with a happy ending: "Then he led me to the couch. He held my hand and asked me to marry him." In hindsight, people find the ending unsurprising and admire the man's and woman's character traits. Others read the same scenario with a terrible ending: "But then he became very rough and pushed me onto the couch. He held me down on the couch and raped me." Given this ending, people see the rape as inevitable and blame the woman for provocative behavior that seems faultless in the first scenario.

This line of research suggests that people are indifferent to social injustice not because they have no concern for justice but because they see no injustice. Those who assume a just world believe that:

- rape victims must have behaved seductively (Culda et al., 2018; Russell & Hand, 2017) and sexual harassment victims must have encouraged the behavior (Bongiorno et al., 2020);
- battered spouses must have provoked their beatings (Valor-Segura et al., 2011);
- people who make less money must not be as competent (Connor et al., 2021);
- sick people are responsible for their illnesses (Gruman & Sloan, 1983); and
- teens who are bullied online deserve it (Chapin & Coleman, 2017).

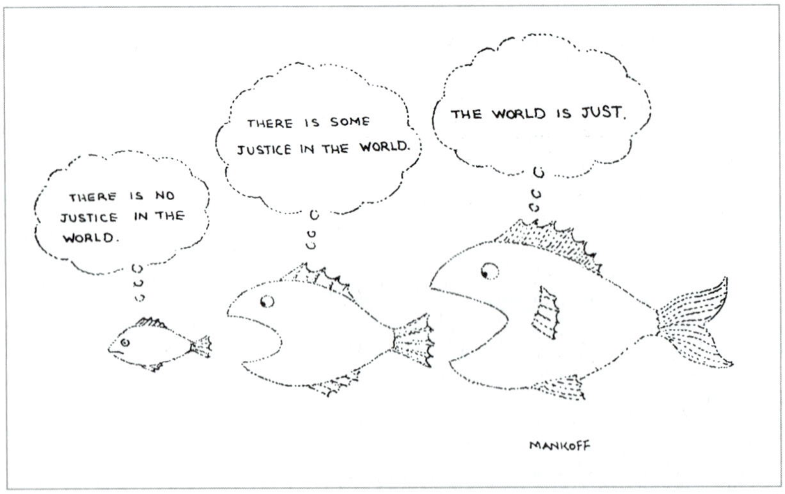

Robert Mankoff

The just-world phenomenon.

Such beliefs enable successful people to reassure themselves that they, too, deserve what they have. The wealthy and healthy can see their own good fortune, and others' misfortune, as justly deserved (Garcia-Sanchez et al., 2022). Linking good fortune with virtue and misfortune with moral failure enables the fortunate to feel pride and to avoid responsibility for the unfortunate. Still, there are some advantages to seeing the world is just. It can be empowering, which can motivate people to invest their energies in long-term goals (Bartholomaeus et al., 2023; Hafer & Sutton, 2016).

People loathe a loser even when the loser's misfortune quite obviously stems substantially from bad luck. Children, for example, tend to view lucky others – such as someone who has found money on a sidewalk – as more likely than unlucky children to do good things and be a nice person (Olson et al., 2008). Adults *know* that gambling outcomes are just good or bad luck and should not affect their evaluations of the gambler. Still, they can't resist judging losers as less competent (Baron & Hershey, 1988). Lawyers and stock market investors may similarly judge themselves by their outcomes, becoming smug after successes and self-reproachful after failures. Talent and initiative matter. But the just-world assumption discounts the uncontrollable factors that can derail good efforts even by talented people.

1. Just-world thinking also leads people to justify their culture's familiar social systems (Jost et al., 2009; Osborne & Sibley, 2013; Vargas-Salfate et al., 2018). From childhood on, we're inclined to think that the way things are is the way things ought to be (Brescoll et al., 2013; Hussak & Cimpian, 2015). Such a belief in the status quo makes it difficult to pass new social policies, such as voting rights laws or tax or health care reform. But after a new policy is in place, our "system justification" works to sustain it.

SUMMING UP: What Are the Cognitive Sources of Prejudice?

- Recent research shows how the stereotyping that underlies prejudice is a by-product of our thinking – our ways of simplifying the world. Clustering people into categories exaggerates the uniformity within a group and the differences between groups.
- A distinctive individual, such as a lone minority person, has a compelling quality that makes us aware of differences that would otherwise go unnoticed. The occurrence of two distinctive events (for example, a distinctive person committing an unusual crime) helps create an illusory correlation between people and behavior. Attributing others' behavior to their dispositions can lead to the *group-serving bias:* assigning outgroup members' negative behavior to their natural character while explaining away their positive behaviors.
- Blaming the victim results from the common presumption that because this is a *just world,* people get what they deserve.

WHAT ARE THE CONSEQUENCES OF PREJUDICE?

Summarize the consequences of prejudice.

How can stereotypes create their own reality? How can prejudice impede performance? Prejudice has consequences as well as causes.

Self-Perpetuating Prejudgments

Prejudice involves preconceived judgments, such as judging someone before we know them. Prejudgments are inevitable: None of us is a dispassionate accountant of social happenings, tallying evidence for and against our biases. And prejudgments matter.

Prejudgments guide our attention and our memories. People who accept gender stereotypes often misremember their own school grades in stereotype-consistent ways. For example, women often recall receiving worse math grades and better art grades than were actually the case (Chatard et al., 2007).

When people violate our stereotypes, we salvage the stereotype by splitting off a new subgroup stereotype, such as "senior Olympians."
Shih-Hao Liao/photoncatcher/123RF

Moreover, after we judge someone as belonging to a category such as a particular race or sex, our memory for it later shifts toward the features we associate with that category. In one experiment, Belgian university students viewed a face that was a blend of 70% of the features of a typical male and 30% female (or vice versa). Later, those shown the 70% male face recalled seeing a male (as you might expect) but misrecalled the face as being even more prototypically male (Huart et al., 2005).

Prejudgments are self-perpetuating. Whenever a group member behaves as expected, we duly note the fact; our prior belief is confirmed. When a group member violates our expectation, we may interpret or explain away the behavior as due to special circumstances (Crocker et al., 1983).

Perhaps you can recall a time when, try as you might, you could not overcome someone's opinion of you, when your actions were misinterpreted no matter what you did. Misinterpretations are likely when someone *expects* an unpleasant encounter with you (Wilder & Shapiro, 1989). William Ickes and his colleagues (1982) demonstrated this in an experiment with pairs of college-age men. As the men arrived, the experimenters falsely forewarned one member of each pair that the other person was "one of the *unfriendliest* people I've talked to lately." The two were then introduced and left alone together for 5 minutes. Students in another experimental condition were led to think the other participant was exceptionally *friendly*.

Those who expected him to be *un*friendly went out of their way to be friendly, and their friendly behavior elicited a warm response. But unlike the positively biased students, their expecting an unfriendly person led them to attribute this reciprocal friendliness to their own "kid-gloves" treatment of him. They afterward expressed more mistrust and dislike for the person and rated his behavior as less friendly. Despite their partner's actual friendliness, the negative bias induced these students to "see" hostility lurking beneath his "forced smiles." They would never have seen it if they hadn't believed it.

We do notice information that is strikingly inconsistent with a stereotype, but even that information has less impact than we might expect. When we focus on an atypical example, we can salvage the stereotype by splitting off a new category (Brewer & Gaertner, 2004; Gershman & Cikara, 2023; Kunda & Oleson, 1995, 1997). The positive image that British schoolchildren form of their friendly school police officers (whom they perceive as a special category) doesn't improve their image of police officers in general (Hewstone et al., 1992). This **subtyping** – seeing people who deviate as exceptions – helps maintain the stereotype that police officers are unfriendly and dangerous. High-prejudice people tend to subtype *positive* outgroup members (seeing them as atypical exceptions); low-prejudice people more often subtype *negative* outgroup members (Hakim et al., 2020; Riek et al., 2013).

subtyping
Accommodating individuals who deviate from one's stereotype by thinking of them as "exceptions to the rule."

A different way to accommodate the inconsistent information is to form a new stereotype for those who don't fit. Recognizing that the stereotype does not apply for everyone in the category, homeowners who have "desirable" Black neighbors can form a new and different stereotype of "professional, middle-class Blacks." This **subgrouping** – forming a subgroup stereotype – tends to lead to a modest change in the stereotype as the stereotype becomes more differentiated (Richards & Hewstone, 2001). Subtypes are *exceptions* to the group; subgroups are acknowledged as a *part* of the overall diverse group (Berthold et al., 2019).

subgrouping
Accommodating individuals who deviate from one's stereotype by forming a new stereotype about this subset of the group.

Discrimination's Impact: The Self-Fulfilling Prophecy

Attitudes may coincide with the social hierarchy not only as a rationalization for it but also because discrimination affects its victims. "One's reputation," wrote Gordon Allport, "cannot be hammered, hammered, hammered into one's head without doing something to one's character" (1958, p. 139). If we could snap our fingers and end all discrimination, it would be naive for the White majority to say to people in marginalized groups, "The tough times are over, folks! You can now all feel fully included." When the oppression ends, its effects linger, like a societal hangover.

In *The Nature of Prejudice,* Allport catalogued 15 possible effects of victimization. Allport believed these reactions were reducible to two basic types: those that involve *blaming oneself* (withdrawal, self-hate, aggression against one's own group) and those that involve *blaming external causes* (fighting back, suspiciousness, increased group pride).

Does discrimination indeed affect its victims? Social beliefs *can* be self-confirming, as demonstrated in a clever pair of experiments by Carl Word, Mark Zanna, and Joel Cooper (1974). In the first experiment, Princeton University White male volunteers interviewed White and Black research assistants posing as job applicants. When the applicant was Black, the interviewers sat farther away, made 50% more speech errors, and ended the interview 25% sooner than when the applicant was White. Imagine being interviewed by someone who sat at a distance, stammered, and ended the interview rather quickly. Would it affect your performance or your feelings about the interviewer?

"It is understandable that the suppressed people should develop an intense hostility towards a culture whose existence they make possible by their work, but in whose wealth they have too small a share."

—Sigmund Freud, *The Future of an Illusion,* 1927.

To find out, the researchers conducted a second experiment in which trained interviewers treated people as the interviewers in the first experiment had treated either the White or the Black applicants. When videotapes of the interviews were later rated, those who were treated like the Blacks in the first experiment seemed more nervous and less effective. Moreover, the interviewees could themselves sense a difference; those treated the way the Blacks had been treated judged their interviewers to be less adequate and less friendly. The experimenters concluded that part of "the 'problem' of Black performance resides . . . within the interaction setting itself." As with other self-fulfilling prophecies, prejudice affects its targets.

Stereotype Threat

Just being sensitive to difference is enough to make us self-conscious when living as a numerical minority – perhaps as an Asian person in a White community or as a White person in an Asian community. As with other circumstances that siphon off our mental energy and attention, the result can be diminished mental and physical stamina (Inzlicht et al., 2006, 2012). Placed in a situation where others expect you to perform poorly, your anxiety may cause you to confirm the belief. As a high school senior, I [JT] was one of only four girls in an advanced math class of 20 students. Looking around on that first day of class, I worried about doing well in the class: Did I really belong there? You might have had a similar experience, feeling that people doubted your ability to do something before you did it. Perhaps the doubt stemmed from your gender, your height, your hair color, your skin color, or your past performance in a sport or a show. If you felt increased pressure as a result, you're not alone. And if that pressure affected your performance, you're not alone either. In fact, this is the base principle behind the concept of **stereotype threat:** an apprehension that one will be evaluated based on a negative stereotype leads to diminished performance (Steele, 2010; Steele et al., 2002).

stereotype threat

A disruptive concern, when facing a negative stereotype, that one will be evaluated based on a negative stereotype. Unlike self-fulfilling prophecies that hammer one's reputation into one's self-concept, stereotype threat situations have immediate effects.

In several experiments, Steven Spencer, Claude Steele, and Diane Quinn (1999) gave a very difficult math test to men and women students who had similar math backgrounds. When told before taking the test that there were *no* gender differences in scores on the test, the women's performance consistently equaled the men's. Told that there *was* a gender difference, the women dramatically confirmed the stereotype (**Figure 6**). Frustrated by the extremely difficult test questions, they apparently felt added apprehension about their gender, which undermined their performances. Stereotype threat can also hamper women's learning math rules and operations even apart from exams (Rydell et al., 2010). The same is true for older people, for whom age-related stereotype threats of diminished cognitive ability (and resulting underperformance) have appeared across nearly three dozen studies (Lamont et al., 2015). The effect may be rooted in cultural views of aging: Stereotype threat underperformance among older adults is larger in Europe than in India, where aging is viewed more positively (Nicolas et al., 2021).

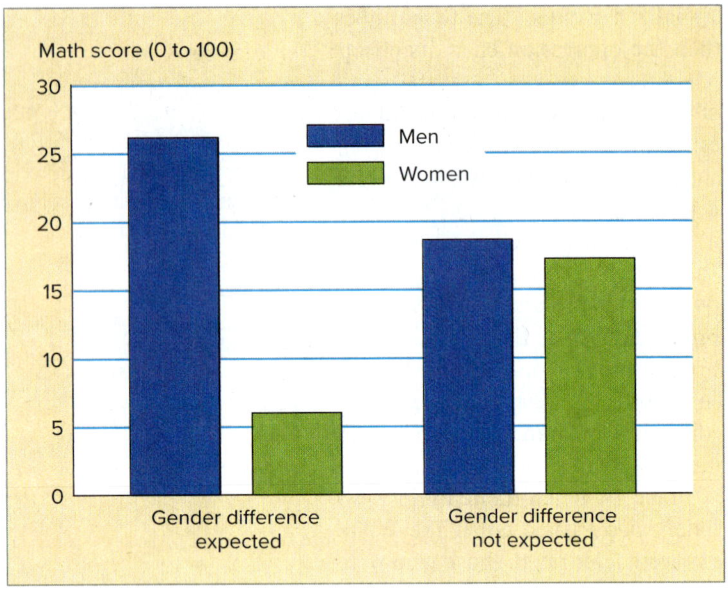

FIGURE 6

Stereotype Vulnerability and Women's Math Performance

Steven Spencer, Claude Steele, and Diane Quinn (1999) gave equally capable men and women a difficult math test. When participants were led to believe there were gender differences in test scores, women scored lower than men. When the threat of confirming the stereotype was removed (when gender differences were not expected), women did just as well as men.

Might racial stereotypes be similarly self-fulfilling? Steele and Joshua Aronson (1995) gave difficult tests of verbal ability to Whites and Blacks. Blacks underperformed Whites only when taking the tests under conditions high in stereotype threat, such as when they were told the test was predictive of future performance. A similar stereotype threat effect has occurred with Hispanic Americans (Nadler & Clark, 2011).

Jeff Stone and his colleagues (1999) reported that stereotype threat affects athletic performance, too. Blacks did worse than usual when a golf task was framed as a test of "sports intelligence," and Whites did worse when it was a test of "natural athletic ability." "When people are reminded of a negative stereotype about themselves – 'White men can't jump' or 'Black men can't think' – it can adversely affect performance," Stone (2000) surmised. The same is true for people with disabilities, for whom concern about others' negative stereotypes can hinder achievement (Silverman & Cohen, 2014). Although stereotype threat effects are not large, they appear fairly consistently across many studies including many different groups (Shewach et al., 2019).

How does stereotype threat undermine performance? It does so in three ways (Schmader et al., 2008):

- *Stress.* fMRI brain scans suggest that the stress of stereotype threat impairs brain activity associated with mathematical processing and increases activity in areas associated with emotion processing (Derks et al., 2008; Krendl et al., 2008; Wraga et al., 2007).
- *Self-monitoring.* Worrying about making mistakes disrupts focused attention (Keller & Dauenheimer, 2003; Seibt & Forster, 2004).
- *Suppressing unwanted thoughts and emotions.* The effort required to regulate one's thinking takes energy and disrupts working memory (Bonnot & Croizet, 2007).

If you tell students they are at risk of failure, the stereotype may erode their performance, said Steele (1997). It may cause them to "disidentify" with school and seek self-esteem elsewhere (**Figure 7**, and see "The Inside Story, Claude Steele on Stereotype Threat"). Indeed, as African American students move from eighth to tenth grade, their school

FIGURE 7

Stereotype Threat

Threat from facing a negative stereotype can produce performance deficits and disidentification.

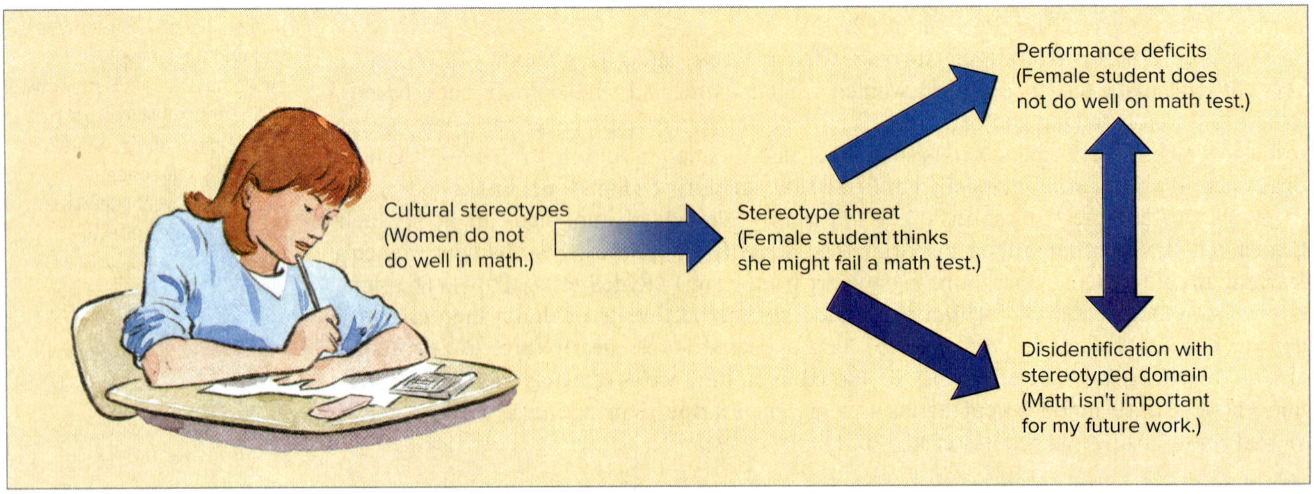

THE inside STORY

Claude Steele on Stereotype Threat

During a committee meeting on campus diversity at the University of Michigan in the late 1980s, I noticed an interesting fact: At every ability level (as assessed by SAT scores), minority students were getting lower college grades than their nonminority counterparts. Soon, Steven Spencer, Joshua Aronson, and I found that this was a national phenomenon; it happened at most colleges and it happened to other groups whose abilities were negatively stereotyped, such as women in advanced math classes. This underperformance wasn't caused by group differences in preparation. It happened at all levels of preparation (as measured by SATs).

Eventually, we produced this underperformance in the laboratory by simply having motivated people perform a difficult task in a domain where their group was negatively stereotyped. We also found that we could eliminate this underperformance by making the same task irrelevant to the stereotype, by removing the "stereotype threat," as we had come to call it. This latter finding spawned more research: figuring out how to reduce stereotype threat and its ill effects. Through this work, we have gained an appreciation for two big things: first, the importance of life context in shaping psychological functioning, and second, the importance of social identities such as age, race, and gender in shaping that context.

Claude Steele
Stanford University
Courtesy of Claude Steele

performance becomes less tied to their self-esteem (Osborne, 1995). Moreover, students who are led to think they have benefited from gender- or race-based preferences when getting into college tend to underperform those who are led to feel competent (Brown et al., 2000).

Better, therefore, to challenge students to believe in their potential, observes Steele. In another of his research team's experiments, Black students responded well to criticism of their writing when also told, "I wouldn't go to the trouble of giving you this feedback if I didn't think, based on what I've read in your letter, that you are capable of meeting the higher standard that I mentioned" (Cohen et al., 1999). Interventions emphasizing coping strategies and ways to alleviate anxiety can also be effective (Liu et al., 2021; O'Brien et al., 2020).

"Values affirmation" – getting people to affirm who they are – also helps (Walton, 2014). A Stanford research team invited African American seventh graders to write about their most important values several times. Compared to their peers, they earned higher grades over the next 2 years (Cohen et al., 2006, 2009). Ensuing studies have extended the values affirmation effect (such as by getting people to recall times they felt successful or proud) to populations ranging from female college physics students to soup kitchen clients (Bowen et al., 2013; Hall et al., 2014; Miyake et al., 2010; Sherman et al., 2013).

If stereotype threats can disrupt performance, could positive stereotypes enhance it? Margaret Shih, Todd Pittinsky, and Nalini Ambady (1999) confirmed that possibility. When Asian American females were asked biographical questions that reminded them of their gender identity before taking a math test, their performance plunged (compared with a control group). When similarly reminded of their Asian identity, their performance rose. Negative stereotypes disrupt performance, and positive stereotypes, it seems, facilitate performance (Rydell et al., 2009).

Do Stereotypes Bias Judgments of Individuals?

Yes, stereotypes bias judgments, but here is some good news: First, *our stereotypes mostly reflect* (though sometimes distort) *reality*. As multiculturalism recognizes, people differ – and can perceive and appreciate those differences. "Stereotype accuracy is one of the largest effects in all of social psychology," argues Lee Jussim (2012; Jussim et al., 2016).

People sometimes maintain general prejudices (such as against gays and lesbians) without applying their prejudice to particular individuals whom they know and respect, such as comedian Bowen Yang.
Kristin Callahan/Shutterstock

Second, *people often evaluate individuals more positively than the individuals' groups* (Miller & Felicio, 1990). Anne Locksley, Eugene Borgida, and Nancy Brekke found that after someone knows a person, "stereotypes may have minimal, if any, impact on judgments about that person" (Borgida et al., 1981; Locksley et al., 1980, 1982). They discovered this by giving University of Minnesota students anecdotal information about recent incidents in the life of "Nancy." In a supposed transcript of a telephone conversation, Nancy told a friend how she responded to three different situations (for example, being harassed by a seedy character while shopping). Some of the students read transcripts portraying Nancy responding assertively (telling the seedy character to leave); others read a report of passive responses (simply ignoring the character until he finally drifts away). Still other students received the same information, except that the person was named "Paul" instead of Nancy. A day later the students predicted how Nancy (or Paul) would respond to other situations.

Did knowing the person's gender have any effect on those predictions? None at all. Expectations of the person's assertiveness were influenced solely by what the students had learned about that individual the day before. Even their judgments of masculinity and femininity were unaffected by knowing the person's gender. Gender stereotypes had been left on the shelf; the students evaluated Nancy and Paul as individuals.

Given both general (base-rate) information about a group and trivial but vivid information about a particular group member, the vivid information usually overwhelms the effect of the general information. This is especially so when the person doesn't fit our image of the typical group member (Fein & Hilton, 1992; Lord et al., 1991). For example, imagine yourself being told how most people in a conformity experiment actually behaved and then viewing a brief interview with one of the supposed participants. Would you, like the typical viewer, guess the person's behavior solely from the interview? Would you ignore the base-rate information on how most people actually behaved?

People often believe stereotypes, yet ignore them when given personalized, anecdotal information. Thus, many people believe "politicians are crooks" but "our Senator Jones has integrity." No wonder many people have a low opinion of politicians yet usually vote to reelect their own representatives. These findings resolve a puzzling set of findings considered early in this chapter. We know that gender stereotypes are strong, yet they have little effect on people's judgments of work attributed to a man or a woman. Now we see why. People may have strong gender stereotypes but ignore them when judging an individual they meet or learn about.

STRONG STEREOTYPES MATTER

However, stereotypes, when *strong,* do color our judgments of individuals (Krueger & Rothbart, 1988). When researchers had students estimate the heights of individually pictured men and women, they judged the individual men as taller than the women – even when their heights were equal, even when they were told that sex didn't predict height in this sample, and even when they were offered cash rewards for accuracy (Nelson et al., 1990).

In a follow-up study, University of Michigan students viewed photos of other students from the university's engineering and nursing departments, along with descriptions of each student's interests (Nelson et al., 1996). Even when informed that the sample contained an equal number of males and females from each department, a description attached to a female face was judged more likely to come from a nursing student. Thus, even when a strong gender stereotype is known to be irrelevant, it has an irresistible force.

Outside the laboratory, strong stereotypes affect everyday experience. For example, men who endorse "hostile sexism" behave more negatively toward their female partners and experience less relationship satisfaction (Hammond & Overall, 2013).

STEREOTYPES BIAS INTERPRETATIONS

Stereotypes also color how we interpret events, noted David Dunning and David Sherman (1997). If people are told, "Some felt the politician's statements were untrue," they will infer that the politician was lying. If told, "Some felt the physicist's statements were untrue," they infer only that the physicist was mistaken. When told two people had an altercation, people perceive it as a fistfight if told it involved two lumberjacks but as a verbal spat if told it involved two marriage counselors. A person concerned about their physical condition seems vain if they are a model but health conscious if they are a triathlete. Like a prison guiding and constraining its inmates, concluded Dunning and Sherman, the "cognitive prison" of our stereotypes guides and constrains our impressions.

Sometimes we make judgments or begin interacting with someone with little to go on but our stereotype. In such cases, stereotypes can strongly bias our interpretations and memories of people. For example, Charles Bond and his colleagues (1988) found that after getting to know their patients, White psychiatric nurses put Black and White patients in physical restraints equally often. But they restrained *incoming* Black patients more often than their White counterparts. With little else to go on, stereotypes mattered.

Stereotypes can also operate subtly. In an experiment by John Darley and Paget Gross (1983), Princeton University students viewed a videotape of a fourth-grade girl, Hannah. The tape depicted her either in a depressed urban neighborhood, supposedly the child of working-class parents, or in an affluent suburban setting, the child of professional parents. Asked to guess Hannah's ability level in various subjects, both groups of viewers refused to use Hannah's class background to prejudge her ability level; each group rated her ability level at her grade level.

Two additional groups of Princeton students also viewed a second videotape, showing Hannah taking an oral achievement test in which she got some questions right and some wrong. Those who had previously been introduced to professional-class Hannah judged her answers as showing high ability and later recalled her getting most questions right; those who had met working-class Hannah judged her ability as below grade level and recalled her missing almost half the questions. But remember: The second videotape was *identical* for the two groups. So, when stereotypes are strong and the information about someone is ambiguous (unlike the cases of Nancy and Paul), stereotypes can *subtly* bias our judgments of individuals.

"Bias can be triggered and can have a devastating impact even when we're not aware of it, even when it's our intention to be fair."

—Social psychologist Jennifer Eberhardt (Frueh, 2019).

Finally, we evaluate people more extremely when their behavior violates our stereotypes (Bettencourt et al., 1997). A woman who rebukes someone cutting in front of her in a movie line ("Shouldn't you go to the end of the line?") may seem more assertive than a man who reacts similarly (Manis et al., 1988). Aided by the testimony of social psychologist Susan Fiske and her colleagues (1991), the U.S. Supreme Court saw such stereotyping at work when Price Waterhouse, one of the nation's top accounting firms, denied Ann Hopkins's promotion to partner. Among the 88 candidates for promotion, Hopkins, the only woman, was number one in the amount of business she brought in to the company and, according to testimony, was hard-working and exacting. But others testified that Hopkins needed a "course at charm school," where she could learn to "walk more femininely, talk more femininely, dress more femininely. . . ." After reflecting on the case and on stereotyping research, the Supreme Court in 1989 decided that encouraging men, but not women, to be aggressive is to act "on the basis of gender":

> We sit not to determine whether Ms. Hopkins is nice, but to decide whether the partners reacted negatively to her personality because she is a woman. . . . An employer who objects to aggressiveness in women but whose positions require this trait places women in an intolerable Catch 22: out of a job if they behave aggressively and out of a job if they don't.

Assertive or aggressive? Perceptions can be influenced by gender.
Fizkes/Shutterstock

SUMMING UP: What Are the Consequences of Prejudice?

- Prejudice and stereotyping have important consequences, especially when strongly held, when judging unknown individuals, and when deciding policies regarding whole groups.
- Once formed, stereotypes tend to perpetuate themselves and resist change. They also create their own realities through self-fulfilling prophecies.
- Prejudice can also undermine people's performance through *stereotype threat*, by making people apprehensive that others will view them stereotypically.
- Stereotypes, especially when strong, can predispose how we perceive people and interpret events.

CONCLUDING THOUGHTS: Can We Reduce Prejudice?

Social psychologists have been more successful in explaining prejudice than in alleviating it. Because the waters of prejudice are fed by many streams, no simple remedy exists. Nevertheless, we can now anticipate techniques for reducing prejudice:

- If unequal status breeds prejudice, we can seek to create cooperative, equal-status relationships.
- If prejudice rationalizes discriminatory behavior, we can mandate nondiscrimination.
- If social institutions support prejudice, we can pull out those supports (for example, with media that model interracial harmony and acceptance of LGBTQ+ individuals).
- If bias and discrimination is perceived as acceptable, we can spread the word that inclusiveness and embracing diversity is the social norm.
- If outgroups seem more homogeneous than they really are, we can make efforts to personalize their members.
- If our automatic prejudices lead us to feel guilt, we can use that guilt to motivate ourselves to break the prejudice habit.

Since the end of World War II in 1945, a number of those antidotes have been applied, and racial, gender, and sexual orientation prejudices have indeed diminished. Social-psychological research also has helped break down discriminatory barriers. The social psychologist Susan Fiske (1999), who testified on behalf of Ann Hopkins (the Price Waterhouse executive denied promotion to partner) later wrote:

> We risked a lot by testifying on Ann Hopkins's behalf, no doubt about it. . . . As far as we knew, no one had ever introduced the social psychology of stereotyping in a gender case before. . . . If we succeeded, we would get the latest stereotyping research out of the dusty journals and into the muddy trenches of legal debate, where it might be useful. If we failed, we might hurt the client, slander social psychology, and damage my reputation as a scientist. At the time I had no idea that the testimony would eventually make it successfully through the Supreme Court.

It now remains to be seen whether, during this century, progress will continue or whether, as could easily happen in a time of increasing population and competition for diminishing resources, antagonisms will increase.

Aggregation

CHAPTER

10

Keith Birmingham/MediaNews Group/Pasadena Star-News/Getty Images

"Our behavior toward each other is the strangest, most unpredictable, and most unaccountable of all the phenomena with which we are obliged to live. In all of nature, there is nothing so threatening to humanity as humanity itself."

—Lewis Thomas, *Notes of a Biology Watcher,* 1981

Since 1900, some 250 wars killed 110 million people, enough to populate a "nation of the dead" with more than the combined population of France, Belgium, the Netherlands, Denmark, Finland, Norway, and Sweden. The death tolls came not only from the two world wars but also from genocides, including the 1915 to 1923 genocide of 1 million Armenians by the Ottoman Empire, the 1937 slaughter of some 250,000 Chinese in Nanking after its surrender to Japanese troops, the 1.5 million Cambodians murdered between 1975 and 1979, the murder of 1 million in Rwanda in 1994 (Sternberg, 2003), and the approximately 200,000 killed in the Russia-Ukraine war since 2022 (Cooper et al., 2023). As Hitler's genocide of millions of Jewish people, Stalin's killing of millions of Russians, and the deaths of millions of Native Americans from the time of Columbus make plain, the human potential for extraordinary cruelty crosses cultures and races.

"Every gun that is made, every warship launched, every rocket fired signifies, in the final sense, a theft from those who hunger and are not fed, those who are cold and are not clothed."

—President Dwight Eisenhower, speech to the American Society of Newspaper Editors, 1953

Even outside of war, human beings have an extraordinary capacity for harming one another. Mass shootings at schools, campuses, and concerts have brought public attention to gun violence. In 2021, 458,000 of the world's people were murdered (UNODC, 2023). In 2022, 16,485 people were murdered in the United States; 106,521 were raped; and an incredible 678,157 — two-thirds of a million people — were shot, stabbed, or assaulted with another weapon (FBI, 2023). In 2021, 2,279 children and teens were murdered with a gun in the United States (Choi, 2023).

These numbers may be only the tip of the iceberg because many rapes and assaults go unreported. An extensive, anonymous survey found that nearly 1 in 5 women in the United States has been sexually assaulted, and 1 out of 4 has been hit, beaten, or slammed against something by an intimate partner (Smith et al., 2018). A 2019 study across 33 campuses found that 13% of U.S. women college students had been raped (Cantor et al., 2020). Worldwide, 30% of women experienced violence at the hands of an intimate partner (WHO, 2021).

Less severe aggression is even more common. One study found that 90% of young couples are verbally aggressive toward each other, including yelling, screaming, and insults (Munoz-Rivas et al., 2007). One out of five U.S. high school students reported being bullied at school in 2019 (NCES, 2023). Many children and adolescents have also experienced bullying via email, texts, social media, or other electronic media (Craig et al., 2020; Dennehy et al., 2020). Bullying can result in depression, drug abuse, dropping out of school, poor physical health, and suicide — even years after the bullying occurred (Kowalski et al., 2014; Schoeler et al., 2018; Sigurdson et al., 2014; Turliuc et al., 2020).

Are we like the mythical Minotaur — half human, half beast? What explains the midsummer day in 1941 when the non-Jewish half of the Polish town of Jebwabne murdered the other half in a macabre frenzy of violence, leaving only a dozen or so survivors among the 1,600 Jews (Gross, 2001)? Why would middle school students bully 12-year-old Andrew Leach so cruelly and relentlessly that he took his own life (Fernandez, 2018)? Why would a gunman kill 14 students and 3 teachers at a high school in Parkland, Florida, in 2018? What explains such monstrous behavior? In this chapter, we ask these questions:

- Is aggression biologically predisposed, or do we learn it?
- What circumstances prompt hostile outbursts?
- Do the media influence aggression?
- How might we reduce aggression?

First, we'll clarify the term "aggression."

WHAT IS AGGRESSION?

Define aggression and describe its different forms.

The original Thugs, members of a sect in northern India, were aggressing when between 1550 and 1850 they strangled more than 2 million people, which they claimed to do in the service of the goddess Kali. But people also use "aggressive" to describe a dynamic salesperson. Social psychologists distinguish such self-assured, energetic, go-getting behavior as the salesperson's from behavior that hurts, harms, or destroys. The salesperson's behavior is assertiveness, but the behavior that hurts or harms is aggression.

To a social psychologist, **aggression** is physical or verbal behavior intended to cause harm. This definition excludes unintentional harm, such as auto accidents or sidewalk collisions; it also excludes actions that may involve pain as an unavoidable side effect of helping someone, such as dental treatments, surgery, or – in the extreme – assisted suicide.

aggression
Physical or verbal behavior intended to hurt someone. In laboratory experiments, this might mean delivering supposed electric shocks or saying something likely to hurt another's feelings.

The definition of aggression includes kicks and slaps, threats and insults, gossip or snide digs, and trolling behavior such as online name-calling and harassment (Cheng et al., 2017). It includes confrontational rudeness, such as giving the finger to another driver or yelling at someone who is walking too slow (Park et al., 2014). It includes decisions during experiments about how much to hurt someone, such as how much electric shock to impose. It also includes destroying property, lying, and other behavior that aims to hurt. As these examples illustrate, aggression includes both **physical aggression** (hurting someone's body) and **social aggression** (such as bullying and cyberbullying, insults, harmful gossip, or social exclusion that hurts feelings [Dehue et al., 2008]). Social aggression can have serious consequences, with victims suffering from depression and sometimes – as has happened in several well-publicized cases – committing suicide. Dan Olweus and Kyrre Breivik (2013), who research bullying, describe the consequences of bullying as "the opposite of well-being."

physical aggression
Hurting someone else's body.

social aggression
Hurting someone else's feelings or threatening their relationships. Sometimes called relational aggression, it includes cyberbullying and some forms of in-person bullying.

However, the social psychology definition of aggression does not include microaggressions, usually defined as words or actions that unintentionally convey prejudice toward marginalized groups; to fit the definition, aggression must be intentional. For that reason and others, some have recommended abandoning the term "microaggressions" and replacing it with another term that better captures their unintentional nature, such as "inadvertent racial slights" (Lilienfeld, 2017).

Psychologists also make a distinction between **hostile aggression** (which springs from anger and aims to injure) and **instrumental aggression** (which aims to injure, too – but is committed in the pursuit of another goal). Both physical and social aggression can be either hostile or instrumental. For example, bullying can be hostile (one teen is angry at another for stealing their boyfriend) or instrumental (a high school student believes they can become popular by rejecting an unpopular girl [Juvonen & Graham, 2014; Prinstein & Cillessen, 2003]).

hostile aggression
Aggression that springs from anger; its goal is to injure.

instrumental aggression
Aggression that aims to injure, but only as a means to some other end.

Most terrorism is instrumental aggression. "What nearly all suicide terrorist campaigns have in common is a specific secular and strategic goal," concludes Robert Pape (2003) after studying all suicide bombings from 1980 to 2001. That goal is "to compel liberal democracies to withdraw military forces from territory that the terrorists consider to be their homeland." Terrorism is rarely committed by someone with a mental illness, noted Arie Kruglanski and his colleagues (2009); instead, terrorists seek personal significance through, for example, attaining hero or martyr status. Terrorism is also a strategic tool used during conflict. In explaining the aim of the 9/11 attacks, Osama bin Laden noted that for a cost of only $500,000, the terrorists inflicted $500 billion worth of damage to the American economy (Zakaria, 2008).

Most wars are instrumental aggression. Russian leader Vladimir Putin said he invaded Ukraine to bring the country back into the Russian fold – a goal disputed by countries around the world, but a mostly instrumental one (BBC, 2022). Aggression in sports, such as checking in hockey or tackling in rugby or football, is usually instrumental; it may hurt, but it is done in pursuit of the goal of winning the game (Sherrill & Bradel, 2017).

Adolescents who bully others – either verbally or physically – are often engaged in instrumental aggression because they seek to demonstrate their dominance and high status. In the strange hierarchy of adolescence, being mean and disliked can sometimes make you popular and revered (Laniga-Wijnen et al., 2020; Salmivalli, 2009). Aggression is not always the output of the hot-headed, berserk maniac, but can be cold, calculated, and controlled (Chester, 2023).

Because it is intended to hurt, online bullying is aggression even though its harm is emotional rather than physical.
oliveromg/Shutterstock

Most murders are hostile aggression, with the majority resulting from intimate partner violence or arguments influenced by alcohol or drugs (Ertl et al., 2019). Such murders are impulsive, emotional outbursts, which helps explain why data from 110 nations showed that having a death penalty did not result in fewer homicides (Costanzo, 1998; Wilkes, 1987). Some murders and many other violent acts of retribution and sexual coercion, however, are instrumental (Felson, 2000). Most of Chicago's more than 1,000 murders carried out by organized crime during the Prohibition era and the years following were cool and calculated instrumental aggression intended for a specific purpose such as eliminating a rival.

WHAT ARE SOME THEORIES OF AGGRESSION?

Compare the important theories of aggression.

In analyzing the causes of aggression, social psychologists have focused on three big ideas: biological influences, frustration, and learned behavior.

Aggression as a Biological Phenomenon

Philosophers have debated whether our human nature is fundamentally that of a benign, contented, "noble savage" or that of a brute. The first view, argued by the 18th-century French philosopher Jean-Jacques Rousseau (1712–1778), blames society, not human nature, for social evils. The second idea, associated with the English philosopher Thomas Hobbes (1588–1679), credits society for restraining the human brute. In the twentieth century, the "brutish" view – that aggressive drive is inborn and thus inevitable – was argued by Sigmund Freud, the founder of psychoanalysis, and Konrad Lorenz, an animal behavior expert.

INSTINCTIVE BEHAVIOR AND EVOLUTIONARY PSYCHOLOGY

Freud speculated that human aggression springs from a self-destructive impulse that redirects the energy of a primitive death urge (the "death instinct") away from the self and toward others. Lorenz, an animal behavior expert, instead saw aggression as adaptive rather than self-destructive. The two agreed that aggressive energy is **instinctive** (innate, unlearned, and universal). If not discharged, aggressive energy supposedly builds up until it explodes or until an appropriate stimulus "releases" it, like a mouse releasing a mousetrap.

instinctive behavior
An innate, unlearned behavior pattern exhibited by all members of a species.

The idea that aggression is an instinct collapsed as the list of supposed human instincts grew to include nearly every conceivable human behavior. Nearly 6,000 supposed instincts were enumerated in one 1924 survey of social science books (Barash, 1979). The social scientists had tried to *explain* social behavior by *naming* it. It's tempting to play this explaining-by-naming game: "Why do sheep stay together?" "Because of their herd instinct." "How do you know they have a herd instinct?" "Just look at them: They're always together!"

The idea that aggression is instinctive also fails to account for the variations in aggressiveness from person to person and culture to culture. How would a shared human instinct for aggression explain the difference between the peaceful Iroquois before White invaders came and the hostile Iroquois after the invasion (Hornstein, 1976)? Although aggression is biologically influenced, the human propensity to aggress does not qualify as instinctive behavior.

However, aggression is sometimes rooted in basic evolutionary impulses. Throughout much of human history, men especially have found aggression adaptive, noted evolutionary psychologists such as John Archer (2006) and Francis McAndrew (2009). Purposeful aggression improved the odds of survival and reproduction. The losers, noted McAndrew, "ran the risk of genetic annihilation."

Mating-related aggression often occurs when males are competing with other males. In one study, men primed to think about mating delivered louder and longer bursts of painful noise against another man who provoked them (Ainsworth & Maner, 2012). Male-on-male aggression may be particularly common in more traditional cultures with less gender equality – perhaps one reason why countries with less gender equality have higher violent crime rates (Corcoran & Stark, 2018).

Men may also become aggressive when their social status is challenged. "Violence committed against the right people at the right time was a ticket to social success," McAndrew observes. Consider former professional basketball player and current sports analyst Charles Barkley, who was drinking in a bar in 1997 when a man threw a glass of water at him. Barkley promptly hurled the man through a plate-glass window – even though Barkley was not hurt by the water, even though the man might have retaliated, and even though Barkley was arrested within minutes of the assault. Nevertheless, witnesses praised Barkley in news reports, seemingly impressed by his aggression. When Barkley was asked if he regretted throwing the man through the window, he replied, "I regret we weren't on a higher floor" (Griskevicius et al., 2009).

Male aggression can be heightened in the context of dating and mating.
View Apart/Shutterstock

Apparently, Barkley is not an isolated example. Across three experiments, college men motivated to increase their status were more aggressive toward others in face-to-face confrontations (Griskevicius et al., 2009). Status-based aggression also helps explain why aggression is highest during adolescence and early adulthood, when the competition for status and mates is the most intense. Although violence is less rewarded than it once was, young men scuffling for status and mates are still very much in evidence at many bars and university campuses around the world. Sometimes that struggle for status is taken to extremes. Ninety-eight percent of mass shooters have been male, a 24-to-1 ratio (Martin & Bowman, 2021).

NEURAL INFLUENCES

Because aggression is a complex behavior, no one spot in the brain controls it. However, researchers have found brain neural systems in both animals and humans that facilitate aggression. When scientists activate these brain areas, hostility increases; when they deactivate them, hostility decreases. Docile animals can thus be provoked into rage and raging animals into submission, usually by stimulating the hypothalamus (Falkner et al., 2016; Flanigan et al., 2020).

In one experiment, researchers placed an electrode in an aggression-inhibiting area of a domineering monkey's brain. A smaller monkey, given a button that activated the electrode, learned to push it every time the tyrant monkey became intimidating. Brain activation works with humans, too. After receiving painless electrical stimulation in her amygdala (a brain core area involved with emotion), one woman became enraged and smashed her guitar against the wall, barely missing her psychiatrist's head (Moyer, 1976, 1983).

Does this mean that violent people's brains are in some way abnormal? To find out, Adrian Raine and his colleagues (1998, 2000, 2008, 2019) used brain scans to measure brain activity in murderers and to measure the amount of gray matter in men with antisocial conduct disorder. They found that the prefrontal cortex, which acts like an emergency brake on deeper brain areas involved in aggressive behavior, was 14% less active than normal in murderers (excluding those who had been abused by their parents) and 15% smaller in the antisocial men. A meta-analysis concluded that aggressive people experience heightened brain activity in the limbic system (including the left amygdala and hippocampus), an area associated with behaviors and emotions linked to survival (Nikolic et al., 2022).

Situational factors can also play a role: Sleep deprivation reduces activity in the prefrontal cortex, an area of the brain responsible for self-control. In aggression-prone individuals, poor sleep can lead to violent and aggressive behavior (Kamphuis et al., 2012; Krizan & Herlache, 2016). Even in samples of normal German and U.S. college students, those who slept less were more physically and verbally aggressive (Chester & Dzierzewski, 2020; Randler & Vollmer, 2013). In a longitudinal study of Chinese college students, poor sleep quality over the past month predicted higher levels of aggression two years later (Zhang & Lei, 2023).

Another reason to get enough sleep: Aggressive people are often tired people.
Lorena Fernandez/Shutterstock

What about mental illness? When news of a mass shooting breaks, politicians often blame mental illness ("The long-term solution" to preventing mass shootings, said Texas governor Greg Abbott, is to "address the mental health issue" [Narea, 2023]). However, being young, male, or drunk are all better predictors of violent crime than being mentally ill (Corrigan et al., 2005; Metzl & MacLeish, 2014). If someone magically cured schizophrenia, bipolar disorder, and depression overnight, violent crime in the U.S. would fall by only 4%, according to Duke University professor Jeffrey Swanson (Swanson, 2016). People with mental illnesses are more likely to be the victims of violence than be the perpetrators (Brekke et al., 2001).

GENETIC INFLUENCES

It has long been known that animals can be bred for aggressiveness, suggesting a role for genetics in aggressive behavior. Finnish psychologist Kirsti Lagerspetz (1979) took normal albino mice and bred the most aggressive ones together; she did the same with the least aggressive ones. After repeating the procedure for 26 generations, she had one set of fierce mice and one set of placid mice.

Aggressiveness also varies among individual people, and some of that variation is likely due to genetic influences (Bettencourt et al., 2006; Denson et al., 2006; Wang et al., 2020). Compared to fraternal twins, identical twins are more likely to be similar in their levels of aggression, such as agreeing on whether they have "a violent temper" or have gotten into fights (Isen et al., 2022; Rowe et al., 1999). Of convicted criminals who are twins, fully half of their identical twins (but only 1 in 5 fraternal twins) also have criminal records (Raine, 1993, 2008).

In a study examining 12.5 million residents of Sweden, those with a genetic sibling convicted of a violent crime were 4 times more likely to be convicted themselves. Conviction rates were much lower for adopted siblings, suggesting a strong genetic component and a more modest environmental influence (Frisell et al., 2011). Recent research has identified a specific gene (MAOA-L) linked to aggression; some even call it the "warrior gene" or the "violence gene" (Smeijers et al., 2020). Among 900 criminals in Finland, those with the gene were 13 times more likely to have repeatedly committed violent crimes, explaining up to 10% of severe violent crime in the country (Tiihonen et al., 2015). Across several lab studies, people with the gene were more likely to act aggressively when provoked (Ficks & Waldman, 2014; McDermott et al., 2009). Long-term studies following several hundred New Zealand children reveal that a recipe for aggressive behavior combines the MAOA-L gene with childhood maltreatment (Caspi et al., 2002; Moffitt et al., 2003). Neither "bad" genes nor a "bad" environment alone predispose later aggressiveness and antisocial behavior; rather, genes predispose some children to be more sensitive and responsive to maltreatment. Nature and nurture interact.

BIOCHEMICAL INFLUENCES

Blood chemistry also influences aggressive behavior.

ALCOHOL Both laboratory experiments and police data indicate that alcohol unleashes aggression when people are provoked (Bushman, 1993; Kuypers et al., 2020; Testa, 2002). A large meta-analysis and a survey with data from 55 countries confirmed that alcohol consumption is associated with higher levels of aggression, especially among men (Duke et al., 2018; Liu et al., 2023). Consider the following:

- When asked to think back on relationship conflicts, intoxicated people administered stronger supposed shocks and felt angrier than sober people during lab experiments (MacDonald et al., 2000).
- College students primed to think about alcohol responded more aggressively to ambiguous insults (Pedersen et al., 2014). Apparently, even thinking about alcohol led to interpreting neutral statements as hostile.

- Forty percent of all violent crimes in the United States and 50% of murders worldwide, involve alcohol (Kuhns et al., 2014). Thirty-seven percent of U.S. rapes and sexual assaults involve alcohol (NCADD, 2014). States with more restrictive laws for alcohol sales also have lower rates of alcohol-involved murder (Naimi et al., 2017).
- College students who kept electronic diaries for 2 months showed a clear pattern: Those who drank alcohol were more likely to act aggressively toward their dating partners. With each drink, rates of abuse went up (Moore et al., 2011). In another day-to-day study, students were more aggressive on days when they drank alcohol (Sheehan & Lau-Barraco, 2019).

One in five college-age women experiences a sexual assault, and many of these crimes involve alcohol.
DC Studio/Shutterstock

- Larger men who drank alcohol were significantly more aggressive after drinking alcohol, but alcohol had little effect on women's or smaller men's aggression. Alcohol, noted the researchers, seemed to encourage larger men "to 'throw their weight around' and intimidate others by behaving aggressively" (DeWall et al., 2010). Apparently, people really are wise to avoid the "big, drunk guy" in the bar.

Alcohol enhances aggressiveness by reducing people's self-awareness, by focusing attention on provocations, and by reducing self-control (Giancola & Corman, 2007; Ito et al., 1996; Meldrum et al., 2023). Alcohol also predisposes people to interpret ambiguous acts (such as a bump in a crowd) as provocations (Begue et al., 2010). Alcohol deindividuates, and it disinhibits.

TESTOSTERONE Hormonal influences on aggression appear to be much stronger in other animals than in humans. But human aggressiveness does correlate with the male sex hormone testosterone. Consider the following:

- Drugs that diminish testosterone levels in violent human males subdue their aggressive tendencies.
- After men reach age 25, their testosterone levels and rates of violent crime decrease together.
- Testosterone levels are higher among prisoners convicted of violent crimes compared with those convicted of nonviolent crimes (Dabbs, 1992; Dabbs et al., 1995, 1997, 2001).
- Boys and men with high testosterone levels are more prone to delinquency, hard drug use, and aggressive responses to provocation, and increases in testosterone levels correlate with increases in aggression (Barzman et al., 2013; Geniole et al., 2020; Grotzinger et al., 2018).
- Men high in dominance or low in self-control who received an administration of testosterone became more aggressive after being provoked (Carré et al., 2017).
- College students reporting higher levels of anger after being ostracized had higher levels of testosterone in their saliva (Peterson & Harmon-Jones, 2012).
- After handling a gun, men's testosterone levels rose, and the more their testosterone rose, the more aggressive they were toward others (Klinesmith et al., 2006).
- People with brain structures indicative of greater testosterone exposure were more aggressive from childhood to adulthood (Nguyen et al., 2016).

"We could avoid two-thirds of all crime simply by putting all able-bodied young men in cryogenic sleep from the age of 12 through 28."

—David Lykken, *The Antisocial Personalities,* 1995

POOR DIET When British researcher Bernard Gesch first tried to study the effect of diet on aggression, he stood in front of hundreds of inmates at an English prison – but no matter how loudly he talked, none of them would listen. Finally, he talked privately to the "daddy" – the inmates' "tough guy" leader – and 231 inmates signed on to receive nutritional supplements or a placebo. Prisoners who got the extra nutrition were later involved in 35% fewer violent incidents (Gesch et al., 2002; Zaalberg et al., 2010). Such programs may eventually help people outside of prison as well because many people have diets

Research suggests eating too much bad food might lead to bad behavior, including aggression.
Olena 1/Shutterstock

deficient in important nutrients, such as omega-3 fatty acids (found in fish and important for brain function) and calcium (which guards against impulsivity).

In another study, researchers surveyed Boston public high school students about their diets and their aggressive or violent actions. Those who drank more than five cans of nondiet soda a week were more likely to have been violent toward peers, siblings, or dating partners and more likely to have carried a weapon, such as a gun or knife. This was true even after the researchers accounted for eight other possible factors (Solnick & Hemenway, 2012). A subsequent study of teens in 64 countries found that each soda consumed a day was linked to an 11% increase in physical fighting (Shi et al., 2020). A longitudinal study confirmed this, finding that soft drink consumption at age 13 predicted aggressive behavior at age 16 (Mrug et al., 2021).

The solution seems to be a better diet. Eleven- and 12-year-old children randomly assigned to take a supplement of omega-3 fatty acids and vitamins behaved less aggressively during the next 3 months (Raine et al., 2016, 2021). Thus, perhaps surprisingly, there may have been at least some truth to the classic "Twinkie defense," in which an accused murderer's attorneys argued he committed the crime because he had been eating a junk food diet of Twinkies and Coca-Cola. The upshot: To lower aggression, eat a diet high in omega-3 fatty acids and vegetables, low in trans fat, and without sweetened drinks (Choy et al., 2020; Marques et al., 2021).

BIOLOGY AND BEHAVIOR INTERACT The traffic between biology and behavior flows both ways. For example, higher levels of testosterone may cause dominant and aggressive behavior, but dominant and aggressive behavior can also lead to higher testosterone levels (Mazur & Booth, 1998). After a World Cup soccer match or a big basketball game between archrivals, testosterone levels rise in the winning fans and fall in the losing fans (Bernhardt et al., 1998). Similarly, men who voted for the winning U.S. presidential candidate in 2008 (Barack Obama) versus the losing candidate (John McCain) experienced rising testosterone (Stanton et al., 2009). The phenomenon also occurs in the laboratory, where socially anxious men exhibit a pronounced drop in their testosterone level after losing a rigged face-to-face competition (Maner et al., 2008). Testosterone surges, plus celebration-related drinking, probably explain why the fans of *winning* soccer and rugby teams – not the fans of losing teams – actually commit more postgame assaults (Sivarajasingam et al., 2005).

So, neural, genetic, and biochemical influences predispose some people to react aggressively to conflict and provocation. But is aggression so much a part of human nature that it makes peace unattainable? The American Psychological Association and the International Council of Psychologists endorsed a statement on violence developed by scientists from a dozen nations (Adams, 1991): "It is scientifically incorrect [to say that] war or any other violent behavior is genetically programmed into our human nature [or that] war is caused by 'instinct' or any single motivation." There are, as we will see, ways to reduce human aggression.

Aggression as a Response to Frustration

It is a warm evening. Tired and hungry after 2 hours of studying, you borrow some change from a friend and head for the nearest vending machine. As the machine devours the change, you can almost taste the salty peanuts you've chosen. But when you push the button, nothing happens. You push it again. Then you flip the coin return button. Still nothing. Again, you hit the buttons. You slam the machine. Alas, no money and no snack. You stomp back to your studies, empty-handed and shortchanged. Should your roommate beware? Are you now more likely to say or do something hurtful?

One of the first psychological theories of aggression, the popular **frustration-aggression theory,** answered yes (Dollard et al., 1939). **Frustration** is anything (such as the malfunctioning vending machine) that blocks us from attaining a goal. Frustration grows when our motivation to achieve a goal is very strong, when we expected gratification, and when the blocking is complete. When Rupert Brown and his colleagues (2001) surveyed British ferry passengers heading to France, they found more aggressive attitudes on a day when French fishing boats blockaded the port and the ferries could not get through. Blocked from obtaining their goal, the passengers became more likely (in responding to various vignettes) to agree with an insult toward a French person who had spilled coffee. Similarly, college students who were frustrated by losing a multiplayer video soccer game blasted their opponents with longer and louder bursts of painful noise (Breuer et al., 2014).

frustration-aggression theory
The theory that frustration triggers a readiness to aggress.

frustration
The blocking of goal-directed behavior.

Frustration-triggered aggression sometimes appears as road rage. Road rage is fed by perceptions of hostile intentions from other drivers, as when one is cut off in traffic (Britt & Garrity, 2006).
ARENA Creative/Shutterstock

Relational aggression is often rooted in frustration, such as after a breakup. Some direct their aggression against the person now dating their ex-partner. One woman described her experience this way: "A girl was upset that I was dating her ex-boyfriend. She would harass me with text messages telling me I was a bad friend and a slut" (Rafferty & Vander Ven, 2014).

Laboratory tests of the frustration-aggression theory have produced mixed results: Sometimes frustration increased aggressiveness, sometimes not. For example, if the frustration was understandable – if, as in one experiment, an accomplice disrupted a group's problem solving because his hearing aid malfunctioned (rather than just because he wasn't paying attention) – frustration led to irritation, not aggression (Burnstein & Worchel, 1962).

Leonard Berkowitz (1978, 1989) realized that the original theory overstated the frustration-aggression connection, so he revised it. Berkowitz theorized that frustration produces aggression only when others' actions seem unjustified; for instance, when someone who frustrated them could have chosen to act otherwise, leading to feelings of anger (Averill, 1983; Weiner, 1981). For example, many people are frustrated in their goals while playing sports, but they usually aren't aggressive unless they are angered by a deliberate, unfair act by an opposing player. Aggression is also influenced by social norms in these situations. Across five experiments, aggression followed frustration only for people whose beliefs or upbringing valued aggression (Leander et al., 2020).

A frustrated person is especially likely to lash out when aggressive cues pull the cork, releasing bottled-up anger (**Figure 1**). Sometimes the cork will blow without such cues. But, as we will see later, cues associated with aggression amplify aggression (Carlson et al., 1990).

DISPLACEMENT THEORY

The aggressive energy brought on by frustration does not need to explode directly against its source. Most people learn to inhibit direct retaliation, especially when others might disapprove or punish; instead, we *displace,* or redirect, our hostilities to safer targets. **Displacement** occurred in an old anecdote about a man who, humiliated by his boss, berates his wife, who yells at their son, who kicks the dog, which bites the mail carrier (who goes home and berates his wife . . .). In experiments and in real life, displaced aggression is most likely

displacement
The redirection of aggression to a target other than the source of the frustration. Generally, the new target is a safer or more socially acceptable target.

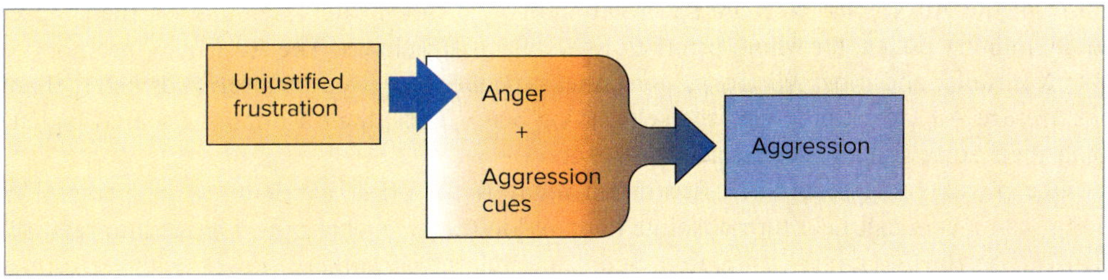

FIGURE 1

A Simplified Synopsis of Leonard Berkowitz's Revised Frustration-Aggression Theory

when the target shares some similarity to the instigator and performs a minor irritating act that unleashes the displaced aggression (Marcus-Newhall et al., 2000; Miller et al., 2003; Pedersen et al., 2000, 2008). When someone is harboring anger from a prior provocation, even a trivial offense may elicit an explosive overreaction (as you may realize if you have ever yelled at your roommate after losing money in a malfunctioning vending machine).

In one experiment, Eduardo Vasquez and his co-researchers (2005) provoked some University of Southern California students (but not others) by having an experimenter insult their performance on an anagram-solving test. Shortly afterward, the participants had to decide how long another student should be required to immerse their hand in painful cold water while completing a task. When the student committed a trivial offense – by giving a mild insult – the previously provoked participants responded punitively, by recommending a longer cold-water treatment than did the unprovoked participants. This phenomenon of displaced aggression helps us understand, noted Vasquez, why a previously provoked and still-angry person might respond to mild highway offenses with road rage or react to spousal criticism with spousal abuse. Displacement also occurs outside the lab. In one analysis of nearly 5 million at-bats from 74,197 games since 1960, Major League Baseball pitchers were most likely to hit batters with the ball when the batter had hit a home run the last time at bat or after the previous batter did so (Timmerman, 2007).

Outgroup targets are especially vulnerable to displaced aggression (Pedersen et al., 2008). Opposites attack. Various commentators have observed that the intense U.S. anger over 9/11 contributed to the eagerness to attack Iraq. Americans were looking for an outlet for their rage and found one in an evil tyrant, Saddam Hussein, who was once their ally. The actual reason for the Iraq war, noted Thomas Friedman (2003), "was that after 9/11 America needed to hit someone in the Arab-Muslim world. . . . We hit Saddam for one simple reason: because we could, and because he deserved it, and because he was right in the heart of that world." One of the war's advocates, Vice President Richard Cheney (2003), seemed to concur. When asked why most others in the world disagreed with the U.S.'s war, he replied, "They didn't experience 9/11."

RELATIVE DEPRIVATION

Frustration is not only caused by complete deprivation; more often, *frustration arises from the gap between expectations and attainments.* The most economically frustrated people are not always impoverished; middle-class people who aspire to more may feel thwarted. When your expectations are fulfilled by your attainments and when your desires are reachable at your income, you feel satisfied rather than frustrated (Solberg et al., 2002). But when being rich feels just out of reach, aggression might be the result.

relative deprivation

The perception that one is less well off than others with whom one compares oneself.

Such feelings, called **relative deprivation,** explain why happiness tends to be lower and crime rates higher in countries with more income inequality (a larger gap between the rich and poor [Coccia, 2017; *The Economist,* 2018]). The greater the income gap, the higher the sense that others are getting something you're not (Cheung & Lucas, 2016). Poor boys with rich neighbors – those most aware of what they were missing – were more aggressive than boys surrounded by concentrated poverty (Odgers et al., 2015). Among college students, those randomly assigned to watch a news story about the poor performance of the economy reported feeling more hostile (Barlett & Anderson, 2014). People who saw themselves as lower in socioeconomic status – whether they actually were or not – were more aggressive, as were those assigned to feel they were relatively deprived compared to others (Greitemeyer & Sagioglou, 2016, 2019).

"A house may be large or small; as long as the surrounding houses are equally small, it satisfies all social demands for a dwelling. But let a palace arise beside the little house, and it shrinks from a little house into a hut."

—Karl Marx, *"Wage Labor and Capital,"* 1847

The term "relative deprivation" was coined by researchers studying the satisfaction felt by U.S. soldiers in World War II (Merton & Kitt, 1950; Stouffer et al., 1949). Ironically, those in the Air Corps felt *more* frustrated about their own rate of promotion than those in the military police, for whom promotions were actually slower. The Air Corps' promotion rate was rapid, and most Air Corps personnel probably perceived themselves as better than the average Air Corps member (the self-serving bias). Thus, their aspirations soared higher than their achievements. The result? Frustration.

One possible source of such frustration today is the affluence depicted in media. TV and social media can help turn absolute deprivation (lacking what others have) into relative deprivation (feeling deprived). Karen Hennigan and her co-workers (1982) analyzed crime rates in U.S. cities around the time television was introduced. In 34 cities where television ownership became widespread in 1951, the 1951 larceny-theft rate (for crimes such as shoplifting and bicycle stealing) took an observable jump. In 34 other cities, where a government freeze had delayed the introduction of television until 1955, a similar jump in the theft rate occurred – in 1955.

"Comparison is the thief of joy."
—Theodore Roosevelt (1858–1919)

Aggression as Learned Social Behavior

Theories of aggression based on instinct and frustration assume that hostile urges erupt from inner emotions, which naturally "push" aggression from within. Social psychologists also contend that learning "pulls" aggression out of us.

Albert Bandura (1997) proposed a **social learning theory** of aggression. He believed that we learn aggression not only by experiencing its payoffs but also by observing others. As with most social behaviors, we acquire aggression by watching others act and noting the consequences.

social learning theory
The theory that we learn social behavior by observing and imitating and by being rewarded and punished.

Picture this scene from one of Bandura's experiments (Bandura et al., 1961). A preschool child is put to work on an interesting art activity. An adult is in another part of the room, where there are Tinker Toys, a mallet, and a big, inflated Bobo doll. After a minute of working with the Tinker Toys, the adult gets up and for almost 10 minutes attacks the inflated doll. She pounds it with the mallet, kicks it, and throws it, while yelling, "Sock him in the nose. . . . Knock him down. . . . Kick him."

After observing this outburst, the child is taken to a different room with many very attractive toys. But after 2 minutes the experimenter interrupts, saying these are her best toys and she must "save them for the other children." The frustrated child now goes into yet another room with various toys designed for aggressive and nonaggressive play, two of which are a Bobo doll and a mallet.

Children who were not exposed to the aggressive adult model rarely displayed any aggressive play or talk. Although frustrated, they nevertheless played calmly. Those who had observed the aggressive adult were much more likely to pick up the mallet and lash out at the doll. Watching the adult's aggressive behavior lowered their inhibitions. Moreover, the children often reproduced the model's specific acts and said her words. Observing aggressive behavior had both lowered their inhibitions and taught them ways to aggress.

Physically aggressive children tend to have had physically punitive parents, who disciplined them by modeling aggression with screaming, slapping, and beating (Goncy et al., 2021; Patterson et al., 1982; Zubizarreta et al., 2019). Even more mild physical punishment from parents, such as spanking, is linked to later aggression among their children (Gershoff, 2002; MacKenzie et al., 2015). These parents often had parents who were themselves physically punitive (Bandura & Walters, 1959; Straus & Gelles, 1980). Such punitive behavior may escalate into abuse, and although most abused children do not become criminals or abusive parents, 30% do later abuse their own children – 4 times the rate of the general population (Kaufman & Zigler, 1987; Widom, 1989). Violence often begets violence.

The social environment outside the home also provides models. Among Chicago adolescents who were otherwise equally at risk for violence, those who observed gun violence were twice as likely to be violent themselves (Bingenheimer et al., 2005). Men from cultures

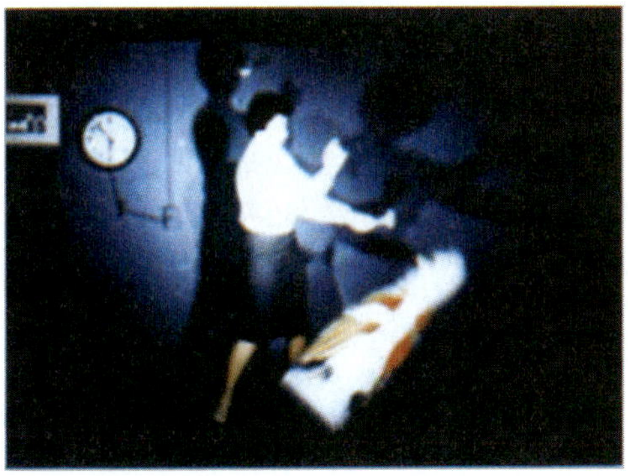

In Bandura's famous experiment, children exposed to an adult's aggression against a Bobo doll became likely to reproduce the observed aggression.
Courtesy of Albert Bandura

A peaceable kingdom. In 2008, a man was convicted of murder in Scotland's Orkney Islands — only the second murder conviction there since the 1800s.
Nicola Colombo/nikokvfrmoto/123RF

that are nondemocratic, high in income inequality, and focused on teaching men to be warriors are more likely to behave aggressively than those from cultures with the opposite characteristics (Bond, 2004).

Richard Nisbett (1990, 1993) and Dov Cohen (1996, 1998) explored the effect of a subculture on attitudes toward violence. They theorized that the U.S. South, settled by Scots-Irish sheepherders ever wary of threats to their flocks, has a "culture of honor," which maintains that insults deserve retaliation (Gul et al., 2021; Henry, 2009). After squeezing by another man in a hallway and hearing him mutter an insult, White Southern men expressed more aggressive thoughts and experienced a surge in testosterone. White Northern men were more likely to find the encounter funny (Cohen et al., 1996).

Even now, cities in the U.S. South have higher than average White homicide rates, particularly using firearms (Lantz & Wenger, 2021; Vandello et al., 2008). More students in "culture of honor" states bring weapons to school, and these states have had 2 to 3 times as many school shootings as others (Brown et al., 2009; Riedman & Desmond, 2023). Domestic violence and sexual assault are also higher in the "culture of honor" states (Brown et al., 2018). For a personal reflection on the "culture of honor," see The Inside Story: Brett Pelham on Growing up in Poverty in a "Culture of Honor."

People learn aggressive responses both by experience and by observing aggressive models. But when will aggressive responses actually occur? Bandura (1979) contended that aggressive acts are motivated by a variety of aversive experiences: frustration, pain, insults (**Figure 2**). Such experiences arouse us emotionally. But whether we act aggressively depends

THE inside STORY

Brett Pelham on Growing Up in Poverty in a "Culture of Honor"

I grew up in extreme poverty in the deep South — in rural Georgia. Most years, my family lived on about two dollars per day. My mother gave birth to her fourth of six kids at age 21. At age 55, after battling the extreme daily stresses that poor people take as a given, she succumbed to cancer. But she left all her children with a legacy of empathy and compassion for others who have suffered. I understand the deep South's "culture of honor" and its associations with inequality, aggression, and prejudice. But, thanks to my mother's example of compassion for others, I believe deeply in empathy.

I have four nephews who have been to jail or prison, and none who have graduated from college. My baby brother was badly beaten twice by the police. These things do *not* give me a free pass on racism or violence. Instead, I hope they give me a little extra empathy for the many ways in which the U.S. health care, educational, and justice systems harm immigrants and people of color.

So I feel sad and frustrated when people say that being disadvantaged in one way gives us no insight about what it's like to be disadvantaged in *another.* Although being poor is not the same as being a sexual minority or person of color, research shows that experiencing one form of stigma or social inequality offers people a glimpse of other forms. People who have suffered often develop increased empathy. Having known the sting of injustice themselves, they understand how even small acts of kindness can reduce human suffering.

Brett Pelham
Montgomery College, Maryland
Courtesy Brett Pelham

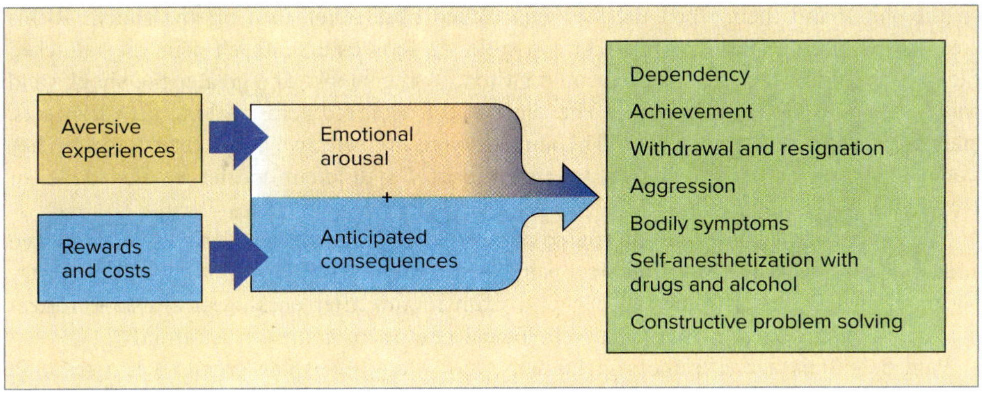

FIGURE 2

The Social Learning View of Aggression

The emotional arousal stemming from an aversive experience motivates aggression. Whether aggression or some other response actually occurs depends on what consequences we have learned to expect.

Source: Based on Bandura, 1979, 1997.

on the consequences we anticipate. Aggression is most likely when we are aroused and it seems safe and rewarding to aggress.

SUMMING UP: What Are Some Theories of Aggression?

- *Aggression* (defined as behavior intended to cause harm) can be *physical* (hurting someone's body) or *social* (hurting their feelings or status).
- *Aggression* (either physical or social) can be *hostile aggression,* which springs from emotions such as anger, and *instrumental aggression,* which aims to injure as a means to some other end.
- There are three broad theories of aggression. The first, the *instinct* view, most commonly associated with Sigmund Freud and Konrad Lorenz, contended that aggressive energy will accumulate from within, like water accumulating behind a dam. Although the available evidence offers little support for that view, it is true that aggression is biologically influenced by heredity, blood chemistry, and the brain.
- According to the second view, *frustration* causes anger and hostility. Given aggressive cues, that anger may provoke aggression. Frustration stems not from deprivation itself but from the gap between expectations and achievements.
- The *social learning* view presents aggression as learned behavior. By experience and by observing others' success, we sometimes learn that aggression pays. Social learning enables family and subcultural influences on aggression, as well as media influences (which we will discuss in the next section).

WHAT ARE SOME INFLUENCES ON AGGRESSION?

Identify the influences on aggression and describe how they work.

Some situations and experiences may provoke aggression. Consider some specific influences: aversive incidents, arousal, the media, and group context.

Aversive Experiences

Recipes for aggression often include some type of aversive experience (Groves & Anderson, 2018). These include pain, uncomfortable heat, an attack, or overcrowding.

PAIN

Researcher Nathan Azrin (1967) was doing experiments with laboratory rats in a cage wired to deliver electric shocks to the animals' feet. Azrin wanted to know if switching off the shocks would reinforce two rats' positive interactions with each other. He planned to turn on the shock and then, when the rats approached each other, turn off the shock. To his great surprise, the experiment proved impossible. As soon as the rats felt pain, they attacked each other before the experimenter could switch off the shock. The greater the shock (and pain), the more violent the attack. The same effect occurred across a long list of species, including cats, turtles, and snakes. The animals were not selective about their targets. They would attack animals of their own species, those of a different species, stuffed dolls, or even tennis balls.

The researchers also varied the source of pain. They found that not only shocks induced attack; intense heat and "psychological pain" – for example, suddenly not rewarding hungry pigeons that have been trained to expect a grain reward after pecking at a disk – brought the same reaction as shocks. This psychological pain is, of course, frustration.

Pain heightens aggressiveness in humans, too. Many of us can recall such a reaction after stubbing a toe or suffering a headache. Leonard Berkowitz and his associates demonstrated this by having University of Wisconsin students hold one hand in either lukewarm water or painfully cold water. Those whose hands were submerged in the cold water reported feeling more irritable and more annoyed, and they were more willing to blast another person with unpleasant noise. Another experiment found that those who rubbed in a cream with capsaicin (the active ingredient in chili peppers) acted more aggressively (Wang et al., 2023). In view of such results, Berkowitz (1983, 1989, 1998) proposed that aversive stimulation rather than frustration is the basic trigger of hostile aggression. Frustration is certainly one important type of unpleasantness. But any aversive event, whether a dashed expectation, a personal insult, or physical pain, can incite an emotional outburst. Even the torment of feeling depressed increases the likelihood of hostile, aggressive behavior (Dugré et al., 2020).

HEAT

Temporary climate variations can affect behavior. Offensive odors, cigarette smoke, and air pollution have all been linked with aggressive behavior (Rotton & Frey, 1985). But the most-studied environmental irritant is heat. William Griffitt (1970; Griffitt & Veitch, 1971) found that students who answered questionnaires in an uncomfortably hot room (over 90 degrees F/32 degrees C) reported feeling more tired and aggressive and expressed more hostility toward a stranger than those in a room with a more moderate temperature. Follow-up experiments revealed that heat also triggers retaliation in response to an attack or injury (Bell, 1980; Rule et al., 1987).

"I pray thee, good Mercutio, let's retire / The day is hot; the Capulets abroad; / And if we meet we shall not 'scape a brawl, / For now, these hot days, is the mad blood stirring."

—Shakespeare, *Romeo and Juliet*, 1597

Does uncomfortable heat increase aggression in the real world as well as in the laboratory? Consider the following:

- In heat-stricken Phoenix, Arizona, the drivers of cars without air conditioning were more likely to honk at a stalled car (Kenrick & MacFarlane, 1986).
- In an analysis of 57,293 Major League Baseball games since 1952, batters were more likely to be hit by a pitch during hot weather – nearly 50% more likely when the temperature was 90 degrees F or above (versus 59 degrees or below) and when three of the pitcher's teammates had previously been hit (Larrick et al., 2011). This wasn't due to reduced accuracy: Pitchers had no more walks or wild pitches. They just clobbered more batters.
- Studies in seven cities have found that when the weather is hot, violent crimes are more likely (Anderson & Anderson, 1984; Cohn, 1993; Harries & Stadler, 1988; Rotton & Cohn, 2004). In Los Angeles, violent crime rates jumped 10% as the temperature rose from the high 60s to the low 90s F – see **Figure 3** (Heilmann et al., 2021).
- Across the Northern Hemisphere, it is not only hotter days that witness more violent crimes but also hotter seasons of the year, hotter summers, hotter years, hotter cities, and hotter regions (Anderson & Delisi, 2010). In a study of 60 countries, each 1 degree C of higher temperatures was associated with a 6% rise in the homicide rate (Mares & Moffett, 2019). Craig Anderson and his colleagues project that if a 4-degree-Fahrenheit (about 2 degrees C) global warming occurs, the United States alone will see at least 50,000 more serious assaults annually (Miles-Novelo &

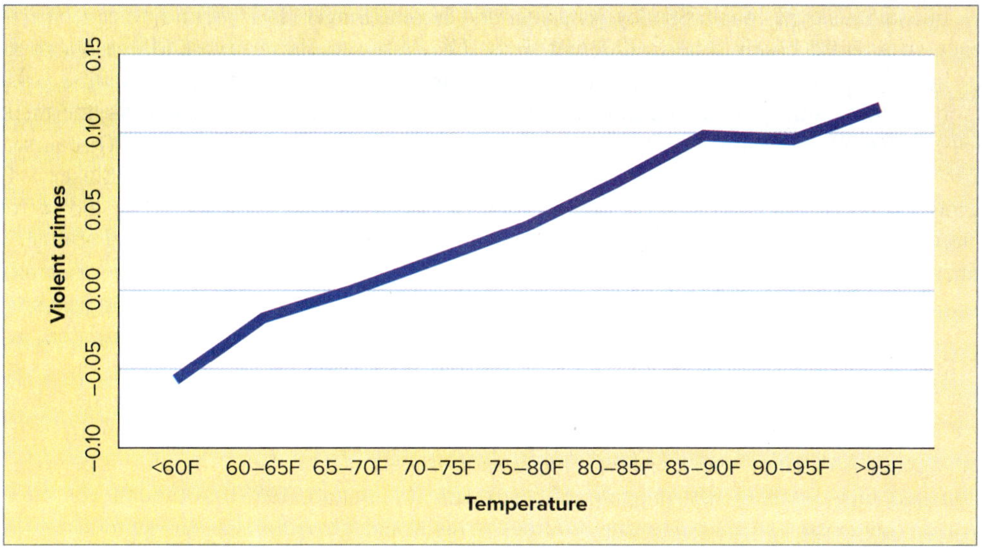

FIGURE 3

Violent Crime and Temperature

In data from Los Angeles 2010–2017, days with higher temperatures saw a higher number of violent crimes committed.
Source: Heilmann et al. (2021)

Anderson, 2019) and possibly more murders as well (Barlett et al., 2020). And that is based on only the direct effects of heat – climate change may also increase violence through other means, such as failed crops, refugee migration, and economic instability (Miles-Novelo & Anderson, 2022).

Do these real-world findings show that heat discomfort directly fuels aggressiveness? Although the conclusion appears plausible, these *correlations* between temperature and aggression don't prove it. People certainly could be more irritable in hot, sticky weather. In the laboratory, hot temperatures do increase arousal and hostile thoughts and feelings (Anderson & Anderson, 1998). Other factors may contribute, though. Perhaps hot summer evenings drive people into the streets, where other influences may well take over. Then again, there may come a point where stifling heat suppresses violence – when it's too hot to do anything, much less hurt someone (Bell, 2005; Bushman et al., 2005a,b; Cohn & Rotton, 2005).

Ferguson, Missouri, August 2014. Riots and looting occur more often during hot summer weather.
Scott Olson/Staff/Getty Images

ATTACKS

Being attacked or insulted is especially likely to provoke aggression. Several experiments confirm that intentional attacks breed retaliatory attacks. In most of these experiments, one person competes with another in a reaction-time contest. After each test trial, the winner chooses how much supposed shock to give the loser. Actually, each person is playing a programmed opponent who steadily escalates the amount of shock. Do the real participants respond charitably? Hardly. Extracting "an eye for an eye" is the more likely response (Ohbuchi & Kambara, 1985).

"An eye for an eye leaves the whole world blind."

—Attributed to Mahatma Gandhi

Arousal

So far, we have seen that various aversive stimulations can arouse anger. Do other types of arousal, such as during exercise or sexual excitement, have a similar effect? Imagine that Lourdes, having just finished a stimulating short run, comes home to discover that her date for the evening has called to say he has made other plans. Will Lourdes be more likely to explode in fury after her run than if she discovered the same message after awakening from a nap? Or, because she has just exercised, will her aggression be diminished? To discover the answer, consider how we interpret and label our bodily states.

In a famous experiment, Stanley Schachter and Jerome Singer (1962) found we can experience an aroused bodily state in different ways. They aroused University of Minnesota men by injecting them with adrenaline. The drug produced body flushing, heart palpitation, and more rapid breathing. When forewarned that the drug would produce those effects, the men felt little emotion, even when sitting next to either a hostile or a euphoric person. Of course, they could readily attribute their bodily sensations to the drug. Schachter and Singer led another group of men to believe the drug produced no such side effects. Then they, too, were placed in the company of either a hostile or a euphoric person. How did they feel and act? They were angry with the hostile person and amused by the euphoric person. The principle seemed to be: *A state of arousal can be interpreted in different ways depending on the context.*

Other experiments indicate that arousal is not as emotionally undifferentiated as Schachter believed. Yet being physically stirred up does intensify just about any emotion (Reisenzein, 1983). For example, people find radio static unpleasant, *especially* when they are aroused by bright lighting (Biner, 1991). People who have just pumped an exercise bike or watched a video of a rock concert find it easy to misattribute their arousal to a provocation and then retaliate with heightened aggression (Zillmann, 1988). Although common sense might lead us to assume that Lourdes's run would have drained her aggressive tensions, it's more likely she would react with more anger and aggression. As these studies show, *arousal fuels emotions.*

Sexual arousal and other forms of arousal, such as anger, can therefore amplify one another (Zillmann, 1989). Love is never so passionate as after a fight or a fright – one reason why it's so popular to take a date to a horror movie. In the laboratory, erotic stimuli are more arousing to people who have just been frightened. Similarly, the arousal of a roller-coaster ride may spill over into a romantic feeling for one's partner.

A frustrating or insulting situation heightens arousal. When it does, the arousal, combined with hostile thoughts and feelings, may form a recipe for aggressive behavior (**Figure 4**).

Aggression Cues

As we noted when considering the frustration-aggression hypothesis, violence is more likely when aggressive cues release pent-up anger. Leonard Berkowitz (1968, 1981, 1995) and others found that the sight of a weapon is such a cue. In one experiment, children who had just played with toy guns became more willing to knock down another child's blocks. In one experiment, people who used a driving simulator while a gun was on the passenger seat drove more aggressively than those driving with a tennis racquet on the seat (Bushman et al., 2017). In a meta-analysis of 78 independent studies, the mere presence of weapons

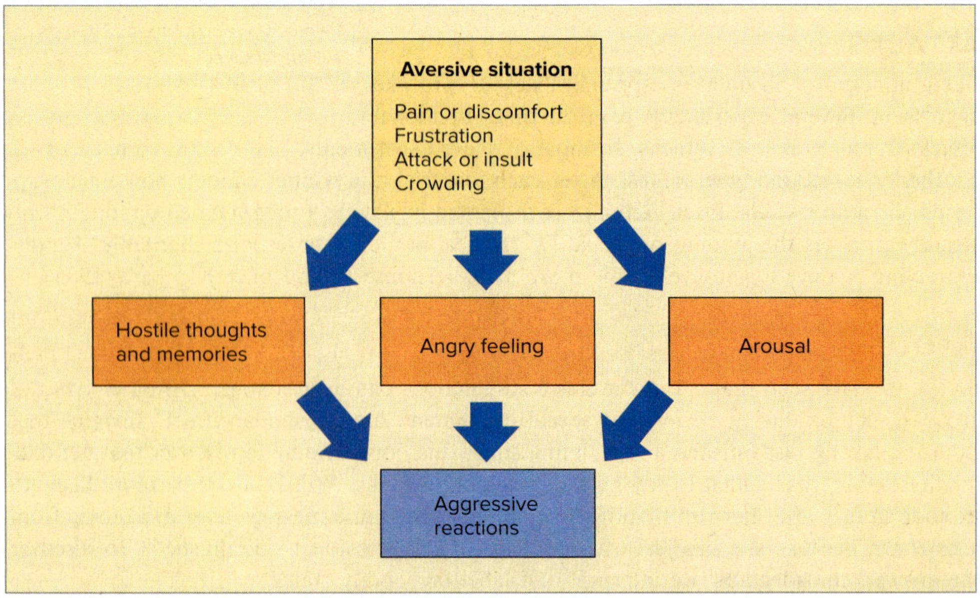

FIGURE 4

Elements of Hostile Aggression

An aversive situation can trigger aggression by provoking hostile cognitions, hostile feelings, and arousal. These reactions make us more likely to perceive harmful intent and to react aggressively.

Source: Simplified from Anderson, Deuser, & DeNeve, 1995. For an updated but more complex version, see Anderson & Bushman, 2018.

increased aggressive thoughts and behaviors, known as the "weapons effect" (Benjamin et al., 2018). What's within sight is within the mind.

The weapons effect might be why in the United States, home to about 300 million privately owned guns, half of all murders are committed with handguns or why handguns in homes are far more likely to kill household members than intruders. "Guns not only permit violence," Berkowitz reported, "they can stimulate it as well. The finger pulls the trigger, but the trigger may also be pulling the finger." Mass shootings may also serve as an aggression cue: Male gun owners expressed more willingness to shoot a home intruder in the weeks following highly publicized shootings (Leander et al., 2019).

Even if it's not touched or used, the mere presence of a gun, such as on a car's passenger seat, can lead to aggression.
KenTannenbaum/Getty Images

Compared with the United States, Britain has one-fifth as many people and 1/26th as many murders. The United States has the most firearms per capita in the world, and its rate of gun murders is 25 times higher than that of other high-income countries (Grinshteyn & Hemenway, 2016). In Japan, it takes about a decade to equal the number of U.S. gun deaths in a day.

In 130 studies across 10 countries, laws restricting firearms sales were followed by reductions in gun crimes (Santaella-Tenorio et al., 2016). When Washington, D.C., adopted a law restricting handgun possession, the number of gun-related murders and suicides each abruptly dropped about 25%. No changes occurred in other methods of murder and suicide, and nearby cities did not show any changes in gun crimes (Loftin et al., 1991). When Australia instituted stricter gun laws and bought back 700,000 guns after a 1996 mass shooting, gun-related murders fell 59% (Howard, 2013). During the 1994–2004 time period when the United States banned assault weapons, the risk of a citizen dying in a mass shooting was 70% lower than the years when assault weapons were legal (DiMaggio et al., 2019).

States with higher gun-ownership rates and fewer restrictions on guns also have higher firearm homicide rates and higher firearm suicide rates (Martinez-Ales et al., 2021; Sanchez et al., 2020; Siegel et al., 2013). Although some have argued that armed citizens might prevent gun violence, more violent crimes – not fewer – occurred in 11 states after they passed "right-to-carry" laws allowing people to carry concealed weapons (Donohue et al., 2019).

Researchers have also examined the risks of violence in homes with and without guns. This research is difficult to conduct because such homes may differ in many ways. Among people of the same gender, race, age, and neighborhood, those who kept a gun in the home (often for protection) were 2.7 times as likely to be murdered – nearly always by a family member or a close acquaintance (Kellermann, 1997; Kellermann et al., 1993). Non-gun-owners who move in with a gun owner – vs. those who did not – were 7 times more likely to be shot and killed by a spouse or partner at home (Studdert et al., 2022). People with guns in their homes were also twice as likely to take their own lives (Anglemyer et al., 2014). A gun in the home is 12 times more likely to kill a household member than an intruder (Narang et al., 2010). A gun in the home has often meant the difference between a fight and a funeral or between temporary suffering and suicide.

Guns not only serve as aggression cues but also put psychological distance between aggressor and victim. As Milgram's obedience studies taught us, remoteness from the victim facilitates cruelty. A knife can kill someone, but a knife attack requires a great deal more personal contact than pulling a trigger from a distance (**Figure 5**).

Media Influences

Most of us are surrounded by media for hours a day – from TV to video games to social media. What impact do those experiences have on levels of aggression? We'll begin with an increasingly common media habit: watching pornography.

FIGURE 5

Weapons Used to Commit Murder in the United States in 2021

Source: FBI (2023).

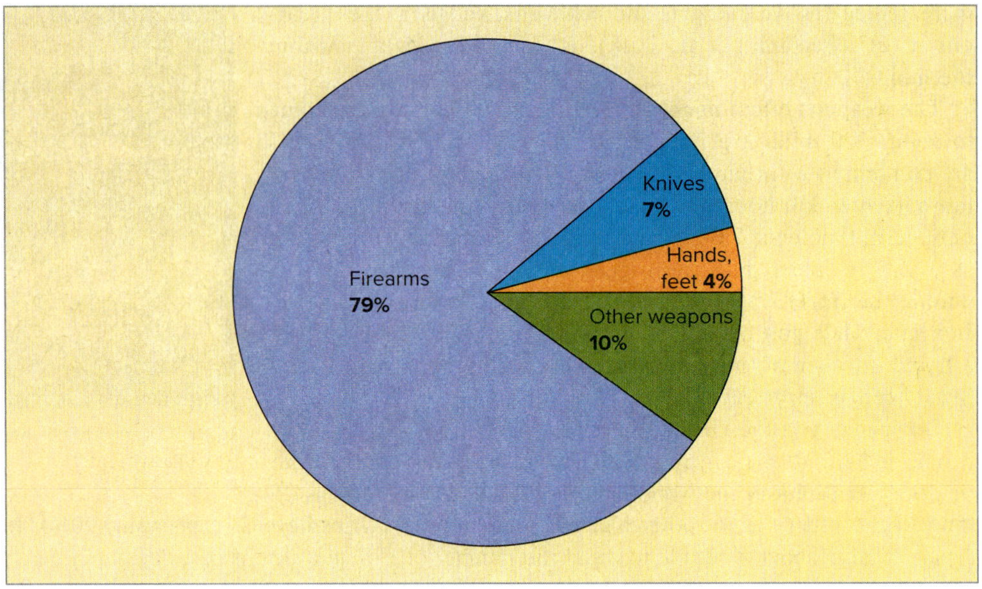

PORNOGRAPHY AND SEXUAL VIOLENCE

Pornography is now a bigger business in the United States than professional football, basketball, and baseball combined. About half of men and 16% of women reported viewing online pornography in the last week, and 2 out of 3 teens have been exposed to online pornography (Regnerus et al., 2016; Wright et al., 2020). Six percent of women and 11% of men reported feeling addicted to pornography (Grubbs et al., 2019). Pornography use is more common among men who are younger, less religious, and have had more sexual partners than average.

Porn videos vary. Some involve two willing partners, but others depict sexual violence and assault (Marshall & Miller, 2019; Sun et al., 2008). A typical sexually violent episode in pornography finds a man forcing himself upon a woman. She at first resists and tries to fight off her attacker. Gradually, as she resists and he persists, she becomes sexually aroused, and her resistance melts. By the end, she is in ecstasy, pleading for more. The problem, of course, is that women do not actually respond this way to sexual assault.

Social psychologists report that viewing such fictional scenes of a man overpowering and arousing a woman can (a) distort men's (and possibly women's) perceptions of how women actually respond to sexual coercion and (b) increase men's aggression against women.

Does viewing sexual violence reinforce the "rape myth" that some women would welcome sexual assault and that "no doesn't really mean no"? Neil Malamuth and James Check (1981) showed University of Manitoba men either two nonsexual movies or two movies depicting a man sexually overcoming a woman. A week later, when surveyed by a different experimenter, those who saw the films with sexual violence were more accepting of violence against women. This was especially true if they were aroused by the films (Hald & Malamuth, 2015).

"Pornography that portrays sexual aggression as pleasurable for the victim increases the acceptance of the use of coercion in sexual relations."

—Social Science Consensus at Surgeon General's Workshop on Pornography and Public Health, 1987

Other studies confirm that exposure to sexual violence increases acceptance of the rape myth (Oddone-Paolucci et al., 2000; Seabrook et al., 2019). For example, while spending three evenings watching sexually violent videos, men became progressively less bothered by rape and violence (Mullin & Linz, 1995). Compared with men not exposed to the videos, the men expressed less sympathy for domestic violence victims and rated the victims' injuries as less severe – even three days later. In fact, noted the researchers, what better way for an evil character to get people to react calmly to the torture and mutilation of women than to show a gradually escalating series of such videos (Donnerstein et al., 1987)?

Evidence also suggests that viewing simulated sexual violence contributes to men's actual aggression toward women. Boys and girls ages 10 to 15 who had seen movies, magazines, or websites with violent sexual content were 6 times more likely to be sexually aggressive toward others (defined as "kissed, touched, or done anything sexual with another person when that person did not want you to do so"), even after adjusting for factors such as gender, aggressive traits, and family background (Ybarra et al., 2011). Across 43 studies, teens and young adults who consumed more sexually explicit and sexually violent media were more likely to have been involved in dating violence and sexual violence (Rodenhizer & Edwards, 2017). A meta-analysis of 22 studies found that people who watch pornography often were more likely to be sexually aggressive, including both physical force and verbal coercion and harassment, including in recent samples (Wright et al., 2016, 2021). They are also more likely to sexually harass others: Belgian university students randomly assigned to play a video game with sexualized female characters were more likely to send sexist jokes to women (Burnay et al., 2019).

Sexual offenders commonly acknowledge pornography use. Among 155 men arrested for child pornography possession, 85% admitted they had molested a child at least once, and the average offender had 13 victims (Bourke & Hernandez, 2009). Rapists, serial killers, and child molesters report using pornography at unusually high rates (Bennett, 1991; Kingston et al., 2008).

But perhaps pornography doesn't actually cause violence; instead, violent men like violent pornography. To rule out this explanation, it is necessary to perform an experiment; for example, to randomly assign some people to watch pornography. In one such experiment, 120 University of Wisconsin men watched a neutral, an erotic, or an aggressive-erotic (rape) film. Then the men, supposedly as part of another experiment, "taught" a male or female accomplice some nonsense syllables by choosing how much supposed shock to administer for incorrect answers. The men who had watched the rape film administered markedly stronger shocks (**Figure 6**), particularly to women and particularly when angered (Donnerstein, 1980).

If the ethics of conducting such experiments trouble you, rest assured that these researchers appreciate the controversial and powerful experience they are giving participants. Only after giving their knowing consent do people participate. Moreover, after the experiment, researchers effectively debunk any myths the videos communicated (Check & Malamuth, 1984).

TV, MOVIES, AND ONLINE VIDEOS

We have seen that watching an aggressive person modeling an attack on a Bobo doll can unleash children's aggressive urges and teach them new ways to aggress. Does everyday television or video viewing have any similar effects?

The content of TV and online videos can be violent. Violent videos mimicking popular cartoons for children sometimes appear on YouTube Kids; one video featuring children setting each other on fire was viewed more than 20 million times (Maheshwari, 2017;

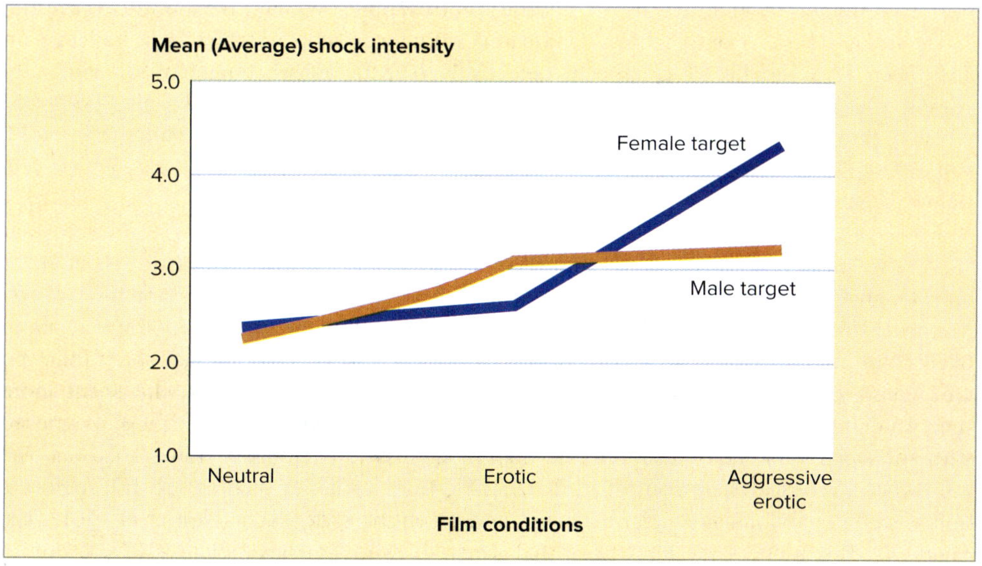

FIGURE 6

Aggression after Watching Pornography

After viewing an aggressive-erotic film, college men delivered stronger shocks than before, especially to a woman.

Source: Data from Donnerstein, 1980.

Orphanides, 2018). Original-content TV shows on streaming sites (such as Netflix or Hulu) feature 6 incidents of violence every hour (Krongard & Tsay-Vogel, 2020). Social aggression (such as bullying and social exclusion) is just as frequent; in the 50 most popular TV shows among 2- to 11-year-olds, 92% featured at least some social aggression. This bullying often came from an attractive perpetrator, was portrayed as funny, and was neither rewarded nor punished (Martins & Wilson, 2012a).

Examples of children reenacting media violence abound, from the 13-year-old who killed his 5-year-old sister imitating wrestling moves he'd seen on TV (AP, 2013) to a boy who died when his brothers imitated a hanging they'd seen in a cartoon (Indo-Asian News Service, 2013). More recently, teens participating in viral TikTok challenges have tricked schoolmates into jumping into the air – and then kicked their legs from behind so they fall full-force onto their faces (Kantor, 2022).

However, single anecdotes of media-inspired violence are not scientific evidence. Researchers, therefore, use correlational and experimental studies to examine the effects of viewing violence. One technique, commonly used with schoolchildren, correlates their TV watching with their aggressiveness. The frequent result: The more violent the content of the child's TV viewing, the more aggressive the child (Eron, 1987; Khurana et al., 2019; Turner et al., 1986). For example, a longitudinal study of 1,715 German adolescents found that those who viewed more violent media were more aggressive 2 years later, even with important other factors controlled (Krahé et al., 2012). The relationship is modest but consistently found in North America, Europe, Asia, and Australia and appears among adults as well (Anderson et al., 2017).

The link also extends to social aggression. Girls who watched more shows featuring gossiping, backbiting, and social exclusion more often displayed such behavior later (Coyne & Archer, 2005), as did elementary school girls in Illinois who watched shows featuring social aggression (Martins & Wilson, 2012b). Girls who watched shows featuring social aggression were more likely to mimic that aggression in text messages; for example, by texting "We're not gonna be friends anymore" (Coyne et al., 2019).

CORRELATIONAL AND LONGITUDINAL STUDIES Can we conclude, then, that a diet of violent TV and videos fuels aggression? Perhaps you are already thinking that because these are correlational studies, the cause-effect relationship could also work in the opposite direction. Maybe aggressive children prefer aggressive videos. Or maybe some underlying third factor, such as lower intelligence, predisposes some children to prefer both aggressive videos and aggressive behavior.

Researchers test these alternative explanations by pulling out the influence of hidden third factors and following people over years in longitudinal studies to determine the sequence of events. Most of the initial studies in this area examined TV, the primary media source consumed by children in past decades. For example, William Belson (1978; Muson, 1978) studied 1,565 London boys. Compared with those who watched little violence on TV, those who watched a great deal (especially realistic rather than cartoon violence) admitted to 50% more violent acts during the preceding 6 months. Belson also examined 22 likely third factors, such as family size. The "heavy violence" and "light violence" viewers still differed after these third factors were included. Belson surmised that the heavy viewers were indeed more violent *because* of their TV exposure.

In longitudinal studies, Leonard Eron and Rowell Huesmann (1980, 1985) found that viewing violence at age 8 predicted aggressiveness at age 19 but that aggressiveness at age 8 did *not* predict viewing violence at age 19. Aggression followed viewing, not the reverse. Moreover, by age 30, those who had watched the most violence in childhood were more likely than others to have been convicted of a crime. Another longitudinal study followed 1,037 New Zealand children from age 5 to age 26. Children and teens who spent more time watching TV were more likely to become young adults convicted of crimes, diagnosed with antisocial personality disorder, and high in aggressive personality traits. This was true even when the researchers controlled for possible third variables such as sex, IQ, socioeconomic status, previous antisocial behavior, and parenting style (Robertson et al., 2013; see **Figure 7**). Researchers are *not* saying that everyone who watches violent media becomes

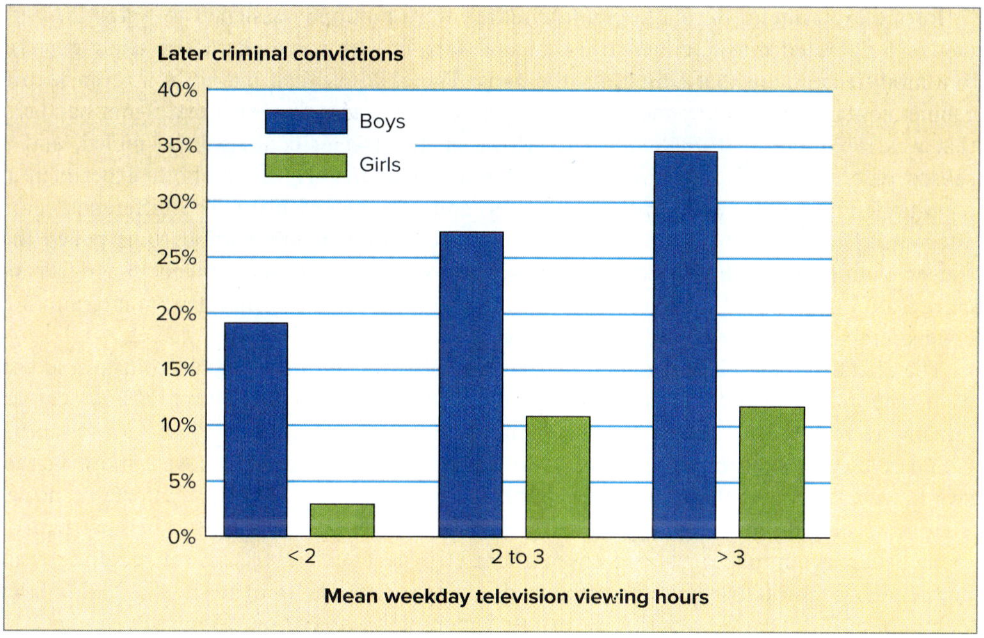

FIGURE 7

TV Viewing and Later Criminal Behavior

Television viewing between ages 5 and 15 predicted having a criminal conviction by age 26.

aggressive in real life; instead, they find it is one of several risk factors for aggressive behavior, combined with family troubles, gender, and being the victim of someone else's aggression. Even after taking these factors into account, however, exposure to violent media is a significant predictor of aggression (Gentile & Bushman, 2012).

Other studies have confirmed these results in various ways, finding that:

- Eight-year-olds' viewing of violence predicted spousal abuse as an adult (Huesmann et al., 1984, 2003).
- Adolescents' violence viewing predicted engaging in assault, robbery, and threats of injury (Johnson et al., 2002).
- Elementary schoolchildren's violent media exposure predicted how often they got into fights 2 to 6 months later (Gentile et al., 2004).
- Adolescents who watched TV shows featuring social aggression were more socially aggressive 1 and 2 years later (Coyne, 2016).

In all these studies, the investigators were careful to adjust for likely third factors, such as intelligence or hostility. Nevertheless, an infinite number of possible third factors could be creating a merely coincidental relation between viewing violence and practicing aggression. Fortunately, the experimental method can control these extraneous factors. If we randomly assign some people to watch a violent video and others a nonviolent video, any later aggression difference between the two groups will be due to the only factor that distinguishes them: what they watched. In the next section, we discuss studies using the experimental method that can prove causation more definitively than correlational and longitudinal studies.

MEDIA-VIEWING EXPERIMENTS The trailblazing Bobo-doll experiments by Albert Bandura and Richard Walters (1963) sometimes had young children view the adult pounding the inflated doll on film instead of observing it live and found children mimicked filmed aggression just as much as live aggression. Then Leonard Berkowitz and Russell Geen (1966) found that angered college students who viewed a violent film acted more aggressively than did similarly angered students who viewed nonaggressive films. Several decades of research later, more than 100 experiments had confirmed the finding that viewing violence amplifies aggression (Anderson et al., 2003).

Watching violent media leads to social and physical aggression in real life.
Maica/Getty Images

In one experiment, 8- to 12-year-old children were randomly assigned to watch 20 minutes of a PG-rated movie, either in its original version with some characters using guns or in a modified version that edited out the guns. The children then played in a room with a cabinet containing Legos, games, Nerf guns, and, hidden in a drawer, a real 9-mm handgun that was modified so it could not fire. However, the trigger could still be pulled, and a sensor recorded how many times the children pulled the trigger. In both experimental conditions, most children found the real gun, and 42% picked it up. The difference came afterward: Hardly any of the children who watched the movie clip without guns pulled the trigger, but children who watched the movie clip that featured guns pulled the trigger an average of 3 times. One of the children put the real (but thankfully disabled) gun to another child's temple and pulled the trigger (Dillon & Bushman, 2017).

The effects appear among adults as well. In another experiment, female college students were randomly assigned to watch portions of a physically aggressive film *(Kill Bill),* a relationally aggressive film *(Mean Girls),* or a nonaggressive control film *(What Lies Beneath).* Compared to the control group, those who watched the aggressive films were more aggressive toward an innocent person, blasting her headphones with loud, uncomfortable noise. They were also more subtly aggressive, giving negative evaluations to another participant (actually an accomplice) who annoyed them (Coyne et al., 2008). Even reading about physical or relational aggression produced the same results (Coyne et al., 2012). Dolf Zillmann and James Weaver (1999) exposed men and women, on 4 consecutive days, to violent or nonviolent feature films. On the fifth day, those exposed to the violent films were more hostile to a (new) research assistant. Fifth graders who watched a tween sitcom featuring social aggression (compared with those watching a control show) were more likely to agree that a student from a different group should be excluded from joining their team for a school competition (Mares & Braun, 2013).

If increased exposure to media violence causes aggression, would less exposure lead to less aggression? One group of researchers found that the answer was yes. German middle school students were randomly assigned to either a control group or an intervention group encouraged to reduce their media use and critically question it. Among those already high in aggressive behavior, the intervention group later reported less aggressive behavior than the control group (Krahé & Busching, 2015; Moller et al., 2012).

All in all, concluded researchers Brad Bushman and Craig Anderson (2001), the evidence for media effects on aggression is now "overwhelming." The research base is large, the methods diverse, and the overall findings consistent, agreed a National Institute of Mental Health task force of leading media violence researchers (Anderson et al., 2003). "Our in-depth review . . . reveals unequivocal evidence that exposure to media violence can increase the likelihood of aggressive and violent behavior in both immediate and long-term contexts." This conclusion has been questioned by some critics (Elson & Ferguson, 2014) but is endorsed by the researchers with the most expertise in the field (Bushman & Huesmann, 2014) and a broad consensus of media researchers, pediatricians, and parents (Bushman et al., 2015). Although viewing violent media is of course only one among many causes of aggression (and thus not *the* cause of aggression), experiments do show that it is *a* cause (Bushman & Anderson, 2015).

"Then shall we simply allow our children to listen to any story anyone happens to make up, and so receive into their minds ideas often the very opposite of those we shall think they ought to have when they are grown up?"

—Plato, *The Republic*, BC 360

WHY DOES MEDIA VIEWING AFFECT BEHAVIOR? Given the convergence of correlational and experimental evidence, researchers have explored *why* viewing violence leads to aggression. Consider three possibilities (Geen & Thomas, 1986). One is the *arousal* watching violence produces (Mueller et al., 1983; Zillmann, 1989). As we noted earlier, arousal tends to spill over: One type of arousal energizes other behaviors.

Other research shows that viewing violence *disinhibits.* In Bandura's experiment, the adult punching the Bobo doll made aggression legitimate and lowered the children's inhibitions. Viewing violence primes the viewer for aggressive behavior by activating violence-related thoughts (Berkowitz, 1984; Bushman & Geen, 1990; Josephson, 1987). Listening to music with sexually violent lyrics seems to have a similar effect (Barongan & Hall, 1995; Johnson et al., 1995; Pritchard, 1998).

Media portrayals also evoke *imitation.* The children in Bandura's experiments reenacted the specific behaviors they had witnessed. The commercial television industry is in a difficult position to dispute that television leads viewers to imitate what they have seen:

Commercials are designed to model consumption of the product. Are media executives right, however, to argue that TV merely holds a mirror to a violent society, that art imitates life, and that the "reel" world, therefore, shows us the real world? Actually, on TV programs, acts of assault outnumber affectionate acts 4 to 1 – thankfully in contrast to a significantly more peaceful world. In other ways as well, television models an unreal world.

But there is good news here, too. If the ways of relating and problem solving modeled on television do trigger imitation, especially among young viewers, then TV modeling of **prosocial behavior** should be socially beneficial. A character who helps others (such as Dora the Explorer or Doc McStuffins) can teach children prosocial behavior.

prosocial behavior
Positive, constructive, helpful social behavior; the opposite of antisocial behavior.

MEDIA INFLUENCES ON THINKING We have focused on television's effect on behavior, but researchers have also examined the cognitive effects of viewing violence: Does prolonged viewing *desensitize* us to cruelty? Does it distort our *perceptions* of reality? Does it *prime* aggressive thoughts?

"Fifty years of research on the effect of TV violence on children leads to the inescapable conclusion that viewing media violence is related to increases in aggressive attitudes, values, and behaviors."

—John P. Murray, "Media Violence: The Effects Are Both Real and Strong," 2008

DESENSITIZATION Repeat an emotion-arousing stimulus, such as an obscene word, over and over. What happens? The emotional response will "extinguish." After witnessing thousands of acts of cruelty, there is good reason to expect a similar emotional numbing. The most common response might well become, "Doesn't bother me at all." Such a response is precisely what Barbara Krahé and her colleagues (2010) observed when they measured the physiological arousal of 303 college students who watched a clip from a violent movie. Regular viewers of violent media showed a lessened response, compared to infrequent viewers, reacting to violence with a shrug rather than concern. A longitudinal study of German adolescents found the same thing: Media violence exposure decreased feelings of empathy for others (Krahé & Moller, 2010).

In a clever experiment, Brad Bushman and Craig Anderson (2009) had a young woman with a taped-up ankle drop her crutches while outside a movie theater and then struggle to retrieve them. Moviegoers who had just seen a violent film took longer to help than those who had just seen a nonviolent film. When the woman dropped her crutches *before* the movie, however, there was no difference in helping – suggesting it was the violent film itself, and not the type of people who watch violent films, that desensitized moviegoers to her dilemma.

"The more fully that any given generation was exposed to television in its formative years, the lower its civic engagement [its rate of voting, joining, meeting, giving, and volunteering]."

—Robert Putnam, *Bowling Alone*, 2000

ALTERED PERCEPTIONS Does television's fictional world also mold conceptions of the real world? George Gerbner and his University of Pennsylvania associates (1979, 1994) suspected this is television's most potent effect. Their surveys of both adolescents and adults showed that heavy viewers (4 hours a day or more) are more likely than light viewers (2 hours or fewer) to exaggerate the frequency of violence in the world around them and to fear being personally assaulted. Similar feelings of vulnerability have been expressed by South African women after viewing video violence against women (Reid & Finchilescu, 1995). A national survey of American 7- to 11-year-old children found that heavy viewers were more likely than light viewers to admit fears "that somebody bad might get into your house" or that "when you go outside, somebody might hurt you" (Peterson & Zill, 1981). For those who watched more television, the world became a scary place. Media portrayals shape perceptions of reality.

COGNITIVE PRIMING Research also reveals that watching violent television primes aggression-related ideas (Bushman, 1998). After viewing violence, people offer more hostile explanations for others' behavior (was the shove intentional?). They interpret spoken homonyms with the more aggressive meaning (interpreting "punch" as a hit rather than a drink). And they recognize aggressive words more quickly. Media portrayals prime thinking.

Children who watch more violent media can become desensitized to cruelty and feel less empathy for others.
MachineHeadz/iStock/Getty Images

First-person shooter games teach and reward aggression, leading to increased aggression after the game is over.
Andrey Popov/Shutterstock

VIDEO GAMES

"Video games are excellent teaching tools," note psychologists Doug Gentile and Craig Anderson. "If health video games can successfully teach health behaviors, and flight simulator video games can teach people how to fly, then what should we expect violent murder-simulating games to teach?"

Research shows that playing violent video games does, on average, increase aggressive behavior, thoughts, and feelings outside the game. A meta-analysis combining data from 1,723 analyses including 360,045 participants (Groves et al., 2021) revealed a clear effect: Violent video-game playing increased aggression – for children, adolescents, and young adults; in North America, Japan, and Western Europe; and across three research designs (correlational, experimental, and longitudinal). That means violent video games caused aggression even when participants were randomly assigned to play them (versus a nonviolent game), which rules out the possibility that (for example) aggressive people like to play aggressive games. A meta-analysis of longitudinal studies found that violent video game play was most strongly linked to aggression in adolescence, around age 14 (Burkhardt & Lenhard, 2022).

In one experiment, for example, French university students were randomly assigned to play either a violent video game *(Condemned 2, Call of Duty 4, The Club)* or a nonviolent video game (*S3K Superbike, Dirt 2,* or *Pure*) for 20 minutes each day for 3 days. Those randomly assigned to play a violent game blasted longer and louder unpleasant noise into the headphones of an innocent person than those who played the nonviolent game, with their aggression increasing each day they played the violent game (Hasan et al., 2013).

Studies examining real-world aggression find similar results. Among 3,372 Finnish adolescents, those who spent more time playing violent video games were more likely to commit real-world aggressive acts such as attacking someone or threatening someone with a weapon (Exelmans et al., 2015). Longitudinal studies also find that playing violent games leads to aggression: A meta-analysis of 24 high-quality studies that followed children and youth for up to 4 years confirmed that "playing violent video games is associated with greater levels of physical violence over time" (Prescott et al., 2018). In 2019, an American Psychological Association task force reviewed hundreds studies between 2005 and 2019 and concluded that the evidence linking violent video-games and aggression warranted recommending that the video-game industry include violence in its game rating system. However, they cautioned against pointing to games as the sole cause of violence such as mass shootings (Suls et al., 2019).

So do most people who play violent video games become aggressive? No. Similarly, most smokers don't die of lung cancer. And most people who spend hundreds of hours rehearsing human slaughter live gentle lives. "I play violent video games," some may protest, "And I'm not aggressive." The problem with this common argument is that video games don't have to change everyone's behavior to have an impact. Even if only some people become more aggressive after playing violent video games, video game players will be more aggressive *on average* compared to others. Similarly, smoking doesn't cause lung cancer for everyone, but smokers are much more likely to get lung cancer than nonsmokers.

Playing violent video games has an array of effects, including:

- *Increases in aggressive behaviors:* After violent gameplay, children and youth play more aggressively with their peers, get into more arguments with their teachers, and participate in more fights. The effect occurs inside and outside the laboratory, across self-reports, teacher reports, and parent reports, and for the reasons illustrated in **Figure 8**. After they started playing violent games, even previously nonhostile kids became more likely to get into fights (Gentile et al., 2004). In Japan, too, playing violent video games early in a school year predicted physical aggressiveness later in the year, even after controlling for gender and prior aggressiveness (Anderson et al., 2008). One experiment randomly assigned children to play a nonviolent version of the game *Minecraft* or a version featuring gun violence. The children then played in

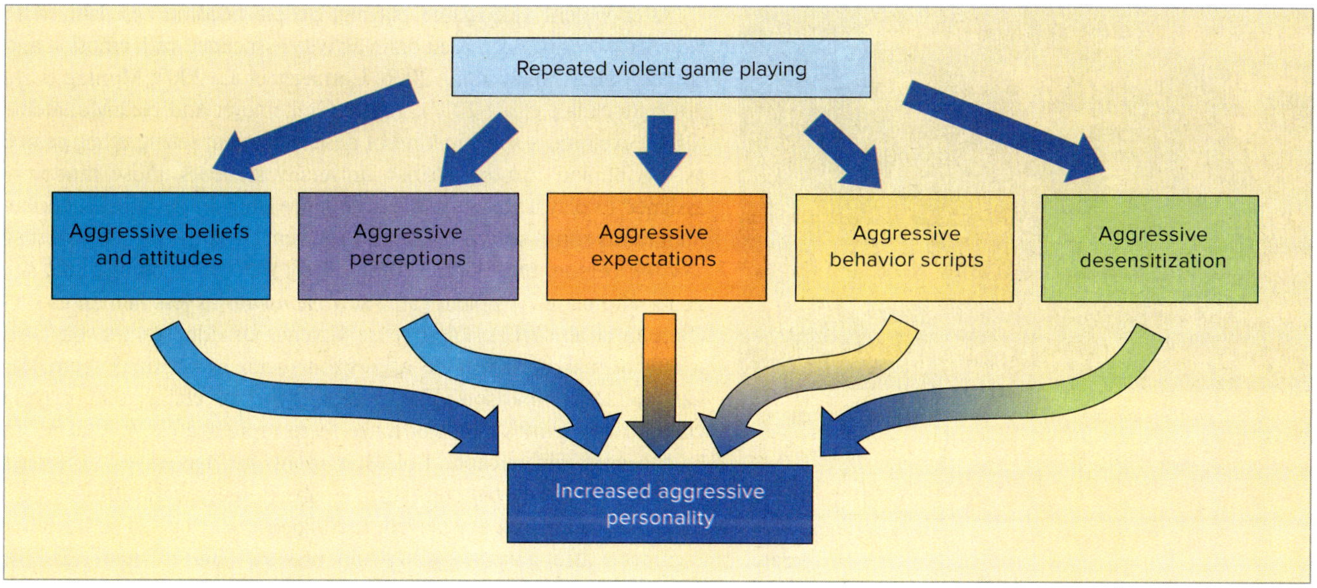

FIGURE 8

Violent Video-Game Influences on Aggressive Tendencies

Source: Adapted from Anderson & Bushman, 2001.

a room that contained toys and games as well as two disabled handguns. The children who had just played the gun violence version pulled the gun trigger 3 times more often than those who had played the nonviolent version (Chang & Bushman, 2019).

- *Increases in aggressive thoughts.* After playing a violent game, students became more likely to guess that a man whose car was just rear-ended would respond aggressively by using abusive language, kicking out a window, or starting a fight (Bushman & Anderson, 2002; Gentile et al., 2017). Those who played violent games were also more likely to have a hostile attribution bias: They expected other people to act aggressively when provoked. Those who play violent games, conclude the researchers, see the world through "blood-red tinted glasses" (Hasan et al., 2012).
- *Increases in aggressive feelings,* including hostility, anger, or revenge. Students who played a violent video game had more aggressive thoughts and feelings than those who watched a recording of someone else playing the same game or who watched a violent video, suggesting that violent video games heighten aggression even more than other violent media – most likely because people actually act aggressively when they play video games instead of acting as passive observers (Lin, 2013).
- *Greater likelihood of carrying a weapon.* Among 9- to 18-year-olds in a U.S. national longitudinal study, those who played violent video games in the past year were 5 times more likely to carry a weapon to school, even when adjusted for other factors (Ybarra et al., 2014).
- *Decreases in self-control and increases in antisocial behavior.* High school students who played a violent video game (compared with a control group who played a nonviolent game) ate 4 times more M&Ms out of a bowl next to the computer, suggesting lowered self-control. They were also more likely to steal, taking more raffle tickets for attractive prizes than they actually earned (Gabbiadini et al., 2014).
- *Decreases in helping others and in empathy for others.* Students randomly assigned to play a violent or nonviolent video game later overheard a loud fight that ended with one person writhing on the floor in pain from a sprained ankle. Students who had just played a violent game took more than a minute on average to come to the person's aid, almost 4 times as long as those who had played a nonviolent game (Bushman & Anderson, 2009).

Is violent video game-playing cathartic? Toxic? Or neutral? Experiments offer some answers.
James Woodson/Digital Vision/Getty Images

After violent video-game playing, people become desensitized to violence, showing decreased brain activity associated with emotion and empathy (Bartholow et al., 2006; Carnagey et al., 2007; Montag et al., 2012; Stockdale et al., 2017). Tobias Greitemeyer and Neil McLatchie (2011) explored a specific kind of desensitization: seeing other people as less human. Among British university students, those randomly assigned to play a violent game were more likely to describe in nonhuman terms someone who had insulted them. And the less human they saw the person, the more aggressive they were. In another study, students who played a violent game saw *themselves* as less human as well (Bastian et al., 2012). The intense violence of video games may also make unambiguous real-life aggression (such as shoving) seem less harmful in comparison. Thus, when someone claims that playing violent video games does not make them more aggressive, that might be because their perception of what counts as "aggressive" no longer includes less severe but still harmful, acts (Greitemeyer, 2014).

Moreover, the more violent the games that are played, the bigger the effects. The bloodier the game, the greater the gamer's after-game hostility and arousal (Barlett et al., 2008). More realistic games that show more real-looking gore produced more aggressive feelings than less realistic games (Bartlett & Rodeheffer, 2009). These studies challenge the **catharsis** hypothesis: the idea that violent games allow people to safely express their aggressive tendencies and "get their anger out" (Kutner & Olson, 2008). Practicing violence breeds rather than releases violence, say catharsis critics. Yet the idea that games might relieve angry feelings is one of the main draws of violent video games for angry people (Bushman & Whitaker, 2010). Unfortunately, say critics, this strategy is likely to backfire, leading to more anger and aggression.

catharsis
Emotional release. The catharsis view of aggression is that the aggressive drive is reduced when one "releases" aggressive energy, either by acting aggressively or by fantasizing aggression.

Video games are not all bad; not all of them are violent, and even violent games improve hand-eye coordination, reaction time, spatial ability, and selective attention (Dye et al., 2009; Sanchez, 2012; Wu et al., 2012), though these effects are limited to those who play frequently and for many hours (Unsworth et al., 2015). In addition, game playing is focused fun that helps satisfy basic needs for a sense of competence, control, and social connection. No wonder an experiment that randomly assigned 6- to 9-year-old boys to receive a game system found them spending an average of 40 minutes a day on it over the next few months. The downside: They spent less time on schoolwork, resulting in lower reading and writing scores than the control group that did not get a game system (Weis & Cerankosky, 2010).

What about playing prosocial games in which people help each other – the conceptual opposite of violent games? In three studies with children and adults in Singapore, Japan, and the United States, those who played prosocial video games helped others, shared, and cooperated more in real-life situations (Gentile et al., 2009). German students randomly assigned to play a prosocial (versus neutral) game were less physically and socially aggressive toward someone who had insulted them (Greitemeyer et al., 2012). A meta-analysis of 98 studies found the same: Violent video games are linked to more antisocial acts and fewer prosocial acts, and prosocial games are linked to fewer antisocial acts and more prosocial acts (Greitemeyer & Mugge, 2014). As Douglas Gentile and Craig Anderson (2011) concluded, "Video games are excellent teachers." Educational games teach children reading and math, prosocial games teach prosocial behavior, and violent games teach violence, they noted. We do what we're taught to do, whether that's to help or to hurt.

As a concerned scientist, Craig Anderson (2003, 2004) (see "The Inside Story: Craig Anderson on Video-Game Violence") therefore encourages parents to discover what their kids are ingesting and to ensure that their media diet, at least in their own home, is healthy. Parents may not be able to control what their child watches, plays, and eats in someone else's home. Nor can they control the media's effect on their children's peer culture. (That is why advising parents to "just say no" to games and media is naive.) But parents can oversee consumption in their own home and provide increased time for alternative activities. Networking with other parents can build a kid-friendly neighborhood. And schools can help by providing media-awareness education.

"It is hard to measure the increasing acceptance of brutality in American life, but its evidence is everywhere, starting with the video games of killing that are a principal entertainment of boys."

—Susan Sontag, *Regarding the Torture of Others*, 2004

THE inside STORY

Craig Anderson on Video Game Violence

Years ago, after learning about and understanding the clearly harmful effects being documented by TV/film violence researchers, I was disturbed as I noticed increasing video game violence. With one of my graduate students, Karen Dill, I therefore began correlational and experimental investigations that led to my testifying before a U.S. Senate subcommittee and consulting for government and public policy groups, including parent and child advocacy organizations.

Although it is gratifying to see one's research have a positive impact, the video-game industry has gone to great lengths to dismiss the research, much as 50 years ago cigarette manufacturers ridiculed basic medical research by asking how many Marlboros a lab rat had to smoke before contracting cancer. I continue to get lots of requests for information about violent video game effects. This led me and some of my colleagues to write and publish a simple-to-read FAQs book, *Game On! Sensible Answers about Video Games and Media Violence*, for teens, parents and others. I also added lots of information at www.craiganderson.org.

Craig A. Anderson
Iowa State University

Group Influences

We have considered what provokes *individuals* to aggress. If frustrations, insults, and aggressive models heighten the aggressive tendencies of isolated people, such factors are likely to prompt the same reaction in groups. As a riot begins, aggressive acts often spread rapidly after the "trigger" example of one antagonistic person. Seeing looters freely helping themselves to TV sets, normally law-abiding bystanders may drop their moral inhibitions and imitate.

Groups can amplify aggressive reactions partly by diffusing responsibility. Decisions to attack in war typically are made by strategists remote from the front lines. They give orders, but others carry them out. Does such distancing make it easier to recommend aggression?

In one experiment, students either *shocked* someone or simply *advised* someone else how much shock to administer. When the recipient had not done anything to provoke the aggressor, characteristic of most victims of mass aggression, the advisers recommended more shock than given by the frontline participants, who felt more directly responsible for any hurt (Gaebelein & Mander, 1978).

Diffusion of responsibility increases not only with distance but also with numbers. Brian Mullen (1986) analyzed information from 60 lynchings between 1899 and 1946 and made an interesting discovery: The greater the number of people in a lynch mob, the more vicious the murder and mutilation.

Through social "contagion," groups magnify aggressive tendencies, much as they polarize other tendencies. Examples are youth gangs, soccer fans, rapacious soldiers, urban rioters, and what Scandinavians call "mobbing"—schoolchildren in groups repeatedly harassing or attacking an insecure, weak schoolmate (Lagerspetz et al., 1982). Mobbing is a group activity.

Youths sharing antisocial tendencies and lacking close family bonds and expectations of academic success may find social identity in a gang. As group identity develops, conformity pressures and deindividuation increase (Staub, 1996). Self-identity diminishes as members give themselves over to the group, often feeling a satisfying oneness with the others. The frequent result is social

Social contagion. When 17 juvenile, orphaned male elephants were relocated during the mid-1990s to a South African park, they became an out-of-control adolescent gang and killed 40 white rhinoceroses. In 1998, concerned park officials relocated 6 older, stronger bull elephants into their midst. The result: The rampaging soon quieted down (Slotow et al., 2000). One of these dominant bulls, at left, faces down several of the juveniles.
Gus van Dyk

contagion — group-fed arousal, disinhibition, and polarization. As gang expert Arnold Goldstein (1994) observed, until gang members marry out, age out, get a job, go to prison, or die, they hang out. They define their turf, display their colors, challenge rivals, and sometimes commit delinquent acts and fight over drugs, territory, honor, sexual partners, or insults.

"As Reinhold Niebuhr has reminded us, groups tend to be more immoral than individuals."

—Martin Luther King, Jr., "Letter from Birmingham Jail," April 13, 1963

The twentieth-century massacres that claimed more than 150 million lives were "not the sums of individual actions," noted Robert Zajonc (2000). *"Genocide is not the plural of homicide."* Massacres are *social* phenomena fed by "moral imperatives" — a collective mentality (including images, rhetoric, and ideology) that mobilizes a group or a culture to extraordinary actions. The massacres of Rwanda's Tutsis, of Europe's Jews, and of America's indigenous population were collective phenomena requiring widespread support, organization, and participation. Before launching the genocidal initiative, Rwanda's Hutu government and business leaders bought and distributed 2 million machetes. Over 3 months, the Hutu attackers reportedly would get up, eat a hearty breakfast, gather together, and then go hunt their former neighbors who had fled. They would hack to death anyone they found, then return home, wash, and socialize over a few beers (Dalrymple, 2007).

Today, violence can result when people are radicalized into violent extremist groups online. Payton Gendron, who killed 10 people at a supermarket in Buffalo in 2022, said his goal was to kill as many Black people as possible. Gendron once admired Black rappers and acknowledged he was not taught racism at home. But after he began consuming 4chan pages, Reddit forums, and YouTube videos promoting White supremacist beliefs, his attitudes became more extreme. "I believed what I read online and acted out of hate," he later admitted (Katersky & Hutchinson, 2022; Morales et al., 2023). Even in simple surveys, people are more likely to support violence when their identities are fused with a group and they believe that violence is morally justifiable (Chinchilla et al., 2022).

Experiments in Israel by Yoram Jaffe and Yoel Yinon (1983) confirm that groups can amplify aggressive tendencies. In one, university men angered by a supposed fellow participant retaliated with decisions to give much stronger shocks when in groups than when alone. In another experiment (Jaffe et al., 1981), people decided, either alone or in groups, how much punishing shock to give someone for incorrect answers on a task. As **Figure 9** shows, individuals gave progressively more of the assumed shock as the experiment proceeded, and group decision making magnified this individual tendency. When circumstances provoke an individual's aggressive reaction, the addition of group interaction will often amplify it. (See "Research Close-Up: When Provoked, Are Groups More Aggressive Than Individuals?")

"The worst barbarity of war is that it forces men collectively to commit acts against which individually they would revolt with their whole being."

—Ellen Key, *War, Peace, and the Future,* 1916

Aggression studies provide an apt opportunity to ask how well social psychology's laboratory findings generalize to everyday life. Do the circumstances that trigger someone to deliver electric shock or allocate hot sauce really tell us anything about the circumstances that trigger verbal abuse or a punch in the face? Craig Anderson and Brad Bushman (1997; Bushman & Anderson, 1998) noted that social psychologists have studied aggression in

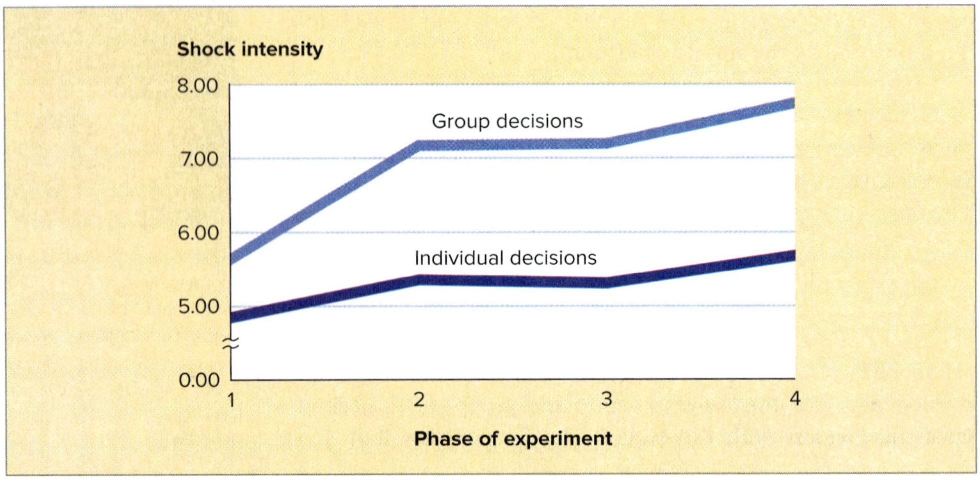

FIGURE 9

Group-Enhanced Aggression

When individuals chose how much shock to administer as punishment for wrong answers, they escalated the shock level as the experiment proceeded. Group decision making further polarized this tendency.

Source: Data from Jaffe et al., 1981.

research CLOSE-UP

When Provoked, Are Groups More Aggressive Than Individuals?

Aggression researchers are noted for their creative methods for measuring aggression, which in various experiments has involved such tactics as administering shock, blasting sound, and hurting people's feelings. Joel Lieberman and his colleagues (1999) took their cue from a cook's arrest for assault after lacing two police officers' food with Tabasco sauce and from child abuse cases in which parents have force-fed hot sauce to their children. This inspired the idea of measuring aggression by having people decide how much hot sauce someone else must consume.

That is what Bruce Meier and Verlin Hinsz (2004) did when comparing aggressive behavior by groups and individuals. They told participants, either as individuals or in groups of three, that they were studying the relationship between personality and food preferences and that they would be tasting and rating hot sauce. The experimenter explained that he needed to remain blind as to how much hot sauce each individual or group would be consuming and so needed the participants to choose the portion. After having the participants sample the intense hot sauce using a wooden stick, the experimenter left to collect the hot sauce that another individual or group had supposedly selected. He returned with a cup filled with 48 grams of the sauce, which each participant expected later to consume. The participants, in turn, were now to spoon as much or as little hot sauce as they wished into a cup for the supposed other people to consume. (In reality, no participant was forced to consume anything.)

The striking result, seen in **Figure 10**, was that groups retaliated by dishing out 24% more hot sauce than did individuals and that group targets were given 24% more than were individuals. Thus, given toxic circumstances, interaction with a group (as a source or target) amplifies individual aggressive tendencies. This finding was particularly evident in the intergroup condition. Group members, after each received a nasty 48 grams of hot sauce, retaliated by dishing out 93 grams of hot sauce for each member of the group that had given them hot sauce. Apparently, surmised Meier and Hinsz, groups not only respond more aggressively to provocation but also perceive more hostility from other groups than they do from individuals.

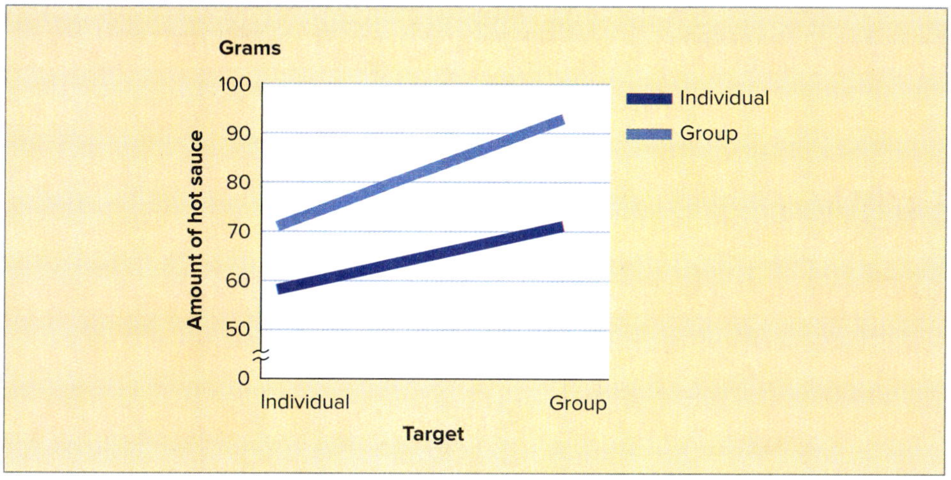

FIGURE 10
Mean Amount of Hot Sauce
Source: Meier & Hinsz, 2004.

both the laboratory and everyday worlds, and the findings are strikingly consistent. In *both* contexts, increased aggression is predicted by the following:

- Being male
- Aggressive or anger-prone personalities
- Alcohol use
- Violence viewing
- Anonymity
- Provocation
- The presence of weapons
- Group interaction

The laboratory allows us to test and revise theories under controlled conditions. Real-world events inspire ideas and provide the venue for applying our theories. Aggression research illustrates how the interplay between studies in the controlled lab and the complex real world advances psychology's contribution to human welfare. Hunches gained from everyday experience inspire theories, which stimulate laboratory research, which then deepens our understanding and our ability to apply psychology to real problems.

SUMMING UP: What Are Some Influences on Aggression?

- Many factors exert influence on aggression. One factor is aversive experiences, which include not only frustrations but also discomfort, pain, and personal attacks, both physical and verbal.
- Arousal from almost any source, even physical exercise or sexual stimulation, can be interpreted as other emotions, such as anger.
- Aggression cues, such as the presence of a gun, increase the likelihood of aggressive behavior.
- Viewing violence (1) breeds a modest increase in aggressive behavior, especially in people who are provoked, (2) desensitizes viewers to aggression, and (3) alters their perceptions of reality. These findings parallel the results of research on the effects of viewing violent pornography, which can increase men's aggression against women and distort their perceptions of women's responses to sexual coercion.
- Violent media permeates the daily life of millions of people and portrays considerable violence. Correlational and experimental studies converge on the conclusion that heavy exposure to video violence correlates with aggressive behavior.
- Playing violent video games may increase aggressive thinking, feelings, and behavior even more than television or movies do because the experience involves much more active participation than those other media.
- Much aggression is committed by groups. Circumstances that provoke individuals may also provoke groups. By diffusing responsibility and polarizing actions, group situations can amplify aggressive reactions.

HOW CAN AGGRESSION BE REDUCED?

Explain how we might counteract the factors that provoke aggression.

Can we reduce aggression? Here we look at how theory and research suggest ways to control aggression.

Catharsis?

In New York City, those who want to vent their anger can pay for the privilege of smashing dishes, laptops, and TVs with a metal bat at an establishment called the Wrecking Club. Dallas, Texas, has an Anger Room, and Toronto, Budapest, Singapore, Australia, and Britain feature Rage Rooms (Green, 2017).

Some believe that these expressions of anger should serve to reduce aggression afterward. If a person "bottles up his rage, we have to find an outlet. We have to give him an opportunity of letting off steam," asserted psychiatrist Fritz Perls (1973). After violent video games were implicated in a 2012 mass shooting, one defender of the games wrote, "Could it be that violent video games are an important outlet for aggression? That, on the whole, these games and 'play violence' let us express anger and aggression in a safe way?"

(Gilsdorf, 2013). Such statements assume the "hydraulic model," which implies accumulated aggressive energy, like dammed-up water, needs a release.

The concept of catharsis is usually credited to Aristotle. Although Aristotle said nothing about aggression, he did argue that we can purge emotions by experiencing them and that viewing tragic plays, therefore, enabled a catharsis (purging) of pity and fear. To have an emotion excited, he believed, is to have that emotion released (Butcher, 1951). The catharsis hypothesis has been extended to include the emotional release supposedly obtained not only by observing drama but also through our recalling and reliving past events, through our expressing emotions, and through our actions.

Does venting your anger online reduce or increase aggression? Studies find it increases it.
TeodorLazarev/Shutterstock

Assuming that aggressive action or fantasy drains pent-up aggression, some therapists and group leaders have encouraged people to ventilate suppressed aggression by acting it out – by whacking one another with foam bats or beating a bed with a tennis racket while screaming. If led to believe that catharsis effectively vents emotions, people will react more aggressively to an insult in an effort to improve their mood (Bushman et al., 2001). Some psychologists, believing that catharsis is therapeutic, advise parents to encourage children's release of emotional tension through aggressive play. But does catharsis work? Do those who vent their anger become less aggressive – or more aggressive?

In laboratory tests of catharsis, angered participants hit a punching bag while either ruminating about someone who angered them or thinking about becoming physically fit. A third group did not hit the punching bag. When given a chance to administer loud blasts of noise to the person who angered them, people in the punching bag plus rumination condition felt angrier and were most aggressive. Moreover, doing nothing at all more effectively reduced aggression than did "blowing off steam" by hitting the bag (Bushman, 2002). Venting anger caused more aggression, not less.

Real-life studies have produced similar results. One study examined internet users who frequently visited "rant" sites where people are encouraged to express their anger. Did the opportunity to express their hostility reduce it? No. Their hostility and anger increased (Martin et al., 2013). Expressing hostility bred more hostility. Contrary to the idea that watching violent sports can be cathartic, Canadian and American spectators of football, wrestling, and hockey games exhibited *more* hostility after viewing the event than before (Arms et al., 1979; Goldstein & Arms, 1971; Russell, 1983). Instead of reducing their anger, viewing these aggressive sports instead increased their anger. As Brad Bushman (2002) noted, "Venting to reduce anger is like using gasoline to put out a fire."

Cruel acts beget cruel attitudes. Furthermore, little aggressive acts can breed their own justification. People derogate their victims, rationalizing further aggression.

"He who gives way to violent gestures will increase his rage."

—Charles Darwin, *The Expression of the Emotions in Man and Animals*, 1872

People who habitually play violent video games are, on average, in a more positive mood afterward, one reason they may believe in catharsis. However, they also experience more aggressive feelings after playing violent vs. non-violent games, suggesting the games improve mood but do nothing to tamp down aggression (Kersten & Greitemeyer, 2022).

Should we therefore bottle up anger and aggressive urges? Silent sulking is hardly more effective because it allows us to continue reciting our grievances as we conduct conversations in our heads. Bushman and his colleagues (2005) experimented with the toxic effect of such rumination. After being insulted, some were given a distraction while the others were induced to ruminate about the insult. Those who had ruminated acted more aggressively than those who had been distracted.

Fortunately, there are nonaggressive ways to express our feelings and to inform others how their behavior affects us. Across cultures, those who reframe accusatory "you" messages as "I" messages – "I feel angry about what you said" or "I get irritated when you leave dirty dishes" – communicate their feelings in a way that better enables the other person to make a positive response (Kubany et al., 1995). We can be assertive without being aggressive.

Most homicides are the result of impulsive actions, not cool and calculated forethought.
Chris Ryan/Getty Images

A Social Learning Approach

If aggressive behavior is learned, then there is hope for its control. How can we do that?

Threatened punishment can deter aggression but only under ideal conditions: when the punishment is strong, prompt, and sure; when it is combined with a reward for the desired behavior; and when the recipient is not angry (Baron, 1977). Generally, punishment for children who engage in aggressive behavior should focus not on physical punishment such as spanking or paddling (which may simply teach more aggression) but instead on strategies such as taking away privileges (Fletcher, 2012).

However, there are limits to punishment's effectiveness. Most homicides are impulsive, hot aggression – the result of an argument, an insult, or an attack. If fatal aggression were cool and instrumental, we could hope that waiting until it happens and severely punishing the criminal afterward would deter such acts. In that world, U.S. states that impose the death penalty might have a lower murder rate than states without the death penalty. But in our world of hot homicide, the reverse is true: death penalty states have *higher* murder rates (DPIC, 2023). As John Darley and Adam Alter (2009) noted, "A remarkable amount of crime is committed by impulsive individuals, frequently young males, who are frequently drunk or high on drugs, and who often are in packs of similar and similarly mindless young men."

Thus, we must *prevent* aggression before it happens. We must teach nonaggressive conflict-resolution strategies. When psychologists Sandra Jo Wilson and Mark Lipsey (2005) assembled data from 249 studies of school violence prevention programs, they found encouraging results, especially for programs focused on selected "problem" students. After students were taught problem-solving skills, emotion-control strategies, and conflict resolution techniques, violent or disruptive behavior was cut nearly in half. When a middle school in Queens, NY instituted a program of peer mediation and anti-bullying training, it saw a substantial decline in the number of students being suspended from school (Prutzman et al., 2022). When an elementary school instituted rewards for prosocial behaviors, aggression was reduced by more than 50% (Yassine & Tipton-Fisler, 2022).

Children whose parents were more permissive were more likely to grow into more aggressive adolescents (Ehrenreich et al., 2014), further suggesting that enforcing rules for behavior might prevent aggression. Bullying is reduced when antibullying programs are interactive (rather than a lecture) and teach children what to do rather than what not to do (Cunningham et al., 2016). Other programs focus on instilling empathy, including feeling sad or angry when other children are bullied (Garandeau et al., 2022).

To foster a gentler world, we could model and reward sensitivity and cooperation from an early age, perhaps by training parents how to discipline without violence and favoring rewards instead of punishments. Training programs encourage parents to reinforce desirable behaviors and to frame statements positively ("When you finish cleaning your room, you can go play," rather than, "If you don't clean your room, you're grounded"). In that way, parents can model non-aggressive behavior. Peers also model behaviors: Teens are significantly more likely to get in physical fights, badly hurt someone else, or brandish a weapon if their friend (or even friend of a friend) had done so (Bond & Bushman, 2017).

If observing aggressive models lowers inhibitions and elicits imitation, we might also reduce brutal, dehumanizing portrayals in media – steps comparable to those already taken to reduce racist and sexist portrayals. We can also inoculate children against the effects of media violence. Eron and Huesmann (1984) taught 170 children that television portrays the world unrealistically, that aggression is less common and less effective than TV suggests, and that aggressive behavior is undesirable. When restudied 2 years later, these children were less influenced by TV violence than were untrained children.

In another study, Stanford University used 18 classroom lessons to persuade children to reduce their TV watching and video game-playing (Robinson et al., 2001). They reduced their TV viewing by a third – and the children's aggressive behavior at school dropped 25% compared with children in a control school. Even music can help reduce aggression when it models the right attitude: German students who were randomly assigned to hear prosocial music like "We Are the World" and "Help" behaved less aggressively than those who heard neutral music (Greitemeyer, 2011).

Other ideas for how to prevent aggression come from studies of differences among people. For example, people who are sensitive to disgust are less aggressive (Pond et al., 2012), suggesting that emphasizing the disgusting aspects of violence might help prevent aggression. People who see moral rules as negotiable (agreeing, for example, "Cheating is appropriate behavior because no one gets hurt") are more aggressive (Gini et al., 2014), suggesting that teaching some nonnegotiable rules and moral reasoning ("It's never okay to hit," "Cheating hurts everyone") might reduce aggressive behavior.

Suggestions such as these can help us minimize aggression. But given the complexity of aggression's causes and the difficulty of controlling them, who can feel the optimism expressed by Andrew Carnegie's forecast that in the twentieth century, "To kill a man will be considered as disgusting as we in this day consider it disgusting to eat one?" Since Carnegie uttered those words in 1900, hundreds of millions of human beings have been killed. It is a sad irony that although today we understand human aggression better than ever before, humanity's inhumanity endures.

Culture Change and World Violence

Nevertheless, cultures can change. "The Vikings slaughtered and plundered," notes science writer Natalie Angier. "Their descendants in Sweden haven't fought a war in nearly 200 years." Indeed, as psychologist Steven Pinker (2011) documented, all forms of violence – including wars, genocide, and murders – became steadily less common over the centuries. We've graduated from plundering neighboring tribes to economic interdependence, from a world in which Western European countries initiated two new wars per year over 600 years to no wars on Western European soil since World War II. Surprisingly, to those of us who love modern British murder mysteries, "a contemporary Englishman has about a 50-fold less chance of being murdered than his compatriot in the Middle Ages," noted Pinker. In all but one Western democracy, the death penalty has been abolished. And the sole exception – the United States – no longer practices it for witchcraft, counterfeiting, and horse theft. In fact, the United States has seen declines in aggressive and violent acts such as

- lynchings,
- rapes,
- and corporal punishment.

We can, Pinker concludes, be grateful "for the institutions of civilization and enlightenment [economic trade, education, government policing and justice] that have made it possible."

SUMMING UP: How Can Aggression Be Reduced?

- How can we minimize aggression? Contrary to the *catharsis* hypothesis, expressing aggression by catharsis tends to breed further aggression, not reduce it.
- The social learning approach suggests controlling aggression by counteracting the factors that provoke it: by reducing aversive stimulation, by rewarding and modeling nonaggression, and by eliciting reactions incompatible with aggression.

CONCLUDING THOUGHTS: Reforming a Violent Culture

Violence and aggression remain all too frequent around the world, including in the United States (apologies to readers elsewhere, but we Americans do have a special problem with violence).

Americans' ideas for protecting ourselves abound:

- Buy a gun for self-protection – the reason mentioned by two-thirds of gun owners (Parker et al., 2017). (We have more than 300 million guns, which puts one at tripled risk of being murdered, often by a family member, and at doubled risk of suicide [Anglemyer et al., 2014].) In assaults where someone had a chance to resist, those who had a gun were more than 5 times more likely to be shot (Branas et al., 2009). Handgun-restricting nations, such as Britain and Canada, are safer.
- Impose a "three strikes and you're out" requirement of lifetime incarceration for those convicted of three violent crimes. (But are we really ready to pay for all the new prisons – and prison hospitals and nursing homes – we would need to house and care for aging former muggers? Prisons in cash-strapped California, where a three strikes has been the law since 1994, are perpetually overcrowded.)
- Deter brutal crime and eliminate the worst offenders as some countries do – by executing the offenders. To show that killing people is wrong – kill people who kill people. (But nearly all the cities and states with the dozen highest violent-crime rates already have the death penalty. Because most homicide is impulsive or under the influence of drugs or alcohol, murderers rarely calculate consequences.)

An alternative approach is suggested by a story about the rescue of a drowning person from a rushing river. Having successfully administered first aid, the rescuer spots another struggling person and pulls them out, too. After a half dozen repetitions, the rescuer suddenly turns and starts running away while the river sweeps yet another floundering person into view. "Aren't you going to rescue that fellow?" asks a bystander. "Heck no," the rescuer shouts. "I'm going upstream to find out what's pushing all these people in."

To be sure, we need police, prisons, and social workers, all of whom help us deal with the social pathologies that plague us. It's fine to swat the mosquitoes but better if we can drain the swamps – by infusing our culture with nonviolent ideals, making the most lethal weapons less available, challenging the social toxins that corrupt youth, and renewing the moral roots of character.

Attraction and Intimacy

Jack Hollingsworth/Blend Images LLC

CHAPTER

11

"The best and most beautiful things in the world cannot be seen nor even touched, but just felt in the heart."

—Letter from 11-year-old Helen Keller, 1891

Our lifelong dependence on one another puts relationships at the core of our existence. Aristotle called humans "the social animal." Indeed, we have what today's social psychologists call a **need to belong**: the desire to connect with others in enduring, close relationships (Baumeister & Leary, 1995; Leary, 2010). This need forms the basis for what we explore in this chapter: How and why we like and love others, both romantically and as friends.

Social attachments are powerful. Consider:

- For our ancestors, mutual attachments enabled group survival. When hunting game or erecting shelter, 10 hands were better than 2.

need to belong
A motivation to bond with others in relationships that provide ongoing, positive interactions.

- The bonds of love can lead to children, whose survival chances are boosted by the nurturing of two bonded parents who support each other (Fletcher et al., 2015).
- In 10,000 recordings of university students' waking hours, they were talking to someone 28% of the time — and that doesn't count the time they spent listening to someone (Mehl & Pennebaker, 2003).
- When not face-to-face, most of the world's 8 billion people connect by voice, texting, and social media sites. In the United States, 98% of entering college students use social media, with 55% spending 6 or more hours a week on the sites (Stolzenberg et al., 2020). The average U.S. teen spends about 2 hours a day sending texts and nearly 5 hours a day on social media (Rothwell, 2023; Twenge, 2017). Our need to belong motivates our desire to be continuously connected.
- When relationships with partners, family, and friends are healthy, self-esteem — a barometer of our relationships — rides high (Denissen et al., 2008). Longing for acceptance and love, we spend billions on cosmetics, clothes, workout supplements, and diets. Even people who say they don't really need others relish being accepted (Carvallo & Gabriel, 2006).
- Exiled, imprisoned, or in solitary confinement, people ache for their own people and places. Rejected, we are at risk for depression (Nolan et al., 2003). Time passes more slowly, and life seems less meaningful (Twenge et al., 2003). There are physical consequences as well: Social isolation increases the risk of death by 32% (Wang et al., 2023).
- For the jilted, the widowed, and the traveler in a strange place, the loss of social bonds triggers pain, loneliness, or withdrawal. Losing a close relationship, adults feel jealous, distraught, or bereaved, as well as mindful of death and life's fragility. After relocating, people — especially those with the strongest need to belong — typically feel homesick (Watt & Badger, 2009). About 30% of first-year college students felt homesick at least occasionally (CollegeData, 2023).
- Reminders of death in turn heighten our need to belong, to be with others, and to hold close those we love (Mikulincer et al., 2003; Wisman & Koole, 2003). The shocking death of a classmate, a co-worker, or a family member brings people together, their differences no longer mattering.

"There's no question in my mind about what stands at the heart of the communication revolution — the human desire to connect."

—Josh Silverman, president of Skype, 2009

As Pope Francis (2017) said, "Each and everyone's existence is deeply tied to that of others: Life is not time merely passing by — life is about interactions." Social bonds are, in many ways, what make life worth living.

HOW IMPORTANT IS THE NEED TO BELONG?

Explain why being rejected or ostracized hurts.

Humans are, as Aristotle said, social animals. We need to belong. As with other motivations, we pursue belonging when we don't have it and seek less when our needs are fulfilled (Baumeister & Leary, 1995; DeWall et al., 2009, 2011). When we do belong – when we feel supported by close, intimate relationships – we tend to be healthier and happier (Cundiff &

Matthews, 2018; Hudson et al., 2020; Sun et al., 2020). When the need to belong is satisfied and balanced with two other human needs — to feel *autonomy* and *competence* — the typical result is a deep sense of well-being (Deci & Ryan, 2002; Milyavskaya et al., 2009; Sheldon & Niemiec, 2006). Happiness is feeling connected, free, and capable.

Social psychologist Kipling Williams (2001, 2011; Hales et al., 2020; Wesselmann & Williams, 2017; Williams & Nida, 2022) has explored what happens when our need to belong is thwarted by *ostracism* (acts of excluding or ignoring). Humans in all cultures, whether in schools, workplaces, or homes, use ostracism to regulate social behavior (Rudert et al., 2023). Many people know what it is like to be shunned — to be avoided, met with averted eyes, or given the silent treatment. The silent treatment is "emotional abuse" and "a terrible, terrible weapon to use," say those who have experienced it from a family member or a co-worker. Ostracism hurts, and the social pain is keenly felt — more than those who are not ostracized ever know (Nordgren et al., 2011).

Ostracism may be even worse than bullying. Bullying, though extremely hurtful, at least acknowledges someone's existence and importance, whereas ostracism treats a person as if they don't exist at all (Williams & Nida, 2009). In one study, children who were ostracized but not bullied felt worse than those who were bullied but not ostracized (Carpenter et al., 2012).

Sometimes deflation turns nasty, as when people lash out at the very people whose acceptance they desire (Reijntjes et al., 2011) or engage in self-defeating behavior. In several experiments, students randomly assigned to be rejected by their peers (versus those who were accepted) became more likely to engage in self-defeating behaviors (such as procrastinating by reading magazines) and less able to regulate their behavior (such as eating cookies [Baumeister et al., 2005; Twenge et al., 2002]). Apparently, the stereotype of someone eating lots of ice cream after a breakup isn't far off. Nor is the trope of the rejected person drowning their sorrows in alcohol: People who were socially rejected by those close to them subsequently drank more alcohol (Laws et al., 2017).

"A man's Social Self is the recognition he gets from his mates. . . . If no one turned round when we entered, answered when we spoke, or minded what we did, but if every person . . . acted as if we were non-existing things, a kind of rage and impotent despair would ere long well up in us."

—William James, *Principles of Psychology*, 1890

Overeating and alcohol use might result from a self-control breakdown: Ostracized people show deficits in brain mechanisms that inhibit unwanted behavior (Otten & Jonas, 2013). Their judgment around other issues also falters: Ostracized people are more likely to believe political conspiracy theories (Poon et al., 2020). Outside of the laboratory, rejected children were, 2 years later, more likely to have self-regulation issues, such as not finishing tasks and not listening to directions and were more likely to act aggressively (Stenseng et al., 2014). In lab experiments, socially rejected people also became more likely to disparage or blast unpleasant noise at someone who had insulted them, were less likely to help others, and were more likely to cheat and steal (Kouchaki & Wareham, 2015; Poon et al., 2013; Twenge et al., 2001, 2007). If a small laboratory experience of being "voted off the island" could produce such aggression, noted the researchers, one wonders what aggressive and antisocial tendencies "might arise from a series of important rejections or chronic exclusion." And in fact, feeling socially isolated is one of the primary risk factors for suicide (Chu et al., 2017).

Williams and Steve Nida (2011) were surprised to discover that even online ostracism also takes a toll. Their experimental procedure was inspired by Williams's experience at a park. When a Frisbee landed near his feet and Williams threw it back to two others, they then included him in the tossing for awhile. When suddenly they stopped tossing the Frisbee his way, Williams was "amazed" at how hurt he felt by the ostracism (Storr, 2018).

Taking this experience into the laboratory, the researchers had more than 5,000 participants from dozens of countries play an internet-based game of throwing a ball with two others (actually computer-generated fellow players), who then suddenly stopped throwing the ball their way.

A recipe for violence. A review of 126 school shootings in 13 countries found that 88% of the shooters experienced social rejection or social conflict at school (Sommer et al., 2014). Seventeen-year-old Dimitrios Pagourtzis, who had just been publicly rejected by the girl he liked, shot and killed 10 people at Santa Fe High School near Houston, Texas, in 2018 (Perez et al., 2018).
Jennifer Reynolds/The Galveston County Daily News/AP Images

Ostracized people experienced more negative emotions and became more likely to conform to others' incorrect judgments. Those left out of the ball-toss game were even more likely to have suicidal thoughts than those who were included (Chen et al., 2020).

Exclusion, whether it's online or in person, hurts longest for anxious people and for those with FoMO – fear of missing out (Holte et al., 2022; Zadro et al., 2006). It hurts more for younger than older adults (Andrews et al., 2022; Hawkley et al., 2011). And it hurts no less when it comes from a group that the rest of society spurns – Australian KKK members in one experiment (Gonsalkorale & Williams, 2006). Exclusion even hurts when the rejection comes from a robot (Nash et al., 2018).

Experiences on social media can also lead to feelings of ostracism. Wouter Wolf and his colleagues (2015) had participants create a personal profile and then, in the ostracism condition, receive a very low number of "likes." Participants ostracized in this way reported just as much negative mood and lack of meaning as those excluded during the online ball-toss game. Further studies have found similar results, with being ignored (ostracism) or being criticized (rejection) both leading to compromised feelings of meaningfulness and control (Lutz & Schneider, 2021). So the next time you feel hurt because you didn't get many likes or found out you weren't included in the group chat, realize you're not the only one who sometimes feels that way.

Ostracized people exhibit heightened activity in a brain cortex area that also activates in response to physical pain (Rotge et al., 2015). Hurt feelings are also embodied in a depressed heart rate (Moor et al., 2010). Heartbreak makes for heart brake.

Indeed, the pain of social rejection is so real in the brain that a pain-relieving Tylenol can reduce hurt feelings, as can sending a light electrical current to the brain region in which rejection is felt (DeWall et al., 2010; Hofman et al., 2021; Riva et al., 2012). Ostracism's opposite – feeling love – activates brain reward systems. When looking at their beloved's picture, university students feel markedly less pain when immersing their hands in cold water (Younger et al., 2010). Ostracism is a real pain, and love is a natural painkiller.

Asked to recall a time when they were socially excluded – perhaps left alone in the dorm when others went out – people in one experiment even perceived the room temperature as 5 degrees colder than did those asked to recall a social acceptance experience (Zhong & Leonardelli, 2008). Ostracizing someone is also not pleasant; students instructed to ostracize others felt dehumanized and reported just as much distress as those who were ostracized (Bastian et al., 2012; Legate et al., 2013).

Roy Baumeister (2005) finds a silver lining in the rejection and ostracism research. When excluded people experience a safe opportunity to make a new friend, they "seem willing and even eager to take it." They become more attentive to smiling, accepting faces (DeWall et al., 2009). An exclusion experience also triggers increased mimicry of others' behavior in an unconscious attempt to build rapport (Lakin et al., 2008). And at a societal level, noted Baumeister (2005), meeting the need to belong should pay dividends:

> My colleagues in sociology have pointed out that minority groups who feel excluded show many of the same patterns that our laboratory manipulations elicit: high rates of aggression and antisocial behavior, decreased willingness to cooperate and obey rules, poorer intellectual performance, more self-destructive acts, short-term focus, and the like. If we could promote a more inclusive society, in which more people feel themselves accepted as valued members, some of these tragic patterns might be reduced.

In other words, prejudice can feel a lot like rejection – yet another reason to work to reduce prejudice based on group membership.

SUMMING UP: How Important Is the Need to Belong?

- Humans have a fundamental *need to belong*. When it is thwarted, such as through exclusion or ostracism, people feel stressed and lose self-control. Social pain mimics physical pain.
- Ostracism hurts even when it comes from a despised group and even when it's online or via social media.

WHAT LEADS TO FRIENDSHIP AND ATTRACTION?

Explain how proximity, physical attractiveness, similarity, and feeling liked nurture liking and loving.

What predisposes one person to like, or to love, another? Few questions about human nature arouse greater interest.

So much has been written about liking and loving that almost every conceivable explanation—and its opposite—has already been proposed. For most people—and for you—what factors nurture liking and loving?

- Does absence make the heart grow fonder? Or is someone who is out of sight also out of mind?
- Do likes attract? Or opposites?
- How much do good looks matter?
- What has fostered your close relationships?

Let's start with those factors that lead to friendship and then consider those that sustain and deepen a relationship.

Proximity

One powerful predictor of whether any two people are friends is sheer **proximity**. Proximity can also breed hostility; most assaults and murders involve people who live close to each other. But much more often, proximity prompts liking. Mitja Back and his University of Leipzig colleagues (2008) confirmed this by randomly assigning students to seats at their first class meeting and then having each make a brief self-introduction to the whole class. One year after this one-time seating assignment, students reported greater friendship with those who happened to be seated next to or near them during that first class gathering. Across three experiments, male students consistently liked female students who sat closer to them more than those who sat further away (Shin et al., 2019).

proximity
Geographical nearness. Proximity (more precisely, "functional distance") powerfully predicts liking.

Though it may seem trivial to those pondering the mysterious origins of romantic love, sociologists long ago found that most people marry someone who lives in the same neighborhood, or works at the same company or job, or sits in the same class, or visits the same favorite place (Bossard, 1932; Burr, 1973; Clarke, 1952; McPherson et al., 2001). In a more recent Pew survey of people married or in long-term relationships, 35% met at work or at school, and some of the rest met when their paths crossed in their neighborhood, church, or gym, or while growing up (Barroso, 2020). Look around. If you marry, it may well be to someone who has lived or worked or studied within walking distance.

INTERACTION

Even more significant than geographic distance is "functional distance"—how often people's paths cross. We become friends with those who use the same entrances, parking lots, and recreation areas. Randomly assigned college roommates who interact frequently are far more likely to become good friends than enemies (Newcomb, 1961). When I [JT] lived in a dorm in college, I passed by the room of another student on my way to the communal bathroom. He usually had his door open, so we'd often talk briefly. We quickly became friends—and are still friends today. Interaction enables people to explore

Close relationships with friends and family contribute to health and happiness.
Don Hammond/Design Pics

their similarities, to sense one another's liking, to learn more about each other, and to perceive themselves as part of a social unit (Arkin & Burger, 1980). In one study, strangers liked each other more the longer they talked (Reis et al., 2011).

So if you're new in town and want to make friends, try to get an apartment near the mailboxes, a desk near the coffeepot, a parking spot near the main buildings, or a room in a dormitory with shared bathroom facilities (Easterbrook & Vignoles, 2015). Such is the architecture of friendship.

The chance nature of such contacts helps explain a surprising finding. Consider this: If you had an identical twin who became engaged to someone, wouldn't you (being in so many ways similar to your twin) expect to share your twin's attraction to that person? But no, reported researchers David Lykken and Auke Tellegen (1993); only half of identical twins recall really liking their twin's selection, and only 5% said, "I could have fallen for my twin's fiancé." Romantic love is often rather like ducklings' imprinting, surmised Lykken and Tellegen. With repeated exposure to and interaction with someone, our infatuation may fix on almost anyone who has roughly similar characteristics and who reciprocates our affection.

"I do not believe that friends are necessarily the people you like best, they are merely the people who got there first."

—Sir Peter Ustinov, *Dear Me*, 1979

Why does proximity breed liking? One factor is availability; obviously, there are fewer opportunities to get to know someone who attends a different school or lives in another town. But there is more to it. Most people like their roommates, or those one door away, better than those two doors away. Those just a few doors away, or even a floor below, hardly live at an inconvenient distance. Moreover, those close by are potential enemies as well as friends. So why does proximity encourage affection more often than animosity?

ANTICIPATION OF INTERACTION

Proximity enables people to discover commonalities and exchange rewards. But merely *anticipating* interaction also boosts liking. John Darley and Ellen Berscheid (1967) discovered this when they gave University of Minnesota women ambiguous information about two other women, one of whom they expected to talk with intimately. After reading the information, the women preferred the person they expected to talk with. Expecting to date someone also boosts liking (Berscheid et al., 1976). Even voters on the losing side of an election will find their opinions of the winning candidate – whom they are now stuck with – rising (Gilbert et al., 1998).

mere-exposure effect
The tendency for novel stimuli to be liked more or rated more positively after the rater has been repeatedly exposed to them.

The phenomenon is adaptive. Anticipatory liking – expecting that someone will be pleasant and compatible – increases the chance of forming a rewarding relationship (Klein & Kunda, 1992; Knight & Vallacher, 1981; Miller & Marks, 1982). It's probably good that we are biased to like those we often see, since our lives are filled with relationships with people whom we may not have chosen but with whom we need to have continuing interactions: roommates, siblings, grandparents, teachers, classmates, co-workers. Liking such people is surely conducive to better relationships and to happier, more productive living.

Feeling close to those close by: People often become attached to, and sometimes fall in love with, those with whom they share activities.
Isaac Koval/Getty Images

MERE EXPOSURE

Proximity leads to liking not only because it enables interaction and anticipatory liking but also for a simpler reason: More than 200 experiments reveal that, contrary to an old proverb, familiarity does not breed contempt. Rather, it fosters fondness (Bornstein, 1989, 1999; Montoya et al., 2017). **Mere exposure** to all sorts of novel stimuli – nonsense syllables, Chinese-like characters, songs, faces – boosts people's ratings of them. Do the "words" *nansoma, saricik,* and *afworbu* mean something better or something worse than the words *iktitaf, biwojni,* and *kadirga?* Told these were Turkish words (they are not), University of Michigan students tested by Robert Zajonc (1968, 1970) preferred whichever of these words they had seen most frequently. The more times they had seen a meaningless word or a

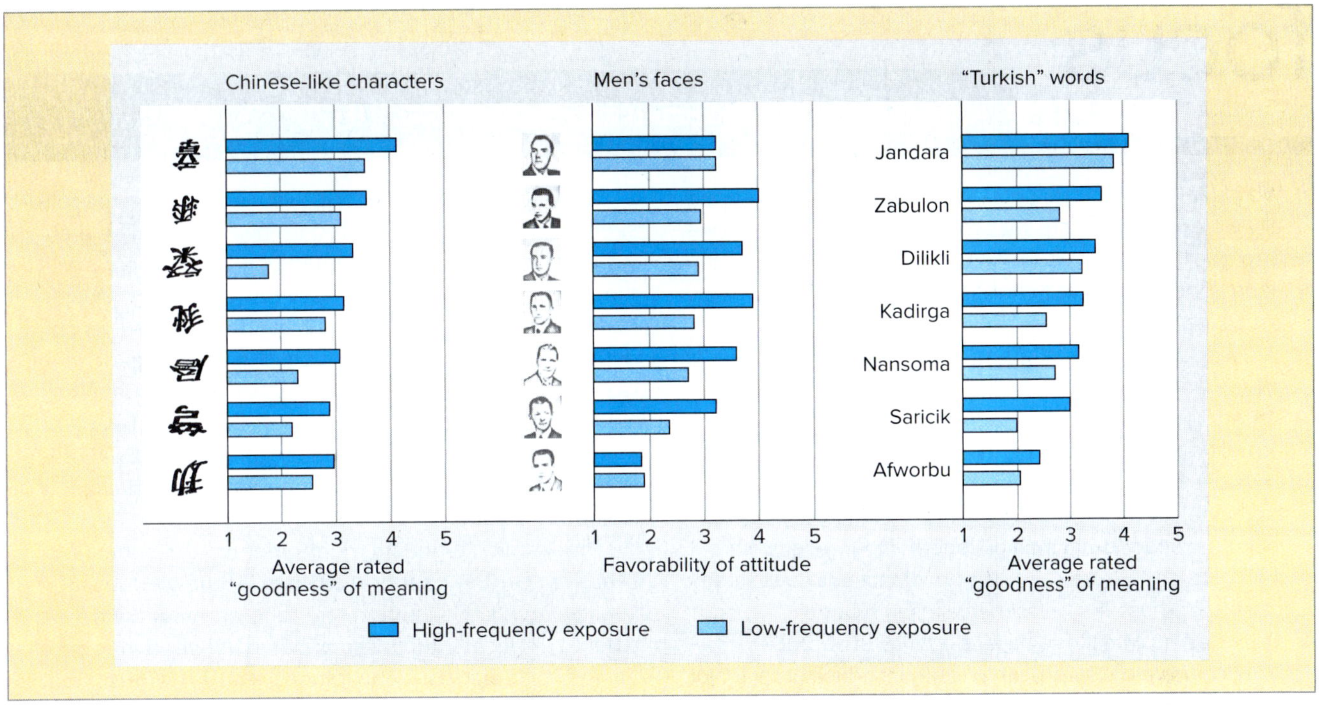

FIGURE 1

The Mere-Exposure Effect

Students rated stimuli — a sample of which is shown here — more positively after being shown them repeatedly.
Source: Zajonc (1968).

Chinese-like character, the more likely they were to say it meant something good **(Figure 1)**, probably because repeated exposure makes the words or characters stand out from others (Mrkva & Van Boven, 2020).

I've [DM] tested this idea with my own students by periodically flashing certain nonsense words on a screen. By the end of the semester, students will rate those "words" more positively than other nonsense words they have never seen before. When hurricanes do significant damage – and thus the hurricane name is mentioned frequently – babies are more likely to receive names starting with that letter, presumably due to mere exposure (Berger et al., 2012). Attitudes toward social groups can also be changed by mere exposure: When people read stories about transgender individuals accompanied by pictures, they become more comfortable and less afraid of transgender people (Flores et al., 2018).

Or consider this: What are your favorite letters of the alphabet? People of differing nationalities, languages, and ages prefer the letters appearing in their own names and those that frequently appear in their own languages (Hoorens et al., 1990; Hoorens & Nuttin, 1993; Kitayama & Karasawa, 1997; Nuttin, 1987). French students rate capital W, the least frequent letter in French, as their least favorite letter. In a stock market simulation study, U.S. business students preferred to buy stocks that shared the same first letter as their name, eBay sellers lowered prices more for customers who had names that started with the same letter as theirs (Knewtson & Sias, 2010; Sherman & Barokas, 2023). Japanese students prefer not only letters from their names but also numbers corresponding to their birth dates. Consumers prefer products whose prices remind them of their birth dates ($49.15 for a birthday on the 15th) and their names (fifty-five dollars for a name starting with F). The preference persists even when the price is higher (Coulter & Grewal, 2014). This "name letter effect" reflects more than mere exposure, however; see "Focus On: Liking Things Associated with Oneself."

When completed in 1889, the Eiffel Tower in Paris was mocked as grotesque (Harrison, 1977). Today, it is the beloved symbol of Paris. Eddie Harmon-Jones and John Allen (2001)

focus ON Liking Things Associated with Oneself

We humans love to feel good about ourselves, and generally we do. Not only are we prone to self-serving bias, we also exhibit what Brett Pelham, Matthew Mirenberg, and John Jones (2002) call *implicit egotism:* We like what we associate with ourselves.

That includes the letters of our name and the people, places, and things that we unconsciously connect with ourselves (Jones et al., 2002; Koole et al., 2001). If a stranger's or politician's face is morphed to include features of our own, we like the new face better (Bailenson et al., 2008; DeBruine, 2004). We are also more attracted to people whose arbitrary experimental code number resembles our birth date, and we are even disproportionately likely to marry someone whose first or last name resembles our own, such as by starting with the same letter (Jones et al., 2004).

Such preferences appear to subtly influence other major life decisions as well, including our locations and careers. Philadelphia, which has more people than Jacksonville, has 2.2 times as many men named Jack. But it has 10.4 times as many people named Philip. Likewise, Virginia Beach has a disproportionate number of people named Virginia.

Compared to the national average, St. Louis has 49% more men named Louis. People named Hill, Park, Beach, Lake, or Rock are disproportionately likely to live in cities with names (such as Park City) that include their names. "People are attracted to places that resemble their names," surmised Pelham, Mirenberg, and Jones (2002).

Weirder yet — we are not making this up — people seem to prefer careers related to their names. There are 2.5 times as many dentists named Denise as there are with the equally popular names Beverly or Tammy. People named George or Geoffrey are overrepresented among geoscientists (geologists, geophysicists, and geochemists). A study using an AI algorithm that scraped data from Google News, Twitter, and other sources replicated these effects, finding that the first letter of one's first name is linked to life decisions including professions and cities of residence (Chatterjee et al., 2023).

The implicit egotism phenomenon does have its skeptics. Uri Simonsohn (2011a,b) acknowledges that implicit egotism occurs in the laboratory, and he was able to replicate the associations between people's names, occupations, and places. But he argues that "reverse causality" sometimes is the explanation. For example, streets are often named after their residents, and towns are often named after their founders (William Allen founded Allentown). And founders' descendants may stick around. In reply, Pelham and Mauricio Carvallo (2011) grant that some of the effects — especially for career choice — are modest. But they contend that implicit egotism is a real, though subtle, unconscious judgmental bias.

If so, perhaps this explains why it was Suzie who sold seashells by the seashore?

explored this phenomenon experimentally. When they showed people a woman's face, their cheek (smiling) muscles typically became more active with repeated viewings. Mere exposure breeds pleasant feelings.

However, there is such a thing as too much exposure; if repetitions are incessant, liking eventually drops (Montoya et al., 2017). Music provides a vivid example: You may grow to like a popular song as you hear it more often, but there eventually comes a point – *ugh* – when you've heard it too much. "Even the best song becomes tiresome if heard too often," says a Korean proverb.

Mostly, though, familiarity increases liking. Mere exposure has an even stronger effect when people receive stimuli without awareness (Bornstein & D'Agostino, 1992; Hansen & Wänke, 2009; Kunst-Wilson & Zajonc, 1980; Willems et al., 2010). In one experiment, women heard a simple melody in one headphone and words in the other; they were asked to repeat the words out loud, focusing attention toward the words and away from the melody (Wilson, 1979). Later, when the women heard the melody interspersed among similar ones not previously played, they did not recognize it. Nevertheless, they *liked best* the melody they had previously heard. Even patients with amnesia – who can consciously recall very little of what they experience – prefer faces they saw recently (Marin-Garcia et al., 2013).

People's instant feelings of liking or disliking were more affected by exposure than by their more considered, conscious judgments (Van Dessel et al., 2019). You can probably recall immediately and intuitively liking or disliking something or someone without consciously knowing why. Zajonc (1980) argues that *emotions are often more instantaneous than thinking*. Zajonc's rather astonishing idea – that emotions are semi-independent of thinking ("affect may precede cognition") – has found support in recent brain research. Emotion and cognition are enabled by distinct brain regions. Lesion a monkey's amygdala (an emotion-related brain structure) and the monkey's emotional responses will be impaired, but its cognitive functions will be intact. Lesion its hippocampus (a memory-related structure) and its cognition will be impaired, but its emotional responses will remain intact (Zola-Morgan et al., 1991).

The mere-exposure effect has "enormous adaptive significance," noted Zajonc (1998). It is a "hardwired" phenomenon that predisposes our attractions and attachments. It helped our ancestors categorize things and people as either familiar and safe or unfamiliar and possibly dangerous. The more two strangers interact, the more attractive they tend to find each other (Reis et al., 2011). The mere-exposure effect colors our evaluations of others: We like familiar people (Swap, 1977) and perceive them as happier (Carr et al., 2017) and more trustworthy (Sofer et al., 2015). "If it's familiar, it has not eaten you yet," Zajonc used to say (Bennett, 2010). It works the other way around, too: Smiling rather than unsmiling strangers seem more familiar, so we like them more (Garcia-Marques et al., 2004).

Mere exposure's negative side is our wariness of the unfamiliar – which may explain the automatic, unconscious prejudice people often feel when confronting those who are different. Infants as young as 3 months exhibit an own-race preference: If they are being raised by others of their race, they prefer to gaze at faces of their own race – presumably because such faces are more familiar (Bar-Haim et al., 2006; Kelly et al., 2005, 2007).

We even like ourselves better the way we're accustomed to seeing ourselves. In a delightful experiment, researchers showed women pictures of themselves and their mirror images. Asked which picture they liked better, most preferred their mirror image – the image they were used to seeing in the mirror. (No wonder our photographs never look quite right.) When close friends of the women were shown the same two pictures, they preferred the true picture – the image *they* were used to seeing (Mita et al., 1977). Even once selfies became common, most people still preferred their mirror image to their selfie image – they preferred the way they saw themselves in the mirror instead of the way others see them (Al-Bitar et al., 2023). Perhaps that should not be a surprise given the shocked reactions of many to social media filters (like TikTok's "Inverted") that flip our mirror image and show us what we look like to others (Garelick, 2022).

Advertisers and politicians exploit the phenomenon of mere exposure. When people have no strong feelings about a product or a candidate, repetition alone can increase sales or votes (McCullough & Ostrom, 1974; Winter, 1973). After endless repetition of a commercial, shoppers often have an unthinking, automatic, favorable response to the product. Students who saw pop-up ads for brand-name products on web pages had a more positive attitude toward the brand, even when they didn't remember seeing the ads (Courbet et al., 2014). If candidates are relatively unknown, those with the most media exposure usually

The mere-exposure effect. If he is like most of us, Chinese President Xi Jinping may prefer his familiar mirror-image (left), which he sees every morning while brushing his teeth, to his actual image (right).
Reynaldo Chaib Paganelli/Alamy Stock Photo

win (Patterson, 1980; Schaffner et al., 1981). Political strategists who understand the mere-exposure effect have replaced reasoned argument with brief ads that hammer home a candidate's name and sound-bite message.

The respected chief of the Washington State Supreme Court, Keith Callow, learned this lesson when in 1990 he lost to a seemingly hopeless opponent, Charles Johnson. Johnson, an unknown attorney who handled minor criminal cases and divorces, filed for the seat on the principle that judges "need to be challenged." Neither man campaigned, and the media ignored the race. On election day, the two candidates' names appeared without any identification – just one name next to the other. The result: a 53% to 47% Johnson victory. "There are a lot more Johnsons out there than Callows," offered the ousted judge afterward to a stunned legal community. Indeed, the state's largest newspaper counted 27 Charles Johnsons in its local phone book. Forced to choose between two unknown names, many voters preferred the comfortable, familiar name of Charles Johnson.

Physical Attractiveness

"We should look to the mind, and not to the outward appearances."

—Aesop, *Fables*

What do (or did) you seek in a potential date? Sincerity? Character? Humor? Good looks? Sophisticated, intelligent people are unconcerned with such superficial qualities as good looks; they know "beauty is only skin deep" and "you can't judge a book by its cover." At least, they know that's how they *ought* to feel. As Cicero counseled, "Resist appearance." (As you'll notice, most research about dating has been done on heterosexual relationships, though that is slowly starting to change; McGorray et al., 2023).

The belief that looks are unimportant may be another instance of how we deny real influences upon us, for there is now an abundance of research studies showing that appearance matters. The consistency and pervasiveness of this effect are astonishing. Good looks are an asset, and people know it: In an analysis of more than 90,000 people across 93 countries, 99% spent at least 10 minutes a day enhancing their physical appearance – and the average person spent 4 hours a day when exercise was included (Kowal et al., 2022).

ATTRACTIVENESS AND DATING

Like it or not, a straight (heterosexual) young woman's physical attractiveness is a moderately good predictor of how frequently she dates, and a straight young man's attractiveness is a modestly good predictor of how frequently he dates (Berscheid et al., 1971; Reis et al., 1980, 1982; Walster et al., 1966). However, women more than men say they would prefer a mate who's homely and warm over one who's attractive and cold (Fletcher et al., 2004). In a worldwide BBC internet survey of nearly 220,000 people, men more than women ranked attractiveness as important in a mate, whereas women more than men assigned importance to honesty, humor, kindness, and dependability (Lippa, 2007). In a longitudinal study following straight married couples for 4 years, the wife's physical attractiveness predicted the husband's marital satisfaction better than the husband's physical attractiveness predicted the wife's satisfaction. In other words, attractive wives led to happier husbands, but attractive husbands had less effect on wives' happiness (Meltzer et al., 2014). Gay men and lesbian women display these sex differences as well, with gay and straight men both valuing appearance more than lesbian or straight women do (Ha et al., 2012).

In one classic study, Elaine Hatfield and co-workers (1966) matched 752 University of Minnesota first-year students for a "Welcome Week" matching dance. The researchers gave each student personality and aptitude tests but then matched the couples randomly. On the night of the dance, the couples danced and talked for 2½ hours and then evaluated their dates. How well did the personality and aptitude tests predict attraction? Did people like someone better who was high in self-esteem, or low in anxiety, or different from themselves in outgoingness? The researchers examined a long list of possibilities. But as far as they could determine, only one thing mattered: how physically attractive the person was (as previously rated by the researchers). The more attractive a woman was, the more the man liked her and wanted to date her again. And the more attractive the man was, the more the woman liked him and wanted to date him again. Pretty pleases.

"Personal beauty is a greater recommendation than any letter of introduction."

—Aristotle, *Diogenes Laertius*

More recent studies have gathered data from speed-dating evenings, during which people interact with a succession of potential dates for only a few minutes each and later indicate which ones they would like to see again (mutual "yeses" are given contact information). In these studies, which focused on straight people, men were more likely than women to predict they would care about a potential date's physical attractiveness, but when it came time to decide whom to date, a prospect's attractiveness was similarly important to both men and women (Eastwick & Finkel, 2008a,b).

The overall importance of physical attractiveness in dating is fairly large – especially when dates stem from first impressions (Eastwick et al., 2014). However, straight men and women may misperceive what the other sex wants in terms of physical attributes. Women tend to overestimate how much men prefer thinness, and men tend to overestimate how much women prefer muscularity (Lei & Perrett, 2021).

Once people have gotten to know each other over months or years through jobs or friendships, they focus more on each person's unique qualities rather than their physical attractiveness and status. In several studies examining liking over time among friends, the more time that went by, the more the friends diverged over who was most attractive as a mate. Among 167 couples, those who knew each other for longer and were friends before dating were less similar in physical attractiveness than those who had known each other a shorter time and were not friends before they dated (Hunt et al., 2015). In a 2012 survey, 43% of women and 33% of men said they had fallen in love with someone they were not initially attracted to (Fisher & Garcia, 2013). In other words, there's someone for everyone – once you get to know them (Eastwick & Hunt, 2014). Pretty pleases, but perhaps only for a paltry period.

Looks even influence voting, or so it seems from a study by Alexander Todorov and colleagues (2005; Todorov, 2011). They showed Princeton University students photographs of the two major candidates in 95 U.S. Senate races since 2000 and in 600 U.S. House of Representatives races. Based on looks alone, the students correctly guessed the winners of 72% of the Senate and 67% of the House races. But gender also mattered: Men were more likely to vote for physically attractive female candidates, and women were more likely to vote for approachable-looking male candidates (Chiao et al., 2008).

matching phenomenon
The tendency for men and women to choose as partners those who are a "good match" in attractiveness and other traits.

THE MATCHING PHENOMENON

Not everyone can end up paired with someone stunningly attractive. So how do people pair off? Judging from research by Bernard Murstein (1986) and others, they get real and pair off with people who are about as attractive as they are. Studies have found a strong correspondence between the rated attractiveness of husbands and wives, of dating partners, and even of those within particular fraternities (Feingold, 1988; Montoya, 2008). People tend to select as friends, and especially to marry, those who are a "good match" not only to their level of intelligence, popularity, and self-worth but also to their level of attractiveness (McClintock, 2014; Taylor et al., 2011).

Physical appearance matters less among couples who were friends before they started dating.
Monkey Business Images/Shutterstock

Experiments confirm this **matching phenomenon**. When choosing whom to approach, knowing the other is free to say yes or no, people often approach and invest more in pursuing someone whose attractiveness roughly matches their own (Berscheid et al., 1971; van Straaten et al., 2009). They seek out someone who seems desirable, but they are mindful of the limits of their own desirability. Good physical matches may be conducive to good relationships, reported Gregory White (1980) from a study of UCLA dating couples. Those who were most similar in physical attractiveness were most likely, 9 months later, to have fallen more deeply in love. When couples are instead dissimilar in attractiveness, they are more likely to consider leaving the relationship for someone else (Davies & Shackelford, 2017).

The relationship between music icon Taylor Swift and NFL star Travis Kelce was plastered all over social media. Was part of their initial attraction due to them being similarly attractive? What do you think?
Michael Owens/Getty Images

Perhaps this research prompts you to think of happy couples who differ in perceived "hotness." In such cases, the less-attractive person often has compensating qualities. Each partner brings assets to the social marketplace, and the value of the respective assets creates an equitable match. Personal advertisements and self-presentations to online dating services exhibit this exchange of assets (Cicerello & Sheehan, 1995; Hitsch et al., 2006; Koestner & Wheeler, 1988; Rajecki et al., 1991). Straight men typically offer wealth or status and seek youth and attractiveness; straight women more often do the reverse: "Attractive, bright woman, 26, slender, seeks warm, professional male." Men who advertise their income and education, and women who advertise their youth and looks, receive more responses to their ads (Baize & Schroeder, 1995). The asset-matching process helps explain why beautiful young women often marry older men of higher social status (Elder, 1969; Kanazawa & Kovar, 2004). The richer the man, the younger and more beautiful the woman.

"If you would marry wisely, marry your equal."

—Ovid (BC 43–AD 17)

"If I weren't beautiful, do you think he'd be with *me*?"

—Melania Trump, when asked "If [Donald Trump] weren't rich, would you be with him?" 2005

THE PHYSICAL-ATTRACTIVENESS STEREOTYPE

In one study, researchers used a makeup artist to give an otherwise attractive accomplice a scarred, bruised, or birthmarked face. Glasgow train commuters of both sexes avoided sitting next to an apparently facially disfigured person (Houston & Bull, 1994). In another experiment, two groups of observers were asked to guess people's traits based on their photographs. Those seeing photos of facially disfigured people judged them as less intelligent, emotionally stable, and trustworthy than did observers seeing photos of those same people after plastic surgery (Jamrozik et al., 2018). Moreover, much as adults are biased toward attractive adults, young children are biased toward attractive children (Dion & Berscheid, 1974; Langlois et al., 2000). Judging by how long they gaze at someone, even 3-month-old infants prefer attractive faces (Langlois et al., 1987). Humans seem to believe that beauty is not only skin deep.

Adults show a similar bias when judging children. Missouri fifth-grade teachers were given identical information about a boy or a girl but with the photograph of an attractive or an unattractive child attached. The teachers perceived the attractive child as more intelligent and successful in school (Clifford & Walster, 1973). Perhaps as a result of these expectations, beautiful children scored higher on tests of academic performance all the way to adolescence, even with other factors controlled (Hamermesh et al., 2023).

Or imagine being a playground supervisor having to discipline an unruly child. Might you, like the women studied by Karen Dion (1972), show less warmth and tact to an unattractive child? The sad truth is that most of us assume that homely children are less able and socially competent than their beautiful peers (see "The Inside Story: Ellen Berscheid on Attractiveness").

What is more, we assume that beautiful people possess certain desirable traits. Other things being equal, we guess beautiful people are happier, sexually warmer, and more outgoing, intelligent, and successful – although not more honest (Eagly et al., 1991; Feingold, 1992; Jackson et al., 1995). In one study, students judged attractive women as more agreeable, open, outgoing, ambitious, and emotionally stable (Segal-Caspi et al., 2012). We are more eager to bond with attractive people, which motivates our projecting desirable attributes such as kindness and reciprocal interest into them (Lemay et al., 2010). When attractive CEOs of companies appear on television, the stock price of their

THE inside STORY

Ellen Berscheid on Attractiveness

I vividly remember the afternoon I began to appreciate the far-reaching implications of physical attractiveness. Graduate student Karen Dion (now a professor at the University of Toronto) learned that some researchers at our Institute of Child Development had collected popularity ratings from nursery school children and taken a photo of each child. Although teachers and caregivers of children had persuaded us that "all children are beautiful" and no physical-attractiveness discriminations could be made, Dion suggested we instruct some people to rate each child's looks and that we correlate these with popularity. After doing so, we realized our long shot had hit home: Attractive children were popular children. Indeed, the effect was far more potent than we and others had assumed, with a host of implications that investigators are still tracing.

Ellen Berscheid
University of Minnesota
Ellen Berscheid

companies rise—but being quoted in a news article, without a photo, has no effect (Halford & Hsu, 2014).

Added together, the findings define a **physical-attractiveness stereotype**: What is beautiful is good. Children learn the stereotype quite early—often through stories told to them by adults. "Disney movies promote the stereotype that what is beautiful is good," reported Doris Bazzini and colleagues (2010) from an analysis of human characters in 21 animated films. Snow White and Cinderella are beautiful—and kind. The witch and the stepsisters are ugly—and wicked. "If you want to be loved by somebody who isn't already in your family, it doesn't hurt to be beautiful," surmised one 8-year-old girl (Dion, 1979). Across six studies, people associated beauty with purity and morality—although other studies find that effect is reduced when beautiful people are perceived to be vain (Han & Laurent, 2023; Klebl et al., 2022).

physical-attractiveness stereotype
The presumption that physically attractive people possess other socially desirable traits as well: What is beautiful is good.

If physical attractiveness is that important, then permanently changing people's attractiveness should change the way others react to them. But is it ethical to alter someone's looks? Such manipulations are performed millions of times a year by cosmetic surgeons and orthodontists. With teeth straightened and whitened, hair replaced and dyed, face lifted, fat liposuctioned, and breasts enlarged, lifted, or reduced, most self-dissatisfied people do express satisfaction with the results of their procedures, though some unhappy patients seek out repeat procedures (Honigman et al., 2004).

To examine the effect of such alterations on others, Michael Kalick (1977) had Harvard students rate their impressions of eight women based on profile photographs taken before or after cosmetic surgery. Not only did they judge the women as more physically attractive after the surgery, but they also saw them as kinder, more sensitive, more sexually warm and responsive, more likable, and so on.

"Even virtue is fairer in a fair body."
—Virgil, *Aeneid*, BC 1st century

FIRST IMPRESSIONS To say that attractiveness is important, other things being equal, is not to say that physical appearance always outranks other qualities. Some people more than others judge people by their looks (Livingston, 2001). Moreover, attractiveness most affects first impressions. But first impressions are important—and have become more so as societies become increasingly mobile and urbanized and as contacts with people become more fleeting (Berscheid, 1981). Your social media profile starts with your face. In speed-dating experiments, the attractiveness effect is strongest when people's choices are superficially made—when meeting lots of people quickly (Lenton & Francesconi, 2010). That helps explain why attractiveness better predicts happiness and social connections for those in urban rather than rural settings (Plaut et al., 2009).

Though interviewers may deny it, attractiveness and personal grooming affect first impressions in job interviews—especially when the evaluator is of the other sex (Agthe et al., 2011; Cash & Janda, 1984; Mack & Rainey, 1990; Marvelle & Green, 1980). People rate new products more favorably when they are associated with attractive inventors (Baron et al., 2006). Such impressions help explain why attractive people and tall people have more prestigious jobs and make more money (Engemann & Owyang, 2003; Persico et al., 2004).

Patricia Roszell and colleagues (1990) looked at the incomes of Canadians whom interviewers had rated on a 1 (homely) to 5 (strikingly attractive) scale. They found that for each additional scale unit of rated attractiveness, people earned, on average, an additional $1,988 annually. Irene Hanson Frieze and associates (1991) did the same analysis with 737 MBA graduates after rating them on a similar 1-to-5 scale, using student yearbook photos. For each additional scale unit of rated attractiveness, men earned an added $2,600 and women earned an added $2,150. In *Beauty Pays,* economist Daniel Hamermesh (2011) argued that, for a man, good looks have the earnings effect of another year and a half of schooling.

The speed with which first impressions form and their influence on thinking help explain why pretty prospers. Even a .013-second exposure—too brief to discern a face—is enough to enable people to guess a face's attractiveness (Olson & Marshuetz, 2005). Moreover, when categorizing subsequent words as either good or bad, an attractive flashed face predisposes people to categorize good words faster. Pretty is perceived promptly and primes positive processing.

IS THE "BEAUTIFUL IS GOOD" STEREOTYPE ACCURATE? Do beautiful people indeed have desirable traits? For centuries, those who considered themselves serious scientists thought so when they sought to identify physical traits (shifty eyes, a weak chin) that would predict criminal behavior. On the other hand, was Leo Tolstoy correct when he wrote that it's "a strange illusion . . . to suppose that beauty is goodness"? Despite others' perceptions, physically attractive people do not differ from others in basic personality traits such as agreeableness, openness, extraversion, ambition, or emotional stability (Segal-Caspi et al., 2012). However, there is some truth to the stereotype. Attractive children and young adults are somewhat more relaxed, outgoing, and socially polished (Feingold, 1992b; Langlois et al., 2000).

In one study, 60 University of Georgia straight men called and talked for 5 minutes with each of three straight women students. Afterward, the men and women rated their telephone partners on social skill and likability. Those who were attractive (even though unseen) were rated higher (Goldman & Lewis, 1977). The same is true online: Even when they hadn't seen the men's photos, women rated the text of attractive men's dating website profiles as more desirable and confident. What is beautiful is good, even online (Brand et al., 2012). Physically attractive individuals tend also to be more popular, more outgoing, and more gender typed—more traditionally masculine if male, more feminine if female (Langlois et al., 1996).

These small average differences between attractive and unattractive people probably result from self-fulfilling prophecies. Attractive people are valued and favored, so many develop more social self-confidence. (Recall from an earlier chapter an experiment in which men evoked a warm response from unseen women they *thought* were attractive.) By that analysis, what's crucial to your social skill is not how you look but how people treat you and how you feel about yourself—whether you accept yourself, like yourself, and feel comfortable with yourself.

WHO IS ATTRACTIVE?

We have described attractiveness as if it were an objective quality like height, which some people have more of, some less. Strictly speaking, attractiveness is whatever the people of any given place and time find attractive. This, of course, varies. People in different places and times have pierced noses, lengthened necks, dyed hair, whitened teeth, painted skin, gorged themselves to become voluptuous, starved to become thin, taken steroids to enhance muscles, gotten hair implants, and bound themselves with leather corsets to make their breasts seem small—or used silicone and padded bras to make them seem big. For cultures

Standards of beauty differ from culture to culture. Yet some people are considered attractive throughout most of the world.
(left to right): Thinkstock Images/Getty Images; Free Agents Limited/Getty Images; Courtesy of Catherine Karnow; Ground Picture/Shutterstock

with scarce resources and for impoverished or hungry people, plumpness seems attractive; for cultures and individuals with abundant resources, beauty more often equals slimness (Nelson & Morrison, 2005). Moreover, attractiveness influences life outcomes less in cultures where relationships are based more on kinship or social arrangement than on personal choice (Anderson et al., 2008). Despite such variations, there remains "strong agreement both within and across cultures about who is and who is not attractive," noted Judith Langlois and colleagues (2000).

To be really attractive is, ironically, to be *perfectly average* (Rhodes, 2006). Researchers have digitized multiple faces and averaged them using a computer. Inevitably, people find the composite faces more appealing than almost all the actual faces (Langlois & Roggman, 1990; Langlois et al., 1994; Perrett, 2010; **Figure 2**). Across 27 nations, an average leg-length-to-body ratio looks more attractive than very short or long legs (Sorokowski et al., 2011). With both humans and animals, averaged looks best embody a typical person and are thus easy for the brain to process and categorize, noted Jamin Halberstadt (2006). Let's face it: Perfectly average is easy on the eyes (and brain).

Computer-averaged faces and bodies also tend to be perfectly *symmetrical*—another characteristic of strikingly attractive (and reproductively successful) people (Brown et al., 2008; Gangestad & Thornhill, 1997). If you could merge either half of your face with its mirror image—thus forming a perfectly symmetrical new face—you would boost your looks (Penton-Voak et al., 2001; Rhodes, 2006; Rhodes et al., 1999). With a few facial features excepted, averaging a number of such attractive, symmetrical faces produces an even better-looking face (Said & Todorov, 2011).

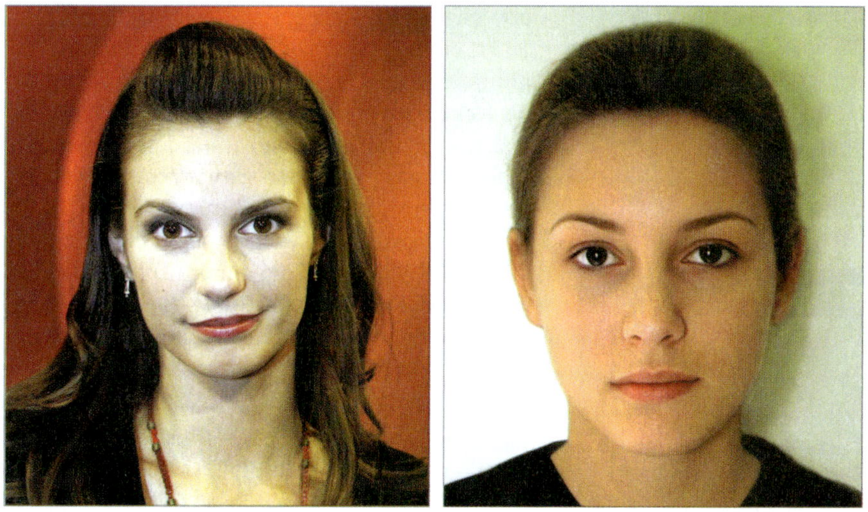

FIGURE 2

Who's the Fairest of Them All?

Each year's selection of "Miss Germany" provides one country's answer. A University of Regensburg student research team, working with a German television channel, offered an alternative. Christoph Braun and his compatriots (Gruendl, 2005) photographed the 22 2002 "Queen of Beauty" finalists, without makeup and with hair tied back, and then created a "Virtual Miss Germany" that was the blended composite of them all. When adults in a local shopping mall were shown the finalists and the Virtual Miss Germany, they easily rated Virtual Miss Germany as the most attractive of them all. Although the winning real Miss Germany (left) may have been disappointed by the news that everyone preferred her virtual competitor to herself, she could reassure herself that she would never meet her virtual competitor.
(left): Oliver Bodmer/Action Press/ZUMA PRESS; (right): Dr. Martin Gruendl

EVOLUTION AND ATTRACTION Psychologists working from the evolutionary perspective explain the human preference for attractive partners in terms of reproductive strategy. They assume that beauty signals biologically important information: health, youth, and fertility. And so it does. Men with attractive faces have higher-quality sperm. Women with hourglass figures have more regular menstrual cycles and are more fertile (Gallup et al., 2008). Over time, men who preferred fertile-looking women fathered more children than those who were as happy to mate with postmenopausal females. That biological outcome of human history, David Buss (1989) believes, explains why straight males in 37 cultures – from Australia to Zambia – did indeed prefer youthful female characteristics that signify reproductive capacity.

"Love is only a dirty trick played on us to achieve a continuation of the species."

—Novelist W. Somerset Maugham (1874–1965)

Evolutionary psychologists also assume that evolution predisposes women to favor male traits that signify an ability to provide and protect resources. In screening potential mates, reported Norman Li and fellow researchers (2002), men require a modicum of physical attractiveness, women require status and resources, and both welcome kindness and intelligence. In a study of 1.8 million online daters from 24 countries, both men and women with higher education and income received more attention, but the effect was 2.5 times larger for men than women (Jonason & Thomas, 2022).

"Power is the great aphrodisiac."

—Henry Kissinger, quoted in *The New York Times*, January 19, 1971

Women's emphasis on men's physical attractiveness may also depend on their goals: Those focused on short-term relationships prefer more symmetrical and thus attractive men, whereas those focused on the long term find this less important, perhaps because physical attractiveness may come with more negative qualities such as infidelity (Quist et al., 2012). Gay, lesbian, and bisexual men and women express preferences similar to their straight peers, with men favoring appearance and women favoring resources (Kostic & Scofield, 2022).

Evolutionary psychologists have also explored men's and women's response to other cues to reproductive success. Straight men everywhere in the world are most attracted to women whose waists are 30% narrower than their hips – a shape associated with peak sexual fertility (Karremans et al., 2010; Perilloux et al., 2010; Platek & Singh, 2010; Zotto & Pegna, 2017). Circumstances that reduce a woman's fertility – malnutrition, pregnancy, menopause – also change her shape.

When judging males as potential marriage partners, women, too, prefer a male waist-to-hip ratio suggesting health and vigor. They rate muscular men as sexier, and muscular men do feel sexier and report more lifetime sex partners (Frederick & Haselton, 2007). This makes evolutionary sense, noted Jared Diamond (1996): A muscular hunk was more likely than a scrawny fellow to gather food, build houses, and defeat rivals. But today's women prefer men with high incomes even more (Muggleton & Fincher, 2017; Singh, 1995).

During ovulation, women show increased accuracy in judging whether men are gay or straight (Rule et al., 2011) and display increased wariness of men outside their own social groups (McDonald et al., 2011). One study found that, when ovulating, young women tend to wear and prefer more revealing outfits than when they are not fertile (Durante et al., 2008). In another study, ovulating lap dancers averaged $70 in tips per hour – double the $35 of those who were menstruating (Miller et al., 2007).

We are, evolutionary psychologists suggest, driven by primal attractions. Like eating and breathing, attraction and mating are based on our biology.

Evolutionary psychology theorizes that strong men would have been more likely to survive and reproduce over the course of human history, explaining women's preference for muscular men.
StockLite/Shutterstock

SOCIAL COMPARISON Although our mating psychology has biological wisdom, attraction is not all hardwired. What's attractive to you also depends on what standard you are using for comparison.

To straight men who have recently looked at pornographic images, average women or even their own wives tend to seem less attractive – particularly their bodies (Kenrick et al., 1989; Sculley & Watkins, 2022). Viewing porn simulating passionate sex similarly decreases satisfaction with one's own partner (Zillmann, 1989). Being sexually aroused may *temporarily* make a person of the other sex seem more attractive. But the lingering effect of exposure to perfect "10s," or of unrealistic sexual depictions, is to make one's own partner seem less appealing – more like a "6" than an "8."

It works the same way with our self-perceptions. After viewing a very attractive person of the same gender, people rate themselves as being less attractive than after viewing a homely person (Brown et al., 1992; Thornton & Maurice, 1997). With social media feeds often filled with supremely attractive people, upward social comparisons and body image issues can be the result (McComb et al., 2023; Pan et al., 2022; Zimmer-Gembeck et al., 2021). Moreover, we often see slim, wrinkle-free, photoshopped people who don't exist. Such extraordinary comparison standards trick us into devaluing our potential mates and ourselves and spending billions on cosmetics, diet aids, and plastic surgery. But even after millions of cosmetic procedures, there may be no net gain in human satisfaction. If others get their teeth straightened, capped, and whitened, and you don't, the social comparison may leave you more dissatisfied with your normal, natural teeth than you would have been if you were surrounded by peers whose teeth were also natural.

Henry James's description of novelist George Eliot (the pen name of Mary Ann Evans): "She is magnificently ugly — deliciously hideous. She has a low forehead, a dull grey eye, a vast pendulous nose, a huge mouth, full of uneven teeth. . . . Now in this vast ugliness resides a most powerful beauty which, in a very few minutes, steals forth and charms the mind, so that you end as I ended, in falling in love with her."

THE ATTRACTIVENESS OF THOSE WE LOVE Let's conclude our discussion of attractiveness on an upbeat note. First, a 17-year-old girl's facial attractiveness is a surprisingly weak predictor of her attractiveness at ages 30 and 50. Sometimes an average-looking adolescent, especially one with a warm, attractive personality, becomes a quite attractive adult (Zebrowitz et al., 1993, 1998).

Second, not only do we perceive attractive people as likable, but we also perceive likable people as attractive. Perhaps you can recall individuals who, as you grew to like them, became more attractive. Their physical imperfections were no longer so noticeable. Alan Gross and Christine Crofton (1977; see also Lewandowski et al., 2007) had students view someone's photograph after reading a favorable or an unfavorable description of the person's personality. Those portrayed as warm, helpful, and considerate also *looked* more attractive to the students. It may be true, then, that "handsome is as handsome does" and that "what is good is beautiful." Discovering someone's similarities to us also makes the person seem more attractive (Beaman & Klentz, 1983; Klentz et al., 1987).

Moreover, love sees loveliness: The more in love a woman is with a man, the more physically attractive she finds him (Price et al., 1974). And the more in love a heterosexual couple is, the less attractive they find those of the other sex (Johnson & Rusbult, 1989; Simpson et al., 1990). "The grass may be greener on the other side," noted Rowland Miller and Jeffry Simpson (1990), "but happy gardeners are less likely to notice." Beauty really *is,* to some extent, in the eye of the beholder.

Similarity versus Complementarity

From our discussion so far, one might surmise Leo Tolstoy was entirely correct: "Love depends . . . on frequent meetings, and on the style in which the hair is done up, and on the color and cut of the dress." Given time, however, other factors influence whether acquaintance develops into friendship.

DO BIRDS OF A FEATHER FLOCK TOGETHER?

Of this much we may be sure: Birds that flock together are of a feather. Friends, engaged couples, and spouses are far more likely than randomly paired people to share common attitudes, beliefs, values, and personality traits (Youyou et al., 2017). Furthermore, the greater the similarity between husband and wife, the happier they are and the less likely they are to divorce (Byrne, 1971; Caspi & Herbener, 1990). Dating couples with more similar political and religious attitudes were more likely to still be together after 11 months (Bleske-Rechek et al., 2009). Such correlational findings are intriguing. But cause and effect remain an enigma. Does similarity lead to liking? Or does liking lead to similarity?

LIKENESS BEGETS LIKING At a campus party, Lakesha has a long discussion of politics, religion, and personal likes and dislikes with Les and Dan. She and Les discover they agree on almost everything, she and Dan on few things. Afterward, she reflects: "Les is really intelligent . . . and so likable. I hope we meet again." In a series of experiments, Donn Byrne (1971) and his colleagues captured the essence of Lakesha's experience. Over and over again, they found that the more similar someone's attitudes are to your own, the more you will like the person.

"Can two walk together except they be agreed?"

—Amos 3:3

Studies have replicated these effects, finding that people like others with similar attitudes (Alves, 2018; Montoya & Horton, 2013; Reid et al., 2013). Facebook friends, fraternity members, and even players on the same community baseball team tend to share facial similarities (Hehman et al., 2018). In both China and the Western world, romantic partners with similar attitudes, traits, and values are more satisfied with their relationships (Chen et al., 2009; Gaunt, 2006; Gonzaga et al., 2007).

The likeness-leads-to-liking effect has been tested across several real-life situations:

- *Roommates and speed daters.* At two of Hong Kong's universities, Royce Lee and Michael Bond (1996) found that roommate friendships flourished when roommates shared values and personality traits but even more so when they *perceived* their roommates as similar. Perceived similarity also mattered more than actual similarity during speed-dating (Tidwell et al., 2013). Reality matters, but perception matters more.
- *Strangers.* In various settings, people entering a room of strangers sit closer to those similar to themselves (Mackinnon et al., 2011). People with glasses sit closer to others with glasses. Long-haired people sit closer to people with long hair. Dark-haired people sit closer to people with dark hair (even after controlling for race and sex). Non-physical attributes also matter: When viewing personal descriptions in online dating profiles, people choose those with similar personality profiles (De La Mare & Lee, 2023).
- *Babies.* Eleven-month-old infants were more likely to choose a stuffed animal that pretended to eat the same food or wore the same color mittens as they did. This suggests that the preference for similar others develops very early, even before babies can talk (Mahajan & Wynn, 2012).
- *Mimicry as behavioral similarity.* People like not only those who think as they do but also those who act as they do. Subtle mimicry fosters fondness. Have you noticed that when someone nods their head as you do or echoes your thoughts, you feel a certain rapport and liking? Liking may then translate into tipping: Dutch restaurant servers who mimicked their customers by merely repeating their order received higher tips (van Baaren et al., 2003). Natural mimicry increases rapport, noted Jessica Lakin and Tanya Chartrand (2003), and desire for rapport increases mimicry.

So, similarity breeds content. Birds of a feather *do* flock together. Surely you have noticed this upon discovering a person who shares your ideas, values, and desires, a special someone who likes the same foods, the same activities, the same music you do.

"And they are friends who have come to regard the same things as good and the same things as evil, they who are friends of the same people, and they who are the enemies of the same people. . . . We like those who resemble us, and are engaged in the same pursuits."

—Aristotle, *Rhetoric*, BC 4th century

The principle that similarity attracts is a key selling point for online dating sites such as chemistry.com and eHarmony.com that match users with similar others via secret formulas based on personality and attitude questionnaires. With that in mind, Samantha Joel and her co-authors (2017) gave college students an exhaustive battery of 100 personality and attitude questionnaires and fed the results into a sophisticated computer program. However, the program couldn't predict who would like each other after they actually met during a series of 4-minute speed dates. So why do so many people not only use online dating sites but find long-term partners on them? Probably because the sites expand your pool of potential dates (Finkel et al., 2012). What happens afterward is much more unpredictable.

DISSIMILARITY BREEDS DISLIKE We have a bias – the false consensus bias – toward assuming that others share our attitudes. We also tend to see those we like as being similar to us (Castelli et al., 2009). Getting to know someone – and discovering that the person is actually dissimilar – tends to decrease liking (Norton et al., 2007). If those dissimilar attitudes pertain to our strong moral convictions, we dislike and distance ourselves from them all the more (Skitka et al., 2005). People in one political party often are not so much fond of fellow party members as they are disdainful of those in the other party (Hoyle, 1993; Mallinas et al., 2018).

In general, dissimilar attitudes depress liking more than similar attitudes enhance it (Singh & Ho, 2000). Within their own groups, where they expect similarity, people find it especially difficult to like someone with dissimilar views (Chen & Kenrick, 2002).

Whether people perceive those of another race as similar or dissimilar influences their racial attitudes. Whenever one group regards another as "other" – as those that speak differently, live differently, think differently – the potential for conflict is high. In fact, the perception of like minds is often more important for attraction than like skins. In one study, liberals expressed dislike of conservatives and conservatives of liberals, but race did not affect liking (Chambers et al., 2012). While 47% of single adults in the United States said they would not consider being in a relationship with someone who voted for Donald Trump, only 15% said they would not consider being in a relationship with someone who was a different race or ethnicity (Brown, 2020).

Despite the popular theory that opposites (for example, a casual dresser and a snappy dresser) complement each other (complementarity), *similar* people — like these two who apparently share a taste for monochromatic plaid — are more likely to be romantically attracted to one another.
Westend61/Getty Images

DO OPPOSITES ATTRACT?

Still we resist: Are we not attracted to people whose needs and personalities complement our own? Would a sadist and a masochist find true love? The common message is that "opposites attract. . . . Socializers pair with loners, novelty-lovers with those who dislike change, free spenders with scrimpers, risk-takers with the very cautious" (Jacoby, 1986). The logic seems compelling, and most of us can think of couples who view their differences as complementary: "My husband and I are perfect for each other. I'm a decisive person. He's not. But he's always happy to go along with arrangements I make."

Given the idea's persuasiveness, the inability of researchers to confirm it is astonishing. For example, perhaps opposites attract when people are feeling depressed; they might then prefer expressive, outgoing people who could cheer them up. However, depressed people are actually less likely to prefer the company of happy people (Locke & Horowitz, 1990; Rosenblatt & Greenberg, 1988, 1991; Wenzlaff & Prohaska, 1989). When you're feeling blue, another's bubbly personality can be aggravating. Sad people may be more conscious of their misery in the company of cheerful people.

Some **complementarity** may evolve as a relationship progresses. Yet, as we've seen, friends and couples are more likely to be similar than different in their needs, attitudes, and personalities. Perhaps one day we will discover some ways in which differences lead to liking. Dominance/submissiveness may be one such set of complementary traits (Dryer & Horowitz, 1997; Markey & Kurtz, 2006). But as a general rule, opposites do not attract.

complementarity
The popularly supposed tendency, in a relationship between two people, for each to complete what is missing in the other.

Liking Those Who Like Us

Liking is usually mutual. Proximity and attractiveness influence our initial attraction to someone, and similarity influences longer-term attraction as well. If we have a deep need to belong and to feel liked and accepted, would we not also take a liking to those who like us? Are the best friendships mutual admiration societies? Indeed, one person's liking for another does predict the other's liking in return (Kenny & Nasby, 1980; Montoya & Insko, 2008). One common way to show interest in someone – asking them questions – is especially effective in increasing liking (Huang et al., 2017). When one person likes another, they tend to look at them more, sit closer, talk more, and smile and laugh more (Montoya et al., 2018).

But does one person's liking another *cause* the other to return the appreciation? People's reports of how they fell in love suggest so (Aron et al., 1989). Discovering that an appealing someone really likes you seems to awaken romantic feelings. Experiments confirm it: Those told that certain others like or admire them usually feel a reciprocal affection (Berscheid & Walster, 1978). And all the better, one speed-dating experiment suggests, when someone likes *you* especially (Eastwick et al., 2007). A dash of uncertainty can also fuel desire. Thinking that someone probably likes you – but you aren't sure – tends to increase your thinking about and feeling attracted to another (Whitechurch et al., 2011).

"The average man is more interested in a woman who is interested in him than he is in a woman with beautiful legs."

—Actress Marlene Dietrich, *The Quotable Woman, 1800–1975*

"I like the pope unless the pope doesn't like me. Then I don't like the pope."

—Donald Trump, February 18, 2016

"If 60,000 people tell me they loved a show, then one walks past and says it sucked, that's the comment I'll hear."

—Musician Dave Matthews, quoted by P. Tolme in *Rock Star Longs for Simple Life*, 2000

And consider this finding: Students like another student who says eight positive things about them better than one who says seven positive things and one negative thing (Berscheid et al., 1969). We are sensitive to the slightest hint of criticism. Writer Larry L. King (1986) speaks for many in noting, "I have discovered over the years that good reviews strangely fail to make the author feel as good as bad reviews make him feel bad."

Whether we are judging ourselves or others, negative information carries more weight because, being less usual, it grabs more attention (Yzerbyt & Leyens, 1991). People's votes are more influenced by their impressions of presidential candidates' weaknesses than by their impressions of strengths, a phenomenon quickly grasped by those who design negative campaign ads (Klein, 1991). It's a general rule of life: Bad is stronger than good (Baumeister et al., 2001). (See "Focus On: Bad Is Stronger Than Good.")

Our liking for those we perceive as liking us was recognized long ago. Observers from the ancient philosopher Hecato ("If you wish to be loved, love") to Ralph Waldo Emerson ("The only way to have a friend is to be one") to Dale Carnegie ("Dole out praise lavishly") anticipated the findings. What they did not anticipate was the precise conditions under which the principle works.

focus ON Bad Is Stronger Than Good

Dissimilar attitudes, we have noted, turn us off to others more than similar attitudes turn us on. And others' criticism captures our attention and affects our emotions more than does their praise. Roy Baumeister, Ellen Bratslavsky, Catrin Finkenauer, and Kathleen Vohs (2001) said this is just the tip of an iceberg: "In everyday life, bad events have stronger and more lasting consequences than comparable good events." Consider the following:

- Destructive acts harm close relationships more than constructive acts build them. (Cruel words linger after kind ones have been forgotten.)
- Bad moods affect our thinking and memory more than do good moods. (Despite our natural optimism, it's easier to recall past bad emotional events than good ones.)
- There are more words for negative than positive emotions, and people asked to think of emotion words mostly come up with negative words. (*Sadness*, *anger*, and *fear* are the three most common.)
- Bad events tend to evoke more misery than good events evoke joy. (In one analysis by Randy Larsen [2009], negative emotional experiences exceeded the intensity of positive emotional experiences by a factor that, coincidentally, equaled pi: 3.14.)
- Single bad events (traumas) have more lasting effects than single very good events. (A death triggers more search for meaning than does a birth.)
- Routine bad events receive more attention and trigger more rumination than do routine good events.
- The negative feelings from being turned down by one's sexual partner last for two days, while the positive feelings from being accepted last just one day (Dobson et al., 2020).
- Losing money upsets people more than gaining the same amount of money makes them happy. Income losses have a bigger influence on life satisfaction and happiness than do income gains (Boyce et al., 2013).
- Very bad family environments override the genetic influence on intelligence more than do very good family environments. (Bad parents can make their genetically bright children less intelligent; good parents are less able to make their unintelligent children smarter.)
- A bad reputation is easier to acquire and harder to shed than a good one. (A single act of lying can destroy one's reputation for integrity.)
- Poor health decreases happiness more than good health increases it. (Pain produces misery far more than comfort produces joy.)

The power of the bad prepares us to deal with threats and protects us from death and disability. For survival, bad can be more bad than good is good. The importance of the bad is one likely reason why the first century of psychology focused so much more on the bad than on the good. From its start through 2023, PsycInfo (a guide to psychology's literature) had 30,300 articles mentioning anger, 276,463 mentioning anxiety, and 349,941 mentioning depression. There were about 10 articles on these topics for every 1 dealing with the positive emotions of joy (7,992), life satisfaction (17,733), or happiness (18,128). Similarly, "fear" (78,544 articles) has triumphed over "courage" (2,848). The strength of the bad is "perhaps the best reason for a positive psychology movement," Baumeister and colleagues surmised. To overcome the strength of individual bad events, "human life needs far more good than bad."

ATTRIBUTION

As we've seen, flattery *will* get you somewhere. But not everywhere. If praise clearly violates what we know is true – if someone says, "Your hair looks great," when we haven't washed it in 3 days – we may lose respect for the flatterer and wonder whether the compliment springs from ulterior motives (Shrauger, 1975). Thus, we often perceive criticism to be more sincere than praise (Coleman et al., 1987). In fact, when someone prefaces a statement with "To be honest," we know we are about to hear a criticism.

"Well-and I'm not just saying this because you're my husband-it stinks."

Robert Mankoff

Laboratory experiments reveal something we've noted in previous chapters: Our reactions depend on our attributions. Do we attribute the flattery to **ingratiation** – to a self-serving strategy? Is the person trying to get us to buy something, to have sex, to do a favor? If so, both the flatterer and the praise lose appeal (Gordon, 1996; Jones, 1964). But if there is no apparent ulterior motive, then we warmly receive both flattery and flatterer.

ingratiation
The use of strategies, such as flattery, by which people seek to gain another's favor.

Aronson (1988) speculated that constant approval can lose value. When a lover says for the five-hundredth time, "You look great," the words carry far less impact than were they now to say, "You look awful in that dress." A loved one you've doted on is hard to reward but easy to hurt. This suggests that an open, honest relationship – one where people enjoy one another's esteem and acceptance yet are honest – is more likely to offer continuing rewards than one dulled by the suppression of unpleasant emotions, one in which people try only, as Dale Carnegie advised, to "lavish praise." Aronson (1988) put it this way:

> As a relationship ripens toward greater intimacy, what becomes increasingly important is authenticity – our ability to give up trying to make a good impression and begin to reveal things about ourselves that are honest even if unsavory. . . . If two people are genuinely fond of each other, they will have a more satisfying and exciting relationship over a longer period of time if they are able to express both positive and negative feelings than if they are completely "nice" to each other at all times. (p. 323)

In most social interactions, we self-censor our negative feelings. Thus, noted William Swann and colleagues (1991), some people receive no corrective feedback. Living in a world of pleasant illusion, they continue to act in ways that alienate their would-be friends. A true friend is one who can let us in on bad news – nicely.

Someone who really loves us will be honest with us but will also tend to see us through rose-colored glasses. The happiest dating and married couples (and those who became happier with time) were those who saw their partners more positively than their partners saw themselves (Murray & Holmes, 1997; Murray et al., 1996a,b). When we're in love, we're biased to find those we love not only physically attractive but also socially attractive, and we're happy to have our partners view us with a similar positive bias (Boyes & Fletcher, 2007). Moreover, the most satisfied married couples tend to have idealized one another as newlyweds and to approach problems without immediately criticizing their partners and finding fault (Karney & Bradbury, 1997; Miller et al., 2006; Murray et al., 2011). Honesty has its place in a good relationship, but so does a presumption of the other's basic goodness.

Relationship Rewards

Asked why they are friends or romantic partners with someone, most people can readily answer. "I like Ashar because she's warm, witty, and well-read." What that explanation leaves out – and what social psychologists believe is most important – is ourselves. Attraction involves the one who is attracted as well as the attractor. Thus, a more psychologically accurate answer might be, "I like Ashar because of how I feel when I'm with her." We are attracted to those we find satisfying and gratifying to be with. Attraction is in the eye (and brain) of the beholder.

"No one is perfect until you fall in love with them."

—Television personality Andy Rooney (1919–2011)

The reward theory of attraction suggests that when we associate our partners with pleasant activities, relationships last.
Ryan Mcvay/Getty Images

reward theory of attraction
The theory that we like those whose behavior is rewarding to us or whom we associate with rewarding events.

The point can be expressed as a simple **reward theory of attraction**: Those who reward us, or whom we associate with rewards, we like. If a relationship gives us more rewards than costs, we will like it and will want it to continue. Canadian children randomly assigned to perform three acts of kindness (versus visit three places) became more socially accepted and were less likely to be bullied: They gained friends as they helped others (Layous et al., 2012). People who received a compliment from a stranger were later more likely to help them, and, in general, compliments from others are received much more positively than most people predict (Boothby & Bohns, 2021; Grant et al., 2022). In his 1665 book of *Maxims,* La Rochefoucauld conjectured, "Friendship is a scheme for the mutual exchange of personal advantages and favors whereby self-esteem may profit."

We not only like people who are rewarding to be with but also, according to the second version of the reward principle, like those we *associate* with good feelings. Conditioning creates positive feelings toward things and people linked with rewarding events (Byrne & Clore, 1970; De Houwer et al., 2001; Lott & Lott, 1974). When, after a strenuous week, we relax in front of a fire, enjoying good food, drink, and music, we will likely feel a special warmth toward those around us. We are less likely to take a liking to someone we meet while suffering a splitting headache.

Experiments confirm this phenomenon of liking – and disliking – by association (Hofmann et al., 2010). When an experimenter was friendly, participants chose to interact with someone who looked similar to her, but if she was unfriendly, they avoided the similar-looking woman (Lewicki, 1985). Elaine Hatfield and William Walster (1978) found a practical tip in these research studies: "Romantic dinners, trips to the theatre, evenings at home together, and vacations never stop being important. . . . If your relationship is to survive, it's important that you *both* continue to associate your relationship with good things."

This simple theory of attraction – we like those who reward us and those we associate with rewards – helps us understand why people everywhere feel attracted to those who are warm, trustworthy, and responsive (Fletcher et al., 1999; Regan, 1998; Wojciszke et al., 1998). The reward theory also helps explain some of the influences on attraction we discussed earlier:

- *Proximity* is rewarding. It costs less time and effort to receive friendship's benefits with someone who lives or works close by.
- We like *attractive* people because we perceive that they offer other desirable traits and because we benefit by associating with them.
- If others have *similar* opinions, we feel rewarded because we presume that they like us in return. Moreover, those who share our views help validate them. We especially like people if we have successfully converted them to our way of thinking (Lombardo et al., 1972; Riordan, 1980; Sigall, 1970).
- We like to be liked and love to be loved. Thus, liking is usually *mutual.* We like those who like us.

SUMMING UP: What Leads to Friendship and Attraction?

- The best predictor of whether any two people are friends is their sheer *proximity* to each other. Proximity is conducive to repeated *exposure* and interaction, which enables us to discover similarities and to feel each other's liking.
- A second determinant of initial attraction is physical attractiveness. Both in laboratory studies and in field experiments involving blind dates, college students tend to prefer attractive people. In everyday life, however, people tend to choose someone whose attractiveness

roughly *matches* their own (or who, if less attractive, has other compensating qualities). Positive attributions about attractive people define a *physical-attractiveness stereotype* – an assumption that what is beautiful is good.

- Liking is greatly aided by similarity of attitudes, beliefs, and values. Likeness leads to liking; opposites rarely attract.
- We are also likely to develop friendships with people who like us.
- According to the *reward theory of attraction,* we like people whose behavior we find rewarding or whom we associate with rewarding events.

WHAT IS LOVE?

Describe the varieties and components of love.

Loving is more complex than liking and thus more difficult to measure and more perplexing to study. People yearn for it, live for it, die for it.

The influences on our initial liking of another – proximity, attractiveness, similarity, being liked, and other rewarding traits – also influence our long-term, close relationships. First impressions are important in dating just as they are in friendships (Berg & McQuinn, 1986).

Nevertheless, long-term loving is not merely an intensification of initial liking. Social psychologists, therefore, study enduring, close relationships.

Passionate Love

The first step in scientifically studying romantic love, as in studying any variable, is to decide how to define and measure it. We have ways to measure aggression, altruism, prejudice, and liking. But how do we measure love?

"How do I love thee? Let me count the ways," wrote Elizabeth Barrett Browning. Social scientists have counted various ways. Psychologist Robert Sternberg (1998) views love as a triangle consisting of three components: passion, intimacy, and commitment **(Figure 3)**. The three components of love are universal enough that they can be reliably measured in 37 languages (Kowal et al., 2023).

Some elements of love are common to all loving relationships: mutual understanding, giving and receiving support, enjoying the loved one's company. Some elements are distinctive. If we experience passionate love, we express it physically, we expect the relationship to be exclusive, and we are intensely fascinated with our partner. You can see it in our eyes.

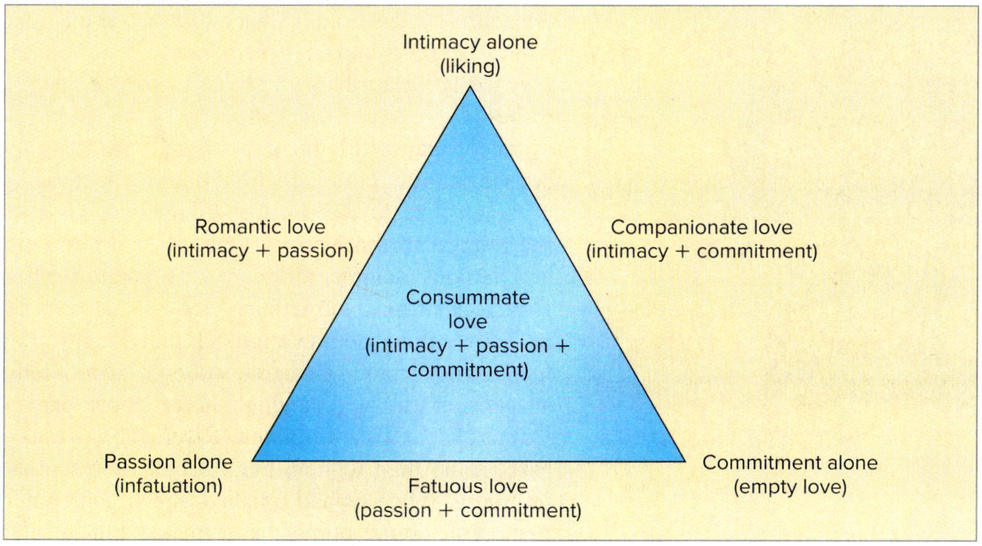

FIGURE 3
Robert Sternberg's Combinations of Three Basic Components of Love

Zick Rubin (1973) confirmed this. He administered a love scale to hundreds of University of Michigan dating couples. Later, from behind a one-way mirror in a laboratory waiting room, he clocked eye contact among "weak-love" and "strong-love" couples (mutual gaze conveys liking and averted eye gaze conveys ostracism [Wirth et al., 2010]). So Rubin's result will not surprise you: The strong-love couples gave themselves away by gazing into each other's eyes for longer. When talking, they also nodded their heads, smiled naturally, and leaned forward (Gonzaga et al., 2001). When observing speed-daters, it takes but a few seconds to make a reasonably accurate guess as to whether one person is interested in another (Place et al., 2009).

passionate love
A state of intense longing for union with another. Passionate lovers are absorbed in each other, feel ecstatic at attaining their partner's love, and are disconsolate on losing it.

Passionate love is emotional, exciting, intense. Elaine Hatfield (1988) defined it as *"a state of intense longing for union with another"* (p. 193). If reciprocated, one feels fulfilled and joyous; if not, one feels empty or despairing. Like other forms of emotional excitement, passionate love involves a roller coaster of elation and gloom, tingling exhilaration and dejected misery. "We are never so defenseless against suffering as when we love," observed Freud. Passionate love preoccupies the lover with thoughts of the other, involving the same reward pathways in the brain as addictions to substances (Fisher et al., 2016; Takahashi et al., 2015).

"Passionate love is in many ways an altered state of consciousness. . . . In many states today, there are laws that a person must not be in an intoxicated condition when marrying. But passionate love is a kind of intoxication."

—Roy Baumeister, *Meanings of Life*, 1991

Passionate love is what you feel when you not only love someone but also are "in love" with them. As Sarah Meyers and Ellen Berscheid (1997) note, we understand that someone who says, "I love you, but I'm not in love with you," means to say, "I like you. I care about you. I think you're marvelous. But I don't feel sexually attracted to you." In other words, they feel friendship but not passion.

A THEORY OF PASSIONATE LOVE

To explain passionate love, Hatfield noted that a given state of arousal can be steered into any of several emotions, depending on how we attribute the arousal. An emotion involves both body and mind—both arousal and the way we interpret and label that arousal. Imagine yourself with a pounding heart and trembling hands: Are you experiencing fear, anxiety, joy? Physiologically, one emotion is quite similar to another. You may therefore experience the arousal as joy if you are in a euphoric situation, anger if your environment is hostile, and passionate love if the situation is romantic. In this view, passionate love is the psychological experience of being biologically aroused by someone we find attractive.

two-factor theory of emotion
Arousal × its label = emotion.

If indeed passion is a revved-up state that's labeled "love," then whatever revs one up should intensify feelings of love. In several experiments, straight college men aroused by reading or viewing erotic materials had a heightened response to a woman—for example, by scoring much higher on a love scale when describing their girlfriend (Carducci et al., 1978; Dermer & Pyszczynski, 1978). Proponents of the **two-factor theory of emotion**, developed by Stanley Schachter and Jerome Singer (1962), argue that when the revved-up men responded to a woman, they easily misattributed some of their own arousal to her.

Although this kiss appears to be purely passionate love, Scott Jones was instead trying to calm his panicked girlfriend Alexandra Thomas, who had been knocked to the ground amidst riots in Vancouver in 2011 (Tran, 2015)—an act of consummate love combining intimacy, passion, and commitment.
Rich Lam/Getty Images

According to this theory, being aroused by *any* source should intensify passionate feelings—provided that the mind is free to attribute some of the arousal to a romantic stimulus. In a dramatic and famous demonstration of this phenomenon, Donald Dutton and Arthur Aron (1974) had an attractive young woman approach individual young men as they crossed a narrow, wobbly, 450-foot-long suspension walkway hanging 230 feet above British Columbia's rocky Capilano River. The woman asked each man to help her fill out a class questionnaire. When he had finished, she scribbled her name and phone number and invited him to call if he wanted to hear more about the project. Most accepted the phone number, and half who did so called. By contrast, men approached by the woman on a low, solid bridge rarely called. Once again, physical arousal accentuated romantic responses.

Scary movies, roller-coaster rides, and physical exercise have the same effect, especially with those we find attractive (Foster et al., 1998; White & Kight, 1984). The effect holds true with married couples, too: Those who do exciting activities together report the best relationships. And after doing an arousing laboratory task (a three-legged race on their hands and knees) versus a more mundane task, couples also reported higher satisfaction with their overall relationship (Aron et al., 2000). Adrenaline makes the heart grow fonder.

According to the two-factor theory of emotion, emotional arousal caused by an exciting experience such as an amusement park ride may be confused for sexual attraction.
Andresr/Getty Images

As this suggests, passionate love is a biological as well as a psychological phenomenon. Research by social psychologist Arthur Aron and colleagues (2005) indicates that passionate love engages dopamine-rich brain areas associated with reward **(Figure 4)**.

Love is also a social phenomenon. Love is more than lust, noted Ellen Berscheid (2010). Supplement sexual desire with a deepening friendship and the result is romantic love. Passionate love = lust + attachment.

"The 'adrenaline' associated with a wide variety of highs can spill over and make passion more passionate. (Sort of a 'Better loving through chemistry' phenomenon.)"

—Elaine Hatfield and Richard Rapson, *Passionate Love*, 1987

VARIATIONS IN LOVE: CULTURE AND GENDER

There is always a temptation to assume that most others share our feelings and ideas. In Western cultures, people assume, for example, that love is a precondition for marriage. Most cultures – 89% in one analysis of 166 cultures – do have a concept of romantic love, as reflected in flirtation or couples running off together (Jankowiak & Fischer, 1992). But in some cultures, notably those practicing arranged marriages, love tends to follow rather than to precede marriage. Even many people in the United States disconnected love and marriage until relatively recently: In the 1960s, only 24% of college women and 65% of college men considered love to be the basis of marriage. More recently, 88% of U.S. adults agree (Geiger & Livingston, 2019). Passionate love tends to be emphasized more in cultures where relationships are more easily broken, perhaps as a strategy to keep one's partner committed when other options are available (Yamada et al., 2017).

Do males and females differ in how they experience passionate love? Studies of men and women falling in and out of love reveal some surprises. Most people, including the writer of the following letter to a newspaper advice columnist, suppose that women fall in love more readily:

> Dear Dr. Brothers:
>
> Do you think it's effeminate for a 19-year-old guy to fall in love so hard it's like the whole world's turned around? I think I'm really crazy because this has happened several times now and love just seems to hit me on the head from nowhere. . . . My father says this is the way girls fall in love and that it doesn't happen this way with guys – at least it's not supposed to. I can't change how I am in this way but it kind of worries me. – P.T. (quoted by Dion & Dion, 1985)

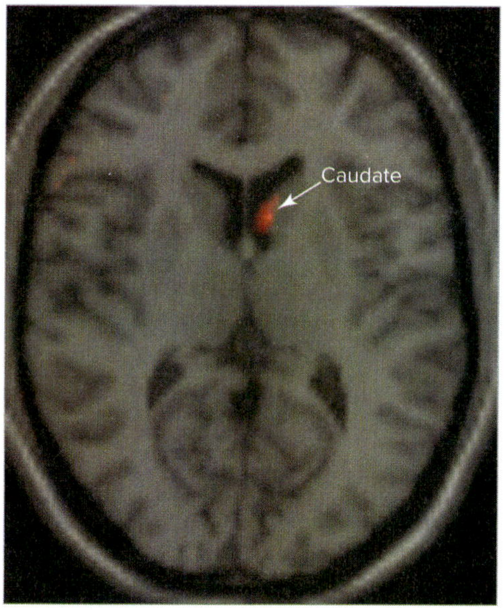

FIGURE 4

This Is Your Brain on Love

MRI scans from young adults intensely in love revealed areas, such as the caudate nucleus, that became more active when gazing at the loved-one's photo (but not when gazing at the photo of another acquaintance).
From Aron et al., 2005. Image courtesy of Lucy L. Brown.

P.T. would be reassured by the repeated finding that it is actually men who tend to fall in love more readily (Ackerman et al., 2011; Dion & Dion, 1985). Men also seem to fall out of love more slowly and are less likely than women to break up a romance before marriage. Surprisingly to most people, in straight relationships, it's men, not women, who most often are first to say "I love you" (Ackerman et al., 2011).

Once in love, however, women are typically as emotionally involved as their partners, or more so. They are more likely to report feeling euphoric

Unlike passionate love, companionate love can last a lifetime.
Steph Chambers/Getty Images

and "giddy and carefree," as if they were "floating on a cloud." Women are also somewhat more likely than men to focus on the intimacy of the friendship and on their concern for their partner. Men are more likely than women to think about the playful and physical aspects of the relationship (Hendrick & Hendrick, 1995).

Companionate Love

Although passionate love burns hot, like a relationship booster rocket, it eventually simmers down once the relationship reaches a stable orbit. The high of romance may be sustained for a few months, even a couple of years. But no high lasts forever. "When you're in love it's the most glorious two-and-a-half days of your life," jested comedian Richard Lewis. The novelty, the intense absorption in the other, the tingly thrill of the romance, the giddy "floating on a cloud" feeling fades. After 2 years of marriage, spouses express affection about half as often as when they were newlyweds (Huston & Chorost, 1994). About 4 years after marriage, the divorce rate peaks in cultures worldwide (Fisher, 1994). If a close relationship is to endure, it will settle to a steadier but still warm afterglow called **companionate love**. The passion-facilitating hormones (testosterone, dopamine, adrenaline) subside, while the hormone oxytocin supports feelings of attachment and trust (Taylor et al., 2010).

companionate love
The affection we feel for those with whom our lives are deeply intertwined.

Unlike the wild emotions of passionate love, companionate love is lower key; it's a deep, affectionate attachment. It activates different parts of the brain (Aron et al., 2005). And it is just as real. Nisa, a !Kung San woman of the African Kalahari Desert, explains: "When two people are first together, their hearts are on fire and their passion is very great. After a while, the fire cools and that's how it stays. They continue to love each other, but it's in a different way – warm and dependable" (Shostak, 1981).

The flow and ebb of romantic love follows the pattern of addictions to caffeine, alcohol, and other drugs (Burkett & Young, 2012). At first, a drug gives a big kick, a high. With repetition, opponent emotions gain strength and tolerance develops. An amount that once was highly stimulating no longer gives a thrill. Stopping the substance, however, does not return you to where you started. Rather, it triggers withdrawal symptoms – malaise, depression, the blahs. The same often happens in love. The passionate high is fated to become lukewarm. The no-longer-romantic relationship becomes taken for granted – until it ends. Then the jilted lover, the widower, the divorcé are surprised at how empty life now seems without the person they long ago stopped feeling passionately attached to. Having focused on what was not working, they stopped noticing what was (Carlson & Hatfield, 1992).

The cooling of passionate love over time and the growing importance of other factors, such as shared values, can be seen in the feelings of those who enter arranged versus love-based marriages in India. Those who married for love reported diminishing feelings of love after a 5-year newlywed period. By contrast, those in arranged marriages reported *more* love after 5 years (Gupta & Singh, 1982; **Figure 5**; for other data on the seeming success of arranged marriages, see Myers et al., 2005, Thakar & Epstein, 2011, and Yelsma & Athappilly, 1988).

The cooling of intense romantic love often triggers a period of disillusion, especially among those who believe that romantic love is essential both for a marriage and for its continuation. Compared with North Americans, Asian people tend to focus less on personal feelings and more on the practical aspects of social attachments (Dion & Dion, 1988; Kito et al., 2017; Sprecher & Toro-Morn, 2002; Sprecher et al., 1994). Thus, they are less vulnerable to disillusionment.

"Grow old along with me! The best is yet to be."
—Robert Browning, "Rabbi ben Ezra," in *Dramatis Personae*, 1864

The decline in intense mutual fascination may be natural and adaptive for species survival. The result of passionate love is often children, whose survival is aided by the parents'

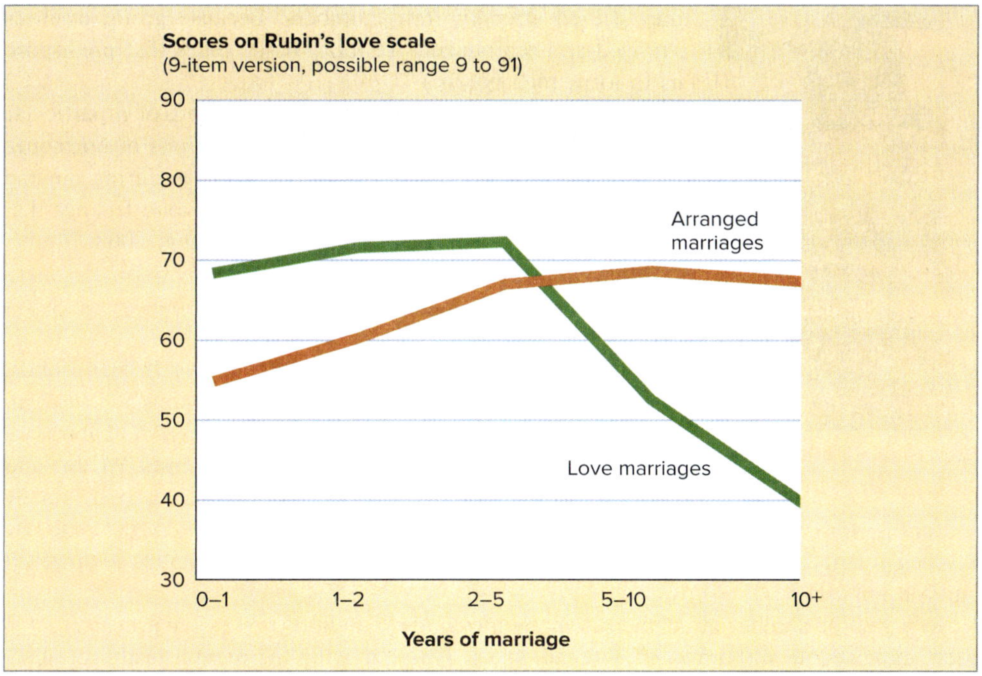

FIGURE 5

Romantic Love Between Partners in Arranged or Love Marriages in Jaipur, India

Source: Gupta & Singh, 1982.

waning obsession with each other (Kenrick & Trost, 1987). Nevertheless, for those married more than 20 years, some of the lost romantic feeling is often renewed as the family nest empties and the parents are once again free to focus their attention on each other (Hatfield & Sprecher, 1986; White & Edwards, 1990). "No man or woman really knows what love is until they have been married a quarter of a century," said Mark Twain. If the relationship has been intimate, mutually rewarding, and rooted in a shared life history, companionate love deepens.

SUMMING UP: What Is Love?

- Researchers have characterized love as having components of intimacy, passion, and commitment. *Passionate love* is experienced as a bewildering confusion of ecstasy and anxiety, elation and pain. The *two-factor theory of emotion* suggests that in a romantic context, arousal from any source, even painful experiences, can be steered into passion.
- In the best of relationships, the initial passionate high settles to a steadier, more affectionate relationship called *companionate love*.

WHAT ENABLES CLOSE RELATIONSHIPS?

Explain how attachment styles, equity, and self-disclosure influence the ups and downs of our close relationships.

Attachment

Love is a biological imperative. We are social creatures, destined to bond with others. Our need to belong is adaptive. Cooperation promotes survival. In solo combat, our early ancestors were not the toughest predators; but as hunter-gatherers, and in fending off predators,

Attachment, especially to caregivers, is a powerful survival impulse.
Juice Images/Alamy Stock Photo

they gained strength from numbers. Because group dwellers survived and reproduced, we today carry genes that predispose us to form such bonds.

Researchers have found that different forms of a particular gene predict mammalian pair bonding. Injections of hormones such as oxytocin (which is released in females during nursing and during mating) and vasopressin produce good feelings that trigger romantic bonding (Donaldson & Young, 2008; Young, 2009). Genes associated with vasopressin activity predict marital stability (Walum et al., 2008). Such is the biology of enduring love.

Our dependence as infants strengthens our human bonds. Soon after birth, we exhibit various social responses: love, fear, anger. But the first and greatest of these is love. As babies, we almost immediately prefer familiar faces and voices. We coo and smile when our parents give us attention. By approximately 8 months, we typically let out a wail when separated from them. Reunited, we cling. By keeping infants close to their caregivers, strong social attachment serves as a powerful survival impulse.

Deprived of familiar attachments, sometimes under conditions of extreme neglect, children may become withdrawn, frightened, silent. After studying the mental health of abandoned children for the World Health Organization, psychiatrist John Bowlby (1980, p. 442) reflected, "Intimate attachments to other human beings are the hub around which a person's life revolves. . . . From these intimate attachments [people draw] strength and enjoyment of life."

Researchers have compared attachment and love in various close relationships: between parents and children, between friends, and between spouses or lovers (Davis, 1985; Maxwell, 1985; Sternberg & Grajek, 1984). Some elements are common to all loving attachments: mutual understanding, giving and receiving support, valuing, and enjoying being with the loved one. The same brain areas associated with maternal attachment are also activated when adults think about their romantic partner (Acevedo et al., 2012). Passionate love is, however, spiced with some added features: physical affection, an expectation of exclusiveness, and an intense fascination with the loved one.

Passionate love is not just for lovers. The intense love of parent and infant for each other qualifies as a form of passionate love. Year-old infants, like young adult lovers, welcome physical affection, feel distress when separated, express intense affection when reunited, and take great pleasure in the significant other's attention and approval (Shaver & Mikulincer, 2011). Of course, infants vary in how they relate to caregivers, and so do adults in how they relate to their romantic partners. This made Phillip Shaver and Cindy Hazan (1993, 1994) wonder whether infant attachment styles might carry over to adult relationships.

ATTACHMENT STYLES

secure attachment
Attachments rooted in trust and marked by intimacy.

Approximately 7 in 10 infants and nearly that many adults exhibit **secure attachment** (Baldwin et al., 1996; Jones & Cunningham, 1996; Mickelson et al., 1997). When placed as infants in a strange situation (usually a laboratory playroom), they play comfortably in their mother's presence, happily exploring this strange environment. If she leaves, they become distressed; when she returns, they run to her, hold her, then relax and return to exploring and playing (Ainsworth, 1973, 1979). This trusting and secure attachment style, many researchers believe, forms a working model of intimacy – a blueprint for one's adult intimate relationships, in which underlying trust sustains relationships through times of conflict (Miller & Rempel, 2004; Oriña et al., 2011; Salvatore et al., 2011). Securely attached adults find it relatively easy to get close to others and don't fret about getting too dependent or being abandoned. As lovers, they enjoy sexuality within the context of a secure, committed relationship. And their relationships tend to be satisfying and enduring (Feeney, 1996; Feeney & Noller, 1990; Simpson et al., 1992).

Approximately 2 in 10 infants and adults exhibit **avoidant attachment**, one of the two types of insecure attachment. Although internally aroused, avoidant infants reveal little distress during separation and little clinging upon reunion. Avoiding closeness, avoidant adults tend to be less invested in relationships and more likely to leave them. They also are more likely to be sexually unfaithful to their partners in both straight and gay relationships (DeWall et al., 2011; Starks & Parsons, 2014). Avoidant individuals may be either *fearful* ("I am uncomfortable getting close to others") or *dismissing* ("It is very important to me to feel independent and self-sufficient" [Bartholomew & Horowitz, 1991]). More college students in the United States had a dismissing attachment style in the 2010s (versus the 1980s), and fewer had a secure attachment style. The researchers speculate that this shift may be rooted in changing family structures and an increasing emphasis on individualism (Konrath et al., 2014).

avoidant attachment
Attachments marked by discomfort over, or resistance to, being close to others. An insecure attachment style.

Approximately 1 in 10 infants and adults has **anxious attachment**, the second type of insecure attachment. In the strange situation, anxiously attached infants are more likely to cling to their mother. When she leaves, they cry; when she returns, they continue to cry and be distressed. As adults, insecure individuals are less trusting, more fearful of a partner's becoming interested in someone else, and therefore more possessive and jealous. They may break up repeatedly with the same person. They are more likely to become emotional when discussing conflicts and their self-esteem fluctuates more based on feedback from others, especially romantic partners (Cassidy, 2000; Hepper & Carnelley, 2012; Simpson et al., 1996). They are also more likely to interpret others' ambiguous behaviors as hostile (Li et al., 2023). Their eagerness to form relationships can hamper their efforts because others perceive their anxiety and the interaction becomes awkward (McClure & Lydon, 2014). Anxiously attached people even transfer their anxious attachment style to their smartphones, causing them to check their phones more often — even while driving (Bodford et al., 2017).

anxious attachment
Attachments marked by anxiety or ambivalence. An insecure attachment style.

Some researchers attribute these varying attachment styles, which have been studied across 62 cultures, to parental responsiveness (Kim et al., 2021; Schmitt et al., 2004). Cindy Hazan (2004) sums up the idea: "Early attachment experiences form the basis of *internal working models* or characteristic ways of thinking about relationships." Thus, sensitive, responsive mothers — mothers who engender a sense of basic trust in the world's reliability — typically have securely attached infants, observed Mary Ainsworth (1979) and Erik Erikson (1963). In fact, one study of 100 Israeli grandmother-daughter-granddaughter threesomes found intergenerational consistency of attachment styles (Besser & Priel, 2005). Those who experienced nurturant and involved parenting as children tend later to have warm and supportive relationships with their romantic partners as young adults (Conger et al., 2000). However, family structure alone was not the important factor: Young adults whose parents were divorced did not differ in attachment style from those whose parents were still married (Washington & Hans, 2013).

There are genetic effects on attachment styles as well. Not surprisingly, people high in neuroticism, usually considered to be about 50% genetic, are also more likely to have anxious or avoidant attachment (Gillath et al., 2008; Marrero-Quevedo et al., 2019). A gene that predisposes prairie voles to cuddle and mate for life (and has the same effect on laboratory mice genetically engineered to have the gene) has varying human forms. This gene is more commonly found in faithful, married men, another gene in those who are unmarried or unfaithful (Caldwell et al., 2008; Walum et al., 2008).

The effects of attachment can last a lifetime: In a 22-year longitudinal study, infants who were insecurely attached to their mothers became adults who struggled to feel more positive emotions (Moutsiana et al., 2014). Attachment styles also have obvious impacts on adult relationships: In an analysis of 188 studies, avoidantly attached people were less satisfied and supported in their relationships, and anxiously attached people experienced more relationship conflict (Li & Chan, 2012). Most life events (including getting married, having a baby, or losing a job) did not lead to enduring changes in attachment style, suggesting attachment style is fairly stable over the lifetime (Fraley et al., 2021).

Which attachment style combinations are the best — and worst? Two securely attached partners would seem to be ideal, and pairings in which at least one partner is insecurely

Couples with an anxiously attached woman and an avoidantly attached man experience more stress.
shisu_ka/Shutterstock

attached may have more issues. The most difficult pairing appears to be an anxious woman and an avoidant man; these couples showed the highest levels of stress hormone when they anticipated talking over a conflict and found it more difficult to give and seek care from their partner (Beck et al., 2013). This makes sense: The anxious woman, uncertain of her partner's love, seeks closeness, while the avoidant man, uncomfortable with closeness, distances himself. For better or for worse, early attachment styles do seem to lay a foundation for future relationships.

Equity

If each partner pursues their personal desires willy-nilly, the relationship will die. Therefore, our society teaches us to exchange rewards by the **equity** principle of attraction: What you and your partner get out of a relationship should be proportional to what you each put into it (Walster et al., 1978). If two people receive equal outcomes, they should contribute equally; otherwise one or the other will feel it is unfair. If both feel their outcomes correspond to the assets and efforts each contributes, then both perceive equity.

equity
A condition in which the outcomes people receive from a relationship are proportional to what they contribute to it. Note: Equitable outcomes needn't always be equal outcomes.

Strangers and casual acquaintances maintain equity by exchanging benefits: You lend me your class notes; later, I'll lend you mine. I invite you to my party; you invite me to yours. Those in an enduring relationship, including roommates and those in love, do not feel bound to trade similar benefits – notes for notes, parties for parties (Berg, 1984). They feel freer to maintain equity by exchanging a variety of benefits ("When you drop by to lend me your notes, why don't you stay for dinner?") and eventually to stop keeping track of who owes whom. A sense of equity underlies nearly all of the qualities that a group of college students identified as "deal-breakers" in considering long-term partners. Most said they would not consider being with someone who was inattentive or uncaring, was dismissive of their interests, or was already in a relationship or married (Jonason et al., 2015).

LONG-TERM EQUITY

Is it crass to suppose that friendship and love are rooted in an equitable exchange of rewards? Don't we sometimes give in response to a loved one's need, without expecting anything in return? Indeed, those involved in an equitable, long-term relationship are unconcerned with short-term equity. Margaret Clark and Judson Mills (1979, 1993; Clark, 1984, 1986) have argued that people even take pains to *avoid* calculating any exchange benefits. When we help a good friend, we do not want instant repayment. If someone invites us for dinner, we wait before reciprocating, lest the person attribute the motive for our return invitation to be merely paying off a social debt. True friends tune into one another's needs even when reciprocation is impossible (Clark et al., 1986, 1989). Similarly, happily married people tend not to keep score of how much they are giving and getting (Buunk & Van Yperen, 1991; Clark et al., 2010). As people observe their partners being self-giving, their sense of trust grows (Wieselquist et al., 1999).

In experiments with University of Maryland students, Clark and Mills confirmed that not being calculating is a mark of friendship. Tit-for-tat exchanges boosted people's liking when the relationship was relatively formal but diminished liking when the two sought friendship. Clark and Mills surmise that marriage contracts, in which each partner specifies what is expected from the other, would more likely undermine than enhance love. Only when the other's positive behavior is voluntary can we attribute it to love.

"Love is the most subtle kind of self-interest."
—Holbrook Johnson

Previously we noted an equity principle at work in the matching phenomenon: People usually bring equal assets to romantic relationships. Often, they are matched for attractiveness, status, and so forth. If they are mismatched in one area, such as attractiveness, they tend to be mismatched in some other area, such as status. But in total assets, they are an equitable match. No one says, and few even think, "I'll trade you my good looks for your big income." But especially in relationships that last, equity is the rule.

PERCEIVED EQUITY AND SATISFACTION

In one survey, "sharing household chores" ranked third (after "having shared interests" and a "satisfying sexual relationship") among the things people saw as marks of successful marriages (Geiger, 2016). Indeed, those in equitable relationships are typically the most content (Carlson, 2022; Fletcher et al., 1987; Hatfield et al., 1985; Van Yperen & Buunk, 1990). Those who perceive their relationship as inequitable feel discomfort: The one who has the better deal may feel guilty, and the one who senses a raw deal may feel strong irritation. (Given the self-serving bias – most husbands perceive themselves as contributing more housework than their wives credit them for – the person who is "overbenefited" is less sensitive to the inequity.)

Couples who share household work equitably enjoy better relationships. If one person feels they are doing more of the heavy lifting, trouble can follow.
fizkes/Shutterstock

Robert Schafer and Patricia Keith (1980) surveyed several hundred married couples of all ages. Partners who felt their marriages were unfair because one spouse contributed too little to the cooking, housekeeping, parenting, or providing felt more distressed and depressed. During the child-rearing years, when wives often feel underbenefited and husbands overbenefited, marital satisfaction tends to dip. In contrast, during the honeymoon and empty-nest stages, spouses are more likely to perceive equity and to feel satisfaction with their marriages (Feeney et al., 1994). When both partners freely give and receive, and make decisions together, the odds of sustained, satisfying love are better (Karney & Bradbury, 2020).

Perceived inequity triggers marital distress, agreed Nancy Grote and Margaret Clark (2001) from their tracking of married couples over time. But they also report that the traffic between inequity and distress runs both ways: Marital distress exacerbates the perception of unfairness (**Figure 6**). One thing that helps: Expressing gratitude for a partner's efforts – in other words, saying "thank you" (Park et al., 2019).

Self-Disclosure

Deep, companionate relationships are intimate. They enable us to be known as we truly are and to feel accepted. We discover this delicious experience in a good marriage or a close friendship – a relationship where trust displaces anxiety and where we are free to open ourselves without fear of losing the other's affection (Holmes & Rempel, 1989). Such relationships are characterized by **self-disclosure** (Derlega et al., 1993). As a relationship grows, self-disclosing partners reveal more and more of themselves to each other; their knowledge of each other penetrates to deeper levels. In relationships that flourish, much of this self-disclosure shares successes and triumphs, and mutual delight over good happenings (Gable et al., 2006). When a friend rejoices with us over good news, it not only increases our joy about the happy event but also helps us feel better about the friendship (Reis et al., 2010).

self-disclosure
Revealing intimate aspects of oneself to others.

Most of us enjoy intimacy. It's gratifying to be singled out for another's disclosure. We feel pleased when a normally reserved person says that something about us "made me feel like opening up" and shares confidential information, whether in person or online (Archer & Cook, 1986; Kashian et al., 2017; Taylor et al., 1981).

Not only do we like those who disclose, we also disclose to those whom we like. And after disclosing to them, we like them more (Collins & Miller, 1994). One way to feed intimacy and love is by talking about your emotions and views. Couples who discussed questions such as "Given the choice of anyone in the world, whom would you want as a dinner guest?" and "What is the greatest accomplishment of your life?" later felt more passionate love for each other (Welker et al., 2014). When we lack opportunities for intimate disclosure, we experience the pain of loneliness (Berg & Peplau, 1982; Solano et al., 1982; Uysal et al., 2010).

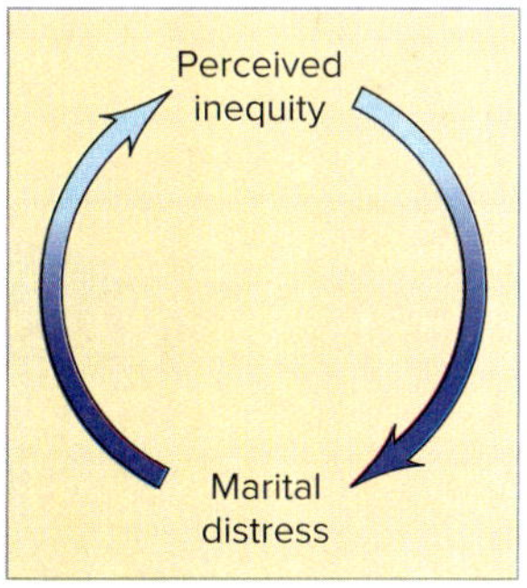

FIGURE 6
Perceived Inequities Trigger Marital Distress, Which Fosters the Perception of Inequities
Source: Adapted from Grote & Clark, 2001.

Experiments have probed both the *causes* and the *effects* of self-disclosure. When are people most willing to disclose intimate information concerning "what you like and don't

Self-disclosure is an effective way to build intimacy.
Tetra Images/Getty Images

like about yourself" or "what you're most ashamed and most proud of"? And what effects do such revelations have on those who reveal and receive them?

The most reliable finding is the **disclosure reciprocity** effect: Disclosure begets disclosure (Chen et al., 2023; Miller, 1990). We reveal more to those who have been open with us. But intimate disclosure is seldom instant. (If it is, the person may seem indiscreet and unstable.) Appropriate intimacy progresses like a dance: I reveal a little, you reveal a little – but not too much. You then reveal more, and I reciprocate.

For those in love, deepening intimacy is exciting. "Rising intimacy will create a strong sense of passion," noted Roy Baumeister and Ellen Bratslavsky (1999). This helps explain why those who remarry after the loss of a spouse tend to begin the new relationship with an increased frequency of sex, and why passion often rides highest when intimacy is restored following severe conflict.

disclosure reciprocity
The tendency for one person's intimacy of self-disclosure to match that of a conversational partner.

Some people – most of them women – are especially skilled "openers"; they easily elicit intimate disclosures from others, even from those who normally don't reveal very much of themselves (Pegalis et al., 1994; Shaffer et al., 1996). Such people tend to be good listeners. During conversation, they maintain attentive facial expressions and appear to be comfortably enjoying themselves (Purvis et al., 1984). They may also express interest by uttering supportive phrases while their conversational partner is speaking. They are what psychologist Carl Rogers (1980) called "growth-promoting" listeners: people who are genuine in revealing their own feelings, who are accepting of others' feelings, and who are empathic, sensitive, reflective listeners.

What are the effects of self-disclosure? People are happier on days when they have more deep or substantive discussions compared to days filled with small talk (Mehl et al., 2010). It is gratifying to open up to another, and then to receive the trust another shows by being open with us. People feel better on days when they have disclosed something significant about themselves, such as their being lesbian or gay, and feel worse when concealing their identity (Beals et al., 2009). Researchers are beginning to explore whether self-disclosure to artificial intelligence (like Alexa or ChatGPT) carries the same benefits as disclosing to a person (Cheng et al., 2023; Zhang & Rau, 2022).

"What is a friend? I will tell you. It is a person with whom you dare to be yourself."

—Writer Frank Crane, "A Definition of Friendship," *Four Minute Essays*, 1919

Having an intimate friend with whom we can discuss threats to our self-image seems to help us survive stress (Swann & Predmore, 1985). A true friendship is a special relationship that helps us cope with our other relationships. "When I am with my friend," reflected the Roman playwright Seneca, "methinks I am alone, and as much at liberty to speak anything as to think it."

Intimate self-disclosure is also one of companionate love's delights. The most self-disclosing dating and married couples tend to enjoy the most satisfying and enduring relationships (Berg & McQuinn, 1986; Hendrick et al., 1988; Sprecher, 1987). For example, in a study of newlywed couples who were all equally in love, those who most deeply and accurately knew each other were most likely to enjoy enduring love (Neff & Karney, 2005). Married partners who most strongly agree that "I try to share my most intimate thoughts and feelings with my partner" tend to have the most satisfying marriages (Sanderson & Cantor, 2001). For very reticent people, marriage may not be as satisfying as it is for those more willing to share their feelings (Baker & McNulty, 2010). When the inevitable disagreements occur, couples who believe that their partner understands their perspective – even if they don't agree with it – report higher relationship satisfaction (Gordon & Chen, 2016).

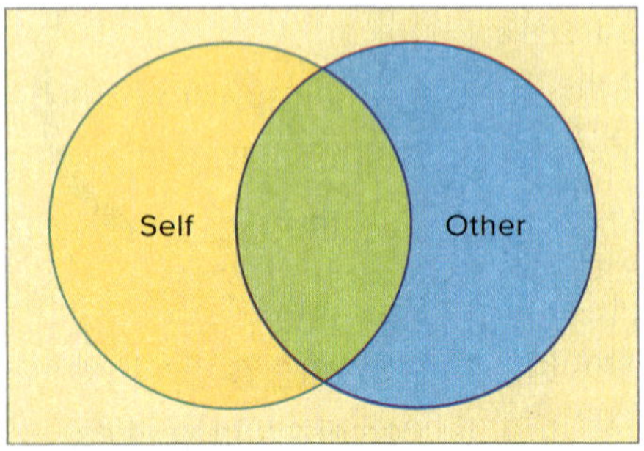

FIGURE 7
Love: An Overlapping of Selves — You Become Part of Me, I Part of You
Source: Weber & Harvey, 1994.

Mutual trust and self-disclosure, argued Arthur Aron and Elaine Aron (1994), are the essence of love – two selves connecting, disclosing, and identifying with each other; two selves, each retaining their individuality, yet sharing activities, delighting in similarities, and mutually supporting. The result for many romantic partners is "self–other integration": intertwined self-concepts (Slotter & Gardner, 2009; **Figure 7**).

Can self-disclosure create closeness even when it's prescribed by others? Arons and their collaborators (1997) wondered. They paired volunteer students who were strangers to each other to interact for 45 minutes. For the first 15 minutes, they shared thoughts on a list of personal but low-intimacy topics such as "When did you last sing to yourself?" The next 15 minutes were spent on more intimate topics such as "What is your most treasured memory?" The last 15 minutes invited even more self-disclosure, with questions such as "Complete this sentence: 'I wish I had someone with whom I could share . . .'" and "When did you last cry in front of another person? By yourself?"

Compared with control participants who spent the 45 minutes in small talk ("What was your high school like?" "What is your favorite holiday?"), those who experienced the escalating self-disclosure ended the hour feeling remarkably close to their conversation partners; in fact, "closer than the closest relationship in the lives of 30% of similar students," reported the researchers. These relationships surely were not yet marked by the loyalty and commitment of true friendship. Nevertheless, the experiment provides a striking demonstration of how readily a sense of closeness to others can grow, given open self-disclosure.

Dating relationships can also benefit from self-disclosure prescriptions. To promote self-disclosure in ongoing dating relationships, Richard Slatcher and James Pennebaker (2006) invited one member of 86 couples to spend 20 minutes on each of 3 days writing their deepest thoughts and feelings about the relationship (or, in a control condition, writing merely about their daily activities). Those who wrote about their feelings expressed more emotion to their partners in the days following. Three months later, 77% were still dating (compared with 52% in the control group). In summary: If you want to be close to others, open up.

SUMMING UP: What Enables Close Relationships?

- From infancy to old age, attachments are central to human life. *Secure attachments,* as in an enduring marriage, mark happy lives.
- Companionate love is most likely to endure when both partners feel the partnership is *equitable,* with both perceiving themselves receiving from the relationship in proportion to what they contribute to it.
- A reward of relationships is the opportunity for intimate *self-disclosure,* a state achieved gradually as each partner reciprocates the other's increasing openness *(disclosure reciprocity).*

HOW DO RELATIONSHIPS END?

Summarize the factors that predict marital dissolution and describe the detachment process.

In 1971, a man wrote a love poem to his bride, slipped it into a bottle, and dropped it into the Pacific Ocean between Seattle and Hawaii (*The New York Times,* 1981). A decade later, a jogger found it on a Guam beach:

> If, by the time this letter reaches you, I am old and gray, I know that our love will be as fresh as it is today.
>
> It may take a week or it may take years for this note to find you. . . . If this should never reach you, it will still be written in my heart that I will go to extreme means to prove my love for you. Your husband, Bob.

The woman to whom the love note was addressed was reached by phone. When the note was read to her, she burst out laughing. And the more she heard, the harder she laughed. "We're divorced," she finally said and slammed down the phone.

"When I was a young man, I vowed never to marry until I found the ideal woman. Well I found her — but alas, she was waiting for the ideal man."

—French Statesman Robert Schuman (1886–1963)

So it often goes. Comparing their unsatisfying relationship with the support and affection they imagine are available elsewhere, many relationships end. Each year, the United States records one divorce for every three marriages. If every relationship went perfectly, half of the music industry would cease to exist.

Divorce

To predict a culture's divorce rates, it helps to know its values (Triandis, 1994). Individualistic cultures (where love is a feeling and people ask, "What does my heart say?") have more divorce than do communal cultures (where love entails obligation and people ask, "What will other people say?"). Individualists marry "for as long as we both shall love," collectivists more often for life. Individualists expect more passion and personal fulfillment in a marriage, which puts greater pressure on the relationship (Dion & Dion, 1993; Yuki & Schug, 2020). Eli Finkel and his colleagues (2014, 2017) argue that marriage has become more challenging in individualistic recent times as couples expect more fulfillment from marriage but invest fewer resources in it – a potentially impossible equation.

Those who enter relationships with a long-term orientation and an intention to persist experience healthier, less turbulent, and more durable partnerships (Arriaga, 2001; Arriaga & Agnew, 2001). Enduring relationships are rooted in enduring love and satisfaction but also in fear of the termination cost, a sense of moral obligation, and inattention to possible alternative partners (Adams & Jones, 1997; Maner et al., 2009; Miller, 1997). For those determined that their marriage last, it usually does.

Those whose commitment to a union outlasts the desires that gave birth to it will endure times of conflict and unhappiness. One national survey found that 86% of those who were unhappily married but who stayed with the marriage were, when reinterviewed 5 years later, now mostly "very" or "quite" happy with their marriages (Popenoe, 2002). Too many ups and downs, though, may spell doom: Married couples with larger fluctuations in marital satisfaction over the years were more likely to divorce (Joiner et al., 2023).

The risk of divorce also depends on who marries whom (Bieber, 2023; Cohen, 2022; Fergusson et al., 1984; Myers, 2000a; Rosenfeld & Roesler, 2023). People usually stay married if they

- married after age 25,
- both grew up in stable, two-parent homes,
- dated for a long while before marriage,
- are well and similarly educated,
- enjoy a stable income from a good job,
- live in a small town or on a farm,
- did not cohabit or become pregnant before marriage,
- have support from family,
- are religiously committed,
- are of similar age, faith, and education.

None of those predictors, by itself, is essential to a stable marriage. Moreover, they are correlates of enduring marriages, not necessarily causes. But if none of those things is true for a couple, marital breakdown is an almost sure bet. If all are true, they are very likely to stay together until death. The English perhaps had it right when, several centuries ago, they presumed that the temporary intoxication of passionate love was a foolish basis for permanent marital decisions. Better, they felt, to choose a mate based on compatible backgrounds, interests, habits, and values (Stone, 1977).

The Detachment Process

Our close relationships help define the social identity that shapes our self-concept (Slotter et al., 2010). Thus, much as we experience life's best moments when relationships begin – when having a baby, making a friend, falling in love – so we experience life's worst

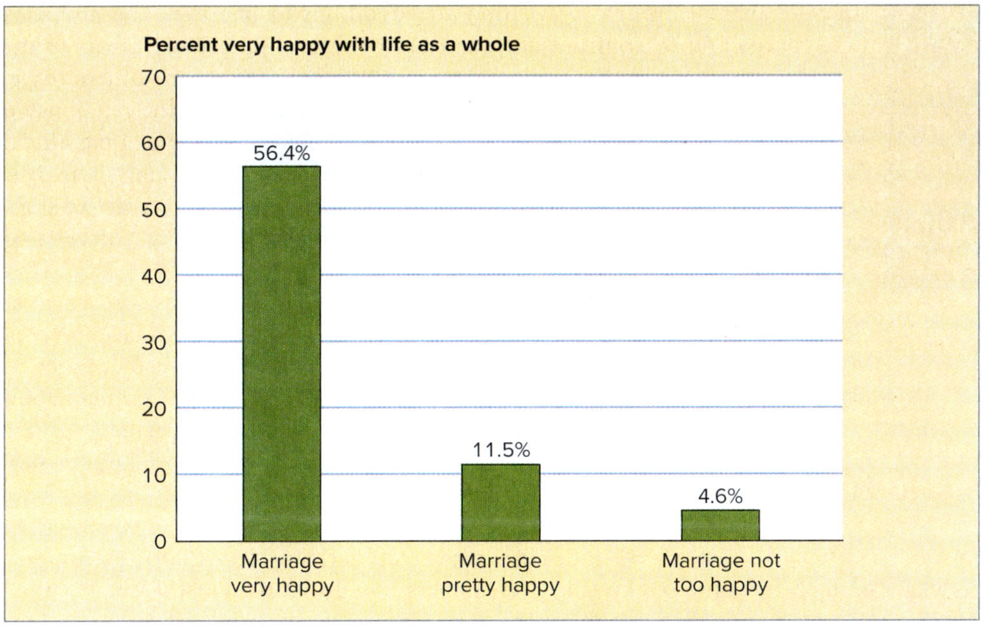

FIGURE 8
Surveys of 38,162 Married Americans, 1972–2022
Source: General Social Survey

moments when relationships end, with a broken bond or death (Jaremka et al., 2011). Severing bonds produces a predictable sequence of agitated preoccupation with the lost partner, followed by deep sadness and, eventually, the beginnings of emotional detachment, a letting go of the old while focusing on something new, and a renewed sense of self (Hazan & Shaver, 1994; Lewandowski & Bizzoco, 2007; Spielmann et al., 2009). Because humans often mate with more than one partner, we must have evolved psychological processes for cutting ties, a mechanism evolutionary psychologists dubbed the "mate ejection module" (Boutwell et al., 2015). However, deep and long-standing attachments seldom break quickly; detaching is a process, not a one-time event.

Among dating couples, the closer and longer the relationship and the fewer the available alternatives, the more painful the breakup (Simpson, 1987). Surprisingly, Roy Baumeister and Sara Wotman (1992) reported that, months or years later, people recall more pain over spurning someone's love than over having been spurned. Their distress arises from guilt over hurting someone, from upset over the heartbroken lover's persistence, or from uncertainty over how to respond. Among married couples, breakup has additional costs: shocked parents and friends, guilt over broken vows, anguish over reduced household income, and possibly less time with children. Still, each year, millions of couples are willing to pay such costs to extricate themselves from what they perceive as the greater costs of continuing a painful, unrewarding relationship. Such costs include depression: In one study, those in unhappy marriages were 10 times more likely to be depressed (O'Leary et al., 1994). When, however, a marriage is "very happy," life as a whole usually seems "very happy" **(Figure 8)**.

When relationships suffer, those without better alternatives or who feel invested in a relationship (through time, energy, mutual friends, possessions, and perhaps children) will seek alternatives to exiting the relationship. Caryl Rusbult and colleagues (1986, 1987, 1998) explored three ways of coping with a failing relationship **(Table 1)**. Some

TABLE 1 Responses to Relationship Distress

	Passive	Active
Constructive	*Loyalty:* Await improvement	*Voice:* Seek to improve relationships
Destructive	*Neglect:* Ignore the partner	*Exit:* End the relationship

Source: Rusbult et al., 1986, 1987, 1998, 2001.

Coldness, disillusionment, and hopelessness are better predictors of divorce than arguing.
PeopleImages.com-Yuri A/Shutterstock

people exhibit *loyalty* – by waiting for conditions to improve. The problems are too painful to confront and the risks of separation are too great, so the loyal partner perseveres, hoping the good old days will return. Others (especially men) exhibit *neglect;* they ignore the partner and allow the relationship to deteriorate. With painful dissatisfactions ignored, an insidious emotional uncoupling ensues as the partners talk less and begin redefining their lives without each other. Still others will *voice* their concerns and take active steps to improve the relationship by discussing problems, seeking advice, and attempting to change.

Study after study – in fact, 115 studies of 45,000 couples – reveal that unhappy couples disagree, command, criticize, and put down. Happy couples more often agree, approve, assent, and laugh (Karney & Bradbury, 1995; Noller & Fitzpatrick, 1990). After observing 2,000 couples, John Gottman (1994, 1998, 2005) noted that healthy marriages were not necessarily devoid of conflict. Rather, they were marked by an ability to reconcile differences and to overbalance criticism with affection. In successful marriages, positive interactions (smiling, touching, complimenting, laughing) outnumbered negative interactions (sarcasm, disapproval, insults) by at least a 5-to-1 ratio. In a paper summarizing more than 1,000 studies on maintaining a romantic relationship, researchers found that the most effective strategies included ignoring other possible partners, interpreting each other's behavior in a positive way, forgiving each other, helping each other, and praying for each other (Ogolsky et al., 2017).

It's not distress and arguments that predict divorce, added Ted Huston and colleagues (2001) from their following of newlyweds through time. (Most newlyweds experience conflict.) Rather, it's coldness, disillusionment, and hopelessness that predict a dim marital future. This is especially so, observed William Swann and associates (2003, 2006), when inhibited men are coupled with critical women.

Successful couples have learned, sometimes aided by communication training, to restrain the poisonous put-downs and gut-level reactions and to think and behave more positively (McNulty, 2010). They fight fairly (by stating feelings without insulting). They depersonalize conflict with comments such as, "I know it's not your fault" (Markman et al., 1988; Notarius & Markman, 1993; Yovetich & Rusbult, 1994). Couples randomly assigned to think less emotionally and more like an observer during fights were later more satisfied with their marriages (Finkel et al., 2013). Would unhappy relationships get better if the partners agreed to *act* more as happy couples do – by complaining and criticizing less? By affirming and agreeing more? By setting aside times to voice their concerns and doing so calmly? By praying or playing together daily? As attitudes trail behaviors, do affections trail actions?

Joan Kellerman, James Lewis, and James Laird (1989) wondered. They knew that among couples passionately in love, eye gazing is typically prolonged and mutual (Rubin, 1973). Would intimate eye gazing similarly stir feelings between those not in love (much as 45 minutes of escalating self-disclosure evoked feelings of closeness among those unacquainted students)? To find out, they asked unacquainted male–female pairs to gaze intently for 2 minutes either at each other's hands or into each other's eyes. When they separated, the eye gazers reported a tingle of attraction and affection toward each other. Simulating love had begun to stir it.

By enacting and expressing love, researcher Robert Sternberg (1988) believes the passion of initial romance can evolve into enduring love:

> "Living happily ever after" need not be a myth, but if it is to be a reality, the happiness must be based upon different configurations of mutual feelings at various times in a relationship. Couples who expect their passion to last forever, or their intimacy to remain unchallenged, are in for disappointment. . . . We must constantly work at understanding, building, and rebuilding our loving relationships. Relationships are constructions, and they decay over time if they are not maintained and improved. We cannot expect a relationship simply to take care of itself, any more than we can expect that of a building. Rather, we must take responsibility for making our relationships the best they can be.

SUMMING UP: How Do Relationships End?

- Often love does not endure. As divorce rates rose in the twentieth century, researchers discerned predictors of marital dissolution. One predictor is an individualistic culture that values feelings over commitment; other factors include the couple's age, education, values, and similarity.
- Researchers are also identifying the process through which couples either detach or rebuild their relationships. And they are identifying the positive and nondefensive communication styles that mark healthy, stable marriages.

CONCLUDING THOUGHTS: Making Love

Two facts of contemporary life seem beyond dispute: First, *close, enduring relationships are hallmarks of a happy life.* One example of a close relationship is marriage. In National Opinion Research Center surveys of 67,546 Americans from 1972 to 2022, 39% of married adults, 21% of those never married, 19% of the divorced, and 15% of the separated declared their lives "very happy." Similar results have come from national surveys in Canada and Europe as well as in East Asia (Hori & Kamo, 2018; Inglehart, 1990).

Second, *close, enduring relationships are in decline.* Increased migration and mobility mean that more people are disconnected from extended family and childhood relationships. Compared with a half-century ago, people today more often move, live alone, divorce, and have a succession of relationships.

Given the psychological ingredients of marital happiness – kindred minds, social and sexual intimacy, equitable giving and receiving of emotional and material resources – it becomes possible to contest the French saying "Love makes the time pass and time makes love pass." But it takes effort to stem love's decay. It takes effort to carve out time each day to talk over the day's happenings. It takes effort to forgo nagging and bickering and instead to disclose and hear each other's hurts, concerns, and dreams. It takes effort to make a relationship into "a classless utopia of social equality" (Sarnoff & Sarnoff, 1989), in which both partners freely give and receive, share decision making, and enjoy life together.

By minding our close relationships, sustained satisfaction is possible, noted John Harvey and Julia Omarzu (1997). Australian relationships researcher Patricia Noller (1996) concurred: "Mature love . . . love that sustains marriage and family as it creates an environment in which individual family members can grow . . . is sustained by beliefs that love involves acknowledging and accepting differences and weaknesses; that love involves an internal decision to love another person and a long-term commitment to maintain that love; and finally that love is controllable and needs to be nurtured and nourished by the lovers."

For those who commit themselves to creating an equitable, intimate, mutually supportive relationship, there may come the security, and the joy, of enduring, companionate love. This is echoed in the classic children's story *The Velveteen Rabbit.* When someone "loves you for a long, long time," explained the wise, old Skin Horse to the Velveteen Rabbit, "not just to play with, but REALLY loves you, then you become Real. . . ."

> "Does it happen all at once, like being wound up," [the rabbit] asked, "or bit by bit?"
>
> "It doesn't happen all at once," said the Skin Horse. "You become. It takes a long time. That's why it doesn't often happen to people who break easily, or have sharp edges, or who have to be carefully kept. Generally, by the time you are Real, most of your hair has been loved off, and your eyes drop out and you get loose in the joints and very shabby. But these things don't matter at all, because once you are Real you can't be ugly, except to people who don't understand."

Helping

CHAPTER

12

Paul Hennessy/SOPA Images/ZUMA Press Wire/Alamy Stock Photo

"Love cures people — both the ones who give it and the ones who receive it."

—Psychiatrist Karl Menninger, "An Autumn Visit with Dr. Karl," 1969

On a hillside in Jerusalem, some 2000 trees form the Garden of the Righteous. Beneath each tree is a plaque with the name of those who gave refuge to one or more Jews during the Nazi Holocaust. These "righteous Gentiles" knew that if the refugees were discovered, Nazi policy dictated that host and refugee would suffer a common fate. Many did (Hellman, 1980; Wiesel, 1985).

One hero who did not survive was Jane Haining, a Church of Scotland missionary who was matron at a school for 400 mostly Jewish girls. On the eve of war, the church, fearing her safety, ordered her to return home. She refused, saying, "If these children need me in days of sunshine, how much more do they need me in days of darkness?" (Barnes, 2008; Brown, 2008). She reportedly cut up her leather luggage to make soles for her girls' shoes. In April 1944, Haining accused a cook of eating sparse food rations intended for the girls. The cook, a Nazi party member, denounced her to the Gestapo, who arrested her for having worked among the Jews. A few weeks later, she was sent to Auschwitz, where she died, suffering the same fate as millions of Jews.

Eight decades later, 21-year-old Riley Howell tackled a gunman who opened fire in a classroom at the University of North Carolina at Charlotte. Howell was shot three times as he charged the gunman, but he brought the assailant to the ground. By ending the shooter's rampage, Riley Howell saved the lives of many, while sacrificing his own (Dwyer & Ward, 2019).

Less dramatic acts of comforting, caring, and compassion abound. Without asking anything in return, people offer directions, donate money, give blood, volunteer time. Most people underestimate just how helpful their fellow humans are willing to be, how good they will feel when they help, and how impactful kindness can be on others (Kumar & Epley, 2023; Zhao & Epley, 2022). Help and kindness go further than we might think. Thus, we ask:

- Why, and when, will people help?
- Who will help?
- What can be done to lessen indifference and increase helping?

These are this chapter's primary questions.

WHY DO WE HELP?

Explain psychology's theories of what motivates helping — and the type of helping each theory seeks to explain.

Altruism is selfishness in reverse. An altruistic person is concerned and helpful even when no benefits are offered or expected in return.

altruism
A motive to increase another's welfare without conscious regard for one's self-interests.

Social Exchange and Social Norms

Several theories of helping agree that, in the long run, helping behavior benefits the helper as well as the helped. Why? One explanation assumes that human interactions are guided by "social economics." We exchange not only material goods and money but also social goods: love, services, information, status (Foa & Foa, 1975). In doing so, we aim to minimize costs and maximize rewards. **Social-exchange theory** does not contend that we consciously monitor costs and rewards, only that such considerations predict our behavior.

social-exchange theory
The theory that human interactions are transactions that aim to maximize one's rewards and minimize one's costs.

Suppose your campus is having a blood drive and someone asks you to participate. You might implicitly weigh the *costs* of donating (needle prick, time, fatigue) against those of not donating (guilt, disapproval). You might also weigh the *benefits* of donating (feeling good about helping someone, free refreshments) against those of not donating (saving the time, discomfort, and anxiety). According to social-exchange theory, such subtle calculations precede decisions to help or not.

INCREASING POSITIVE EMOTION

Rewards that motivate helping may be external or internal. A New Yorker who jumped onto subway tracks to save a man who had fainted was motivated by the external rewards of his time-and-a-half Sunday pay. "I was thinking, if he gets hit, I can't go to work," he said (Weischelbaum et al., 2010). When businesses donate money to improve their corporate images or when someone offers a ride hoping to receive appreciation or friendship, the reward is external. We give to get. Thus, we are most eager to help someone attractive to us, someone whose approval we desire (Krebs, 1970; Unger, 1979). In experiments and in everyday life, public generosity boosts one's status, while selfish behavior can lead to punishment (Hardy & Van Vugt, 2006; Henrich et al., 2006). Around the world, people who help others earn

Schoolchildren packing donations for disaster survivors. As children mature, they usually come to take pleasure in helping others.
Pamela Moore/fstop123/E+/Getty Images

more money, perform better at their jobs, and have more children (Allen et al., 2023; Eriksson et al., 2018; Kosse & Tincani, 2020; Liao et al., 2022).

Rewards may also be internal, often focused on increasing positive emotions. Nearly all blood donors agree that giving blood "makes you feel good about yourself" and "gives you a feeling of self-satisfaction" (Piliavin, 2003; Piliavin et al., 1982). "Give blood," advises an old Red Cross poster. "All you'll feel is good." Feeling good helps explain why people far from home will do kindnesses for strangers whom they will never see again.

Helping's boost to self-worth explains this *do-good/feel-good effect*. One month-long study of 85 couples found that giving emotional support to one's partner was positive for the *giver* by boosting the giver's mood (Gleason et al., 2003). Bereaved spouses recover from their depressed feelings faster when they are engaged in helping others (Brown et al., 2008, 2009). People who volunteer and help others report finding more meaning in life, experience more happiness and life satisfaction, and increase in self-confidence (Eskreis-Winkler et al., 2018; Hui et al., 2020; Joshanloo & Bond, 2022; Klein, 2017; Weinstein & Ryan, 2010).

Some have even suggested that health care providers should actually prescribe volunteering to improve mood and physical health (Johnson & Post, 2017). It might be good advice: In one experiment, depressed people who were randomly assigned to be kind to others later felt less depressed and more satisfied with their lives (Cregg & Cheavens, 2023). And among older adults, those who volunteered were not only happier and less lonely but were also 32% to 40% less likely to die over the next 4 years (Kim et al., 2020; Nakamura et al., 2023).

Jane Piliavin (2003) and Susan Andersen (1998) reviewed studies that showed that youth who engaged in community service projects, participated in school-based "service learning," or tutored children developed social skills and positive social values. Such young people are at markedly less risk for delinquency, pregnancy, and school dropout and are more likely to become engaged citizens. Those who do good tend to do well.

Same for giving money. Making donations activates brain areas linked with reward (Harbaugh et al., 2007). Generous people are happier than those whose spending is self-focused. In one experiment, some people given an envelope of cash were told to spend it on themselves, while others were directed to spend the money on other people. At the day's end, those who spent their money on others were happier (Aknin et al., 2020; Dunn et al., 2008; Dunn & Norton, 2013; Geenen et al., 2014). People instructed to help others experienced an immune system boost, while those asked to engage in self-focused kindness did not (Nelson-Coffey et al., 2017). Other research confirms that *giving increases happiness:*

- In a survey of more than 200,000 people in 136 countries, people felt happier after spending money on others rather than on themselves (Aknin et al., 2013, 2015). Even those once incarcerated for violent crimes feel more happiness when giving to others rather than to themselves (Hanniball et al., 2019). Givers are also less prone to depression than nongivers (Smith & Davidson, 2014).
- Giving employees "prosocial bonuses" – charitable donations to spend on others or on teammates rather than themselves – produces "happier and more satisfied employees" and higher-performing work teams (Anik et al., 2013).
- Purchasing a goody bag for a sick child improves people's mood enough for others to notice their increased happiness (Aknin et al., 2014).
- While the happiness boost of *receiving* money or gifts declines over time, the happiness boost of *giving* to others remains high (O'Brien & Kassirer, 2019).

Giving to others feels better than spending money on ourselves.
Blue Jean Images/Alamy Stock Photo

This cost-benefit analysis – people help because it makes them feel good – can seem cold. In defense of the theory, however, it is a credit to humanity that helping can be inherently rewarding, that much of our behavior is not antisocial but "prosocial," and that we can find fulfillment in the giving of love. The human race would be worse off if we gained pleasure only by serving ourselves.

"For it is in giving that we receive."

—Saint Francis of Assisi, (1181–1226)

REDUCING NEGATIVE EMOTION

The benefits of helping also include reducing or avoiding negative emotions. Near someone in distress, we may feel distress. Someone's scream outside your window arouses and distresses you. Horror movies distress us because we empathize with the frightened victims. If you cannot reduce your arousal by interpreting the scream as a playful shriek, then you may investigate or give aid, thereby reducing your distress (Piliavin & Piliavin, 1973). Altruism researcher Dennis Krebs (1975; see "The Inside Story: Dennis Krebs on Life Experience and the Study of Altruism") found that Harvard University men who were the most upset at another's distress also gave the most help to the person. Sure enough, the brains of "extraordinary altruists" – people who donated a kidney to a stranger, for example – reacted more strongly to images of fearful faces. Their amygdala (the part of the brain that reacts to fear) was also larger than average (Marsh et al., 2014).

GUILT

Distress is not the only negative emotion we act to reduce. Throughout recorded history, guilt has been a painful emotion that people avoid and seek to relieve (Ty et al., 2017). As Everett Sanderson remarked after heroically saving a child who had fallen onto subway tracks in front of an approaching train, "If I hadn't tried to save that little girl, if I had just stood there like the others, I would have died inside. I would have been no good to myself from then on."

Cultures have institutionalized ways to relieve guilt: animal and human sacrifices, offerings of grain and money, penitent behavior, confession, denial. In ancient Israel, the sins of the people were periodically laid on a "scapegoat" animal – usually a goat, and thus the term – that was then led into the wilderness to carry away the people's guilt.

THE inside STORY

Dennis Krebs on Life Experience and the Study of Altruism

At age 14, I was traumatized when my family moved from Vancouver, B.C., to California. I fell from president of my junior high school to an object of social ridicule because of my clothes, accent, and behavior. The fighting skills I had acquired boxing soon generated a quite different reputation from the one I enjoyed in Canada. I sank lower and lower until, after several visits to juvenile detention homes, I was arrested and convicted for driving under the influence of drugs. I escaped from jail, hitchhiked to a logging camp in Oregon, and eventually made my way back to British Columbia. I was admitted to university on probation, graduated at the top of my class, won a Woodrow Wilson Fellowship, and was accepted to a psychology doctoral program at Harvard.

Attending Harvard required moving back to the United States. Concerned about my escapee record in California, I turned myself in and suffered through the ensuing publicity. I was pardoned, in large part because of the tremendous support I received from many people. After 3 years at Harvard, I was hired as an assistant professor. Eventually I returned to British Columbia to chair the Psychology Department at Simon Fraser University.

Though it makes me somewhat uncomfortable, I disclose this history as a way of encouraging people with two strikes against them to remain in the game. A great deal of the energy I have invested in understanding morality has stemmed from a need to understand why I went wrong, and my interest in altruism has been fueled by the generosity of those who helped me overcome my past.

Dennis Krebs
Simon Fraser University
Courtesy of Dennis Krebs

To examine the consequences of guilt, social psychologists have induced people to transgress: to lie, to deliver shock, to knock over a table loaded with alphabetized cards, to break a machine, to cheat. Afterward, the guilt-laden participants may be offered a way to relieve their guilt – by confessing, by disparaging the one harmed, or by doing a good deed to offset the bad one. The results are remarkably consistent: People will do whatever can be done to expunge the guilt, relieve their bad feelings, and restore their self-image (Ding et al., 2016; Ilies et al., 2013; Sachdeva et al., 2009; Xu et al., 2011).

Picture yourself as a participant in one such experiment conducted with Mississippi State University students (McMillen & Austin, 1971). You and another student, each seeking to earn credit toward a course requirement, arrive for the experiment. Soon after, an accomplice enters, portraying himself as a previous participant looking for a lost book. He mentions that the experiment involves taking a multiple-choice test and that most of the correct answers are "B." After the accomplice departs, the experimenter arrives, explains the experiment, and then asks, "Have you been in this experiment before or heard anything about it?"

Would you lie? The behavior of those who have gone before you in this experiment – 100% of whom told a little lie by answering no – suggests that you would. After you have taken the test (without receiving any feedback on it), the experimenter says, "You are free to leave. However, if you have some spare time, I could use your help in scoring some questionnaires." Assuming you have told the lie, do you think you would now be more or less willing to volunteer some time? Those who had lied were apparently eager to redeem their self-images; on average, they offered a whopping 63 minutes – compared to only 2 minutes for those who had not been induced to lie. One moral of this experiment was well expressed by a 7-year-old girl, who, in one of my [DM] own experiments, wrote: "Don't Lie or youl Live with gilt."

Our eagerness to do good after doing bad reflects our need to reduce *private* guilt and restore a shaken self-image. It also reflects our desire to reclaim a positive *public* image. We are more likely to redeem ourselves with helpful behavior when other people know about our misdeeds (Carlsmith & Gross, 1969).

All in all, guilt leads to much good. By motivating people to confess, apologize, help, and avoid repeated harm, guilt boosts sensitivity and sustains close relationships.

EXCEPTIONS TO THE FEEL-BAD/DO-GOOD SCENARIO Should we always expect to find the "feel-bad/do-good" phenomenon? No, because there are different types of negative emotions. One negative mood, anger, produces anything but compassion. Another exception is profound grief. People who suffer the loss of a spouse or a child, whether through death or separation, often undergo a period of intense self-preoccupation, which restrains giving to others (Aderman & Berkowitz, 1983; Gibbons & Wicklund, 1982).

In a powerful laboratory simulation of self-focused grief, William Thompson, Claudia Cowan, and David Rosenhan (1980) had Stanford University students listen privately to a taped description of a person (whom they were to imagine was their best friend) dying of cancer. The experiment focused some students' attention on their own worry and grief:

> He (she) could die and you would lose him, never be able to talk to him again. Or worse, he could die slowly. You would know every minute could be your last time together. For months you would have to be cheerful for him while you were sad. You would have to watch him die in pieces, until the last piece finally went, and you would be alone.

For others, it focused their attention on the friend:

> He spends his time lying in bed, waiting those interminable hours, just waiting and hoping for something to happen. Anything. He tells you that it's not knowing that is the hardest.

When given a chance to help a graduate student with their research, 25% of those whose attention had been self-focused helped. Of those whose attention was other-focused, 83% helped. The two groups were equally touched, but only the other-focused participants found helping someone especially rewarding. The same applies in more everyday scenarios: In a study of heterosexual couples, husbands experiencing chronic stress – often a self-focused state of mind – were less likely to notice when their wives needed help and support (Neff et al., 2021).

In short, the feel-bad/do-good effect occurs with people whose attention is on others, not on themselves – a state of mind that apparently makes altruism more rewarding (Barnett et al., 1980; McMillen et al., 1977). If they are not self-preoccupied by depression, grief, or stress, sad people are often sensitive, helpful people.

FEEL GOOD, DO GOOD *Positive* emotions can also lead to helping. There are few more consistent findings in psychology: Happy people are helpful people. This effect occurs with both children and adults, regardless of whether the good mood comes from a success, from thinking happy thoughts, or from any of several other positive experiences (Salovey et al., 1991). One woman recalled her experience after falling in love:

> At the office, I could hardly keep from shouting out how deliriously happy I felt. The work was easy; things that had annoyed me on previous occasions were taken in stride. And I had strong impulses to help others; I wanted to share my joy. When Mary's typewriter broke down, I virtually sprang to my feet to assist. Mary! My former "enemy"! (Tennov, 1979, p. 22)

"It's curious how, when you're in love, you yearn to go about doing acts of kindness to everybody."

—P. G. Wodehouse, *The Mating Season*, 1949

In experiments on happiness and helpfulness, the person who is helped may be someone seeking a donation, an experimenter seeking help with paperwork, or a woman who drops papers. Here are three examples.

In Sydney, Australia, Joseph Forgas and colleagues (2008) had an accomplice offer either a mood-boosting compliment or a mood-deflating criticism to a salesperson. Moments later, a second accomplice arrived and sought the salesperson's help in locating a nonexistent item. Those receiving the mood boost made the greatest effort to help.

In Opole, Poland, Dariusz Dolinski and Richard Nawrat (1998) found that a positive mood of relief can dramatically boost helping. Imagine yourself as one of their unwitting participants. After illegally parking your car for a few moments, you return to discover what looks like a parking ticket under your windshield wiper. Groaning inwardly, you pick up the apparent ticket and then are much relieved to discover it is only an ad. Moments later, a university student approaches you and asks you to spend 15 minutes answering questions – to "help me complete my M.A. thesis." Would your positive, relieved mood make you more likely to help? Indeed, 62% of people whose fear had just turned to relief agreed willingly. That was nearly double the number who did so when no ticketlike paper was left or when it was left on the car door (not a place for a ticket).

In the United States, back when pay phones were used, Alice Isen, Margaret Clark, and Mark Schwartz (1976) had an accomplice call people who had just received a free sample of stationery 0 to 20 minutes earlier. The accomplice said she had used her last dime to dial this (supposedly wrong) number and asked each person to relay a message by phone. As **Figure 1** shows, the individuals' willingness to relay the phone message rose during the 5 minutes after getting the free sample. Then, as the good mood wore off, helpfulness dropped.

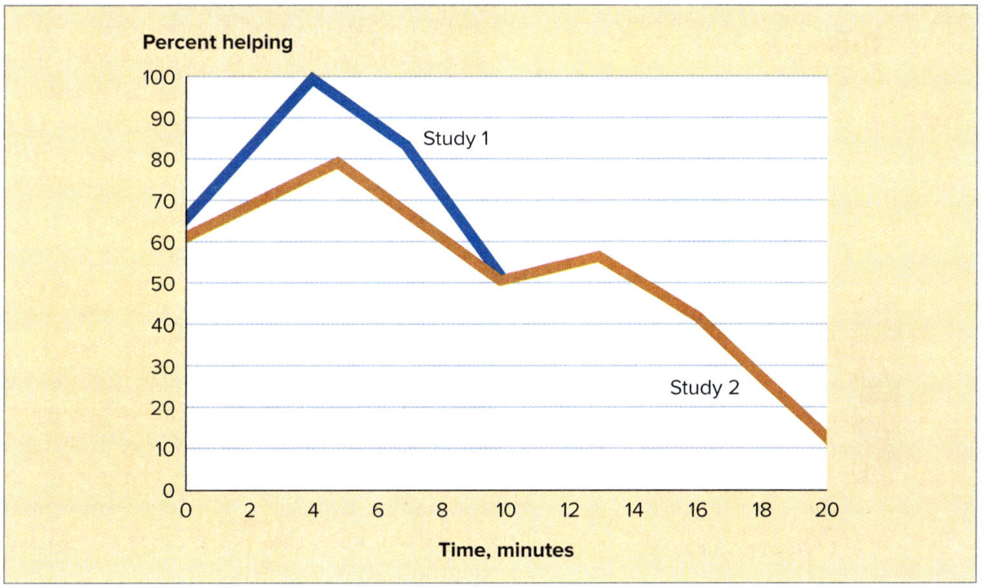

FIGURE 1

Percentage of Participants Willing to Relay a Phone Message 0 to 20 Minutes after Receiving a Free Sample

Of control subjects who did not receive a gift, only 10% helped.

Source: Data from Isen et al., 1976.

Why are happy people helpful? Experiments reveal several factors at work (Carlson et al., 1988). Helping softens a bad mood and sustains a good mood. (Perhaps you can recall feeling good after giving someone directions.) A positive mood is, in turn, conducive to positive thoughts and positive self-esteem, which predispose us to positive behavior (Berkowitz, 1987; Cunningham et al., 1990; Isen et al., 1978). In a good mood – after receiving a gift or while feeling the warm glow of success – people are more likely to have positive thoughts. And positive thinkers are likely to be positive actors . . . which helps explain why, even after controlling for other demographic factors, extraordinary acts of altruism tend to come from happy places. The areas of the United States with the happiest people are also the places with the highest rates of kidney donations (Brethel-Haurwitz & Marsh, 2014). Sunny days in New York City – when people were presumably in sunnier moods – were also days when riders tipped their taxi drivers more (Deveraj & Patel, 2017).

SOCIAL NORMS

Often, we help others not because we have calculated consciously that such behavior is in our self-interest but because of a subtler form of self-interest: we *ought* to. We ought to help a new neighbor move in. We ought to return the wallet we found. We ought to protect our combat buddies from harm. Norms, the *oughts* of our lives, are social expectations. They *prescribe* proper behavior. Researchers who study helping behavior have identified two social norms that motivate altruism: the reciprocity norm and the social-responsibility norm.

reciprocity norm
An expectation that people will help, not hurt, those who have helped them.

social capital
The mutual support and cooperation enabled by a social network.

"If you don't go to somebody's funeral, they won't come to yours."

—Yogi Berra

THE RECIPROCITY NORM One universal moral code is a **reciprocity norm:** *We should return help, not harm, to those who help us* (Gouldner, 1960; Melamed et al., 2020). We "invest" in others and expect dividends. Politicians know that the one who gives a favor can later expect a favor. Mail surveys and solicitations sometimes include a little gift of money or personalized address labels, assuming some people will reciprocate the favor. Even 21-month-old infants display reciprocity by being more willing to help someone who has tried to give them a toy (Dunfield & Kuhlmeier, 2010). The reciprocity norm also applies within a marriage. At times, you may give more than you receive, but in the long run, the exchange should balance out. In all such interactions, to receive without giving in return violates the reciprocity norm.

Reciprocity within social networks helps define the **social capital** – the supportive connections, information flow, trust, and cooperative actions – that keep a community healthy. Neighbors keeping an eye on one another's homes is social capital in action.

The norm operates most effectively as people respond publicly to deeds earlier done to them. In laboratory games as in everyday life, fleeting one-shot encounters produce greater selfishness than sustained relationships. But even when people respond anonymously, they sometimes do the right thing and repay the good done to them (Burger et al., 2009). In one experiment, university students more willingly made a charity pledge when they were asked by someone who had previously bought them some candy (Whatley et al., 1999; **Figure 2**).

When people cannot reciprocate, they may feel threatened and demeaned by accepting aid. Thus, proud, high-self-esteem people are often reluctant to seek help (Nadler & Fisher, 1986). Receiving unsolicited help can take one's self-esteem down a notch (Schneider et al., 1996; Shell & Eisenberg, 1992). People in Asia, for whom social ties and the reciprocity norm are stronger than for North Americans, are more likely to refuse a gift from a casual acquaintance to avoid the perceived need to reciprocate (Shen et al., 2011).

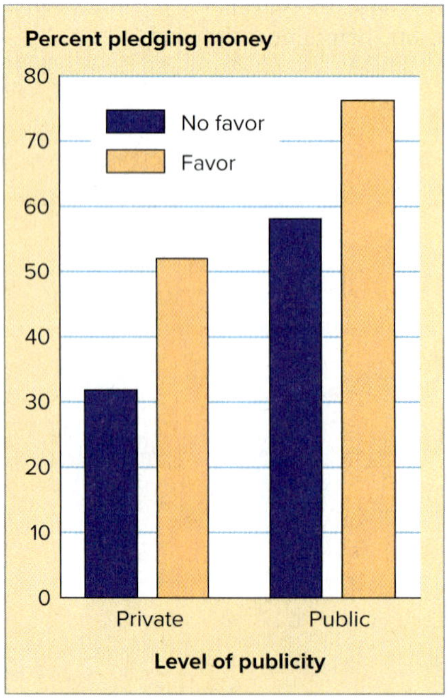

FIGURE 2

Private and Public Reciprocation of a Favor

People were more willing to give to an experimental accomplice's charity if the accomplice had done a small favor for them earlier, especially when their reciprocation was made known to the accomplice.
Source: Whatley et al., 1999.

The practical moral is that we should offer our children and our friends needed support but not provide so much support that we undermine their sense of competence (Finkel & Fitzsimmons, 2013). Support should supplement, rather than substitute for, others' actions.

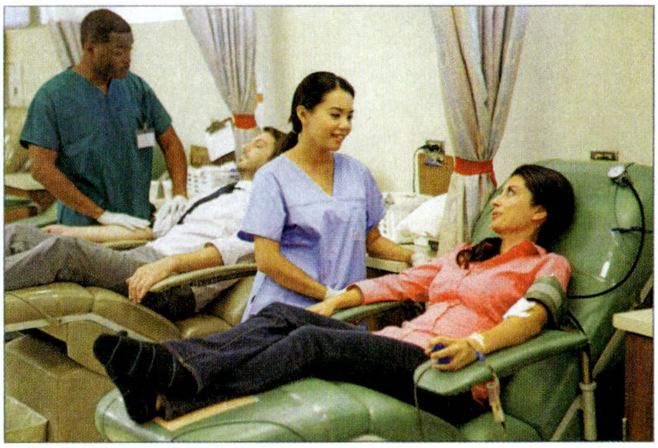

Blood donors respond to the social responsibility norm.
stockbroker/123RF

THE SOCIAL-RESPONSIBILITY NORM The reciprocity norm reminds us to balance giving and receiving. With people who are unable to reciprocate, such as children, the severely impoverished, and those with disabilities, however, a different social norm motivates helping. The **social-responsibility** norm decrees that people should help those who need help, without regard to future exchanges (Berkowitz, 1972; Schwartz, 1975). This social responsibility norm has a long history, as evident from archeological discoveries of 7,500-year-old skeletons of people who were severely crippled and unable to feed or care for themselves, yet able to survive thanks to others' compassionate care (Gorman, 2012). If a person on crutches drops a book, you honor the social responsibility norm as you pick it up. In India, a relatively collectivistic culture, people support the social-responsibility norm more strongly than in the individualistic West (Baron & Miller, 2000). They voice an obligation to help even when the need is not life threatening or the needy person – perhaps a stranger needing a bone marrow transplant – is outside their family circle.

social-responsibility norm
An expectation that people will help those needing help.

Even when helpers in Western countries remain anonymous and have no expectation of any reward, they often help people in need (Shotland & Stebbins, 1983). However, they usually apply the social-responsibility norm selectively to those whose need appears not to be due to their own negligence. Especially among political conservatives (Skitka & Tetlock, 1993), the norm seems to be: Give people what they deserve. If they are victims of circumstance, such as natural disaster, then by all means be compassionate (Goetz et al., 2010; Zagefka et al., 2011). If they seem to have created their own problems (by laziness, immorality, or lack of foresight, for example), then, the norm suggests, they don't deserve help.

Responses are thus closely tied to *attributions.* If we attribute the need to an uncontrollable predicament, we help. If we attribute the need to the person's choices, fairness does not require us to help; we say it's the person's own fault (Weiner, 1980). Attributions affect public policy as well as individual helping decisions. The key is whether your attributions evoke sympathy, which in turn motivates helping (Rudolph et al., 2004; **Figure 3**).

For example, imagine yourself as one of the University of Wisconsin students receiving a call from "Tony Freeman," who explains that he is in your introductory psychology class (Barnes et al., 1979). He says that he needs help for the upcoming exam and that he has gotten your name from the class roster. "I don't know. I just don't seem to take good notes in there," Tony explains. "I know I can, but sometimes I just don't feel like it, so most of the notes I have aren't very good to study with." How sympathetic would you feel toward Tony? How much of a sacrifice would you make to lend him your notes? If you are like the students in this experiment, you would probably be much less inclined to help in this

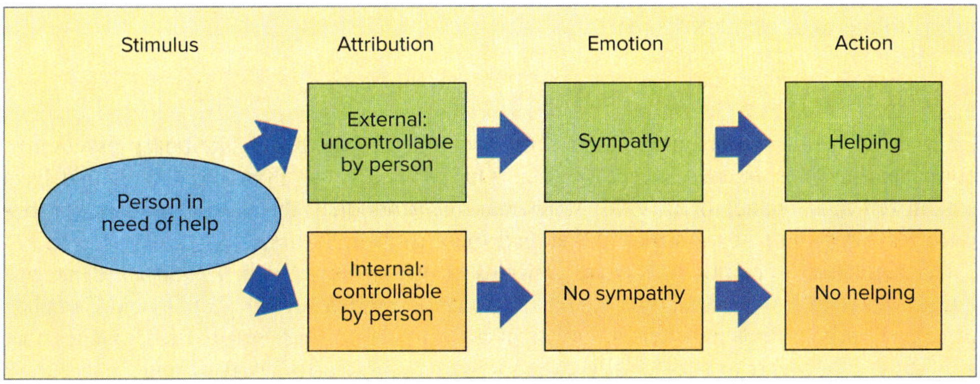

FIGURE 3

Attributions and Helping
In this model, proposed by German researcher Udo Rudolph and colleagues (2004), helping is mediated by people's perceptions of the predicament and their resulting degree of sympathy.

When the *Titanic* sank, 70% of the females and 20% of the males survived. The chances of survival were 2.5 times better for a first- than a third-class passenger. Yet, thanks to gender norms for altruism, the survival odds were better for third-class passengers who were women (47%) than for first-class passengers who were men (31%).
Everett Historical/Shutterstock

situation, with Tony sounding lazy and unmotivated, than if Tony had explained that his troubles were beyond his control – such as missing classes due to illness. Thus, the social-responsibility norm compels us to help those most in need and those most deserving.

GENDER AND RECEIVING HELP Do women receive more help than men? Alice Eagly and Maureen Crowley (1986) located 35 studies that compared help received by men and women in need and found women received more help. (Virtually all the studies involved short-term encounters with strangers in need – the very situations in which people expect males to be chivalrous, noted Eagly and Crowley.)

Women offered help equally to males and females, whereas men offered more help when the persons in need were females. Several experiments in the 1970s found that women with a car that had a flat tire got many more offers of help than did men (Penner et al., 1973; Pomazal & Clore, 1973; West et al., 1975). Of course, men's chivalry toward lone women may have been motivated by something other than altruism. And men more frequently helped attractive than unattractive women (Mims et al., 1975; Pazhoohi & Burriss, 2016; Stroufe et al., 1977; West & Brown, 1975), including when the request for help came via social media (Schwarz & Baßfeld, 2019). There may also be a gendered power dynamic at work: About two-thirds of men were willing to give money to a woman whose house had burned down, but less than half were willing to give money to a woman whose business had burned down, with no differences in donations for house vs. business when the recipient was male (Bareket et al., 2022).

Women not only receive more offers of help in certain situations but also seek more help (Addis & Mahalik, 2003; Liddon et al., 2018; Nagai et al., 2023). They are twice as likely to seek medical and psychiatric help. They more often welcome help from friends. Arie Nadler (1991), a Tel Aviv University expert on help seeking, attributed this to gender differences in individualism versus collectivism: women are more collectivistic and thus more willing to ask others to help.

Evolutionary Psychology

"Fallen heroes do not have children. If self-sacrifice results in fewer descendants, the genes that allow heroes to be created can be expected to disappear gradually from the population."

—E. O. Wilson, *On Human Nature*, 1978

Another explanation of helping comes from evolutionary theory. Evolutionary psychology contends that life's essence is gene survival. Our genes drive us in adaptive ways that have maximized their chance of survival. When our ancestors died, their genes lived on, predisposing us to behave in ways that will spread them into the future.

As suggested by the title of Richard Dawkins's (1976) popular book *The Selfish Gene,* evolutionary psychology offers a humbling human image – one that psychologist Donald Campbell (1975a,b) called a biological reaffirmation of a deep, self-serving "original sin." Genes that predispose individuals to self-sacrifice in the interests of strangers' welfare would not survive in the evolutionary competition. Evolutionary success does, however, come from cooperation. Humans are the animal kingdom's supercooperators because we exhibit multiple mechanisms for overcoming selfishness (Nowak & Highfield, 2011; Pfaff, 2014), including the following:

- *Kin selection:* If you carry my genes, I'll favor you.
- *Reciprocity:* We scratch each other's backs.
- *Group selection:* Back-scratching groups survive.

We consider each of these mechanisms below.

KIN SELECTION

Our genes dispose us to care for relatives. Thus, one form of self-sacrifice that *would* increase gene survival is devotion to one's children, a primal form of altruism embedded in parents' brains (Preston, 2013). Compared with neglectful parents, parents who prioritize their children's welfare are more likely to pass their genes on. As evolutionary psychologist David Barash (1979, p. 153) wrote, "Genes help themselves by being nice to themselves, even if they are enclosed in different bodies." Genetic egoism (at the biological level) fosters parental altruism (at the psychological level). Although evolution favors self-sacrifice for one's children, children have less at stake in the survival of their parents' genes. Thus, parents will generally be more devoted to their children than their children are to them.

"When people ask me how I'm doing, I say, 'I'm only as good as my most sad child.'"
—Michelle Obama, October 24, 2008

Other relatives share genes in proportion to their biological closeness. You share one-half of your genes with your brothers and sisters and one-eighth with your cousins. **Kin selection** – favoritism toward those who share our genes – led the evolutionary biologist J. B. S. Haldane to jest that although he would not give up his life for his brother, he would sacrifice himself for *three* brothers – or for nine cousins. Haldane would not have been surprised that genetic relatedness predicts helping and that genetically identical twins are noticeably more mutually supportive than fraternal twins (Segal, 1984; Stewart-Williams, 2007). In one laboratory game experiment, identical twins were twice as likely as fraternal twins to cooperate with their twin for a shared gain when playing for money (Segal & Hershberger, 1999).

kin selection
The idea that evolution has selected altruism toward one's close relatives to enhance the survival of mutually shared genes.

The kin selection principle implies that nature (as well as culture) programs us to care about close relatives (Lynch et al., 2020). When Carlos Rogers of the Toronto Raptors NBA basketball team volunteered to end his career and donate a kidney to his sister, people applauded his self-sacrificial love. But such acts for close kin are not totally unexpected. What we do not expect (and therefore honor) is the altruism of those who risk themselves to save a stranger.

Also, in evolutionary history, genes were shared more with neighbors than with foreigners. In the aftermath of natural disasters and other life-and-death situations, the order of who gets helped would not surprise an evolutionary psychologist: the children before the old, family members before friends, neighbors before strangers (Burnstein et al., 1994; Form & Nosow, 1958). We feel more empathy for a distressed or tortured person in our ingroup and even *Schadenfreude* (secret pleasure at another's misfortune) for rival or outgroup members (Batson et al., 2009; Cikara et al., 2011; Tarrant et al., 2009). People consistently donate more to individuals and organizations that are close by (Touré-Tillery & Fishbach, 2017). Helping stays close to home.

Some evolutionary psychologists note that kin selection predisposes ethnic ingroup favoritism – the root of countless historical and contemporary conflicts (Rushton, 1991). E. O. Wilson (1978) noted that kin selection is "the enemy of civilization. If human beings are to a large extent guided . . . to favor their own relatives and tribe, only a limited amount of global harmony is possible" (p. 167).

"Let's say you're walking by a pond and there's a drowning baby. If you said, 'I've just paid $200 for these shoes and the water would ruin them, so I won't save the baby,' you'd be an awful, horrible person. But there are millions of children around the world in the same situation, where just a little money for medicine or food could save their lives. And yet we don't consider ourselves monsters for having this dinner rather than giving the money to Oxfam. Why is that?"
—Philosopher-psychologist Joshua Greene, quoted by C. Zimmer in "The Neurobiology of the Self," 2005.

RECIPROCITY

Genetic self-interest also predicts reciprocity. An organism helps another, biologist Robert Trivers argued, because it expects help in return (Binham, 1980). The giver expects later to be the getter. Failure to reciprocate gets punished. People despise the cheat, the turncoat, the traitor.

Reciprocity works best in small, isolated groups in which people often see the others for whom they do favors. Sociable female baboons – those who groom and stay in close

Reciprocity: If you help me, I will help you.
Westend61/SuperStock

contact with their peers – gain a reproductive advantage: Their infants more often live to see a first birthday (Silk et al., 2003). If a vampire bat has gone a day or two without food, a well-fed nestmate will regurgitate food for a meal (Wilkinson, 1990). The donor bat does so willingly, losing fewer hours until starvation than the recipient gains. But such favors occur only among familiar nestmates who share in the give-and-take. Those who always take and never give and those who have no relationship with the donor bat go hungry. It pays to have friends.

GROUP SELECTION

If individual self-interest inevitably wins in genetic competition, then why will we help strangers? Why will we help those whose limited resources or abilities preclude their reciprocating? And what causes soldiers to throw themselves on grenades? One answer, initially favored by Darwin, is *group selection:* Groups of mutually supportive altruists outlast groups of nonaltruists (Krebs, 1998; McAndrew, 2002; Wilson, 2015). This is most dramatically evident with the social insects, which function like cells in a body. Bees and ants will labor sacrificially for their colony's survival.

To a much lesser extent, humans exhibit ingroup loyalty by sacrificing to support "us," sometimes against "them." We are like employees who compete with one another to move up the corporate ladder, but also cooperate to help the business succeed against competing businesses (Nowak, 2012). Natural selection is therefore "multilevel," say some researchers (Mirsky, 2009). It operates at *both* individual and group levels.

Donald Campbell (1975a,b) offered another basis for unreciprocated altruism: Human societies evolved ethical and religious rules that serve as brakes on the biological bias toward self-interest. Commandments such as "love your neighbor as yourself" admonish us to balance self-concern with concern for the group and so contribute to the survival of the group. Those internal rules work to promote group selection even when no one is watching (Odouard et al., 2023). Richard Dawkins (1976) offered a similar conclusion: "Let us try to *teach* generosity and altruism, because we are born selfish. Let us understand what our selfish genes are up to, because we may then at least have the chance to upset their designs, something no other species has ever aspired to" (p. 3).

Comparing and Evaluating Theories of Helping

By now, you may have noticed similarities among the social-exchange, social norm, and evolutionary views of altruism. As **Table 1** shows, each proposes two types of prosocial behavior: a tit-for-tat reciprocal exchange and a more unconditional helpfulness. They do so at three complementary levels of explanation. If the evolutionary view is correct, then our genetic predispositions *should* manifest themselves in psychological and sociological phenomena.

Each theory appeals to logic, yet each is vulnerable to charges of being speculative and after the fact. When we start with a known effect (the give-and-take of everyday life) and explain it by conjecturing a social-exchange process, a "reciprocity norm," or an evolutionary origin, we might merely be explaining-by-naming. The argument that a behavior occurs

TABLE 1 Comparing Theories of Altruism

How Is Altruism Explained?

Theory	Level of Explanation	Externally Rewarded Helping	Intrinsic Helping
Social-exchange	Psychological	External rewards for helping	Distress → inner rewards for helping
Social norms	Sociological	Reciprocity norm	Social-responsibility norm
Evolutionary	Biological	Reciprocity	Kin selection

because of its survival function is hard to disprove. With hindsight, it's easy to think it had to be that way. If we can explain *any* conceivable behavior after the fact as the result of a social exchange, a norm, or natural selection, then we cannot disprove the theories. Each theory's task is therefore to generate predictions that enable us to test it.

An effective theory also provides a coherent scheme for summarizing a variety of observations. On this criterion, our three altruism theories get higher marks. Each offers us a broad perspective that illuminates both enduring commitments and spontaneous help.

Genuine Altruism and Empathy

One day, Abraham Lincoln was having a philosophical discussion with another passenger in a horse-drawn coach. Lincoln was arguing that selfishness prompts all good deeds, when they heard a sow making a terrible noise. Her piglets had gotten into a marshy pond and were in danger of drowning. Lincoln called the coach to a halt, jumped out, and lifted the little pigs to safety. Upon his return, his companion remarked, "Now, Abe, where does selfishness come in on this little episode?" Lincoln replied, "Why, bless your soul, Ed, that was the very essence of selfishness. I should have had no peace of mind all day had I gone and left that suffering old sow worrying over those pigs. I did it to get peace of mind, don't you see?" (Batson et al., 1986). Until recently, psychologists would have sided with Lincoln.

Daniel Batson (2011) has devoted much of his career to discerning whether helpfulness also contains a streak of genuine altruism – helping when there is no benefit to the self. Batson theorized that our willingness to help is influenced by *both* self-serving and selfless considerations **(Figure 4)**. Distress over someone's suffering motivates us to relieve our upset feelings, either by escaping the distressing situation or by helping (as Lincoln did). Especially when we feel securely attached to someone, we also feel **empathy,** a more other-focused emotion (Mikulincer et al., 2005). For example, loving parents suffer when their children suffer and rejoice over their children's joys.

empathy
The vicarious experience of another's feelings; putting oneself in another's shoes.

When we feel empathy, we focus not so much on our own distress as on that of the sufferer. Genuine sympathy and compassion motivate us to help others for their own sakes. When we value another's welfare, perceive the person as needing help, and take the person's perspective, we feel *empathic concern* (Batson, 2023; Batson et al., 2007). We naturally

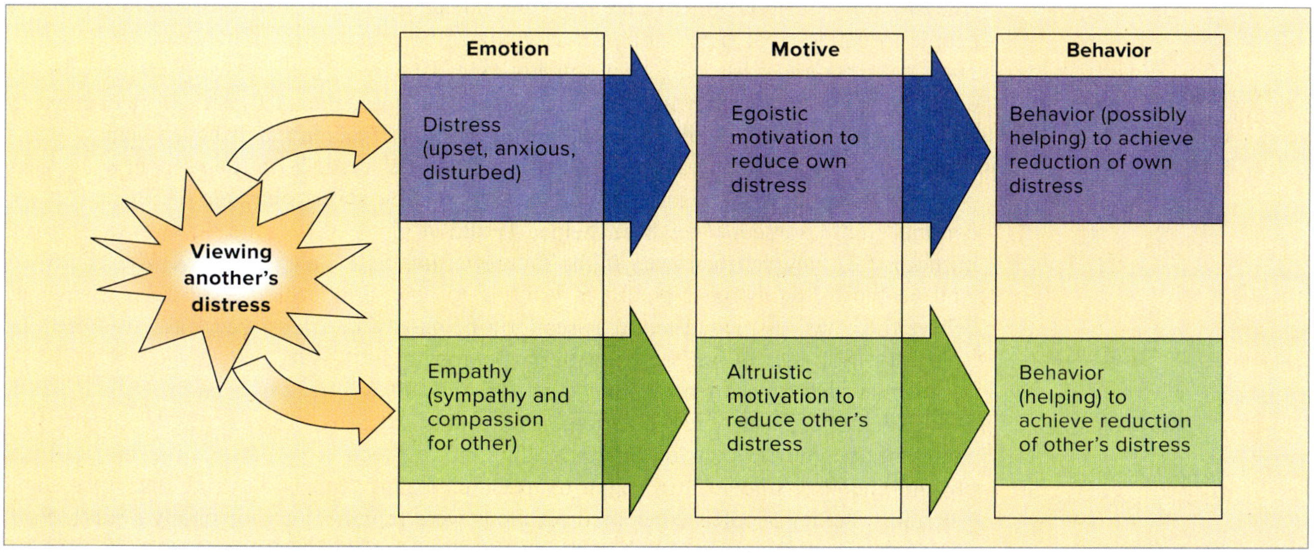

FIGURE 4

Egoistic and Altruistic Routes to Helping

Viewing another's distress can evoke a mixture of self-focused distress and other-focused empathy. Researchers agree that distress triggers egoistic motives. But they debate whether empathy can trigger a pure altruistic motive.
Source: Adapted from Batson et al., 1987.

Might genuine altruism motivate health educators leading exercise with children in Uganda? Daniel Batson believes it might.
Courtesy of Laura Myers

help those whose distress directly affects us, like family members and close friends, but empathic concern prompts us to help those outside of our circle as well (Guevara Beltran et al., 2023).

To increase empathy, it helps to get a small dose of what another feels. For example, people become more likely to say that, yes, extreme sleep deprivation is torture when they are moderately sleep-deprived themselves (Nordgren et al., 2011).

In humans, empathy comes naturally. Even day-old infants cry more when they hear another infant cry (Hoffman, 1981). In hospital nurseries, one baby's crying sometimes evokes a chorus of crying. Most 18-month-old infants, after observing an unfamiliar adult accidentally drop a marker or clothespin and have trouble reaching it, will readily help (Tomasello, 2009). Two-year-olds display arousal when observing someone who needs help (Hepach et al., 2012). And with 6- to 9-year-olds, the greater their empathy, the greater their helpfulness (Li et al., 2013). To some, all this suggests that humans are hardwired for empathy.

"We are made for goodness . . . Why else do we get so outraged by wrong? When we hear of any egregious act, we are appalled."

—Archbishop Desmond Tutu, *Made for Goodness: And Why This Makes All the Difference*, 2011

Primates, elephants, dogs, parrots, rats, and mice also display empathy, indicating that the building blocks of altruism predate humanity (Brucks & von Bayern, 2020; de Waal, 2014a,b; Langford et al., 2006). Chimpanzees will share banana pellets or choose a token that gives both themselves and another chimp a food treat over a token that gratifies only themselves (Horner et al., 2011; Schmelz et al., 2018).

To separate egoistic distress reduction from empathy-based altruism, Batson's research group conducted studies that aroused empathy. Then the researchers noted whether the aroused people would reduce their own distress by escaping the situation or whether they would go out of their way to aid the person. The results were consistent: With their empathy aroused, people usually helped. For example, in one experiment, participants observed a young woman (who had said a childhood accident made her unusually sensitive to shocks) suffering while she supposedly received electric shocks. Most volunteered to take her place (Batson et al., 1981).

Is this genuine altruism? Mark Schaller and Robert Cialdini (1988) doubted it. Feeling empathy for a sufferer makes one sad, they noted. In one of their experiments, they led people to believe that their sadness was going to be relieved by a different sort of mood-boosting experience: listening to a comedy tape. Under such conditions, people who felt empathy were not especially helpful. Schaller and Cialdini concluded that if we feel empathy but know that something else will make us feel better, we aren't as likely to help.

But other findings suggest that genuine altruism does exist: With their empathy aroused, people will help even when they believe no one will know about their helping. Their concern continues until someone *has* been helped (Fultz et al., 1986). If their efforts to help are unsuccessful, they feel bad even if the failure is not their fault (Batson & Weeks, 1996). And people will sometimes persist in wanting to help a suffering person even when they believe their own distressed mood arises from being given a drug – suggesting that helping isn't just a response to one's own distress (Schroeder et al., 1988).

"As I see it, there are two great forces of human nature: self-interest, and caring for others."

—Bill Gates, *A New Approach to Capitalism in the 21st Century*, 2008

After 25 such experiments testing self-interested versus altruistic empathy, Batson (2001, 2006, 2011, 2021) and others (Dovidio, 1991; Staub, 2015; Stocks et al., 2009) believe that sometimes people do focus on others' welfare, not on their own. Batson, a former philosophy and theology student, had begun his research feeling "excited to think that if we could ascertain whether people's concerned reactions were genuine, and not simply a subtle form of selfishness, then we could shed new light on a basic issue regarding human nature" (1999a). Two decades later, he believes he has his answer: Genuine "empathy-induced altruism is part of human nature" (1999b). And that, says Batson, raises the hope – confirmed by research – that inducing empathy might improve attitudes toward stigmatized people such as the unhoused and the imprisoned. (See "Focus On: The Benefits – and the Costs – of Empathy-Induced Altruism.")

focus ON The Benefits — and the Costs — of Empathy-Induced Altruism

People do most of what they do, including much of what they do for others, for their own benefit, acknowledges altruism researcher Daniel Batson (2011). But self-interest is not the whole story of helping, he believes; there is also a genuine altruism rooted in empathy, in feelings of sympathy and compassion for others' welfare. We are supremely social creatures. Consider:

Empathy-induced altruism

- *produces sensitive helping.* Where there is empathy, it's not just the thought that counts; it's alleviating the other's suffering.
- *inhibits aggression.* Show Batson someone who feels empathy for a target of potential aggression and he'll show you someone who's unlikely to favor attack — someone who's as likely to forgive as to harbor anger. In general, women report more empathic feelings than men, and they are less likely to support war and other forms of aggression (Jones, 2003).
- *increases cooperation.* In laboratory experiments, Batson and Nadia Ahmad found that people in potential conflict are more trusting and cooperative when they feel empathy for the other. Personalizing an outgroup, by getting to know people in it, helps people understand their perspective. For example, people who read about a woman who survived being in a coma from COVID-19 — and were thus induced to feel empathy — were more likely to say they would wear a mask in public, compared with those who only learned facts about the virus (Pfattheicher et al., 2020). College students dispositionally higher in empathic concern were more likely to report adhering to health and safety guidelines during the pandemic (Shrestha et al., 2023).
- *improves attitudes toward stigmatized groups.* Take others' perspective, allow yourself to feel what they feel, and you may become more supportive of others in difficult situations.

But empathy-induced altruism comes with liabilities, note Batson and colleagues.

- *It can be harmful.* People who risk their lives on behalf of others sometimes lose them. People who seek to do good can also do harm, sometimes by unintentionally humiliating or demotivating the recipient.
- *It can't address all needs.* It's easier to feel empathy for a needy individual than, say, for Mother Earth, whose environment is being stripped and warmed at the peril of our descendants.
- *It burns out.* Feeling others' pain is painful, which may cause us to avoid situations that evoke our empathy or to experience "burnout" or "compassion fatigue."
- *It can feed favoritism, injustice, and indifference to the larger common good* (Decety & Cowell, 2014). Empathy, being particular, produces partiality — toward a single child or family. When their empathy for someone is aroused, people will violate their own standards of fairness and justice by giving that person favored treatment (Batson et al., 1997; Oceja, 2008). For example, people give more money to a needy child if they see their name and picture — even if that means giving less to eight unnamed and unseen children (Kogut & Ritov, 2005). Ironically, noted Batson and colleagues (1999), empathy-induced altruism can, therefore, "pose a powerful threat to the common good [by leading] me to narrow my focus of concern to those for whom I especially care — the needing friend — and in so doing to lose sight of the bleeding crowd." No wonder charity so often stays close to home. Instead, authors such as Paul Bloom (2016) suggest a strategy of "rational compassion" that helps others more equally.

SUMMING UP: Why Do We Help?

- Three theories explain helping behavior. The *social-exchange theory* assumes that helping, like other social behaviors, is motivated by a desire to maximize rewards, which may be external or internal. Thus, after wrongdoing, people often become more willing to offer help. Sad, but not depressed or stressed, people also tend to be helpful. Finally, there is a striking feel-good/do-good effect: Happy people are helpful people. Social norms also mandate helping. The *reciprocity norm* stimulates us to help those who have helped us. The *social-responsibility norm* beckons us to help needy people, even if they cannot reciprocate, as long as they are deserving. Women in crisis, partly because they may be seen as more needy, receive more offers of help than men, especially from men.

- Evolutionary psychology assumes two types of helping: devotion to kin (rooted in *kin selection*) and reciprocity. Most evolutionary psychologists, however, believe that the genes of selfish individuals are more likely to survive than the genes of self-sacrificing individuals. Thus, selfishness is our natural tendency and society must therefore teach helping.
- We can evaluate these three theories according to the ways in which they characterize prosocial behavior as based on tit-for-tat exchange and/or unconditional helpfulness. Each can be criticized for using speculative or after-the-fact reasoning, but they do provide a coherent scheme for summarizing observations of prosocial behavior.
- In addition to helping that is motivated by external and internal rewards and the evading of punishment or distress, there appears also to be a genuine, *empathy-based altruism.* With their empathy aroused, many people are motivated to assist others in need or distress, even when their helping is anonymous or their own mood will be unaffected.

WHEN WILL WE HELP?

Explain how and why helping is influenced by the number and behavior of other bystanders, by mood states, and by traits and values.

Bystander inaction. What influences our interpretations of a scene such as this and our decisions to help or not to help?
Janine Wiedel Photolibrary/Alamy Stock Photo

On March 13, 1964, 28-year-old bar manager Kitty Genovese was attacked by a man with a knife as she returned from work to her Queens, New York, apartment house at 3:00 A.M. Her screams of terror and pleas for help – "Oh my God, he stabbed me! Please help me! Please help me!" – aroused some of her neighbors. Some supposedly came to their windows and caught fleeting glimpses as the attacker left and then returned to attack again. Not until her attacker departed for the second time did anyone call the police. Soon after, Kitty Genovese died.

Later analyses disputed the initial *New York Times* report that 38 witnesses observed the murder yet remained inactive; it was probably closer to a dozen. Two actually did call the police, and one neighbor held her as she bled (Cook, 2014; Pelonero, 2014; Roberts, 2020). Nevertheless, the initial story helped inspire research on bystander inaction, which is illustrated in other incidents. Eleanor Bradley tripped and broke her leg while shopping. Dazed and in pain, she pleaded for help. For 40 minutes, the stream of sidewalk pedestrians simply parted and flowed around her. Finally, a cab driver helped her to a doctor (Darley & Latané, 1968). In 2021, a woman was harassed, groped, and finally raped on a commuter train in suburban Philadelphia as passengers recorded the attack but did nothing to intervene. "We don't know . . . if they were scared or if they were confused or if they were hoping someone else would take action," said Laura Palumbo of the National Sexual Violence Resource Center (Dastagir, 2021).

"The only thing necessary for the triumph of evil is that good men do nothing."

—Attributed to British statesman Edmund Burke (1729–1797)

Consider how you might respond if you saw someone being sexually assaulted on a train, or lying on the sidewalk, or being bullied on social media. Although it's tempting to believe we would all intervene, we tend to overestimate our own bravery and underestimate the power of social constraints (Swim & Hyers, 1999). Intervening can have costs.

Social psychologists were curious and concerned about bystanders' inaction. So they undertook experiments to identify when people will help in an emergency. Then they broadened the question to "Who is likely to help in nonemergencies – by such deeds as giving money, donating blood, or contributing time?" Let's see what they have learned, looking first at the *circumstances* that enhance helpfulness and then at the *people* who help.

Number of Bystanders

Bystander passivity during emergencies prompted social commentators to lament people's "alienation," "apathy," "indifference," and "unconscious sadistic impulses." By attributing the nonintervention to the bystanders' dispositions, we can reassure ourselves that, as caring people, we would have helped. But were the bystanders really so inhuman?

THE inside STORY

John M. Darley on Bystander Reactions

Shocked by the Kitty Genovese murder, Bibb Latané and I met over dinner and began to analyze the bystanders' reactions. Being social psychologists, we thought not about the personality flaws of the "apathetic" individuals but rather about how anyone in that situation might react as did these people. By the time we finished our dinner, we had formulated several factors that together could lead to the surprising result: no one helping. Then we set about conducting experiments that isolated each factor and demonstrated its importance in an emergency situation.

John M. Darley, 1938–2018
Princeton University

Courtesy of John M. Darley, Princeton University

Social psychologists Bibb Latané and John Darley (1970) were unconvinced (see "The Inside Story: John M. Darley on Bystander Reactions"). They staged ingenious emergencies and found that a single situational factor – the presence of other bystanders – greatly decreased intervention. By 1980, they had conducted four dozen experiments that compared help given by bystanders who believed they were either alone or with others. Bystanders who were part of a group were less likely to help than lone bystanders, a phenomenon known as the **bystander effect** (Latané & Nida, 1981; Stalder, 2008). In online communication, too, people are more likely to respond helpfully to a request for help if they believe the request has come to them alone and not to several others as well (Blair et al., 2005). This might be one reason why social media users rarely intervene when they witness cyberbullying: They know others are seeing the bullying as well – and are doing nothing (Dillon & Bushman, 2015; Kazerooni et al., 2018).

bystander effect
The finding that a person is less likely to provide help when there are other bystanders.

Sometimes the victim was actually less likely to get help when many people were around. When research assistants "accidentally" dropped coins or pencils during 1,497 elevator rides, they were helped 40% of the time when one other person was on the elevator and less than 20% of the time when there were six passengers (Latané & Dabbs, 1975). In a meta-analysis of 105 studies, the presence of more people during critical situations lowered the chances that people would help (Fischer et al., 2011). Children as young as 5 are less likely to help when other children are present (Plötner et al., 2015). Even rats are less likely to help a trapped rat when other rats are present and not helping (Havlik et al., 2020).

Why does the presence of other bystanders sometimes inhibit helping? Latané and Darley surmised that as the number of bystanders increases, any given bystander is less likely to *notice* the incident, less likely to *interpret* the incident as a problem or an emergency, and less likely to *assume responsibility* for taking action **(Figure 5)**.

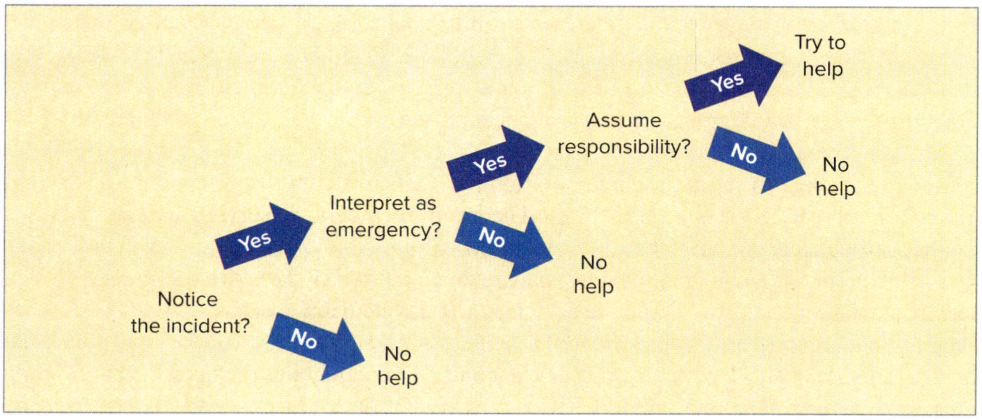

FIGURE 5
Latané and Darley's Decision Tree
Only one path up the tree leads to helping. At each fork of the path, the presence of other bystanders may divert a person down a branch toward not helping.
Source: Adapted from Darley & Latané, 1968.

Wildfire or safe controlled burn? If you saw this scene from the highway, would you call emergency services if everyone else were just driving by, seemingly unconcerned?
WeatherVideoHD.TV

NOTICING

Twenty minutes after Eleanor Bradley – whose story we told earlier – has fallen and broken her leg on a crowded city sidewalk, you come along. Your eyes are on the backs of the pedestrians in front of you (it is bad manners to stare at those you pass) and your private thoughts are on the day's events. Would you therefore be less likely to notice the injured woman than if the sidewalk were virtually deserted?

To find out, Latané and Darley (1968) had Columbia University men fill out a questionnaire in a room, either by themselves or with two strangers. While they were working (and being observed through a one-way mirror), there was a staged emergency: Smoke poured into the room through a wall vent. Solitary students, who often glanced idly about the room while working, noticed the smoke almost immediately, usually in less than 5 seconds. Those in groups kept their eyes on their work, and it typically took them about 20 seconds to notice the smoke.

INTERPRETING

Once we notice an ambiguous event, we must interpret it. Try putting yourself in that room with two strangers. The room is filling with smoke. Though worried, you don't want to embarrass yourself by appearing flustered. You glance at the others. They look calm, indifferent. Assuming everything must be okay, you shrug it off and go back to work. Then one of the others notices the smoke and, noting your apparent unconcern, reacts similarly. This is yet another example of informational influence. Each person uses others' behavior as clues to reality. Such misinterpretations can contribute to a delayed response to actual fires in offices, restaurants, and other places with many people (Canter et al., 1980).

The misinterpretations are fed by what Thomas Gilovich, Kenneth Savitsky, and Victoria Husted Medvec (1998) called an *illusion of transparency*: a tendency to overestimate others' ability to "read" our internal states. In their experiments, people facing an emergency presumed their concern was more visible than it was. More than we usually suppose, our concern or alarm is not very noticeable. Keenly aware of our emotions, we presume they leak out and that others see right through us. Sometimes others do read our emotions, but often we effectively keep our cool. The result is "pluralistic ignorance": ignorance that others are thinking and feeling what we are (Sargent & Newman, 2021). In emergencies, each person may think, "I'm very concerned," but perceive others as calm – "so maybe it's not an emergency."

So it happened in Latané and Darley's experiment. When those working alone noticed the smoke, they usually hesitated a moment, then got up, walked over to the vent, felt, sniffed, and waved at the smoke, hesitated again, and then went to report it. In dramatic contrast, those in groups of 3 did not move. Among the 24 men in 8 groups, only 1 person reported the smoke within the first 4 minutes **(Figure 6)**. By the end of the 6-minute experiment, the smoke was so thick, it was obscuring the men's vision and they were rubbing their eyes and coughing. Still, in only 3 of the 8 groups did even a single person leave to report the problem.

Equally interesting, the group's passivity affected its members' interpretations. What caused the smoke? "A leak in the air conditioning." "Chemistry labs in the building." "Steam pipes." "Truth gas." Not one said, "Fire." The group members, by serving as nonresponsive models, influenced one another's interpretation of the situation.

That experimental dilemma parallels real-life dilemmas we all face. Are the shrieks outside merely playful antics or the desperate screams of someone being assaulted? Is the boys' scuffling a friendly tussle or a vicious fight? Is the person slumped in the doorway sleeping, high on drugs, or seriously ill, perhaps in a diabetic coma? That surely was the question confronting those who passed by Hugo Alfredo Tale-Yax as he lay on a Queens, New York, sidewalk,

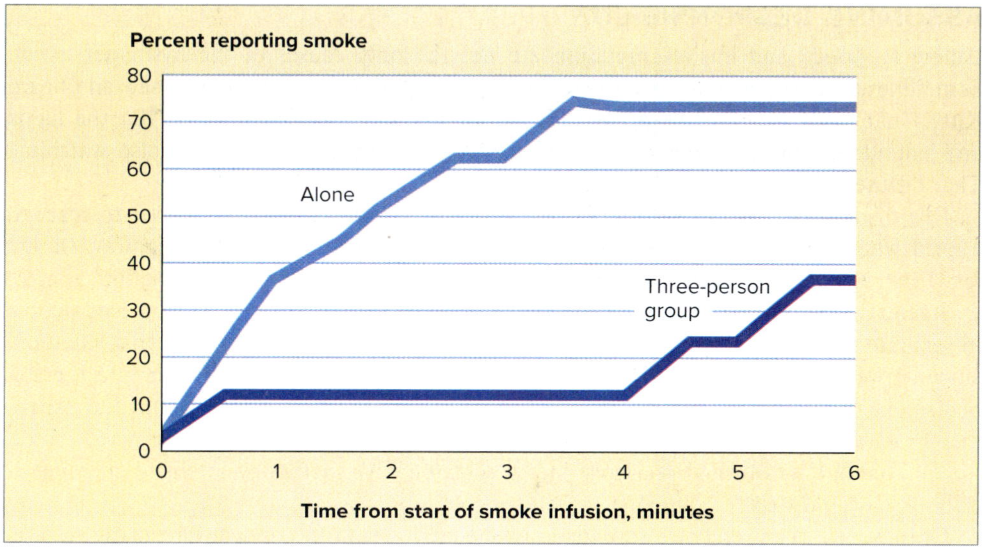

FIGURE 6

The Smoke-Filled-Room Experiment

Smoke pouring into the testing room was much more likely to be reported by individuals working alone than by three-person groups.

Source: Data from Darley & Latané, 1968.

facedown and bleeding to death from multiple stab wounds. A surveillance video showed that for more than an hour, people walked by the homeless man, until finally one passerby shook him and then turned him over to reveal his wounds (Sulzberger & Meenan, 2010).

Unlike the smoke-filled-room experiment, each of these everyday situations involves the desperate need of another person. In such situations, a bystander effect occurs: People are less likely to help someone when other bystanders are present. Latané and Judith Rodin (1969) staged an experiment around a woman in distress. A female researcher asked Columbia University men to work on a questionnaire and then left to work in an adjacent office. Four minutes later, she could be heard (from a tape recorder) climbing on a chair to reach some papers. This was followed by a scream and a loud crash as the chair collapsed and she fell to the floor. "Oh, my God, my foot ... I ... I ... can't move it," she sobbed. "Oh ... my ankle ... I ... can't get this ... thing ... off me." Only after 2 minutes of moaning did she manage to make it out her office door.

Seventy percent of those who were alone when they overheard the "accident" came into the room or called out to offer help. Among pairs of strangers confronting the emergency, only 40% of the time did either person offer help. Those who did nothing apparently interpreted the situation as a nonemergency. "A mild sprain," said some. "I didn't want to embarrass her," explained others. This again demonstrates the bystander effect. As the number of people known to be aware of an emergency increases, any given person becomes less likely to help. For the victim, there is no safety in numbers.

People's interpretations also affect their reactions to street crimes. In staging physical fights in which a man violently shook a woman as she struggled and screamed, Lance Shotland and Margaret Straw (1976) found that bystanders intervened 65% of the time when the woman shouted, "Get away from me; I don't know you" but only 19% of the time when she shouted, "Get away from me; I don't know why I ever married you." Assumed spousal abuse, it seems, triggers less intervention than stranger abuse.

In such dangerous situations with a perpetrator present and intervention requiring physical risk, the bystander effect is less – people are just as willing to help when others are present (Fischer et al., 2011). Indeed, sometimes bystanders provide physical support in intervening. This was dramatically evident on 9/11 as passengers, led by Todd Beamer ("Let's roll!"), collectively intervened as four al Qaeda hijackers headed United Flight 93 toward its presumed target of the U.S. Capitol. This also happens in day-to-day life. During public fights captured on street cameras in three cities around the world, at least one bystander intervened 90% of the time (Philpot et al., 2020).

Interpretations matter. Is this man locked out of his car, or is he a burglar? Our interpretation affects our response.

Peter Dazeley/Photographer's Choice/Getty Images

ASSUMING RESPONSIBILITY

Failing to notice and misinterpretation are not the only causes of the bystander effect. Sometimes an emergency is obvious. According to initial reports, those who saw and heard Kitty Genovese's pleas for help correctly interpreted what was happening. But the lights and silhouetted figures in neighboring windows told them that others were also watching. That diffused the responsibility for action.

Few of us have observed a murder. But all of us have at times been slower to react to a need when others were present. Passing a stranded motorist on a busy highway, we are less likely to offer help than if on a country road. To explore bystander inaction in clear emergencies, Darley and Latané (1968) simulated the Genovese drama. They placed people in separate rooms where they would hear a victim crying for help. To create that situation, students were asked to converse over a laboratory intercom. The researchers told the students that to guarantee their anonymity, no one would be visible, nor would the experimenter eavesdrop. During the ensuing discussion, the participants heard one person, after his microphone was turned on, lapse into a seizure. With increasing intensity and speech difficulty, he pleaded for someone to help.

Of those led to believe they were the only one talking with the student having the seizure, 85% left their room to seek help. Of those who believed four others also overheard the victim, only 31% went for help. Were those who didn't respond apathetic and indifferent? When the experimenter came in to end the experiment, most immediately expressed concern. Many had trembling hands and sweating palms. They believed an emergency had occurred but were undecided whether to act. Some of the indecision of those in the larger group may have stemmed from self-interest: They kept hoping someone else would help so the responsibility wouldn't fall on them (Thomas et al., 2016).

After the smoke-filled room, the woman-in-distress, and the seizure experiments, Latané and Darley asked the participants whether the presence of others had influenced them. We know their presence had a dramatic effect. Yet the participants almost invariably denied the influence. They typically replied, "I was aware of the others, but I would have reacted just the same if they weren't there." That response reinforces a familiar point: *We often do not know why we do what we do.* That is why experiments are revealing. A survey of uninvolved bystanders following a real emergency would have left the bystander effect hidden.

In the "Conformity and Obedience" chapter, we noted other examples of people's inability to predict their own actions. Although university students predicted they would respond with moral courage to sexist remarks, a racial slur, or the theft of someone's phone, few of their comparable classmates (when facing the actual situations) did so. Thus, it takes research to see how people in fact behave.

Urban dwellers are seldom alone in public places, which helps account for why city people often are less likely to intervene than country people. "Compassion fatigue" and "sensory overload" from encountering so many needy people further restrain helping in large cities across the world (Levine et al., 1994; Yousif & Korte, 1995). In large cities, bystanders are also more often strangers – whose increasing numbers depress helping. When bystanders are friends or people who share a group identity, increased numbers may, instead, increase helping (Levine & Crowther, 2008). When college undergraduates imagined witnessing someone lead a drunk woman into a bedroom at a party, they were more willing to intervene when the woman was a friend instead of a stranger (Katz et al., 2015).

Training programs can also change attitudes toward intervening in situations of sexual assault, harassment, or bullying (Edwards et al., 2020; Katz & Moore, 2013). As the #MeToo movement that began in 2017 demonstrated, sexual harassment can often continue for years when bystanders do nothing. When college students learned about how to intervene in these situations through a "Bringing in the Bystander" program, they became more positive about stepping in when they witnessed behavior that might lead to sexual violence (such as watching a drunk person be led into a bedroom by a group of people [Cares et al., 2015; Inman et al., 2018]). The same program was also effective in the military, with soldiers who participated more likely than a control group to take action to stop sexual assault or stalking (Potter & Moynihan, 2011). When high school teachers helped students internalize messages around using respectful language, students became more likely to step in to defend those who were being bullied and bullying incidents declined sharply (Cheon et al., 2023).

Even when bystanders don't intervene directly, they can make a difference by reporting the incident immediately, by interrupting the interaction by talking to the potential victim, or by just being very distracting. One man on a New York subway used distraction to great effect: He stood between a man and woman who were fighting, calmly munching on chips – earning him the nickname "The Snackman" (Dwyer, 2012).

Smartphone video captured the brutal death of George Floyd as Minneapolis police officer Derek Chauvin suffocated him while three other police officers looked on. If one of these officers had successfully practiced active bystandership, perhaps Floyd would still be alive today.
From Facebook

In 2015, three New Orleans police officers watched as their fellow officer Alfred Moran repeatedly hit a handcuffed man who had been arrested for public drunkenness. The bystander officers did nothing to stop the incident and did not report it to their supervisors; two of them, along with Moran, were fired (Bullington, 2016). In response to this and other incidents, the New Orleans Police Department began educating officers about bystander intervention, teaching them techniques to intervene when their fellow officers might be on the verge of violence (Robertson, 2016) – a strategy known as "active bystandership" (Novotney, 2017). It seemed to work: When New Orleans police confronted screaming demonstrators defending a Confederate monument in 2017, officers intervened when they observed another officer about to erupt in anger, reports altruism researcher Ervin Staub, who helped design the training (Staub, 2018, 2019).

In May 2020, three Minneapolis police officers watched as officer Derek Chauvin knelt on citizen George Floyd's neck for over 9 minutes – a clear example of bystander nonintervention. In the aftermath of Floyd's death, there were strong calls for police reform and retraining. Social psychology research suggests that active bystandership training might be a key part of such reform.

REVISITING RESEARCH ETHICS

The bystander intervention experiments raise an ethical issue. Is it right to force unwitting people to overhear someone's apparent collapse? Were the researchers in the seizure experiment ethical when they forced people to decide whether to interrupt their discussion to report the problem? Would you object to being in such a study? Note that it would have been impossible to get your "informed consent"; doing so would have destroyed the experiment's cover.

The researchers were always careful to debrief the laboratory participants. After explaining the seizure experiment, the experimenter gave the participants a questionnaire. All said the deception was justified and that they would be willing to take part in similar experiments in the future. None reported feeling angry at the experimenter. Other researchers confirm that the overwhelming majority of participants in such experiments say that their participation was both instructive and ethically justified (Schwartz & Gottlieb, 1981). In field experiments, an accomplice assisted the victim if no one else did, thus reassuring bystanders that the problem was being dealt with.

Remember that the social psychologist has a twofold ethical obligation: to protect the participants and to enhance human welfare by discovering influences upon human behavior. Such discoveries can alert us to unwanted influences and show us how we might exert positive influences. The ethical principle seems to be: After protecting participants' welfare, social psychologists fulfill their responsibility to society by giving us insight into our behavior.

Helping When Someone Else Does

If observing aggressive models can heighten aggression and if unresponsive models can heighten nonresponding, then will helpful models promote helping? Imagine hearing a crash followed by sobs and moans. If another bystander said, "Uh-oh. This is an emergency! We've got to do something," would it stimulate others to help?

Everybody's doing it: Seeing other people helping often spurs people to help.
JUPITERIMAGES/Brand X/Alamy Stock Photo

The evidence is clear: Prosocial models do promote altruism. Across 88 studies of more than 25,000 people, people were more likely to help when they saw others helping (Jung et al., 2020). Some specific examples:

- Los Angeles drivers were more likely to offer help to a female driver with a flat tire if a quarter mile earlier they had witnessed someone helping another woman change a tire. Similarly, New Jersey Christmas shoppers were more likely to drop money in a Salvation Army kettle if they had just seen someone else do the same (Bryan & Test, 1967).
- British adults were more willing to donate blood if they were approached after observing someone else say they would donate (Rushton & Campbell, 1977).
- A glimpse of extraordinary human kindness and charity – such as the examples of heroic altruism at this chapter's outset – often triggers what Jonathan Haidt (2003) called *elevation,* "a distinctive feeling in the chest of warmth and expansion" that may provoke chills, tears, and throat clenching. Such elevation often inspires people to become more self-giving (Schnall et al., 2010).

Time Pressures

In the parable of the Good Samaritan, two people pass by a man slumped on the road, while a third (the Samaritan) stops to help. Perhaps the first two rushed by without stopping because they were busy and in a hurry. To see whether time pressure impacts helping, Darley and Batson (1973) cleverly staged the situation described in the parable.

After collecting their thoughts before recording a brief extemporaneous talk (which, for half the participants, was actually about the Good Samaritan parable), Princeton Theological Seminary students were directed to a recording studio in an adjacent building. En route, they passed a man sitting slumped in a doorway, head down, coughing and groaning. Some of the students had been sent off nonchalantly: "It will be a few minutes before they're ready for you, but you might as well head on over." Of those, almost two-thirds stopped to offer help. Others were told, "Oh, you're late. They were expecting you a few minutes ago . . . so you'd better hurry." Of these, only 1 out of 10 offered help.

Reflecting on these findings, Darley and Batson noted that the hurried participants passed on by the person in distress even when en route "to speak on the parable of the Good Samaritan, thus inadvertently confirming the point of the parable. (Indeed, on several occasions, seminary students going to give their talk on the parable of the Good Samaritan literally stepped over the victim as they hurried on his way!)"

Are we being unfair to the seminary students, who were, after all, hurrying to *help* the experimenter? Perhaps they keenly felt the social-responsibility norm but found it pulling them two ways: toward the experimenter and toward the victim. In another enactment of the Good Samaritan situation, Batson and associates (1978) directed 40 University of Kansas students to an experiment in another building. Half were told they were late, half that they had plenty of time. Half of each of these groups thought their participation was vitally important to the experimenter; half thought it was not essential. The results: Those leisurely on their way to an unimportant appointment usually stopped to help. But people seldom stopped to help if, like the White Rabbit in *Alice's Adventures in Wonderland,* they were late for a very important date. Thus, they were trying to help the experimenter – but in their hurry, they simply did not take time to tune in to a person in need. As social psychologists have so often observed, their behavior was influenced more by context than by conviction.

Similarity

Because similarity is conducive to liking and liking is conducive to helping, we are more empathic and helpful toward those *similar* to us (Miller et al., 2001). The similarity bias applies to both appearance and to beliefs. Tim Emswiller and his fellow researchers (1971) had accomplices, dressed either conservatively or in the disheveled garb favored by hippies of the time, ask "conservative" and "hip" Purdue University students for a dime for a phone call. Fewer than half the students did the favor for those dressed differently from themselves. Two-thirds did so for those dressed similarly. (See "Research Close-Up: Ingroup Similarity and Helping.")

research CLOSE-UP

Ingroup Similarity and Helping

Likeness breeds liking, and liking elicits helping. So, do people offer more help to others who display similarities to themselves? To explore the similarity-helping relationship, Mark Levine, Amy Prosser, and David Evans at Lancaster University joined with Stephen Reicher at St. Andrews University (2005) to study the behavior of Manchester United soccer football team fans. Taking their cue from John Darley and Daniel Batson's (1973) famous Good Samaritan experiment, they directed each newly arrived student participant to the laboratory in an adjacent building. En route, a jogger working for the experimenter — wearing a shirt from either nearby Manchester United or rival Liverpool — seemingly slipped on a grass bank just in front of them, grasped his ankle, and groaned in apparent pain. As **Figure 7** shows, the Manchester fans routinely paused to offer help to their fellow Manchester supporter but usually did not offer such help to a supposed Liverpool supporter.

But, the researchers wondered, what if we remind Manchester fans of the identity they share with Liverpool supporters — as football fans rather than as those who dislike football fans? So they repeated the experiment, but with one difference: Before participants witnessed the jogger's fall, the researcher explained that the study concerned the positive aspects of being a football fan. Given that only a small minority of fans are troublemakers, this research aimed to explore what fans get out of their love for "the beautiful game." Now a jogger wearing a football club shirt, whether for Manchester or Liverpool, became one of "us fans." And as **Figure 8** shows, the grimacing jogger was helped regardless of which team he supported — and more so than if wearing a plain shirt.

The principle in the two cases is the same, noted the researchers. People are predisposed to help their fellow group members, whether those are defined more narrowly (as "us Manchester fans") or more inclusively (as "us football fans"). If even rival fans can be persuaded to help one another by thinking about what unites them, then surely other antagonists can as well. One way to increase people's willingness to help others is to promote social identities that are inclusive rather than exclusive.

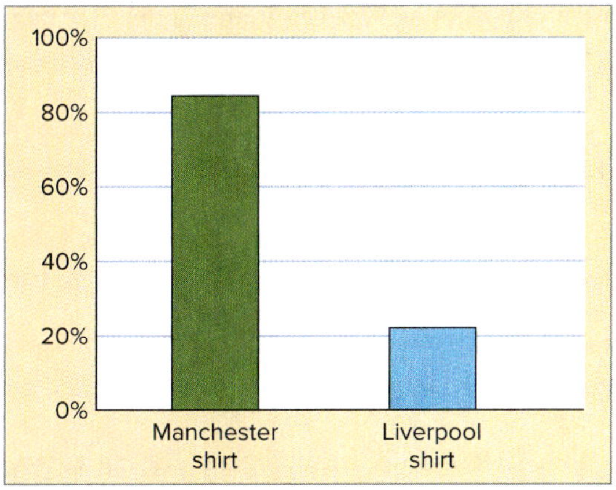

FIGURE 7

Percentage of Manchester United Fans Who Helped Victim Wearing Manchester or Liverpool Shirt

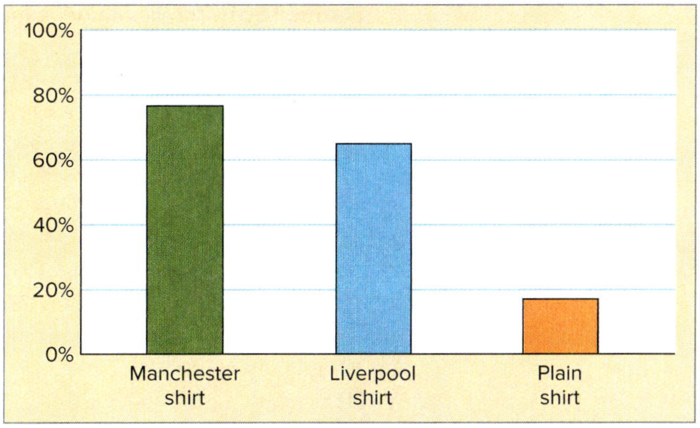

FIGURE 8

Common Fan Identity Condition: Percentage of Manchester United Fans Who Helped Victim Wearing Manchester or Liverpool Shirt

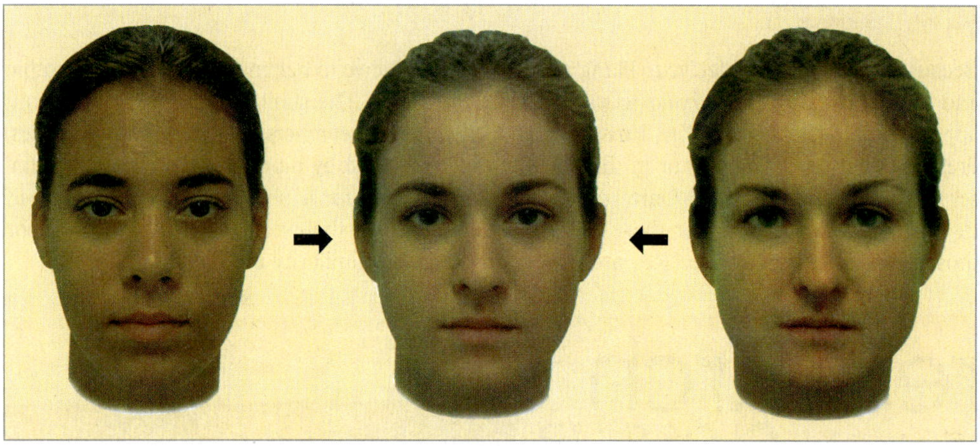

FIGURE 9

Similarity Breeds Cooperation

Lisa DeBruine (2002) morphed participants' faces (left) with strangers' faces (right) to make the composite center faces—toward whom the participants were more generous than toward the stranger.

Courtesy of Lisa DeBruine

Like similarity, familiarity breeds compassion. No face is more familiar than one's own. That explains why, when Lisa DeBruine (2002) had McMaster University students play an interactive game with a supposed other player, they were more trusting and generous when the other person's pictured face had some features of their own face morphed into it **(Figure 9)**. In me I trust. Even just believing they shared a birthday, a first name, or a fingerprint pattern with someone leads people to more frequently respond to a request for help (Burger et al., 2004).

Does the similarity bias extend to race? During the 1970s, researchers explored that question with confusing results: Some studies found that people were more willing to help those of the same race, some that people were more willing to help those of a different race, and some found no effect (Benson et al., 1976; Dutton & Lake, 1973; Lerner & Frank, 1974).

Is there a general rule that resolves these seemingly contradictory findings?

Few people want to appear prejudiced. Perhaps, then, people favor their own race but keep that bias secret to preserve a positive image. If so, the same-race bias should appear only when people can attribute failure to help to factors other than race. That is what happened in experiments by Samuel Gaertner and John Dovidio (1977, 1986). For example, University of Delaware White women were less willing to help a Black woman than a White woman in distress *if* their responsibility could be diffused among the bystanders ("I didn't help the Black woman because there were others who could"). When there were no other bystanders, the women were equally helpful to the Black and the White woman. The rule seems to be: When norms for appropriate behavior are well-defined, Whites don't discriminate; when norms are ambiguous or conflicting and providing help is more difficult or riskier, racial similarity may bias responses (Saucier et al., 2005).

For me [DM], the laboratory came to life one night as I walked from a dinner meeting in Washington, D.C., to my hotel. On a deserted sidewalk, a well-dressed, distraught-seeming man about my age approached me and begged for a dollar. He explained that he had just come over from London and, after visiting the Holocaust Museum, had accidentally left his wallet in a taxi. So here he was, stranded and needing a $24 taxi fare to a friend's home in suburban D.C.

"So how's one dollar going to get you there?" I asked.

"I asked people for more, but no one would help me," he nearly sobbed, "so I thought maybe if I asked for less I could collect taxi fare."

"But why not take the Metro?" I challenged.

"It stops about 5 miles from Greenbriar, where I need to go," he explained. "Oh my, how am I ever going to get there? If you could help me out, I will mail you back the money on Monday."

Here I was, as if a participant in an on-the-street altruism experiment. Having grown up in a city and as a frequent visitor to New York and Chicago, I am accustomed to panhandling and have never rewarded it. But I also consider myself a caring person. Moreover, this fellow was unlike any panhandler I had ever met. He was dressed sharply. He was intelligent. He had a convincing story. And he looked like me! If he's lying, he's a slimeball, I said to myself, and giving him money would be stupid, naive, and rewarding slimeballism. If he's a truth-teller and I turn my back on him, then *I'm* a slimeball.

He had asked for $1. I gave him $30, along with my name and address, which he took gratefully and disappeared into the night.

As I walked on, I began to suspect – correctly, as it turned out – that I had been a patsy. Having lived in Britain, why had I not tested his knowledge of England? Why had I not taken him to a phone to call his friend? Why had I at least not offered to pay a taxi driver and send him on his way, rather than give him the money? And why, after a lifetime of resisting scams, had I succumbed to this one?

Sheepishly, because I like to think myself not influenced by ethnic stereotypes, I had to admit that it was not only his socially skilled, personal approach but also the mere fact of his similarity to me.

SUMMING UP: When Will We Help?

- Several situational influences work to inhibit or to encourage altruism. As the number of bystanders at an emergency increases, any given bystander is (1) less likely to notice the incident, (2) less likely to interpret it as an emergency, and (3) less likely to assume responsibility – a phenomenon called the *bystander effect*. Experiments on helping behavior pose an ethical dilemma but fulfill the researcher's mandate to enhance human life by uncovering important influences on behavior.
- When are people most likely to help? One circumstance is when they have just observed someone else helping.
- Another circumstance that promotes helping is having at least a little spare time; those in a hurry are less likely to help.
- We tend to help those whom we perceive as being similar to us.

WHO WILL HELP?

Identify some traits and values that predict helping.

We have considered internal influences on the decision to help (such as guilt and mood) and external influences as well (such as social norms, number of bystanders, time pressures, and similarity). We also need to consider the helpers' dispositions, including, for example, their personality traits, gender, and religious values.

Personality Traits and Status

Surely some traits must distinguish the Mother Teresa types from others. Faced with identical situations, some people will respond helpfully, while others won't bother. Who are the likely helpers?

Personality researchers have summarized the effect of personality on altruism:

- There are *individual differences* in helpfulness that persist over time and are noticed by one's peers (Demedardi et al., 2021; Hampson, 1984; Penner, 2002). Five-year-olds who most readily shared their treats were, at ages 23 and 32, most socially progressive in their political views (Dunkel, 2014). Some people *are* reliably more helpful and stay that way. These individual differences even appear in the brain: The brains of people who demonstrated the extraordinary altruism of donating a kidney to a stranger were more reactive to observing another person's pain (Brethel-Haurwitz et al., 2018).
- The personality trait that best predicts willingness to help – especially willingness to help strangers – is *agreeableness*, indicative of someone who highly values getting along with others (Habashi et al., 2016; Oda & Matsumoto-Oda, 2022). Not surprisingly, those with callous traits such as psychopathy or narcissism (who are usually noticeably low in agreeableness) are less helpful and empathic (Beussink et al., 2017; Nehrlich et al., 2019).

Outgoing, friendly people who value harmonious social relationships are the most likely to help others.
Steve Debenport/E+/Getty Images

- Personality influences *how particular people react to particular situations* (Carlo et al., 1991; Romer et al., 1986; Wilson & Petruska, 1984). Those high in self-monitoring are attuned to others' expectations and are therefore helpful *if* they think helpfulness will be socially rewarded (White & Gerstein, 1987). Others' opinions matter less to internally guided, low-self-monitoring people.

Status and social class also affect altruism. Across several studies, Paul Piff and his colleagues (2010; Robinson & Piff, 2017) found that less privileged people were more generous, trusting, and helpful than more privileged people, likely because they felt more compassion for others and felt less entitled to special treatment (Piff, 2014; Stellar et al., 2012). Especially in private situations – when no one was "looking" – those lower in social class were more likely to help others (Kraus & Callaghan, 2016). People lower in social status showed more reaction in brain areas linked to sensitivity to others (Muscatell et al., 2016) and were better at judging others' emotions (Kraus et al., 2010). Even people randomly assigned to feel more powerful showed brain activity suggesting lower empathy (Hogeveen et al., 2014). This research suggests that the stereotype of the callous rich person might have some truth to it.

Gender

The interaction of person and situation also appears in 172 studies comparing the helpfulness of nearly 50,000 male and female individuals. When faced with potentially dangerous situations in which strangers need help (such as with a flat tire or a fall in a subway), men more often help (Eagly & Crowley, 1986). Alice Eagly (2009) noted that among recipients of the Carnegie medal for heroism in saving human life, 91% have been men.

In safer situations, such as volunteering to help with an experiment or spend time with children with developmental disabilities, women are slightly more likely to help. In a 2019 national survey of 95,505 entering American college students, 74% of men – and 85% of women – rated "helping others in difficulty" as "very important" or "essential" (Stolzenberg et al., 2020). Women are more likely to describe themselves as helpful and focused on altruism, and among children, girls are slightly more likely to say they would stop to help a fellow soccer player who fell down (Nielson et al., 2017; Van Lange et al., 2018; Xi et al., 2022). Faced with a friend's problems, women respond with greater empathy and spend more time helping (George et al., 1998). Women also have been as likely as, or more likely than, men to risk death as Holocaust rescuers, to donate a kidney, and to volunteer with the Peace Corps and Doctors of the World (Becker & Eagly, 2004). Thus, the gender difference depends on the situation.

Finally, women tend to be more generous. They are more supportive of government programs that distribute wealth and are more likely to distribute their own wealth. Indiana University's Women's Philanthropy Institute reports that: (1) single women donate more than single men, (2) men donate more if married to a woman, and (3) at every income level, female-headed households donate more than male-headed households (Mesch & Pactor, 2015). Small wonder, noted Adam Grant (2013), that 20 years ago, philanthropist Bill Gates rejected advice to set up a charitable foundation – until marrying, having two daughters, and recalling his mother who "never stopped pressing me to do more for others."

Religious Faith

In 1943, with Nazi submarines sinking ships faster than the Allied forces could replace them, the troop ship *SS Dorchester* steamed out of New York harbor with 902 men headed for Greenland (Elliott, 1989; Kurzman, 2004; Parachin, 1992). Among those leaving anxious families behind were four chaplains: Methodist preacher George Fox, Rabbi Alexander Goode, Catholic priest John Washington, and Reformed Church minister Clark Poling. Some 150 miles from its destination, on a moonless night, a German U-boat caught the *Dorchester* in its crosshairs. Within moments of the torpedo's impact, stunned men were pouring out of their bunks as the ship began listing. With power cut, the ship's radio was useless; its escort vessels, unaware of the unfolding tragedy, pushed on in the darkness. On board, chaos reigned as panicky men came up from the hold without life jackets and leaped into overcrowded lifeboats.

The four chaplains' ultimate selflessness inspired this painting, which hangs in Valley Forge, Pennsylvania's Chapel of the Four Chaplains.
Lynn Burkholder/First Impressions

As the four chaplains arrived on the steeply sloping deck, they began guiding the men to their boat stations. They opened a storage locker, distributed life jackets, and coaxed the men over the side. When Petty Officer John Mahoney turned back to retrieve his gloves, Rabbi Goode responded, "Never mind. I have two pairs." Only later did Mahoney realize that the Rabbi was not conveniently carrying an extra pair; he was giving up his own.

In the icy, oil-smeared water, as Private William Bednar heard the chaplains preaching courage, he found the strength to swim out from under the ship until reaching a life raft. Still on board, Grady Clark watched in awe as the chaplains handed out the last life jacket and then, with ultimate selflessness, gave away their own. As Clark slipped into the waters, he looked back at an unforgettable sight: The four chaplains were standing—their arms linked—praying, in Latin, Hebrew, and English. Other men joined them in a huddle as the *Dorchester* slid beneath the sea. "It was the finest thing I have ever seen or hope to see this side of heaven," said John Ladd, another of the 230 survivors. None of the chaplains survived.

Does the chaplains' heroic example imply that faith promotes courage and caring? The world's four largest religions—Christianity, Islam, Hinduism, and Buddhism—all teach compassion and charity (Steffen & Masters, 2005). But do their followers walk the talk? Religiosity is a mixed bag, reported Ariel Malka and colleagues (2011). It is often associated with conservative opposition to government initiatives, including support for the poor, yet it also promotes prosocial values.

Consider what happens when people are subtly "primed" with spiritual thoughts. With God on their minds—after unscrambling sentences with words such as *spirit, divine, God,* and *sacred*—people become much more generous in their donations (Pichon et al., 2007; Schumann et al., 2014; Shariff et al., 2016). When Moroccan Muslim shopkeepers were given money in a game, 100% gave it all to charity when the call to prayer was sounding across the city, compared to 60% when it was not (Duhaime, 2015). Follow-up studies have found that religious priming increases other "good" behaviors, such as persistence on an assigned task and actions consistent with one's moral beliefs (Carpenter & Marshall, 2009; Toburen & Meier, 2010). But "religion" and "God" have somewhat different priming effects. "Religion" primes helpfulness toward ingroup members and "God" toward outgroup members—even outgroup members of a different religion (Karatas & Gurhan-Canli, 2020; Pasek et al., 2023; Preston & Ritter, 2013).

In studies of college students and the general public, the religiously committed have reported volunteering more hours—as tutors, relief workers, and campaigners for social justice—than have the religiously uncommitted (Hansen et al., 1995; Penner, 2002; Petrovic et al., 2021). Nearly half of religious Americans said they volunteered in the last week, compared to 1 out of 4 less religious Americans (Pew, 2016). Worldwide surveys confirm the correlation between faith engagement and volunteering. One analysis of 117,007 people responding to World Values Surveys in 53 countries reported that twice-weekly religious attenders "are more than five times more likely to volunteer" than nonattenders (Ruiter & De Graaf, 2006).

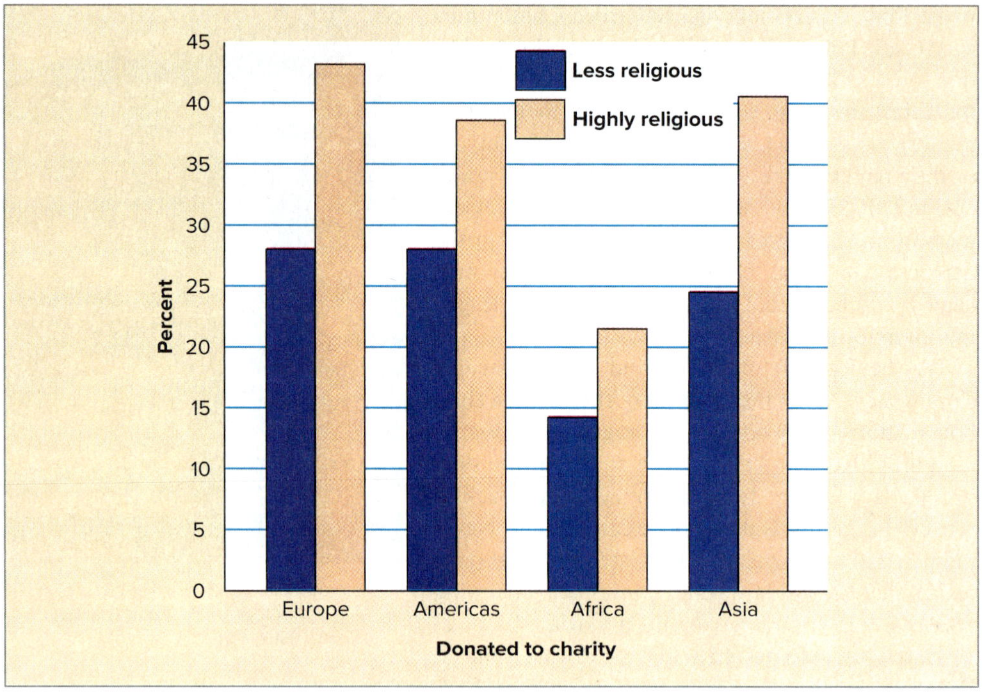

FIGURE 10

Helping and Religious Engagement

Worldwide, reported Gallup researchers Brett Pelham and Steve Crabtree (2008), highly religious people are — despite averaging lower incomes — more likely to report having given away money in the last month and having volunteered and helped a stranger. Highly religious people said religion is important in their daily life and attended a service in the last week. Less religious are all others.

Moreover, Sam Levenson's jest – "When it comes to giving, some people stop at nothing" – is seldom true of those who are most actively religious. A massive Gallup World Poll surveyed 2,000 or more people in each of 140 countries. Despite having lower incomes, highly religious people (who reported that religion is important to their daily lives and that they had attended a religious service in the prior week) reported markedly higher than average rates of charitable giving, volunteerism, and helping a stranger in the previous month **(Figure 10)**.

"Religion is the mother of philanthropy."

—Frank Emerson Andrews, *Attitudes Toward Giving*, 1953

One might wonder if this occurs because religious people have a ready outlet for their donations and volunteer opportunities via their churches, synagogues, or mosques. However, religious people were also more likely to be generous with others in an online game or by agreeing to spend 30 minutes filling out a questionnaire to help a student with their thesis project (Blogowska et al., 2013; Everett et al., 2016).

In addition, the links between religion and planned helping seem to be relatively unique among communal organizations. Robert Putnam (2000) analyzed national survey data from 22 types of organizations, including hobby clubs, professional associations, self-help groups, and service clubs. "It was membership in religious groups," he reported, "that was most closely associated with other forms of civic involvement, like voting, jury service, community projects, talking with neighbors, and giving to charity" (p. 67).

An analysis across 70 countries confirmed that "religious individuals were more likely to be members of charitable organizations" and less likely to engage in self-serving lies or fraud. But this seeming prosocial effect of religiosity was strongest "in countries in which religious behavior is a matter of personal choice" rather than imposed by strong social norms (Stavrova & Siegers, 2014). Religion promotes helping – if it's your idea.

SUMMING UP: Who Will Help?

- Some people, especially those high in the personality trait of agreeableness, are consistently more helpful than others.
- The effect of personality or gender may depend on the situation. Men, for example, have been observed to help more in dangerous situations, while women are more likely to be volunteers and charitable givers.
- Religious faith predicts altruism, as reflected in volunteerism and charitable contributions.

HOW CAN WE INCREASE HELPING?

Suggest how helping might be increased by reversing the factors that inhibit helping, by teaching norms of helping, and by socializing people to see themselves as helpful.

As social scientists, our goal is to understand human behavior, thus also suggesting ways to improve it. One way to promote altruism is to reverse the factors that decrease it. Given that hurried, preoccupied people help less, can we think of ways to slow people down and turn their attention outward? If the presence of others diminishes each bystander's sense of responsibility, how can we enhance responsibility?

Reduce Ambiguity, Increase Responsibility

If Latané and Darley's decision tree (see Figure 5) describes the dilemmas bystanders face, then helping should increase if we can prompt people to correctly *interpret an incident* and to *assume responsibility*. Leonard Bickman and colleagues (Bickman, 1975, 1979; Bickman & Green, 1977) tested that presumption in a series of experiments on crime reporting. In each, they staged a shoplifting incident. In some of the stores, they placed signs aimed at sensitizing bystanders to shoplifting and informing them how to report it. The researchers found that the signs had little effect. In other cases, witnesses heard a bystander interpret the incident: "Say, look at her. She's shoplifting. She put that into her purse." Still others heard this person add, "We saw it. We should report it. It's our responsibility." Both comments substantially boosted reporting of the crime. Similarly, training programs that aim to help college students intervene in possible situations of sexual assault or sexual harassment teach techniques such as learning how to interpret situations and speaking up (Katz & Moore, 2013).

PERSONALIZED APPEAL

The potency of personal influence is strong. New blood donors, unlike repeat donors, were usually there at someone's personal invitation (Foss, 1978). Leonard Jason and collaborators (1984) confirmed that personal appeals for blood donation are much more effective than posters and media announcements – if the personal appeals come from friends.

To reduce anonymity, researchers have had bystanders identify themselves to one another – by name, age, and so forth – after which they were more likely to offer aid to a sick person (Solomon & Solomon, 1978; Solomon et al., 1981). Similarly, when a female experimenter caught the eye of another shopper and gave her a warm smile before stepping on an elevator, that shopper was far more likely than other shoppers to offer help when the experimenter later said, "Damn. I've left my glasses. Can anyone tell me what floor the umbrellas are on?" Even a trivial momentary conversation with someone ("Excuse me, aren't you Suzie Spear's sister?" "No, I'm not") dramatically increased the person's later helpfulness.

The personal touch might also explain why people are more likely to help when asked face-to-face than when asked via email – a stunning 34 times more likely. Phone and Zoom requests for help are also less effective than asking in person (Roghanizad & Bohns, 2017, 2022).

Helpfulness also increases when one expects to meet the victim and other witnesses again. Using a laboratory intercom system, Jody Gottlieb and Charles Carver (1980) led University of Miami students to believe they were discussing problems of college living with other students. (Actually, the other discussants were tape-recorded.) When one of the supposed fellow discussants had a choking fit and cried out for help, students who believed they would soon be meeting her face-to-face more quickly rushed to help. In short, *anything that personalizes bystanders* – a personal request, eye contact, stating one's name, anticipating interaction – increases willingness to help. In experiments, restaurant patrons have tipped more when their servers introduced themselves by name, wrote friendly messages on checks, touched guests on the arm or shoulder, or squatted at the table during the service encounter (Leodoro & Lynn, 2007; Schirmer et al., 2011).

Personal treatment makes bystanders more self-aware, and self-aware people are more attuned to their own altruistic ideals. Note that people made self-aware by acting in front of a mirror or a TV camera exhibit increased consistency between attitudes and actions. By contrast, "deindividuated" people are less responsible. Thus, circumstances that promote self-awareness – name tags, being watched and evaluated, undistracted quiet – should also increase helping.

Shelley Duval, Virginia Duval, and Robert Neely (1979) confirmed this. They showed some University of Southern California women their own images on a TV screen or had them complete biographical questionnaires just before giving them a chance to contribute time and money to people in need. Those made self-aware contributed more. Similarly, pedestrians who have just had their pictures taken by someone became more likely to help another pedestrian pick up dropped envelopes (Hoover et al., 1983). And among Italian pedestrians who had just seen themselves in a mirror, 70% helped a stranger by mailing a postcard – compared to 13% of those who did not see their own reflection (Abbate et al., 2006). Social media users more focused on how they were coming across to their online audience were more likely to donate to a charity cause (Lavertu et al., 2020). Self-aware people more often live out their ideals.

Guilt and Concern for Self-Image

Previously, we noted that people who feel guilty will act to reduce guilt and restore their self-worth. Can awakening people's guilt therefore increase their desire to help?

A Reed College research team led by Richard Katzev (1978) experimented with guilt-induced helping. When visitors to the Portland Art Museum disobeyed a "Please do not touch" sign, experimenters reprimanded some of them: "Please don't touch the objects. If everyone touches them, they will deteriorate." Likewise, when visitors to the Portland Zoo fed unauthorized food to the bears, some of them were admonished with, "Hey, don't feed unauthorized food to the animals. Don't you know it could hurt them?" In both cases, 58% of the now guilt-laden individuals shortly thereafter offered help to another experimenter who had "accidentally" dropped something. Of those not reprimanded, only one-third helped. Guilt-laden people are helpful people.

That was my [DM's] experience after passing a man struggling to get up from a busy city sidewalk as I raced to catch a train. His glazed eyes brought to mind the many drunken people I had assisted during my college days as an emergency room attendant. Or . . . I wondered after walking by . . . was he actually experiencing a health crisis? Plagued by guilt, I later picked up sidewalk litter, offered my train seat to an elderly couple looking for seats together, and vowed that the next time I faced such an uncertain situation in an unfamiliar city, I would think to call 911.

Robert Cialdini and David Schroeder (1976) offered another practical way to trigger concern for self-image: Ask for a contribution so small that it's hard to say no without feeling like a Scrooge. Cialdini (1995) discovered this when a United Way canvasser came to his door. As she asked for a donation, he was mentally preparing his refusal – until she said magic words that demolished his financial excuse: "Even a penny will help." "I had been neatly finessed into compliance," recalled Cialdini. "And there was another interesting feature of our exchange as well. When I stopped coughing (I really had choked on my attempted rejection), I gave her not the penny she had mentioned but the amount I usually allot to legitimate charity solicitors. At that, she thanked me, smiled innocently, and moved on."

The guilt many people feel after passing by this homeless man might motivate them to help someone in the next situation they encounter.
Vitaliipixels/Shutterstock

Was Cialdini's response atypical? To find out, he and Schroeder had a solicitor approach suburbanites. When the solicitor said, "I'm collecting money for the American Cancer Society," 29% contributed an average of $1.44 each. When the solicitor added, "Even a penny will help," 50% contributed and gave an average of $1.54 each. When James

Weyant (1984) repeated this experiment, he found similar results: The "even a penny will help" boosted the number contributing from 39 to 57%. And when 6,000 people were solicited by mail for the American Cancer Society, those asked for small amounts were more likely to give – and gave no less on average – than those asked for larger amounts (Weyant & Smith, 1987). A qualification: When those who had previously donated are approached, bigger requests (within reason) do elicit bigger donations (Doob & McLaughlin, 1989). But with door-to-door solicitation, there is more success with requests for small contributions, which are difficult to turn down and still allow the person to maintain an altruistic self-image.

Labeling people as helpful can also strengthen a helpful self-image. After they had made charitable contributions, Robert Kraut (1973) told some female study participants, "You are a generous person." Two weeks later, these women were more willing than those not so labeled to contribute to a different charity.

Socializing Altruism

How might we socialize altruism? Here are practical ways to do so **(Figure 11)**.

TEACHING MORAL INCLUSION

Rescuers of Jews in Nazi Europe, leaders of the antislavery movement, and medical missionaries shared at least one common trait: They were *morally inclusive.* Their moral concern encircled diverse people. One rescuer faked a pregnancy on behalf of a pregnant hidden Jew – thus including the soon-to-be-born child within the circle of her own children's identities (Fogelman, 1994).

Moral exclusion – omitting certain people from one's circle of moral concern, often via dehumanization – has the opposite effect. It justifies all sorts of harm, from discrimination to genocide (Landry et al., 2022; Opotow, 1990; Staub, 2005a; Tyler & Lind, 1990). Exploitation or cruelty becomes acceptable, even appropriate, toward those whom we regard as undeserving or as nonpersons. The Nazis excluded Jews from their moral community. Anyone who participates in enslavement, death squads, or torture practices a similar exclusion. To a lesser extent, moral exclusion describes those of us who concentrate our concerns, favors, and financial inheritance upon "our people" (for example, our children) to the exclusion of others.

moral exclusion

The perception of certain individuals or groups as outside the boundary within which one applies moral values and rules of fairness. *Moral inclusion* is regarding others as within one's circle of moral concern.

Moral exclusion also describes restrictions in the public empathy for the human costs of war. Reported war deaths are typically "our deaths." Many Americans, for example, know that more than 58,000 Americans died in the Vietnam War (their 58,248 names are inscribed on the Vietnam War Memorial). But few Americans know that the war also left some 2 million Vietnamese dead. During the Iraq war, news of American fatalities – nearly 4,500 – caused much more concern than the 150,000+ Iraqi deaths (Alkhuzai et al., 2008).

"We consider humankind our family."

—Parliament of the World Religions, *Towards a Global Ethic*, 1993

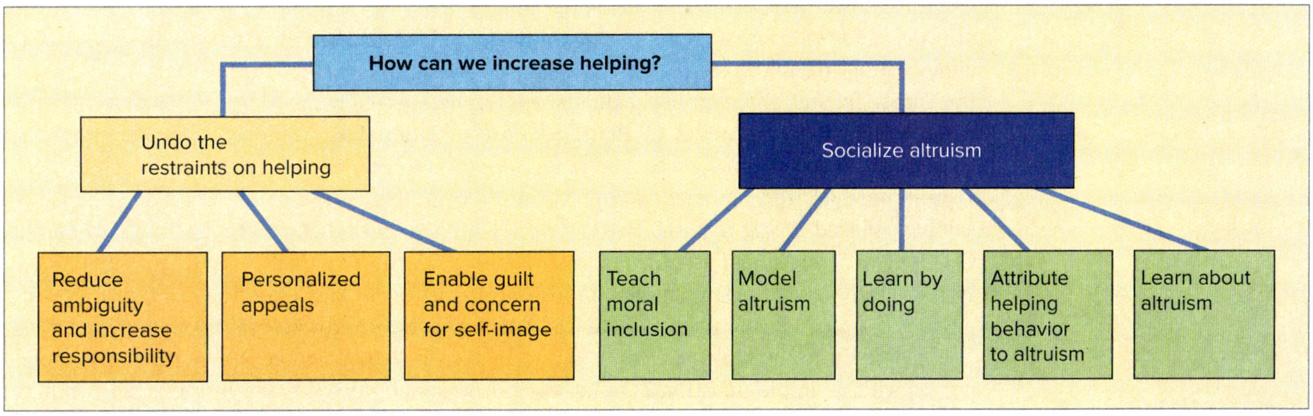

FIGURE 11

Practical Ways to Increase Helping

One way to practice moral inclusion is to believe "all humanity is my ingroup" (McFarland et al., 2012).
John Lund/Blend Images LLC

We easily become numbed by impersonal big numbers of outgroup fatalities (Dunn & Ashton-James, 2008; Slovic, 2007). People presumed that they would be more upset about a hurricane that killed 5,000 rather than 50 people, but they were not. When a heartbreaking photograph of a drowned Syrian toddler flashed around the world in 2015, donations to help refugees suddenly spiked – even though the crisis had been going on for 4 years and had already cost 250,000 lives (Slovic et al., 2017). "If I look at the mass, I will never act," said Mother Teresa. "If I look at the one, I will." Shown a single victim, a 7-year-old girl named Rokia, people responded with more money for a hunger charity than when told the organization was working to save millions (Slovic & Västfjäll, 2010). In laboratory games simulating altruism, people are generally prosocial toward individuals, but more willing to steal from a large, anonymous group of victims (Alos-Ferrer et al., 2022).

A first step toward socializing altruism is therefore to counter the natural ingroup bias favoring kin and tribe by personalizing and broadening the range of people whose well-being should concern us. Daniel Batson (1983) noted how religious teachings do this. They extend the reach of kin-linked altruism by urging "brotherly and sisterly" love toward all "children of God" in the whole human "family." As research with an "Identification with All Humanity Scale" shows, if everyone is part of our family, then everyone is in the same group (McFarland et al., 2013). The boundaries between "we" and "they" fade. Inviting advantaged people to put themselves in others' shoes, to imagine how they feel, also helps (Batson et al., 2003). White students who learned more about the experiences of racial minority students developed more empathy toward them (Lu et al., 2020). To "do unto others as you would have them do unto you," one must take the others' perspective.

MODELING ALTRUISM

Previously, we noted that seeing unresponsive bystanders makes us less likely to help. What makes us more like to help?

REAL-LIFE MODELING If we see or read about someone helping, we become more likely to offer assistance. If they had earlier witnessed someone helping a woman who'd dropped books, female shoppers were more likely to assist someone who had dropped a dollar (Burger et al., 2014). Across 88 studies of more than 25,000 people, those who saw someone else help were more likely to help, too (Jung et al., 2020).

It's better, noted Robert Cialdini and co-workers (2003), *not* to publicize rampant tax cheating, littering, and teen drinking and instead to emphasize – to define a norm of – people's widespread honesty, cleanliness, and abstinence. Tell people of others recycling, voting, paying taxes on time, reusing hotel towels, or not littering, and more will do the same. In one of many experiments, researchers asked visitors not to remove petrified wood from along the paths of Petrified Forest National Park. Some were also told that "past visitors have removed the petrified wood." Other people who were told that "past visitors have left the petrified wood" to preserve the park were much less likely to pick up samples placed along a path. Better yet, tell people how norms are favorably changing. Given a "dynamic norm" such as being told that 30% of people have begun eating less meat in the last 5 years, people express more interest in doing the same than if given a "static norm" of a steady 30% trying to eat less meat (Sparkman & Walton, 2018).

Brief nudges about norms can also be effective. When people are reminded of social norms with a simple question ("What do you personally think is the morally right thing to do?"), they donate 50% more to charity than those not reminded (Capraro et al., 2019). Thinking about God or karma – call it a supernatural social norm – also increased prosocial behavior (White et al., 2019).

MEDIA MODELING Do media's positive models promote helping, much as its aggressive portrayals promote aggression? Prosocial models have actually had even greater effects than antisocial models. Susan Hearold (1986) meta-analyzed 108 comparisons of prosocial TV programs with neutral programs or no program. She found that, on average, "If the viewer watched prosocial programs instead of neutral programs, he would [at least temporarily] be elevated from the 50th to the 74th percentile in prosocial behavior."

In one such study, researchers Lynette Friedrich and Aletha Stein (1973; Stein & Friedrich, 1972) showed preschool children *Mister Rogers' Neighborhood* episodes each day for 4 weeks as part of their nursery school program. (*Mister Rogers' Neighborhood* aimed to enhance young children's social and emotional development.) During the viewing period, children became more cooperative, helpful, and likely to state their feelings. In a follow-up study, kindergartners who viewed four *Mister Rogers'* programs were able to state the show's prosocial content, both on a test and in puppet play (Coates et al., 1976; Friedrich & Stein, 1975). More recent studies have also found that children who watched prosocial shows (vs. a control show) were better at taking someone else's perspective (Cingel & Krcmar, 2019).

Do adults also respond to prosocial role modeling on-screen? Graeme Blair and his colleagues (2019) tested this idea in a society-wide intervention in Nigeria, a country suffering from widespread corruption. The researchers worked with a Nigerian anticorruption group to make a feature film starring well-known actors. The film had two versions: one showing the characters reporting corruption via a (real) toll-free hotline, and one that did not include that scene. Residents in communities seeing the film with the corruption-reporting role models were more likely to report corruption using the hotline. Psychologist Ervin Staub and his colleagues employed a similar technique in Rwanda, a country scarred by genocide in the 1990s. Along with local writers, they penned a radio drama about conflict among two villages in which the warring groups eventually made peace and forgave each other. Rwandans who listened to the radio drama about reconciliation expressed more empathy for varied groups than those who listened to an alternative drama (Staub, 2018).

Other media also effectively model prosocial behavior, partly by increasing empathy. Recent studies from across the world show positive effects on attitudes or behavior from prosocial media, including playing prosocial video games and listening to prosocial music lyrics (Coyne et al., 2018; Gentile et al., 2009; Halbrook et al., 2019; Prot et al., 2014). For example, playing *Lemmings,* a video game in which the goal is to help others, increases later real-life empathy and helping in response to another's misfortune (Greitemeyer & Osswald, 2010; Greitemeyer et al., 2010). Listening to prosocial songs, like the Beatles song "Help," made listeners more likely to help someone pick up dropped pencils (Greitemeyer, 2009a,b, 2011). Brief interventions – such as asking people to take the perspective of a person in a story or being prompted to think about someone experiencing a tough situation – can also increase empathy for others (Fry & Runyan, 2018).

Children who help usually learn to like helping and are more likely to be helpful in the future.
wavebreakmedia/Shutterstock

LEARNING BY DOING

Ervin Staub (2005b, 2015) has shown that just as immoral behavior fuels immoral attitudes, helping increases future helping. Children and adults learn by doing. In a series of studies with children near age 12, Staub and his students found that after children were asked to make toys for hospitalized children or for an art teacher, they became more helpful. So did children after teaching younger children to make puzzles or use first aid.

When children act helpfully, they develop helping-related values, beliefs, and skills, notes Staub. Helping also helps satisfy their needs for a positive self-concept. On a larger scale, "service learning" and volunteer programs woven into a school curriculum have been shown to increase later citizen involvement, social responsibility, cooperation, and leadership (Andersen, 1998; Putnam, 2000). Attitudes follow behavior. Helpful actions therefore promote the self-perception that one is caring and helpful. And that compassionate positive self-perception in turn promotes further helping.

LEARNING ABOUT BYSTANDER INTERVENTION

Researchers have found another way to boost altruism that provides a happy conclusion to our chapter. In one experiment, some students heard about how bystander inaction can affect the interpretation of an emergency and feelings of responsibility. Other students heard either a different lecture or no lecture at all. Two weeks later, the participants found themselves walking (with an unresponsive accomplice) past someone slumped over. Of those who had not heard the bystander intervention lecture, only one-fourth paused to offer help, but half of those who had heard the bystander intervention lecture stopped to help (Beaman et al., 1978).

I [JT] witnessed this firsthand when Gina, a student in my social psychology class, told me what happened one day after our lecture on bystander intervention. Gina was walking down the steps outside the classroom when a woman fell down right behind her, apparently having a seizure. Gina called 911, and she and another bystander helped the woman until the paramedics arrived. But, she said, "I was the only one with my phone out and there were maybe 15 people just watching." Having just learned about bystander intervention, Gina took action while most of the bystanders did not.

Having read this chapter, perhaps you, too, have changed. As you come to understand what influences people's responses, will your attitudes and your behavior be the same?

SUMMING UP: How Can We Increase Helping?

Research suggests that we can enhance helpfulness in two ways.

- First, we can reverse those factors that inhibit helping. We can take steps to reduce the ambiguity of an emergency, to make a personal appeal, and to increase feelings of responsibility.
- Second, we can teach altruism. Research into portrayals of prosocial models shows the media's power to teach positive behavior. Children who view helpful behavior tend to act helpfully. Learning about altruism, as you have just done, can also prepare people to perceive and respond to others' needs.

CONCLUDING THOUGHTS: Taking Social Psychology into Life

Those of us who research, teach, and write about social psychology do so believing that our work matters. It engages humanly significant phenomena. Studying social psychology can therefore expand our thinking and prepare us to live and act with greater awareness and compassion, or so we presume.

How good it feels, then, when students and former students confirm our presumptions with stories of how they have related social psychology to their lives. As it turns out, both of us authors have had this experience. As related in the last section, one of my [JT] students helped a woman having a seizure after my lecture on bystander intervention as other bystanders stood watching. Shortly before I [DM] wrote these sentences, a former student, now living in Washington, D.C., stopped by. She mentioned that she recently found herself part of a stream of pedestrians striding past a man lying unconscious on the sidewalk. "It took my mind back to our social psych class and the accounts of why people fail to help in such situations. Then I thought, "Well, if I just walk by, too, who's going to help him?" So she made a call to an emergency help number and waited with the victim – and other bystanders who now joined her – until help arrived.

Conflict and Peacemaking

CHAPTER

13

Probal Rashid/LightRocket/Getty Images

"If you want peace, work for justice."

—Pope Paul VI, *Message for the Celebration of the Day of Peace*, 1972

There is a speech that has been spoken in many languages by the leaders of many countries. It goes like this: "The intentions of our country are entirely peaceful. But other nations threaten us. Thus we must defend ourselves against attack. By so doing, we shall protect our way of life and preserve the peace" (Richardson, 1960). Almost every nation claims concern only for peace but, mistrusting other nations, arms itself in self-defense. The result is a world that has been spending more than $6 billion a day on arms and armies while millions die of malnutrition and untreated disease (SIPRI, 2023).

The elements of such **conflict** (a perceived incompatibility of actions or goals) are similar at many levels, from nations to individuals. People in conflict perceive that one side's gain is the other's loss:

- "We want peace and security." "So do we, but you threaten us."

What creates conflict?

How can peace be achieved?

Concluding Thoughts: The conflict between individual and communal rights

conflict
A perceived incompatibility of actions or goals.

peace
A condition marked by low levels of hostility and aggression and by mutually beneficial relationships.

- "We want more pay." "We can't afford it."
- "I'd like the music off." "I'd like it on."

If we can manage conflict through mutual understanding, we can not only resolve disputes but make peace. Genuine **peace** is the outcome of a creatively managed conflict, when the parties reconcile their perceived differences and reach genuine accord. In this chapter, we explore why people and nations are often in conflict and what can be done to achieve peace.

WHAT CREATES CONFLICT?

Explain the sources of conflict.

Social psychology studies have identified several ingredients of conflict. Strikingly, these ingredients are common to all levels of social conflict, whether intergroup (us versus them) or interpersonal (me versus us).

Social Dilemmas

Many problems that threaten our future – nuclear arms, climate change, overpopulation, low stocks of ocean fish – arise as various parties pursue their self-interests, often (ironically) to their collective detriment. One individual may think, "It would cost me a lot to buy an electric car. Besides, the greenhouse gases I personally generate are trivial." Many others reason similarly, and the result is a warming climate, melting ice cover, rising seas, and more extreme weather – collective disasters.

When individually rewarding choices become collectively punishing, we have a dilemma: How can we reconcile individual self-interest with communal well-being?

To isolate and study that dilemma, social psychologists have used laboratory games that expose real social conflicts. "Social psychologists who study conflict are in much the same position as the astronomers," noted conflict researcher Morton Deutsch (1999). "We cannot conduct true experiments with large-scale social events. But we can identify the conceptual similarities between the large scale and the small, as the astronomers have between the planets and Newton's apple. That is why the games people play as subjects in our laboratory may advance our understanding of war, peace, and social justice."

social trap
A situation in which the conflicting parties, by each rationally pursuing its self-interest, become caught in mutually destructive behavior. Examples include the prisoner's dilemma and the tragedy of the commons.

Let's consider two such games, both examples of a **social trap** (a situation when conflicting parties are caught in mutually destructive behavior): the prisoner's dilemma and the tragedy of the commons.

THE PRISONER'S DILEMMA

The prisoner's dilemma originated from a story about two suspects questioned separately by the district attorney (DA), the lawyer who can bring criminal charges against suspects (Rapoport, 1960). The DA knows they are both guilty but has only enough evidence to convict them of a lesser offense. So the DA creates an incentive for each one to confess privately:

- If Prisoner A confesses and Prisoner B doesn't, the DA will grant immunity to A and will use A's confession to convict B of a maximum offense (and vice versa if B confesses and A doesn't).
- If both confess, each will receive a moderate sentence.
- If neither prisoner confesses, each will be convicted of a lesser crime and receive a light sentence.

The matrix of **Figure 1** summarizes the choices. If you were a prisoner faced with such a dilemma, with no chance to talk to the other prisoner, would you confess?

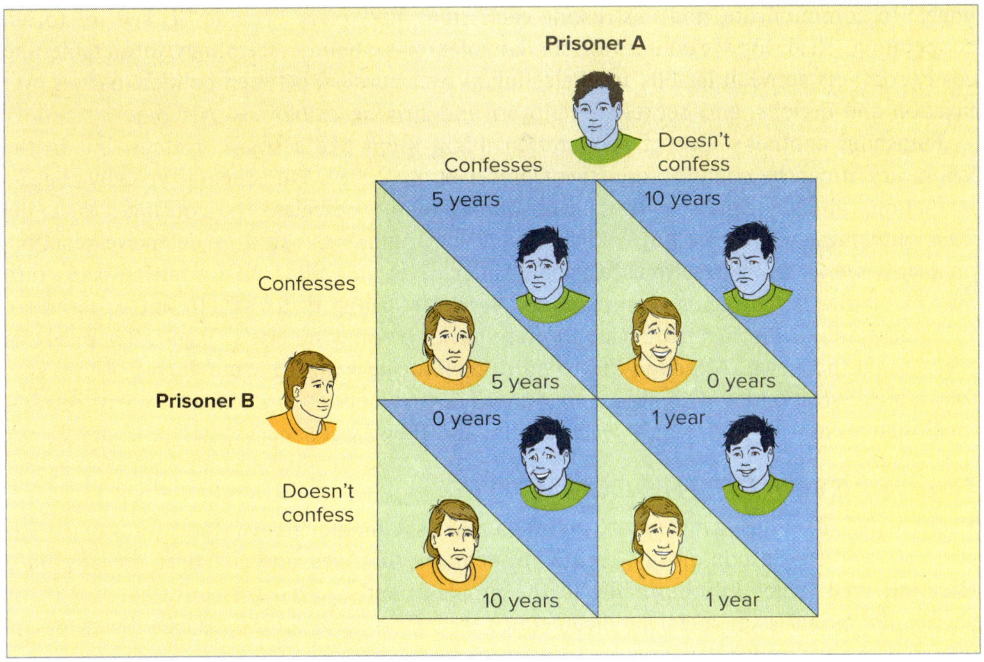

FIGURE 1

The Classic Prisoner's Dilemma

In each box, the number above the diagonal is prisoner A's outcome. Thus, if both prisoners confess, both get 5 years. If neither confesses, each gets 1 year. If one confesses, that prisoner is set free in exchange for evidence used to convict the other of a crime bringing a 10-year sentence. If you were one of the prisoners, unable to communicate with your fellow prisoner, would you confess?

Many people say they would confess, even though mutual *non*confession elicits lighter sentences than mutual confession. Perhaps this is because (as shown in the Figure 1 matrix) no matter what the other prisoner decides, each is better off confessing than being convicted individually.

Researchers have presented variations of the prisoner's dilemma in lab experiments, with the choices being to defect (choosing not to cooperate) or to cooperate, and the outcomes being chips, money, or grade points instead of criminal sentences (Chakraborty, 2023). As **Figure 2** illustrates, on any given decision, a person is better off defecting (because such behavior exploits the other's cooperation or protects against the other's exploitation). However (and here's the rub), by not cooperating, both parties end up far worse off than if they had trusted each other and thus had gained a joint profit. This dilemma often traps each one in a maddening predicament in which both realize they *could* mutually profit. But

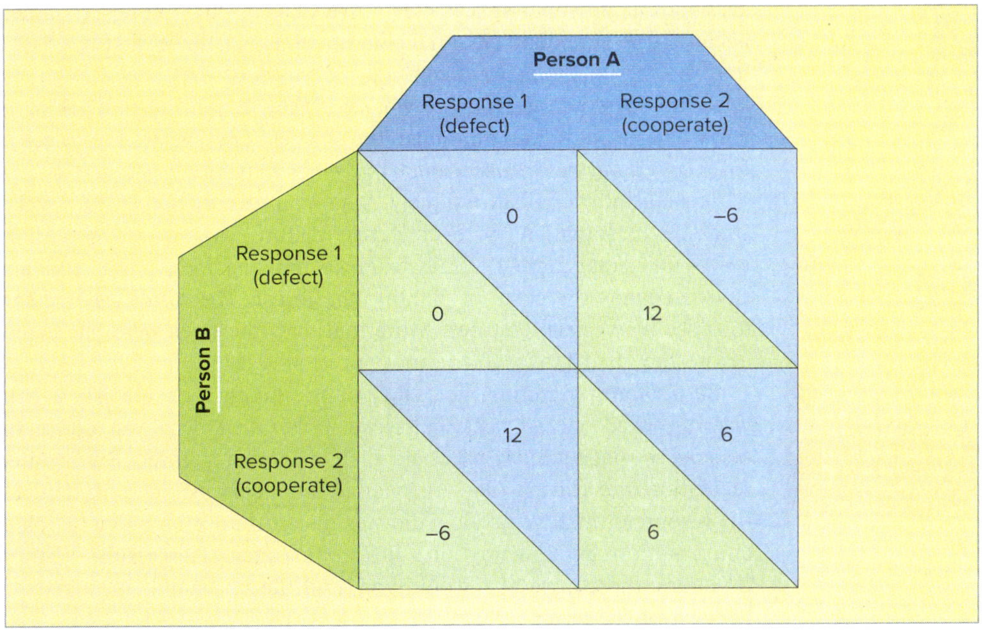

FIGURE 2

Laboratory Version of the Prisoner's Dilemma

The numbers represent some reward, such as money. In each box, the number above the diagonal lines is the outcome for person A. Unlike the classic prisoner's dilemma (a one-shot decision), most laboratory versions involve repeated plays.

unable to communicate, and mistrusting each other, they often become "locked in" to not cooperating. Real-world examples of similar dilemmas abound: seemingly intractable and costly conflicts between Israelis and Palestinians over borders, between political parties over taxation and deficits, and between employers and striking employees over pay.

Punishing another's lack of cooperation might seem like a smart strategy, but in the laboratory, it can be counterproductive (Dreber et al., 2008). Punishment typically triggers retaliation, which means that those who punish tend to escalate the conflict, worsening their outcomes, while nice guys finish first. What punishers see as a defensive reaction, recipients see as an aggressive escalation (Anderson et al., 2008). When hitting back, they may hit harder while seeing themselves as merely returning tit for tat. In one experiment, volunteers used a mechanical device to press back on someone else's finger after receiving pressure on their own. Although they tried to reciprocate with the same degree of pressure, they typically responded with 40% more force. Thus, touches soon escalated to hard presses, much like a child saying "I only *touched* him, and then he *hit* me!" (Shergill et al., 2003).

THE TRAGEDY OF THE COMMONS

Many social dilemmas involve more than two parties. Climate change stems from deforestation and from the carbon dioxide emitted by vehicles, furnaces, and coal-fired power plants. Each car contributes infinitesimally to the problem, and the harm is diffused over many people. To model such social predicaments, researchers have developed laboratory dilemmas that involve multiple people.

A metaphor for the insidious nature of social dilemmas is what ecologist Garrett Hardin (1968) called the **tragedy of the commons.** He derived the name from the centrally located grassy pasture in old English towns. Imagine 100 farmers surrounding a commons capable of sustaining 100 cows. When each grazes one cow, the common feeding ground is optimally used. But then a farmer reasons, "If I put a second cow in the pasture, I'll double my output, minus the mere 1% overgrazing" and adds a second cow. So does each of the other farmers. The inevitable result? The tragedy of the commons: a mud field and famished cows.

tragedy of the commons
The "commons" is any shared resource, including air, water, energy sources, and food supplies. The tragedy occurs when individuals consume more than their share, with the cost of their doing so dispersed among all, causing the ultimate collapse — the tragedy — of the commons.

In today's world, the "commons" can be air, water, fish, or any shared and limited resource. If all use the resource in moderation, it may replenish itself as rapidly as it's harvested. The grass will grow, the fish will reproduce, and the water reservoir will reload. If not, a tragedy of the commons occurs.

Likewise, environmental pollution is the sum of many minor pollutions, each of which benefits the individual polluters much more than they could benefit themselves (and the environment) if they stopped polluting. We litter public places – dorm lounges, parks, zoos – while keeping our personal spaces clean. We deplete our natural resources because the immediate personal benefits of, for instance, taking a long, hot shower outweigh the seemingly inconsequential costs. Whalers knew others would exploit the whales if they didn't and that taking a few whales would hardly diminish the species. Therein lies the tragedy. *Everybody's business (conservation) becomes nobody's business.*

Is such individualism uniquely American? Kaori Sato (1987) gave students in Japan, a more collective culture, opportunities to harvest – for actual money – trees from a simulated forest. The students shared equally the costs of planting the forest. The result was similar to those in Western cultures: More than half the trees were harvested before they had grown to the most profitable size.

Sato's forest reminds me [DM] of my family's cookie jar, which was restocked once a week. What we *should* have done was conserve cookies so that each day we could each enjoy two or three. But lacking regulation and fearing that other family members would soon deplete the resource, what we actually did was maximize our individual cookie consumption by downing one after the other. The result: Within 24 hours, the cookie glut would end, and the jar would sit empty for the rest of the week.

It's tempting to hoard a resource that other people will also want. But if everyone hoards, the resource is soon depleted. You're not going to be able to carry all of those cookies anyway.
Sean Justice/Corbis Premium RF/Alamy Stock Photo

When resources are more difficult to quantify, people often consume more than they realize (Herlocker et al., 1997). As a bowl of mashed potatoes is passed around a table of 10, the first few diners are more likely to scoop out a disproportionate share than when a platter of 10 chicken drumsticks is passed.

THE FUNDAMENTAL ATTRIBUTION ERROR

The prisoner's dilemma and the tragedy of the commons games have several similar features. First, both games tempt people to explain their own behavior as due to external forces ("I had to protect myself against exploitation by my opponent") and to explain their partners' behavior as due to internal forces ("she was greedy," "he was untrustworthy"). Most never realize that their counterparts are viewing them with the same fundamental attribution error (Gifford & Hine, 1997; Hine & Gifford, 1996).

When Muslims have killed Americans, Western media have attributed the killings to evil dispositions (internal forces) – to the primitive, fanatical, hateful terrorists. When an American soldier killed 16 Afghans, including 9 children, he was said to be experiencing financial stress, suffering from marital problems, and frustrated by being passed over for a promotion – external forces (Greenwald, 2012). Violence explanations vary by whether the act is by or toward one's side.

EVOLVING MOTIVES

Second, *motives often change.* At first, people are eager to make some easy money, then to minimize their losses, and finally to save face and avoid defeat (Brockner et al., 1982; Teger, 1980). These shifting motives are strikingly similar to the shifting motives during the buildup of the Vietnam War. At first, President Lyndon Johnson's speeches expressed concern for democracy, freedom, and justice. As the conflict escalated, his concern became protecting America's honor and avoiding the national humiliation of losing a war. The same happened in the Iraq war, which initially was justified as destroying Saddam Hussein's weapons of mass destruction and then (when none were found) as deposing Hussein. Conflict can even become its own motive, as people can find purpose in conflict, as both soldiers and civilians sometimes do in times of war. In a series of experiments, people reminded of past violent conflicts (for example, the American Revolutionary War) or more recent violent conflicts (the November 2015 terrorist attacks in Paris) found more meaning in life *and* more meaning in violent conflict (Rovenpor et al., 2019). Conflict became a self-perpetuating cycle.

OUTCOMES NEED NOT SUM TO ZERO

Third, most real-life conflicts, like the prisoner's dilemma and the tragedy of the commons, are **non-zero-sum games.** The two sides' profits and losses need not add up to zero. Both can win; both can lose. Each game pits the immediate interests of individuals against the well-being of the group. Each is a diabolical social trap that shows how, even when each individual behaves rationally, harm can result. No malicious person planned for the earth's atmosphere to be warmed by a carbon dioxide blanket.

non-zero-sum games
Games in which outcomes need not sum to zero. With cooperation, both can win; with competition, both can lose (also called *mixed-motive situations*).

Not all self-serving behavior leads to collective doom. In plentiful commons – as in the world of the eighteenth-century capitalist economist Adam Smith (1776, p. 18) – individuals who seek to maximize their own profit may also give the community what it needs: "It is not from the benevolence of the butcher, the brewer, or the baker, that we expect our dinner," he observed, "but from their regard to their own interest."

RESOLVING SOCIAL DILEMMAS

In real-life situations, many people approach commons dilemmas with a cooperative outlook and expect similar cooperation from others, thus enabling their collective betterment (Krueger et al., 2012; Ostrom, 2014). Research with laboratory dilemmas has identified several ways to further encourage such mutual betterment (Gifford & Hine, 1997; Nowak, 2012).

REGULATION If taxes were entirely voluntary, how many would pay their full share? Modern societies do not depend on charity to pay for schools, parks, and social and military security; they require and enforce it. We also develop rules to safeguard our common good.

At the beginning of the COVID-19 pandemic in 2020, many cities imposed stay-at-home orders, ordered restaurants and bars to close, and required people to wear masks when around others to try to limit the spread of the virus. In addition, fishing and hunting have long been regulated by local seasons and limits; at the global level, an International Whaling Commission sets an agreed-upon "harvest" that enables whales to regenerate. Likewise, overfishing has been greatly reduced where fishing industries have guaranteed each fisher a percentage of each year's allowable catch (Costello et al., 2008).

However, regulation has costs: costs of administering and enforcing the regulations, costs of diminished personal freedom. This was evident during the pandemic when many restaurants and bars went out of business. A volatile political question thus arises: At what point does a regulation's cost exceed its benefits?

SMALL IS BEAUTIFUL There is another way to resolve social dilemmas: Make the group small. In a small commons, each person feels more responsible and effective (Kerr, 1989). As a group grows larger, people become more likely to think, "I couldn't have made a difference anyway" – a common excuse for noncooperation (Kerr & Kaufman-Gilliland, 1997).

In small groups, people also feel more identified with a group's success. Residential stability – when the same families stay in a neighborhood – also strengthens communal identity and procommunity behavior (Oishi et al., 2007). On the Pacific Northwest island where I [DM] grew up, our small neighborhood shared a communal water supply. On hot summer days when the reservoir ran low, a light came on, signaling our 15 families to conserve. Recognizing our responsibility to one another and feeling that our conservation really mattered, each of us conserved. The reservoir never ran dry.

"For that which is common to the greatest number has the least care bestowed upon it."
—Aristotle (BC 384–322)

In a much larger commons – say, a city – voluntary conservation is less successful. As Cape Town was facing becoming the world's first major city to run out of water in 2018, its nearly 4 million people were admonished to take extreme measures to conserve. Yet it was easy for any individual to think, "my flushing the toilet or taking a shower won't make a noticeable difference in the city's reservoir." Thus, residents and businesses did not conserve as much as anticipated, hastening the reservoir near-depletion (Maxmen, 2018).

Evolutionary psychologist Robin Dunbar (1992, 2010) noted that tribal villages and clans often have averaged about 150 people – enough to afford mutual support and protection but not more people than one can monitor. Thus, 150 has become known as "Dunbar's

Small is cooperative. On Scotland's Isle of Muck, Constable Lawrence MacEwan had an easy time policing the island's 33 residents. Over his half century on the job, there was only one crime (Boyle, 2019). In 2010, a row between two friends who had been drinking at a wedding became the first recorded crime in 50 years, but the next morning, they shook hands and all was well (Cameron, 2010). In 2015, the nearby island of Canna experienced its "crime of the century" (its first crime since the 1960s) when thieves stole crafts, food, and money from its shop. The shop was left unlocked so that fishing people resting at the pier overnight could buy what they needed, paying via an "honesty box."
Catherine Karnow

number" – the maximum number of people someone can maintain relationships with. This seemingly natural group size is also, he believes, the optimum size for business organizations, religious congregations, and military fighting units. When groups grow beyond 150 members, it's difficult for people to know and keep track of everyone. Even on social media, most people cannot interact in a meaningful way with more than 150 others (Dunbar, 2016; Koltsova et al., 2021).

COMMUNICATION To resolve a social dilemma, people must communicate. In the laboratory as in real life, group communication sometimes degenerates into threats and name-calling (Deutsch & Krauss, 1960). More often, communication enables cooperation (Bornstein et al., 1988, 1989). Discussing the dilemma forges a group identity, which enhances concern for everyone's welfare. It devises group norms and expectations and pressures members to follow them. It enables them to commit themselves to cooperation (Bouas & Komorita, 1996; Drolet & Morris, 2000; Kerr et al., 1994, 1997; Pruitt, 1998). Thanks to language, humans are the most cooperative, reciprocally helpful species (Nowak, 2012).

Imagine that an experimenter offered you and six strangers a choice: You can each have $6, or you can donate your $6 to the other six. If you give away your money, the experimenter will double your gift. No one will be told whether you chose to give or keep your $6. Thus, if all seven give, everyone pockets $12. If you alone keep your $6 and all the others give theirs, you pocket $18. If you give and all the others don't, you pocket nothing. In this experiment, cooperation is mutually advantageous, but it requires risk. Psychologist Robyn Dawes found that, without discussion, about 30% of people gave. With discussion, in which they could establish trust and cooperation, about 80% gave (Dawes, 1980, 1994). Communication leads to cooperation.

Without communication, those who expect others not to cooperate will usually refuse to cooperate themselves (Messé & Sivacek, 1979; Pruitt & Kimmel, 1977). People who mistrust others are often uncooperative, as they feel they need to protect themselves against exploitation. Noncooperation, in turn, feeds further mistrust ("What else could I do? It's a dog-eat-dog world"). In experiments, communication reduces mistrust, enabling people to reach agreements that lead to their common betterment (Dannals et al., 2022).

"My own belief is that Russian and Chinese behavior is as much influenced by suspicion of our intentions as ours is by suspicion of theirs. This would mean that we have great influence on their behavior — that, by treating them as hostile, we assure their hostility."

—U.S. Senator J. William Fulbright, *A New Internationalism,* 1971

CHANGING THE PAYOFFS In the laboratory, cooperation rises when experimenters change the payoff matrix to reward cooperation and punish exploitation (Balliet et al., 2011). Changing payoffs also helps resolve actual dilemmas. In some cities, freeways clog and skies smog because people prefer the convenience of driving to work by themselves. Each knows that one more car does not add noticeably to the congestion and pollution. To alter the personal cost-benefit calculations, many cities now give carpoolers and electric car drivers incentives, such as designated freeway lanes or reduced tolls.

APPEALING TO ALTRUISTIC NORMS We have seen that increasing bystanders' feelings of responsibility for others boosts altruism. Will appeals to altruistic motives similarly prompt people to act for the common good?

The evidence is mixed. On the one hand, just *knowing* the dire consequences of noncooperation has little effect. People may realize that their self-serving choices are mutually destructive yet continue to make them. People know that climate change is occurring yet continue buying gas-slurping SUVs. As we have seen many times in this book, attitudes sometimes fail to influence behavior. *Knowing* what is good does not necessarily lead to *doing* what is good.

To change behavior, many cities have changed the payoff matrix. Fast carpool-only lanes increase the benefits of carpooling and clean air vehicles, and the costs of driving alone.
Ted Foxx/Alamy Stock Photo

Norms and expectations matter: Cooperation is not usually emphasized on the stock market trading floor but is in many community groups and other workplaces.
Geber86/Getty Images

Still, most people do adhere to norms of social responsibility, reciprocity, equity, and keeping one's commitments (Kerr, 1992). The problem is how to tap such feelings. One way is through the influence of a charismatic leader who inspires others to cooperate (De Cremer, 2002). In China, those who were educated during Mao's "planned economy" era – an era that emphasized equal wealth distribution – made more cooperative social dilemma game choices than those who were not (Zhu et al., 2013).

Another way to increase altruism is by defining situations in ways that invoke cooperative norms. In one experiment, only a third of participants cooperated in a simulation labeled the "Wall Street Game." But two-thirds did so when the same social dilemma was labeled the "Community Game" (Liberman et al., 2004). There may also be a biological component: When White European university students were reminded of altruistic norms and received a dose of the bonding hormone oxytocin, they gave 74% more to help refugees than did the control group (Marsh et al., 2017).

Could such appeals work in large-scale dilemmas? In the 1960s struggle for civil rights for Black Americans, many marchers willingly agreed, for the sake of the larger group, to suffer harassment, beatings, and jail. In wartime, people make great personal sacrifices for the good of their group. As Winston Churchill said of the Battle of Britain, the actions of the Royal Air Force pilots were genuinely altruistic: Many people owed a great deal to those who flew into battle knowing there was a high probability – 70% for those on a standard tour of duty – that they would not return (Levinson, 1950).

"Never in the field of human conflict was so much owed by so many to so few."

—Sir Winston Churchill, House of Commons, August 20, 1940

To summarize, we can minimize destructive entrapment in social dilemmas by establishing rules that regulate self-serving behavior, by keeping groups small, by enabling people to communicate, by changing payoffs to make cooperation more rewarding, and by invoking compelling altruistic norms.

Competition

Hostilities often arise when groups compete for scarce jobs, housing, or resources. When interests clash, conflict erupts (Krupp & Cook, 2018). When Dutch citizens felt threatened, such as by economic or terrorist threats, they became higher in right-wing authoritarianism (believing in absolute authority and harsh punishments – a philosophy that can increase conflict [Onraet et al., 2014]). Across 17 countries, the threat of the COVID-19 pandemic led to the desire for authoritarian leadership and the instituting of martial law, especially among those high in right-wing authoritarianism (Pizarro et al., 2023). Similarly, terrorist bombings in London increased anti-Muslim and anti-immigrant sentiments (Van de Vyver et al., 2016). Not only do perceived threats feed prejudice and conflict, prejudice – in a vicious cycle – also amplifies the perception of a threat (Bahns, 2017).

To experiment on competition's effect, we could randomly divide people into two groups, have the groups compete for a scarce resource, and see what happens. That is precisely what Muzafer Sherif (1966) and his colleagues did in a famous series of experiments with 11- and 12-year-old boys. The inspiration for those experiments dated back to Sherif's witnessing, as a teenager, Greek troops invading his Turkish province in 1919.

They started killing people right and left. [That] made a great impression on me. There and then I became interested in understanding why these things were happening among human beings. . . . I wanted to learn whatever science or specialization was needed to understand this intergroup savagery. (Quoted by Aron & Aron, 1989, p. 131.)

Sherif introduced the seeming essentials for savagery into several 3-week summer camping experiences. In one study, he divided 22 unacquainted Oklahoma City boys into two groups, took them to a Boy Scout camp in separate buses, and settled them in bunkhouses about a half-mile apart at Oklahoma's Robber's Cave State Park. For most of the first week, each group was unaware of the other's existence. By cooperating in various activities – preparing meals, camping out, fixing up a swimming hole, building a rope bridge – each group soon became close-knit. They gave themselves names: "Rattlers" and "Eagles." Typifying the good feeling, a sign appeared in one cabin: "Home Sweet Home."

Group identity thus established, the stage was set for the conflict. Near the end of the first week, the Rattlers discovered the Eagles "on 'our' baseball field." When the camp staff then proposed a tournament of competitive activities between the two groups (baseball games, tugs-of-war, cabin inspections, treasure hunts, and so forth), both groups responded enthusiastically. This was a win-lose competition. The spoils (medals, knives) would all go to the tournament victor.

The result? The camp degenerated into open warfare. It was like a scene from William Golding's novel *Lord of the Flies,* which depicts the social disintegration of boys marooned on an island. In Sherif's study, the conflict began with each side calling the other names during the competitive activities. Soon it escalated to dining hall "garbage wars," flag burnings, cabin ransackings, even fistfights. Asked to describe the other group, the boys said they were "sneaky," "smart alecks," "stinkers" but referred to their own group as "brave," "tough," "friendly." It was a difficult experience, driving some of the boys to bedwetting, running away, homesickness, and later recollections of an unhappy experience (Perry, 2014).

The win-lose competition had produced intense conflict, negative images of the outgroup, and strong ingroup cohesiveness and pride. Group polarization no doubt exacerbated the conflict. In competition-fostering situations, groups behave more competitively than do individuals (Wildschut et al., 2003, 2007). Even after hearing tolerance-advocating messages, ingroup discussion often exacerbates dislike of the conflicting group (Paluck, 2010).

All this occurred without any cultural, physical, or economic differences between the two groups and with boys who were their communities' "cream of the crop." Sherif noted that, had we visited the camp at that point, we would have concluded these "were wicked, disturbed, and vicious bunches of youngsters" (Sherif, 1966, p. 85). Actually, their evil behavior was triggered by an evil situation. Or so Sherif contended, though a recent criticism asserts that his research team encouraged the conflict in order to illustrate their belief that competition is often socially toxic (Perry, 2018). Sherif also believed in the reconciling power of cooperation. And, as we will see, his camp experiment not only made strangers into enemies; it also then made the enemies into friends.

Competition kindles conflict. In competition-fostering situations, groups act more competitively, as in this raid by boys during the Robber's Cave experiment, than do individuals.
The Drs. Nicholas and Dorothy Cummings Center for the History of Psychology. The University of Akron.

Perceived Injustice

"That's unfair!" "What a ripoff!" "We deserve better!" Such comments typify conflicts bred by perceived injustice.

"Do unto others 25 percent better than you would expect them to do unto you, to correct for subjective error."

—Linus Pauling, response to audience question at Monterey Peninsula College, 1961.

But what is just? The answer may vary depending on your cultural perspective. In collectivistic cultures, such as China, India, and rural Africa, justice is defined as *equality* or *need fulfillment:* everyone getting the same share or everyone getting the share they need (Hui et al., 1991; Leung & Bond, 1984; Schäfer et al., 2015). As Karl Marx wrote, "From each according to his abilities, to each according to his needs."

In Western capitalist nations, however, people are more likely to follow the principle of *equity:* the distribution of rewards in proportion to individuals' contributions (Huppert et al., 2019; Starmans et al., 2017; Walster et al., 1978). Imagine you and "Jamie" are work colleagues. If you contribute more than Jamie (put in more effort in your joint projects) and benefit more than Jamie (are paid more money), the relationship is equitable. However, if you contribute more and benefit less than Jamie does, you will feel exploited and irritated; Jamie may feel guilty. Chances are, though, that you will be more sensitive to the inequity than Jamie will be, due to self-serving bias (Greenberg, 1986; Messick & Sentis, 1979).

Even if someone agrees with the equity principle's definition of justice, they might disagree about how to measure each person's contributions. For example, older people may favor basing pay on seniority, and younger people might argue for the importance of current productivity. Given such a disagreement, whose definition is likely to prevail? Those with social power usually convince themselves and others that they deserve what they're getting (Guinote, 2017; Mikula, 1984). This has been called a "golden" rule: Whoever has the gold makes the rules.

Misperception

Recall that conflict is a *perceived* incompatibility of actions or goals. Many conflicts contain only a small core of truly incompatible goals; the bigger problem is the misperceptions of the other's motives and goals. The Eagles and the Rattlers did indeed have some genuinely incompatible aims. But their perceptions subjectively magnified their differences (**Figure 3**).

In earlier chapters, we considered the seeds of such misperception:

- *Self-serving bias* leads individuals and groups to accept credit for their good deeds and shirk responsibility for bad deeds.
- A tendency to *self-justify* inclines people to deny the wrong of their evil acts. ("You call that hitting? I hardly touched him!")
- Thanks to the *fundamental attribution error,* each side sees the other's hostility as reflecting an evil disposition.
- Groups then filter the information and interpret it to fit their *preconceptions.*
- Groups frequently *polarize* these self-serving, self-justifying, biasing tendencies.
- One symptom of *groupthink* is the tendency to perceive one's own group as moral and strong, and the opposition as evil and weak. Acts of terrorism that in most people's eyes are despicable brutality are seen by others as a "holy war."
- Indeed, the mere fact of being in a group triggers an *ingroup bias.*
- Negative *stereotypes* of the outgroup, once formed, are often resistant to contradictory evidence.

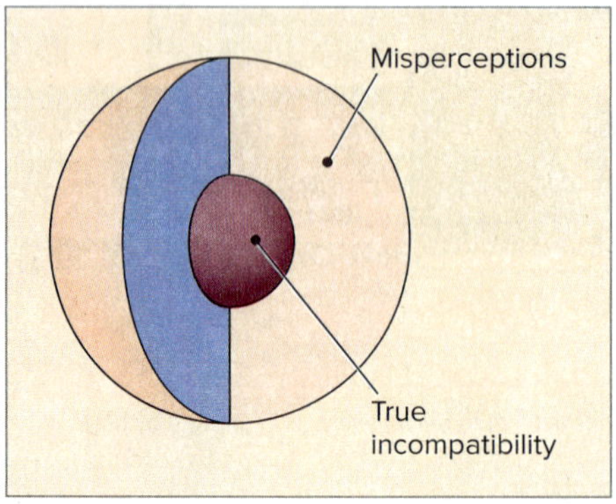

FIGURE 3
Many conflicts contain a core of truly incompatible goals surrounded by a larger exterior of misperceptions.

So it should not surprise us, though it should sober us, to discover that people in conflict form distorted images of one another. Wherever in the world you live, was it not true that when your country was last at war, it clothed itself in moral virtue? That it prepared for war by demonizing the enemy? That most of its people accepted their government's case for war and rallied 'round its flag? Show social psychologists Ervin Staub and Daniel Bar-Tal (2003) a group in intractable conflict, and they will show you a group that:

- sees its own goals as supremely important,
- takes pride in "us" and devalues "them,"
- believes itself victimized,
- elevates patriotism, solidarity, and loyalty to their group's needs,
- celebrates self-sacrifice, and
- suppresses criticism.

"Aggression breeds patriotism, and patriotism curbs dissent."

—Maureen Dowd, "The Iceman Cometh," 2003

Although one side to a conflict may indeed be acting with greater moral virtue, the point is that enemy images are predictable. Even the types of misperception are intriguingly predictable. This might be worth considering the next time you read the latest opinion piece about a politician from an opposing party.

MIRROR-IMAGE PERCEPTIONS

To a striking degree, the misperceptions of those in conflict are mutual. People in conflict attribute similar virtues to themselves and vices to the other. When U.S. psychologist Urie Bronfenbrenner (1961) visited the Soviet Union in 1960 and conversed with many ordinary citizens, he was astonished to hear them saying the same things about the United States that Americans were saying about the Soviets. The Soviets said that the U.S. government was militarily aggressive; that it exploited and deluded the American people; that in diplomacy, it was not to be trusted. "Slowly and painfully, it forced itself upon one that the Russians' distorted picture of us was curiously similar to our view of them – a mirror image." That mirror image persists: In 2022–2023 polls, 75% of Russians view the U.S. in a negative light, and 70% of Americans see Russia as the enemy (Shedd & Strandner, 2022; Wike et al., 2023).

The negative perceptions may also become a self-fulfilling prophecy. If A expects B to be hostile, A may treat B in such a way that B fulfills A's expectations, thus beginning a vicious cycle (Kennedy & Pronin, 2008). Morton Deutsch (1986) explained:

> You hear the false rumor that a friend is saying nasty things about you; you snub him; he then badmouths you, confirming your expectation. Similarly, if the policymakers of East and West believe that war is likely and either attempts to increase its military security vis-à-vis the other, the other's response will justify the initial move.

Negative **mirror-image perceptions** have been an obstacle to peace in many places:

mirror-image perceptions
Reciprocal views of each other often held by parties in conflict; for example, each may view itself as moral and peace-loving and the other as evil and aggressive.

- *Middle East perceptions.* Both sides of the Palestinian-Israeli conflict insist that "we" are motivated by our need to protect our security and our territory, whereas "they" want to obliterate us and gobble up our land. "We" are the indigenous people here, "they" are the invaders. "We" are the victims; "they" are the aggressors, and that message begins in early childhood (Bar-Tal, 2004, 2013; Heradstveit, 1979; Kelman, 2007; Nasie et al., 2021). Given such intense mistrust, negotiation is difficult.
- *What defines terrorism?* Terrorism is in the eye of the beholder. Ninety-eight percent of Palestinians agreed that the killing of 29 Palestinians by an assault-rifle-bearing Israeli at a mosque was terrorism, but 82% did not believe that the killing of 21 Israeli youths by a Palestinian suicide bomb was terrorism (Kruglanski & Fishman, 2006). Israelis likewise have responded to violence with intensified perceptions of Palestinian evil intent (Bar-Tal, 2004, 2013).
- *"Myside" bias.* People also display a "myside" bias. In one experiment, American students were much more likely to favor banning an accident-prone German car from U.S. roads than a comparably accident-prone American car from German roads (Stanovich et al., 2013). Even torture seems more morally justified when "we" rather than "they" do it (Tarrant et al., 2012).

Self-confirming, mirror-image perceptions are a hallmark of intense conflict.
Steve Debenport/Getty Images

- *Political polarization.* In the polarized United States, both Democrats and Republicans see love and benevolence on their side and hatred and evil on the other (Pew, 2019; Waytz et al., 2014). They also misperceive each other's positions: 93% of Republicans believe Americans have a responsibility to learn from the country's past mistakes, but Democrats think only 35% of Republicans believe that (Hawkins, 2022). In the United Kingdom, those on either side of political disagreements were the most divided when they believed the other side didn't understand them and their motives. "They just don't understand us" is a common belief across political divides (Livingstone et al., 2020).

Such conflicts, noted Philip Zimbardo (2004), engage "a two-category world – of good people, like US, and of bad people, like THEM." In fact, noted Daniel Kahneman and Jonathan Renshon (2007), all the biases uncovered in 40 years of psychological research are conducive to war. They "incline national leaders to exaggerate the evil intentions of adversaries, to misjudge how adversaries perceive them, to be overly sanguine when hostilities start, and overly reluctant to make necessary concessions in negotiations."

Opposing sides in a conflict tend to exaggerate their differences. On issues related to abortion and politics, partisans perceive exaggerated differences from their adversaries – who actually agree with them more often than they would guess (Chambers et al., 2006; Hoerst & Drury, 2021; Jerit & Zhao, 2020). Opposing sides also tend to have a "bias blind spot," noted psychologist Cynthia McPherson Frantz (2006). They see their own understandings as not biased by their liking or disliking for others, but those who disagree with them seem unfair and biased. This might be one reason why people protesting for social change sometimes feel justified in using extreme actions such as vandalizing property or physically fighting with police or counterprotesters. However, violent actions have the opposite effect, reducing popular support for their cause (Feinberg et al., 2020). Vandalism and violence may garner attention, but they undermine victory.

"The American people are good, but the leaders are bad."

—Baghdad grocer Adul Gesan after 1998 American bombing of Iraq

Group conflicts are often fueled by an illusion that the enemy's top leaders are evil but their people, though controlled and manipulated, are pro-"us." This *evil leader-good people* perception characterized Americans' and Russians' views of each other during the Cold War. The United States entered the Vietnam War believing that in areas dominated by the Communist Vietcong "terrorists," many of the people were allies-in-waiting. As suppressed information later revealed, those beliefs were mere wishful thinking. In 2022, many Russians believed that Ukrainians would welcome their troops as liberators (Harding, 2022). Instead, Ukraine strenuously fought the invasion (See "Research Close-Up: Misperceptions and War".)

SIMPLISTIC THINKING

When tension rises – as happens during an international crisis – rational thinking becomes more difficult (Janis, 1989). Views of the enemy become more simplistic and stereotyped, and seat-of-the-pants judgments become more likely. Even the mere expectation of conflict can serve to freeze thinking and impede creative problem solving (Carnevale & Probst, 1998). Social psychologist Philip Tetlock (1988) observed inflexible thinking when he analyzed Russian and American rhetoric since 1945. During the Berlin blockade, the Korean War, and the Russian invasion of Afghanistan, political statements became simplified into good-versus-bad terms.

Researchers have also analyzed political rhetoric preceding the outset of major wars, surprise military attacks, Middle Eastern conflicts, and revolutions (Conway et al., 2001). In nearly every case, attacking leaders displayed increasingly simplistic we-are-good/

research CLOSE-UP Misperception and War

Most research that we report in this book offers numerical data drawn from laboratory or survey observations of people's behavior, thoughts, and attitudes. But there are other ways to do research. Some social psychologists, especially in Europe, analyze natural human discourse; they study written texts or spoken conversation to glimpse how people interpret and construct the events of their lives (Edwards & Potter, 2005). Others have analyzed human behavior in historical contexts, as did Irving Janis (1972) in exploring groupthink in historical fiascoes and Philip Tetlock (2005) in exploring the judgment failures of supposed political experts.

In what was arguably social psychology's longest career, Ralph K. White, legendary for his late 1930s studies of democratic versus autocratic leadership (with pioneering social psychologists Kurt Lewin and Ronald Lippitt), published in 2004 — at age 97 — a capstone article summarizing his earlier analyses of how misperceptions feed war. In reviewing 10 wars from the past century, White reported that each was marked by at least one of three misperceptions: *underestimating* the strength of one's enemy, *rationalizing* one's own motives and behavior, and, especially, *demonizing* the enemy.

Underestimating one's adversary, he observed, emboldened Hitler to attack Russia, Japan to attack the United States, and the United States to enter the Korean and Vietnam wars. And rationalization of one's own actions and demonization of the adversary are the hallmark of war. In the early twenty-first century, as the United States and Iraq threatened war, each said the other was "evil." To George W. Bush, Saddam Hussein was a "murderous tyrant" and a "madman" who threatened the civilized world with weapons of mass destruction. To Iraq's government, the Bush government was a "gang of evil" (Preston, 2002). And in the months prior to the 2020 U.S. presidential election, each party painted the other as posing a threat to democracy (Viser & Olorunnipa, 2020).

The truth need not lie midway between such clashing perceptions. Yet "valid perception is an antidote to hate," concluded White as he reflected on his lifetime as a peace psychologist. Empathy — accurately perceiving the other's thoughts and feelings — is "one of the most important factors for preventing war. . . . Empathy can help two or more nations avoid the dangers of misperception that lead to the wars most would prefer not to fight."

they-are-bad thinking immediately prior to their aggressive action. Russian president Vladimir Putin, for example, argued without evidence that Ukraine's government was "pro-Nazi" in the weeks after Russia's invasion of the country (Troianovski, 2022).

SHIFTING PERCEPTIONS

If misperceptions accompany conflict, they should appear and disappear as conflicts wax and wane. And they do, with startling regularity. The same processes that create the enemy's image can reverse that image when the enemy becomes an ally. Thus, the "bloodthirsty, cruel, treacherous" Japanese of World War II soon became – in North American minds and in the media – our "intelligent, hard-working, self-disciplined, resourceful allies" (Gallup, 1972).

The Germans, who after two world wars were hated, then admired, and then again hated, were once again admired – apparently no longer plagued by what earlier was presumed to be cruelty in their national character. As long as Iraq was attacking unpopular Iran, even while using chemical weapons to massacre its own Kurds, many nations supported it. Our enemy's enemy is our friend. When Iraq ended its war with Iran and invaded oil-rich Kuwait, Iraq's behavior suddenly became "barbaric." Images of our enemies change with amazing ease.

Misperceptions during conflict provide a chilling reminder that people need not be insane or abnormally malicious to form distorted images of their antagonists. When we experience conflict with another nation, another group, or simply a roommate or a parent, we readily misperceive our own motives as good and the other's as evil. And just as readily, our antagonists form a mirror-image perception of us.

So, with antagonists trapped in a social dilemma, competing for scarce resources, or perceiving injustice, the conflict continues until something enables both parties to peel away

"[There is] a psychological barrier between us, a barrier of suspicion, a barrier of rejection; a barrier of fear, of deception, a barrier of hallucination. . . ."

—Former Egyptian President Anwar Al-Sadat to the Israeli Knesset, 1977 their misperceptions and work at reconciling their actual differences. Good advice, then, is this: When in conflict, do not assume that the other fails to share your values and morality. Rather, share and compare perceptions, assuming that the other perceives the situation differently.

SUMMING UP: What Creates Conflict?

- Whenever two or more people, groups, or nations interact, their perceived needs and goals may conflict. Many social dilemmas arise as people pursue individual self-interest to their collective detriment. Two *non-zero sum* laboratory games, the *prisoner's dilemma* and the *tragedy of the commons,* exemplify such dilemmas. In real life, we can avoid such traps by establishing rules that regulate self-serving behavior; by keeping social groups small so people feel responsibility for one another; by enabling communication, thus reducing mistrust; by changing payoffs to make cooperation more rewarding; and by invoking altruistic norms.
- When people compete for scarce resources, human relations often sink into prejudice and hostility. In his famous experiments, Muzafer Sherif found that win-lose competition quickly made strangers into enemies, triggering outright warfare even among normally upstanding boys.
- *Conflicts* also arise when people perceive injustice. According to equity theory, people define justice as the distribution of rewards in proportion to one's contributions. Conflicts occur when people disagree on the extent of their contributions and thus on the equity of their outcomes.
- Conflicts frequently contain a small core of truly incompatible goals, surrounded by a thick layer of misperceptions of the adversary's motives and goals. Often, conflicting parties have *mirror-image perceptions*. When both sides believe "We are peace-loving – they are hostile," each may treat the other in ways that provoke confirmation of its expectations. International conflicts are sometimes also fed by an evil leader-good people illusion.

HOW CAN PEACE BE ACHIEVED?

Explain the processes that enable the achievement of peace.

"We know more about war than we do about peace — more about killing than we know about living."

—General Omar Bradley (1893–1981), former U.S. Army Chief of Staff

We have seen how conflicts are ignited by social traps, competition, perceived injustices, and misperceptions. Although the picture is grim, it is not hopeless. Sometimes hostilities transform into friendship. To explore the transition from closed fists to open arms, social psychologists have focused on four peacemaking strategies. We can remember these as the four Cs of peacemaking: contact, cooperation, communication, and conciliation.

Contact

Might putting two conflicting individuals or groups into close contact enable them to know and like each other? Perhaps not: We have seen how negative expectations can bias judgments and create self-fulfilling prophecies. When tensions run high, contact may fuel a fight.

But we have also seen that proximity – and the accompanying interaction, anticipation of interaction, and mere exposure – boosts liking. And we noted how blatant racial prejudice declined following desegregation, showing that *attitudes follow behavior.* If this social-psychological principle now seems obvious, remember: That's how things usually seem after you know them. To the U.S. Supreme Court in 1896, the idea that desegregated behavior might reduce prejudicial attitudes was anything but obvious. What seemed obvious at the time was "that legislation is powerless to eradicate racial instincts" *(Plessy v. Ferguson).* What does modern research show?

DOES CONTACT PREDICT ATTITUDES?

In general, contact between those of different groups predicts tolerance (Tropp et al., 2022). In a painstaking analysis, researchers assembled data from 516 studies of 250,555 people in

38 nations (Pettigrew & Tropp, 2008, 2011; Tropp & Pettigrew, 2005). In 94% of studies, *increased contact predicted decreased prejudice.* This is especially so for majority group attitudes toward minorities and especially true in individualistic cultures (Durrheim et al., 2011; Gibson & Claassen, 2010; Kende et al., 2018). Contact between groups even reduced prejudice when people perceived high levels of threat or discrimination (Van Assche et al., 2023).

Even simple exposure to other-race faces improves attitudes toward other races (Zebrowitz et al., 2008). Online exposure via social media sites can also decrease prejudice, especially when people perceive similarity with outgroup members (Kim & Harwood, 2020; Neubaum et al., 2020). This occurs partially because contact reduces dehumanization of outgroups—getting to know people who seem different often communicates their common humanity (Bruneau et al., 2021).

Many studies—in Bosnia, Israel and Palestine, Iraq, Turkey, Northern Ireland, Lebanon, Liberia, South Africa, and Britain (Wright et al., 2017)—find links between contact and positive attitudes:

- *Sexual orientation and transgender identity.* The more contact straight people have with gays and lesbians, the more accepting they become (Collier et al., 2012; DellaPosta, 2018; Earle et al., 2021; Górska et al., 2017; Smith et al., 2009). The more contact people have with transgender individuals, the less trans-prejudice they express and the warmer they feel toward transgender people (Michelson & Harrison, 2023; Norton & Herek, 2013). What matters is not just what you know about gay or transgender people, but *who* you know.
- *Immigrants.* Residents of urban U.S. counties, where 15% of people are immigrants, have more positive attitudes toward immigrants than those in rural U.S. counties, where only 2% of people are immigrants (Sacchetti & Guskin, 2017). In Germany, districts with the most immigrants have the *fewest* hate crimes (Wagner et al., 2020).
- *Religion.* The more contact Dutch adolescents have with Muslims, the more accepting of Muslims they are (González et al., 2008). Iraqi Christians randomly assigned to play on a soccer team with Muslims (rather than playing on an all-Christian team) were more likely to vote for a Muslim player from another team to receive an award (Mousa, 2020). In Northern Ireland, Catholic and Protestant teens felt more positive toward the other religious group when they had more contact with each other (Merrilees et al., 2023).
- *Race.* For White students in the United States or South Africa, having a Black roommate improves racial attitudes and leads to greater comfort with those of another race (Corno et al., 2022; Gaither & Sommers, 2013).
- *Socioeconomic status (SES).* Children and teens who had more contact with lower SES peers were less likely to support favoritism of higher SES peers (Gonul et al., 2023).
- *Age.* The more contact younger people have with older adults, the more favorable their attitudes toward older people (Drury et al., 2016). The same was true in the other direction: Older adults who had more contact with younger adults viewed young adults more warmly (Kuball et al., 2023).
- *Indirect contact.* Even vicarious indirect contact, via story reading or imagination, or through a friend's having an outgroup friend, tends to reduce prejudice (Zhou et al., 2019). This indirect contact effect, also called the *extended-contact effect,* can spread more positive attitudes through a peer group (Christ et al., 2010).

In the United States, segregation and expressed prejudice have diminished together since the 1960s. But was interracial contact the *cause* of these improved attitudes? Were those who actually experienced desegregation affected by it?

School desegregation produced measurable benefits, such as leading to more Black youth attending and succeeding in college (Stephan, 1988). Does the desegregation of schools, neighborhoods, and workplaces also produce favorable *social* results? The evidence is mixed.

On the one hand, many studies conducted during and shortly after desegregation found Whites' attitudes toward Blacks improving markedly. Among department store clerks and customers, merchant marines, government workers, police officers, neighbors, and students,

In some studies, school desegregation improved racial attitudes. Further research identified interracial situations that produce the most positive outcomes.
lisegagne/E+/Getty Images

racial contact led to diminished prejudice (Amir, 1969; Pettigrew, 1969). For example, near the end of World War II, the U.S. Army partially desegregated some of its rifle companies (Stouffer et al., 1949). When asked their opinions of such desegregation, 11% of the White soldiers in segregated companies approved. Of those in desegregated companies, 60% approved.

Morton Deutsch and Mary Collins (1951) took advantage of a made-to-order natural experiment. In accord with state law, New York City desegregated its public housing units, assigning families to apartments without regard to race. In a similar development across the river in Newark, New Jersey, Black people and White people were assigned to separate buildings. White women in the desegregated development were far more likely than those in the segregated development to favor interracial housing and to say their attitudes toward Black people had improved. Exaggerated stereotypes had wilted in the face of reality.

Such findings influenced the Supreme Court's 1954 decision to desegregate schools and helped fuel the 1960s civil rights movement (Pettigrew, 1986, 2004). Yet initial studies of the effects of school desegregation were less encouraging. After reviewing all the available studies, Walter Stephan (1986) concluded that racial attitudes had not changed with desegregation. For Black youth, desegregated schooling increased the likelihood of attending integrated (or predominantly White) colleges, living in integrated neighborhoods, and working in integrated settings, but did not influence attitudes as much.

Thus, we can see that sometimes desegregation improves racial attitudes, and sometimes – especially when there is anxiety or perceived threat (Pettigrew, 2004) – it doesn't. Such disagreements excite the scientist's detective spirit. What explains the difference? So far, we've been lumping all kinds of desegregation together. Actual desegregation occurs in many ways and under vastly different conditions. We'll explore these conditions next.

DOES DESEGREGATION IMPROVE RACIAL ATTITUDES?

WHEN DESEGREGATION DOES NOT IMPROVE RACIAL ATTITUDES Researchers have gone into dozens of desegregated schools and observed with whom children of a given race eat, talk, and loiter. Race influences contact. White people disproportionately associated with White people, Black people with Black people (Schofield, 1982, 1986). On college campuses, students often self-segregate by race, including in social groups such as fraternities and sororities (Combs et al., 2017; Kim et al., 2015). The same self-imposed segregation was evident in a South African desegregated beach, as John Dixon and Kevin Durrheim (2003) discovered when they recorded the location of Black, White, and Indian beachgoers one midsummer afternoon (**Figure 4**).

Desegregated neighborhoods, cafeterias, and restaurants may likewise fail to produce integrated interactions (Clack et al., 2005; Dixon et al., 2005a,b). In school cafeterias, people may wonder, "Why are all the Black kids sitting together?" (a question that could just as easily be asked of the White kids). One study observed 119 class sessions of 26 University of Cape Town tutorial groups (Alexander & Tredoux, 2010). On average, the researchers calculated, 71% of Black students would have needed to change seats to achieve a fully integrated seating pattern. Even within the same race, people tend to self-segregate based on other factors. In universities in Northern Ireland, Catholic students sat with other Catholic students in the lecture hall, and Protestant students sat with other Protestants (Orr et al., 2012). And in the Northern Ireland city of Belfast, Catholics and Protestants even use different entrances to public parks and grocery stores (Dixon et al., 2020).

Anxiety around interracial interaction may explain why desegregation doesn't always lead to better attitudes. When students of different races are paired as roommates or as partners

FIGURE 4

Desegregation Needn't Mean Contact

After this Scottburgh, South Africa, beach became "open" and desegregated in the new South Africa, Blacks (represented by red dots), Whites (blue dots), and Indians (yellow dots) tended to cluster with their own race.

Source: From Dixon & Durrheim, 2003.

in an experiment, they are less likely to engage in intimate self-disclosure than those in same-race relationships (Johnson et al., 2009; Trail et al., 2009).

Efforts to facilitate contact sometimes help but sometimes fall flat. "We had one day when some of the Protestant schools came over," explained one Catholic youngster after a Northern Ireland school exchange (Cairns & Hewstone, 2002). "It was supposed to be like . . . mixing, but there was very little mixing. It wasn't because we didn't want to; it was just really awkward." The lack of mixing stems partly from *pluralistic ignorance.* Many White people and Black people say they would like more contact but misperceive that the other does not reciprocate their feelings. (See "Research Close-Up: Relationships That Might Have Been" and "The Inside Story: Nicole Shelton and Jennifer Richeson on Cross-Racial Friendships.")

WHEN DESEGREGATION IMPROVES RACIAL ATTITUDES

FRIENDSHIP The encouraging older studies of store clerks, soldiers, and housing-project neighbors involved considerable interracial contact, more than enough to reduce the anxiety that marks initial intergroup contact. Other studies show similar benefits for prolonged, personal contact – between Black and White prison inmates, between Black and White girls at a summer camp, between Black and White university roommates, between Black, Coloured, and White South Africans, and between U.S.-born people and immigrants (Al Ramiah & Hewstone, 2013; Beelmann & Heinemann, 2014; Tropp et al., 2018). The same has been true of intergroup contact programs in Northern Ireland, Cyprus, and Bosnia (Hewstone et al., 2014). One program that brought Israeli and Palestinian youth to a 3-week camp in the United States produced significant and sustained improvement in their attitudes toward the other group (Schroeder & Risen, 2014).

So how does intergroup contact reduce prejudice and increase support for racial equality? It does so, report contact researchers (Al Ramiah & Hewstone, 2013; Killen et al., 2022; Tropp & Barlow, 2018), by:

- *reducing anxiety* (more contact brings greater comfort),
- *increasing empathy* (contact helps people put themselves in the others' shoes),
- *humanizing others* (enabling people to discover their similarities), and
- *decreasing perceived threats* (alleviating overblown fears and increasing trust).

research CLOSE-UP Relationships That Might Have Been

Perhaps you can recall a time when you really would have liked to reach out to someone. Maybe it was someone of another race whom you wanted to welcome to the open seat at your dining hall or library table. But you worried that the person might be wary of sitting with you. On some such occasions, the other person shared your wish to connect but assumed that your distance signified indifference or even prejudice. Alas, thanks to pluralistic ignorance — shared false impressions of another's feelings — you passed like ships in the night.

These types of misunderstandings may stand in the way of cross-racial friendships. To find out, Nicole Shelton and Jennifer Richeson (2005; Richeson & Shelton, 2012) asked White Princeton University students to imagine how they would react upon entering their dining hall and noticing several Black (or White) "students who live near you sitting together." How interested would you be in joining them? And how likely is it that one of them would beckon you to join them? White students believed that they, more than Black students, would be interested in the contact — even though Black students express desire for cross-racial friendships in surveys.

And how do people explain failures to make interracial contact? Shelton and Richeson next invited Princeton White and Black students to contemplate a dining hall situation in which they notice a table with familiar-looking students of the other race, but neither they nor the seated students reach out to the other. The study participants, regardless of race, attributed their own inaction in such a situation primarily to fear of rejection and more often attributed the seated students' inaction to lack of interest.

Do these social misperceptions constrain actual interracial contact? They do: White Princeton students who were most prone to pluralistic ignorance — to presuming that they feared interracial rejection more than did Black students — were also the most likely to experience diminishing cross-racial contacts in the ensuing seven weeks.

Shelton and Richeson were not contending that misperceptions alone impede romances and cross-racial friendships. But misperceptions do restrain people from risking an overture. Understanding this phenomenon — recognizing that others' coolness may actually reflect motives and feelings similar to our own — may help us reach out to others and sometimes to transform potential friendships into real ones.

Cross-racial friendships can reduce prejudice if people see their friends both as individuals *and* as members of their groups. Saying "I don't see color" is both inaccurate and often counterproductive.
Felix Sanchez/Blend Images LLC

Among American students who have studied in Germany or in Britain, the more their contact with people in their host country, the more positive their attitudes (Stangor et al., 1996). Exchange students' hosts also are changed by the experience; they become more open to new experiences and more likely to see things from the visitor's cultural perspective (Sparkman et al., 2016; Vollhardt, 2010). In general, people who have contact with those of other cultures or races become more flexible and creative in their thinking (Hodson et al., 2018).

Group salience (visibility) also helps bridge divides between people. If you always think of that friend solely as an individual, your positive feelings may not extend to other members of the friend's group (Miller, 2002). For example, if you are Asian and have a Black friend but don't really think of your friend as Black, that friendship won't have much of an impact on your attitudes toward Black people in general. Ideally, then, we should form trusting friendships across group lines but also recognize that the friend represents those in another group (Brown et al., 2007; Davies & Aron, 2016).

We are especially likely to befriend dissimilar people when their outgroup identity is initially minimized. If our liking for our new friends is going to generalize to others, their group identity must at some point become salient. So, to reduce prejudice and conflict, we had best initially minimize group diversity, then acknowledge it, then transcend it. In other words, make friends regardless of race, but don't deny the existence of race during the friendship.

Surveys of nearly 4,000 Europeans reveal that friendship is a key to successful contact: If you have a minority-group friend, you become much more likely to express sympathy and support for the friend's group and even somewhat more support for immigration by that group. That has been shown for West Germans' attitudes toward Turks, French people's attitudes toward Asians and North Africans, Netherlanders' attitudes toward Surinamers and Turks, British attitudes toward West Indians and Asians, and Northern Ireland Protestants' and Catholics' attitudes toward each other (Brown et al., 1999; Hamberger & Hewstone, 1997; Paolini et al., 2004; Pettigrew, 1997).

EQUAL-STATUS CONTACT The social psychologists who advocated desegregation never claimed that all contact would improve attitudes. Just as positive contact boosts liking, negative contact increases *disliking* (Guffler & Wagner, 2017; Hayward et al., 2017, 2018; McKeown & Psaltis, 2017). Positive contact is more commonplace, but negative experiences have a greater effect (Graf et al., 2014; Paolini et al., 2014).

Social psychologists had expected poor results when contacts were competitive, unsupported by authorities, and unequal (Pettigrew, 1988; Stephan, 1987). Before 1954, many prejudiced White people had frequent contacts with Black people—as shoeshine men and domestic workers. As we have seen, such unequal contacts breed attitudes that merely justify the continuation of inequality. So it's important that the contact be **equal-status contact,** like that between the store clerks, the soldiers, the neighbors, the prisoners, and the summer campers.

equal-status contact
Contact on an equal basis. Just as a relationship between people of unequal status breeds attitudes consistent with their relationship, so do relationships between those of equal status. Thus, to reduce prejudice, interracial contact should ideally be between persons equal in status.

Cooperation

Although equal-status contact can help, it is sometimes not enough. It didn't help when Muzafer Sherif stopped the Eagles versus Rattlers competition and brought the groups together for noncompetitive activities, such as watching movies, shooting off fireworks, and eating. By that time, their hostility was so strong that mere contact only provided opportunities for taunts and attacks. When an Eagle was bumped by a Rattler, his fellow Eagles urged him to "brush off the dirt." Desegregating the two groups hardly promoted their social integration.

THE inside STORY

Nicole Shelton and Jennifer Richeson on Cross-Racial Friendships

We noticed that both White and ethnic minority students in our classes often indicated that they genuinely wanted to interact with people outside of their ethnic group but were afraid that they would not be accepted. However, they assumed that members of other groups simply did not want to connect. This sounded very much like Dale Miller's work on pluralistic ignorance. Over the course of a few weeks, we designed a series of studies to explore pluralistic ignorance during interracial interactions.

Since the publication of our article, we have had researchers tell us that we should use our work in new student orientation sessions in order to reduce students' fears about reaching across racial lines. We are delighted that when we present this work in our courses, students of all racial backgrounds tell us that it indeed has opened their eyes about making the first move to develop interracial friendships.

Nicole Shelton
Princeton University
Courtesy of Nicole Shelton

Jennifer Richeson
Yale University
Courtesy of Jennifer Richeson

Given entrenched hostility, what can a peacemaker do? Think back to the successful and the unsuccessful desegregation efforts. The army's racial mixing of rifle companies didn't just bring Blacks and Whites into equal-status contact, it made them depend on each other. Together, they were fighting a common enemy, striving toward a shared goal.

Does that suggest a second factor that predicts whether the effect of desegregation will be favorable? Does competitive contact divide and *cooperative* contact unite? Consider what happens to people who together face a common predicament. In conflicts at all levels, from couples to rival teams to nations, *shared threats* and *common goals* breed unity.

COMMON EXTERNAL THREATS BUILD COHESIVENESS

Have you ever been caught in a blizzard, punished by a teacher, or persecuted and ridiculed because of your social, racial, or religious identity when with others sharing the same experience? If so, you may recall feeling close to them. Perhaps previous social barriers fell as you helped one another dig out of the snow or struggled to cope with your common enemy. Survivors of shared pain or more extreme crises, such as a bombing, also often report a spirit of cooperation and solidarity rather than everyone-for-themselves panic (Bastian et al., 2014; Drury et al., 2009).

"I couldn't help but say to [Mr. Gorbachev], just think how easy his task and mine might be in these meetings that we held if suddenly there was a threat to this world from some other species from another planet. [We'd] find out once and for all that we really are all human beings here on this earth together."

—Former U.S. President Ronald Reagan, December 4, 1985, speech

Such friendliness is common among those who experience a shared threat. John Lanzetta (1955) observed this when he put four-man groups of naval ROTC cadets to work on problem-solving tasks and then began informing them over a loudspeaker that their answers were wrong, their productivity inexcusably low, their thinking stupid. Other groups did not receive this harassment. Lanzetta observed that the group members under duress became friendlier to one another, more cooperative, less argumentative, less competitive. They were in it together. And the result was a cohesive spirit. Recent experiments confirm a silver lining of mistreatment by a boss: Mistreated employees become more cohesive (Stoverink et al., 2014). Misery loves company.

In many experiments and real-world situations, having a common enemy has unified groups (Dion, 1979; Greenaway & Cruwys, 2019). Just being reminded of an outgroup (say, a rival school) heightens people's responsiveness to their own group (Wilder & Shapiro, 1984). To perceive discrimination against one's racial or religious group is to feel more bonded and identified with it (Craig & Richeson, 2012; Martinovic & Verkuyten, 2012; Ramos et al., 2012). Recognizing that one's group and another group have both faced discrimination boosts closeness (Cortland et al., 2017). When keenly conscious of who "they" are, we also know who "we" are.

When facing a well-defined external threat during wartime, we-feeling soars. The membership of civic organizations mushrooms (Putnam, 2000). Children who survive a war later display a more cooperative spirit toward their ingroup (Bauer et al., 2014). Even just imagining or fearing the extinction of one's group often serves to strengthen ingroup solidarity (Wohl et al., 2010). Likewise, just imagining the globally shared climate change threat reduced antagonism toward other nations (Pyszczynski et al., 2012).

Shared predicaments trigger cooperation, as these Walmart workers on strike in Chicago demonstrate.
Marie Kanger Born/Shutterstock

When two groups face a common threat, their differences often don't seem that large anymore. In a set of experiments, Black and White Americans and Israelis and Palestinians were slower to categorize each other into groups when they faced a common threat (Flade et al., 2019). When Russia invaded Ukraine in 2022, Ukrainian citizens united against the threat, raising money, donating blood, and coordinating groups of people to reload Russian and Belarusian websites until they crashed (Lapatina, 2022). Use of the word "we" doubled from before to after the terrorist attacks of 9/11 in everyday conversations as well as in the New York mayor's press conferences (Liehr et al., 2004; Pennebaker & Lay, 2002).

Shared threats also produce a political "rally 'round the flag" effect, where support for leaders spikes dramatically (Lambert et al., 2011). George W. Bush's job-performance ratings reflected this threat-bred spirit of unity after 9/11. In the public eye, the mediocre-seeming president of 9/10 had become the exalted president of 9/12 – "our leader" in the fight against "those who hate us." Thereafter, his ratings gradually declined but then jumped again as the war in Iraq began (**Figure 5**).

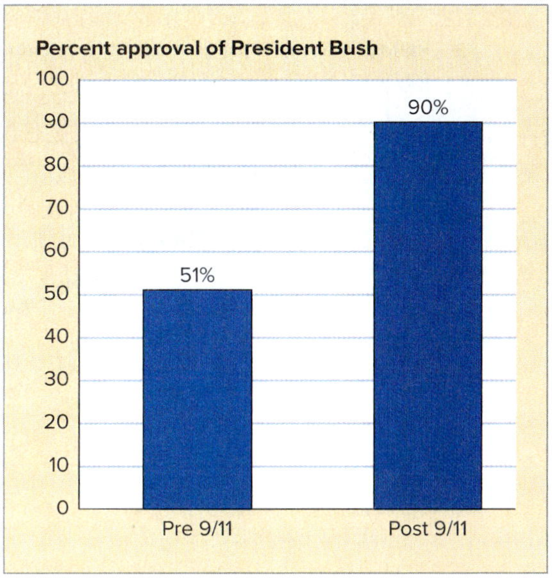

FIGURE 5

External Threats Breed Internal Unity

As former U.S. President George W. Bush's approval ratings illustrated, national conflicts mold public attitudes.
Source: Gallup, 2006.

Leaders may therefore *create* a threatening external enemy as a technique for building group cohesiveness. George Orwell's novel *1984* illustrates the tactic: The leader of the protagonist nation uses border conflicts with the other two major powers to lessen internal strife. From time to time the enemy shifts, but there is always an enemy. Indeed, the nation seems to *need* an enemy. For the world, for a nation, for a group, having a common enemy is powerfully unifying. Sunni and Shia Muslim differences that feel large in Iraq will not seem so large to Muslims in countries where both sects must cope with anti-Muslim attitudes.

Might the world likewise find unity if facing a common enemy? In 1987, U.S. President Ronald Reagan observed, "In our obsession with antagonisms of the moment, we often forget how much unites all the members of humanity. Perhaps we need some outside, universal threat to recognize this common bond." Two decades later, former U.S. vice president and environmental activist Al Gore (2007) agreed, suggesting that, with the specter of climate change, "We – all of us – now face a universal threat. Though it is not from outside this world, it is nevertheless cosmic in scale."

SUPERORDINATE GOALS FOSTER COOPERATION

Closely related to the unifying power of an external threat is the unifying power of **superordinate goals,** goals that unite all in a group and require cooperative effort. To promote harmony among his warring campers, Sherif introduced such goals. He created a problem with the camp water supply, necessitating both groups' cooperation to restore the water. When a truck "broke down" on a camp excursion, a staff member casually left the tug-of-war rope nearby, prompting one boy to suggest that everyone from both groups pull the truck to get it started. When it started, a backslapping celebration ensued over their victorious "tug-of-war against the truck."

superordinate goal
A shared goal that necessitates cooperative effort; a goal that overrides people's differences from one another.

After working together to achieve such superordinate goals, the boys ate together and enjoyed themselves around a campfire. Friendships sprouted across group lines. Hostilities plummeted (**Figure 6**). On the last day, the boys decided to travel home together on one bus. During the trip, they no longer sat by groups. As the bus approached Oklahoma City and home, they, as one, spontaneously sang "Oklahoma" and then bade their friends farewell. With isolation and competition, Sherif made strangers into bitter enemies. With superordinate goals, he made enemies into friends.

Are Sherif's experiments mere child's play? Or can pulling together to achieve superordinate goals be similarly beneficial with conflicting adults? Robert Blake and Jane Mouton (1979) wondered. In a series of 2-week experiments involving more than 1,000 executives in 150 different groups, they re-created the essential features of the situation experienced by the Rattlers and the Eagles. Each group first engaged in activities by itself, then competed with another group, and then cooperated with the other group in working toward jointly chosen superordinate goals. Their results provided "unequivocal evidence that adult reactions parallel those of Sherif's younger subjects." Business school students who represented opposing businesses in a negotiation process trusted each other more and made more progress when they first discussed common superordinate goals such as what each side could achieve from the discussion (Swaab et al., 2021).

FIGURE 6

Unfavorable Ratings of Outgroups After Conflict vs. Cooperation

After competition, the Eagles and the Rattlers rated each other unfavorably. After they worked cooperatively to achieve superordinate goals, hostility dropped sharply.

Source: Data from Sherif (1966).

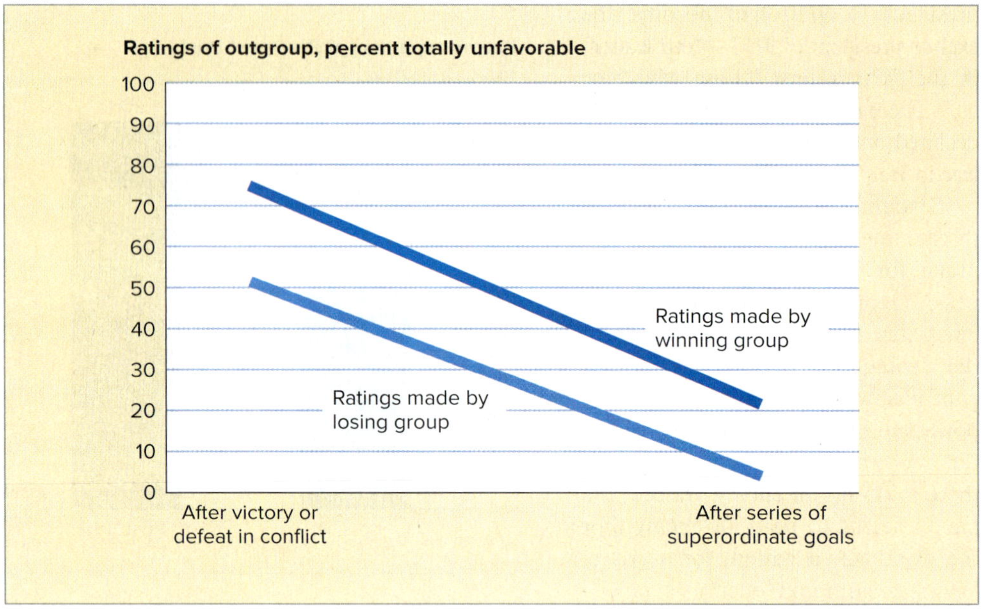

John Dovidio, Samuel Gaertner, and their collaborators (2005, 2009) reported that working cooperatively has especially favorable effects under conditions that lead people to define a new, inclusive group that dissolves their former subgroups. Old feelings of bias against another group diminish when members of the two groups sit alternately around a table (rather than on opposite sides), give their new group a single name, and then work together under conditions that foster a good mood. "Us" and "them" become "we."

From Amazon tribes to European countries, peace arises when groups become interconnected and interdependent and develop an overarching social identity (Fry, 2012). To reduce Muslim-Christian tension in Central African Republic, Catholic Relief Services has paid people to dig drainage ditches, with one condition: that Muslims and Christians work together (Kristof, 2018).

The cooperative efforts by the Rattlers and the Eagles ended in success. Would the same harmony have emerged if the water had remained off and the truck still stalled? Likely not. Experiments with university students confirmed that *successful* cooperation between two groups boosts their attraction for each other. If previously conflicting groups *fail* in a cooperative effort, however, and if conditions allow them to attribute their failure to each other, the conflict may worsen (Worchel et al., 1977, 1978; Worchel & Norvell, 1980). Sherif's groups were already feeling hostile to each other. Thus, failure to fix the water supply could have been blamed on one group or the other. That would have exacerbated rather than alleviated their conflict. Unity is fed by striving for and reaching superordinate goals.

Promoting "common ingroup identity." The banning of gang colors and the common European practice of school uniforms — an increasing trend in the United States, as well — aim to change "us" and "them" to "we."
Cultura Exclusive/DUEL/Getty Images

COOPERATIVE LEARNING IMPROVES RACIAL ATTITUDES

So far we have noted that desegregation has only modest social benefits when it does not involve equal-status friendships. We have also noted the dramatic social benefits of successful, cooperative contacts between members of rival groups. Several research teams therefore wondered: Could interracial friendships be promoted by replacing competitive learning situations with cooperative ones?

In one experiment, White youth on 2- to 3-week Outward Bound expeditions (involving intimate contact and cooperation) expressed improved attitudes toward Black peers a month after the expedition *if* they had been randomly assigned to an interracial expedition group (Green & Wong, 2008). Working together as equals seemed to reduce prejudice.

Robert Slavin and Nancy Madden (1979) analyzed survey data from 2,400 students in 71 U.S. high schools and found similarly encouraging results. Students of different races who played and worked together were more likely to report having friends of another race and to express positive racial attitudes. Charles Green and his colleagues (1988) confirmed this in a study of 3,200 Florida middle-school students. Compared with students at schools promoting competition, those at schools with interracial "learning teams" had more positive racial attitudes.

Interracial cooperation — on athletic teams, in class projects and extracurricular activities — melts differences and improves racial attitudes. White teen athletes who play cooperative team sports (such as basketball) with Black teammates express more liking and support for Blacks than do their counterparts involved in individual sports (such as wrestling) (Brown et al., 2003).
sirtravelalot/Shutterstock

From such correlational findings, can we conclude that cooperative interracial activity improves racial attitudes? To find out, we experiment: We can randomly designate some students, but not others, to work together in racially mixed groups. For example, Slavin (1985; Slavin et al., 2003, 2009) and his colleagues divided classes into interracial teams, each composed of four or five students from all achievement levels. Team members sat together, studied a variety of subjects together, and at the end of each week competed with the other teams in a class tournament. All members contributed to their team's score by doing well, sometimes by competing with other students, and sometimes by competing with their own previous scores. Everyone had a chance to succeed. Moreover, team members were motivated to help one another prepare for the weekly tournament – by drilling each other on fractions, spelling, or historical events – whatever was the next event. Rather than isolating students from one another, team competition brought them into closer contact and drew out mutual support.

Another research team, led by Elliot Aronson (2004; Aronson & Gonzalez, 1988), elicited similar group cooperation with a "jigsaw classroom" technique. In experiments in Texas and California elementary schools, the researchers assigned children to racially and academically diverse six-member groups. The topic of study was then divided into six parts, with each student becoming the expert on his or her part. In a unit on Chile, one student might be the expert on Chile's history, another on its geography, another on its culture. First, the various "historians," "geographers," and so forth got together to master their material. Then they returned to the home groups to teach it to their classmates. Each group member held, so to speak, a piece of the jigsaw. Self-confident students therefore had to listen to and learn from reticent students who, in turn, soon realized they had something important to offer their peers.

"This was truly an exciting event. My students and I had found a way to make desegregation work the way it was intended to work!"

—Elliot Aronson, "Drifting My Own Way," 2003

Other research teams have devised additional methods for cooperative learning. As shown in 148 studies across 11 countries, adolescents, too, have more positive peer relationships and achieve more when working cooperatively rather than competitively (Lemmer & Wagner, 2015; Roseth et al., 2008). For a historic example of effective desegregation, see "Focus On: Jackie Robinson, Branch Rickey, and the Integration of Baseball."

What can we conclude from this research? With cooperative learning, students learn not only the material but other lessons. Cooperative learning, said Slavin and Cooper (1999), promotes "the academic achievement of all students while simultaneously improving intergroup relations." Aronson reported that "children in the interdependent, jigsaw classrooms grow to like each other better, develop a greater liking for school, and develop greater self-esteem than children in traditional classrooms" (Aronson, 1980, p. 232).

To sum up, cooperative, equal-status contacts exert a positive influence on campers, industrial executives, college students, and schoolchildren. Does the principle extend to all

focus ON Jackie Robinson, Branch Rickey, and the Integration of Baseball

On April 10, 1947, a 19-word announcement forever changed the face of baseball and put social-psychological principles to the test: "The Brooklyn Dodgers today purchased the contract of Jackie Roosevelt Robinson from the Montreal Royals. He will report immediately." Five days later, Robinson became the first African American since 1887 to play major league baseball. In the fall, Dodger fans realized their dreams of going to the World Series. Robinson, after enduring racial taunts and balls pitched at his head, was voted *Sporting News* rookie of the year and in a poll finished second to Bing Crosby as the most popular man in America. Baseball's racial barrier was forever broken.

Motivated by both his Methodist morality and a drive for baseball success, Major League Baseball executive Branch Rickey had been planning the integration for some time, reported social psychologists Anthony Pratkanis and Marlene Turner (1994a,b). Three years earlier, Rickey had been asked by the sociologist-chair of the Mayor's Committee on Unity to desegregate his team. His response was to ask for time (so the hiring would not be attributed to pressure) and for advice on how best to do it. In 1945 Rickey was the only owner voting for allowing Black players in Major League Baseball. In 1947 he made his move using these principles identified by Pratkanis and Turner:

- *Create a perception that change is inevitable.* Leave little possibility that protest or resistance can turn back the clock. The team's radio announcer, Red Barber, a traditional Southerner, recalled that in 1945 Rickey took him to lunch and explained very slowly and strongly that his scouts were searching for "the first Black player I can put on the White Dodgers. I don't know who he is or where he is, but he is coming." An angered Barber at first intended to quit but in time decided to accept the inevitable and keep the world's "best sports announcing job." Rickey was equally matter-of-fact with the players in 1947, offering to trade any player who didn't want to play with Robinson.
- *Establish equal-status contact with a superordinate goal.* One sociologist explained to Rickey that when relationships focus on an overarching goal, such as winning the pennant, "the people involved would adjust appropriately." One of the players who had been initially opposed later helped Robinson with his hitting, explaining, "When you're on a team, you got to pull together to win."
- *Puncture the norm of prejudice.* Rickey led the way, but others helped. Team leader shortstop Pee Wee Reese, a Southerner, began regularly eating meals with Robinson. One day in Cincinnati, as the crowd was hurling slurs, Reese left his shortstop position, walked over to Robinson at first base, smiled and spoke to him, and then — with a hushed crowd watching — put his arm around Robinson's shoulder.
- *Cut short the spiral of violence by practicing nonviolence.* Rickey, wanting "a ballplayer with guts enough not to fight back," role-played for Robinson the kind of insults and dirty play he would experience and gained Robinson's commitment not to return violence with violence. When Robinson was taunted and spiked, he allowed his teammates to respond. Team cohesion was thereby increased.

Robinson and Bob Feller later became the first players in baseball history elected to the Hall of Fame in their first year of eligibility. As he received the award, Robinson asked three persons to stand beside him: his mother, his wife, and his friend Branch Rickey.

Jackie Robinson and Branch Rickey
JH/AP Images

levels of human relations? Are families unified by pulling together to farm the land, restore an old house, or sail a sloop? Are communal identities forged by barn raisings, group singing, or cheering on the football team? Is international understanding bred by international collaboration in science and space, by joint efforts to feed the world and conserve resources, by friendly personal contacts between people of different nations? Indications are that the answer to all of those questions is yes (Brewer & Miller, 1988; Desforges et al., 1991, 1997; Deutsch, 1985, 1994). Thus, an important challenge facing our divided world is to identify and agree on our superordinate goals and to structure cooperative efforts to achieve them.

Cooperation and peace. Researchers have identified more than 40 peaceful societies where people live with no, or virtually no, recorded instances of violence. An analysis of 25 of these societies, including the cooperative, barn-building of Amish folks shown here, reveals that most base their worldviews on cooperation rather than competition (Bonta, 1997).
George Sheldon/Shutterstock

GROUP AND SUPERORDINATE IDENTITIES

In everyday life, we often reconcile multiple identities (Gaertner et al., 2000, 2001). We acknowledge our subgroup identity (as parent or child) and then transcend it (sensing our superordinate identity as a family). Pride in our ethnic heritage can complement our larger communal or national identity. Being mindful of our *multiple* social identities enables social cohesion (Brewer & Pierce, 2005; Crisp & Hewstone, 1999, 2000): "I am many things, some of which you are, too."

But in ethnically diverse cultures, how do people balance their ethnic identities with their national identities? They may have a "bicultural" or "omnicultural" identity, one that identifies with both the larger culture and one's own ethnic and religious culture (Moghaddam, 2009, 2010; Phinney, 1990). Someone with a bicultural identity might say, "In many ways, I am like everyone around me, but I also affirm my own cultural heritage." Americans who retain a strong sense of being Cuban, Mexican, Puerto Rican, Chinese, Vietnamese, or Korean may also feel strongly American (Meca et al., 2023; Nguyen & Rule, 2020; Roger et al., 1991). As W. E. B. DuBois (1903, p. 17) explained in *The Souls of Black Folk,* "The American Negro [longs] . . . to be both a Negro and an American."

Over time, identification with a new culture often grows. The children of Chinese immigrants to Australia and the United States feel their Chinese ethnic identity somewhat less keenly and their new national identity more strongly than do immigrants who were born in China (Rosenthal & Feldman, 1992). Often, however, the *grand*children of immigrants feel more comfortable identifying with their ethnicity (Triandis, 1994).

Researchers have wondered whether pride in one's group competes with identification with the larger culture. We evaluate ourselves partly in terms of our social identities. Seeing our own group (our school, our employer, our family, our race, our nation) as good helps us feel good about ourselves. A positive ethnic identity can therefore contribute to positive self-esteem. So can a positive mainstream culture identity. "Marginal" people, who have neither a strong ethnic nor a strong mainstream cultural identity (**Table 1**), often have low self-esteem. Bicultural people, who affirm both identities, typically have a strongly positive self-concept (Abu-Rayya & Sam, 2017; Meca et al., 2023; Phinney, 1990). Often, they alternate between their two cultures, adapting their language and behavior to the group they are with (LaFromboise et al., 1993), sometimes known as "code-switching" (Johnson et al., 2022; Loureiro-Rodriguez et al., 2018; Wu et al., 2022).

"Most of us have overlapping identities which unite us with very different groups. We can love what we are, without hating what — and who — we are not. We can thrive in our own tradition, even as we learn from others, and come to respect their teachings."

—Former Secretary General of the United Nations, Kofi Annan, Nobel Peace Prize lecture, 2001

TABLE 1 Ethnic and Cultural Identity

	Ethnic Group Identification	
Majority Group Identification	**Strong**	**Weak**
Strong	Bicultural	Assimilated
Weak	Separated	Marginal

Source: Adapted from Phinney (1990).

Diversity within unity. Soccer players of different ethnicities take a knee to show support for the Black Lives Matter movement during a championship game in Spain in August 2020.
Alex Caparros - UEFA/UEFA/Getty Images

Is it better to recognize and affirm group differences or to look beyond them (Hahn et al., 2015)? Debate continues over the ideals of multiculturalism (celebrating diversity) versus colorblind assimilation (meshing one's values and habits with the prevailing culture without as much attention to racial or ethnic identity). Those in the majority racial group at a university – whether White or Black – are more likely to favor colorblind assimilation. They more often agree, for example, that "there should be a single center on campus for all students, rather than separate cultural centers for students of different racial groups" (Hehman et al., 2012). Those in the minority, however, may argue that colorblind assimilation ignores important differences in the experiences of historically disadvantaged groups – and thus may favor a multicultural approach (Rios, 2022).

On the multiculturalism side, the Department of Canadian Heritage (2006) declared that "multiculturalism ensures that all citizens can keep their identities, can take pride in their ancestry and have a sense of belonging. Acceptance gives Canadians a feeling of security and self-confidence, making them open to and accepting of diverse cultures."

On the colorblind assimilation side are those who concur with Britain's Commission for Racial Equality, worrying that multiculturalism separates people (Phillips, 2004). In threatening situations, highlighting multicultural differences can enhance hostility between groups. In a series of experiments, focusing on differences prompted people to see more malice in outgroup members' threatening behaviors (Vorauer & Sasaki, 2011). Multiculturalism may encourage the view that differences among groups are fixed and unchangeable, undermining efforts to work toward equality (Wilton et al., 2018). Highlighting genetic differences between ethnic groups increases the risk of violence, while learning about genetic similarities helps foster peace (Kimel et al., 2016). After Rwanda's ethnic bloodbath in the 1990s, government documents and government-controlled media no longer mentioned Hutu and Tutsi, saying "there is no ethnicity here. We are all Rwandan" (Lacey, 2004). Focusing on common heritage is effective for religious harmony as well: Emphasizing the shared biblical history between Jews, Muslims, and Christians reduced adherents' prejudice toward members of other faiths (Kunst et al., 2019).

"Nothing inspires greater tolerance from the intolerant than an abundance of common and unifying beliefs, practices, rituals, institutions, and processes."

—Jonathan Haidt, *When and Why Nationalism Beats Globalism*, 2016

How can we resolve this debate? In the space between multiculturalism and assimilation lies "diversity within unity," an omnicultural perspective advocated by cultural psychologist Fathali Moghaddam (2009, 2010) and by sociologist Amitai Etzioni and others (2005): "It presumes that all members of a given society will fully respect and adhere to those basic values and institutions that are considered part of the basic shared framework of the society. At the same time, every group in society is free to maintain its distinct subculture – those policies, habits, and institutions that do not conflict with the shared core." Completely denying the existence of group identity is not a viable strategy for peace and harmony; however, emphasizing common humanity and multiple identities can be effective (Staub, 2018).

Immigrant nations like the United States and Australia still struggle between separation and wholeness, between people's pride in their distinct heritage and unity as one nation, between acknowledging the reality of diversity and the quest for shared values and identity. The ideal of diversity within unity forms the United States motto: *E pluribus unum.* Out of many, one.

Communication

What is the role of communication in resolving conflicts? There are three primary strategies. When husband and wife, labor and management, or nation X and nation Y disagree, they can **bargain** with each other directly. They can ask a third party to **mediate** by making suggestions and facilitating their negotiations. Or they can choose to **arbitrate** by submitting their disagreement to someone who will study the issues and impose a settlement. We explore these three possibilities below.

bargaining
Seeking an agreement to a conflict through direct negotiation between parties.

mediation
An attempt by a neutral third party to resolve a conflict by facilitating communication and offering suggestions.

arbitration
Resolution of a conflict by a neutral third party who studies both sides and imposes a settlement.

BARGAINING

If you want to buy or sell a car, are you better off adopting a tough bargaining stance – opening with an extreme offer so that splitting the difference will yield a favorable result? Or are you better off beginning with a sincere "good-faith" offer?

Experiments suggest no simple answer. On the one hand, those who demand more will often get more. Robert Cialdini, Leonard Bickman, and John Cacioppo (1979) provide a typical result. In a control condition, they approached various Chevrolet dealers and asked the price of a new Monte Carlo sports coupe. In the experimental condition, they approached other dealers and first struck a tough bargaining stance, asking for and rejecting a price on a *different* car ("I need a lower price than that. That's a lot."). When they then asked the price of the Monte Carlo, they were quoted a price that averaged some $200 lower – $850 in today's dollars – than what the control group was offered.

Tough bargaining may lower the other party's expectations, making the other side willing to settle for less (Yukl, 1974). But toughness can sometimes backfire. Many conflicts are not over a pie of fixed size but over a pie that shrinks if the conflict continues. A time delay is often a lose-lose scenario. When a labor strike is prolonged, employees lose wages and management loses revenue. Being tough is therefore a potential lose-lose scenario. If the other party responds with an equally tough stance, both may be locked into positions from which neither can back down without losing face.

In the weeks before the 1991 Persian Gulf War, then-President George H. W. Bush threatened, in the full glare of publicity, to "kick Saddam's ass." Saddam Hussein, no less macho, threatened to make "infidel" Americans "swim in their own blood." After such belligerent statements, it was difficult for each side to avoid war and save face.

MEDIATION

A third-party mediator may offer suggestions that enable conflicting parties to make concessions and still save face (Pruitt, 1998). If my concession can be attributed to a mediator who is also getting concessions from the other side, neither of us will be viewed as weakly caving in.

TURNING WIN-LOSE INTO WIN-WIN Mediators' first task is to help the parties rethink the conflict and gain information about the others' interests. Typically, people on both sides have a competitive "win-lose" orientation: They think they are successful if their opponent is unhappy with the result and unsuccessful if their opponent is pleased (Thompson et al., 1995). The mediator aims to replace this win-lose orientation with a cooperative "win-win" orientation by prodding both sides to set aside their conflicting demands and instead think about each other's underlying needs, interests, and goals.

A classic win-win story concerns two sisters who quarreled over an orange (Follett, 1940). Finally they compromised and split the orange in half, whereupon one sister squeezed her half for juice while the other used the peel on her half to make a cake. If the sisters had each explained *why* they wanted the orange, they very likely would have agreed to share it differently, giving one sister all the juice and the other all the peel. This is an example of an **integrative agreement** (Pruitt & Lewis, 1975, 1977). Compared with compromises, in which each party sacrifices something important, integrative agreements are more enduring. Because they are mutually rewarding, they also lead to better ongoing relationships (Pruitt, 1986).

integrative agreements
Win-win agreements that reconcile both parties' interests to their mutual benefit.

UNRAVELING MISPERCEPTIONS WITH CONTROLLED COMMUNICATIONS Communication often helps reduce self-fulfilling misperceptions. Perhaps you can recall experiences similar to that of this college student:

> Often, after a prolonged period of little communication, I perceive Martha's silence as a sign of her dislike for me. She, in turn, thinks that my quietness is a result of my being mad at her.

TABLE 2 How Couples Can Argue Constructively

Do Not	Do
• evade the argument, give the silent treatment, or walk out on it	• clearly define the issue and repeat the other's arguments in your own words
• use your intimate knowledge of the other person to hit below the belt and humiliate	• share your positive and negative feelings
• bring in unrelated issues	• welcome feedback about your behavior
• feign agreement while harboring resentment	• clarify where you agree and disagree and what matters most to each of you
• tell the other party how they are feeling	• ask questions that help the other find words to express the concern
• attack indirectly by criticizing someone or something the other person values	• wait for spontaneous explosions to subside, without retaliating
• undermine the other by intensifying their insecurity or threatening disaster	• offer positive suggestions for mutual improvement

Communication facilitators work to break down barriers, as in this diversity training exercise. In work organizations, too, diversity training can improve attitudes (Kalinoski et al., 2013).
edhar/123rf

> My silence induces her silence, which makes me even more silent . . . until this snowballing effect is broken by some occurrence that makes it necessary for us to interact. And the communication then unravels all the misinterpretations we had made about one another.

The outcome of such conflicts often depends on *how* people communicate their feelings. Psychologists Ian Gotlib and Catherine Colby (1988) offered advice to couples on how to avoid destructive quarrels and how to have good quarrels (**Table 2**).

In addition, children can learn that conflict is normal, that people can learn to get along with those who are different, that most disputes can be resolved with two winners, and that nonviolent communication strategies are an alternative to a world of bullies and victims. The "violence prevention curriculum . . . is not about passivity," noted Deborah Prothrow-Stith (1991, p. 183). "It is about using anger not to hurt oneself or one's peers, but to change the world."

David Johnson and Roger Johnson (1995, 2000, 2003) put 6- to 14-year-old children through about a dozen hours of conflict resolution training in six schools. Before the training, most students were involved in daily conflicts – put-downs and teasing, playground turn-taking conflicts, arguments over possessions – that nearly always resulted in a winner and a loser. After training, the children more often found win-win solutions, better mediated friends' conflicts, and retained and applied their new skills in and out of school throughout the school year.

Conflict researchers report that a key factor is *trust* (Balliet & Van Lange, 2013; Tarabeih et al., 2022). If you believe the other person is well intentioned, you are more likely to divulge your needs and concerns. Lacking trust, you may fear that being open will give the other party information that might be used against you. Even simple behaviors can enhance trust. In experiments, negotiators who were instructed to mimic the others' mannerisms, as naturally empathic people often do, elicited more trust and greater discovery of compatible interests and mutually satisfying deals (Maddux et al., 2008). Meeting people face to face and hearing their views in their own voice (rather than in writing or online) also helps humanize them (Schroeder et al., 2017).

When the two parties mistrust each other and communicate unproductively, a third-party mediator – a marriage counselor, a labor mediator, a diplomat – can help. Most human societies rely on mediators of one sort or another to resolve conflicts (Garfield & Glowacki, 2023). Often the mediator is someone trusted by both sides. In the 1980s, it took an Algerian Muslim to mediate the conflict between Iran and Iraq, and the Pope to resolve a geographical dispute between Argentina and Chile (Carnevale & Choi, 2000).

Trust, like other social behaviors, is also a biological phenomenon. Social neuroscientists have found that individuals with lowered levels of serotonin, the brain neurotransmitter, become more likely to see a low offer in a laboratory game as unfair and to reject it (Bilderbeck et al., 2014; Colzato et al., 2013; Crockett et al., 2008). Infusions of the hormone oxytocin have something of an opposite effect, increasing people's trust of strangers when they play games (Zak, 2008).
Jupiterimages/Getty Images

After coaxing the conflicting parties to rethink their perceived win-lose conflict, the mediator often has each party identify and rank its goals. When goals are compatible, the ranking procedure makes it easier for each to concede on less-important goals so that both groups can achieve their primary goals (Erickson et al., 1974; Schulz & Pruitt, 1978). South Africa achieved internal peace when Black and White South Africans granted each other's top priorities: replacing apartheid with majority rule and safeguarding the security, welfare, and rights of Whites (Kelman, 1998). The same technique can work in labor negotiations. For example, if workers will forgo benefits less important to them but very costly to management (perhaps company-provided dental care) and if management will forgo moderately valuable arrangements that workers very much resent (perhaps inflexible working hours), both sides may gain (Ross & Ward, 1995).

The mediator may ask the conflicting parties to restrict their arguments to statements of fact, including statements of how they feel and how they respond when the other acts in a given way: "I enjoy music. But when you play it loud, I find it hard to concentrate. That makes me crabby." Such statements using "I" can feel less hostile than accusatory "you" statements ("You don't care about me when you play your music.") To increase empathy, the mediator may ask people to reverse roles and argue the other's position or to imagine and explain what the other person is experiencing (Yaniv, 2012). The mediator may have them restate one another's positions before replying with their own: "It annoys you when I play my music and you're trying to study." Experiments show that taking another's perspective and inducing empathy decreases stereotyping and increases cooperation (Galinsky & Moskowitz, 2000; Gutenbrunner & Wagner, 2016; Todd et al., 2011).

"We can be frank and outspoken without being reckless or abusive, polite without cringing, we can attack radicalism and its evils without ourselves fostering feelings of hostility between different racial groups."

—Nelson Mandela, letter from prison, July 1, 1970

When parties – perhaps two colleagues or two partners – are at an impasse and need to move on from their standstill, one simple strategy is literally to take steps forward together . . . *to go for a walk*. Walking together, like other forms of movement synchrony, engages people in jointly attending to their environment and coordinating their steps. Doing so increases their empathy and rapport, softens the boundary between them, and engenders cooperation (Good et al., 2017; Webb et al., 2017).

The simple act of walking can sometimes be effective in overcoming an impasse and bridging a divide between parties in conflict.
monzenmachi/Getty Images

These peacemaking principles – based partly on laboratory experiments, partly on practical experience – have helped mediate both international and industrial conflicts (Blake & Mouton, 1962, 1979; Fisher, 1994; Wehr, 1979). One small team of Arab and Jewish Americans, led by social psychologist Herbert Kelman (1997, 2010), conducted workshops bringing together influential Arabs and Israelis. Isolated, the participants were free to speak directly to their adversaries without fear that their constituents were second-guessing what they were saying. The result? Those from both sides typically came to understand the other's perspective and how the other side responds to their own group's actions.

ARBITRATION

Some conflicts are so intractable, the underlying interests so divergent, that a mutually satisfactory resolution is unattainable. In a divorce dispute over custody of a child, both parents cannot enjoy full custody. In such cases, a third-party mediator may – or may not – be able to help resolve the conflict.

If not, the parties may turn to *arbitration* by having the mediator or another third party *impose* a settlement. Disputants usually prefer to settle their differences without arbitration so that they retain control over the outcome. Neil McGillicuddy and others (1987) observed this preference in an experiment involving those coming to a dispute settlement center. When people knew they would face an arbitrated settlement if mediation failed, they tried harder to resolve the problem, exhibited less hostility, and thus were more likely to reach agreement.

In cases where differences seem large and irreconcilable, the prospect of arbitration may cause the disputants to freeze their positions, hoping to gain an advantage when the arbitrator chooses a compromise. To combat that tendency, some disputes, such as those involving the salaries of individual baseball players, are settled with "final-offer arbitration," in which the third party chooses one of the two final offers. Final-offer arbitration motivates each party to make a reasonable proposal.

Typically, however, the final offer is not as reasonable as it would be if each party, free of self-serving bias, saw its own proposal through others' eyes. Negotiation researchers report that most disputants are made stubborn by "optimistic overconfidence" (Kahneman & Tversky, 1995). Successful mediation is hindered when, as often happens, both parties believe they have a two-thirds chance of winning a final-offer arbitration (Bazerman, 1986, 1990).

Conciliation

Sometimes tension and suspicion run so high that even communication, let alone resolution, becomes all but impossible. Each party may threaten, coerce, or retaliate against the other. Unfortunately, this behavior escalates the conflict. So, would a strategy of appeasing the other party by being unconditionally cooperative produce a satisfying result? Often not. In laboratory games, those who are 100% cooperative often are exploited. Politically, a one-sided pacifism is usually out of the question.

GRIT

Social psychologist Charles Osgood (1962, 1980) advocated a third alternative, one that is conciliatory yet strong enough to discourage exploitation. Osgood called it "graduated and reciprocated initiatives in tension reduction." He nicknamed it **GRIT,** a label that suggests the determination it requires. GRIT aims to reverse the "conflict spiral" by triggering reciprocal de-escalation. To do so, it draws upon social-psychological concepts, such as the norm of reciprocity and the attribution of motives.

GRIT
Acronym for "*G*raduated and *R*eciprocated *I*nitiatives in *T*ension reduction," a strategy designed to de-escalate international tensions.

GRIT requires one side to initiate a few small de-escalatory actions, after *announcing a conciliatory intent.* The initiator states their desire to reduce tension, declares each conciliatory act before making it, and invites the adversary to reciprocate. Such announcements create a framework that helps the adversary correctly interpret what otherwise might be seen as weak or tricky actions. They also bring public pressure to bear on the adversary to follow the reciprocity norm. For example, when police de-escalate conflicts with street protesters by refraining from using tear gas and riot gear, protests are more likely to stay peaceful. In contrast, when police begin with a show of force, protests are more likely to become violent (Koerth & Lartey, 2020; Maguire, 2015).

Next, the initiator establishes credibility and genuineness by carrying out, exactly as announced, several verifiable *conciliatory acts.* This intensifies the pressure to reciprocate. Making conciliatory acts diverse – perhaps offering medical help, closing a military base, or lifting a trade ban – keeps the initiator from making a significant sacrifice in any one area and leaves the adversary freer to choose its own means of reciprocation. If the adversary reciprocates voluntarily, its own conciliatory behavior may soften its attitudes.

GRIT *is* conciliatory. But it is not "surrender on the installment plan." The remaining aspects of the plan protect each side's self-interest by *maintaining retaliatory capability.* The initial conciliatory steps entail some small risk but do not jeopardize either side's security; rather, they are calculated to begin edging both sides down the tension ladder. If one side takes an aggressive action, the other side reciprocates in kind, making clear it will not tolerate exploitation. Yet the reciprocal act is not an overresponse that would re-escalate the conflict. If the adversary offers its own conciliatory acts, these, too, are matched or even slightly exceeded. Morton Deutsch (1993) captured the spirit of GRIT in advising negotiators to be "'firm, fair, and friendly': *firm* in resisting intimidation, exploitation, and dirty tricks; *fair* in holding to one's moral principles and not reciprocating the other's immoral behavior despite his or her provocations; and *friendly* in the sense that one is willing to initiate and reciprocate cooperation."

Does GRIT really work? In an extensive series of experiments at Ohio University, Svenn Lindskold and his associates (1976, 1986, 1988) found "strong support for the various steps in the GRIT proposal." In laboratory games, announcing cooperative intent *does* boost cooperation. Repeated conciliatory or generous acts *do* breed greater trust (Klapwijk & Van Lange, 2009; Shapiro, 2010). Maintaining an equality of power *does* protect against exploitation.

Lindskold was not contending that the world of the laboratory experiment mirrors the more complex world of everyday life. Rather, experiments enable us to formulate and verify powerful theoretical principles, such as the reciprocity norm and the self-serving bias. As Lindskold (1981) noted, "It is the theories, not the individual experiments, that are used to interpret the world."

"I am not suggesting that principles of individual behavior can be applied to the behavior of nations in any direct, simpleminded fashion. What I am trying to suggest is that such principles may provide us with hunches about international behavior that can be tested against experience in the larger arena."

—Charles E. Osgood, *Our Crisis in Perspective*, 1966

REAL-WORLD APPLICATIONS

GRIT-like strategies have occasionally been tried outside the laboratory, with promising results. During the Berlin crisis of the early 1960s, U.S. and Soviet tanks faced each other barrel to barrel. The crisis was defused when the Americans pulled back their tanks step-by-step. At each step, the Soviets reciprocated. Similarly, in the 1970s, small concessions by Israel and Egypt (for example, Israel allowing Egypt to open up the Suez Canal, Egypt allowing ships bound for Israel to pass through) helped reduce tension to a point where the negotiations became possible (Rubin, 1981).

To many, the most significant attempt at GRIT was the so-called Kennedy experiment (Etzioni, 1967). On June 10, 1963, U.S. President John F. Kennedy gave a major speech, "A Strategy for Peace [with the Soviet Union]." He noted that "Our problems are man-made . . . and can be solved by man" and then announced his first conciliatory act: The United States was stopping all atmospheric nuclear tests and would not resume them unless another country did. Kennedy's entire speech was published in the Soviet press. Five days later Premier Nikita Khrushchev reciprocated, announcing he had halted production of strategic bombers. There soon followed further reciprocal gestures: The United States agreed to sell wheat to the Soviet Union, the Soviets agreed to a "hot line" between the two countries, and the two countries soon achieved a test-ban treaty. For a time, these conciliatory initiatives eased relations between the two countries.

Might conciliatory efforts also help reduce tension between individuals? There is every reason to expect so. When a relationship is strained and communication nonexistent, it sometimes takes only a conciliatory gesture – a soft answer, a warm smile, a gentle touch – for both parties to begin easing down the tension ladder to a rung where contact, cooperation, and communication again become possible.

SUMMING UP: How Can Peace Be Achieved?

- Although conflicts are readily kindled and fueled by social dilemmas, competition, and misperceptions, some equally powerful forces, such as contact, cooperation, communication, and conciliation, can transform hostility into harmony. Despite some encouraging early studies, other studies show that mere contact (such as mere desegregation in schools) has little effect upon racial attitudes. But when contact encourages emotional ties with individuals identified with an outgroup and when it is structured to convey *equal status,* hostilities often lessen.
- Contacts are especially beneficial when people work together to overcome a common threat or to achieve a *superordinate goal.* Taking their cue from experiments on cooperative contact, several research teams have replaced competitive classroom learning situations with opportunities for cooperative learning, with heartening results.
- Conflicting parties often have difficulty communicating. A third-party *mediator* can promote communication by prodding the antagonists to replace their competitive win-lose view of their conflict with a more cooperative win-win orientation via *bargaining,* leading to an *integrative agreement.* Mediators can also structure communications that will peel away misperceptions and increase mutual understanding and trust. When a negotiated settlement is not reached, the conflicting parties may defer the outcome to an *arbitrator,* who either dictates a settlement or selects one of the two final offers.
- Sometimes tensions run so high that genuine communication is impossible. In such cases, small conciliatory gestures by one party may elicit reciprocal conciliatory acts by the other party. One such conciliatory strategy, graduated and reciprocated initiatives in tension reduction *(GRIT),* aims to alleviate tense international situations. Those who mediate tense labor-management and international conflicts sometimes use another peacemaking strategy. They instruct the participants, as this chapter instructed you, in the dynamics of conflict and peacemaking in the hope that understanding can help former adversaries establish and enjoy peaceful, rewarding relationships.

CONCLUDING THOUGHTS: The Conflict Between Individual and Communal Rights

Many social conflicts are a contest between individual and collective rights. One person's right to smoke conflicts with others' rights to a smoke-free environment. One industrialist's right to do unregulated business conflicts with a community's right to clean air. One person's right to own handguns conflicts with a neighborhood's right to safe schools.

"This is the age of the individual."

—U.S. President Ronald Reagan, address on Wall Street, 1982

Hoping to blend the best of individualist and collectivist values, some social scientists have advocated a *communitarian* synthesis that aims to balance individual rights with the collective right to communal well-being. Communitarians welcome incentives for individual initiative and appreciate why Marxist economies have crumbled. "If I were, let's say, in Albania at this moment," said communitarian sociologist Amitai Etzioni (1991), "I probably would argue that there's too much community and not enough individual rights." But communitarians also question the other extreme: the self-indulgence of the 1960s ("Do your own thing"), the 1970s (the "Me decade"), the 1980s ("Greed is good"), the 1990s ("Follow your bliss"), the 2000s ("An Army of One"), the 2010s ("Never compromise"), and the 2020s ("I did my own research.") Unrestrained personal freedom, they say, destroys a culture's social fabric; unregulated commercial freedom, they add, has plundered our shared environment.

During the last half-century, Western individualism has intensified. Parents have become more likely to prize self-reliance in their children and are less concerned with obedience (Alwin, 1990; Park et al., 2014). Children more often have uncommon or unique names instead of common ones (Twenge et al., 2010, 2016). Clothing and grooming styles have become more diverse, personal freedoms have increased, and strict social rules have waned (Huynh & Grossmann, 2021; Putnam, 2000; Santos et al., 2017).

Communitarians are not advocating a nostalgia trip — a return, for example, to the more restrictive and unequal gender and racial roles of the 1950s. Rather, they propose a middle ground between the individualism of the West and the collectivism of the East, between macho independence and caregiving connectedness, between concerns for individual rights and for communal well-being, between liberty and fraternity, between me-thinking and we-thinking.

As with luggage searches at airports, smoking bans on planes, sobriety checkpoints and speed limits on highways, and mask mandates during pandemics, societies accept some adjustments to individual rights in order to protect the public good. Environmental restraints on individual freedoms (to spew greenhouse gases, to hunt whales, to deforest) similarly exchange certain short-term liberties for long-term communal gain. Some individualists warn that such constraints on individual liberties may plunge us down a slippery slope leading to the loss of more important liberties. (If today we let them search our luggage, tomorrow they'll be knocking down the doors of our houses. If today we remove books from libraries, tomorrow they'll burn all of the copies. If today we ban assault rifles, tomorrow they'll take our hunting rifles.) In protecting the interests of the majority, do we risk suppressing the basic rights of minorities? Communitarians reply that if we don't balance concern for individual rights with concern for our collective well-being, we risk worse civic disorder, which in turn *will* fuel cries for an autocratic crackdown.

This much is sure: As the conflict between individual and collective rights continues, scholarship and research can illuminate alternative cultural values and make visible our own assumed values.

Applying Social Psychology

PART FOUR

Social Psychology in the Clinic

CHAPTER

14

wavebreakmedia/Shutterstock

What influences the accuracy of clinical judgments?

What cognitive processes accompany mental health issues?

What are some social-psychological approaches to treatment?

How do social relationships support health and happiness?

Concluding Thoughts: Enhancing happiness

"Life does not consist mainly, or even largely, of facts and happenings. It consists mainly of the storm of thoughts that are forever blowing through one's mind."

—Mark Twain, *Mark Twain's Autobiography*, 1924

Throughout this book, we have linked laboratory and life by relating social psychology's principles and findings to everyday happenings. In these chapters, we recall many of these principles and apply them in practical contexts. "Social Psychology in the Clinic" applies social psychology to evaluating and promoting mental and physical health. "Social Psychology in Court" explores the social thinking of, and social influences on, jurors and juries. "Social Psychology and the Sustainable Future" explores how social psychological principles might help avert the ecological crisis of increasing population, consumption, and climate change.

If you are a typical college student, you occasionally feel mildly depressed. Perhaps you have at times felt dissatisfied with life, discouraged about the future, sad, lacking appetite and energy, unable to concentrate, perhaps even wondering if life is worth living. Maybe disappointing grades have jeopardized your career goals. Perhaps the breakup of a relationship has left you downcast. At such times, you may fall into self-focused brooding that only worsens your feelings. In one survey of U.S. collegians, 1 out of 4 said that feelings of depression had interfered with their schoolwork (ACHA, 2023), and in another, 43% said they "felt overwhelmed by all I had to do" (Stolzenberg et al., 2020). In 2022, 20% of U.S. 18- to 25-year-olds experienced depression severe enough to meet clinical criteria (SAMHSA, 2023), double the 2010 depression rates (Twenge, 2017).

Among the many thriving areas of applied social psychology is one that relates social psychology's concepts to depression and loneliness and to their opposites, happiness and well-being. This bridge-building research between social psychology and **clinical psychology** seeks answers to four important questions:

clinical psychology
The study, assessment, and treatment of people with psychological difficulties.

- As laypeople or as professional psychologists, how can we improve our judgments and predictions about others?
- How do the ways in which we think about ourselves and others contribute to depression, loneliness, anxiety, and ill health?
- How might people reverse maladaptive thought patterns?
- What part do close, supportive relationships play in health and happiness?

WHAT INFLUENCES THE ACCURACY OF CLINICAL JUDGMENTS?

Describe biases that clinicians and their clients should be wary of.

A parole board talks with a convicted rapist and ponders whether to release him. A clinical psychologist considers whether her patient is seriously suicidal. A physician notes a patient's symptoms and decides whether to recommend an invasive test. A school social worker wonders if a child's overheard threat was a joke, a one-time outburst, or a signal indicating a potential school assassin.

All these professionals must decide whether to make their judgments subjectively or objectively. Should they listen to their subjective gut instincts, their hunches, their inner wisdom? Or should they rely on the objective wisdom embedded in formulas, statistical analyses, and computerized predictions?

In the contest between heart and head, most psychological clinicians vote with their hearts. They listen to the whispers from their experience, a still, small voice that clues them. They prefer not to let cold calculations decide the futures of warm human beings. As **Figure 1** indicates, they are far more likely than nonclinical (and more research-oriented) psychologists to welcome nonscientific "ways of knowing." Feelings trump formulas.

Clinical judgments are also *social* judgments, noted social-clinical psychologist James Maddux (2008). The social construction of mental illness works like this, he said: Someone observes a pattern of atypical or unwanted thinking and acting. A powerful group sees the desirability or profitability of diagnosing and treating this problem and thus gives it a name. News about this "disease" spreads, and people begin seeing it in themselves or family

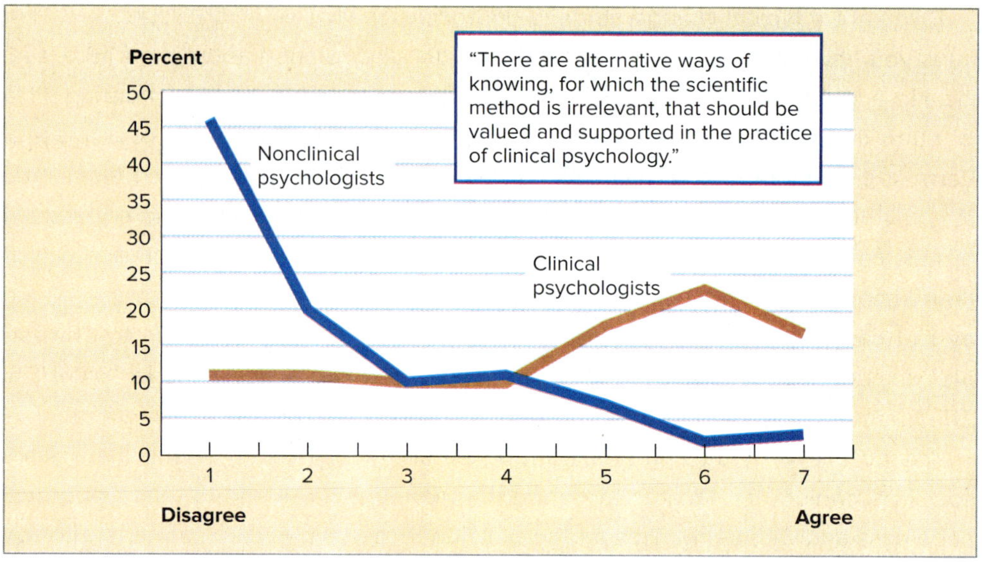

FIGURE 1

Clinical Intuition

When Narina Nunez, Debra Ann Poole, and Amina Memon (2003) surveyed a national sample of clinical and nonclinical psychologists, they discovered "two cultures": one mostly skeptical of "alternative ways of knowing," the other mostly accepting.

Source: Nunez, Poole, & Memon, 2003.

members. And thus is born body dysmorphic disorder (for those preoccupied with a supposed appearance defect), oppositional defiant disorder (for toddlers throwing tantrums), hypoactive sexual desire disorder (for those not wanting sex "often enough"), or orgasmic disorder (for those having orgasms too seldom or too soon). "The science of medicine is not diminished by acknowledging that the notions of *health* and *illness* are socially constructed," noted Maddux, "nor is the science of economics diminished by acknowledging that the notions of *poverty* and *wealth* are socially constructed."

As social phenomena, clinical judgments are vulnerable to illusory correlations, overconfidence bred by hindsight, and self-confirming diagnoses (Garb, 2005; Maddux, 1993). For example, in one survey of 129 practicing clinicians, most believed that their performance was at the 80th percentile, and none believed they were below the 50th percentile – a classic example of social psychological concepts such as *overconfidence* and *self-serving bias* (Walfish et al., 2012). Let's see why alerting mental health workers to how people form impressions (and misimpressions) might help avert serious misjudgments (McFall, 1991, 2000).

Illusory Correlations

It's tempting to see correlations where none exist. If we expect two things to be associated – if, for example, we believe that premonitions predict events – it's easy to perceive *illusory correlations*. Even when shown random data, we may notice and remember instances when premonitions and events are coincidentally related and soon forget all the instances when premonitions aren't borne out and when events happen without a prior premonition.

Clinicians, like all of us, may perceive illusory correlations. Imagine that Imani, a therapist, expects people with sexual disorders to give certain responses to the Rorschach inkblots (in which people are asked to say what they think an inkblot pattern looks like). In thinking about her own experience with clients, she might believe she has witnessed such an association – but she might be forgetting the responses that did not fit her expectations.

To discover when such a perception is an illusory correlation, psychological science offers a simple method: Have one clinician administer and interpret the test. Have another clinician assess the same person's traits or symptoms. Repeat this process with many people. Are test outcomes in fact correlated with reported symptoms? Some tests are indeed predictive. Others, such as the Rorschach inkblots and the Draw-a-Person test (in which someone is asked to draw a picture of a person, which presumably reveals their attitudes), have correlations far weaker than the clinicians who use them suppose (Lilienfeld et al., 2000, 2005).

Why, then, do clinicians continue to express confidence in uninformative or ambiguous tests? Pioneering experiments by Loren Chapman and Jean Chapman (1969, 1971) helped us see why. They invited college students and professional clinicians to study some test performances and diagnoses. If the students or clinicians *expected* a particular association, they generally *perceived* it. For example, clinicians who believed that only suspicious people draw peculiar eyes on the Draw-a-Person test perceived such a relationship – even when shown cases in which suspicious people drew peculiar eyes *less* often than nonsuspicious people. If they believed in a connection, they were more likely to notice confirming instances.

In fairness to clinicians, illusory thinking also occurs among political analysts, historians, sportscasters, personnel directors, stockbrokers, and many other professionals, including research psychologists. As researchers, we have often been unaware of the shortcomings of our theoretical analyses. We so eagerly presume that our idea of truth is *the* truth that, no matter how hard we try, we cannot see our own errors. We authors have read dozens of reviews of our own manuscripts and have been reviewers for dozens of others. It is far easier to spot someone else's sloppy thinking than to perceive our own.

Courtesy of Elizabeth Louden

What does this drawing of a person say about the child who drew it? According to research, not much: The Draw-a-Person test is not very predictive.

Hindsight and Overconfidence

If someone we know takes their own life, how do we react? One common reaction is to think that we, or those close to the person, should have been able to predict and therefore to prevent the suicide: "We should have known!" In hindsight, we can see the suicidal signs and the pleas for help. One experiment gave participants a description of a depressed person. Some participants were told that the person took their own life; other participants were not told this. Compared with those not informed of the suicide, those who had been informed became more likely to say they "would have expected" it (Goggin & Range, 1985). Moreover, they viewed the victim's family more negatively. After a tragedy, an I-should-have-known-it-all-along phenomenon can leave family, friends, and therapists feeling guilty. And the more expertise someone has, the more likely they are to think they should have known (Knoll & Arkes, 2017). The same is often true when someone commits violence against others; for example, when a teen opens fire at their school and observers assume their teachers and parents should have known what they were going to do.

Self-Confirming Diagnoses

So far we've seen that mental health clinicians sometimes perceive illusory correlations and that hindsight explanations can err. A third possible problem with clinical judgment is that patients may supply information that fulfills clinicians' expectations. To get a feel for how this phenomenon might be tested experimentally, imagine yourself on a blind date with someone who has been told that you are an uninhibited, outgoing person. To see whether this is true, your date slips questions into the conversation, such as "Have you ever done anything crazy in front of other people?" As you answer such questions, will you reveal a different "you" than if your date thought you were shy and reserved and asked questions that would reveal that side of you?

In a clever series of experiments, Mark Snyder (1984) gave University of Minnesota students some hypotheses to test concerning individuals' traits. The finding: People often test for a trait by looking for information that confirms it. As in the blind-date example, if people are trying to find out if someone is an extravert, they often solicit instances of extraversion ("What would you do if you wanted to liven things up at a party?"). Testing for introversion, they are more likely to ask, "What factors make it hard for you to really open up to people?" In response, those probed for extraversion *seem* more sociable, and those probed for introversion seem shyer. Our assumptions about another help elicit the behavior we expect.

Seen here in a courtroom in 2018, Jesse Osborne was 14 when he shot and killed his father and then a 6-year-old boy at an elementary school in South Carolina. *After* school shootings, people look back and see signs of the coming violence — such as Osborne's interest in guns and bombs and his desire for infamy. Yet many teen boys have such interests and do not murder others, making it difficult to predict who will commit violence and who will not.
Ken Ruinard/The Independent-Mail/AP Images

At Indiana University, Russell Fazio and his colleagues (1981) discovered that people who were asked the "extraverted" questions not only seemed more extraverted to their conversation partner but also started to see themselves as more extraverted than those who were asked the introverted questions. Even after the conversation was over, an accomplice of the experimenter was able to guess which condition they'd been assigned to 70% of the time.

"As is your sort of mind, so is your sort of search: You'll find what you desire."

—English poet Robert Browning, "Christmas-Eve and Easter-Day," 1850

Given such experiments, you can see why confirmation bias can lead to misdiagnoses and the behaviors of people undergoing psychotherapy come to fit their therapists' theories (Koyama et al., 2018; Mendel et al., 2011). When Harold Renaud and Floyd Estess (1961) conducted life-history interviews of 100 healthy, successful men, they were startled to discover that their subjects' childhood experiences were loaded with "traumatic events," tense relations with certain people, and bad decisions by their parents — the very factors usually used to explain psychiatric problems. If therapists go fishing for traumas in early childhood experiences, they will often find them.

Clinical Intuition versus Statistical Prediction

"A very bright young man who is likely to succeed in life. He is intelligent enough to achieve lofty goals as long as he stays on task and remains motivated."

—Probation officer's clinical intuition in response to Eric Harris's "homicidal thoughts" — 2½ months before he committed the Columbine High School shootings in April 1999

Given these hindsight- and diagnosis-confirming tendencies, most clinicians and interviewers express more confidence in their intuitive assessments than in statistical data (such as using past grades and aptitude scores to predict success in graduate or professional school). Yet when researchers pit statistical prediction against intuitive prediction, statistics usually wins. Statistical predictions can indeed be unreliable. But human intuition — even expert intuition — is even more unreliable (Faust & Ziskin, 1988; Meehl, 1954; Swets et al., 2000). In a meta-analysis of 36 studies of clinicians' judgments, there was only a weak correlation between the confidence they had in their judgments and the accuracy of their judgments (Miller et al., 2015).

Three decades after demonstrating the superiority of statistical over intuitive prediction, Paul Meehl (1986) found the evidence stronger than ever. "There is no controversy in social science which shows [so many] studies coming out so uniformly in the same direction as this one. [When you] can hardly come up with a half dozen studies showing even a weak tendency in favor of the clinician, it is time to draw a practical conclusion."

"The effect of Meehl's work on clinical practice in the mental health area can be summed up in a single word: zilch. He was honored, elected to the presidency of [the American Psychological Association] at a very young age in 1962, recently elected to the National Academy of Sciences, and ignored."

—Robyn M. Dawes, resignation letter to the American Psychological Association, 1989

One University of Minnesota research team conducted a meta-analysis of 134 studies in which practitioners tried to predict human behavior or make psychological or medical diagnoses (Grove et al., 2000). Only in eight of the studies (6%) did clinical prediction surpass "mechanical" (statistical) prediction. In 8 times as many (63 studies, or 47%), statistical prediction fared better. (The rest were a virtual draw.) Ah, but would clinicians fare differently when given the opportunity for a firsthand clinical interview? Yes, reported the researchers: Allowed interviews, the clinicians fared substantially *worse.* "It is fair to say that 'the ball is in the clinicians' court,'" the researchers concluded. "Given the overall deficit in clinicians' accuracy relative to mechanical prediction, the burden falls on advocates of clinical prediction to show that clinicians' predictions are more [accurate or cost-effective]."

Many studies show that therapy is effective (Duncan & Reese, 2013). However, for predicting behavior, statistical techniques win over clinical intuition.
Prostock-studio/Shutterstock

Daniel Kahneman (2011, p. 223) notes that we now have some 200 studies comparing clinical/intuitive and statistical prediction. These include efforts to predict medical outcomes such as cardiac diagnoses, economic outcomes such as the success of a new business, and other outcomes such as the winners of football games. In most of these cases, statistical prediction won; for the rest, intuitive and statistical predictions performed about the same.

What if we combined statistical prediction with clinical intuition — for example, by giving professional clinicians the statistical prediction of someone's parole violation or suicide and then asked them to refine or improve on the prediction? Alas, in the few studies in which that has been done, prediction was better if the "improvements" were ignored; prediction based on just the statistics was better (Dawes, 1994). Such results have led some clinical psychologists to suggest the field adopt evidence-based approaches to diagnosis and treatment (Youngstrom et al., 2015). In 2005, the American Psychological Association adopted evidence-based practice as standard policy, publishing a comprehensive set of guidelines for its use in 2021 (Melchert et al., 2023).

Why, then, do so many clinicians continue to interpret Rorschach inkblot tests and offer intuitive predictions about parolees, suicide risk, and likelihood of child abuse? Partly out of sheer ignorance, said Paul Meehl, but also partly out of "mistaken conceptions of ethics":

> If I try to forecast something important about a college student, or a criminal, or a depressed patient by inefficient rather than efficient means, meanwhile charging this person or the taxpayer 10 times as much money as I would need to achieve greater predictive accuracy, that is not a sound ethical practice. That it feels better, warmer, and cuddlier to me as predictor is a shabby excuse indeed.

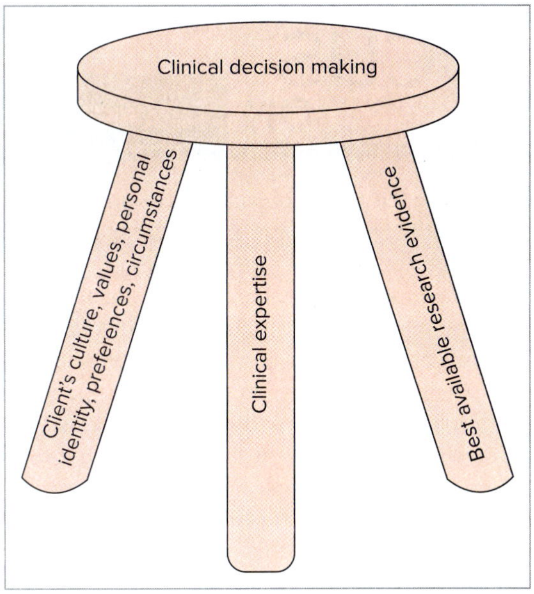

Evidence-Based Practice

Such words are shocking. Did Meehl (who did not completely dismiss clinical expertise) underestimate experts' intuitions? To see why his findings are apparently valid, consider the assessment of human potential by graduate school admissions interviewers. Dawes (1976) explained why statistical prediction is so often superior to an interviewer's intuition when predicting certain outcomes such as graduate school success:

> What makes us think that we can do a better job of selection by interviewing (students) for a half hour, than we can by adding together relevant (standardized) variables, such as undergraduate GPA, GRE score, and perhaps ratings of letters of recommendation? The most reasonable explanation to me lies in our overevaluation of our cognitive capacity. And it is really cognitive conceit. Consider, for example, what goes into a GPA. Because for most graduate applicants it is based on at least 3½ years of undergraduate study, it is a composite measure arising from a minimum of 28 courses and possibly, with the popularity of the quarter system, as many as 50. . . . Yet you and I, looking at a folder or interviewing someone for a half hour, are supposed to be able to form a better impression than one based on 3½ years of the cumulative evaluations of 20–40 different professors. . . . Finally, if we do wish to ignore GPA, it appears that the only reason for doing so is believing that the candidate is particularly brilliant even though his or her record may not show it. What better evidence for such brilliance can we have than a score on a carefully devised aptitude test? Do we really think we are better equipped to assess such aptitude than is the Educational Testing Service, whatever its faults?

The bottom line, contended Dawes (2005) after three decades pressing his point, is that, lacking evidence, using clinical intuition rather than statistical prediction "is simply unethical." (And similar principles may apply in medicine as well: see "Focus On: A Physician's View: The Social Psychology of Medicine").

However, psychologists can offer useful predictions based on research studies examining specific past behaviors. Such was the case when psychologists Melissa Dannelet and Carl Redick assessed Maurice Clemmons, who was in a Tacoma, Washington, jail on rape and assault charges. Based partly on "previous violence, young age at first violent incident, relationship instability and prior supervision failure," Dannelet and Redick predicted that Clemmons was at "risk for future dangerous behavior and for committing future criminal acts jeopardizing public safety and security due to past illicit behaviors" (AP, 2009; Logan, 2016). Six weeks later, after being released on bond, Clemmons came upon four police officers working on their laptops in a coffee shop and shot and killed them. If only the psychologists' warnings were heeded.

"'I beseech ye in the bowels of Christ, think that ye may be mistaken.' I should like to have that written over the portals of every church, every school, and every courthouse, and, may I say, of every legislative body in the United States."

—Judge Learned Hand, *Morals in Public Life,* 1951, echoing Oliver Cromwell's 1650 plea to the Church of Scotland

Implications for Better Clinical Practice

Professional clinicians are human; they are "vulnerable to insidious errors and biases," concluded James Maddux (1993). They are, as we have seen,

- frequently the victims of illusory correlation.
- too readily convinced of their own after-the-fact analyses.
- often unaware that erroneous diagnoses can be self-confirming.
- likely to overestimate the accuracy of their clinical intuition.

focus ON A Physician's View: The Social Psychology of Medicine

Reading this text helped me understand the human behaviors I observe in my work as a cancer specialist and as medical director of a large staff of physicians. A few examples:

Reviews of medical records illustrate the "I-knew-it-all-along phenomenon." Physician reviewers who assess the medical records of their colleagues often believe, in hindsight, that problems such as cancer or appendicitis should clearly have been recognized and treated much more quickly. Once you know the correct diagnosis, it's easy to look back and interpret the early symptoms accordingly.

For many physicians I have known, the intrinsic motives behind their entering the profession — to help people, to be scientifically stimulated — soon become "overjustified" by the high pay. Before long, the joy is lost. The extrinsic rewards become the reason to practice, and the physician, having lost the altruistic motives, works to increase "success," measured in income.

"Self-serving bias" is ever present. We physicians gladly accept personal credit when things go well. When they don't — when the patient is misdiagnosed or doesn't get well or dies — we attribute the failure elsewhere. We were given inadequate information or the case was ill-fated from the beginning.

Indeed, as I observe medical attitudes and decision making I feel myself submerged in a giant practical laboratory of social psychology. To understand the goings-on around me, I find social psychological insights invaluable and would strongly advise premed students to study the field.

Burton F. VanderLaan
Grand Rapids, Michigan
Courtesy of Dr. Burton F Vanderlaan

The implications for mental health workers are easily stated: Be mindful that clients' verbal agreement with what you say does not prove its validity. Beware of the tendency to see correlations that you expect to see or that are supported by striking examples readily available in your memory. Rely on your notes more than on your memory. Recognize that hindsight is seductive: It can lead you to feel overconfident and sometimes to judge yourself too harshly for not having foreseen outcomes. Guard against the tendency to ask questions that assume your preconceptions are correct; consider opposing ideas and test them, too (Garb, 1994).

SUMMING UP: What Influences the Accuracy of Clinical Judgments?

- As psychiatrists and *clinical psychologists* diagnose and treat their clients, they may perceive illusory correlations.
- Hindsight explanations of people's difficulties are sometimes too easy. Indeed, after-the-fact explaining can breed overconfidence in clinical judgment.
- In interaction with clients, erroneous diagnoses are sometimes self-confirming because interviewers tend to seek and recall information that verifies what they are looking for.
- Research on the errors that so easily creep into intuitive judgments illustrates the need for rigorous testing of intuitive conclusions and the use of statistics to make predictions.
- Statistical prediction cannot answer all questions. Thankfully, however, it can help us sift truth from falsehood if we are aware of the biases that tend to cloud judgments that are made "from the heart."

WHAT COGNITIVE PROCESSES ACCOMPANY MENTAL HEALTH ISSUES?

Describe the cognitive processes that accompany psychological disorders.

Let's next consider how people's thinking affects their feelings. What are the memories, attributions, and expectations of depressed, lonely, shy, or illness-prone people?

Depression

People who feel depressed tend to think in negative terms. They view life through the dark glasses of low self-esteem and see the world in a negative light (Belmans et al., 2023; Kuster et al., 2012; Sowislo & Orth, 2013; van Tuijl et al., 2020). With seriously depressed people – those who are feeling worthless, lethargic, indifferent toward friends and family, and unable to sleep or eat normally – the negative thinking is self-defeating. Their intensely pessimistic outlook leads them to magnify every bad experience and minimize every good one. They may view advice to "count your blessings" or "look on the bright side" as hopelessly unrealistic. As one depressed young woman reported, "The real me is worthless and inadequate. I can't move forward with my work because I become frozen with doubt" (Burns, 1980, p. 29). Depression can be caused by events and circumstances, but some people are also genetically predisposed to be more likely to experience depression at some point in their lives.

DISTORTION OR REALISM?

Are all depressed people unrealistically negative? To find out, Lauren Alloy and Lyn Abramson (1979; Alloy et al., 2004) studied college students who were either mildly depressed or not depressed. They had the students press a button and observe whether the button controlled a light coming on. Surprisingly, the depressed students were quite accurate in estimating their degree of control. It was the nondepressed people whose judgments were distorted; they exaggerated their control. Despite their self-preoccupation, mildly depressed people also are more attuned to others' feelings and often more accurate in their memories and judgments (Forgas, 2014; Harkness et al., 2005). For example, depressed people are more accurate than nondepressed people at judging whether someone likes them back (Moritz & Roberts, 2020). Depressed people even excel at accurately estimating time intervals (Kornbrot et al., 2013).

"Life is the art of being well deceived."

—William Hazlitt, *The Round Table: A Collection of Essays*, 1817

This surprising phenomenon of **depressive realism,** nicknamed the "sadder-but-wiser effect," shows up in various judgments of one's control or skill (Ackermann & DeRubeis, 1991; Alloy et al., 1990).

depressive realism
The tendency of mildly depressed people to make accurate rather than self-serving judgments, attributions, and predictions.

As Shelley Taylor (1989) explains:

> Normal [nondepressed] people exaggerate how competent and well liked they are. Depressed people do not. Normal people remember their past behavior with a rosy glow. Depressed people [unless severely depressed] are more evenhanded in recalling their successes and failures. Normal people describe themselves primarily positively. Depressed people describe both their positive and their negative qualities. Normal people take credit for successful outcomes and tend to deny responsibility for failure. Depressed people accept responsibility for both success and failure. Normal people exaggerate the control they have over what goes on around them. Depressed people are less vulnerable to the illusion of control. Normal people believe to an unrealistic degree that the future holds a bounty of good things and few bad things. Depressed people are more realistic in their perceptions of the future. In fact, on virtually every point on which normal people show enhanced self-regard, illusions of control, and unrealistic visions of the future, depressed people fail to show the same biases. "Sadder but wiser" does indeed appear to apply to depression.

(For more on this, see "The Inside Story: Shelley Taylor on Positive Illusions.")

THE inside STORY

Shelley Taylor on Positive Illusions

Some years ago, I was conducting interviews with people who had cancer for a study on adjustment to intensely stressful events. I was surprised to learn that, for some people, the cancer experience actually seemed to have brought benefits, as well as the expected liabilities. Many people told me that they thought they were better people for the experience, they felt they were better adjusted to cancer than other people, they believed that they could exert control over their cancer in the future, and they believed their futures would be cancer-free, even when we knew from their medical histories that their cancers were likely to recur.

As a result, I became fascinated by how people can construe even the worst of situations as good, and I've studied these "positive illusions" ever since. Through our research, we learned quickly that you don't have to experience trauma to demonstrate positive illusions. Most people, including the majority of college students, think of themselves as somewhat better than average, as more in control of the circumstances around them than may actually be true, and as likely to experience more positive future outcomes in life than may be realistic. These illusions are not a sign of maladjustment — quite the contrary. Good mental health may depend on the ability to see things as somewhat better than they are and to find benefits even when things seem most bleak.

Shelley Taylor
University of California – Los Angeles

Courtesy of Shelley Taylor

However, moderate to severe depression may cross from realism to pessimism. When followed over several weeks, people low in depressive symptoms recalled feeling less stress than they actually had, while those with mild depression recalled their previous stress accurately — consistent with depressive realism. But people with very high levels of depressive symptoms recalled experiencing more stress than they actually had (Chang & Overall, 2022).

In addition, depressed people are also more likely to believe that they are to blame for negative events. For example, if you fail an exam and blame yourself, you may conclude that you are stupid or lazy; consequently, you may feel depressed. If you attribute the failure to an unfair exam or to other circumstances beyond your control, you may instead feel angry. In more than 100 studies of 15,000 participants, depressed people have been more likely than nondepressed people to exhibit a negative **explanatory style** (Haeffel et al., 2008; Peterson & Steen, 2002; Sweeney et al., 1986). As shown in **Figure 2,** this explanatory style attributes failure and setbacks to causes that are *stable* ("It's going to last forever"), *global* ("It's going to affect everything I do"), and *internal* ("It's all my fault"). The result of this

explanatory style
One's habitual way of explaining life events. A negative, pessimistic, depressive explanatory style attributes failure to stable, global, and internal causes.

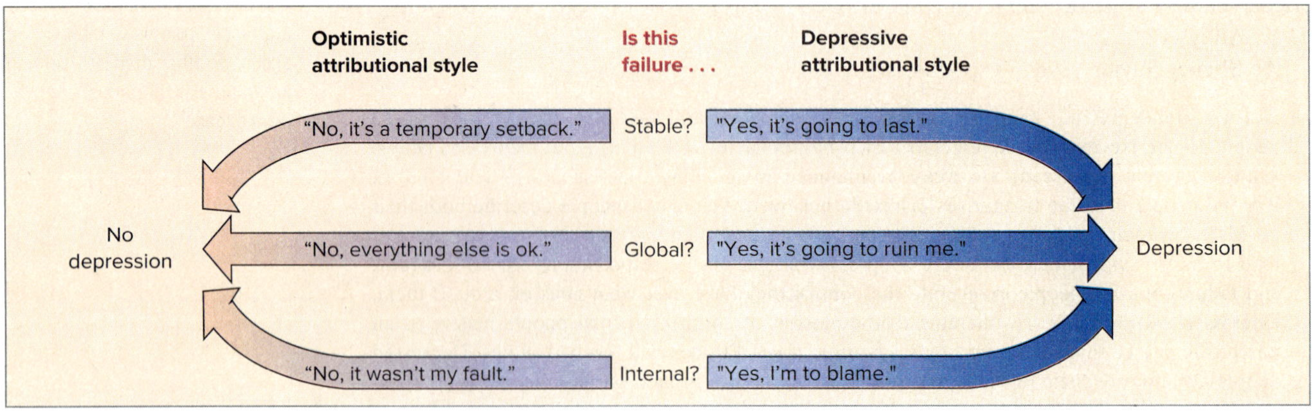

FIGURE 2
Depressive Explanatory Style
Depression is linked with a negative, pessimistic way of explaining and interpreting failures.

pessimistic, overgeneralized, self-blaming thinking, said Abramson and her colleagues (1989), is a depressing sense of hopelessness.

IS NEGATIVE THINKING A CAUSE OR A RESULT OF DEPRESSION?

The cognitive accompaniments of depression raise a chicken-and-egg question: Do depressed moods cause negative thinking, or does negative thinking cause depression?

DEPRESSED MOODS CAUSE NEGATIVE THINKING Our moods color our thinking. When we *feel* happy, we *think* happy. We see and recall a good world. But let our mood turn gloomy, and our thoughts switch to a different track. Off come the rose-colored glasses; on come the dark glasses. Now the bad mood primes our recollections of negative events (Johnson & Magaro, 1987). Our relationships seem to sour, our self-images tarnish, our hopes dim, others seem more sinister (Brown & Taylor, 1986). As depression increases, memories and expectations plummet. When U.S. adults recorded their emotions every day for 8 days and were then asked to recall these experiences on the final day, depressed people remembered being sad or angry on more days than they actually were (Urban et al., 2018).

"To the man who is enthusiastic and optimistic, if what is to come should be pleasant, it seems both likely to come about and likely to be good, while to the indifferent or depressed man it seems the opposite."

—Aristotle,
The Art of Rhetoric, BC fourth century

When depression lifts, thinking brightens (Barnett & Gotlib, 1988; Kuiper & Higgins, 1985). Thus, *currently* depressed people recall their parents as having been rejecting and punitive. But *formerly* depressed people recall their parents in the same positive terms that never-depressed people do (Lewinsohn & Rosenbaum, 1987). Even when depressed people recall happy memories, these memories bring them less happiness than they do for nondepressed people (Kim & Yoon, 2020). Remember: *Moods modify memories.*

By studying Indiana University basketball fans, Edward Hirt and his colleagues (1992) demonstrated that even a temporary bad mood can darken thinking. After fans were either depressed by watching their team lose or elated by a victory, researchers asked them to predict the team's future performance and their own. After a loss, people offered bleaker assessments not only of the team's future but also of their own likely performance at throwing darts, solving anagrams, and getting a date. When things aren't going our way, it may seem as though they never will.

A depressed mood also affects behavior. When depressed, we tend to be withdrawn, glum, and quick to complain. Depressed people are somewhat realistic in realizing that others don't always like their behavior; their pessimism and bad moods can trigger social rejection (Carver et al., 1994; Strack & Coyne, 1983). They may also expect to be socially rejected, which can become a self-fulfilling prophecy (Kirchner et al., 2022).

Depressed behavior can also trigger depression in others. College students who have depressed roommates tend to become a little depressed themselves (Burchill & Stiles, 1988; Joiner, 1994; Sanislow et al., 1989). In dating couples, too, depression is often contagious (Katz et al., 1999). Better news comes from a study that followed nearly 5,000 residents of one Massachusetts city for 20 years: Happiness is also contagious. When surrounded by happy people, people often become happier (Fowler & Christakis, 2008).

We can see, then, that being depressed has cognitive and behavioral effects. Does it also work the other way around: Does depression have cognitive *origins?*

NEGATIVE THINKING CAUSES DEPRESSED MOODS Depression is natural when experiencing severe stress – losing a job, getting divorced or rejected, or suffering any experience that disrupts our sense of who we are and why we are worthy human beings. The brooding that comes with this short-term depression can be adaptive. Just as nausea and pain protect the body from toxins, depression protects us by slowing us down, causing us to reassess, and then redirecting our energy in new ways (Andrews & Thomson, 2009, 2010; Watkins, 2008). Insights gained during times of depressed inactivity may later result in better strategies for interacting with the world.

Although all of us may be temporarily depressed by bad events, some people are more enduringly depressed. Depression-prone people respond to bad events with intense rumination and self-blame (Mor & Winquist, 2002; Pyszczynski et al., 1991). Their self-esteem fluctuates more rapidly up with boosts and down with threats (Butler et al., 1994).

Why are some people so affected by *minor* stresses? Evidence suggests that when stress-induced rumination is filtered through a negative explanatory style, the frequent outcome is depression (Robinson & Alloy, 2003). In other words, they keep thinking about negative events and believe they caused those events to happen. Colin Sacks and Daphne Bugental (1987) asked some young women to get acquainted with a stranger who sometimes acted cold and unfriendly, creating an awkward social situation. Unlike optimistic women, those with a pessimistic explanatory style – who characteristically offered stable, global, and internal attributions for bad events – reacted to the social failure by feeling depressed. Moreover, they then behaved more antagonistically toward the next people they met. Their negative thinking led to a negative mood, which led to negative behavior.

Such depressing rumination is more common among women, reported Susan Nolen-Hoeksema (2003). When trouble strikes, men tend to act, women tend to think – and often to "overthink," she observed. And that helps explain why, beginning in adolescence, women worldwide have, compared with men, a nearly doubled risk of depression (Bromet et al., 2011; CDC, 2018).

Outside the laboratory, studies of children, teenagers, and adults confirm that pessimistic people more often become depressed when bad things happen. One study monitored university students every 6 weeks for two-and-a-half years (Alloy et al., 1999). Seventeen percent of pessimists became depressed, compared to only 1% of optimists. "A recipe for severe depression is preexisting pessimism encountering failure," noted Martin Seligman (1991, p. 78).

Researcher Peter Lewinsohn and his colleagues (1985) assembled these findings into a coherent psychological understanding of depression. The negative self-image, attributions, and expectations of a depressed person are, they reported, an essential link in a vicious circle that is triggered by negative experience – perhaps academic or vocational failure, family conflict, or social rejection **(Figure 3).** Such ruminations create a depressed mood that alters how a person thinks and acts, which then fuels further negative experiences, self-blame, and depressed mood. In experiments, mildly depressed people's moods brighten when a task diverts their attention to something external (Nix et al., 1995). Depression is therefore *both* a cause and a result of negative cognitions.

Martin Seligman (1991, 1998, 2002) believes that self-focus and self-blame help explain the high levels of depression in today's Western world. He contends that the decline of religion and family, plus the growth of individualism, breeds hopelessness and self-blame when things don't go well. Failed classes, careers, and marriages produce despair when we stand alone, with nothing and no one to fall back on. If, as a macho *Fortune* ad declared, you can "make it on your own," on "your own drive, your own guts, your own energy, your own ambition," then whose fault is it if you *don't* make it? In non-Western cultures, in which close-knit relationships and cooperation are the norm, major depression is less common and less tied to guilt and self-blame over perceived personal failure. In Japan, for example, depressed people instead tend to report feeling shame over letting down their family or co-workers (Draguns, 1990).

These insights into the thinking style linked with depression have prompted social psychologists to study thinking patterns associated with other problems. How do those who are plagued with excessive loneliness, shyness, or substance abuse view themselves? How well do they recall their successes and their failures? And to what do they attribute their ups and downs?

Loneliness

If depression is the common cold of psychological disorders, then loneliness is the headache. Loneliness is a painful awareness that our social relationships are less numerous or meaningful than we desire. Loneliness tends to increase between the early teen years and one's mid-20s, and then declines (von Soest et al., 2020a). Loneliness increases later in life with the loss of loved ones but is not as emotionally painful as it is earlier in life (Böger & Huxhold, 2018; Russo, 2018).

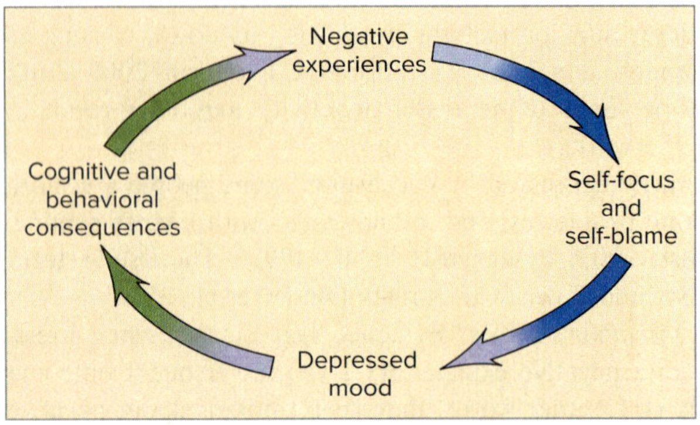

FIGURE 3
The Vicious Cycle of Depression
Source: Lewinsohn et al., 1985.

Social connectedness and identity help protect people from

depression (Cruwys et al., 2014). Yet in modern cultures, close social relationships are less numerous and in-person social interaction less frequent. Teens and young adults in the late 2010s spent less time interacting in person than those in the 1980s – in one set of surveys, an hour a day less (Twenge et al., 2019; Twenge & Spitzberg, 2020). Another analysis found that social engagement with friends declined by 20 hours a month between 2003 and 2020, with the majority of the decline before the COVID-19 pandemic (Kannan & Veazie, 2022).

Moreover, the number of one-person U.S. households increased from 5% in the 1920s to 28% in 2020 (Anderson et al., 2023; Census Bureau, 2019). Canada, Australia, Europe have experienced a similar multiplication of one-person households (Charnie, 2017). In 2018, the British prime minister responded to a report of 9 million lonely Brits by appointing a government "Minister for Loneliness" (BBC, 2018).

Like depression, loneliness is also genetically influenced (Spithoven et al., 2019). For example, identical twins are much more likely than fraternal twins to share moderate to extreme loneliness (Bartels et al., 2008; Boomsma et al., 2006). However, loneliness is also linked to how much time people spend with others in their daily lives. Loneliness among teens increased markedly after 2012, in tandem with declines in in-person social interaction (Twenge et al., 2019). Men, younger people, and people living in individualist societies – all groups more likely to be socially isolated – are also the most likely to be lonely (Barretto et al., 2021).

FEELING LONELY AND EXCLUDED

But loneliness need not coincide with aloneness. One can feel lonely in the middle of a party. "In America, there is loneliness but no solitude," lamented Mary Pipher (2003). "There are crowds but no community." In Los Angeles, observed Pipher's daughter, "There are 10 million people around me but nobody knows my name." Lonely people may compensate by seeing humanlike qualities in things, animals, and supernatural beings, with which they find companionship (Epley et al., 2008).

One can be utterly alone – as I [DM] am while writing these words in the solitude of an isolated turret office at a British university 5,000 miles from home – without feeling lonely. To feel lonely is to feel excluded from a group, unloved by those around you, unable to share your private concerns, different and alienated from those in your surroundings (Beck & Young, 1978; Davis & Franzoi, 1986). Small wonder, then, that loneliness increases one's risk of future depression, pain, and fatigue (Jaremka et al., 2013).

Loneliness also increases the risk of health problems. Loneliness affects stress hormones, immune activity, and inflammation. Loneliness, therefore, puts people at increased risk not only for depression and suicide but also high blood pressure, heart disease, cognitive decline, cancer, and sleep impairment (Cacioppo et al., 2014; Kraav et al., 2020). Among more than 300,000 people in 148 studies, social isolation increased the risk of death as much as smoking up to 15 cigarettes a day (Holt-Lunstad et al., 2010, 2017).

Loneliness – which may be evoked by an icy stare or a cold shoulder – feels, quite literally, cold. When recalling an experience of exclusion, people estimate a lower room temperature than when thinking of being included. After being excluded in a ball game in a lab, people show a heightened preference for warm foods and drinks (Zhong & Leonardelli, 2008). Such feelings can be adaptive. Loneliness signals people to seek social connections, which facilitates survival. Even when loneliness triggers nostalgia – a longing for the past – it serves to remind people of their social connections (Zhou et al., 2008).

Face-to-face social interaction appears to better relieve loneliness than the electronic connection of social media, which may actually increase

Ignoring someone else while looking at your phone — known as "phubbing" (a term combining the words "phone" and "snubbing") increases feelings of social exclusion (David & Roberts, 2017) and depression (Roberts & David, 2016; Wang et al., 2020) among those ignored. Why do people continue to "phub" others? Probably because they underestimate how much their own phone use impacts those around them (Barrick et al., 2022).
IKO/123RF

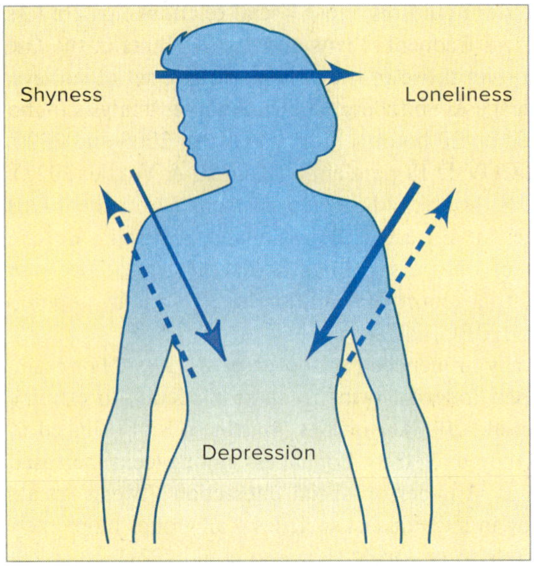

FIGURE 4
The Interplay of Chronic Shyness, Loneliness, and Depression
Solid arrows indicate a primary cause-effect direction, as summarized by Jody Dill and Craig Anderson (1999). Dotted lines indicate additional effects.

loneliness. People who spent more time on social media also felt more socially isolated and lonelier (Bonsaksen et al., 2023; Primack et al., 2017; Song et al., 2014). A longitudinal study found that Facebook use led to loneliness, rather than loneliness leading to Facebook use (Kross et al., 2013). When friends communicate in person, they feel significantly more emotional closeness than when communicating electronically (Sherman et al., 2013).

PERCEIVING OTHERS NEGATIVELY

Like depressed people, chronically lonely people seem caught in a vicious cycle of self-defeating social thinking and social behaviors. They have some of the negative explanatory style of the depressed; they perceive their interactions as making a poor impression, blame themselves for their poor social relationships, and see most things as beyond their control (Anderson et al., 1994; Christensen & Kashy, 1998; Snodgrass, 1987). Moreover, they perceive others in negative ways. When paired with a stranger of the same gender or with a first-year college roommate, lonely students are more likely to perceive the other person negatively (Jones et al., 1981; Wittenberg & Reis, 1986). Ironically, reported Danu Stinson and her co-researchers (2011), socially insecure people therefore often behave in ways that produce the very social rejection they fear. As **Figure 4** illustrates, loneliness, depression, and shyness sometimes feed one another.

These negative views may both reflect and color the lonely person's experience. Believing in their social unworthiness and feeling pessimistic about others inhibit lonely people from acting to reduce their loneliness. Lonely people often find it hard to introduce themselves, make phone calls, and participate in groups (Nurmi et al., 1996, 1997; Rook, 1984; Spitzberg & Hurt, 1987). Once someone becomes lonely, it can become a spiral, with lonely people more anxious about social interaction and thus more likely to "choke" in social situations (Cacioppo & Cacioppo, 2014; Knowles et al., 2015). Yet, like mildly depressed people, they are attuned to others and skilled at recognizing emotional expression (Gardner et al., 2005).

Anxiety and Shyness

Shyness is social anxiety marked by self-consciousness and worry about what others think (Anderson & Harvey, 1988; Asendorpf, 1987; Carver & Scheier, 1986). Being interviewed for a much-wanted job, dating someone for the first time, stepping into a roomful of strangers, performing before an important audience, or giving a speech (one of the most common phobias) can make almost anyone feel anxious. But some people feel anxious in almost any situation in which they may feel they are being evaluated, even having lunch with a co-worker. They tend to interpret ambiguous social interactions negatively and dwell on even mildly negative incidents (Chen et al., 2020). For these people, anxiety is more a personality trait than a temporary state.

DOUBTING OUR ABILITY IN SOCIAL SITUATIONS

self-presentation theory
A theory positing that we are eager to present ourselves in ways that make a good impression.

What causes us to feel anxious or shy in social situations? Why are some people shackled in the prison of their own social anxiety? Barry Schlenker and Mark Leary (1982, 1985; Leary & Kowalski, 1995) answered those questions by applying **self-presentation theory**. Self-presentation theory assumes that we are eager to present ourselves in ways that make a good impression. Thus, *we feel social anxiety when we are motivated to impress others but* *have self-doubts.* This simple principle helps explain a variety of research findings, each of which may ring true in your experience. We feel most anxious when we are

- with powerful, high-status people – people whose impressions of us matter.
- in an evaluative context, such as when having a first interview.
- self-conscious (as shy people often are), with our attention focused on ourselves and how we are coming across.
- focused on something central to our self-image, as when a college professor presents research before peers at a professional convention.
- in novel or unstructured situations, such as a first school dance or first formal dinner, where we are unsure of the social rules.

For most people, the tendency in all such situations is to be cautiously self-protective: to talk less; to avoid topics that reveal one's ignorance; to be guarded about oneself; to be unassertive, agreeable, and smiling. Ironically, such anxious concern with making a good impression often makes a bad impression (Broome & Wegner, 1994; Meleshko & Alden, 1993). With time, however, shy people often become well-liked. Their lack of egotism and their modesty, sensitivity, and discretion wear well (Gough & Thorne, 1986; Paulhus & Morgan, 1997; Shepperd et al., 1995).

OVERPERSONALIZING SITUATIONS

Compared with outgoing people, shy, self-conscious people see incidental events as somehow relevant to themselves (Fenigstein, 1984; Fenigstein & Vanable, 1992). Shy, anxious people overpersonalize situations, a tendency that breeds anxious concern and, in extreme cases, paranoia. They are especially prone to *the spotlight effect;* they overestimate the extent to which other people are watching and evaluating them. If their hair won't comb right or they have a facial blemish, they assume everyone else notices and judges them accordingly (Brown & Stopa, 2007). Shy people may even be conscious of their self-consciousness. They wish they could stop worrying about blushing, about what others are thinking, or about what to say next.

To reduce social anxiety, some people turn to alcohol. Alcohol lowers anxiety and reduces self-consciousness (Hull & Young, 1983). Thus, chronically self-conscious people are especially likely to drink following a failure. If recovering from alcoholism, they are more likely than those low in self-consciousness to relapse when they again experience stress or failure.

Symptoms as diverse as anxiety and alcohol abuse can serve a self-handicapping function. Labeling oneself as anxious, shy, depressed, or under the influence of alcohol can provide an excuse for failure (Snyder & Smith, 1986). Behind a barricade of symptoms, the person's ego stands secure. "Why don't I date? Because I'm shy, so people don't easily get to know the real me." The symptom is an unconscious strategic ploy to explain away negative outcomes.

What if we were to remove the need for such a ploy by providing people with a handy alternative explanation for their anxiety and therefore for possible failure? Would a shy person no longer need to be shy? That is precisely what Susan Brodt and Philip Zimbardo (1981) found when they brought shy and not-shy college women to the laboratory and had them converse with a handsome man who posed as another participant. Before the conversation, the women were cooped up in a small chamber and blasted with loud noise. Some of the shy women (but not others) were told that the noise would leave them with a pounding heart, a common symptom of social anxiety. Thus, when these women later talked with the man, they could attribute their pounding hearts and any conversational difficulties to the noise, not to their shyness or social inadequacy. Compared with the shy women who were not given this handy explanation for their pounding hearts, these women were no longer so shy. They talked fluently once the conversation got going and asked questions of the man. In fact, unlike the other shy women (whom the man could easily spot as shy), these women were indistinguishable from the not-shy women.

What do you think: Do people drink at parties mostly to relieve social anxiety?
Dragos Condrea/Alamy Stock Photo

Emotions and Physical Health

behavioral medicine
An interdisciplinary field that integrates and applies behavioral and medical knowledge about health and disease.

health psychology
The study of the psychological roots of health and illness. Offers psychology's contribution to behavioral medicine.

In the industrialized world, at least half of all deaths are linked with lifestyle behaviors – with consuming cigarettes, alcohol, drugs, and harmful foods; with reactions to stress; with lack of exercise; with not following a doctor's advice. The interdisciplinary field of **behavioral medicine** studies these behavioral contributions to illness. Psychology's contribution to this interdisciplinary science is its subfield, **health psychology.** One of the primary topics of interest in health psychology is how emotions influence health.

PERSONALITY, MOOD, AND HEALTH

For example, do our emotions predict our susceptibility to heart disease, stroke, cancer, and other ailments? Consider the following.

Heart disease has been linked with a competitive, impatient, and – the aspect that matters most – *anger-prone* personality (Chida & Steptoe, 2009; Kupper & Denollet, 2007). Under stress, reactive, anger-prone *Type A* people secrete more of the stress hormones believed to accelerate the buildup of plaque in the heart's arteries. It's the impatient anger of some Type A people, not their drive to achieve, that is linked to heart disease.

Depression also increases the risk of various ailments. Depressed and anxious people are twice as likely to develop heart disease, even after controlling for differences in smoking and other disease-related factors (Boehm et al., 2011; Nakada et al., 2023; Whang et al., 2009). Those who experienced depression as teens were more likely to develop heart disease decades later (Park et al., 2023). In the year after a heart attack, depressed people have a doubled risk of further heart problems compared with the nondepressed (Frasure-Smith et al., 1995, 1999; Frasure-Smith & Lespérance, 2005). The association between depression and heart disease may result from stress-related inflammation of the arteries (O'Donovan et al., 2012). Stress hormones enhance protein production that contributes to inflammation, which helps fight infections. But inflammation also can exacerbate asthma, clogged arteries, and depression, which is linked to health issues. Among more than 5,000 older adults in Norway, those in the top 33% for negative mood were twice as likely to die in the course of 17 years (Petrie et al., 2018). The bottom line: Anger, depression, and stress are heartfelt emotions (see **Figure 5**).

HOPELESSNESS, STRESS, AND HEALTH

Stories abound of people who take a sudden turn for the worse when something makes them lose hope or who suddenly improve when hope is renewed. As cancer attacks the liver of 9-year-old Jeff, his doctors fear the worst. But Jeff remains optimistic. He is determined to grow up to be a cancer research scientist. One day Jeff is elated. A specialist who has taken a long-distance interest in his case is planning to stop off while on a cross-country trip. There is so much Jeff wants to tell the doctor and to show him from the diary he has kept since

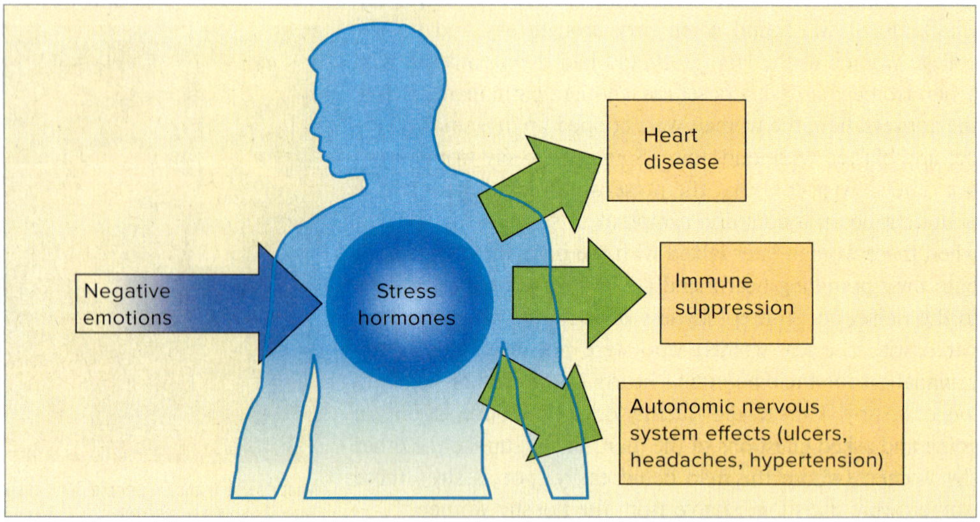

FIGURE 5
The Effects of Negative Emotions on Health
Stress-caused negative emotions may impact several body systems and compromise physical health. This is especially so for depressed or anger-prone people.

he got sick. On the anticipated day, fog blankets his city. The doctor's plane is diverted to another city, from which the doctor flies on to his final destination. Hearing the news, Jeff cries quietly. The next morning, pneumonia and fever have developed, and Jeff lies listless. By evening he is in a coma. The next afternoon he dies (Visintainer & Seligman, 1983).

Understanding the links between attitudes and disease requires more than dramatic true stories. If hopelessness coincides with cancer, we are left to wonder: Does cancer breed hopelessness, or does hopelessness also hinder resistance to cancer? To resolve this chicken-and-egg riddle, researchers have (1) experimentally created hopelessness by subjecting organisms to uncontrollable stresses and (2) correlated a hopeless explanatory style with future illnesses.

The clearest indication of the effects of hopelessness comes from experiments that subject animals to mild but uncontrollable electric shocks, loud noises, or crowding. Such experiences do not directly cause diseases such as cancer, but they do lower the body's resistance. Rats injected with live cancer cells more often develop and die of tumors if they also receive inescapable shocks (rather than escapable shocks or no shocks). Moreover, compared with juvenile rats given controllable shocks, those given uncontrollable shocks are twice as likely in adulthood to develop tumors if given cancer cells and another round of shocks (Visintainer & Seligman, 1985).

It's a big leap from rats to humans. But a growing body of evidence reveals that people who undergo highly stressful experiences become more vulnerable to disease (Segerstrom & Miller, 2004). Stress doesn't make us sick, but it does increase inflammation and divert energy from our disease-fighting immune system, leaving us more vulnerable to infections and malignancy (Cohen, 2002, 2004; Yuan et al., 2022). The death of a spouse and even the strain of an exam week have been associated with depressed immune defenses (Jemmott & Locke, 1984).

Consider the following:

- Stress magnifies the severity of respiratory infections and of symptoms experienced by volunteers who are knowingly infected with a cold virus (Cohen et al., 2003, 2006, 2012; Pedersen et al., 2010).
- Newlywed couples who became angry while discussing problems suffered more immune system suppression the next day (Kiecolt-Glaser et al., 1993). When people are stressed by marital conflict, puncture wounds inflicted in the laboratory take longer to heal (Kiecolt-Glaser et al., 2005).
- Especially among men and younger adults, divorce – often a stressful experience – increases the risk of early death (Sbarra et al., 2011).
- Middle-aged adults with increasing levels of stress experienced more hardening of the arteries, a significant risk factor for heart attacks (Spencer et al., 2023).
- Work stress can literally be disheartening. In one study that followed 17,415 middle-aged U.S. women, researchers found that significant work stress predicted an 88% increased risk of heart attacks (Slopen et al., 2010). In Denmark, a study of 12,116 female nurses found that those reporting significant work pressures had a 40% increased risk of heart disease (Allesøe et al., 2010).
- Stress increases the production of inflammation-producing proteins. Those who experience social stress, including children reared in abusive families, are therefore more prone to inflammation responses (Dickerson et al., 2009; Miller et al., 2011).

Have you ever noticed you're more likely to get sick right after final exams? That might occur because stress can compromise the immune system.
Eldar Nurkovic/123RF

If uncontrollable stress affects health, depresses immune functioning, increases inflammation, and generates a passive, hopeless resignation, then will people who exhibit such pessimism be more vulnerable to illness? Indeed, a pessimistic style of explaining bad events (saying, "It's going to last, it's going to undermine everything, and it's my fault") makes illness more likely (Carver et al., 2010). Christopher Peterson and Martin Seligman (1987) studied the press quotations of 94 members of baseball's Hall of Fame and gauged how often they offered pessimistic explanations for bad events, such as losing big games. Those who routinely did so were more likely to die younger. The optimists outlived the pessimists. Follow-up research has found that the absence of pessimism predicts good physical health better than the presence of optimism (Scheier et al., 2021).

Other studies have followed lives through time:

- Harvard graduates who expressed the most optimism in 1946 were the healthiest when restudied 34 years later (Peterson et al., 1988).
- Among older adults followed for 10 years, only 30% of the optimists died, compared to 57% of the pessimists (Giltay et al., 2004, 2007).
- Older adults with more social connections were less likely to develop dementia orcognitive impairment (Mahalingam et al., 2023).
- Catholic nuns who expressed the most positive feelings at age 22 outlived their more dour counterparts by an average of 7 years over the ensuing 50 years (Danner et al., 2001).

The healing power of positive belief is evident in the well-known *placebo effect,* referring to the healing power of *believing* that one is getting an effective treatment. (If you *think* a treatment is going to be effective, it just may be – even if it's actually inert.) But every silver lining has a cloud. Optimists may see themselves as invulnerable and thus fail to take sensible precautions; for example, those who smoke cigarettes too optimistically underestimate the risks involved (Segerstrom et al., 1993). And when things go wrong in a big way – when the optimist encounters a devastating illness – adversity can be shattering. Optimism is good for health. But even optimists have a mortality rate of 100% – eventually.

SUMMING UP: What Cognitive Processes Accompany Mental Health Issues?

- Social psychologists are actively exploring the attributions and expectations of depressed, lonely, socially anxious, and physically ill people. Depressed people have a negative *explanatory style,* interpreting negative events as being stable, global, and internally caused. Despite their more negative judgments, mildly depressed people in laboratory tests tend to be surprisingly realistic (known as *depressive realism*). Depression can be a vicious circle in which negative thoughts elicit self-defeating behaviors, and vice versa.
- Loneliness involves feelings of isolation or not fitting in and is common in individualistic societies. Like depression, it can be a vicious cycle in which feelings of aloofness lead to socially undesirable behaviors.
- Most people experience anxiety in situations where they are being evaluated, but shy individuals are extremely prone to anxiety even in friendly, casual situations. This can be another vicious cycle in which anxious feelings elicit awkward, off-putting behavior.
- The mushrooming field of *health psychology* is exploring the effects of negative emotions and the links among illness, stress, and a pessimistic explanatory style.

WHAT ARE SOME SOCIAL-PSYCHOLOGICAL APPROACHES TO TREATMENT?

Describe treatments for maladaptive thought patterns linked to mental and physical illness.

There is no social-psychological therapy. But therapy is a social encounter, and social psychologists have suggested how their principles might be integrated into existing treatment techniques (Forsyth & Leary, 1997; Strong et al., 1992). Consider three approaches:

- To promote internal changes, change one's external behavior.
- Break negative, self-defeating thought-behavior cycles.
- Attribute improvements to one's own self-control, rather than to the treatment.

Inducing Internal Change Through External Behavior

Our actions affect our attitudes. The roles we play, the things we say and do, and the decisions we make influence who we are.

Consistent with this attitudes-follow-behavior principle, several psychotherapy techniques prescribe action:

- Behavior therapists try to shape behavior on the theory that the client's inner disposition will also change after the behavior changes.
- People asked to publicly advocate a healthy behavior (such as exercise or restrained eating and drinking) and then reminded of their own unhealthy behaviors experienced *cognitive dissonance* and later changed their behavior (Freijy & Kothe, 2013).
- In assertiveness training, people first role-play assertiveness in a supportive context, then gradually implement assertive behaviors in everyday life.
- Rational-emotive behavior therapy assumes that we generate our own emotions. Clients receive "homework" assignments to talk and act in new ways that will generate new emotions: Challenge that overbearing relative. Stop telling yourself you're an unattractive person and ask someone out (Al-Roubaiy, 2020).
- Self-help groups subtly induce participants to behave in new ways in front of the group—to express anger, cry, act with high self-esteem, express positive feelings.

All these techniques share a common assumption: If we cannot directly control our feelings by sheer willpower, we can influence them indirectly through our behavior.

Experiments confirm that what we say about ourselves can affect how we feel. Those induced to present themselves in self-enhancing (rather than self-deprecating) ways later feel better about themselves (Jones et al., 1981; Rhodewalt & Agustsdottir, 1986). Those who performed kind acts for a month became happier (Alden & Trew, 2013). Public displays—whether positive or negative—carry over to later self-esteem. Saying is believing, even when we talk about ourselves.

In experiments, people internalized their behavior most when they thought they had a choice. For example, Pamela Mendonca and Sharon Brehm (1983) invited one group of overweight children who were about to begin a weight-loss program to choose the treatment they preferred. Then they reminded them periodically that they had chosen their treatment. Compared with children in the same program who were not given a choice, those who felt responsible for their treatment lost more weight during the program and kept more weight off 3 months later.

Breaking Vicious Cycles

If depression, loneliness, and social anxiety maintain themselves through a vicious cycle of negative experiences, negative thinking, and self-defeating behavior, it should be possible to break the cycle at any of several points—by changing the environment, by training the person to behave more constructively, or by reversing negative thinking. And it is. Several therapy methods help free people from depression's vicious cycle.

SOCIAL SKILLS TRAINING

Depression, loneliness, and shyness are not just problems in someone's mind. Being around a depressed person can be irritating and depressing. As lonely and shy people suspect, they

The most effective treatment for phobias, including social phobia, is exposure: engaging in the activity in a safe environment and learning that it can be pleasant.
Rawpixel.com/Shutterstock

may indeed come across poorly in social situations. Ironically, the more self-preoccupied people seek to make a good impression, the more their effort may backfire (Lun et al., 2011). Those who instead focus on supporting others often enjoy others' regard in return.

In these cases, social-skills training may help. By observing and then practicing new behaviors in safe situations, the person may develop the confidence to behave more effectively in other situations. As the person begins to enjoy the rewards of behaving more skillfully, a more positive self-perception develops. Frances Haemmerlie and Robert Montgomery (1982, 1984, 1986) demonstrated this in several heartwarming studies with straight college students who were shy or anxious. Those who were inexperienced and nervous around those of the other sex may say to themselves, "I don't date much, so I must be socially inadequate, so I shouldn't try reaching out to anyone." To reverse this negative sequence, Haemmerlie and Montgomery enticed such students into pleasant interactions with people of the other sex.

In one of their experiments, college men completed social anxiety questionnaires and then came to the laboratory on two different days. Each day they enjoyed 12-minute conversations with each of six young women. The men thought the women were also participants. Actually, the women were accomplices who had been asked to carry on a natural, positive, friendly conversation with each of the men.

The effect of these two-and-a-half hours of conversation was remarkable. As one participant wrote afterward, "I had never met so many girls that I could have a good conversation with. After a few girls, my confidence grew to the point where I didn't notice being nervous like I once did." Such comments were supported by a variety of measures. Unlike men in a control condition, those who experienced the conversations reported considerably less anxiety around women when retested 1 week and then 6 months later. Placed alone in a room with an attractive female stranger, they also became much more likely to start a conversation. Outside the laboratory, they began dating occasionally.

These types of interventions are also effective for children and teens. In a meta-analysis of 97 studies, social-skills training programs significantly improved interpersonal and emotional skills among youth. The most effective programs used 11 to 20 skill-building exercises to help young people practice social interaction in a safe setting, often at school (Cordier et al., 2021; de Mooij et al., 2020).

Stresses challenge some people and defeat others — for example, some athletes thrive under pressure while others crumble. Researchers have sought to understand the "explanatory style" that makes some people more vulnerable to depression.
Sean Prior/Alamy Stock Photo

EXPLANATORY STYLE THERAPY

The vicious cycles that maintain depression, loneliness, and shyness can be broken by social-skills training, by positive experiences that alter self-perceptions, *and* by changing negative thought patterns. Some people have good social skills, but their experiences with hypercritical friends and family have convinced them otherwise. For such people, it may be enough to help them reverse their negative beliefs about themselves and their futures. Among the cognitive therapies with this aim is an *explanatory style therapy* proposed by social psychologists (Abramson, 1988; Gillham et al., 2000; Masi et al., 2011).

One such program trained depressed college students to change their typical attributions. Mary Anne Layden (1982) first taught the students the advantages of explaining outcomes optimistically by accepting credit for successes and seeing how circumstances can make things go wrong. She helped the students see how they typically interpreted success and failure. Then came the treatment phase: Layden instructed them to keep a diary of daily successes and failures, noting how the students contributed to their own successes and noting external reasons for their failures. Compared with an untreated control group, the trained students' self-esteem had risen and their attributional style had become more positive. The more their explanatory style improved, the more their depression lifted. By changing their attributions, they had changed their emotions.

Maintaining Change Through Internal Attributions for Success

Two of the principles considered so far – that internal change may follow behavior change and that changed self-perceptions and self-attributions can help break a vicious cycle – converge on a corollary principle: After improvement is achieved, it endures best if people attribute it to factors under their own control rather than to a treatment program. We have seen how interventions can help with depression and social anxiety; what about behavioral changes associated with weight loss?

As a rule, coercive techniques trigger the most dramatic and immediate behavior changes (Brehm & Smith, 1986). By making the unwanted behavior extremely costly or embarrassing and the healthier behavior extremely rewarding, a therapist may achieve impressive results. The problem, as 50 years of social-psychological research reminds us, is that coerced changes in behavior soon fade.

Consider the experience of Marta, who is concerned with her mild obesity and frustrated with her inability to do anything about it. Marta is considering several commercial weight-control programs. Each claims it achieves the best results. She chooses one and is ordered onto a strict 1,200-calorie-a-day diet. Moreover, she is required to record and report her calorie intake each day and to come in once a week to be weighed so she and her instructor can know precisely how she is doing. Confident of the program's value and not wanting to embarrass herself, Marta adheres to the program and is delighted to find the unwanted pounds gradually disappearing. As she reaches her target weight, Marta thinks, "This unique program really does work!"

Sadly, however, after graduating from the program, Marta experiences the fate of most weight-control graduates (Hall & Kahan, 2018; Jeffery et al., 2000): She regains the lost weight. On the street, she sees her instructor approaching. Embarrassed, she moves to the other side of the sidewalk and looks away. Alas, she is recognized by the instructor, who warmly invites her back into "the program." Admitting that the program achieved good results for her the first time, Marta grants her need of it and agrees to return, beginning a second round of yo-yo dieting.

Marta's experience typifies that of the participants in several weight-control experiments, including one by Janet Sonne and Dean Janoff (1979). Half the participants were led, like Marta, to attribute their changed eating behavior to the program. The others were led to credit their own efforts. Both groups lost weight during the program. But when reweighed 11 weeks later, those in the self-credit condition had maintained the weight loss better. These people, like those in the shy-man-meets-women study described earlier, illustrate the benefits of self-efficacy. Having learned to cope successfully and believing that *they did it,* they felt more confident and were more effective. Further research, including 16 studies of 1,663 people, has confirmed that weight loss programs that focus on self-efficacy and self-motivation are more effective (Comşa et al., 2020).

Coercive weight-loss techniques, like those used in reality TV shows, work quickly but do not last. Six years after being on "The Biggest Loser," most participants gained nearly all of the weight back (Fothergill et al., 2016). Weight loss programs tend to work better if people feel more in control of their actions.
Jamie Grill/JGI/Blend Images

Having emphasized what changed behavior and thought patterns can accomplish, we do well to remind ourselves of their limits. Social-skills training and positive thinking cannot transform us into consistent winners who are always loved and admired. Bad things will still happen, and temporary depression, loneliness, and shyness are perfectly appropriate responses to bad events. It is when such feelings exist chronically and without any discernible cause that there is reason for concern and a need to change the self-defeating thoughts and behaviors.

Using Therapy as Social Influence

Psychologists more and more accept the idea that social influence – one person affecting another – is at the heart of therapy. Stanley Strong (1991) offered a prototypical example: A thirtyish woman comes to a therapist saying she feels depressed. The therapist gently probes her feelings and her situation. She explains her helplessness and her husband's demands. Although admiring her devotion, the therapist helps her see how she takes responsibility for her husband's problems. She protests. But the therapist persists. In time, she realizes that her husband may not be as fragile as she presumed. She begins to see how she can respect both her husband and herself. With the therapist, she plans strategies for each new week. At the end of a long stream of reciprocal influences between therapist and client, she emerges no longer depressed and equipped with new ways of behaving.

Analyses of psychotherapeutic influence have focused on how therapists establish credible expertise and trustworthiness, how their credibility enhances their influence, and how the interaction affects the client's thinking (Connolly Gibbons et al., 2023; McNeill & Stoltenberg, 1988; Neimeyer et al., 1991; Strong, 1968). Peripheral cues, such as therapist credibility, may open the door for ideas that the therapist can now get the client to think about. But the thoughtful *central route to persuasion* provides the most enduring attitude and behavior change. Therapists should therefore aim not to elicit a client's superficial agreement with their expert judgment but to help clients change their own thinking.

Fortunately, most clients entering therapy are motivated to take the central route – to think deeply about their problems under the therapist's guidance. The therapist's task is to offer arguments and raise questions that elicit favorable thoughts. The therapist's insights matter less than the thoughts they evoke in the client. Questions such as "How do you respond to what I just said?" can stimulate the client's thinking.

Martin Heesacker (1989) illustrated how a therapist can help a client reflect with the case of Dave, a 35-year-old male graduate student. Having seen what Dave denied – an underlying substance abuse problem – the counselor drew on his knowledge of Dave, an intellectual person who liked hard evidence, in persuading him to accept the diagnosis and join a treatment-support group. The counselor said, "OK, if my diagnosis is wrong, I'll be glad to change it. But let's go through a list of the characteristics of a substance abuser to check out my accuracy." The counselor then went through each criterion slowly, giving Dave time to think about each point. As he finished, Dave sat back and exclaimed, "I don't believe it: I'm a damned alcoholic."

In his 1620 *Pensées,* the philosopher Pascal foresaw this principle: "People are usually more convinced by reasons they discover themselves than by those found by others." It's a principle worth remembering.

SUMMING UP: What Are Some Social-Psychological Approaches to Treatment?

- Changes in external behavior can trigger internal change.
- A self-defeating cycle of negative attitudes and behaviors can be broken by training more skillful behavior, by positive experiences that alter self-perceptions, and by changing negative thought patterns.
- Improved states are best maintained after treatment if people attribute their improvement to internal factors under their continued control rather than to the treatment program itself.
- Mental health workers, aided by their image as expert, trustworthy communicators, recognize that changing clients' attitudes and behaviors requires persuasion that stimulates healthier thinking by offering cogent arguments and raising questions.

HOW DO SOCIAL RELATIONSHIPS SUPPORT HEALTH AND HAPPINESS?

Identify evidence suggesting that supportive, close relationships predict both physical health and mental well-being.

Our relationships are fraught with stress. "Hell is – other people!" wrote Jean-Paul Sartre (1946). When Peter Warr and Roy Payne (1982) asked a representative sample of British adults what, if anything, had emotionally strained them the day before, "family" was their most frequent answer. And stress, as we have seen, aggravates health problems such as coronary heart disease, hypertension, and suppression of our disease-fighting immune system.

Still, on balance, close relationships are more likely to lead to health and happiness than to illness. Asked what prompted yesterday's times of pleasure, the same British sample, by an even larger margin, again answered "family." Close relationships provide our greatest heartaches but also our greatest joys. As social animals, people need people.

Relationships and Physical Health

Extensive investigations, each interviewing thousands of people across years, have reached a common conclusion: Close relationships predict health (Berkman, 1995; MacNeil-Vroomen et al., 2018; Pantell et al., 2013; Ryff & Singer, 2000). In one digest of 148 studies worldwide, older people with ample social connections were 50% more likely to be alive 8 years later than those with meager connections (Holt-Lunstad et al., 2010). People who are socially isolated, live alone, or who are lonely are 30% to 70% more likely to die prematurely (Holt-Lunstad et al., 2015; Smith et al., 2018). "It takes a village to raise a centenarian," noted Susan Pinker (2014). "Longevity is a team sport."

Across 139 countries worldwide, people who "have friends or family you can count on" are also much more likely to report being satisfied with their personal health (Kumar et al., 2012). In experiments, highly-sociable people are less susceptible to cold viruses (Cohen et al., 1997, 2003; **Figure 6**). (If you're wondering how this study was done, people volunteered to get a solution including a cold virus sprayed up their noses, and the researchers then saw who got sick and who didn't over the coming days.)

Married people likewise tend to live healthier, longer lives than their unmarried counterparts (Denney & Boardman, 2021; Zella, 2017). The National Center for Health Statistics reports that people, regardless of age, sex, race, and income, tend to be healthier and live longer if married (Curtin & Tejada-Vera, 2019). Living alone, which is more common among unmarried people, is one of the primary predictors of loneliness (Lasgaard et al., 2016). Married folks experience less pain from headaches and backaches, suffer less stress, and drink and smoke less. One experiment subjected married women to the threat of electric shocks to their lower leg as they lay in an fMRI brain-scanning machine. Some of the women held their husband's hand, some held an anonymous person's hand, and some held no one's hand. While awaiting the shocks, the threat-responsive areas of the women's brains were less active if they held their husband's hand (Coan et al., 2006). Consistent with findings that it's happy and

The need to belong — to have close social relationships — is a fundamental human motivation linked to health (Baumeister & Leary, 1995).
Monkey Business Images/Shutterstock

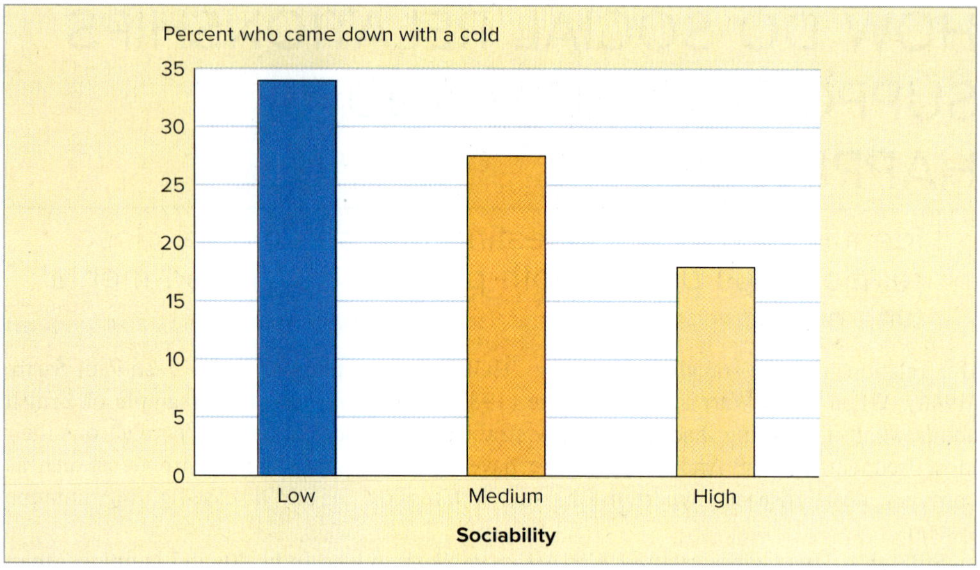

FIGURE 6

Rate of Colds by Sociability

After a cold virus injection, highly sociable people were less vulnerable to catching colds.

Source: Cohen et al., 2003.

supportive marriages that are conducive to health (De Vogli et al., 2007), the soothing hand-holding benefit was greatest for those reporting the happiest marriages.

More than marriage per se, it's marital *quality* that predicts health (Lawrence et al., 2019; Whisman et al., 2018). One study found that at age 50, a good marriage predicted healthy aging better than low cholesterol levels did (Vaillant, 2002). And divorce increases the risk of ill health, as evident in 32 studies of 6.5 million people (Sbarra et al., 2011), partially because divorced people smoked more and exercised less (Bourassa et al., 2019). One review of studies concluded that the association between marriage quality and physical health "is similar in size to associations between health behaviors (diet, physical activity) and health outcomes" (Robles, 2015; Robles et al., 2014). Moreover, over time, marital quality predicts future health (rather than the reverse).

But why? What mediates and explains the effect of marriage quality on health? Theodore Robles and others offer some possibilities:

- *Biological* mediators: Social support calms us and reduces stress (Hostinar et al., 2014). In contrast, our cardiovascular, hormonal, and immune systems respond negatively to marital strain (Uchino et al., 2014).
- *Social-cognitive* mediators: How spouses think about each other influences their emotional control and their anxiety and sadness.
- *Health* mediators: Social support promotes healthier eating and better sleep, whereas marital tension increases unhealthy eating and substance use.

Giving social support also helps. In one 5-year study of 423 elderly married couples, those who gave the most social support (from rides and errands for friends and neighbors to emotional support of their spouse) enjoyed greater longevity, even after controlling for age, sex, initial health, and economic status (Brown et al., 2003). Especially among women, suggested a Finnish study that tracked more than 700 people's illnesses, it is better to give than only to receive (Väänänen et al., 2005).

Moreover, losing social ties heightens the risk of disease:

- A Finnish study of 96,000 newly-widowed people found their risk of death doubled in the week following their partner's death (Kaprio et al., 1987). Some call this "broken heart syndrome." Overall, recently widowed people are more vulnerable to disease and death (Caputo et al., 2021; Dohrenwend et al., 1982).
- The recently widowed are also more likely to develop dementia (Wu-Chung et al., 2022).
- A study of 30,000 men revealed that when a marriage ends, men drink and smoke more and eat fewer vegetables and more fried foods (Eng et al., 2001).

CONFIDING AND HEALTH

Thus, there is a link between social support and health. Why? Perhaps because close relationships give us people to confide in, bolstering our self-esteem and helping us overcome stressful events (Taylor et al., 1997). When we are wounded by someone's dislike or the loss of a job, a friend's advice, help, and reassurance may indeed be good medicine (Cutrona, 1986; Rook, 1987). People who confide a personal secret to someone else are then happier (Slepian & Moulton-Tetlock, 2019). Even when we're not discussing our problems, friends provide us with distraction and a sense that we're accepted, liked, and respected.

With someone we consider a close friend, we also may confide painful feelings. In one study, James Pennebaker and Robin O'Heeron (1984) contacted the surviving spouses of suicide or car accident victims. Those who bore their grief alone had more health problems than those who expressed it openly. When Pennebaker (1990) surveyed more than 700 college women, he found 1 in 12 reported a traumatic sexual experience in childhood. Compared with women who had experienced nonsexual traumas, such as parental death or divorce, the sexually-abused women reported more headaches, stomach ailments, and other health problems, *especially if they had kept their abuse history secret.*

To isolate the confiding, confessional side of close relationships, Pennebaker asked the bereaved spouses to relate the upsetting events that had been preying on their minds. If they were first asked to describe a trivial event, they were physically tense. But once they confided their troubles, they relaxed. Writing about personal traumas in a journal also seems to help. When volunteers in another experiment did so, they had fewer health problems during the next 6 months (Pennebaker, 2016). One participant explained, "Although I have not talked with anyone about what I wrote, I was finally able to deal with it, work through the pain instead of trying to block it out. Now it doesn't hurt to think about it." Even if it's only "talking to my diary" and even if the writing is about one's future dreams and life goals, it helps to be able to confide (Burton & King, 2008; Lyubomirsky et al., 2006). In one experiment, writing therapy was as effective for 633 trauma victims as psychotherapy (van Emmerick et al., 2013). In everyday life, self-disclosures are healing (Kelly & Macready, 2009).

"Friendship is a sovereign antidote against all calamities."

—Seneca, BC 5–AD 65

POVERTY, INEQUALITY, AND HEALTH

We have seen connections between close relationships and health. What about economic status, another aspect of social relations? In Scotland, the United States, Canada, and elsewhere, impoverished people are at greater risk for premature death (Park et al., 2022; Wilkinson & Pickett, 2009). Those in the top 1% of income in the United States can expect to live 14.6 years longer than those in the lowest 1% of income (Chetty et al., 2016). In a 23-year longitudinal study, women living in lower-income neighborhoods were 39% more likely to die of cancer than those in better-off areas (Marcus et al., 2017). Poverty predicts perishing. Wealthy predicts healthy.

The correlation between poverty and ill health could run either way. Bad health isn't good for one's income. But most evidence indicates that the arrow runs from poverty toward ill health (Major et al., 2013; Sapolsky, 2005). So how *does* poverty "get under the skin"? The answers include (a) reduced access to quality health care, (b) unhealthier lifestyles (smoking and opioid abuse are much more common among less-educated and lower-income people), and, to a striking extent, (c) increased stress. To be impoverished is to be at risk for increased stress, negative emotions, and a toxic environment (Adler & Snibbe, 2003; Chen, 2004; Gallo & Matthews, 2003; Nunes et al., 2022). To be poor is to more

Wealthy and healthy. A 2008 *Scotsman* article illustrated the striking disparity in life expectancy in lower-income Calton, on the east end of Glasgow, and in affluent Lenzie, 8 miles away.
Spindrift Photo Agency

FIGURE 7

Income inequality and health

Social and physical health problems are greater in countries with higher income inequality. This health problems index is a composite of lower life expectancy, infant mortality, obesity, teen births, mental illness, imprisonment, and lower levels of literacy, social trust, and social mobility.

Source: Wilkinson & Pickett, 2011.

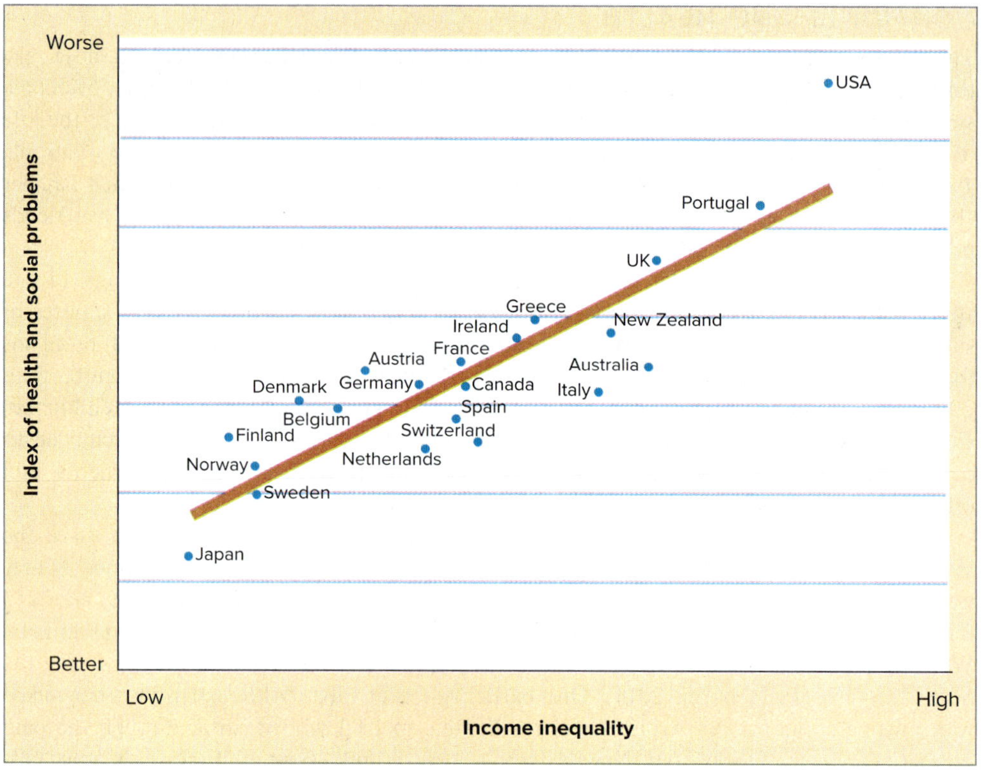

often be sleep-deprived after working a second job, earning paychecks that don't cover the bills, commuting on crowded public transit, living in a high-pollution area, and doing hard labor that's controlled by someone else.

People also die younger in regions with great income inequality (Kawachi et al., 1999; Lynch et al., 1998; see **Figure 7**). People in Britain and the United States, where income inequality is high, have lower life expectancies than people in Japan and Sweden, where income inequality is less pronounced. Within the United States, states and cities with more income inequality have higher rates of death from suicide and heart disease, with each $250 spent on welfare and education linked to a 1.6 percentage point reduction in deaths from heart disease (Kim, 2016). In countries where inequality has grown over the last decade, as in Eastern Europe and Russia, life expectancy has been falling. As income inequality continued to rise in the United States, deaths during midlife increased among White Americans; at the same time, they declined in countries with less income discrepancy, such as Sweden and Canada. Many of these excess deaths were due to suicide and drug overdoses (Case & Deaton, 2015). During the COVID-19 pandemic, countries with more income inequality had more deaths from the virus (Elgar et al., 2020).

Is inequality merely an indicator of greater poverty? The mixed evidence indicates that poverty matters but that inequality matters, too. John Lynch and his colleagues (1998, 2000) reported that people at every income level are at greater risk of early death if they live in a community with great income inequality. It's not just being poor, it's also *feeling* poor relative to one's surroundings, that proves toxic. And that, Robert Sapolsky (2005) suggested, helps explain why the United States, which has the greatest income inequality of Westernized nations, has simultaneously ranked number 1 in the world on health care expenditures, yet number 29 on life expectancy.

Relationships and Happiness

So far, we've seen how close relationships and social status are linked to physical health. What about connections to mental health and happiness?

FRIENDSHIPS AND HAPPINESS

Being attached to friends with whom we can share intimate thoughts has two effects, observed the seventeenth-century philosopher Francis Bacon (1612): "It redoubleth joys, and cutteth griefs in half." In other words, close relationships are good not just for the body but for the soul.

In one study, college students wore an audio recorder for a week so researchers could gain an understanding of their social interactions. Those who talked with other people more often and disclosed more about themselves were happier, both on the day of the interactions and in general (Sun et al., 2020). In another study, people were happiest when they were with their friends (Hudson et al., 2020). Generally, real-time interactions are superior to social media exchanges. The happiest teens are those who spend more time than average with their friends face-to-face, and less time than average on social media (Twenge et al., 2018). In a longitudinal study of Facebook users, adults who interacted with their friends face-to-face later reported feeling happier, but those who spent more time on Facebook felt less happy (Shakya & Christakis, 2017). Real-life friends bring many benefits; Facebook friends may not.

MARITAL ATTACHMENT AND HAPPINESS

For the nearly 9 in 10 people who are married or eventually will marry, a primary example of a close relationship is marriage. Does marriage correlate positively with happiness? Or is there more happiness in the pleasure-seeking single life than in the "bondage," "chains," and "yoke" of marriage?

A mountain of data reveals that most people are happier attached than unattached (Wilcox, 2024). Survey after survey of many tens of thousands of Europeans and Americans have produced a consistent result: Compared with those single or widowed, and especially compared with those divorced or separated, married people report being happier and more satisfied with life, as well as less lonely (Gove et al., 1990; Inglehart, 1990; von Soest et al., 2020). In the U.S. General Social Survey between 2010 and 2018, for example, 22% of never-married adults, but 40% of married adults, reported being "very happy" (Wolfinger, 2019). Lesbian couples, too, report greater well-being than those who are unpartnered (Peplau & Fingerhut, 2007). There are multiple ways to satisfy the human need to belong (DePaulo, 2006). Nevertheless, there are few stronger predictors of happiness than a close, nurturing, equitable, intimate, lifelong companionship with a romantic partner.

Similar to the findings for physical health, the marriage's quality is more important for happiness than simply being married. People who say their marriages are satisfying – who find themselves still in love with their partners – rarely report being unhappy, discontented with life, or depressed (Robles, 2015). Fortunately, most married people *do* declare their marriages happy ones. In the General Social Survey, almost two-thirds say their marriages are "very happy." Three out of 4 say their spouses are their best friends. Four out of 5 people say they would marry the same people again. As a consequence, most such people feel quite happy with life as a whole (Lawrence et al., 2019).

"The sun looks down on nothing half so good as a household laughing together over a meal."

—C. S. Lewis, "Membership," 1949

Why are married people generally happier (as well as healthier)? Does marriage promote happiness, or does happiness promote marriage? Are happy people more appealing as marriage partners? Do depressed people more often stay single or suffer divorce (**Figure 8**)? Certainly, happy people are more fun to be with. They are also more outgoing, trusting, compassionate, and focused on others (Myers, 1993). Unhappy people, as we have noted, are more often socially rejected. Depression often triggers marital stress, which deepens the depression (Davila et al., 1997). So, positive, happy people do more readily form happy relationships.

But "the prevailing opinion of researchers," reported University of Oslo sociologist Arne Mastekaasa (1995), is that the marriage-happiness connection is "mainly due" to the beneficial effects of marriage. A study following 1,380 New Jersey adults over 15 years found that the tendency for married people to be less depressed occurred even after controlling for premarital happiness (Horwitz et al., 1997).

Marriage enhances happiness for at least two reasons. First, married people are more likely to enjoy an enduring, supportive, intimate relationship and are less likely to suffer loneliness. Second, marriage can offer the roles of spouse and parent, which can provide

FIGURE 8

Marital Status and Depression in the Last Year

An analysis of nearly 1 million Canadians found depression rates were significantly lower among married adults than unmarried adults.

Source: Bulloch et al., 2017

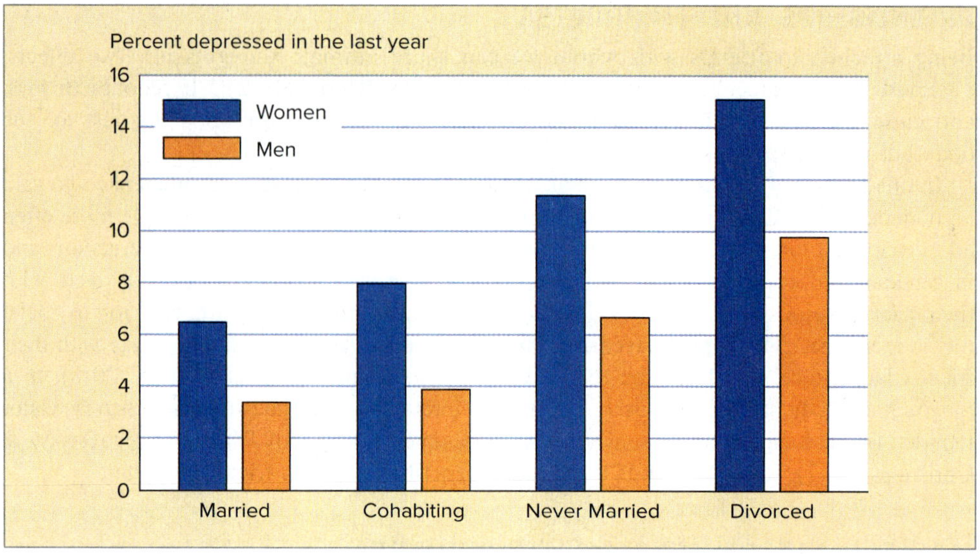

additional sources of self-esteem and social identity (Crosby, 1987; Cruwys et al., 2014). It is true that multiple roles can multiply stress. Our circuits can and do overload. Yet each role also provides rewards, status, avenues to enrichment, and escape from stress faced in other parts of one's life. A self with many identities is like a mansion with many rooms. When fire struck one wing of Windsor Castle, most of the castle still remained for royals and tourists to enjoy. When our personal identity stands on several legs, it, too, holds up under the loss of any one. If we [DM and JT] mess up at work, well, we can tell ourselves that we're still good spouses and parents, and, in the final analysis, these parts of our identities are what matter most.

SUMMING UP: How Do Social Relationships Support Health and Happiness?

- People who enjoy close, supportive relationships are at less risk for illness and premature death. Such relationships help people cope with stress, especially by enabling people to confide their intimate emotions. Social status is also linked to physical health.
- Close relationships also foster happiness. People who have intimate, long-term attachments with friends and family members cope better with loss and report greater happiness. Compared with unmarried adults, those who are married, for example, are much more likely to report being very happy and are at less risk for depression. This appears due both to the greater social success of happy people and to the well-being engendered by a supportive life companion.

CONCLUDING THOUGHTS: Enhancing Happiness

Thirty+ years ago I [DM] wrote a book, *The Pursuit of Happiness,* that reported key findings from new research studies of happiness. When the editors wanted to subtitle the book *What Makes People Happy?* I cautioned them: That's not a question this or any book can answer. What we have learned is simply what correlates with – and therefore predicts – happiness. Thus, the book's eventual subtitle was *Who Is Happy – and Why?*

Nevertheless, in 400+ subsequent media interviews concerning happiness, the most frequent question has been "What can people do to be happy?" Without claiming any easy formula for health and happiness, I assembled 10 research-based points to ponder:

1. *Realize that enduring happiness doesn't come from "making it."* People adapt to changing circumstances – even to wealth or a disability. Thus, wealth is like health: Its utter absence breeds misery, but having it (or any circumstance we long for) doesn't guarantee happiness.
2. *Take control of your time.* Happy people feel in control of their lives, often aided by mastering their use of time. It helps to set goals and divide them into daily aims. Although we often overestimate how much we will accomplish in any given day (leaving us frustrated), we generally underestimate how much we can accomplish in a year, given just a little progress every day.
3. *Act happy.* We can sometimes act ourselves into a frame of mind. Manipulated into a smiling expression, people feel better; when they scowl, the whole world seems to scowl back. So put on a happy face. Talk as if you feel positive self-esteem, are optimistic, and are outgoing. Going through the motions can trigger the emotions.
4. *Seek work and leisure that engage your skills.* Happy people often are in a zone called *flow* – absorbed in a task that challenges them without overwhelming them. The most expensive forms of leisure (sitting on a yacht) often provide less flow experience than gardening, socializing, or craft work.
5. *Join the "movement" movement.* An avalanche of research reveals that aerobic exercise not only promotes health and energy but also is an antidote for mild depression and anxiety. Sound minds reside in sound bodies.
6. *Give your body the sleep it wants.* Happy people live active, vigorous lives yet reserve time for renewing sleep and solitude. Many people suffer from a sleep debt, with resulting fatigue, diminished alertness, and gloomy moods.
7. *Give priority to close relationships.* Intimate friendships with those who care deeply about you can help you weather difficult times. Confiding is good for soul and body. Resolve to nurture your closest relationships: to *not* take those closest to you for granted, to display to them the sort of kindness that you display to others, to affirm them, to share, and to play together. To rejuvenate your affections, resolve in such ways to *act* lovingly.
8. *Focus beyond the self.* Reach out to those in need. Happiness increases helpfulness. (Those who feel good do good.) But doing good also makes one feel good.
9. *Keep a gratitude journal.* Those who pause each day to reflect on some positive aspect of their lives (their health, friends, family, freedom, education, senses, natural surroundings, and so on) experience heightened well-being.
10. *Nurture your spiritual self.* For many people, faith provides a support community, a reason to focus beyond self, and a sense of purpose and hope. Study after study finds that actively religious people are happier and that they cope better with crises.

Social Psychology in Court

CHAPTER

15

Scott Olson/Getty Images

How reliable is eyewitness testimony?

What other factors influence juror judgments?

What influences the individual juror?

How do group influences affect juries?

Concluding Thoughts: Thinking smart with psychological science

"A courtroom is a battleground where lawyers compete for the minds of jurors."

—James Randi, *Commentary: Science in the Courts*, 1999

On a hot August day in Ferguson, Missouri, police officer Darren Wilson shot and killed 18-year-old Michael Brown. Peaceful protests over Brown's death soon became heated, and Ferguson erupted into violence and rioting. At the center of the unrest was a question: Was Wilson justified in shooting Brown?

A grand jury convened in Ferguson in December 2014 did not indict Wilson, so he did not stand trial. The case featured several issues addressed in social psychology studies:

- Eyewitnesses provided varying accounts of Brown's behavior before he was shot. How influential is eyewitness testimony? How trustworthy are eyewitness recollections? What makes a credible witness?

- Darren Wilson is White and Michael Brown was Black. What impact do victims' and defendants' race, attractiveness, and social status have on jury judgments?
- The grand jury included three Blacks and nine Whites, and seven men and five women. Do jurors' characteristics bias their verdicts? If so, can lawyers use the jury selection process to stack a jury in their favor?
- During deliberations, how do jurors influence one another? Can a minority win over the majority? Do 12-member juries reach the same decisions as 6-member juries?

Such questions fascinate lawyers, judges, and defendants. They are questions to which social psychology can suggest answers, as law schools recognize by hiring professors of "law and social science" and as trial lawyers recognize when hiring psychological consultants.

We can think of a courtroom as a miniature social world, one that magnifies everyday social processes with major consequences for those involved. In criminal cases, psychological factors may influence decisions involving arrest, interrogation, prosecution, plea bargaining, sentencing, and parole. Whether or not a case reaches a jury verdict, the social dynamics of the courtroom matter.

HOW RELIABLE IS EYEWITNESS TESTIMONY?

Explain the accuracy of eyewitness testimony and ways to increase eyewitness accuracy and educate jurors.

As the courtroom drama unfolds, jurors hear testimony, form impressions of the defendant, listen to instructions from the judge, and render a verdict. Let's take these steps one at a time, starting with eyewitness testimony.

Although never previously in trouble with the law, Kirk Bloodsworth was convicted for the sexual assault and slaying of a 9-year-old girl after five eyewitnesses identified him at his trial. During his 2 years on death row and 7 more under a sentence of life imprisonment, he maintained his innocence. Then DNA testing proved it was not his semen on the girl's underwear. Released from prison, he still lived under a cloud of doubt until 2003, 19 years after his conviction, when DNA testing identified the actual killer (Wells et al., 2006).

In the vast majority of cases of people exonerated by DNA evidence, mistaken eyewitness identification was the reason for their conviction. The average wrongly convicted person served 17 years in prison; the average was 27 when convicted and 44 when exonerated (Innocence Project, 2023). Thus, as Gary Wells and Laura Smalarz put it, lives are "destroyed by distorted recollections" (2022). What can go wrong in eyewitness testimony to cause these tragedies?

The Power of Persuasive Eyewitnesses

Vivid anecdotes and personal testimonies can be powerfully persuasive and often more compelling than abstract information. There's no better way to end an argument than to say, "I saw it with my own eyes!"

Memory researcher Elizabeth Loftus (1974, 1979a, 2011b) found that those who had "seen" were indeed believed, even when their testimony was shown to be useless. When students were presented with a hypothetical robbery-murder case with circumstantial evidence but no eyewitness testimony, only 18% voted for conviction. Other students received the same information but with the addition of a single eyewitness. Now, knowing that

Joseph Mirachi

"As it turned out, my battery of lawyers was no match for their battery of eyewitnesses."

someone had declared, "That's the one!" 72% voted for conviction. For a third group, the defense attorney discredited the eyewitness testimony (the witness had bad vision and was not wearing glasses). Did that discrediting reduce the effect of the testimony? In this case, not much: 68% still voted for conviction.

Later experiments revealed that discrediting may reduce somewhat the number of guilty votes (Whitley, 1987). But unless contradicted by another eyewitness, a vivid eyewitness account is difficult to erase from jurors' minds (Leippe, 1985). That helps explain why, compared with criminal cases lacking eyewitness testimony, those that have eyewitness testimony are more likely to produce convictions (Visher, 1987).

But can't jurors spot erroneous testimony? To find out, researchers staged hundreds of eye-witnessed thefts of a calculator. Afterward, they asked each eyewitness to identify the culprit from a photo lineup. Other people, acting as jurors, observed the eyewitnesses being questioned and then evaluated their testimony. Are incorrect eyewitnesses believed less often than those who are accurate? As it happened, both correct and incorrect eyewitnesses were believed 80% of the time (Wells et al., 1979). That led the researchers to speculate that "human observers have absolutely no ability to discern eyewitnesses who have mistakenly identified an innocent person" (Wells et al., 1980).

In a follow-up experiment, the staged theft sometimes allowed witnesses a good long look at the thief and sometimes didn't. The jurors believed the witnesses more when conditions were good. But even when conditions were so poor that two-thirds of the witnesses had actually misidentified an innocent person, 62% of the jurors still usually believed the witnesses (Lindsay et al., 1981).

Later studies found that jurors were more skeptical of eyewitnesses whose memory of trivial details was poor—though these tended to be the most *accurate* witnesses (Wells & Leippe, 1981). Jurors think a witness who can remember that there were three pictures hanging in the room must have "really been paying attention" (Bell & Loftus, 1988, 1989). Actually, those who pay attention to surrounding details are *less* likely to attend to the culprit's face.

The persuasive power of three eyewitnesses sent Chicagoan James Newsome, who had never been arrested before, to prison on a life sentence for supposedly gunning down a convenience store owner. Fifteen years later, he was released after fingerprint analysis revealed the real culprit to be Dennis Emerson, a career criminal who was 3 inches taller and had longer hair (*Chicago Tribune,* 2002).

When Eyes Deceive

Is eyewitness testimony often inaccurate? Stories abound of innocent people who have wasted away for years in prison because of the testimony of eyewitnesses who were sincere but wrong (Doyle, 2005; Wells et al., 2006). Among 375 convictions overturned by DNA evidence in the United States, 69% were wrongful convictions influenced by mistaken eyewitnesses. Of these, 42% involved a cross-racial misidentification: a person of one race misidentifying a suspect of another race.

Richard Anthony Jones (right), spent 17 years in prison for aggravated robbery due to mistaken eyewitness testimony, even though he was at a birthday party at the time of the crime. Jones bore a strong resemblance to Ricky Amos (left), who investigators believe actually committed the crime.
Kansas Department of Corrections

To assess the accuracy of eyewitness recollections, we need to learn their overall rates of "hits" and "misses." One way for researchers to gather such information is to stage crimes comparable to those in everyday life and then solicit eyewitness reports.

During the past century, this has been done many times, sometimes with disconcerting results (Sporer, 2008). For example, 141 students witnessed an "assault" on a professor at California State University, Hayward. Seven weeks later, when Robert Buckhout (1974) asked them to identify the assailant from a group of six photographs, 60% chose an innocent person. No wonder eyewitnesses to actual crimes sometimes disagree about what they saw. Later studies have confirmed that eyewitnesses often are more confident than correct. In one study, students felt, on average, 74% sure of their later recollections of a classroom visitor but were only 55% correct (Bornstein & Zickafoose, 1999).

"Certitude is not the test of certainty."

—Oliver Wendell Holmes, *Collected Legal Papers*, 1920

Three studies conducted in England and Wales showed remarkable consistency. Roughly 40% of witnesses identified the suspect in a lineup of possible suspects, and another 40% said they did not see the suspect in the lineup. Despite having been cautioned that the person they witnessed might not be in the lineup, 20% chose an innocent person (Valentine et al., 2003). Young adult (versus older) eyewitnesses and those who had viewed the culprit for more than 1 minute at a distance of less than 5 meters (about 16 feet) were also more accurate than older eyewitnesses and those who viewed the person more briefly and from farther away (Horry et al., 2014). Child witnesses – who may be eager to please adults – are more likely to choose an innocent person in a lineup, especially if the culprit is not in the lineup (Fitzgerald & Price, 2015).

Jurors find confident witnesses the most believable (Cash & Lane, 2020; Wells et al., 2002, 2006). Unless their credibility is punctured by an obvious error, confident witnesses seem more credible (Jules & McQuiston, 2013; Tenney et al., 2007). And more confident witnesses *are* more accurate when police follow certain procedures for the initial identification, such as including only one suspect per lineup and cautioning that the offender might not be in the lineup (Wixted & Wells, 2017). Under these conditions, the witness who is confident in their first judgment *is* more accurate, especially when the witness makes their decision quickly (Quigley-McBride & Wells, 2023; Smalarz et al., 2021; Wixted et al., 2015).

When these conditions are not met, however, an unconfident identification can become a confident – and often inaccurate – one by the time of the trial as it is reinforced over and over. For example, being told "Good, you picked the suspect" increases witnesses' confidence – even if they actually picked the wrong person. By the trial, witnesses could be fully confident in their incorrect judgment (Smalarz & Wells, 2015; Steblay et al., 2014). To guard against the officer influencing the witness's identification or memory, the U.S. Department of Justice now recommends that witness confidence during the initial identification should be documented and that the officer who shows the lineup to the witness should not know who the suspect is (Johnson, 2017). In 57% of DNA exoneration cases that included eyewitness testimony, the eyewitnesses were initially uncertain (Garrett, 2011).

Why can eyewitness identifications be inaccurate? Errors sneak into our perceptions and our memories because our minds are not video recorders. Many errors are understandable, as revealed by *change blindness* experiments in which people fail to detect that an innocent person entering a scene differs from another person exiting the scene (Davis et al., 2008). People are quite good at recognizing a pictured face when later shown the same picture alongside a new face. But researcher Vicki Bruce (1998) was surprised to discover that subtle differences in views, expressions, or lighting "are hard for human vision to deal with." We construct our memories based partly on what we perceived at the time and partly on our expectations, beliefs, and current knowledge (**Figure 1**).

The strong emotions that accompany witnessed crimes and traumas may further corrupt eyewitness memories. In one experiment, visitors wore heart rate monitors while in the London Dungeon's Horror Labyrinth. Those whose heart rates increased the most later made the most mistakes in identifying someone they had encountered (Valentine & Mesout, 2009).

FIGURE 1

Expectations Affect Perception

People will see what they expect in this image — either an old or a young woman.

Photo Researchers/Science History Images/Alamy Stock Photo

One study documented the effect of stress on memory with more than 500 soldiers at survival schools: mock prisoner of war camps training the soldiers to withstand deprivation of food and sleep and intense, confrontational interrogation, which resulted in a high heart rate and a flood of stress hormones. A day after release from the camp, when the participants were asked to identify their intimidating interrogators from a 15-person lineup, only 30% could do so, although 62%

could recall a low-stress interrogator. Thus, concluded the researchers, "contrary to the popular conception that most people would never forget the face of a clearly seen individual who had physically confronted them and threatened them for more than 30 minutes, [many] were unable to correctly identify their perpetrator" (Morgan et al., 2004). We are most at risk for false recollections made with high confidence with faces of another race (Brigham et al., 2006; Meissner et al., 2005).

Research also indicates that harsh "enhanced" interrogation techniques, sometimes using torture, are ineffective (Vrij et al., 2017). With uncooperative terrorist suspects, brutal interrogation increases resistance, impedes accurate information retrieval, and makes lie detection more difficult.

The Misinformation Effect

Can false memories be created? In a pioneering study on that question, Elizabeth Loftus and associates (1978) showed University of Washington students 30 slides depicting successive stages of an automobile-pedestrian accident. One critical slide showed a red Datsun stopped at a stop sign or a yield sign. Afterward they asked half the students, among other questions, "Did another car pass the red Datsun while it was stopped at the stop sign?" They asked the other half the same question, but with the words "stop sign" replaced by "yield sign." Later, all viewed both slides in **Figure 2** and recalled which one they had seen previously. Those who had been asked the question consistent with what they had seen were 75% correct. Those previously asked the misleading question were only 41% correct; more often than not, they denied seeing what they had actually seen and instead "remembered" the picture they had never seen!

misinformation effect
Incorporating "misinformation" into one's memory of the event after witnessing an event and receiving misleading information about it.

Other studies of this **misinformation effect** found that after suggestive questions, witnesses may believe that a red light was actually green or that a robber had a mustache when he didn't (Loftus, 1979a,b, 2001; Loftus & Klemfuss, 2023). When questioning eyewitnesses, police and attorneys commonly ask questions framed by their own understanding of what happened. So it is troubling to discover how easily witnesses incorporate misleading information into their memories, especially when they believe the questioner is well informed, when shown fabricated evidence, when suggestive questions are repeated, or when they have discussed events with other witnesses (Frenda et al., 2011; Wade et al., 2010; Wright et al., 2009; Zaragoza & Mitchell, 1996). This effect can be reduced by explicitly telling people that a piece of information was incorrect ("there was no stop sign" or "some of what you heard might not be correct") or implying it might be ("the police cadet was inexperienced at detailing observed crimes") (Blank & Launay, 2014; Bulevich et al., 2022; Echterhoff et al., 2005; Greene et al., 1982).

FIGURE 2

The Misinformation Effect

When shown one of these two pictures and then asked a question suggesting the sign from the other photo, most people later "remembered" seeing the sign they had never actually seen.

Source: Loftus et al., 1978. (photos): Courtesy of Elizabeth Loftus

It also is troubling to realize that false memories feel and look like real memories. They can be as persuasive as real memories — convincingly sincere, yet sincerely wrong. This is true of young children (who are especially susceptible to misinformation) as well as adults. In one study, children were told once a week for 10 weeks, "Think real hard, and tell me if this ever happened to you: Can you remember going to the hospital with the mousetrap on your finger?" Remarkably, when later interviewed by a new adult who asked the same question, 58% of preschoolers produced false and often detailed stories about the fictitious event (Ceci & Bruck, 1993a,b, 1995). One boy explained that his brother had pushed him into a basement woodpile, where his finger got stuck in the trap. "And then we went to the hospital, and my mommy, daddy, and Colin drove me there, to the hospital in our van because it was far away. And the doctor put a bandage on this finger."

Given such vivid stories, professional psychologists were often fooled. They could not reliably separate real from false memories — nor could the children. Told the incident never actually happened, some protested, "But it really did happen. I remember it!" Such findings raise the possibility of false accusations, as in alleged child sex abuse cases in which children's memories may have been contaminated by repeated suggestive questioning and in which there is no corroborating evidence. Given suggestive interview questions, most preschoolers and many older children will produce false reports, such as seeing a thief steal food in their day-care center (Bruck & Ceci, 1999, 2004).

In other studies, university students were asked to imagine childhood events, such as breaking a window or having a nurse remove a skin sample. This led one-fourth to recall that the imagined event actually happened (Garry et al., 1996; Mazzoni & Memom, 2003). This *imagination inflation* happens partly because visualizing something activates similar areas in the brain as does actually experiencing it (Gonsalves et al., 2004). Imagining inputs incorrect information.

Fortunately, researchers have found some ways to tell — or at least predict — whether someone is recalling a true or false memory. People who were recalling false memories were more likely to use filler words such as "um" and "you know" and were more likely to pause as they were talking (Gustafsson et al., 2019; Lindholm et al., 2018).

Misinformation-induced false memories provide one explanation for a peculiar phenomenon: *false confessions* (Gudjonsson, 2021; Kassin et al., 2010, 2018; Lassiter, 2010; Loftus, 2011a). Among convictions overturned by DNA evidence in the United States, 27% involved false confessions: confessions people made to a crime even though DNA later proved them innocent (Innocence Project, 2023). Many of these were *compliant confessions:* confessions made by people who were worn down and often sleep deprived ("If you will just tell us you accidentally rather than deliberately set the fire, you can go home"). Many people who falsely confess have a naive faith that their innocence will be obvious, are easily influenced or otherwise vulnerable, or may just want to get the interview over with (Otgaar et al., 2021; Scherr et al., 2020). Other confessions are *internalized confessions:* false memories believed after people were fed misinformation (Kassin & Kiechel, 1996). A teen whose parents were murdered was told that his father accused him of the crime before he died (which wasn't true; the father died before he could talk to the police). Shocked, the teen confessed and spent 19 years in prison before the real murderers were found (Starr, 2019).

After 43 hours of questioning by Italian police, the last 8 hours conducted overnight without food, water, or sleep, American exchange student Amanda Knox confessed to killing her roommate Meredith Kercher. She later recanted, and no physical evidence tied her to the crime. After 4 years in jail in Italy, she was acquitted in 2011 and returned home to the United States.
Federico Zirilli/AFP/Getty Images

Confessions, even when coerced, can set off a chain reaction. Police make more errors with evidence and eyewitness identifications when a suspect has confessed (Kassin, 2014; Kassin et al., 2012). Sixty percent of judges and 50% of juries will convict a suspect who confessed, even if the confession was coerced and other evidence is weak (Stevenson et al., 2023;

Wallace & Kassin, 2012). Even with DNA evidence suggesting a suspect's innocence, mock jurors will often still vote to convict a suspect who has confessed (Appleby & Kassin, 2016). It is difficult for people to believe that people would confess to a crime they didn't commit (Alceste et al., 2021; Kassin, 2017).

It's tempting to believe that false confessions happen to other people and that we ourselves would never do such a thing. Research suggests otherwise. In one experiment, researchers told students they had committed a crime as a young teen, such as assault or theft (in reality, none had ever had any police contact). After three interviews using memory-enhancing techniques such as visualization, an incredible 70% believed that they had actually committed a crime (Shaw & Porter, 2015), and 30% had false memories of the crime (Wade et al., 2018). Follow-up studies showed that observers watching videos of these false confessions were able to identify the confessions as false only about half the time (Shaw, 2020).

Retelling

Retelling events commits people to their recollections, accurate or not. An accurate retelling helps them later resist misleading suggestions (Bregman & McAllister, 1982). Other times, the more we retell a story, the more we convince ourselves of a falsehood. Another study had eyewitnesses to a staged theft rehearse their answers to questions before taking the witness stand. Doing so increased the confidence of those who were wrong and thus made jurors who heard their false testimony more likely to convict the innocent person (Wells et al., 1981).

We often adjust what we say to please our listeners. Moreover, having done so, we come to believe the altered message. Imagine witnessing an argument that erupts into a fight in which one person injures the other. Afterward, the injured party sues. Before the trial, a smooth lawyer for one of the two parties interviews you. Might you slightly adjust your testimony, giving a version of the fight that supports this lawyer's client? If you did so, might your later recollections in court be similarly slanted?

Blair Sheppard and Neil Vidmar (1980) reported that the answer to both questions is yes. At the University of Western Ontario, they had some students serve as witnesses to a fight and others as lawyers and judges. When interviewed by lawyers for the defendant, the witnesses later gave the judge testimony that was more favorable to the defendant. In a follow-up experiment, witnesses did not omit important facts from their testimony; they just changed their tone of voice and choice of words depending on whether they thought they were witnesses for the defendant or for the plaintiff (Vidmar & Laird, 1983). However, even this was enough to bias the impressions of those who heard the testimony. So it's not only suggestive questions that can distort eyewitness recollections but also their own retellings, which may be adjusted subtly to suit their audience. How police officers and others respond to witness statements can also have an impact (see "Research Close-up: Feedback to Witnesses").

"Witnesses probably ought to be taking a more realistic oath: 'Do you swear to tell the truth, the whole truth, or whatever it is you think you remember?'"

—Elizabeth F. Loftus, "Memory In Canadian Courts of Law," 2003

research CLOSE-UP
Feedback to Witnesses

Eyewitness to a crime on viewing a lineup: "Oh, my God . . . I don't know . . . It's one of those two . . . but I don't know . . . Oh, man . . . the guy a little bit taller than number two . . . It's one of those two, but I don't know. . . ."

Months later at trial: "You were positive it was number two? It wasn't a maybe?"

Eyewitness's answer: "There was no maybe about it . . . was absolutely positive."

(*Missouri v. Hutching,* 1994, reported by Wells & Bradfield, 1998)

What explains witnesses misrecalling their original uncertainty? Gary Wells and Amy Bradfield (1998, 1999) wondered. Research had shown that one's confidence gains a boost from (a) learning that another witness has fingered the same person, (b) being asked the same question repeatedly, and (c) preparing for cross-examination (Lüüs & Wells, 1994; Shaw, 1996; Wells et al., 1981). Might the lineup interviewer's feedback also influence not just confidence but also recollections of earlier confidence ("I knew it all along")?

To find out, Wells and Bradfield conducted two experiments in which 352 Iowa State University students viewed a grainy security camera video of a man entering a store. Moments later, off camera, he murders a security guard. The students then viewed the photo spread from the actual criminal case, minus the gunman's photo, and were asked to identify the gunman. All 352 students made a false identification, following which the experimenter gave confirming feedback ("Good. You identified the actual suspect"), disconfirming feedback ("Actually, the suspect was number _____"), or no feedback. Finally, all were later asked, "At the time that you identified the person in the photo spread, how certain were you that the person you identified from the photos was the gunman that you saw in the video?" (from 1, not at all certain, to 7, totally certain).

The experiment produced two striking results: First, the effect of the experimenter's casual comment was huge. In the confirming feedback condition, 58% of the eyewitnesses rated their certainty as 6 or 7 when making their initial judgments. This was 4 times the 14% who said the same in the no-feedback condition and 11 times the 5% in the disconfirming condition. What's striking is that those were their confident recollections *before* they received any feedback.

It wasn't obvious to the participants that their judgments were affected because the second rather amazing finding is that when asked if the feedback had influenced their answers, 58% said no. Moreover, as a group, those who felt uninfluenced were influenced just as much as those who said they were (**Figure 3**).

This phenomenon — increased witness confidence after supportive feedback — is both big and reliable enough, across 21 studies of 7,000 participants, to have gained a name: the *post-identification feedback effect* (Douglass & Steblay, 2006; Smalarz & Wells, 2014; Steblay et al., 2014). It is understandable that eyewitnesses would be curious about the accuracy of their recollections and that interrogators would want to satisfy the eyewitnesses' curiosity ("you did identify the actual suspect"). But the possible later effect of inflated eyewitness confidence points to the need to keep interrogators blind (ignorant) of which person is the suspect. Alternatively, witness certainty can be assessed before any feedback is given (Steblay et al., 2014).

The inability of eyewitnesses to appreciate the post-identification feedback effect points to a lesson that runs deeper than jury research. Again, we see why we need social psychological research. As social psychologists have so often found — recall Milgram's obedience experiments — simply asking people how they would act or asking what explains their actions sometimes gives us wrong answers. Benjamin Franklin was right: "There are Three things extremely [sic] hard, Steel, a Diamond, and to know one's self" (1750). That is why we need not only surveys that ask people to explain themselves but also experiments in which we see what they actually do.

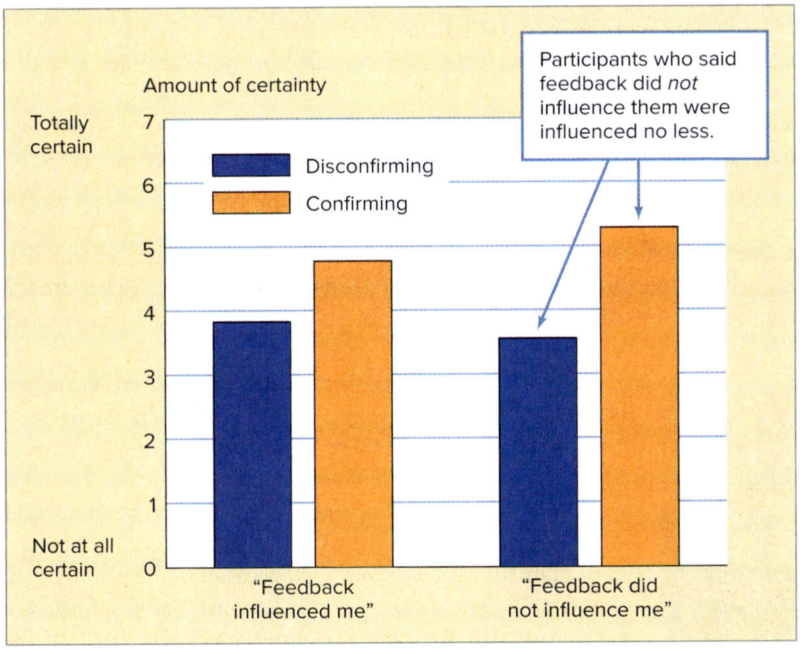

FIGURE 3

Recalled Certainty of Eyewitnesses' False Identification after Receiving Confirming or Disconfirming Feedback (Experiment 2)

Source: Data from Wells & Bradfield, 1998.

Reducing Error

One survey of British law enforcement professionals found that even experienced police officers harbor misconceptions about interrogation and eyewitness memory (Chaplin & Shaw, 2016). Given these error-prone tendencies, what constructive steps can be taken to increase the accuracy of eyewitnesses and jurors? The U.S. Department of Justice convened a panel of researchers, attorneys, and law enforcement officers to hammer out *Eyewitness Evidence: A Guide for Law Enforcement* (Technical Working Group for Eyewitness Evidence, 1999; Wells et al., 2000). Their suggestions parallel many of those from a Canadian review of eyewitness identification procedures (Yarmey, 2003a) and were updated in 2017 (U.S. Department of Justice, 2017) with an additional consensus statement from researchers issued in 2020 (Wells et al., 2020). They include the best and fairest ways to (a) train police interviewers and (b) administer lineups or photo arrays of suspects. This "forensic science of mind" seeks to preserve rather than contaminate the eyewitness memory aspect of the crime scene. Research evidence has successfully altered how police officers interview witnesses and conduct lineups of possible suspects (Wells, 2020).

TRAINING POLICE INTERVIEWERS

When Ronald Fisher and colleagues (1987, 1989, 2011) examined tape-recorded interviews of eyewitnesses conducted by experienced Florida police detectives, they found a typical pattern. Following an open-ended beginning ("Tell me what you recall"), the detectives would occasionally interrupt with follow-up questions, including questions eliciting terse answers ("How tall was he?").

The *Eyewitness Evidence* guide instructs interviewers to begin by allowing eyewitnesses to offer their own unprompted recollections. The recollections will be most complete if the interviewer jogs the memory by first guiding people to reconstruct the setting by having them visualize the scene and what they were thinking and feeling at the time. Even showing pictures of the setting – of, say, the store checkout lane with a clerk standing where she was robbed – can promote accurate recall (Cutler & Penrod, 1988). After giving witnesses ample, uninterrupted time to report everything that comes to mind, the interviewer then jogs their memory with evocative questions ("Was there anything unusual about the voice? Was there anything unusual about the person's appearance or clothing?"). Such open-ended questions are better than those asking witnesses to focus on particular characteristics (such as hair color), which can lead them to forget other details (Camp et al., 2012). It is most effective when questions are clustered together by topic, such as people, objects, and location (Paulo et al., 2021).

When detectives were trained to question in this way, the eyewitnesses' information increased 25 to 50% without increasing the false memory rate (Fisher et al., 1989, 1994, 2011). A later meta-analysis of 46 published studies confirmed that this type of "cognitive interview" substantially increases details recalled, with no loss in accuracy (Memon et al., 2011). In response to such results, most police agencies in North America and Britain have adopted the cognitive interview procedure (Dando et al., 2009). (The procedure also shows promise for enhancing information gathered in oral histories and medical surveys.)

Eyewitness recollections are the most accurate when witnesses are asked open-ended questions that allow them to recall details.
Aaron Roeth Photography

Accurate identifications of suspects tend to be automatic and effortless (Sauer et al., 2010). The right face just pops out. Eyewitnesses who made their identifications in fewer than 10 to 12 seconds were nearly 90% accurate; those taking longer were only about 50% accurate (Dunning & Perretta, 2002). Although other studies challenge a neat 10- to 12-second rule, they confirm that quicker identifications are generally more accurate (Weber et al., 2004). In an analysis of 640 eyewitness viewings of London police lineups, nearly 9 in 10 "fast" identifications were of the actual suspect, as were fewer than 4 in 10 slower identifications (Valentine et al., 2003).

Identification attempts should also not be repeated. Witnesses who viewed a sequential lineup more than once were more likely to choose a "filler" photograph of an innocent person – possibly because they recognized the person from seeing them in the lineup previously (Horry et al., 2012a).

Thus, researchers advise investigators to "test a witness's memory of a suspect only once" (Wixted et al., 2021).

MINIMIZING FALSE LINEUP IDENTIFICATIONS

After a suburban Toronto department store robbery, the cashier involved could recall only that the culprit was not wearing a tie and was "very neatly dressed and rather good looking." When police put the good-looking Ron Shatford in a lineup with 11 unattractive men, the cashier readily identified him as the culprit. Only after he had served 15 months of a long sentence did another person confess, allowing Shatford to be retried and found not guilty (Doob & Kirshenbaum, 1973). In another case, a witness said the perpetrator had curly hair and a beard. When the lineup included a man, Leonard Callace, with straight hair and a beard and 5 men with only mustaches, the witness confidently identified the bearded Callace. Callace spent 6 years in prison before being exonerated by DNA evidence (Coloff et al., 2016). Stacking the police lineup with dissimilar people can clearly promote misidentification.

If a suspect has a distinguishing feature – a tie, a tattoo, or an eye patch – false identifications are reduced by putting a similar feature on other lineup foils (Zarkadi et al., 2009) or by obscuring the feature (Coloff et al., 2016). Suspects with angry expressions are also identified as the culprit more often, particularly if the foils have neutral or happy expressions (Flowe et al., 2014). Another way to reduce misidentifications is to remind witnesses that the person they saw may or may not be in the lineup. That reminder reduced wrong choices by 45% (Wells, 1984, 1993, 2005, 2008). Alternatively, eyewitnesses can be given a "blank" lineup that contains only foil pictures. Those who falsely identify a suspect in a blank lineup are more likely to make errors when they later face the actual lineup with the suspect included.

Mistakes also subside when witnesses make individual yes or no judgments in response to a *sequence* of people, as shown in dozens of studies in Europe, North America, Australia, and South Africa (Kellen & McAdoo, 2022; Lindsay & Wells, 1985; Meissner et al., 2005; Steblay et al., 2001). A simultaneous lineup tempts people to pick the person who, among the lineup members, most resembles the perpetrator. Witnesses viewing just one suspect at a time are less likely to make false identifications, especially if they are not told in advance how many photos they will view and are not given limitations such as "only your first yes will count" (Horry et al., 2012b; 2021).

If witnesses view several photos or people simultaneously, they are more likely to choose whoever most resembles the culprit. (When not given a same-race lineup, witnesses may pick someone of the culprit's race, especially when it's a race different from their own [Wells & Olson, 2001].) With a *sequential lineup,* eyewitnesses compare each person, one at a time, with their memory of the culprit and make an absolute decision: match or no-match (Goodsell et al., 2010; Gronlund, 2004a,b). One experiment randomly assigned crime eyewitnesses to view lineups simultaneously or sequentially. The sequential lineup reduced the misidentification of foils from 18 to 12%, with no reduction in accurate identifications of suspects (Wells et al., 2015).

Whether the lineup is sequential or not, it also helps if witnesses can view lineup photos from any angle – front, left side, right side – often facilitated with a computer program (Colloff et al., 2022). Another technique is to have witnesses rate their confidence in how much each lineup member matches their memory of the offender. Lineup members with higher ratings were more likely to be the actual offender, even if overall ratings were low (Brewer et al., 2019).

Simultaneous suspect lineups like this one may increase the chance of false identifications. For example, if the perpetrator had glasses and a beard, a witness might choose #2 even if he is not actually the perpetrator.

Rich Legg/Getty Images

Troy Davis (1968–2011). Despite error-prone procedures for screening eyewitness testimonies, the state of Georgia argued that Davis, who maintained his innocence to his last breath, was guilty of murder and executed him in 2011.
Georgia Department of Corrections/Tribune News Service/Columbus Ledger-Enquirer/Getty Images

These no-cost procedures make police lineups more like good experiments. They contain a *control group* (a no-suspect lineup or a lineup in which mock witnesses try to guess the suspect based merely on a general description). They have an experimenter who is *blind* to the hypothesis and who therefore won't subtly influence witnesses or challenge the identification of someone who is not the favored suspect (Charman et al., 2019; Kovera & Evelo, 2017, 2020; Rodriguez & Berry, 2020). Questions are *scripted* and *neutral,* so they don't subtly demand a particular response (the procedure doesn't imply the culprit is in the lineup). And they prohibit confidence-inflating post-lineup comments ("you got him") prior to trial testimony. Such procedures greatly reduce the natural human *confirmation bias* (having an idea and seeking confirming evidence).

When Troy Davis was arrested for the 1989 killing of a Georgia police officer, the police showed some of the witnesses Davis's photo before they viewed the lineup. His lineup picture had a different background than the other photos. The lineup was administered by an officer who knew that Davis was the suspect. Later, seven of the nine witnesses against Davis recanted, with six saying the police threatened them if they did not identify Davis. The man who first told police that Davis was the shooter later confessed to the crime. Despite court appeals and pleas from the Pope, a former FBI director, and 630,000 others, Georgia executed Troy Davis in 2011 (*The New York Times,* 2011).

Mindful of all this research, New Jersey's attorney general mandated statewide blind testing in lineups (when the officer administering the lineup does not know who the suspect is, to avoid steering witnesses toward suspects) and sequential lineups (to minimize simply comparing people and choosing the person who most resembles the one they saw commit a crime) (Kolata & Peterson, 2001; Wells et al., 2002). In 2011, the New Jersey Supreme Court, in response to research on eyewitness identification procedures, overhauled its state's rule for treating lineup evidence. By making it easier for defendants to challenge flawed evidence, the court attached consequences to the use of lineup procedures that are most likely to produce mistaken identifications (Goode & Schwartz, 2011). As of 2022, 14 U.S. states had revised their jury instructions or admissibility frameworks on the basis of the scientific research on eyewitness evidence (Kafadar et al., 2022).

EDUCATING JURORS

Do jurors evaluate eyewitness testimony rationally? Do they understand how the circumstances of a lineup determine its reliability? Do they know whether or not to take an eyewitness's self-confidence into account? Do they realize how memory can be influenced – by earlier misleading questions, by stress at the time of the incident, by the interval between the event and the questioning, by whether the suspect is the same or a different race, by whether recall of other details is sharp or hazy? Studies in Canada, Great Britain, Norway, and the United States reveal that although juror knowledge is increasing, jurors still fail to fully appreciate some of these factors known to influence eyewitness testimony (Desmarais & Read, 2011; Magnussen et al., 2010; Wise & Safer, 2010). In one national survey, for example, more than half falsely believed that "Human memory works like a video camera, accurately recording the events we see and hear so that we can review and inspect them later" (Simons & Chabris, 2011). Jurors – as well as many attorneys and police officers – often have mistaken beliefs, such as: police officers are more accurate eyewitnesses than civilians, stress improves memory, and officers can accurately detect who is lying – all beliefs that research has shown to be wrong (Pezdek & Reisberg, 2022).

To educate jurors, experts now are asked (usually by defense attorneys) to testify about the fallibility of eyewitness testimony (Cutler & Kovera, 2011). Starting in 2012, New Jersey required that jurors be instructed on factors that can influence eyewitness testimony: "Human memory is not foolproof. Research has shown that human memory is not at all like a video recording . . . people may have greater difficulty identifying members of a different race . . . high levels of stress can reduce an eyewitness's ability to recall and make an accurate identification" (quoted in Schacter & Loftus, 2013). The aim is to offer jurors the sort of information covered here to help them evaluate the testimony of both prosecution and defense witnesses. **Table 1** shows how much 64 expert researchers, compared to 111 jurors, agree on influences on eyewitness testimony.

TABLE 1 Influences on Eyewitness Testimony

Phenomenon	Eyewitness Experts Agreeing*	Jurors Agreeing*
Question wording. An eyewitness's testimony about an event can be affected by how the questions put to that eyewitness are worded.	98%	85%
Lineup instructions. Police instructions can affect an eyewitness's willingness to make an identification.	98%	41%
Confidence malleability. An eyewitness's confidence can be influenced by factors that are unrelated to identification accuracy.	95%	50%
Mug-shot-induced bias. Exposure to mug shots of a suspect increases the likelihood that the witness will later choose that suspect in a lineup.	95%	59%
Postevent information. Eyewitnesses' testimony about an event often reflects not only what they actually saw but also information they obtained later on.	94%	60%
Attitudes and expectations. An eyewitness's perception and memory of an event may be affected by their attitudes and expectations.	92%	81%
Cross-race bias. Eyewitnesses are more accurate when identifying members of their own race than members of other races.	90%	47%
Accuracy versus confidence. An eyewitness's confidence is not a good predictor of his or her identification accuracy.	87%	38%

*"This phenomenon is reliable enough for psychologists to present it in courtroom testimony."

Source: Experts from Kassin et al., 2001. Jurors from Benton et al., 2006.

When taught the conditions under which eyewitness accounts are trustworthy, jurors become more discerning (Devenport et al., 2002; Pawlenko et al., 2013) and more likely to convict on the basis of eyewitness evidence collected using unbiased, scientifically validated techniques (Safer et al., 2016). Moreover, attorneys and judges are recognizing the importance of some of these factors when deciding when to ask for or permit suppression of lineup evidence (Stinson et al., 1996, 1997).

SUMMING UP: How Reliable Is Eyewitness Testimony?

- In hundreds of experiments, social psychologists have found that the accuracy of eyewitness testimony can be impaired by a host of factors involving the ways people form judgments and memories.
- Some eyewitnesses express themselves more assertively than others. The assertive witness is more likely to be believed, although assertiveness is actually a trait of the witness that does not reflect the certainty of the information.
- When false information is given to a witness, the *misinformation effect* may result in the witness coming to believe that the false information is true.
- As the sequence of events in a crime is told repeatedly, errors may creep in and become embraced by the witness as part of the true account.
- To reduce such errors, interviewers are advised to let the witness tell what they remember without interruption and to encourage the witness to visualize the scene of the incident and the emotional state the witness was in when the incident occurred.
- Educating jurors about the pitfalls of eyewitness testimony can improve the way testimony is received and, ultimately, the accuracy of the verdict.
- Photo lineups should be *sequential* (one at a time) rather than simultaneous (shown all at once).

WHAT OTHER FACTORS INFLUENCE JUROR JUDGMENTS?

Explain how defendants' attractiveness and similarity to jurors may bias jurors, and how faithfully jurors follow judges' instructions.

The Defendant's Characteristics

According to the famed trial lawyer Clarence Darrow (1933), jurors seldom convict a person they like or acquit one they dislike. He argued that the main job of the trial lawyer is to make a jury like the defendant. Was he right? And is it true, as Darrow also said, that "facts regarding the crime are relatively unimportant"?

Darrow overstated the case. One classic study of more than 3,500 criminal cases and 4,000 civil cases found that about 4 times in 5 the judge agreed with the jury's decision, a result replicated in later analyses (Kalven & Zeisel, 1966; Spencer, 2007). In the first 3 years of a new jury trial system in South Korea, judges and juries agreed on the verdict 91% of the time (Kim et al., 2013). Although it's possible both the jury and the judge may have been wrong, the evidence usually is clear enough that jurors can set aside their biases, focus on the facts, and agree on a verdict (Saks & Hastie, 1978; Visher, 1987). Facts matter.

But facts are not all that matter. Communicators are more persuasive if they seem credible and attractive. Likewise, in courtrooms, high-status defendants often receive more leniency (McGillis, 1979). In 2016, Stanford University athlete Brock Turner was sentenced to only 6 months in prison after sexually assaulting an unconscious woman, prompting widespread outrage on the belief that his higher status led to leniency (Stack, 2016). In one study, mock jurors were less likely to believe victims who had drunk any amount of alcohol (Martin & Monds, 2023). In another, mock jurors perceived sexual assault victims as having more control over the situation – a version of saying "she asked for it" – when the accused perpetrator was a star quarterback (Pica et al., 2018).

Actual cases vary in so many ways – in the type of crime, in the status, age, gender, and race of the defendant – that it's difficult to isolate the factors that influence jurors. So experimenters have controlled such factors by giving mock jurors the same basic facts of a case while varying, for instance, the defendant's attractiveness or similarity to the jurors.

Defendants seen as high-status or attractive are less likely to be found guilty and more likely to escape harsh punishment.
Hero Images/Image Source

PHYSICAL APPEARANCE

The *physical attractiveness stereotype* holds that beautiful people are good people. Michael Efran (1974) wondered whether that stereotype would bias students' judgments of someone accused of cheating. He asked some of his University of Toronto students whether attractiveness should affect the presumption of guilt. They answered, "No, it shouldn't." But did it? Yes. When Efran gave another group of students a description of the case with a photograph of either an attractive or an unattractive defendant, they judged the more attractive person as less guilty and recommended a lesser punishment.

Other experimenters have confirmed that when the evidence is meager or ambiguous, justice is not blind to a defendant's looks (Maeder et al., 2015; Mazzella & Feingold, 1994). Baby-faced adults (people with large, round eyes and small chins) are judged as more naive and are found guilty more often of crimes of mere negligence but less often of intentional criminal acts (Berry & Zebrowitz-McArthur, 1988). When researchers asked people to rate the trustworthiness of 742 convicted murderers from photographs of their faces, they found that these ratings predicted which defendants had received the death penalty instead of life in prison – suggesting the defendants' appearance significantly influenced the jurors who had sentenced them to death (Wilson & Rule, 2015).

In a mammoth experiment conducted with BBC Television, Richard Wiseman (1998) showed viewers evidence about a burglary with just one variation. Some viewers saw the defendant played by an actor who fit what a panel of 100 people judged as the stereotypical criminal: unattractive, crooked nose, small eyes. Among 64,000 people phoning in their verdict, 41% judged him guilty. British viewers elsewhere saw an attractive, baby-faced defendant with large blue eyes. Only 31% found him guilty.

To see if these findings extend to the real world, one study had police officers rate the physical attractiveness of 1,742 defendants appearing before 40 Texas judges in misdemeanor cases that were serious (such as forgery), moderate (such as harassment), or minor (such as public intoxication). In each type of case, the judges set higher bails and fines for less attractive defendants (Downs & Lyons, 1991; **Figure 4**). Being pretty pays.

SIMILARITY TO THE JURORS

If Clarence Darrow was even partly right in his declaration that liking or disliking a defendant colors judgments, other factors that influence liking may also matter. Among such influences is the principle that similarity leads to liking. Mock jurors are more sympathetic to a defendant who shares their attitudes, religion, race, or (in cases of sexual assault), gender (Selby et al., 1977; Towson & Zanna, 1983; Ugwuegbu, 1979).

Some examples:

- In 1,748 small claims court cases in Israel, Jewish plaintiffs received more favorable outcomes when their cases were randomly assigned to Jewish judges, and Arab plaintiffs received more favorable outcomes when assigned to Arab judges (Shayo & Zussman, 2011).
- When a defendant's race fits a crime stereotype – say, a White defendant charged with embezzlement or a Black defendant charged with auto theft – mock jurors offer more negative verdicts and punishments (Jones & Kaplan, 2003; Mazzella & Feingold, 1994). Whites who espouse nonprejudiced views are more likely to demonstrate racial bias in trials in which race issues are not blatant (Sommers & Ellsworth, 2000, 2001).
- Australian students read evidence concerning a left- or right-wing person accused of a politically motivated burglary. The students judged less guilt when the defendant's political views were similar to their own (Amato, 1979).

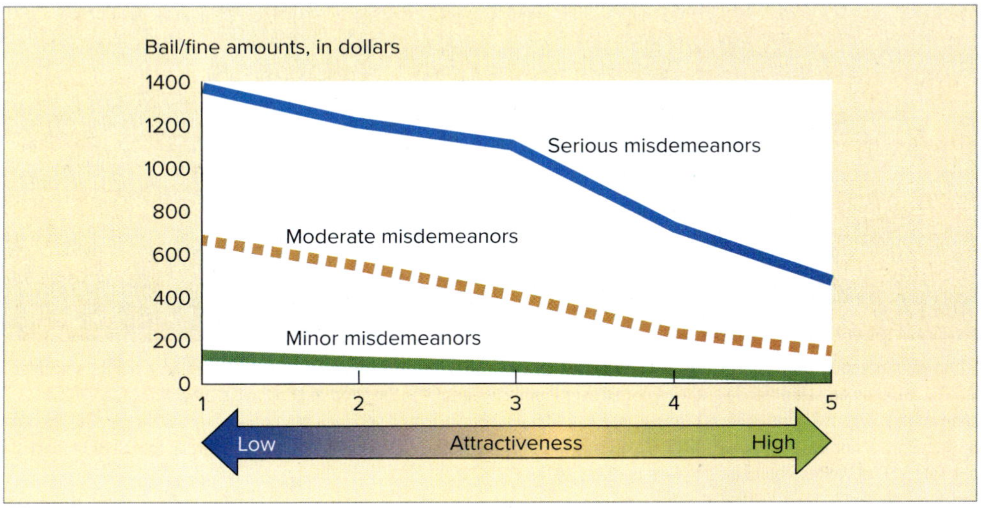

FIGURE 4

Attractiveness and Legal Judgments

Texas judges set higher bails and fines for less attractive defendants.

Source: Data from Downs & Lyons, 1991.

- English-speaking participants were more likely to think someone accused of assault was not guilty if the defendant's testimony was in English rather than translated from Spanish or Thai (Stephan & Stephan, 1986).

This principle appears to be especially strong in matters of race. In 83,924 cases in Florida's Miami-Dade County between 2012 and 2015, Black defendants were 4 to 10% more likely than White defendants to receive a jail sentence, even when controlling for type of crime and previous convictions (Omori & Petersen, 2020). A U.S. Sentencing Commission analysis of criminal convictions between 2007 and 2011 found that Black men received sentences 20% longer than those of White men in cases with the same seriousness and criminal history. Judges were also 25% less likely to show Black (versus White) defendants leniency by giving a sentence shorter than suggested by federal sentencing guidelines (Palazzolo, 2013). In South Carolina, sentences for Black juveniles were more punitive than those for White juveniles – especially in counties with larger Black populations and larger populations of adolescents, creating a heightened perception of threat (Lowery et al., 2018).

A newspaper's analysis found that Blacks were sentenced to 68% more prison time than Whites in first-degree felony cases in Florida, even when factors such as the defendant's prior criminal record and the severity of the crime were equal. In one Florida county, sentences were three times as long for Black defendants as for White defendants convicted of armed robbery. "That's like running a red light in a white car and your ticket is $100 and running a red light in a black car and your ticket is $300," observed a former city commissioner (Salman et al., 2016).

Likewise, Blacks who kill Whites are more often sentenced to death than Whites who kill Blacks (Baumgartner et al., 2015, 2017; Butterfield, 2001). Killing a White person is 17 times more likely to lead to an execution than killing a Black person (Phillips & Marceau, 2020). As Craig Haney (1991) put it, "Blacks are overpunished as defendants or undervalued as victims, or both."

In two studies, harsher sentences were also given to those who looked more stereotypically Black. Given similar criminal histories, Black and White inmates in Florida received similar sentences, but within each race, those with more "Afrocentric" facial features were given longer sentences (Blair et al., 2004). Among Blacks convicted of murdering White victims over a 20-year period in Philadelphia, defendants whose appearance was more stereotypically Black were more likely to be sentenced to death (Eberhardt et al., 2006). Even names made a difference, with Black defendants with more stereotypically Black names

When neighborhood watch volunteer George Zimmerman (standing) fatally shot Black teen Trayvon Martin during a scuffle in 2012, he claimed self-defense and was not arrested until 6 weeks after the shooting, following a public outcry. Polls showed that 73% of Blacks believed Zimmerman would have been arrested sooner if Martin had been White, a view shared by only 35% of non-Blacks (Gallup, 2012). At his trial in 2013, Zimmerman was found not guilty, a verdict that 86% of Blacks, but only 30% of Whites, found dissatisfactory (Pew, 2013).
Orlando Sentinel/Tribune News Service/Getty Images

(like Jamal) receiving longer sentences than those with more stereotypically White names (like James) (Kenthirarajah et al., 2023).

Ideally, jurors would leave their biases outside the courtroom and begin a trial with open minds. So implies the Sixth Amendment to the U.S. Constitution: "The accused shall enjoy the right to a speedy and public trial by impartial jury." In its concern for objectivity, the judicial system is similar to science. Both scientists and jurors are supposed to sift and weigh the evidence. Both the courts and science have rules about what evidence is relevant. Both are to keep careful records and assume that others given the same evidence would decide similarly.

There is good news: When the evidence is clear and individuals focus on it (as when they reread and debate the meaning of testimony), their biases based on similarity or race are minimal (Kaplan & Scherschting, 1980; Lieberman, 2011). Fortunately, the quality of the evidence matters more than the prejudices of the individual jurors.

"You look like this sketch of someone who's thinking about committing a crime."

David Sipress

The Judge's Instructions

Most of us can recall courtroom dramas in which an attorney exclaimed, "Your honor, I object!" whereupon the judge sustains the objection and instructs the jury to ignore the other attorney's suggestive question or the witness's remark. How effective are such instructions?

For example, many locales have "rape shield" statutes that prohibit or limit testimony concerning the victim's prior sexual activity. If such reliable, illegal, or prejudicial testimony is nevertheless slipped in by the defense or blurted out by a witness, will jurors follow a judge's instruction to ignore it? And is it enough for the judge to remind jurors, "The issue is not whether you like or dislike the defendant but whether the defendant committed the offense"?

Very possibly not. Several experimenters report that jurors show concern for due process (Fleming et al., 1999) but find it difficult to ignore inadmissible evidence. In one study, University of Washington students heard a description of a grocery store robbery-murder and a summary of the prosecution's case and the defense's case. When the prosecution's case was weak, no one judged the defendant guilty. When a tape recording of an incriminating phone call made by the defendant was added to the weak case, approximately one-third judged the person guilty. The judge's instructions that the tape was not legal evidence and should be ignored did nothing to erase the effect of the damaging testimony (Sue et al., 1973).

Indeed, a judge's order to ignore testimony – "It must play no role in your consideration of the case. You have no choice but to disregard it" – can even boomerang, adding to the testimony's impact (Wolf & Montgomery, 1977). Perhaps such statements create **reactance** in the jurors. Or perhaps they sensitize jurors to the inadmissible testimony, as when we warn you not to notice your nose as you finish this sentence. Judges can more easily strike inadmissible testimony from the court records than from the jurors' minds. As trial lawyers sometimes say, "You can't unring a bell."

reactance
A motive to protect or restore one's sense of freedom. Reactance arises when someone threatens our freedom of action.

This is especially so with emotional information (Edwards & Bryan, 1997). Jurors are less able to ignore an emotionally provocative description of a defendant's record ("hacking up a woman") compared to a less emotional, dry legal description ("assault with a deadly weapon"). Even if jurors later claim to have ignored the inadmissible information, it may alter how they construe other information.

Pretrial publicity is also difficult for jurors to ignore, with negative publicity increasing guilty verdicts and positive publicity decreasing guilty verdicts (Hoetger et al., 2022; Ruva & Coy, 2020; Steblay et al., 1999). In one large-scale experiment, 800 mock jurors saw incriminating news reports about the criminal record of a man accused of robbing a supermarket. Some heard the judge's instructions to disregard the pretrial publicity, and others did not. The effect of the judicial admonition? Nil. Those told to ignore it were just as likely to vote to convict – it's difficult to ignore what you already have heard (Kramer et al., 1990).

With a 24-hour news cycle, pretrial publicity often occurs before a jury is selected. Will jurors be biased by what they learned before they entered the courtroom? Although they deny being influenced, experiments have shown otherwise.
cdrin/Shutterstock

People whose opinions are biased by pretrial publicity typically deny its effect on them, and that denial makes it difficult to eliminate biased jurors (Moran & Cutler, 1991). In experiments, even getting mock jurors to pledge their impartiality and their willingness to disregard prior information has not eliminated the pretrial publicity effect (Dexter et al., 1992; Ruva & Guenther, 2015; Ruva & Coy, 2020).

In some cases, jurors who bring up inadmissible evidence during deliberations will be chastised by other jury members for doing so, thus limiting its influence on jury verdicts (London & Nunez, 2000). To minimize the effects of inadmissible testimony, judges also can forewarn jurors that certain types of evidence, such as a rape victim's sexual history, are irrelevant. Once jurors form impressions based on such evidence, a judge's admonitions have much less effect (Borgida & White, 1980; Kassin & Wrightsman, 1979). Thus, reported Vicki Smith (1991), a pretrial training session pays dividends. Teaching jurors legal procedures and standards of proof improves their understanding of the trial procedure and their willingness to withhold judgment until after they have heard all the trial information.

Better yet, judges could cut inadmissible testimony before the jurors hear it – by videotaping testimonies and removing the inadmissible parts. Live and videotaped testimonies have much the same impact as do live and videotaped lineups (Cutler et al., 1989; Miller & Fontes, 1979). Videotaping not only enables the judge to edit out inadmissible testimony but also speeds up the trial and allows witnesses to talk about crucial events before memories fade.

SUMMING UP: What Other Factors Influence Juror Judgments?

- The facts of a case are usually compelling enough that jurors can lay aside their biases and render a fair judgment. When the evidence is ambiguous, however, jurors are more likely to interpret it with their preconceived biases and to feel sympathetic to a defendant who is attractive or similar to themselves.
- When jurors are exposed to damaging pretrial publicity or to inadmissible evidence, will they follow a judge's instruction to ignore it? In simulated trials, the judge's orders were sometimes followed, but often, especially when the judge's admonition came *after* an impression was made, they were not.
- Researchers have also explored the influence of other factors, such as the severity of the potential sentence and various characteristics of the victim.

WHAT INFLUENCES THE INDIVIDUAL JUROR?

Describe how verdicts depend on how the individual jurors process information.

Courtroom influences on "the average juror" are worth pondering. But no juror is the average juror; each carries into the courthouse individual attitudes and personalities. And when they deliberate, jurors influence one another. So two key questions are (1) How are verdicts influenced by individual jurors' characteristics? and (2) How are verdicts influenced by jurors' deliberations with each other? We will begin with the first question and then move on to the second, on group influences, in the next section.

Juror Comprehension

To gain insight into juror comprehension, researchers had mock jurors recruited from courthouse jury pools view reenactments of actual trials. Almost always, jurors first constructed a story that made sense of all the evidence before making their decision on whether to convict. After observing one murder trial, for example, some jurors concluded that a quarrel had made the defendant angry, triggering him to get a knife, search for the victim, and stab him to death. Others surmised that the frightened defendant picked up a knife that he used to defend himself when he later encountered the victim. When jurors begin deliberating, they often discover that others have constructed different stories (Pennington & Hastie, 1993). This implies – and research confirms – that jurors are best persuaded when attorneys present evidence in narrative fashion – a story.

UNDERSTANDING INSTRUCTIONS

After they have come up with a plausible story to explain the evidence, jurors must grasp the judge's instructions about the verdicts they can render. For those instructions to be effective, jurors must first understand them. Not surprisingly, many people do not understand the complex legalese of judicial instructions (Baguley et al., 2017). Depending on the type of case, a jury may be told that the standard of proof is a "preponderance of the evidence," "clear and convincing evidence," or "beyond a reasonable doubt." Such statements may have one meaning for the legal community and different meanings to jurors (Kagehiro, 1990; Mueller-Johnson et al., 2018; Wright & Hall, 2007).

A judge may also remind jurors to avoid premature conclusions as they weigh each new item of presented evidence. But research with both college students and mock jurors chosen from prospective jury pools shows that human beings do form premature opinions, and those leanings do influence how they interpret new information (Carlson & Russo, 2001).

INCREASING JURORS' UNDERSTANDING

Understanding how jurors misconstrue judicial instructions is the first step toward better jury decisions. A next step might be giving jurors access to transcripts rather than forcing them to rely on their memories in processing complex information (Bourgeois et al., 1993). A further step would be devising and testing clearer, more effective ways to present information – something several social psychologists have studied. For example, when a judge provides a number for the required standard of proof (as, for instance, 51, 71, or 91% certainty), jurors understand and respond appropriately (Kagehiro, 1990). And surely there must be a simpler way to tell jurors, as required by the Illinois Death Penalty Act, not to impose the death sentence in murder cases when there are justifying circumstances: "If you do not unanimously find from your consideration of all the evidence that there are no mitigating factors sufficient to preclude imposition of a death sentence, then you should sign the verdict requiring the court to impose a sentence other than death" (Diamond, 1993). When jury instructions are instead written in more understandable "plain language," comprehension increases (for example, instead of "innocent misrecollection is not uncommon," writing "people sometimes honestly forget things or make mistakes about what they remember."). Even better are instructions that define key terms (such as noting "preponderance of the evidence" means "more likely than not"), eliminate information irrelevant to the particular case, and use names instead of terms such as "the defendant" (Smith & Haney, 2011).

Similarly, a "fact-based" approach asks jurors a series of plain-language questions ("Are you satisfied beyond a reasonable doubt that Mr. X consciously and voluntarily shot Mr. Y?") and explains how the answers translate into verdicts ("If 'no,' you should find the accused not guilty."). This approach appears to lead to jury members better comprehending the law (Spivak et al., 2020).

Jury Selection

In thousands of American trials a year, consultants – some of them social scientists – help lawyers pick juries and plot strategy (Gavzer, 1997; Hutson, 2007; Miller, 2001; Nance, 2015). Many trial attorneys now use scientific jury selection to write survey questions they can use to exclude potential jurors who might be biased against their clients. Most lawyers have reported satisfaction with the results (Moran et al., 1994). Most jurors, when asked by a judge to "raise your hand if you've read anything about this case that would prejudice you," don't directly acknowledge their preconceptions. But if, for example, the judge allows an attorney to survey prospective jurors' attitudes toward drugs, the attorney can often guess their verdicts in a drug-trafficking case (Moran et al., 1990). Likewise, people who acknowledge they "don't put much faith in the testimony of psychiatrists" are less likely to accept an insanity defense (Cutler et al., 1992).

"Beware of the Lutherans, especially the Scandinavians; they are almost always sure to convict."

—Clarence Darrow, "How to Pick a Jury," 1936

Individuals react differently to specific case features. Racial prejudice becomes relevant in racially charged cases; gender seems linked with felony verdicts only in rape and domestic violence cases; belief in personal responsibility versus corporate responsibility relates to personal injury awards in suits against businesses (Ellsworth & Mauro, 1998). Jurors who believe myths about rape – such as believing that a woman inviting a man inside her apartment is necessarily an invitation to sex – are significantly less likely to vote to convict an accused rapist (Hafer & Jacquin, 2022; Lilley et al., 2023; Willmott et al., 2018). Conversely, jurors who have been sexually abused are more likely to believe sexual abuse victims and to vote to convict accused sexual abusers (Jones et al., 2020).

Despite the excitement – and ethical concern – about scientific jury selection, experiments reveal that attitudes and personal characteristics do not predict verdicts as strongly as some might believe (Lieberman, 2011). There are "no magic questions to be asked of prospective jurors," cautioned Steven Penrod and Brian Cutler (1987). Researchers Michael Saks and Reid Hastie (1978) agreed: "The studies are unanimous in showing that evidence is a substantially more potent determinant of jurors' verdicts than the individual characteristics of jurors" (p. 68).

Jury Selection and the Death Penalty

A *close* case can, however, be decided by who is selected for the jury. In criminal cases, people who would oppose the death penalty under any circumstances cannot serve on the jury of cases where the death penalty may be imposed. The rest, who believe the death penalty is sometimes justified, are known as death-qualified jurors. These jurors are more likely to favor the prosecution, to feel that courts coddle criminals, and to oppose protecting the constitutional rights of defendants (Bersoff, 1987). Jurors who are willing to impose the death penalty are more punitive and less willing to consider mitigating factors (Haney et al., 2022). Dismissing jurors because they are opposed to the death penalty results in a jury that is more likely to vote guilty (West et al., 2017).

The attitudes and experiences of jury members, especially around sexuality, may influence their verdicts in sexual assault cases.
Image Source/Getty Images

Because the legal system operates on tradition and precedent, such research findings only slowly alter judicial practice. In 1986, the U.S. Supreme Court, in a split decision, overturned a lower court ruling (and thus disagreed) that death-qualified jurors are indeed a biased sample. Ellsworth (1989) believed the Court, in this case, disregarded the compelling and consistent evidence partly because of its "ideological commitment to capital punishment" and partly because of the havoc that would result if the convictions of thousands of people on death row had to be reconsidered. The solution, should the Court ever wish to adopt it for future cases, is to convene separate juries to (a) decide guilt in capital murder cases, and, given a guilty verdict, to (b) hear additional evidence on factors motivating the murder and to decide between death or imprisonment.

But a deeper issue is at stake here: whether the death penalty itself falls under the U.S. Constitution's ban on "cruel and unusual punishment." Canada, Australia, New Zealand, Western Europe, and most countries in South America prohibit capital punishment. In addition, Americans' pro-death penalty attitudes seem to be softening. After reaching 80% in 1994, support for the death penalty fell to 56% in 2019 (Gallup, 2020).

In wrestling with the death penalty, U.S. courts have considered whether courts inflict the penalty arbitrarily, whether they apply it with racial bias, and whether legal killing deters illegal killing. The social science answers to these questions are clear (Alvarez & Miller, 2017; Costanzo, 1997; Haney & Logan, 1994). Consider the deterrence issue. States with the death penalty do not have lower homicide rates. Homicide rates did not drop when states initiated the death penalty, and they have not risen when states have abolished it. When committing a crime of passion, people don't pause to calculate the consequences (which include life in prison without parole as another potent deterrent). Moreover, the death penalty is applied inconsistently (in Texas, 40 times as often as in New York). And it is applied more often with low-income defendants, who often receive a weak defense (Johnson & Johnson, 2001; *The Economist,* 2000). Nevertheless, the Supreme Court determined that admitting only death-qualified jurors provides a representative jury of one's peers and that "the death penalty undoubtedly is a significant deterrent." Social science still has work to do.

SUMMING UP: What Influences the Individual Juror?

- Social psychologists are interested in not only the interactions among witnesses, judges, and juries, but also what happens within and between individual jurors. One major concern is jurors' ability to comprehend the evidence, especially when it involves statistics indicating the probability that a given person committed the crime.
- Trial lawyers often use jury consultants to help them select jurors most sympathetic to their case.
- In cases in which the death penalty may be applied, lawyers can disqualify any prospective juror who opposes the death penalty on principle. Social psychology research argues that this in itself produces a biased jury, but the U.S. Supreme Court has ruled otherwise.

HOW DO GROUP INFLUENCES AFFECT JURIES?

Explain how individual jurors' prejudgments coalesce into a group decision and what can influence the outcome.

Imagine a jury that has just finished a trial and has entered the jury room to begin its deliberations. Chances are approximately two in three that the jurors will *not* initially agree on a verdict. Yet, after discussion, about 95% emerge with a consensus (Hans et al., 2002; Kalven & Zeisel, 1966). One-third of jurors say that they would have voted against their jury's decision had they been a jury of one (Waters & Hans, 2009). Clearly, group influence has occurred.

Are juries subject to the social influences that mold other decision groups – to patterns of majority and minority influence? To *group polarization?* To *groupthink?* Let's start with a simple question: If we knew the jurors' initial leanings, could we predict their verdict?

The law prohibits observing actual jury deliberations, so researchers simulate the jury process by presenting cases to mock juries and having them deliberate as a real jury would (Ruva & Guenther, 2017). In a series of such studies, researchers tested various mathematical schemes for predicting group decisions, including decisions by mock juries (Davis et al., 1975, 1977, 1989; Kerr et al., 1976). Will some mathematical combination of initial decisions predict the final group decision? Across several experiments, a "two-thirds-majority" scheme fared best: The group verdict was usually the alternative favored by at least two-thirds of the jurors at the outset. Without such a majority, a hung jury was likely.

Likewise, in a survey of juries, 9 in 10 reached the verdict favored by the majority on the first ballot (Kalven & Zeisel, 1966). Although we might fantasize about someday being the courageous lone juror who sways the majority, it seldom happens.

Minority Influence

A typical 12-person jury is like a typical small college class: The three quietest people rarely talk, and the three most vocal people contribute more than half the speaking time (Hastie et al., 1983). In one trial, the four jurors who favored acquittal persisted, were vocal, and eventually prevailed. From the research on minority influence, we know that jurors in the minority will be most persuasive when they are consistent, persistent, and self-confident. This is especially so if they can begin to trigger some defections from the majority (Gordijn et al., 2002; Kerr, 1981).

Group Polarization

Jury deliberation shifts people's opinions in other intriguing ways as well. In experiments, deliberation often magnifies initial sentiments (Takada & Murata, 2014). For example, University of Kentucky students listened to a 30-minute tape of a murder trial and were asked to recommend a prison sentence. Groups with several students high in authoritarian attitudes initially recommended strong punishments (56 years) and were even more punitive after deliberation (68 years). Groups with fewer authoritarians were initially more lenient (38 years) and after deliberation became even more lenient (29 years) (Bray & Noble, 1978). By contrast, group diversity often moderates judgments. Compared with Whites who judge Black defendants on all-White mock juries, those serving on racially mixed mock juries enter deliberation expressing more leniency, exhibit openness to a wider range of information, make more high-quality contributions to the deliberations, and think over information more thoroughly (Bergold & Kovera, 2022; Sommers, 2006; Stevenson et al., 2017).

Confirmation of group polarization in juries comes from an ambitious study of 69 12-person mock juries. Each was shown a reenactment of an actual murder case trial, with roles played by an experienced judge and actual attorneys. Then they were given unlimited time to deliberate the case in a jury room. As **Figure 5** shows, the evidence was

FIGURE 5

Group Polarization in Juries

In highly realistic simulations of a murder trial, 828 Massachusetts jurors stated their initial verdict preferences, then deliberated the case for periods ranging from 3 hours to 5 days. Deliberation strengthened initial tendencies that favored the prosecution.

Source: Hastie et al., 1983.

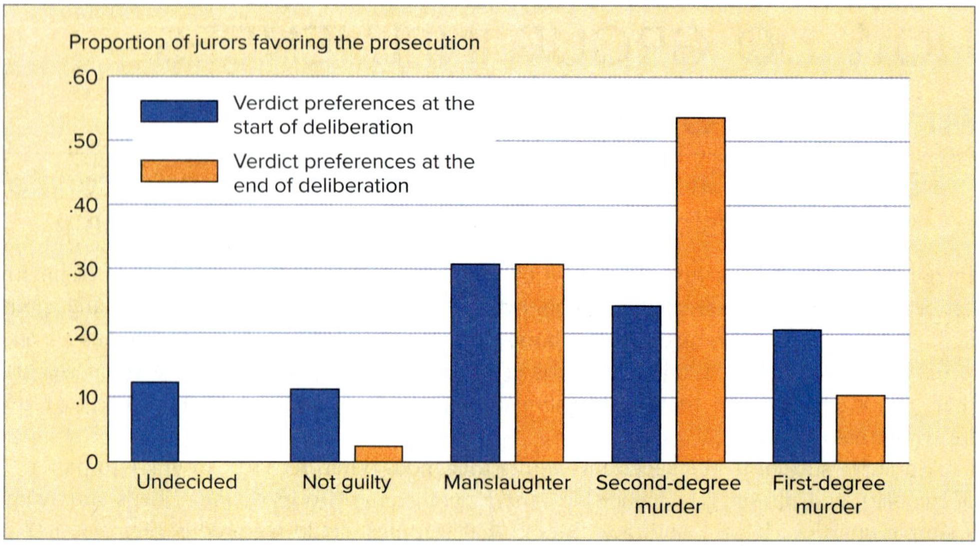

incriminating: Before deliberation, 4 out of 5 jurors voted guilty but felt unsure enough that a weak verdict of manslaughter was their most popular preference. After deliberation, nearly all agreed the accused was guilty, and most now preferred a stronger verdict: second-degree murder (Hastie et al., 1983). Through deliberation, the jury's initial leanings had grown stronger – a classic example of group polarization. (For another example, see "Research Close-up: Group Polarization in a Natural Court Setting".)

research CLOSE-UP

Group Polarization in a Natural Court Setting

In simulated juries, deliberation often amplifies jurors' individual inclinations. Does such group polarization occur in actual courts? Cass Sunstein, David Schkade, and Lisa Ellman (2004) showed us how researchers can harvest data from natural settings when exploring social psychological phenomena. Their data were 14,874 votes by judges on 4,958 three-judge U.S. circuit court panels. (On these federal courts of appeals, an appeal is almost always heard by three of the court's judges.)

Sunstein and his colleagues first asked whether judges' votes tended to reflect the ideology of the Republican or Democratic president who appointed them. Indeed, when voting on ideologically tinged cases involving affirmative action, environmental regulation, campaign finance, and abortion, Democrat-appointed judges more often supported the liberal position than did Republican-appointed judges. No surprise there. That's what presidents and their party members assume when seeking congressional approval of their kindred-spirited judicial nominees.

Would such tendencies be amplified when the panel had three judges appointed by the same party? Would three Republican-appointed judges be even more often conservative than the average Republican appointee? And would three Democrat-appointed judges be more often liberal than the average Democrat appointee? Or would judges vote their convictions uninfluenced by their fellow panelists? **Table 2** presents their findings.

Note that when three appointees from the same party formed a panel (RRR or DDD), they became more likely to vote their party's ideological preference than did the average individual judge — very consistent with the principle of group polarization. The polarization exhibited by like-minded threesomes was, the Sunstein team reported, "confirmed in many areas, including affirmative action, campaign finance, sex discrimination, sexual harassment, piercing the corporate veil, disability discrimination, race discrimination, and review of environmental regulations" (although not in the politically volatile cases of abortion and capital punishment, where judges voted their well-formed convictions).

Sunstein and colleagues offered an example: If all three judges "believe that an affirmative action program is unconstitutional, and no other judge is available to argue on its behalf, then the exchange of arguments in the room will suggest that the program is genuinely unconstitutional." This is group polarization in action, they concluded — an example of "one of the most striking findings in modern social science: Groups of like-minded people tend to go to extremes."

TABLE 2 Proportion of "Liberal" Voting by Individual Judges and by Three-Judge Panels

	Individual Judges' Votes		Individual Judges' Votes, by Panel Composition			
	Party					
Examples of Case Type	**R***	**D***	**RRR**	**RRD**	**RDD**	**DDD**
Campaign finance	.28	.46	.23	.30	.35	.80
Affirmative action	.48	.74	.37	.50	.83	.85
Environmental	.46	.64	.27	.55	.62	.72
Sex discrimination	.35	.51	.31	.38	.49	.75
Average across 13 case types	.38	.51	.34	.39	.50	.61

*R, Republican appointee; *D, Democrat appointee.

Leniency

In many experiments, another curious effect of deliberation has surfaced: Especially when the evidence is not highly incriminating, jurors often become more lenient over the course of deliberations, becoming more likely to render a not guilty verdict (MacCoun & Kerr, 1988). Even if only a bare majority initially favors finding the defendant not guilty, that bare majority will usually prevail (Stasser et al., 1981). Moreover, a minority that favors a not-guilty verdict stands a better chance of prevailing than one that favors conviction (Tindale et al., 1990).

Again, a survey of actual juries confirms the laboratory results. When the majority does not prevail, the shift is usually from guilty to not guilty (Kalven & Zeisel, 1966). When a judge disagrees with the jury's decision, it is usually because the jury acquits someone the judge would have convicted.

"It is better that ten guilty persons escape than one innocent suffer."

—William Blackstone, *Commentaries on the Laws of England*, 1769

Might *informational influence* (stemming from others' persuasive arguments) account for the increased leniency? The "innocent-unless-proved-guilty" and "proof-beyond-a-reasonable-doubt" rules put the burden of proof on those who favor conviction. Perhaps this makes evidence of the defendant's innocence more persuasive. Or perhaps *normative influence* creates the leniency effect, as jurors who view themselves as fair-minded confront other jurors who are even more concerned with protecting a possibly innocent defendant.

Are Twelve Heads Better Than One?

When a problem has an objective right answer, group judgments surpass those by most individuals. Does the same hold true in juries? When deliberating, jurors exert normative pressure by trying to shift others' judgments by the sheer weight of their own. But they also share information, thus enlarging one another's understanding. So, does informational influence produce superior collective judgment?

The evidence, though meager, is encouraging. Groups recall information from a trial better than do their individual members (Vollrath et al., 1989). Deliberation also tends to cancel out certain biases and draws jurors' attention away from their own prejudgments and to the evidence. Twelve heads can be, it seems, better than one.

Are Six Heads as Good as Twelve?

In keeping with their British heritage, juries in the United States and Canada have traditionally been composed of 12 people whose task is to reach a unanimous verdict. However, in civil cases and state criminal cases not involving a potential death penalty, the U.S. Supreme Court ruled in the early 1970s that courts could use six-person juries. Do such juries operate the same as 12-person juries?

Many legal scholars and social psychologists argue that the answer is no (Saks, 1974, 1996). First, consider the statistics. For example, if 10% of a community's total jury pool is Black, then 72% of 12-member juries but only 47% of six-member juries may be expected to have at least one Black person. So smaller juries may be less likely to include a community's diversity.

And if, in a given case, one-sixth of the jurors initially favor acquittal, that would be a single individual in a six-member jury and two people in a 12-member jury. The Court assumed that, psychologically, the two situations would be identical. But as you may recall from our discussion of conformity, resisting group pressure is far more difficult for a minority of one than for a minority of two. Psychologically speaking, a jury split 10 to 2 is not equivalent to a jury split 5 to 1. Not surprisingly, then, 12-person juries are twice as likely as six-person juries to have hung verdicts (Ellsworth & Mauro, 1998; Saks & Marti, 1997).

Jury researcher Michael Saks (1998) summed up the research findings: "Larger juries are more likely than smaller juries to contain members of minority groups, more accurately recall trial testimony, give more time to deliberation, hang [become a hung jury] more often, and appear more likely to reach 'correct' verdicts."

Twelve-member juries are more diverse and deliberate longer than six-member juries.
bikeriderlondon/Shutterstock

From Lab to Life: Simulated and Real Juries

Perhaps while reading this chapter, you have wondered what some critics (Tapp, 1980; Vidmar, 1979) have wondered: Isn't there an enormous gulf between mock jurors discussing a hypothetical case and real jurors deliberating a real person's fate? Indeed there is. It is one thing to ponder a pretend decision with minimal information and quite another to agonize over the complexities and profound consequences of an actual case. So Reid Hastie, Martin Kaplan, James Davis, Eugene Borgida, and others asked their participants, who sometimes were drawn from actual juror pools, to view enactments of actual trials. The enactments were so realistic that sometimes participants forgot the trial they were watching on television was staged (Thompson et al., 1981).

Student mock jurors become engaged, too. "As I eavesdropped on the mock juries," recalled researcher Norbert Kerr (1999), "I became fascinated by the jurors' insightful arguments, their mix of amazing recollections and memory fabrications, their prejudices, their attempts to persuade or coerce, and their occasional courage in standing alone. Here brought to life before me were so many of the psychological processes I had been studying! Although our student jurors understood they were only simulating a real trial, they really cared about reaching a fair verdict." A meta-analysis of 53 studies found that student and nonstudent mock juries were similar in their verdicts and in the amount of damages they awarded (Bornstein et al., 2017).

Researchers also defend the laboratory simulations by noting that the laboratory offers a practical, inexpensive method of studying important issues under controlled conditions (Dillehay & Nietzel, 1980; Kerr & Bray, 2005). As researchers have begun testing these questions in more realistic situations, findings from the laboratory studies have often held up quite well. No one contends that the simplified world of the jury experiment mirrors the complex world of the real courtroom. Rather, the experiments help us formulate theories with which we interpret the complex world.

Come to think of it, are these jury simulations any different from social psychology's other experiments, all of which create simplified versions of complex realities? By varying just one or two factors at a time in this simulated reality, the experimenter pinpoints how changes in one or two aspects of a situation can affect us. And that is the essence of social psychology's experimental method.

Attorneys are using new technology to present crime stories in ways jurors can easily grasp, as in this computer simulation of a homicide generated on the basis of forensic evidence.
Silas Stein/dpa/Alamy Stock Photo

SUMMING UP: How Do Group Influences Affect Juries?

- Juries are groups, and they are swayed by the same influences that bear upon other types of groups. For example, the most vocal members of a jury tend to do most of the talking, and the quietest members say little.
- As a jury deliberates, opposing views may become more entrenched and polarized.
- Especially when evidence is not highly incriminating, deliberation may make jurors more lenient than they originally were.
- The 12-member jury is a tradition stemming from English Common Law. Researchers find that a jury this size allows for reasonable diversity among jurors, a mix of opinions and orientations, and better recall of information.
- Researchers have also examined and questioned the assumptions underlying several U.S. Supreme Court decisions permitting smaller juries.
- Simulated juries are not real juries, so we must be cautious in generalizing research findings to actual courtrooms. Yet, like all experiments in social psychology, laboratory jury experiments help us formulate theories and principles that we can use to interpret the more complex world of everyday life.

CONCLUDING THOUGHTS: Thinking Smart with Psychological Science

An intellectually fashionable idea, sometimes called "postmodernism," contends that truth is socially constructed; knowledge always reflects the cultures that form it. Indeed, as we have often noted in this book, we do often follow our hunches, our biases, our cultural bent. Social scientists are not immune to *confirmation bias, belief perseverance, overconfidence,* and the biasing power of preconceptions. Our preconceived ideas and values guide our theory development, our interpretations, our topics of choice, and our language.

Being mindful of hidden values within psychological science should motivate us to clean the cloudy spectacles through which we view the world. Mindful of our vulnerability to bias and error, we can steer between the two extremes: of being naive about a value-laden psychology that pretends to be value-neutral or of being tempted to an unrestrained subjectivism that dismisses evidence as nothing but collected biases. In the spirit of humility, we can put testable ideas to the test. If we think the death penalty does (or does not) deter crime more than other available punishments, we can utter our personal opinions and we can ask whether states with a death penalty have lower homicide rates, whether their rates have dropped after instituting the death penalty, and whether they have risen when abandoning the penalty.

As we have seen, the U.S. Supreme Court considered pertinent social science evidence when disallowing five-member juries and ending school desegregation. But it has discounted research when offering opinions on whether the death penalty deters crime, whether courts inflict the penalty arbitrarily, whether they apply it with racial bias, and whether potential jurors selected by virtue of their accepting capital punishment are biased toward conviction.

Beliefs and values do guide the perceptions of judges as well as scientists and laypeople. And that is why we need to think smarter – to rein in our hunches and biases by testing them against available evidence. If our beliefs find support, so much the better for them. If not, so much the worse for them. That's the humble spirit that underlies both psychological science and everyday critical thinking.

Social Psychology and the Sustainable Future

CHAPTER

16

maxstockphoto/Shutterstock

"We do not inherit the earth from our ancestors; we borrow it from our children."

—Haida (Native North American) proverb

Imagine yourself on a huge spaceship traveling through our galaxy. To sustain your community, a spacecraft biosphere grows plants and breeds animals. By recycling waste and managing resources, the mission has, until recently, been sustainable over time and across generations of people born onboard.

The spaceship's name is Planet Earth, and its expanding crew now numbers 8+ billion. Alas, it increasingly consumes its resources at an unsustainable rate — 50% beyond the spaceship's capacity. Thus, it now takes the Earth 1.7 years to regenerate what we use in a year (FootPrintNetwork.org, 2021). With the growing population and consumption have come deforestation, depletion of wild fish stocks, and climate destabilization. Not all people consume resources equally; the United States, for example, uses 4 times as much per person as the rest of the world.

In 1960, the spaceship Earth carried 3 billion people and 127 million motor vehicles. Today, with more than 8 billion people, it has more than 1 billion motor vehicles. The greenhouse gases emitted by motor vehicles, along with the burning of coal and oil to generate electricity and heat homes and buildings, are changing the Earth's climate. To ascertain how much and how fast climate change is occurring, several thousand scientists worldwide have collaborated to create and review the evidence via the Intergovernmental Panel on Climate Change (IPCC). The past chair of its scientific assessment committee, John Houghton (2011), said that the report's conclusions — supported by the national academies of science of the world's 11 most developed countries — are undergirded by the most "thoroughly researched and reviewed" scientific effort in human history.

The IPCC (2014, 2019, 2022), the American Association for the Advancement of Science (2014), the United Nations (2020), and the U.S. government Climate Science Special Report (Wuebbles et al., 2017) offer massive evidence of climate change, as illustrated in **Figure 1:**

FIGURE 1

Scientific Indicators of Global Climate Change

Source: Adapted from Cook, 2010.

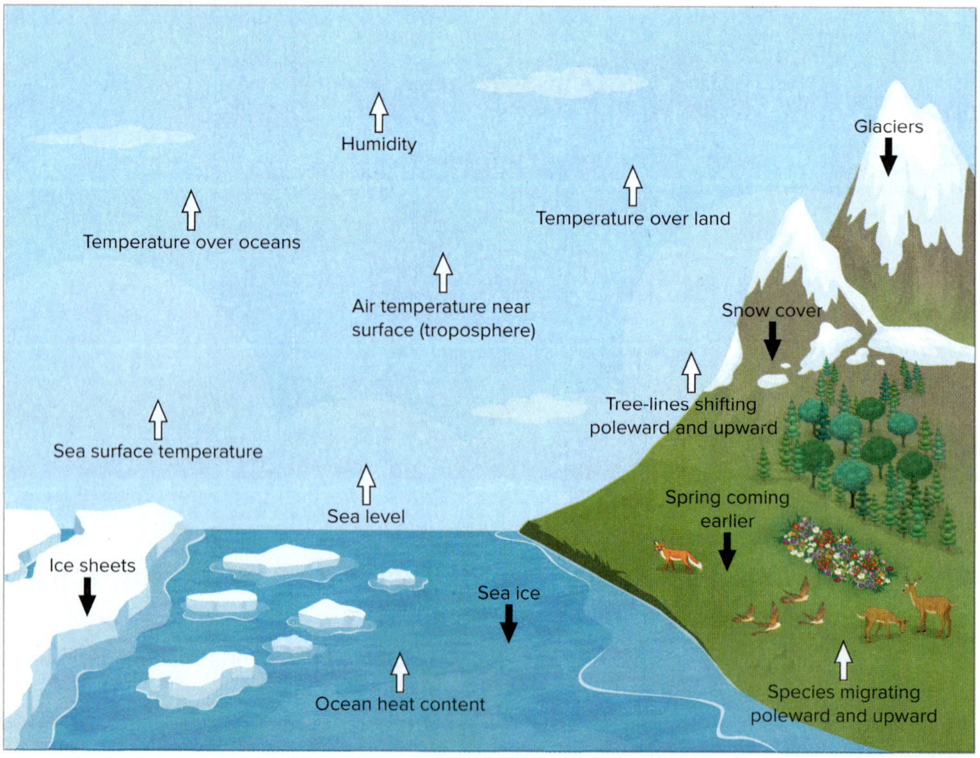

- *A warming greenhouse gas blanket is growing.* About half the carbon dioxide emitted by human activity since the Industrial Revolution (since 1750) remains in the atmosphere (Royal Society, 2010). There is now 45% more atmospheric carbon dioxide and 157% more atmospheric methane than before industrial times (World Meteorological Organization, 2017). As the permafrost thaws, methane gas release threatens to compound the problem (Carey, 2012).
- *Sea and air temperatures are rising.* Since 1901, the global air temperature has increased 1.8° F (1.0° C). Across 98% of the Earth's surface, temperatures were hotter at the end of the twentieth century than at any time in the previous 2,000 years (Gramling, 2019). 2023 was the hottest year on record, and the increase in average temperatures has accelerated in the last 15 years (Hausfather, 2023; Pulver et al., 2024) (**Figure 2**).

"The evidence is overwhelming: levels of greenhouse gases in the atmosphere are rising. Temperatures are going up. Springs are arriving earlier. Ice sheets are melting. Sea level is rising. The patterns of rainfall and drought are changing. Heat waves are getting worse as is extreme precipitation. The oceans are acidifying."

—American Association for the Advancement of Science, *What We Know: The Reality, Risks and Response to Climate Change*, 2014

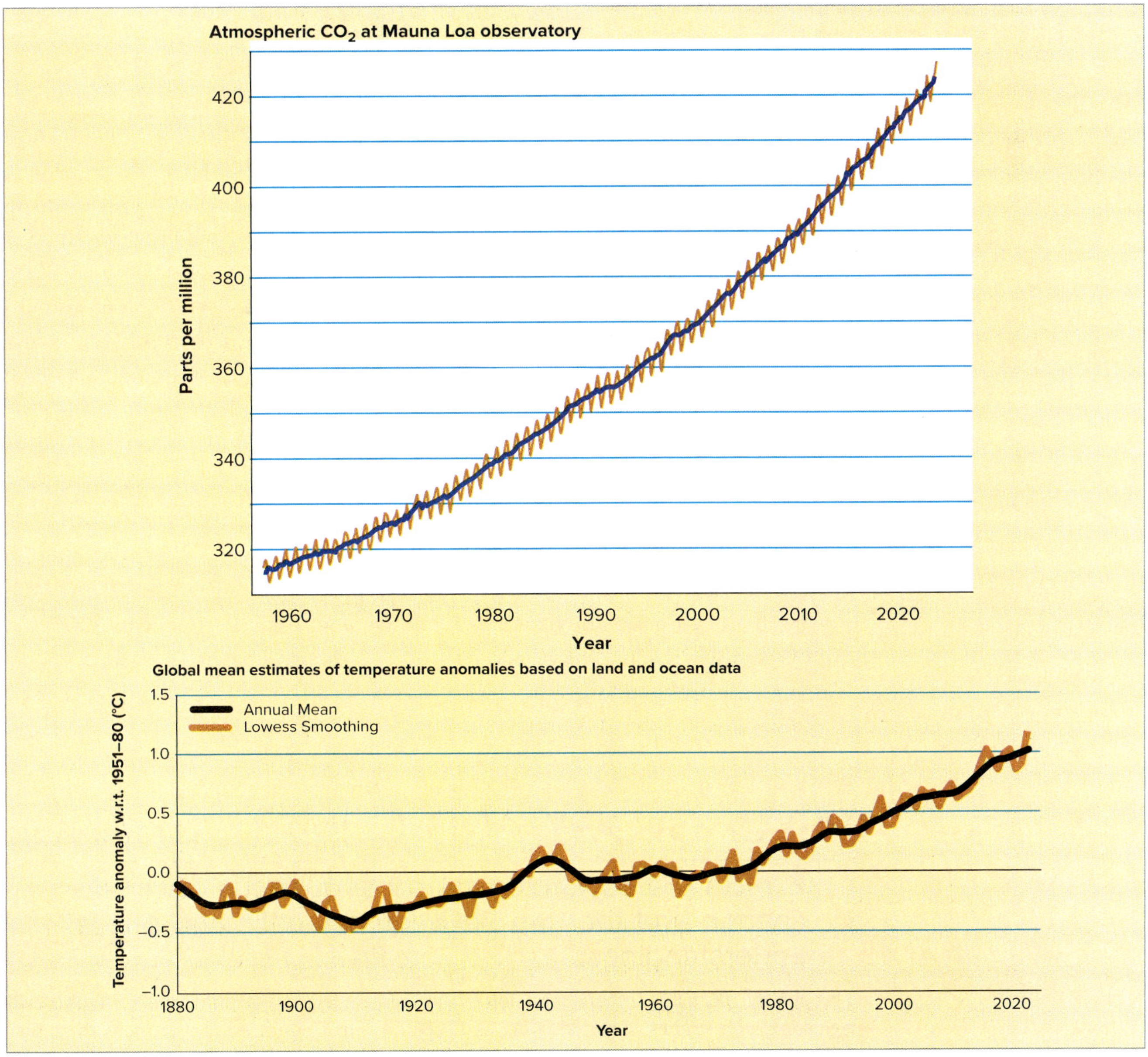

FIGURE 2

Global Climate on Steroids

As atmospheric CO_2 has risen, so have global temperatures.

Sources: Top graph: NOAA, 2024; Bottom graph: NASA, 2024.

FIGURE 3

The Shrinking Ice Cap

National Aeronautics and Space Administration (NASA) photos show the September 1979 and September 2020 Arctic ice sheets.
(both photos): *Source:* NASA/Goddard Space Flight Center Scientific Visualization Studio. NASA Global Climate Change, 2023 (graph)

- *Ice and snow packs are melting, causing sea levels to rise.* As polar bears know, Arctic ice cover has shrunk substantially (**Figure 3**). Most of the glaciers of Glacier National Park in Montana are now gone, and Greenland's are shrinking, pouring billions of gallons of water into the North Atlantic (Freedman & Samenow, 2019). This makes sea levels rise, endangering coastal and low-lying areas, including in Pakistan, southern China, Indian and Pacific Ocean islands, and the Arctic (Cornwall, 2016; Houghton, 2011; Nerem et al., 2018). In the United States, daily tidal flooding is accelerating in 25 Atlantic and Gulf coast cities (Wuebbles et al., 2017).
- *Extreme weather is increasing.* Any single weather event — a heatwave here, a hurricane there — cannot be attributed to climate change. Weird weather happens. But it is happening more often and is now "beyond the bounds of natural variability" (AMS, 2017; NASEM, 2016). Climate events costing more than a billion (inflation-adjusted) dollars have more than tripled since 1980 (NCEI, 2024). With more than 1.23 million humans dead from weather disasters between 2000 and 2019 and the number increasing (UN, 2020), climate change is a larger life-or-death concern than terrorism.

"If present trends continue, this century may well witness extraordinary climate change and an unprecedented destruction of ecosystems, with serious consequences for all of us."

—Pope Francis, *Laudato Si*, 2015

PSYCHOLOGY AND CLIMATE CHANGE

Explain the psychological consequences of climate change and the gap between scientific and public understandings.

Throughout its history, social psychology has responded to current events — to the civil rights era with studies of stereotyping and prejudice, to civil unrest and crime with studies of aggression, to the women's movement with studies of gender and gender-related attitudes. Now that global climate change is "the greatest problem the world faces" (Houghton, 2011), psychological science is studying (a) its effects on human behavior, (b) public opinion about climate change, and (c) ways to modify the human sources of climate change (Clayton et al., 2016).

Psychological Effects of Climate Change

It's a national security issue, say some: Terrorist bombs and climate change are both weapons of mass destruction. "If we learned that al Qaeda was secretly developing a new terrorist technique that could disrupt water supplies around the globe, force tens of millions from their homes, and potentially endanger our entire planet, we would be aroused into a frenzy and deploy every possible asset to neutralize the threat," observed essayist Nicholas Kristof (2007). "Yet that is precisely the threat that we're creating ourselves, with our greenhouse gases." Consider the human consequences.

DISPLACEMENT AND TRAUMA

If temperatures increase by the expected 2° to 4° Celsius (3.5° to 7° Fahrenheit) this century, the resulting changes in water availability, agriculture, disaster risk, and sea level will necessitate massive resettlement (de Sherbinin et al., 2011). When drought or floods force people to leave their land, shelter, and work, as when sub-Saharan African farming and grazing lands become desert, the frequent result is increased poverty and hunger, earlier death, and loss of cultural identity. If an extreme weather event or climate change disrupted your ties to a place and its people, you could expect to feel grief, anxiety, and a sense of loss (Doherty & Clayton, 2011; Henderson & Mulder, 2015; Hrabok et al., 2020). In a global survey 10,000 teens and young adults, half said that their anxiety around climate change negatively impacted their daily life (Hickman et al., 2021). For social and mental health, climate matters.

CLIMATE AND CONFLICT

Got war? Blame the climate. Such is often the case. Many human maladies – from economic downturns to wars – have been traced to climate fluctuations (Zhang et al., 2011). When the climate changes, agriculture often suffers, leading to increased famine, epidemics, and overall misery. Poorer countries, with fewer resources, are especially vulnerable (Fischer & Van de Vliert, 2011). And when miserable, people become more prone to anger with their governments and with one another, leading to war. For social stability, climate matters.

One analysis of 60 quantitative studies revealed conflict spikes throughout history and across the globe in response to climate events. The conclusion: Higher temperatures and rainfall extremes, such as drought and flood, predicted increased domestic violence, ethnic aggression, land invasions, and civil conflicts (Hsiang et al., 2013). The researchers project that a 2° Celsius temperature rise – as is predicted by 2040 – could increase intergroup conflicts by more than 50% (see **Figure 4**).

Studies both in the laboratory and in everyday life reveal that heat also amplifies short-term aggression. On hot days, neighborhood violence becomes more frequent. Violence is also more common in hotter seasons of the year, hotter summers, hotter years, hotter cities, hotter days, and hotter regions (Anderson & Delisi, 2011; Kim et al., 2023; Rinderu et al., 2018). One study estimated that about 7% of all shootings in U.S. cities were due to higher-than-normal temperatures (Lyons et al., 2022). Craig Anderson and Matt Delisi (2011) project that if a 4° Fahrenheit (>2°C) warming occurs, the United States will suffer at least 50,000 more serious assaults each year.

Is the weather getting weirder? No single weather event can be attributed to climate change. But climate scientists warn that global warming is producing increasing extreme weather events and increased human displacement, such as the flooding in the Northeast U.S. in 2023.
U.S. Air National Guard photo by Senior Master Sgt. Michael Davis/ APFootage/Alamy Stock Photo

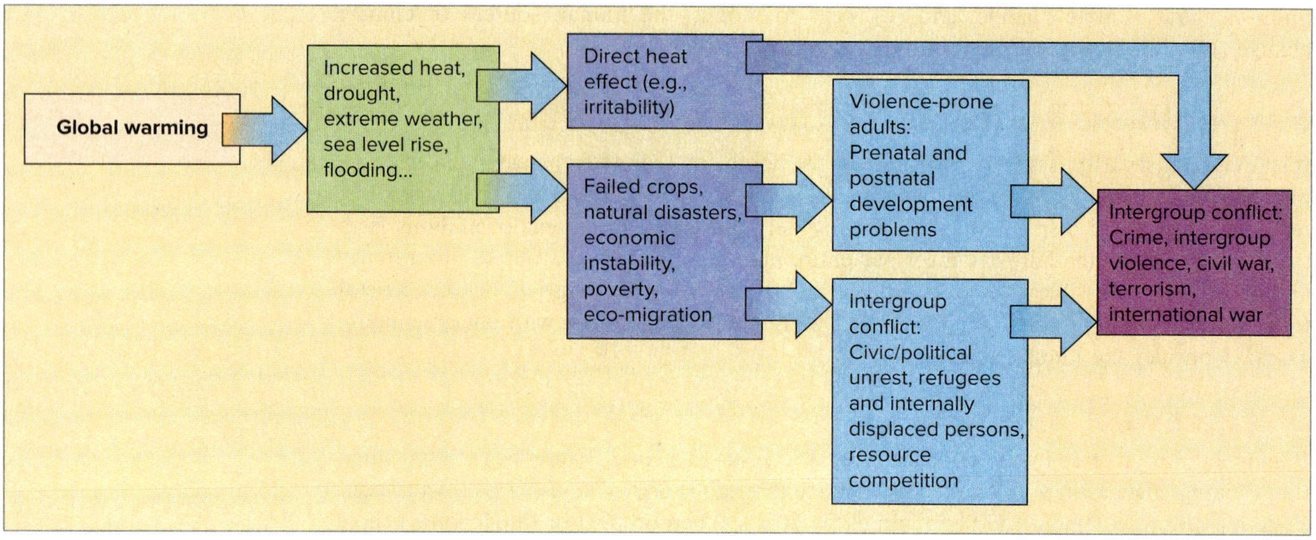

FIGURE 4

Three Routes via Which Climate Change May Increase Violence and Conflict

Source: Miles-Novelo & Anderson, 2018.

Public Opinion about Climate Change

Is the Earth getting hotter? Are humans responsible? Will it matter to our grandchildren? Yes, yes, and yes, say climate scientists – 97% of whom agree, in repeated surveys, that climate change is occurring and is human caused (Cook, 2016). The findings of 88,125 climate science publications are even more definitive: 99% find evidence of climate change (Lynas et al., 2021). As one report in *Science* explained, "Almost all climate scientists are of one mind about the threat of global warming: It's real, it's dangerous, and the world needs to take action immediately" (Kerr, 2009).

Yet many folks don't know about that scientific consensus. Only 65% of Americans in 2019 agreed that "most scientists believe global warming is occurring" (Saad, 2019). Only about a third of Americans think climate scientists understand "very well" whether climate change is occurring, and only a fourth say climate scientists understand the causes of climate change very well (Pasquini & Kennedy, 2023). The majority of Americans (54%) are "extremely" or "very" certain that climate change is occurring (Schwartz, 2020), but that is still considerably less than the consensus of climate scientists.

The gulf between the scientific and U.S. public understandings of climate change intrigues social psychologists. Why the gap? Why is global warming not a hotter topic? And what might be done to align scientific and public understandings?

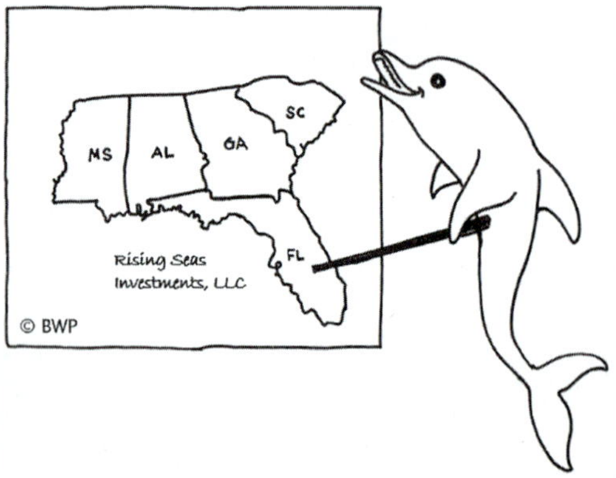

"Well, yes, Jason, there's always a very small risk it will still be dry land in 100 years, but if we're going to base our long term investments on the data, it's hard to find a safer bet for ocean growth."

PERSONAL EXPERIENCE AND THE AVAILABILITY HEURISTIC

By now, it's a familiar lesson: Vivid and recent experiences often overwhelm abstract statistics. Despite knowing the statistical rarity of shark attacks and plane crashes, vivid images of such – being readily available in memory – often hijack our emotions and distort our judgments. We make our intuitive judgments under the influence of the *availability heuristic,* and thus we often focus on the wrong things. If an airline misplaces our bag, we likely will ignore data on the airline's overall lost-bag rate and belittle the airline. Our ancient brain comes designed to attend to the immediate situation, not out-of-sight data and beyond-the-horizon dangers (Gifford, 2011). Experience overrides analysis. The dangers of increases in global temperatures seem abstract compared to our daily experience of the weather.

For this reason, people often confuse temporary local weather with long-term global climate change. One climate skeptic declared a record East Coast blizzard "a coup de grace" for global warming – meaning he thought one blizzard meant global warming wasn't really occurring (Breckler, 2010). He was not alone: In a May 2011 survey, 47% of Americans agreed that "The record snowstorms this winter in the eastern United States make me question whether global warming is occurring." But then after the ensuing blistering summer, 67% of Americans agreed that global warming worsened the "record high summer temperatures in the U.S. in 2011" (Leiserowitz et al, 2011).

In 2018, 74% of Americans said that the last 5 years' extreme weather – floods, blistering heat, and wildfires – influenced their climate change opinions (Leiserowitz et al., 2018). After their vivid experiences with Hurricane Irene, New Jersey residents became more likely to agree with statements such as, "When humans interfere with nature it often produces disastrous consequences" (Rudman et al., 2013). As in so many life realms, our local and temporary experience distorts our global, long-term judgments. But as you've learned in this book, representative data – like the data showing increasing global temperatures – are more accurate than our own individual and sometimes distorted perceptions.

"Global warming isn't real because I was cold today! Also great news: world hunger is over because I just ate."

—Stephen Colbert on Twitter, November 18, 2014

PERSUASION

Today's local weather biases people's understanding of tomorrow's global warming. But that only scratches the surface of public skepticism about climate change. Resistance to climate science also stems from simple *misinformation* and from *motivated reasoning.*

MISINFORMATION People may discount climate threat because they are natural optimists or because they misinterpret uncertainty about the *extent* of temperature and sea-level rise as uncertainty about the *fact* of climate change (Gifford, 2011). Especially in the United States, some groups seek to sow doubt about taking action around climate change by discrediting scientists and emphasizing the short-term costs of action rather than the long-term costs of inaction (CRED, 2014). People who doubt other scientific findings also tend to doubt the climate science consensus (Lewandowsky et al., 2013). (For a compelling and graphic 7-minute synopsis of "Why People Don't Believe in Climate Change," see tinyurl.com/ClimateBeliefs.) One set of researchers developed a game called "Cranky Uncle" to help people learn about climate change by refuting common misunderstandings (Cook et al., 2023).

Journalistic "false balance" can further distort public perceptions (Koehler, 2016). In one study, citizens were told (correctly) that expert economists agree by nearly a 50-to-1 margin that a carbon tax would control CO_2 emissions less expensively than would an automotive fuel economy standard. But if also given an argument from "both sides," people then believed that expert conclusions were more ambiguous (Imundo & Rapp, 2021). Imagine if people heard that medical experts agree that vaccines do not cause autism but then also read arguments from both pro- and antivaccine people. The "false balance" – there is no evidence that vaccines cause autism – will likely weaken their perception of the medical consensus.

MOTIVATED REASONING Our desire to avoid negative emotions such as fear may motivate denial of climate threat. Moreover, we have a natural tendency to believe in and justify the way things are. We like our habitual ways of traveling, eating, and heating and cooling our spaces. When comfortable, we're motivated not to change what's familiar (Feygina et al., 2010; Kahan, 2014). Thus, if a solution to a climate problem is costly, people will tend to deny the problem itself (Campbell & Kay, 2014). And our natural confirmation bias may lead us to attend more to data that confirm our preexisting views.

So, to overcome misinformation, motivated reasoning, and the human tendency to consider personal experience before analysis, how might climate educators apply social psychology's principles?

- *Connect the message to the audience's values.* In the United States, 85% of those on the political left, but only 22% on the right, consider global climate change a major threat (Poushter et al., 2022). So how might one persuade each group? A left-leaning audience might respond more to information about climate effects on the world's impoverished. A right-leaning audience might respond more to information

Vivid images, such as polar bears on melting ice, often make a bigger impression than statistics.
FloridaStock/Shutterstock

about clean energy boosting national security by diminishing dependence on foreign energy, and conserving the planet for our grandchildren (PE, 2024). Although messages about the consensus around climate change can lead some on the right to push back, the messages still increased conservatives' acknowledgment of climate change (Rode et al., 2022).

- *Use credible communicators.* People are more open to messengers whose identities and affiliations are like their own – someone they trust and respect (CRED, 2014). For example, Mothers Against Drunk Driving succeeds by having mothers communicate with other mothers. For climate change, it would likely be best to use credible communicators similar in social background or education to the audience they are trying to reach.
- *Think local.* Although climate change is a global issue, people respond more to threats that are near in place or time. In Australia, Texas, or California, the prospects of worsening drought or wildfires may awaken concern. In Florida or the Netherlands, rising seas will seem more pertinent.
- *Make communications vivid and memorable.* Mindful of the availability heuristic, and of the effectiveness of cigarette warnings with graphic photos, make messages vivid. Rather than warn of "future climate change," explain that "the Earth has a fever."
- *Use effective language* (Bertolotti & Catellani, 2014). Rather than describe "a greenhouse effect," describe "a heat-trapping blanket." Instead of a "theory" of climate change, offer "an understanding of how this works" (CRED, 2014). Instead of proposing a politically unpopular "carbon tax," suggest "carbon offsets" (Cordes et al., 2024). Liken the risk management to people's own decisions – buying fire insurance on their dwelling and liability insurance on their driving, and putting on seat belts – to spare themselves worst-case outcomes.
- *Frame energy savings in attention-getting ways.* An information sheet about energy savings might use longer time periods. Instead of saying, "This Energy Star refrigerator will save you $120 a year on your electric bills," say, "It will save you $2,400 in wasted energy bills over the next 20 years" (Hofmeister, 2010).
- *Nudge people by using "green defaults."* Set printers to double-sided printing unless single-sided is chosen, and have building lights turn off when motion sensors do not detect a human presence (Byerly et al., 2018; Scott et al., 2015).

SUMMING UP: Psychology and Climate Change

- Scientists report that exploding population and increasing consumption and greenhouse gas emissions have together exceeded the Earth's carrying capacity. We now are seeing the predicted global warming, melting polar ice, rising seas, and more extreme weather.
- Expected social consequences of climate change include human displacement, trauma, and conflict stemming from competition over scarce resources.
- Social psychologists are also exploring the gap between scientific and public understandings of climate change. And they are suggesting ways to educate and persuade the public to support a sustainable future.

ENABLING SUSTAINABLE LIVING

Identify new technologies and strategies for reducing consumption that together may enable sustainable living.

What shall we do? Eat, drink, and be merry, for tomorrow is doom? Behave as do so many in prisoners' dilemma games, by pursuing self-interest to our collective detriment? ("Heck, on a global scale, my consumption is teeny; it makes my life comfortable and costs the world practically nothing.") Wring our hands, dreading that fertility plus prosperity equals calamity, and vow never to bring children into a doomed world?

Those more optimistic about the future see two routes to environmentally sustainable lifestyles: (a) increasing technological efficiency and agricultural productivity, and (b) moderating consumption and population.

"No one made a greater mistake than he who did nothing because he could only do a little."

—English cleric Sydney Smith, "*Elementary Sketches of Moral Philosophy*," 1850

New Technologies

With the world's population expected to grow another 2.5 billion by 2050 – and with more and more people wanting to drive, eat, and live like North Americans – one of the world's great challenges is how to power our human future without further polluting and warming it.

One component in a sustainable future is improved technologies. We have not only replaced incandescent bulbs with LED lights but also replaced printed letters and catalogs with e-mail and e-commerce, and coal burning with solar panels and wind farms. We've also replaced commuter miles with working remotely – a practice that became even more popular after 2020. Commuting every weekday may never again return to 2019 levels.

Today's middle-aged adults drive cars that get twice the mileage and produce a twentieth of the pollution of the ones they drove as teenagers, and new hybrid and battery-powered cars offer even greater efficiency.

New technology may also help combat climate change, including more powerful solar panels, longer-lasting batteries, carbon capture, remote sensing of greenhouse gas emissions, and meat grown in laboratories instead of from animals (McLellan, 2023; Muhumuza, 2022).

Capturing light in a bottle. Illac Diaz inspects a new solar light bulb sealed into the corrugated roof of a Manila apartment.
JAY DIRECTO/AFP/Getty Images

Reducing Consumption

The second component of a sustainable future is controlling consumption. As today's poorer countries develop, their consumption will increase. As it does, developed countries must consume less.

Carpooling seems more attractive if it means bypassing traffic in congested urban areas such as Los Angeles.
P_Wei/iStock/Getty Images Plus/Getty Images

With 8 billion people on the planet, humans have already overshot the Earth's carrying capacity, so consumption must become more sustainable. With our material appetites swelling – as more people seek personal computers, refrigeration, air-conditioning, jet travel – what can be done to moderate consumption by those who can afford to overconsume?

INCENTIVES

One way is through public policies that harness the motivating power of incentives (Swim et al., 2014; White et al., 2019). As a general rule, we do less of what is taxed and more of what is rewarded. Tax credits for solar panels convince many who would otherwise not install them. On jammed highways, high-occupancy vehicle lanes reward carpooling and penalize driving solo. Europe leads the way in incentivizing mass transit and bicycle use over personal vehicle use. In addition to the small vehicles incentivized by high fuel taxes, cities such as Vienna, Munich, Zurich, and Copenhagen have closed many city center streets to car traffic. London, Stockholm, Singapore, and Milan drivers pay congestion fees when entering the heart of the city. Amsterdam is a bicycle haven. Dozens of German cities have "environmental zones" where only low CO_2 cars may enter (Rosenthal, 2011).

Another idea is carbon taxes, which levy an extra fee on energy sources such as airplane fuel and gas for cars. Some free-market proponents object to carbon taxes because they are taxes. Others respond that carbon taxes are simply payment for external damage to today's health and tomorrow's environment, and they can be offset by corresponding reductions of other taxes (Roser, 2021). If not today's CO_2 emitters, who should pay for the cost of tomorrow's more threatening floods, tornadoes, hurricanes, droughts, and sea rise? Without carbon taxes, people in developing nations, who have the smallest emissions, will likely suffer the greatest consequences from climate change. "Markets are truly free only when everyone pays the full price for his or her actions," contends Environmental Defense Fund economist Gernot Wagner (2011). "Anything else is socialism." (See "The Inside Story: Janet Swim on Psychology's Response to Climate Change.")

FEEDBACK AND SOCIAL NORMS

Another way to encourage greener homes and businesses is to harness the power of immediate feedback to the consumer by installing "smart meters" that provide a continuous readout of electricity use and its cost. Turn off a computer monitor or the lights in an empty room, and the meter displays the decreased wattage. Turn on the air-conditioning, and you immediately know the usage and cost. When the electric company sticks a "smiley" or "frowny" face on home energy bills when the consumer's energy use is less or more than the neighborhood average – thus informing people of the social norm – energy use is reduced (Karlin et al., 2015). Applying such social psychological findings, one company now gives energy reports with personalized, neighborhood-comparing feedback to more than 60 million households worldwide (Schultz et al., 2018).

Experiments can also manipulate social norms and study the results. In one, Gregg Sparkman and Gregory Walton (2017) placed signs communicating an improving social norm ("Stanford Residents Are Changing: Now Most Use Full Loads!") on the washing machines of one building in a graduate student housing complex. Compared to the residents of another building with no signs on the washing machines, those who saw the social-norm signs used 28% less water. "If you start seeing other people change, it can give you a reason to question psychological barriers to change," noted Sparkman (Armstrong, 2019). In a large

THE inside STORY

Janet Swim on Psychology's Response to Climate Change

While watching Al Gore's climate change movie, I had an epiphany. As I reflected on its message — that we must take action to avert impending climate change — I realized that psychology could help explain people's denial of climate change and could help motivate action. I then led an American Psychological Association task force that connected psychological research to understanding the human causes and responses to climate change. I was stunned by the attention given to our report by the national press, government officials, and scholars worldwide.

What I learned refocused my career, with support from like-minded psychologists and fellow Pennsylvania State University researchers who study climate change and how we might avert or adapt to it. Over the last decade, we have observed increased anxiety, anger, and talking about climate change, especially among younger people. Our interdisciplinary team has also helped zoo and aquarium educators to communicate effectively about climate science.

Janet K. Swim
Pennsylvania State University
Courtesy of Janet Swim

meta-analysis of climate-change interventions, those focusing on social comparisons — seeing that others were recycling or turning lights off — changed their behavior the most (Bergquist et al., 2023). Social-norm interventions generally work best when they emphasize that an increasing number of people are engaging in the behavior, that those people are similar to them, and are specific about what actions people need to take (Constantino et al., 2022).

IDENTITY

In one survey, the top reason people gave for buying a hybrid car was that it "makes a statement about me" (Clayton & Myers, 2009, p. 9). Indeed, argued Tom Crompton and Tim Kasser (2010), our sense of who we are — our identity — has profound implications for our climate-related behaviors. Does our social identity, the ingroup that defines our circle of concern, include only those around us now? Or does it encompass vulnerable people in places unseen, our descendants and others in the future, and even the creatures in the planet's natural environment?

Support for new energy policies will require a shift in public consciousness on the scale of the 1960s civil rights movement and the 1970s women's movement. Yale University environmental science dean James Gustave Speth (2008, 2012) has called for an enlarged identity — a "new consciousness" — in which people

- see humanity as part of nature;
- see nature as having intrinsic value that we must steward;
- value the future and its inhabitants as well as our present;
- appreciate our human interdependence, by thinking "we" and not just "me";
- define quality of life in relational and spiritual rather than materialistic terms;
- value equity, justice, and the human community.

As climate change affects the environment, we can consider that the future of humans and the future of the planet go hand in hand.
xfilephotos/Shutterstock

One way to do this is by tying these collective goals to more personal goals. If you have the personal goal of saving money, you might be able to connect that goal to the larger cause of saving the environment — by, say, not wasting food and driving less. Across three studies,

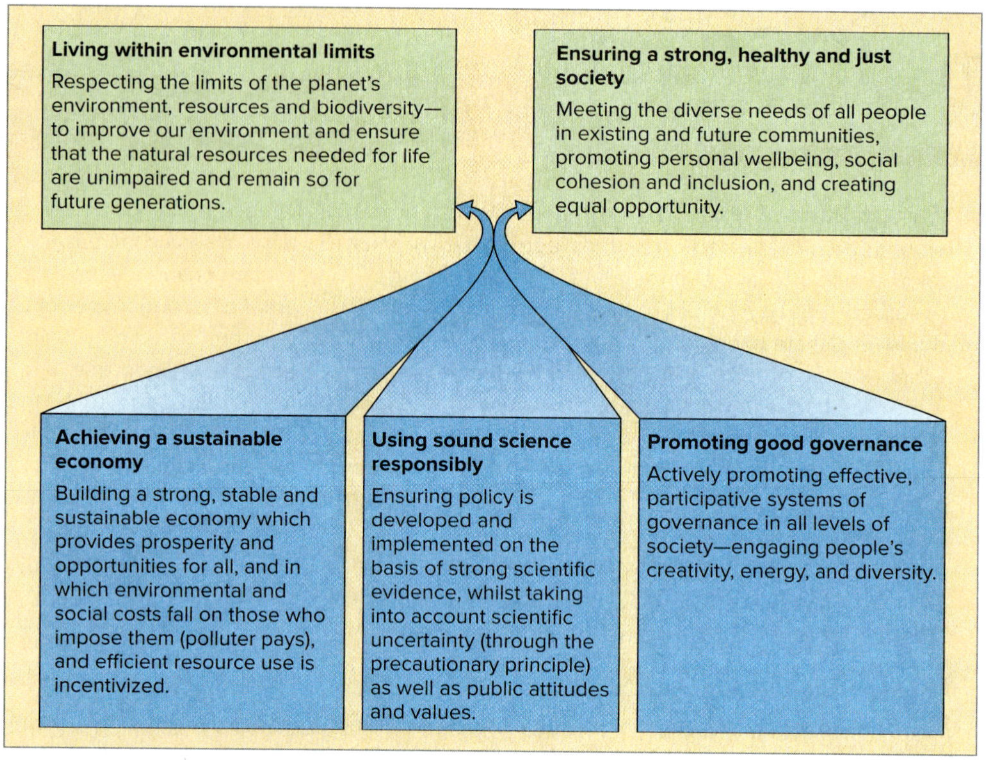

FIGURE 5

"Five Principles of Sustainable Development" in the U.K. Government's Framework for Sustainable Development

The British government defines sustainable development as development that meets present needs without compromising future generations' abilities to meet their needs. "We want to live within environmental limits and achieve a just society, and we will do so by means of sustainable economy, good governance, and sound science." Social psychology's contribution will be to help influence behaviors that enable people to live within environmental limits and to enjoy personal and social well-being.

Source: Five principles of sustainable development. Sustainable Development Commission. www.sd-commission.org.uk

people who were able to make these connections between their individual desires and the greater good increased their intentions to engage in sustainable behaviors (Unsworth & McNeill, 2017). Another way is by promoting discussion of climate change among family and friend groups. When people learn that their family and friends care about climate change, even those more politically opposed to the idea are more convinced (Goldberg et al., 2020).

Is there any hope that human priorities might shift from accumulating money to finding meaning and from aggressive consumption to nurturing connections? The British government's plan for achieving sustainable development includes an emphasis on promoting personal well-being and social health (**Figure 5**).

Social psychology can help by suggesting ways to reduce consumption and exploring why materialism does not routinely lead to happiness. We consider these topics next.

SUMMING UP: Enabling Sustainable Living

- Humanity can prepare for a sustainable future by increasing technological efficiency.
- We can also create incentives, give feedback, and promote identities that will support more sustainable consumption. Rapid cultural change has happened in the past 50 years, and there is hope that in response to the global crisis, it can happen again.

THE SOCIAL PSYCHOLOGY OF MATERIALISM AND WEALTH

Explain social psychology's contribution to our understanding of materialism.

Life for most people in Western countries is good. Today the average North American and Western European enjoys luxuries unknown even to royalty in centuries past: hot showers, flush toilets, central air-conditioning, microwave ovens, jet travel, fresh fruit even in the winter, big-screen digital television, email, smartphones, and Post-it notes. But does money – and its associated luxuries – necessarily *buy* happiness? Few of us would answer yes. But ask a different question – "Would a *little* more money make you a *little* happier?" – and most of us will say yes. What does that mean for the environment?

Increased Materialism

Although the Earth asks that we live more lightly upon it, materialism – a focus on money and possessions – undermines proenvironmental attitudes (Hurst et al., 2013; Kasser, 2016, 2018). Materialism also erodes empathy and inclines people to treat others as objects (Wang & Krumhuber, 2017).

Nevertheless, materialism has surged, most clearly in the United States. Think of it as today's American dream: life, liberty, and the purchase of happiness. Evidence of rising materialism comes from the Higher Education Research Institute annual survey of nearly a quarter-million entering collegians. The proportion considering it "very important or essential" that they become "very well-off financially" rose from 39% in 1970 to 84% in 2019 (**Figure 6**). Those proportions virtually flip-flopped with those who considered it very important to "develop a meaningful philosophy of life." Materialism was up, spirituality down.

What a change in values! Among 19 listed objectives, Americans entering college in recent years have ranked becoming "very well-off financially" number 1. That outranks not

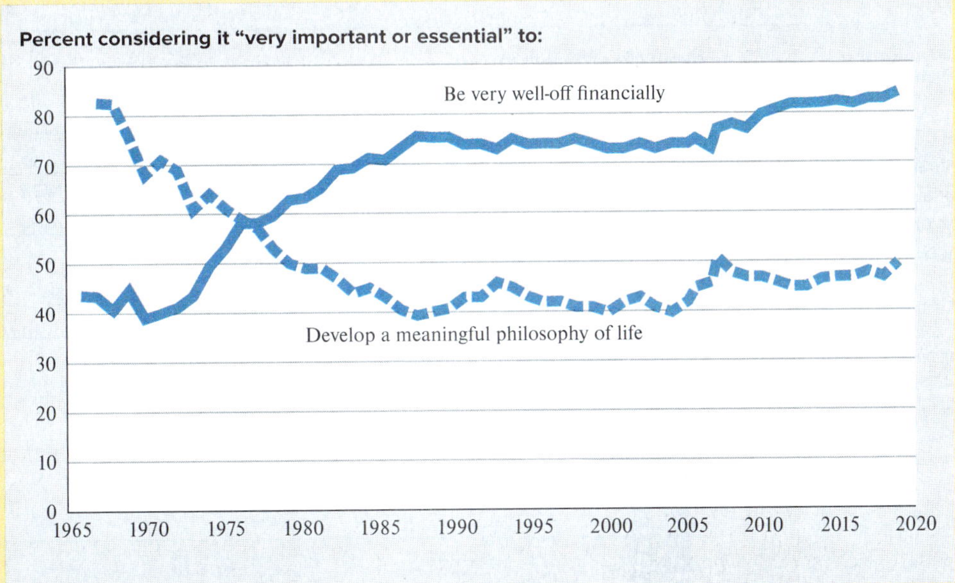

FIGURE 6

Values of U.S. College Students, 1966–2019

Changing materialism, from annual surveys of 13 million students

Source: Stolzenberg et al., 2020.

only developing a life philosophy but also "becoming an authority in my own field," "helping others in difficulty," and "raising a family." This change in values may be partially due to increases in income inequality, leading to the idea that it's necessary to have much more to be successful.

In addition, the desire for material goods has increased: Compared to those in the 1970s, more recent high school students were more likely to believe it was important to own one's own home and have a new car every 2 to 3 years (Twenge & Kasser, 2013; Twenge, 2023). Although younger adults are more concerned than older adults about climate change, many wear "fast fashion" clothing only a few times, contributing to the global burden of waste (Swim et al., 2022; Willett et al., 2022).

Wealth and Well-Being

Does unsustainable consumption indeed enable "the good life"? Does being well-off enable – or at least correlate with – psychological well-being? Would people be happier if they could exchange a simple lifestyle for one with palatial surroundings, ski vacations in the Alps, private housekeepers, and executive-class travel? Social-psychological theory and evidence offer some answers.

ARE WEALTHY COUNTRIES HAPPIER?

We can observe the traffic between wealth and well-being by asking, first, if rich nations are happier places. There is, indeed, some correlation between national wealth and well-being (measured as self-reported happiness and life satisfaction). The Scandinavians have been mostly prosperous and satisfied; the Bulgarians, neither (Diener & Tay, 2015; **Figure 7**). People in richer countries and postal-code regions also live longer (Payne, 2017). But after nations reach above $20,000 GDP per person, higher levels of national wealth are not predictive of increased life satisfaction.

ARE WEALTHIER INDIVIDUALS HAPPIER?

We can ask, second, whether within any given nation, rich people are happier. Are people who drive their BMWs to work happier than those who take the bus?

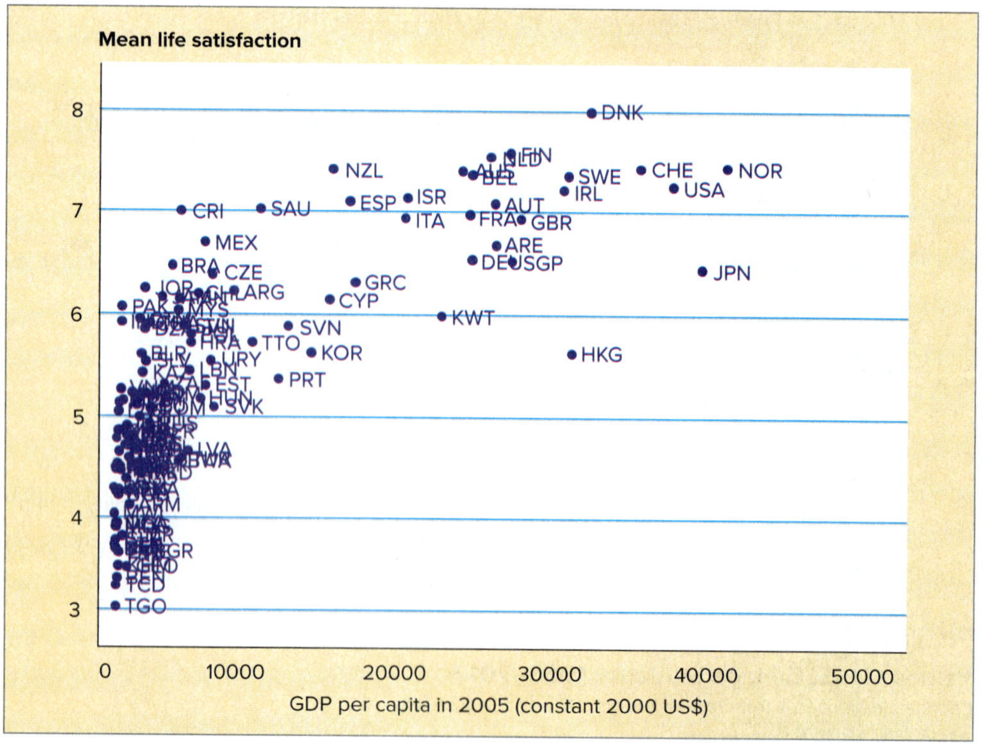

FIGURE 7

National Wealth and Well-Being

Life satisfaction (on a 0 to 10 scale) across 132 countries, as a function of national wealth (2005 gross domestic product [GDP], adjusted to the 2000 U.S. dollar value).

Source: Di Tella & MacCulloch, 2010. (Technical note: Some economists prefer to display income on a log scale, which then indicates a more linear relationship between national income and happiness.)

In developing countries – where low income threatens basic needs – being relatively well-off does predict greater well-being (Howell & Howell, 2008). In affluent countries, where most can afford life's necessities, affluence (and financial satisfaction) still matters – partly because people with more money perceive more control over their lives (Johnson & Krueger, 2006; Tan et al., 2020).

Among U.S. residents, more income means more happiness (Killingsworth, 2021; Killingsworth et al., 2022; Twenge & Cooper, 2020). It helps to comfortably afford life's necessities. But, beyond about $100,000 a year, there's a diminished rate of increased happiness as income rises from high to super high (Jebb et al., 2018). Once a millionaire, accumulating more millions provides little additional boost to happiness (Donnelly et al., 2018).

Part of the happiness-income correlation is attributable to happier (and more optimistic and outgoing) people being more likely to graduate from college, get hired and promoted, and have higher incomes (De Neve & Oswald, 2012). Moreover, having one's psychological needs met (for respect, relationship, and empowerment) predicts positive, happy feelings better than does income (Fischer & Boer, 2011; Ng & Diener, 2014; Tay & Diener, 2011).

DOES ECONOMIC GROWTH INCREASE HAPPINESS?

We can ask, third, whether, over time, a culture's happiness rises with its affluence. Does our collective well-being float upward with a rising economic tide?

In 1957, as economist John Kenneth Galbraith was describing the United States as *The Affluent Society,* Americans' per-person income was (in 2024 dollars) $17,000. Today, as **Figure 8** indicates, the United States is a triply affluent society. With increasing inequality, this rising tide has lifted the yachts faster than the dinghies. Yet, most boats have risen. With double the spending power, thanks partly to the surge in married women's employment, we now own twice as many cars per person, eat out twice as often, and are supported by a whole new world of technology.

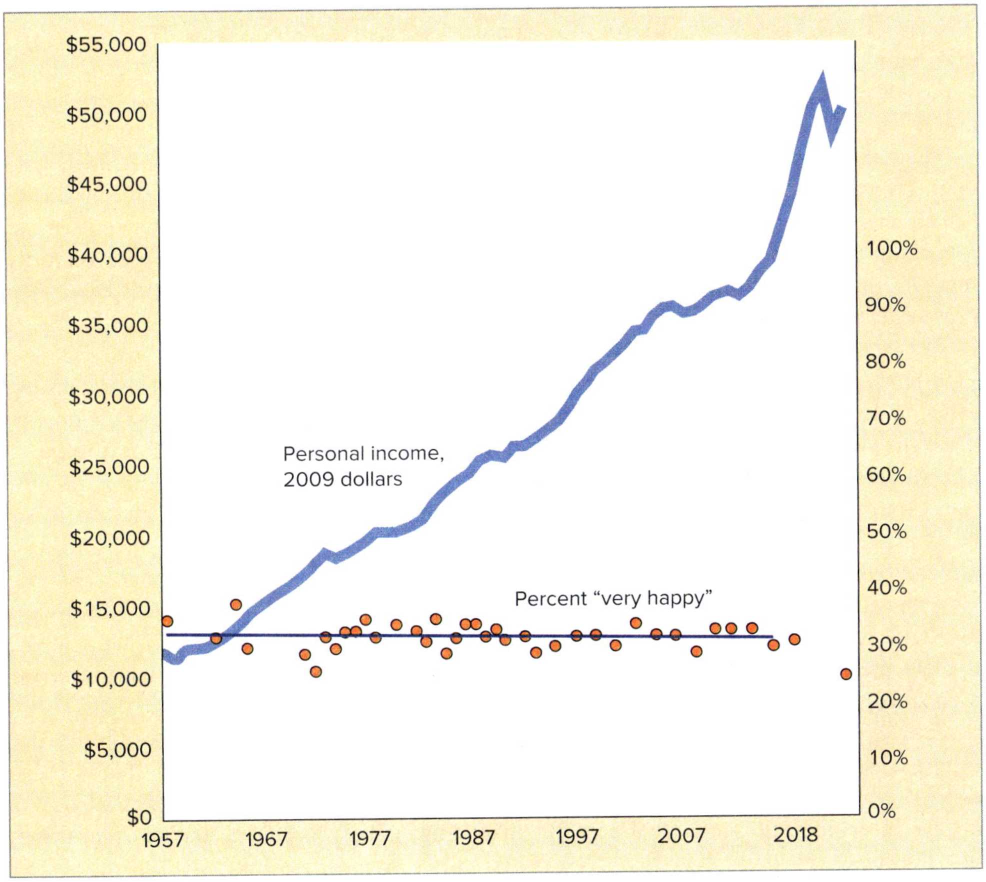

FIGURE 8

Has Economic Growth Advanced Human Morale?

While inflation-adjusted income has risen, self-reported happiness has not.

Sources: Happiness data from General Social Surveys, National Opinion Research Center, University of Chicago (and Niemi et al., 1989 for pre-1972 data). Income data from Bureau of the Census (1975) and U.S. Bureau of Economic Analysis (2024).

People are shopping for more and more valuable goods in China. Although living standards have risen, life satisfaction has not.
Sorbis/Shutterstock

So, believing that it's "very important" to "be very well-off financially" and having become better off financially, are today's Americans happier? Are they happier than previous generations were?

They are not. From 1957 to 2022, the number of adult Americans who said they were "very happy" declined from 35% to 25% (Niemi et al., 1989; Twenge et al., 2016; Twenge, 2023). Twice as rich and less happy. The same has been true of many other countries as well (Easterlin et al., 2010). After a decade of extraordinary economic growth in China – from few owning a phone and only 40% owning a color television to most people now having such things – Gallup surveys revealed a *decreasing* proportion of Chinese satisfied "with the way things are going in your life today" (Burkholder, 2005; Davey & Rato, 2012; Easterlin et al., 2012).

The findings are startling because they challenge modern materialism: *Economic growth has provided no apparent boost to human morale.* We excel at making a living but often fail at making a life. We celebrate our prosperity but yearn for purpose. We cherish our freedoms but long for connection.

Materialism Fails to Satisfy

It is striking that economic growth in affluent countries has failed to increase life satisfaction and happiness. It is further striking that individuals who strive the most for wealth tend to be less happy and less satisfied with life (Dittmar et al., 2014). This materialism-dissatisfaction correlation "comes through very strongly in every culture I've looked at," reported Richard Ryan (1999).

Seek *extrinsic* goals – wealth, beauty, popularity, prestige, or anything else centered on external rewards or approval – and you may experience anxiety, depression, and psychosomatic ills (Eckersley, 2005; Sheldon et al., 2004). Focusing on money makes people less attuned to others, less caring, and less warm (Vohs, 2015).

Those who instead strive for *intrinsic* goals such as "intimacy, personal growth, and contribution to the community" experience a higher quality of life, concluded Tim Kasser (2000, 2002). Intrinsic values, Kasser (2011, 2016) added, promote personal and social well-being and help immunize people against materialistic values. Those focused on close relationships, meaningful work, and concern for others enjoy inherent rewards that often prove elusive to those more focused on things or on their status and image.

Pause a moment and think: What was the most personally satisfying event that you experienced in the last month? Kennon Sheldon and his colleagues (2001) put that question (and similar questions about the last week and semester) to samples of university students. Then they asked them to rate how well 10 different needs were met by the satisfying event. The students rated self-esteem, relatedness (feeling connected with others), and autonomy (feeling in control) as the emotional needs that most strongly accompanied the satisfying event. At the bottom of the list of factors predicting satisfaction were money and luxury.

Materialists tend to report a relatively large gap between what they want and what they have and to enjoy fewer close, fulfilling relationships. Wealthier people and world travelers also tend to savor life's simpler pleasures less (Quoidbach et al., 2010, 2015). Next to the opulent pleasures enabled by wealth, simple pleasures – sipping tea with a friend, savoring a chocolate, or finishing a project – may pale.

"Why do you spend your money for that which is not bread, and your labor for that which does not satisfy?"

—Isaiah 55:2

People focused on extrinsic and material goals also "focus less on caring for the Earth," reported Kasser (2011). "As materialistic values go up, concern for nature tends to go down. . . . When people strongly endorse money, image, and status, they are less likely to engage in ecologically beneficial activities like riding bikes, recycling, and re-using things in new ways."

But why do yesterday's luxuries, such as air-conditioning, so quickly become today's requirements? Two principles drive this psychology of consumption: our ability to adapt and our need to compare.

OUR HUMAN CAPACITY FOR ADAPTATION

The **adaptation-level phenomenon** is our tendency to judge our experience (for example, of sounds, temperatures, or income) relative to a neutral level defined by our prior experience. We adjust our neutral levels – the points at which sounds seem neither loud nor soft, temperatures neither hot nor cold, events neither pleasant nor unpleasant – on the basis of our experience. We then notice and react to up or down changes from those levels.

adaptation-level phenomenon
The tendency to adapt to a given level of stimulation and thus to notice and react to changes from that level.

Thus, as our achievements rise above past levels, we feel successful and satisfied. As our social prestige, income, or technology improves, we feel pleasure. Before long, however, we adapt. What once felt good comes to register as neutral, and what formerly was neutral now feels like deprivation.

Would it ever, then, be possible to create a social paradise? Donald Campbell (1975b) answered no: If you woke up tomorrow to your utopia – perhaps a world with no bills, no ills, someone who loves you unreservedly – you would feel euphoric, for a time. Yet before long, you would recalibrate your adaptation level and again sometimes feel gratified (when achievements surpass expectations), sometimes feel deprived (when they fall below), and sometimes feel neutral.

"From time to time in the years to come, I hope you will be treated unfairly, so that you will come to know the value of justice. I hope that you will suffer betrayal because that will teach you the importance of loyalty. Sorry to say, but I hope you will be lonely from time to time so that you don't take friends for granted . . . and I hope you will have just enough pain to learn compassion."

—U.S. Supreme Court Chief Justice John Roberts, address to his son's ninth-grade graduating class, 2017

To be sure, adaptation to some events, such as the death of a spouse, may be incomplete, as the sense of loss lingers (Diener et al., 2006). Yet we generally underestimate our adaptive capacity. People have difficulty predicting the intensity and duration of their future positive and negative emotions (Wilson & Gilbert, 2003; **Figure 9**). The anguish of those paralyzed by spinal cord injuries returns to a near-normal mix of joy with occasional sadness or frustration after a time (Boyce & Wood, 2011; Hall et al., 1999). The elation from getting what we want – riches, top exam scores, our national team winning the World Cup – evaporates more rapidly than we expect.

We also sometimes "miswant." When first-year university students predicted their satisfaction with various housing possibilities shortly before entering their school's housing lottery, they focused on physical features. "I'll be happiest in a beautiful and well-located dorm," many students seemed to think. But they were wrong. When contacted a year later, it was the social features, such as a sense of community, that predicted happiness, reported Elizabeth Dunn and her colleagues (2003).

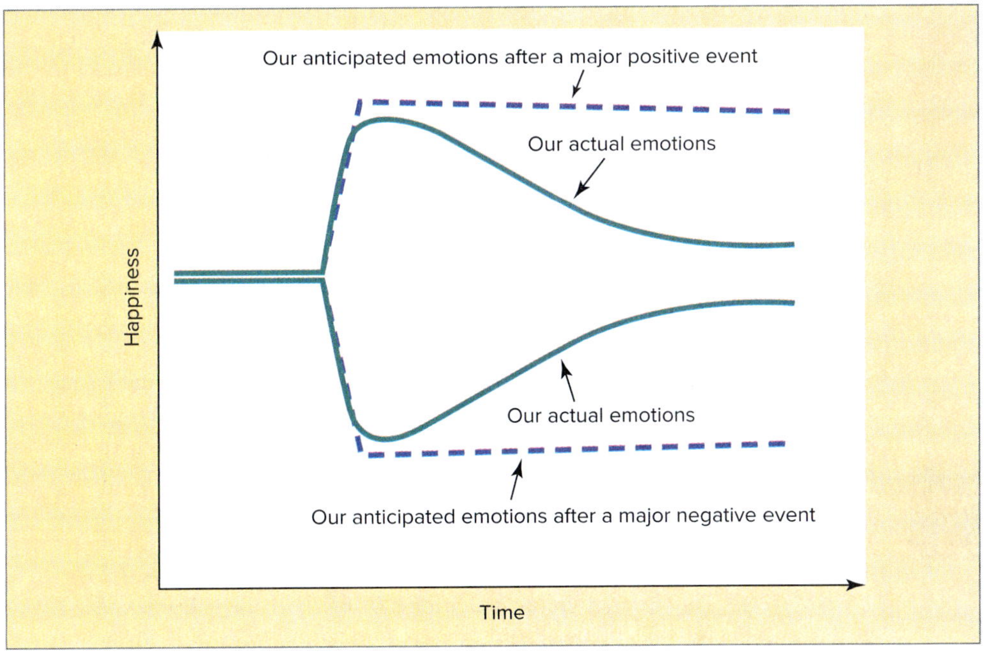

FIGURE 9
The Impact Bias
People generally overestimate the enduring impact of significant positive and negative life events.
Source: Figure inspired by de Botton, 2004.

The best things in life are not things. Research indicates that happiness grows more from spending on experiences than on stuff — especially when spent on anticipated then recollected experiences that foster relationships and identity, such as my hiking Scotland's West Highland Way with two of my children [DM] or spending time at the beach with mine [JT]. (top): Dave Myers; (bottom): Courtesy of Jean Twenge and Pam Davis

Other surveys and experiments have repeatedly confirmed that positive experiences leave us happier, especially experiences that build relationships, foster meaning, and identity, and are not deflated by comparisons with what others have (Dunn & Norton, 2013; Gilovich & Kumar, 2015; Pchelin & Howell, 2014). More than our material purchases, experiences give us something to talk about with others (Kumar & Gilovich, 2015). Even buying *time* (a cab ride, paying someone to run an errand, using a laundry service) brings more happiness than material purchases (Whillans et al., 2017). The best things in life are not things.

OUR WANTING TO COMPARE

social comparison
Evaluating one's opinions and abilities by comparing oneself with others.

Much of life revolves around **social comparison,** a point made by the old joke about two hikers who come upon a hungry bear. One reaches into his backpack and pulls out a pair of sneakers. "Why bother putting those on?" asks the other. "You can't outrun a bear." "I don't have to outrun the bear," answers the first. "I just have to outrun you."

Similarly, happiness is relative to our comparisons with others, especially those within our own groups (Lyubomirsky, 2001; Zagefka & Brown, 2005). As the satirist H. L. Mencken (1916) jested, a wealthy man is one whose income "is at least $100 more a year" than that of "his wife's sister's husband."

Whether we feel good or bad depends on whom we're comparing ourselves with. We are slow-witted or clumsy only when others are smart or agile. Let one professional athlete sign a new contract for $15 million a year and an $8-million-a-year teammate may now feel less satisfied. "Our poverty became a reality. Not because of our having less, but by our neighbors having more," recalled Will Campbell in *Brother to a Dragonfly.* Perhaps you can recall being on a stationary train (or boat) when an adjacent train departed, giving you a sense that you were moving backward. That perceptual phenomenon parallels the experience of people on fixed incomes who feel poorer when seeing others around them becoming richer (Payne, 2017).

As we climb the ladder of success or affluence, we mostly compare ourselves with peers who are at or above our current level, not with those who have less (Gerber et al., 2018). People living in communities where other residents are very wealthy tend to feel envy and less satisfaction as they compare upward (Fiske, 2011). The saying that "comparison is the thief of joy" applies to *upward* comparison – as perhaps you have noticed when comparing your everyday life to friends' happy social media posts or your body to the perfection you see online (Bissell & Chou, 2023 Steers et al., 2014).

Times of increased inequality tend, for many, to be times of diminished perceived fairness and happiness. Glynnis Jones/Shutterstock

INCOME INEQUALITY

In developed and emerging economies worldwide, income inequality has been growing. In data from 34 countries around the world, the richest 10% average 9.5 times the income of the poorest 10% (OECD, 2020). Countries with greater income inequality not only have greater health and social problems but also higher rates of dissatisfaction and mental health issues (Burkhauser et al.,2016; Payne, 2017; Scholten et al., 2018; Wilkinson & Pickett, 2017a,b). Over time, years with more income inequality – and associated increases in perceived unfairness and lack of trust – are also years with less happiness, especially among those with lower incomes (Oishi et al., 2011). As income inequality grew in the United States and Europe between the 1970s and 2010s, higher-income people's happiness stayed about the same, but lower-income people's happiness declined, so that income was a stronger predictor of happiness over time (Oishi et al., 2022; Twenge & Cooper, 2020). In German states, reductions in income inequality via taxes were linked to increases in life satisfaction in the population (Cheung, 2018).

Airline travel, with its boarding priorities and seating tiers, is a miniature world of such inequality. Who commit acts of air rage? Most often, say researchers who have combed through millions of flights, it's coach passengers on planes with first-class sections – and especially planes on which the coach passengers must pass through the roomy first-class section on the way to their cramped seating (DeCelles & Norton, 2016). For those of lower status, inequality + comparison = dissatisfaction.

"O.K., if you can't see your way to giving me a pay raise, how about giving Parkerson a pay cut?"

Social comparisons foster negative feelings.

Although people often prefer the economic policies in place, a national survey found that Americans overwhelmingly preferred the income distribution on the right of **Figure 10** (which, unbeknownst to the respondents, is Sweden's income distribution) to the one on the left (which is the U.S. income distribution). Moreover, people preferred (in an ideal world) a top 20% income share of about 30 and 40% (rather than the actual 84%). And there was general agreement about this among Republicans and Democrats, and among those making less than \$50,000 and more than \$100,000 (Norton & Ariely, 2011).

Moreover, the pay gap between big-company CEOs and typical workers is much larger than most people would prefer. In the United States, for example, the actual pay ratio of S&P 500 CEOs to typical workers (about 300:1) far exceeds the ideal ratio (7:1). The researchers' conclusion: "People all over the world and from all walks of life would prefer smaller pay gaps between the rich and poor" (Kuziemko et al., 2015; Mishel & Kandra, 2020).

In China, income inequality has also grown. This may be why rising affluence has not produced increased happiness – there or elsewhere (Ding et al., 2021; Easterlin et al., 2012; Helliwell et al., 2013). Rising income inequality makes for more people having rich neighbors, one reason why economic growth has not increased overall happiness (Cheung & Lucas, 2016; Hagerty, 2000; Oishi & Kesebir, 2015).

The adaptation-level and social-comparison phenomena give us pause. They imply that the quest for happiness through material achievement requires continually expanding affluence. They also help us understand why rich people are, on average, less generous, less compassionate, and less empathic (Marsh, 2012; Mathewes & Sandsmark, 2017).

The good news: Adaptation to a simpler life can also happen. If we shrink our consumption by choice or by necessity, we will initially feel a pinch, but the pain likely will pass. Indeed, thanks to our capacity to adapt and to adjust comparisons, the emotional impact of significant life events – losing a job or having a disabling accident – dissipates sooner than most people suppose (Gilbert et al., 1998).

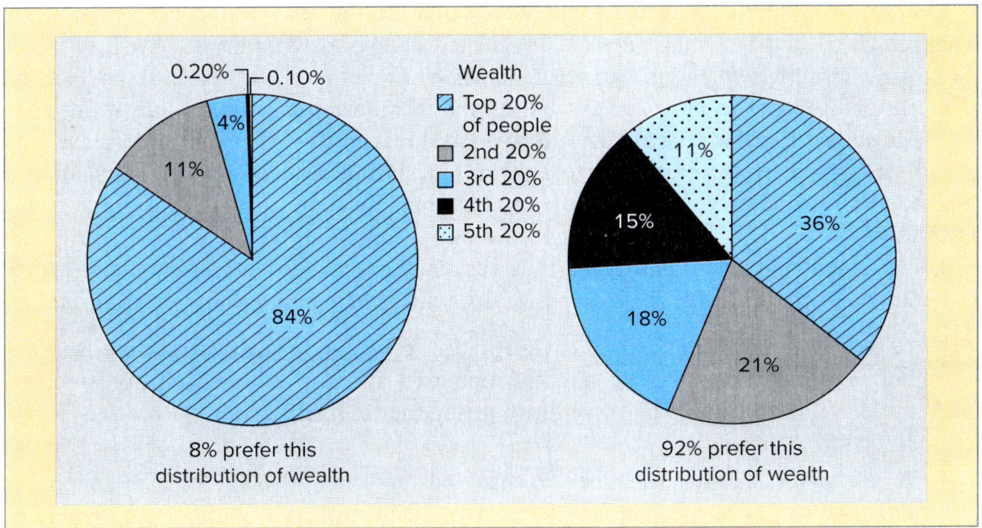

FIGURE 10

In an Ideal Society, What Would Be the Level of Income Inequality?

A survey of Americans provided a surprising consensus that a more equal distribution of wealth — like that shown on the right (which happened to be Sweden's distribution) — would be preferable to the American status quo (shown on the left).
Source: Norton & Ariely, 2011.

Toward Sustainability and Survival

As individuals and as a global society, we face difficult social and political issues. How might a democratic society induce people to adopt values that emphasize psychological well-being over materialism? How might a thriving market economy mix incentives for economic growth with restraints that preserve a habitable planet? How much can technological innovations, such as solar panels and electric cars, reduce our ecological footprints? And to what extent does the overarching goal of preserving the Earth for our grandchildren call us each to limit our own liberties – our freedom to drive, burn, and dump whatever we wish?

A shift to postmaterialist values will gain momentum as people, governments, and corporations take these steps:

- Face the implications of population and consumption growth for climate change and environmental destruction.
- Realize that extrinsic, materialist values make for *less* happy lives.
- Identify and promote the things in life that can enable sustainable human flourishing.

"All our wants, beyond those which a very moderate income will supply, are purely imaginary."

—Henry St. John,
letter to Jonathan Swift, 1719

"If the world is to change for the better it must have a change in human consciousness," said Czech President and writer Václav Havel (1990). We must discover "a deeper sense of responsibility toward the world, which means responsibility toward something higher than self." If people were to believe that ever-bigger houses, closets full of seldom-worn clothes, and garages with luxury cars do not define the good life, then might a shift in consciousness become possible? Instead of being an indicator of social status, might conspicuous consumption become unfashionable?

Social psychology's contribution to a sustainable, flourishing future will come partly through its consciousness-transforming insights into adaptation and comparison. These insights also come from experiments that lower people's comparison standards and thereby cool luxury fever and renew contentment. In two such experiments, Marshall Dermer and his colleagues (1979) put university women through imaginative exercises in deprivation. After viewing depictions of the grimness of Milwaukee life in 1900 or after imagining and writing about being burned and disfigured, the women expressed greater satisfaction with their own lives.

In another experiment, Jennifer Crocker and Lisa Gallo (1985) found that people who completed the sentence "I'm glad I'm not a . . ." in five different ways later felt less depressed and more satisfied with their lives than did those who completed sentences beginning "I wish I were a. . . ." Realizing that others have it worse helps us count our blessings. "I cried because I had no shoes," says a Persian proverb, "until I met a man who had no feet." *Downward* social comparison facilitates contentment.

Downward comparison to a hypothetical worse-off self also enhances contentment. Minkyung Koo and her colleagues (2008) invited people to write about how they might never have met their romantic partner. Compared with others who wrote about meeting their partner, those who imagined not having the relationship expressed more satisfaction with it. Can you likewise imagine how some good things in *your* life might never have happened? It's very easy for me [DM] to imagine not having chanced into an acquaintance that led to an invitation to author this book. Just thinking about that reminds me to count my blessings.

Social psychology also contributes to a sustainable and survivable future through its explorations of the good life. If materialism does not enhance life quality, what does?

- *Close, supportive relationships.* Our deep need to belong is satisfied by close, supportive relationships. People who are supported by intimate friendships or a committed marriage are much more likely to say they are very happy (Grover & Helliwell, 2017).
- *Faith communities* and volunteer organizations are often a source of such connections, as well as of meaning and hope. That helps explain a finding from General

Social Surveys of more than 50,000 Americans since 1972: 26% of those rarely or never attending religious services declared themselves very happy, as did 48% of those attending multiple times weekly. The high religiosity of most poor countries also enables their people to live with surprisingly high levels of meaning in life (Oishi & Diener, 2014).

- *Positive thinking habits.* Optimism, self-esteem, perceived control, and extraversion also mark happy experiences and happy lives. One analysis of 638 studies of 420,000+ people in 63 countries found that a sense of autonomy – feeling free and independent – consistently predicts people's sense of well-being more than wealth does (Fischer & Boer, 2011).
- *Experiencing nature.* University students randomly assigned to a nature walk near their campus ended up (to their and others' surprise) happier, less anxious, and more focused than students who took a similar-length walk through campus walking tunnels or on a busy street (Bratman et al., 2015; Grassini, 2022; Nisbet & Zelenski, 2011). Japanese researchers report that "forest bathing" – walks in the woods – also helps lower stress hormones and blood pressure (Phillips, 2011).
- *Flow.* Work and leisure experiences that engage one's skills mark happy lives. Between the anxiety of being overwhelmed and stressed, and the apathy of being underwhelmed and bored, noted Mihaly Csikszentmihalyi (1990, 1999), lies a zone in which people experience *flow.* Flow is an optimal state in which, absorbed in an activity, we lose consciousness of self and time. When people's experience is sampled using electronic pagers, they report the greatest enjoyment not when they are mindlessly passive but when they are unself-consciously absorbed in a mindful challenge. In fact, the less expensive (and generally more involving) a leisure activity, the *happier* people are while doing it. Most people are happier gardening than powerboating, happier talking to friends than watching TV. Low-consumption recreations prove the most satisfying.

That is good news indeed. Those things that make for the genuinely good life – close relationships, social networks based on belief, positive thinking habits, engaging activity – are enduringly sustainable. And that is an idea close to the heart of Jigme Singye Wangchuk, former king of Bhutan. "Gross national happiness is more important than gross national product," he said. Writing from the Center of Bhutan Studies in Bhutan, Sander Tideman (2003) explained: "Gross National Happiness . . . aims to promote real progress and sustainability by measuring the quality of life, rather than the mere sum of production and consumption." Now other nations, too, are assessing national quality of life. (See "Research Close-Up: Measuring National Well-Being.")

"We have failed to see how our economy, our environment and our society are all one. And that delivering the best possible quality of life for us all means more than concentrating solely on economic growth."

—British Prime Minister Tony Blair, foreword to *A Better Quality of Life*, 1999

research CLOSE-UP Measuring National Well-Being

"A city is successful not when it's rich, but when its people are happy." So said Bogotá, Colombia, former Mayor Enrique Peñalosa, in explaining his campaign to improve his city's quality of life — by building schools and increasing school enrollment 34%, building or rebuilding more than 1,200 parks, creating an effective transit system, and reducing the murder rate dramatically (Gardner & Assadourian, 2004).

Peñalosa's idea of national success is shared by a growing number of social scientists and government planners. In Britain, the New Economics Foundation (2009, 2011) developed "National Accounts of Well-Being" that track national social health and has published a *Well-Being Manifesto for a Flourishing Society.* The foundation's motto: "We believe in economics as if people and the planet mattered." To assess national progress, they urge, we should measure not just financial progress but also the kinds of growth that enhance people's life satisfaction and happiness.

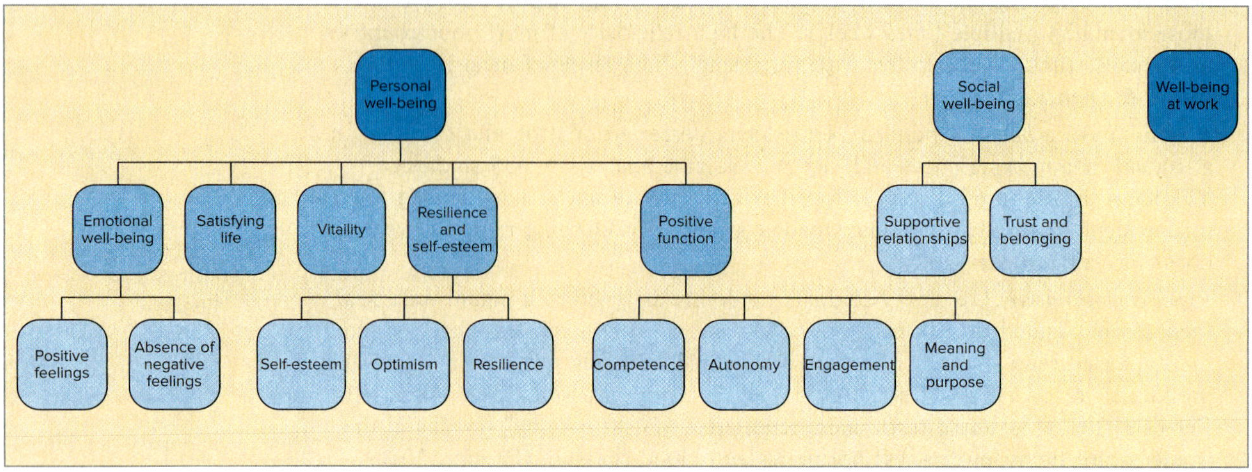

FIGURE 11

Components of Well-Being

In its 2009 *National Accounts of Well-Being* report, Britain's New Economics Foundation urged governments to "directly measure people's subjective well-being: their experiences, feelings and perceptions of how their lives are going." What matters, this think tank argued, is not so much the overall size of the economy as people's experienced quality of life. Categories for assessing national well-being include personal well-being, social well-being, and work-related well-being.

Source: NEF. (2009). Reprinted by permission.

The "Guidelines for National Indicators of Subjective Well-Being and Ill-Being" developed by University of Illinois psychologist Ed Diener (2005, 2013; Diener et al., 2008, 2009, 2015) and signed by four dozen of the world's leading researchers aim to promote new ways of measuring human progress (**Figure 11**). It notes that "global measures of subjective well-being, such as assessments of life satisfaction and happiness, can be useful for policy debates," such as by detecting the human effects of any policy interventions. More specifically, questions are now available for assessing these indicators:

- *Positive emotions,* including those involving low arousal (contentment), moderate arousal (pleasure), and high arousal (euphoria), and those involving positive responses to others (affection) and to activities (interest and engagement).
- *Negative emotions,* including anger, sadness, anxiety, stress, frustration, envy, guilt and shame, loneliness, and helplessness. Measures may ask people to recall or record the frequency of their experiencing positive and negative emotions.
- *Happiness,* which often is taken to mean a general positive mood, such as indicated by people's answers to a widely used survey question: "Taking all things together, how would you say things are these days — would you say that you are very happy, pretty happy, or not too happy?"
- *Life satisfaction,* which engages people in appraising their life as a whole.
- *Domain satisfactions,* which invites people to indicate their satisfaction with their physical health, work, leisure, relationships, family, and community.
- *Quality of life,* a broader concept that includes one's environment and health, and one's perceptions of such.

Such well-being measures can assist governments as they debate economic and tax policies, family protection laws, health care, and community planning — a point now affirmed by more than 40 nations that now are assessing citizen well-being (Diener et al., 2015; Krueger & Stone, 2014). In a lab experiment asking people to pretend to be the mayor of a small city, participants who received information on well-being made different and more sustainable decisions than those who only received economic information (Kasser et al., 2019).

Well-being indicators are also part of worldwide Gallup surveys in more than 150 countries encompassing more than 98% of the world's people. The surveys compare countries (revealing, for example, that people in some high-income countries such as Israel and Saudi Arabia have reported lower levels of positive emotion than people in some low-income countries such as Kenya and India).

SUMMING UP: The Social Psychology of Materialism and Wealth

- To judge from the expressed values of college students and the desire for expensive items so common today, today's Americans – and to a lesser extent people in other Western countries – live in a highly materialistic age.
- People in rich nations report greater happiness and life satisfaction than those in poor nations (though with diminishing returns as one moves from moderately to very wealthy countries). Rich people within a country are somewhat happier than working-class people, though after a certain limit, money provides diminishing returns. Does economic growth over time make people happier? Not at all, it seems, from the slight decline in self-reported happiness and the increasing rate of depression during the post-1960 years of increasing affluence.
- Two principles help explain why materialism fails to satisfy: the *adaptation-level phenomenon* and *social comparison.* When incomes and consumption rise, we soon adapt. And comparing ourselves with others, we may find our relative position unchanged. Comparing upward breeds dissatisfaction, which helps explain the more frequent sense of unfairness and unhappiness in times and places of great inequality.
- To build a sustainable and satisfying future, we can individually seek and, as a society, promote close relationships, supportive social networks, positive thinking habits, and engaging activity.

CONCLUDING THOUGHTS: How Does One Live Responsibly in the Modern World?

> We must recognize that . . . we are one human family and one Earth community with a common destiny. We must join together to bring forth a sustainable global society founded on respect for nature, universal human rights, economic justice, and a culture of peace. Towards this end, it is imperative that we, the peoples of the Earth, declare our responsibility to one another, to the greater community of life, and to future generations.
>
> –*Preamble.* The Earth Charter. www.earthcharter.org

Reading and writing about population growth, climate change, materialism, consumption, adaptation, comparison, and sustainability provokes my [DM's] reflection: Am I part of the answer or part of the problem? I can talk a good line. But do I walk my own talk?

If I'm to be honest, my record is mixed.

I ride a bike to work year-round. But in one recent year, I also flew 100,000 miles on fuel-guzzling jets.

I have insulated my 124-year-old home, installed an efficient furnace, and turned the winter daytime thermostat down to 68. But having grown up in a cool summer climate, I can't imagine living without my air-conditioning on sweltering summer days.

To control greenhouse gas production, I routinely turn off lights and the computer monitor when away from my office and have planted trees around my house. But I've helped finance South American deforestation with the coffee I've sipped.

I applauded in 1973 when the United States established an energy-conserving 55 miles per hour national maximum speed limit and was disappointed when it was abandoned in 1995. But now that speed limits on the highway around my town are back up to 70 mph, I drive 70 mph.

At my house, we recycle all our paper, cans, and bottles. But each week we receive enough mail, newspapers, and periodicals to fill a 3-cubic-foot paper recycling bin.

For me [JT], it's a similar story. I read psychology journals and magazines online instead of on paper, but the work involved in rinsing jars and containers means not everything ends up in the recycling bin that could. Frequently working at home means using less gasoline, but I regularly fly to give talks at colleges, businesses, and conferences. My San Diego pool is heated by solar panels 9 months out of the year but relies on a heat pump and gas heat the other 3 months.

It's hardly a bold response to the looming crisis. Our great-grandchildren will not thrive on this planet if all of today's more than 8 billion humans demand a similar-sized ecological footprint. Plus, it will take more than just individual action to solve this problem. We need governments and corporations to change practices and laws to turn climate change around.

How, then, does one participate in the modern world, welcoming its beauties and conveniences, yet remain mindful of our environmental legacy? Even the leaders of the simpler-living movement – who, like me [DM], flew gas-guzzling jets to our three conferences in luxurious surroundings – struggle with how to live responsibly in the modern world.

"The best time to plant a tree is 20 years ago. The second best time is now."

—Chinese proverb

So what do you think? What regulations do you favor or oppose? Higher fuel-efficiency requirements for cars and trucks? Auto-pollution checks? Leaf-burning bans to reduce smog? If you live in a country where high fuel taxes motivate people to drive small, fuel-efficient cars, do you wish you could have the much lower fuel taxes and cheaper petrol that have enabled Americans to drive big cars? If you are an American, would you favor higher gasoline and oil taxes to help conserve resources and restrain climate change?

"The great dilemma of environmental reasoning stems from this conflict between short-term and long-term values."

—E. O. Wilson, *The Future of Life*, 2002

Will humanity be able to curb climate change and resource depletion? If the biologist E. O. Wilson (2002) was right that humans evolved to commit themselves only to their own small piece of geography, their own kin, and their own time, can we hope that our species will exhibit "extended altruism" by caring for our distant descendants? Will today's envied Instagram-influencer lifestyles become unfashionable in a future where sustainability becomes necessity? Or will people's concern for themselves and for displaying the symbols of success always trump their concerns for their unseen great-grandchildren?

Epilogue

If you have read this entire book, your introduction to social psychology is complete. As we wrote at the beginning of this book, we hoped the book would be at once solidly scientific and warmly human, factually rigorous and intellectually provocative. You are the judge of whether that goal has been achieved. But we can tell you that sharing the discipline has been a joy for us as your authors. If receiving our gift has brought you any measure of pleasure, stimulation, and enrichment, then our joy is multiplied.

A knowledge of social psychology, we do believe, has the power to restrain intuition with critical thinking, illusion with understanding, and judgmentalism with compassion. In these 16 chapters, we have assembled social psychology's insights into belief and persuasion, love and hate, conformity and independence. We have glimpsed incomplete answers to intriguing questions: How do our attitudes feed and get fed by our actions? What leads people sometimes to hurt and sometimes to help one another? What kindles social conflict, and how can we transform closed fists into helping hands?

Answering such questions expands our minds. And "once expanded to the dimensions of a larger idea," noted Oliver Wendell Holmes, the mind "never returns to its original size." Such has been our experience, and perhaps yours, as you, through this and other courses, become an educated person.

David G. Myers
davidmyers.org / @DavidGMyers

Jean M. Twenge
jeantwenge.com / @jean_twenge

References

AAAS. (2014). *What we know: The reality, risks and response to climate change* [PDF file]. Washington, DC: The American Association for the Advancement of Science Climate Science Panel. https://whatweknow.aaas.org/wp-content/uploads/2014/07/whatweknow_website.pdf

AAMC (American Association of Medical Colleges). (2023). The majority of U.S. medical students are women, new data show. https://www.aamc.org/news-insights/press-releases/majority-us-medical-students-are-women-new-data-show

ABA (American Bar Association). (2023). Women in the legal profession: Demographics.

Abbate, C. S., Isgro, A., Wicklund, R. A., & Boca, S. (2006). A field experiment on perspective-taking, helping, and self-awareness. *Basic and Applied Social Psychology, 28,* 283–287.

Abbey, A. (1987). Misperceptions of friendly behavior as sexual interest: A survey of naturally occurring incidents. *Psychology of Women Quarterly, 11,* 173–194.

Abbey, A. (1991). Misperception as an antecedent of acquaintance rape: A consequence of ambiguity in communication between women and men. In A. Parrot (Ed.), *Acquaintance rape.* New York: Wiley.

Abbey, A. (2011). Alcohol and dating risk factors for sexual assault: Double standards are still alive and well entrenched. *Psychology of Women Quarterly, 35,* 362–368.

Abbey, J. (2012). "Pregnant man" Thomas Beatie separates from wife. *ABCNews.com.*

ABC News. (2004, December 28). Whistleblower revealed abuse at Abu Ghraib prison. *ABCnews.go.com.*

Abrams, D., Wetherell, M., Cochrane, S., Hogg, M. A., & Turner, J. C. (1990). Knowing what to think by knowing who you are: Self-categorization and the nature of norm formation, conformity and group polarization. *British Journal of Social Psychology, 29,* 97–119.

Abramson, L. Y. (Ed.). (1988). *Social cognition and clinical psychology: A synthesis.* New York: Guilford.

Abramson, L. Y., Metalsky, G. I., & Alloy, L. B. (1989). Hopelessness depression: A theory-based subtype. *Psychological Review, 96,* 358–372.

Abu-Rayya, H. M., & Sam, D. L. (2017). Is integration the best way to acculturate? A reexamination of the bicultural-adaptation relationship in the "ICSEY dataset" using the bilineal method. *Journal of Cross-Cultural Psychology, 48,* 287–293.

Acevedo, B. P., Aron, A., Fisher, H. E., & Brown, L. L. (2012). Neural correlates of long-term intense romantic love. *Scan, 7,* 145–159.

Ackerman, J. M., Griskevicius, V., & Li, N. P. (2011). Let's get serious: Communicating commitment in romantic relationships. *Journal of Personality and Social Psychology, 100,* 1079–1094.

Ackermann, R., & DeRubeis, R. J. (1991). Is depressive realism real? *Clinical Psychology Review, 11,* 565–584.

Adams, D. (1991). (Ed. and Commentator). *The Seville statement on violence: Preparing the ground for the constructing of peace.* Paris: UNESCO.

Adams, G., Garcia, D. M., Purdie-Vaughns, V., & Steele, C. M. (2006). The detrimental effects of a suggestion of sexism in an instruction situation. *Journal of Experimental Social Psychology, 42,* 602–615.

Adams, J. M., & Jones, W. H. (1997). The conceptualization of marital commitment: An integrative analysis. *Journal of Personality and Social Psychology, 72,* 1177–1196.

Addis, M. E., & Mahalik, J. R. (2003). Men, masculinity, and the contexts of help seeking. *American Psychologist, 58,* 5–14.

Aderman, D., & Berkowitz, L. (1983). Self-concern and the unwillingness to be helpful. *Social Psychology Quarterly, 46,* 293–301.

Adler, N. E., & Snibbe, A. C. (2003). The role of psychosocial processes in explaining the gradient between socioeconomic status and health. *Current Directions in Psychological Science, 12,* 119–123.

Adler, N. E., Boyce, T., Chesney, M. A., Cohen, S., Folkman, S., Kahn, R. L., & Syme, S. L. (1993). Socioeconomic inequalities in health: No easy solution. *Journal of the American Medical Association, 269,* 3140–3145.

Adler, N. E., Boyce, T., Chesney, M. A., Cohen, S., Folkman, S., Kahn, R. L., & Syme, S. L. (1994). Socioeconomic status and health: The challenge of the gradient. *American Psychologist, 49,* 15–24.

Adler, R. P., Lesser, G. S., Meringoff, L. K., Robertson, T. S., & Ward, S. (1980). *The effects of television advertising on children.* Lexington, MA: Lexington Books.

Adorno, T., Frenkel-Brunswik, E., Levinson, D., & Sanford, R. N. (1950). *The authoritarian personality.* New York: Harper.

Agiesta, J. (2020, May 12). CNN Poll: Negative ratings for government handling of coronavirus persist. *CNN.* Retrieved May 13, 2020 from https://www.cnn.com/2020/05/12/politics/cnn-poll-federal-government-handling-of-coronavirus/index.html.

Agthe, M., Spörrle, M., & Maner, J. K. (2011). Does being attractive always help? Positive and negative effects of attractiveness on social decision making. *Personality and Social Psychology Bulletin, 37,* 1042–1054.

Aiello, J. R., & Douthitt, E. Z. (2001). Social facilitation from Triplett to electronic performance monitoring. *Group Dynamics: Theory, Research, and Practice, 5,* 163–180.

Aiello, J. R., Thompson, D. E., & Brodzinsky, D. M. (1983). How funny is crowding anyway? Effects of room size, group size, and the introduction of humor. *Basic and Applied Social Psychology, 4,* 193–207.

Ainsworth, M. D. S. (1973). The development of infant-mother attachment. In B. Caldwell & H. Ricciuti (Eds.), *Review of child development research* (Vol. 3). Chicago: University of Chicago Press.

Ainsworth, M. D. S. (1979). Infant-mother attachment. *American Psychologist, 34,* 932–937.

Ainsworth, S. E., & Maner, J. K. (2012). Sex begets violence: Mating motives, social dominance, and physical aggression in men. *Journal of Personality and Social Psychology, 103,* 819–829.

Ainsworth, S. E., & Maner, J. K. (2014). Assailing the competition: Sexual selection, proximate mating motives, and aggressive behavior in men. *Personality and Social Psychology Bulletin, 40,* 1648–1658.

Aisch, G., et al. (2016, November 10). The divide between red and blue America grew even deeper in 2016. *The New York Times.* https://www.nytimes.com/interactive/2016/11/10/us/politics/red-blue-divide-grew-stronger-in-2016.html

Ajzen, I., & Fishbein, M. (1977). Attitude-behavior relations: A theoretical analysis and review of empirical research. *Psychological Bulletin, 84,* 888–918.

Ajzen, I., & Fishbein, M. (2005). The influence of attitudes on behavior. In D. Albarracin, B. T. Johnson, & M. P. Zanna (Eds.), *The handbook of attitudes.* Mahwah, NJ: Erlbaum.

Aknin, L. B., Barrington-Leigh, C., Dunn, E. W., Helliwell, J. F., Burns, J., Biswas-Diener, R., Kemeza, I., Nyende, P., Ashton-James, C. E., & Norton, M. I. (2013). Prosocial spending and well-being: Cross-cultural evidence for a psychological universal. *Journal of Personality and Social Psychology, 104,* 635–652.

Aknin, L. B., Broesch, T., Hamlin, J. K., Van de Vondervoort, J. W. (2015). Prosocial behavior leads to happiness in a small-scale rural society. *Journal of Experimental Psychology: General, 144,* 788–795.

Aknin, L. B., Dunn, E. W., Proulx, J., Lok, I., & Norton, M. I. (2020). Does spending money on others promote happiness?: A registered replication report. *Journal of Personality and Social Psychology, 119,* e15–e26.

Aknin, L. B., Fleerackers, A. L., & Hamlin, J. K. (2014). Can third-party observers detect the emotional rewards of generous spending? *The Journal of Positive Psychology, 9,* 198–203.

Akrami, N., Ekehammar, B., & Bergh, R. (2011). Generalized prejudice: Common and specific components. *Psychological Science, 22,* 57–59.

Al-Bitar, Z. B., Hamdan, A. M., Shqaidef, A., Garagiola, U., & Naini, F. B. (2023). Perception of frontal facial images compared with their mirror images: chirality, enantiomorphic discrimination, and relevance to clinical practice. *Maxillofacial Plastic and Reconstructive Surgery, 45,* 29.

Alceste, F., Luke, T., Redlich, A., Hellgren, J., Amrom, A., & Kassin, S. (2021). The psychology of confessions: A comparison of expert and lay opinions. *Applied Cognitive Psychology, 35*(1), 39–51.

Alden, L. E., & Trew, J. L. (2013). If it makes you happy: Engaging in kind acts increases positive affect in socially anxious individuals. *Emotion, 13,* 64–75.

Alexander, L., & Tredoux, C. (2010). The spaces between us: A spatial analysis of informal segregation at a South African university. *Journal of Social Issues, 66,* 367–386.

Alexopoulos, C. (2021). Justify my love: Cognitive dissonance reduction among perpetrators of online and offline infidelity. *Journal of Social and Personal Relationships, 38,* 3669–3691.

Alkhuzai, A. H., et al. (2008). Violence-related mortality in Iraq from 2002 to 2006. *New England Journal of Medicine, 358,* 484–493.

Allee, W. C., & Masure, R. M. (1936). A comparison of maze behavior in paired and isolated shell-parakeets (*Melopsittacus undulatus Shaw*) in a two-alley problem box. *Journal of Comparative Psychology, 22,* 131–155.

Allen, M. S., Knipler, S. J., & Chan, A. Y. C. (2019). Happiness and counterfactual thinking at the 2016 Summer Olympic Games. *Journal of Sports Sciences, 37,* 1762–1769.

Allen, M. S., Robson, D. A., Martin, L. J., & Laborde, S. (2020). Systematic review and meta-analysis of self-serving attribution biases in the competitive context of organized sport. *Personality and Social Psychology Bulletin, 46,* 1027–1043.

Allen, M. S., Robson, D. A., Mishra, M., & Laborde, S. (2023). A prospective and retrospective 10-year study of altruism and reproductive success. *Evolutionary Behavioral Sciences.*

Allen, V. L., & Levine, J. M. (1969). Consensus and conformity. *Journal of Experimental Social Psychology, 5,* 389–399.

Allesøe, K., Hundrup, V. A., Thomsen, J. F., & Osler, M. (2010). Psychosocial work environment and risk of ischaemic heart disease in women: The Danish Nurse Cohort Study. *Occupational and Environmental Medicine, 67,* 318–322.

Alloy, L., Abramson, L. Y., Gibb, B. E., Crossfield, A. G., Pieracci, A. M., Spasojevic, J., & Steinberg, J. A. (2004). Developmental antecedents of cognitive vulnerability to depression: Review of findings from the cognitive vulnerability to depression project. *Journal of Cognitive Psychotherapy, 18,* 115–133.

Alloy, L. B., & Abramson, L. Y. (1979). Judgment of contingency in depressed and nondepressed students: Sadder but wiser? *Journal of Experimental Psychology: General, 108,* 441–485.

Alloy, L. B., Abramson, L. Y., Whitehouse, W. G., Hogan, M. E., Tashman, N. A., Steinberg, D. L., Rose, D. T., & Donovan, P. (1999). Depressogenic cognitive styles: Predictive validity, information processing and personality characteristics, and developmental origins. *Behaviour Research and Therapy, 37,* 503–531.

Alloy, L. B., Albright, J. S., Abramson, L. Y., & Dykman, B. M. (1990). Depressive realism and nondepressive optimistic illusions: The role of the self. In R. E. Ingram (Ed.), *Contemporary psychological approaches to depression: Theory, research and treatment.* New York: Plenum.

Allport, F. H. (1920). The influence of the group upon association and thought. *Journal of Experimental Psychology, 3,* 159–182.

Allport, G. W. (1958). *The nature of prejudice* (abridged). Garden City, NY: Anchor Books.

Alquist, J. L., Ainsworth, S. E., & Baumeister, R. F. (2013). Determined to conform: Disbelief in free will increases in conformity. *Journal of Experimental Social Psychology, 49,* 80–86.

Al Ramiah, A., & Hewstone, M. (2013). Intergroup contact as a tool for reducing, resolving, and preventing intergroup conflict: Evidence, limitations, and potential. *American Psychologist, 68,* 527–542.

Al-Roubaiy, N. S. (2020). One pathway to cognitive behaviour therapy integration: Introducing assimilative integrative rational emotive behaviour therapy. *The Cognitive Behaviour Therapist, 13,* e7.

Alvarez, M. J., & Miller, M. K. (2017). How defendants' legal status and ethnicity and participants' political orientation relate to death penalty sentencing decisions. *Translational Issues in Psychological Science, 3,* 298–311.

Alves, H. (2018). Sharing rare attitudes attracts. *Personality and Social Psychology Bulletin, 44,* 1270–1283.

Alwin, D. F. (1990). Historical changes in parental orientations to children. In N. Mandell (Ed.), *Sociological studies of child development* (Vol. 3). Greenwich, CT: JAI Press.

Alós-Ferrer, C., García-Segarra, J., & Ritschel, A. (2022). Generous with individuals and selfish to the masses. *Nature Human Behaviour, 6,* 88–96.

Amato, P. R. (1979). Juror-defendant similarity and the assessment of guilt in politically motivated crimes. *Australian Journal of Psychology, 31,* 79–88.

American College Health Association. (2023). *American College Health Association-National College Health Assessment III: Undergraduate Reference group report Spring 2023.* Silver Spring, MD: Author.

American Psychological Association. (2017). *Ethical principles of psychologists and code of conduct: 2010 and 2016 amendments.* Washington, DC: APA. http://www.apa.org/ethics/code

American Psychological Association (2023, June 6). Understanding transgender people, gender identity and gender expression. apa.org

Amir, Y. (1969). Contact hypothesis in ethnic relations. *Psychological Bulletin, 71,* 319–342.

AMS (American Meteorological Society). (2017, December 13). *Human influence on climate lead to several major weather extremes in 2016.* https://bit.ly/3luB3LK

Andersen, S. M., & Chen, S. (2002). The relational self: An interpersonal social-cognitive theory. *Psychological Review, 109,* 619–645.

Andersen, S. M. (1998). *Service learning: A national strategy for youth development. A position paper issued by the Task Force on Education Policy.* Washington, DC: Institute for Communitarian Policy Studies, George Washington University.

Anderson, C. A., & Anderson, D. C. (1984). Ambient temperature and violent crime: Tests of the linear and curvilinear hypotheses. *Journal of Personality and Social Psychology, 46,* 91–97.

Anderson, C. A., & Anderson K. B. (1998). Temperature and aggression: Paradox, controversy, and a (fairly) clear picture. In R. G. Geen & E. Donnerstein (Eds.), *Human aggression: Theories, research, and implications for social policy.* San Diego: Academic Press.

Anderson, C. A., & Bushman, B. J. (1997). External validity of "trivial" experiments: The case of laboratory aggression. *Review of General Psychology, 1,* 19–41.

Anderson, C. A., & Bushman, B. J. (2001). Effects of violent video games on aggressive behavior, aggressive cognition,aggressive affect, physiological arousal, and prosocial behavior: QA meta-analytic review of the scientific literature. *Psychological Science, 12,* 35–359.

Anderson, C. A., & Bushman, B. J. (2018). Media violence and the general aggression model. *Journal of Social Issues, 74*(2), 386–413.

Anderson, C. A., & Delisi, M. (2010). Implications of global climate change for violence in developed and developing countries. In J. P. Forgas, A. W. Kruglanski, & K. D. Williams (Eds.), *The psychology of social conflict and aggression.* New York: Psychology Press.

Anderson, C. A., & Delisi, M. (2011). Implications of global climate change for violence in developed and developing countries. In J. P. Forgas, A. W., Kruglanski, & K. D. Williams (Eds.), *The psychology of social conflict and aggression.* New York: Psychology Press.

Anderson, C. A., & Harvey, R. J. (1988). Discriminating between problems in living: An examination of measures of depression, loneliness, shyness, and social anxiety. *Journal of Social and Clinical Psychology, 6,* 482–491.

Anderson, C. A. (2003). Video games and aggressive behavior. In D. Ravitch & J. P. Viteritti (Eds.), *Kids stuff: Marking violence and vulgarity in the popular culture.* Baltimore, MD: Johns Hopkins University Press.

Anderson, C. A. (2004). An update on the effects of violent video games. *Journal of Adolescence, 27,* 113–122.

Anderson, C. A., Allen, J. J., Plante, C., Quigley-McBride, A., Lovett, A., & Rokkum, J. N. (2019). The MTurkification of social and personality psychology. *Personality and Social Psychology Bulletin, 45,* 842–850.

Anderson, C. A., Buckley, K. E., & Carnagey, N. L. (2008). Creating your own hostile environment: A laboratory examination of trait aggressiveness and the violence escalation cycle. *Personality and Social Psychology Bulletin, 34,* 462–473.

Anderson, C. A., Deuser, W. E., & DeNeve, K. M. (1995). Hot temperatures, hostile affect, hostile cognition, and arousal: Tests of a general model of affective aggression. *Personality and Social Psychology Bulletin, 21,* 434–448.

Anderson, C. A., Lindsay, J. J., & Bushman, B. J. (1999). Research in the psychological laboratory: Truth or triviality? *Current Directions in Psychological Science, 8,* 3–9.

Anderson, C. A., Miller, R. S., Riger, A. L., Dill, J. C., & Sedikides, C. (1994). Behavioral and characterological attributional styles as predictors of depression and loneliness: Review, refinement, and test. *Journal of Personality and Social Psychology, 66,* 549–558.

Anderson, C. A., Suzuki, K., Swing, E. L., Groves, C. L., Gentile, D. A., Prot, S., & . . . Petrescu, P. (2017). Media violence and other aggression risk factors in seven nations. *Personality and Social Psychology Bulletin, 43,* 986–998.

Anderson, C., Brion, S., Moore, D. A., & Kennedy, J. A. (2012). A status-enhancement account of overconfidence. *Journal of Personality and Social Psychology, 103,* 718–735.

Anderson, C., Keltner, D., & John, O. P. (2003). Emotional convergence between people over time. *Journal of Personality and Social Psychology, 84,* 1054–1068.

Anderson, C., Srivastava, S., Beer, J. S., Spataro, S. E., & Chatman, J. A. (2006). Knowing your place: Self-perceptions of status in face-to-face groups. *Journal of Personality and Social Psychology, 91,* 1094–1110.

Anderson, L., Washington, C., Kreider, R. M., & Gryn, T. (2023, June 8). Home Alone: More than a quarter of all households have one person. https://www.census.gov/library/stories/2023/06/more-than-a-quarter-all-households-have-one-person.html

Anderson, V. N. (2017). Cisgender men and trans prejudice: Relationships with sexual orientation and gender self-esteem. *Psychology of Men & Masculinity, 19*(3), 373–384.

Andrews, J. L., Khin, A. C., Crayn, T., Humphreys, K., & Schweizer, S. (2022). Measuring online and offline social rejection sensitivity in the digital age. *Psychological Assessment, 34,* 742–751.

Andrews, P. W., & Thomson, Jr., J. A. (2009). The bright side of being blue: Depression as an adaptation for analyzing complex problems. *Psychological Review, 116,* 620–654.

Andrews, P. W., & Thomson, Jr., J. A. (2010, January/February). Depression's evolutionary roots. *Scientific American Mind,* 57–61.

Anglemyer, A., Horvath, T., & Rutherford, G. (2014). The accessibility of firearms and risk for suicide and homicide victimization among household members: A systematic review and meta-analysis. *Annals of Internal Medicine, 160,* 101–110.

Anglin, S. M. (2019). Do beliefs yield to evidence? Examining belief perseverance vs. Change in response to congruent empirical findings. *Journal of Experimental Social Psychology, 82,* 176–199.

Anik, L., Aknin, L. B., Norton, M. I., Dunn, E. W., & Quoidbach, J. (2013). Prosocial bonuses increase employee satisfaction and team performance. *PLOS ONE, 8,* e75509.

Annan, K. (2002, December 29). *In Africa, AIDS has a woman's face.* United Nations. https://www.un.org/sg/en/content/sg/articles/2002-12-29/africa-aids-has-womans-face

An, S., & Kang, H. (2013). Do online ad breaks clearly tell kids that advergames are advertisements that intend to sell things? *International Journal of Advertising, 32,* 655–678.

AP. (2013, November 25). Man breaks woman's jump from Oakland stadium deck. *Associated Press release.* https://bit.ly/30RLGzE

AP (Associated Press). (2012, January 29. Accessed April 1, 2015). Maria Hoefl-Riesch edges Lindsey Vonn. *ESPN.* http://espn.go.com/olympics/skiing/story/_/id/7516020/lindsey-vonn-denied-weekend-sweep-003-seconds

AP (Associated Press). (2019, January 23). *AP-NORC poll: Disasters influence thinking on climate change.* https://www.telegraphherald.com/ap/national/article_a38a2a9a-0612-5e25-91b0-358b5d8341d3.html

Apicella, C., Norenzayan, A., & Henrich, J. (2020). Beyond weird: A review of the last decade and a look ahead to the global laboratory of the future. *Evolution and Human Behavior, 41,* 319–329.

Appleby, S. C., & Kassin, S. M. (2016). When self-report trumps science: Effects of confessions, DNA, and prosecutorial theories on perceptions of guilt. *Psychology, Public Policy, and Law, 22,* 127–140.

Aratini, L. (2020, June 29). How did face masks become a political issue in America? *The Guardian.* https://www.theguardian.com/world/2020/jun/29/face-masks-us-politics-coronavirus

Archer, D., Iritani, B., Kimes, D. B., & Barrios, M. (1983). Face-ism: Five studies of sex differences in facial prominence. *Journal of Personality and Social Psychology, 45,* 725–735.

Archer, J. (2000). Sex differences in aggression between heterosexual partners: A meta-analytic review. *Psychological Bulletin, 126,* 651–680.

Archer, J. (2006). Testosterone and human aggression: An evaluation of the challenge hypothesis. *Neuroscience and Biobehavioral Reviews, 30,* 319–345.

Archer, J. (2009). Does sexual selection explain human sex differences? *Behavioral and Brain Sciences, 32,* 249–311.

Archer, R. L., & Cook, C. E. (1986). Personalistic self-disclosure and attraction: Basis for relationship or scarce resource. *Social Psychology Quarterly, 49,* 268–272.

Argyle, M., & Henderson M. (1985). *The anatomy of relationships.* London: Heinemann.

Arieff, A. (2011, August 22). It's not about the furniture: Cubicles, continued. *The New York Times Opinionator.* https://opinionator.blogs.nytimes.com/2011/08/22/its-not-about-the-furniture-cubicles-continued/

Arkes, H. R. (1990). *Some practical judgment/decision making research.* Paper presented at the American Psychological Association convention.

Arkin, R. M., & Burger, J. M. (1980). Effects of unit relation tendencies on interpersonal attraction. *Social Psychology Quarterly, 43,* 380–391.

Arkin, R. M., Appleman, A., & Burger, J. M. (1980). Social anxiety, self-presentation, and the self-serving bias in causal attribution. *Journal of Personality and Social Psychology, 38,* 23–35.

Arkin, R. M., Lake, E. A., & Baumgardner, A. H. (1986). Shyness and self-presentation. In W. H. Jones, J. M. Cheek, & S. R. Briggs (Eds.), *Shyness: Perspectives on research and treatment.* New York: Plenum.

Armitage, C. J., & Conner, M. (2001). Efficacy of the theory of planned behaviour: A meta-analytic review. *British Journal of Social Psychology, 40,* 471–499.

Armor, D. A., & Taylor, S. E. (1996). Situated optimism: Specific outcome expectancies and self-regulation. In M. P. Zanna (Ed.), *Advances in experimental social psychology* (Vol. 30). San Diego: Academic Press.

Arms, R. L., Russell, G. W., & Sandilands, M. L. (1979). Effects on the hostility of spectators of viewing aggressive sports. *Social Psychology Quarterly, 42,* 275–279.

Armstrong, K. (2019, December 23). The social dynamics of environmentalism. *APS Observer.* https://www.psychologicalscience.org/observer/the-social-dynamics-of-environmentalism

Army Technology. (2018, November 30). Women in the army: Female fighters in the world's seven biggest armies. https://www.army-technology.com/uncategorised/women-in-the-army/

Aron, A., & Aron, E. (1989). *The heart of social psychology* (2nd ed.; p. 131). Lexington, MA: Lexington Books.

Aron, A., & Aron, E. N. (1994). Love. In A. L. Weber & J. H. Harvey (Eds.), *Perspective on close relationships.* Boston: Allyn & Bacon.

Aron, A., Dutton, D. G., Aron, E. N., & Iverson, A. (1989). Experiences of falling in love. *Journal of Social and Personal Relationships, 6,* 243–257.

Aron, A., Fisher, H., Mashek, D. J., Strong, G., Li, H., & Brown, L. L. (2005). Reward, motivation, and emotion systems associated with early-stage intense romance love. *Journal of Neurophysiology, 94,* 327–337.

Aron, A., Melinat, E., Aron, E. N., Vallone, R. D., & Bator, R. J. (1997). The experimental generation of interpersonal closeness: A procedure and some preliminary findings. *Personality and Social Psychology Bulletin, 23,* 363–377.

Aron, A., Norman, C. C., Aron, E. N., McKenna, C., & Heyman, R. E. (2000). Couples' shared participation in novel and arousing activities and experienced relationship quality. *Journal of Personality and Social Psychology, 78,* 273–284.

Aronson, E., & Gonzalez, A. (1988). Desegregation, jigsaw, and the Mexican-American experience. In P. A. Katz & D. Taylor (Eds.), *Towards the elimination of racism: Profiles in controversy.* New York: Plenum.

Aronson, E. (1980). *The social animal.* 3rd edition. New York: Freeman.

Aronson, E. (1988). *The social animal* (5th ed.). New York: Freeman, p. 323.

Aronson, E. (2004). Reducing hostility and building compassion: Lessons from the jigsaw classroom. In A. G. Miller (Ed.), *The social psychology of good and evil.* New York: Guilford.

Aronson, E., Brewer, M., & Carlsmith, J. M. (1985). Experimentation in social psychology. In G. Lindzey & E. Aronson (Eds.), *Handbook of social psychology* (Vol. 1). Hillsdale, NJ: Erlbaum.

Arriaga, X. B., & Agnew, C. R. (2001). Being committed: Affective, cognitive, and conative components of relationship commitment. *Personality and Social Psychology Bulletin, 27,* 1190–1203.

Arriaga, X. B. (2001). The ups and downs of dating: Fluctuations in satisfaction in newly formed romantic relationships. *Journal of Personality and Social Psychology, 80,* 754–765.

Asch, S. E. (1946). Forming impressions of personality. *The Journal of Abnormal and Social Psychology, 41*(3), 258–290.

Asch, S. E. (1955, November). Opinions and social pressure. *Scientific American,* 31–35.

Asendorpf, J. B. (1987). Videotape reconstruction of emotions and cognitions related to shyness. *Journal of Personality and Social Psychology, 53,* 541–549.

Ashton-James, C., & Tracy, J. L. (2012). Pride and prejudice: How feelings about the self influence judgments of others. *Personality and Social Psychology Bulletin, 38,* 466–476.

Associated Press. (2009, December 1). Psychiatric report found Clemmons a risk, but not enough to commit him. *Heraldnet.* https://www.heraldnet.com/news/psychiatric-report-found-clemmons-a-risk-but-not-enough-to-commit-him/

Atari, M., Davani, A. M., Kogon, D., Kennedy, B., Ani Saxena, N., Anderson, I., & Dehghani, M. (2022). Morally homogeneous networks and radicalism. *Social Psychological and Personality Science, 13,* 999–1009.

Atari, M., Haidt, J., Graham, J., Koleva, S., Stevens, S. T., & Dehghani, M. (2023). Morality beyond the WEIRD: How the nomological network of morality varies across cultures. *Journal of Personality and Social Psychology.*

Athota, V. S., & O'Connor, P. J. (2014). How approach and avoidance constructs of personality and trait emotional intelligence predict core human values. *Learning and Individual Differences, 31,* 51–58.

Auyeung, B., Lombardo, M. V., & Baron-Cohen, S. (2013). Prenatal and postnatal hormone effects on the human brain and cognition. *Pflügers Archiv-European Journal of Physiology, 465,* 557–571.

Averill, J. R. (1983). Studies on anger and aggression: Implications for theories of emotion. *American Psychologist, 38,* 1145–1160.

Axsom, D., Yates, S., & Chaiken, S. (1987). Audience response as a heuristic cue in persuasion. *Journal of Personality and Social Psychology, 53,* 30–40.

Ayers, J. W., Althouse, B. M., Leas, E. C., Dredze, M., & Allem, J. (2017). Internet searches for suicide following the release of *13 Reasons Why. JAMA Internal Medicine, 177,* 1527–1529.

Azrin, N. H. (1967, May). Pain and aggression. *Psychology Today,* pp. 27–33.

Baars, B. J., & McGovern, K. A. (1994). Consciousness. In V. Ramachandran (Ed.), *Encyclopedia of human behavior.* Orlando, FL: Academic Press.

Babad, E., Bernieri, F., & Rosenthal, R. (1991). Students as judges of teachers' verbal and nonverbal behavior. *American Educational Research Journal, 28,* 211–234.

Bachman, J. G., & O'Malley, P. M. (1977). Self-esteem in young men: A longitudinal analysis of the impact of educational and occupational attainment. *Journal of Personality and Social Psychology, 35,* 365–380.

Back, M. D., Schmukle, S. C., & Egloff, B. (2008). Becoming friends by chance. *Psychological Science, 19,* 439–440.

Bacon, F. (1612). *Essays.* XXVII. Of friendship. London.

Baguley, C. M., McKimmie, B. M., & Masser, B. M. (2017). Deconstructing the simplification of jury instructions: How simplifying the features of complexity affects jurors' application of instructions. *Law and Human Behavior, 41,* 284–304.

Bahns, A. (2017). Threat as justification of prejudice. *Group Processes & Intergroup Relations, 20,* 52–74.

Bail, C. A., Argyle, L. P., Brown, T. W., Bumpus, J. P., Chen, H., Hunzaker, M. B. F., Lee, J., Mann, M., Merhout, F., & Volfovsky, A. (2018). Exposure to opposing views on social media can increase political polarization. *PNAS, 115,* 9216–9221.

Bailenson, J. N., Iyengar, S., Yee, N., & Collins, N. (2008). Facial similarity between voters and candidates causes influence. *Public Opinion Quarterly, 72*(5), 935–961.

Bailey, J. M., Kirk, K. M., Zhu, G., Dunne, M. P., & Martin, N. G.(2000). Do individual differences in sociosexuality represent genetic or environmentally contingent strategies? Evidence from the Australian Twin Registry. *Journal of Personality and Social Psychology, 78,* 537–545.

Baize, H. R., Jr., & Schroeder, J. E. (1995). Personality and mate selection in personal ads: Evolutionary preferences in a public mate selection process. *Journal of Social Behavior and Personality, 10,* 517–536.

Baker, L., & McNulty, J. K. (2010). Shyness and marriage: Does shyness shape even established relationships? *Personality and Social Psychology Bulletin, 36,* 665–676.

Baldwin, M. W., Keelan, J. P. R., Fehr, B., Enns, V., & Koh-Rangarajoo, E. (1996). Social-cognitive conceptualization of attachment working models: Availability and accessibility effects. *Journal of Personality and Social Psychology, 71,* 94–109.

Balliet, D., & Van Lange, P. A. M. (2013). Trust, conflict. and cooperation: A meta-analysis. *Psychological Bulletin, 139,* 1090–1112.

Balliet, D., Mulder, L. B., & Van Lange, P. A. M. (2011). Reward, punishment, and cooperation: A meta-analysis. *Psychological Bulletin, 137,* 594–615.

Balliet, D., Wu, J., & De Dreu, Carsten, K. W. (2014). Ingroup favoritism in cooperation: A meta-analysis. *Psychological Bulletin, 140,* 1556–1581.

Balsa, A. I., Homer, J. F., French, M. T., & Norton, E. C. (2010). Alcohol use and popularity: Social payoffs from conforming to peers' behavior. *Journal of Research on Adolescence, 21,* 559–568.

Banaji, M. R., & Greenwald, A. G. (2013). *Blindspot: Hidden biases of good people.* New York: Delacorte Press.

Bandura, A., & Walters, R. H. (1959). *Adolescent aggression.* New York: Ronald Press.

Bandura, A., & Walters, R. H. (1963). *Social learning and personality development.* New York: Holt, Rinehart & Winston.

Bandura, A. (1979). The social learning perspective: Mechanisms of aggression. In H. Toch (Ed.), *Psychology of crime and criminal justice.* New York: Holt, Rinehart & Winston.

Bandura, A. (1997). *Self-efficacy: The exercise of control.* New York: Freeman.

Bandura, A. (2000). Social cognitive theory: An agentic perspective. *Annual Review of Psychology, 52,* 1-26.

Bandura, A. (2004). Swimming against the mainstream: The early years from chilly tributary to transformative mainstream. *Behaviour Research and Therapy, 42,* 613-630.

Bandura, A. (2008). Reconstrual of "free will" from the agentic perspective of social cognitive theory. In J. Baer, J. C. Kaufman, & R. F. Baumeister (Eds.), *Are we free? Psychology and free will.* New York: Oxford University Press.

Bandura, A. (2018). Toward a psychology of human agency: Pathways and reflections. *Perspectives on Psychological Science, 13,* 130-136.

Bandura, A., Pastorelli, C., Barbaranelli, C., & Caprara, G. V. (1999). Self-efficacy pathways to childhood depression. *Journal of Personality and Social Psychology, 76,* 258-269.

Bandura, A., Ross, D., & Ross, S. A. (1961). Transmission of aggression through imitation of aggressive models. *Journal of Abnormal and Social Psychology, 63,* 575-582.

Banks, G. C., Field, J. G., Oswald, F. L., O'Boyle, E. H., Landis, R. S., Rupp, D. E., & Rogelberg, S. G. (2019). Answers to 18 questions about open science practices. *Journal of Business and Psychology, 34,* 257-270.

Banks, S. M., Salovey, P., Greener, S., Rothman, A. J., Moyer, A., Beauvais, J., & Epel, E. (1995). The effects of message framing on mammography utilization. *Health Psychology, 14,* 178-184

Baranowski, A. M., & Hecht, H. (2015). Gender differences and similarities in receptivity to sexual invitations: Effects of location and risk perception. *Archives of Sexual Behavior, 44,* 2257-2265.

Barash, D. (1979). *The whisperings within.* New York: Harper Row.

Barash, D. P. (2003, November 7). Unreason's seductive charms. *Chronicle of Higher Education.* www.chronicle.com/free/v50/i11/11b00601.htm

Barber, B. M., & Odean, T. (2001a). Boys will be boys: Gender, overconfidence and common stock investment. *Quarterly Journal of Economics, 116,* 261-292.

Barber, N. (2000). On the relationship between country sex ratios and teen pregnancy rates: A replication. *Cross-Cultural Research, 34,* 327-333.

Barberá, P., Jost, J. T., Nagler, J., Tucker, J. A., & Bonneau, R. (2015). Tweeting from left to right: Is online political communication more than an echo chamber? *Psychological Science, 26,* 1531-1542.

Bareket, O., Ein-Gar, D., & Kogut, T. (2022). I will help you survive but not thrive: Helping decisions in situations that empower women. *Group Processes and Intergroup Relations, 26.*

Bargh, J. A., & Raymond, P. (1995). The naive misuse of power: Nonconscious sources of sexual harassment. *Journal of Social Issues, 51,* 85-96.

Bargh, J. A. (2006). What have we been priming all these years? On the development, mechanisms, and ecology of nonconscious social behavior. *European Journal of Social Psychology, 36,* 147-168.

Bargh, J. A., Schwader, K. L., Hailey, S. E., Dyer, R. L., & Boothby, E. J. (2012). Automaticity in social-cognitive processes. *Trends in Cognitive Sciences, 16,* 593-605.

Bar-Haim, Y., Ziv, T., Lamy, D., & Hodes, R. M. (2006). Nature and nurture in own-race face processing. *Psychological Science, 17,* 159-163.

Barlett, C. P., & Anderson, C. A. (2014). Bad news, bad times, and violence: The link between economic distress and aggression. *Psychology of Violence, 4,* 309-321.

Barlett, C. P., DeWitt, C. C., Madison, C. S., Heath, J. B., Maronna, B., & Kirkpatrick, S. M. (2020). Hot temperatures and even hotter tempers: Sociological mediators in the relationship between global climate change and homicide. *Psychology of Violence, 10,* 1-7.

Barlett, C. P., Harris, R. J., & Bruey, C. (2008). The effect of the amount of blood in a violence video game on aggression, hostility, and arousal. *Journal of Experimental Social Psychology, 44,* 539-546.

Barnes, E. (2008, August 24). Scots heroine of Auschwitz who gave her life for young Jews. *Scotland on Sunday,* 3.

Barnes, R. (2020, June 15). Supreme Court says gay, transgender workers protected by federal law forbidding discrimination. *The Washington Post.* washingtonpost.com.

Barnes, R. D., Ickes, W., & Kidd, R. F. (1979). Effects of the perceived intentionality and stability of another's dependency on helping behavior. *Personality and Social Psychology Bulletin, 5,* 367-372.

Barnett, M. A., King, L. M., Howard, J. A., & Melton, E. M. (1980). *Experiencing negative affect about self or other: Effects on helping behavior in children and adults.* Paper presented at the Midwestern Psychological Association convention, Montreal, Quebec.

Barnett, P. A., & Gotlib, I. H. (1988). Psychosocial functioning and depression: Distinguishing among antecedents, concomitants, and consequences. *Psychological Bulletin, 104,* 97-126.

Barongan, C., & Hall, G. C. N. (1995). The influence of misogynous rap music on sexual aggression against women. *Psychology of Women Quarterly, 19,* 195-207.

Baron, J., & Hershey, J. C. (1988). Outcome bias in decision evaluation. *Journal of Personality and Social Psychology, 54,* 569-579.

Baron, J., & Miller, J. G. (2000). Limiting the scope of moral obligations to help: A cross-cultural investigation. *Journal of Cross-Cultural Psychology, 31,* 703-725.

Baron, R. A. (1977). *Human aggression.* New York: Plenum.

Baron, R. A., Markman, G. D., & Bollinger, M. (2006). Exporting social psychology: Effects of attractiveness on perceptions of entrepreneurs, their ideas for new products, and their financial success. *Journal of Applied Social Psychology, 36,* 467-492.

Baron, R. S. (1986). Distraction-conflict theory: Progress and problems. In L. Berkowitz (Ed.), *Advances in experimental social psychology,* Orlando, FL: Academic Press.

Barreto, M., & Doyle, D. M. (2023). Benevolent and hostile sexism in a shifting global context. *Nature Reviews Psychology, 2,* 98-111.

Barreto, M., Victor, C., Hammond, C., Eccles, A., Richins, M. T., & Qualter, P. (2020). Loneliness around the world: Age, gender, and cultural differences in loneliness. *Personality and Individual Differences, 169,* 110066.

Barrick, E. M., Barasch, A., & Tamir, D. I. (2022). The unexpected social consequences of diverting attention to our phones. *Journal of Experimental Social Psychology, 101,* 1-14.

Barroso, A. (2020, August 20). Key takeaways on Americans' views of and experiences with dating and relationships. *Pew Research Center.* https://pewrsr.ch/3kXVLTB

Barry, D. (1995, January). Bored stiff. *Funny Times,* p. 5.

Barry, D. (1998). *Dave Barry turns 50.* New York: Crown.

Bar-Tal, D. (2004). The necessity of observing real life situations: Palestinian-Israeli violence as a laboratory for learning about social behaviour. *European Journal of Social Psychology, 34,* 677-701.

Bar-Tal, D. (2013). *Intractable conflicts: Socio-psychological foundations and dynamics.* New York: Cambridge University Press.

Bartels, M., Cacioppo, J. T., Hudziak, J. J., & Boomsma, D. I. (2008). Genetic and environmental contributions to stability in loneliness throughout childhood. *American Journal of Medical Genetics Part B, 147B,* 385-391.

Bartholomaeus, J., Burns, N., & Strelan, P. (2023). The empowering function of the belief in a just world for the self: Trait-level and experimental tests of its association with positive and negative affect. *Personality and Social Psychology Bulletin, 49,* 510–526.

Bartholomew, K., & Horowitz, L. (1991). Attachment styles among young adults: A test of a four-category model. *Journal of Personality and Social Psychology, 61,* 226–244.

Bartholow, B. D., Bushman, B. J., & Sestir, M. A. (2006). Chronic violent video game exposure and desensitization: Behavioral and event-related brain potential data. *Journal of Experimental Social Psychology, 42*(4), 532–539.

Bartlett, C. P., & Rodeheffer, C. (2009). Effects of realism on extended violent and nonviolent video game play on aggressive thoughts, feelings, and physiological arousal. *Aggressive Behavior, 35,* 213–224.

Bartlett, R. (2019). *Consumer-lending discrimination in the fintech era.* https://faculty.haas.berkeley.edu/morse/research/papers/discrim.pdf

Bartonicek, A., & Colombo, M. (2020). Claw-in-the-door: Pigeons, like humans, display the foot-in-the-door effect. *Animal Cognition, 23*(5), 893–900.

Barzman, D. H., Mossman, D., Appel, K., Blom, T. J., Strawn, J. R., Ekhator, N. N., Patel, B., DelBello, M. P., Sorter, M., Kein, D., & Geracioti, T. D. (2013). The association between salivary hormone levels and children's inpatient aggression: A pilot study. *Psychiatry Quarterly, 84,* 475–484.

Barzun, J. (1975). *Simple and direct* (pp. 173–174). New York: Harper & Row.

Basol, M., Roozenbeek, J., & van der Linden, S. (2020). Good news about Bad news: Gamified inoculation boosts confidence and cognitive immunity against fake news. *Journal of Cognition, 3*(1).

Bassili, J. N. (2003). The minority slowness effect: Subtle inhibitions in the expression of views not shared by others. *Journal of Personality and Social Psychology, 84,* 261–276.

Bastian, B., & Haslam, N. (2006). Psychological essentialism and stereotype endorsement. *Journal of Experimental Social Psychology, 42,* 228–235.

Bastian, B., Jetten, J., & Ferris, L. J. (2014). Pain as social glue: Shared pain increased cooperation. *Psychological Science, 25,* 2079–2085.

Bastian, B., Jetten, J., Chen, H., Radke, H. R. M., Harding, J. F., & Fasoli, F. (2012). Losing our humanity: The self-dehumanizing consequences of social ostracism. *Personality and Social Psychology Bulletin, 39,* 156–169.

Batson, C. D., & Thompson, E. R. (2001). Why don't moral people act morally? Motivational considerations. *Current Directions in Psychological Science, 10,* 54–57.

Batson, C. D., & Weeks, J. L. (1996). Mood effects of unsuccessful helping: Another test of the empathy-altruism hypothesis. *Personality and Social Psychology Bulletin, 22,* 148–157.

Batson, C. D. (1983). Sociobiology and the role of religion in promoting prosocial behavior: An alternative view. *Journal of Personality and Social Psychology, 45,* 1380–1385.

Batson, C. D. (1999a). Behind the scenes. In D. G. Myers, *Social Psychology,* 6th edition. New York: McGraw Hill.

Batson, C. D. (1999b). *Addressing the altruism question experimentally.* Paper presented at the Templeton Foundation/Fetzer Institute Symposium on Empathy, Altruism, and Agape, Cambridge, MA.

Batson, C. D. (2001). Addressing the altruism question experimentally. In S. G. Post, L. B. Underwood, J. P. Schloss, & W. B. Hurlbut (Eds.), *Altruism and altruistic love: Science, philosophy, and religion in dialogue.* New York: Oxford University Press.

Batson, C. D. (2006). "Not all self-interest after all": Economics of empathy-induced altruism. In D. De Cremer, M. Zeelenberg, & J. K. Murnighan (Eds.), *Social psychology and economics.* Mahwah, NJ: Erlbaum.

Batson, C. D. (2011). *Altruism in humans.* New York: Oxford University Press.

Batson, C. D. (2021). The empathy-altruism hypothesis. In A. Kostić & D. Chadee (Eds.), *Positive psychology: An international perspective.* (pp. 12–32). Wiley Blackwell.

Batson, C. D. (2023). *Empathic concern: What it is and why it's important.* Oxford University Press.

Batson, C. D., Bolen, M. H., Cross, J. A., & Neuringer-Benefiel, H. E. (1986). Where is the altruism in the altruistic personality? *Journal of Personality and Social Psychology, 50,* 212–220.

Batson, C. D., Chao, M. C., & Givens, J. M. (2009). Pursuing moral outrage: Anger at torture. *Journal of Experimental Social Psychology, 45,* 155–160.

Batson, C. D., Coke, J. S., Jasnoski, M. L., & Hanson, M. (1978). Buying kindness: Effect of an extrinsic incentive for helping on perceived altruism. *Personality and Social Psychology Bulletin, 4,* 86–91.

Batson, C. D., Duncan, B. D., Ackerman, P., Buckley, T., & Birch, K. (1981). Is empathic emotion a source of altruistic motivation? *Journal of Personality and Social Psychology, 40,* 290–302.

Batson, C. D., Eklund, J. H., Chermok, V. L., Hoyt, J. L., & Ortiz, B. G. (2007). An additional antecedent of empathic concern: Valuing the welfare of the person in need. *Journal of Personality and Social Psychology, 93,* 65–74.

Batson, C. D., Fultz, J., & Schoenrade, P. A. (1987). Distress and empathy: Two qualitatively distinct vicarious emotions with different motivational consequences. *Journal of Personality, 55,* 19–40.

Batson, C. D., Kobrynowicz, D., Dinnerstein, J. L., Kampf, H. C., & Wilson, A. D. (1997). In a very different voice: Unmasking moral hypocrisy. *Journal of Personality and Social Psychology, 72,* 1335–1348.

Batson, C. D., Lishner, D. A., Carpenter, A., Dulin, L., Harjusola-Webb, S., Stocks, E. L., Gale, S., Hassan, O., & Sampat, B. (2003). ". . . As you would have them do unto you": Does imagining yourself in the other's place stimulate moral action? *Personality and Social Psychology Bulletin, 29,* 1190–1201.

Batson, C. D., Sympson, S. C., Hindman, J. L., Decruz, P., Todd, R. M., Jennings, G., & Burris, C. T. (1996). "I've been there, too": Effect on empathy of prior experience with a need. *Personality and Social Psychology Bulletin, 22,* 474–482.

Batson, C. D., Thompson, E. R., & Chen, H. (2002). Moral hypocrisy: Addressing some alternatives. *Journal of Personality and Social Psychology, 83,* 330–339.

Batson, C. D., Thompson, E. R., Seuferling, G., Whitney, H., & Strongman, J. A. (1999). Moral hypocrisy: Appearing moral to oneself without being so. *Journal of Personality and Social Psychology, 77,* 525–537.

Batz-Barbarich, C., Tay, L., Kuykendall, L., & Cheung, H. K. (2018). A meta-analysis of gender differences in subjective well-being: Estimating effect sizes and associations with gender inequality. *Psychological Science, 29,* 1491–1503.

Bauer, M., Cassar, A., Chytilová, J., & Henrich, J. (2014). War's enduring effects on the development of egalitarian motivations and in-group biases. *Psychological Science, 25,* 47–57.

Bauman, C. W., & Skitka, L. J. (2010). Making attributions for behaviors: The prevalence of correspondence bias in the general population. *Basic and Applied Social Psychology, 32,* 269–277.

Baumeister, R. F., & Bratslavsky, E. (1999). Passion, intimacy, and time: Passionate love as a function of change in intimacy. *Personality and Social Psychology Review, 3,* 49–67.

Baumeister, R. F., & Leary, M. R. (1995). The need to belong: Desire for interpersonal attachments as a fundamental human motivation. *Psychological Bulletin, 117,* 497–529.

Baumeister, R. F., & Scher, S. J. (1988). Self-defeating behavior patterns among normal individuals: Review and analysis of common self-destructive tendencies. *Psychological Bulletin, 104,* 3–22.

Baumeister, R. F., & Vohs, K. (2004). Sexual economics: Sex as female resource for social exchange in heterosexual interactions. *Personality and Social Psychology Bulletin, 8,* 339–363.

Baumeister, R. F., & Vohs, K. D. (2018). Revisiting our reappraisal of the (surprisingly few) benefits of high self-esteem. *Perspectives on Psychological Science, 13,* 137–140.

Baumeister, R. F., & Wotman, S. R. (1992). *Breaking hearts: The two sides of unrequited love.* New York: Guilford.

Baumeister, R. F. (2005). *The cultural animal: Human nature, meaning, and social life.* New York: Oxford University Press.

Baumeister, R. F., Ainsworth, S. E., & Vohs, K. D. (2016). Are groups more or less than the sum of their members? the moderating role of individual identification. *Behavioral and Brain Sciences, 39,* e137.

Baumeister, R. F., Campbell, J. D., Krueger, J. I., & Vohs, K. D. (2003). Does high self-esteem cause better performance, interpersonal success, happiness, or healthier lifestyles? Psychological Science in the Public Interest, 4, 1-44.

Baumeister, R. F., Catanese, K. R., & Vohs, K. D. (2001). Is there a gender difference in strength of sex drive? Theoretical views, conceptual distinctions, and a review of relevant evidence. *Personality and Social Psychology Review, 5,* 242-273.

Baumeister, R. F., DeWall, C. N., Ciarocco, N. J., & Twenge, J. M. (2005). Social exclusion impairs self-regulation. *Journal of Personality and Social Psychology, 88,* 589-604.

Baumgardner, A. H., & Brownlee, E. A. (1987). Strategic failure in social interaction: Evidence for expectancy disconfirmation process. *Journal of Personality and Social Psychology, 52,* 525-535.

Baumgartner, F., Davidson, M., Johnson, K., Krishnamurthy, A., & Wilson, C. (2017). *Deadly justice: A statistical portrait of the death penalty.* Oxford: Oxford University Press.

Baumgartner, F. R., Grigg, A. J., & Mastro, A. (2015). #BlackLivesDon'tMatter: race-of-victim effects in US executions, 1976-2013. *Politics, Groups, and Identities, 3,* 209-221.

Baumrind, D. (1964). Some thoughts on the ethics of research: After reading Milgram's "Behavioral study of obedience." *American Psychologist, 19,* 421-423.

Baumrind, D. (2015). When subjects become objects: The lies behind the Milgram legend. *Theory & Psychology, 25,* 690-696.

Baxter, T. L., & Goldberg, L. R. (1987). Perceived behavioral consistency underlying trait attributions to oneself and another: An extension of the actor-observer effect. *Personality and Social Psychology Bulletin, 13,* 437-447.

Bayer, E. (1929). Beitrage zur zeikomponenten theorie des hungers. *Zeitschrift fur Psychologie, 112,* 1-54.

Bazerman, M. H. (1986, June). Why negotiations go wrong. *Psychology Today,* pp. 54-58.

Bazerman, M. H. (1990). *Judgment in managerial decision making* (2nd ed.). New York: John Wiley.

Bazzini, D., Curtin, L., Joslin, S., Regan, S., & Martz, D. (2010). Do animated Disney characters portray and promote the beauty-goodness stereotype? *Journal of Applied Social Psychology, 40,* 2687-2709.

BBC. (2018, January 17). Minister for loneliness appointed to continue Jo Cox's work. https://www.bbc.com/news/uk-42708507

BBC. (2023, March 31). Homosexuality: The countries where it is illegal to be gay. BBC.com.

BBC News. (2022, February 24). Ukraine conflict: Russian forces attack from three sides. BBC.com.

Beals, K. P., Peplau, L. A., & Gable, S. L. (2009). Stigma management and well-being: The role of perceived social support, emotional processing, and suppression. *Personality and Social Psychology Bulletin, 35,* 867-879.

Beaman, A. L., & Klentz, B. (1983). The supposed physical attractiveness bias against supporters of the women's movement: A meta-analysis. *Personality and Social Psychology Bulletin, 9,* 544-550.

Beaman, A. L., Barnes, P. J., Klentz, B., & McQuirk, B. (1978). Increasing helping rates through information dissemination: Teaching pays. *Personality and Social Psychology Bulletin, 4,* 406-411.

Beaman, A. L., Klentz, B., Diener, E., & Svanum, S. (1979). Self-awareness and transgression in children: Two field studies. *Journal of Personality and Social Psychology, 37,* 1835-1846.

Beaman, L., Duflo, E., Pande, R., & Topalova, P. (2012). Female leadership raises aspirations and educational attainment for girls: A policy experiment in India. *Science, 335,* 582-586.

Bearak, B. (2010, July 9). South Africa braces for new attacks on immigrants. *The New York Times.* https://www.nytimes.com/2010/07/10/world/africa/10safrica.html

Beaulieu, C. M. J. (2004). Intercultural study of personal space: A case study. *Journal of Applied Social Psychology, 34,* 794-805.

Becatoros, E. (2012, November 13). On streets of Athens, racist attacks increase. *Associated Press* news.yahoo.com

Beck, A. T., & Young, J. E. (1978, September). College blues. *Psychology Today,* pp. 80-92.

Becker, D. V., Neel, R., & Anderson, U. S. (2010). Illusory conjunctions of angry facial expressions follow intergroup biases. *Psychological Science, 21,* 938-940.

Becker, S. W., & Eagly, A. H. (2004). The heroism of women and men. *American Psychologist, 59,* 163-178.

Beck, L. A., Pietrimonoco, P. R., DeBuse, C. J., Powers, S. I., & Sayer, A. G. (2013). Spouses' attachment pairings predict neuroendocrine, behavioral, and psychological responses to marital conflict. *Journal of Personality and Social Psychology, 105,* 388-424.

Beelmann, A., & Heinemann, K. S. (2014). Preventing prejudice and improving intergroup attitudes: A meta-analysis of child and adolescent training programs. *Journal of Applied Developmental Psychology, 35,* 10-24.

Begue, L., Beauvois, J-L., Courbet, D., Oberle, D., Lepage, J., & Duke, A. A. (2015). Personality predicts obedience in a Milgram paradigm. *Journal of Personality, 83,* 299-306.

Begue, L., Bushman, B., Giancola, P., Subra, B., & Rosset, E. (2010). "There is no such thing as an accident," especially when people are drunk. *Personality and Social Psychology Bulletin, 36,* 1301-1304.

Bekafigo, M. A., Stepanova, E. V., Eiler, B. A., Noguchi, K., & Ramsey, K. L. (2019). The effect of group polarization on opposition to Donald Trump. *Political Psychology, 40*(5), 1163-1178.

Bellah, R. N. (1995/1996, Winter). Community properly understood: A defense of "democratic communitarianism." *The Responsive Community,* pp. 49-54.

Bell, B. E., & Loftus, E. F. (1988). Degree of detail of eyewitness testimony and mock juror judgments. *Journal of Applied Social Psychology, 18,* 1171-1192.

Bell, B. E., & Loftus, E. F. (1989). Trivial persuasion in the courtroom: The power of (a few) minor details. *Journal of Personality and Social Psychology, 56,* 669-679.

Belletier, C., Normand, A., & Huguet, P. (2019). Social-facilitation-and-impairment effects: From motivation to cognition and the social brain. *Current Directions in Psychological Science, 28,* 260-265.

Bellezza, S., Gino, F., & Keinan, A. (2014). The red sneakers effect: Inferring status and competence from signals of nonconformity. *Journal of Consumer Research, 41,* 35-54.

Bellmore, A., Calvin, A. J., Xu, J., & Zhu, X. (2015). The five W's of "bullying" on Twitter: Who, what, why, where, and when. *Computers in Human Behavior, 44,* 305-314.

Bell, P. A. (1980). Effects of heat, noise, and provocation on retaliatory evaluative behavior. *Journal of Social Psychology, 110,* 97-100.

Bell, P. A. (2005). Reanalysis and perspective in the heat-aggression debate. *Journal of Personality and Social Psychology, 89,* 71-73.

Belmans, E., Raes, F., Vervliet, B., & Takano, K. (2023). Depressive symptoms and persistent negative self-referent thinking among adolescents: A learning account. *Acta Psychologica, 232,* 1-7.

Belson, W. A. (1978). *Television violence and the adolescent boy.* Westmead, England: Saxon House, Teakfield Ltd.

Beltz, A. M., Swanson, J. L., & Berenbaum, S. A. (2011). Gendered occupational interests: Prenatal androgen effects on psychological orientation to Things versus People. *Hormones and Behavior, 60,* 313-317.

Bem, D. J., & McConnell, H. K. (1970). Testing the self-perception explanation of dissonance phenomena: On the salience of premanipulation attitudes. *Journal of Personality and Social Psychology, 14,* 23–31.

Bem, D. J. (1972). Self-perception theory. In L. Berkowitz (Ed.), *Advances in experimental social psychology* (Vol. 6). New York: Academic Press.

Benartzi, S., & Thaler, R. H. (2013). Behavioral economics and the retirement savings crisis. *Science, 339,* 1152–1153.

Bender, M. (2021, July 27). The Olympics without fans is harming athletes' performance. *Scientific American.*

Benenson, J. F., Markovits, H., Fitzgerald, C., Geoffroy, D., Flemming, J., Kahlenberg, S. M., & Wrangham, R. W. (2009). Males' greater tolerance of same-sex peers. *Psychological Science, 20,* 184–190.

Benjamin, A. J., Kepes, S., & Bushman, B. J. (2018). Effects of weapons on aggressive thoughts, angry feelings, hostile appraisals, and aggressive behavior: A meta-analytic review of the weapons effect. *Personality and Social Psychology Review, 22,* 347–377.

Benjamin, Jr., L. T., & Simpson, J. A. (2009). The power of the situation: The impact of Milgram's obedience studies on personality and social psychology. *American Psychologist, 64,* 12–19.

Bennett, D. (2010, January 31). Easy = true: How "cognitive fluency" shapes what we believe, how we invest, and who will become a supermodel. *Boston Globe.* http://archive.boston.com/bostonglobe/ideas/articles/2010/01/31/easy__true/

Bennett, R. (1991, February). Pornography and extrafamilial child sexual abuse: Examining the relationship. Unpublished manuscript, Los Angeles Police Department Sexually Exploited Child Unit.

Benningstad, N. C. G., & Kunst, J. R. (2020). Dissociating meat from its animal origins: A systematic literature review. *Appetite, 147.*

Bennis, W. (1984). Transformative power and leadership. In T. J. Sergiovani & J. E. Corbally (Eds.), *Leadership and organizational culture.* Urbana: University of Illinois Press.

Benson, P. L., Karabenick, S. A., & Lerner, R. M. (1976). Pretty pleases: The effects of physical attractiveness, race, and sex on receiving help. *Journal of Experimental Social Psychology, 12,* 409–415.

Benton, S. L., Downey, R. G., Gilder, P. J., & Benton, S. A. (2008). College students' norm perception predicts reported use of protective behavioral strategies for alcohol consumption. *Journal of Studies on Alcohol and Drugs, 69,* 859–866.

Benton, T. R., Ross, D. F., Bradshaw, E., Thomas, W. N., & Bradshaw, G. S. (2006). Eyewitness memory is still not common sense: Comparing jurors, judges and law enforcement to eyewitness experts. *Applied Cognitive Psychology, 20,* 115–129.

Berenbaum, S. A., Beltz, A. M., Bryk, K., & McHale, S. (2018). Gendered peer involvement in girls with congenital adrenal hyperplasia: Effects of prenatal androgens, gendered activities, and gender cognitions. *Archives of Sexual Behavior, 47,* 915–929.

Berger, J., & Le Mens, G. (2009). How adoption speed affects the abandonment of cultural tastes. *Proceedings of the National Academy of Sciences, 106,* 8146–8150.

Berger, J., Bradlow, E. T., Braumstein, A., & Zhang, Y. (2012). From Karen to Katie: Using baby names to understand cultural evolution. *Psychological Science, 23,* 1067–1073.

Bergh, R., & Brandt, M. J. (2022). Mapping principal dimensions of prejudice in the United States. *Journal of Personality and Social Psychology, 123,* 154–173.

Berg, J. H., & McQuinn, R. D. (1986). Attraction and exchange in continuing and noncontinuing dating relationships. *Journal of Personality and Social Psychology, 50,* 942–952.

Berg, J. H., & Peplau, L. A. (1982). Loneliness: The relationship of self-disclosure and androgyny. *Personality and Social Psychology Bulletin, 8,* 624–630.

Berg, J. H. (1984). Development of friendship between roommates. *Journal of Personality and Social Psychology, 46,* 346–356.

Berglas, S., & Jones, E. E. (1978). Drug choice as a self-handicapping strategy in response to noncontingent success. *Journal of Personality and Social Psychology, 36,* 405–417.

Bergold, A. N., & Bull Kovera, M. (2022). Diversity's impact on the quality of deliberations. *Personality and Social Psychology Bulletin, 48,* 1406–1420.

Bergold, S., & Steinmayr, R. (2023). Teacher judgments predict developments in adolescents' school performance, motivation, and life satisfaction. *Journal of Educational Psychology, 115,* 642–664.

Bergquist, M. (2020). Most people think they are more pro-environmental than others: A demonstration of the Better-than-Average Effect in perceived pro-environmental behavioral engagement. *Basic & Applied Social Psychology, 42,* 50–61.

Bergquist, M., Thiel, M., Goldberg, M. H., & van der Linden, S. (2023). Field interventions for climate change mitigation behaviors: A second-order meta-analysis. *PNAS Proceedings of the National Academy of Sciences of the United States of America, 120,* 1–10.

Bergsieker, H. B., Leslie, L. M., Constantine, V. S., & Fiske, S. T. (2012). Stereotyping by omission: Eliminate the negative, accentuate the positive. *Journal of Personality and Social Psychology, 102,* 1214–1238.

Berkman, L. F. (1995). The role of social relations in health promotion. *Psychosomatic Medicine, 57,* 245–254.

Berkowitz, L., & Geen, R. G. (1966). Film violence and the cue properties of available targets. *Journal of Personality and Social Psychology, 3,* 525–530.

Berkowitz, L. (1968, September). Impulse, aggression and the gun. *Psychology Today,* pp. 18–22.

Berkowitz, L. (1972). Social norms, feelings, and other factors affecting helping and altruism. In L. Berkowitz (Ed.), *Advances in experimental social psychology* (Vol. 6). New York: Academic Press.

Berkowitz, L. (1978). Whatever happened to the frustration-aggression hypothesis? *American Behavioral Scientists, 21,* 691–708.

Berkowitz, L. (1981, June). How guns control us. *Psychology Today,* 11–12.

Berkowitz, L. (1983). Aversively stimulated aggression: Some parallels and differences in research with animals and humans. *American Psychologist, 38,* 1135–1144.

Berkowitz, L. (1984). Some effects of thoughts on anti- and prosocial influences of media events: A cognitive-neoassociation analysis, *Psychological Bulletin, 95,* 410–427.

Berkowitz, L. (1987). Mood, self-awareness, and willingness to help. *Journal of Personality and Social Psychology, 52,* 721–729.

Berkowitz, L. (1989). Frustration-aggression hypothesis: Examination and reformulation. *Psychological Bulletin, 106,* 59–73.

Berkowitz, L. (1995). A career on aggression. In G. G. Brannigan & M. R. Merrens (Eds.), *The social psychologists: Research adventures.* New York: McGraw Hill.

Berkowitz, L. (1998). Affective aggression: The role of stress, pain, and negative affect. In R. G. Geen & E. Donnerstein (Eds.), *Human aggression: Theories, research, and implications for social policy.* San Diego: Academic Press.

Bernardo, A. B. I., & Liu, J. H. (2018). Socially engaged social psychology in Asia: Sustaining research progress in diverse directions. *Journal of Pacific Rim Psychology, 12.*

Berndsen, M., Spears, R., van der Pligt, J., & McGarty, C. (2002). Illusory correlation and stereotype formation: Making sense of group differences and cognitive biases. In C. McGarty, V. Y. Yzerbyt, & R. Spears (Eds.), *Stereotypes as explanations: The formation of meaningful beliefs about social groups.* New York: Cambridge University Press.

Bernhardt, P. C., Dabbs, J. M., Jr., Fielden, J. A., & Lutter, C. D. (1998). Testosterone changes during vicarious experiences of winning and losing among fans at sporting events. *Physiology and Behavior, 65,* 59–62.

Berns, G. S., Chappelow, J., Zink, C. F., Pagnoni, G., Martin-Skurski, M. E., & Richards, J. (2005). Neurobiological correlates of social conformity and independence during mental rotation. *Biological Psychiatry, 58,* 245–253.

Bernstein, M. J., Young, S. G., & Claypool, H. M. (2010). Is Obama's win a gain for Blacks? Changes in implicit racial prejudice following the 2008 election. *Social Psychology, 41,* 147–151.

Berry, D. S., & Zebrowitz-McArthur, L. (1988). What's in a face: Facial maturity and the attribution of legal responsibility. *Personality and Social Psychology Bulletin, 14,* 23–33.

Berscheid, E., & Walster (Hatfield), E. (1978). *Interpersonal attraction.* Reading, MA: Addison-Wesley.

Berscheid, E. (1981). An overview of the psychological effects of physical attractiveness and some comments upon the psychological effects of knowledge of the effects of physical attractiveness. In W. Lucker, K. Ribbens, & J. A. McNamera (Eds.), *Logical aspects of facial form (craniofacial growth series).* Ann Arbor: University of Michigan Press.

Berscheid, E. (2010). Love in the fourth dimension. *Annual Review of Psychology, 61,* 1–25.

Berscheid, E., Boye, D., & Walster (Hatfield), E. (1968). Retaliation as a means of restoring equity. *Journal of Personality and Social Psychology, 10,* 370–376.

Berscheid, E., Dion, K., Walster (Hatfield), E., & Walster, G. W. (1971). Physical attractiveness and dating choice: A test of the matching hypothesis. *Journal of Experimental Social Psychology, 7,* 173–189.

Berscheid, E., Graziano, W., Monson, T., & Dermer, M. (1976). Outcome dependency: Attention, attribution, and attraction. *Journal of Personality and Social Psychology, 34,* 978–989.

Berscheid, E., Walster, G. W., & Hatfield (was Walster), E. (1969). *Effects of accuracy and positivity of evaluation on liking for the evaluator.* Unpublished manuscript. Summarized by E. Berscheid and E. Walster (Hatfield) (1978), *Interpersonal attraction.* Reading, MA: Addison-Wesley.

Bersoff, D. N. (1987). Social science data and the Supreme Court: Lockhart as a case in point. *American Psychologist, 42,* 52–58.

Berthold, A., Steffens, M. C., & Mummendey, A. (2019). What did they say? How subgroup stereotypes influence memory for superordinate groups. *Journal of Experimental Social Psychology, 83,* 23–36.

Bertolotti, M., & Catellani, P. (2014). Effects of message framing in policy communication on climate change. *European Journal of Social Psychology, 44,* 474–486.

Bertrand, M., & Mullainathan, S. (2004). Are Emily and Greg more employable than Lakisha and Jamal? A field experiment on labor market discrimination. *American Economic Review, 94,* 991–1013.

Besser, A., & Priel, B. (2005). The apple does not fall far from the tree: Attachment styles and personality vulnerabilities to depression in three generations of women. *Personality and Social Psychology Bulletin, 31,* 1052–1073.

Bettencourt, B. A., & Kernahan, C. (1997). A meta-analysis of aggression in the presence of violent cues: Effects of gender differences and aversive provocation. *Aggressive Behavior, 23,* 447–456.

Bettencourt, B. A., Dill, K. E., Greathouse, S. A., Charlton, K., & Mulholland, A. (1997). Evaluations of ingroup and outgroup members: The role of category-based expectancy violation. *Journal of Experimental Social Psychology, 33,* 244–275.

Bettencourt, B. A., Talley, A., Benjamin, A. J., & Valentine, J. (2006). Personality and aggressive behavior under provoking and neutral conditions: A meta-analytic review. *Psychological Bulletin, 132,* 751–777.

Beussink, C. N., Hackney, A. A., & Vitacco, M. J. (2017). The effects of perspective taking on empathy-related responses for college students higher in callous traits. *Personality and Individual Differences, 11,* 986–991.

Bianchi, E. (2016). American individualism rises and falls with the economy: Cross-temporal evidence that individualism declines when the economy falters. *Journal of Personality and Social Psychology, 111,* 567–584.

Bianchi, E. C., Hall, E. V., & Lee, S. (2018). Reexamining the link between economic downturns and racial antipathy: Evidence that prejudice against blacks rises during recessions. *Psychological Science, 29,* 1584–1597.

Bickman, L., & Green, S. K. (1977). Situational cues and crime reporting: Do signs make a difference? *Journal of Applied Social Psychology, 7,* 1–18.

Bickman, L. (1975). Bystander intervention in a crime: The effect of a mass-media campaign. *Journal of Applied Social Psychology, 5,* 296–302.

Bickman, L. (1979). Interpersonal influence and the reporting of a crime. *Personality and Social Psychology Bulletin, 5,* 32–35.

Bieber, C. (2023, August 15). Leading causes of divorce: 43% report lack of family support. Forbes.com.

Bilali, R. (2022). Fighting violent extremism with narrative intervention: Evidence from a field experiment in West Africa. *Psychological Science, 33,* 184–195.

Bilderbeck, A. C., Brown, G. D. A., Read, J., Woolrich, M., Cowen, P. J., Behrens, T. E. J., & Rogers, R. D. (2014). Serotonin and social norms: Tryptophan depletion impairs social comparison and leads to resource depletion in a multiplayer harvesting game. *Psychological Science, 25,* 1303–1313.

Billig, M., & Tajfel, H. (1973). Social categorization and similarity in intergroup behaviour. *European Journal of Social Psychology, 3,* 27–52.

Biner, P. M. (1991). Effects of lighting-induced arousal on the magnitude of goal valence. *Personality and Social Psychology Bulletin, 17,* 219–226.

Bingenheimer, J. B., Brennan, R. T., & Earls, F. J. (2005). Firearm violence exposure and serious violent behavior. *Science, 308,* 1323–1326.

Binham, R. (1980, March–April). Trivers in Jamaica. *Science, 80,* 57–67.

Bishop, B. (2020, December 17). For most Americans, the local presidential vote was a landslide. *Daily Yonder.*

Bissell, K., & Chou, S. (2023). Living for the likes: Social media use, fear of missing out, and body and life satisfaction in women. *Psychology of Popular Media.*

Björkqvist, K. (1994). Sex differences in physical, verbal, and indirect aggression: A review of recent research. *Sex Roles, 30,* 177–188.

Blair, C. A., Thompson, L. F., & Wuensch, K. L. (2005). Electronic helping behavior: The virtual presence of others makes a difference. *Basic and Applied Social Psychology, 27,* 171–178.

Blair, G., Littman, R., & Paluck, E. L. (2019). Motivating the adoption of new community-minded behaviors: An empirical test in Nigeria. *Science Advances, 5,* eaau5175.

Blair, I. V., Judd, C. M., & Chapleau, K. M. (2004). The influence of Afrocentric facial features in criminal sentencing. *Psychological Science, 15,* 674–679.

Blaker, N. M., Rompa, I., Dessing, I. H., Vriend, A. F., Herschberg, C., & van Vugt, M. (2013). The height leadership advantage in men and women: Testing evolutionary psychology predictions about the perceptions of tall leaders. *Group Processes & Intergroup Relations, 16,* 17–27.

Blake, R. R., & Mouton, J. S. (1962). The intergroup dynamics of win-lose conflict and problem-solving collaboration in union-management relations. In M. Sherif (Ed.), *Intergroup relations and leadership.* New York: Wiley.

Blake, R. R., & Mouton, J. S. (1979). Intergroup problem solving in organizations: From theory to practice. In W. G. Austin & S. Worchel (Eds.), *The Social Psychology of Intergroup Relations.* Monterey, CA: Brooks/Cole.

Blanchard, F. A., & Cook, S. W. (1976). Effects of helping a less competent member of a cooperating interracial group on the development of interpersonal attraction. *Journal of Personality and Social Psychology, 34,* 1245–1255.

Blank, H., & Launay, C. (2014). How to protect eyewitness memory against the misinformation effect: A meta-analysis of post-warning studies. *Journal of Applied Research in Memory and Cognition, 3,* 77–88.

Blank, H., Nestler, S., von Collani, G., & Fischer, V. (2008). How many hindsight biases are there? *Cognition, 106,* 1408–1440.

Blanton, H., Jaccard, J., Gonzales, P. M., & Christie, C. (2006). Decoding the implicit association test: Implications for criterion prediction. *Journal of Experimental Social Psychology, 42,* 192–212.

Blanton, H., Jaccard, J., Klick, J., Mellers, B., Mitchell, G., & Tetlock P. E. (2009). Strong claims and weak evidence: reassessing the predictive validity of the IAT. *Journal of Applied Psychology, 94,* 583–603.

Blanton, H., Jaccard, J., Strauts, E., Mitchell, G., & Tetlock, P. E. (2015). Toward a meaningful metric of implicit prejudice. *Journal of Applied Psychology, 100,* 1468–1481.

Blanton, H., Pelham, B. W., DeHart, T., & Carvallo, M. (2001). Overconfidence as dissonance reduction. *Journal of Experimental Social Psychology, 37,* 373–385.

Blass, T. (2000). The Milgram paradigm after 35 years: Some things we now know about obedience to authority. In T. Blass (Ed.), *Obedience to authority: Current perspectives on the Milgram paradigm.* Mahwah, NJ: Erlbaum.

Bleske-Rechek, A., Remiker, M. W., & Baker, J. P. (2009). Similar from the start: Assortment in young adult dating couples and its link to relationship stability over time. *Individual Differences Research, 7,* 142–158.

Block, J., & Funder, D. C. (1986). Social roles and social perception: Individual differences in attribution and error. *Journal of Personality and Social Psychology, 51,* 1200–1207.

Blogowska, J., Saroglou, V., & Lambert, C. (2013). Religious prosociality and aggression: It's real. *Journal for the Scientific Study of Religion, 52,* 524–536.

Bloom, M. (2017). Constructing expertise: Terrorist recruitment and "talent spotting" in the PIRA, Al Qaeda, and ISIS. *Studies in Conflict & Terrorism, 40,* 603–623.

Bloom, P. (2010, May 6). The moral life of babies. *The New York Times Magazine.* www.nytimes.com

Bloom, P. (2016). *Against empathy: The case for rational compassion.* New York: Ecco.

BLS (Bureau of Labor Statistics). (2017). Average hours per day parents spent caring for and helping household children. https://www.bls.gov/charts/american-time-use/activity-by-parent.htm

Boccanfuso, E., White, F. A., & Maunder, R. D. (2021). Reducing transgender stigma via an e-contact intervention. *Sex Roles: A Journal of Research, 84,* 326–336.

Bodenhausen, G. V., & Macrae, C. N. (1998). Stereotype activation and inhibition. In R. S. Wyer, Jr., *Stereotype activation and inhibition: Advances in social cognition* (Vol. 11). Mahwah, NJ: Erlbaum.

Bodenhausen, G. V. (1990). Stereotypes as judgmental heuristics: Evidence of circadian variations in discrimination. *Psychological Science, 1,* 319–322.

Bodenhausen, G. V. (1993). Emotions, arousal, and stereotypic judgments: A heuristic model of affect and stereotyping. In D. M. Mackie & D. L. Hamilton (Eds.), *Affect, cognition, and stereotyping: Interactive processes in group perception.* San Diego: Academic Press.

Bodenhausen, G. V., Sheppard, L. A., & Kramer, G. F. (1994). Negative affect and social judgment: The differential impact of anger and sadness. *European Journal of Social Psychology, 24,* 45–62.

Boden, J. M., Fergusson, D. M., & Horwood, L. J. (2008). Does adolescent self-esteem predict later life outcomes? A test of the causal role of self-esteem. *Development and Psychopathology, 20,* 319–339.

Bodford, J. E., Kwan, V. Y., & Sobota, D. S. (2017). Fatal attractions: Attachment to smartphones predicts anthropomorphic beliefs and dangerous behaviors. *Cyberpsychology, Behavior, and Social Networking, 20,* 320–326.

Boecker, L., Loschelder, D. D., & Topolinski, S. (2022). How individuals react emotionally to others' (mis)fortunes: A social comparison framework. *Journal of Personality and Social Psychology, 123,* 55–83.

Boehm, J. K., Peterson, C., Kivimaki, M., & Kubzansky, L. (2011). A prospective study of positive psychological well-being and coronary heart disease. *Health Psychology, 30,* 259–267.

Böger, A., & Huxhold, O. (2018). Do the antecedents and consequences of loneliness change from middle adulthood into old age? *Developmental Psychology, 54,* 181–197.

Boggiano, A. K., & Ruble, D. N. (1985). Children's responses to evaluative feedback. In R. Schwarzer (Ed.), *Self-related cognitions in anxiety and motivation.* Hillsdale, NJ: Erlbaum.

Böheim, R., Grübl, D., & Lackner, M. (2019). Choking under pressure—evidence of the causal effect of audience size on performance. *Journal of Economic Behavior & Organization,* 168, 76–93.

Boice, J. (2020, March 20). Infectious disease experts don't know how bad the coronavirus is going to get, either. *Five Thirty Eight.* https://fivethirtyeight.com/features/infectious-disease-experts-dont-know-how-bad-the-coronavirus-is-going-to-get-either/

Bonam, C. M., Bergieker, H. B., & Eberhardt, J. L. (2016). Polluting Black space. *Journal of Experimental Psychology: General, 145,* 1561–1582.

Bond, C. F., Jr., & Titus, L. J. (1983). Social facilitation: A meta-analysis of 241 studies. *Psychological Bulletin, 94,* 265–292.

Bond, C. F., Jr., DiCandia, C. G., & MacKinnon, J. R. (1988). Responses to violence in a psychiatric setting: The role of patient's race. *Personality and Social Psychology Bulletin, 14,* 448–458.

Bond, M. H. (2004). Culture and aggression: From context to coercion. *Personality and Social Psychology Review, 8,* 62–78.

Bond, R., & Smith, P. B. (1996). Culture and conformity: A meta-analysis of studies using Asch's (1952b, 1956) line judgment task. *Psychological Bulletin, 119,* 111–137.

Bond, R. M., & Bushman, B. J. (2017). The contagious spread of violence among US adolescents through social networks. *American Journal of Public Health, 107,* 288–294.

Bond, R. M., Fariss, C. J., Jones, J. J., Kramer, A. I., Marlow, C., Settle, J. E., & Fowler, J. H. (2012). A 61-million-person experiment in social influence and political mobilization. *Nature, 489,* 295–298.

Bongiorno, R., Langbroek, C., Bain, P. G., Ting, M., & Ryan, M. K. (2020). Why women are blamed for being sexually harassed: The effects of empathy for female victims and male perpetrators. *Psychology of Women Quarterly, 44,* 11–27.

Bonner, B. L., & Baumann, M. R. (2012). Leveraging member expertise to improve knowledge transfer and demonstrability in groups. *Journal of Personality and Social Psychology, 102,* 337–350.

Bonnot, V., & Croizet, J.-C. (2007). Stereotype internalization and women's math performance: The role of interference in working memory. *Journal of Experimental Social Psychology, 43,* 857–866.

Bono, J. E., & Judge, T. A. (2004). Personality and transformational and transactional leadership: A meta-analysis. *Journal of Applied Psychology, 89,* 901–910.

Bonsaksen, T., Ruffolo, M., Price, D., Leung, J., Thygesen, H., Lamph, G., Kabelenga, I., & Geirdal, A. Ø. (2023). Associations between social media use and loneliness in a cross-national population: Do motives for social media use matter? *Health Psychology and Behavioral Medicine, 11.*

Bonta, B. D. (1997). Cooperation and competition in peaceful societies. *Psychological Bulletin, 121,* 299–320.

Boomsma, D. I., Cacioppo, J. T., Slagboom, P. E., & Posthuma, D. (2006). Genetic linkage and association analysis for loneliness in Dutch twin and sibling pairs points to a region on chromosome 12q23-24. *Behavior Genetics, 36,* 137–146.

Boothby, E. J., & Bohns, V. K. (2021). Why a simple act of kindness is not as simple as it seems: Underestimating the positive impact of our compliments on others. *Personality and Social Psychology Bulletin, 47,* 826–840.

Booth, R., & Mohdin, A. (2018, December 2). Revealed: The stark evidence of everyday racial bias in Britain. *The Guardian.* https://www.theguardian.com/uk-news/2018/dec/02/revealed-the-stark-evidence-of-everyday-racial-bias-in-britain

Booth, R. W., Aydin, C., Ulupunar, E., & Nadeem, M. (2023). Probability bias is an independent correlate of depressive symptoms. *Motivation and Emotion.*

Borgida, E., & White, P. (1980). *Judgmental bias and legal reform.* Unpublished manuscript, University of Minnesota.

Borgida, E. (1981). Legal reform of rape laws. In L. Bickman (Ed.), *Applied social psychology annual.* (Vol. 2, pp. 211–241). Beverly Hills, CA: Sage.

Bor, J., Venkataramani, A. S., Williams, D.R., & Tsai, A. C. (2018). Police killings and their spillover effects on the mental health of Black Americans: A population-based, quasi-experimental study. *The Lancet, 392,* 302–310.

Bornstein, B. H., & Zickafoose, D. J. (1999). "I know I know it, I know I saw it": The stability of the confidence-accuracy relationship across domains. *Journal of Experimental Psychology: Applied, 5,* 76–88.

Bornstein, B. H., Golding, J. M., Neuschatz, J., Kimbrough, C., Reed, K., Magyarics, C., & Luecht, K. (2017). Mock juror sampling issues in jury simulation research: A meta-analysis. *Law and Human Behavior, 41,* 13–28.

Bornstein, G., & Rapoport, A. (1988). Intergroup competition for the provision of step-level public goods: Effects of preplay communication. *European Journal of Social Psychology, 18,* 125–142.

Bornstein, G., Rapoport, A., Kerpel, L., & Katz, T. (1989). Within- and between-group communication in intergroup competition for public goods. *Journal of Experimental Social Psychology, 25,* 422–436.

Bornstein, R. F., & D'Agostino, P. R. (1992). Stimulus recognition and the mere exposure effect. *Journal of Personality and Social Psychology, 63,* 545–552.

Bornstein, R. F. (1989). Exposure and affect: Overview and meta-analysis of research, 1968–1987. *Psychological Bulletin, 106,* 265–289.

Bornstein, R. F. (1999). Source amnesia, misattribution, and the power of unconscious perceptions and memories. *Psychoanalytic Psychology, 16,* 155–178.

Bos, P. A., Terburg, D., & van Honk, J. (2010). Testosterone decreases trust in socially naïve humans. *Proceedings of the National Academy of Sciences, 107,* 11149–11150.

Bossard, J. H. S. (1932). Residential propinquity as a factor in marriage selection. *American Journal of Sociology, 38,* 219–224.

Bosson, J. K., & Michniewicz, K. S. (2013). Gender dichotimization at the level of ingroup identify: What it is, and why men use it more than women. *Journal of Personality and Social Psychology, 105,* 425–442.

Bosson, J. K., Jurek, P., Vandello, J. A., Kosakowska-Berezecka, N., Olech, M., Besta, T., Bender, M., Hoorens, V., Becker, M., Timur Sevincer, A., Best, D. L., Safdar, S., Włodarczyk, A., Zawisza, M., Żadkowska, M., Abuhamdeh, S., Badu Agyemang, C., Akbaş, G., Albayrak-Aydemir, N., . . . et al. (2021). Psychometric properties and correlates of Precarious Manhood Beliefs in 62 nations. *Journal of Cross-Cultural Psychology, 52,* 231–258.

Bothwell, R. K., Brigham, J. C., & Malpass, R. S. (1989). Cross-racial identification. *Personality and Social Psychology Bulletin, 15,* 19–25.

Botvin, G. J., Epstein, J. A., & Griffin, K. W. (2008). A social influence model of alcohol use for inner-city adolescents: Family drinking, perceived drinking norms, and perceived social benefits of drinking. *Journal of Studies on Alcohol and Drugs, 69,* 397–405.

Botvin, G. J., Schinke, S., & Orlandi, M. A. (1995). School-based health promotion: Substance abuse and sexual behavior. *Applied & Preventive Psychology, 4,* 167–184.

Bouas, K. S., & Komorita, S. S. (1996). Group discussion and cooperation in social dilemmas. *Personality and Social Psychology Bulletin, 22,* 1144–1150.

Bourassa, K. J., Ruiz, J. M., & Sbarra, D. A. (2019). Smoking and physical activity explain the increased mortality risk following marital separation and divorce: Evidence from the English Longitudinal Study of Ageing. *Annals of Behavioral Medicine, 53,* 255–266.

Bourgeois, M. J., Horowitz, I. A., & Lee, L. F. (1993). Effects of technicality and access to trial transcripts on verdicts and information processing in a civil trial. *Personality and Social Psychology Bulletin, 19,* 219–226.

Bourke, M. L., & Hernandez, A. E. (2009). The "Butner study" redux: A report of the incidence of hands-on child victimization by child pornography offenders. *Journal of Family Violence, 24,* 183–191.

Boutwell, B. B., Barnes, J. C., & Beaver, K. M. (2015). When love dies: Further elucidating the existence of a mate ejection module. *Review of General Psychology, 19,* 30–38.

Bouwman, E. P., Bolderdijk, J. W., Onwezen, M. C., & Taufik, D. (2022). "Do you consider animal welfare to be important?" activating cognitive dissonance via value activation can promote vegetarian choices. *Journal of Environmental Psychology, 83,* 1–11.

Bowen, E. (1988, April 4). Whatever became of Honest Abe? *Time.*

Bowen, N. K., Wegmann, K. M., & Webber, K. C. (2013). Enhancing a brief writing intervention to combat stereotype threat among middle-school students. *Journal of Educational Psychology, 105,* 427–435.

Bowes, S. M., Costello, T. H., & Tasimi, A. (2023). The conspiratorial mind: A meta-analytic review of motivational and personological correlates. *Psychological Bulletin.*

Bowlby, J. (1980). *Loss, sadness and depression, Vol. III of Attachment and loss.* (p. 422). London: Basic Books.

Boyce, C. J., & Wood, A. M. (2011). Personality prior to disability determines adaptation: Agreeable individuals recover lost life satisfaction faster and more completely. *Psychological Science, 22,* 1397–1402.

Boyce, C. J., Wood, A. M., Banks, J., Clark, A. E., & Brown, G. D. A. (2013). Money, well-being, and loss aversion: Does an income loss have a greater effect on well-being than an equivalent income gain? *Psychological Science, 24,* 2557–2562.

Boyes, A. D., & Fletcher, G. J. O. (2007). Metaperceptions of bias in intimate relationships. *Journal of Personality and Social Psychology, 92,* 286–306.

Boyle, G. (2019, September 21). Where there's Muck. . . . https://www.gdnonline.com/Details/609219

Boynton, M. H., Portnoy, D. B., & Johnson, B. T. (2013). Exploring the ethics and psychological impact of deception in psychological research. *IRB: Ethics & Human Research, 35,* 7–13.

Bradford, T. W., Grier, S. A., & Henderson, G. R. (2017). Weight loss through virtual support communities: A role for identity-based motivation in public commitment. *Journal of Interactive Marketing, 40,* 9–23.

Bradley, W., & Mannell, R. C. (1984). Sensitivity of intrinsic motivation to reward procedure instructions. *Personality and Social Psychology Bulletin, 10,* 426–431.

Brady, W. J., Wills, J. A., Burkart, D., Jost, J. T., & Van Bavel, J. J. (2019). An ideological asymmetry in the diffusion of moralized content on social media among political leaders. *Journal of Experimental Psychology: General, 148,* 1802–1813.

Branas, C. C., Richmond, T. S., Culhane, D. P., Have, T. R. T., & Wiebe, D. J. (2009). Investigating the link between gun possession and gun assault. *American Journal of Public Health, 99,* 2034–2040.

Brand, R. J., Bonatsos, A., D'Orazio, R., & DeShong, H. (2012). What is beautiful is good, even online: Correlations between photo attractiveness and text attractiveness in men's online dating profiles. *Computers in Human Behavior, 28,* 166–170.

Brandt, M. J., & Van Tongeren, D. R. (2017). People both high and low on religious fundamentalism are prejudiced toward dissimilar groups. *Journal of Personality and Social Psychology, 112,* 76–97.

Brandt, M. J., IJzerman, H., Dijksterhuis, A., Farach, F. J., Geller, J., Giner-Sorolla, R., Grange, J. A., Perugini, M., Spies, J. R., & van't Veer, A. (2014). The replication recipe: What makes for a convincing replication? *Journal of Experimental Social Psychology, 50,* 217–224.

Bratman, G. N., Daily, G. C., Levy, B. J., & Gross, J. J. (2015). The benefits of nature experience: Improved affect and cognition. *Landscape and Urban Planning, 138,* 41–50.

Bratt, C., Sidanius, J., & Sheehy-Skeffington, J. (2016). Shaping the development of prejudice: Latent growth modeling of the influence of social dominance orientation on outgroup affect in youth. *Personality and Social Psychology Bulletin, 42,* 1617–1634.

Brauer, M., Judd, C. M., & Gliner, M. D. (1995). The effects of repeated expressions on attitude polarization during group discussions. *Journal of Personality and Social Psychology, 68,* 1014–1029.

Brauer, M., Judd, C. M., & Jacquelin, V. (2001). The communication of social stereotypes: The effects of group discussion and information distribution on stereotypic appraisals. *Journal of Personality and Social Psychology, 81,* 463–475.

Braverman, J. (2005). The effect of mood on detection of covariation. *Personality and Social Psychology Bulletin, 31,* 1487–1497.

Bray, R. M., & Noble, A. M. (1978). Authoritarianism and decisions of mock juries: Evidence of jury bias and group polarization. *Journal of Personality and Social Psychology, 36,* 1424–1430.

Breckler, S. J. (2010, April). In the heat of the moment. *Monitor on Psychology,* p. 39.

Bregman, N. J., & McAllister, H. A. (1982). Eyewitness testimony: The role of commitment in increasing reliability. *Social Psychology Quarterly, 45,* 181–184.

Brehm, J. W. (1956). Postdecision changes in the desirability of alternatives. *The Journal of Abnormal and Social Psychology, 52,* 384–389.

Brehm, J. W. (1999). *Would the real dissonance theory please stand up?* American Psychological Society convention, 1999.

Brehm, S., & Brehm, J. W. (1981). *Psychological reactance: A theory of freedom and control.* New York: Academic Press.

Brehm, S. S., & Smith, T. W. (1986). Social psychological approaches to psychotherapy and behavior change. In S. L. Garfield & A. E. Bergin (Eds.), *Handbook of psychotherapy and behavior change,* (3rd ed.). New York: Wiley.

Brekke, J. S., Prindle, C., Bae, S. W., & Long, J. D. (2001). Risks for individuals with schizophrenia who are living in the community. *Psychiatric Services, 52,* 1358–1366.

Brescoll, V. L., Uhlmann, E. L., & Newman, G. E. (2013). The effects of system-justifying motives on endorsement of essentialist explanations for gender differences. *Journal of Personality and Social Psychology, 105,* 891–908.

Brethel-Haurwitz, K., & Marsh, A. A. (2014). Geographical differences in subjective well-being predict extraordinary altruism. *Psychological Science, 25,* 762–771.

Brethel-Haurwitz, K. M., Cardinale, E. M., Vekaria, K. M., Robertson, E. L., Walitt, B., VanMeter, J. W., & Marsh, A. A. (2018). Extraordinary altruists exhibit enhanced self-other overlap in neural responses to distress. *Psychological Science, 29,* 1631–1641.

Bretter, C., Unsworth, K. L., & Robinson, M. A. (2023). Watching the mimickers: Mimicry and identity in observed interactions. *Journal of Experimental Psychology: Applied, 29,* 398–413.

Breuer, J., Scharkow, M., & Quandt, T. (2014). Sore losers? A reexamination of the frustration-aggression hypothesis for collocated video game play. *Psychology of Popular Media Culture, 4*(2), 126–137.

Brewer, M. B., & Gaertner, S. L. (2004). Toward reduction of prejudice: Intergroup contact and social categorization. In M. B. Brewer & M. Hewstone (Eds.), *Self and social identity.* Malden, MA: Blackwell.

Brewer, M. B., & Miller, N. (1988). Contact and cooperation: When do they work? In P. A. Katz & D. Taylor (Eds.), *Towards the elimination of racism: Profiles in controversy.* New York: Plenum.

Brewer, M. B., & Pierce, K. P. (2005). Social identity complexity and outgroup tolerance. *Personality and Social Psychology Bulletin, 31,* 428–437.

Brewer, M. B., & Silver, M. (1978). In-group bias as a function of task characteristics. *European Journal of Social Psychology, 8,* 393–400.

Brewer, N. T., Hall, M. G., Noar, S. M., Parada, H., Stein-Seroussi, A., Bach, L. E., & . . . Ribisl, K. M. (2016). Effect of pictorial cigarette pack warnings on changes in smoking behavior: A randomized clinical trial. *JAMA Internal Medicine, 176,* 905–912

Brewer, N., Weber, N., & Guerin, N. (2019). Police lineups of the future? *American Psychologist, 75,* 76–91.

Bridger, E. K., Tufte, H. A., & Comerford, D. A. (2023). Dispositional and situational attributions for why the rich live longer than the poor. *Journal of Applied Social Psychology*. 53, 469–481.

Brigham, J. C., Bennett, L. B., Meissner, C. A., & Mitchell, T. L. (2006). The influence of race on eyewitness testimony. In R. Lindsay, M. Toglia, D. Ross, & J. D. Read (Eds.), *Handbook of eyewitness psychology.* Mahwah, NJ: Erlbaum.

British Psychological Society. (2018). *Code of human research ethics.* Leicester, UK: Author. https://www.bps.org.uk/news-and-policy/bps-code-ethics-and-conduct

Britt, T. W., & Garrity, M. J. (2006). Attributions and personality as predictors of the road rage response. *British Journal of Social Psychology, 45,* 127–147.

Briñol, P., Petty, R. E., & Wagner, B. (2009). Body posture effects on self-evaluation: A self-validation approach. *European Journal of Social Psychology, 39,* 1053–1064.

Brockner, J., Rubin, J. Z., Fine, J., Hamilton, T. P., Thomas, B., & Turetsky, B. (1982). Factors affecting entrapment in escalating conflicts: The importance of timing. *Journal of Research in Personality, 16,* 247–266.

Brodt, S. E., & Zimbardo, P. G. (1981). Modifying shyness-related social behavior through symptom misattribution. *Journal of Personality and Social Psychology, 41,* 437–449.

Brody, J. (2017, August 21). Fat bias starts early and takes a serious toll. *The New York Times.* https://www.nytimes.com/2017/08/21/well/live/fat-bias-starts-early-and-takes-a-serious-toll.html

Bromet, E., Andrade, L. H., Hwang, I., Sampson, N. A., Alonso, J., de Girolamo, G., de Graaf, R., Demyttenaere, K., Hu, C., Iwata, N., Karam, A. N., Kaur, J., Kostyuchenko, S., Lépine, J. P., Levinson, D., Matschinger, H., Mora, M. E., Browne, M. O., Posada-Villa, J., Viana, M. C., . . . & Kessler, R. C. (2011). Cross-national epidemiology of DSM-IV major depressive episode. *BMC Medicine, 9,* 90.

Bronfenbrenner, U. (1961). The mirror image in Soviet-American relations. *Journal of Social Issues, 17*(3), 45–56.

Broockman, D., & Kalla, J. (2016). Durably reducing transphobia: A field experiment on door-to-door canvassing. *Science, 352,* 220–224.

Brooks, D. (2005, August 10). All cultures are not equal. *The New York Times.* www.nytimes.com

Brooks, D. (2011, September 29). The limits of empathy. *The New York Times.* www.nytimes.com

Brooks, R. (2012). "Asia's missing women" as a problem in applied evolutionary psychology? *Evolutionary Psychology, 12,* 910–925.

Broome, A., & Wegner, D. M. (1994). Some positive effects of releasing socially anxious people from the need to please. Paper presented to the American Psychological Society convention.

Broussard, K. A., Warner, R. H., & Pope, A. D. (2018). Too many boxes, or not enough? Preferences for how we ask about gender in cisgender, LGB, and gender-diverse samples. *Sex Roles, 78*(9–10), 606–624.

Brown, A. (2019, June 18). Bisexual adults are far less likely than gay men and lesbians to be "out" to the people in their lives. *Pew Research Center.* https://pewrsr.ch/3rmTN2E

Brown, A. (2020, August 20). Nearly half of U.S. adults say dating has gotten harder for most people in the last 10 years. *Pew Research Center.* https://pewrsr.ch/30jOXri

Brown, D. E. (1991). *Human universals.* New York: McGraw Hill.

Brown, D. E. (2000). Human universals and their implications. In N. Roughley (Ed.), *Being humans: Anthropological universality and particularity in transdisciplinary perspectives.* New York: Walter de Gruyter.

Brown, G. (2008). *Wartime courage: Stories of extraordinary bravery in World War II.* London: Bloomsbury.

Brown, H. J., Jr. (1990). *P.S. I love you.* Nashville: Rutledge Hill.

Brown, J. D., & Dutton, K. A. (1994). *From the top down: Self-esteem and self-evaluation.* Unpublished manuscript, University of Washington.

Brown, J. D., & Taylor, S. E. (1986). Affect and the processing of personal information: Evidence for mood-activated self-schemata. *Journal of Experimental Social Psychology, 22,* 436–452.

Brown, J. D., Novick, N. J., Lord, K. A., & Richards, J. M. (1992). When Gulliver travels: Social context, psychological closeness, and self-appraisals. *Journal of Personality and Social Psychology, 62,* 717–727.

Brown, M. A., & Stopa, L. (2007). The spotlight effect and the illusion of transparency in social anxiety. *Journal of Anxiety Disorders, 21,* 804–819.

Brown, R., & Wootton-Millward, L. (1993). Perceptions of group homogeneity during group formation and change. *Social Cognition, 11,* 126–149.

Brown, R. (1965). *Social psychology.* New York: Free Press.

Brown, R. (1987). *Theory of politeness: An exemplary case.* Paper presented to the Society of Experimental Social Psychology meeting. Cited by R. O. Kroger & L. A. Wood (1992), Are the rules of address universal? IV: Comparison of Chinese, Korean, Greek, and German usage. *Journal of Cross-Cultural Psychology, 23,* 148–162.

Brown, R., Eller, A., Leeds, S., & Stace, K. (2007). Intergroup contact and intergroup attitudes: A longitudinal study. *European Journal of Social Psychology, 37,* 692–703.

Brown, R., Maras, P., Masser, B., Vivian, J., & Hewstone, M. (2001). Life on the ocean wave: Testing some intergroup hypotheses in a naturalistic setting. *Group Processes and Intergroup Relations, 4,* 81–97.

Brown, R. P., Baughman, K., & Carvallo, M. (2018). Culture, masculine honor, and violence toward women. *Personality and Social Psychology Bulletin, 44,* 538–549.

Brown, R. P., Charnsangavej, T., Keough, K. A., Newman, M. L., & Rentfrom, P. J. (2000). Putting the "affirm" into affirmative action: Preferential selection and academic performance. *Journal of Personality and Social Psychology, 79,* 736–747.

Brown, R. P., Osterman, L. L., & Barnes, C. D. (2009). School violence and the culture of honor. *Psychological Science, 20,* 1400–1405.

Brown, R., Vivian, J., & Hewstone, M. (1999). Changing attitudes through intergroup contact: The effects of group membership salience. *European Journal of Social Psychology, 29,* 741–764.

Brown, S. L., Brown, R. M., House, J. S., & Smith, D. M. (2008). Coping with spousal loss: Potential buffering effects of self-reported helping behavior. *Personality and Social Psychology Bulletin, 34,* 849–861.

Brown, S. L., Nesse, R. M., Vinokur, A. D., & Smith, D. M. (2003). Providing social support may be more beneficial than receiving it. *Psychological Science, 14,* 320–327.

Brown, S. L., Smith, D. M., Schulz, R., Kabeto, M. U., Ubel, P. A., Poulin, M., Yi, J., Kim, C., & Langa, K. M. (2009). Caregiving behavior is associated with decreased mortality risk. *Psychological Science, 20,* 488–494.

Brown, V. R., & Paulus, P. B. (2002). Making group brainstorming more effective: Recommendations from an associative memory perspective. *Current Directions in Psychological Science, 11,* 208–212.

Bruce, V. (1998, July). Identifying people caught on video. *The Psychologist,* pp. 331–335.

Bruck, M., & Ceci, S. J. (1999). The suggestibility of children's memory. *Annual Review of Psychology, 50,* 419–439.

Bruck, M., & Ceci, S. J. (2004). Forensic developmental psychology: Unveiling four common misconceptions. *Current Directions in Psychological Science, 15,* 229–232.

Brucks, D., & von Bayern, A. M. P. (2020). Parrots voluntarily help each other to obtain food rewards. *Current Biology, 30,* 292.

Brummelman, E., Thomaes, S., & Sedikides, C. (2016). Separating narcissism from self-esteem. *Current Directions in Psychological Science, 25,* 8–13.

Brummelman, E., Thomaes, S., Nelemans, S. A., de Castro, B. O., Overbeek, G., & Bushman, B. J. (2015). Origins of narcissism in children. *Proceedings of the Natural Academy of Sciences, 112,* 3659–3662.

Bruneau, E., Hameiri, B., Moore-Berg, S. L., & Kteily, N. (2021). Intergroup contact reduces dehumanization and meta-dehumanization: Cross-sectional, longitudinal, and quasi-experimental evidence from 16 samples in five countries. *Personality and Social Psychology Bulletin, 47,* 906–920.

Brunell, A. B., Gentry, W. A., Campbell, W. K., Hoffman, B. J., Kuhnert, K. W., & DeMarree, K. G. (2008). Leader emergence: The case of the narcissistic leader. *Personality and Social Psychology Bulletin, 34,* 1663–1676.

Bruni, F. (2018, October 30). The Internet will be the death of us. *The New York Times.* https://www.nytimes.com/2018/10/30/opinion/internet-violence-hate-prejudice.html

Bryan, C. J., Master, A., & Walton, G. M. (2014). "Helping" versus "being a helper": Invoking the self to increase helping in young children. *Child Development, 85*(5), 1836–1842.

Bryan, C. J., Yeager, D. S., Hinojosa, C. P., Chabot, A., Bergen, H., Kawamura, M., & Steubing, F. (2016). Harnessing adolescent values to motivate healthier eating. *Proceedings of the National Academy of Sciences, 113,* 10830–10835.

Bryan, J. H., & Test, M. A. (1967). Models and helping: Naturalistic studies in aiding behavior. *Journal of Personality and Social Psychology, 6,* 400–407.

Bränström, R., Pachankis, J. E., Jin, J., Klein, D. N., & Hatzenbuehler, M. L. (2023). Self-schemas and information processing biases as mechanisms underlying sexual orientation disparities in depressive symptoms: Results from a longitudinal, population-based study. *Journal of Psychopathology and Clinical Science.*

Buckhout, R. (1974, December). Eyewitness testimony. *Scientific American,* pp. 23–31.

Buehler, R., Griffin, D., & Ross, M. (2002). Inside the planning fallacy: The causes and consequences of optimistic time predictions. In T. Gilovich, D. Griffin, & D. Kahneman (Eds.), *Heuristics and biases: The psychology of intuitive judgment.* Cambridge: Cambridge University Press.

Bugental, D. B., & Hehman, J. A. (2007). Ageism: A review of research and policy implications. *Social Issues and Policy Review, 1,* 173–216.

Bui, Q. (2016, September 12). The Most Detailed Map of Gay Marriage in America. *New York Times.*

Bulevich, J. B., Gordon, L. T., Hughes, G. I., & Thomas, A. K. (2022). Are witnesses able to avoid highly accessible misinformation? Examining the efficacy of different warnings for high and low accessibility postevent misinformation. *Memory & Cognition, 50,* 45–58.

Bullington, J. (2016, June 15). NOPD fires 3 officers after body cam catches 1 hitting handcuffed man. *New Orleans Times-Picayune.* https://www.nola.com/news/crime_police/article_00bc034b-ec90-5322-8087-c19ffff17c8c.html

Bulloch, A. G. M., Williams, J. V. A., Lavorato, D. H., & Patten, S. B. (2017). The depression and marital status relationship is modified by both age and gender. *Journal of Affective Disorders, 223,* 65–68.

Bullock, J. (2006, March 17). *The enduring importance of false political beliefs.* Paper presented at the annual meeting of the Western Political Science Association, Albuquerque. https://www.allacademic.com/meta/p97459_index.html

Bump, P. (2023, August 22). Why do Republicans disproportionately believe health misinformation? *Washington Post.*

Burchill, S. A. L., & Stiles, W. B. (1988). Interactions of depressed college students with their roommates: Not necessarily negative. *Journal of Personality and Social Psychology, 55,* 410–419.

Bureau of Labor Statistics (2023, June 22). American Time Use Survey – 2022 results. https://www.bls.gov/news.release/atus.nr0.htm

Bureau of the Census. (1975). *Historical abstract of the United States: Colonial times to 1970.* Washington, DC: Superintendent of Documents.

Bureau of the Census. (2020). *Citizen voting-age population and voting rates for Congressional Districts: 2018.* https://www.census.gov/data/tables/time-series/demo/voting-and-registration/congressional-voting-tables.html

Burger, J. M., & Cornelius, T. (2003). Raising the price of agreement: Public commitment and the lowball compliance procedure. *Journal of Applied Social Psychology, 33,* 923–934.

Burger, J. M., & Guadagno, R. E. (2003). Self-concept clarity and the foot-in-the-door procedure. *Basic and Applied Social Psychology, 25,* 79–86.

Burger, J. M. (1987). Increased performance with increased personal control: A self-presentation interpretation. *Journal of Experimental Social Psychology, 23,* 350–360.

Burger, J. M. (2009, January). Replicating Milgram: Would people still obey today? *American Psychologist, 64,* 1–11.

Burger, J. M. (2014). Situational features in Milgram's experiment that kept his participants shocking. *Journal of Social Issues, 70,* 489–500.

Burger, J. M., Bender, T. J., Day, L., DeBolt, J. A., Guthridge, L., How, H. W., Meyer, M., Russell, K. A., & Taylor, S. (2014). The power of one: The relative influence of helpful and selfish models. *Social Influence, 10*(2), 77–84.

Burger, J. M., Messian, N., Patel, S., del Prade, A., & Anderson, C. (2004). What a coincidence! The effects of incidental similarity on compliance. *Personality and Social Psychology Bulletin, 30,* 35–43.

Burger, J. M., Sanchez, J., Imberi, J. E., & Grande, L. R. (2009). The norm of reciprocity as an internalized social norm: Returning favors even when no one finds out. *Social Influence, 4,* 11–17.

Burger, J. M., Soroka, S., Gonzago, K., Murphy, E., & Somervell, E. (2001). The effect of fleeting attraction on compliance to requests. *Personality and Social Psychology Bulletin, 27,* 1578–1586.

Burkett, J. P., & Young, L. J. (2012). The behavioral, anatomical and pharmacological parallels between social attachment, love, and addiction. *Psychopharmacology, 224,* 1–26.

Burkhardt, J., & Lenhard, W. (2022). A meta-analysis on the longitudinal, age-dependent effects of violent video games on aggression. *Media Psychology, 25,* 499–512.

Burkhauser, R. V., De Neve, J-E., & Powdthavee, N. (2016, January). *Top incomes and human well-being around the world* [PDF file]. Discussion paper 9677. IZA, Bonn, Germany. ftp.iza.org/dp9677.pdf

Burkholder, R. (2005, January 11). Chinese far wealthier than a decade ago, but are they happier? *Gallup.* https://news.gallup.com/poll/14548/Chinese-Far-Wealthier-Than-Decade-Ago-They-Happier.aspx

Burnay, J., Bushman, B. J., & Larøi, F. (2019). Effects of sexualized video games on online sexual harassment. *Aggressive Behavior, 45,* 214–223.

Burns, D. D. (1980). *Feeling good: The new mood therapy.* New York: Signet. pp. 29

Burns, K. (2019, May 11). Caster Semenya and the twisted politics of testosterone. *Wired.* https://www.wired.com/story/caster-semenya-and-the-twisted-politics-of-testosterone/

Burnstein, E., & Vinokur, A. (1977). Persuasive argumentation and social comparison as determinants of attitude polarization. *Journal of Experimental Social Psychology, 13,* 315–332.

Burnstein, E., & Worchel, P. (1962). Arbitrariness of frustration and its consequences for aggression in a social situation. *Journal of Personality, 30,* 528–540.

Burnstein, E. (2009). Robert B. Zajonc (1923–2008). *American Psychologist, 64,* 558–559.

Burnstein, E., Crandall, R., & Kitayama, S. (1994). Some neo-Darwinian decision rules for altruism: Weighing cues for inclusive fitness as a function of the biological importance of the decision. *Journal of Personality and Social Psychology, 67,* 773–789.

Burr, W. R. (1973). *Theory construction and the sociology of the family.* New York: Wiley.

Burton, C. M., & King, L. A. (2008). Effects of (very) brief writing on health: The two-minute miracle. *British Journal of Health Psychology, 13,* 9–14.

Bushman, B. J., & Anderson, C. A. (1998). Methodology in the study of aggression: Integrating experimental and nonexperimental findings. In R. Geen & E. Donnerstein (Eds.), *Human aggression: Theories, research and implications for policy.* San Diego: Academic Press.

Bushman, B. J., & Anderson, C. A. (2001). Media violence and the American public: Scientific facts versus media misinformation. *American Psychologist, 56,* 477–489.

Bushman, B. J., & Anderson, C. A. (2002). Violent video games and hostile expectations: A test of the general aggression model. *Personality and Social Psychology Bulletin, 28,* 1679–1686.

Bushman, B. J., & Anderson, C. A. (2009). Comfortably numb: Desensitizing effects of violent media on helping others. *Psychological Science, 20,* 273–277.

Bushman, B. J., & Anderson, C. A. (2015). Understanding causality in the effects of media violence. *American Behavioral Scientist, 59,* 1807–1821.

Bushman, B. J., & Baumeister, R. F. (1998). Threatened egotism, narcissism, self-esteem, and direct and displaced aggression: Does self-love or self-hate lead to violence? *Journal of Personality and Social Psychology, 75,* 219–229.

Bushman, B. J., & Geen, R. G. (1990). Role of cognitive-emotional mediators and individual differences in the effects of media violence on aggression. *Journal of Personality and Social Psychology, 58,* 156–163.

Bushman, B. J., & Huesmann, L. R. (2014). Twenty-five years of research on violence in digital games and aggression revisited. *European Psychologist, 19,* 47–55.

Bushman, B. J., & Whitaker, J. L. (2010). Like a magnet: Catharsis beliefs attract angry people to violent video games. *Psychological Science, 21,* 790–792.

Bushman, B. J. (1993). Human aggression while under the influence of alcohol and other drugs: An integrative research review. *Current Directions in Psychological Science, 2,* 148–152.

Bushman, B. J. (1998). Priming effects of media violence on the accessibility of aggressive constructs in memory. *Personality and Social Psychology Bulletin, 24,* 537–545.

Bushman, B. J. (2002). Does venting anger feed or extinguish the flame? Catharsis, rumination, distraction, anger, and aggressive responding. *Personality and Social Psychology Bulletin, 28,* 724–731.

Bushman, B. J. (2005). Violence and sex in television programs do not sell products in advertisements. *Psychological Science, 16,* 702–708.

Bushman, B. J. (2007). That was a great commercial, but what were they selling? Effects of violence and sex on memory for products in television commercials. *Journal of Applied Social Psychology, 37,* 1784–1796.

Bushman, B. J., Baumeister, R. F., & Phillips, C. M. (2001). Do people aggress to improve their mood? Catharsis beliefs, affect regulation opportunity, and aggressive responding. *Journal of Personality and Social Psychology, 81,* 17–32.

Bushman, B. J., Baumeister, R. F., Thomaes, S., Ryu, E., Begeer, S., & West, S. G. (2009). Looking again, and harder, for a link between low self-esteem and aggression. *Journal of Personality,* published online February 2, 2009.

Bushman, B. J., Bonacci, A. M., Pedersen, W. C., Vasquez, E. A., & Miller, N. (2005). Chewing on it can chew you up: Effects of rumination on triggered displaced aggression. *Journal of Personality and Social Psychology, 88,* 969–983.

Bushman, B. J., Gollwitzer, M., & Cruz, C. (2015). There is broad consensus: Media researchers agree that violent media increase aggression in children, and pediatricians and parents concur. *Psychology of Popular Media Culture, 4,* 200–214.

Bushman, B. J., Moeller, S. J., & Crocker, J. (2011). Sweets, sex, or self-esteem? Comparing the value of self-esteem boosts with other pleasant rewards. *Journal of Personality, 79,* 993–1012.

Bushman, B. J., Wang, M. C., & Anderson, C. A. (2005a). Is the curve relating temperature to aggression linear or curvilinear? Assaults and temperature in Minneapolis reexamined. *Journal of Personality and Social Psychology, 89,* 62–66.

Bushman, B. J., Wang, M. C., & Anderson, C. A. (2005b). Is the curve relating temperature to aggression linear or curvilinear? A response to Bell (2005) and to Cohn and Rotton (2005). *Journal of Personality and Social Psychology, 89,* 74–77.

Bushman, B., Kerwin, T., Whitlock, T., Weisenberger, J. M. (2017). The weapons effect on wheels: Motorists drive more aggressively when there is a gun in the vehicle. *Journal of Experimental Social Psychology, 73,* 82–85.

Buss, D. M., & Schmitt, D. P. (2019). Mate preferences and their behavioral manifestations. *Annual Review of Psychology, 70,* 77–110.

Buss, D. M. (1989). Sex differences in human mate preferences: Evolutionary hypotheses tested in 37 cultures. *Behavioral and Brain Sciences, 12,* 1–49.

Buss, D. M. (1995). Psychological sex differences: Origins through sexual selection. *American Psychologist, 50,* 164–168.

Buss, D. M. (1999). Behind the scenes. In D. G. Myers, *Social psychology* (6th ed.). New York: McGraw Hill.

Buss, D. M. (2009). The great struggles of life: Darwin and the emergence of evolutionary psychology. *American Psychologist, 64,* 140–148.

Buss, D. M., Durkee, P. K., Shackelford, T. K., Bowdle, B. F., Schmitt, D. P., Brase, G. L., Choe, J. C., & Trofimova, I. (2020). Human status criteria: Sex differences and similarities across 14 nations. *Journal of Personality and Social Psychology, 119,* 979–998.

Butcher, S. H. (1951). *Aristotle's theory of poetry and fine art.* New York: Dover.

Butler, A. C., Hokanson, J. E., & Flynn, H. A. (1994). A comparison of self-esteem lability and low trait self-esteem as vulnerability factors for depression. *Journal of Personality and Social Psychology, 66,* 166–177.

Butler, D. M., & Broockman, D. E. (2011). Do politicians racially discriminate against constituents? A field experiment on state legislators. *American Journal of Political Science, 55,* 463–477.

Butler, L. H., Fay, N., & Ecker, U. K. H. (2023). Social endorsement influences the continued belief in corrected misinformation. *Journal of Applied Research in Memory and Cognition, 12,* 364–375

Buttelmann, D., & Böhm, R. (2014). The ontogeny of the motivation that underlies in-group bias. *Psychological Science, 25,* 921–927.

Butterfield, F. (2001, April 20). Victims' race affects decisions on killers' sentence, study finds. *The New York Times.* https://www.nytimes.com/2001/04/20/us/victims-race-affects-decisions-on-killers-sentence-study-finds.html

Butz, D. A., & Plant, E. A. (2006). Perceiving outgroup members as unresponsive: Implications for approach-related emotions, intentions, and behavior. *Journal of Personality and Social Psychology, 91,* 1066–1079.

Buunk, B. P., & Van Yperen, N. W. (1991). Referential comparisons, relational comparisons, and exchange orientation: Their relation to marital satisfaction. *Personality and Social Psychology Bulletin, 17,* 709–717.

Byerly, H., Balmford, A., Ferraro, P. J., Wagner, C. H., Palchak, E., Polasky, S., Ricketts, T. H., Schwartz, A. J., & Fisher, B. (2018). Nudging pro-environmental behavior: evidence and opportunities. *Frontiers in Ecology and the Environment, 16,* 159–168.

Byrne, D., & Clore, G. L. (1970). A reinforcement model of evaluative responses. *Personality: An International Journal, 1,* 103–128.

Byrne, D. (1971). *The attraction paradigm.* New York: Academic Press.

Byrnes, J. P., Miller, D. C., & Schafer, W. D. (1999). Gender differences in risk taking: A meta-analysis. *Psychological Bulletin, 125,* 367–383.

Cacioppo, J. T., & Cacioppo, S. (2013). Social neuroscience. *Perspectives on Psychological Science, 8,* 667–669.

Cacioppo, J. T., & Cacioppo, S. (2014). Social relationships and health: The toxic effects of perceived social isolation. *Social and Personality Psychology Compass, 8,* 58–72.

Cacioppo, J. T., & Petty, R. E. (1986). Social processes. In M. G. H. Coles, E. Donchin, & S. W. Porges (Eds.), *Psychophysiology.* New York: Guilford.

Cacioppo, J. T., Claiborn, C. D., Petty, R. E., & Heesacker, M. (1991). General framework for the study of attitude change in psychotherapy. In C. R. Snyder & D. R. Forsyth (Eds.), *Handbook of social and clinical psychology.* New York: Pergamon.

Cacioppo, J. T., Petty, R. E., & Morris, K. J. (1983). Effects of need for cognition on message evaluation, recall, and persuasion. *Journal of Personality and Social Psychology, 45,* 805–818.

Cacioppo, J. T., Petty, R. E., Feinstein, J. A., & Jarvis, W. B. G. (1996). Dispositional differences in cognitive motivation: The life and times of individuals varying in need for cognition. *Psychological Bulletin, 119,* 197–253.

Cafferty, J. (2011, March 15). Why is there no looting in Japan? *CNN.* www.caffertyfile.blogs.cnn.com

Cairns, E., & Hewstone, M. (2002). The impact of peacemaking in Northern Ireland on intergroup behavior. In S. Gabi & B. Nevo (Eds.), *Peace education: The concept, principles, and practices around the world.* Mahwah, NJ: Erlbaum.

Caldwell, H. K., Lee, H.-J., MacBeth, A. H., & Young, W. S. (2008). Vasopressin: Behavioral roles of an "original" neuropeptide. *Progress in Neurobiology, 84,* 1–24.

Caluori, N., Brown-Iannuzzi, J. L., & Cipolli, W., III. (2021). Economic inequality shapes the relationship between globalization and prejudice. *Social Psychological and Personality Science, 12,* 1082–1091.

Calvillo, D. P., Harris, J. D., & Hawkins, W. C. (2023). Partisan bias in false memories for misinformation about the 2021 U.S. Capitol riot. *Memory, 31,* 137–146.

Camerer, C., Dreber, A., Holzmeister, F., Ho, T.-H., Huber, J., Johannesson, M., . . . Wu, H. (2018). Evaluating the replicability of social science experiments in *Nature* and *Science* between 2010 and 2015. *Nature Human Behavior, 2,* 637–644.

Cameron, C. (2022, October 13). These are the people who died in connection with the capitol riot. *New York Times.*

Cameron, G. (2010, May 7). The Muck files. *The Scottish Sun.* www.thesun.co.uk/scotsol

Cameron, L. D., Pepper, J. K., & Brewer, N. T. (2015). Responses of young adults to graphic warning labels for cigarette packages. *Tobacco Control, 24,* e14–e22.

Campbell, D. T. (1975a). The conflict between social and biological evolution and the concept of original sin. *Zygon, 10,* 234–249.

Campbell, D. T. (1975b). On the conflicts between biological and social evolution and between psychology and moral tradition. *American Psychologist, 30,* 1103–1126.

Campbell, M. A. (2005). Cyberbulling: An old problem in a new guise? *Australian Journal of Guidance and Counselling, 15,* 68–76.

Campbell, M. R., & Brauer, M. (2021). Is discrimination widespread? Testing assumptions about bias on a university campus. *Journal of Experimental Psychology: General, 150,* 756–777.

Campbell, T. H., & Kay, A. C. (2014). Solution aversion: On the relation between ideology and motivated disbelief. *Journal of Personality and Social Psychology, 107,* 809–824.

Campbell, W. K., & Sedikides, C. (1999). Self-threat magnifies the self-serving bias: A meta-analytic integration. *Review of General Psychology, 3,* 23–43.

Campbell, W. K., Bosson, J. K., Goheen, T. W., Lakey, C. E., & Kernis, M. H. (2007). Do narcissists dislike themselves "deep down inside"? *Psychological Science, 18,* 227–229.

Camp, G., Wesstein, H., & deBruin, A. B. H. (2012). Can questioning induce forgetting? Retrieval-induced forgetting of eyewitness information. *Applied Cognitive Psychology, 26,* 431–435.

Canadian Psychological Association. (2017). *Canadian code of ethics for psychologists.* Ottawa: Canadian Psychological Association. http://www.cpa.ca/docs/File/Ethics/CPA_Code_2017_4thEd.pdf

Canevello, A., & Crocker, J. (2011). Interpersonal goals, others' regard for the self, and self-esteem: The paradoxical consequences of self-image and compassionate goals. *European Journal of Social Psychology, 41,* 422–434.

Canter, D., Breaux, J., & Sime, J. (1980). Domestic, multiple occupancy, and hospital fires. In D. Canter (Ed.), *Fires and human behavior.* Hoboken, NJ: Wiley.

Cantor, D., Fisher, B., Chibnall, S., Harps, S., Townsend, R., . . . Madden, K. (2020). *Report on the AAU campus climate survey on sexual assault and misconduct.* Washington, DC: Association of American Universities.

Cantril, H., & Bumstead, C. H. (1960). *Reflections on the human venture.* New York: New York University Press.

Cantu, S. M., Simpson, J. A., Griskevicius, V., Weisberg, Y. J., Durante, K. M., & Beal, D. J. (2014). Fertile and selectively flirty: Women's behavior toward men changes across the ovulatory cycle. *Psychological Science, 25,* 431–438.

Capraro, V., Jagfeld, G., Klein, R., Mul, M., & van de Pol, I. (2019). Increasing altruistic and cooperative behaviour with simple moral nudges. *Scientific Reports, 9,* 11880.

Caprioli, M., & Boyer, M. A. (2001). Gender, violence, and international crisis. *Journal of Conflict Resolution, 45,* 503–518.

Caputo, J., Li, P., Kühn, M., Brønnum-Hansen, H., & Oksuzyan, A. (2021). Immigration background and the widowhood effect on mortality. *The Journals of Gerontology: Series B: Psychological Sciences and Social Sciences, 76,* 2155–2168.

Carducci, B. J., Cosby, P. C., & Ward, D. D. (1978). Sexual arousal and interpersonal evaluations. *Journal of Experimental Social Psychology, 14,* 449–457.

Cares, A. C., Banyard, V. L., Moynihan, M. M., Williams, L. M., Potter, S. J., & Stapleton, J. G. (2015). Changing attitudes about being a bystander to violence: Translating an in-person sexual violence prevention program to a new campus. *Journal of Violence Against Women, 21,* 165–187.

Carey, J. (2012, November). Global warming faster than expected? *Scientific American,* 51–55.

Carli, L. L., & Leonard, J. B. (1989). The effect of hindsight on victim derogation. *Journal of Social and Clinical Psychology, 8,* 331–343.

Carli, L. L. (1999). Cognitive reconstruction, hindsight, and reactions to victims and perpetrators. *Personality and Social Psychology Bulletin, 25,* 966–979.

Carlo, G., Eisenberg, N., Troyer, D., Switzer, G., & Speer, A. L. (1991). The altruistic personality: In what contexts is it apparent? *Journal of Personality and Social Psychology, 61,* 450–458.

Carlsmith, J. M., & Gross, A. E. (1969). Some effects of guilt on compliance. *Journal of Personality and Social Psychology, 11,* 232–239.

Carlson, D. L. (2022). Reconceptualizing the gendered division of housework: Number of shared tasks and partners' relationship quality. *Sex Roles: A Journal of Research.*

Carlson, E. N., Vazire, S., & Oltmanns, T. F. (2011). You probably think this paper's about you: Narcissists' perceptions of their personality and reputation. *Journal of Personality and Social Psychology, 101,* 185–201.

Carlson, J., & Hatfield, E. (1992). *The psychology of emotion.* Fort Worth, TX: Holt, Rinehart & Winston.

Carlson, K. A., & Russo, J. E. (2001). Biased interpretation of evidence by mock jurors. *Journal of Experimental Psychology: Applied, 7,* 91–103.

Carlson, L., E., Beattie, T. L., Giese-Davis, J., Faris, P., Tamagawa, R., Fick, L. J., Degelman, E. S., & Speca, M. (2015). Mindfulness-based cancer recovery and supportive-expressive therapy to maintain telomere length relative to controls in distressed breast cancer survivors. *Cancer, 121*(3), 476–484.

Carlson, M., Charlin, V., & Miller, N. (1988). Positive mood and helping behavior: A test of six hypotheses. *Journal of Personality and Social Psychology, 55,* 211–229.

Carlson, M., Marcus-Newhall, A., & Miller, N. (1990). Effects of situational aggression cues: A quantitative review. *Journal of Personality and Social Psychology, 58,* 622–633.

Carnagey, N. L., Anderson, C. A., & Bushman, B. J. (2007). The effect of video game violence on physiological desensitization to real-life violence. *Journal of Experimental Social Psychology, 43,* 489–496.

Carnaghi, A., Maass, A., & Fasoli, F. (2011). Enhancing masculinity by slandering homosexuals: The role of homophobic epithets in heterosexual gender identity. *Personality and Social Psychology Bulletin, 37,* 1655–1665.

Carnevale, P. J., & Choi, D-W. (2000). Culture in the mediation of international disputes. *International Journal of Psychology, 35,* 105–110.

Carnevale, P. J., & Probst, T. M. (1998). Social values and social conflict in creative problem solving and categorization. *Journal of Personality and Social Psychology, 74,* 1300–1309.

Carney, D. R., & Banaji, M. R. (2008). *First is best.* Unpublished manuscript, Harvard University.

Carothers, B. J., & Reis, H. T. (2013). Men and women are from Earth: Examining the latent structure of gender. *Journal of Personality and Social Psychology, 104,* 385–407.

Carpenter, C. J. (2012). A meta-analysis and an experiment investigating the effects of speaker disfluency on persuasion. *Western Journal of Communication, 76,* 552–569.

Carpenter, J., Nida, S., Saylor, C., & Taylor, C. (2012, February). *Consequences: Bullying versus ostracism in middle school students.* Poster presented at the Southeastern Psychological Association annual conference, New Orleans, LA.

Carpenter, T. F., & Marshall, M. A. (2009). An examination of religious priming and intrinsic religious motivation in the moral hypocrisy paradigm. *Journal for the Scientific Study of Religion, 48,* 386–393.

Carpusor, A. G., & Loges, W. E. (2006). Rental discrimination and ethnicity in names. *Journal of Applied Social Psychology, 36,* 934–952.

Carr, E. W., Brady, T. F., & Winkielman, P. (2017). Are you smiling, or have I seen you before? Familiarity makes faces look happier. *Psychological Science, 28,* 1087–1102.

Carroll, D., Davey Smith, G., & Bennett, P. (1994, March). Health and socioeconomic status. *The Psychologist,* pp. 122–125.

Carroll, J. S., Busby, D. M., Willoughby, B. J., & Brown, C. C. (2017). The porn gap: Differences in men's and women's pornography patterns in couple relationships. *Journal of Couple & Relationship Therapy, 16,* 146–163.

Carroll, L. (2014, August 12). The Robin Williams effect: Could suicides follow star's death? *NBCnews.com.* http://www.nbcnews.com/storyline/robin-williams-death/robin-williams-effect-could-suicides-follow-stars-death-n178961

Carré, J. M., Geniole, S. N., Ortiz, T. L., Bird, B. M., Videto, A., & Bonin, P. L. (2017). Exogenous testosterone rapidly increases aggressive behavior in dominant and impulsive men. *Biological Psychiatry, 82,* 249–256.

Cartwright, D. S. (1975). The nature of gangs. In D. S. Cartwright, B. Tomson, & H. Schwartz (Eds.), *Gang delinquency.* Monterey, CA: Brooks/Cole.

Carvallo, M., & Gabriel, S. (2006). No man is an island: The need to belong and dismissing avoidant attachment style. *Personality and Social Psychology Bulletin, 32,* 697–709.

Carver, C. S., & Scheier, M. F. (1981). *Attention and self-regulation.* New York: Springer-Verlag.

Carver, C. S., & Scheier, M. F. (1986). Analyzing shyness: A specific application of broader self-regulatory principles. In W. H. Jones, J. M. Cheek, & S. R. Briggs (Eds.), *Shyness: Perspectives on research and treatment.* New York: Plenum.

Carver, C. S., Kus, L. A., & Scheier, M. F. (1994). Effect of good versus bad mood and optimistic versus pessimistic outlook on social acceptance versus rejection. *Journal of Social and Clinical Psychology, 13,* 138–151.

Carver, C. S., Scheier, M. F., & Segerstrom, S. C. (2010). Optimism. *Clinical Psychology Review, 30,* 879–889.

Case, A., & Deaton, A. (2015). Rising morbidity and mortality in midlife among white non-Hispanic Americans in the 21st century. *Proceedings of the National Academy of Sciences, 112,* 15078–15083.

Casey, K. (2022). Snap judgments: Predicting politician competence from photos. *The Journal of Politics, 84,* 698–713.

Cash, D. K., & Lane, S. M. (2020). Judging memory: Strong verbal confidence and lineup context influence inferences about eyewitnesses. *Psychology, Crime & Law, 27*(4), 1–21.

Cash, T. F., & Janda, L. H. (1984, December). The eye of the beholder. *Psychology Today,* pp. 46–52.

Caspi, A., & Herbener, E. S. (1990). Continuity and change: Assortative marriage and the consistency of personality in adulthood. *Journal of Personality and Social Psychology, 58,* 250–258.

Caspi, A., McClay, J., Moffitt, T., Mill, J., Martin, J., Craig, I. W., Taylor, A., & Poulton, R. (2002). Role of genotype in the cycle of violence in maltreated children. *Science, 297,* 851–854.

Caspi, A., Sugden, K., Moffitt, T. E., Taylor, A., Craig, I. W., Harrington, H. L., McClay, J., Mill, J., Martin, J., Braithwaite, A., & Poulton, R. (2003). Influence of life stress on depression: Moderation by a polymorphism in the 5-HTT gene. *Science, 30,* 386–389.

Cassidy, J. (2000). Adult romantic attachments: A developmental perspective on individual differences. *Review of General Psychology, 4,* 111–131.

Castelli, L., Arcuri, L., & Carraro, L. (2009). Projection processes in the perception of political leaders. *Basic and Applied Social Psychology, 31,* 189–196.

Castelli, L., Carraro, L., Tomelleri, S., & Amari, A. (2007). White children's alignment to the perceived racial attitudes of the parents: Closer to the mother than father. *British Journal of Developmental Psychology, 25,* 353–357.

CDC: Centers for Disease Control. (2018). Prevalence of depression among adults aged 20 and over: United States, 2013–2016. *NCHS Data Brief No. 303,* February 2018.

Ceci, S. J., & Bruck, M. (1993a). Child witnesses: Translating research into policy. *Social Policy Report* (Society for Research in Child Development), *7*(3), 1–30.

Ceci, S. J., & Bruck, M. (1993b). Suggestibility of the child witness: A historical review and synthesis. *Psychological Bulletin, 113,* 403–439.

Ceci, S. J., & Bruck, M. (1995). *Jeopardy in the courtroom: A scientific analysis of children's testimony.* Washington, DC: American Psychological Association.

Ceci, S. J., & Williams, W. M. (2018). Who decides what is acceptable speech on campus? Why restricting free speech is not the answer. *Perspectives on Psychological Science, 13,* 299–323.

Ceci, S. J., Kahn, S., & Williams, W. M. (2023). Exploring Gender Bias in Six Key Domains of Academic Science: An Adversarial Collaboration. *Psychological Science in the Public Interest, 24,* 15–73.

Chaiken, S., & Eagly, A. H. (1976). Communication modality as a determinant of message persuasiveness and message comprehensibility. *Journal of Personality and Social Psychology, 34,* 605–614.

Chaiken, S., & Eagly, A. H. (1983). Communication modality as a determinant of persuasion: The role of communicator salience. *Journal of Personality and Social Psychology, 45,* 241–256.

Chaiken, S., & Maheswaran, D. (1994). Neuristic processing can bias systematic processing: Effects of source credibility, argument ambiguity, and task importance on attitude judgment. *Journal of Personality and Social Psychology, 66,* 460–473.

Chaiken, S. (1979). Communicator physical attractiveness and persuasion. *Journal of Personality and Social Psychology, 37,* 1387–1397.

Chaiken, S. (1980). Heuristic versus systematic information processing and the use of source versus message cues in persuasion. *Journal of Personality and Social Psychology, 39,* 752–766.

Chakraborty, A. (2023). Motives behind cooperation in finitely repeated prisoner's dilemma. *Games and Economic Behavior, 141,* 105–132.

Chambers, J. R., & Windschitl, P. D. (2004). Biases in social comparative judgments: The role of nonmotivated factors in above-average and comparative-optimism effects. *Psychological Bulletin, 130,* 813–838.

Chambers, J. R., Baron, R. S., & Inman, M. L. (2006). Misperceptions in intergroup conflict: Disagreeing about what we disagree about. *Psychological Science, 17,* 38–45.

Chambers, J. R., Schlenker, B. R., & Collisson, B. (2012). Ideology and prejudice: The role of value conflicts. *Psychological Science, 24,* 140–149.

Champagne, F. A., & Mashoodh, R. (2009). Genes in context: Gene-environment interplay and the origins of individual differences in behavior. *Current Directions in Psychological Science, 18,* 127–131.

Chang, J. H., & Bushman, B. J. (2019). Effect of exposure to gun violence in video games on children's dangerous behavior with real guns: A randomized controlled trial. *JAMA Network Open, 2,* e194319.

Chang, V. T., & Overall, N. C. (2022). Biased memories contribute to the links between stress and depressive symptoms. *Emotion, 22,* 227–243.

Chang, Y., Hou, R.-J., Wang, K., Cui, A. P., & Zhang, C.-B. (2020). Effects of intrinsic and extrinsic motivation on social loafing in online travel communities. *Computers in Human Behavior, 109.*

Chan, M. K. H., Louis, W. R., & Jetten, J. (2010). When groups are wrong and deviants are right. *European Journal of Social Psychology, 40,* 1103–1109.

Chan, M. S., Jones, C. R., Jamieson, K. H., & Albarracin, D. (2017). Debunking: A meta-analysis of the psychological efficacy of messages countering misinformation. *Psychological Science, 28,* 1531–1546.

Chapin, J., & Coleman, G. (2017). The cycle of cyberbullying: Some experience required. *The Social Science Journal, 54,* 314–318.

Chaplin, C., & Shaw, J. (2016). Confidently wrong: Police endorsement of psycho-legal misconceptions. *Journal of Police and Criminal Psychology, 31,* 208–216.

Chapman, L. J., & Chapman, J. P. (1969). Genesis of popular but erroneous psychodiagnostic observations. *Journal of Abnormal Psychology, 74,* 272–280.

Chapman, L. J., & Chapman, J. P. (1971, November). Test results are what you think they are. *Psychology Today,* pp. 18–22, 106–107.

Charlesworth, T. E. S., & Banaji, M. R. (2019). Patterns of implicit and explicit attitudes: I. Long-term change and stability from 2007 to 2016. *Psychological Science, 30*(2), 174–192.

Charlesworth, T. E. S., & Banaji, M. R. (2022). Patterns of implicit and explicit attitudes: IV Change and stability from 2007 to 2020. *Psychological Science, 33,* 1347–1371.

Charman, S. D., Matuku, K., & Mook, A. (2019). Non-blind lineup administration biases administrators' interpretations of ambiguous witness statements and their perceptions of the witness. *Applied Cognitive Psychology, 33,* 1260–1270.

Charnie, J. (2017, February 22). *The rise of one-person households.* Inter Press Service News Agency. With data from Eurostat, OECD, and national estimates. https://www.ipsnews.net/2017/02/the-rise-of-one-person-households

Chartrand, T. L., & Bargh, J. A. (1999). The chameleon effect: The perception-behavior link and social interaction. *Journal of Personality and Social Psychology,* 76, 893–910.

Chatard, A., Guimond, S., & Selimbegovic, L. (2007). "How good are you in math?" The effect of gender stereotypes on students' recollection of their school marks. *Journal of Experimental Social Psychology, 43,* 1017–1024.

Chatterjee, P., Mishra, H., & Mishra, A. (2023). Does the first letter of one's name affect life decisions? A natural language processing examination of nominative determinism. *Journal of Personality and Social Psychology.*

Check, J., & Malamuth, N. (1984). Can there be positive effects of participation in pornography experiments? *Journal of Sex Research, 20,* 14–31.

Chen, E. (2004). Why socioeconomic status affects the health of children: A psychosocial perspective. *Current Directions in Psychological Science, 13,* 112–115.

Cheney, R. (2003, March 16). Comments on Face the Nation, *CBS News.*

Chen, F. F., & Kenrick, D. T. (2002). Repulsion or attraction? Group membership and assumed attitude similarity. *Journal of Personality and Social Psychology, 83,* 111–125.

Cheng, J., Bernstein, M., Danescu-Niculescu-Mizil, C., & Leskovec, J. (2017, February). *Anyone can become a troll: Causes of trolling behavior in online discussions.* Paper presented at the Proceedings of the 2017 ACM Conference on Computer Supported Cooperative Work and Social Computing.

Cheng, S., Chang, C., Chang, W., Wang, H., Liang, C., Kishimoto, T., Chang, J. P., Kuo, J. S., & Su, K. (2023). The now and future of ChatGPT and GPT in psychiatry. *Psychiatry and Clinical Neurosciences, 77,* 592–596.

Chen, H., Luo, S., Yue, G., Xu, D., & Zhaoyang, R. (2009). Do birds of a feather flock together in China? *Personal Relationships, 16,* 167–186.

Chen, J., Short, M., & Kemps, E. (2020). Interpretation bias in social anxiety: A systematic review and meta-analysis. *Journal of Affective Disorders, 276,* 1119–1130.

Chen, J., Teng, L., Yu, Y., & Yu, X. (2016). The effect of online information sources on purchase intentions between consumers with high and low susceptibility to informational influence. *Journal of Business Research, 69,* 467–475.

Chen, L.-H., Baker, S. P., Braver, E. R., & Li, G. (2000). Carrying passengers as a risk factor for crashes fatal to 16- and 17-year-old drivers. *Journal of the American Medical Association, 283,* 1578–1582.

Chen, Q., Zhang, Q., Zhao, S., & Li, C. (2023). Trusting strangers: The benefits of reciprocal self-disclosure during online computer-mediated communication and mediating role of interpersonal liking. *International Journal of Psychology*.

Chen, S., Boucher, H. C., & Tapias, M. P. (2006). The relational self revealed: Integrative conceptualization and implications for interpersonal life. *Psychological Bulletin, 132,* 151–179.

Chen, S. C. (1937). Social modification of the activity of ants in nest-building. *Physiological Zoology, 10,* 420–436.

Chen, Y., & Biswas, M. I. (2022). Impact of national culture on the severity of the covid-19 pandemic. *Current Psychology: A Journal for Diverse Perspectives on Diverse Psychological Issues*.

Chen, Z., Poon, K.-T., DeWall, C. N., & Jiang, T. (2020). Life lacks meaning without acceptance: Ostracism triggers suicidal thoughts. *Journal of Personality and Social Psychology, 119*(6), 1423–1443.

Cheon, S. H., Reeve, J., Marsh, H. W., & Jang, H.-R. (2023). Cluster randomized control trial to reduce peer victimization: An autonomy-supportive teaching intervention changes the classroom ethos to support defending bystanders. *American Psychologist, 78,* 856–872.

Chester, D. (2023). Aggression as successful self-control. *Social and Personality Psychology Compass,* e12832.

Chester, D. S., & Dzierzewski, J. M. (2020). Sour sleep, sweet revenge? Aggressive pleasure as a potential mechanism underlying poor sleep quality's link to aggression. *Emotion, 20,* 842–853.

Chetty, R., Stepner, M., Abraham, S., Lin, S., Scuderi, B., Turner, N., Bergeron, A., & Cutler, D. (2016). The association between income and life expectancy in the United States, 2001–2014. *JAMA, 315,* 1750–1766.

Cheung, F., & Lucas, R. E. (2016). Income inequality is associated with stronger social comparison effects: The effect of relative income on life satisfaction. *Journal of Personality and Social Psychology, 110*(2), 332–341.

Cheung, F. (2018). Income redistribution predicts greater life satisfaction across individual, national, and cultural characteristics. *Journal of Personality and Social Psychology, 115,* 867–882.

Cheung, G., & Lucas, R. E. (2016). Income inequality is associated with stronger social comparison effects: The effect of relative income on life satisfaction. *Journal of Personality and Social Psychology, 110,* 332–341.

Chiao, J. Y., Bowman, N. E., & Gill, H. (2008). The political gender gap: Gender bias in facial inferences that predict voting behavior. *PLOS ONE, 3*(10), e3666.

Chicago Tribune. (2002, September 30). When believing isn't seeing. www.chicagotribune.com

Chida, Y., & Steptoe, A. (2009). The association of anger and hostility with future coronary heart disease: A meta-analytic review of prospective evidence. *Journal of the American College of Cardiology, 17,* 936–946.

Chinchilla, J., Vazquez, A., & Gómez, Á. (2022). Identity fusion predicts violent pro-group behavior when it is morally justifiable. *The Journal of Social Psychology, 162,* 701–715.

Ching, B. H.-H. (2022). The effect of masculinity threat on transprejudice: Influence of different aspects of masculinity contingent self-worth. *Psychology & Sexuality, 13,* 550–564.

Chodorow, N. J. (1978). *The reproduction of mother: Psychoanalysis and the sociology of gender.* Berkeley, CA: University of California Press.

Chodorow, N. J. (1989). *Feminism and psychoanalytic theory.* New Haven, CT: Yale University Press.

Choi, A. (2023, October 2). Gun homicides and suicides in US children and teens are at a record high. CNN.com.

Choi, I., & Choi, Y. (2002). Culture and self-concept flexibility. *Personality & Social Psychology Bulletin, 28,* 1508–1517.

Choi, I., Nisbett, R. E., & Norenzayan, A. (1999). Causal attribution across cultures: Variation and universality. *Psychological Bulletin, 125,* 47–63.

Choi, S., Won, J., Park, K., & Kim, S. (2023). Hemispheric differences in self-evaluation errors of upper extremity movement in patients with chronic stroke. *Journal of the International Neuropsychological Society, 29,* 59–67.

Chopik, W. J., O'Brien, E., & Konrath, S. H. (2017). Differences in empathic concern and perspective taking across 63 countries. *Journal of Cross-Cultural Psychology, 48,* 23–38.

Chou, W. S., Prestin, A., & Kunath, S. (2014). Obesity in social media: A mixed methods analysis. *Translational Behavioral Medicine, 4,* 314–323.

Choy, O., Focquaert, F., & Raine, A. (2020). Benign biological interventions to reduce offending. *Neuroethics, 13,* 29–41.

Christakis, N. A., & Fowler, J. H. (2009). *Connected: The surprising power of social networks and how they shape our lives.* New York: Little, Brown.

Christensen, P. N., & Kashy, D. A. (1998). Perceptions of and by lonely people in initial social interaction. *Personality and Social Psychology Bulletin, 24,* 322–329.

Christ, O., Hewstone, M., Tausch, N., Wagner, U., Voci, A., Hughes, J., & Cairns, E. (2010). Direct contact as a moderator of extended contact effects: Cross-sectional and longitudinal impact on outgroup attitudes, behavioral intentions, and attitude certainty. *Personality and Social Psychology Bulletin, 36,* 1662–1674.

Christy, A. G., Schlegel, R. J., & Cimpian, A. (2019). Why do people believe in a "true self?" The role of essentialist reasoning about personal identity and the self. *Journal of Personality and Social Psychology, 117,* 386–416.

Chua, H. F., Boland, J. E., & Nisbett, R. E. (2005). Cultural variation in eye movements during scene perception. *Proceedings of the National Academy of Sciences, 102,* 12629–12633.

Chu, C., Buchman-Schmitt, J. M., Stanley, I. H., Hom, M. A., Tucker, R. P., Hagan, C. R., . . . Joiner, T. E., Jr. (2017). The interpersonal theory of suicide: A systematic review and meta-analysis of a decade of cross-national research. *Psychological Bulletin, 143,* 1313–1345.

Chulov, M. (2014, December 11). ISIS: The inside story. *The Guardian.* https://www.theguardian.com/world/2014/dec/11/-sp-isis-the-inside-story

Church, A. T., Aria, R. M., Rincon, B. C., Vargas-Flores, J. J., Ibanez-Eyes, J., Wang, L., Alvarez, J. M., Wang, C., & Ortiz, F. A. (2014). A four-culture study of self-enhancement and adjustment using the social relations model: Do alternative conceptualizations and indices make a difference? *Journal of Personality and Social Psychology, 106,* 997–1014.

Church, G. J. (1986, January 6). China. *Time,* pp. 6–19.

CIA. (2017, accessed October 20). Sex ratio. *The world fact book.* www.cia.gov

Cialdini, R. B., & Schroeder, D. A. (1976). Increasing compliance by legitimizing paltry contributions: When even a penny helps. *Journal of Personality and Social Psychology, 34,* 599–604.

Cialdini, R. B. (1984). *Influence: How and why people agree to things.* New York: William Morrow.

Cialdini, R. B. (1988). *Influence: Science and practice.* Glenview, IL: Scott, Foresman/Little, Brown.

Cialdini, R. B. (1995). A full-cycle approach to social psychology. In G. G. Brannigan & M. R. Merrens (Eds.), *The social psychologists: Research adventures.* New York: McGraw Hill.

Cialdini, R. B. (2005). Basic social influence is underestimated. *Psychological Inquiry, 16,* 158–161.

Cialdini, R. B. (2021). *Influence, new and expanded: The psychology of persuasion.* New York: Harper Business.

Cialdini, R. B., Bickman, L., & Cacioppo, J. T. (1979). An example of consumeristic social psychology: Bargaining tough in the new car showroom. *Journal of Applied Social Psychology, 9,* 115–126.

Cialdini, R. B., Borden, R. J., Thorne, A., Walker, M. R., Freeman, S., & Sloan, L. R. (1976). Basking in reflected glory: Three (football) field studies. *Journal of Personality and Social Psychology, 39,* 406–415.

Cialdini, R. B., Cacioppo, J. T., Bassett, R., & Miller, J. A. (1978). Lowball procedure for producing compliance: Commitment then cost. *Journal of Personality and Social Psychology, 36,* 463–476.

Cialdini, R. B., Demaine, L. J., Barrett, D. W., Sagarin, B. J., & Rhoads, K. L. V. (2003). *The poison parasite defense: A strategy for sapping a stronger opponent's persuasive strength.* Unpublished manuscript, Arizona State University.

Cialdini, R. B., Lasky-Fink, J., Demaine, L. J., Barrett, D. W., Sagarin, B. J., & Rogers, T. (2021). Poison parasite counter: Turning duplicitous mass communications into self-negating memory-retrieval cues. *Psychological Science, 32,* 1811–1829.

Cialdini, R. B., Vincent, J. E., Lewis, S. K., Catalan, J., Wheeler, D., & Danby, B. L. (1975). Reciprocal concessions procedure for inducing compliance: The door-in-the-face technique. *Journal of Personality and Social Psychology, 31,* 206–215.

Cicerello, A., & Sheehan, E. P. (1995). Personal advertisements: A content analysis. *Journal of Social Behavior and Personality, 10,* 751–756.

Cikara, M., & Van Bavel, J. J. (2014). The neuroscience of intergroup relations: An integrative review. *Perspectives on Psychological Science, 9,* 245–274.

Cikara, M., Botvinick, M. M., & Fiske, S. T. (2011). Us versus them: Social identity shapes neural responses to intergroup competition and harm. *Psychological Science, 22,* 306–313.

Cingel, D. P., & Krcmar, M. (2019). Prosocial television, preschool children's moral judgments, and moral reasoning: The role of social moral intuitions and perspective-taking. *Communication Research, 46,* 355–374.

Clack, B., Dixon, J., & Tredoux, C. (2005). Eating together apart: Patterns of segregation in a multi-ethnic cafeteria. *Journal of Community and Applied Social Psychology, 15,* 1–16.

Clarke, A. C. (1952). An examination of the operation of residual propinquity as a factor in mate selection. *American Sociological Review, 27,* 17–22.

Clark, K., & Clark, M. (1947). Racial identification and preference in Negro children. In T. M. Newcomb & E. L. Hartley (Eds.), *Readings in social psychology.* New York: Holt.

Clark, M. S., & Mills, J. (1979). Interpersonal attraction in exchange and communal relationships. *Journal of Personality and Social Psychology, 37,* 12–24.

Clark, M. S., & Mills, J. (1993). The difference between communal and exchange relationships: What it is and is not. *Personality and Social Psychology Bulletin, 19,* 684–691.

Clark, M. S. (1984). Record keeping in two types of relationships. *Journal of Personality and Social Psychology, 47,* 549–557.

Clark, M. S. (1986). Evidence for the effectiveness of manipulations of desire for communal versus exchange relationships. *Personality and Social Psychology Bulletin, 12,* 414–425.

Clark, M. S., Lemay, E. P., Jr., Graham, S. M., Pataki, S. P., & Finkel, E. J. (2010). Ways of giving benefits in marriage: Norm use, relationship satisfaction, and attachment-related variability. *Psychological Science, 21,* 944–951.

Clark, M. S., Mills, J., & Corcoran, D. (1989). Keeping track of needs and inputs of friends and strangers. *Personality and Social Psychology Bulletin, 15,* 533–542.

Clark, M. S., Mills, J., & Powell, M. C. (1986). Keeping track of needs in communal and exchange relationships. *Journal of Personality and Social Psychology, 51,* 333–338.

Clark, R. D., & Hatfield, E. (1989). Gender differences in receptivity to sexual offers. *Journal of Psychology and Human Sexuality, 2,* 39–55.

Clark, R. D. (1990). The impact of AIDS on gender differences in willingness to engage in casual sex. *Journal of Applied Social Psychology, 20,* 771–782.

Clark, R. D., III, & Maass, S. A. (1988). The role of social categorization and perceived source credibility in minority influence. *European Journal of Social Psychology, 18,* 381–394.

Clayton, S., & Myers, G. (2009). *Conservation Psychology: Understanding and Promoting Human Care for Nature* (p. 9). Hoboken, NJ: Wiley-Blackwell.

Clayton, S., Devine-Wright, P., Swim, J., Bonnes, M., Steg, L., Whitmarsh, L., & Carrico, A. (2016). Expanding the role for psychology in addressing environmental challenges. *American Psychologist, 71,* 199–215.

Clegg, J. M., Wen, N. J., & Legare, C. H. (2017). Is non-conformity WEIRD? Cultural variation in adults' beliefs about children's competency and conformity. *Journal of Experimental Psychology: General, 146,* 428–441.

Clifford, M. M., & Walster, E. H. (1973). The effect of physical attractiveness on teacher expectation. *Sociology of Education, 46,* 248–258.

Coan, J. A., Schaefer, H. S., & Davidson, R. J. (2006). Lending a hand: Social regulation of the neural response to threat. *Psychological Science, 17,* 1032–1039.

Coates, B., Pusser, H. E., & Goodman, I. (1976). The influence of "Sesame Street" and "Mister Rogers' Neighborhood" on children's social behavior in the preschool. *Child Development, 47,* 138–144.

Coats, E. J., & Feldman, R. S. (1996). Gender differences in nonverbal correlates of social status. *Personality and Social Psychology Bulletin, 22,* 1014–1022.

Coccia, M. (2017). A theory of general causes of violent crime: Homicides, income inequality and deficiencies of the heat hypothesis and of the model of CLASH. *Aggression and Violent Behavior, 37,* 199–200.

Cohen, D. (1996). Law, social policy, and violence: The impact of regional cultures. *Journal of Personality and Social Psychology, 70,* 961–978.

Cohen, D. (1998). Culture, social organization, and patterns of violence. *Journal of Personality and Social Psychology, 75,* 408–419.

Cohen, D., Nisbett, R. E., Bowdle, B. F., & Schwarz, N. (1996). Insult, aggression, and the Southern culture of honor: An "experimental ethnography." *Journal of Personality and Social Psychology, 70,* 945–960.

Cohen, G. L., Garcia, J., Purdie-Vaugns, V., Apfel, N., & Brzustoski, P. (2009). Recursive processes in self-affirmation: Intervening to close the minority achievement gap. *Science, 324,* 400–403.

Cohen, G. L., Steele, C. M., & Ross, L. D. (1999). The mentor's dilemma: Providing critical feedback across the racial divide. *Personality and Social Psychology Bulletin, 5,* 1302–1318.

Cohen, J. (2016, June 3). Let smokers see the warning they need. *The New York Times.* https://www.nytimes.com/2016/06/03/opinion/let-smokers-see-the-warning-they-need.html

Cohen, M., & Davis, N. (1981). *Medication errors: Causes and prevention.* Philadelphia: G. F. Stickley Co. Cited by R. B. Cialdini (1989), *Agents of influence: Bunglers, smugglers, and sleuths.* Paper presented at the American Psychological Association convention.

Cohen, P. (2022, May 29). Science says: Get married at age Whatever You Want (and these are the odds of divorce). Family Inequality blog. https://familyinequality.wordpress.com/2022/05/29/science-says-get-married-at-age-whatever-you-want-and-these-are-the-odds-of-divorce/

Cohen, R. (2011, January 13). Mohammed the Brit. *The New York Times.*

Cohen, S. (2002). Psychosocial stress, social networks, and susceptibility to infection. In H. G. Koenig & H. J. Cohen (Eds.), *The link between religion and health: Psychoneuroimmunology and the faith factor.* New York: Oxford University Press.

Cohen, S. (2004). Social relationships and health. *American Psychologist, 59,* 676–684.

Cohen, S., Alper, C. M., Doyle, W. J., Treanor, J. J., & Turner, R. B. (2006). Positive emotional style predicts resistance to illness after experimental exposure to rhinovirus or influenza A virus. *Psychosomatic Medicine, 68,* 809–815.

Cohen, S., Doyle, W. J., Skoner, D. P., Rabin, B. S., & Gwaltney, J. M., Jr. (1997). Social ties and susceptibility to the common cold. *Journal of the American Medical Association, 277,* 1940–1944.

Cohen, S., Doyle, W. J., Turner, R., Alper, C. M., & Skoner, D. P. (2003). Sociability and susceptibility to the common cold. *Psychological Science, 14,* 389–395.

Cohen, S., Janicki-Deverts, D., Doyle, W. J., Miller, G. E., Frank, E., Rabin, B. S., & Turner, R. B. (2012). Chronic stress, glucocorticoid receptor resistance, inflammation, and disease risk. *PNAS, 109,* 5995–5999.

Cohn, E. G., & Rotton, J. (2005). The curve is still out there: A reply to Bushman, Wang, and Anderson (2005), Is the curve relating temperature to aggression linear or curvilinear? *Journal of Personality and Social Psychology, 89,* 67–70.

Cohn, E. G. (1993). The prediction of police calls for service: The influence of weather and temporal variables on rape and domestic violence. *Environmental Psychology, 13,* 71–83.

Coker, B. (2012). Seeking the opinions of others online: Evidence of evaluation overshoot. *Journal of Economic Psychology, 33,* 1033–1042.

Colarelli, S. M., Spranger, J. L., Hechanova, M. R. (2006). Women, power, and sex composition in small groups: An evolutionary perspective. *Journal of Organizational Behavior Special Issue: Darwinian Perspectives on Behavior in Organizations, 27,* 163–184.

Cole, J. C., Gillis. A. J., van der Linden, S., Cohen, M. A., & Vandenbergh, M. P. (2023). Social psychological perspectives on political polarization: Insights and implications for climate change. *Perspectives on Psychological Science, in press.*

Coleman, L. M., Jussim, L., & Abraham, J. (1987). Students' reactions to teachers' evaluations: The unique impact of negative feedback. *Journal of Applied Social Psychology, 17,* 1051–1070.

Coles, N. A., Gaertner, L., Frohlich, B., Larsen, J. T., & Basnight-Brown, D. M. (2023). Fact or artifact? Demand characteristics and participants' beliefs can moderate, but do not fully account for, the effects of facial feedback on emotional experience. *Journal of Personality and Social Psychology, 124,* 287–310.

Coles, N. A., Larsen, J. T., & Lench, H. C. (2019). A meta-analysis of the facial feedback literature: Effects of facial feedback on emotional experience are small and variable. *Psychological Bulletin, 145,* 610–651.

Coles, N. A., March, D. S., Marmolejo-Ramos, F., Larsen, J. T., Arinze, N. C., Ndukaihe, I. L. G., Willis, M. L., Foroni, F., Reggev, N., Mokady, A., Forscher, P. S., Hunter, J. F., Kaminski, G., Yüvrük, E., Kapucu, A., Nagy, T., Hajdu, N., Tejada, J., Freitag, R. M. K., . . . Liuzza, M. T. (2022). A multi-lab test of the facial feedback hypothesis by the Many Smiles Collaboration. *Nature Human Behaviour, 6,* 1731–1742.

CollegeData.com (2023). Transition to college: Here's what students have to say about it. https://www.collegedata.com/resources/transition-to-college/transition-to-college-survey-results

Colliander, J. (2019). "This is fake news": Investigating the role of conformity to other users' views when commenting on and spreading disinformation in social media. *Computers in Human Behavior, 97,* 202–215.

Collier, K. L., Bos, H. M. W., & Sandfort, T. G. M. (2012). Intergroup contact, attitudes toward homosexuality, and the role of acceptance of gender non-conformity in young adolescents. *Journal of Adolescence, 35,* 899–907.

Collins, N. L., & Miller, L. C. (1994). Self-disclosure and liking: A meta-analytic review. *Psychological Bulletin, 116,* 457–475.

Colloff, M. F., Flowe, H. D., Smith, H. M. J., Seale-Carlisle, T. M., Meissner, C. A., Rockey, J. C., Pande, B., Kujur, P., Parveen, N., Chandel, P., Singh, M. M., Pradhan, S., & Parganiha, A. (2022). Active exploration of faces in police lineups increases discrimination accuracy. *American Psychologist, 77,* 196–220.

Coloff, M. F., Wade, K. A., & Strange, D. (2016). Unfair lineups make witnesses more likely to confuse innocent and guilty suspects. *Psychological Science, 27,* 1227–1239.

Colt, J. (2021, January 7). Quoted in Boise man who stormed U.S. Capitol building: "I got caught up in the moment." *Idaho News.* https://idahonews.com/more-to-watch/boise-man-goes-viral-after-making-his-way-onto-senate-floor

Columb, C., & Plant, E. A. (2016). The Obama effect six years later: The effect of exposure to Obama on implicit anti-black evaluative bias and implicit racial stereotyping. *Social Cognition, 34,* 523–543.

Colzato, L. S., Steenbergen, L., de Kwaadsteniet, E. W., Sellaro, R., Liepelt, R., & Hommel, B. (2013). Tryptophan promotes interpersonal trust. *Psychological Science, 24,* 2575–2577.

Combs, B. H., Stewart, T. L., & Sonnett, J. (2017). People like us: Dominance-oriented racial affiliation preferences and the White Greek system on a southern US campus. *Sociological Spectrum, 37,* 27–47.

Comer, D. R. (1995). A model of social loafing in a real work group. *Human Relations, 48,* 647–667.

Comşa, L., David, O., & David, D. (2020). Outcomes and mechanisms of change in cognitive-behavioral interventions for weight loss: A meta-analysis of randomized clinical trials. *Behaviour Research and Therapy, 132,* Article 103654.

Confer, J. C., Easton, J. A., Fleischman, D. S., Goetz, C. D., Lewis, D. M. G., Perilloux, C., & Buss, D. M. (2010). Evolutionary psychology: Controversies, questions, prospects, and limitations. *American Psychologist, 65,* 110–126.

Conger, R. D., Cui, M., Bryant, C. M., & Elder, G. H. (2000). Competence in early adult romantic relationships: A developmental perspective on family influences. *Journal of Personality and Social Psychology, 79,* 224–237.

Connolly Gibbons, M. B., Duong, L., Zoupou, E., Kashden, J., Fisher, J., & Crits-Christoph, P. (2023). Randomized controlled trial evaluating feedback to community-based therapists based on patient reports of trust and respect. *Journal of Consulting and Clinical Psychology, 91,* 337–349.

Connor, P., Varney, J., Keltner, D., & Chen, S. (2021). Social Class Competence Stereotypes Are Amplified by Socially Signaled Economic Inequality. *Personality & Social Psychology Bulletin, 47,* 89–105.

Conroy-Beam, D., Buss, D. M., Pham, M. N., & Shackelford, T. K. (2015). How sexually dimorphic are human mate preferences? *Personality and Social Psychology Bulletin, 41,* 1082–1093.

Constantino, S. M., Sparkman, G., Kraft-Todd, G. T., Bicchieri, C., Centola, D., Shell-Duncan, B., Vogt, S., & Weber, E. U. (2022). Scaling up change: A critical review and practical guide to harnessing social norms for climate action. *Psychological Science in the Public Interest, 23,* 50–97.

Contrada, R. J., Ashmore, R. D., Gary, M. L., Coups, E., Egeth, J. D., Sewell, A., Ewell, K., Goyal, T. M., & Chasse, V. (2000). Ethnicity-related sources of stress and their effects on well-being. *Current Directions in Psychological Science, 9,* 136–139.

Conway, J. R., Noë, N., Stulp, G., & Pollet, T. V. (2015). Finding your soulmate: Homosexual and heterosexual age preferences in online dating. *Personal Relationships, 22,* 666–678.

Conway, L. G., III, Suedfeld, P., & Tetlock, P. E. (2001). Integrative complexity and political decisions that lead to war or peace. In D. J. Christie, R. V. Wagner, & D. Winter (Eds.), *Peace, conflict, and violence: Peace psychology for the 21st century.* Englewood Cliffs, NJ: Prentice-Hall.

Conway, L. G., McFarland, J. D., Costello, T. H., & Lilienfeld, S. O. (2021). The curious case of left-wing authoritarianism: When authoritarian persons meet anti-authoritarian norms. *Journal of Theoretical Social Psychology, 5,* 423–442.

Conway, M., & Ross, M. (1986). Remembering one's own past: The construction of personal histories. In R. Sorrentino & E. T. Higgins (Eds.), *Handbook of motivation and cognition.* New York: Guilford.

Cooke, L., Chambers, L., Anez, E., Croker, H., Boniface, D., Yeomans, M., & Wardle, J. (2011). Eating for pleasure or profit: The effect of incentives on children's enjoyment of vegetables. *Psychological Science, 22,* 190–196.

Cook, J. (2010, December 30). The many lines of evidence for global warming in a single graphic. *SkepticalScience.* https://skepticalscience.com/The-many-lines-of-evidence-for-global-warming-in-a-single-graphic.html

Cook, J. (2016, July/August). A skeptical response to science denial. *Skeptical Inquirer.* https://skepticalinquirer.org/2016/11/a-skeptical-response-to-science-denial/

Cook, J., Ecker, U. K. H., Trecek-King, M., Schade, G., Jeffers-Tracy, K., Fessmann, J., Kim, S. C., Kinkead, D., Orr, M., Vraga, E., Roberts, K., & McDowell, J. (2023). The cranky uncle game—combining humor and gamification to build student resilience against climate misinformation. *Environmental Education Research, 29,* 607–623.

Cook, K. (2014). *Kitty Genovese: The murder, the bystanders, the crime that changed America.* New York: Norton.

Cooley, C. H. (1902). *Human nature and the social order.* New York: Schocken Books.

Cooper, H. (1983). Teacher expectation effects. In L. Bickman (Ed.), *Applied social psychology annual* (Vol. 4). Beverly Hills, CA: Sage.

Cooper, H., Gibbons-Neff, T., Schmitt, E., & Barnes, J. E. (2023, August 18). Troop Deaths and Injuries in Ukraine War Near 500,000, U.S. Officials Say. *New York Times.*

Cooper, J., & Feldman, L. A. (2019). Does cognitive dissonance occur in older age? A study of induced compliance in a healthy elderly population. *Psychology and Aging, 34,* 709–713.

Cooper, J. (1999). Unwanted consequences and the self: In search of the motivation for dissonance reduction. In E. Harmon-Jones & J. Mills (Eds.), *Cognitive dissonance: Progress on a pivotal theory in social psychology.* Washington, DC: American Psychological Association.

Corcoran, K. E., & Stark, R. (2018). Culture, region, and cross-national violent crime. *Sociological Forum, 33,* 310–333.

Cordes, H., Baumeister, S., & Käyrä, M. (2024). Factors influencing the willingness to pay for aviation voluntary carbon offsets: A literature review. *European Journal of Tourism Research, 36,* 1–23.

Cordier, R., Speyer, R., Mahoney, N., Arnesen, A., Mjelve, L. H., & Nyborg, G. (2021). Effects of interventions for social anxiety and shyness in school-aged children: A systematic review and meta-analysis. *PLoS ONE, 16*(7).

Corno, L., La Ferrara, E., & Burns, J. (2022). Interaction, stereotypes, and performance: Evidence from South Africa. *American Economic Review, 112,* 3848–3875.

Cornwall, W. (2016). Sea ice shrinks in step with carbon emissions. *Science, 354,* 533.

Correll, J., Park, B., Judd, C. M., & Wittenbrink, B. (2002). The police officer's dilemma: Using ethnicity to disambiguate potentially threatening individuals. *Journal of Personality and Social Psychology, 83,* 1314–1329.

Correll, J., Park, B., Judd, C. M., & Wittenbrink, B. (2007). The influence of stereotypes on decisions to shoot. *European Journal of Social Psychology, 37,* 1102–1117.

Correll, J., Wittenbrink, B., Crawford, M. T., & Sadler, M. S. (2015). Stereotypic vision: How stereotypes disambiguate visual stimuli. *Journal of Personality and Social Psychology, 108,* 219–233.

Corrigan, P. W., Watson, A. C., Byrne, P., & Davis, K. E. (2005). Mental illness stigma: Problem of public health or social justice? *Social Work, 50,* 363–368.

Cortland, C. I., Craig, M. A., Shapiro, J. R., Richeson, J. A., Neel, R., & Goldstein, N. J. (2017). Solidarity through shared disadvantage: Highlighting shared experiences of discrimination improves relations between stigmatized groups. *Journal of Personality and Social Psychology, 113,* 547–567.

Costa-Lopes, R., Dovidio, J. F., Pereira, C., & Jost, J. T. (2013). Social psychological perspectives on the legitimation of social inequality: Past, present and future. *European Journal of Social Psychology, 43,* 229–237.

Costanzo, M. (1997). *Just revenge: Costs and consequences of the death penalty.* New York: St. Martin's.

Costanzo, M. (1998). *Just revenge.* New York: St. Martins.

Costello, C., Gaines, S. D., & Lynham, J. (2008). Can catch shares prevent fisheries' collapse? *Science, 321,* 1678–1682.

Costello, T. H., & Patrick, C. J. (2023). Development and initial validation of two brief measures of left-wing authoritarianism: A machine learning approach. *Journal of Personality Assessment, 105,* 187–202.

Costello, T. H., Bowes, S. M., Stevens, S. T., Waldman, I. D., Tasimi, A., & Lilienfeld, S. O. (2022). Clarifying the structure and nature of left-wing authoritarianism. *Journal of Personality and Social Psychology, 122,* 135–170.

Coster, H. (2014, May 14). Peer pressure can be a lifesaver [Blog post]. *The New York Times.* https://opinionator.blogs.nytimes.com/2014/05/14/peer-pressure-can-be-a-lifesaver/

Cota, A. A., & Dion, K. L. (1986). Salience of gender and sex composition of ad hoc groups: An experimental test of distinctiveness theory. *Journal of Personality and Social Psychology, 50,* 770–776.

Cottrell, N. B., Wack, D. L., Sekerak, G. J., & Rittle, R. M. (1968). Social facilitation of dominant responses by the presence of an audience and the mere presence of others. *Journal of Personality and Social Psychology, 9,* 245–250.

Coulter, K. S., & Grewal, D. (2014). Name-letters and birthday-numbers: Implicit egotism effects in pricing. *Journal of Marketing, 78,* 102–120.

Courbet, D., Fourquet-Courbet, M. P., Kazan, R., & Intartaglia, J. (2014). The long-term effects of e-advertising: The influence of Internet pop-ups viewed at a low level of attention in implicit memory. *Journal of Computer-Mediated Communication, 19,* 274–293.

Courtice, E. L., Quinn-Nilas, C., Bickram, D. A., Witoski, S., Hoskin, R. A., & Blair, K. L. (2023). Is the messenger the message? Canadian political affiliation and other predictors of mask wearing frequency & attitudes during the COVID-19 pandemic. *Canadian Journal of Behavioural Science/ Revue Canadienne Des Sciences Du Comportement, 55,* 1–13.

Cousins, N. (1978, September 16). The taxpayers revolt: Act two. *Saturday Review,* 56.

Cox, C. R., Van Enkevort, E. A., Hicks, J. A., Kahn-Weintraub, M., & Morin, A. (2014). The relationship between alcohol cues, alcohol expectancies, and physical balance. *Experimental and Clinical Psychopharmacology, 22,* 307–315.

Coyne, S. M., & Archer, J. (2005). The relationship between indirect and physical aggression on television and in real life. *Social Development, 14,* 324–338.

Coyne, S. M. (2016). Effects of viewing relational aggression on television on aggressive behavior in adolescents: A three-year longitudinal study. *Developmental Psychology, 52,* 284–295.

Coyne, S. M., Ehrenreich, S. E., Holmgren, H. G., & Underwood, M. K. (2019). "We're not gonna be friends anymore": Associations between viewing relational aggression on television and relational aggression in text messaging during adolescence. *Aggressive Behavior, 45*(3), 319–326.

Coyne, S. M., Nelson, D. A., Lawton, F., Haslam, S., Rooney, L., Titterington, L., & . . . Ogunlaja, L. (2008). The effects of viewing physical and relational aggression in the media: Evidence for a cross-over effect. *Journal of Experimental Social Psychology, 44,* 1551–1554.

Coyne, S. M., Padilla-Walker, L. M., Holmgren, H. G., Davis, E. J., Collier, K. M., Memmott-Elison, M. K., & Hawkins, A. J. (2018). A meta-analysis of prosocial media on prosocial behavior, aggression, and empathic concern: A multidimensional approach. *Developmental Psychology, 54,* 331–347.

Coyne, S. M., Ridge, R., Stevens, M., Callister, M., & Stockdale, L. (2012). Backbiting and bloodshed in books: Short-term effects of reading physical and relational aggression in literature. *British Journal of Social Psychology, 51,* 188–196.

Crabtree, S. (2002, January 22). Gender roles reflected in teen tech use. *Gallup Tuesday Briefing.* www.gallup.com

Cracco, E., Bardi, L., Desmet, C., Genschow, O., Rigoni, D., De Coster, L., . . . Brass, M. (2018). Automatic imitation: A meta-analysis. *Psychological Bulletin, 144,* 453–500.

Craig, M. A., & Richeson, J. A. (2012). Coalition or derogation? How perceived discrimination influences intraminority intergroup relations. *Journal of Personality and Social Psychology, 102,* 759–777.

Craig, W., Boniel-Nissim, M., King, N., Walsh, S. D., Boer, M., . . . Pickett, W. (2020). Social media use and cyber-bullying: A cross-national analysis of young people in 42 countries. *Journal of Adolescent Health, 66*(6, Suppl), S100–S108.

Crandall, C. S., & Eshleman, A. (2003). A justification-suppression model of the expression and experience of prejudice. *Psychological Bulletin, 129,* 414–446.

Crandall, C. S. (1988). Social contagion of binge eating. *Journal of Personality and Social Psychology, 55,* 588–598.

Crano, W. D., & Mellon, P. M. (1978). Causal influence of teachers' expectations on children's academic performance: A cross-legged panel analysis. *Journal of Educational Psychology, 70,* 39–49.

Crawford, J. T., Brandt, M. J., Inbar, Y., Chambers, J. R., & Motyl, M. (2017). Social and economic ideologies differentially predict prejudice across the political spectrum, but social issues are most divisive. *Journal of Personality and Social Psychology, 112,* 383–412.

CRED (Center for Research on Environmental Decisions). (2014). *Connecting on climate: A guide to effective climate change communication* [PDF file]. https://ecoamerica.org/wp-content/uploads/2014/12/ecoAmerica-CRED-2014-Connecting-on-Climate.pdf

Cregg, D. R., & Cheavens, J. S. (2023). Healing through helping: An experimental investigation of kindness, social activities, and reappraisal as well-being interventions. *The Journal of Positive Psychology, 18,* 924–941.

Crisp, R. J., & Hewstone, M. (1999). Differential evaluation of crossed category groups: Patterns, processes, and reducing intergroup bias. *Group Processes & Intergroup Relations, 2,* 307–333.

Crisp, R. J., & Hewstone, M. (2000). Multiple categorization and social identity. In D. Capozza & R. Brown (Eds.), *Social identity theory: Trends in theory and research.* Beverly Hills, CA: Sage.

Crocetti, E., Albarello, F., Prati, F., & Rubini, M. (2021). Development of prejudice against immigrants and ethnic minorities in adolescence: A systematic review with meta-analysis of longitudinal studies. *Developmental Review, 60.*

Crocker, J., & Gallo, L. (1985). *The self-enhancing effect of downward comparison.* Paper presented at the American Psychological Association convention, Los Angeles, California.

Crocker, J., & Luhtanen, R. (1990). Collective self-esteem and ingroup bias. *Journal of Personality and Social Psychology, 58,* 60–67.

Crocker, J., & Luhtanen, R. (2003). Level of self-esteem and contingencies of self-worth: Unique effects on academic, social, and financial problems in college students. *Personality and Social Psychology Bulletin, 29,* 701–712.

Crocker, J., & McGraw, K. M. (1984). What's good for the goose is not good for the gander: Solo status as an obstacle to occupational achievement for males and females. *American Behavioral Scientist, 27,* 357–370.

Crocker, J., & Park, L. E. (2004). The costly pursuit of self-esteem. *Psychological Bulletin, 130,* 392–414.

Crocker, J., & Wolfe, C. (2001). Contingencies of self-worth. *Psychological Review, 85*(5), 894–908.

Crocker, J. (1981). Judgment of covariation by social perceivers. *Psychological Bulletin, 90,* 272–292.

Crocker, J. (2002). The costs of seeking self-esteem. *Journal of Social Issues, 58,* 597–615.

Crocker, J. (2011). Presidential address: Self-image and compassionate goals and construction of the social self: Implications for social and personality psychology. *Personality and Social Psychology Review, 15,* 394–407.

Crocker, J., Hannah, D. B., & Weber, R. (1983). Personal memory and causal attributions. *Journal of Personality and Social Psychology, 44,* 55–56.

Crocker, J., Thompson, L. L., McGraw, K. M., & Ingerman, C. (1987). Downward comparison, prejudice, and evaluations of others: Effects of self-esteem and threat. *Journal of Personality and Social Psychology, 52,* 907–916.

Crockett, M. J., Clark, L., Tabibnia, G., Lieberman, M. D., & Robbins, T. W. (2008). Serotonin modulates behavioral reactions to unfairness. *Science, 320,* 1739.

Crompton, T., & Kasser, T. (2010, July/August). Human identity: A missing link in environmental campaigning. *Environment Magazine,* pp. 23–33.

Crosby, F. J. (Ed.) (1987). *Spouse, parent, worker: On gender and multiple roles.* New Haven, CT: Yale University Press.

Crosby, J. R., & Monin, B. (2007). Failure to warn: How student race affects warnings of potential academic difficulty. *Journal of Experimental Social Psychology, 43,* 663–670.

Crosby, J. R., King, M., & Savitsky, K. (2014). The minority spotlight effect. *Social Psychological and Personality Science, 5,* 743–750.

Cross, C. P., Copping, L. T., & Campbell, A. (2011). Sex differences in impulsivity: A meta-analysis. *Psychological Bulletin, 137,* 97–130.

Croxton, J. S., Eddy, T., & Morrow, N. (1984). Memory biases in the reconstruction of interpersonal encounters. *Journal of Social and Clinical Psychology, 2,* 348–354.

Croyle, R. T., & Cooper, J. (1983). Dissonance arousal: Physiological evidence. *Journal of Personality and Social Psychology, 45,* 782–791.

Cruwys, T., Haslam, S. A., Dingle, G. A., Haslam, C., & Jetten, J. (2014). Depression and social identity: An integrative review. *Personality and Social Psychology Review, 18,* 215–238.

Cruz, T. (2018, August 13). Quoted by M. Flegenheimer. Beto O'Rourke dreams of one Texas. Ted Cruz sees another clearly. *The New York Times.* https://www.nytimes.com/2018/08/31/us/politics/beto-orourke-dreams-of-one-texas-ted-cruz-sees-another-clearly.html

Csikszentmihalyi, M. (1990). *Flow: The psychology of optimal experience.* New York: Harper & Row.

Csikszentmihalyi, M. (1999). If we are so rich, why aren't we happy? *American Psychologist, 54,* 821–827.

Cuddy, A. J. C., & 23 others. (2009). Stereotype content model across cultures: Towards universal similarities and some differences. *British Journal of Social Psychology,* 48, 1–33.

Culda, G. L., Opre, A. N., & Dobrin, A. D. (2018). Victim blaming by women and men who believe the world is a just place. *Cognition, Brain, Behavior: An Interdisciplinary Journal, 22*(2), 99–110.

Cundiff, J. M., & Matthews, K. A. (2018). Friends with health benefits: The long-term benefits of early peer social integration for blood pressure and obesity in midlife. *Personality and Social Psychology Bulletin, 29,* 814–823.

Cunningham, C. E., Mapp, C., Rimas, H., Cunningham, L., Mielko, S., Vaillancourt, T., & Marcus, M. (2016). What limits the effectiveness of antibullying programs? A thematic analysis of the perspective of students. *Psychology of Violence, 6,* 596–606.

Cunningham, M. R., Shaffer, D. R., Barbee, A. P., Wolff, P. L., & Kelley, D. J. (1990). Separate processes in the relation of elation and depression to helping: Social versus personal concerns. *Journal of Experimental Social Psychology, 26,* 13–33.

Cupp, S. E. (2018, December 19). It's high time we confront online bullies who urge others to kill themselves. *Tribune Content Agency.* https://tribunecontentagency.com/article/its-high-time-we-confront-online-bullies-who-urge-others-to-kill-themselves/

Curtin, S. C., & Tejada-Vera, B. (2019). *Mortality among adults aged 25 and over by martial status: United States, 2010–2017.* National Center for Health Statistics. https://www.cdc.gov/nchs/data/hestat/mortality/mortality_marital_status_10_17.htm

Cutler, B. L., & Kovera, M. B. (2011). Expert psychological testimony. *Current Directions in Psychological Science, 20,* 53–57.

Cutler, B. L., & Penrod, S. D. (1988). Context reinstatement and eyewitness identification. In G. M. Davies & D. M. Thomson (Eds.), *Context reinstatement and eyewitness identification.* New York: Wiley.

Cutler, B. L., Moran, G., & Narvy, D. J. (1992). Jury selection in insanity defense cases. *Journal of Research in Personality, 26,* 165–182.

Cutler, B. L., Penrod, S. D., & Dexter, H. R. (1989). The eyewitness, the expert psychologist and the jury. *Law and Human Behavior, 13,* 311–332.

Cutrona, C. E. (1986). Behavioral manifestations of social support: A microanalytic investigation. *Journal of Personality and Social Psychology, 51,* 201–208.

Cyr, D., Head, M., Lim, E., & Stibe, A. (2018). Using the elaboration likelihood model to examine online persuasion through website design. *Information & Management, 55,* 807–821.

Czyz, S. H., Szmajke, A., Kruger, A., & Kubler, M. (2016). Participation in team sports can eliminate the effect of social loafing. *Perceptual and Motor Skills, 123,* 754–768.

Dabbs, J. M., Jr. (1992). Testosterone measurements in social and clinical psychology. *Journal of Social and Clinical Psychology, 11,* 302–321.

Dabbs, J. M., Jr. (2000). *Heroes, rogues, and lovers: Testosterone and behavior.* New York: McGraw Hill.

Dabbs, J. M., Jr., Carr, T. S., Frady, R. L., & Riad, J. K. (1995). Testosterone, crime, and misbehavior among 692 male prison inmates. *Personality and Individual Differences, 18,* 627–633.

Dabbs, J. M., Jr., Riad, J. K., & Chance, S. E. (2001). Testosterone and ruthless homicide. *Personality and Individual Differences, 31,* 599–603.

Dabbs, J. M., Jr., Strong, R., & Milun, R. (1997). Exploring the mind of testosterone: A beeper study. *Journal of Research in Personality, 31,* 577–588.

Dabiriyan Tehrani, H., & Yamini, S. (2022). Gender differences concerning the horizontal and vertical individualism and collectivism: A meta-analysis. *Psychological Studies.*

da Costa, S., Delfino, G., Murattori, M., Zubieta, E., García, L., Páez, D., Beramendi, M., & Sosa, F. (2021). Obedience to authority, cognitive and affective responses and leadership style in relation to a non-normative order: The Milgram experiment. *Revista de Psicología, 39,* 717–744.

Dai, H. D., Ratnapradipa, K., Michaud, T. L., King, K. M., Guenzel, N., Tamrakar, N., Puga, T., & Sussman, S. (2022). Vaping media literacy, harm perception, and susceptibility of E-cigarette use among youth. *American Journal of Preventive Medicine, 63,* 852–860.

Dale, S. (2015). Heuristics and biases: The science of decision-making. *Business Information Review, 32,* 93–99.

Dalrymple, T. (2007). On evil. *New English Review.* https://www.newenglishreview.org/Theodore_Dalrymple/On_Evil/

Dambrun, M., & Vatiné, E. (2010). Reopening the study of extreme social behaviors: Obedience to authority within an immersive video environment. *European Journal of Social Psychology, 40,* 760–773.

Damon, W. (1995). *Greater expectations: Overcoming the culture of indulgence in America's homes and schools.* New York: Free Press.

Dando, C., Wilcock, R., & Milne, R. (2009). The cognitive interview: The efficacy of a modified mental reinstatement of context procedure for frontline police investigators. *Applied Cognitive Psychology, 23,* 138–147.

Dannals, J. E., Halali, E., Kopelman, S., & Halevy, N. (2022). Power, constraint, and cooperation in groups: The role of communication. *Journal of Experimental Social Psychology, 100,* 1–9.

Danner, D. D., Snowdon, D. A., & Friesen, W. V. (2001). Positive emotions in early life and longevity: Findings from the Nun Study. *Journal of Personality and Social Psychology, 80,* 804–813.

Daou, M., Hutchison, Z., Bacelar, M., Rhoads, J. A., Lohse, K. R., & Miller, M. W. (2019). Learning a skill with the expectation of teaching it impairs the skill's execution under psychological pressure. *Journal of Experimental Psychology: Applied, 25,* 219–229.

Dapp, L. C., Krauss, S., & Orth, U. (2023). Testing the bottom-up and top-down models of self-esteem: A meta-analysis of longitudinal studies. *Journal of Personality and Social Psychology, 124,* 1111–1131.

Dardenne, B., Dumont, M., & Bollier, T. (2007). Insidious dangers of benevolent sexism: Consequences for women's performance. *Journal of Personality and Social Psychology, 93,* 764–779.

Darley, J., & Alter, A. (2009). Behavioral issues of punishment and deterrence. In E. Shafir (Ed.), *The behavioral foundations of policy.* Princeton, NJ: Princeton University Press.

Darley, J. M., & Batson, C. D. (1973). "From Jerusalem to Jericho": A study of situational and dispositional variables in helping behavior. *Journal of Personality and Social Psychology, 27*(1), 100.

Darley, J. M., & Berscheid, E. (1967). Increased liking as a result of the anticipation of personal contact. *Human Relations, 20,* 29–40.

Darley, J. M., & Gross, P. H. (1983). A hypothesis-confirming bias in labelling effects. *Journal of Personality and Social Psychology, 44,* 20–33.

Darley, J. M., & Latané, B. (1968). Bystander intervention in emergencies: Diffusion of responsibility. *Journal of Personality and Social Psychology, 8,* 377–383.

Darrow, C. (1933). Cited by Sutherland, E. H., & Cressy, D. R. (1966). *Principles of criminology.* (p. 442). Philadelphia: Lippincott.

Darwin, C. (1859/1988). *On the origin of species,* Vol. 15 of *The Works of Charles Darwin* (P. H. Barrett, R. B. Freeman, Eds.). New York: New York University Press.

Dasgupta, N., & Rivera, L. M. (2006). From automatic antigay prejudice to behavior: The moderating role of conscious beliefs about gender and behavioral control. *Journal of Personality and Social Psychology, 91,* 268–280.

Dashiell, J. F. (1930). An experimental analysis of some group effects. *Journal of Abnormal and Social Psychology, 25,* 190–199.

Dastagir, A. E. (2021, October 21). Rape on Philadelphia train was horrific, but experts say we're missing something in our outrage. *USA Today.*

Davey, G., & Rato, R. (2012). Subjective well-being in China: A review. *Journal of Happiness Studies, 13,* 333–346.

Davidai, S., & Gilovich, T. (2016). The headwinds/tailwinds asymmetry: An availability bias in assessments of barriers and blessings. *Journal of Personality and Social Psychology, 111,* 835–851.

Davidai, S., & Walker, J. (2022). Americans misperceive racial disparities in economic mobility. *Personality and Social Psychology Bulletin, 48,* 793–806.

David, M. E., & Roberts, J. A. (2017). Phubbed and alone: Phone snubbing, social exclusion, and attachment to social media. *Journal of the Association of Consumer Research, 2,* 155–163.

Davies, A. C., & Shackelford, T. K. (2017). Don't you wish your partner was hot like me? The effectiveness of mate poaching across relationship types considering the relative mate-values of the poacher and the partner of the poached. *Personality and Individual Differences, 106,* 32–35.

Davies, K., & Aron, A. (2016). Friendship development and intergroup attitudes: The role of interpersonal and intergroup friendship processes. *Journal of Social Issues, 72,* 489–510.

Davies, P. (2004, April 14). Into the 21st century. *Metaviews.* www.metanexus.net

Davies, P. (2007). *Cosmic jackpot: Why our universe is just right for life.* Boston: Houghton-Mifflin.

Davila, J., Bradbury, T. N., Cohan, C. L., & Tochluk, S. (1997). Marital functioning and depressive symptoms: Evidence for a stress generation model. *Journal of Personality and Social Psychology, 73,* 849–861.

Davis, C. G., Lehman, D. R., Silver, R. C., Wortman, C. B., & Ellard, J. H. (1996). Self-blame following a traumatic event: The role of perceived avoidability. *Personality and Social Psychology Bulletin, 22,* 557–567.

Davis, C. G., Lehman, D. R., Wortman, C. B., Silver, R. C., & Thompson, S. C. (1995). The undoing of traumatic life events. *Personality and Social Psychology Bulletin, 21,* 109–124.

Davis, D., Loftus, E. F., Vanous, S., & Cucciare, M. (2008). "Unconscious transference" can be an instance of "change blindness." *Applied Cognitive Psychology, 22,* 605–623.

Davis, J. H., Kameda, T., Parks, C., Stasson, M., & Zimmerman, S. (1989). Some social mechanics of group decision making: The distribution of opinion, polling sequence, and implications for consensus. *Journal of Personality and Social Psychology, 57,* 1000–1012.

Davis, J. H., Kerr, N. L., Atkin, R. S., Holt, R., & Meek, D. (1975). The decision processes of 6- and 12-person mock juries assigned unanimous and two-thirds majority rules. *Journal of Personality and Social Psychology, 32,* 1–14.

Davis, J. H., Kerr, N. L., Stasser, G., Meek, D., & Holt, R. (1977). Victim consequences, sentence severity, and decision process in mock juries. *Organizational Behavior and Human Performance, 18,* 346–365.

Davis, J. T. M., & Hines, M. (2020). How large are gender differences in toy preferences? A systematic review and meta-analysis of toy preference research. *Archives of Sexual Behavior, 49*(2), 373–394.

Davis, K. E., & Jones, E. E. (1960). Changes in interpersonal perception as a means of reducing cognitive dissonance. *Journal of Abnormal and Social Psychology, 61,* 402–410.

Davis, K. E. (1985, February). Near and dear: Friendship and love compared. *Psychology Today,* pp. 22–30.

Davis, M. H., & Franzoi, S. L. (1986). Adolescent loneliness, self-disclosure, and private self-consciousness: A longitudinal investigation. *Journal of Personality and Social Psychology, 51,* 595–608.

Dawes, R. M. (1976). Shallow psychology. In J. S. Carroll & J. W. Payne (Eds.), *Cognition and social behavior.* Hillsdale, NJ: Erlbaum.

Dawes, R. M. (1980). Social dilemmas. *Annual Review of Psychology, 31,* 169–193.

Dawes, R. M. (1990). The potential nonfalsity of the false consensus effect. In R. M. Hogarth (Ed.), *Insights in decision making: A tribute to Hillel J. Einhorn.* Chicago: University of Chicago Press.

Dawes, R. M. (1994). *House of cards: Psychology and psychotherapy built on myth.* New York: Free Press.

Dawes, R. M. (2005). The ethical implications of Paul Meehl's work on comparing clinical versus actuarial prediction methods. *Journal of Clinical Psychology, 61,* 1245–1255.

Dawkins, R. (1976). *The selfish gene.* New York: Oxford University Press.

Dawkins, R. (1993). Gaps in the mind. In P. Cavalieri & P. Singer (Eds.), *The Great Ape Project: Equality beyond humanity* (pp. 80–87). London: Fourth Estate.

Dawson, N. V., Arkes, H. R., Siciliano, C., Blinkhorn, R., Lakshmanan, M., & Petrelli, M. (1988). Hindsight bias: An impediment to accurate probability estimation in clinicopathologic conferences. *Medical Decision Making, 8,* 259–264.

de Assis, S., Warri, A., Cruz, M. I., Laja, O., Tian, Y., Zhang, B., Wang, Y., Huang, T. H., & Hilakivi-Clarke, L. (2012). High-fat or ethinyl-oestradiol intake during pregnancy increases mammary cancer risk in several generations of offspring. *Nature Communications, 3,* 1053.

de Botton, A. (2004). *Status anxiety.* London: Hamish Hamilton Limited.

DeBruine, L. M. (2002). Facial resemblance enhances trust. *Proceedings of the Royal Society of London, 269,* 1307–1312.

DeBruine, L. M. (2004). Facial resemblance increases the attractiveness of same-sex faces more than other-sex faces. *Proceedings of the Royal Society of London, B, 271*(1552), 2085–2090.

DeCelles, K. A., & Norton, M. I. (2016). Physical and situational inequality on airplanes predicts air rage. *PNAS , 113*(20), 5588–5591.

Decety, J., & Cowell, J. M. (2014). Friends or foes: Is empathy necessary for moral behavior? *Perspectives on Psychological Science, 9,* 525–537.

Decety, J., & Sommerville, J. A. (2003). Shared representations between self and other: A social cognitive neuroscience view. *Trends in Cognitive Sciences, 7,* 527–533.

Dechêne, A., Stahl, C., Hansen, J., & Wänke, M. (2010). The truth about the truth: A meta-analysis review of the truth effect. *Personality and Social Psychology Review, 14,* 238–257.

Deci, E. L., & Ryan, R. M. (1985). *Intrinsic motivation and self-determination in human behavior.* New York: Plenum.

Deci, E. L., & Ryan, R. M. (1991). A motivational approach to self: Integration in personality. In R. Dienstbier (Ed.) *Perspectives on motivation: Nebraska Symposium on Motivation* (Vol. 38, pp. 237–288). Lincoln, NE: University of Nebraska Press.

Deci, E. L., & Ryan, R. M. (2008). Facilitating optimal motivation and psychological well-being across life's domains. *Canadian Psychology, 49,* 14–23.

Deci, E. L., & Ryan, R. M. (2012). Self-determination theory. In P. A. Van Lange, A. W. Kruglanski, & E. T. Higgins (Eds.), *Handbook of theories of social psychology* (Vol. 1). Thousand Oaks, CA: Sage.

Deci, E. L., & Ryan, R. M. (Eds.), (2002). *Handbook of self-determination research.* Rochester, NY: University of Rochester Press.

De Cremer, D. (2002). Charismatic leadership and cooperation in social dilemmas: A matter of transforming motives? *Journal of Applied Social Psychology, 32,* 997–1016.

Defranza, D., Mishra, H., & Mishra, A. (2020). How language shapes prejudice against women: An examination across 45 world languages. *Journal of Personality and Social Psychology, 119*(1), 7–22.

de Hoogh, A. H. B., den Hartog, D. N., Koopman, P. L., Thierry, H., van den Berg, P. T., van der Weide, J. G., & Wilderom, C. P. M. (2004). Charismatic leadership, environmental dynamism, and performance. *European Journal of Work and Organisational Psychology, 13,* 447–471.

de Hoog, N., Stroebe, W., & de Wit, J. F. (2007). The impact of vulnerability to and severity of a health risk on processing and acceptance of fear-arousing communications: A meta-analysis. *Review of General Psychology, 11,* 258–285.

De Houwer, J., Thomas, S., & Baeyens, F. (2001). Associative learning of likes and dislikes: A review of 25 years of research on human evaluative conditioning. *Psychological Bulletin, 127,* 853–869.

Dehue, F., Bolman, C., & Vollink, T. (2008). Cyberbulling: Youngsters' experiences and parental perception. *Cyberpsychology & Behavior, 11,* 217–223.

De Keersmaecker, J., Dunning, D., Pennycook, G., Rand, D. G., Sanchez, C., Unkelbach, C., & Roets, A. (2020). Investigating the robustness of the illusory truth effect across individual differences in cognitive ability, need for cognitive closure, and cognitive style. *Personality and Social Psychology Bulletin, 46,* 204–215.

De La Mare, J. K., & Lee, A. J. (2023). Assortative preferences for personality and online dating apps: Individuals prefer profiles similar to themselves on agreeableness, openness, and extraversion. *Personality and Individual Differences, 208,* 1–9.

de Lange, M. A., Debets, L. W., Ruitenburg, K., & Holland, R. W. (2012). Making less of a mess: Scent exposure as a tool for behavioral change. *Social Influence, 7,* 90–97.

Delgado, J. (1973). In M. Pines, *The brain changers.* New York: Harcourt Brace Jovanovich.

DellaPosta, D. (2018). Gay acquaintanceship and attitudes toward homosexuality: A conservative test. *Socius, 4,* 1–12.

Del Vicario, M., Zollo, F., Caldarelli, G., Scala, A., & Quattrociocchi, W. (2017). Mapping social dynamics on Facebook: The Brexit debate. *Social Networks, 50,* 6–16.

Demedardi, M.-J., Stephan, Y., & Monnier, C. (2021). On the importance of being agreeable: The impact of personality traits on prosocial lying in children. *International Journal of Behavioral Development, 45,* 484–491.

de Meza, D., & Dawson, C. (2021). Neither an optimist nor a pessimist be: Mistaken expectations lower well-being. *Personality and Social Psychology Bulletin, 47,* 540–550.

de Mooij, B., Fekkes, M., Scholte, R. H. J., & Overbeek, G. (2020). Effective components of social skills training programs for children and adolescents in nonclinical samples: A multilevel meta-analysis. *Clinical Child and Family Psychology Review, 23,* 250–264.

de Moor, E. L., Denissen, J. J. A., Emons, W. H. M., Bleidorn, W., Luhmann, M., Orth, U., & Chung, J. M. (2021). Self-esteem and satisfaction with social relationships across time. *Journal of Personality and Social Psychology, 120,* 173–191.

Demoulin, S., Saroglou, V., & Van Pachterbeke, M. (2008). Infra-humanizing others, supra-humanizing gods: The emotional hierarchy. *Social Cognition, 26,* 235–247.

De Neve, J., & Oswald, A. J. (2012). Estimating the influence of life satisfaction and positive affect on later income using sibling fixed effects. *PNAS, 109*(49), 19953–19958.

Denissen, J. J. A., Penke, L., Schmitt, D. P., & van Aken, M. A. G. (2008). Self-esteem reactions to social interactions: Evidence for sociometer mechanisms across days, people, and nations. *Journal of Personality and Social Psychology, 95,* 181–196.

Dennehy, R., Meaney, S., Walsh, K. A., Sinnott, C., Cronin, M., & Arensman, E. (2020). Young people's conceptualizations of the nature of cyberbullying: A systematic review and synthesis of qualitative research. *Aggression and Violent Behavior, 51*(4), 101379.

Dennett, D. (2005, December 26). *Der Spiegel* interview with evolution philosopher Daniel Dennett: Darwinism completely refutes intelligent design. *Der Spiegel.* www.service.dspiegel.de.

Denney, J. T., & Boardman, J. D. (2021). Hearing impairment, household composition, marital status, and mortality among US adults. *The Journals of Gerontology: Series B: Psychological Sciences and Social Sciences, 76,* 201–208.

Denrell, J., & Le Mens, G. (2007). Interdependent sampling and social influence. *Psychological Review, 114,* 398–422.

Denrell, J. (2008). Indirect social influence. *Science, 321,* 47–48.

Denson, T. F., Pedersen, W. C., & Miller, N. (2006). The displaced aggression questionnaire. *Journal of Personality and Social Psychology, 90,* 1032–1051.

Denyer, S., & Gowen, A. (2018, April 18). Too many men. *The Washington Post.* www.washingtonpost.com

Department of Canadian Heritage. (2006). What is multiculturalism? Retrieved from www.pch.gc.ca

DePaulo, B. (2006). *Singled out: How singles are stereotyped, stigmatized, and ignored, and still live happily ever after.* New York: St. Martin's.

DePinto, J. (2022, June 9). A look at how Americans have viewed the Jan. 6 Capitol attack – CBS poll analysis. CBSnews.com.

De Pinto, J. (2022, June 9). A look at how Americans have viewed the Jan. 6 Capitol attack—CBS News poll analysis. CBSnews.com.

Derks, B., Inzlicht, M., & Kang, S. (2008). The neuroscience of stigma and stereotype threat. *Group Processes and Intergroup Relations, 11,* 163–181.

Derlega, V., Metts, S., Petronio, S., & Margulis, S. T. (1993). *Self-disclosure.* Newbury Park, CA: Sage.

Dermer, M., & Pyszczynski, T. A. (1978). Effects of erotica upon men's loving and liking responses for women they love. *Journal of Personality and Social Psychology, 36,* 1302–1309.

Dermer, M., Cohen, S. J., Jacobsen, E., & Anderson, E. A. (1979). Evaluative judgments of aspects of life as a function of vicarious exposure to hedonic extremes. *Journal of Personality and Social Psychology, 37,* 247–260.

Desforges, D. M., Lord, C. G., Pugh, M. A., Sia, T. L., Scarberry, N. C., & Ratcliff, C. D. (1997). Role of group representativeness in the generalization part of the contact hypothesis. *Basic and Applied Social Psychology, 19,* 183–204.

Desforges, D. M., Lord, C. G., Ramsey, S. L., Mason, J. A., Van Leeuwen, M. D., West, S. C., & Lepper, M. R. (1991). Effects of structured cooperative contact on changing negative attitudes toward stigmatized social groups. *Journal of Personality and Social Psychology, 60,* 531–544.

de Sherbinin, A., & 17 others. (2011). Preparing for resettlement associated with climate change. *Science, 334,* 456–457.

Desilver, D. (2018, September 26). Few women lead large U.S. companies, despite modest gains over past decade. *Pew Research Center.* https://www.pewresearch.org/fact-tank/2018/09/26/few-women-lead-large-u-s-companies-despite-modest-gains-over-past-decade/

DeSilver, D. (2019, April 23). Fewer than a third of countries currently have a military draft; most exclude women. *Pew Research Center.* https://www.pewresearch.org/fact-tank/2019/04/23/fewer-than-a-third-of-countries-currently-have-a-military-draft-most-exclude-women/

DeSilver, D. (2022, March 10). The polarization in today's Congress has roots that go back decades. Pew Research Center.

DeSilver, D. (2023, June 13). In places where same-sex marriages are legal, how many married same-sex couples are there? Pew Research Center.

Desmarais, S. L., & Read, J. D. (2011). After 30 years, what do we know about what jurors know? A meta-analytic review of lay knowledge regarding eyewitness factors. *Law and Human Behavior, 35,* 200–210.

DeSteno, D., Petty, R. E., Wegener, D. T., & Rucker, D. D. (2000). Beyond valence in the perception of likelihood: The role of emotion specificity. *Journal of Personality and Social Psychology, 78,* 397–416.

Deutsch, M., & Collins, M. E. (1951). *Interracial housing: A psychological evaluation of a social experiment.* Minneapolis: University of Minnesota Press.

Deutsch, M., & Gerard, H. B. (1955). A study of normative and informational social influence upon individual judgment. *Journal of Abnormal and Social Psychology, 51,* 629–636.

Deutsch, M., & Krauss, R. M. (1960). The effect of threat upon interpersonal bargaining. *Journal of Abnormal and Social Psychology, 61,* 181–189.

Deutsch, M. (1985). *Distributive justice: A social psychological perspective.* New Haven: Yale University Press.

Deutsch, M. (1986). Folie à deux: A psychological perspective on Soviet-American relations. In M. P. Kearns (Ed.), *Persistent patterns and emergent structures in a waning century.* New York: Praeger.

Deutsch, M. (1993). Educating for a peaceful world. *American Psychologist, 48,* 510–517.

Deutsch, M. (1994). Constructive conflict resolution: Principles, training, and research. *Journal of Social Issues, 50,* 13–32.

Deutsch, M. (1999). Behind the scenes. In D. G. Myers (Ed.), *Social psychology* (6th ed.). New Yor: McGraw Hill.

Devenport, J. L., Stinson, V., Cutler, B. L., & Kravitz, D. A. (2002). How effective are the cross-examination and expert testimony safeguards? Jurors' perceptions of the suggestiveness and fairness of biased lineup procedures. *Journal of Applied Psychology, 87,* 1042–1054.

Deveraj, S., & Patel, P. C. (2017). Taxicab tipping and sunlight. *PLOS ONE, 12*(6), e0179193.

Devine, P. A., Brodish, A. B., & Vance, S. L. (2005). Self-regulatory processes in interracial interactions: The role of internal and external motivation to respond without prejudice. In J. P. Forgas, K. D. Williams, & S. M. Laham (Eds.), *Social motivation: Conscious and unconscious processes.* New York: Cambridge University Press.

Devine, P. G., & Malpass, R. S. (1985). Orienting strategies in differential face recognition. *Personality and Social Psychology Bulletin,* 11, 33–40.

Devine, P. G. (1989). Stereotypes and prejudice: Their automatic and controlled components. *Journal of Personality and Social Psychology, 56,* 5–18.

Devine, P. G., Evett, S. R., & Vasquez-Suson, K. A. (1996). Exploring the interpersonal dynamics of intergroup contact. In R. Sorrentino & E. T. Higgins (Eds.), *Handbook of motivation and cognition: The interpersonal content* (Vol. 3). New York: Guilford.

Devine, P. G., Forscher, P. S., Austin, A. J., & Cox, W. T. L. (2012). Long-term reduction in implicit race bias: A prejudice habit-breaking intervention. *Journal of Experimental Social Psychology, 48,* 1267–1278.

De Vogli, R., Chandola, T., & Marmot, M. G. (2007). Negative aspects of close relationships and heart disease. *Archives of Internal Medicine, 167,* 1951–1957.

Devos-Comby, L., & Salovey, P. (2002). Applying persuasion strategies to alter HIV-relevant thoughts and behavior. *Review of General Psychology, 6,* 287–304.

Devries, K. M., & 13 others. (2013). The global prevalence of intimate partner violence against women. *Science, 340,* 1527.

De Waal, F. (2014a, September). One for all. *Scientific American,* 69–71.

De Waal, F. (2014b). *The Bonobo and the atheist: In search of humanism among the primates.* New York: Norton.

DeWall, C. N., Bushman, B. J., Giancola, P. R. & Webster, G. D. (2010). The big, the bad, and the boozed-Up: Weight moderates the effect of alcohol on aggression. *Journal of Experimental Social Psychology, 46*(4), 619–623.

DeWall, C. N., Lambert, N. M., Slotter, E. B., Pond, R. S., Deckman, T., Finkel, E. J., Luchies, L. B., & Fincham, F. D. (2011). So far away from one's partner, yet so close to romantic alternatives: Avoidant attachment, interest in alternatives, and infidelity. *Journal of Personality and Social Psychology, 101,* 1302–1316.

DeWall, C. N., Maner, J. K., & Rouby, D. A. (2009). Social exclusion and early-stage interpersonal perception: Selective attention to signs of acceptance. *Journal of Personality and Social Psychology, 96,* 729–741.

Dexter, H. R., Cutler, B. L., & Moran, G. (1992). A test of voir dire as a remedy for the prejudicial effects of pretrial publicity. *Journal of Applied Social Psychology, 22,* 819–832.

de Zavala, A. G., Cichocka, A., & Iskra-Golec, I. (2013). Collective narcissism moderates the effect of in-group image threat on intergroup hostility. *Journal of Personality and Social Psychology, 104,* 1019–1039.

Diamond, J. (1996, December). The best ways to sell sex. *Discover,* 78–86.

Diamond, S. S. (1993). Instructing on death: Psychologists, juries, and judges. *American Psychologist, 48,* 423–434.

Díaz, R., & Cova, F. (2022). Reactance, morality, and disgust: The relationship between affective dispositions and compliance with official health recommendations during the COVID-19 pandemic. *Cognition and Emotion, 36,* 120–136.

Dickerson, S. S., Gable, S. L., Irwin, M. R., Aziz, N., & Kemeny, M. E. (2009). Social-evaluative threat and proinflammatory cytokine regulation: An experimental laboratory investigation. *Psychological Science, 20,* 1237–1243.

Diekman, A. B., Brown, E. R., Johnston, A. M., & Clark, E. K. (2010). Seeking congruity between goals and roles: A new look at why women opt out of science, technology, engineering, and mathematics careers. *Psychological Science, 21,* 1051–1057.

Diekmann, K. A., Samuels, S. M., Ross, L., & Bazerman, M. H. (1997). Self-interest and fairness in problems of resource allocation: Allocators versus recipients. *Journal of Personality and Social Psychology, 72,* 1061–1074.

Diener, E., & Tay, L. (2015). Subjective well-being and human welfare around the world as reflected in the Gallup world poll. *International Journal of Psychology, 50*(2), 135–149.

Diener, E., & Wallbom, M. (1976). Effects of self-awareness on antinormative behavior. *Journal of Research in Personality, 10,* 107–111.

Diener, E. (1976). Effects of prior destructive behavior, anonymity, and group presence on deindividuation and aggression. *Journal of Personality and Social Psychology, 33,* 497–507.

Diener, E. (1979). Deindividuation, self-awareness, and disinhibition. *Journal of Personality and Social Psychology, 37,* 1160–1171.

Diener, E. (1980). Deindividuation: The absence of self-awareness and self-regulation in group members. In P. Paulus (Ed.), *The psychology of group influence.* Hillsdale, NJ: Erlbaum.

Diener, E. (2005, December 1). *Guidelines for national indicators of subjective well-being and ill-being.* Department of Psychology, University of Illinois.

Diener, E. (2013). The remarkable changes in the science of well-being. *Perspectives on Psychological Science, 8,* 663–666.

Diener, E., Fraser, S. C., Beaman, A. L., & Kelem, R. T. (1976). Effects of deindividuation variables on stealing among Halloween trick-or-treaters. *Journal of Personality and Social Psychology, 33*(2), 178–183.

Diener, E., Kesebir, P., & Lucas, R. (2008). Benefits of accounts of well-being—for societies and for psychological science. *Applied Psychology, 57,* 37–53.

Diener, E., Lucas, R. E., & Schimmack, U. (2009). *Well-being for public policy.* Oxford, UK: Oxford University Press.

Diener, E., Lucas, R. E., & Scollon, C. N. (2006). Beyond the hedonic treadmill: Revising the adaptation theory of well-being. *American Psychologist, 61,* 305–314.

Diener, E., Oishi, S., & Lucas, R. E. (2015). National accounts of subjective well-being. *American Psychologist, 70,* 234–242.

Dijksterhuis, A., Smith, P. K., van Baaren, R. B., & Wigboldus, D. H. J. (2005). The unconscious consumer: Effects of environment on consumer behavior. *Journal of Consumer Psychology, 15,* 193–202.

Dillard, A. J., & Meier, B. P. (2023). Getting COVID-19: Anticipated negative emotions are worse than experienced negative emotions. *Social Science & Medicine, 320,* 1–7.

Dillard, A. J., Dean, K. K., Gilbert, H., & Lipkus, I. M. (2021). You won't regret it (or love it) as much as you think: Impact biases for everyday health behavior outcomes. *Psychology & Health, 36,* 761–786.

Dillehay, R. C., & Nietzel, M. T. (1980). Constructing a science of jury behavior. In L. Wheeler (Ed.), *Review of personality and social psychology* (Vol. 1). Beverly Hills, CA: Sage.

Dill, J. C., & Anderson, C. A. (1999). Loneliness, shyness, and depression: The etiology and interrelationships of everyday problems in living. In T. Joiner & J. C. Coyne (Eds.) *The interactional nature of depression: Advances in interpersonal approaches.* Washington, DC: American Psychological Association.

Dillon, K. P., & Bushman, B. J. (2015). Unresponsive or un-noticed?: Cyberbystander intervention in an experimental cyberbullying context. *Computers in Human Behavior, 45,* 144–150.

Dillon, K. P., & Bushman, B. J. (2017). Effects of Exposure to Gun Violence in Movies on Children's Interest in Real Guns. *JAMA Pediatrics, 171,* 1057–1062.

DiMaggio, C., Avraham, J., Berry, C., Bukur, M., Feldman, J., Klein, M., Shah, N., Tandon, M., & Frangos, S. (2019). Changes in US mass shooting deaths associated with the 1994–2004 federal assault weapons ban: Analysis of open-source data. *The Journal of Trauma and Acute Care Surgery, 86,* 11–19.

Di, M., Wang, X., Zhao, J., Feng, W., Zhao, J., Nguyen, K., & Wang, Y. (2021). Correspondence bias of Chinese and American undergraduates: Similar initial trait attributions but different situational corrections. *Journal of General Psychology, 148,* 105–123.

Dindia, K., & Allen, M. (1992). Sex differences in self-disclosure: A meta-analysis. *Psychological Bulletin, 112,* 106–124.

Ding, J., Salinas-Jiménez, J., & Salinas-Jiménez, M. del M. (2021). The impact of income inequality on subjective well-being: The case of China. *Journal of Happiness Studies: An Interdisciplinary Forum on Subjective Well-Being, 22,* 845–866.

Ding, W., Xie, R., Sun, B., Li, W., Wang, D., & Zhen, R. (2016). Why does the "sinner" act prosocially? The mediating role of guilt and the moderating role of moral identity in motivating moral cleansing. *Frontiers in Psychology, 7,* 1317.

Dion, K. K., & Berscheid, E. (1974). Physical attractiveness and peer perception among children. *Sociometry, 37,* 1–12.

Dion, K. K., & Dion, K. L. (1985). Personality, gender, and the phenomenology of romantic love. In P. R. Shaver (Ed.), *Review of personality and social psychology* (Vol. 6). Beverly Hills, CA: Sage.

Dion, K. K., & Dion, K. L. (1993). Individualistic and collectivistic perspectives on gender and the cultural context of love and intimacy. *Journal of Social Issues, 49,* 53–69.

Dion, K. K., & Stein, S. (1978). Physical attractiveness and interpersonal influence. *Journal of Experimental Social Psychology, 14,* 97–109.

Dion, K. K. (1972). Physical attractiveness and evaluations of children's transgressions. *Journal of Personality and Social Psychology, 24,* 207–213.

Dion, K. L., & Dion, K. K. (1988). Romantic love: Individual and cultural perspectives. In R. J. Sternberg & M. L. Barnes (Eds.), *The psychology of love.* New Haven, CT: Yale University Press.

Dion, K. L. (1979). Intergroup conflict and intragroup cohesiveness. In W. G. Austin & S. Worchel (Eds.), *The social psychology of intergroup relations.* Monterey, CA: Brooks/Cole.

Dishion, T. J., McCord, J., & Poulin, F. (1999). When interventions harm: Peer groups and problem behavior. *American Psychologist, 54,* 755–764.

Di Tella, R., & MacCulloch, R. (2010). Happiness adaptation to income beyond "basic needs." Chapter 8. In E. Diener, J. Helliwell, & D. Kahneman (Eds.), *International differences in well-being.* New York: Oxford University Press.

Dittmar, H., Bond, R., Hurst, M., & Kasser, T. (2014). The relationship between materialism and personal well-being: A meta-analysis. *Journal of Personality and Social Psychology, 107,* 879–924.

Ditto, P. H., Liu, B. S., Clark, C. J., Wojcik, S. P., Chen, E. E., Grady, R. H., & Celniker, J. B., & Zinger, J. F. (2019). At least bias is bipartisan: A meta-analytic comparison of partisan bias in liberals and conservatives. *Perspectives on Psychological Science, 14*(2), 273–291.

Dixon, J., & Durrheim, K. (2003). Contact and the ecology of racial division: Some varieties of informal segregation. *British Journal of Social Psychology, 42,* 1–23.

Dixon, J., Durrheim, K., & Tredoux, C. (2005a). Beyond the optimal contact strategy: A reality check for the contact hypothesis. *American Psychologist, 60,* 697–711.

Dixon, J., Tredoux, C., & Clack, B. (2005b). On the micro-ecology of racial division: A neglected dimension of segregation. *South African Journal of Psychology, 35,* 395–411.

Dixon, J., Tredoux, C., Davies, G., Huck, J., Hocking, B., Sturgeon, B., Whyatt, D., Jarman, N., & Bryan, D. (2020). Parallel lives: Intergroup contact, threat, and the segregation of everyday activity spaces. *Journal of Personality and Social Psychology, 118,* 457–480.

Dobson, K., Zhu, J., Balzarini, R. N., & Campbell, L. (2020). Responses to sexual advances and satisfaction in romantic relationships: Is yes good and no bad? *Social Psychological and Personality Science, 11,* 801–811.

Dobzhansky, T. (1973, March). Nothing in biology makes sense except in the light of evolution. *American Biology Teacher, 35*(3), 125129.

Doherty, C., & Kiley, J. (2016, June 22). Key facts about partisanship and political animosity in America. *Pew Research Center.* https://www.pewresearch.org/fact-tank/2016/06/22/key-facts-partisanship/

Doherty, T. J., & Clayton, S. (2011). The psychological impacts of global climate change. *American Psychologist, 66,* 265–276.

Dohrenwend, B., Pearlin, L., Clayton, P., Hamburg, B., Dohrenwend, B. P., Riley, M., & Rose, R. (1982). Report on stress and life events. In G. R. Elliott & C. Eisdorfer (Eds.), *Stress and human health: Analysis and implications of research* (A study by the Institute of Medicine/National Academy of Sciences). New York: Springer.

Dolinski, D., & Grzyb, T. (2016). One serious shock versus gradated series of shocks: Does "multiple feet-in-the-door" explain obedience in Milgram studies? *Basic and Applied Social Psychology, 38,* 276–283.

Dolinski, D., & Nawrat, R. (1998). "Fear-then-relief" procedure for producing compliance: Beware when the danger is over. *Journal of Experimental Social Psychology, 34,* 27–50.

Dolinski, D., & Szczucka, K. (2012). Fear-then-relief-then-argument: How to sell goods using the EDTR technique of social influence. *Social Influence, 7,* 251–267.

Doliński, D., Grzyb, T., Folwarczny, M., Grzybała, P., Krzyszycha, K., Martynowska, K., & Trojanowski, J. (2017). Would you deliver an electric shock in 2015? Obedience in the experimental paradigm developed by Stanley Milgram in the 50 years following the original studies. *Social Psychological and Personality Science, 8,* 927–933.

Dollard, J., Doob, L., Miller, N., Mowrer, O. H., & Sears, R. R. (1939). *Frustration and aggression.* New Haven, CT: Yale University Press.

Dolnik, L., Case, T. I., & Williams, K. D. (2003). Stealing thunder as a courtroom tactic revisited: Processes and boundaries. *Law and Human Behavior, 27,* 265–285.

Dominus, S. (2012, May 7). What happened to the girls in Le Roy. *New York Times Magazine.* Retrieved March 28, 2015, from http://www.nytimes.com/2012/03/11/magazine/teenage-girls-twitching-le-roy.html?_r=0.

Donaldson, Z. R., & Young, L. J. (2008). Oxytocin, vasopressin, and the neurogenetics of sociality. *Science, 322,* 900–904.

Don, B. P., Girme, Y. U., & Hammond, M. D. (2019). Low self-esteem predicts indirect support seeking and its relationship consequences in intimate relationships. *Personality and Social Psychology Bulletin, 45,* 1028–1041.

Dong, M., Kupfer, T. R., Yuan, S., & van Prooijen, J. (2023). Being good to look good: Self-reported moral character predicts moral double standards among reputation-seeking individuals. *British Journal of Psychology, 114,* 244–261.

Dong P., Huang X., & Zhong C. (2015). Ray of hope: Hopelessness increases preferences for brighter lighting. *Social Psychological and Personality Science, 6,* 84–91.

Donnelly, G. E., Zheng, T., Haisley, & Norton, M. I. (2018). The amount and source of millionaires' wealth (moderately) predict their happiness. *Personality and Social Psychology Bulletin, 44,* 684–699.

Donnelly, K., & Twenge, J. M. (2017). Masculine and feminine traits on the Bem Sex-Role Inventory, 1993–2012: A cross-temporal meta-analysis. *Sex Roles: A Journal of Research, 76,* 556–565.

Donnelly, K., Twenge, J. M., Clark, M. A., Shaikh, S. K., Beiler, A., & Carter N. T. (2015). Americans' attitudes towards women's work and family roles, 1976–2013. *Psychology of Women Quarterly,* 1–14.

Donnelly, K., Twenge, J. M., Clark, M. A., Shaikh, S. K., Beiler-May, A., & Carter, N. T. (2016). Attitudes toward women's work and family roles in the United States, 1976–2013. *Psychology of Women Quarterly, 40,* 41–54.

Donnerstein, E. (1980). Aggressive erotica and violence against women. *Journal of Personality and Social Psychology, 39,* 269–277.

Donnerstein, E., Linz, D., & Penrod, S. (1987). *The question of pornography.* London: Free Press.

Donohue, J. J., Aneja, A., & Weber, K. D. (2019). Right-to-carry laws and violent crime: A comprehensive assessment using panel data and a state-level synthetic controls analysis. *Journal of Empirical Legal Studies, 16,* 198–247.

Doob, A. N., & Kirshenbaum, H. M. (1973). Bias in police lineups—Partial remembering. *Journal of Police Science and Administration, 1,* 287–293.

Doob, A. N., & McLaughlin, D. S. (1989). Ask and you shall be given: Request size and donations to a good cause. *Journal of Applied Social Psychology, 19,* 1049–1056.

Dorrance-Hall, E., Wilcox, S., Holmstrom, A., McGraw, J., & Schmälzle, R. (2021). Reactance to healthy eating and physical activity messages: Face threat and face management strategies in memorable daily conversations among couples. *Health Communication.*

Dorrough, A. R., Leszczyńska, M., Werner, S., Schaeffer, L., Galley, A.-S., Akin, E., Bachmann, J., Bruske, M., Burghardt, U., & Simandi, F. (2022). Equal performance, different grade: Women's performance in discussion perceived worse than men's. *Personality and Social Psychology Bulletin, 48,* 222–238.

Doubek, J., & Taylor, J. (2017, October). Anti-abortion Rep. Tim Murphy will resign after report on abortion request. *National Public Radio.*

Douglas, K. M., & Sutton, R. M. (2023). What are conspiracy theories? A definitional approach to their correlates, consequences, and communication. *Annual Review of Psychology, 74,* 271–298.

Douglas, K. M., Sutton, R. M., & Cichocka, A. (2017). The psychology of conspiracy theories. *Current Directions in Psychological Science, 26,* 538–542.

Douglass, A. B., & Steblay, N. (2006). Memory distortion in eyewitnesses: A meta-analysis of the post-identification feedback effect. *Applied Cognitive Psychology, 20,* 859–869.

Douglass, F. (1845/1960). *Narrative of the life of Frederick Douglass, an American slave: Written by himself.* (B. Quarles, Ed.). Cambridge, MA: Harvard University Press.

Dovidio, J. F. (1991). The empathy-altruism hypothesis: Paradigm and promise. *Psychological Inquiry, 2,* 126–128.

Dovidio, J. F., Gaertner, S. L., & Saguy, T. (2009). Commonality and the complexity of "we": Social attitudes and social change. *Personality and Social Psychology Bulletin, 13,* 3–20.

Dovidio, J. F., Gaertner, S. L., Anastasio, P. A., & Sanitioso, R. (1992). Cognitive and motivational bases of bias: Implications of aversive racism for attitudes toward Hispanics. In S. Knouse, P. Rosenfeld, & A. Culbertson (Eds.), *Hispanics in the workplace.* Newbury Park, CA: Sage.

Dovidio, J. F., Gaertner, S. L., Hodson, G., Houlette, M., & Johnson, K. M. (2005). Social inclusion and exclusion: Recategorization and the perception of intergroup boundaries. In D. Abrams, M. A. Hogg, & J. M. Marques (Eds.), *The social psychology of inclusion and exclusion.* New York: Psychology Press.

Downs, A. C., & Lyons, P. M. (1991). Natural observations of the links between attractiveness and initial legal judgments. *Personality and Social Psychology Bulletin, 17,* 541–547.

Doyle, J. M. (2005). *True witness: Cops, courts, science, and the battle against misidentification.* New York: Palgrave Macmillan.

DPIC (2023). DPIC analysis: Pandemic murder rates highest in death penalty states. Death Penalty Information Center (https://deathpenaltyinfo.org/stories/dpic-analysis-pandemic-murder-rates-highest-in-death-penalty-states).

Draguns, J. G. (1990). Normal and abnormal behavior in cross-cultural perspective: Specifying the nature of their relationship. *Nebraska Symposium on Motivation 1989, 37,* 235–277.

Dreber, A., Rand, D. G., Fudenberg, D., & Nowak, M. A. (2008). Winners don't punish. *Nature, 452,* 348–351.

Driskell, J. E., & Mullen, B. (1990). Status, expectations, and behavior: A meta-analytic review and test of the theory. *Personality and Social Psychology Bulletin, 16,* 541–553.

Drolet, A. L., & Morris, M. W. (2000). Rapport in conflict resolution: Accounting for how face-to-face contact fosters mutual cooperation in mixed-motive conflicts. *Journal of Experimental Social Psychology, 36,* 26–50.

Drury, J., Cocking, C., & Reicher, S. (2009). Everyone for themselves? A comparative study of crowd solidarity among emergency survivors. *British Journal of Social Psychology, 48,* 487–506.

Drury, L., Hutchison, P., & Abrams, D. (2016). Direct and extended intergenerational contact and young people's attitudes towards older adults. *British Journal of Social Psychology, 55,* 522–543.

Drydakis, N. (2009). Sexual orientation discrimination in the labour market. *Labour Economics, 16,* 364–372.

Dryer, D. C., & Horowitz, L. M. (1997). When do opposites attract? Interpersonal complementarity versus similarity. *Journal of Personality and Social Psychology, 72,* 592–603.

DuBois, W. E. B. (1903/1961). *The souls of Black folk.* Greenwich, CT: Fawcett Books.

Duffy, C. (2023, July 17). With the rise of AI, social media platforms could face perfect storm of misinformation in 2024. CNN.com

Duffy, K. (2021, January 7). A newly elected West Virginia GOP lawmaker live-streamed himself on Facebook storming the US Capitol, shouting: "We're in baby!" *Business Insider.*

Dufner, M., Gebauer, J. E., Sedikides, C., & Denissen, J. J. A. (2019). Self-enhancement and psychological adjustment: A meta-analytic review. *Personality and Social Psychology Review, 23,* 48–72.

Dugré, J. R., Dumais, A., Dellazizzo, L., & Potvin, S. (2020). Developmental joint trajectories of anxiety-depressive trait and trait-aggression: Implications for co-occurrence of internalizing and externalizing problems. *Psychological Medicine, 50,* 1338–1347.

Duhaime, E. P. (2015). Is the call to prayer a call to cooperate? A field experiment on the impact of religious salience on prosocial behavior. *Judgment and Decision Making, 10,* 593–596.

Duke, A. A., Smith, K. Z., Oberleitner, L. S., Westphal, A., & McKee, S. A. (2018). Alcohol, drugs, and violence: A meta-meta-analysis. *Psychology of Violence, 8,* 238–249.

Dumas, T. M., Davis, J. P., Merrin, G. J., Puccia, M., & Blustein, D. (2018). If you're high status and you know it: Teasing apart the within- and between-person effects of peer- and self-reported status in the drinking group on alcohol-related outcomes. *Psychology of Addictive Behaviors, 32,* 327–337.

Dunbar, R. (1992). Neocortex size as a constraint on group size in primates. *Journal of Human Evolution, 22,* 469–493.

Dunbar, R. (2010, December 25). You've got to have (150) friends. *The New York Times.* https://www.nytimes.com/2010/12/26/opinion/26dunbar.html

Dunbar, R. I. M. (2016). Do online social media cut through the constraints that limit the size of offline social networks? *Royal Society Open Science, 3*(1), Article 150292.

Duncan, B. L., & Reese, R. J. (2013). Empirically supported treatments, evidence-based treatments, and evidence-based practice. In G. Stricker, T. A. Widiger, & I. B. Weiner (Eds.) , *Handbook of psychology: Clinical psychology* (pp. 489–513). Hoboken, NJ, US: John Wiley & Sons Inc.

Duncan, B. L. (1976). Differential social perception and attribution of intergroup violence: Testing the lower limits of stereotyping of blacks. *Journal of Personality and Social Psychology, 34,* 590–598.

Dunfield, K. A., & Kuhlmeier, V. A. (2010). Intention-mediated selective helping in infancy. *Psychological Science, 21,* 523–527.

Dunham, Y., Chen, E. E., & Banaji, M. R. (2013). Two signatures of implicit intergroup attitudes: Developmental invariance and early enculturation. *Psychological Science, 24,* 860–868.

Dunkel, C. S. (2014). Sharing in childhood as precursor to support for national health insurance. *Basic and Applied Social Psychology, 36,* 515–519.

Dunlosky, J., & Rawson, K. A. (2012). Overconfidence produces underachievement: Inaccurate self evaluations undermine students' learning and retention. *Learning and Instruction, 22,* 271–280.

Dunn, A. (2020, July 14). As the U.S. copes with multiple crises, partisans disagree sharply on severity of problems facing the nation. *Pew Research Center.* https://pewrsr.ch/305mkO7

Dunn, E., & Ashton-James, C. (2008). On emotional innumeracy: Predicted and actual affective response to grand-scale tragedies. *Journal of Experimental Social Psychology, 44,* 692–698.

Dunn, E., & Norton, M. (2013). *Happy money: The science of smarter spending.* New York: Simon & Schuster.

Dunn, E. W., Aknin, L. B., & Norton, M. I. (2008). Spending money on others promotes happiness. *Science, 319,* 1687–1688.

Dunn, E. W., Wilson, T. D., & Gilbert, D. T. (2003). Location, location, location: The misprediction of satisfaction in housing lotteries. *Personality and Social Psychology Bulletin, 29,* 1421–1432.

Dunning, D., & Perretta, S. (2002). Automaticity and eyewitness accuracy: A 10- to 12-second rule for distinguishing accurate from inaccurate positive identifications. *Journal of Applied Psychology, 87,* 951–962.

Dunning, D., & Sherman, D. A. (1997). Stereotypes and tacit inference. *Journal of Personality and Social Psychology, 73,* 459–471.

Dunning, D. (1995). Trait importance and modifiability as factors influencing self-assessment and self-enhancement motives. *Personality and Social Psychology Bulletin, 21,* 1297–1306.

Dunning, D. (2005). *Self-insight: Roadblocks and detours on the path to knowing thyself.* London: Psychology Press.

Dunning, D. (2006). Strangers to ourselves? *The Psychologist, 19,* 600-603.

Dunning, D., Meyerowitz, J. A., & Holzberg, A. D. (1989). Ambiguity and self-evaluation. *Journal of Personality and Social Psychology, 57,* 1082-1090.

Dunning, D., Perie, M., & Story, A. L. (1991). Self-serving prototypes of social categories. *Journal of Personality and Social Psychology, 61,* 957-968.

Dunning, D., & Perretta, S. (2002).

Dunn, M., & Searle, R. (2010). Effect of manipulated prestige-car ownership on both sex attractiveness ratings. *British Journal of Psychology, 101,* 69-80.

Durante, K. M., Li, N. P., & Haselton, M. G. (2008). Changes in women's dress across the ovulatory cycle: Naturalistic and laboratory task-based evidence. *Personality and Social Psychology Bulletin, 34,* 1451-1460.

Durkee, M. I., Perkins, T. R., & Smith, R. E. (2022). Longitudinal effects of the "acting White" accusation and racial identity development among Black college students. *Journal of Research on Adolescence, 32,* 191-207.

Durrheim, K., Tredoux, C., Foster, D., & Dixon, J. (2011). Historical trends in South African race attitudes. *South African Journal of Psychology, 41,* 263-278.

Dutton, D. (2006, January 13). Hardwired to seek beauty. *The Australian.* www.theastralian.news.com.au

Dutton, D. G., & Aron, A. P. (1974). Some evidence for heightened sexual attraction under conditions of high anxiety. *Journal of Personality and Social Psychology, 30,* 510-517.

Dutton, D. G., & Lake, R. A. (1973). Threat of own prejudice and reverse discrimination in interracial situations. *Journal of Personality and Social Psychology, 28,* 94-100.

Duval, S., Duval, V. H., & Neely, R. (1979). Self-focus, felt responsibility, and helping behavior. *Journal of Personality and Social Psychology, 37,* 1769-1778.

Dwyer, J., & Ward, M. (2019, May 6). Riley Howell's parents say he was shot 3 times while tackling the U.N.C. Charlotte gunman. *The New York Times.* https://www.nytimes.com/2019/05/06/us/riley-howell-uncc-shooting.html

Dwyer, J. (2012, April 12). When fists and kicks fly on the subway, it's Snackman to the rescue. *The New York Times.* https://www.nytimes.com/2012/04/13/nyregion/stopping-a-fight-on-the-subway-and-winning-internet-fame.html

Dye, M. W. G., Green, C. S., & Bavelier, D. (2009). Increasing speed of processing with action video games. *Current Directions in Psychological Science, 18,* 321-326.

Dylko, I., Dolgov, I., Hoffman, W., Eckhart, N., Molina, M., & Aaziz, O. (2017). The dark side of technology: An experimental investigation of the influence of customizability technology on online political selective exposure. *Computers in Human Behavior, 73,* 181-190.

Eagly, A. (2017, August 15). Does biology explain why men outnumber women in tech? *The Conversation.* www.theconversation.com

Eagly, A. H., & Chaiken, S. (1993). *The psychology of attitudes.* San Diego: Harcourt Brace Jovanovich.

Eagly, A. H., & Chaiken, S. (1998). *The handbook of social psychology* (4th ed.). New York: McGraw Hill.

Eagly, A. H., & Chaiken, S. (2005). Attitude research in the 21st century: The current state of knowledge. In D. Albarracin, B. T. Johnson, & M. P. Zanna (Eds.), *The handbook of attitudes.* Mahwah, NJ: Erlbaum.

Eagly, A. H., & Crowley, M. (1986). Gender and helping behavior: A meta-analytic review of the social psychological literature. *Psychological Bulletin, 100,* 283-308.

Eagly, A. H., & Revelle, W. (2022). Understanding the magnitude of psychological differences between women and men requires seeing the forest and the trees. *Perspectives on Psychological Science, 17,* 1339-1358.

Eagly, A. H., & Wood, W. (2013). The nature-nurture debates: 25 years of challenges in understanding the psychology of gender. *Perspective on Psychological Science, 8,* 340-357.

Eagly, A. H. (1987). *Sex differences in social behavior: A social-role interpretation.* Hillsdale, NJ: Erlbaum.

Eagly, A. H. (1994). *Are people prejudiced against women?* Donald Campbell Award invited address, American Psychological Association convention, Los Angeles, CA.

Eagly, A. H. (2009). The his and hers of prosocial behavior: An examination of the social psychology of gender. *American Psychologist, 64,* 644-658.

Eagly, A. H., Ashmore, R. D., Makhijani, M. G., & Longo, L. C. (1991). What is beautiful is good, but . . . : A meta-analytic review of research on the physical attractiveness stereotype. *Psychological Bulletin, 110,* 109-128.

Eagly, A. H., Nater, C., Miller, D. I., Kaufmann, M., & Sczesny, S. (2020). Gender stereotypes have changed: A cross-temporal meta-analysis of U.S. public opinion polls From 1946 to 2018. *American Psychologist, 75,* 301-315.

Earle, M., Hoffarth, M. R., Prusaczyk, E., MacInnis, C., & Hodson, G. (2021). A multilevel analysis of LGBT (Lesbian, Gay, Bisexual, Transgender) rights support across 77 countries: The role of contact and country laws. *British Journal of Social Psychology, 60*(3), 851-869.

Easterbrook, M., & Vignoles, V. (2015). When friendship formation goes down the toilet: Design features of share accommodation influence interpersonal bonds and well-being. *British Journal of Social Psychology, 54,* 125-139.

Easterlin, R. A., McVey, L. A., Switek, M., Sawangfa, O., & Zweig, J. S. (2010). The happiness-income paradox revisited. *PNAS, 107,* 22463-22468.

Easterlin, R. A., Morgan, R., Switek, M., & Wang, F. (2012). China's life satisfaction, 1990-2010. *PNAS, 109,* 9670-9671.

Eastwick, P. W., & Finkel, E. J. (2008a). Speed-dating as a methodological innovation. *The Psychologist, 21,* 402-403.

Eastwick, P. W., & Finkel, E. J. (2008b). Sex differences in mate preferences revisited: Do people know what they initially desire in a romantic partner? *Journal of Personality and Social Psychology, 94,* 245-264.

Eastwick, P. W., & Hunt, L. L. (2014). Relational mate value: Consensus and uniqueness in romantic evaluations. *Journal of Personality and Social Psychology, 106,* 728-751.

Eastwick, P. W., Finkel, E. J., Krishnamurti, T., & Loewenstein, G. (2007). Mispredicting distress following romantic breakup: Revealing the time course of the affective forecasting error. *Journal of Experimental Social Psychology, 44,* 800-807.

Eastwick, P. W., Luchies, L. B., Finkel, E. J., & Hunt, L. L. (2014). The predictive validity of ideal partner preferences: A review and meta-analysis. *Psychological Bulletin, 140,* 623-665.

Eberhardt, J. L. (2005). Imaging race. *American Psychologist, 60,* 181-190.

Eberhardt, J. L. (2019). *Biased: Uncovering the hidden prejudice that shapes what we see, think, and do.* New York: Viking.

Eberhardt, J. L., Davies, P. G., Purdie-Vaughns, V. J., & Johnson, S. L. (2006). Looking deathworthy: Perceived stereotypicality of Black defendants predicts capital-sentencing outcomes. *Psychological Science, 17,* 383-386.

Eberhardt, J. L., Goff, P. A., Purdie, V. J., & Davies, P. G. (2004). Seeing black: Race, crime, and visual processing. *Journal of Personality and Social Psychology, 87,* 876-893.

Eberle, D., Berens, G., & Li, T. (2013). The impact of interactive corporate social responsibility communication on corporate reputation. *Journal of Business Ethics, 118,* 731-746.

Echterhoff, G., Hirst, W., & Hussy, W. (2005). How eyewitnesses resist misinformation: Social postwarnings and the monitoring of memory characteristics. *Memory & Cognition, 33,* 770-782.

Eckersley, R. (2005). Is modern Western culture a health hazard? *International Journal of Epidemiology, 35*(2), 252-258.

Ecker, U. K. H., Lewandowsky, S., Swire, B., & Chang, D. (2011). Correcting false information in memory: Manipulating the strength of information encoding and its retraction. *Psychonomic Bulletin & Review, 18,* 570-578.

Eck, J., & Gebauer, J. E. (2022). A sociocultural norm perspective on Big Five prediction. *Journal of Personality and Social Psychology, 122*(3), 554–575.

Economist. (2000, June 10). America's death-penalty lottery.

Economist. (2018, July 7). The stark relationship between income inequality and crime. https://www.economist.com/graphic-detail/2018/06/07/the-stark-relationship-between-income-inequality-and-crime

Edelman, B., Luca, M., & Svirsky, D. (2017). Racial discrimination in the sharing economy: Evidence from a field experiment. *American Economic Journal: Applied Economics, 9,* 1–22.

Edelson, M., Sharot, T., Dolan, R. J., & Dudai, Y. (2011). Following the crowd: Brain substrates of long-term memory conformity. *Science, 333,* 108–111.

Edwards, D., & Potter, J. (2005). Discursive psychology, mental states and descriptions. In H. te Molder & J. Potter (Eds.), *Conversation and cognition.* New York: Cambridge University Press.

Edwards, K., & Bryan, T. S. (1997). Judgmental biases produced by instructions to disregard: The (paradoxical) case of emotional information. *Personality and Social Psychology Bulletin, 23,* 849–864.

Edwards, K. (1990). The interplay of affect and cognition in attitude formation and change. *Journal of Personality and Social Psychology, 59,* 202–216.

Edwards, K. M., Sessarego, S. N., Mitchell, K. J., Chang, H., Waterman, E. A., & Banyard, V. L. (2020). Preventing teen relationship abuse and sexual assault through bystander training: Intervention outcomes for school personnel. *American Journal of Community Psychology, 65,* 160–172.

Effron, D. A., & Raj, M. (2020). Misinformation and morality: Encountering fake-news headlines makes them seem less unethical to publish and share. *Psychological Science, 31,* 75–87.

Efran, M. G. (1974). The effect of physical appearance on the judgment of guilt, interpersonal attraction, and severity of recommended punishment in a simulated jury task. *Journal of Research in Personality, 8,* 45–54.

Egebark, J., & Ekström, M. (2018). Liking what others "Like": Using Facebook to identify determinants of conformity. *Experimental Economics, 21,* 793–814.

Ehrenreich, S. E., Beron, K. J., Brinkley, D. Y., & Underwood, M. K. (2014). Family predictors of continuity and change in social and physical aggression from ages 9 to 18. *Aggressive Behavior, 40,* 421–439.

Ehrlich, P., & Feldman, M. (2003). Genes and cultures: What creates our behavioral phenome? *Current Anthropology, 44,* 87–95.

Eibach, R. P., & Ehrlinger, J. (2006). "Keep your eyes on the prize": Reference points and racial differences in assessing progress toward equality. *Personality and Social Psychology Bulletin, 32,* 66–77.

Eich, E., Reeves, J. L., Jaeger, B., & Graff-Radford, S. B. (1985). Memory for pain: Relation between past and present pain intensity. *Pain, 23,* 375–380.

Eisenberg, N. (2014, September). Is our focus becoming overly narrow? *Observer,* pp. 5, 46.

Eiser, J. R., Sutton, S. R., & Wober, M. (1979). Smoking, seat-belts, and beliefs about health. *Addictive Behaviors, 4,* 331–338.

Ekstrom, P. D., Le Forestier, J. M., & Lai, C. K. (2022). Racial demographics explain the link between racial disparities in traffic stops and county-level racial attitudes. *Psychological Science, 33,* 497–509.

Elder, G. H., Jr. (1969). Appearance and education in marriage mobility. *American Sociological Review, 34,* 519–533.

Elgar, F. J., Stefaniak, A., & Wohl, M. J. A. (2020). The trouble with trust: Time-series analysis of social capital, income inequality, and COVID-19 deaths in 84 countries. *Social Science & Medicine, 263.*

Elkjær, E., Mikkelsen, M. B., Michalak, J., Mennin, D. S., & O'Toole, M. S. (2022). Expansive and contractive postures and movement: A systematic review and meta-analysis of the effect of motor displays on affective and behavioral responses. *Perspectives on Psychological Science, 17,* 276–304.

Ellemers, N., Van Rijswijk, W., Roefs, M., & Simons, C. (1997). Bias in intergroup perceptions: Balancing group identity with social reality. *Personality and Social Psychology Bulletin, 23,* 186–198.

Elliot, A. J., & Devine, P. G. (1994). On the motivational nature of cognitive dissonance: Dissonance as psychological discomfort. *Journal of Personality and Social Psychology, 67,* 382–394.

Elliott, L. (1989, June). Legend of the four chaplains. *Reader's Digest,* pp. 66–70.

Ellis, B. J., & Symons, D. (1990). Sex difference in sexual fantasy: An evolutionary psychological approach. *Journal of Sex Research, 27,* 490–521.

Ellison, P. A., Govern, J. M., Petri, H. L., & Figler, M. H. (1995). Anonymity and aggressive driving behavior: A field study. *Journal of Social Behavior and Personality, 10,* 265–272.

Ellsworth, P. (1989, March 6). Supreme Court ignores social science research on capital punishment. Quoted by *Behavior Today,* pp. 7–8.

Ellsworth, P. C., & Mauro, R. (1998). Psychology and law. In D. Gilbert, S. T. Fiske, & G. Lindzey (Eds.), *Handbook of social psychology* (4th edition). New York: McGraw Hill.

Elms, A. (2009). Obedience lite. *American Psychologist, 64,* 32–36.

Elsaadawy, N., & Carlson, E. N. (2022). Do you make a better or worse impression than you think? *Journal of Personality and Social Psychology, 123,* 1407–1420.

Elson, M., & Ferguson, C. J. (2014). Twenty-five years of research on violence in digital games and aggression: Empirical evidence, perspectives, and a debate gone astray. *European Psychologist, 19,* 33–46.

Emerson, R. W. (1863/2001). "The scholar." Address before the United Literary Societies of Dartmouth College, Hanover, New Hampshire. In J. Myerson, & R. A. Bosco (Eds.), *The later lectures of Ralph Waldo Emerson, 1843–1871* (p. 315). Athens, GA: University of Georgia Press.

Emswiller, T., Deaux, K., & Willits, J. E. (1971). Similarity, sex, and requests for small favors. *Journal of Applied Social Psychology, 1,* 284–291.

Engel, C., Timme, S., & Glöckner, A. (2020). Coherence-based reasoning and order effects in legal judgments. *Psychology, Public Policy, and Law, 26*(3), 333–352.

Engemann, K. M., & Owyang, M. T. (2003, April). So much for that merit raise: The link between wages and appearance. *The Regional Economist.* https://bit.ly/2OFoIcy

English, A. S., & Geeraert, N. (2020). Crossing the rice-wheat border: Not all intra-cultural adaptation is equal. *PloS One, 15,* e0236326.

Eng, P. M., Kawachi, I., Fitzmaurice, G., & Rimm, E. B. (2001). *Effects of marital transitions on changes in dietary and other health behaviors in men.* Paper presented to the American Psychosomatic Society meeting.

Enisman, M., Shpitzer, H., & Kleiman, T. (2021). Choice changes preferences, not merely reflects them: A meta-analysis of the artifact-free free-choice paradigm. *Journal of Personality and Social Psychology, 120,* 16–29.

Enos, R. D., & Fowler, A. (2016). Aggregate effects of large-scale campaigns on voter turnout. *Political Science Research and Methods,* 1–19.

Epley, N., & Dunning, D. (2006). The mixed blessings of self-knowledge in behavioral prediction: Enhanced discrimination but exacerbated bias. *Personality and Social Psychology Bulletin, 32,* 641–655.

Epley, N., & Huff, C. (1998). Suspicion, affective response, and educational benefit as a result of deception in psychology research. *Personality and Social Psychology Bulletin, 24,* 759–768.

Epley, N., & Whitchurch, E. (2008). Mirror, mirror on the wall: Enhancement in self-recognition. *Personality and Social Psychology Bulletin, 34,* 1159–1170.

Epley, N., Akalis, S., Waytz, A., & Cacioppo, J. T. (2008). Creating social connection through inferential reproduction: Loneliness and perceived agency in gadgets, gods, and greyhounds. *Psychological Science, 19,* 114–120.

Epley, N., Savitsky, K., & Kachelski, R. A. (1999, September/October). What every skeptic should know about subliminal persuasion. *Skeptical Inquirer,* 40–45.

Epstude, K., & Roese, N. J. (2008). The functional theory of counterfactual thinking. *Personality and Social Psychology Review, 12,* 168–192.

Erickson, B., Holmes, J. G., Frey, R., Walker, L., & Thibaut, J. (1974). Functions of a third party in the resolution of conflict: The role of a judge in pretrial conferences. *Journal of Personality and Social Psychology, 30,* 296–306.

Erickson, B., Lind, E. A. Johnson, B. C., & O'Barr, W. M. (1978). Speech style and impression formation in a court setting: The effects of powerful and powerless speech. *Journal of Experimental Social Psychology, 14,* 266–279.

Erikson, E. H. (1963). *Childhood and society.* New York: Norton.

Eriksson, K., Vartanova, I., Strimling, P., & Simpson, B. (2018). Generosity pays: Selfish people have fewer children and earn less money. *Journal of Personality and Social Psychology, 118,* 532–544.

Erlangsen, A., Drefahl, S., Haas, A., Bjorkenstam, C., Nordentoft, M., & Andersson, G. (2020). Suicide among persons who entered same-sex and opposite-sex marriage in Denmark and Sweden, 1989-2016: A binational, register-based cohort study. *Journal of Epidemiology and Community Health, 74,* 78–83.

Eron, L. D., & Huesmann, L. R. (1980). Adolescent aggression and television. *Annals of the New York Academy of Sciences, 347,* 319–331.

Eron, L. D., & Huesmann, L. R. (1984). The control of aggressive behavior by changes in attitudes, values, and the conditions of learning. In R. J. Blanchard & C. Blanchard (Eds.), *Advances in the study of aggression* (Vol. 1). Orlando, FL: Academic Press.

Eron, L. D., & Huesmann, L. R. (1985). The role of television in the development of prosocial and antisocial behavior. In D. Olweus, M. Radke-Yarrow, & J. Block (Eds.), *Development of antisocial and prosocial behavior.* Orlando, FL: Academic Press.

Eron, L. D. (1987). The development of aggressive behavior from the perspective of a developing behaviorism. *American Psychologist, 42,* 425–442.

Ertl, A. Sheats, K. J., Petrosky, E., Betz, C. J., Yuan, K., & Fowler, K. A. (2019). Surveillance for violent deaths—National violent death reporting system, 32 States, 2016. *Surveillance Summaries, 68,* 1–36.

Eskreis-Winkler, L., Fishbach, A., & Duckworth, A. L. (2018). Dear Abby: Should I give advice or receive it? *Psychological Science, 29,* 1797–1806.

Esses, V. M., Haddock, G., & Zanna, M. P. (1993a). Values, stereotypes, and emotions as determinants of intergroup attitudes. In D. Mackie & D. Hamilton (Eds.), *Affect, cognition and stereotyping: Interactive processes in intergroup perception.* San Diego, CA: Academic Press.

Esses, V. M., Haddock, G., & Zanna, M. P. (1993b). The role of mood in the expression of intergroup stereotypes. In M. P. Zanna & J. M. Olson (Eds.), *The psychology of prejudice: The Ontario symposium* (Vol. 7). Hillsdale, NJ: Erlbaum.

Etzioni, A. (1967). The Kennedy experiment. *The Western Political Quarterly, 20,* 361–380.

Etzioni, A. (1991, May–June). The community in an age of individualism (interview). *The Futurist,* pp. 35–39.

Etzioni, A. (1993). *The spirit of community.* New York: Crown.

Etzioni, A. (2005). *The diversity within unity platform.* Washington, DC: The Communitarian Network.

Evans, G. W. (1979). Behavioral and physiological consequences of crowding in humans. *Journal of Applied Social Psychology, 9,* 27–46.

Evans, R. I., Smith, C. K., & Raines, B. E. (1984). Deterring cigarette smoking in adolescents: A psycho-social-behavioral analysis of an intervention strategy. In A. Baum, J. Singer, & S. Taylor (Eds.), *Handbook of psychology and health: Social psychological aspects of health* (Vol. 4). Hillsdale, NJ: Erlbaum.

Everett, J. A. C., Haque, O. S., & Rand, D. G. (2016). How good is the Samaritan, and why? An experimental investigation of the extent and nature of religious prosociality using economic games. *Social Psychological and Personality Science, 7,* 248–255.

Ewing, L. (2023, July 16). While women's soccer boasts fierce LGBT advocates, FIFA reviews transgender rules. Reuters.

Exelmans, L., Custers, K., & van den Bulck, J. (2015). Violent video game and delinquent behavior in adolescents. *Aggressive Behavior, 41,* 267–279.

Exline, J. J., Zell, A. L., Bratslavsky, E., Hamilton, M., & Swenson, A. (2012). People-pleasing through eating: Sociotropy predicts greater eating in response to perceived social pressure. *Journal of Social and Clinical Psychology, 31,* 169–193.

Fabrigar, L. R., & Petty, R. E. (1999). The role of the affective and cognitive bases of attitudes in susceptibility to affectively and cognitively based persuasion. *Personality and Social Psychology Bulletin, 25,* 363–381.

Faircloth, R. (2020, May 30). Minnesota Gov. Tim Walz: "This is about chaos" as new fires, looting hit Minneapolis. *Minneapolis StarTribune.* https://www.startribune.com/walz-bolsters-guard-troops-after-4th-destructive-night/570882282/

Falk, C. F., Heine, S. J., Yuki, M., & Takemura, K. (2009). Why do Westerners self-enhance more than East Asians? *European Journal of Personality, 23,* 183–203.

Falkner, A. L., Grosenick, L., Davidson, T., Deisseroth, K., & Lin, D. (2016). Hypothalamic control of male aggression-seeking behavior. *Nature Neuroscience, 19,* 596–604.

Farb, N. A. S., Segal, Z. V., Mayberg, H., Bean, J., & McKeon, D. (2007). Attending to the present: Mindfulness meditation reveals distinct neural modes of self-reference. *Social Cognitive and Affective Neuroscience, 2,* 313–322.

Farquhar, J. W., Maccoby, N., Wood, P. D., Alexander, J. K., Breitrose, H., Brown, B. W., Jr., Haskell, W. L., McAlister, A. L., Meyer, A. J., Nash, J. D., & Stern, M. P. (1977, June 4). Community education for cardiovascular health. *Lancet,* 1192–1195.

Farris, C., Treat, T. A., Viken, R. J., & McFall, R. M. (2008). Perceptual mechanisms that characterize gender differences in decoding women's sexual intent. *Psychological Science, 19,* 348–354.

Farrow, R. (2019). *Catch and kill: Lies, spies, and a conspiracy to protect predators.* New York: Little, Brown.

Farwell, L., & Weiner, B. (2000). Bleeding hearts and the heartless: Popular perceptions of liberal and conservative ideologies. *Personality and Social Psychology Bulletin, 26,* 845–852.

Faulkner, S. L., & Williams, K. D. (1996). *A study of social loafing in industry.* Paper presented at the Midwestern Psychological Association convention, Chicago, IL.

Faust, D., & Ziskin, J. (1988). The expert witness in psychology and psychiatry. *Science, 241,* 31–35.

Fazio, L. K., & Sherry, C. L. (2020). The effect of repetition on truth judgments across development. *Psychological Science, 31,* 1150–1160.

Fazio, L. K., Rand, D. G., & Pennycook, G. (2019). Repetition increases perceived truth equally for plausible and implausible statements. *Psychonomic Bulletin & Review, 26,* 1705–1710.

Fazio, R. (1987). Self-perception theory: A current perspective. In M. P. Zanna, J. M. Olson, & C. P. Herman (Eds.), *Social influence: The Ontario symposium* (Vol. 5). Hillsdale, NJ: Erlbaum.

Fazio, R. H., Effrein, E. A., & Falender, V. J. (1981). Self-perceptions following social interaction. *Journal of Personality and Social Psychology, 41,* 232–242.

Fazio, R. H., Zanna, M. P., & Cooper, J. (1977). Dissonance versus self-perception: An integrative view of each theory's proper domain of application. *Journal of Experimental Social Psychology, 13,* 464–479.

Fazio, R. H., Zanna, M. P., & Cooper, J. (1979). On the relationship of data to theory: A reply to Ronis and Greenwald. *Journal of Experimental Social Psychology, 15,* 70–76.

FBI (2023). Crime Data Explorer, 2021, Homicide. https://cde.ucr.cjis.gov/LATEST/webapp/#/pages/explorer/crime/crime-trend

FBI. (2023). Crime Data Explorer. https://cde.ucr.cjis.gov/LATEST/webapp/#/pages/home

FBI (Federal Bureau of Investigation). (2020). *Uniform crime reports: 2019. Crime in the United States.* Retrieved from https://ucr.fbi.gov/crime-in-the-u.s/2019/preliminary-report/tables/table-4/table-4.xls/view

Feeney, J. A., & Noller, P. (1990). Attachment style as a predictor of adult romantic relationships. *Journal of Personality and Social Psychology, 58,* 281–291.

Feeney, J. A. (1996). Attachment, caregiving, and marital satisfaction. *Personal Relationships, 3,* 401–416.

Feeney, J., Peterson, C., & Noller, P. (1994). Equity and marital satisfaction over the family life cycle. *Personality Relationships, 1,* 83–99.

Feinberg, J. M., & Aiello, J. R. (2006). Social facilitation: A test of competing theories. *Journal of Applied Social Psychology, 36,* 1–23.

Feinberg, M., & Willer, R. (2011). Apocalypse soon? Dire messages reduce belief in global warming by contradicting just-world beliefs. *Psychological Science, 22,* 34–38.

Feinberg, M., & Willer, R. (2015). From gulf to bridge: When do moral arguments facilitate political influence? *Personality & Social Psychology Bulletin, 41,* 1665–1681.

Feinberg, M., & Willer, R. (2019). Moral reframing: A technique for effective and persuasive communication across political divides. *Social and Personality Psychology Compass, 13*(12), e12501.

Feinberg, M., Fang, R., Liu, S., & Peng, K. (2019). A world of blame to go around: Cross-cultural determinants of responsibility and punishment judgments. *Personality and Social Psychology Bulletin, 45,* 634–651.

Feinberg, M., Willer, R., & Kovacheff, C. (2020). The activist's dilemma: Extreme protest actions reduce popular support for social movements. *Journal of Personality and Social Psychology, 119*(5), 1086–1111.

Feingold, A. (1988). Matching for attractiveness in romantic partners and same-sex friends: A meta-analysis and theoretical critique. *Psychological Bulletin, 104,* 226–235.

Feingold, A. (1992b). Good-looking people are not what we think. *Psychological Bulletin, 111,* 304–341.

Fein, S., & Hilton, J. L. (1992). Attitudes toward groups and behavioral intentions toward individual group members: The impact of nondiagnostic information. *Journal of Experimental Social Psychology, 28,* 101–124.

Fein, S., & Spencer, S. J. (1997). Prejudice as self-image maintenance: Affirming the self through derogating others. *Journal of Personality and Social Psychology, 73,* 31–44.

Feldman, L., & Chattoo, C. B. (2019). Comedy as a route to social change: The effects of satire and news on persuasion about Syrian refugees. *Mass Communication & Society, 22,* 277–300.

Feldman, R. S., & Prohaska, T. (1979). The student as Pygmalion: Effect of student expectation on the teacher. *Journal of Educational Psychology, 71,* 485–493.

Feldman, R. S., & Theiss, A. J. (1982). The teacher and student as Pygmalions: Joint effects of teacher and student expectations. *Journal of Educational Psychology, 74,* 217–223.

Felson, R. B. (2000). A social psychological approach to interpersonal aggression. In V. B. Van Hasselt & M. Hersen (Eds.), *Aggression and violence: An introductory text.* Boston: Allyn & Bacon.

Feng, Z., Zou, K., & Savani, K. (2023). Cultural antecedents of virus transmission: Individualism is associated with lower compliance with social distancing rules during the COVID-19 pandemic. *Journal of Personality and Social Psychology, 124,* 461–482.

Fenigstein, A., & Vanable, P. A. (1992). Paranoia and self-consciousness. *Journal of Personality and Social Psychology, 62,* 129–138.

Fenigstein, A. (1984). Self-consciousness and the overperception of self as a target. *Journal of Personality and Social Psychology, 47,* 860–870.

Fenigstein, A. (2015). Milgram's shock experiments and the Nazi perpetrators: A contrarian perspective on the role of obedience pressures during the Holocaust. *Theory & Psychology, 25,* 581–598.

Fennis, B. M., & Aarts, H. (2012). Revisting the agentic shift: Weakening personal control increases susceptibility to social influence. *European Journal of Social Psychology, 42,* 824–831.

Fergusson, D. M., Horwood, L. J., & Shannon, F. T. (1984). A proportional hazards model of family breakdown. *Journal of Marriage and the Family, 46,* 539–549.

Fernandez, A. (2018, March 13). Mom shares photos of son's casket after he killed himself because he was allegedly bullied. *People.* https://people.com/human-interest/mississippi-sixth-grader-suicide-after-bullying/

Fernbach, P. M., & Bogard, J. E. (2023). Conspiracy theory as individual and group behavior: Observations from the flat earth international conference. *Topics in Cognitive Science.*

Ferriday, C., Vartanian, O., & Mandel, D. R. (2011). Public but not private ego threat triggers aggression in narcissists. *European Journal of Social Psychology, 41,* 564–568.

Ferriman, K., Lubinski, D., & Benbow, C. P. (2009). Work preferences, life values, and personal views of top math/science graduate students and the profoundly gifted: Developmental changes and gender differences during emerging adulthood and parenthood. *Journal of Personality and Social Psychology, 97,* 517–522.

Feshbach, S. (1980). *Television advertising and children: Policy issues and alternatives.* Paper presented at the American Psychological Association convention.

Festinger, L., & Carlsmith, J. M. (1959). Cognitive consequences of forced compliance. *Journal of Abnormal and Social Psychology, 58,* 203–210.

Festinger, L., & Maccoby, N. (1964). On resistance to persuasive communications. *Journal of Abnormal and Social Psychology, 68,* 359–366.

Festinger, L. (1954). A theory of social comparison processes. *Human Relations, 7,* 117–140.

Festinger, L. (1957). *A theory of cognitive dissonance.* Stanford: Stanford University Press.

Festinger, L., Pepitone, A., & Newcomb, T. (1952). Some consequences of deindividuation in a group. *Journal of Abnormal and Social Psychology, 47,* 382–389.

Festinger, L., Riecken, H. W., & Schachter, S. (1956). *When prophecy fails.* Minneapolis: University of Minnesota Press.

Fetterman, A. K., Baker, C. D., & Meier, B. P. (2023). Crime in your area: Use of neighborhood apps is associated with inaccurate perceptions of higher local crime rates. *Psychology of Popular Media.*

Feygina, I., Jost, J. T., & Goldsmith, R. E. (2010). System justification, the denial of global warming, and the possibility of "system-sanctioned change." *Personality and Social Psychology Bulletin, 36,* 326–338.

Feynman, R. (1967). *The character of physical law.* Cambridge, MA: MIT Press.

Ficks, C. A., & Waldman, I. D. (2014). Candidate genes for aggression and antisocial behavior: A meta-analysis of association studies of the 5HTTLPR and MAOA-uVNTR. *Behavior Genetics, 44,* 427–444.

Fiedler, F. E. (1987, September). When to lead, when to stand back. *Psychology Today,* pp. 26–27.

Figl, K., Kießling, S., & Remus, U. (2023). Do symbol and device matter? The effects of symbol choice of fake news flags and device on human interaction with fake news on social media platforms. *Computers in Human Behavior, 144,* 1–16.

Filieri, R., Acikgoz, F., Li, C., & Alguezaui, S. (2023). Influencers' "organic" persuasion through electronic word of mouth: A case of sincerity over brains and beauty. *Psychology & Marketing, 40,* 347–364.

Fincham, F. D., Lambert, N. M., & Beach, S. R. H. (2010). Faith and unfaithfulness: Can praying for your partner reduce infidelity? *Journal of Personality and Social Psychology, 99,* 649–659.

Finez, L., Berjot, S., Rosnet, E., Cleveland, C., & Tice, D. M. (2012). Trait self-esteem and claimed self-handicapping motives in sports situations. *Journal of Sports Sciences, 30*(16), 1757–1765.

Finkel, E., & Fitzsimmons, G. (2013). When helping hurts. *The New York Times.* https://www.nytimes.com/2013/05/12/opinion/sunday/too-much-helicopter-parenting.html

Finkel, E. J. (2017). *The all-or-nothing marriage: How the best marriages work.* New York: Dutton.

Finkel, E. J., Bail, C. A., Cikara, M., Ditto, P. H., Iyengar, S., Klar, S., Mason, L., McGrath, M. C., Nyhan, B., Rand, D. G., Skitka, L. J., Tucker, J. A., Van Bavel, J. J., Wang, C. S., & Druckman, J. N. (2020). Political sectarianism in America. *Science, 370,* 533–536.

Finkel, E. J., Eastwick, P. W., Karney, B. R., Reis, H. T., & Sprecher, S. (2012). Online dating: A critical analysis from the perspective of psychological science. *Psychological Science in the Public interest, 13,* 3–66.

Finkel, E. J., Hui, C. M., Carswell, K. L., & Larson, G. M. (2014). The suffocation of marriage: Climbing Mount Maslow without enough oxygen. *Psychological Inquiry, 25,* 1–41.

Finkel, E. J., Slotter, E. B., Luchies, L. B., Walton, G. M., & Gross, J. J. (2013). A brief intervention to promote conflict reappraisal preserves marital quality over time. *Psychological Science, 24,* 1595–1601.

Fischer, A., & LaFrance, M. (2015). What drives the smile and the tear: Why women are more emotionally expressive than men. *Emotion Review, 7,* 22–29.

Fischer, P., & Greitemeyer, T. (2010). A new look at selective-exposure effects: An integrative model. *Current Directions in Psychological Science, 19,* 384–389.

Fischer, P., Krueger, J., Greitemeyer, T., Kastenmüller, A., Vogrincic, C., Frey, D., Heene, M., Wicher, M., & Kainbacher, M. (2011). The bystander-effect: A meta-analytic review on bystander intervention in dangerous and non-dangerous emergencies. *Psychological Bulletin, 137,* 517–537.

Fischer, R., & Boer, D. (2011). What is more important for national well-being: Money or autonomy? A meta-analysis of well-being, burnout, and anxiety across 63 societies. *Journal of Personality and Social Psychology, 101,* 164–184.

Fischer, R., & Chalmers, A. (2008). Is optimism universal? A meta-analytical investigation of optimism levels across 22 nations. *Personality and Individual Differences, 45,* 378–382.

Fischer, R., & Van de Vliert, E. (2011). Does climate undermine subjective well-being? A 58-nation study. *Personality and Social Psychology Bulletin, 37,* 1031–1041.

Fischhoff, B., & Bar-Hillel, M. (1984). Diagnosticity and the base rate effect. *Memory and Cognition, 12,* 402–410.

Fischhoff, B. (1982). Debiasing. In D. Kahneman, P. Slovic, & A. Tversky (Eds.), *Judgment under uncertainty: Heuristics and biases.* New York: Cambridge University Press.

Fishbein, M., & Ajzen, I. (1974). Attitudes toward objects as predictive of single and multiple behavioral criteria. *Psychological Review, 81,* 59–74.

Fisher, H., & Garcia, J. R. (2013, February 5). *Singles in America.* Match.com survey of single population. https://prn.to/30lEFqU

Fisher, H. (1994, April). The nature of romantic love. *Journal of NIH Research,* 59–64.

Fisher, H. E., Xu, X., Aron, A., & Brown, L. L. (2016). Intense, passionate, romantic love: A natural addiction? How the fields that investigate romance and substance abuse can inform each other. *Frontiers in Psychology, 7*(40), 687.

Fisher, K., Egerton, M., Gershuny, J. I., & Robinson, J. P. (2007). Gender convergence in the American Heritage Time Use Study (AHTUS). *Social Indicators Research, 82,* 1–33.

Fisher, M., Cox, J. W., & Hermann, P. (2016, December 6). Pizzagate: From rumor, to hashtag, to gunfire in D.C. *Washington Post.*

Fisher, R. (1981, March). Preventing nuclear war. *Bulletin of the Atomic Scientists,* 11–17.

Fisher, R. P., Geiselman, R. E., & Amador, M. (1989). Field test of the cognitive interview: Enhancing the recollection of actual victims and witnesses of crime. *Journal of Applied Psychology, 74,* 722–727.

Fisher, R. P., Geiselman, R. E., & Raymond, D. S. (1987). Critical analysis of police interview techniques. *Journal of Police Science and Administration, 15,* 177–185.

Fisher, R. P., McCauley, M. R., & Geiselman, R. E. (1994). Improving eyewitness testimony with the Cognitive Interview. In D. F. Ross, J. D. Read, & M. P. Toglia (Eds.), *Adult eyewitness testimony: Current trends and developments.* Cambridge, UK: Cambridge University Press.

Fisher, R. P., Milne, R., & Bull, R. (2011). Interviewing cooperative witnesses. *Current Directions in Psychological Science, 20,* 20–23.

Fisher, T. D., Moore, Z. T., & Pittinger, M. J. (2012). Sex on the brain? An examination of frequency of sexual cognitions as a function of gender, erotophilia, and social desirability. *Journal of Sex Research, 49,* 69–77.

Fiske, S. T., & Hauser, R. M. (2014). Protecting human research participants in the age of big data. *Proceedings of the National Academic of Sciences, 111,* 13675–13676.

Fiske, S. T., & Markus, H. R. (2012). *Facing social class: How societal rank influences interaction.* Atlanta, GA: Sage.

Fiske, S. T. (1989). *Interdependence and stereotyping: From the laboratory to the Supreme Court (and back).* Invited address, American Psychological Association convention, New Orleans, Louisiana.

Fiske, S. T. (1992). Thinking is for doing: Portraits of social cognition from daguerreotype to laserphoto. *Journal of Personality and Social Psychology, 63,* 877–889.

Fiske, S. T. (1999). Behind the scenes. In D. G. Myers. *Social psychology,* 6th edition. New York: McGraw Hill.

Fiske, S. T. (2004). Mind the gap: In praise of informal sources of formal theory. *Personality and Social Psychology Review, 8,* 132–137.

Fiske, S. T. (2011). *Envy up, scorn down: How status divides us.* New York: Sage Foundation.

Fiske, S. T., Bersoff, D. N., Borgida, E., Deaux, K., & Heilman, M. E. (1991). Social science research on trial: The use of sex stereotyping research in *Price Waterhouse v. Hopkins. American Psychologist, 46,* 1049–1060.

Fiske, S. T., Harris, L. T., & Cuddy, A. J. C. (2004). Why ordinary people torture enemy prisoners. *Science, 306,* 1482–1483.

Fitzgerald, R. J., & Price, H. L. (2015). Eyewitness identification across the life span: A meta-analysis of age differences. *Psychological Bulletin, 141,* 1228–1265.

Flade, F., Klar, Y., & Imhoff, R. (2019). Unite against: A common threat invokes spontaneous decategorization between social categories. *Journal of Experimental Social Psychology, 85,* 103890.

Flanigan, M. E., Aleyasin, H., Li, L., Burnett, C. J., Chan, K. L., . . . Russo, S. J. (2020). Orexin signaling in GABAaergic lateral habenula neurons modulates aggressive behavior in male mice. *Nature Neuroscience, 23,* 638–650.

Flay, B. R., Ryan, K. B., Best, J. A., Brown, K. S., Kersell, M. W., d'Avernas, J. R., & Zanna, M. P. (1985). Are social-psychological smoking prevention programs effective? The Waterloo study. *Journal of Behavioral Medicine, 8,* 37–59.

Fleming, M. A., Wegener, D. T., & Petty, R. E. (1999). Procedural and legal motivations to correct for perceived judicial biases. *Journal of Experimental Social Psychology, 35,* 186–203.

Fletcher, G. J. O., & Ward, C. (1989). Attribution theory and processes: A cross-cultural perspective. In M. H. Bond (Ed.), *The cross-cultural challenge to social psychology.* Newbury Park, CA: Sage.

Fletcher, G. J. O., Fincham, F. D., Cramer, L., & Heron, N. (1987). The role of attributions in the development of dating relationships. *Journal of Personality and Social Psychology, 53,* 481–489.

Fletcher, G. J. O., Simpson, J. A., Campbell, L., & Overall, N. C. (2015). Pair-bonding, romantic love, and evolution: The curious case of *Homo sapiens. Perspectives on Psychological Science, 10,* 20–36.

Fletcher, G. J. O., Simpson, J. A., Thomas, G., & Giles, L. (1999). Ideals in intimate relationships. *Journal of Personality and Social Psychology, 76,* 72–89.

Fletcher, G. J. O., Tither, J. M., O'Loughlin, C., Friesen, M., & Overall, N. (2004). Warm and homely or cold and beautiful? Sex differences in trading off traits in mate selection. *Personality and Social Psychology Bulletin, 30,* 659–672.

Fletcher, J. (2012). Positive parenting, not physical punishment. *Canadian Medical Association Journal, 184,* 1339.

Flores, A. R., Brown, T. N. T., & Park, A. S. (2016). *Public support for transgender rights: A twenty-three country survey* [PDF file]. The Williams Institute, UCLA School of Law. https://williamsinstitute.law.ucla.edu/wp-content/uploads/23-Country-Survey.pdf

Flores, A. R., Haider-Markel, D. P., Lewis, D. C., Miller, P. R., Tadlock, B. L., & Taylor, J. K. (2018). Challenged expectations: Mere exposure effects on attitudes about transgender people and rights. *Political Psychology, 39*(1), 197–216.

Flowe, H. D., Klatt, T., & Colloff, M. F. (2014). Selecting fillers on emotional appearance improves lineup identification accuracy. *Law and Human Behavior, 38,* 509–519.

Foa, U. G., & Foa, E. B. (1975). *Resource theory of social exchange.* Morristown, NJ: General Learning Press.

Fogelman, E. (1994). *Conscience and courage: Rescuers of Jews during the Holocaust.* New York: Doubleday Anchor.

Folberg, A. M., Zhu, M., He, Y., & Ryan, C. S. (2022). The primacy of nurturance and dominance/assertiveness: Unidimensional measures of the big two mask gender differences in subdimensions. *International Review of Social Psychology, 35*(1).

Follett, M. P. (1940). Constructive conflict. In H. C. Metcalf & L. Urwick (Eds.), *Dynamic administration: The collected papers of Mary Parker Follett.* New York: Harper.

FootPrintNetwork.org. (2021). World ecological footprint. *Global Footprint Network.* https://data.footprintnetwork.org/?_ga=2.41957350.213018028.1618336463-1971561093.1618336463#/countryTrends?cn=5001&type=earth

Ford, T. E., Boxer, C. F., Armstrong, J., & Edel, J. R. (2008). More than "just a joke": The prejudice-releasing function of sexist humor. *Personality and Social Psychology Bulletin, 34,* 159–170.

Forgas, J. P. (2007). When sad is better than happy: Negative affect can improve the quality and effectiveness of persuasive messages and social influence strategies. *Journal of Experimental Social Psychology, 43,* 513–528.

Forgas, J. P. (2008). Affect and cognition. *Perspectives on Psychological Science, 3,* 94–101.

Forgas, J. P. (2010). Affective influences on the formation, expression, and change of attitudes. In J. P. Forgas, J. Cooper, & W. D. Crano (Eds.), *The psychology of attitudes and attitude change.* New York: Psychology Press.

Forgas, J. P. (2011). Affect and global versus local processing: The processing benefits of negative affect for memory, judgments, and behavior. *Psychological Inquiry, 21,* 216–224.

Forgas, J. P. (2013). Don't worry, be sad! On the cognitive, motivational, and interpersonal benefits of negative mood. *Current Directions in Psychological Science, 22,* 225–232.

Forgas, J. P. (2014, June 4). Four ways sadness may be good for you. *Greater Good Magazine.* www.greatergood.berkeley.edu

Forgas, J. P. (2022). Mood effects on sociability: How affect regulates relationship behaviors. In J. P. Forgas, W. Crano, & K. Fiedler (Eds.), *The psychology of sociability: Understanding human attachment.* (pp. 258–283). Routledge.

Forgas, J. P., Bower, G. H., & Krantz, S. E. (1984). The influence of mood on perceptions of social interactions. *Journal of Experimental Social Psychology, 20,* 497–513.

Forgas, J. P., Dunn, E., & Granland, S. (2008). Are you being served . . . ? An unobtrusive experiment of affective influences on helping in a department store. *European Journal of Social Psychology, 38,* 333–342.

Forgas, J. P., Goldenberg, L. & Unkelbach, C. (2009). Can bad weather improve your memory? An unobtrusive field study of natural mood effects on real-life memory. *Journal of Experimental Social Psychology,* 254–259.

Form, W. H., & Nosow, S. (1958). *Community in disaster.* New York: Harper.

Forrester, R. L., Slater, H., Jomar, K., Mitzman, S., & Taylor, P. J. (2017). Self-esteem and non-suicidal self-injury in adulthood: A systematic review. *Journal of Affective Disorders, 221,* 172–183.

Forscher, P. S., Cox, W. T. L., Graetz, N., & Devine, P. G. (2015). The motivation to express prejudice. *Journal of Personality and Social Psychology, 109,* 791–812.

Forscher, P. S., Lai, C. K., Axt, J. R., Ebersole, C. R., Herman, M., Devine, P. G., & Nosek, B. A. (2019). A meta-analysis of procedures to change implicit measures. *Journal of Personality and Social Psychology, 117,* 522–559.

Forsyth, D. R., & Leary, M. R. (1997). Achieving the goals of the scientist-practitioner model: The seven interfaces of social and counseling psychology. *The Counseling Psychologist, 25,* 180–200.

Foss, R. D. (1978). *The role of social influence in blood donation.* Paper presented at the American Psychological Association convention, Toronto, Ontario.

Foster, C. A., Witcher, B. S., Campbell, W. K., & Green, J. D. (1998). Arousal and attraction: Evidence for automatic and controlled processes. *Journal of Personality and Social Psychology, 74,* 86–101.

Fothergill, E., Guo, J., Howard, L., Kerns, J. C., Knuth, N. D., Brychta, R., & . . . Hall, K. D. (2016). Persistent metabolic adaptation 6 years after "The Biggest Loser" competition. *Obesity, 24,* 1612–1619.

Fourie, M. M., Deist, M., & Moore-Berg, S. L. (2022). Hierarchies of being human: Intergroup dehumanization and its implication in present-day South Africa. *Peace and Conflict: Journal of Peace Psychology, 28,* 345–360.

Fowler, J. H., & Christakis, N. A. (2008). Dynamic spread of happiness in a large social network: Longitudinal analysis over 20 years in the Framingham Heart Study. *British Medical Journal, 337* (doi: 10.1136/bmj.a2338).

Fox, J., Vendemia, M. A., Smith, M. A., & Brehm, N. R. (2021). Effects of taking selfies on women's self-objectification, mood, self-esteem, and social aggression toward female peers. *Body Image, 36,* 193–200.

Fraley, R. C., Gillath, O., & Deboeck, P. R. (2021). Do life events lead to enduring changes in adult attachment styles? A naturalistic longitudinal investigation. *Journal of Personality and Social Psychology, 120,* 1567–1606.

Fraley, R. C., Griffin, B. N., Belsky, J., & Roisman, G. I. (2012). Developmental antecedents of political ideology: A longitudinal investigation from birth to age 18 years. *Psychological Science, 23,* 1425–1431.

Francis, E., & Goodwin, L. (2022, December 27). Democrats call for George Santos to resign seat over résumé 'lies.' *Washington Post.*

Francis, P. (2017). "The future you." Talk delivered at TED 2017 conference. Retrieved from https://time.com/4755663/pope-francis-ted-talk-transcript/

Frankel, A., & Snyder, M. L. (1987). *Egotism among the depressed: When self-protection becomes self-handicapping.* Paper presented at the American Psychological Association convention, New York.

Frankenbach, J., Weber, M., Loschelder, D. D., Kilger, H., & Friese, M. (2023). Sex drive: Theoretical conceptualization and meta-analytic review of gender differences. *Psychological Bulletin.*

Franklin, B. (1750). *Poor Richard's almanack.* Philadelphia.

Frantz, C. M. (2006). I AM being fair: The bias blind spot as a stumbling block to seeing both sides. *Basic and Applied Social Psychology,* 28, 157–167.

Frasure-Smith, N., & Lespérance, F. (2005). Depression and coronary heart disease: Complex synergism of mind, body, and environment. *Current Directions in Psychological Science, 14,* 39–43.

Frasure-Smith, N., Lesperance, F., & Talajic, M. (1995). The impact of negative emotions on prognosis following myocardial infarction: Is it more than depression? *Health Psychology, 14,* 388–398.

Frasure-Smith, N., Lesperance, F., Juneau, M., Talajic, M., & Bourassa, M. G. (1999). Gender, depression, and one-year prognosis after myocardial infarction. *Psychosomatic Medicine, 61,* 26–37.

Frederick, D. A., & Haselton, M. G. (2007). Why is muscularity sexy? Tests of the fitness indicator hypothesis. *Personality and Social Psychology Bulletin, 8,* 1167–1183.

Freedman, A., & Samenow, J. (2019, August 3). The Greenland ice sheet poured 197 billion tons of water into the North Atlantic in July alone. *The Washington Post.* https://wapo.st/36xSeph

Freedman, J. L., & Fraser, S. C. (1966). Compliance without pressure: The foot-in-the-door technique. *Journal of Personality and Social Psychology, 4,* 195–202.

Freedman, J. L., & Perlick, D. (1979). Crowding, contagion, and laughter. *Journal of Experimental Social Psychology, 15,* 295–303.

Freedman, J. L., & Sears, D. O. (1965). Warning, distraction, and resistance to influence. *Journal of Personality and Social Psychology, 1,* 262–266.

Freedman, J. L. (1965). Long-term behavioral effects of cognitive dissonance. *Journal of Experimental Social Psychology, 1,* 145–155.

Freedman, J. L., Birsky, J., & Cavoukian, A. (1980). Environmental determinants of behavioral contagion: Density and number. *Basic and Applied Social Psychology, 1,* 155–161.

Freijy, T., & Kothe, E. J. (2013). Dissonance-based interventions for health behaviour change: A systematic review. *British Journal of Health Psychology, 18,* 310–337.

Frenda, S. J., Nichols, R. M., & Loftus, E. F. (2011). Current issues and advances in misinformation research. *Current Directions in Psychological Science, 20,* 20–23.

Freund, B., Colgrove, L. A., Burke, B. L., & McLeod, R. (2005). Self-rated driving performance among elderly drivers referred for driving evaluation. *Accident Analysis and Prevention, 37,* 613–618.

Friebel, G., & Seabright, P. (2011). Do women have longer conversations? Telephone evidence of gendered communication strategies. *Journal of Economic Psychology, 32,* 348–356.

Friedman, T. L. (2003, June 4). Because we could. *The New York Times.* https://www.nytimes.com/2003/06/04/opinion/because-we-could.html

Friedrich, L. K., & Stein, A. H. (1973). Aggressive and prosocial television programs and the natural behavior of preschool children. *Monographs of the Society of Research in Child Development, 38* (4, Serial No. 151).

Friedrich, L. K., & Stein, A. H. (1975). Prosocial television and young children: The effects of verbal labeling and role playing on learning and behavior. *Child Development, 46,* 27–38.

Frieze, I. H., Olson, J. E., & Russell, J. (1991). Attractiveness and income for men and women in management. *Journal of Applied Social Psychology, 21,* 1039–1057.

Frimer, J. A., Skitka, L. J., & Motyl, M. (2017). Liberals and conservatives are similarly motivated to avoid exposure to one another's opinions. *Journal of Experimental Social Psychology, 7,* 21–12.

Frisell, T., Lichtenstein, P., & Långström, N. (2011). Violent crime runs in families: A total population study of 12.5 million individuals. *Journal of Research in Psychiatry and the Allied Sciences, 41,* 97–105.

Froming, W. J., Walker, G. R., & Lopyan, K. J. (1982). Public and private self-awareness: When personal attitudes conflict with societal expectations. *Journal of Experimental Social Psychology, 18,* 476–487.

Frueh, S. (2019, October 15). *Uncovering unconscious racial bias: Lecture examines stereotypes and their impacts.* National Academies of Sciences, Engineering, and Medicine. https://www.nationalacademies.org/news/2019/10/uncovering-unconscious-racial-bias-lecture-examines-stereotypes-and-their-impacts

Fry, B. N., & Runyan, J. D. (2018). Teaching empathic concern and altruism in the smartphone age. *Journal of Moral Education, 47,* 1–16.

Fry, D. P. (2012). Life without war. *Science, 336,* 879–884.

Fryer, R. G. (2016). *An empirical analysis of racial differences in police use of force.* NBER Working Paper no. 22399. http://www.nber.org/papers/w22399

Fry, R., Aragao, C., Hurst, K., & Parker, K. (2023, April 13). In a Growing Share of U.S. Marriages, Husbands and Wives Earn About the Same. Pew Research Center.

Fulgoni, G. M., & Mörn, M. (2009). Whither the click: How online advertising works. *Journal of Advertising Research, 49,* 134–142.

Fultz, J., Batson, C. D., Fortenbach, V. A., McCarthy, P. M., & Varney, L. L. (1986). Social evaluation and the empathy-altruism hypothesis. *Journal of Personality and Social Psychology, 50,* 761–769.

Fumento, M. (2014). Runaway hysteria: The Toyota panic, with the federal government's seal of approval. *Skeptical Inquirer, 38*(5), 42–49.

Furnham, A. (2016). Whether you think you can, or you think you can't—you're right. In R. J. Sternberg, S. T. Fiske, & D. J. Foss (Eds.), *Scientists making a difference: One hundred eminent behavioral and brain scientists talk about their most important contributions.* New York: Cambridge University Press.

Fürst, G., Ghisletta, P., & Lubart, T. (2014). Toward an integrative model of creativity and personality: Theoretical suggestions and preliminary empirical testing. *Journal of Creative Behavior, 50*(2), 87–108.

Gabbiadini, A., Riva, P., Andrighetto, L., Volpato, C., & Bushman, B. J. (2014). Interactive effect of moral disengagement and violent video games on self-control, cheating, and aggression. *Social Psychological and Personality Science, 5,* 451–458.

Gable, S. L., Gonzaga, G. C., & Strachman, A. (2006). Will you be there for me when things go right? Supportive responses to positive event disclosures. *Journal of Personality and Social Psychology, 91,* 904–917.

Gabrenya, W. K., Jr., Wang, Y.-E., & Latané, B. (1985). Social loafing on an optimizing task: Cross-cultural differences among Chinese and Americans. *Journal of Cross-Cultural Psychology, 16,* 223–242.

Gabriel, S., & Gardner, W. L. (1999). Are there "his" and "hers" types of interdependence? The implications of gender differences in collective versus relational interdependence for affect, behavior, and cognition. *Journal of Personality and Social Psychology, 77,* 642–655.

Gaebelein, J. W., & Mander, A. (1978). Consequences for targets of aggression as a function of aggressor and instigator roles: Three experiments. *Personality and Social Psychology Bulletin, 4,* 465–468.

Gaertner, L., Iuzzini, J., Witt, M. G., & Oriña, M. M. (2006). Us without them: Evidence for an intragroup origin of positive in-group regard. *Journal of Personality and Social Psychology, 90,* 426–439.

Gaertner, L., Sedikides, C., & Chang, K. (2008). On pancultural self-enhancement: Well-adjusted Taiwanese self-enhance on personally valued traits. *Journal of Cross-Cultural Psychology, 39,* 463–477.

Gaertner, L., Sedikides, C., & Graetz, K. (1999). In search of self-definition: Motivational primacy of the individual self, motivational primacy of the collective self, or contextual primacy? *Journal of Personality and Social Psychology, 76,* 5–18.

Gaertner, S. L., & Dovidio, J. F. (1977). The subtlety of white racism, arousal, and helping behavior. *Journal of Personality and Social Psychology, 35,* 691–707.

Gaertner, S. L., & Dovidio, J. F. (1986). The aversive form of racism. In J. F. Dovidio & S. L. Gaertner (Eds.), *Prejudice, discrimination, and racism.* Orlando, FL: Academic Press.

Gaertner, S. L., & Dovidio, J. F. (2005). Understanding and addressing contemporary racism: From aversive racism to the Common Ingroup Identity Model. *Journal of Social Issues, 61,* 615–639.

Gaertner, S. L., Dovidio, J. F., Nier, J. A., Banker, B. S., Ward, C. M., Houlette, M., & Loux, S. (2000). The common ingroup identity model for reducing intergroup bias: Progress and challenges. In D. Capozza & R. Brown (Eds.), *Social identity processes: Trends in theory and research.* London: Sage.

Gaertner, S. L., Mann, J., Murrell, A., & Dovidio, J. F. (2001). Reducing intergroup bias: The benefits of recategorization. In M. A. Hogg & D. Abrams (Eds.), *Intergroup relations: Essential readings.* Philadelphia: Psychology Press.

Gaither, S. E., & Sommers, S. R. (2013). Living with an other-race roommate shapes Whites' behavior in subsequent diverse settings. *Journal of Experimental Social Psychology, 49,* 272–276.

Galak, J., Gray, K., Elbert, I., & Strohminger, N. (2016). Trickle-down preferences: Preferential conformity to high status peers in fashion choices. *PLOS ONE, 11*(5), e0153448.

Gal, D., & Rucker, D. D. (2010). When in doubt, shout! Paradoxical influences of doubt on proselytizing. *Psychological Science, 21,* 1701–1707.

Galinsky, A. D., & Moskowitz, G. B. (2000). Perspective-taking: Decreasing stereotype expression, stereotype accessibility, and in-group favoritism. *Journal of Personality and Social Psychology, 78,* 708–724.

Galinsky, E., Aumann, K., & Bond, J. T. (2009). *Times are changing: Gender and generation at work and at home.* New York: Families and Work Institute.

Gallo, L. C., & Matthews, K. A. (2003). Understanding the association between socioeconomic status and physical health: Do negative emotions play a role? *Psychological Bulletin, 129,* 10–51.

Gallup. (1996). *Gallup survey of scientists sampled from the 1995 edition of American Men and Women of Science.* Reported by National Center for Science Education www.ncseweb.org

Gallup. (2006). Presidential approval rating–George W. Bush. https://news.gallup.com/poll/116500/presidential-approval-ratings-george-bush.aspx

Gallup. (2012). Blacks, Nonblacks hold sharply different views of Trayvon Martin case. https://www.gallup.com/poll/153776/blacks-nonblacks-hold-sharply-different-views-martin-case.aspx

Gallup. (2020). Death penalty. http://www.gallup.com/poll/1606/death-penalty.aspx

Gallup. (2021). The presidency. https://news.gallup.com/poll/4729/presidency.aspx

Gallup (2023). Environment. https://news.gallup.com/poll/1615/environment.aspx

Gallup, G. G., Jr., & Frederick, M. J., & Pipitone, R. N. (2008). Morphology and behavior: Phrenology revisited. *Review of General Psychology, 12,* 297–304.

Gallup, G. H. (1972). *The Gallup Poll: Public Opinion 1935–1971* (Vol. 3, pp. 551, 1716). New York: Random House.

Gangestad, S. W., & Snyder, M. (2000). Self-monitoring: Appraisal and reappraisal. *Psychological Bulletin, 126,* 530–555.

Gangestad, S. W., & Thornhill, R. (1997). Human sexual selection and developmental stability. In J. A. Simpson & D. T. Kenrick (Eds.), *Evolutionary social psychology.* Mahwah, NJ: Erlbaum.

Garandeau, C. F., Laninga-Wijnen, L., & Salmivalli, C. (2022). Effects of the KiVa anti-bullying program on affective and cognitive empathy in children and adolescents. *Journal of Clinical Child and Adolescent Psychology, 51,* 515–529.

Garb, H. N. (1994). Judgment research: Implications for clinical practice and testimony in court. *Applied and Preventive Psychology, 3,* 173–183.

Garb, H. N. (2005). Clinical judgment and decision making. *Annual Review of Clinical Psychology, 1,* 67–89.

Garcia-Marques, T., Mackie, D. M., Claypool, H. M., & Garcia-Marques, L. (2004). Positivity can cue familiarity. *Personality and Social Psychology Bulletin, 30,* 585–593.

García-Sánchez, E., Correia, I., Pereira, C. R., Willis, G. B., Rodríguez-Bailón, R., & Vala, J. (2022). How fair is economic inequality? Belief in a Just World and the legitimation of economic disparities in 27 European countries. *Personality and Social Psychology Bulletin, 48,* 382–395.

Gardner, G., & Assadourian, E. (2004). Rethinking the good life. Chapter 8 in *State of the World 2004.* Washington, DC: WorldWatch Institute.

Gardner, W. L., Pickett, L., Jefferis, V., & Knowles, M. (2005). On the outside looking in: Loneliness and social monitoring. *Personality and Social Psychology Bulletin, 31,* 1549–1560.

Garfield, Z. H., & Glowacki, L. (2023). Interpersonal conflicts and third-party mediation in a pastoralist society. *Evolution and Human Behavior.*

Garlick, R. (2022, August 23). When did we become so obsessed with being "symmetrical?" *New York Times.*

Garrett, B. L. (2011, April 12). Getting it wrong: Convicting the innocent. *Slate.* https://slate.com/tag/getting-it-wrong-convicting-the-innocent

Garry, M., Manning, C. G., Loftus, E. F., & Sherman, S. J. (1996). Imagination inflation: Imagining a childhood event inflates confidence that it occurred. *Psychonomic Bulletin & Review, 3,* 208–214.

Gates, M. (2020). Bill and Melinda Gates Foundation website. https://www.gatesfoundation.org/Who-We-Are

Gates, M. F., & Allee, W. C. (1933). Conditioned behavior of isolated and grouped cockroaches on a simple maze. *Journal of Comparative Psychology, 15,* 331–358.

Gati, I., & Perez, M. (2014). Gender differences in career preferences from 1990 to 2010: Gaps reduced but not eliminated. *Journal of Counseling Psychology, 61,* 63–80.

Gaube, S., Fischer, P., Windl, V., & Lermer, E. (2020). The effect of persuasive messages on hospital visitors' hand hygiene behavior. *Health Psychology, 39,* 471–481.

Gaucher, D., Friesen, J., & Kay, A. C. (2011). Evidence that gendered wording in job advertisements exists and sustains gender inequality. *Journal of Personality and Social Psychology, 101,* 109–128.

Gaunt, R. (2006). Couple similarity and marital satisfaction: Are similar spouses happier? *Journal of Personality, 74,* 1401–1420.

Gavanski, I., & Hoffman, C. (1987). Awareness of influences on one's own judgments: The roles of covariation detection and attention to the judgment process. *Journal of Personality and Social Psychology, 52,* 453–463.

Gavzer, B. (1997, January 5). Are trial consultants good for justice? *Parade,* p. 20.

Gawande, A. (2002). *Complications: A surgeon's notes on an imperfect science.* New York: Metropolitan Books, Holt.

Gawronski, B., & Bodenhausen, G. V. (2006). Associative and propositional processes in evaluation: An integrative review of implicit and explicit attitude change. *Psychological Bulletin, 132,* 692–731.

Gazzaniga, M. (1998). *The mind's past.* Berkeley, CA: University of California Press.

Gazzaniga, M. (2008). *Human: The science behind what makes us unique.* New York: Ecco.

Gazzaniga, M. S. (1985). *The social brain: Discovering the networks of the mind.* New York: Basic Books.

Gazzaniga, M. S. (1992). *Nature's mind: The biological roots of thinking, emotions, sexuality, language, and intelligence.* New York: Basic Books.

Gebauer, J. E., Sedikides, C., Wagner, J., Bleidorn, W., Rentfrow, P. J., Potter, J., & Gosling, S. D. (2015). Cultural norm fulfillment, interpersonal belonging, or getting ahead? A large-scale, cross-cultural test of three perspectives on the function of self-esteem. *Journal of Personality and Social Psychology, 109,* 526–548.

Geenen, N. Y. R., Hohelüchter, M., Langholf, V., & Walther, E. (2014). The beneficial effects of prosocial spending on happiness: Work hard, make money, and spend it on others? *The Journal of Positive Psychology, 9,* 204–208.

Geen, R. G., & Thomas, S. L. (1986). The immediate effects of media violence on behavior. *Journal of Social Issues, 42*(3), 7–28.

Geiger, A. W., & Livingston, G. (2019, February 13). 8 facts about love and marriage in America. *Pew Research Center.* https://www.pewresearch.org/fact-tank/2019/02/13/8-facts-about-love-and-marriage/

Geiger, A. W. (2016, November 30). Sharing chores a key to good marriage, say majority of married adults. *Pew Research Center.* https://www.pewresearch.org/fact-tank/2016/11/30/sharing-chores-a-key-to-good-marriage-say-majority-of-married-adults/

Gelfand, M. J. & 44 others. (2011). Differences between tight and loose cultures: A 33-nation study. *Science, 332,* 1100–1104.

Gelfand, M., Li, R., Stamkou, E., Pieper, D., Denison, E., Fernandez, J., Choi, V., Chatman, J., Jackson, J., & Dimant, E. (2022). Persuading Republicans and Democrats to comply with mask wearing: An intervention tournament. *Journal of Experimental Social Psychology, 101,* 1–23.

Geniole, S. N., Bird, B. M., McVittie, J. S., Purcell, R. B., Archer, J., & Carré, J. M. (2020). Is testosterone linked to human aggression? A meta-analytic examination of the relationship between baseline, dynamic, and manipulated testosterone on human aggression. *Hormones and Behavior, 123,* 104644.

Genschow, O., Westfal, M., Crusius, J., Bartosch, L., Feikes, K. I., Pallasch, N., & Wozniak, M. (2021). Does social psychology persist over half a century? A direct replication of Cialdini et al's (1975) classic door-in-the-face technique. *Journal of Personality and Social Psychology, 120,* e1-e7.

Gentile, B. C., Twenge, J. M., & Campbell, W. K. (2009). *Birth cohort differences in self-esteem, 1988-2008: A cross-temporal meta-analysis.* Unpublished manuscript.

Gentile, D. A., & Anderson, C. A. (2011). Don't read more into the Supreme Court's ruling on the California video game law. *newswise.* https://www.newswise.com/articles/don-t-read-more-into-the-supreme-court-s-ruling-on-the-california-video-game-law

Gentile, D. A., & Bushman, B. J. (2012). Reassessing media violence effects using a risk and resilence approach to understanding aggression. *Psychology of Popular Media Culture, 1,* 138-151.

Gentile, D. A., Bender, P. K., & Anderson, C. A. (2017). Violent video game effects on salivary cortisol, arousal, and aggressive thoughts in children. *Computers in Human Behavior, 70,* 39-43.

Gentile, D. A., Lynch, P. J., Linder, J. R., & Walsh, D. A. (2004). The effects of violent video game habits on adolescent hostility, aggressive behaviors, and school performance. *Journal of Adolescence, 27,* 5-22.

George, D., Carroll, P., Kersnick, R., & Calderon, K. (1998). Gender-related patterns of helping among friends. *Psychology of Women Quarterly, 22,* 685-704.

Georgiou, N., Delfabbro, P., & Balzan, R. (2023). The effectiveness of a scientific reasoning intervention for conspiracy theory beliefs. *Applied Cognitive Psychology.*

Gerard, H. B. (1999). A social psychologist examines his past and looks to the future. In A. Rodrigues & R. Levine (Eds.), *Reflections on 100 years of experimental social psychology.* New York: Basic Books.

Gerard, H. B., Wilhelmy, R. A., & Conolley, E. S. (1968). Conformity and group size. *Journal of Personality and Social Psychology, 8,* 79-82.

Gerber, J. P., Wheeler, L., & Suls, J. (2018). A social comparison theory meta-analysis 60+ years on. *Psychological Bulletin, 144*(2), 177-197.

Gerbner, G. (1994). The politics of media violence: Some reflections. In C. Hamelink & O. Linne (Eds.), *Mass communication research: On problems and policies.* Norwood, NJ: Ablex.

Gerbner, G., Gross, L., Signorielli, N., Morgan, M., & Jackson-Beeck, M. (1979). The demonstration of power: Violence profile No. 10. *Journal of Communication, 29,* 177-196.

Gershman, S. J., & Cikara, M. (2023). Structure learning principles of stereotype change. *Psychonomic Bulletin & Review, 30*(4), 1273-1293.

Gershoff, E. T. (2002). Corporal punishment by parents and associated child behaviors and experiences: A meta-analytic and theoretical review. *Psychological Bulletin, 128,* 539-579.

Gerson, M. (2022, April 22). There's a reason Russian soldiers can't look their victims in the face. *Washington Post.*

Gerstenfeld, P. B., Grant, D. R., & Chiang, C.-P. (2003). Hate online: A content analysis of extremist Internet sites. *Analyses of Social Issues and Public Policy, 3,* 29-44.

Gesch, C. B., Hammond, S. M., Hampson, S. E., Eves, A., & Crowder, M. J. (2002). Influence of supplementary vitamins, minerals and essential fatty acids on the antisocial behavior of young adult prisoners. Randomised, placebo-controlled trial. *British Journal of Psychiatry, 181,* 22-28.

Gettler, L., McDade, T. W., Feranil, A., & Kuzawa, C. W. (2011). Longitudinal evidence that fatherhood decreases testosterone in human males. *PNAS, 108,* 16194-16199.

Ge, Y., Knittel, C. R., MacKenzie, D., & Zoepf, S. (2016). *Racial and gender discrimination in transportation network companies.* National Bureau of Economic Research, Inc., NBER Working Papers: 22776.

Ghitza, Y., Gelman, A., & Auerbach, J. (2019). The Great Society, Reagan's Revolution, and generations of presidential voting [PDF file]. http://www.stat.columbia.edu/~gelman/research/unpublished/cohort_voting_20191017.pdf

Ghosh, T., S., S., & Dwivedi, Y. K. (2022). Brands in a game or a game for brands? Comparing the persuasive effectiveness of in-game advertising and advergames. *Psychology & Marketing, 39,* 2328-2348.

Ghumman, S., & Barnes, C. M. (2013). Sleep and prejudice: A resource recovery approach. *Journal of Applied Social Psychology, 43,* E166-E178.

Giancola, P. R., & Corman, M. D. (2007). Alcohol and aggression: A test of the attention-allocation model. *Psychological Science, 18,* 649-655.

Gibbons, F. X., & Wicklund, R. A. (1982). Self-focused attention and helping behavior. *Journal of Personality and Social Psychology, 43,* 462-474.

Gibbons, F. X. (1978). Sexual standards and reactions to pornography: Enhancing behavioral consistency through self-focused attention. *Journal of Personality and Social Psychology, 36,* 976-987.

Gibson, C., & Guskin, E. (2017, October 17). A majority of Americans now say that sexual harassment is a "serious problem." *The Washington Post.* https://wapo.st/3uSmC9j

Gibson, J. I., & Claassen, C. (2010). Racial reconciliation in South Africa: Interracial contact. *Journal of Social Issues, 66,* 255-272.

Gibson, S. (2013). Milgram's obedience experiments: A rhetorical analysis. *British Journal of Social Psychology, 52,* 290-309.

Gibson, S. (2019). Obedience without orders: Expanding social psychology's conception of "obedience." *British Journal of Social Psychology, 58,* 241-259.

Giedinghagen, A. (2023). The tic in TikTok and (where) all systems go: Mass social media induced illness and Munchausen's by internet as explanatory models for social media associated abnormal illness behavior. *Clinical Child Psychology and Psychiatry, 28,* 270-278.

Gifford, R., & Hine, D. W. (1997). Toward cooperation in commons dilemmas. *Canadian Journal of Behavioural Science, 29,* 167-179.

Gifford, R. (2011). The dragons of inaction: Psychological barriers that limit climate change mitigation and adaptation. *American Psychologist, 66,* 290-302.

Gigerenzer, G. (2004). Dread risk, September 11, and fatal traffic accidents. *Psychological Science, 15,* 286-287.

Gigerenzer, G. (2007). *Gut feelings: The intelligence of the unconscious.* New York: Viking.

Gigerenzer, G. (2010). *Rationality for mortals: How people cope with uncertainty.* New York: Oxford University Press.

Gigone, D., & Hastie, R. (1993). The common knowledge effect: Information sharing and group judgment. *Journal of Personality and Social Psychology, 65,* 959-974.

Gilbert, D. T., & Ebert, J. E. J. (2002). *Decisions and revisions: The affective forecasting of escapable outcomes.* Unpublished manuscript, Harvard University.

Gilbert, D. T., & Hixon, J. G. (1991). The trouble of thinking: Activation and application of stereotypic beliefs. *Journal of Personality and Social Psychology, 60,* 509-517.

Gilbert, D. T., & Jones, E. E. (1986). Perceiver-induced constraint: Interpretations of self-generated reality. *Journal of Personality and Social Psychology, 50,* 269-280.

Gilbert, D. T., & Malone, P. S. (1995). The correspondence bias. *Psychological Bulletin, 117,* 21-38.

Gilbert, D. T., & Wilson, T. D. (2000). Miswanting: Some problems in the forecasting of future affective states. In J. Forgas (Ed.), *Feeling and thinking: The role of affect in social cognition.* Cambridge, England: Cambridge University Press.

Gilbert, D. T., Giesler, R. B., & Morris, K. A. (1995). When comparisons arise. *Journal of Personality and Social Psychology, 69,* 227-236.

Gilbert, D. T., Krull, D. S., & Malone, P. S. (1990). Unbelieving the unbelievable: Some problems in the rejection of false information. *Journal of Personality and Social Psychology, 59,* 601-613.

Gilbert, D. T., Lieberman, M. D., Morewedge, C. K., & Wilson, T. D. (2004). The peculiar longevity of things not so bad. *Psychological Science, 15,* 14-19.

Gilbert, D. T., Pinel, E. C., Wilson, T. D., Blumberg, S. J., & Wheatley, T. P. (1998). Immune neglect: A source of durability bias in affective forecasting. *Journal of Personality and Social Psychology, 75,* 617–638.

Gilbert, D. T., Tafarodi, R. W., & Malone, P. S. (1993). You can't not believe everything you read. *Journal of Personality and Social Psychology, 65,* 221–233.

Gildersleeve, K., Haselton, M. G., & Fales, M. R. (2014). Do women's mate preferences change across the ovulatory cycle? A meta-analytic review. *Psychological Bulletin, 140,* 1205–1259.

Gilead, M., Sela, M., & Maril, A. (2019). That's my truth: Evidence for involuntary opinion confirmation. *Social Psychological and Personality Science, 10,* 393–401.

Giletta, M., Choukas-Bradley, S., Maes, M., Linthicum, K. P., Card, N. A., & Prinstein, M. J. (2021). A meta-analysis of longitudinal peer influence effects in childhood and adolescence. *Psychological Bulletin, 147,* 719–747.

Gillath, O. M., Shaver, P. R., Baek, J.-M., & Chun, D. S. (2008). Genetic correlates of adult attachment. *Personality and Social Psychology Bulletin, 34,* 1396–1405.

Gillham, J. E., Shatte, A. J., Reivich, K. J., & Seligman, M. E. P. (2000). Optimism, pessimism, and explanatory style. In E. C. Chang (Ed.), *Optimism and pessimism.* Washington, DC: APA Books.

Gilligan, C. (1982). *In a different voice: Psychological theory and women's development.* Cambridge, MA: Harvard University Press.

Gilligan, C., Lyons, N. P., & Hanmer, T. J. (Eds.) (1990). *Making connections: The relational worlds of adolescent girls at Emma Willard School.* Cambridge, MA: Harvard University Press.

Gill, J. (2022, July 12). Analysis: Can an EU law save children from harmful content online? Reuters.com

Gilovich, T., & Eibach, R. (2001). The fundamental attribution error where it really counts. *Psychological Inquiry, 12,* 23–26.

Gilovich, T., & Kumar, A. (2015). We'll always have Paris: The hedonic payoff from experiential and material investments. In M. Zanna & J. Olson (Eds.), *Advances in experimental social psychology, 51.* New York: Elsevier.

Gilovich, T., & Medvec, V. H. (1994). The temporal pattern to the experience of regret. *Journal of Personality and Social Psychology, 67,* 357–365.

Gilovich, T., Kerr, M., & Medvec, V. H. (1993). Effect of temporal perspective on subjective confidence. *Journal of Personality and Social Psychology, 64,* 552–560.

Gilovich, T., Medvec, V. H., & Savitsky, K. (2000). The spotlight effect in social judgment: An egocentric bias in estimates of the salience of one's own actions and appearance. *Journal of Personality and Social Psychology, 78,* 211–222.

Gilovich, T., Savitsky, K., & Medvec, V. H. (1998). The illusion of transparency: Biased assessments of others' ability to read one's emotional states. *Journal of Personality and Social Psychology, 75,* 332–346.

Gilsdorf, E. (2013, January 17). Why we need violent video games. *Cognoscenti.* http://cognoscenti.wbur.org/2013/01/17/video-gamesethan-gilsdo

Giltay, E. J., Geleijnse, J. M., Zitman, F. G., Buijsse, B., & Kromhout, D. (2007). Lifestyle and dietary correlates of dispositional optimism in men: The Zutphen Elderly Study. *Journal of Psychosomatic Research, 63,* 483–490.

Giltay, E. J., Geleijnse, J. M., Zitman, F. G., Hoekstra, T., & Schouten, E. G. (2004). Dispositional optimism and all-cause and cardiovascular mortality in a prospective cohort of elderly Dutch men and women. *Archives of General Psychiatry, 61,* 1126–1135.

Gini, G., Pozzoli, T., & Hymel, S. (2014). Moral disengagement among children and youth: A meta-analytic review of links to aggressive behavior. *Aggressive Behavior, 40,* 56–68.

Gino, F., Ayal, S., & Ariely, D. (2009). Contagion and differentiation in unethical behavior: The effect of one bad apple on the barrel. *Psychological Science, 20,* 393–398.

Glasman, L. R., & Albarracin, D. (2006). Forming attitudes that predict future behavior: A meta-analysis of the attitude-behavior relation. *Psychological Bulletin, 132,* 778–822.

Glass, D. C. (1964). Changes in liking as a means of reducing cognitive discrepancies between self-esteem and aggression. *Journal of Personality, 32,* 531–549.

Gleason, M. E. J., Iida, M., Bolger, N., & Shrout, P. E. (2003). Daily supportive equity in close relationships. *Personality and Social Psychology Bulletin, 29,* 1036–1045.

Glick, P., & Fiske, S. T. (1996). The ambivalent sexism inventory: Differentiating hostile and benevolent sexism. *Journal of Personality and Social Psychology, 70,* 491–512.

Glick, P., & Fiske, S. T. (2007). Sex discrimination: The psychological approach. In F. J. Crosby, M. S. Stockdale, & S. Ropp (Eds.), *Sex discrimination in the workplace: Multidisciplinary perspectives.* Malden, MA: Blackwell.

Glick, P., & Fiske, S. T. (2011). Ambivalent sexism revisited. *Psychology of Women Quarterly, 35,* 530–535.

Glick, P., Gangl, C., Gibb, S., Klumpner, S., & Weinberg, E. (2007). Defensive reactions to masculinity threat: More negative affect toward effeminate (but not masculine) gay men. *Sex Roles, 57,* 55–59.

GLSEN. (2022). *The 2021 national school climate survey.* New York: Gay, Lesbian & Straight Education Network. glsen.org.

Gluck, J., Bluck, S., & Weststrate, N. M. (2019). More on the MORE life experience model: What we have learned (so far). *Journal of Value Inquiry, 53,* 349–370.

Gluszek, A., & Dovidio, J. F. (2010). The way *they* speak: A social psychological perspective on the stigma of nonnative accents in communication. *Personality and Social Psychology Review, 14,* 214–237.

Gnambs, T., & Appel, M. (2017). Narcissism and social networking behavior: A meta-analysis. *Journal of Personality, 86*(2), 200–212.

Gockel, C., Kerr, N. L., Seok, D-H., & Harris, D. W. (2008). Indispensability and group identification as sources of task motivation. *Journal of Experimental Social Psychology, 44,* 1316–1321.

Goethals, G. R., Messick, D. M., & Allison, S. T. (1991). The uniqueness bias: Studies of constructive social comparison. In J. Suls & T. A. Wills (Eds.), *Social comparison: Contemporary theory and research.* Hillsdale, NJ: Erlbaum.

Goetz, J. L., Keltner, D., & Simon-Thomas, E. (2010). Compassion: An evolutionary analysis and empirical review. *Psychological Bulletin, 136,* 351–374.

Goggin, W. C., & Range, L. M. (1985). The disadvantages of hindsight in the perception of suicide. *Journal of Social and Clinical Psychology, 3,* 232–237.

Goldbaum, C., Stack, L., & Traub, A. (2020, June 2). After peaceful protests, looters strike at Macy's and across Midtown. *The New York Times.* https://www.nytimes.com/2020/06/02/nyregion/nyc-looting-protests.html

Goldberg, M. H., van der Linden, S., Leiserowitz, A., & Maibach, E. (2020). Perceived social consensus can reduce ideological biases on climate change. *Environment and Behavior, 52,* 495–517.

Goldman, S. K. (2012). Effects of the 2008 Obama presidential campaign on White racial prejudice. *Public Opinion Quarterly, 76,* 663–687.

Goldman, W., & Lewis, P. (1977). Beautiful is good: Evidence that the physically attractive are more socially skillful. *Journal of Experimental Social Psychology, 13,* 125–130.

Goldstein, A. P. (1994). Delinquent gangs. In A. P. Goldstein, B. Harootunian, & J. C. Conoley (Eds.), *Student aggression: Prevention, control, and replacement.* New York: Guilford.

Goldstein, D. (2019, April 20). 20 years after Columbine, schools have gotten safer. But fears have only grown. *The New York Times.* https://www.nytimes.com/2019/04/20/us/columbine-anniversary-school-violence-statistics.html?

Goldstein, J. H., & Arms, R. L. (1971). Effects of observing athletic contests on hostility. *Sociometry, 34,* 83–90.

Gómez, Á., Brooks, M. L., Buhrmeister, M. D., Váquez, A., Jetten, J., & Swann, Jr., W. B. (2011). On the nature of identity fusion: Insights into the construct and a new measure. *Journal of Personality and Social Psychology, 100,* 918–933.

Goncy, E. A., Basting, E. J., & Dunn, C. B. (2021). A meta-analysis linking parent-to-child aggression and dating abuse during adolescence and young adulthood. *Trauma, Violence, & Abuse, 22,* 1248–1261.

Gonsalkorale, K., & Williams, K. D. (2006). The KKK would not let me play: Ostracism even by a despised outgroup hurts. *European Journal of Social Psychology, 36,* 1–11.

Gonsalves, B., Reber, P. J., Gitelman, D. R., Parrish, T. B., Mesulam, M.-M., & Paller, K. A. (2004). Neural evidence that vivid imagining can lead to false remembering. *Psychological Science, 15,* 655–659.

Gönül, B., Sahin, A. B., & Killen, M. (2023). Perceived contact with friends from lower socioeconomic status reduces exclusion based on social class. *Developmental Science.*

Gonzaga, G. C., Campos, B., & Bradbury, T. (2007). Similarity, convergence, and relationship satisfaction in dating and married couples. *Journal of Personality and Social Psychology, 93,* 34–48.

Gonzaga, G. C., Keltner, D., Londahl, E. A., & Smith, M. D. (2001). Love and the commitment problem in romantic relations and friendship. *Journal of Personality and Social Psychology, 81,* 247–262.

Gonzalez-Barrera, A., & Connor, P. (2019, March 14). Around the world, more say immigrants are a strength than a burden. *Pew Research Center.* https://blogs.worldbank.org/peoplemove/around-world-more-say-immigrants-are-strength-burden

Gonzalez-Franco, M., Slater, M., Birney, M. E., Swapp, D., Haslam, S. A., & Reicher, S. D. (2018). Participant concerns for the Learner in a virtual reality replication of the Milgram obedience study. *PLOS ONE, 13*(12), e0209704.

González, K. V., Verkuyten, M., Weesie, J., & Poppe, E. (2008). Prejudice towards Muslims in the Netherlands: Testing integrated threat theory. *British Journal of Social Psychology, 47,* 667–685.

Good, A., Choma, B., & Russo, F. A. (2017). Movement synchrony influences intergroup relations in a minimal groups paradigm. *Basic and Applied Social Psychology, 39,* 231–238.

Goode, E., & Schwartz, J. (2011, August 28). Police lineups start to face fact: Eyes can lie. *The New York Times.* https://www.nytimes.com/2011/08/29/us/29witness.html

Goodhart, D. E. (1986). The effects of positive and negative thinking on performance in an achievement situation. *Journal of Personality and Social Psychology, 51,* 117–124.

Goodsell, C. A., Gronlund, S. D., & Carlson, C. A. (2010). Exploring the sequential lineup advantage using WITNESS. *Law and Human Behavior, 34,* 445–459.

Gordijn, E. H., De Vries, N. K., & De Dreu, C. K. W. (2002). Minority influence on focal and related attitudes: Change in size, attributions and information processing. *Personality and Social Psychology Bulletin, 28,* 1315–1326.

Gordon, A. M., & Chen, S. (2016). Do you get where I'm coming from? Perceived understanding buffers against the negative impact of conflict on relationship satisfaction. *Journal of Personality and Social Psychology, 110,* 239–260.

Gordon, R. A. (1996). Impact of ingratiation on judgments and evaluations: A meta-analytic investigation. *Journal of Personality and Social Psychology, 71,* 54–70.

Gore, A. (2007, July 1). Moving beyond Kyoto. *The New York Times.* www.nytimes.com

Gorman, J. (2012, December 17). In Vietnam, ancient bones tell a story of compassion. *The New York Times.* https://bit.ly/2OFRyJP

Gorrese, A., & Ruggieri, R. (2012). Peer attachment: A meta-analytic review of gender and age differences and associations with parent attachment. *Journal of Youth and Adolescence, 41,* 650–672.

Górska, P., van Zomeren, M., & Bilewicz, M. (2017). Intergroup contact as the missing link between LGB rights and sexual prejudice. *Social Psychology,* 48, 321–334.

Gotlib, I. H., & Colby, C. A. (1988). How to have a good quarrel. In P. Marsh (Ed.), *Eye to eye: How people interact.* Topsfield, MA: Salem House.

Gottlieb, J., & Carver, C. S. (1980). Anticipation of future interaction and the bystander effect. *Journal of Experimental Social Psychology, 16,* 253–260.

Gottman, J. (2005, April 14). The mathematics of love. *Edge.* https://www.edge.org/conversation/john_gottman-the-mathematics-of-love

Gottman, J. M. (1998). Psychology and the study of marital processes. *Annual Review of Psychology, 49,* 169–197.

Gottman, J. (with N. Silver). (1994). *Why marriages succeed or fail.* New York: Simon & Schuster.

Gough, H. G., & Thorne, A. (1986). Positive, negative, and balanced shyness. In W. H. Jones, J. M. Cheek, & S. R. Briggs (Eds.), *Shyness: Perspectives on research and treatment.* New York: Plenum.

Gough, S. (2003). A word from our founder Stephen Gough. Naked Rambler Organisation. http://www.nakedrambler.org/about_us.html

Gouldner, A. W. (1960). The norm of reciprocity: A preliminary statement. *American Sociological Review, 25*(2), 161–178.

Gove, W. R., Style, C. B., & Hughes, M. (1990). The effect of marriage on the well-being of adults: A theoretical analysis. *Journal of Family Issues, 11,* 4–35.

Gracia, P., Garcia-Roman, J., Oinas, T., & Anttila, T. (2022). Gender differences in child and adolescent daily activities: A cross-national time use study. *Acta Sociologica, 65,* 41–65.

Graf, S., Paolini, S., & Rubin, M. (2014). Negative intergroup contact is more influential, but positive intergroup contact is more common: Assessing contact prominence and contact prevalence in five Central European countries. *European Journal of Social Psychology, 44,* 536–547.

Graham, J., Nosek, B. A., & Haidt, J. (2012, December 12). The moral stereotypes of liberals and conservatives: Exaggeration of differences across the political spectrum. *PLOS ONE, 7,* e50092.

Graham, R., & Stack, L. (2021, May 26). U.S. faces outbreak of anti-Semitic threats and violence. *New York Times.*

Gramlich, J. (2020, February 11). Democrats, Republicans each expect made-up news to target their own party more than the other in 2020. *Pew Research Center.* https://www.pewresearch.org/fact-tank/2020/02/11/democrats-republicans-each-expect-made-up-news-to-target-their-own-party-more-than-the-other-in-2020/

Gramling, C. (2019, August 17). Current warming is unprecedented. *Science News.* https://bit.ly/38G5NFS

Granberg, D., & Bartels, B. (2005). On being a lone dissenter. *Journal of Applied Social Psychology, 35,* 1849–1858.

Granstrom, K., & Stiwne, D. (1998). A bipolar model of groupthink: An expansion of Janis's concept. *Small Group Research, 29,* 32–56.

Grant, A. (2013, July 20). Why men need women. *The New York Times.* https://www.nytimes.com/2013/07/21/opinion/sunday/why-men-need-women.html

Grant, A. (2017, November 4). Kids, would you please start fighting? *The New York Times.* https://www.nytimes.com/2017/11/04/opinion/sunday/kids-would-you-please-start-fighting.html

Grant, D. (2017). The ballot order effect is huge: evidence from Texas. *Public Choice, 172*(3/4), 421–442.

Grant, N. K., Krieger, L. R., Nemirov, H., Fabrigar, L. R., & Norris, M. E. (2022). I'll scratch your back if you give me a compliment: Exploring psychological mechanisms underlying compliments' effects on compliance. *British Journal of Social Psychology, 61,* 37–54.

Grant, S., Perlman, M. D., & Grant, D. (2020). Targeted testing for bias in order assignment, with an application to Texas election ballots. *Journal of Statistical Planning & Inference, 206,* 12–28.

Grapsas, S., Brummelman, E., Dufner, M., & Denissen, J. J. A. (2022). Affective contingencies of narcissism. *Journal of Personality and Social Psychology, 123,* 444–462.

Grassini, S. (2022). A Systematic Review and Meta-Analysis of Nature Walk as an Intervention for Anxiety and Depression. *Journal of Clinical Medicine, 11.*

Gray, J. D., & Silver, R. C. (1990). Opposite sides of the same coin: Former spouses' divergent perspectives in coping with their divorce. *Journal of Personality and Social Psychology, 59,* 1180–1191.

Greenaway, K. H., & Cruwys, T. (2019). The source model of group threat: Responding to internal and external threats. *American Psychologist, 74,* 218–231.

Greenaway, K. H., Cruwys, T., Haslam, S. A., & Jetten, J. (2016). Social identities promote well-being because they satisfy global psychological needs. *European Journal of Social Psychology, 46,* 294–307.

Greenberg, D. M., Warrier, V., Abu-Akel, A., Allison, C., Gajos, K. Z., Reinecke, K., Rentfrow, P. J., Radecki, M. A., & Baron-Cohen, S. (2023). Sex and age differences in "theory of mind" across 57 countries using the English version of the "Reading the Mind in the Eyes" Test. *PNAS Proceedings of the National Academy of Sciences of the United States of America, 120,* 1–12.

Greenberg, J. (1986). Differential intolerance for inequity from organizational and individual agents. *Journal of Applied Social Psychology, 16,* 191–196.

Green, C. W., Adams, A. M., & Turner, C. W. (1988). Development and validation of the school interracial climate scale. *American Journal of Community Psychology, 16,* 241–259.

Green, D. P., & Wong, J. S. (2008). Tolerance and the contact hypothesis: A field experiment. In E. Borgida (Ed.), *The political psychology of democratic citizenship.* London: Oxford University Press.

Greene, E., Flynn, M. S., & Loftus, E. F. (1982). Inducing resistance to misleading information. *Journal of Verbal Learning & Verbal Behavior, 21,* 207–219.

Greenfield, P. M. (2013). The changing psychology of culture from 1800 through 2000. *Psychological Science, 24,* 1722–1731.

Green, P. (2017, August 10). Anger rooms are all the rage. Timidly, we gave one a whack. *The New York Times.* https://www.nytimes.com/2017/08/09/style/anger-rooms-the-wrecking-club.html

Greenwald, A. G., & Banaji, M. R. (2017). The implicit revolution: Reconceiving the relation between conscious and unconscious. *American Psychologist, 72,* 861–871.

Greenwald, A. G., & Pettigrew, T. F. (2014). With malice toward none and charity for some: Ingroup favoritism enables discrimination. *American Psychologist, 69,* 669–684.

Greenwald, A. G. (1975). On the inconclusiveness of crucial cognitive tests of dissonance versus self-perception theories. *Journal of Experimental Social Psychology, 11,* 490–499.

Greenwald, A. G. (1980). The totalitarian ego: Fabrication and revision of personal history. *American Psychologist, 35,* 603–618.

Greenwald, A. G. (1992). *Subliminal semantic activation and subliminal snake oil.* Paper presented to the American Psychological Association Convention, Washington, DC.

Greenwald, A. G., Banaji, M. R., & Nosek, B. A. (2015). Statistically small effects of the implicit association test can have societally large effects. *Journal of Personality and Social Psychology, 108,* 553–561.

Greenwald, A. G., Nosek, B. A., & Banaji, M. R. (2003). Understanding and using the implicit association test: I. An improved scoring algorithm. *Journal of Personality and Social Psychology, 85,* 197–216.

Greenwald, G. (2012, March 19). Discussing the motives of the Afghan shooter: The contrast is glaring in how we talk about violence by Americans versus violence toward Americans. *Salon.* https://www.salon.com/2012/03/19/discussing_the_motives_of_the_afghan_shooter/

Greitemeyer, T., & McLatchie, N. (2011). Denying humanness to others: A newly discovered mechanism by which violent video games increase aggressive behavior. *Psychological Science, 22,* 659–665.

Greitemeyer, T., & Mugge, D. O. (2014). Video games do affect social outcomes: A meta-analytic review of the effects of violent and prosocial video game play. *Personality and Social Psychology Bulletin, 40,* 578–589.

Greitemeyer, T., & Osswald, S. (2010). Effects of prosocial video games on prosocial behavior. *Journal of Personality and Social Psychology, 98,* 211–221.

Greitemeyer, T., & Sagioglou, C. (2016). Subjective socioeconomic status causes aggression: A test of the theory of social deprivation. *Journal of Personality and Social Psychology, 111,* 178–194.

Greitemeyer, T., & Sagioglou, C. (2019). The experience of deprivation: Does relative more than absolute status predict hostility? *British Journal of Social Psychology, 58,* 515–533.

Greitemeyer, T. (2009a). Effects of songs with prosocial lyrics on prosocial thoughts, affect, and behavior. *Journal of Experimental Social Psychology, 45,* 186–190.

Greitemeyer, T. (2009b). Effects of songs with prosocial lyrics on prosocial behavior: Further evidence and a mediating mechanism. *Personality and Social Psychology Bulletin, 35,* 1500–1511.

Greitemeyer, T. (2009c). Effects of songs with prosocial lyrics on prosocial thoughts, affect, and behavior. *Journal of Experimental Social Psychology, 45,* 186–190.

Greitemeyer, T. (2011). Exposure to music with prosocial lyrics reduces aggression: First evidence and test of the underlying mechanism. *Journal of Experimental Social Psychology, 47,* 28–36.

Greitemeyer, T. (2014). Intense acts of violence during video game play make daily life aggression appear innocuous: A new mechanism why violent video games increase aggression. *Journal of Experimental Social Psychology, 50,* 52–56.

Greitemeyer, T., Agthe, M., Turner, R., & Gschwendtner, C. (2012). Acting prosocially reduces retaliation: Effects of prosocial video games on aggressive behavior. *European Journal of Social Psychology, 42,* 235–242.

Greitemeyer, T., Osswald, S., & Brauer, M. (2010). Playing prosocial games increases empathy and decreases Schadenfreude. *Emotion, 10,* 796–802.

Grieshaber, K. (2023, June 27). Germany saw 2,480 antisemitic incidents in 2022, monitoring group says. Associated Press.

Griffith, S. (2012, February 1). Hold the extra burgers and fries when people pleasers arrive. *Think blog.* blog.case.edu

Griffitt, W., & Veitch, R. (1971). Hot and crowded: Influences of population density and temperature on interpersonal affective behavior. *Journal of Personality and Social Psychology, 17,* 92–98.

Griffitt, W. (1970). Environmental effects on interpersonal affective behavior. Ambient effective temperature and attraction. *Journal of Personality and Social Psychology, 15,* 240–244.

Griffitt, W. (1987). Females, males, and sexual responses. In K. Kelley (Ed.), *Females, males, and sexuality: Theories and research.* Albany: State University of New York Press.

Griggs, R. A. (2015). The disappearance of independence in textbook coverage of Asch's social pressure experiments. *Teaching of Psychology, 42,* 137–142.

Griggs, R. A., Blyler, J., & Jackson, S. L. (2021). Using research ethics as a springboard for teaching Milgram's obedience study as a contentious classic. *Scholarship of Teaching and Learning in Psychology, 6*(4), 350–356.

Grigoryan, L., Seo, S., Simunovic, D., & Hofmann, W. (2023). Helping the ingroup versus harming the outgroup: Evidence from morality-based groups. *Journal of Experimental Social Psychology, 105,* 1–10.

Grinshteyn, E., & Hemenway, D. (2016). Violent death rates: The US compared with other high-income OECD countries, 2010. *American Journal of Medicine, 129,* 266–273.

Griskevicius, V., Tybur, J. M., Gangestad, S. W., Perea, E. F., Shapiro, J. R., & Kenrick, D. T. (2009). Aggress to impress: Hostility as an evolved context-dependent strategy. *Journal of Personality and Social Psychology, 96,* 980–994.

Groenenboom, A., Wilke, H. A. M., & Wit, A. P. (2001). Will we be working together again? The impact of future interdependence on group members' task motivation. *European Journal of Social Psychology, 31,* 369–378.

Gronlund, S. D. (2004a). Sequential lineups: Shift in criterion or decision strategy? *Journal of Applied Psychology, 89,* 362–368.

Gronlund, S. D. (2004b). Sequential lineup advantage: Contributions of distinctiveness and recollection. *Applied Cognitive Psychology, 19,* 23–37.

Gross, A. E., & Crofton, C. (1977). What is good is beautiful. *Sociometry, 40,* 85–90.

Gross, J. T. (2001). *Neighbors: The destruction of the Jewish community in Jedwabne, Poland.* Princeton: Princeton University Press.

Grossmann, I., & Varnum, M. E. W. (2015). Social structure, infectious diseases, disasters, secularism, and cultural change in America. *Psychological Science, 26,* 311–324.

Grossman, S. (2014, February 16). 1 in 4 Americans apparently unaware the Earth orbits the Sun. *Time.* http://time.com/7809/1-in-4-americans-thinks-sun-orbits-earth/

Gross, T. F. (2009). Own-ethnicity bias in the recognition of Black, East Asian, Hispanic, and White faces. *Basic and Applied Social Psychology, 31,* 128–135.

Grote, N. K., & Clark, M. S. (2001). Perceiving unfairness in the family: Cause or consequence of marital distress? *Journal of Personality and Social Psychology, 80,* 281–293.

Grotzinger, A. D., Mann, F. D., Patterson, M. W., Tackett, J. L., Tucker-Drob, E. M., & Harden, K. P. (2018). Hair and salivary testosterone, hair cortisol, and externalizing behaviors in adolescents. *Psychological Science, 29,* 688–699.

Grove, J. R., Hanrahan, S. J., & McInman, A. (1991). Success/failure bias in attributions across involvement categories in sport. *Personality and Social Psychology Bulletin, 17,* 93–97.

Grover, S., & Helliwell, J. F. (2019). How's life at home? New evidence on marriage and the set point for happiness. *Journal of Happiness Studies, 20,* 373–390.

Groves, C. L., & Anderson, C. A. (2018). Aversive events and aggression. *Current Opinion in Psychology, 19,* 144–148.

Groves, C. L., Plante, C., Anderson, C. A., & Allen, J. J. (2021). Rabbit ears to virtual reality: A comprehensive meta-analysis of sixty years of media violence research. Manuscript under review.

Groves, K. S. (2020). Testing a moderated mediation model of transformational leadership, values, and organization change. *Journal of Leadership & Organizational Studies, 27,* 35–48.

Grove, W. M., Zald, D. H., Lebow, B. S., Snitz, B. E., & Nelson, C. (2000). Clinical versus mechanical prediction: A meta-analysis. *Psychological Assessment, 12,* 19–30.

Grubbs, J. B., Kraus, S. W., & Perry, S. L. (2019). Self-reported addiction to pornography in a nationally representative sample: The roles of use habits, religiousness, and moral incongruence. *Journal of Behavioral Addictions, 8,* 88–93.

Grube, J. W., Kleinhesselink, R. R., & Kearney, K. A. (1982). Male self-acceptance and attraction toward women. *Personality and Social Psychology Bulletin, 8,* 107–112.

Gruendl, M. (2005, accessed December 14). Virtual Miss Germany. *Beautycheck.* https://bit.ly/3cL5zh5

Gruman, J. C., & Sloan, R. P. (1983). Disease as justice: Perceptions of the victims of physical illness. *Basic and Applied Social Psychology, 4,* 39–46.

Grzyb, T., & Dolinski, D. (2023). You and I are alike, so I will hold back—The effect of directed empathy on the behavior of participants of Stanley Milgram's obedience paradigm. *Acta Psychologica, 234,* 103859.

Gudjonsson, G. H. (2021). The science-based pathways to understanding false confessions and wrongful convictions. *Frontiers in Psychology, 12.*

Guerin, B. (1993). *Social facilitation.* Paris: Cambridge University Press.

Guerin, B. (1999). Social behaviors as determined by different arrangements of social consequences: Social loafing, social facilitation, deindividuation, and a modified social loafing. *The Psychological Record, 49,* 565–578.

Guevara Beltran, D., Shiota, M. N., & Aktipis, A. (2023). Empathic concern motivates willingness to help in the absence of interdependence. *Emotion.*

Guffler, K., & Wagner, U. (2017). Backfire of good intentions: Unexpected long-term contact intervention effects in an intractable conflict area. *Peace and Conflict: Journal of Peace Psychology, 23,* 383–391.

Guimond, S., Dambrun, N., Michinov, N., & Duarte, S. (2003). Does social dominance generate prejudice? Integrating individual and contextual determinants of intergroup cognitions. *Journal of Personality and Social Psychology, 84,* 697–721.

Guinote, A. (2017). How power affects people: Activating, wanting, and goal seeking. *Annual Review of Psychology, 68,* 353–381.

Gul, P., Cross, S. E., & Uskul, A. K. (2021). Implications of culture of honor theory and research for practitioners and prevention researchers. *American Psychologist, 76,* 502–515.

Gupta, M. D. (2017, September). Return of the missing daughters. *Scientific American,* pp. 78–85.

Gupta, U., & Singh, P. (1982). Exploratory study of love and liking and type of marriages. *Indian Journal of Applied Psychology, 19,* 92–97.

Güss, C. D., & Tuason, M. T. (2021). Individualism and egalitarianism can kill: How cultural values predict coronavirus deaths across the globe. *Frontiers in Psychology, 12.*

Gustafsson, P. U., Lindholm, T., & Jönsson, F. U. (2019). Predicting accuracy in eyewitness testimonies with memory retrieval effort and confidence. *Frontiers in Psychology, 10,* 703.

Gutenbrunner, L., & Wagner, U. (2016). Perspective-taking techniques in the mediation of intergroup conflict. *Peace and Conflict: Journal of Peace Psychology, 22,* 298–305.

Haas, B. W., Abney, D. H., Eriksson, K., Potter, J., & Gosling, S. D. (2023). Person-culture personality fit: Dispositional traits and cultural context explain country-level personality profile conformity. *Social Psychological and Personality Science, 14*(3), 275–285.

Habashi, M. M., Graziano, W. G., & Hoover, A. E. (2016). Searching for the prosocial personality: A big five approach to linking personality and prosocial behavior. *Personality and Social Psychology Bulletin, 42,* 1177–1192.

Hacker, H. M. (1951). Women as a minority group. *Social Forces, 30,* 60–69.

Hackman, J. R. (1986). The design of work teams. In J. Lorsch (Ed.), *Handbook of organizational behavior.* Englewood Cliffs, NJ: Prentice-Hall.

Haddock, G., & Zanna, M. P. (1994). Preferring "housewives" to "feminists." *Psychology of Women Quarterly, 18,* 25–52.

Haddock, G., Maio, G. R., Arnold, K., & Huskinson, T. (2008). Should persuasion be affective or cognitive? The moderating effects of need for affect and need for cognition. *Personality and Social Psychology Bulletin, 34,* 769–778.

Haeffel, G. J., Gibb, B. E., Metalsky, G. I., Alloy, L. B., Abramson, L. Y., Hankin, B. L., Joiner, T. E., Jr., & Swendsen, J. D. (2008). Measuring cognitive vulnerability to depression: Development and validation of the cognitive style questionnaire. *Clinical Psychology Review, 28,* 824–836.

Haemmerlie, F. M., & Montgomery, R. L. (1982). Self-perception theory and unobtrusively biased interactions: A treatment for heterosocial anxiety. *Journal of Counseling Psychology, 29,* 362–370.

Haemmerlie, F. M., & Montgomery, R. L. (1984). Purposefully biased interventions: Reducing heterosocial anxiety through self-perception theory. *Journal of Personality and Social Psychology, 47,* 900–908.

Haemmerlie, F. M., & Montgomery, R. L. (1986). Self-perception theory and the treatment of shyness. In W. H. Jones, J. M. Cheek, & S. R. Briggs (Eds.), *A sourcebook on shyness: Research and treatment.* New York: Plenum.

Hafer, A., & Jacquin, K. M. (2022). The impact of victim and offender military association and gender on judgments in a rape trial. *American Journal of Forensic Psychology, 40,* 5–34.

Hafer, C. L., & Rubel, A. N. (2015). The why and how of defending belief in a just world. *Advances in Experimental Social Psychology, 51,* 41–96.

Hafer, C.L., & Sutton, R. (2016). Belief in a just world. In C. Sabbagh & M. Schmitt (Eds.), *Handbook of social justice theory and research.* New York: Springer.

Hagerty, M. R. (2000). Social comparisons of income in one's community: Evidence from national surveys of income and happiness. *Journal of Personality and Social Psychology, 78,* 764–771.

Hagger, M. S., Cheung, M. W.-L., Ajzen, I., & Hamilton, K. (2022). Perceived behavioral control moderating effects in the theory of planned behavior: A meta-analysis. *Health Psychology, 41,* 155–167.

Hahn, A., & Gawronski, B. (2019). Facing one's implicit biases: From awareness to acknowledgment. *Journal of Personality and Social Psychology, 116,* 769–794.

Hahn, A., Banchefsky, S., Park, B., & Judd, C. M. (2015). Measuring intergroup ideologies: Positive and negative aspects of emphasizing versus looking beyond group differences. *Personality and Social Psychology Bulletin, 41,* 1646–1664.

Haidt, J. (2003). The moral emotions. In R. J. Davidson (Ed.), *Handbook of affective sciences.* Oxford: Oxford University Press.

Haidt, J. (2006). *The happiness hypothesis: Finding modern truth in ancient wisdom.* Basic Books.

Haines, E. L., Deaux, K., & Lofaro, N. (2016). The times they are a-changing . . . or are they not? A comparison of gender stereotypes, 1983–2014. *Psychology of Women Quarterly, 40,* 353–363.

Haines, M. P. (1996). *A social norms approach to preventing binge drinking at colleges and universities* [PDF file]. Higher Education Center for Alcohol and Other Drug Prevention. http://www.socialnormsresources.org/pdf/socnormapproach.pdf

Hakim, N. H., Zhao, X., & Bharj, N. (2020). The paradox of the moderate Muslim discourse: Subtyping promotes support for anti-Muslim policies. *Frontiers in Psychology, 11.*

Halberstadt, A. G., & Saitta, M. B. (1987). Gender, nonverbal behavior, and perceived dominance: A test of the theory. *Journal of Personality and Social Psychology, 53,* 257–272.

Halberstadt, A. G., Cooke, A. N., Garner, P. W., Hughes, S. A., Oertwig, D., & Neupert, S. D. (2022). Racialized emotion recognition accuracy and anger bias of children's faces. *Emotion, 22,* 403–417.

Halberstadt, J. (2006). The generality and ultimate origins of the attractiveness of prototypes. *Personality and Social Psychology Review, 10,* 166–183.

Halbrook, Y. J., O'Donnell, A. T., & Msetfi, R. M. (2019). When and how video games can be good: A review of the positive effects of video games on well-being. *Perspectives on Psychological Science, 14,* 1096–1104.

Hald, G. M., & Malamuth, N. N. (2015). Experimental effects of exposure to pornography: The moderating effect of personality and mediating effect of sexual arousal. *Archives of Sexual Behavior, 44,* 99–109.

Hales, A. H., McIntyre, M. M., Rudert, S. C., Williams, K. D., & Thomas, H. (2020). Ostracized and observed: The presence of an audience affects the experience of being excluded. *Self and Identity, 20*(1), 1–22.

Halevy, N., Berso, Y., & Galinsky, A. D. (2011). The mainstream is not electable: When vision triumphs over representativeness in leader emergence and effectiveness. *Personality and Social Psychology Bulletin, 37,* 893–904.

Halfmann, E., Bredehöft, J., & Häusser, J. A. (2020). Replicating roaches: A preregistered direct replication of Zajonc, Heingartner, and Herman's (1969) social-facilitation study. *Psychological Science, 31,* 332–337.

Halford, J. T., & Hsu, H.-C. (2014). *Beauty is wealth: CEO appearance and shareholder value* [PDF file]. China International Conference in Finance. http://www.cicfconf.org/sites/default/files/paper_868.pdf

Halko, M-L., Kaustia, M., & Alanko, E. (2012). The gender effect in risky asset holdings. *Journal of Economic Behavior and Organization, 83,* 66–81.

Hall, C. C., Zhao, J., & Shafir, E. (2014). Self-affirmation among the poor: Cognitive and behavioral implications. *Psychological Science, 25,* 619–625.

Hall, J. A., & Pennington, N. (2013). Self-monitoring, honesty, and cue use on Facebook: The relationship with user extraversion and conscientiousness. *Computers in Human Behavior, 29,* 1556–1564.

Hall, J. A. (1984). *Nonverbal sex differences: Communication accuracy and expressive style.* Baltimore: Johns Hopkins University Press.

Hall, J. A. (2006). Nonverbal behavior, status, and gender: How do we understand their relations? *Psychology of Women Quarterly, 30,* 384–391.

Hall, K. D., & Kahan, S. (2018). Maintenance of lost weight and long-term management of obesity. *Medical Clinics of North America, 102,* 183–197.

Hall, K. M., Knudson, S. T., Wright, J., Charlifue, S. W., Graves, D. E., & Warner, P. (1999). Follow-up study of individuals with high tetraplegia (C1-C4) 14 to 24 years postinjury. *Archives of Physical Medicine and Rehabilitation, 80,* 1507–1513.

Hamberger, J., & Hewstone, M. (1997). Inter-ethnic contact as a predictor of blatant and subtle prejudice: Tests of a model in four West European nations. *British Journal of Social Psychology, 36,* 173–190.

Hamermesh, D. S. (2011). *Beauty pays: Why attractive people are more successful.* Princeton, NJ: Princeton University Press.

Hamermesh, D. S., Gordon, R. A., & Crosnoe, R. (2023). "O youth and beauty:" children's looks and children's cognitive development. *Journal of Economic Behavior & Organization, 212,* 275–289.

Hamilton, D. L., & Gifford, R. K. (1976). Illusory correlation in interpersonal perception: A cognitive basis of stereotypic judgments. *Journal of Experimental Social Psychology, 12,* 392–407.

Hamilton, D. L., & Rose, T. L. (1980). Illusory correlation and the maintenance of stereotypical beliefs. *Journal of Personality and Social Psychology, 39*(5), 832–845.

Hamilton, L. (2022, April 25). Conspiracy vs. Science: A Survey of U.S. Public Beliefs. University of New Hampshire Carsey School of Public Policy.

Hammond, M. D., & Overall, N. C. (2013). Men's hostile sexism and biased perceptions of intimate partners: Fostering dissatisfaction and negative behavior in close relationships. *Personality and Social Psychology Bulletin, 39,* 1585–1599.

Hampson, R. B. (1984). Adolescent prosocial behavior: Peer-group and situational factors associated with helping. *Journal of Personality and Social Psychology, 46,* 153–162.

Hampton, K., Rainie, L., Lu, W., Dwyer, M., Shin, I., & Purcell, K. (2014, August 26). Social media and the "spiral of silence." *Pew Research Center.* https://www.pewresearch.org/internet/2014/08/26/social-media-and-the-spiral-of-silence/

Han, D. E., & Laurent, S. M. (2023). Beautiful seems good, but perhaps not in every way: Linking attractiveness to moral evaluation through perceived vanity. *Journal of Personality and Social Psychology, 124,* 264–286.

Hanel, P. H. P., Maio, G. R., & Manstead, A. S. R. (2019). A new way to look at the data: Similarities between groups of people are large and important. *Journal of Personality and Social Psychology, 116,* 541–562.

Haney, C., & Logan, D. D. (1994). Broken promise: The Supreme Court's response to social science research on capital punishment. *Journal of Social Issues, 50,* 75–101.

Haney, C. (1991). The fourteenth amendment and symbolic legality: Let them eat due process. *Law and Human Behavior, 15,* 183–204.

Haney, C., Zurbriggen, E. L., & Weill, J. M. (2022). The continuing unfairness of death qualification: Changing death penalty attitudes and capital jury selection. *Psychology, Public Policy, and Law, 28,* 1–31.

Han, K., & Kim, M. Y. (2022). Mechanism of the better-than-average effect in moral issues: Asymmetrical causal attribution across moral (vs. immoral) contexts. *Acta Psychologica, 226,* 103575.

Hanniball, K. B., Aknin, L. B., Douglas, K. S., & Viljoen, J. L. (2019). Does helping promote well-being in at-risk youth and ex-offender samples? *Journal of Experimental Social Psychology, 82,* 307–317.

Hansen, D. E., Vandenberg, B., & Patterson, M. L. (1995). The effects of religious orientation on spontaneous and nonspontaneous helping behaviors. *Personality and Individual Differences, 19,* 101–104.

Hansen, J., & Wänke, M. (2009). Liking what's familiar: The importance of unconscious familiarity in the mere-exposure effect. *Social Cognition, 27,* 161–182.

Hansen, J., Hanewinkel, R., & Morgenstern, M. (2020). Electronic cigarette advertising and teen smoking initiation. *Addictive Behaviors, 103,* 106243.

Hans, V. P., Mott, N. L., & Munsterman, G. T. (2002). *Are hung juries a problem?* Williamsburg, VA: National Center for State Courts.

Harbaugh, W. T., Mayr, U., & Burghart, D. R. (2007). Neural responses to taxation and voluntary giving reveal motives for charitable donations. *Science, 316,* 1622–1625.

Harber, K. D. (1998). Feedback to minorities: Evidence of a positive bias. *Journal of Personality and Social Psychology, 74,* 622–628.

Harber, K. D., Stafford, R., & Kennedy, K. A. (2010). The positive feedback bias as a response to a self-image threat. *Journal of Social Psychology, 49,* 207–218.

Hardin, G. (1968). The tragedy of the commons. *Science, 162,* 1243–1248.

Harding, L. (2022, March 4). Demoralised Russian soldiers tell of anger at being 'duped' into war. *The Guardian.*

Hardy, C., & Latané, B. (1986). Social loafing on a cheering task. *Social Science, 71,* 165–172.

Hardy, C. L., & Van Vugt, M. (2006). Nice guys finish first: The competitive altruism hypothesis. *Personality and Social Psychology Bulletin, 32,* 1402–1413.

Haritos-Fatouros, M. (1988). The official torturer: A learning model for obedience to the authority of violence. *Journal of Applied Social Psychology, 18,* 1107–1120.

Haritos-Fatouros, M. (2002). *Psychological origins of institutionalized torture.* New York: Routledge.

Harkins, S. G., & Jackson, J. M. (1985). The role of evaluation in eliminating social loafing. *Personality and Social Psychology Bulletin, 11,* 457–465.

Harkins, S. G., & Petty, R. E. (1982). Effects of task difficulty and task uniqueness on social loafing. *Journal of Personality and Social Psychology, 43,* 1214–1229.

Harkins, S. G., & Petty, R. E. (1987). Information utility and the multiple source effect. *Journal of Personality and Social Psychology, 52,* 260–268.

Harkins, S. G., Latané, B., & Williams, K. (1980). Social loafing: Allocating effort or taking it easy? *Journal of Experimental Social Psychology, 16,* 457–465.

Harkness, K. L., Sabbagh, M. A., Jacobson, J. A., Chowdrey, N. K., & Chen, T. (2005). Enhanced accuracy of mental state decoding in dysphoric college students. *Cognition & Emotion, 19,* 999–1025.

Harmon-Jones, E., & Allen, J. J. B. (2001). The role of affect in the mere exposure effect: Evidence from psychophysiological and individual differences approaches. *Personality and Social Psychology Bulletin, 27,* 889–898.

Harmon-Jones, E., Gerdjikov, T., & Harmon-Jones, C. (2008). The effect of induced compliance on relative left frontal cortical activity: A test of the action-based model of dissonance. *European Journal of Social Psychology, 38,* 35–45.

Harries, K. D., & Stadler, S. J. (1988). Heat and violence: New findings from Dallas field data, 1980–1981. *Journal of Applied Social Psychology, 18,* 129–138.

Harris, C. R., Jenkins, M., & Glaser, D. (2006). Gender differences in risk assessment: Why do women take fewer risks than men? *Judgment and Decision Making, 1,* 48–63.

Harris, J. R. (1996). Quoted from an article by Jerome Burne for the *Manchester Observer* (via Harris: 72073.1211@CompuServe.com).

Harris, J. R. (1998). *The nurture assumption.* New York: Free Press.

Harris, J. R. (2007). *No two alike: Human nature and human individuality.* New York: Norton.

Harris, L. T., & Fiske, S. T. (2006). Dehumanizing the lowest of the low: Neuroimaging responses to extreme out-groups. *Psychological Science, 17*(10), 847–853.

Harris, M. A., & Orth, U. (2020). The link between self-esteem and social relationships: A meta-analysis of longitudinal studies. *Journal of Personality and Social Psychology, 119,* 1459–1477.

Harris, M. J., & Rosenthal, R. (1985). Mediation of interpersonal expectancy effects: 31 meta-analyses. *Psychological Bulletin, 97,* 363–386.

Harris, M. J., & Rosenthal, R. (1986). Four factors in the mediation of teacher expectancy effects. In R. S. Feldman (Ed.), *The social psychology of education.* New York: Cambridge University Press.

Harrison, A. A. (1977). Mere exposure. In L. Berkowitz (Ed.), *Advances in experimental social psychology* (Vol. 10, pp. 39–83). New York: Academic Press.

Hart, A. J., & Morry, M. M. (1997). Trait inferences based on racial and behavioral cues. *Basic and Applied Social Psychology, 19,* 33–48.

Hart, W., Albarracin, D., Eagly, A. H., Brechan, I., Lindberg, M. J., & Merrill, L. (2009). Feeling validated versus being correct: A meta-analysis of selective exposure to information. *Psychological Bulletin, 135,* 555–588.

Harvard Business School. (2022). Admissions class of 2024 profile. https://www.hbs.edu/mba/admissions/class-profile/Pages/default.aspx

Harvey, J. H., & Omarzu, J. (1997). Minding the close relationship. *Personality and Social Psychology Review, 1,* 224–240.

Hasan, Y., Begue, L., & Bushman, B. J. (2012). Viewing the world through "blood-red tinted glasses": The hostile expectation bias mediates the link between violent video game exposure and aggression. *Journal of Experimental Social Psychology, 48,* 953–956.

Hasan, Y., Begue, L., Scharkow, M., & Bushman, B. J. (2013). The more you play, the more aggressive you become: A long-term experimental study of cumulative violent video game effects on hostile expectations and aggressive behavior. *Journal of Experimental Social Psychology, 49,* 224–227.

Haselton, M. G., & Gildersleeve, K. (2011). Can men detect ovulation? *Current Directions in Psychological Science, 20,* 87–92.

Haslam, N., & Kashima, Y. (2010). The rise and rise of social psychology in Asia: A bibliometric analysis. *Asian Journal of Social Psychology, 13,* 202–207.

Haslam, S. A. (2014). Making good theory practical: Five lessons for an applied social identity approach to challenges of organizational, health, and clinical psychology. *British Journal of Social Psychology, 53,* 1–20.

Haslam, S. A., Adarves-Yorno, I., & Postmes, T. (2014, July/August). Creative is collective. *Scientific American Mind,* pp. 31–35.

Haslam, S. A., Reicher, S. D., & Platow, M. J. (2010). *The new psychology of leadership: Identity, influence and power.* London: Psychology Press.

Haslam, S. A., Reicher, S., Millard, K., & McDonald, R. (2015). "Happy to have been of service": The Yale archive as window into the engaged followership of participants in Milgram's "obedience" experiments. *British Journal of Social Psychology, 54,* 55–83.

Hass, R. G., Katz, I., Rizzo, N., Bailey, J., & Eisenstadt, D. (1991). Cross-racial appraisal as related to attitude ambivalence and cognitive complexity. *Personality and Social Psychology Bulletin, 17,* 83–92.

Hastie, R., Penrod, S. D., & Pennington, N. (1983). *Inside the jury.* Cambridge, MA: Harvard University Press.

Hatcher, J. W., Cares, S., Detrie, R., Dillenbeck, T., Goral, E., Troisi, K., & Whirry-Achten, A. M. (2017). Conformity, arousal, and the effect of arbitrary information. *Group Processes and Intergroup Relations, 21*(4), 631–645.

Hatch, H. A., Warner, R. H., Broussard, K. A., & Harton, H. C. (2023). Predictors of transgender prejudice: A meta-analysis. *Sex Roles: A Journal of Research.*

Hatfield, E., & Sprecher, S. (1986). *Mirror, mirror: The importance of looks in everyday life.* Albany, NY: SUNY Press.

Hatfield, E., & Walster, G. W. (1978). *A new look at love.* Reading, MA: Addison-Wesley. (Note: originally published as Walster, E., & Walster, G. W.)

Hatfield, E. (1988). Passionate and compassionate love. In R. J. Sternberg & M. L. Barnes (Eds.), *The psychology of love* (p. 193). New Haven, CT: Yale University Press.

Hatfield, E., Cacioppo, J. T., & Rapson, R. (1992). The logic of emotion: Emotional contagion. In M. S. Clark (Ed.), *Review of Personality and Social Psychology.* Newbury Park, CA: Sage.

Hatfield, E., Traupmann, J., Sprecher, S., Utne, M., & Hay, J. (1985). Equity and intimate relations: Recent research. In W. Ickes (Ed.), *Compatible and incompatible relationships.* New York: Springer-Verlag.

Hatfield (Walster), E., Aronson, V., Abrahams, D., & Rottman, L. (1966). Importance of physical attractiveness in dating behavior. *Journal of Personality and Social Psychology, 4,* 508–516.

Ha, T., van denBerg, J. E. M., Engels, R. C., & Lichtwarck-Aschoff, A. (2012). Effects of attractiveness and status in dating desire in homosexual and heterosexual men and women. *Archives of Sexual Behavior, 41,* 673–682.

Hatzenbuehler, M. L. (2014). Structural stigma and the health of lesbian, gay, and bisexual populations. *Current Directions in Psychological Science, 23,* 127–132.

Hatzfeld, J. (2006). *Machete season: The killers in Rwanda speak.* New York: Farrar, Straus and Giroux.

Haugtvedt, C. P., & Wegener, D. T. (1994). Message order effects in persuasion: An attitude strength perspective. *Journal of Consumer Research, 21,* 205–218.

Hauser, M. (2006). *Moral minds: How nature designed our universal sense of right and wrong.* New York: Ecco.

Hauser, M. (2009). It seems biology (not religion) equals morality. *The Edge.* www.edge.org

Hausfather, Z. (2023, October 13). I study climate change. The data is telling us something new. *New York Times.*

Hausmann, L. M., Levine, J. M., & Higgins, E. T. (2008). Communication and group perception: Extending the "saying is believing" effect. *Group Processes & Intergroup Relations, 11,* 539–554.

Havas, D. A., Glenberg, A. M., Gutowski, K. A., Lucarelli, M. J., & Davidson, R. J. (2010). Cosmetic use of Botulinum Toxin-A affects processing of emotional language. *Psychological Science, 21,* 895–900.

Havel, V. (1990). *Disturbing the peace.* New York: Knopf.

Havlik, J. L., Sugano, Y. Y. V., Jacobi, M. C., Kukreja, R. R., Jacobi, J. H. C., & Mason, P. (2020). The bystander effect in rats. *Science Advances, 6,* eabb4205.

Hawkins, S., et al. (2022, December). Defusing the history wars: Finding common ground in teaching America's national story. https://www.moreincommon.com/media/y4rpsigy/defusing-the-history-wars_more-in-common-1.pdf

Hawkley, L. C., Williams, K. D., & Cacioppo, J. T. (2011). Responses to ostracism across adulthood. *Social, Cognitive, and Affective Neuroscience, 6,* 234–243.

Hayward, L. E., Tropp, L. R., Hornsey, M. J., & Barlow, F. K. (2017). Toward a comprehensive understanding of intergroup contact: Descriptions and mediators of positive and negative contact among majority and minority groups. *Personality and Social Psychology Bulletin, 43,* 347–364.

Hayward, L. E., Tropp, L. R., Hornsey, M. J., & Barlow, F. K. (2018). How negative contact and positive contact with whites predict collective action among racial and ethnic minorities. *British Journal of Social Psychology, 57,* 1–20.

Hazan, C., & Shaver, P. R. (1994). Attachment as an organizational framework for research on close relationships. *Psychological Inquiry, 5,* 1–22.

Hazan, C. (2004). Intimate attachment/capacity to love and be loved. In C. Peterson & M. E. P. Seligman (Eds.), *The values in action classification of strengths and virtues.* Washington, DC: American Psychological Association.

Headey, B., & Wearing, A. (1987). The sense of relative superiority—central to well-being. *Social Indicators Research, 20,* 497–516.

Hearold, S. (1986). A synthesis of 1043 effects of television on social behavior. In G. Comstock (Ed.), *Public communication and behavior* (Vol. 1). Orlando, FL: Academic Press.

Hedgecock, W. M., Luangrath, A. W., & Webster, R. (2021). Counterfactual thinking and facial expressions among Olympic medalists: A conceptual replication of Medvec, Madey, and Gilovich's (1995) findings. *Journal of Experimental Psychology: General, 150,* e13–e21.

Heesacker, M. (1989). Counseling and the elaboration likelihood model of attitude change. In J. F. Cruz, R. A. Goncalves, & P. P. Machado (Eds.), *Psychology and Education: Investigations and Interventions.* Porto, Portugal: Portugese Psychological Association. (Proceedings of the International Conference on Interventions in Psychology and Education, Porto, Portugal, July 1987.)

Hegarty, P., Watson, N., Fletcher, L., & McQueen, G. (2010). When gentlemen are first and ladies are last: Effects of gender stereotypes on the order of romantic partners' names. *British Journal of Social Psychology, 50,* 21–35.

Hehman, E., Flake, J. K., & Calanchini, J. (2018). Disproportionate use of lethal force in policing is associated with regional racial biases of residents. *Social Psychological and Personality Science, 9*(4), 393–401.

Hehman, E., Flake, J. K., & Freeman, J. B. (2018). The faces of group members share physical resemblance. *Personality and Social Psychology Bulletin, 44,* 3–15.

Hehman, E., Gaertner, S. L., Dovidio, J. F., Mania, E. W., Guerra, R., Wilson, D. C., & Friel, B. M. (2012). Group status drives majority and minority integration preferences. *Psychological Science, 23*(1), 46–52.

Heider, F. (1958). *The psychology of interpersonal relations.* New York: Wiley.

Heilmann, K., Kahn, M. E., & Tang, C. K. (2021). The urban crime and heat gradient in high and low poverty areas. *Journal of Public Economics, 197.*

Heilmann, K., Kahn, M. E., & Tang, C. K. (2021). The urban crime and heat gradient in high and low poverty areas. *Journal of Public Economics,* 14

Heim, J., Moyer, J. W., & Lang, M. J. (2022, December 4). Walmart gunman showed troubling behavior before attack, ex-colleagues say. *Washington Post.*

Heine, S. J., & Hamamura, T. (2007). In search of East Asian self-enhancement. *Personality and Social Psychology Review, 11,* 4–27.

Heine, S. J., & Lehman, D. R. (1997). The cultural construction of self-enhancement: An examination of group-serving biases. *Journal of Personality and Social Psychology, 72,* 1268–1283.

Heine, S. J., Kitayama, S., Lehman, D. R., Takata, T., Ide, E., Leung, C., & Matsumoto, H. (2001). Divergent consequences of success and failure in Japan and North America: An investigation of self-improving motivations and malleable selves. *Journal of Personality and Social Psychology, 81,* 599–615.

Heine, S. J., Lehman, D. R., Markus, H. R., & Kitayama, S. (1999). Is there a universal need for positive self-regard? *Psychological Review, 106,* 766–794.

Heine, S. J., Takemoto, T., Moskalenko, S., Lasaleta, J., & Heinrich, J. (2008). Mirrors in the head: Cultural variation in objective self-awareness. *Personality and Social Psychology Bulletin, 34,* 879–887.

Heleven, E., & Van Overwalle, F. (2019). The neural representation of the self in relation to close others using fMRI repetition suppression. *Social Neuroscience, 14,* 717–728.

Helliwell, J., Layard, R., & Sachs, J. (Eds.) (2013). *World happiness report.* New York: The Earth Institute, Columbia University.

Hellman, P. (1980). *Avenue of the righteous of nations.* New York: Atheneum.

Helminen, E. C., Ducar, D. M., Scheer, J. R., Parke, K. L., Morton, M. L., & Felver, J. C. (2023). Self-compassion, minority stress, and mental health in sexual and gender minority populations: A meta-analysis and systematic review. *Clinical Psychology: Science and Practice, 30,* 26–39.

Helzer, E. G., & Dunning, D. (2012). Why and when peer prediction is superior to self-prediction: The weight given to future aspiration versus past achievement. *Journal of Personality and Social Psychology Bulletin, 103,* 38–53.

Henderson-King, E. I., & Nisbett, R. E. (1996). Anti-black prejudice as a function of exposure to the negative behavior of a single black person. *Journal of Personality and Social Psychology, 71,* 654–664.

Henderson, S., & Mulder, R. (2015). Climate change and mental disorders. *Australian and New Zealand Journal of Psychiatry, 49,* 1061–1062.

Hendrick, S. S., & Hendrick, C. (1995). Gender differences and similarities in sex and love. *Personal Relationships, 2,* 55-65.

Hendrick, S. S., Hendrick, C., & Adler, N. L. (1988). Romantic relationships: Love, satisfaction, and staying together. *Journal of Personality and Social Psychology, 54,* 980-988.

Hennenlotter, A., Dresel, C., Castrop, F., Ceballos Baumann, A., Wohschlager, A., & Haslinger, B. (2008). The link between facial feedback and neural activity within central circuitries of emotion: New insights from Botulinum Toxin-induced denervation of frown muscles. *Cerebral Cortex, 19,* 537-542.

Hennigan, K. M., Del Rosario, M. L., Health, L., Cook, T. D., Wharton, J. D., & Calder, B. J. (1982). Impact of the introduction of television on crime in the United States: Empirical findings and theoretical implications. *Journal of Personality and Social Psychology, 42,* 461-477.

Henrich, J., Heine, S. J., & Norenzayan, A. (2010). The weirdest people in the world? *Behavioral and Brain Sciences, 33,* 61-135.

Henrich, J., McElreath, R., Barr, A., Ensminger, J., Barrett, C., Bolyanatz, A., Cardenas, J. C., Gurven, M., Gwako, E., Henrich, N., Lerorogol, C., Marlowe, F., Tracer, D., & Ziker, J. (2006). Costly punishment across human societies. *Science, 312,* 1767-1770.

Henry, P. J. (2008). College sophomores in the laboratory redux: Influences of a narrow data base on social psychology's view of the nature of prejudice. *Psychological Inquiry, 19,* 49-71.

Henry, P. J. (2009). Low-status compensation: A theory for understanding the role of status in cultures of honor. *Journal of Personality and Social Psychology, 97,* 451-466.

Hepach, R., Vaish, A., & Tomasello, M. (2012). Young children are intrinsically motivated to see others helped. *Psychological Science, 23,* 967-972.

Hepper, E. G., & Carnelley, K. B. (2012). The self-esteem roller coaster: Adult attachment moderates the impact of daily feedback. *Personal Relationships, 19,* 504-520.

Hepworth, J. T., & West, S. G. (1988). Lynchings and the economy: A time-series reanalysis of Hovland and Sears (1940). *Journal of Personality and Social Psychology, 55,* 239-247.

Heradstveit, D. (1979). *The Arab-Israeli conflict: Psychological obstacles to peace* (Vol. 28). Oslo, Norway: Universitetsforlaget. Distributed by Columbia University Press. Reviewed by R. K. White (1980), *Contemporary Psychology, 25,* 11-12.

Herlocker, C. E., Allison, S. T., Foubert, J. D., & Beggan, J. K. (1997). Intended and unintended overconsumption of physical, spatial, and temporal resources. *Journal of Personality and Social Psychology, 73,* 992-1004.

Herman, C. P. (2015). The social facilitation of eating. A review. *Appetite, 86,* 61-73.

Herman, C. P. (2017). The social facilitation of eating or the facilitation of social eating? *Journal of Eating Disorders, 5,* 16.

Hernandez, I., & Preston, J. L. (2013). Disfluency disrupts the confirmation bias. *Journal of Experimental Social Psychology, 49,* 178-182.

Hernandez, M., Avery, D. R., Volpone, S. D., & Kaiser, C. R. (2019). Bargaining while Black: The role of race in salary negotiations. *Journal of Applied Psychology, 104,* 581-592.

Hernández-Serrano, O., Griffin, K. W., García-Fernández, J. M., Orgilés, M., & Espada, J. P. (2013). Public commitment, resistance to advertising, and leisure promotion in a school-based drug abuse prevention program: A component dismantling study. *Journal of Drug Education, 43,* 331-351.

Herring, D. R., White, K. R., Jabeen, L. N., Hinojos, M., Terrazas, G., Reyes, S. M., & . . . Crites, S. J. (2013). On the automatic activation of attitudes: A quarter century of evaluative priming research. *Psychological Bulletin, 139,* 1062-1089.

Herzmann, G., Ogle, O., & Curran, T. (2022). More elaborate processing of own-race faces and less elaborate processing of other-race faces contribute to the other-race effect in face memory. *British Journal of Psychology, 113,* 1033-1055.

Hess, U. (2021). Who to whom and why: The social nature of emotional mimicry. *Psychophysiology, 58*(1).

Hetey, R. C., & Eberhardt, J. L. (2018). The numbers don't speak for themselves: Racial disparities and the persistence of inequality in the criminal justice system. *Current Directions in Psychological Science, 27,* 183-187.

Hewstone, M., & Fincham, F. (1996). Attribution theory and research: Basic issues and applications. In M. Hewstone, W. Stroebe, & G. M. Stephenson (Eds.), *Introduction to social psychology: A European perspective.* Oxford, UK: Blackwell.

Hewstone, M. (1990). The "ultimate attribution error"? A review of the literature on intergroup causal attribution. *European Journal of Social Psychology,* 20, 311-335.

Hewstone, M., Hopkins, N., & Routh, D. A. (1992). Cognitive models of stereotype change: Generalization and subtyping in young people's views of the police. *European Journal of Social Psychology, 22,* 219-234.

Hewstone, M., Lolliot, S., Swart, H., Myers, E., Voci, A., Al Ramiah, A., & Cairns, E. (2014). Intergroup contact and intergroup conflict. *Peace and Conflict: Journal of Peace Psychology, 20,* 39-53.

He, Y., Ebner, N. C., & Johnson, M. K. (2011). What predicts the own-age bias in face recognition memory? *Social Cognition, 29,* 97-109.

Hickman, C., Marks, E., Pihkala, P., Clayton, S., Lewandowski, R. E., Mayall, E. E., Wray, B., Mellor, C., & van Susteren, L. (2021). Climate anxiety in children and young people and their beliefs about government responses to climate change: a global survey. *The Lancet. Planetary Health, 5,* e863-e873.

Hideg, I., & Ferris, D. L. (2016). The compassionate sexist? How benevolent sexism promotes and undermines gender equality in the workplace. *Journal of Personality and Social Psychology, 111,* 706-727.

Higgins, E. T., & McCann, C. D. (1984). Social encoding and subsequent attitudes, impressions and memory: "Context-driven" and motivational aspects of processing. *Journal of Personality and Social Psychology, 47,* 26-39.

Higgins, E. T., & Rholes, W. S. (1978). Saying is believing: Effects of message modification on memory and liking for the person described. *Journal of Experimental Social Psychology, 14,* 363-378.

Hilmert, C. J., Kulik, J. A., & Christenfeld, N. J. S. (2006). Positive and negative opinion modeling: The influence of another's similarity and dissimilarity. *Journal of Personality and Social Psychology, 90,* 440-452.

Himelboim, I., Borah, P., Lee, D. K. L., Lee, J., Su, Y., Vishnevskaya, A., & Xiao, X. (2023). What do 5G networks, Bill Gates, Agenda 21, and QAnon have in common? Sources, distribution, and characteristics. *New Media & Society.*

Hine, D. W., & Gifford, R. (1996). Attributions about self and others in commons dilemmas. *European Journal of Social Psychology, 26,* 429-445.

Hinkle, S., Brown, R., & Ely, P. G. (1992). Social identity theory processes: Some limitations and limiting conditions. *Revista de Psicologia Social,* pp. 99-111.

Hinsz, V. B., & Jackson, J. W. (2022). The relevance of group dynamics for understanding the US Capitol insurrection. *Group Dynamics: Theory, Research, and Practice, 26,* 288-308.

Hinsz, V. B. (1990). Cognitive and consensus processes in group recognition memory performance. *Journal of Personality and Social Psychology, 59,* 705-718.

Hinsz, V. B., Tindale, R. S., & Vollrath, D. A. (1997). The emerging conceptualization of groups as information processors. *Psychological Bulletin, 121,* 43-64.

Hirschman, R. S., & Leventhal, H. (1989). Preventing smoking behavior in school children: An initial test of a cognitive-development program. *Journal of Applied Social Psychology, 19,* 559-583.

Hirt, E. R., Zillmann, D., Erickson, G. A., & Kennedy, C. (1992). Costs and benefits of allegiance: Changes in fans' self-ascribed competencies after team victory versus defeat. *Journal of Personality and Social Psychology, 63,* 724-738.

Hitsch, G. J., Hortacsu, A., & Ariely, D. (2006, February). *What makes you click? Mate preferences and matching outcomes in online dating.* MIT Sloan Research Paper No. 4603-06 (ssrn.com/abstract=895442).

Ho, A. K., Sidanius, J., Kteily, N., Sheehy-Skeffington, J., Pratto, F., Henkel, K. E., & . . . Stewart, A. L. (2015). The nature of social dominance orientation: Theorizing and measuring preferences for intergroup inequality using the new SDO_7 scale. *Journal of Personality and Social Psychology, 109,* 1003–1028.

Hobden, K. L., & Olson, J. M. (1994). From jest to antipathy: Disparagement humor as a source of dissonance-motivated attitude change. *Basic and Applied Social Psychology, 15,* 239–249.

Hodges, B. H., & Geyer, A. L. (2006). A nonconformist account of the Asch experiments: Values, pragmatics, and moral dilemmas. *Personality and Social Psychology Review,* 102–119.

Hodson, G., Crisp, R. J., Meleady, R., & Earle, M. (2018). Intergroup contact as an agent of cognitive liberalization. *Perspectives on Psychological Science, 13,* 523–548.

Hoerst, C., & Drury, J. (2021). Social norms misperception among voters in the 2020 US presidential election. *Analyses of Social Issues and Public Policy, 21,* 312–346.

Hoetger, L. A., Devine, D. J., Brank, E. M., Drew, R. M., & Rees, R. (2022). The impact of pretrial publicity on mock juror and jury verdicts: A meta-analysis. *Law and Human Behavior, 46,* 121–139.

Hoffman, M. L. (1981). Is altruism part of human nature? *Journal of Personality and Social Psychology, 40,* 121–137.

Hofling, C. K., Brotzman, E., Dairymple, S., Graves, N., & Pierce, C. M. (1966). An experimental study in nurse-physician relationships. *Journal of Nervous and Mental Disease, 143,* 171–180.

Hofmann, W., De Houwer, J., Perugini, M., Baeyens, F., & Crombez, G. (2010). Evaluative conditioning in humans: A meta-analysis. *Psychological Review, 136,* 390–421.

Hofman, S., Wieser, M. J., & van der Veen, F. M. (2021). Acetaminophen does not affect cardiac and brain responses to social rejection but seems to attenuate behavioral adaptation in a social judgment task. *Social Neuroscience, 16,* 362–374.

Hofmeister, B. (2010). Bridging the gap: Using social psychology to design market interventions to overcome the energy efficiency gap in residential energy markets. *Southeastern Environmental Law Journal, 19,* p. 1.

Hogan, R., Curphy, G. J., & Hogan, J. (1994). What we know about leadership: Effectiveness and personality. *American Psychologist, 49,* 493–504.

Hogeveen, J., Inzlicht, M., & Obhi, S. S. (2014). Power changes how the brain responds to others. *Journal of Experimental Psychology: General, 143,* 755–762.

Hogg, M. (2014). From uncertainty to extremism: Social categorization and identity formation. *Current Directions in Psychological Science, 23,* 338–342.

Hogg, M. A., & Hains, S. C. (1998). Friendship and group identification: A new look at the role of cohesiveness in groupthink. *European Journal of Social Psychology, 28,* 323–341.

Hogg, M. A. (1992). *The social psychology of group cohesiveness: From attraction to social identity.* London: Harvester Wheatsheaf.

Hogg, M. A. (2010). Human groups, social categories, and collective self: Social identity and the management of self-uncertainty. In R. M. Arkin, K. C. Oleson, & P. J. Carroll (Eds.), *Handbook of the uncertain self.* New York: Psychology Press.

Hogg, M. A. (2021). Uncertain self in a changing world: A foundation for radicalisation, populism, and autocratic leadership. *European Review of Social Psychology, 32,* 235–268.

Hogg, M. A., Hains, S. C., & Mason, I. (1998). Identification and leadership in small groups: Salience, frame of reference, and leader stereotypicality effects on leader evaluations. *Journal of Personality and Social Psychology, 75,* 1248–1263.

Hogg, M. A., Turner, J. C., & Davidson, B. (1990). Polarized norms and social frames of reference: A test of the self-categorization theory of group polarization. *Basic and Applied Social Psychology, 11,* 77–100.

Hollander, E. P. (1958). Conformity, status, and idiosyncrasy credit. *Psychological Review, 65,* 117–127.

Hollander, M. M., & Turowetz, J. (2017). Normalizing trust: Participants' immediately post-hoc explanations of behaviour in Milgram's "obedience" experiments. *British Journal of Social Psychology, 56,* 655–674.

Holland, R. W., Hendriks, M., & Aarts, H. (2005). Smells like clean spirit: Nonconscious effect of scent on cognition and behavior. *Psychological Science, 16,* 689–693.

Holmberg, D., & Holmes, J. G. (1994). Reconstruction of relationship memories: A mental models approach. In N. Schwarz & S. Sudman (Eds.), *Autobiographical memory and the validity of retrospective reports.* New York: Springer-Verlag.

Holmes, J. G., & Rempel, J. K. (1989). Trust in close relationships. In C. Hendrick (Ed.), *Review of personality and social psychology* (Vol. 10). Newbury Park, CA: Sage.

Holoien, D. S., & Fiske, S. T. (2013). Downplaying positive impressions: Compensation between warmth and competence in impression management. *Journal of Experimental Social Psychology, 49,* 33–41.

Holte, A. J., Fisher, W. N., & Ferraro, F. R. (2022). Afraid of social exclusion: Fear of missing out predicts cyberball-induced ostracism. *Journal of Technology in Behavioral Science, 7,* 315–324.

Holtgraves, T. (1997). Styles of language use: Individual and cultural variability in conversational indirectness. *Journal of Personality and Social Psychology, 73,* 624–637.

Holt-Lunstad, J., Robles, T. F., & Sbarra, D. A. (2017). Advancing social connection as a public health priority in the United States. *American Psychologist, 72,* 517–530.

Holt-Lunstad, J., Smith, T. B., & Layton, J. B. (2010). Social relationships and mortality risk: A meta-analytic review. *PLOS Medicine, 7*(7), e1000316.

Holt-Lunstad, J., Smith, T. B., Baker, M., Harris, T., & Stephenson, D. (2015). Loneliness and social isolation as risk factors for mortality: A meta-analytic review. *Perspectives on Psychological Science, 10,* 227–237.

Holtzworth, A., & Jacobson, N. S. (1988). An attributional approach to marital dysfunction and therapy. In J. E. Maddux, C. D. Stoltenberg, & R. Rosenwein (Eds.), *Social processes in clinical and counseling psychology.* New York: Springer-Verlag.

Hong, S., & Na, J. (2018). How Facebook is perceived and used by people across cultures: The implications of cultural differences in the use of Facebook. *Social Psychological and Personality Science, 9,* 435–443.

Hong, S., & Park, H. S. (2012). Computer-mediated persuasion in online reviews: Statistical versus narrative evidence. *Computers in Human Behavior, 28,* 906–919.

Honigman, R. J., Phillips, K. A., & Castle, D. J. (2004). A review of psychosocial outcomes for patients seeking cosmetic surgery. *Plastic and Reconstructive Surgery, 113,* 1229–1237.

Hoon, W. C. (2023, March 14). 5 fast facts: The gender wage gap. US Department of Labor Blog.

Hoorens, V., & Nuttin, J. M. (1993). Overvaluation of own attributes: Mere ownership or subjective frequency? *Social Cognition, 11,* 177–200.

Hoorens, V., Nuttin, J. M., Herman, I. E., & Pavakanun, U. (1990). Mastery pleasure versus mere ownership: A quasi-experimental cross-cultural and cross-alphabetical test of the name letter effect. *European Journal of Social Psychology, 20,* 181–205.

Hoorens, V., Smits, T., & Shepperd, J. A. (2008). Comparative optimism in the spontaneous generation of future life-events. *British Journal of Social Psychology, 47,* 441–451.

Hoover, C. W., Wood, E. E., & Knowles, E. S. (1983). Forms of social awareness and helping. *Journal of Experimental Social Psychology, 19,* 577–590.

Hooykaas, R. (1972). *Religion and the rise of modern science.* Grand Rapids, MI: Eerdmans.

Hori, M., & Kamo, Y. (2018). Gender differences in happiness: The effects of marriage, social roles, and social support in East Asia. *Applied Research in Quality of Life, 13,* 839–857.

Horner, V., Carter, J. D., Suchak, M., & de Waal, F. B. M. (2011). Spontaneous prosocial choice by chimpanzees. *PNAS, 108,* 13847–13851.

Horner, V., Proctor, D., Bonnie, K. E., Whiten, A., & de Waal, F. B. M. (2010). Prestige affects cultural learning in chimpanzees. *PLOS ONE, 5,* e10625.

Horne, Z., Powell, D., Hummel, J. E., & Holyoak, K. J. (2015). Countering antivaccination attitudes. *Proceedings of the National Academy of Sciences, 112,* 10321–10324.

Hornsey, M. J., Edwards, M., Lobera, J., Díaz, C. C., & Barlow, F. K. (2021). Resolving the small-pockets problem helps clarify the role of education and political ideology in shaping vaccine scepticism. *British Journal of Psychology, 112,* 992–1011.

Hornstein, H. (1976). *Cruelty and kindness.* Englewood Cliffs, NJ: Prentice-Hall.

Horowitz, J. M. (2019, May 8). Americans see advantages and challenges in country's growing racial and ethnic diversity. *Pew Research Center.* https://www.pewresearch.org/social-trends/2019/05/08/americans-see-advantages-and-challenges-in-countrys-growing-racial-and-ethnic-diversity/

Horowitz, J. M., Brown, A., & Cox, K. (2019, April 9). Race in America 2019. *Pew Research Center.* https://www.pewsocialtrends.org/2019/04/09/race-in-america-2019

Horry, R., Fitzgerald, R. J., & Mansour, J. K. (2021). "Only your first yes will count": The impact of prelineup instructions on sequential lineup decisions. *Journal of Experimental Psychology: Applied, 27,* 170–186.

Horry, R., Halford, P., Brewer, N., Milne, R., & Bull, R. (2014). Archival analyses of eyewitness identification test outcomes: What can they tell us about eyewitness memory? *Law and Human Behavior, 38,* 94–108.

Horry, R., Memon, A., Wright, D. B., & Milne, R. (2012a). Predictors of eyewitness identification decisions from video lineups in England: A field study. *Law and Human Behavior, 36,* 257–265.

Horry, R., Palmer, M. A., & Brewer, N. (2012b). Backloading in the sequential lineup prevents within-lineup criterion shifts that undermine eyewitness identification performance. *Journal of Experimental Psychology: Applied, 18,* 346–360.

Horwitz, A. V., White, H. R., & Howell-White, S. (1997). Becoming married and mental health: A longitudinal study of a cohort of young adults. *Journal of Marriage and the Family, 58,* 895–907.

Hostinar, C. E., Sullivan, R. M., & Gunnar, M. R. (2014). Psychobiological mechanisms underlying the social buffering of the hypothalamic-pituitary-adrenocortical axis: A review of animal models and human studies across development. *Psychological Bulletin, 140,* 256–282.

Houghton, J. (2011). *Global warming, climate change and sustainability: A challenge to scientists, policymakers and religious believers.* Cambridge, England: The International Society for Science and Religion. https://www.issr.org.uk/latest-news/global-warming

Hou, R., & Zhang, C. (2021). Reducing social loafing in online brand communities: Insights from social exchange theory. *Social Behavior and Personality: An International Journal, 49,* 1–10.

House, R. J., & Singh, J. V. (1987). Organizational behavior: Some new directions for I/O psychology. *Annual Review of Psychology, 38,* 669–718.

Houston, V., & Bull, R. (1994). Do people avoid sitting next to someone who is facially disfigured? *European Journal of Social Psychology, 24,* 279–284.

Hovland, C. I., & Sears, R. (1940). Minor studies of aggression: Correlation of lynchings with economic indices. *Journal of Psychology, 9,* 301–310.

Hovland, C. I., Lumsdaine, A. A., & Sheffield, F. D. (1949). *Experiments on mass communication. Studies in social psychology in World War II* (Vol. III). Princeton, NJ: Princeton University Press.

Howard, D. J. (1997). Familiar phrases as peripheral persuasion cues. *Journal of Experimental Social Psychology, 33,* 231–243.

Howard, J. (2013, January 16). I went after guns. Obama can, too. *The New York Times.*

Howard, R. M., & Perilloux, C. (2017). Is mating psychology most closely tied to biological sex or preferred partner's sex? *Personality and Individual Differences, 115,* 83–89.

Howell, R. T., & Howell, C. J. (2008). The relation of economic status to subjective well-being in developing countries: A meta-analysis. *Psychological Bulletin, 134,* 536–560.

Hoyle, R. H. (1993). Interpersonal attraction in the absence of explicit attitudinal information. *Social Cognition, 11,* 309–320.

Hrabok, M., Delorme, A., & Agyapong, V. I. O. (2020). Threats to mental health and well-being associated with climate change. *Journal of Anxiety Disorders, 76,* 102295.

Hsiang, S. M., Burke, M., & Miguel, E. (2013). Quantifying the influence of climate on human conflict. *Science, 341,* 1212.

Hsu, N., Badura, K. L., Newman, D. A., & Speach, M. E. P. (2021). Gender, "masculinity," and "femininity": A meta-analytic review of gender differences in agency and communion. *Psychological Bulletin, 147,* 987–1011.

Huang, C., & Park, D. (2012). Cultural influences on Facebook photographs. *International Journal of Psychology,* 1–10.

Huang, C. (2017). Time spent on social network sites and psychological well-being: A meta-analysis. *Cyberpsychology, Behavior, and Social Networking, 20,* 346–354.

Huang, J., Su, S., Zhou, L., & Liu, X. (2013). Attitude toward the viral ad: Expanding traditional advertising models to interactive advertising. *Journal of Interactive Marketing, 27,* 36–46.

Huang, K., Yeomans, M., Brooks, A. W., Minson, K., & Gino, F. (2017). It doesn't hurt to ask: Question-asking increases liking. *Journal of Personality and Social Psychology, 113,* 430–452.

Huang, Y., Kendrick, K. M., & Yu, R. (2014). Conformity to the opinions of other people lasts for no more than 3 days. *Psychological Science, 25,* 1388–1393.

Huang, Y., Osborne, D., & Sibley, C. G. (2019). The gradual move toward gender equality: A 7-year latent growth model of ambivalent sexism. *Social Psychological and Personality Science, 10,* 335–344.

Huart, J., Corneille, O., & Becquart, E. (2005). Face-based categorization, context-based categorization, and distortions in the recollection of gender ambiguous faces. *Journal of Experimental Social Psychology, 41,* 598–608.

Huddy, L., & Virtanen, S. (1995). Subgroup differentiation and subgroup bias among Latinos as a function of familiarity and positive distinctiveness. *Journal of Personality and Social Psychology, 68,* 97–108.

Hudson, N. W., Lucas, R. E., & Donnellan, M. B. (2020). Are we happier with others? An investigation of the links between spending time with others and subjective well-being. *Journal of Personality and Social Psychology, 119,* 672–694.

Hudson, N. W., Lucas, R. E., & Donnellan, M. B. (2020). The highs and lows of love: Romantic relationship quality moderates whether spending time with one's partner predicts gains or losses in well-being. *Personality and Social Psychology Bulletin, 46,* 572–589.

Huesmann, L. R., Lagerspetz, K., & Eron, L. D. (1984). Intervening variables in the TV violence-aggression relation: Evidence from two countries. *Developmental Psychology, 20,* 746–775.

Huesmann, L. R., Moise-Titus, J., Podolski, C. L., & Eron, L. D. (2003). Longitudinal relations between children's exposure to TV violence and their aggressive and violent behavior in young adulthood: 1977–1992. *Developmental Psychology, 39,* 201–221.

Hüffmeier, J., Krumm, S., Kanthak, J., & Hertel, G. (2012). "Don't let the group down": Facets of instrumentality moderate the motivating effects of groups in a field experiment. *European Journal of Social Psychology, 42,* 533–538.

Hughes, B. L., Camp, N. P., Gomez, J., Natu, V. S., Grill-Spector, K., & Eberhardt, J. L. (2019). Neural adaptation to faces reveals racial outgroup homogeneity effects in early perception. *PNAS, 116,* 14532–14537.

Hui, B. P. H., Ng, J. C. K., Berzaghi, E., Cunningham-Amos, L. A., & Kogan, A. (2020). Rewards of kindness? A meta-analysis of the link between prosociality and well-being. *Psychological Bulletin, 146,* 1084–1116.

Hui, C. H., Triandis, H. C., & Yee, C. (1991). Cultural differences in reward allocation: Is collectivism the explanation? *British Journal of Social Psychology, 30,* 145–157.

Hull, J. G., & Young, R. D. (1983). The self-awareness-reducing effects of alcohol consumption: Evidence and implications. In J. Suls & A. G. Greenwald (Eds.), *Psychological perspectives on the self* (Vol. 2). Hillsdale, NJ: Erlbaum.

Hull, J. G., Brunelle, T. J., Prescott, A. T., & Sargent, J. D. (2014). A longitudinal study of risk-glorifying video games and behavioral deviance. *Journal of Personality and Social Psychology, 107,* 300–325.

Hull, J. G., Levenson, R. W., Young, R. D., & Sher, K. J. (1983). Self-awareness-reducing effects of alcohol consumption. *Journal of Personality and Social Psychology, 44,* 461–473.

Humprecht, E. (2019). Where "fake news" flourishes: A comparison across four Western democracies. *Information, Communication & Society, 22,* 1973–1988.

Hunt, L. L., Eastwick, P. W., & Finkel, E. J. (2015). Leveling the playing field: Longer acquaintance predicts reduced assortative mating on attractiveness. *Psychological Science, 26,* 1046–1053.

Hunt, M. (1990). *The compassionate beast: What science is discovering about the humane side of humankind.* New York: William Morrow.

Hunt, M. G., Marx, R., Lipson, C., & Young, J. (2018). No more FOMO: Limiting social media decreases loneliness and depression. *Journal of Social and Clinical Psychology, 37,* 751–768.

Hunt, M. G., Xu, E., Fogelson, A., & Rubens, J. (2023). Follow friends one hour a day: Limiting time on social media and muting strangers improves well-being. *Journal of Social & Clinical Psychology, 42,* 187–213.

Hunt, P. J., & Hillery, J. M. (1973). Social facilitation in a location setting: An examination of the effects over learning trials. *Journal of Experimental Social Psychology, 9,* 563–571.

Hupbach, A., Olcaysoy Okten, I., & Horn, P. (2022). Directed forgetting in the social domain: Forgetting behaviors but not inferred traits. *Journal of Applied Research in Memory and Cognition, 11,* 522–533.

Huppert, E., Cowell, J. M., Cheng, Y., Contreras, I. C., Gomez, S. N., Gonzalez, G. M. L., Huepe, D., Ibanez, A., Lee, K., Mahasneh, R., Malcolm, S. S., Salas, N., Selcuk, B., Tungodden, B., Wong, A., Zhou, X., & Decety, J. (2019). The development of children's preferences for equality and equity across 13 individualistic and collectivist cultures. *Developmental Science, 22,* 1–15.

Hurst, M., Dittmar, H., Bond, R., & Kasser, T. (2013). The relationship between materialistic values and environmental attitudes and behaviors: A meta-analysis. *Journal of Environmental Psychology, 36,* 257–269.

Hussak, L. J., & Cimpian, A. (2015). An early-emerging explanatory heuristic promotes support for the status quo. *Journal of Personality and Social Psychology, 109,* 739–752.

Huston, T. L., & Chorost, A. F. (1994). Behavioral buffers on the effect of negativity on marital satisfaction: A longitudinal study. *Personal Relationships, 1,* 223–239.

Huston, T. L., Niehuis, S., & Smith, S. E. (2001). The early marital roots of conjugal distress and divorce. *Current Directions in Psychological Science, 10,* 116–119.

Hutson, M. (2007, March/April). Unnatural selection. *Psychology Today,* pp. 90–95.

Huynh, A. C., & Grossmann, I. (2021). Rising ethnic diversity in the United States accompanies shifts toward an individualistic culture. *Social Psychological and Personality Science, 12,* 1316–1325.

Hyatt, C. S., Sleep, C. E., Lamkin, J., Maples-Keller, J. L., Sedikides, C., Campbell, W. K., & Miller, J. D. (2018). Narcissism and self-esteem: A nomological network analysis. *PLOS ONE, 13,* e0201088.

Hyde, J. S. (2005). The gender similarities hypothesis. *American Psychologist, 60,* 581–592.

Hyde, J. S. (2018). Gender similarities. In C. B. Travis, J. W. White, A. Rutherford, W. S. Williams, S. L. Cook, K. F. Wyche, . . . K. F. Wyche (Eds.), *APA handbook of the psychology of women: History, theory, and battlegrounds* (pp. 129–143). Washington, DC: American Psychological Association.

Ickes, W., Layden, M. A., & Barnes, R. D. (1978). Objective self-awareness and individuation: An empirical link. *Journal of Personality, 46,* 146–161.

Ickes, W., Patterson, M. L., Rajecki, D. W., & Tanford, S. (1982). Behavioral and cognitive consequences of reciprocal versus compensatory responses to preinteraction expectancies. *Social Cognition, 1,* 160–190.

Igielnik, R. (2023, August 19). These voters share almost no political beliefs, but they agree on one thing: We're failing as a nation. *New York Times.*

Ilies, R., Peng, A. C., Savani, K., & Dimotakis, N. (2013). Guilty and helpful: An emotion-based reparatory model of voluntary work behavior. *Journal of Applied Psychology, 98,* 1051–1059.

Imai, Y. (1994). Effects of influencing attempts on the perceptions of powerholders and the powerless. *Journal of Social Behavior and Personality, 9,* 455–468.

Imhoff, R., & Banse, R. (2009). Ongoing victim suffering increases prejudice: The case of secondary anti-Semitism. *Psychological Science, 20,* 1443–1447.

Imhoff, R., & Erb, H. (2009). What motivates nonconformity? Uniqueness seeking blocks majority influence. *Personality and Social Psychology Bulletin, 35,* 309–320.

Imhoff, R., Dotsch, R., Bianchi, M., Banse, R., & Wigboldus, D. (2011). Facing Europe: Visualizing spontaneous ingroup projection. *Psychological Science, 22,* 1583–1590.

Imundo, M. N., & Rapp, D. N. (2021). When fairness is flawed: Effects of false balance reporting and weight-of-evidence statements on beliefs and perceptions of climate change. *Journal of Applied Research in Memory and Cognition.*

Indo-Asian News Service. (2013, March 13). Child killed after imitating TV hanging scene. *NDTV.* http://www.ndtv.com/article/cities/child-killed-after-imitating-tv-hanging-scene-346554

Ingham, A. G., Levinger, G., Graves, J., & Peckham, V. (1974). The Ringelmann effect: Studies of group size and group performance. *Journal of Experimental Social Psychology, 10,* 371–384.

Inglehart, R., & Welzel, C. (2005). *Modernization, cultural change, and democracy: The human development sequence.* New York: Cambridge University Press.

Inglehart, R. (1990). *Culture shift in advanced industrial society.* Princeton, NJ: Princeton University Press.

Inman, E. M., Chaudoir, S. R., Galvinhill, P. R., & Sheehy, A. M. (2018). The effectiveness of the Bringing in the Bystander™ program among first-year students at a religiously-affiliated liberal arts college. *Journal of Social and Political Psychology, 6,* 511–525.

Innis, M. (2014, June 11). Australia's graphic cigarette pack warnings appear to work. *The New York Times.* https://www.nytimes.com/2014/06/12/business/international/australias-graphic-cigarette-pack-warnings-appear-to-work.html

Innocence Project. (2023). Explore the numbers: Innocence Project's impact. https://innocenceproject.org/exonerations-data/

Inzlicht, M., Gutsell, J. N., & Legault, L. (2012). Mimicry reduces racial prejudice. *Journal of Experimental Social Psychology, 48,* 361–365.

Inzlicht, M., McKay, L., & Aronson, J. (2006). Stigma as ego depletion: How being the target of prejudice affects self-control. *Psychological Science, 17,* 262–269.

IPCC. (2014). *AR5 climate change 2014: Impacts, adaptation, and vulnerability.* Geneva: Intergovernmental Panel on Climate Change. https://www.ipcc.ch/report/ar5/wg2/

IPCC. (2019). *The ocean and cyrosphere in a changing climate: Summary for policymakers.* https://www.ipcc.ch/srocc/

IPCC. (2022). Climate change 2022: Impacts, adaptation, and vulnerability. https://www.ipcc.ch/report/ar6/wg2/

IPU (International Parliamentary Union). (2023). *New IPU report shows that women MPs have never been so diverse.* https://www.ipu.org/news/press-releases/2023-03/new-ipu-report-shows-women-mps-have-never-been-so-diverse

Ireland, M. E., & Pennebaker, J. W. (2010). Language style matching in writing: Synchrony in essays, correspondence, and poetry. *Journal of Personality and Social Psychology, 99,* 549–571.

Isen, A. M., & Means, B. (1983). The influence of positive affect on decision-making strategy. *Social Cognition, 2,* 28–31.

Isen, A. M., Clark, M., & Schwartz, M. F. (1976). Duration of the effect of good mood on helping: Footprints on the sands of time. *Journal of Personality and Social Psychology, 34,* 385–393.

Isen, A. M., Shalker, T. E., Clark, M., & Karp, L. (1978). Affect, accessibility of material in memory, and behavior: A cognitive loop. *Journal of Personality and Social Psychology, 36,* 1–12.

Isen, J., Tuvblad, C., Younan, D., Ericson, M., Raine, A., & Baker, L. A. (2022). Developmental trajectories of delinquent and aggressive behavior: Evidence for differential heritability. *Child Psychiatry and Human Development, 53,* 199–211.

Iso-Ahola, S. E. (2013). Exercise: Why it is a challenge for both the nonconscious and conscious mind. *Psychological Bulletin, 17,* 93–110.

Isozaki, M. (1984). The effect of discussion on polarization of judgments. *Japanese Psychological Research, 26,* 187–193.

Ito, T. A., Miller, N., & Pollock, V. E. (1996). Alcohol and aggression: A meta-analysis on the moderating effects of inhibitory cues, triggering events, and self-focused attention. *Psychological Bulletin, 120,* 60–82.

Ivanov, A., & Zelchenko, P. (2020). Designing an electronic brainstorming environment for engaging East-Asian teams. *International Journal of Human-Computer Interaction, 36*(5), 414–428.

Jäckle, S., & Wenzelburger, G. (2015). Religion, religiosity, and the attitudes toward homosexuality—A multilevel analysis of 79 countries. *Journal of Homosexuality, 62,* 207–241.

Jackman, M. R., & Senter, M. S. (1981). Beliefs about race, gender, and social class different, therefore unequal: Beliefs about trait differences between groups of unequal status. In D. J. Treiman & R. V. Robinson (Eds.), *Research in stratification and mobility* (Vol. 2). Greenwich, CT: JAI Press.

Jackman, T. (2021, January 27). Police union says 140 officers injured in Capitol riot. *The Washington Post.* https://wapo.st/2PskfKd

Jackson, J. J., Thoemmes, F., Jonkmann, K., Lüdtke, O., & Trautwien, U. (2012). Military training and personality trait development: Does the military make the man, or does the man make the military? *Psychological Science, 23,* 270–277.

Jackson, J. M., & Latané, B. (1981). All alone in front of all those people: Stage fright as a function of number and type of co-performers and audience. *Journal of Personality and Social Psychology, 40,* 73–85.

Jackson, J. W., Kirby, D., Barnes, L., & Shepard, L. (1993). Institutional racism and pluralistic ignorance: A cross-national comparison. In M. Wievorka (Ed.), *Racisme et modernite.* Paris: Editions la Découverte.

Jackson, L. A., Hunter, J. E., & Hodge, C. N. (1995). Physical attractiveness and intellectual competence: A meta-analytic review. *Social Psychology Quarterly, 58,* 108–123.

Jacobi, T., & Schweers, D. (2017). Justice, interrupted: The effect of gender, ideology, and seniority at Supreme Court oral arguments. *Virginia Law Review, 103*(7), 1379–1496.

Jacobs, R. C., & Campbell, D. T. (1961). The perpetuation of an arbitrary tradition through several generations of a laboratory microculture. *Journal of Abnormal and Social Psychology, 62,* 649–658.

Jacoby, S. (1986, December). When opposites attract. *Reader's Digest,* pp. 95–98.

Jaffe, Y., & Yinon, Y. (1983). Collective aggression: The group-individual paradigm in the study of collective antisocial behavior. In H. H. Blumberg, A. P. Hare, V. Kent, & M. Davies (Eds.), *Small groups and social interaction* (Vol. 1). Cambridge: Wiley.

Jaffe, Y., Shapir, N., & Yinon, Y. (1981). Aggression and its escalation. *Journal of Cross-Cultural Psychology, 12,* 21–36.

James, W. (1899). *Talks to teachers on psychology: And to students on some of life's ideals* (p. 33). New York: Holt, 1922. Cited by W. J. McKeachie, Psychology in America's bicentennial year. *American Psychologist, 31,* 819–833.

Jamieson, D. W., Lydon, J. E., Stewart, G., & Zanna, M. P. (1987). Pygmalion revisited: New evidence for student expectancy effects in the classroom. *Journal of Educational Psychology, 79,* 461–466.

Jamieson, J. P. (2010). The home field advantage in athletics: A meta-analysis. *Journal of Applied Social Psychology, 40,* 1819–1848.

Jamrozik, A., Oraa Ali, M., Sarwer, D. B., & Chatterjee, A. (2018). More than skin deep: Judgments of individuals with facial disfigurement. *Psychology of Aesthetics, Creativity, and the Arts, 13*(1), 117–129.

Janes, L. M., & Olson, J. M. (2000). Jeer pressure: The behavioral effects of observing ridicule of others. *Personality and Social Psychology Bulletin, 26,* 474–485.

Jang, K. L., Dick, D. M., Wolf, H., Livesley, W. J., & Paris, J. (2005). Psychosocial adversity and emotional instability: An application of gene-environment interaction models. *European Journal of Personality, 19,* 359–372.

Janis, I. L., & Mann, L. (1977). *Decision-making: A psychological analysis of conflict, choice and commitment.* New York: Free Press.

Janis, I. L. (1971, November). Groupthink. *Psychology Today,* pp. 43–46.

Janis, I. L. (1972). *Victims of groupthink.* New York: Houghton Mifflin.

Janis, I. L. (1982). Counteracting the adverse effects of concurrence-seeking in policy-planning groups: Theory and research perspectives. In H. Brandstatter, J. H. Davis, & G. Stocker-Kreichgauer (Eds.), *Group decision making.* New York: Academic Press.

Janis, I. L. (1989). *Crucial decisions: Leadership in policymaking and crisis management.* New York: Free Press.

Jankowiak, W. R., & Fischer, E. F. (1992). A cross-cultural perspective on romantic love. *Ethnology, 31,* 149–155.

Jansen, R. A., Rafferty, A. N., & Griffiths, T. L. (2021). A rational model of the Dunning-Kruger effect supports insensitivity to evidence in low performers. *Nature Human Behaviour, 5,* 756–763.

Jaremka, L. M., Fagundes, C. P., Glaser, R., Bennett, J. M., Malarkey, W. B., & Kiecolt-Glaser, J. (2013). Loneliness predicts pain, depression, and fatigue: Understanding the role of immune dysregulation. *Psychoneuroendocrinology, 38,* 1310–1317.

Jaremka, L. M., Gabriel, S., & Carvallo, M. (2011). What makes us feel the best also makes us feel the worst: The emotional impact of independent and interdependent experiences. *Self and Identity, 10,* 44–63.

Jarvis, S. N., Ebersole, C. R., Nguyen, C. Q., Zhu, M., & Kray, L. J. (2022). Stepping up to the mic: Gender gaps in participation in live question-and-answer sessions at academic conferences. *Psychological Science, 33,* 1882–1893.

Jasko, K., Webber, D., Kruglanski, A. W., Gelfand, M., Taufiqurrohman, M., Hettiarachchi, M., & Gunaratna, R. (2020). Social context moderates the effects of quest for significance on violent extremism. *Journal of Personality and Social Psychology, 118,* 1165–1187.

Jason, L. A., Rose, T., Ferrari, J. R., & Barone, R. (1984). Personal versus impersonal methods for recruiting blood donations. *Journal of Social Psychology, 123,* 139–140.

Jebb, A. T., Tay, L., Diener, E., & Oishi, S. (2018). Happiness, income satiation, and turning points around the world. *Nature Human Behaviour, 2,* 33–38.

Jeffery, R. W., Drewnowski, A., Epstein, L. H., Stunkard, A. J., Wilson, G. T., Wing, R. R., & Hill, D. R. (2000). Long-term maintenance of weight loss: Current status. *Health Psychology, 19,* no. 1 (Supplement), 5–16.

Jellison, J. M., & Green, J. (1981). A self-presentation approach to the fundamental attribution error: The norm of internality. *Journal of Personality and Social Psychology, 40,* 643–649.

Jemmott, J. B., III., & Locke, S. E. (1984). Psychosocial factors, immunologic mediation, and human susceptibility to infectious diseases: How much do we know? *Psychological Bulletin, 95,* 78–108.

Jeong, S-H., & Hwang, Y. (2012). Does multitasking increase or decrease persuasion? Effects of multitasking on comprehension and counterarguing. *Journal of Communication, 62,* 571–587.

Jerit, J., & Zhao, Y. (2020). Political misinformation. *Annual Review of Political Science, 23,* 77–94.

Jervis, R. (1985). Perceiving and coping with threat: Psychological perspectives. In R. Jervis, R. N. Lebow, & J. Stein (Eds.), *Psychology and deterrence.* Baltimore: Johns Hopkins University Press.

Jetten, J., Mols, F., & Steffens, N. K. (2021). Prosperous But Fearful of Falling: The Wealth Paradox, Collective Angst, and Opposition to Immigration. *Personality & Social Psychology Bulletin, 47,* 766–780.

Joel, S., Eastwick, P. W., & Finkel, E. J. (2017). Is romantic desire predictable? Machine learning applied to initial romantic attraction. *Psychological Science, 28,* 1478–1489.

Johnen, M., Jungblut, M., & Ziegele, M. (2018). The digital outcry: What incites participation behavior in an online firestorm? *New Media & Society, 20*(9), 3140–3160.

Johnson, A. L., Crawford, M. T., Sherman, S. J., Rutchick, A. M., Hamilton, D. L., Ferreira, M. B., & Petrocelli, J. V. (2006). A functional perspective on group memberships: Differential need fulfillment in group typology. *Journal of Experimental Social Psychology, 42,* 707–719.

Johnson, B. K., Neo, R. L., Heijnen, M. E. M., Smits, L., & van Veen, C. (2020). Issues, involvement, and influence: Effects of selective exposure and sharing on polarization and participation. *Computers in Human Behavior, 104.*

Johnson, C. (2017, January 6). Justice Department issues new guidelines on securing eyewitness IDs. *NPR.* https://n.pr/2UnhnNO

Johnson, C. S., Olson, M. A., & Fazio, R. H. (2009). Getting acquainted in interracial interactions: Avoiding intimacy but approaching race. *Personality and Social Psychology Bulletin, 35,* 557–571.

Johnson, D. G., Mattan, B. D., Flores, N., Lauharatanahirun, N., & Falk, E. B. (2022). Social-cognitive and affective antecedents of code switching and the consequences of linguistic racism for Black people and people of color. *Affective Science, 3,* 5–13.

Johnson, D. J., & Rusbult, C. E. (1989). Resisting temptation: Devaluation of alternative partners as a means of maintaining commitment in close relationships. *Journal of Personality and Social Psychology, 57,* 967–980.

Johnson, D. W., & Johnson, R. T. (1995). Teaching students to be peacemakers: Results of five years of research. *Peace and Conflict: Journal of Peace Psychology, 1,* 417–438.

Johnson, D. W., & Johnson, R. T. (2000). The three Cs of reducing prejudice and discrimination. In S. Oskamp (Ed.), *Reducing prejudice and discrimination.* Mahwah, NJ: Erlbaum.

Johnson, D. W., & Johnson, R. T. (2003). Student motivation in co-operative groups: Social interdependence theory. In R. M. Gillies & A. F. Ashman (Eds.), *Co-operative learning: The social and intellectual outcomes of learning in groups.* New York: Routledge.

Johnson, J. D., Jackson, L. A., & Gatto, L. (1995). Violent attitudes and deferred academic aspirations: Deleterious effects of exposure to rap music. *Basic and Applied Social Psychology, 16,* 27–41.

Johnson, J. G., Cohen, P., Smailes, E. M., Kasen, S., & Brook, J. S. (2002). Television viewing and aggressive behavior during adolescence and adulthood. *Science, 295,* 2468–2471.

Johnson, J. L., & Johnson, C. F. (2001). Poverty and the death penalty. *Journal of Economic Issues, 2,* 517–523.

Johnson, M. H., & Magaro, P. A. (1987). Effects of mood and severity on memory processes in depression and mania. *Psychological Bulletin, 101,* 28–40.

Johnson, R. D., & Downing, L. L. (1979). Deindividuation and valence of cues: Effects of prosocial and antisocial behavior. *Journal of Personality and Social Psychology, 37,* 1532–1538.

Johnson, S. L., Kitchens, B., & Gray, P. (2020, October 26). Facebook srves as an echo chamber, especially for conservatives. Blame its algorithm. *Washington Post* (www.washingtonpost.com).

Johnson, S. S., & Post, S. G. (2017). Rx It's good to be good (G2BG) 2017 commentary: Prescribing volunteerism for health, happiness, resilience, and longevity. *American Journal of Health Promotion, 31,* 163–172.

Johnson, W., & Krueger, R. F. (2006). How money buys happiness: Genetic and environmental processes linking finances and life satisfaction. *Journal of Personality and Social Psychology, 90,* 680–691.

Joiner, R. J., Bradbury, T. N., Lavner, J. A., Meltzer, A. L., McNulty, J. K., Neff, L. A., & Karney, B. R. (2023). Are changes in marital satisfaction sustained and steady, or sporadic and dramatic? *American Psychologist.*

Joiner, T. E., Jr. (1994). Contagious depression: Existence, specificity to depressed symptoms, and the role of reassurance seeking. *Journal of Personality and Social Psychology, 67,* 287–296.

Joly-Mascheroni, R. M., Senju, A., & Shepherd, A. J. (2008). Dogs catch human yawns. *Biology Letters, 4,* 446–448.

Jonason, P. K., & Thomas, A. G. (2022). Being more educated and earning more increases romantic interest: Data from 18 M online daters from 24 nations. *Human Nature, 33,* 115–131

Jonason, P. K., Garcia, J. R., Webster, G. D., Li, N. P., & Fisher, H. E. (2015). Relationship dealbreakers: Traits people avoid in potential mates. *Personality and Social Psychology Bulletin, 41,* 1697–1711.

Jones, C. R., Fazio, R. H., & Olson, M. A. (2009). Implicit misattribution as a mechanism underlying evaluative conditioning. *Journal of Personality and Social Psychology, 96,* 933–948.

Jones, C. S., & Kaplan, M. F. (2003). The effects of racially stereotypical crimes on juror decision-making and information-processing strategies. *Basic and Applied Social Psychology, 25,* 1–13.

Jones, E. E., & Davis, K. E. (1965). From acts to dispositions: The attribution process in person perception. In L. Berkowitz (Ed.), *Advances in experimental social psychology* (Vol. 2). New York: Academic Press.

Jones, E. E., & Harris, V. A. (1967). The attribution of attitudes. *Journal of Experimental Social Psychology, 3,* 2–24.

Jones, E. E., & Nisbett, R. E. (1971). *The actor and the observer: Divergent perceptions of the causes of behavior.* Morristown, NJ: General Learning Press.

Jones, E. E. (1964). *Ingratiation.* New York: Appleton-Century-Crofts.

Jones, E. E. (1976). How do people perceive the causes of behavior? *American Scientist, 64,* 300–305.

Jones, E. E., Rhodewalt, F., Berglas, S., & Skelton, J. A. (1981). Effects of strategic self-presentation on subsequent self-esteem. *Journal of Personality and Social Psychology, 41,* 407–421.

Jones, J. M. (2003, April 4). Blacks show biggest decline in support for war compared with 1991. *Gallup.* https://news.gallup.com/poll/8122/blacks-show-biggest-decline-support-war-compared-1991.aspx

Jones, J. M. (2023, April 13). *Record Party Gap on Environment-Economic Growth Tradeoff.* Gallup.com.

Jones, J. T., & Cunningham, J. D. (1996). Attachment styles and other predictors of relationship satisfaction in dating couples. *Personal Relationships, 3,* 387–399.

Jones, J. T., Pelham, B. W., & Mirenberg, M. C. (2002). Name letter preferences are not merely mere exposure: Implicit egotism as self-regulation. *Journal of Experimental Social Psychology, 38,* 170–177.

Jones, J. T., Pelham, B. W., Carvallo, M., & Mirenberg, M. C. (2004). How do I love thee? Let me count the Js: Implicit egotism and interpersonal attraction. *Journal of Personality and Social Psychology, 87,* 665–683.

Jones, L. L., & Brunell, A. B. (2014). Clever and crude but not kind: Narcissism, self-esteem, and the self-reference effect. *Memory, 22,* 307–322.

Jones, M. B. (2015). The home advantage in major league baseball. *Perceptual & Motor Skills, 121,* 791–804.

Jones, T. M., Bottoms, B. L., & Stevenson, M. C. (2020). Child victim empathy mediates the influence of jurors' sexual abuse experiences on child sexual abuse case judgments: Meta-analyses. *Psychology, Public Policy, and Law, 26,* 312–332.

Josephson, W. L. (1987). Television violence and children's aggression: Testing the priming, social script, and disinhibition predictions. *Journal of Personality and Social Psychology, 53,* 882–890.

Joshanloo, M., & Bond, M. H. (2022). National wealth, individualism, generalised trust, and religiosity as moderators of the relationship between helping strangers and life satisfaction in 137 societies. *International Journal of Psychology.*

Jost, J. T. (2019). The IAT is dead, long live the IAT: Context-sensitive measures of implicit attitudes are indispensable to social and political psychology. *Current Directions in Psychological Science, 28,* 10–19.

Jost, J. T., Kay, A. C., & Thorisdottir, H. (Eds.), (2009). *Social and psychological bases of ideology and system justification.* New York: Oxford University Press.

Jouffre, S., & Croizet, J. (2016). Empowering and legitimizing the fundamental attribution error: Power and legitimization exacerbate the translation of role-constrained behaviors into ability differences. *European Journal of Social Psychology, 46,* 621–631.

Joyal-Desmarais, K., Scharmer, A. K., Madzelan, M. K., See, J. V., Rothman, A. J., & Snyder, M. (2022). Appealing to motivation to change attitudes, intentions, and behavior: A systematic review and meta-analysis of 702 experimental tests of the effects of motivational message matching on persuasion. *Psychological Bulletin, 148,* 465–517.

Judd, C. M., Blair, I. V., & Chapleau, K. M. (2004). Automatic stereotypes vs. automatic prejudice: Sorting out the possibilities in the Payne (2001) weapon paradigm. *Journal of Experimental Social Psychology, 40,* 75–81.

Jugert, P., Cohrs, J., & Duckitt, J. (2009). Inter- and intrapersonal processes underlying authoritarianism: The role of social conformity and personal need for structure. *European Journal of Personality, 23,* 607–621.

Jules, S. J., & McQuiston, D. E. (2013). Speech style and occupational status affect assessments of eyewitness testimony. *Journal of Applied Social Psychology, 43,* 741–748.

Jung, H., Seo, E., Han, E., Henderson, M. D., & Patall, E. A. (2020). Prosocial modeling: A meta-analytic review and synthesis. *Psychological Bulletin, 146,* 635–663.

Jung, J., Bramson, A., & Crano, W. D. (2018). An agent-based model of indirect minority influence on social change and diversity. *Social Influence, 13*(1), 18–38.

Jussim, L. (1986). Self-fulfilling prophecies: A theoretical and integrative review. *Psychological Review, 93,* 429–445.

Jussim, L. (2012). *Social perception and social reality: Why accuracy dominates bias and self-fulfilling prophecy.* New York: Oxford University Press.

Jussim, L. (2017). Accuracy, bias, self-fulfilling prophecies, and scientific self-correction. *Behavioral and Brain Sciences, 40,* 1–65.

Jussim, L., Crawford, J. T., Anglin, S. M., Chambers, J. R., Stevens, S. T., & Cohen, F. (2016). Stereotype accuracy: One of the largest and most replicable effects in all of social psychology. In T. D. Nelson (Ed.), *Handbook of prejudice, stereotyping, and discrimination., 2nd ed.* (pp. 31–63).

Jussim, L., Robustelli, S. L., & Cain, T. R. (2009). Teacher expectations and self-fulfilling prophecies. In K. R. Wenzel & A. Wigfield (Eds.), *Handbook of motivation at school.* New York: Routledge/Taylor & Francis.

Jussim, L., Stevens, S. T., & Honeycutt, N. (2018). Unasked questions about stereotype accuracy. *Archives of Scientific Psychology, 6,* 214–229.

Juvonen, J., & Graham, S. (2014). Bullying in schools: The power of bullies and the plight of victims. *Annual Review of Psychology, 65,* 159–185.

Kafadar, K., Dodson, C., Garrett, B., & Yaffe, J. (2022). New directions in eyewitness evidence. Wilson Center for Science and Justice.

Kagehiro, D. K. (1990). Defining the standard of proof in jury instructions. *Psychological Science, 1,* 194–200.

Kahan, D. M. (2014). Making climate-science communication evidence-based—All the way down. In M. Boykoff & D. Crow (Eds.), *Culture, politics and climate change.* New York: Routledge Press.

Kahan, D. M., Hoffman, D. A., Braman, D., Evans, D., & Rachlinski, J. J. (2012). They saw a protest: Cognitive illiberalism and the speech-conduct distinction. *Stanford Law Review, 64,* 851–906.

Kahan, D. M., Jenkins-Smith, H., & Braman, D. (2011). Cultural cognition of scientific consensus. *Journal of Risk Research, 14,* 147–174.

Kahan, D. M., Peters, E., Dawson, E. C., & Slovic, P. (2014). *Motivated numeracy and enlightened self-government.* The Cultural Cognition Project, Yale University, Working Paper No. 116.

Kahle, L. R., & Berman, J. (1979). Attitudes cause behaviors: A cross-lagged panel analysis. *Journal of Personality and Social Psychology, 37,* 315–321.

Kahn, C. (2019, August 19). For Trump, appeals to White fears about race may be a tougher sell in 2020. Reuters/Ipsos poll. https://reut.rs/3sHCgm6

Kahneman, D., & Deaton, A. (2010). High income improves evaluation of life but not emotional well-being. *PNAS, 107,* 16489–16493.

Kahneman, D., & Miller, D. T. (1986). Norm theory: Comparing reality to its alternatives. *Psychological Review, 93,* 75–88.

Kahneman, D., & Renshon, J. (2007, January/February). Why hawks win. *Foreign Policy.* www.foreignpolicy.com

Kahneman, D., & Tversky, A. (1979). Intuitive prediction: Biases and corrective procedures. *Management Science, 12,* 313–327.

Kahneman, D., & Tversky, A. (1995). Conflict resolution: A cognitive perspective. In K. Arrow, R. Mnookin, L. Ross, A. Tversky, & R. Wilson (Eds.), *Barriers to the negotiated resolution of conflict.* New York: Norton.

Kahneman, D. (2011). *Thinking, fast and slow.* New York: Farrar, Straus, and Giroux.

Kaiser, C. R., & Pratt-Hyatt, J. S. (2009). Distributing prejudice unequally: Do Whites direct their prejudice toward strongly identified minorities? *Journal of Personality and Social Psychology, 96,* 432–445.

Kalenkoski, C. M., Ribar, D. C., & Stratton, L. S. (2009). *How do adolescents spell time use?* Institute for the Study of Labor, Bonn, Germany, Discussion Paper 4374.

Kalick, S. M. (1977). *Plastic surgery, physical appearance, and person perception.* Unpublished doctoral dissertation, Harvard University. Cited by E. Berscheid in An overview of the psychological effects of physical attractiveness and some comments upon the psychological effects of knowledge of the effects of physical attractiveness. In W. Lucker, K. Ribbens, & J. A. McNamera (Eds.), *Logical aspects of facial form* (craniofacial growth series). Ann Arbor: University of Michigan Press, 1981.

Kalinoski, Z. T., Steele-Johnson, D., Peyton, E. J., Leas, K. A., Steinke, J., & Bowling, N. A. (2013). A meta-analytic evaluation of diversity training outcomes. *Journal of Organizational Behavior, 34,* 1076–1104.

Kalkstein, D. A., Hook, C. J., Hard, B. M., & Walton, G. M. (2023). Social norms govern what behaviors come to mind—And what do not. *Journal of Personality and Social Psychology, 124,* 1203–1229.

Kalven, H., Jr., & Zeisel, H. (1966). *The American jury.* Chicago: University of Chicago Press.

Kameda, T., & Sugimori, S. (1993). Psychological entrapment in group decision making: An assigned decision rule and a groupthink phenomenon. *Journal of Personality and Social Psychology, 65,* 282–292.

Kaminski, K. S., & Sporer, S. L. (2018). Observer judgments of identification accuracy are affected by non valid cues: A Brunswikian lens model analysis. *European Journal of Social Psychology, 48,* 47–61.

Kammer, D. (1982). Differences in trait ascriptions to self and friend: Unconfounding intensity from variability. *Psychological Reports, 51,* 99–102.

Kämmer, J. E., Hautz, W. E., Herzog, S. M., Kunina-Habenicht, O., & Kurvers, R. H. J. M. (2017). The potential of collective intelligence in emergency medicine: Pooling medical students' independent decisions improves diagnostic performance. *Medical Decision Making, 37*(6), 715–724.

Kampf, M. S., Liebermann, H., Kerschreiter, R., Krause, S., Nestler, S., & Schmukle, S. C. (2018). Disentangling the sources of mimicry: Social relations analyses of the link between mimicry and liking. *Psychological Science, 29,* 131–138.

Kamphuis, J., Meerlo, P., Koolhaas, J. M., & Lancel, M. (2012). Poor sleep as a potential causal factor in aggression and violence. *Sleep Medicine, 13,* 327–334.

Kanagawa, C., Cross, S. E., & Markus, H. R. (2001). "Who am I?" The cultural psychology of the conceptual self. *Personality and Social Psychology Bulletin, 27,* 90–103.

Kanazawa, S., & Kovar, J. L. (2004). Why beautiful people are more intelligent. *Intelligence, 32,* 227–243.

Kannan, V. D., & Veazie, P. J. (2022). US trends in social isolation, social engagement, and companionship—nationally and by age, sex, race/ethnicity, family income, and work hours, 2003–2020. *SSM–Population Health, 21,* 101331.

Kanten, A. B., & Teigen, K. H. (2008). Better than average and better with time: Relative evaluations of self and others in the past, present, and future. *European Journal of Social Psychology, 38,* 343–353.

Kantor, W. G. (2022, March 18). Teen who suffered concussion in TikTok 'Skullbreaker Challenge' now works to make social media safer. People.com.

Kaplan, M. F., & Schersching, C. (1980). Reducing juror bias: An experimental approach. In P. D. Lipsitt & B. D. Sales (Eds.), *New directions in psycholegal research* (pp. 149–170). New York: Van Nostrand Reinhold.

Kaplan, M. F. (1989). Task, situational, and personal determinants of influence processes in group decision making. In E. J. Lawler (Ed.), *Advances in group processes* (Vol. 6). Greenwich, CT: JAI Press.

Kaplan, M. F., Wanshula, L. T., & Zanna, M. P. (1993). Time pressure and information integration in social judgment: The effect of need for structure. In O. Svenson & J. Maule (Eds.), *Time pressure and stress in human judgment and decision making.* Cambridge, England: Cambridge University Press.

Kaposi, D. (2022). The second wave of critical engagement with Stanley Milgram's 'obedience to authority' experiments: What did we learn? *Social and Personality Psychology Compass, 16*(6).

Kappes, A., Harvey, A. H., Lohrenz, T., Montague, P. R., & Sharot, T. (2020). Confirmation bias in the utilization of others' opinion strength. *Nature Neuroscience, 23,* 130–137.

Kaprio, J., Koskenvuo, M., & Rita, H. (1987). Mortality after bereavement: A prospective study of 95,647 widowed persons. *American Journal of Public Health, 77,* 283–287.

Karatas, M., & Gurhan-Canli, Z. (2020). A construal level account of the impact of religion and God on prosociality. *Personality and Social Psychology Bulletin, 46*(7), 1107–1120.

Karau, S. J., & Williams, K. D. (1993). Social loafing: A meta-analytic review and theoretical integration. *Journal of Personality and Social Psychology, 65,* 681–706.

Karau, S. J., & Williams, K. D. (1997). The effects of group cohesiveness on social loafing and compensation. *Group Dynamics: Theory, Research, and Practice, 1,* 156–168.

Karlin, B., Zinger, J. F., & Ford, R. (2015). The effects of feedback on energy conservation: A meta-analysis. *Psychological Bulletin, 141,* 1205–1227.

Karney, B. R., & Bradbury, T. N. (1995). The longitudinal course of marital quality and stability: A review of theory, method, and research. *Psychological Bulletin, 118,* 3–34.

Karney, B. R., & Bradbury, T. N. (1997). Neuroticism, marital interaction, and the trajectory of marital satisfaction. *Journal of Personality and Social Psychology, 72,* 1075–1092.

Karney, B. R., & Bradbury, T. N. (2020). Research on marital satisfaction and stability in the 2010s: Challenging conventional wisdom. *Journal of Marriage and Family, 82,* 100–116.

Karremans, J. C., Frankenhis, W. E., & Arons, S. (2010). Blind men prefer a low waist-to-hip ratio. *Evolution and Human Behavior, 31,* 182–186.

Kasen, S., Chen, H., Sneed, J., Crawford, T., & Cohen, P. (2006). Social role and birth cohort influences on gender-linked personality traits in women: A 20-year longitudinal analysis. *Journal of Personality and Social Psychology, 91,* 944–958.

Kashian, N., Jang, J., Shin, S. Y., Dai, Y., & Walther, J. B. (2017). Self-disclosure and liking in computer-mediated communication. *Computers in Human Behavior, 71,* 275–283.

Kashima, E. S., & Kashima, Y. (1998). Culture and language: The case of cultural dimensions and personal pronoun use. *Journal of Cross-Cultural Psychology, 29,* 461–486.

Kashima, Y., & Kashima, E. S. (2003). Individualism, GNP, climate, and pronoun drop: Is individualism determined by affluence and climate, or does language use play a role? *Journal of Cross-Cultural Psychology, 34,* 125–134.

Kasser, T. (2000). Two versions of the American dream: Which goals and values make for a high quality of life? In E. Diener & D. Rahtz (Eds.), *Advances in quality of life: Theory and research.* Dordrecht, Netherlands: Kluwer.

Kasser, T. (2002). *The high price of materialism.* Cambridge, MA: MIT Press.

Kasser, T. (2011). *High price of materialism* [Animated video]. YouTube. https://www.youtube.com/watch?v=oGab38pKscw

Kasser, T. (2016). Materialistic values and goals. *Annual Review of Psychology, 67,* 489–514.

Kasser, T. (2018). Materialism and living well. In E. Diener, S. Oishi, & L. Tay (Eds.), *Handbook of well-being.* Salt Lake City, UT: DEF Publishers.

Kasser, T., Maynard, D., & Perry, A. (2019). An experimental laboratory test of the effects of alternative indicators of progress. *Social Indicators Research, 143,* 901–915.

Kassin, S. (2014). False confessions: Causes, consequences, and implications for reform. *Policy Insights from the Behavioral and Brain Sciences, 1,* 112–121.

Kassin, S. M., & Kiechel, K. L. (1996). The social psychology of false confessions: Compliance, internalization, and confabulation. *Psychological Science, 7,* 125–128.

Kassin, S. M., & Wrightsman, L. S. (1979). On the requirements of proof: The timing of judicial instruction and mock juror verdicts. *Journal of Personality and Social Psychology, 37,* 1877–1887.

Kassin, S. M. (2017). False confessions: How can psychology so basic be so counterintuitive? *American Psychologist, 72*(9), 951–964.

Kassin, S. M., Bogart, D., & Kerner, J. (2012). Confessions that corrupt: Evidence from the DNA exoneration case files. *Psychological Science, 23,* 41–45.

Kassin, S. M., Drizin, S. A., Grisso, T., Gudjonsson, G. H., Leo, R. A., & Redlich, A. D. (2010). Police-induced confessions: Risk factors and recommendations. *Law and Human Behavior, 34,* 3–38.

Kassin, S. M., Goldstein, C. C., & Savitsky, K. (2003). Behavioral confirmation in the interrogation room: On the dangers of presuming guilt. *Law and Human Behavior, 27,* 187–203.

Kassin, S. M., Redlich, A. D., Alceste, F., & Luke, T. J. (2018). On the general acceptance of confessions research: Opinions of the scientific community. *American Psychologist, 73,* 63–80.

Kassin, S. M., Tubb, V. A., Hosch, H. M., & Memon, A. (2001). On the "general acceptance" of eyewitness testimony research: A new survey of the experts. *American Psychologist, 56,* 405–416.

Katersky, A., & Hutchinson, B. (2022, October 18). Buffalo mass shooting suspect 'radicalized' by fringe social media: NY attorney general. ABCNews.com.

Katz, E. (1957). The two-step flow of communication: An up-to-date report on a hypothesis. *Public Opinion Quarterly, 21,* 61–78.

Katzev, R., & Wang, T. (1994). Can commitment change behavior? A case study of environmental actions. *Journal of Social Behavior and Personality, 9,* 13–26.

Katzev, R., Edelsack, L., Steinmetz, G., & Walker, T. (1978). The effect of reprimanding transgressions on subsequent helping behavior: Two field experiments. *Personality and Social Psychology Bulletin, 4,* 126–129.

Katz, J., & Moore, J. (2013). Bystander education training for campus sexual assault prevention: An initial meta-analysis. *Violence and Victims, 28,* 1054–1067.

Katz, J., Beach, S. R. H., & Joiner, T. E., Jr. (1999). Contagious depression in dating couples. *Journal of Social and Clinical Psychology, 18,* 1–13.

Katz, J., Pazienza, R., Olin, R., & Rich, H. (2015). That's what friends are for: Bystander responses to friends or strangers at risk for party rape victimization. *Journal of Interpersonal Violence, 30,* 2775–2792.

Katz, R. (2018, October 29). Inside the online cesspool of anti-Semitism that housed Robert Bowers. *Politico.* https://www.politico.com/magazine/story/2018/10/29/inside-the-online-cesspool-of-anti-semitism-that-housed-robert-bowers-221949

Katz-Wise, S. L., Priess, H. A., & Hyde, J. S. (2010). Gender-role attitudes and behavior across the transition to parenthood. *Developmental Psychology, 46,* 18–28.

Kaufman, J., & Zigler, E. (1987). Do abused children become abusive parents? *American Journal of Orthopsychiatry, 57,* 186–192.

Kaur-Ballagan, K. (2020, June 15). *Attitudes to race and inequality in Great Britain.* Ipsos MORI. https://www.ipsos.com/ipsos-mori/en-uk/attitudes-race-and-inequality-great-britain

Kawachi, I., Kennedy, B. P., & Wilkinson, R. G. (1999). Crime: Social disorganization and relative deprivation. *Social Science and Medicine, 48,* 719–731.

Kawakami, K., Dovidio, J. F., Moll, J., Hermsen, S., & Russin, A. (2000). Just say no (to stereotyping): Effects of training in the negation of stereotypic associations on stereotype activation. *Journal of Personality and Social Psychology, 78,* 871–888.

Kawakami, K., Dunn, E., Kiarmali, F., & Dovidio, J. F. (2009). Mispredicting affective and behavioral responses to racism. *Science, 323,* 276–278.

Kawakami, K., Friesen, J. P., Williams, A., Vingilis-Jaremko, L., Sidhu, D. M., Rodriguez-Bailón, R., Cañadas, E., & Hugenberg, K. (2021). Impact of perceived interpersonal similarity on attention to the eyes of same-race and other-race faces. *Cognitive Research: Principles and Implications, 6.*

Kay, A. C., & Eibach, R. P. (2013). Compensatory control and its implications for ideological extremism. *Journal of Social Issues, 69,* 564–585.

Kazerooni, F., Taylor, S. H., Bazarova, N. N., & Whitlock, J. (2018). Cyberbullying bystander intervention: The number of offenders and retweeting predict likelihood of helping a cyberbullying victim. *Journal of Computer-Mediated Communication, 23,* 146–162.

Kearl, H. (2018). *The facts behind the #MeToo movement: A national study on sexual harassment and assault.* Stop Street Harassment. http://www.stopstreetharassment.org/wp-content/uploads/2018/01/Full-Report-2018-National-Study-on-Sexual-Harassment-and-Assault.pdf

Keating, J. P., & Brock, T. C. (1974). Acceptance of persuasion and the inhibition of counterargumentation under various distraction tasks. *Journal of Experimental Social Psychology, 10,* 301–309.

Keating, J., Van Boven, L., & Judd, C. M. (2016). Partisan underestimation of the polarizing influence of group discussion. *Journal of Experimental Social Psychology, 65,* 52–58.

Kellen, D., & McAdoo, R. M. (2022). Toward a more comprehensive modeling of sequential lineups. *Cognitive Research: Principles and Implications, 7.*

Keller, E. B., & Berry, B. (2003). *The influentials: One American in ten tells the other nine how to vote, where to eat, and what to buy.* New York: Free Press.

Keller, J., & Dauenheimer, D. (2003). Stereotype threat in the classroom: Dejection mediates the disrupting threat effect on women's math performance. *Personality and Social Psychology Bulletin, 29,* 371–381.

Kellerman, J., Lewis, J., & Laird, J. D. (1989). Looking and loving: The effects of mutual gaze on feelings of romantic love. *Journal of Research in Personality, 23,* 145–161.

Kellermann, A. L. (1997). Comment: Gunsmoke—changing public attitudes toward smoking and firearms. *American Journal of Public Health, 87,* 910–912.

Kellermann, A. L., Rivara, F. P., Rushforth, N. B., Banton, J. G., Reay, D. T., Francisco, J. T., Locci, A. B., Prodzinski, J., Hackman, B. B., & Somes, G. (1993). Gun ownership as a risk factor for homicide in the home. *New England Journal of Medicine, 329,* 1984–1991.

Kelley, H. H., & Stahelski, A. J. (1970). The social interaction basis of cooperators' and competitors' beliefs about others. *Journal of Personality and Social Psychology, 16,* 66–91.

Kelly, A. E., & Macready, D. E. (2009). Why disclosing to a confidant can be so good (or bad) for us. In W. & T. Afifi (Eds.), *Uncertainty and information regulation in interpersonal contexts: Theories and applications* (pp. 384–402). New York: Routledge.

Kelly, D. J., Liu, S., Ge, L., Quinn, P. C., Slater, A. M., Lee, K., Liu, Q., & Pascalis, O. (2007). Cross-race preferences for same-race faces extended beyond the African versus Caucasian contrast in 3-month-old infants. *Infancy, 11,* 87–95.

Kelly, D. J., Quinn, P. C., Slater, A. M., Lee, K., Ge, L., & Pascalis, O. (2007). The other-race effect develops during infancy: Evidence of perceptual narrowing. *Psychological Science, 18,* 1084–1089.

Kelly, D. J., Quinn, P. C., Slater, A. M., Lee, K., Gibson, A., Smith, M., Ge, L., & Y Pascalis, O. (2005). Three-month-olds, but not newborns prefer own-race faces. *Developmental Science, 8,* F31–F36.

Kelman, H. C. (1997). Group processes in the resolution of international conflicts: Experiences from the Israeli-Palestinian case. *American Psychologist, 52,* 212–220.

Kelman, H. C. (1998). Building a sustainable peace: The limits of pragmatism in the Israeli-Palestinian negotiations. Address to the American Psychological Association convention, San Francisco, California.

Kelman, H. C. (2007). The Israeli-Palestinian peace process and its vicissitudes: Insights from attitude theory. *American Psychologist, 62,* 287–303.

Kelman, H. C. (2010). Looking back at my work on conflict resolution in the Middle East. *Peace and Conflict: Journal of Peace Psychology, 16,* 361–387.

Kende, J., Phalet, K., Van den Noortgate, W., Kara, A., & Fischer, R. (2018). Equality revisited: A cultural meta-analysis of intergroup contact and prejudice. *Social Psychological and Personality Science, 9,* 887–895.

Kendrick, R. V., & Olson, M. A. (2012). When feeling right leads to being right in the reporting of implicitly-formed attitudes, or how I learned to stop worrying and trust my gut. *Journal of Experimental Social Psychology, 48,* 1316–1321.

Kennedy, C., & Hartig, H. (2019, February 27). Response rates in telephone surveys have resumed their decline. Pew Research Center.

Kennedy, J. A., Anderson, C., & Moore, D. A. (2013). When overconfidence is revealed to others: Testing the status-enhancement theory of overconfidence. *Organizational Behavior and Human Decision Processes, 122,* 266–279.

Kennedy, J. F. (1956). *Profiles in courage* (p. 4). New York: Harper.

Kennedy, K. A., & Pronin, E. (2008). When disagreement gets ugly: Perceptions of bias and the escalation of conflict. *Personality and Social Psychology Bulletin, 34,* 833–848.

Kenny, D. A., & Nasby, W. (1980). Splitting the reciprocity correlation. *Journal of Personality and Social Psychology, 38,* 249–256.

Kenrick, D. T., & MacFarlane, S. W. (1986). Ambient temperature and horn-honking: A field study of the heat/aggression relationship. *Environment and Behavior, 18,* 179–191.

Kenrick, D. T., & Trost, M. R. (1987). A biosocial theory of heterosexual relationships. In K. Kelly (Ed.), *Females, males, and sexuality.* Albany: State University of New York Press.

Kenrick, D. T., Gutierres, S. E., & Goldberg, L. L. (1989). Influence of popular erotica on judgments of strangers and mates. *Journal of Experimental Social Psychology, 25,* 159–167.

Kenrick, D. T., Nieuweboer, S., & Buunk, A. P. (2009). Universal mechanisms and cultural diversity: Replacing the blank slate with a coloring book. In M. Schaller, A. Norenzayan, S. Heine, T. Yamagishi, & T. Kameda (Eds.), *Evolution, culture, and the human mind.* New York: Psychology Press.

Kenthirarajah, D. (Toni), Camp, N. P., Walton, G. M., Kay, A. C., & Cohen, G. L. (2023). Does "Jamal" receive a harsher sentence than "James"? First-name bias in the criminal sentencing of Black men. *Law and Human Behavior, 47,* 169–181.

Kenworthy, J. B., Hewstone, M., Levine, J. M., Martin, R., & Willis, H. (2008). The phenomenology of minority-majority status: Effects of innovation in argument generation. *European Journal of Social Psychology, 38,* 624–636.

Kern, M. L., & Sap, M. (2015, February). *Do you feel what I feel? Cultural variations in linguistic expressions of emotion.* Symposium talk presented at the 16th annual meeting of the Society of Personality and Social Psychology, Long Beach, CA.

Kerr, N. (1999). Behind the scenes. In D. G. Myers (Ed.), *Social Psychology* (6th ed.). New York: McGraw Hill.

Kerr, N. L., & Bray, R. M. (2005). Simulation, realism, and the study of the jury. In N. Brewer & K. D. Williams (Eds.), *Psychology and law: An empirical perspective.* New York: Guilford.

Kerr, N. L., & Bruun, S. E. (1981). Ringelmann revisited: Alternative explanations for the social loafing effect. *Personality and Social Psychology Bulletin, 7*(2), 224–231.

Kerr, N. L., & Kaufman-Gilliland, C. M. (1994). Communication, commitment, and cooperation in social dilemmas. *Journal of Personality and Social Psychology, 66,* 513–529.

Kerr, N. L. & Kaufman-Gilliland, C. M. (1997). ". . . and besides, I probably couldn't have made a difference anyway": Justification of social dilemma defection via perceived self-inefficacy. *Journal of Experimental Social Psychology, 33,* 211–230.

Kerr, N. L., & MacCoun, R. J. (1985). The effects of jury size and polling method on the process and product of jury deliberation. *Journal of Personality and Social Psychology, 48,* 349–363.

Kerr, N. L. (1981). Social transition schemes: Charting the group's road to agreement. *Journal of Personality and Social Psychology, 41,* 684–702.

Kerr, N. L. (1983). Motivation losses in small groups: A social dilemma analysis. *Journal of Personality and Social Psychology, 45,* 819–828.

Kerr, N. L. (1989). Illusions of efficacy: The effects of group size on perceived efficacy in social dilemmas. *Journal of Experimental Social Psychology, 25,* 287–313.

Kerr, N. L. (1992). Norms in social dilemmas. In D. Schroeder (Ed.), *Social dilemmas: Psychological perspectives.* New York: Praeger.

Kerr, N. L., Atkin, R. S., Stasser, G., Meek, D., Holt, R. W., & Davis, J. H. (1976). Guilt beyond a reasonable doubt: Effects of concept definition and assigned decision rule on the judgments of mock jurors. *Journal of Personality and Social Psychology, 34,* 282–294.

Kerr, N. L., Messé, L. A., Seok, D.-H., Sambolec, E. J., Lount, R. B., Jr., & Park, E. S. (2007). Psychological mechanisms underlying the Köhler motivation gain. *Personality and Social Psychology Bulletin, 33,* 828–841.

Kerr, R. A. (2009). Amid worrisome signs of warming, "climate fatigue" sets in. *Science, 326,* 926–928.

Kersten, R., & Greitemeyer, T. (2022). Why do habitual violent video game players believe in the cathartic effects of violent video games? A misinterpretation of mood improvement as a reduction in aggressive feelings. *Aggressive Behavior, 48,* 219–231.

Kesebir, S., & Oishi, S. (2010). A spontaneous self-reference effect in memory: Why some birthdays are harder to remember than others. *Psychological Science, 21,* 1525–1531.

Keynes, J. M. (1936). *The general theory of employment, interest, and money.* Palgrave Macmillan.

Khurana, A., Bleakley, A., Ellithorpe, M. E., Hennessy, M., Jamieson, P. E., & Weitz, I. (2019). Media violence exposure and aggression in adolescents: A risk and resilience perspective. *Aggressive Behavior, 45,* 70–81.

Kiecolt-Glaser, J. K., Loving, T. J., Stowell, J. R., Malarkey, W. B., Lemeshow, S., Dickinson, S. L., & Glaser, R. (2005). Hostile marital interactions, proinflammatory cytokine production, and wound healing. *Archives of General Psychiatry, 62,* 1377–1384.

Kiecolt-Glaser, J. K., Malarkey, W. B., Chee, M., Newton, T., Cacioppo, J. T., Mao, H.-Y., & Glaser, R. (1993). Negative behavior during marital conflict is associated with immunological down-regulation. *Psychosomatic Medicine, 55,* 395–409.

Kierkegaard, S. (1844). *The journals of Søren Kierkegaard,* IV A, 164.

Kihlstrom, J. F., & Cantor, N. (1984). Mental representations of the self. In L. Berkowitz (Ed.), *Advances in experimental social psychology* (Vol. 17). New York: Academic Press.

Kihlstrom, J. F. (1994). *The social construction of memory.* Address to the American Psychological Society Convention, Washington, DC.

Kille, D. R., Forest, A. L., & Wood, J. V. (2013). Tall, dark, and stable: Embodiment motivates mate selection preferences. *Psychological Science, 24,* 112–114.

Killen, M., Luken Raz, K., & Graham, S. (2022). Reducing prejudice through promoting cross-group friendships. *Review of General Psychology, 26,* 361–376.

Killingsworth, M. (2021). Experienced well-being rises with income, even above $75,000 per year. *Proceedings of the National Academy of Sciences, 118,* e2016976118.

Killingsworth, M., Kahneman, D., & Mellers, B. (2022). Income and emotional well-being: A conflict resolved. *Proceedings of the National Academies of Science, 120,* e2208661120.

Kim, D., & Yoon, K. L. (2020). Emotional response to autobiographical memories in depression: Less happiness to positive and more sadness to negative memories. *Cognitive Behaviour Therapy.* Advance online publication. https://doi.org/10.1080/16506073.2020.1765859

Kim, D. (2016). The associations between US state and local social spending, income inequality, and individual all-cause and cause-specific mortality: The National Longitudinal Mortality Study. *Preventive Medicine, 84,* 62–68.

Kim, D. A., Hwong, A. R., Stafford, D., Hughes, D. A., O'Malley, A. J., Fowler, J. H., & Christakis, N. A. (2015). Social network targeting to maximise population behaviour change: A cluster randomised controlled trial. *The Lancet, 386*(9989), 145–153.

Kimel, S. Y., Huesmann, R., Kunst, J. R., & Halperin, E. (2016). Living in a genetic world: How learning about interethnic genetic similarities and differences affects peace and conflict. *Personality and Social Psychology Bulletin, 42,* 688–700.

Kim, E. S., Whillans, A. V., Lee, M. T., Chen, Y., & VanderWeele, T. J. (2020). Volunteering and subsequent health and well-being in older adults: An outcome-wide longitudinal approach. *American Journal of Preventive Medicine, 59,* 176–186.

Kim, H., & Markus, H. R. (1999). Deviance of uniqueness, harmony or conformity? A cultural analysis. *Journal of Personality and Social Psychology, 77,* 785–800.

Kim, H. S., & Sherman, D. K. (2007). "Express yourself": Culture and the effect of self-expression on choice. *Journal of Personality and Social Psychology, 92,* 1–11.

Kimmel, A. J. (1998). In defense of deception. *American Psychologist, 53,* 803–805.

Kim, S., & Harwood, J. (2020). Facebook contact: The effect of an outgroup member's language proficiency on desire for future intergroup contact. *International Journal of Intercultural Relations, 77,* 160–168.

Kim, S., Baek, M., & Park, S. (2021). Association of parent–child experiences with insecure attachment in adulthood: A systematic review and meta-analysis. *Journal of Family Theory & Review, 13,* 58–76.

Kim, S. E., Kim, Y., Hashizume, M., Honda, Y., Kazutaka, O., Hijioka, Y., & Kim, H. (2023). Positive Association of Aggression with Ambient Temperature. *The Yale Journal of Biology and Medicine, 96,* 189–196.

Kim, S., Park, J., Park, K., & Eom, J. (2013). Judge-jury agreement in criminal cases: The first three years of the Korean jury system. *Journal of Empirical Legal Studies, 10,* 35–53.

Kim, S., Stavrova, O., & Vohs, K. D. (2022). Do voting and election outcomes predict changes in conspiracy beliefs? Evidence from two high-profile US Elections. *Journal of Experimental Social Psychology, 103,* 1–8.

Kim, Y. K., Park, J. J., & Koo, K. K. (2015). Testing self-segregation: Multiple-group structural modeling of college students' interracial friendship by race. *Research in Higher Education, 56,* 57–77.

Kinder, D. R., & Sears, D. O. (1985). Public opinion and political action. In G. Lindzey & E. Aronson (Eds.), *The handbook of social psychology,* (3rd ed.). New York: Random House.

Kingdon, J. W. (1967). Politicians' beliefs about voters. *The American Political Science Review, 61,* 137–145.

Kingston, D. A., Fedoroff, P., Firestone, P., Curry, S., & Bradford, J. M. (2008). Pornography use and sexual aggression: The impact of frequency and type of pornography use on recidivism among sexual offenders. *Aggressive Behavior, 34,* 341–351.

Kinias, Z., Kim, H. S., Hafenbrack, A. C., & Lee, J. J. (2014). Standing out as a signal to selfishness: Culture and devaluation of non-normative characteristics. *Organizational Behavior and Human Decision Processes, 124,* 190–203

Kinnier, R. T., & Metha, A. T. (1989). Regrets and priorities at three stages of life. *Counseling and Values, 33,* 182–193.

Kinzler, K. D., Shutts, K., Dejesus, J., & Spelke, E. S. (2009). Accent trumps race in guiding children's social preferences. *Social Cognition, 27,* 623–634.

Kirchner, L., Schummer, S. E., Krug, H., Kube, T., & Rief, W. (2022). How social rejection expectations and depressive symptoms bi-directionally predict each other–A cross-lagged panel analysis. *Psychology and Psychotherapy: Theory, Research and Practice, 95,* 477–492.

Kirzinger, A., Kearney, A., Montero, A., Sparks, G., Dawson, L., & Brodie, M. (2023, March 24). KFF/The Washington Post Trans Survey. KFF.org.

Kitayama, S., & Karasawa, M. (1997). Implicit self-esteem in Japan: Name letters and birthday numbers. *Personality and Social Psychology Bulletin, 23,* 736–742.

Kitayama, S., & Markus, H. R. (2000). The pursuit of happiness and the realization of sympathy: Cultural patterns of self, social relations, and well-being. In E. Diener & E. M. Suh (Eds.), *Subjective well-being across cultures.* Cambridge, MA: MIT Press.

Kitayama, S. (1999). Behind the scenes. In D. G. Myers (Ed.), *Social psychology* (6th ed.). New York: McGraw Hill.

Kitayama, S., Salvador, C. E., Nanakdewa, K., Rossmaier, A., San Martin, A., & Savani, K. (2022). Varieties of interdependence and the emergence of the Modern West: Toward the globalizing of psychology. *American Psychologist, 77,* 991–1006.

Kite, M. E. (2001). Changing times, changing gender roles: Who do we want women and men to be? In R. K. Unger (Ed.), *Handbook of the psychology of women and gender.* New York: Wiley.

Kito, M., Yuki, M., & Thomson, R. (2017). Relational mobility and close relationships: a socioecological approach to explain cross-cultural differences. *Personal Relationships, 24,* 114–130.

Kivikangas, J. M., Fernández-Castilla, B., Järvelä, S., Ravaja, N., & Lönnqvist, J.-E. (2021). Moral foundations and political orientation: Systematic review and meta-analysis. *Psychological Bulletin, 147,* 55–94.

Kjaervik, S. L., & Bushman, B. J. (2021). The link between narcissism and aggression: A meta-analytic review. *Psychological Bulletin, 147,* 477–503.

Klaas, E. T. (1978). Psychological effects of immoral actions: The experimental evidence. *Psychological Bulletin, 85,* 756–771.

Klapwijk, A., & Van Lange, P. A. M. (2009). Promoting cooperation and trust in "noisy" situations: The power of generosity. *Journal of Personality and Social Psychology, 96,* 83–103.

Klebl, C., Luo, Y., & Bastian, B. (2022). Beyond aesthetic judgment: Beauty increases moral standing through perceptions of purity. *Personality and Social Psychology Bulletin, 48,* 954–967.

Kleck, R. E., & Strenta, A. (1980). Perceptions of the impact of negatively valued physical characteristics on social interaction. *Journal of Personality and Social Psychology, 39,* 861–873.

Klein, A., & Golub, S. A. (2016). Family rejection as a predictor of suicide attempts and substance misuse among transgender and gender nonconforming adults. *LGBT Health, 3,* 193–199.

Klein, J. G. (1991). Negative effects in impression formation: A test in the political arena. *Personality and Social Psychology Bulletin, 17,* 412–418.

Kleinke, C. L. (1977). Compliance to requests made by gazing and touching experimenters in field settings. *Journal of Experimental Social Psychology, 13,* 218–223.

Klein, N., & Epley, N. (2017). Less evil than you: Bounded self-righteousness in character inferences, emotional reactions, and behavioral extremes. *Personality and Social Psychology Bulletin, 43,* 1202–1212.

Klein, N. (2017). Prosocial behavior increases perceptions of meaning in life. *Journal of Positive Psychology, 12,* 354–361.

Klein, R. A., Vianello, M., Hasselman, F., Adams, B. G., Adams, R. B., . . . Nosek, B. A. (2018). Many Labs 2: Investigating variation in replicability across samples and settings. *Advances in Methods and Practices in Psychological Science, 1,* 443–490.

Klein, W. M., & Kunda, Z. (1992). Motivated person perception: Constructing justifications for desired beliefs. *Journal of Experimental Social Psychology, 28,* 145–168.

Klentz, B., Beaman, A. L., Mapelli, S. D., & Ullrich, J. R. (1987). Perceived physical attractiveness of supporters and nonsupporters of the women's movement: An attitude-similarity-mediated error (ASME). *Personality and Social Psychology Bulletin, 13,* 513–523.

Klinesmith, J., Kasser, T., & McAndrew, F. T. (2006). Guns, testosterone, and aggression. *Psychological Science, 17*(7), 568–571.

Klopfer, P. H. (1958). Influence of social interaction on learning rates in birds. *Science, 128,* 903.

Kluger, J. (2020). The science of love. In *The Science of Gender.* Time special edition.

Knewtson, H. S., & Sias, R. W. (2010). Why Susie owns Starbucks: The name letter effect in security selection. *Journal of Business Research, 63,* 1324–1327.

Knight, G. P., Guthrie, I. K., Page, M. C., & Fabes, R. A. (2002). Emotional arousal and gender differences in aggression: A meta-analysis. *Aggressive Behavior, 28,* 366–393.

Knight, J. A., & Vallacher, R. R. (1981). Interpersonal engagement in social perception: The consequences of getting into the action. *Journal of Personality and Social Psychology, 40,* 990–999.

Knoblock-Westerwick, S., Liu, L., Hino, A., Westerwick, A., & Johnson, B. K. (2019). Context impacts on confirmation bias: Evidence from the 2017 Japanese snap election compared with American and German findings. *Human Communication Research, 45,* 427–449.

Knoll, M. A. Z., & Arkes, H. R. (2017). The effects of expertise on the hindsight bias. *Journal of Behavioral Decision Making, 30,* 389–399.

Knowles, E. D., & Peng, K. (2005). White selves: Conceptualizing and measuring a dominant-group identity. *Journal of Personality and Social Psychology, 89,* 223–241.

Knowles, E. S. (1983). Social physics and the effects of others: Tests of the effects of audience size and distance on social judgment and behavior. *Journal of Personality and Social Psychology, 45,* 1263–1279.

Knowles, M. (2020, July 18.) A med-school staffer dived into online groups to debunk coronavirus conspiracy theories. Would anyone listen? *The Washington Post.* https://www.washingtonpost.com/nation/2020/07/18/coronavirus-online-groups-misinformation/

Knowles, M. L., Lucas, G. M., Baumeister, R. F., & Gardner, W. L. (2015). Choking under social pressure: Social monitoring among the lonely. *Personality and Social Psychology Bulletin, 41,* 805–821.

Knox, R. E., & Inkster, J. A. (1968). Postdecision dissonance at post-time. *Journal of Personality and Social Psychology, 8,* 319–323.

Koehler, D. J. (1991). Explanation, imagination, and confidence in judgment. *Psychological Bulletin, 110,* 499–519.

Koehler, D. J. (2016). Can journalistic "false balance" distort public perception of consensus in expert opinion? *Journal of Experimental Psychology: Applied, 22,* 24–38.

Koenig, A. M., Eagly, A. H., Mitchell, A. A., & Ristikari, T. (2011). Are leader stereotypes masculine? A meta-analysis of three research paradigms. *Psychological Bulletin, 137,* 616–642.

Koenig, L. B., McGue, M., & Iacono, W. G. (2008). Stability and change in religiousness during emerging adulthood. *Developmental Psychology, 44,* 531–543.

Koerth, M., & Lartey, J. (2020, June 1). De-escalation keeps protesters and police safer. Departments respond with force anyway. *Five Thirty-Eight.* https://fivethirtyeight.com/features/de-escalation-keeps-protesters-and-police-safer-heres-why-departments-respond-with-force-anyway/

Koestner, R., & Wheeler, L. (1988). Self-presentation in personal advertisements: The influence of implicit notions of attraction and role expectations. *Journal of Social and Personal Relationships, 5,* 149–160.

Kogut, T., & Ritov, I. (2005). The "identified victim" effect: An identified group, or just a single individual? *Journal of Behavioral Decision Making, 18,* 157–167.

Koklic, M. K., Golob, U., Podnar, K., & Zabkar, V. (2019). The interplay of past consumption, attitudes and personal norms in organic food buying. *Appetite, 137,* 27–34.

Kolata, G., & Peterson, I. (2001, July 21). New way to insure eyewitnesses can ID the right bad guy. *The New York Times.* http://www.crimelynx.com/newway.html

Kolivas, E. D., & Gross, A. M. (2007). Assessing sexual aggression: Addressing the gap between rape victimization and perpetration prevalence rates. *Aggression and Violent Behavior, 12,* 315–328.

Koltsova, O. Y., Mararitsa, L. V., Terpilovskii, M. A., & Sinyavskaya, Y. E. (2021). Social signature in an online environment: Stability and cognitive limits. *Computers in Human Behavior, 122.*

Konrad, A. M., Ritchie, J. E., Jr., Lieb, P., & Corrigall, E. (2000). Sex differences and similarities in job attribute preferences: A meta-analysis. *Psychological Bulletin, 126,* 593–641.

Konrath, S., Au, J., & Ramsey, L. R. (2012). Cultural differences in face-ism: Male politicians have bigger heads in more gender-equal cultures. *Psychology of Women Quarterly, 36,* 476–487.

Konrath, S. H., Chopik, W. J., Hsing, C. K., & O'Brien, E. (2014). Changes in adult attachment styles in American college students over time: A meta-analysis. *Personality and Social Psychology Review, 18,* 326–348.

Koole, S. L., Dijksterhuis, A., & van Knippenberg, A. (2001). What's in a name? Implicit self-esteem and the automatic self. *Journal of Personality and Social Psychology, 80,* 669–685.

Koo, M., Algoe, S. B., Wilson, T. D., & Gilbert, D. T. (2008). It's a wonderful life: Mentally subtracting positive events improves people's affective states, contrary to their affective forecasts. *Journal of Personality and Social Psychology, 95,* 1217–1224.

Koomen, W., & Dijker, A. J. (1997). Ingroup and outgroup stereotypes and selective processing. *European Journal of Social Psychology,* 27, 589–601.

Koppel, L., Andersson, D., Tinghog, G., Vastfjall, D., & Feldman, G. (2023). We are all less risky and more skillful than our fellow drivers: Replication and extension of Svenson (1981). *Meta-Psychology, 7.*

Koppel, M., Argamon, S., & Shimoni, A. R. (2002). Automatically categorizing written texts by author gender. *Literary and Linguistic Computing, 17,* 401–412.

Kopp, L., Atance, C. M., & Pearce, S. (2017). 'Things aren't so bad!': Preschoolers overpredict the emotional intensity of negative outcomes. *British Journal of Developmental Psychology, 35,* 623–627.

Koriat, A., Lichtenstein, S., & Fischhoff, B. (1980). Reasons for confidence. *Journal of Experimental Social Psychology: Human Learning and Memory, 6,* 107–118.

Kornbrot, D. E., Msetfi, R. M., & Grimwood, M. J. (2013). Time perception and depressive realism: Judgment type, psychophysical functions and bias. *PLoS ONE, 8,* e71585.

Kosse, F., & Tincani, M. M. (2020). Prosociality predicts market success around the world. *Nature Communications, 11,* 5298.

Kostic, B., & Scofield, J. E. (2022). Sex and sexual orientation differences in sexuality and mate choice criteria. *Archives of Sexual Behavior, 51,* 2855–2865.

Koterba, E. A., Ponti, F., & Ligman, K. (2021). "Get out of my selfie!" Narcissism, gender, and motives for self-photography among emerging adults. *Psychology of Popular Media, 10*(1), 98–104.

Kouchaki, M., & Wareham, J. (2015). Excluded and behaving unethically: Social exclusion, physiological responses, and unethical behavior. *Journal of Applied Psychology, 100,* 547–556.

Koudenburg, N., Greijdanus, H., & Scheepers, D. (2019). The polarizing effects of group discussion in a negative normative context: Integrating societal-, group-, and individual-level factors. *British Journal of Social Psychology, 58,* 150–174.

Kovera, M. B., & Evelo, A. J. (2017). The case for double-blind lineup administration. *Psychology, Public Policy, and Law, 23,* 421–437.

Kovera, M. B., & Evelo, A. J. (2020). Improving eyewitness-identification evidence through double-blind lineup administration. *Current Directions in Psychological Science, 29,* 563–568.

Kowal, M., Sorokowski, P., Dinić, B. M., Pisanski, K., Gjoneska, B., Frederick, D. A., Pfuhl, G., Milfont, T. L., Bode, A., Aguilar, L., García, F. E., Roberts, S. C., Abad-Villaverde, B., Kavčič, T., Miroshnik, K. G., Ndukaihe, I. L. G., Šafárová, K., Valentova, J. V., Aavik, T., . . . Sternberg, R. J. (2023). Validation of the short version (tls-15) of the triangular love scale (tls-45) across 37 languages. *Archives of Sexual Behavior.*

Kowal, M., Sorokowski, P., Pisanski, K., Valentova, J. V., Varella, M. A. C., Frederick, D. A., Al-Shawaf, L., García, F. E., Giammusso, I., Gjoneska, B., Kozma, L., Otterbring, T., Papadatou-Pastou, M., Pfuhl, G., Stöckli, S., Studzinska, A., Toplu-Demirtaş, E., Touloumakos, A. K., Bakos, B. E., . . . et al. (2022). Predictors of enhancing human physical attractiveness: Data from 93 countries. *Evolution and Human Behavior.*

Kowalski, R. M., Guimetti, G. W., Schroeder, A. N., & Lattanner, M. R. (2014). Bullying in the digital age: A critical review and meta-analysis of cyberbulling research among youth. *Psychological Bulletin, 140,* 1073–1137.

Koyama, A., Ohtake, Y., Yasuda, K., Sakai, K., Sakamoto, R., Matsuoka, H., Okumi, H., & Yasuda, T. (2018). Avoiding diagnostic errors in psychosomatic medicine: A case series study. *BioPsychoSocial Medicine, 12,* 4.

Kraav, S.-L., Awoyemi, O., Junttila, N., Vornanen, R., Kauhanen, J., Toikko, T., Lehto, S. M., Hantunen, S., & Tolmunen, T. (2020). The effects of loneliness and social isolation on all-cause, injury, cancer, and CVD mortality in a cohort of middle-aged Finnish men A prospective study. *Aging & Mental Health.* Online publication. https://doi.org/10.1080/13607863.2020.1830945

Krackow, A., & Blass, T. (1995). When nurses obey or defy inappropriate physician orders: Attributional differences. *Journal of Social Behavior and Personality, 10,* 585–594.

Kraft, T. L., & Pressman, S. D. (2012). Grin and bear it: The influence of manipulated facial expression on the stress response. *Psychological Science, 23,* 1372–1378.

Krahe, B., Busching, R., & Moller, I. (2012). Media violence use and aggression among German adolescents: Associations and trajectories of change in a three-wave longitudinal study. *Psychology of Popular Media Culture, 1,* 152–166.

Krahe, B., Moller, I., Huesmann, L. R., Kirwil, L., Felber, J., & Berger, A. (2010). Desensitization to media violence: Links with habitual media violence exposure, aggressive cognitions, and aggressive behavior. *Journal of Personality and Social Psychology, 100,* 630–646.

Krahé, B., & Busching, R. (2015). Breaking the vicious cycle of media violence use and aggression: A test of intervention effects over 30 months. *Psychology of Violence, 5,* 217–226.

Krahé, B., & Möller, I. (2010). Longitudinal effects of media violence on aggression and empathy among German adolescents. *Journal of Applied Developmental Psychology, 31,* 401–409.

Kramer, A. D. I., & Chung, C. K. (2011). *Dimensions of self-expression in Facebook status updates.* Proceedings of the Fifth International AAAI Conference on Weblogs and Social Media (www.aaai.org).

Kramer, A. D. I., Guillory, J. E., & Hancock, J. T. (2014). Experimental evidence of massive-scale emotional contagion through social networks. *Proceedings of the National Academy of Sciences, 111,* 8788–8790.

Kramer, A. E. (2008, August 32). Russia's collective farms: Hot capitalist property. *The New York Times.* https://www.nytimes.com/2008/08/31/business/worldbusiness/31food.html

Kramer, G. P., Kerr, N. L., & Carroll, J. S. (1990). Pretrial publicity, judicial remedies, and jury bias. *Law and Human Behavior, 14,* 409–438.

Kramer, R. S. S., & Jones, A. L. (2023). Wanting or having children predicts age preferences in online dating. *Evolutionary Behavioral Sciences, 17,* 16–30.

Kraus, M. W., & Callaghan, B. (2016). Social class and prosocial behavior: The moderating role of public versus private contexts. *Social Psychological and Personality Science, 7,* 769–777.

Kraus, M. W., & Keltner, D. (2013). Social class rank, essentialism, and punitive judgment. *Journal of Personality and Social Psychology, 105,* 247–261.

Kraus, M. W., Côté, S., & Keltner, D. (2010). Social class, contextualism, and empathic accuracy. *Psychological Science, 21,* 1716–1723.

Kraus, M. W., Onyeador, I. N., Daumeyer, N. M., Rucker, J. M., & Richeson, J. A. (2019). The misperception of racial economic inequality. *Perspectives on Psychological Science, 14,* 899–921.

Kraus, M. W., Piff, P. K., Mendoza-Denton, R., Rheinschmidt, M. L., & Keltner, D. (2012). Social class, solipsism, and contextualism: How the rich are different from the poor. *Psychological Review, 119,* 546–572.

Kraus, S. J. (1995). Attitudes and the prediction of behavior: A meta-analysis of the empirical literature. *Personality and Social Psychology Bulletin, 21,* 58–75.

Krauss, S., & Orth, U. (2022). Work Experiences and Self-Esteem Development: A Meta-Analysis of Longitudinal Studies. *European Journal of Personality, 36*(6), 849–869.

Krauss, S., Orth, U., & Robins, R. W. (2020). Family environment and self-esteem development: A longitudinal study from age 10 to 16. *Journal of Personality and Social Psychology, 119*(2), 457–478.

Kraut, R. E. (1973). Effects of social labeling on giving to charity. *Journal of Experimental Social Psychology, 9*(6), 551–562.

Kravitz, D. A., & Martin, B. (1986). Ringelmann rediscovered: The original article. *Journal of Personality and Social Psychology, 50,* 936–941.

Krebs, D. (1970). Altruism—An examination of the concept and a review of the literature. *Psychological Bulletin, 73,* 258–302.

Krebs, D. (1975). Empathy and altruism. *Journal of Personality and Social Psychology, 32,* 1134–1146.

Krebs, D. (1998). The evolution of moral behaviors. In C. Crawford & D. L. Krebs (Eds.), *Handbook of evolutionary psychology: Ideas, issues, and applications.* Mahwah, NJ: Erlbaum.

Krendl, A. C., Richeson, J. A., Kelley, W. M., & Heatherton, T. F. (2008). The negative consequences of threat: A functional magnetic resonance imaging investigation of the neural mechanisms underlying women's underperformance in math. *Psychological Science, 19,* 168–175.

Kristof, N. (2018, March 23). Conflict is more profitable than peace. *The New York Times.* https://www.nytimes.com/2018/03/23/opinion/sunday/central-african-republic-conflict.html

Kristof, N. (2023, January 24). A smarter way to reduce gun deaths. *New York Times.*

Kristof, N. D. (2007, August 16). The big melt. *The New York Times.* https://www.nytimes.com/2007/08/16/opinion/16kristof.html

Krizan, Z., & Herlache, A. D. (2016). Sleep disruption and aggression: Implications for violence and its prevention. *Psychology of Violence, 6,* 542–552.

Krizan, Z., & Herlache, A. D. (2017). The narcissism spectrum model: A synthetic view of narcissistic personality. *Personality and Social Psychology Review, 21,* 1–29.

Kroeper, K. M., Sanchez, D. T., & Himmelstein, M. S. (2014). Heterosexual men's confrontation of sexual prejudice: The role of precarious manhood. *Sex Roles, 70,* 1–13.

Kroger, R. O., & Wood, L. A. (1992). Are the rules of address universal? IV: Comparison of Chinese, Korean, Greek, and German usage. *Journal of Cross-Cultural Psychology, 23,* 148–162.

Krongard, S., & Tsay-Vogel, M. (2020). Online original TV series: Examining portrayals of violence in popular binge-watched programs and social reality perceptions. *Psychology of Popular Media, 9,* 155–164.

Krosnick, J. A., & Alwin, D. F. (1989). Aging and susceptibility to attitude change. *Journal of Personality and Social Psychology, 57,* 416–425.

Krosnick, J. A., & Schuman, H. (1988). Attitude intensity, importance, and certainty and susceptibility to response effects. *Journal of Personality and Social Psychology, 54,* 940–952.

Kross, E., Verduyn, P., Demiralp, E., Park, J., Lee, D. S., Lin, N., & . . . Ybarra, O. (2013). Facebook use predicts declines in subjective well-being in young adults. *PLOS ONE, 8*(8), e69841.

Krueger, A. B., & Stone, A. A. (2014). Progress in measuring subjective well-being: Moving toward national indicators and policy evaluations. *Science, 346,* 42–43.

Krueger, J., & Clement, R. W. (1994a). Memory-based judgments about multiple categories: A revision and extension of Tajfel's accentuation theory. *Journal of Personality and Social Psychology, 67,* 35–47.

Krueger, J., & Clement, R. W. (1994b). The truly false consensus effect: An ineradicable and egocentric bias in social perception. *Journal of Personality and Social Psychology, 67,* 596–610.

Krueger, J., & Rothbart, M. (1988). Use of categorical and individuating information in making inferences about personality. *Journal of Personality and Social Psychology, 55,* 187–195.

Krueger, J. I., Baumeister, R. F., & Vohs, K. D. (2022). Feeling good without doing good: Comment on Orth and Robins (2022). *American Psychologist, 77,* 18–19.

Krueger, J. I., DiDonato, T. E., & Freestone, D. (2012). Social projection can solve social dilemmas. *Psychological Inquiry, 23,* 1–27.

Kruger, J., & Dunning, D. (1999). Unskilled and unaware of it: How difficulties in recognizing one's own incompetence lead to inflated self-assessments. *Journal of Personality and Social Psychology, 76,* 743–753.

Kruger, J., & Gilovich, T. (1999). "I cynicism" in everyday theories of responsibility assessment: On biased assumptions of bias. *Journal of Personality and Social Psychology, 76,* 743–753.

Kruger, J., Wirtz, D., & Miller, D. T. (2005). Counterfactual thinking and the first instinct fallacy. *Journal of Personality and Social Psychology, 88,* 725–735.

Kruglanski, A. W., & Fishman, S. (2006). The psychology of terrorism: "Syndrome" versus "tool" perspective. *Journal of Terrorism and Political Violence, 18(2),* 193–215.

Kruglanski, A. W., & Gigerenzer, G. (2011). Intuitive and deliberate judgments are based on common principles. *Psychological Review, 118,* 97–109.

Kruglanski, A. W., & Webster, D. M. (1991). Group members' reactions to opinion deviates and conformists at varying degrees of proximity to decision deadline and of environmental noise. *Journal of Personality and Social Psychology, 61,* 212–225.

Kruglanski, A. W., Chen, X., Dechesne, M., Fishman, S., & Orehek E. (2009). Fully committed: Suicide bombers' motivation and the quest for personal significance. *Political Psychology, 30,* 331–357.

Kruglanski, A. W., Ellenberg, M., Szumowska, E., Molinario, E., Speckhard, A., Leander, N. P., Pierro, A., Di Cicco, G., & Bushman, B. J. (2023). Frustration-aggression hypothesis reconsidered: The role of significance quest. *Aggressive Behavior, 49,* 445–468.

Kruglanski, A. W., Jasko, K., Chernikova, M., Milyavasky, M., Babush, M., Baldner, C., & Perro, A. (2015). The rocky road from attitudes to behaviors: Charting the goal systemic course of actions. *Psychological Review, 122,* 598–620.

Krull, D. S., Loy, M. H.-M., Lin, J., Wang, C.-F., Chen, S., & Zhao, X. (1999). The fundamental fundamental attribution error: Correspondence bias in individualist and collectivist cultures. *Personality and Social Psychology Bulletin, 25,* 1208–1219.

Krupp, D. B., & Cook, T. R. (2018). Local competition amplifies the corrosive effects of inequality. *Psychological Science, 29,* 824–833.

Krys, K., Capaldi, C. A., van Tilburg, W., Lipp, O. V., Bond, M. H., Vauclair, C. -Melani., Manickam, L. S. S., Domínguez, E. A., Torres, C., Lun, V. M., Teyssier, J., Miles, L. K., Hansen, K., Park, J., Wagner, W., Yu, A. A., Xing, C., Wise, R., Sun, C., & Siddiqui, R. S. (2018). Catching up with wonderful women: The women-are-wonderful effect is smaller in more gender egalitarian societies. *International Journal of Psychology, 53,* 21–26.

KSTP. (2020, May 28). Floyd family attorney issues statement following protests in Minneapolis. *KSTP.* https://kstp.com/minnesota-news/george-floyd-family-attorney-issues-statement-following-minneapolis-protests/5743758/

Kteily, N., Hodson, G., & Bruneau, E. (2016). They see us as less than human: Metadehumanization predicts intergroup conflict via reciprocal dehumanization. *Journal of Personality and Social Psychology, 110,* 343–370.

Kteily, N. S., & Bruneau, E. (2017). Darker demons of our nature: The need to (re) focus attention on blatant forms of dehumanization. *Current Directions in Psychological Science, 26,* 487–494.

Kuball, T., Pollmanns, C., Asbrock, F., & Jahn, G. (2023). Older adults' stereotypes of and attitudes toward younger adults and intergenerational contact frequency. *Journal of Intergenerational Relationships.*

Kubany, E. S., Bauer, G. B., Pangilinan, M. E., Muroka, M. Y., & Enriquez, V. G. (1995). Impact of labeled anger and blame in intimate relationships. *Journal of Cross-Cultural Psychology, 26,* 65–83.

Kugihara, N. (1999). Gender and social loafing in Japan. *Journal of Social Psychology, 139,* 516–526.

Kuhns, J. B., Exum, M. L., Clodfelter, T. A., & Bottia, M. C. (2014). The prevalence of alcohol-involved homicide offending: A meta-analytic review. *Homicide Studies, 18,* 251–270.

Kuiper, N. A., & Higgins, E. T. (1985). Social cognition and depression: A general integrative perspective. *Social Cognition, 3,* 1–15.

Kulesza, W., Dolinski, D., Muniak, P., Winner, D., Izydorczak, K., Derakhshan, A., & Rizulla, A. (2023). Biased social comparison in the moment of crisis: The better-than-average effect and COVID-19. *Social Psychology, 54,* 40–51.

Kulig, J. W. (2012). What's in a name? Our false uniqueness! *British Journal of Social Psychology, 52,* 173–179.

Kumar, A., & Epley, N. (2023). A little good goes an unexpectedly long way: Underestimating the positive impact of kindness on recipients. *Journal of Experimental Psychology: General, 152,* 236–252.

Kumar, A., & Gilovich, T. (2015). Some "thing" to talk about? Differential story utility from experiential and material purchases. *Personality and Social Psychology Bulletin, 41,* 1320–1331.

Kumar, R. (2021). Impact of societal culture on Covid-19 morbidity and mortality across countries. *Journal of Cross-Cultural Psychology, 52,* 643–662

Kumar, S., Calvo, R., Avendano, M., Sivaramakrishnan, K., & Berkman, L. F. (2012). Social support, volunteering and health around the world: Cross-national evidence from 139 countries. *Social Science and Medicine, 74,* 696–706.

Kumkale, G. T., & Albarracin, D. (2004). The sleeper effect in persuasion: A meta-analytic review. *Psychological Bulletin, 130,* 143–172.

Kunda, Z., & Oleson, K. C. (1995). Maintaining stereotypes in the face of disconfirmation: Constructing grounds for subtyping deviants. *Journal of Personality and Social Psychology, 68,* 565–579.

Kunda, Z., & Oleson, K. C. (1997). When exceptions prove the rule: How extremity of deviance determines the impact of deviant examples on stereotypes. *Journal of Personality and Social Psychology, 72,* 965–979.

Kunda, Z., & Spencer, S. J. (2003). When do stereotypes come to mind and when do they color judgment? A goal-based theoretical framework for stereotype activation and application. *Psychological Bulletin, 129,* 522–544.

Kunst, J. R., Kimel, S. Y., Shani, M., Alayan, R., & Thomsen, L. (2019). Can Abraham bring peace? The relationship between acknowledging shared religious roots and intergroup conflict. *Psychology of Religion and Spirituality, 11,* 417–432.

Kunst-Wilson, W. R., & Zajonc, R. B. (1980). Affective discrimination of stimuli that cannot be recognized. *Science, 207,* 557–558.

Kuper-Smith, B. J., Doppekhofter, L., Oganian, Y., Rosenblau, G., & Korn, C. W. (2020). Optimistic beliefs about the personal impact of COVID-19. Manuscript in preparation. Preprint doi: 10.31234/osf.io/epcyb

Kupper, N., & Denollet, J. (2007). Type D personality as a prognostic factor in heart disease: Assessment and mediating mechanisms. *Journal of Personality Assessment, 89,* 265–276.

Kurzman, D. (2004). *No greater glory: The four immortal chaplains and the sinking of the Dorchester in World War II.* New York: Random House.

Kuster, F., Orth, U., & Meier, L. L. (2012). Rumination mediates the prospective effect of low self-esteem on depression: A five-wave longitudinal study. *Personality and Social Psychology Bulletin, 38,* 747–759.

Kutner, L., & Olson, C. (2008). *Grand Theft childhood: The surprising truth about violent video games and what parents can do.* New York: Simon & Schuster.

Kuypers, K. P. C., Verkes, R. J., van den Brink, W., van Amsterdam, J. G. C., & Ramaekers, J. G. (2020). Intoxicated aggression: Do alcohol and stimulants cause dose-related aggression? A review. *European Neuropsychopharmacology, 30,* 114–147.

Kuziemko, I., Norton, M. I., Saez, E., Stantcheva, S. (2015). How elastic are preferences for redistribution? Evidence from randomized survey experiments. *American Economic Review, 105,* 1478–1508.

Kwan, L. Y.-Y., & Hung, Y. S. (2023). Why self-proclaimed environmentalists commit non sustainable behaviors?: Using normative motivation to understand personal attitudes and choices. *Current Psychology: A Journal for Diverse Perspectives on Diverse Psychological Issues.*

Lacassagne, D., Béna, J., & Corneille, O. (2022). Is Earth a perfect square? Repetition increases the perceived truth of highly implausible statements. *Cognition, 223,* 1–5.

Lacey, M. (2004, April 9). A decade after massacres, Rwanda outlaws ethnicity. *The New York Times.* https://www.nytimes.com/2004/04/09/world/a-decade-after-massacres-rwanda-outlaws-ethnicity.html

LaFrance, M. (1985). Does your smile reveal your status? *Social Science News Letter, 70* (Spring), 15–18.

LaFrance, M., Hecht, M. A., & Paluck, E. L. (2003). The contingent smile: A meta-analysis of sex differences in smiling. *Psychological Bulletin, 129,* 305–334.

LaFromboise, T., Coleman, H. L. K., & Gerton, J. (1993). Psychological impact of biculturalism: Evidence and theory. *Psychological Bulletin, 114,* 395–412.

Lagerspetz, K. (1979). Modification of aggressiveness in mice. In S. Feshbach & A. Fraczek (Eds.), *Aggression and behavior change.* New York: Praeger.

Lagerspetz, K. M. J., Bjorkqvist, K., Berts, M., & King, E. (1982). Group aggression among school children in three schools. *Scandinavian Journal of Psychology, 23,* 45–52.

Lai, C. K., Marini, M., Lehr, S. A., Cerruti, C., Shin, J. E., Joy-Gaba, J. A., Ho, A. K., Teachman, B. A., Wojcik, S. P., Koleva, S. P., Frazier, R. S., Heiphetz, L., Chen, E. E., Turner, R. N., Haidt, J., Kesebir, S., Hawkins, C. B., Schaefer, H. S., Rubichi, S., Sartori, G., . . . & Nosek, B. A. (2014). Reducing implicit racial preferences: I. A comparative investigation of 17 interventions. *Journal of Experimental Psychology: General, 143,* 1765–1785.

Laird, J. D. (1974). Self-attribution of emotion: The effects of expressive behavior on the quality of emotional experience. *Journal of Personality and Social Psychology, 29,* 475–486.

Laird, J. D. (1984). The real role of facial response in the experience of emotion: A reply to Tourangeau and Ellsworth, and others. *Journal of Personality and Social Psychology, 47,* 909–917.

Lakin, J. L., & Chartrand, T. L. (2003). Using nonconscious behavioral mimicry to create affiliation and rapport. *Psychological Science, 14,* 334–339.

Lakin, J. L., Chartrand, T. L., & Arkin, R. M. (2008). I am too just like you: Nonconscious mimicry as an automatic behavioral responses to social exclusion. *Psychological Science, 19,* 816–821.

Lalonde, R. N. (1992). The dynamics of group differentiation in the face of defeat. *Personality and Social Psychology Bulletin, 18,* 336–342.

Lalwani, A. K., Shavitt, S., & Johnson, T. (2006). What is the relation between cultural orientation and socially desirable responding? *Journal of Personality and Social Psychology, 90,* 165–178.

Lamal, P. A. (1979). College student common beliefs about psychology. *Teaching of Psychology, 6,* 155–158.

Lamb, A. (2020, June 2). *"Destruction is not the answer:" After Raleigh riots, those arrested express regret. WRAL.* https://www.wral.com/destruction-is-not-the-answer-after-raleigh-riots-those-arrested-express-regret/19126202/

Lamb, C. S., & Crano, W. D. (2014). Parents' beliefs and children's marijuana use: Evidence for a self-fulfilling prophecy effect. *Addictive Behaviors, 39,* 127–132.

Lambert, A. J., Schott, J. P., & Scherer, L. (2011). Threat, politics, and attitudes: Toward a greater understanding of rally-'round-theflag effects. *Current Directions in Psychological Science, 20,* 343–348.

Lamer, S. A., Dvorak, P., Biddle, A. M., Pauker, K., & Weisbuch, M. (2022). The transmission of gender stereotypes through televised patterns of nonverbal bias. *Journal of Personality and Social Psychology, 123,* 1315–1335.

Lammers, J., & Baldwin, M. (2018). Past-focused temporal communication overcomes conservatives' resistance to liberal political ideas. *Journal of Personality and Social Psychology, 114,* 599–619.

Lamont, R. A., Swift, H. J., & Abrams, D. (2015). A review and meta-analysis of age-based stereotype threat: Negative stereotypes, not facts, do the damage. *Psychology and Aging, 30,* 180–193.

Lamp, S. J., Cugle, A., Silverman, A. L., Thomas, M. T., Liss, M., & Erchull, M. J. (2019). Picture perfect: The relationship between selfie behaviors, self-objectification, and depressive symptoms. *Sex Roles: A Journal of Research, 81,* 704–712.

Landrum, A. R., Lull, R. B., Akin, H., Hasell, A., & Jamieson, K. H. (2017). Processing the papal encyclical through perceptual filters: Pope Francis, identity-protective cognition, and climate change concern. *Cognition, 166,* 1–12.

Landry, A. P., Orr, R. I., & Mere, K. (2022). Dehumanization and mass violence: A study of mental state language in Nazi propaganda (1927–1945). *PLoS ONE, 17*(11).

Landry, A. P., Schooler, J. W., Willer, R., & Seli, P. (2023). Reducing explicit blatant dehumanization by correcting exaggerated meta-perceptions. *Social Psychological and Personality Science, 14,* 407–418.

Lane, D. J., Gibbons, F. X., O'Hara, R. E., & Gerrard, M. (2011). Standing out from the crowd: How comparison to prototypes can decrease health-risk behavior in young adults. *Basic and Applied Social Psychology, 33,* 228–238.

Langer, E. J., & Imber, L. (1980). The role of mindlessness in the perception of deviance. *Journal of Personality and Social Psychology, 39,* 360–367.

Langford, D. J., Crager, S. E., Shehzad, Z., Smith, S. B., Sotocinal, S. G., Levenstadt, J. S., Chanda, M. L., Levitin, D. J., & Mogil, J. S. (2006). Social modulation of pain as evidence for empathy in mice. *Science, 312,* 1967–1970.

Langlois, J. H., & Roggman, L. A. (1990). Attractive faces are only average. *Psychological Science, 1,* 115–121.

Langlois, J. H., Kalakanis, L., Rubenstein, A. J., Larson, A., Hallam, M., & Smoot, M. (2000). Maxims or myths of beauty? A meta-analytic and theoretical review. *Psychological Bulletin, 126,* 390–423.

Langlois, J. H., Kalakanis, L., Rubenstein, A., Larson, A., Hallam, M., & Smoot, M. (1996). *Maxims and myths of beauty: A meta-analytic and theoretical review.* Paper presented at the American Psychological Society convention, San Francisco, CA.

Langlois, J. H., Roggman, L. A., & Musselman, L. (1994). What is average and what is not average about attractive faces? *Psychological Science, 5,* 214–220.

Langlois, J. H., Roggman, L. A., Casey, R. J., Ritter, J. M., Rieser-Danner, L. A., & Jenkins, V. Y. (1987). Infant preferences for attractive faces: Rudiments of a stereotype? *Developmental Psychology, 23,* 363–369.

Laninga-Wijnen, L., Harakeh, Z., Dijkstra, J. K., Veenstra, R., & Vollebergh, W. (2020). Who sets the aggressive popularity norm in classrooms? It's the number and strength of aggressive, prosocial, and bi-strategic adolescents. *Journal of Abnormal Child Psychology, 48,* 13–27.

Lankford, A. (2009). Promoting aggression and violence at Abu Ghraib: The U.S. military's transformation of ordinary people into torturers. *Aggression and Violent Behavior, 14,* 388–395.

Lantz, B., & Wenger, M. R. (2021). Guns, groups, and the Southern culture of honor: Considering the role of co-offenders in Southern firearm violence. *Psychology of Violence, 11,* 405–416.

Lanzetta, J. T. (1955). Group behavior under stress. *Human Relations, 8,* 29–53.

Lapantina, A. (2022, March 5). Putin picked the wrong country to mess with. *New York Times.*

Larrick, R. P., Timmerman, T. A., Carton, A. M., & Abrevaya, J. (2011). Temper, temperature, and temptation: Heat-related retaliation in baseball. *Psychological Science, 22,* 423–428.

Larsen, B., Hetherington, M. J., Greene, S. H., Ryan, T. J., Maxwell, R. D., & Tadelis, S. (2022). *Using Donald Trump's COVID-19 Vaccine Endorsement to Give Public Health a Shot in the Arm: A Large-Scale Ad Experiment.* National Bureau of Economic Research, Inc, NBER Working Papers: 29896.

Larsen, R. (2009). The contributions of positive and negative affect to emotional well-being. *Psychological Topics, 18,* 247–266.

Larson, J. R., Jr., Foster-Fishman, P. G., & Keys, C. B. (1994). Discussion of shared and unshared information in decision-making groups. *Journal of Personality and Social Psychology, 67,* 446–461.

Larsson, K. (1956). *Conditioning and sexual behavior in the male albino rat.* Stockholm: Almqvist & Wiksell.

Lasgaard, M., Friis, K., & Shevlin, M. (2016). "Where are all the lonely people?" A population-based study of high-risk groups across the life span. *Social Psychiatry and Psychiatric Epidemiology, 51,* 1373–1384.

Lassiter, G. D., & Dudley, K. A. (1991). The *a priori* value of basic research: The case of videotaped confessions. *Journal of Social Behavior and Personality, 6,* 7–16.

Lassiter, G. D., & Irvine, A. A. (1986). Videotaped confessions: The impact of camera point of view on judgments of coercion. *Journal of Applied Social Psychology, 16,* 268–276.

Lassiter, G. D. (2010). Psychological science and sound public policy: Video recording of custodial interrogations. *American Psychologist, 65,* 768–779.

Lassiter, G. D., Diamond, S. S., Schmidt, H. C., & Elek, J. K. (2007). Evaluating videotaped confessions. *Psychological Science, 18,* 224–226.

Lassiter, G. D., Geers, A. L., Handley, I. M., Weiland, P. E., & Munhall, P. J. (2002). Videotaped interrogations and confessions: A simple change in camera perspective alters verdicts in simulated trials. *Journal of Applied Psychology, 87,* 867–874.

Lassiter, G. D., Munhall, P. J., Berger, I. P., Weiland, P. E., Handley, I. M., & Geers, A. L. (2005). Attributional complexity and the camera perspective bias in videotaped confessions. *Basic and Applied Social Psychology, 27,* 27–35.

Latané, B., & Dabbs, J. M., Jr. (1975). Sex, group size and helping in three cities. *Sociometry, 38,* 180–194.

Latané, B., & Darley, J. M. (1968). Group inhibition of bystander intervention in emergencies. *Journal of Personality and Social Psychology, 10,* 215–221.

Latané, B., & Darley, J. M. (1970). *The unresponsive bystander: Why doesn't he help?* New York: Appleton-Century Crofts.

Latané, B., & Nida, S. (1981). Ten years of research on group size and helping. *Psychological Bulletin, 89,* 308–324.

Latané, B., & Rodin, J. (1969). A lady in distress: Inhibiting effects of friends and strangers on bystander intervention. *Journal of Experimental Social Psychology, 5,* 189–202.

Latané, B., Williams, K., & Harkins. S. (1979). Many hands make light the work: The causes and consequences of social loafing. *Journal of Personality and Social Psychology, 37,* 822–832.

Laughlin, P. R., & Adamopoulos, J. (1980). Social combination processes and individual learning for six-person cooperative groups on an intellective task. *Journal of Personality and Social Psychology, 38,* 941–947.

Laughlin, P. R., Hatch, E. C., Silver, J. S., & Boh, L. (2006). Groups perform better than the best individuals on letters-to-numbers problems: Effects of group size. *Journal of Personality and Social Psychology, 90,* 644–651.

Laughlin, P. R., Zander, M. L., Knievel, E. M., & Tan, T. K. (2003). Groups perform better than the best individuals on letters-to-numbers problems: Informative equations and effective strategies. *Journal of Personality and Social Psychology, 85,* 684–694.

Lavertu, L., Marder, B., Erz, A., & Angell, R. (2020). The extended warming effect of social media: Examining whether the cognition of online audiences offline drives prosocial behavior in "real life." *Computers in Human Behavior, 110.*

Lawrence, E. M., Rogers, R. G., Zajacova, A., & Wadsworth, T. (2019). Marital happiness, marital status, health, and longevity. *Journal of Happiness Studies, 20,* 1539–1561.

Laws, H. B., Ellerbeck, N. E., Rodrigues, A. S., Simmons, J. A., & Ansell, E. B. (2017). Social rejection and alcohol use in daily life. *Alcoholism: Clinical and Experimental Research, 41,* 820–827.

Lawson, T. J. (2010). The social spotlight increases blindness to change blindness. *Basic and Applied Social Psychology, 32,* 360–368.

Layden, M. A. (1982). Attributional therapy. In C. Antaki & C. Brewin (Eds.), *Attributions and psychological change: Applications of attributional theories to clinical and educational practice.* London: Academic Press.

Layous, K., Nelson, S. K., Oberle, E., Schonert-Reichl, K. A., & Lyubomirsky, S. (2012). Kindness counts: Prompting prosocial behavior in preadolescents boosts peer acceptance and well-being. *PLOS ONE, 7,* e51380.

Lazarsfeld, P. F. (1949). The American soldier—an expository review. *Public Opinion Quarterly, 13,* 377–404.

Lazer, D., & others. (2009). Computational social science. *Science, 323,* 721–723.

Leach, S., & Weick, M. (2018). Can people judge the veracity of their intuitions? *Social Psychological and Personality Science, 9,* 40–49.

Leader, T., Mullen, B., & Abrams, D. (2007). Without mercy: The immediate impact of group size on lynch mob atrocity. *Personality and Social Psychology Bulletin, 33,* 1340–1352.

Leander, N. P., Agostini, M., Stroebe, W., Kreienkamp, J., Spears, R., Kuppens, T., Van Zomeren, M., Otten, S., & Kruglanski, A. W. (2020). Frustration-affirmation? Thwarted goals motivate compliance with social norms for violence and nonviolence. *Journal of Personality and Social Psychology, 119,* 249–271.

Leander, N. P., Stroebe, W., Kreienkamp, J., Agostini, M., Gordijn, E., & Kruglanski, A. W. (2019). Mass shootings and the salience of guns as means of compensation for thwarted goals. *Journal of Personality and Social Psychology, 116,* 704–723.

Leaper, C., & Ayres, M. M. (2007). A meta-analytic review of gender variations in adults' language use: Talkativeness, affiliative speech, and assertive speech. *Personality and Social Psychology Review, 11,* 328–363.

Leaper, C., & Robnett, R. D. (2011). Women are more likely than men to use tentative language, aren't they? A meta-analysis testing for gender differences and moderators. *Psychology of Women Quarterly, 35,* 129–142.

Leary, M. (1994). *Self-presentation: Impression management and interpersonal behavior.* Pacific Grove, CA: Brooks/Cole.

Leary, M. R., & Kowalski, R. M. (1995). *Social anxiety.* New York: Guilford.

Leary, M. R. (1998). The social and psychological importance of self-esteem. In R. M. Kowalski & M. R. Leary (Eds.), *The social psychology of emotional and behavioral problems.* Washington, DC: American Psychological Association.

Leary, M. R. (2004a). *The curse of the self: Self-awareness, egotism, and the quality of human life.* New York: Oxford University Press.

Leary, M. R. (2004b). The self we know and the self we show: Self-esteem, self-presentation, and the maintenance of interpersonal relationships. In M. Brewer & M. Hewstone (Eds.), *Emotion and motivation.* Malden, MA: Usishers.

Leary, M. R. (2007). Motivational and emotional aspects of the self. *Annual Review of Psychology, 58,* 317–344.

Leary, M. R. (2010). Affiliation, acceptance, and belonging: The pursuit of interpersonal connection. In S. T. Fiske, D. T. Gilbert, & G. Lindzey (Eds.), *Handbook of social psychology* (5th ed.). Hoboken, NJ: Wiley.

Leary, M. R. (2012). Sociometer theory. In P. A. M. Van Lange, A. W. Kruglanski, & E. T. Higgins (Eds.), *Handbook of theories of social psychology* (Vol. 2, pp. 151–159). Thousand Oaks, CA: Sage.

Leary, M. R., Nezlek, J. B., Radford-Davenport, D., Martin, J., & McMullen, A. (1994). Self-presentation in everyday interactions: Effects of target familiarity and gender composition. *Journal of Personality and Social Psychology, 67,* 664–673.

Leary, M. R., Raimi, K. T., Jongman-Sereno, K. P., & Diebels, K. J. (2015). Distinguishing intrapsychic from interpersonal motives in psychological theory and research. *Perspectives on Psychological Science, 10,* 497–517.

Leckelt, M., Kufner, A. C. P., Nestler, S., & Back, M. D. (2015). Behavioral processes underlying the decline of narcissists' popularity over time. *Journal of Personality and Social Psychology, 109,* 856–871.

LeCroy, V. R., & Rodefer, J. S. (2019). The influence of job candidate LGBT association on hiring decisions. *North American Journal of Psychology, 21,* 373–386.

LeDoux, J. (2002). *Synaptic self: How our brains become who we are.* New York: Viking.

LeDoux, J. (2014). Low roads and higher order thoughts in emotion. *Cortex: A Journal Devoted to the Study of the Nervous System and Behavior, 59,* 214–215.

LeDoux, J. E. (1996). *The emotional brain: The mysterious underpinnings of emotional life.* Simon & Schuster.

Lee, A. J., Sidari, M. J., Murphy, S. C., Sherlock, J. M., & Zietsch, B. P. (2020). Sex differences in misperceptions of sexual interest can be explained by sociosexual orientation and men projecting their own interest onto women. *Psychological Science, 31,* 184–192.

Lee, F., Hallahan, M., & Herzog, T. (1996). Explaining real-life events: How culture and domain shape attributions. *Personality and Social Psychology Bulletin, 22,* 732–741.

Lee, I.-C., Pratto, F., & Johnson, B. T. (2011). Intergroup consensus/disagreement in support of group-based hierarchy: An examination of socio-structural and psycho-cultural factors. *Psychological Bulletin, 137,* 1029–1064.

Lee, J., & Penrod, S. D. (2022). Three-level meta-analysis of the other-race bias in facial identification. *Applied Cognitive Psychology.*

Lee, R. Y.-P., & Bond, M. H. (1996). *How friendship develops out of personality and values: A study of interpersonal attraction in Chinese culture.* Unpublished manuscript, Chinese University of Hong Kong.

Lee, S. A., & Liang, Y. (Jake). (2019). Robotic foot-in-the-door: Using sequential-request persuasive strategies in human-robot interaction. *Computers in Human Behavior, 90,* 351–356.

Lee, S., Rotman, J. D., & Perkins, A. W. (2014). Embodied cognition and social consumption: Self-regulating temperature through social products and behaviors. *Journal of Consumer Psychology,* 24, 234–240.

Lee, T. K., Kim, Y., & Coe, K. (2018). When social media become hostile media: An experimental examination of news sharing, partisanship, and follower count. *Mass Communication & Society, 21,* 450–472.

Legate, N., DeHaan, C. R., Weinstein, N., & Ryan, R. M. (2013). Hurting you hurts me too: The psychological costs of complying with ostracism. *Psychological Science, 24,* 583–588.

Legrain, P. (2003, May 9). Cultural globalization is not Americanization. *Chronicle of Higher Education.* www.chronicle.com/free

Lehmann-Haupt, C. (1986, February 6). Larry King quoted in the Books of the Times. *The New York Times,* p. 21.

Leippe, M. R. (1985). The influence of eyewitness nonidentification on mock-jurors. *Journal of Applied Social Psychology, 15,* 656–672.

Leiserowitz, A., Maibach, E., Rosenthal, S., Kotcher, J., Ballew, M., . . . Gustafson, A. (2018). *Climate change in the American mind: December 2018.* Yale University and George Mason University. New Haven, CT: Yale Program on Climate Change Communication.

Leiserowitz, A., Maibach, E., Roser-Renouf, C. & Smith, N. (2011). *Global Warming's Six Americas, May 2011.* Yale University and George Mason University. New Haven, CT: Yale Project on Climate Change Communication.

Lei, X., & Perrett, D. (2021). Misperceptions of opposite-sex preferences for thinness and muscularity. *British Journal of Psychology, 112,* 247–264.

Lemay, E. P., Jr., Clark, M. S., & Greenberg, A. (2010). What is beautiful is good because what is beautiful is desired: Physical attractiveness stereotyping as projection of interpersonal goals. *Personality and Social Psychology Bulletin, 36,* 339–353.

Lemmer, G., & Wagner, U. (2015). Can we really reduce ethnic prejudice outside the lab? A meta-analysis of direct and indirect contact interventions. *European Journal of Social Psychology, 45,* 152–168.

Lemyre, L., & Smith, P. M. (1985). Intergroup discrimination and self-esteem in the minimal group paradigm. *Journal of Personality and Social Psychology, 49,* 660–670.

Lenhart, A. (2010, April 20). Teens, cell phones and texting. Pew Internet and American Life Project. *Pew Research Center.* www.pewresearch.org

Lenton, Å. P., & Francesconi, M. (2010). How humans cognitively manage an abundance of mate options. *Psychological Science, 21,* 528–533.

Leodoro, G., & Lynn, M. (2007). The effect of server posture on the tips of Whites and Blacks. *Journal of Applied Social Psychology, 37,* 201–209.

Leone, C., & Hawkins, L. B. (2006). Self-monitoring and close relationships. *Journal of Personality, 74,* 739–778.

Leone, C., & Yoho, M. J. (2022). Self-monitoring and former best friends: Individual differences in friendship dissolution. *Journal of General Psychology.*

Leonhardt, D. (2022, March 18). Covid and the 'Very Liberal'. *New York Times.*

Lepper, M. R., & Greene, D. (Eds.) (1979). *The hidden costs of reward.* Hillsdale, NJ: Erlbaum.

Lerner, M. J., & Miller, D. T. (1978). Just world research and the attribution process: Looking back and ahead. *Psychological Bulletin, 85,* 1030–1051.

Lerner, M. J., & Simmons, C. H. (1966). Observer's reaction to the "innocent victim": Compassion or rejection? *Journal of Personality and Social Psychology, 4,* 203–210.

Lerner, M. J. (1980). *The belief in a just world: A fundamental delusion.* New York: Plenum.

Lerner, R. M., & Frank, P. (1974). Relation of race and sex to supermarket helping behavior. *Journal of Social Psychology, 94,* 201–203.

Leshner, A. I. (2005, October). Science and religion should not be adversaries. *APS Observer.* www.psychologicalscience.org

Le, T. P. (2019). The association of conformity to feminine norms with women's food consumption after a negative mood induction. *Appetite, 133,* 123–129.

Leung, K., & Bond, M. H. (1984). The impact of cultural collectivism on reward allocation. *Journal of Personality and Social Psychology, 47,* 793–804.

Levav, J., & Fitzsimons, G. J. (2006). When questions change behavior: The role of ease of representation. *Psychological Science, 17,* 207–213.

Levesque, M. J., Nave, C. S., & Lowe, C. A. (2006). Toward an understanding of gender differences in inferring sexual interest. *Psychology of Women Quarterly, 30,* 150–158.

Levine, J. M. (1989). Reaction to opinion deviance in small groups. In P. Paulus (Ed.), *Psychology of group influence: New perspectives.* Hillsdale, NJ: Erlbaum.

Levine, M., & Crowther, S. (2008). The responsive bystander: How social group membership and group size can encourage as well as inhibit bystander intervention. *Journal of Personality and Social Psychology, 95,* 1429–1439.

Levine, M., Prosser, A., Evans, D., & Reicher, S. (2005). Identity and emergency intervention: How social group membership and inclusiveness of group boundaries shape helping behavior. *Personality and Social Psychology Bulletin, 31,* 443–453.

Levine, R. V., & Norenzayan, A. (1999). The pace of life in 31 countries. *Journal of Cross-Cultural Psychology, 30,* 178–205.

Levine, R. V., Martinez, T. S., Brase, G., & Sorenson, K. (1994). Helping in 36 U.S. cities. *Journal of Personality and Social Psychology, 67,* 69–82.

Levinson, H. (1950). *The science of chance: From probability to statistics.* New York: Rinehart.

Levitan, L. C., & Verhulst, B. (2016). Conformity in groups: The effects of others' views on expressed attitudes and attitude change. *Political Behavior, 38,* 277–315.

Levitan, L. C., & Visser, P. S. (2008). The impact of the social context on resistance to persuasion: Effortful versus effortless responses to counter-attitudinal information. *Journal of Experimental Social Psychology, 44,* 640–649.

Levy-Leboyer, C. (1988). Success and failure in applying psychology. *American Psychologist, 43,* 779–785.

Levy, S. R., Stroessner, S. J., & Dweck, C. S. (1998). Stereotype formation and endorsement: The role of implicit theories. *Journal of Personality and Social Psychology, 74,* 1421–1436.

Lewandowski, G. W., & Bizzoco, N. M. (2007). Addition through subtraction: Growth following the dissolution of a low-quality relationship. *Journal of Positive Psychology, 2,* 40–54.

Lewandowski, G. W., Jr., Aron, A., & Gee, J. (2007). Personality goes a long way: The malleability of opposite-sex physical attractiveness. *Personal Relationships, 14,* 571–585

Lewandowsky, S., Ecker, U. K. H., Seifert, C. M., Schwarz, N., & Cooke, J. (2012). Misinformation and its correction: Continued influence and successful debasing. *Psychological Science in the Public Interest, 13,* 106–131.

Lewandowsky, S., Oberauer, K., & Gignac, G. E. (2013). NASA faked the moon landing—therefore, (climate) science is a hoax: An anatomy of the motivated rejection of science. *Psychological Science, 24,* 622–633.

Lewicki, P. (1985). Nonconscious biasing effects of single instances on subsequent judgments. *Journal of Personality and Social Psychology, 48,* 563–574.

Lewinsohn, P. M., & Rosenbaum, M. (1987). Recall of parental behavior by acute depressives, remitted depressives, and nondepressives. *Journal of Personality and Social Psychology, 52,* 611–619.

Lewinsohn, P. M., Hoberman, H., Teri, L., & Hautziner, M. (1985). An integrative theory of depression. In S. Reiss & R. Bootzin (Eds.), *Theoretical issues in behavior therapy.* New York: Academic Press.

Lewis, C. S. (1952). *Mere Christianity.* New York: Macmillan.

Lewis, C. S. (1954). *The horse and his boy.* London: Geoffrey Bles.

Leyens, J.-P., Cortes, B., Demoulin, S., Dovidio, J. F., Fiske, S. T., Gaunt, R., Paladino, M.-P., Rodriquez-Perez, A., Rodriquez-Torrez, R., & Vaes, J. (2003). Emotional prejudice, essentialism, and nationalism. *European Journal of Social Psychology, 33,* 703–717.

Leyens, J.-P., Demoulin, S., Vaes, J., Gaunt, R., & Paladino, M. P. (2007). Infra-humanization: The wall of group differences. *Social Issues and Policy Review, 1,* 139–172.

Liao, H., Su, R., Ptashnik, T., & Nielsen, J. (2022). Feeling good, doing good, and getting ahead: A meta-analytic investigation of the outcomes of prosocial motivation at work. *Psychological Bulletin, 148,* 158–198.

Liberman, V., Samuels, S. M., & Ross, L. (2004). The name of the game: Predictive power of reputations vs. situational labels in determining Prisoner's Dilemma game moves. *Personality and Social Psychology Bulletin, 30,* 1175–1185.

Liberman, Z., Woodward, A. L., & Kinzler, K. D. (2017). The origins of social categorization. *Trends in Cognitive Sciences, 21,* 556–568.

Li, C. (2010). Primacy effect or recency effect? A long-term memory test of Super Bowl commercials. *Journal of Consumer Behaviour, 9,* 32–44.

Li, D., Carnelley, K. B., & Rowe, A. C. (2023). Insecure attachment orientation in adults and children and negative attribution bias: A meta-analysis. *Personality and Social Psychology Bulletin, 49,* 1679–1694.

Liddon, L., Kingerlee, R., & Barry, J. A. (2018). Gender differences in preferences for psychological treatment, coping strategies, and triggers to help-seeking. *British Journal of Clinical Psychology, 57,* 42–58.

Lieberman, J. D. (2011). The utility of scientific jury selection: Still murky after 30 years. *Current Directions in Psychological Science, 20,* 48–52.

Lieberman, J. D., Solomon, S., Greenberg, J., & McGregor, H. A. (1999). A hot new way to measure aggression: Hot sauce allocation. *Aggressive Behavior, 25*(5), 331–348.

Liehr, P., Mehl, M. R., Summers, L. C., & Pennebaker, J. W. (2004). Connecting with others in the midst of stressful upheaval on September 11, 2001. *Applied Nursing Research, 17,* 2–9.

Likowski, K. U., Muhlberger, A., Gerdes, A. B. M., Wieser, M. J., Pauli, P., & Weyers, P. (2012). Facial mimicry and the mirror neuron system: Simultaneous acquisition of facial electromyography and functional magnetic resonance imaging. *Frontiers in Human Neuroscience, 6,* Article 214, 1–10.

Lilienfeld, S. O. (2017). Microaggressions: Strong claims, inadequate evidence. *Perspectives on Psychological Science, 12,* 138–169.

Lilienfeld, S. O. (2020). Embracing unpopular ideas: Introduction to the special section on heterodox issues in psychology. *Archives of Scientific Psychology, 8,* 1–4.

Lilienfeld, S. O., Fowler, K. A., Lohr, J. M., & Lynn, S. J. (2005). Pseudoscience, nonscience, and nonsense in clinical psychology: Dangers and remedies. In R. H. Wright & N. A. Cummings (Eds.), *Destructive trends in mental health: The well-intentioned path to harm.* New York: Routledge.

Lilienfeld, S. O., Wood, J. M., & Garb, H. N. (2000). The scientific status of projective techniques. *Psychological Science in the Public Interest, 1,* 27–66.

Lilley, C., Willmott, D., & Mojtahedi, D. (2023). Juror characteristics on trial: Investigating how psychopathic traits, rape attitudes, victimization experiences, and juror demographics influence decision-making in an intimate partner rape trial. *Frontiers in Psychiatry, 13.*

Lind, A., Hall, L., Breidegard, B., Balkenius, C., & Johansson, P. (2014). Speakers' acceptance of real-time speech exchange indicates that we use auditory feedback to specify the meaning of what we say. *Psychological Science, 25,* 1198–1205.

Lindholm, T., Jönsson, F. U., & Liuzza, M. T. (2018). Retrieval effort cues predict eyewitness accuracy. *Journal of Experimental Psychology: Applied, 24,* 534–542.

Lindsay, R. C. L., & Wells, G. L. (1985). Improving eyewitness identifications from lineups: Simultaneous versus sequential lineup presentation. *Journal of Applied Psychology, 70,* 556–564.

Lindsay, R. C. L., Wells, G. L., & Rumpel, C. H. (1981). Can people detect eyewitness-identification accuracy within and across situations? *Journal of Applied Psychology, 66,* 79–89.

Lindskold, S., & Han, G. (1988). GRIT as a foundation for integrative bargaining. *Personality and Social Psychology Bulletin, 14,* 335–345.

Lindskold, S. (1981). *The laboratory evaluation of GRIT: Trust, cooperation, aversion to using conciliation.* Paper presented at the American Association for the Advancement of Science convention.

Lindskold, S., Bennett, R., & Wayner, M. (1976). Retaliation level as a foundation for subsequent conciliation. *Behavioral Science, 21,* 13–18.

Lindskold, S., Han, G., & Betz, B. (1986). The essential elements of communication in the GRIT strategy. *Personality and Social Psychology Bulletin, 12,* 179–186.

Lin, J.-H. (2013). Do video games exert stronger effects on aggression than film? The role of media interactivity and identification on the association of violent content and aggressive outcomes. *Computers in Human Behavior, 29,* 535–543.

Lin, L. Y., Sidani, J. E., Shensa, A., Radovic, A., Miller, E., Colditz, J. B., & . . . Primack, B. A. (2016). Association between social media use and depression among U.S. young adults. *Depression and Anxiety, 33,* 323–331.

Li, N. P., Bailey, J. M., Kenrick, D. T., & Linsenmeier, J. A. W. (2002). The necessities and luxuries of mate preferences: Testing the tradeoffs. *Journal of Personality and Social Psychology, 82,* 947–955.

Linville, P. W., Fischer, G. W., & Salovey, P. (1989). Perceived distributions of the characteristics of in-group and out-group members: Empirical evidence and a computer simulation. *Journal of Personality and Social Psychology, 57,* 165–188.

Lippa, R. A. (2007). The preferred traits of mates in a cross-national study of heterosexual and homosexual men and women: An examination of biological and cultural influences. *Archives of Sexual Behavior, 36,* 193–208.

Lippa, R. A. (2010). Sex differences in personality traits and gender-related occupational preferences across 53 nations: Testing evolutionary and social-environmental theories. *Archives of Sexual Behavior, 39,* 619–636.

Li, T., & Chan, D. K.-S. (2012). How anxious and avoidant attachment affect romantic relationship quality differently: A meta-analytic review. *European Journal of Social Psychology, 42,* 406–419.

Lit, L., Schweitzer, J. B., & Oberbauer, A. M. (2011). Handler beliefs affect scent detection dog outcomes. *Animal Cognition, 14,* 387–394.

Liu, D., & Baumeister, R. F. (2016). Social networking online and personality of self-worth: A meta-analysis. *Journal of Research in Personality, 64,* 79–89.

Liu, H., Ma, X., Shi, L., Wang, J., Juan, J. T. H., Ma, D., & Sun, J. (2023). Associations between tobacco and alcohol use and aggressive behavior among adolescents in 55 low- and middle-income countries. *Journal of Affective Disorders, 329,* 519–524.

Liu, J., Zhao, S., Chen, X., Falk, E., & Albarracín, D. (2017). The influence of peer behavior as a function of social and cultural closeness: A meta-analysis of normative influence on adolescent smoking initiation and continuation. *Psychological Bulletin, 143,* 1082–1115.

Liu, S., Liu, P., Wang, M., & Zhang, B. (2021). Effectiveness of stereotype threat interventions: A meta-analytic review. *Journal of Applied Psychology, 106,* 921–949.

Livingstone, A. G., Fernández Rodríguez, L., & Rothers, A. (2020). "They just don't understand us": The role of felt understanding in intergroup relations. *Journal of Personality and Social Psychology, 119,* 633–656.

Livingston, G., & Parker, K. (2019). 8 facts about American dads. *Pew Research Center.* https://www.pewresearch.org/fact-tank/2019/06/12/fathers-day-facts/

Livingston, R. W. (2001). What you see is what you get: Systematic variability in perceptual-based social judgment. *Personality and Social Psychology Bulletin, 27,* 1086–1096.

Li, Y., Johnson, E. J., & Zaval, L. (2011). Local warming: Daily temperature change influences belief in global warming. *Psychological Science, 22,* 454–459.

Li, Y., Li, H., Decety, J., & Lee, K. (2013). Experiencing a natural disaster alters children's altruistic giving. *Psychological Science, 24,* 1686–1695.

Locke, E. A., & Latham, G. P. (1990). Work motivation and satisfaction: Light at the end of the tunnel. *Psychological Science, 1,* 240–246.

Locke, E. A., & Latham, G. P. (2002). Building a practically useful theory of goal setting and task performance. *American Psychologist, 57,* 705–717.

Locke, E. A., & Latham, G. P. (2009). Has goal setting gone wild, or have its attackers abandoned good scholarship? *Academy of Management Perspectives, 23,* 17–23.

Locke, K. D., & Horowitz, L. M. (1990). Satisfaction in interpersonal interactions as a function of similarity in level of dysphoria. *Journal of Personality and Social Psychology, 58,* 823–831.

Locksley, A., Borgida, E., Brekke, N., & Hepburn, C. (1980). Sex stereotypes and social judgment. *Journal of Personality and Social Psychology, 39,* 821–831.

Locksley, A., Hepburn, C., & Ortiz, V. (1982). Social stereotypes and judgments of individuals: An instance of the base-rate fallacy. *Journal of Experimental Social Psychology, 18,* 23–42.

Lockwood, P. (2002). Could it happen to you? Predicting the impact of downward comparisons on the self. *Journal of Personality and Social Psychology, 87,* 343–358.

Loewenstein, G., & Schkade, D. (1999). Wouldn't it be nice? Predicting future feelings. In D. Kahneman, E. Diener, & N. Schwarz (Eds.), *Understanding well-being: Scientific perspectives on enjoyment and suffering* (pp. 85–105). New York: Russell Sage Foundation.

Loftin, C., McDowall, D., Wiersema, B., & Cottey, T. J. (1991). Effects of restrictive licensing of handguns on homicide and suicide in the District of Columbia. *New England Journal of Medicine, 325,* 1615–1620.

Loftus, E. F., & Bernstein, D. M. (2005). Rich false memories: The royal road to success. In A. F. Healy (Ed.), *Experimental cognitive psychology and its applications.* Washington, DC: American Psychological Association.

Loftus, E. F., & Klemfuss, J. Z. (2023). Misinformation—past, present, and future. *Psychology, Crime & Law.*

Loftus, E. F., & Klinger, M. R. (1992). Is the unconscious smart or dumb? *American Psychologist, 47,* 761–765.

Loftus, E. F. (1974, December). Reconstructing memory: The incredible eyewitness. *Psychology Today,* pp. 117–119.

Loftus, E. F. (1979a). *Eyewitness testimony.* Cambridge, MA: Harvard University Press.

Loftus, E. F. (1979b). The malleability of human memory. *American Scientist, 67,* 312–320.

Loftus, E. F. (2001, November). Imagining the past. *The Psychologist, 14,* 584–587.

Loftus, E. F. (2003). Make-believe memories. *American Psychologist, 58,* 867–873.

Loftus, E. F. (2007). Memory distortions: Problems solved and unresolved. In M. Garry & H. Hayne (Eds.), *Do justice and let the sky fall: Elizabeth Loftus and her contributions to science, law, and academic freedom.* Mahway, NJ: Erlbaum.

Loftus, E. F. (2011a, August 31). The risk of ill-informed juries. *The New York Times.*

Loftus, E. F. (2011b). How I got started: From semantic memory to expert testimony. *Applied Cognitive Psychology, 25,* 347–348.

Loftus, E. F., Miller, D. G., & Burns, H. J. (1978). Semantic integration of verbal information into a visual memory. *Journal of Experimental Social Psychology: Human Learning and Memory, 4,* 19–31.

Logan, M. (2016). Threat to criminal justice officials: If it is predictable, it is preventable. *Violence and Gender, 3,* 171–176.

Lombardo, J. P., Weiss, R. F., & Buchanan, W. (1972). Reinforcing and attracting functions of yielding. *Journal of Personality and Social Psychology, 21,* 359–368.

London, K., & Nunez, N. (2000). The effect of jury deliberations on jurors' propensity to disregard inadmissible evidence. *Journal of Applied Psychology, 85,* 932–939.

Lonner, W. J. (1980). The search for psychological universals. In H. C. Triandis & W. W. Lambert (Eds.), *Handbook of cross-cultural psychology* (Vol. 1). Boston: Allyn & Bacon.

Lonsdale, A. J., & North, A. C. (2012). Musical taste and the representativeness heuristic. *Psychology of Music, 40,* 131–142.

Lonsdorf, E. V. (2017). Sex differences in nonhuman primate behavioral development. *Journal of Neuroscience Research, 95,* 213–221.

Lordan, G., & Pischke, J. (2022). Does Rosie like riveting? Male and female occupational choices. *Economica, 89,* 110–130.

Lord, C. G., Desforges, D. M., Ramsey, S. L., Trezza, G. R., & Lepper, M. R. (1991). Typicality effects in attitude-behavior consistency: Effects of category discrimination and category knowledge. *Journal of Experimental Social Psychology, 27,* 550–575.

Losch, M. E., & Cacioppo, J. T. (1990). Cognitive dissonance may enhance sympathetic tonus, but attitudes are changed to reduce negative affect rather than arousal. *Journal of Experimental Social Psychology, 26,* 289–304.

Lott, A. J., & Lott, B. E. (1974). The role of reward in the formation of positive interpersonal attitudes. In T. Huston (Ed.), *Foundations of interpersonal attraction.* New York: Academic Press.

Loughman, S., & Haslam, N. (2007). Animals and androids: Implicit associations between social categories and nonhumans. *Psychological Science, 18,* 116–121.

Loukas, A., Paddock, E. M., Li, X., Harrell, M. B., Pasch, K. E., & Perry, C. L. (2019). Electronic nicotine delivery systems marketing and initiation among youth and young adults. *Pediatrics, 144*(3).

Lount, R. B., Jr., & Wilk, S. L. (2014). Working harder or hardly working? posting performance eliminates social loafing and promotes social laboring in workgroups. *Management Science, 60,* 1098–1106.

Loureiro-Rodríguez, V., Moyna, M. I., & Robles, D. (2018). Hey, baby, ¿Qué pasó?: Performing bilingual identities in Texan popular music. *Language & Communication, 60,* 120–135.

Lovett, F. (1997). Thinking about values (report of December 13, 1996 *Wall Street Journal* national survey). *The Responsive Community, 7*(2), 87.

Lowery, B. (2023). *Selfless: The Social Creation of "You."* New York: Harper.

Lowery, P. G., Burrow, J. D., & Kaminski, R. J. (2018). A multilevel test of the racial threat hypothesis in one state's juvenile court. *Crime & Delinquency, 64,* 53–87.

Lowery, W. (2014, April 4). 91% of the time the better-financed candidate wins. *The Washington Post.* http://www.washingtonpost.com/blogs/the-fix/wp/2014/04/04/think-money-doesnt-matter-in-elections-this-chart-says-youre-wrong/

Loy, J. W., & Andrews, D. S. (1981). They also saw a game: A replication of a case study. *Replications in Social Psychology, 1*(2), 45–59.

Lubinski, D., & Benbow, C. P. (2006). Study of mathematically precocious youth after 35 years: Uncovering antecedents for math science expertise. *Perspectives on Psychological Science, 1,* 316–345.

Lucidi, F., Girelli, L., Chirico, A., Alivernini, F., Cozzolino, M., Violani, C., & Mallia, L. (2019). Personality traits and attitudes toward traffic safety predict risky behavior across young, adult, and older drivers. *Frontiers in Psychology, 10.*

Lücken, M., & Simon, B. (2005). Cognitive and affective experiences of minority and majority members: The role of group size, status, and power. *Journal of Experimental Social Psychology, 41,* 396–413.

Lu, J. G., Jin, P., & English, A. S. (2021). Collectivism predicts mask use during COVID-19. *PNAS Proceedings of the National Academy of Sciences of the United States of America, 118*(23).

Lumsden, A., Zanna, M. P., & Darley, J. M. (1980). *When a newscaster presents counter-additional information: Education or propaganda?* Paper presented at the Canadian Psychological Association annual convention.

Lum, T. S., Yan, E. W., Ho, A. Y., Shum, M. Y., Wong, G. Y., Lau, M. Y., & Wang, J. (2016). Measuring filial piety in the 21st century: Development, factor structure, and reliability of the 10-item contemporary filial piety scale. *Journal of Applied Gerontology, 35,* 1235–1247.

Lun, J., Mesquita, B., & Smith, B. (2011). Self- and other-presentation styles in the Southern and Northern United States: An analysis of personal ads. *European Journal of Social Psychology, 41,* 435–445.

Luscombe, B. (2020). Matters of sex. In *The science of gender.* Time special edition.

Lutsky, L. A., Risucci, D. A., & Tortolani, A. J. (1993). Reliability and accuracy of surgical resident peer ratings. *Evaluation Review, 17,* 444–456.

Luttrell, A., Philipp-Muller, A., & Petty, R. E. (2019). Challenging moral attitudes with moral messages. *Psychological Science, 30,* 1136–1150.

Lutz, S., & Schneider, F. M. (2021). Is receiving dislikes in social media still better than being ignored? The effects of ostracism and rejection on need threat and coping responses online. *Media Psychology, 24,* 741–765.

Lüüs, C. A. E., & Wells, G. L. (1994). Determinants of eyewitness confidence. In D. F. Ross, J. D. Read, & M. P. Toglia (Eds.), *Adult eyewitness testimony: Current trends and developments* (pp. 348-362). New York: Cambridge University Press.

Lu, Y., Hill, C. E., Hancock, G. R., & Keum, B. T. (2020). The effectiveness of helping skills training for undergraduate students: Changes in ethnocultural empathy. *Journal of Counseling Psychology, 67,* 14–24.

Lykken, D. T., & Tellegen, A. (1993). Is human mating adventitious or the result of lawful choice? A twin study of mate selection. *Journal of Personality and Social Psychology, 65,* 56–68.

Lykken, D. T. (1997). The American crime factory. *Psychological Inquiry, 8,* 261–270.

Lynas, M., Houlton, B. Z., & Perry, S. (2021). Greater than 99% consensus on human caused climate change in the peer-reviewed scientific literature. *Environmental Research Letters, 16,* 114005.

Lynch, J. W., Kaplan, G. A., Pamuk, E. R., Cohen, R. D., Heck, K. E., Balfour, J. L., & Yen, I. H. (1998). Income inequality and mortality in metropolitan areas of the United States. *American Journal of Public Health, 88,* 1074–1080.

Lynch, J. W., Smith, G. D., Kaplan, G. A., & House, J. S. (2000). Income inequality and health: A neo-material interpretation. *British Medical Journal, 320,* 1200–1204.

Lynch, R., Lummaa, V., & Loehr, J. (2020). Self sacrifice and kin psychology in war: Threats to family predict decisions to volunteer for a women's paramilitary organization. *Evolution and Human Behavior, 40*(6), 543–550.

Lyons, V. H., Gause, E. L., Spangler, K. R., Wellenius, G. A., & Jay, J. (2022). Analysis of daily ambient temperature and firearm violence in 100 US cities. *JAMA Network Open, 5,* e2247207.

Lyubomirsky, S. (2001). Why are some people happier than others? The role of cognitive and motivational processes in well-being. *American Psychologist, 56,* 239–249.

Lyubomirsky, S., Sousa, L., & Dickerhoof, R. (2006). The costs and benefits of writing, talking, and thinking about life's triumphs and defeats. *Journal of Personality and Social Psychology, 90,* 692–708.

Ma, A., Savani, K., Liu, F., Tai, K., & Kay, A. C. (2023). The mutual constitution of culture and psyche: The bidirectional relationship between individuals' perceived control and cultural tightness-looseness. *Journal of Personality and Social Psychology, 124,* 901–916.

Maass, A. (1998). Personal communication from Universita degli Studi di Padova.

Maass, A. (1999). Linguistic intergroup bias: Stereotype perpetuation through language. In M. P. Zanna (Ed.), *Advances in Experimental Social Psychology, 31,* 79–121.

Maass, A., Milesi, A., Zabbini, S., & Stahlberg, D. (1995). Linguistic intergroup bias: Differential expectancies or in-group protection? *Journal of Personality and Social Psychology, 68,* 116–126.

Maass, A., Volparo, C., & Mucchi-Faina, A. (1996). Social influence and the verifiability of the issue under discussion: Attitudinal versus objective items. *British Journal of Social Psychology, 35,* 15–26.

Maccoby, E. E. (2002). Gender and group process: A developmental perspective. *Current Directions in Psychological Science, 11,* 54–58.

Maccoby, N., & Alexander, J. (1980). Use of media in lifestyle programs. In P. O. Davidson & S. M. Davidson (Eds.), *Behavioral medicine: Changing health lifestyles.* New York: Brunner/Mazel.

Maccoby, N. (1980). Promoting positive health behaviors in adults. In L. A. Bond & J. C. Rosen (Eds.), *Competence and coping during adulthood.* Hanover, NH: University Press of New England.

MacCoun, R. J., & Kerr, N. L. (1988). Asymmetric influence in mock jury deliberation: Jurors' bias for leniency. *Journal of Personality and Social Psychology, 54,* 21–33.

MacDonald, G., Zanna, M. P., & Holmes, J. G. (2000). An experimental test of the role of alcohol in relationship conflict. *Journal of Experimental Social Psychology, 36,* 182–193.

MacDonald, T. K., & Ross, M. (1997). Assessing the accuracy of predictions about dating relationships: How and why do lovers' predictions differ from those made by observers? Unpublished manuscript, University of Lethbridge.

Mack, D., & Rainey, D. (1990). Female applicants' grooming and personnel selection. *Journal of Social Behavior and Personality, 5,* 399–407.

MacKenzie, M. J., Nicklas, E., Brooks-Gunn, J., & Waldfogel, J. (2015). Spanking and children's externalizing behavior across the first decade of life: Evidence for transactional processes. *Journal of Youth and Adolescence, 44,* 658–669.

Mackinnon, S. P., Jordan, C. H., & Wilson, A. E. (2011). Birds of a feather sit together: Physical similarity predicts seating choice. *Personality and Social Psychology Bulletin, 37,* 879–892.

MacNeil-Vroomen, J., Schulz, R., Doyle, M., Murphy, T. E., Ives, D. G., & Monin, J. K. (2018). Time-varying social support and time to death in the cardiovascular health study. *Health Psychology, 37,* 1000–1005.

Macrae, C. N., & Bodenhausen, G. V. (2000). Social cognition: Thinking categorically about others. *Annual Review of Psychology, 51,* 93–120.

Macrae, C. N., & Bodenhausen, G. V. (2001). Social cognition: Categorical person perception. *British Journal of Psychology, 92,* 239–255.

Macrae, C. N., Bodenhausen, G. V., Milne, A. B., & Jetten, J. (1994). Out of mind but back in sight: Stereotypes on the rebound. *Journal of Personality and Social Psychology, 67,* 808–817.

Maddux, J. E., & Gosselin, J. T. (2003). Self-efficacy. In M. R. Leary, & J. P. Tangney (Eds.), *Handbook of self and identity.* New York: Guilford.

Maddux, J. E., & Rogers, R. W. (1983). Protection motivation and self-efficacy: A revised theory of fear appeals and attitude change. *Journal of Experimental Social Psychology, 19,* 469–479.

Maddux, J. E. (1993). The mythology of psychopathology: A social cognitive view of deviance, difference, and disorder. *The General Psychologist, 29 (2),* 34–45.

Maddux, J. E. (2008). Positive psychology and the illness ideology: Toward a positive clinical psychology. *Applied Psychology: An International Review, 57,* 54–70.

Maddux, W. W., Galinsky, A. D., Cuddy, A. J. C., & Polifroni, M. (2008). When being a model minority is good . . . and bad: Realistic threat explains negativity towards Asian Americans. *Personality and Social Psychology Bulletin, 34,* 74–89.

Madera, J. M., Hebl, M. R., & Martin, R. C. (2009). Gender and letters of recommendation for academia: Agentic and communal differences. *Journal of Applied Psychology, 94,* 1591–1599.

Ma, D. S., Correll, J., Wittenbrink, B., Bar-Anan, Y., Sriram, N., & Nosek, B. A. (2013). When fatigue turns deadly: The association between fatigue and racial bias in the decision to shoot. *Basic and Applied Social Psychology, 35,* 515–524.

Maeder, E. M., Yamamoto, S., & Saliba, P. (2015). The influence of defendant race and victim physical attractiveness on juror decision-making in a sexual assault trial. *Psychology, Crime & Law, 21,* 62–79.

Maertens, R., Roozenbeek, J., Basol, M., & van der Linden, S. (2021). Long-term effectiveness of inoculation against misinformation: Three longitudinal experiments. *Journal of Experimental Psychology: Applied, 27,* 1–16.

Magnussen, S., Melinder, A., Stridbeck, U., & Raja, A. (2010). Beliefs about factors affecting the reliability of eyewitness testimony: A comparison of judges, jurors and the general public. *Applied Cognitive Psychology, 24,* 122–133.

Maguire, E. R. (2015) New directions in protest policing. *Saint Louis University Public Law Review, 35,* Article 6.

Mahadevan, N., & Jordan, C. (2022). Desperately seeking status: How desires for, and perceived attainment of, status and inclusion relate to grandiose and vulnerable narcissism. *Personality and Social Psychology Bulletin, 48,* 704–717.

Mahadevan, N., Gregg, A. P., & Sedikides, C. (2018). Is self-regard a sociometer or a hierometer? Self-esteem tracks status and inclusion, narcissism tracks status. *Journal of Personality and Social Psychology, 116,* 444–466.

Mahajan, N., & Wynn, K. (2012). Origins of "us" versus "them": Prelinguistic infants prefer similar others. *Cognition, 124,* 227–233.

Mahalingam, G., Samtani, S., Lam, B. C. P., Lipnicki, D. M., Lima, C. M. F., Blay, S. L., Castro, C. E., Shifu, X., Guerchet, M., Preux, P., Gbessemehlan, A., Skoog, I., Najar, J., Sterner, T. R., Scarmeas, N., Yannakoulia, M., Dardiotis, T., Kim, K., Riedel, H. S., . . . Brodaty, H. (2023). Social connections and risk of incident mild cognitive impairment, dementia, and mortality in 13 longitudinal cohort studies of ageing. *Alzheimer's & Dementia: The Journal of the Alzheimer's Association, 19,* 5114–5128.

Maheshwari, S. (2017, November 4). On YouTube Kids, startling videos slip past filters. *The New York Times.* https://www.nytimes.com/2017/11/04/business/media/youtube-kids-paw-patrol.html

Maimaran, M., & Fishbach, A. (2014). If it's useful and you know it, do you eat? Preschoolers refrain from instrumental food. *Journal of Consumer Research, 41,* 642–655.

Maitner, A. T., & Summerville, A. (2022). "What was meant to be" versus "what might have been": Effects of culture and control on counterfactual thinking. *Journal of Personality and Social Psychology, 123,* 1–27.

Major, B., Kaiser, C. R., & McCoy, S. K. (2003). It's not my fault: When and why attributions to prejudice protect self-esteem. *Personality and Social Psychology Bulletin, 29,* 772–781.

Major, B., Mendes, W. B., & Dovidio, J. F. (2013). Intergroup relations and health disparities: A social psychological perspective. *Health Psychology, 32,* 514–524.

Ma-Kellams, C. (2020). Cultural variation and similarities in cognitive thinking styles versus judgment biases: A review of environmental factors and evolutionary forces. *Review of General Psychology, 24,* 238–253.

Malamuth, N. M., & Check, J. V. P. (1981). The effects of media exposure on acceptance of violence against women: A field experiment. *Journal of Research in Personality, 15,* 436–446.

Malka, A., Soto, C. J., Cohen, A. B., & Miller, D. T. (2011). Religiosity and social welfare: Competing influences of cultural conservatism and prosocial value orientation. *Journal of Personality, 79,* 763–792.

Malkiel, B. G. (2016). *A random walk down Wall Street.* New York: W. W. Norton.

Malle, B. F. (2006). The actor–observer asymmetry in attribution: A (surprising) meta-analysis. *Psychological Bulletin, 132,* 895–919.

Mallinas, S. R., Crawford, J. T., & Cole, S. (2018). Political opposites do not attract: The effects of ideological dissimilarity on impression formation. *Journal of Social and Political Psychology, 6,* 49–75.

Mallinckrodt, V., & Mizerski, D. (2007). The effects of playing an advergame on young children's perceptions, preferences, and requests. *Journal of Advertising, 36,* 87–100.

Malthouse, E. (2023). Confirmation bias and vaccine-related beliefs in the time of COVID-19. *Journal of Public Health, 45,* 523–528.

Maner, J. K., Gailliot, M. T., & Miller, S. L. (2009). The implicit cognition of relationship maintenance: Inattention to attractive alternatives. *Journal of Experimental Social Psychology, 45,* 174–179.

Maner, J. K., Miller, S. L., Schmidt, N. B., & Eckel, L. A. (2008). Submitting to defeat: Social anxiety, dominance threat, and decrements in testosterone. *Psychological Science, 19,* 764–768.

Manis, M., Cornell, S. D., & Moore, J. C. (1974). Transmission of attitude-relevant information through a communication chain. *Journal of Personality and Social Psychology, 30,* 81–94.

Manis, M., Nelson, T. E., & Shedler, J. (1988). Stereotypes and social judgment: Extremity, assimilation, and contrast. *Journal of Personality and Social Psychology, 55,* 28–36.

Mannes, A. E., & Moore, D. A. (2013). A behavioral demonstration of overconfidence in judgment. *Psychological Science, 24*(7), 1190–1197.

Mann, L. (1981). The baiting crowd in episodes of threatened suicide. *Journal of Personality and Social Psychology, 41,* 703–709.

March, D. S., Gaertner, L., & Olson, M. A. (2021). Danger or dislike: Distinguishing threat from negative valence as sources of automatic anti-Black bias. *Journal of Personality and Social Psychology, 121,* 984–1004.

Marcus, A. F., Illescas, A. H., Hohl, B. C., & Llanos, A. M. (2017). Relationships between social isolation, neighborhood poverty, and cancer mortality in a population-based study of US adults. *PLOS ONE, 12*(3), e0173370.

Marcus-Newhall, A., Pedersen, W. C., Carlson, M., & Miller, N. (2000). Displaced aggression is alive and well: A meta-analytic review. *Journal of Personality and Social Psychology, 78,* 670–689.

Marcus, S. (1974, January 13). Review of *Obedience to Authority. The New York Times Book Review,* pp. 1–2.

Mares, D. M., & Moffett, K. W. (2019). Climate change and crime revisited: An exploration of monthly temperature anomalies and UCR crime data. *Environment and Behavior, 51,* 502–529.

Mares, M-L., & Braun, M. T. (2013). Effects of conflict in tween sitcoms on U.S. students' moral reasoning about social exclusion. *Journal of Children and Media, 7,* 428–445.

Margolis, S., & Lyubomirsky, S. (2020). Experimental manipulation of extraverted and introverted behavior and its effects on well-being. *Journal of Experimental Psychology: General, 149,* 719–731.

Marigold, D. C., Holmes, J. G., Wood, J. V., & Cavallo, J. V. (2014). You can't always give what you want: The challenge of providing social support to low self-esteem individuals. *Journal of Personality and Social Psychology, 107,* 56–80.

Marin-Garcia, E., Ruiz-Vargas, J. M., & Kapur, N. (2013). Mere exposure effect can be elicited in transient global amnesia. *Journal of Clinical and Experimental Neuropsychology, 35,* 1007–1014.

Markey, P. M., & Kurtz, J. E. (2006). Increasing acquaintanceship and complementarity of behavioral styles and personality traits among college roommates. *Personality and Social Psychology Bulletin, 32,* 907–916.

Markman, H. J., Floyd, F. J., Stanley, S. M., & Storaasli, R. D. (1988). Prevention of marital distress: A longitudinal investigation. *Journal of Consulting and Clinical Psychology, 56,* 210–217.

Marks, G., & Miller, N. (1987). Ten years of research on the false-consensus effect: An empirical and theoretical review. *Psychological Bulletin, 102,* 72–90.

Markus, H., & Wurf, E. (1987). The dynamic self-concept: A social psychological perspective. *Annual Review of Psychology, 38,* 299–337.

Markus, H. (2001, October 7). *Culture and the good life.* Address to the Positive Psychology Summit conference, Washington, DC.

Markus, H. R., & Kitayama, S. (1991). Culture and the self: Implications for cognition, emotion, and motivation. *Psychological Review, 98,* 224–253.

Markus, H. R., & Kitayama, S. (1994). A collective fear of the collective: Implications for selves and theories of selves. *Personality and Social Psychology Bulletin, 20,* 568–579.

Markus, H. R., & Kitayama, S. (2010). Cultures and selves: A cycle of mutual constitution. *Perspectives on Psychological Science, 5,* 420–430.

Markus, H. R. (2005). On telling less than we can know: The too tacit wisdom of social psychology. *Psychological Inquiry, 16,* 180–184.

Marlon, J., Neyens, L., Jefferson, M., Howe, P., Mildenberger, M., & Leiserowitz, A. (2022, February 23). Yale Climate Opinion Maps 2021. Yale Program on Climate Change Communication.

Marques, E. S., Leite, T. H., de Oliveira, A. G. e S., Cunha, D. B., Verly Júnior, E., & Azeredo, C. M. (2021). Association between family physical violence victimization and food consumption among Brazilian adolescents. *Journal of Interpersonal Violence, 36,* 10182–10197.

Marrero-Quevedo, R. J., Blanco-Hernández, P. J., & Hernández-Cabrera, J. A. (2019). Adult attachment and psychological well-being: The mediating role of personality. *Journal of Adult Development, 26,* 41–56.

Marsh, A. A., Rhoads, S. A., & Ryan, R. M. (2019). A multi-semester classroom demonstration yields evidence in support of the facial feedback effect. *Emotion, 19,* 1500–1504.

Marsh, A. A., Stoycos, S. A., Brethel-Haurwitz, K. M., Robinson, P., VanMeter, J. W., & Cardinale, E. M. (2014). Neural and cognitive characteristics of extraordinary altruists. *PNAS, 111,* 15036–15041.

Marshall, E. A., & Miller, H. A. (2019). Consistently inconsistent: A systematic review of the measurement of pornography use. *Aggression and Violent Behavior, 48,* 169–179.

Marshall, T. C., Ferenczi, N., Lefringhausen, K., Hill, S., & Deng, J. (2020). Intellectual, narcissistic, or Machiavellian? How Twitter users differ from Facebook-only users, why they use Twitter, and what they tweet about. *Psychology of Popular Media, 9,* 14–30.

Marsh, H. W., Kong, C-K., & Hau, K.-T. (2000). Longitudinal multilevel models of the big-fish-little-pond effect on academic self-concept: Counterbalancing contrast and reflected-glory effects in Hong Kong schools. *Journal of Personality and Social Psychology, 78,* 337–349.

Marsh, J. (2012, September 25). Why inequality is bad for the one percent. *Greater Good Magazine.* https://greatergood.berkeley.edu/article/item/why_inequality is_bad_for_the_one_percent

Marsh, N., Scheele, D., Feinstein, J. S., Gerhardt, H., Strang, S., Maier, W., & Hurlemann, R. (2017). Oxytocin-enforced norm compliance reduces xenophobic outgroup rejection. *PNAS Proceedings of the National Academy of Sciences of the United States of America, 114,* 9314–9319.

Martens, A., & Kosloff, S. (2012). Evidence that killing escalates within-subjects in a bug-killing paradigm. *Aggressive Behavior, 38,* 170–174.

Martens, A., Kosloff, S., & Jackson, L. E. (2010). Evidence that initial obedient killing fuels subsequent volitional killing beyond effects of practice. *Social Psychological and Personality Science, 1,* 268–273.

Martens, A., Kosloff, S., Greenberg, J., Landau, M. J., & Schmader, R. (2007). Killing begets killing: Evidence from a bug-killing paradigm that initial killing fuels subsequent killing. *Personality and Social Psychology Bulletin, 33,* 1251–1264.

Martin, E., & Monds, L. A. (2023). The effect of victim intoxication and crime type on mock jury decision-making. *Psychology, Crime & Law.*

Martin, M., & Bowman, E. (2021, March 27). Why nearly all mass shooters are men. NPR.org.

Martinovic, B., & Verkuyten, M. (2012). Host national and religious identification among Turkish Muslims in Western Europe: The role of ingroup norms, perceived discrimination and value incompatibility. *European Journal of Social Psychology, 42,* 893–903.

Martin, R. C., Coyier, K. R., VanSistine, L. M., & Schroeder, K. L. (2013). Anger on the Internet: The perceived value of rant-sites. *Cyberpsychology, Behavior, and Social Networking, 16,* 119–122.

Martin, R., Hewstone, M., & Martin, P. Y. (2008). Majority versus minority influence: The role of message processing in determining resistance to counter-persuasion. *European Journal of Social Psychology, 38,* 16–34.

Martin, R., Martin, P. Y., Smith, J. R., & Hewstone, M. (2007). Majority versus minority influence and prediction of behavioural intentions and behaviour. *Journal of Experimental Social Psychology, 43,* 763–771.

Martin, S. J., Goldstein, N. J., & Cialdini, R. B. (2014). *The small big: Small changes that spark big influence.* New York: Grand Central Publishing.

Martins, N., & Wilson, B. J. (2012a). Mean on the screen: Social aggression in programs popular with children. *Journal of Communication, 62,* 991–1009.

Martins, N., & Wilson, B. J. (2012b). Social aggression on television and its relationship to children's aggression in the classroom. *Human Communication Research, 38,* 48–71.

Marty, M. (1988, December 1). Graceful prose: Your good deed for the day. *Context,* p. 2.

Martínez-Alés, G., Gimbrone, C., Rutherford, C., Kandula, S., Olfson, M., Gould, M. S., Shaman, J., & Keyes, K. M. (2021). Role of firearm ownership on 2001–2016 trends in US firearm suicide rates. *American Journal of Preventive Medicine, 61,* 795–803.

Maruyama, G., Rubin, R. A., & Kingbury, G. (1981). Self-esteem and educational achievement: Independent constructs with a common cause? *Journal of Personality and Social Psychology, 40,* 962–975.

Marvelle, K., & Green, S. (1980). Physical attractiveness and sex bias in hiring decisions for two types of jobs. *Journal of the National Association of Women Deans, Administrators, and Counselors, 44*(1), 3–6.

Masi, C. M., Chen, H-Y., Hawkley, L. C., & Cacioppo, J. T. (2011). A meta-analysis of interventions to reduce loneliness. *Personality and Social Psychology Review, 15,* 219–266.

Mastekaasa, A. (1995). Age variations in the suicide rates and self-reported subjective well-being of married and never-married persons. *Journal of Community & Applied Social Psychology, 5,* 21–39.

Mast, M. S., & Hall, J. A. (2006). Women's advantage at remembering others' appearance: A systematic look at the why and when of a gender difference. *Personality and Social Psychology Bulletin, 32,* 353–364.

Mastroianni, G. R. (2015). Obedience in perspective: Psychology and the Holocaust. *Theory & Psychology, 25,* 657–669.

Masuda, T., & Kitayama, S. (2004). Perceiver-induced constraint and attitude attribution in Japan and the U.S.: A case for the cultural dependence of the correspondence bias. *Journal of Experimental Social Psychology, 40,* 409–416.

Masuda, T., Gonzalez, R., Kwan, L., & Nisbett, R. E. (2008). Culture and aesthetic preference: Comparing the attention to context of East Asians and Americans. *Personality and Social Psychology Bulletin, 34,* 1260–1275.

Mathieu, M. T., & Gosling, S. D. (2012). The accuracy or inaccuracy of affective forecasts depends on how accuracy is indexed: A meta-analysis of past studies. *Psychological Science, 23,* 161–162.

Mattan, B. D., Kubota, J. T., Dang, T. P., & Cloutier, J. (2018). External motivation to avoid prejudice alters neural responses to targets varying in race and status. *Social Cognitive and Affective Neuroscience, 13,* 22–31.

Matthewes, C., & Sandsmark, E. (2017, July 28). Being rich wrecks your soul. We used to know that. *The Washington Post.* washingtonpost.com

Ma, V., & Schoeneman, T. J. (1997). Individualism versus collectivism: A comparison of Kenyan and American self-concepts. *Basic and Applied Social Psychology, 19,* 261–273.

Maxmen, A. (2018, January 24). As Cape Town water crisis deepens, scientists prepare for "Day Zero". *Nature.* https://www.nature.com/articles/d41586-018-01134-x

Maxwell, G. M. (1985). Behaviour of lovers: Measuring the closeness of relationships. *Journal of Personality and Social Psychology, 2,* 215–238.

Mazur, A., & Booth, A. (1998). Testosterone and dominance in men. *Behavioral and Brain Sciences, 21,* 353–363.

Mazzella, R., & Feingold, A. (1994). The effects of physical attractiveness, race, socioeconomic status, and gender of defendants and victims on judgments of mock jurors: A meta-analysis. *Journal of Applied Social Psychology, 24,* 1315–1344.

Mazzoni, G., & Memon, A. (2003). Imagination can create false autobiographical memories. *Psychological Science, 14,* 186–188.

Mazzurega, M., Marisa, J., Zampini, M., & Pavani, F. (2018). Thinner than yourself: Self-serving bias in body size estimation. *Psychological Research, 84*(4), 932–949.

McAlister, A., Perry, C., Killen, J., Slinkard, L. A., & Maccoby, N. (1980). Pilot study of smoking, alcohol and drug abuse prevention. *American Journal of Public Health, 70,* 719–721.

McAndrew, F. T. (2002). New evolutionary perspectives on altruism: Multilevel-selection and costly-signaling theories. *Current Directions in Psychological Science, 11,* 79–82.

McAndrew, F. T. (2009). The interacting roles of testosterone and challenges to status in human male aggression. *Aggression and Violent Behavior, 14,* 330–335.

McArdle, M. (2020, July 10). The real problem with "cancel culture." *The Washington Post.* https://www.washingtonpost.com/opinions/2020/07/10/real-problem-with-cancel-culture/

McCain, J. L., & Campbell, W. K. (2018). Narcissism and social media use: A meta-analytic review. *Psychology of Popular Media Culture, 7*(3), 308–327.

McCann, C. D., & Hancock, R. D. (1983). Self-monitoring in communicative interactions: Social cognitive consequences of goal-directed message modification. *Journal of Experimental Social Psychology, 19,* 109–121.

McCarthy, J. (2019, June 27). Americans still greatly overestimate U.S. gay population. *Gallup.* https://news.gallup.com/poll/259571/americans-greatly-overestimate-gay-population.aspx

McCarthy, J. (2021, September 10). U.S. approval of interracial marriage at new high of 94%. Gallup.com.

McCarthy, J. (2023, June 5). U.S. Same-Sex Marriage Support Holds at 71% High. Gallup.com

McCauley, C., & Moskalenko, S. (2017). Understanding political radicalization: The two-pyramids model. *American Psychologist, 72,* 205–216.

McCauley, C. (1989). The nature of social influence in groupthink: Compliance and internalization. *Journal of Personality and Social Psychology, 57,* 250–260.

McCauley, C. (1998). Group dynamics in Janis's theory of groupthink: Backward and forward. *Organizational Behavior and Human Decision Processes, 73,* 142–163.

McCauley, C. R. (2002). Psychological issues in understanding terrorism and the response to terrorism. In C. E. Stout (Ed.) *The psychology of terrorism* (Vol 3). Westport, CT: Praeger/Greenwood.

McClean, E. J., Martin, S. R., Emich, K. J., & Woodruff, T. (2018). The social consequences of voice: An examination of voice type and gender on status and subsequent leader emergence. *Academy of Management Journal, 61,* 1869–1891.

McClintock, E. A. (2014). Beauty and status: The illusion of exchange in partner selection? *American Sociological Review, 79,* 575–604.

McClure, M. J., & Lydon, J. E. (2014). Anxiety doesn't become you: How attachment anxiety compromises relational opportunities. *Journal of Personality and Social Psychology, 106,* 89–111.

McCluskey, M., Dean, S., & Voilovych, O. (2023, June 15). Ukrainians were 'ready to eliminate' Russian soldier before dramatic surrender, commander says. CNN.com.

McComb, C. A., Vanman, E. J., & Tobin, S. J. (2023). A meta-analysis of the effects of social media exposure to upward comparison targets on self-evaluations and emotions. *Media Psychology, 26,* 612–635.

McCrae, R. R., & Costa, Jr., P. T. (2008). The Five-Factor Theory of personality. In O. P. John, R. W., Robins, & L. A. Pervin (Eds.), *Handbook of personality: Theory and research* (3rd ed.). New York: Guilford.

McCullough, J. L., & Ostrom, T. M. (1974). Repetition of highly similar messages and attitude change. *Journal of Applied Psychology, 59,* 395–397.

McCurry, J. (2017, October 27). Japanese student sues over school's order to dye hair black. *The Guardian.* https://www.theguardian.com/world/2017/oct/27/japanese-student-sues-over-schools-order-to-dye-hair-black

McDermott, R., Tingley, D. Cowden, J., Frazzetto, G., & Johnson, D. D. P. (2009). Monoamine oxidase A gene (MAOA) predicts behavioral aggression following provocation. *PNAS, 106,* 2118–2123.

McDonald, M. M., Asher, B. D., Kerr, N. L., & Navarrete, C. D. (2011). Fertility and intergroup bias in racial and minimal-group contexts: Evidence for shared architecture. *Psychological Science, 22,* 860–865.

McDowell, A., Raifman, J., Progovac, A. M., & Rose, S. (2020). Association of Nondiscrimination Policies With Mental Health Among Gender Minority Individuals. *JAMA Psychiatry, 77,* 952–958.

McFall, R. M. (1991). Manifesto for a science of clinical psychology. *The Clinical Psychologist, 44,* 75–88.

McFall, R. M. (2000). Elaborate reflections on a simple manifesto. *Applied and Preventive Psychology, 9,* 5–21.

McFarland, C., & Ross, M. (1985). *The relation between current impressions and memories of self and dating partners.* Unpublished manuscript, University of Waterloo.

McFarland, L. A., Hendricks, J. L., & Ward, W. B. (2023). A contextual framework for understanding impression management. *Human Resource Management Review, 33,* 1–18.

McFarland, S., Brown, D., & Webb, M. (2013). "Identification with all humanity" as a moral concept and psychological construct. *Current Directions in Psychological Science, 22,* 192–196.

McFarland, S., Webb, M., & Brown, D. (2012). All humanity is my ingroup: A measure and studies of identification with all humanity. *Journal of Personality and Social Psychology, 103,* 830–853.

McGillicuddy, N. B., Welton, G. L., & Pruitt, D. G. (1987). Third-party intervention: A field experiment comparing three different models. *Journal of Personality and Social Psychology, 53,* 104–112.

McGillis, D. (1979). Biases and jury decision making. In I. H. Frieze, D. Bar-Tal, & J. S. Carroll (Eds.), *New approaches to social problems.* San Francisco: Jossey-Bass.

McGlone, M. S., & Tofighbakhsh, J. (2000). Birds of a feather flock conjointly (?): Rhyme as reason in aphorisms. *Psychological Science, 11,* 424–428.

McGlynn, R. P., Tubbs, D. D., & Holzhausen, K. G. (1995). Hypothesis generation in groups constrained by evidence. *Journal of Experimental Social Psychology, 31,* 64–81.

McGorray, E. L., Emery, L. F., Garr-Schultz, A., & Finkel, E. J. (2023). "Mostly White, heterosexual couples": Examining demographic diversity and reporting practices in relationship science research samples. *Journal of Personality and Social Psychology, 125,* 316–344.

McGowan, P. O., Sasaki, A., D'Alessio, A. C., Dymov, S., Labonté, B., Szyl, M., Turecki, G., & Meaney, M. J. (2010). Epigenetic regulation of the glucocorticoid receptor in human brain associates with childhood abuse. *Nature Neuroscience, 12,* 342–348.

McGrath, J. E. (1984). *Groups: Interaction and performance.* Englewood Cliffs, NJ: Prentice-Hall.

McGrath, R. E. (2015). Character strengths in 75 nations: An update. *Journal of Positive Psychology, 10,* 41–52.

McGraw, A. P., Mellers, B. A., & Tetlock, P. E. (2005). Expectations and emotions of Olympic athletes. *Journal of Experimental Social Psychology, 41,* 438–446.

McGuire, W. J., & Padawer-Singer, A. (1978). Trait salience in the spontaneous self-concept. *Journal of Personality and Social Psychology, 33,* 743–754.

McGuire, W. J. (1964). Inducing resistance to persuasion: Some contemporary approaches. In L. Berkowitz (Ed.), *Advances in experimental social psychology* (Vol. 1). New York: Academic Press.

McGuire, W. J. (1978). An information-processing model of advertising effectiveness. In H. L. Davis & A. J. Silk (Eds.), *Behavioral and management sciences in marketing.* New York: John Wiley & Sons.

McGuire, W. J., McGuire, C. V., & Winton, W. (1979). Effects of household sex composition on the salience of one's gender in the spontaneous self-concept. *Journal of Experimental Social Psychology, 15,* 77–90.

McGuire, W. J., McGuire, C. V., Child, P., & Fujioka, T. (1978). Salience of ethnicity in the spontaneous self-concept as a function of one's ethnic distinctiveness in the social environment. *Journal of Personality and Social Psychology, 36,* 511–520.

McKenna, K. Y. A., & Bargh, J. A. (1998). Coming out in the age of the Internet: Identity demarginalization through virtual group participation. *Journal of Personality and Social Psychology, 75,* 681–694.

McKenna, K. Y. A., & Bargh, J. A. (2000). Plan 9 from cyberspace: The implications of the Internet for personality and social psychology. *Personality and Social Psychology Review, 4,* 57–75.

McKeown, S., & Psaltis, C. (2017). Intergroup contact and the mediating role of intergroup trust on outgroup evaluation and future contact intentions in Cyprus and Northern Ireland. *Peace and Conflict: Journal of Peace Psychology, 23,* 392–404.

McKone, E., Dawel, A., Robbins, R. A., Shou, Y., Chen, N., & Crookes, K. (2023). Why the other-race effect matters: Poor recognition of other-race faces impacts everyday social interactions. *British Journal of Psychology, 114,* 230–252.

McLeish, A. C., Hart, J. L., Wood, L. A., & Walker, K. L. (2022). Differences in young adults' perceptions of e-cigarettes by history of use. *Journal of American College Health.*

McLellan, C. (2023, February 8). Fighting climate change: These 5 technologies are our best weapons. ZNet.com.

McMillen, D. L., & Austin, J. B. (1971). Effect of positive feedback on compliance following transgression. *Psychonomic Science, 24,* 59–61.

McMillen, D. L., Sanders, D. Y., & Solomon, G. S. (1977). Self-esteem, attentiveness, and helping behavior. *Journal of Personality and Social Psychology, 3,* 257–261.

McNamarah, C. T. (2019). White caller crime: Racialized police communication and existing while Black. *Michigan Journal of Race and Law, 24,* 335–415.

McNeill, B. W., & Stoltenberg, C. D. (1988). A test of the elaboration likelihood model for therapy. *Cognitive Therapy and Research, 12,* 69–79.

McNulty, J. K. (2010). When positive processes hurt relationships. *Current Directions in Psychological Science, 19,* 167–171.

McNulty, J. K., O'Mara, E. M., & Karney, B. R. (2008). Benevolent cognitions as a strategy of relationship maintenance: "Don't sweat the small stuff" . . . . But it is not all small stuff. *Journal of Personality and Social Psychology, 94,* 631–646.

McPherson, M., Smith-Lovin, L., & Cook, J. M. (2001). Birds of a feature: Homophily in social networks. *Annual Review of Sociology, 27,* 415–444.

Mead, G. H. (1934). *Mind, self, and society.* Chicago: University of Chicago Press.

Meca, A., Cruz, B., Veniegas, T. K., Allison, K. K., Santibanez, L., & Gonzales-Backen, M. A. (2023). Cultural identity configurations: A latent profile analysis of ethnic/racial and US identity process and content. *Journal of Youth and Adolescence, 52,* 105–121.

Media Insight Project. (2017, March). *"Who shared it?": How Americans decide what news to trust on social media.* http://mediainsight.org/Pages/%27Who-Shared-It%27-How-Americans-Decide-What-News-to-Trust-on-Social-Media.aspx

Medin, D. L. (2011, September). Fields for psychology. APS *Observer,* pp. 5, 36.

Medvec, V. H., & Savitsky, K. (1997). When doing better means feeling worse: The effects of categorical cutoff points on counterfactual thinking and satisfaction. *Journal of Personality and Social Psychology, 72,* 1284–1296.

Meehl, P. E. (1954). *Clinical vs. statistical prediction: A theoretical analysis and a review of evidence.* Minneapolis: University of Minnesota Press.

Meehl, P. E. (1986). Causes and effects of my disturbing little book. *Journal of Personality Assessment, 50,* 370–375.

Meeusen, C., Barlow, F. K., & Sibley, C. G. (2017). Generalized and specific components of prejudice: The decomposition of intergroup context effects. *European Journal of Social Psychology, 47,* 443–456.

Mehl, M. R., & Pennebaker, J. W. (2003). The sounds of social life: A psychometric analysis of students' daily social environments and natural conversations. *Journal of Personality and Social Psychology, 84,* 857–870.

Mehl, M. R., Vazire, S., Holleran, S. E., & Clark, C. S. (2010). Eavesdropping on happiness: Well-being is related to having less small talk and more substantive conversations. *Psychological Science, 21,* 539–541.

Meier, B. P., & Hinsz, V. B. (2004). A comparison of human aggression committed by groups and individuals: An interindividual-intergroup discontinuity. *Journal of Experimental Social Psychology, 40*(4), 551–559.

Meissner, C. A., & Brigham, J. C. (2001). Thirty years of investigating the own-race bias in memory for faces: A meta-analytic review. *Psychology, Public Policy, & Law, 7,* 3–35.

Meissner, C. A., Brigham, J. C., & Butz, D. A. (2005). Memory for own- and other-race faces: A dual-process approach. *Applied Cognitive Psychology, 19,* 545–567.

Melamed, D., Simpson, B., & Abernathy, J. (2020). The robustness of reciprocity: Experimental evidence that each form of reciprocity is robust to the presence of other forms of reciprocity. *Science Advances, 6*(23), eaba0504.

Melander, E. (2005), Gender equality and intrastate armed conflict. *International Studies Quarterly, 49,* 695–714.

Melchert, T. P., Halfond, R. W., Hamdi, N. R., Bufka, L. F., Hollon, S. D., & Cuttler, M. J. (2023). Evidence-based practice in psychology: Context, guidelines, and action. *American Psychologist.*

Meldrum, R. C., Mindthoff, A., Evans, J. R., & Piquero, A. R. (2023). Experimental evidence that alcohol intoxication diminishes the inhibitory effect of self-control on reactive aggression. *Journal of Experimental Criminology.*

Meleshko, K. G. A., & Alden, L. E. (1993). Anxiety and self-disclosure: Toward a motivational model. *Journal of Personality and Social Psychology, 64,* 1000–1009.

Mellers, B. A., & Tetlock, P. E. (2019). From discipline-centered rivalries to solution-centered science: Producing better probability estimates for policy makers. *American Psychologist, 74,* 290–300.

Mellers, B., Hertwig, R., & Kahneman, D. (2001). Do frequency representations eliminate conjunction effects: An exercise in adversarial collaboration. *Psychological Science, 12,* 269–275.

Mellers, B., Stone, E., Atanasov, P., Rohrbaugh, N., Metz, S. E., Ungar, L., . . . Tetlock, P. (2015). The psychology of intelligence analysis: Drivers of prediction accuracy in world politics. *Journal of Experimental Psychology: Applied, 21,* 1–14.

Mellers, B., Ungar, L., Baron, J., Ramos, J., Gurcay, B., Fincher, K., Scott, S. E., Moore, D. Atanasov, P., Swift, S. A., Murray, T., Stone, E., & Tetlock, P. E. (2014). Psychological strategies for winning a geopolitical forecasting tournament. *Psychological Science, 25,* 1106–1115.

Meltzer, A. L., McNulty, J. K., Jackson, G. L., & Karney, B. R. (2014). Sex differences in the implications of partner physical attractiveness for the trajectory of marital satisfaction. *Journal of Personality and Social Psychology, 106,* 418–428.

Memon, A., Meissner, C. A., & Fraser, J. (2011). The cognitive interview: A meta-analytic review and study space analysis of the past 25 years. *Psychology, Public Policy, and Law, 16,* 340–372.

Mencken, H. L. (1916). *A book of burlesques* (p. 210). New York: Knopf.

Mendel, R., Traut-Mattausch, E., Jonas, E., Leucht, S., Kane, J. M., Maino, K., Kissling, W., & Hamann, J. (2011). Confirmation bias: Why psychiatrists stick to wrong preliminary diagnoses. *Psychological Medicine, 41,* 2651–2659.

Mendez, M. F. (2023). A functional and neuroanatomical model of dehumanization. *Cognitive and Behavioral Neurology, 36*(1), 42–47.

Mendonca, P. J., & Brehm, S. S. (1983). Effects of choice on behavioral treatment of overweight children. *Journal of Social and Clinical Psychology, 1,* 343–358.

Meppelink, C. S., Smit, E. G., Fransen, M. L., & Diviani, N. (2019). "I was right about vaccination": Confirmation bias and health literacy in online health information seeking. *Journal of Health Communication, 24,* 129–140.

Merari, A. (2002). *Explaining suicidal terrorism: Theories versus empirical evidence.* Invited address to the American Psychological Association, Chicago, Illinois.

Merikle, P. M., Smilek, D., & Eastwood, J. D. (2001). Perception without awareness: Perspectives from cognitive psychology. *Cognition, 79,* 115–134.

Merrilees, C. E., Taylor, L. K., Klotz, M., Goeke-Morey, M. C., Shirlow, P., & Cummings, E. M. (2023). Timing is everything: Developmental changes in the associations between intergroup contact and bias. *International Journal of Behavioral Development, 47,* 243–252.

Mertens, S., Herberz, M., Hahnel, U. J. J., & Brosch, T. (2022). The effectiveness of nudging: A meta-analysis of choice architecture interventions across behavioral domains. *PNAS Proceedings of the National Academy of Sciences of the United States of America, 119.*

Merton, R. K., & Kitt, A. S. (1950). Contributions to the theory of reference group behavior. In R. K. Merton & P. F. Lazarsfeld (Eds.), *Continuities in social research: Studies in the scope and method of the American soldier.* Glencoe, IL: Free Press.

Merton, R. K. (1938; reprinted 1970). *Science, technology and society in seventeenth-century England.* New York: Fertig.

Merton, R. K. (1948). The self-fulfilling prophecy. *Antioch Review, 8,* 193–210.

Mesch, D. J., & Pactor, A. (2015). Women and philanthropy: A literature review. In T. Jung, S. Phillips, & J. Harlow (Eds.), *The Routledge companion to philanthropy.* New York: Routledge.

Mesmer-Magnus, J. R., & DeChurch, L. A. (2009). Information sharing and team performance: A meta-analysis. *Journal of Applied Psychology, 94,* 535–546.

Messé, L. A., & Sivacek, J. M. (1979). Predictions of others' responses in a mixed-motive game: Self-justification or false consensus? *Journal of Personality and Social Psychology, 37,* 602–607.

Messick, D. M., & Sentis, K. P. (1979). Fairness and preference. *Journal of Experimental Social Psychology, 15,* 418–434.

Metzl, J. M., & MacLeish, K. T. (2014). Mental illness, mass shootings, and the politics of American firearms. *American Journal of Public Health, 105,* 240–249.

Meyers, S. A., & Berscheid, E. (1997). The language of love: The difference a preposition makes. *Personality and Social Psychology Bulletin, 23,* 347–362.

Mezulis, A. H., Abramson, L. Y., Hyde, J. S., & Hankin, B. L. (2004). Is there a universal positivity bias in attributions? A meta-analytic review of individual, developmental, and cultural differences in the self-serving attributional bias. *Psychological Bulletin, 130,* 711–747.

Michaels, J. W., Blommel, J. M., Brocato, R. M., Linkous, R. A., & Rowe, J. S. (1982). Social facilitation and inhibition in a natural setting. *Replications in Social Psychology, 2,* 21–24.

Michelson, M. R., & Harrison, B. F. (2023). Ties that bind: The effects of transgender contact on transphobia. *Journal of Homosexuality, 70,* 2848–2900.

Mickelson, K. D., Kessler, R. C., & Shaver, P. R. (1997). Adult attachment in a nationally representative sample. *Journal of Personality and Social Psychology, 73,* 1092–1106.

Midgley, C., Thai, S., Lockwood, P., Kovacheff, C., & Page-Gould, E. (2021). When every day is a high school reunion: Social media comparisons and self-esteem. *Journal of Personality and Social Psychology, 121,* 285–307.

Miech, R. A., Johnston, L. D., Bachman, J. G., O'Malley, P. M., & Schulenberg, J. E. (2018). *Monitoring the future: A continuing study of American youth (12th-Grade Survey), 2017.* Ann Arbor, MI: Inter-university Consortium for Political and Social Research [distributor], 2018-10-29. https://doi.org/10.3886/ICPSR37183.v1

Miech, R. A., Johnston, L. D., Patrick, M. E., O'Malley, P. M., Bachman, J. G., & Schulenberg, J. E. (2022). *Monitoring the future: National survey results on drug use, 1975-2022: Secondary school students.* Ann Arbor: Institute for Social Research, University of Michigan.

Miguel, E., Camerer, C., Casey, K., Cohen, J., Esterling, K. M., Gerber, A., Glennerster, R., Green, D. P., Humphreys, M., Imbens, G., Laitin, D., Madon, T., Nelson, L., Nosek, B. A., Petersen, M., Sedlmayr, R., Simmons, J. P., Simonsohn, U., & Van der Laan, M. (2014). Promoting transparency in social science research. *Science, 343,* 30–31.

Miklikowska, M. (2017). Development of anti-immigrant attitudes in adolescence: The role of parents, peers, intergroup friendships, and empathy. *British Journal of Psychology, 108,* 626–648.

Mikula, G. (1984). Justice and fairness in interpersonal relations: Thoughts and suggestions. In H. Taijfel (Ed.), *The social dimension: European developments in social psychology* (Vol. 1). Cambridge: Cambridge University Press.

Mikulincer, M., & Shaver, P. R. (2001). Attachment theory and intergroup bias: Evidence that priming the secure base schema attenuates negative reactions to out-groups. *Journal of Personality and Social Psychology, 81,* 97–115.

Mikulincer, M., Florian, V., & Hirschberger, G. (2003). The existential function of close relationships: Introducing death into the science of love. *Personality and Social Psychology Review, 7,* 20–40.

Mikulincer, M., Shaver, P. R., Gillath, O., & Nitzberg, R. A. (2005). Attachment, caregiving, and altruism: Boosting attachment security increases compassion and helping. *Journal of Personality and Social Psychology, 89,* 817–839.

Miles-Novelo, A., & Anderson, C. (2018). *The effects of climate change on aggression and violence.* Unpublished manuscript. http://www.craiganderson.org/wp-content/uploads/caa/abstracts/2015-2019/18M-NA.pdf

Miles-Novelo, A., & Anderson, C. A. (2019). Climate change and psychology: Effects of rapid global warming on violence and aggression. *Current Climate Change Reports, 5,* 36–46.

Miles-Novelo, A., & Anderson, C. A. (2022). *Climate change and human behavior: Impacts of a rapidly changing climate on aggression and violence.* Cambridge, UK: Cambridge University Press.

Milgram, A. (2000). My personal view of Stanley Milgram. In T. Blass (Ed.), *Obedience to authority: Current perspectives on the Milgram paradigm.* Mahwah, NJ: Erlbaum.

Milgram, S. (1965). Some conditions of obedience and disobedience to authority. *Human Relations, 18,* 57–76.

Milgram, S. (1974). *Obedience to authority.* New York: Harper and Row.

Milgram, S., Bickman, L., & Berkowitz, L. (1969). Note on the drawing power of crowds of different size. *Journal of Personality and Social Psychology, 13,* 79–82.

Miller, A. G. (1986). *The obedience experiments: A case study of controversy in social science.* New York: Praeger.

Miller, A. G. (2004). What can the Milgram obedience experiments tell us about the Holocaust? Generalizing from the social psychological laboratory. In A. G. Miller (Ed.), *The social psychology of good and evil.* New York: Guilford.

Miller, A. G. (2006). *Exonerating harm-doers: Some problematic implications of social-psychological explanations.* Paper presented to the Society of Personality and Social Psychology convention.

Miller, C. E., & Anderson, P. D. (1979). Group decision rules and the rejection of deviates. *Social Psychology Quarterly, 42,* 354–363.

Miller, C. T., & Felicio, D. M. (1990). Person-positivity bias: Are individuals liked better than groups? *Journal of Experimental Social Psychology, 26,* 408–420.

Miller, D. J., Spengler, E. S., & Spengler, P. M. (2015). A meta-analysis of confidence and judgment accuracy in clinical decision making. *Journal of Counseling Psychology, 62,* 553–567.

Miller, D. W. (2001, November 23). Jury consulting on trial. *Chronicle of Higher Education,* pp. A15, A16.

Miller, G. E., Chen, E., & Parker, K. J. (2011). Psychological stress in childhood and susceptibility to the chronic diseases of aging: Moving toward a model of behavioral and biological mechanisms. *Psychological Bulletin, 137,* 959–997.

Miller, G. R., & Fontes, N. E. (1979). *Videotape on trial: A view from the jury box.* Beverly Hills, CA: Sage.

Miller, G., Tybur, J. M., & Jordan, B. D. (2007). Ovulatory cycle effects on tip earnings by lap dancers: Economic evidence for human estrus? *Evolution and Human Behavior, 28,* 375–381.

Miller, J. G. (1984). Culture and the development of everyday social explanation. *Journal of Personality and Social Psychology, 46,* 961–978.

Miller, L. C. (1990). Intimacy and liking: Mutual influence and the role of unique relationships. *Journal of Personality and Social Psychology, 44,* 1234–1244.

Miller, M. G., & Sutherland, J. L. (2023). The Effect of Gender on Interruptions at Congressional Hearings. *American Political Science Review, 117,* 103–121.

Miller, N., & Campbell, D. T. (1959). Recency and primacy in persuasion as a function of the timing of speeches and measurements. *Journal of Abnormal and Social Psychology, 59,* 1–9.

Miller, N., & Marks, G. (1982). Assumed similarity between self and other: Effect of expectation of future interaction with that other. *Social Psychology Quarterly, 45,* 100–105.

Miller, N. (2002). Personalization and the promise of contact theory. *Journal of Social Issues, 58,* 387–410.

Miller, N., Pedersen, W. C., Earleywine, M., & Pollock, V. E. (2003). A theoretical model of triggered displaced aggression. *Personality and Social Psychology Review, 7,* 75–97.

Miller, P. A., Kozu, J., & Davis, A. C. (2001). Social influence, empathy, and prosocial behavior in cross-cultural perspective. In W. Wosinska, R. B. Cialdini, D. W. Barrett, & J. Reykowski (Eds.), *The practice of social influence in multiple cultures.* Mahwah, NJ: Erlbaum.

Miller, P. J. E., & Rempel, J. K. (2004). Trust and partner-enhancing attributions in close relationships. *Personality and Social Psychology Bulletin, 30,* 695–705.

Miller, P. J. E., Niehuis, S., & Huston, T. L. (2006). Positive illusions in marital relationships: A 13-year longitudinal study. *Personality and Social Psychology Bulletin, 32,* 1579–1594.

Miller, R. L., Brickman, P., & Bolen, D. (1975). Attribution versus persuasion as a means for modifying behavior. *Journal of Personality and Social Psychology, 31,* 430–441.

Miller, R. S., & Simpson, J. A. (1990). *Relationship satisfaction and attentiveness to alternatives.* Paper presented at the American Psychological Association convention, Boston, MA.

Miller, R. S. (1997). Inattentive and contented: Relationship commitment and attention to alternatives. *Journal of Personality and Social Psychology, 73,* 758–766.

Miller, S. L., Zielaskowski, K., & Plant, E. A. (2012). The basis of shooter biases: Beyond cultural stereotypes. *Personality and Social Psychology Bulletin, 38,* 1358–1366.

Millman, A. (2022, June 22). Former West Virginia lawmaker sentenced for role in January 6 riot. CNN.com

Mills, J. S., Musto, S., Williams, L., & Tiggemann, M. (2018). "Selfie" harm: Effects on mood and body image in young women. *Body Image, 27,* 86–92.

Milyavskaya, M., Gingras, I., Mageau, G. A., Koestner, R., Gagnon, H., Fang, J., & Boiché, J. (2009). Balance across contexts: Importance of balanced need satisfaction across various life domains. *Personality and Social Psychology Bulletin, 35,* 1031–1045.

Mims, P. R., Hartnett, J. J., & Nay, W. R. (1975). Interpersonal attraction and help volunteering as a function of physical attractiveness. *Journal of Psychology, 89,* 125–131.

Min, K. S., & Arkes, H. R. (2012). When is difficult planning good planning? The effects of scenario-based planning on optimistic prediction bias. *Journal of Applied Social Psychology, 42,* 2701–2729.

Minson, J. A., & Dorison, C. A. (2022). Why is exposure to opposing views aversive? Reconciling three theoretical perspectives. *Current Opinion in Psychology, 47.*

Mirsky, S. (2009, January). What's good for the group. *Scientific American,* p. 51.

Miscenko, D., Guenter, H., & Day, D. V. (2017). Am I a leader? Examining leader identity development over time. *The Leadership Quarterly, 28*(5), 605–620.

Mishel, L., & Kandra, J. (2020, August 18). *CEO compensation surged 14% in 2019 to $21.3 million: CEOs now earn 320 times as much as a typical worker.* Economic Policy Institute. https://www.epi.org/publication/ceo-compensation-surged-14-in-2019-to-21-3-million-ceos-now-earn-320-times-as-much-as-a-typical-worker/

Mita, T. H., Dermer, M., & Knight, J. (1977). Reversed facial images and the mere-exposure hypothesis. *Journal of Personality and Social Psychology, 35,* 597–601.

Mitchell, A., Jurkowitz, M., Oliphant, J. B., & Shearer, E. (2020, July 30). Americans Who Mainly Get Their News on Social Media Are Less Engaged, Less Knowledgeable. Pew Research Center.

Mitchell, G. (2012). Revisiting truth or triviality: The external validity of research in the psychological laboratory. *Perspectives on Psychological Science, 7,* 109–117.

Mitchell, T. R., & Thompson, L. (1994). A theory of temporal adjustments of the evaluation of events: Rosy prospection and rosy retrospection. In C. Stubbart, J. Porac, & J. Meindl (Eds.), *Advances in managerial cognition and organizational information processing.* Greenwich, CT: JAI Press.

Mitchell, T. R., Thompson, L., Peterson, E., & Cronk, R. (1997). Temporal adjustments in the evaluation of events: The "rosy view." *Journal of Experimental Social Psychology, 33,* 421–448.

Miyake, A., Kost-Smith, L., Finkelstein, N. D., Pollock, S. J., Cohen, G. L., & Ito, T. A. (2010). Reducing the gender achievement gap in college science: A classroom study of values affirmation. *Science, 330,* 1234–1237.

Moffitt, T., Caspi, A., Sugden, K., Taylor, A., Craig, I. W., Harrington, H., McClay, J., Mill, J., Martin, J., Braithwaite, A., & Poulton, R. (2003). Influence of life stress on depression: Moderation by a polymorphism in the 5-HTT gene. *Science, 301,* 386–389.

Moghaddam, F. M. (2005). The staircase to terrorism: A psychological exploration. *American Psychologist, 60,* 161–169.

Moghaddam, F. M. (2009). Omniculturalism: Policy solutions to fundamentalism in the era of fractured globalization. *Culture and Psychology, 15,* 337–347.

Moghaddam, F. M. (2010). *The new global insecurity.* New York: Praeger.

Mojzisch, A., & Schulz-Hardt, S. (2010). Knowing others' preferences degrades the quality of group decisions. *Journal of Personality and Social Psychology, 98,* 784–808.

Mojzisch, A., Elster, C., & Germar, M. (2022). People perceive themselves to adhere more strictly to COVID-19 guidelines than others. *Psychology, Health & Medicine, 27,* 325–332.

Moller, A. C., & Sheldon, K. M. (2020). Athletic scholarships are negatively associated with intrinsic motivation for sports, even decades later: Evidence for long-term undermining. *Motivation Science, 6,* 43–48.

Moller, I., Krahe, B., Busching, R., & Krause, C. (2012). Efficacy of an intervention to reduce the use of media violence and aggression: An experimental evaluation with adolescents in Germany. *Journal of Youth and Adolescence, 41,* 105–120.

Montag, C., Weber, B., Trautner, P., Newport, B., Markett, S., Walter, N. T., Felten, A., & Reuter, M. (2012). Does excessive play of violent first-person-shooter-video-games dampen brain activity in response to emotional stimuli? *Biological Psychology, 89,* 107–111.

Montanaro, D. (2022, July 21). A majority thinks Trump is to blame for Jan. 6 but won't face charges, poll finds. NPR.org.

Montoya, R. M., & Horton, R. S. (2013). A meta-analytic investigation of the processes underlying the similarity-attraction effect. *Journal of Social and Personal Relationships, 30,* 64–94.

Montoya, R. M., & Insko, C. A. (2008). Toward a more complete understanding of the reciprocity of liking effect. *European Journal of Social Psychology, 38,* 477–498.

Montoya, R. M. (2008). I'm hot, so I'd say you're not: The influence of objective physical attractiveness on mate selection. *Personality and Social Psychology Bulletin, 34,* 1315–1331.

Montoya, R. M., Horton, R. S., Vevea, J. L., Citkowicz, M., & Lauber, E. A. (2017). A re-examination of the mere exposure effect: The influence of repeated exposure on recognition, familiarity, and liking. *Psychological Bulletin, 143,* 459–498.

Montoya, R. M., Kershaw, C., & Prosser, J. L. (2018). A meta-analytic investigation of the relation between interpersonal attraction and enacted behavior. *Psychological Bulletin, 144,* 673–709.

Moons, W. G., & Mackie, D. M. (2007). Thinking straight while seeing red: The influence of anger on information processing. *Personality and Social Psychology Bulletin, 33,* 706–720.

Moor, B. G., Crone, E. A., & van der Molen, M. W. (2010). The heartbrake of social rejection: Heart rate deceleration in response to unexpected peer rejection. *Psychological Science, 21,* 1326–1333.

Moore, D. A., & Swift, S. A. (2011). The three faces of overconfidence in organizations. In D. DeCremer, R. van Dick, & J. K. Murnighan (Eds.), *Social psychology and organizations.* New York: Routledge/Taylor & Francis.

Moore, D. W. (2004, April 20). Ballot order: Who benefits? *Gallup Poll Tuesday Briefing.* www.gallup.com

Moore, T. M., Elkins, S. R., McNulty, J. K., Kivisto, A. J., & Handsel, V. A. (2011). Alcohol use and intimate partner violence perpetration among college students: Assessing the temporal association using electronic diary technology. *Psychology of Violence, 1,* 315–328.

Morales, M., Levenson, E., Ly, L., & Elamroussi, A. (2023, February 15). Buffalo grocery store mass shooter apologizes for racist attack and receives sentence of life in prison. CNN.com.

Morand, S., & Walther, B. A. (2018). Individualistic values are related to an increase in the outbreaks of infectious diseases and zoonotic diseases. *Scientific Reports, 8,* 3866.

Moran, G., & Cutler, B. L. (1991). The prejudicial impact of pretrial publicity. *Journal of Applied Social Psychology, 21,* 345–367.

Moran, G., Cutler, B. L., & De Lisa, A. (1994). Attitudes toward tort reform, scientific jury selection, and juror bias: Verdict inclination in criminal and civil trials. *Law and Psychology Review, 18,* 309–328.

Moran, G., Cutler, B. L., & Loftus, E. F. (1990). Jury selection in major controlled substance trials: The need for extended voir dire. *Forensic Reports, 3,* 331–348.

Morgan, C. A., III, Hazlett, G., Doran, A., Garrett, S., Hoyt, G., Thomas, P., Baranoski, M., & Southwick, & S. M. (2004). Accuracy of eyewitness memory for persons encountered during exposure to highly intense stress. *International Journal of Law and Psychiatry, 27,* 265–279.

Moritz, D., & Roberts, J. E. (2020). Depressive symptoms and self-esteem as moderators of metaperceptions of social rejection versus acceptance: A truth and bias analysis. *Clinical Psychological Science, 8,* 252–265.

Morling, B., & Lamoreaux, M. (2008). Measuring culture outside the head: A meta-analysis of individualism-collectivism in cultural products. *Personality and Social Psychology Bulletin, 12,* 199–221.

Mor, N., & Winquist, J. (2002). Self-focused attention and negative affect: A meta-analysis. *Psychological Bulletin, 128,* 638–662.

Morris, W. N., & Miller, R. S. (1975). The effects of consensus-breaking and consensus-preempting partners on reduction of conformity. *Journal of Experimental Social Psychology, 11,* 215–223.

Moscatelli, S., Albarello, F., Prati, F., & Rubini, M. (2014). Badly off or better off than them? The impact of relative deprivation and relative gratification on intergroup discrimination. *Journal of Personality and Social Psychology, 107,* 248–264.

Moscovici, S., & Zavalloni, M. (1969). The group as a polarizer of attitudes. *Journal of Personality and Social Psychology, 12,* 124–135.

Moscovici, S. (1985). Social influence and conformity. In G. Lindzey & E. Aronson (Eds.), *The handbook of social psychology,* (3rd ed.). Hillsdale, NJ: Erlbaum.

Moscovici, S., Lage, S., & Naffrechoux, M. (1969). Influence of a consistent minority on the responses of a majority in a color perception task. *Sociometry, 32,* 365–380.

Moskowitz, T. J., & Wertheim, L. J. (2011). *Scorecasting: The hidden influences behind how sports are played and games are won.* New York: Crown Archetype.

Moss, J. H., & Maner, J. K. (2016). Biased sex ratios influence fundamental aspects of human mating. *Personality and Social Psychology Bulletin, 42,* 72–80.

Motherhood Project. (2001, May 2). *Watch out for children: A mothers' statement to advertisers* [PDF file]. Institute for American Values. http://americanvalues.org/catalog/pdfs/watchout.pdf

Mousa, S. (2020). Building social cohesion between Christians and Muslims through soccer in post-ISIS Iraq. *Science, 369,* 866–870.

Moutsiana, C., Fearon, P., Murray, L., Cooper, P., Goodyer, I., Johnstone, T., & Halligan, S. (2014). Making an effort to feel positive: Insecure attachment in infancy predicts the neural underpinnings of emotion regulation in adulthood. *Journal of Child Psychology and Psychiatry, 55,* 999–1008.

Moyer-Gusé, E., Robinson, M. J., & Mcknight, J. (2018). The role of humor in messaging about the MMR vaccine. *Journal of Health Communication, 23,* 514–522.

Moyer, K. E. (1976). *The psychobiology of aggression.* New York: Harper & Row.

Moyer, K. E. (1983). The physiology of motivation: Aggression as a model. In C. J. Scheier & A. M. Rogers (Eds.), *G. Stanley Hall Lecture Series* (Vol. 3). Washington, DC: American Psychological Association.

Mrkva, K., & Van Boven, L. (2020). Salience theory of mere exposure: Relative exposure increases liking, extremity, and emotional intensity. *Journal of Personality and Social Psychology, 118*(6), 1118–1145.

Mrug, S., Jones, L. C., Elliott, M. N., Tortolero, S. R., Peskin, M. F., & Schuster, M. A. (2021). Soft drink consumption and mental health in adolescents: A longitudinal examination. *Journal of Adolescent Health, 68,* 155–160.

Mueller, C. M., & Dweck, C. S. (1998). Praise for intelligence can undermine children's motivation and performance. *Journal of Personality and Social Psychology, 75,* 33–52.

Mueller, C. W., Donnerstein, E., & Hallam, J. (1983). Violent films and prosocial behavior. *Personality and Social Psychology Bulletin, 9,* 83–89.

Mueller-Johnson, K., Dhami, M. K., & Lundrigan, S. (2018). Effects of judicial instructions and juror characteristics on interpretations of beyond reasonable doubt. *Psychology, Crime & Law, 24,* 117–133.

Muggleton, N. K., & Fincher, C. L. (2017). Unrestricted sexuality promotes distinctive short- and long-term mate preferences in women. *Personality and Individual Differences, 111,* 169–173.

Muhumuza, J. (2022, October 5). Four emerging technologies that could help tackle climate change. CPI.com.

Mujcic, R., & Frijters, P. (2020). The colour of a free ride. *The Economic Journal,* ueaa090.

Mullen, B., & Baumeister, R. F. (1987). Group effects on self-attention and performance: Social loafing, social facilitation, and social impairment. In C. Hendrick (Ed.), *Group processes and intergroup relations: Review of personality and social psychology* (Vol. 9). Newbury Park, CA: Sage.

Mullen, B. (1986a). Atrocity as a function of lynch mob composition: A self-attention perspective. *Personality and Social Psychology Bulletin, 12,* 187–197.

Mullen, B. (1986b). Stuttering, audience size, and the other-total ratio: A self-attention perspective. *Journal of Applied Social Psychology, 16,* 139–149.

Mullen, B., Bryant, B., & Driskell, J. E. (1997). Presence of others and arousal: An integration. *Group Dynamics: Theory, Research, and Practice, 1,* 52–64.

Mullen, B., Copper, C., & Diskell, J. E. (1990). Jaywalking as a function of model behavior. *Personality and Social Psychology Bulletin, 16,* 320–330.

Muller, S., & Johnson, B. T. (1990). *Fear and persuasion: A linear relationship?* Paper presented at the Eastern Psychological Association convention.

Mullin, C. R., & Linz, D. (1995). Desensitization and resensitization to violence against women: Effects of exposure to sexually violent films on judgments of domestic violence victims. *Journal of Personality and Social Psychology, 69,* 449–459.

Munoz-Rivas, M. J., Grana, J. L., O'Leary, K. D., & Gonzalez, M. P. (2007). Aggression in adolescent dating relationships: Prevalence, justification, and health consequences. *Journal of Adolescent Health, 40,* 298–304.

Munro, G. D., Ditto, P. H., Lockhart, L. K., Fagerlin, A., Gready, M., & Peterson, E. (1997). *Biased assimilation of sociopolitical arguments: Evaluating the 1996 U.S. presidential debate.* Unpublished manuscript, Hope College.

Murphy, C. (1990, June). New findings: Hold on to your hat. *The Atlantic,* pp. 22–23.

Murphy, S. C., von Hippel, W., Dubbs, S. L., Angilletta, M. J., Wilson, R. S., Trivers, R., & Barlow, F. K. (2015). The role of overconfidence in romantic desirability and competition. *Personality and Social Psychology Bulletin, 41,* 1036–1052.

Murrar, S., Campbell, M. R., & Brauer, M. (2020). Exposure to peers' pro-diversity attitudes increases inclusion and reduces the achievement gap. *Nature Human Behaviour, 4,* 889–897.

Murray, D. R., & Schaller, M. (2012). Threat(s) and conformity deconstructed: Perceived threat of infectious disease and its implications for conformist attitudes and behavior. *European Journal of Social Psychology, 42,* 180–188.

Murray, D. R. (2014). Direct and indirect implications of pathogen prevalence for scientific and technological innovation. *Journal of Cross-Cultural Psychology, 45,* 971–985.

Murray, K. E., & Marx, D. M. (2013). Attitudes toward unauthorized immigrants, authorized immigrants, and refugees. *Cultural Diversity and Ethnic Minority Psychology, 19,* 332–341.

Murray, S. L., & Holmes, J. G. (1997). A leap of faith? Positive illusions in romantic relationships. *Personality and Social Psychology Bulletin, 23,* 586–604.

Murray, S. L., Gellavia, G. M., Rose, P., & Griffin, D. W. (2003). Once hurt, twice hurtful: How perceived regard regulates daily marital interactions. *Journal of Personality and Social Psychology, 84,* 126–147.

Murray, S. L., Griffin, D. W., Derrick, J. L., Harris, B., Aloni, M., & Leder, S. (2011). *Psychological Science, 22*(5), 619–626.

Murray, S. L., Holmes, J. G., & Griffin, D. W. (1996a). The benefits of positive illusions: Idealization and the construction of satisfaction in close relationships. *Journal of Personality and Social Psychology, 70,* 79–98.

Murray, S. L., Holmes, J. G., & Griffin, D. W. (1996b). The self-fulfilling nature of positive illusions in romantic relationships: Love is not blind, but prescient. *Journal of Personality and Social Psychology, 71,* 1155–1180.

Murray, S. L., Holmes, J. G., & Griffin, D. W. (2000). Self-esteem and the quest for felt security: How perceived regard regulates attachment processes. *Journal of Personality and Social Psychology, 78,* 478–498.

Murray, S. L., Holmes, J. G., Gellavia, G., Griffin, D. W., & Dolderman, D. (2002). Kindred spirits? The benefits of egocentrism in close relationships. *Journal of Personality and Social Psychology, 82,* 563–581.

Murstein, B. L. (1986). *Paths to marriage.* Newbury Park, CA: Sage.

Muscatell, K. A., Dedovic, K., Slavich, G. M., Jarcho, M. R., Breen, E. C., Bower, J. E., & . . . Eisenberger, N. I. (2016). Neural mechanisms linking social status and inflammatory responses to social stress. *Social Cognitive and Affective Neuroscience, 11,* 915–922.

Muschalla, B., & Schönborn, F. (2021). Induction of false beliefs and false memories in laboratory studies–a systematic review. *Clinical Psychology & Psychotherapy.*

Muson, G. (1978, March). Teenage violence and the telly. *Psychology Today,* 50–54.

Myers, D. G., & Bishop, G. D. (1970). Discussion effects on racial attitudes. *Science, 169,* 778–789.

Myers, D. G. (1978). Polarizing effects of social comparison. *Journal of Experimental Social Psychology, 14,* 554–563.

Myers, D. G. (1993). *The pursuit of happiness.* New York: Avon.

Myers, D. G. (2000a). *The American paradox: Spiritual hunger in an age of plenty.* New Haven, CT: Yale University Press.

Myers, D. G. (2000b). The funds, friends, and faith of happy people. *American Psychologist, 55,* 56–67.

Myers, D. G. (2001, December). Do we fear the right things? *American Psychological Society Observer,* 3.

Myers, D. G. (2010). Group polarization. In J. Levine & M. Hogg (Eds.), *Encyclopedia of group processes and intergroup relations.* Thousand Oaks, CA: Sage.

Myers, J. E., Madathil, J., & Tingle, L. R. (2005). Marriage satisfaction and wellness in India and the United States: A preliminary comparison of arranged marriages and marriages of choice. *Journal of Counseling and Development, 83,* 183–190.

Myers, J. N. (1997, December). Quoted by S. A. Boot, Where the weather reigns. *World Traveler,* pp. 86, 88, 91, 124.

Nadler, A., & Fisher, J. D. (1986). The role of threat to self-esteem and perceived control in recipient reaction to help: Theory development and empirical validation. In L. Berkowitz (Ed.), *Advances in Experimental Social Psychology* (Vol. 19). Orlando, FL: Academic Press.

Nadler, A. (1991). Help-seeking behavior: Psychological costs and instrumental benefits. In M. S. Clark (Ed.), *Prosocial behavior.* Newbury Park, CA: Sage.

Nadler, J. T., & Clark, M. H. (2011). Stereotype threat: A meta-analysis comparing African Americans to Hispanic Americans. *Journal of Applied Social Psychology, 41,* 872–890.

Nagai, S., Kimura, M., Honda, M., Iida, T., & Mizuno, H. (2023). Gender differences in help-seeking: A meta-analysis of Japanese studies, including unreported data1. *Japanese Psychological Research.*

Nagar, D., & Pandey, J. (1987). Affect and performance on cognitive task as a function of crowding and noise. *Journal of Applied Social Psychology, 17,* 147–157.

Nail, P. R., MacDonald, G., & Levy, D. A. (2000). Proposal of a four-dimensional model of social response. *Psychological Bulletin, 126,* 454–470.

Naimi, T. S., Xuan, Z., Coleman, S. M., Lira, M. C., Hadland, S. E., Cooper, S. E., & . . . Swahn, M. H. (2017). Alcohol policies and alcohol-involved homicide victimization in the United States. *Journal of Studies on Alcohol and Drugs, 78,* 781–788.

Nair, H., Manchanda, P., & Bhatia, T. (2008, May). *Asymmetric social interactions in physician prescription behavior: The role of opinion leaders.* Stanford University Graduate School of Business Research Paper No. 1970 (ssrn.com/abstract5937021).

Nakada, S., Ho, F. K., Celis-Morales, C., Jackson, C. A., & Pell, J. P. (2023). Individual and joint associations of anxiety disorder and depression with cardiovascular disease: A UK Biobank prospective cohort study. *European Psychiatry, 66.*

Nakamura, D. (2023, March 13). Hate crimes in U.S. rose to highest level in 2021, FBI says. *Washington Post.*

Nakamura, J. S., Lee, M. T., VanderWeele, T. J., & Kim, E. S. (2023). Informal helping and subsequent health and well-being in older U.S. Adults. *International Journal of Behavioral Medicine.*

Nance, A. R. (2015). Social media selection: How jury consultants can use: Social media to build a more favorable jury. *Law & Psychology Review, 39,* 267–286.

NAP. (2016). *Attribution of extreme weather events in the context of climate change.* Washington, DC: Committee on Extreme Weather Events and Climate Change Attribution, National Academies of Sciences, Engineering, and Medicine.

Napier, K., & Shamir, L. (2019). Quantitative sentiment analysis of lyrics in popular music. *Journal of Popular Music Studies, 30,* 161–176.

Narang, P., Paladugu, A., Manda, S. R., Smock, W., Cosnay, C., & Lippmann, S. (2010). Do guns provide safety? At what cost? *Southern Medical Journal, 103,* 151–153.

Narea, N. (2023, May 8). Mental illness is not responsible for America's guns crisis. Vox.com.

Nario-Redmond, M. R. (2010). Cultural stereotypes of disabled and non-disabled men and women: Consensus for global category representations and diagnostic domains. *British Journal of Social Psychology, 49,* 471–488.

NASA. (2024). https://data.giss.nasa.gov/gistemp/graphs/

NASA Global Climate Change. (2023). Arctic sea ice minimum. https://climate.nasa.gov/vital-signs/arctic-sea-ice/

Nash, K., Lea, J. M., Davies, T., & Yogeeswaran, K. (2018). The bionic blues: Robot rejection lowers self-esteem. *Computers in Human Behavior, 78,* 59–63.

Nasie, M., Reifen Tagar, M., & Bar, T. D. (2021). Ethno-political socialization of young children in societies involved in intractable conflict: The case of Israel. *Journal of Social Issues, 77,* 1257–1281

National Centers for Environmental Information (2024). Billion-dollar weather and climate disasters. https://www.ncei.noaa.gov/access/billions/time-series/US

National Safety Council (2023). Deaths by transportation mode. injuryfacts.nsc.org

National Safety Council. (2023). *Deaths by transportation mode, United States 2007-2021.* https://injuryfacts.nsc.org/home-and-community/safety-topics/deaths-by-transportation-mode/

Navarrete, C. D., McDonald, M. M., Molina, L. E., & Sidanius, J. (2010). Prejudice at the nexus of race and gender: An outgroup male target hypothesis. *Journal of Personality and Social Psychology, 98,* 933–945.

NCADD (National Council of Alcoholism and Drug Dependence). (2014). *Alcohol and crime.* https://ncadd.org/learn-about-alcohol/alcohol-and-crime

NCES (National Center for Education Statistics). (2023). *Indicators of school crime and safety. Indicator 10: Bullying at school and electronic bullying.* https://nces.ed.gov/fastfacts/display.asp?id=719

Neff, K. D. (2011). Self-compassion, self-esteem, and well-being. *Social and Personality Psychology Compass, 5,* 1–12.

Neff, K. D. (2023). Self-compassion: Theory, method, research, and intervention. *Annual Review of Psychology, 74,* 193–218.

Neff, L. A., & Karney, B. R. (2005). To know you is to love you: The implications of global adoration and specific accuracy for marital relationships. *Journal of Personality and Social Psychology, 88,* 480–497.

Neff, L. A., Nguyen, T. T. T., & Williamson, H. C. (2021). Too stressed to help? The effects of stress on noticing partner needs and enacting support. *Personality and Social Psychology Bulletin, 47,* 1565–1579.

Nehrlich, A. D., Gebauer, J. E., Sedikides, C., & Schoel, C. (2019). Agentic narcissism, communal narcissism, and prosociality. *Journal of Personality and Social Psychology, 117,* 142–165.

Neimeyer, G. J., MacNair, R., Metzler, A. E., & Courchaine, K. (1991). Changing personal beliefs: Effects of forewarning, argument quality, prior bias, and personal exploration. *Journal of Social and Clinical Psychology, 10,* 1–20.

Neimeyer, R. A., Pitcho-Prelorentzos, S., & Mahat-Shamir, M. (2021). "If only . . .": Counterfactual thinking in bereavement. *Death Studies, 45,* 692–701.

Nelson-Coffey, S. K., Fritz, M. M., Lyubomirsky, S., & Cole, S. W. (2017). Kindness in the blood: A randomized controlled trial of the gene regulatory impact of prosocial behavior. *Psychoneuroendocrinology, 81,* 8–13.

Nelson, L., & LeBoeuf, R. (2002). *Why do men overperceive women's sexual intent? False consensus vs. evolutionary explanations.* Paper presented to the annual meeting of the Society for Personality and Social Psychology, Savannah, GA.

Nelson, L. D., & Morrison, E. L. (2005). The symptoms of resource scarcity: Judgments of food and finances influence preferences for potential partners. *Psychological Science, 16,* 167–173.

Nelson, L. J., & Miller, D. T. (1995). The distinctiveness effect in social categorization: You are what makes you unusual. *Psychological Science, 6,* 246.

Nelson, T. E., Acker, M., & Manis, M. (1996). Irrepressible stereotypes. *Journal of Experimental Social Psychology, 32,* 13–38.

Nelson, T. E., Biernat, M. R., & Manis, M. (1990). Everyday base rates (sex stereotypes): Potent and resilient. *Journal of Personality and Social Psychology, 59,* 664–675.

Nemeth, C., & Chiles, C. (1988). Modelling courage: The role of dissent in fostering independence. *European Journal of Social Psychology, 18,* 275–280.

Nemeth, C., & Wachtler, J. (1974). Creating the perceptions of consistency and confidence: A necessary condition for minority influence. *Sociometry, 37,* 529–540.

Nemeth, C. (1979). The role of an active minority in intergroup relations. In W. G. Austin & S. Worchel (Eds.), *The social psychology of intergroup relations.* Monterey, CA: Brooks/Cole.

Nemeth, C. J., & Ormiston, M. (2007). Creative idea generation: Harmony versus stimulation. *European Journal of Social Psychology, 37,* 524–535.

Nemeth, C. J. (1997). Managing innovation: When less is more. *California Management Review, 40,* 59–74.

Nemeth, C. J. (1999). Behind the scenes. In D. G. Myers (Ed.), *Social psychology* (6th ed.). New York: McGraw Hill.

Nemeth, C. J. (2011). Minority influence theory. In P. Van Lange, A. Kruglanski, & E. T. Higgins (Eds.), *Handbook of theories in social psychology.* New York: Sage.

Nemeth, C. J., Brown, K., & Rogers, J. (2001a). Devil's advocate versus authentic dissent: Stimulating quantity and quality. *European Journal of Social Psychology, 31,* 1–13.

Nemeth, C. J., Connell, J. B., Rogers, J. D., & Brown, K. S. (2001b). Improving decision making by means of dissent. *Journal of Applied Social Psychology, 31,* 48–58.

Nerem, R. S., Beckley, B. D., Fasulla, J. T., Hamlington, B. D., Masters, D., & Mitchum, G. T. (2018). Climate-change-driven accelerated sea-level rise. *Proceedings of the National Academy of Sciences, 115,* 2022–2025.

Nestler, S., Blank, H., & Egloff, B. (2010). Hindsight ≠ hindsight: Experimentally induced dissociations between hindsight components. *Journal of Experimental Psychology: Learning, Memory, and Cognition, 36,* 1399–1413.

Netchaeva, E., Kouchaki, M., & Sheppard, L. D. (2015). A man's (precarious) place: Men's experienced threat and self-assertive reactions to female superiors. *Personality and Social Psychology Bulletin, 41,* 1247–1259.

Neubaum, G., Sobieraj, S., Raasch, J., & Riese, J. (2020). Digital destigmatization: How exposure to networking profiles can reduce social stereotypes. *Computers in Human Behavior, 112,* 106461.

Neumann, R., & Strack, F. (2000). Approach and avoidance: The influence of proprioceptive and exteroceptive cues on encoding of affective information. *Journal of Personality and Social Psychology, 79,* 39–48.

Neuman, S. (2013, January 25). Around the globe, women already serve in combat units. *NPR.* https://www.npr.org/2013/01/24/170184589/around-the-globe-women-already-serve-in-combat-units

Newcomb, T. M. (1961). *The acquaintance process.* New York: Holt, Rinehart & Winston.

New Economics Foundation. (2009). *National accounts of well-being: Bring real wealth onto the balance sheet* [PDF file]. London: New Economics Foundation. https://neweconomics.org/uploads/files/2027fb05fed1554aea_uim6vd4c5.pdf

New Economics Foundation. (2011). *Measuring our progress: The power of well-being* [PDF file]. London: New Economics Foundation. https://neweconomics.org/uploads/files/Measuring_our_Progress.pdf

Newman, D., Lewandowsky, S., & Mayo, R. (2022). Believing in nothing and believing in everything: The underlying cognitive paradox of anti-COVID-19 vaccine attitudes. *Personality and Individual Differences, 189,* 111522.

Newman, L. S. (1993). How individualists interpret behavior: Idiocentrism and spontaneous trait inference. *Social Cognition, 11,* 243–269.

Newman, M. L., Groom, C. J., Handelman, L. D., & Pennebaker, J. W. (2008). Gender differences in language use: An analysis of 14,000 text samples. *Discourse Processes, 45,* 211–236.

Newport, F. (2018, July 5). Slight preference for having boy children persists in U.S. *Gallup.* https://news.gallup.com/poll/236513/slight-preference-having-boy-children-persists.aspx

Newton, P., & Meyer, D. (2013). Exploring the attitudes-action gap in household resource consumption: Does "environmental lifestyle" segmentation align with consumer behaviour? *Sustainability, 5,* 1211–1233.

New York Times. (1981, August 28). Notes on people: A message of hope travels the high seas. https://www.nytimes.com/1981/08/28/nyregion/notes-on-people-a-message-of-love-travels-the-high-seas.html

New York Times. (2011, September 20). A grievous wrong. www.nytimes.com

Ng, T. W. H. (2017). Transformational leadership and performance outcomes: Analyses of multiple mediation pathways. *The Leadership Quarterly, 28,* 385–417.

Nguyen, A.-M., & Rule, N. O. (2020). Implicit biculturalism theories: How bicultural individuals perceive others and organize their own cultures. *Identity: An International Journal of Theory and Research, 20*(4), 258–271.

Nguyen, T., McCracken, J. T., Albaugh, M. D., Botteron, K. N., Hudziak, J. J., & Ducharme, S. (2016). A testosterone-related structural brain phenotype predicts aggressive behavior from childhood to adulthood. *Psychoneuroendocrinology, 63,* 109–118.

Ng, W., & Diener, E. (2014). What matters to the rich and the poor? Subjective well-being, financial satisfaction, and postmaterialist needs across the world. *Journal of Personality and Social Psychology, 107,* 326–338.

Nicholson, I. (2011). "Torture at Yale": Experimental subjects, laboratory torment, and the "rehabilitiation" of Milgram's "Obedience to authority." *Theory and Psychology, 21,* 737–761.

Nicolas, P., Régner, I., & Lemaire, P. (2021). Cultural differences in susceptibility to stereotype threat: France versus India. *The Journals of Gerontology: Series B: Psychological Sciences and Social Sciences, 76,* 1329–1339.

Nielsen, M. E. (1998). Social psychology and religion on a trip to Ukraine. *Psych Web.* http://psychwww.com/psyrelig/ukraine/index.htm

Nielson, M. G., Padilla-Walker, L., & Holmes, E. K. (2017). How do men and women help? Validation of a multidimensional measure of prosocial behavior. *Journal of Adolescence, 56,* 91–106.

Niemi, R. G., Mueller, J., & Smith, T. W. (1989). *Trends in public opinion: A compendium of survey data.* New York: Greenwood Press.

Nigbur, D., Lyons, E., & Uzzell, D. (2010). Attitudes, norms, identity and environmental behaviour: Using an expanded theory of planned behaviour to predict participation in a kerbside recycling programme. *British Journal of Social Psychology, 49,* 259–284.

Nigro, G. N., Hill, D. E., Gelbein, M. E., & Clark, C. L. (1988). Changes in the facial prominence of women and men over the last decade. *Psychology of Women Quarterly, 12,* 225–235.

Nijstad, B. A., & Stroebe, W. (2006). How the group affects the mind: A cognitive model of idea generation in groups. *Personality and Social Psychology Review, 10,* 186–213.

Nikolic, M., Pezzoli, P., Jaworska, N., & Seto, M. C. (2022). Brain responses in aggression-prone individuals: A systematic review and meta-analysis of functional magnetic resonance imaging (fMRI) studies of anger- and aggression-eliciting tasks. *Progress in Neuro-Psychopharmacology & Biological Psychiatry, 119,* 1–14.

Nisbet, E. K., & Zelenski, J. M. (2011). Underestimating nearby nature: Affective forecasting errors obscure the happy path to sustainability. *Psychological Science, 22,* 1101–1106.

Nisbett, R. E., & Masuda, T. (2003). Culture and point of view. *Proceedings of the National Academy of Sciences, 100,* 11163–11170.

Nisbett, R. E. (1990). Evolutionary psychology, biology, and cultural evolution. *Motivation and emotion, 14,* 255–263.

Nisbett, R. E. (1993). Violence and U.S. regional culture. *American Psychologist, 48,* 441–449.

Nisbett, R. E. (2003). *The geography of thought: How Asians and Westerners think differently . . . and why.* New York: Free Press.

Niu, G., Sun, L., Liu, Q., Chai, H., Sun, X., & Zhou, Z. (2020). Selfie-posting and young adult women's restrained eating: The role of commentary on appearance and self-objectification. *Sex Roles, 82,* 232–240.

Nix, G., Watson, C., Pyszczynski, T., & Greenberg, J. (1995). Reducing depressive affect through external focus of attention. *Journal of Social and Clinical Psychology, 14,* 36–52.

NOAA. (2024). *Atmospheric CO_2.* https://www.esrl.noaa.gov/gmd/webdata/ccgg/trends/co2_data_mlo.png

Noah, T., Schul, Y., & Mayo, R. (2018). When both the original study and its failed replication are correct: Feeling observed eliminates the facial-feedback effect. *Journal of Personality and Social Psychology, 114,* 657–664.

Nolan, S. A., Flynn, C., & Garber, J. (2003). Prospective relations between rejection and depression in young adolescents. *Journal of Personality and Social Psychology, 85,* 745–755.

Nolen-Hoeksema, S. (2003). *Women who think too much: How to break free of overthinking and reclaim your life.* New York: Holt.

Noller, P., & Fitzpatrick, M. A. (1990). Marital communication in the eighties. *Journal of Marriage and Family, 52,* 832–843.

Noller, P. (1996). What is this thing called love? Defining the love that supports marriage and family. *Personal Relationships, 3,* 97–115.

NORC. (1996). General social survey. National Opinion Research Center. sda.berkeley.edu/sdaweb/analysis/?dataset=gss12

Nordgren, L. F., Banas, K., & MacDonald, G. (2011). Empathy gaps for social pain: Why people underestimate the pain of social suffering. *Journal of Personality and Social Psychology, 100,* 120–128.

Nordgren, L. F., van Harreveld, F., & van der Pligt, J. (2009). The restraint bias: How the illusion of self-restraint promotes impulsive behavior. *Psychological Science, 20,* 1523–1528.

Norem, J. K., & Cantor, N. (1986). Defensive pessimism: Harnessing anxiety as motivation. *Journal of Personality and Social Psychology, 51,* 1208–1217.

Norem, J. K. (2000). Defensive pessimism, optimism, and pessimism. In E. C. Chang (Ed.), *Optimism and pessimism.* Washington, DC: APA Books.

North, A. C., Hargreaves, D. J., & McKendrick, J. (1997). In-store music affects product choice. *Nature, 390,* 132.

Norton, A. T., & Herek, G. M. (2013). Heterosexuals' attitudes toward transgender people: Findings from a national probability sample of U.S. adults. *Sex Roles, 68,* 738–753.

Norton, M. I., & Ariely, D. (2011). Building a better America-One wealth quintile at a time. *Perspectives on Psychological Science, 6,* 9–12.

Norton, M. I., Frost, J. H., & Ariely, D. (2007). Less is more: The lure of ambiguity, or why familiarity breeds contempt. *Journal of Personality and Social Psychology, 92,* 97–105.

Nosek, B. A. (2007). Implicit-explicit relations. *Current Directions in Psychological Science, 16,* 65–69.

Nosek, B. A., Hardwicke, T. E., Moshontz, H., Allard, A., Corker, K. S., Dreber, A., Fidler, F., Hilgard, J., Struhl, M. K., Nuijten, M. B., Rohrer, J. M., Romero, F., Scheel, A. M., Scherer, L. D., Schönbrodt, F. D., & Vazire, S. (2022). Replicability, robustness, and reproducibility in psychological science. *Annual Review of Psychology, 73,* 719–748.

Notarius, C., & Markman, H. J. (1993). *We can work it out.* New York: Putnam.

Novelli, D., Drury, J., & Reicher, S. (2010). Come together: Two studies concerning the impact of group relations on "personal space." *British Journal of Social Psychology, 49,* 223–236.

Novotney, A. (2017, October). Preventing police misconduct. *Monitor on Psychology, 48*(9), 30.

Nowak, M. A., & Highfield, R. (2011). *Supercooperators: Altruism, evolution, and why we need each other to succeed.* New York: Free Press.

Nowak, M. A. (2012, July). Why we help. *Scientific American,* 34–39.

Nunes, J. C., Carroll, M. K., Mahaffey, K. W., Califf, R. M., Doraiswamy, P. M., Short, S., Shah, S. H., Swope, S., Williams, D., Hernandez, A. F., & Hong, D. S. (2022). General Anxiety Disorder-7 Questionnaire as a marker of low socioeconomic status and inequity. *Journal of Affective Disorders, 317,* 287–297.

Nunez, N., Poole, D. A., & Memon, A. (2003). Psychology's two cultures revisited: Implications for the integration of science with practice. *Scientific Review of Mental Health Practice, 2,* 8–19.

Nurmi, J-E., & Salmela-Aro, K. (1997). Social strategies and loneliness: A prospective study. *Personality and Individual Differences, 23,* 205–215.

Nurmi, J-E., Toivonen, S., Salmela-Aro, K., & Eronen, S. (1996). Optimistic, approach-oriented, and avoidance strategies in social situations: Three studies on loneliness and peer relationships. *European Journal of Personality, 10,* 201–219.

Nuttin, J. M., Jr. (1987). Affective consequences of mere ownership: The name letter effect in twelve European languages. *European Journal of Social Psychology, 17,* 318–402.

Nyer, P. U., & Dellande, S. (2010). Public commitment as a motivator for weight loss. *Psychology & Marketing, 27,* 1–12.

Nyhan, B., & Reifler, J. (2008). *When corrections fail: The persistence of political misperceptions.* Unpublished manuscript, Duke University.

Obama, B. (2015, June 26). Funeral for Clementa Pinkney, Charleston, SC.

Obama, M. (2016). Speech given in New Hampshire. https://www.theguardian.com/us-news/2016/oct/14/michelle-obama-speech-transcript-donald-trump

O'Brien, E., & Kassirer, S. (2019). People are slow to adapt to the warm glow of giving. *Psychological Science, 30,* 193–204.

O'Brien, E., Konrath, S. H., Grühn, D., & Hagen, A. (2013). Empathic concern and perspective taking: Linear and quadratic effects of age across the adult life span. *The Journals of Gerontology: Series B: Psychological Sciences and Social Sciences, 68B,* 168–175.

O'Brien, L. T., Garcia, D. M., Blodorn, A., Adams, G., Hammer, E., & Gravelin, C. (2020). An educational intervention to improve women's academic STEM outcomes: Divergent effects on well-represented vs. underrepresented minority women. *Cultural Diversity and Ethnic Minority Psychology, 26,* 163–168.

Oceja, L. (2008). Overcoming empathy-induced partiality: Two rules of thumb. *Basic and Applied Social Psychology, 30,* 176–182.

O'Connor, A. (2004, May 14). Pressure to go along with abuse is strong, but some soldiers find strength to refuse. *The New York Times.* www.nytimes.com

Oda, R., & Matsumoto-Oda, A. (2022). HEXACO, Dark Triad and altruism in daily life. *Personality and Individual Differences, 185.*

Oddone-Paolucci, E., Genuis, M., & Violato, C. (2000). A meta-analysis of the published research on the effects of pornography. In C. Violata (Ed.), *The changing family and child development.* Aldershot, England: Ashgate Publishing.

Odgers, C. L., Donley, S., Caspi, A., Bates, C. J., & Moffitt, T. E. (2015). Living alongside more affluent neighbors predicts greater involvement in antisocial behavior among low-income boys. *Journal of Child Psychology and Psychiatry, 56,* 1055–1064.

Odouard, V. V., Smirnova, D., & Edelman, S. (2023). Polarize, catalyze, and stabilize: How a minority of norm internalizers amplify group selection and punishment. *Behavioral Ecology and Sociobiology, 77.*

OECD. (2020). *Inequality.* http://www.oecd.org/social/inequality.htm

Ofosu, E. K., Chambers, M. K., Chen, J. M., & Hehman, E. (2019). Same-sex marriage legalization associated with reduced implicit and explicit antigay bias. *PNAS, 116,* 8846–8851.

Ogolsky, B. G., Monk, J. K., Rice, T. M., Theisen, J. C., & Maniotes, C. R. (2017). Relationship maintenance: A review of research on romantic relationships. *Journal of Family Theory & Review, 9,* 275–306.

Ohbuchi, K., & Kambara, T. (1985). Attacker's intent and awareness of outcome, impression management, and retaliation. *Journal of Experimental Social Psychology, 21,* 321–330.

Ohtaki, P. (1999, March 24). Internment-camp reporter makes homecoming visit. Associated Press. Reprinted in P. T. Ohtaki (Ed.), *It was the right thing to do!* (Self-published collection of Walt and Mildred Woodward-related correspondence and articles).

Oishi, S., & Diener, E. (2014). Residents of poor nations have a greater sense of meaning in life than residents of wealthy nations. *Psychological Science, 25,* 422–430.

Oishi, S., & Kesebir, S. (2015). Income inequality explains why economic growth does not always translate to an increase in happiness. *Psychological Science, 26,* 1630–1638.

Oishi, S., Cha, Y., Komiya, A., & Ono, H. (2022). Money and happiness: the income-happiness correlation is higher when income inequality is higher. *PNAS Nexus, 1,* 224.

Oishi, S., Kesebir, S., & Diener, E. (2011). Income inequality and happiness. *Psychological Science, 22,* 1095–1100.

Oishi, S., Rothman, A. J., Snyder, M., Su, J., Zehm, K., Hertel, A. W., Gonzales, M. H., & Sherman, G. D. (2007). The socioecological model of procommunity action: The benefits of residential stability. *Journal of Personality and Social Psychology, 93,* 831–844.

Okimoto, T. G., Wenzel, M., & Hendrick, K. (2013). Refusing to apologize can have psychological benefits (and we issue no mea culpa for this research finding). *European Journal of Social Psychology, 43,* 22–31.

O'Leary, K. D., Christian, J. L., & Mendell, N. R. (1994). A closer look at the link between marital discord and depressive symptomatology. *Journal of Social and Clinical Psychology, 13,* 33–41.

Olmstead, S. B. (2020). A decade review of sex and partnering in adolescence and young adulthood. *Journal of Marriage and Family, 82,* 769–795.

Olson, I. R., & Marshuetz, C. (2005). Facial attractiveness is appraised in a glance. *Emotion, 5,* 498–502.

Olson, J. M., & Cal, A. V. (1984). Source credibility, attitudes, and the recall of past behaviours. *European Journal of Social Psychology, 14,* 203–210.

Olson, J. M., Roese, N. J., & Zanna, M. P. (1996). Expectancies. In E. T. Higgins & A. W. Kruglanski (Eds.), *Social psychology: Handbook of basic principles* (pp. 211–238). New York: Guilford.

Olson, K. R., Dunham, Y., Dweck, C. S., Spelke, E. S., & Banaji, M. R. (2008). Judgments of the lucky across development and culture. *Journal of Personality and Social Psychology, 94,* 757–776.

Olvera, C., Stebbins, G. T., Goetz, C. G., & Kompoliti, K. (2021). TikTok Tics: A Pandemic Within a Pandemic. *Movement Disorders Clinical Practice, 8,* 1200–1205.

Olweus, D., & Breivik, K. (2013). The plight of victims of school bullying: The opposite of well-being. In B. A. Asher, F. Casas, I. Frones, & J. E., Korbin (Eds.), *International handbook of child well-being.* Heidelberg, Germany: Springer.

O'Mahony C., Brassil, M., Murphy, G., Linehan, C. (2023) The efficacy of interventions in reducing belief in conspiracy theories: A systematic review. *PLoS ONE, 18,* e0280902.

Omori, M., & Petersen, N. (2020). Institutionalizing inequality in the courts: Decomposing racial and ethnic disparities in detention, conviction, and sentencing. *Criminology, 58*(4), 678–713.

Onraet, E., Dhont, K., & Van Hiel, A. (2014). The relationships between internal and external threats and right-wing attitudes: A three-wave longitudinal study. *Personality and Social Psychology Bulletin, 40,* 712–725.

Open Secrets (2023). Did money win? Website accessed September 8, 2023. https://www.opensecrets.org/elections-overview/winning-vs-spending

Opotow, S. (1990). Moral exclusion and injustice: An introduction. *Journal of Social Issues, 46,* 1–20.

Oppenheimer, D. M., & Trail, T. E. (2010). Why leaning to the left makes you lean to the left: Effect of spatial orientation on political attitudes. *Social Cognition, 28,* 651–661.

Orenstein, P. (2003, July 6). Where have all the Lisas gone? *The New York Times.* www.nytimes.com

Orive, R. (1984). Group similarity, public self-awareness, and opinion extremity: A social projection explanation of deindividuation effects. *Journal of Personality and Social Psychology, 47,* 727–737.

Oriña, M. M., Collins, W. A., Simpson, J. A., Salvatore, J. E., Haydon, K. C., & Kim, J. S. (2011). Developmental and dyadic perspectives on commitment in adult romantic relationships. *Psychological Science, 22,* 908–915.

Ornstein, R. (1991). *The evolution of consciousness: Of Darwin, Freud, and cranial fire: The origins of the way we think.* New York: Prentice-Hall.

Orphanides, K. G. (2018, March 23). Children's YouTube is still churning out blood, suicide and cannibalism. *Wired UK.* https://www.wired.co.uk/article/youtube-for-kids-videos-problems-algorithm-recommend

Orr, R., McKeown, S., Cairns, E., & Stringer, M. (2012). Examining non-racial segregation: A micro-ecological approach. *British Journal of Social Psychology, 51,* 717–723.

Orth, U., & Robins, R. W. (2013). Understanding the link between low self-esteem and depression. *Current Directions in Psychological Science, 22,* 455–460.

Orth, U., & Robins, R. W. (2022). Is high self-esteem beneficial? Revisiting a classic question. *American Psychologist, 77,* 5–17.

Osborne, D., & Sibley, C. G. (2013). Through rose-colored glasses: System-justifying beliefs dampen the effects of relative deprivation on well-being and political mobilization. *Personality and Social Psychology Bulletin, 39,* 991–1004.

Osborne, D., Costello, T. H., Duckitt, J., & Sibley, C. G. (2023). The psychological causes and societal consequences of authoritarianism. *Nature Reviews Psychology, 2,* 220–232.

Osborne, J. W. (1995). Academics, self-esteem, and race: A look at the underlying assumptions of the disidentification hypothesis. *Personality and Social Psychology Bulletin, 21,* 449–455.

Osbourne, L., Barnett, J., & Blackwood, L. (2021). "you never feel so black as when you're contrasted against a white background": Black students' experiences at a predominantly white institution in the uk. *Journal of Community & Applied Social Psychology.*

Osgood, C. E. (1962). *An Alternative to War or Surrender.* Urbana, IL: University of Illinois Press.

Osgood, C. E. (1980). GRIT: A strategy for survival in mankind's nuclear age? Paper presented at the Pugwash Conference on New Directions in Disarmament, Racine, WI.

Oskamp, S. (1991). *Curbside recycling: Knowledge, attitudes, and behavior.* Paper presented at the Society for Experimental Social Psychology meeting, Columbus, OH.

Osofsky, M. J., Bandura, A., & Zimbardo, P. G. (2005). The role of moral disengagement in the execution process. *Law and Human Behavior, 29,* 371–393.

Osterhouse, R. A., & Brock, T. C. (1970). Distraction increases yielding to propaganda by inhibiting counterarguing. *Journal of Personality and Social Psychology, 15,* 344–358.

Ostrom, E. (2014). Do institutions for collective action evolve? *Journal of Bioeconomics, 16,* 3–30.

Ostrom, T. M., & Sedikides, C. (1992). Out-group homogeneity effects in natural and minimal groups. *Psychological Bulletin, 112,* 536–552.

Oswald, F. L., Mitchell, G., Blanton, H., Jaccard, J., & Tetlock, P. E. (2013). Predicting ethnic and racial discrimination: A meta-analysis of IAT criterion studies. *Journal of Personality and Social Psychology, 105,* 171–192.

Oswald, F. L., Mitchell, G., Blanton, H., Jaccard, J., & Tetlock, P. E. (2015). Using the IAT to predict ethnic and racial discrimination: Small effect sizes of unknown societal significance. *Journal of Personality and Social Psychology, 108,* 562–571.

Otgaar, H., Schell, L. J. M., Howe, M. L., Vilar, A. D. L. F., Houben, S. T. L., & Merckelbach, H. (2021). The link between suggestibility, compliance, and false confessions: A review using experimental and field studies. *Applied Cognitive Psychology, 35,* 445–455.

Otten, M., & Jonas, K. J. (2013). Out of the group, out of control? The brain responds to social exclusion with changes in cognitive control. *Scan, 8,* 789–794.

OurWorldinData.org. (2019). Sex ratio at birth, 2017. Chart. https://ourworldindata.org/gender-ratio

Oyserman, D., Coon, H. M., & Kemmelmeier, M. (2002a). Rethinking individualism and collectivism: Evaluation of theoretical assumptions and meta-analyses. *Psychological Bulletin, 128,* 3–72.

Oyserman, D., Kemmelmeier, M., & Coon, H. M. (2002b). Cultural psychology, a new look: Reply to Bond (2002), Fiske (2002), Kitayama (2002), and Miller (2002). *Psychological Bulletin, 128,* 110–117.

Packer, D. J. (2008). Identifying systematic disobedience in Milgram's obedience experiments: A meta-analytic review. *Perspectives on Psychological Science, 3*(4), 301–304.

Padgett, V. R. (1989). *Predicting organizational violence: An application of 11 powerful principles of obedience.* Paper presented at the American Psychological Association convention.

Padon, A. A., Lochbuehler, K., Maloney, E. K., & Cappella, J. N. (2018). A randomized trial of the effect of youth appealing e-cigarette advertising on susceptibility to use e-cigarettes among youth. *Nicotine & Tobacco Research, 20*(8), 954–961.

Page, S. E. (2007). *The difference: How the power of diversity creates better groups, firms, schools, and societies.* Princeton, NJ: Princeton University Press.

Palazzolo, J. (2013, February 14). Racial gap in men's sentencing. *The Wall Street Journal.* http://www.wsj.com/articles/SB10001424127887324432004578304463789858002

Pallak, S. R., Murroni, E., & Koch, J. (1983). Communicator attractiveness and expertise, emotional versus rational appeals, and persuasion: A heuristic versus systematic processing interpretation. *Social Cognition, 2,* 122–141.

Palmer, D. L. (1996). Determinants of Canadian attitudes toward immigration: More than just racism? *Canadian Journal of Behavioural Science, 28,* 180–192.

Palmer, E. L., & Dorr, A. (Eds.) (1980). *Children and the faces of television: Teaching, violence, selling.* New York: Academic Press.

Paluck, E. L. (2010). Is it better not to talk? Group polarization, extended contact, and perspective taking in Eastern Democratic Republic of Congo. *Personality and Social Psychology Bulletin, 36,* 1170–1185.

Pandey, J., Sinha, Y., Prakash, A., & Tripathi, R. C. (1982). Right-left political ideologies and attribution of the causes of poverty. *European Journal of Social Psychology, 12,* 327–331.

Pantell, M., Rehkopf, D., Jutte, D., Syme, S. L., Balmes, J., & Adler, N. (2013). Social isolation: A predictor of mortality comparable to traditional clinical risk factors. *American Journal of Public Health, 103,* 2056–2062.

Pan, W., Mu, Z., Zhao, Z., & Tang, Z. (2022). Female users' tiktok use and body image: Active versus passive use and social comparison processes. *Cyberpsychology, Behavior, and Social Networking.*

Paolini, S., Harwood, J., Rubin, M., Husnu, S., Joyce, N., Hewstone, M. (2014). Positive and extensive intergroup contact in the past buffers against the disproportionate impact of negative contact in the present. *European Journal of Social Psychology, 44,* 548–562.

Paolini, S., Hewstone, M., Cairns, E., & Voci, A. (2004). Effects of direct and indirect cross-group friendships on judgments of Catholics and Protestants in Northern Ireland: The mediating role of an anxiety-reduction mechanism. *Personality and Social Psychology Bulletin, 30,* 770–786.

Pape, R. A. (2003, September 22). Dying to kill us. *The New York Times.* https://www.nytimes.com/2003/09/22/opinion/dying-to-kill-us.html

Parachin, V. M. (1992, December). Four brave chaplains. *Retired Officer Magazine,* pp. 24–26.

Paramita, W., & Septianto, F. (2021). The benefits and pitfalls of humblebragging in social media advertising: The moderating role of the celebrity versus influencer. *International Journal of Advertising: The Review of Marketing Communications, 40,* 1294–1319.

Parent, M. C., Kalenkoski, C. M., & Cardella, E. (2017). Risky business: Precarious manhood and investment portfolio decisions. *Psychology of Men & Masculinity, 19(2),* 195–202.

Parikh, N., Ruzic, L., Stewart, G. W., Spreng, R. N., & De Brigard, F. (2018). What if? Neural activity underlying semantic and episodic counterfactual thinking. *NeuroImage, 178,* 332–345.

Park, A., Ickes, W., & Robinson, R. L. (2014). More f#!%ing rudeness: Reliable personality predictors of verbal rudeness and other ugly confrontational behaviors. *Journal of Aggression, Conflict, and Peace Research, 6,* 26–43.

Park, B., & Rothbart, M. (1982). Perception of out-group homogeneity and levels of social categorization: Memory for the subordinate attributes of in-group and out-group members. *Journal of Personality and Social Psychology, 42,* 1051–1068.

Parker, K., Horowitz, J. M., Igielnik, R., Oliphant, B., & Brown, A. (2017, June 22). Protection tops the list of reasons for owning a gun. *Pew Research Center.* https://www.pewresearch.org/politics/psdt_2017-06-22-guns-01-07/

Park, G.-R., Grignon, M., Young, M., & Dunn, J. R. (2022). How do housing asset and income relate to mortality? A population-based cohort study of 881220 older adults in Canada. *Social Science & Medicine, 314,* 1–8.

Park, G., Yaden, D. B., Schwartz, H. A., Kern, M. L., Eichstaedt, J. C., Kosinski, M., & . . . Seligman, M. P. (2016). Women are warmer but no less assertive than men: Gender and language on Facebook. *PLOS ONE, 11*(5), e0155885.

Park, H., Coello, J. A., & Lau, A. S. (2014). Child socialization goals in East Asian versus Western nations from 1989 to 2010: Evidence for social change in parenting. *Parenting: Science and Practice, 14,* 69–91.

Park, H., Kim, T., & Kim, J. (2023). Longitudinal pathways from adolescent depressive symptoms to cardiovascular disease risk in adulthood. *Social Science & Medicine, 318,* 1–8.

Park, J.-Y., & Jang, S. (2018). Did I get the best discount? Counterfactual thinking of tourism products. *Journal of Travel Research, 57,* 17–30.

Park, Y., Impett, E. A., MacDonald, G., & Lemay, E. P. (2019). Saying "Thank you": Partners' expressions of gratitude protect relationship satisfaction and commitment from the harmful effects of attachment insecurity. *Journal of Personality and Social Psychology, 117,* 773–806.

Pascarella, E. T., & Terenzini, P. T. (1991). *How college affects students: Findings and insights from twenty years of research.* San Francisco: Jossey-Bass.

Pascual, A., Carpenter, C. J., Guéguen, N., & Girandola, F. (2016). A meta-analysis of the effectiveness of the low-ball compliance-gaining procedure. *European Review of Applied Psychology, 66,* 261–267.

Pasek, M. H., Kelly, J. M., Shackleford, C., White, C. J. M., Vishkin, A., Smith, J. M., Norenzayan, A., Shariff, A., & Ginges, J. (2023). Thinking about god encourages prosociality toward religious outgroups: A cross-cultural investigation. *Psychological Science, 34,* 657–669.

Pasquini, G. & Kennedy, B. (2023, October 25). Americans continue to have doubts about climate scientists' understanding of climate change. Pew Research Center.

Patterson, G. R., Chamberlain, P., & Reid, J. B. (1982). A comparative evaluation of parent training procedures. *Behavior Therapy, 13,* 638–650.

Patterson, M. L. (2008). Back to social behavior: Mining the mundane. *Basic and Applied Social Psychology, 30,* 93–101.

Patterson, M. L., Iizuka, Y., Tubbs, M., Ansel, J., Tsutsumi, M., & Anson, J. (2007). Passing encounters east and west: comparing japanese and american pedestrian interactions. *Journal of Nonverbal Behavior, 31,* 155–166.

Patterson, T. E. (1980). The role of the mass media in presidential campaigns: The lessons of the 1976 election. *Items, 34,* 25–30.

Paulhus, D. (1982). Individual differences, self-presentation, and cognitive dissonance: Their concurrent operation in forced compliance. *Journal of Personality and Social Psychology, 43,* 838–852.

Paulhus, D. L., & Lim, D. T. K. (1994). Arousal and evaluative extremity in social judgments: A dynamic complexity model. *European Journal of Social Psychology, 24,* 89–99.

Paulhus, D. L., & Morgan, K. L. (1997). Perceptions of intelligence in leaderless groups: The dynamic effects of shyness and acquaintance. *Journal of Personality and Social Psychology, 72,* 581-591.

Paulhus, D. L., & Williams, K. M. (2002). The Dark Triad of personality: Narcissism, Machiavellianism and psychopathy. *Journal of Research in Personality, 36,* 556–563.

Paulhus, D. L. (1998). Interpersonal and intrapsychic adaptiveness of trait self-enhancement: A mixed blessing? *Journal of Personality and Social Psychology, 74,* 1197–1208.

Paulhus, D. L., Westlake, B. G., Calvez, S. S., & Harms, P. D. (2013). Self-presentation style in job interviews: The role of personality and culture. *Journal of Applied Social Psychology, 43,* 2042–2059.

Paulo, R. M., Jones, E., & Mendes, R. (2021). Testing two retrieval strategies to enhance eyewitness memory: Category and location clustering recall. *Psychology, Public Policy, and Law, 27,* 140–149.

Paulus, P. B., & Coskun, H. (2012). Group creativity: Understanding collaborative creativity processes. In J. M. Levine (Ed.), *Group processes.* Boca Raton, FL: Psychology Press.

Paulus, P. B., & Kenworthy, J. B. (2022). The crowd dynamics and collective stupidity of the January 6 riot: Theoretical analyses and prescriptions for a collectively wiser future. *Group Dynamics: Theory, Research, and Practice, 26,* 199–219.

Paulus, P. B., & Korde, R. (2014). How to get the most creativity and innovation out of groups and teams. In K. Thomas & J. Chan (Eds.), *Handbook of research on creativity.* Northhampton, MA: Edward Elgar Publishing.

Paulus, P. B., Dzindolet, M., & Kohn, N. W. (2011). Collaborative creativity–Group creativity and team innovation. In M. D. Mumford (Ed.), *Handbook of organizational creativity.* New York: Elsevier.

Paulus, P. B., Larey, T. S., & Dzindolet, M. T. (2000). Creativity in groups and teams. In M. Turner (Ed.), *Groups at work: Advances in theory and research.* Hillsdale, NJ: Hampton.

Paulus, P. B., Larey, T. S., & Ortega, A. H. (1995). Performance and perceptions of brainstormers in an organizational setting. *Basic and Applied Social Psychology, 17,* 249–265.

Pawlenko, N. B., Safer, M. A., Wise, R. A., & Holfeld, B. (2013). A teaching aid for improving jurors' assessments of eyewitness accuracy. *Applied Cognitive Psychology, 27,* 190–197.

Payne, B. K. (2001). Prejudice and perception: The role of automatic and controlled processes in misperceiving a weapon. *Journal of Personality and Social Psychology, 81,* 181–192.

Payne, B. K. (2006). Weapon bias: Split-second decisions and unintended stereotyping. *Current Directions in Psychological Science, 15,* 287–291.

Payne, K. (2017). *The broken ladder: How inequality affects the way we think, live, and die.* New York: Viking.

Pazhoohi, F., & Burriss, R. P. (2016). Hijab and "hitchhiking": A field study. *Evolutionary Psychological Science, 2,* 32–37.

PBS News Hour (2020, October 16). Most Americans say nation is deeply divided over values, poll says. pbs.org

Pchelin, P., & Howell, R. T. (2014). The hidden cost of value-seeking: People do not accurately forecast the economic benefits of experiential purchases. *The Journal of Positive Psychology, 9,* 322–334.

PE (2024). Later is too late to act on climate change. Potential Energy Coalition. https://potentialenergycoalition.org/global-report/?utm_source=newsletter&utm_medium=email&utm_campaign=wp_climatecoach&wpisrc=nl_climatecoach

Pearce, L., & Cooper, J. (2021). Fostering COVID-19 safe behaviors using cognitive dissonance. *Basic and Applied Social Psychology, 43,* 267–282.

Pedersen, A., Zachariae, R., & Bovbjerg, D. H. (2010). Influence of psychological stress on upper respiratory infection—A meta-analysis of prospective studies. *Psychosomatic Medicine, 72,* 823–832.

Pedersen, W. C., Bushman, B. J., Vasquez, E. A., & Miller, N. (2008). Kicking the (barking) dog effect: The moderating role of target attributes on triggered displaced aggression. *Personality and Social Psychology Bulletin, 34,* 1382–1395.

Pedersen, W. C., Gonzales, C., & Miller, N. (2000). The moderating effect of trivial triggering provocation on displaced aggression. *Journal of Personality and Social Psychology, 78,* 913–927.

Pedersen, W. C., Vasquez, E. A., Bartholow, B. D., Grosvenor, M., & Truong, A. (2014). Are you insulting me? Exposure to alcohol primes increases aggression following ambiguous provocation. *Personality and Social Psychology Bulletin, 40,* 1037–1049.

Peetz, J., & Buehler, R. (2009). Is there a budget fallacy? The role of savings goals in the prediction of personal spending. *Personality and Social Psychology Bulletin, 35,* 1579–1591.

Pegalis, L. J., Shaffer, D. R., Bazzini, D. G., & Greenier, K. (1994). On the ability to elicit self-disclosure: Are there gender-based and contextual limitations on the opener effect? *Personality and Social Psychology Bulletin, 20,* 412–420.

Pekrun, R., Murayama, K., Marsh, H. W., Goetz, T., & Frenzel, A. C. (2019). Happy fish in little ponds: Testing a reference group model of achievement and emotion. *Journal of Personality and Social Psychology, 117,* 166–185.

Pelham, B., & Carvallo, M. (2011). The surprising potency of implicit egotism: A reply to Simonsohn. *Journal of Personality and Social Psychology, 101,* 25–30.

Pelham, B., & Crabtree, S. (2008, October 8). Worldwide, highly religious more likely to help others: Pattern holds throughout the world and across major religions. *Gallup.* https://news.gallup.com/poll/111013/worldwide-highly-religious-more-likely-help-others.aspx

Pelham, B. W., Mirenberg, M. C., & Jones, J. T. (2002). Why Susie sells seashells by the seashore: Implicit egotism and major life decisions. *Journal of Personality and Social Psychology, 82,* 469–487.

Pelonero, C. (2014). *Kitty Genovese: A true account of a public murder and its private consequences.* New York: Skyhorse.

Pennebaker, J. (1990). *Opening up: The healing power of confiding in others.* New York: William Morrow.

Pennebaker, J. W., & Lay, T. C. (2002). Language use and personality during crises: Analyses of Mayor Rudolph Giuliani's press conferences. *Journal of Research in Personality, 36,* 271–282.

Pennebaker, J. W., & O'Heeron, R. C. (1984). Confiding in others and illness rate among spouses of suicide and accidental death victims. *Journal of Abnormal Psychology, 93,* 473–476.

Pennebaker, J. W. (2016). Expressive writing. In R. J. Sternberg, S. T. Fiske, & D. J. Foss (Eds.), *Scientists making a difference: One hundred eminent behavioral and brain scientists talk about their most important contributions.* (pp. 461–465). New York: Cambridge University Press.

Penner, L. A. (2002). Dispositional and organizational influences on sustained volunteerism: An interactionist perspective. *Journal of Social Issues, 58,* 447–467.

Penner, L. A., Dertke, M. C., & Achenbach, C. J. (1973). The "flash" system: A field study of altruism. *Journal of Applied Social Psychology, 3,* 362–370.

Pennington, N., & Hastie, R. (1993). The story model for juror decision making. In R. Hastie (Ed.), *Inside the juror: The psychology of juror decision making.* New York: Cambridge University Press.

Pennycook, G., Binnendyk, J., & Rand, D. G. (2023). Overconfidently conspiratorial: Conspiracy believers are dispositionally overconfident and massively overestimate how much others agree with them. PsyArXiv.

Penrod, S., & Cutler, B. L. (1987). Assessing the competence of juries. In I. B. Weiner & A. K. Hess (Eds.), *Handbook of forensic psychology.* New York: Wiley.

Pentland, A. (2010). To signal is human. *American Scientist, 98,* 204–211.

Penton-Voak, I. S., Jones, B. C., Little, A. C., Baker, S., Tiddeman, B., Burt, D. M., & Perrett, D. I. (2001). Symmetry, sexual dimorphism in facial proportions and male facial attractiveness. *Proceedings of the Royal Society of London, 268,* 1–7.

Peplau, L. A., & Fingerhut, A. W. (2007). The close relationships of lesbians and gay men. *Annual Review of Psychology, 58,* 405–424.

Pereira, A., Harris, E., & Van Bavel, J. J. (2023). Identity concerns drive belief: The impact of partisan identity on the belief and dissemination of true and false news. *Group Processes & Intergroup Relations, 26,* 24–47.

Pereira, C., Vala, J., & Costa-Lopes, R. (2010). From prejudice to discrimination: The legitimizing role of perceived threat in discrimination against immigrants. *European Journal of Social Psychology, 40,* 1231–1250.

Perez, E., Morris, J., & Ellis, R. (2018, May 21). What we know about Dimitrios Pagourtzis, the alleged Santa Fe high school shooter. *CNN.* https://www.cnn.com/2018/05/18/us/dimitrios-pagourtzis-santa-fe-suspect

Perfumi, S. C., Bagnoli, F., Caudek, C., & Guazzini, A. (2019). Deindividuation effects on normative and informational social influence within computer-mediated-communication. *Computers in Human Behavior, 92,* 230–237.

Perilloux, H. K., Webster, G. D., & Gaulin, S. J. C. (2010). Signals of genetic quality and maternal investment capacity: The dynamic effects of fluctuating asymmetry and waist-to-hip ratio on men's ratings of women's attractiveness. *Social Psychology and Personality Science, 1,* 34–42.

Perls, F. S. (1973, July). *Ego, hunger and aggression: The beginning of Gestalt therapy.* Random House, 1969. Cited by Berkowitz in The case for bottling up rage. *Psychology Today,* 24–30.

Perrett, D. (2010). *In your face: The new science of human attraction.* New York: Palgrave Macmillan.

Perrin, P. B. (2016). Translating psychological science: Highlighting the media's contribution to contagion in mass shootings: Comment on Kaslow (2015). *American Psychologist, 71,* 71–72.

Perry, A., Rubinsten, O., Peled, L., & Shamay-Tsoory, S. G. (2013). Don't stand so close to me: A behavioral and ERP study of preferred interpersonal distance. *NeuroImage, 83,* 761–769.

Perry, G. (2013). *Behind the shock machine: The untold story of the notorious Milgram psychology experiments.* New York: New Press.

Perry, G. (2014). The view from the boys. *Psychologist, 27,* 834–836.

Perry, G. (2018). *The lost boys: Inside Muzafer Sherif's Robbers Cave experiment.* Royal Oak, MI: Scribe.

Perry, G., Brannigan, A., Wanner, R. A., & Stam, H. (2020). Credibility and incredulity in Milgram's obedience experiments: A reanalysis of an unpublished test. *Social Psychology Quarterly, 83,* 88–106.

Persico, N., Postlewaite, A., & Silverman, D. (2004). The effect of adolescent experience on labor market outcomes: The case of height. *Journal of Political Economy, 112,* 1019–1053.

Pessin, J., & Husband, R. W. (1933). Effects of social stimulation on human maze learning. *Journal of Abnormal and Social Psychology, 28,* 148–154.

Pessin, J. (1933). The comparative effects of social and mechanical stimulation on memorizing. *American Journal of Psychology, 45,* 263–270.

Petersen, J. L., & Hyde, J. S. (2011). Gender differences in sexual attitudes and behaviors: A review of meta-analytic results and large datasets. *Journal of Sex Research, 48,* 149–165.

Peterson, C., & Seligman, M. E. P. (1987). Explanatory style and illness. *Journal of Personality, 55,* 237–265.

Peterson, C., & Steen, T. A. (2002). Optimistic explanatory style. In C. R. Snyder & S. J. Lopez (Ed.), *Handbook of positive psychology.* London: Oxford University Press.

Peterson, C., Bishop, M. P., Fletcher, C. W., Kaplan, M. R., Yesko, E. S., Moon, C. H., et al. (2001). Explanatory style as a risk factor for traumatic mishaps. *Cognitive Therapy and Research, 25,* 633–649.

Peterson, C. K., & Harmon-Jones, E. (2012). Anger and testosterone: Evidence that situationally-induced anger relates to situationally-induced testosterone. *Emotion, 12,* 899–902.

Peterson, C., Seligman, M. E. P., & Vaillant, G. E. (1988). Pessimistic explanatory style is a risk factor for physical illness: A thirty-five-year longitudinal study. *Journal of Personality and Social Psychology, 55,* 23–27.

Peterson, E. (1992). *Under the unpredictable plant.* Grand Rapids, MI: Eerdmans.

Peterson, J. L., & Zill, N. (1981). Television viewing in the United States and children's intellectual, social, and emotional development. *Television and Children, 2,* 21–28.

Petraitis, J. M., Lampman, C. B., Boeckmann, R. J., & Falconer, E. M (2014). Sex differences in the attractiveness of hunter-gatherer and modern risks. *Journal of Applied Social Psychology, 44,* 442–453.

Petrie, K. J., Pressman, S. D., Pennebaker, J. W., Øverland, S., Tell, G. S., & Sivertsen, B. (2018). Which aspects of positive affect are related to mortality? Results from a general population longitudinal study. *Annals of Behavioral Medicine, 52, 571–581.*

Petrocelli, J. V., Percy, E. J., Sherman, S. J., & Tormala, Z. L. (2011). Counterfactual potency. *Journal of Personality and Social Psychology, 100,* 30–46.

Petrovic, K., Chapman, C. M., & Schofield, T. P. (2021). Religiosity and volunteering over time: Religious service attendance is associated with the likelihood of volunteering, and religious importance with time spent volunteering. *Psychology of Religion and Spirituality, 13,* 136–146.

Pettigrew, T. F., & Tropp, L. R. (2008). How does intergroup contact reduce prejudice? Meta-analytic tests of three mediators. *European Journal of Social Psychology, 38,* 922–934.

Pettigrew, T. F., & Tropp, L. R. (2011). *When groups meet: The dynamics of intergroup contact.* New York: Psychology Press.

Pettigrew, T. F. (1958). Personality and socio-cultural factors in intergroup attitudes: A cross-national comparison. *Journal of Conflict Resolution, 2,* 29–42.

Pettigrew, T. F. (1969). Racially separate or together? *Journal of Social Issues, 2,* 43–69.

Pettigrew, T. F. (1979). The ultimate attribution error: Extending Allport's cognitive analysis of prejudice. *Personality and Social Psychology Bulletin, 55,* 461–476.

Pettigrew, T. F. (1980). Prejudice. In S. Thernstrom et al. (Eds.), *Harvard encyclopedia of American ethnic groups.* Cambridge, MA: Harvard University Press.

Pettigrew, T. F. (1986). The intergroup contact hypothesis reconsidered. In M. Hewstone & R. Brown (Eds.), *Contact and conflict in intergroup encounters.* Oxford: Blackwell.

Pettigrew, T. F. (1988). *Advancing racial justice: Past lessons for future use.* Paper for the University of Alabama conference "Opening Doors: An appraisal of Race Relations in America."

Pettigrew, T. F. (1997). Generalized intergroup contact effects on prejudice. *Personality and Social Psychology Bulletin, 23,* 173–185.

Pettigrew, T. F. (2004). Intergroup contact: Theory, research, and new perspectives. In J. A. Banks & C. A. McGee Banks (Eds.), *Handbook of research on multicultural education.* San Francisco: Jossey-Bass.

Pettigrew, T. F. (2006). A two-level approach to anti-immigrant prejudice and discrimination. In R. Mahalingam (Ed.), *Cultural psychology of immigrants.* Mahwah, NJ: Erlbaum.

Pettigrew, T. F., Christ, O., Wagner, U., Meertens, R. W., van Dick, R., & Zick, A. (2008). Relative deprivation and intergroup prejudice. *Journal of Social Issues, 64,* 385–401.

Pettigrew, T. F., Jackson, J. S., Brika, J. B., Lemaine, G., Meertens, R. W., Wagner, U., & Zick, A. (1998). Outgroup prejudice in western Europe. *European Review of Social Psychology, 8,* 241–273.

Pettigrew, T. F., Wagner, U., & Christ, O. (2010). Population ratios and prejudice: Modeling both contact and threat effects. *Journal of Ethnic and Migration Studies, 36,* 635–650.

Petty, R. E., & Briñol, P. (2008). Persuasion: From single to multiple to metacognitive processes. *Perspectives on Psychological Science, 3,* 137–147.

Petty, R. E., & Briñol, P. (2015). Emotion and persuasion: cognitive and meta-cognitive processes impact attitudes. *Cognition and Emotion, 29,* 1–26.

Petty, R. E., & Cacioppo, J. T. (1986). *Communication and persuasion: Central and peripheral routes to attitude change.* New York: Springer-Verlag.

Petty, R. E., Barden, J., & Wheeler, S. C. (2009). The Elaboration Likelihood Model of persuasion: Developing health promotions for sustained behavioral change. In R. J. DiClemente, R. A. Crosby, & M. C. Kegler (Eds.), *Emerging theories in health promotion practice and research* (2nd ed.). San Francisco: Jossey-Bass.

Petty, R. E., Cacioppo, J. T., & Goldman, R. (1981). Personal involvement as a determinant of argument-based persuasion. *Journal of Personality and Social Psychology, 41,* 847–855.

Petty, R. E., Haugtvedt, C. P., & Smith, S. M. (1995). Elaboration as a determinant of attitude strength: Creating attitudes that are persistent, resistant, and predictive of behavior. In R. E. Petty & J. A. Krosnick (Eds.), *Attitude strength: Antecedents and consequences.* Hillsdale, NJ: Erlbaum.

Petty, R. E., Schumann, D. W., Richman, S. A., & Strathman, A. J. (1993). Positive mood and persuasion: Different roles for affect under high and low elaboration conditions. *Journal of Personality and Social Psychology, 64,* 5–20.

Pew Center for Research (2022, August 9). As partisan hostility grows, signs of frustration with the two-party system. https://www.pewresearch.org/politics/2022/08/09/as-partisan-hostility-grows-signs-of-frustration-with-the-two-party-system/

Pew (Pew Research Center). (2010). Gender equality universally embraced, but inequalities acknowledged. *Global Attitudes Project.* https://www.pewresearch.org/global/2010/07/01/gender-equality/

Pew Research Center. (2013). Big racial divide over Zimmerman verdict. https://www.pewresearch.org/politics/2013/07/22/big-racial-divide-over-zimmerman-verdict/

Pew Research Center. (2016, April 12). Religion in everyday life. https://www.pewforum.org/2016/04/12/religion-in-everyday-life/

Pew Research Center. (2017, December 5). On gender differences, no consensus on nature vs. nurture. https://www.pewsocialtrends.org/2017/12/05/on-gender-differences-no-consensus-on-nature-vs-nurture/

Pew Research Center. (2019, December 17). In a politically polarized era, sharp divides in both partisan coalitions. https://www.pewresearch.org/politics/2019/12/17/in-a-politically-polarized-era-sharp-divides-in-both-partisan-coalitions/

Pew Research Center. (2019, October 10). Partisan antipathy: More intense, more personal. https://www.pewresearch.org/politics/2019/10/10/partisan-antipathy-more-intense-more-personal/

Pew Research Center (2022, August 9). As partisan hostility grows, signs of frustration with the two-party system. PewResearch.org.

Pezdek, K., & Reisberg, D. (2022). Psychological myths about evidence in the legal system: How should researchers respond? *Journal of Applied Research in Memory and Cognition, 11,* 143–156.

Peña-Alves, S., Greene, K., Ray, A. E., Glenn, S. D., Hecht, M. L., & Banerjee, S. C. (2019). "Choose today, live tomorrow": A content analysis of anti-substance use messages produced by adolescents. *Journal of Health Communication, 24,* 592–602.

Pfaff, D. W. (2014). *The altruistic brain: How we are natural good.* New York: Oxford University Press.

Pfaff, L. A., Boatwright, K. J., Potthoff, A. L., Finan, C., Ulrey, L. A., & Huber, D. M. (2013). Perceptions of women and men leaders following 360-degree feedback evaluations. *Performance Improvement Quarterly, 26,* 35–56.

Pfattheicher, S., Nockur, L., Bohm, R., Sassenrath, C., & Petersen, M. B. (2020). The emotional path to action: Empathy promotes physical distancing and wearing of face masks during the COVID-19 pandemic. *Psychological Science, 31*(11), 1363–1373.

Phillips, A. L. (2011). A walk in the woods. *American Scientist, 69,* 301–302.

Phillips, L. T., Stephens, N. M., Townsend, S. S. M., & Goudeau, S. (2020). Access is not enough: Cultural mismatch persists to limit first-generation students' opportunities for achievement throughout college. *Journal of Personality and Social Psychology, 119,* 1112–1131.

Phillips, S., & Marceau, J. (2020). Whom the state kills. *Harvard Civil Rights - Civil Liberties Law Review, 55.*

Phillips, T. (2004, April 3). Quoted by T. Baldwin & D. Rozenberg, "Britain 'must scrap multiculturalism.'" *The Times,* p. A1.

Phills, C. E., Hahn, A., & Gawronski, B. (2020). The bidirectional causal relation between implicit stereotypes and implicit prejudice. *Personality and Social Psychology Bulletin, 46,* 1318–1330.

Philpot, R., Liebst, L. S., Levine, M., Bernasco, W., & Lindegaard, M. R. (2020). Would I be helped? Cross-national CCTV footage shows that intervention is the norm in public conflicts. *American Psychologist, 75,* 66–75.

Phinney, J. S. (1990). Ethnic identity in adolescents and adults: Review of research. *Psychological Bulletin, 108,* 499–514.

Phua, J., Jun, S. V., & Hahm, J. M. (2018). Celebrity-endorsed e-cigarette brand Instagram advertisements: Effects on young adults' attitudes towards e-cigarettes and smoking intentions. *Journal of Health Psychology, 23*(4), 550–560.

Pica, E., Sheahan, C., & Pozzulo, J. (2018). "But he's a star football player!": How social status influences mock jurors' perceptions in a sexual assault case. *Journal of Interpersonal Violence, 35*(19–20), 3963–3985.

Pichon, I., Boccato, G., & Saroglou, V. (2007). Nonconscious influences of religion on prosociality: A priming study. *European Journal of Social Psychology, 37,* 1032–1045.

Pierson, B. (2022, December 8). FDA rule mandating graphic warnings on cigarettes blocked by judge. Reuters.com

Piff, P. K. (2014). Wealth and the inflated self: Class, entitlement, and narcissism. *Personality and Social Psychology Bulletin, 40,* 34–43.

Piff, P. K., Kraus, M. W., Côté, S., Cheng, B. H., & Keltner, D. (2010). Having less, giving more: The influence of social class on prosocial behavior. *Journal of Personality and Social Psychology, 99,* 771–784.

Pilditch, T. D., Roozenbeek, J., Madsen, J. K., & van der Linden, S. (2022). Psychological inoculation can reduce susceptibility to misinformation in large rational agent networks. *Royal Society Open Science, 9,* 211953.

Piliavin, J. A., & Piliavin, I. M. (1973). *The Good Samaritan: Why* does *he help?* Unpublished manuscript, University of Wisconsin.

Piliavin, J. A. (2003). Doing well by doing good: Benefits for the benefactor. In C. L. M. Keyes & J. Haidt (Eds.), *Flourishing: Positive psychology and the life well-lived.* Washington, DC: American Psychological Association.

Piliavin, J. A., Evans, D. E., & Callero, P. (1982). Learning to "Give to unnamed strangers": The process of commitment to regular blood donation. In E. Staub, D. Bar-Tal, J. Karylowski, & J. Reykawski (Eds.), *The development and maintenance of prosocial behavior: International perspectives.* New York: Plenum.

Pinker, S. (1997). *How the mind works.* New York: Norton.

Pinker, S. (2002). *The blank slate* (p. 143). New York: Viking.

Pinker, S. (2008). *The sexual paradox: Men, women, and the real gender gap.* New York: Scribner.

Pinker, S. (2011, September 27). A history of violence. *Edge.* https://www.edge.org/3rd_culture/pinker07/pinker07_index.html

Pinker, S. (2014). *The village effect: How face-to-face contact can make us healthier, happier, and smarter.* New York: Spiegel & Grau.

Piper, K. (2020, April 8). Predictions are hard, especially about the coronavirus. *Vox.* https://www.vox.com/future-perfect/2020/4/8/21210193/coronavirus-forecasting-models-predictions

Pipher, M. (2003). *The middle of everywhere: The world's refugees come to our town.* Houghton Mifflin Harcourt: Boston.

Pizarro, J. J., Cakal, H., Méndez, L., Zumeta, L. N., Gracia, L. M., Basabe, N., Navarro, C. G., Cazan, A., Keshavarzi, S., López, L. W., Yahiiaiev, I., Alzugaray, P. C., Villagrán, L., Moyano, D. E., Petrović, N., Mathias, A., Techio, E. M., Wlodarczyk, A., Alfaro, B. L., . . . Páez, D. (2023). Sociopolitical consequences of covid-19 in the americas, europe, and asia: A multilevel, multicountry investigation of risk perceptions and support for antidemocratic practices. *Political Psychology.*

Pizzutti, C., Basso, K., & Albornoz, M. (2016). The effect of the discounted attribute importance in two-sided messages. *European Journal of Marketing, 50,* 1703–1725.

Place, S. S., Todd, P. M., Penke, L., & Asendorpf, J. B. (2009). The ability to judge the romantic interest of others. *Psychological Science, 20,* 22–26.

Plant, E. A., Goplen, J., & Kunstman, J. W. (2011). Selective responses to threat: The roles of race and gender in decisions to shoot. *Personality and Social Psychology, 37,* 1274–1281.

Platek, S. M., & Singh, D. (2010). Optimal waist-to-hip ratios in women activate neural reward centers in men. *PLOS ONE, 5*(2), e9042.

Platow, M. J., Haslam, S. A., Both, A., Chew, I., Cuddon, M., Goharpey, N., Måurer, J., Rosini, S., Tsekouras, A., & Grace, D. M. (2004). "It's not funny if *they're* laughing": Self-categorization, social influence, and responses to canned laughter. *Journal of Experimental Social Psychology, 41,* 542–550.

Plaut, V. C., Adams, G., & Anderson, S. L. (2009). Does attractiveness buy happiness? "It depends on where you're from." *Personal Relationships, 16,* 619–630.

Plaut, V. C., Markus, H. R., & Lachman, M. E. (2002). Place matters: Consensual features and regional variation in American wellbeing and self. *Journal of Personality and Social Psychology, 83,* 160–184.

Plötner, M., Over, H., Carpenter, M., & Tomasello, M. (2015). Young children show the bystander effect in helping situations. *Psychological Science, 26,* 499–506.

Poincaré, J. H. (1905). *Science and hypothesis.* Chapter IX, "Hypothesis in Physics" (p. 101). New York: The Science Press.

Pollet, T. V., & Saxton, T. K. (2019). How diverse are the samples used in the journals 'evolution & human behavior' and 'evolutionary psychology'? *Evolutionary Psychological Science, 5,* 357–368.

Pomazal, R. J., & Clore, G. L. (1973). Helping on the highway: The effects of dependency and sex. *Journal of Applied Social Psychology, 3,* 150–164.

Pond, R. S., DeWall, C. N., Lambert, N. M., Deckman, T., Bonser, I. M., & Fincham, F. D. (2012). Repulsed by violence: Disgust sensitivity buffers trait, behavioral, and daily aggression. *Journal of Personality and Social Psychology, 102,* 175–188.

Poniewozik, J. (2003, November 24). All the news that fits your reality. *Time,* 90.

Poon, K.-T., Chen, Z., & DeWall, C. N. (2013). Feeling entitled to more: Ostracism increases dishonest behavior. *Personality and Social Psychology Bulletin, 39,* 1227–1239.

Poon, K.-T., Chen, Z., & Wong, W.-Y. (2020). Beliefs in conspiracy theories following ostracism. *Personality and Social Psychology Bulletin, 46*(8), 1234–1246.

Popenoe, D. (2002). *The top ten myths of divorce.* Unpublished manuscript. National Marriage Project, Rutgers University.

Post, J. M. (2005). The new face of terrorism: Socio-cultural foundations of contemporary terrorism. *Behavioral Sciences and the Law, 23,* 451–465.

Postmes, T., & Spears, R. (1998). Deindividuation and antinormative behavior: A meta-analysis. *Psychological Bulletin, 123,* 238–259.

Potter, S. J., & Moynihan, M. M. (2011). Bringing in the Bystander in-person prevention program to a U.S. military installation: Results from a pilot study. *Military Medicine, 176,* 870–875.

Poushter, J., & Kent, N. (2020, June 25). The global divide on homosexuality persists. *Pew Research Center.* https://www.pewresearch.org/global/2020/06/25/global-divide-on-homosexuality-persists/

Poushter, J., Fagan, M., & Gubbala, S. (2022, August 31). Climate change remains top global threat across 19-country survey. Pew Research Center.

PPRI. (2019, October 20). *Fractured nation: Widening partisan polarization and key issues in 2020 presidential elections.* American Values Survey. https://www.prri.org/research/fractured-nation-widening-partisan-polarization-and-key-issues-in-2020-presidential-elections/

Pratkanis, A. R., & Turner, M. E. (1994a). The year cool Papa Bell lost the batting title: Mr. Branch Rickey and Mr. Jackie Robinson's plea for affirmative action. *Nine: A Journal of Baseball History and Social Policy Perspectives,* 2, 260–276.

Pratkanis, A. R., & Turner, M. E. (1994b). Nine principles of successful affirmative action: Mr. Branch Rickey, Mr. Jackie Robinson, and the integration of baseball. *Nine: A Journal of Baseball History and Social Policy Perspectives, 3,* 36–65.

Pratkanis, A. R., Greenwald, A. G., Leippe, M. R., & Baumgardner, M. H. (1988). In search of reliable persuasion effects: III. The sleeper effect is dead. Long live the sleeper effect. *Journal of Personality and Social Psychology, 54,* 203–218.

Pratt, M. W., Pancer, M., Hunsberger, B., & Manchester, J. (1990). Reasoning about the self and relationships in maturity: An integrative complexity analysis of individual differences. *Journal of Personality and Social Psychology, 59,* 575–581.

Pratto, F. (1996). Sexual politics: The gender gap in the bedroom, the cupboard, and the cabinet. In D. M. Buss & N. M. Malamuth (Eds.), *Sex, power, conflict: Evolutionary and feminist perspectives.* New York: Oxford University Press.

Pratto, F., Sidanius, J., Stallworth, L. M., & Malle, B. F. (1994). Social dominance orientation: A personality variable predicting social and political attitudes. *Journal of Personality and Social Psychology, 67,* 741–763.

Pratto, F., Stallworth, L. M., & Sidanius, J. (1997). The gender gap: Differences in political attitudes and social dominance orientation. *British Journal of Social Psychology, 36,* 49–68.

Prentice, D. A., & Carranza, E. (2002). What women and men should be, shouldn't be, are allowed to be, and don't have to be: The contents of prescriptive gender stereotypes. *Psychology of Women Quarterly, 26,* 269–281.

Prentice-Dunn, S., & Rogers, R. W. (1980). Effects of deindividuating situational cues and aggressive models on subjective deindividuation and aggression. *Journal of Personality and Social Psychology, 39,* 104–113.

Prentice-Dunn, S., & Rogers, R. W. (1989). Deindividuation and the self-regulation of behavior. In P. B. Paulus (Ed.), *Psychology of group influence* (2nd ed.). Hillsdale, NJ: Erlbaum.

Prescott, A. T., Sargent, J. D., & Hull, J. G. (2018). Meta-analysis of the relationship between violent video game play and physical aggression over time. *PNAS, 115,* 9882–9888.

Preston, J. (2002, November 14). Threats and responses: Baghdad. Iraq tells the U.N. arms inspections will be permitted. *The New York Times.* https://www.nytimes.com/2002/12/10/world/threats-responses-baghdad-s-declaration-us-first-get-copy-report-iraqi-weapons.html

Preston, J. L., & Ritter, R. S. (2013). Different effects of religion and God on prosociality with the ingroup and outgroup. *Personality and Social Psychology Bulletin, 39,* 1471–1483.

Preston, S. D. (2013). The origins of altruism in offspring care. *Psychological Bulletin, 139,* 1305–1341.

Price, G. H., Dabbs, J. M., Jr., Clower, B. J., & Resin, R. P. (1974). *At first glance—Or, is physical attractiveness more than skin deep?* Paper presented at the Eastern Psychological Association convention. Cited by K. L. Dion & K. K. Dion (1979). Personality and behavioral correlates of romantic love. In M. Cook & G. Wilson (Eds.), *Love and attraction.* Oxford: Pergamon.

Primack, B. A., Shensa, A., Sidani, J. E., Whaite, E. O., Lin, L. Y., Rosen, D., & . . . Miller, E. (2017). Social media use and perceived social isolation among young adults in the U.S. *American Journal of Preventive Medicine, 53,* 1–8.

Prinsen, S., de Ridder, D. T. D., & de Vet, E. (2013). Eating by example: Effects of environmental cues on dietary decisions. *Appetite, 70,* 1–5.

Prinstein, M. J., & Cillessen, A. N. (2003). Forms and functions of adolescent peer aggression associated with high levels of peer status. *Merrill-Palmer Quarterly, 49,* 310–342.

Priolo, D., Pelt, A., Bauzel, R. S., Rubens, L., Voisin, D., & Fointiat, V. (2019). Three decades of research on induced hypocrisy: A meta-analysis. *Personality and Social Psychology Bulletin, 45*(12), 1681–1701.

Pritchard, I. L. (1998). *The effects of rap music on aggressive attitudes toward women.* Master's thesis, Humboldt State University.

Prochnow, T., Patterson, M. S., Bridges Hamilton, C. N., Delgado, H., Craig, S., & Umstattd Meyer, M. R. (2021). Sex differences in play networks and self-reported physical activity among children at summer care programs. *Child & Youth Services, 42,* 136–149.

Prohaska, V. (1994). "I know I'll get an A": Confident overestimation of final course grades. *Teaching of Psychology, 21,* 141–143.

Pronin, E., & Ross, L. (2006). Temporal differences in trait self-ascription: When the self is seen as an other. *Journal of Personality and Social Psychology, 90,* 197–209.

Pronin, E. (2008). How we see ourselves and how we see others. *Science, 320,* 1177–1180.

Pronin, E., Berger, J., & Molouki, S. (2007). Alone in a crowd of sheep: Asymmetric perceptions of conformity and their roots in an introspection illusion. *Journal of Personality and Social Psychology, 92,* 585–595.

Pronin, E., Lin, D. Y., & Ross, L. (2002). The bias blind spot: Perceptions of bias in self versus others. *Personality and Social Psychology Bulletin, 28,* 369–381.

Prothrow-Stith, D. (with M. Wiessman) (1991). *Deadly consequences.* New York: HarperCollins, p. 183.

Prot, S., Gentile, D. A., Anderson, C. A., Suzuki, K., Swing, E., Lim, K. M., Horiuchi, Y., Jelic, M., Krahé, B., Liuqing, W., Liau, A. K., Khoo, A., Petrescu, P. D., Sakamoto, A., Tajima, S., Toma, R. A., Warburton, W., Zhang, X., & Lam, B. C. (2014). Long-term relations among prosocial-media use, empathy, and prosocial behavior. *Psychological Science, 25,* 358–368.

Proudfoot, D., & Kay, A. C. (2023). Communal expectations conflict with autonomy motives: The western drive for autonomy shapes women's negative responses to positive gender stereotypes. *Journal of Personality and Social Psychology, 124,* 1–21.

Provine, R. R. (2005). Yawning. *American Scientist, 93,* 532–539.

Pruitt, D. G., & Kimmel, M. J. (1977). Twenty years of experimental gaming: Critique, synthesis, and suggestions for the future. *Annual Review of Psychology, 28,* 363–392.

Pruitt, D. G., & Lewis, S. A. (1975). Development of integrative solutions in bilateral negotiation. *Journal of Personality and Social Psychology, 31,* 621–633.

Pruitt, D. G., & Lewis, S. A. (1977). The psychology of integrative bargaining. In D. Druckman (Ed.), *Negotiations: A social-psychological analysis.* New York: Halsted.

Pruitt, D. G. (1986). Achieving integrative agreements in negotiation. In R. K. White (Ed.), *Psychology and the prevention of nuclear war.* New York: New York University Press.

Pruitt, D. G. (1998). Social conflict. In D. Gilbert, S. T. Fiske, & G. Lindzey (Eds.), *Handbook of social psychology* (4th ed.). New York: McGraw Hill.

Prutzman, P., Roberts, E., Fishler, T., & Jones, T. (2022). The story of a model restorative school: Creative response to conflict at MS 217 in Queens, NY. *Journal of Aggression, Conflict and Peace Research, 14,* 346–362.

Pryor, J. B., DeSouza, E. R., Fitness, J., Hutz, C., Kumpf, M., Lubbert, K., Pesonen, O., & Erber, M. W. (1997). Gender differences in the interpretation of social-sexual behavior: A cross-cultural perspective on sexual harassment. *Journal of Cross-Cultural Psychology, 28,* 509–534.

Puhl, R. M., & Heuer, C. A. (2009). The stigma of obesity: A review and update. *Obesity, 17,* 941–964.

Puhl, R. M., & Heuer, C. A. (2010). Obesity stigma: Important considerations for public health. *American Journal of Public Health, 100,* 1019–1028.

Pulver, D. V., Rice, D., & Padilla, R. (2024, January 1). It's over: 2023 was Earth's hottest year, experts say. *USA Today.*

Purvis, J. A., Dabbs, J. M., Jr., & Hopper, C. H. (1984). The "opener": Skilled user of facial expression and speech pattern. *Personality and Social Psychology Bulletin, 10,* 61–66.

Putnam, R. (2000). *Bowling alone.* New York: Simon & Schuster.

Pyszczynski, T., Hamilton, J. C., Greenberg, J., & Becker, S. E. (1991). Self-awareness and psychological dysfunction. In C. R. Snyder & D. O. Forsyth (Eds.), *Handbook of social and clinical psychology: The health perspective.* New York: Pergamon.

Pyszczynski, T., Motyl, M., Vail, Kenneth E., I., II, Hirschberger, G., Arndt, J., & Kesebir, P. (2012). Drawing attention to global climate change decreases support for war. *Peace and Conflict: Journal of Peace Psychology, 18,* 354–368.

Qirko, H. N. (2004). "Fictive kin" and suicide terrorism. *Science, 304,* 49–50.

Quartz, S. R., & Sejnowski, T. J. (2002). *Liars, lovers, and heroes: What the new brain science reveals about how we become who we are.* New York: Morrow.

Quigley-McBride, A., & Wells, G. L. (2023). Eyewitness confidence and decision time reflect identification accuracy in actual police lineups. *Law and Human Behavior, 47,* 333–347.

Quillian, L., & Lee, J. J. (2023). Trends in racial and ethnic discrimination in hiring in six Western countries. *PNAS Proceedings of the National Academy of Sciences of the United States of America, 120,* 1–10.

Quillian, L., Lee, J. J., & Honore, B. (2020). Racial discrimination in the U.S. housing and mortgage lending markets: A quantitative review of trends, 1976–2016. *Race and Social Problems, 12,* 13–28.

Quillian, L., Pager, D., Hexel, O., & Midtbøen, A. H. (2017). Meta-analysis of field experiments shows no change in racial discrimination in hiring over time. *PNAS, 114,* 10870–10875.

Quist, M. C., Watkins, C. D., Smith, F. G., Little, A. C., Debruine, L. M., & Jones, B. C. (2012). Sociosexuality predicts women's preferences for symmetry in men's faces. *Archives of Sexual Behavior, 41,* 1415–1421.

Quoidbach, J., & Dunn, E. W. (2010). Personality neglect: The unforeseen impact of personal dispositions on emotional life. *Psychological Science, 21,* 1783–1786.

Quoidbach, J., Dunn, E., Petrides, K., & Mikolajczak, M. (2010). Money giveth, money taketh away: The dual effect of wealth on happiness. *Psychological Science, 21,* 759–763.

Quoidbach, J., Dunn, E. W., Hansenne, M., & Bustin, G. (2015). The price of abundance: How a wealth of experiences impoverishes savoring. *Personality and Social Psychology Bulletin, 41,* 393–404.

Rabinovich, A., Morton, T. A., & Birney, M. E. (2012). Communicating climate science: The role of perceived communicator's motives. *Journal of Environmental Psychology, 32,* 11–28.

Rafferty, R., & Vander Ven, T. (2014). "I hate everything about you": A qualitative examination of cyberbullying and on-line aggression in a college sample. *Deviant Behavior, 35,* 364–377.

Raifman, J., Charlton, B. M., Arrington-Sanders, R., Chan, P. A., Rusley, J., Mayer, K. H., Stein, M. D., Austin, S. B., & McConnell, M. (2020). Sexual orientation and suicide attempt disparities among US adolescents: 2009–2017. *Pediatrics, 145*(3).

Raifman, J., Moscoe, E., & Austin, S. B. (2017). Difference-in-differences analysis of the association between state same-sex marriage policies and adolescent suicide attempts. *Journal of the American Medical Association, 171,* 350–356.

Raine, A. (1993). *The psychopathology of crime: Criminal behavior as a clinical disorder.* San Diego, CA: Academic Press.

Raine, A. (2008). From genes to brain to antisocial behavior. *Current Directions in Psychological Science, 17,* 323–328.

Raine, A. (2019). The neuromoral theory of antisocial, violent, and psychopathic behavior. *Psychiatry Research, 277,* 64–69.

Raine, A., Cheney, R. A., Ho, R., Portnoy, J., Liu, J., Soyfer, L., Hibbeln, J., & Richmond, T. S. (2016). Nutritional supplementation to reduce child aggression: A randomized, stratified, single-blind, factorial trial. *Journal of Child Psychology and Psychiatry, 57,* 1038–1046.

Raine, A., Fung, A. L. C., Gao, Y., & Lee, T. M. C. (2021). Omega-3 supplementation, child antisocial behavior, and psychopathic personality: A randomized, double-blind, placebo-controlled, stratified, parallel group trial. *European Child & Adolescent Psychiatry, 30,* 303–312.

Raine, A., Lencz, T., Bihrle, S., LaCasse, L., & Colletti, P. (2000). Reduced prefrontal gray matter volume and reduced autonomic activity in antisocial personality disorder. *Archives of General Psychiatry, 57,* 119–127.

Raine, A., Stoddard, J., Bihrle, S., & Buchsbaum, M. (1998). Prefrontal glucose deficits in murderers lacking psychosocial deprivation. *Neuropsychiatry, Neuropsychology, & Behavioral Neurology, 11,* 1–7.

Rains, S. A. (2013). The nature of psychological reactance revisited: A meta-analytic review. *Human Communication Research, 39,* 47–73.

Rajagopal, P., Raju, S., & Unnava, H. R. (2006). Differences in the cognitive accessibility of action and inaction regrets. *Journal of Experimental Social Psychology, 42,* 302–313.

Rajecki, D. W., Bledsoe, S. B., & Rasmussen, J. L. (1991). Successful personal ads: Gender differences and similarities in offers, stipulations, and outcomes. *Basic and Applied Social Psychology, 12,* 457–469.

Ramos, M. R., Cassidy, C., Reicher, S., & Haslam, S. A. (2012). A longitudinal investigation of the rejection–identification hypothesis. *British Journal of Social Psychology, 51,* 642–660.

Randler, C., & Vollmer, C. (2013). Aggression in young adults–A matter of short sleep and social jetlag? *Psychological Reports: Disability and Trauma, 113,* 754–765.

Rank, S. G., & Jacobson, C. K. (1977). Hospital nurses' compliance with medication overdose orders: A failure to replicate. *Journal of Health and Social Behavior, 18,* 188–193.

Rapoport, A. (1960). *Fights, games, and debates.* Ann Arbor, MI: University of Michigan Press.

Ratcliff, C. L., & Sun, Y. (2020). Overcoming resistance through narratives: Findings from a meta-analytic review. *Human Communication Research, 46,* 412–443.

Ratliff, K. A., & Nosek, B. A. (2010). Creating distinct implicit and explicit attitudes with an illusory correlation paradigm. *Journal of Experimental Social Psychology, 46,* 721–728.

Ravary, A., Baldwin, M. W., & Bartz, J. A. (2019). Shaping the body politic: Mass media fat-shaming affects implicit anti-fat attitudes. *Personality and Social Psychology Bulletin, 45,* 1580–1589.

Rawn, C. D., & Vohs, K. D. (2011). People use self-control to risk personal harm: An intra-interpersonal dilemma. *Personality and Social Psychology Review, 15,* 267–289.

Reece, R. L. (2017, Fall). Fighting fat stigma with science. *Teaching Tolerance,* pp. 35–37. https://www.tolerance.org/magazine/fall-2017/fighting-fat-stigma-with-science

Reed, D. R., & Knaapila, A. (2010). Genetics of taste and smell: poisons and pleasures. *Progress in Molecular Biology and Translational Science, 94,* 213–240.

Reed, S., & Meggs, J. (2017). Examining the effect of prenatal testosterone and aggression on sporting choice and sporting longevity. *Personality and Individual Differences, 116,* 11–15.

Regan, D. T., & Cheng, J. B. (1973). Distraction and attitude change: A resolution. *Journal of Experimental Social Psychology, 9,* 138–147.

Regan, D. T., & Fazio, R. (1977). On the consistency between attitudes and behavior: Look to the method of attitude formation. *Journal of Experimental Social Psychology, 13,* 28–45.

Regan, P. C. (1998). What if you can't get what you want? Willingness to compromise ideal mate selection standards as a function of sex, mate value, and relationship context. *Personality and Social Psychology Bulletin, 24,* 1294–1303.

Regnerus, M., Gordon, D., & Price, J. (2016). Documenting pornography use in America: A comparative analysis of methodological approaches. *Journal of Sex Research, 53,* 873–881.

Reicher, S. D., & Haslam, S. A. (2011, November/December). Culture of shock. *Scientific American Mind,* 57–61.

Reicher, S. D., & Haslam, S. A. (2016, May/June). Fueling extremes. *Scientific American Mind,* pp. 35–39.

Reicher, S. D., Haslam, S. A., & Smith, J. R. (2012). Working toward the experimenter: Reconceptualizing obedience within the Milgram paradigm as identification-based followership. *Perspectives on Psychological Science, 7,* 315–324.

Reicher, S., Spears, R., & Postmes, T. (1995). A social identity model of deindividuation phenomena. In W. Storebe & M. Hewstone (Eds.), *European review of social psychology* (Vol. 6). Chichester, UK: Wiley.

Reid, C. A., Davis, J. L., & Green, J. D. (2013). The power of change: Interpersonal attraction as a function of attitude similarity and attitude alignment. *Journal of Social Psychology, 153,* 700–719.

Reid, P., & Finchilescu, G. (1995). The disempowering effects of media violence against women on college women. *Psychology of Women Quarterly, 19,* 397–411.

Reijntjes, A., Thomaes, S., Kamphuis, J. H., Bushman, B. J., de Castro, B. O., & Telch, M. J. (2011). Explaining the paradoxical rejection–aggression link: The mediating effects of hostile intent attributions, anger, and decreases in state self-esteem on peer rejection-induced aggression on youth. *Personality and Social Psychology Bulletin, 37,* 955–963.

Reilly, E. B., & Stuyvenberg, C. L. (2022). A meta-analysis of loving-kindness meditations on self-compassion. *Mindfulness.*

Reinero, D. A., Harris, E. A., Rathje, S., Duke, A., & Van Bavel, J. J. (2024). Partisans are more likely to entrench their beliefs in misinformation when political outgroup members fact-check claims. PsyArxiv preprint.

Reisenzein, R. (1983). The Schachter theory of emotion: Two decades later. *Psychological Bulletin, 94,* 239–264.

Reis, H. T., Maniaci, M. R., Caprariello, P. A., Eastwick, P. W., & Finkel, E. J. (2011). Familiarity does indeed promote attraction in live interaction. *Journal of Personality and Social Psychology, 101,* 557–570.

Reis, H. T., Nezlek, J., & Wheeler, L. (1980). Physical attractiveness in social interaction. *Journal of Personality and Social Psychology, 38,* 604–617.

Reis, H. T., O'Keefe, S. D., & Lane, R. D. (2017). Fun is more fun when others are involved. *The Journal of Positive Psychology, 12,* 547–557.

Reis, H. T., Smith, S. M., Carmichael, C. L., Caprariello, P. A., Tsa, F.-F., Rodrigues, A., & Maniaci, M. R. (2010). Are you happy for me? How sharing positive events with others provides personal and interpersonal benefits. *Journal of Personality and Social Psychology, 99,* 311–329.

Reis, H. T., Wheeler, L., Spiegel, N., Kernis, M. H., Nezlek, J., & Perri, M. (1982). Physical attractiveness in social interaction: II. Why does appearance affect social experience? *Journal of Personality and Social Psychology, 43,* 979–996.

Renaud, H., & Estess, F. (1961). Life history interviews with one hundred normal American males: "Pathogenecity" of childhood. *American Journal of Orthopsychiatry, 31,* 786–802.

Ren, Z., Dimant, E., & Schweitzer, M. (2023). Beyond belief: How social engagement motives influence the spread of conspiracy theories. *Journal of Experimental Social Psychology, 104,* 1–12.

Reuters (2023, February 28). Women make up 40% of boards at top UK companies for first time. Reuters.com

Rhodes, G. (2006). The evolutionary psychology of facial beauty. *Annual Review of Psychology, 57,* 199–226.

Rhodes, G., Sumich, A., & Byatt, G. (1999). Are average facial configurations attractive only because of their symmetry? *Psychological Science, 10,* 52–58.

Rhodes, M. G., & Anastasi, J. S. (2012). The own-age bias in face recognition: A meta-analytic and theoretical review. *Psychological Bulletin, 138,* 146–174.

Rhodewalt, F., & Agustsdottir, S. (1986). Effects of self-presentation on the phenomenal self. *Journal of Personality and Social Psychology, 50,* 47–55.

Rhodewalt, F. (1987). Is self-handicapping an effective self-protective attributional strategy? Paper presented at the American Psychological Association convention.

Rhodewalt, F., Saltzman, A. T., & Wittmer J. (1984). Self-handicapping among competitive athletes: The role of practice in self-esteem protection. *Basic and Applied Social Psychology, 5,* 197–209.

Rholes, W. S., Newman, L. S., & Ruble, D. N. (1990). Understanding self and other: Developmental and motivational aspects of perceiving persons in terms of invariant dispositions. In E. T. Higgins & R. M. Sorrentino (Eds.), *Handbook of motivation and cognition: Foundations of social behavior* (Vol. 2). New York: Guilford.

Rice, B. (1985, September). Performance review: The job nobody likes. *Psychology Today,* pp. 30–36.

Richardson, D. S. (2005). The myth of female passivity: Thirty years of revelations about female aggression. *Psychology of Women Quarterly, 29,* 238–247.

Richardson, J. D., Huddy, W. P., & Morgan, S. M. (2008). The hostile media effect, biased assimilation, and perceptions of a presidential debate. *Journal of Applied Social Psychology, 38,* 1255–1270.

Richardson, L. F. (1960). Generalized foreign policy. *British Journal of Psychology Monographs Supplements, 23.* Cited by A. Rapoport in *Fights, games, and debates* (p. 15). Ann Arbor, MI: University of Michigan Press.

Richardson, M., Abraham, C., & Bond, R. (2012). Psychological correlates of university students' academic performance: A systematic review and meta-analysis. *Psychological Bulletin, 138,* 353–387.

Richards, Z., & Hewstone, M. (2001). Subtyping and subgrouping: Processes for the prevention and promotion of stereotype change. *Personality and Social Psychology Review, 5,* 52–73.

Richeson, J. A., & Shelton, J. N. (2012). Stereotype threat in interracial interactions. In M. Inzlicht & T. Schmader (eds.), *Stereotype threat: Theory, process, and application* (pp. 231–245). New York: Oxford University Press.

Richeson, J. A., & Trawalter, S. (2008). The threat of appearing prejudiced, and race-based attentional biases. *Psychological Science, 19,* 98–102.

Ridge, R. D., & Reber, J. S. (2002). "I think she's attracted to me": The effect of men's beliefs on women's behavior in a job interview scenario. *Basic and Applied Social Psychology, 24,* 1–14.

Riedman, D., & Desmond, O. (2023). Shooting incidents at K-12 schools. CHDS School Shooting Safety Compendium. Naval Postgraduate School Center for Homeland Defense and Security. Retrieved from www.chds.us/ssdb

Riek, B. M., Mania, E. W., & Gaertner, S. L. (2013). Reverse subtyping: The effects of prejudice level on the subtyping of counterstereotypic outgroup members. *Basic and Applied Social Psychology, 35,* 409–417.

Riess, M., Rosenfeld, P., Melburg, V., & Tedeschi, J. T. (1981). Self-serving attributions: Biased private perceptions and distorted public descriptions. *Journal of Personality and Social Psychology, 41,* 224–231.

Rietzschel, E. F., Nijstad, B. A., & Stroebe, W. (2006). Productivity is not enough: A comparison of interactive and nominal brainstorming groups on idea generation and selection. *Journal of Experimental Social Psychology, 42,* 244–251.

Rijnbout, J. S., & McKimmie, B. M. (2012). Deviance in group decision making: Group-member centrality alleviates negative consequences for the group. *European Journal of Social Psychology, 42,* 915–923.

Rime, B., & Paez, D. (2023). Why we gather: A new look, empirically documented, at Emile Durkheim's theory of collective assemblies and collective effervescence. *Perspectives on Psychological Science.*

Rinderu, M. I., Bushman, B. J., & Van Lange, P. A. M. (2018). Climate, aggression, and violence (CLASH): A cultural-evolutionary approach. *Current Opinion in Psychology, 19,* 113–118.

Riordan, C. A. (1980). *Effects of admission of influence on attributions and attraction.* Paper presented at the American Psychological Association convention, Montreal, Quebec.

Rios, K. (2022). Multiculturalism and colorblindness as threats to the self: A framework for understanding dominant and non-dominant group members' responses to interethnic ideologies. *Personality and Social Psychology Review, 26,* 315–341.

Risen, J. L., & Critcher, C. R. (2011). Visceral fit: While in a visceral state, associated states of the world seem more likely. *Journal of Personality and Social Psychology, 100,* 777–793.

Risen, J. L., Gilovich, T., & Dunning, D. (2007). One-shot illusory correlations and stereotype formation. *Personality and Social Psychology Bulletin, 33,* 1492–1502.

Ritchey, A. J., & Ruback, R. B. (2018). Predicting lynching atrocity: The situational norms of lynchings in Georgia. *Personality and Social Psychology Bulletin, 44,* 619–637.

Riva, P., Romero Lauro, L. J., DeWall, C. N., & Bushman, B. J. (2012). Buffer the pain away: Stimulating the right ventrolateral prefrontal cortex reduces pain following social exclusion. *Psychological Science, 23,* 1473–1475.

Riva, P., Williams, K. D., Torstrick, A. M., & Montali, L. (2014). Orders to shoot (a camera): Effects of ostracism on obedience. *Journal of Social Psychology, 154,* 208–216.

Rivera, G. N., Christy, A. G., Kim, J., Vess, M., Hicks, J. A., & Schlegel, R. J. (2019). Understanding the relationship between perceived authenticity and well-being. *Review of General Psychology, 23,* 113–126.

Rivers, A. M., Sherman, J. W., Rees, H. R., Reichardt, R., & Klauer, K. C. (2020). On the roles of stereotype activation and application in diminishing implicit bias. *Personality and Social Psychology Bulletin, 46,* 349–364.

Robberson, M. R., & Rogers, R. W. (1988). Beyond fear appeals: Negative and positive persuasive appeals to health and self-esteem. *Journal of Applied Social Psychology, 18,* 277–287.

Roberts, J. A., & David, M. E. (2016). My life has become a major distraction from my cell phone: Partner phubbing and relationship satisfaction among romantic partners. *Computers in Human Behavior, 54,* 134–141.

Roberts, L. J., Jackson, M. S., & Grundy, I. H. (2019). Choking under pressure: Illuminating the role of distraction and self-focus. *International Review of Sport and Exercise Psychology, 12,* 49–69.

Robertson, C. (2016, August 28). New Orleans program teaches officers to police one another. *The New York Times.* https://www.nytimes.com/2016/08/29/us/a-new-orleans-program-teaches-officers-to-police-each-other.html

Robertson, I. (1987). *Sociology* (p. 67). New York: Worth Publishers.

Robertson, L. A., McAnally, H. M., & Hancox, R. J. (2013). Childhood and adolescent television viewing and antisocial behavior in early adulthood. *Pediatrics, 131,* 439–446.

Roberts, S. (2020, September 2). Sophia Farrar dies at 92; belied indifference to Kitty Genovese attack. *New York Times.*

Robinson, A. R., & Piff, P. K. (2017). Deprived, but not depraved: Prosocial behavior is an adaptive response to lower socioeconomic status. *Behavioral and Brain Sciences, 40,* e341.

Robinson, M. D., & Ryff, C. D. (1999). The role of self-deception in perceptions of past, present, and future happiness. *Personality and Social Psychology Bulletin, 25,* 595–606.

Robinson, M. S., & Alloy, L. B. (2003). Negative cognitive styles and stress-reactive rumination interact to predict depression: A prospective study. *Cognitive Therapy and Research, 27,* 275–291.

Robinson, T. N., Wilde, M. L., Navracruz, L. C., Haydel, F., & Varady, A. (2001). Effects of reducing children's television and video game use on aggressive behavior. *Archives of Pediatric and Adolescent Medicine, 155,* 17–23.

Robins, R. W., & Beer, J. S. (2001). Positive illusions about the self: Short-term benefits and long-term costs. *Journal of Personality and Social Psychology, 80,* 340–352.

Robins, R. W., Mendelsohn, G. A., Connell, J. B., & Kwan, V. S. Y. (2004). Do people agree about the causes of behavior? A social relations analysis of behavior ratings and causal attributions. *Journal of Personality and Social Psychology, 86,* 334–344.

Robles, T. F. (2015). Marital quality and health: Implications for marriage in the 21st century. *Current Directions in Psychological Science, 23,* 427–432.

Robles, T. F., Slatcher, R. B., Trombello, J. M., & McGinn, M. M. (2014). Marital quality and health: A meta-analytic review. *Psychological Bulletin, 140,* 140–187.

Rochat, F., & Modigliani, A. (1995). The ordinary quality of resistance: From Milgram's laboratory to the village of Le Chambon. *Journal of Social Issues, 51,* 195–210.

Rochat, F. (1993). *How did they resist authority? Protecting refugees in Le Chambon during World War II.* Paper presented at the American Psychological Association convention.

Rocklage, M. D., & Luttrell, A. (2021). Attitudes based on feelings: Fixed or fleeting? *Psychological Science, 32,* 364–380.

Rode, J. B., Dent, A. L., & Ditto, P. H. (2023). Climate change consensus messages may cause reactance in conservatives, but there is no meta-analytic evidence that they backfire. *Environmental Communication, 17,* 60–66.

Rodenhizer, K. A. E., & Edwards, K. M. (2017). The impacts of sexual media exposure on adolescent and emerging adults' dating and sexual violence attitudes and behaviors: A critical review of the literature. *Trauma, Violence, and Abuse, 20*(4), 439–452.

Rodriguez, D. N., & Berry, M. A. (2020). Administrator blindness affects the recording of eyewitness lineup outcomes. *Law and Human Behavior, 44,* 71–87.

Roehling, M. V. (2000). Weight-based discrimination in employment: Psychological and legal aspects. *Personnel Psychology, 52,* 969–1016.

Roese, N. J., & Hur, T. (1997). Affective determinants of counterfactual thinking. *Social Cognition, 15,* 274–290.

Roese, N. J., & Vohs, K. D. (2012). Hindsight bias. *Perspectives on Psychological Science, 7,* 411–426.

Roese, N. L., & Olson, J. M. (1994). Attitude importance as a function of repeated attitude expression. *Journal of Experimental Social Psychology, 66,* 805–818.

Roessel, J., Schoel, C., & Stahlberg, D. (2018). What's in an accent? General spontaneous biases against nonnative accents: An investigation with conceptual and auditory IATs. *European Journal of Social Psychology, 48,* 535–550.

Roger, L. H., Cortes, D. E., & Malgady, R. B. (1991). Acculturation and mental health status among Hispanics: Convergence and new directions for research. *American Psychologist, 46,* 585–597.

Rogers, C. R. (1980). *A way of being.* Boston: Houghton Mifflin.

Rogers, C. R. (1985, February). Quoted by Michael A. Wallach and Lise Wallach in How psychology sanctions the cult of the self. *Washington Monthly,* pp. 46–56.

Roghanizad, M. M., & Bohns, V. K. (2017). Ask in person: You're less persuasive than you think over email. *Journal of Experimental Social Psychology, 69,* 223–226.

Roghanizad, M. M., & Bohns, V. K. (2022). Should I ask over Zoom, phone, email, or in-person? Communication channel and predicted versus actual compliance. *Social Psychological and Personality Science, 13,* 1163–1172.

Rohrer, J. H., Baron, S. H., Hoffman, E. L., & Swander, D. V. (1954). The stability of autokinetic judgments. *Journal of Abnormal and Social Psychology, 49,* 595–597.

Romer, D., Gruder, D. L., & Lizzadro, T. (1986). A person-situation approach to altruistic behavior. *Journal of Personality and Social Psychology, 51,* 1001–1012.

Romo, V. (2023, March 22). Antisemitic incidents are at an all-time high, the ADL reports. NPR.org.

Ronay, R., Oostrom, J. K., Lehmann-Willenbrock, N., & Van Vugt, M. (2017). Pride before the fall: (Over)confidence predicts escalation of public commitment. *Journal of Experimental Social Psychology, 69,* 13–22.

Roney, J. R. (2003). Effects of visual exposure to the opposite sex: Cognitive aspects of mate attraction in human males. *Personality and Social Psychology Bulletin, 29,* 393–404.

Rook, K. S. (1984). Promoting social bonding: Strategies for helping the lonely and socially isolated. *American Psychologist, 39,* 1389–1407.

Rook, K. S. (1987). Social support versus companionship: Effects on life stress, loneliness, and evaluations by others. *Journal of Personality and Social Psychology, 52,* 1132–1147.

Roose, K. (2021, September 3). What Is QAnon, the Viral Pro-Trump Conspiracy Theory? *New York Times.*

Rosander, M., & Eriksson, O. (2012). Conformity on the Internet–the role of task difficulty and gender differences. *Computers in Human Behavior, 28,* 1587–1595.

Rose, A. J., & Rudolph, K. D. (2006). A review of sex differences in peer relationship processes: Potential trade-offs for the emotional and behavioral development of girls and boys. *Psychological Bulletin, 132,* 98–131.

Rosenberg, B. D., & Siegel, J. T. (2018). A 50-year review of psychological reactance theory: Do not read this article. *Motivation Science, 4,* 281–300.

Rosenberg, L. A. (1961). Group size, prior experience and conformity. *Journal of Abnormal and Social Psychology, 63,* 436–437.

Rosenberg, T. (2010, November 1). The opt-out solution. *The New York Times.*

Rosenblatt, A., & Greenberg, J. (1988). Depression and interpersonal attraction: The role of perceived similarity. *Journal of Personality and Social Psychology, 55,* 112–119.

Rosenblatt, A., & Greenberg, J. (1991). Examining the world of the depressed: Do depressed people prefer others who are depressed? *Journal of Personality and Social Psychology, 60,* 620–629.

Rosenbloom, S. (2008, January 3). Putting your best cyberface forward. *The New York Times.* www.nytimes.com/2008/01/03/fashion/03impression.html

Rosenbusch, H., Evans, A. M., & Zeelenberg, M. (2019). Multilevel emotion transfer on YouTube: Disentangling the effects of emotional contagion and homophily on video audiences. *Social Psychological and Personality Science, 10,* 1028–1035.

Rosenfeld, M. J., & Roesler, K. (2023). Stability and change in predictors of marital dissolution in the us 1950–2017. *Journal of Marriage and Family.*

Rosenthal, D. A., & Feldman, S. S. (1992). The nature and stability of ethnic identity in Chinese youth: Effects of length of residence in two cultural contexts. *Journal of Cross-Cultural Psychology, 23,* 214–227.

Rosenthal, E. (2011, June 26). Europe stifles drivers in favor of alternatives. *The New York Times.* www.nytimes.com

Rosenthal, R., & Jacobson, L. (1968). *Pygmalion in the classroom: Teacher expectation and pupils' intellectual development.* New York: Holt, Rinehart & Winston.

Rosenthal, R. (1985). From unconscious experimenter bias to teacher expectancy effects. In J. B. Dusek, V. C. Hall, & W. J. Meyer (Eds.), *Teacher expectancies.* Hillsdale, NJ: Erlbaum.

Rosenthal, R. (1991). Teacher expectancy effects: A brief update 25 years after the Pygmalion experiment. *Journal of Research in Education, 1,* 3–12.

Rosenthal, R. (2002). Covert communication in classrooms, clinics, courtrooms, and cubicles. *American Psychologist, 57,* 839–849.

Rosenthal, R. (2003). Covert communication in laboratories, classrooms, and the truly real world. *Current Directions in Psychological Science, 12,* 151–154.

Rosenthal, R. (2006). Applying psychological research on interpersonal expectations and covert communication in classrooms, clinics, corporations, and courtrooms. In S. I. Donaldson, D. E. Berger, & K. Pezdek (Eds.), *Applied psychology: New frontiers and rewarding careers.* Mahwah, NJ: Erlbaum.

Rosenthal, S. A., & Pittinsky, T. L. (2006). Narcissistic leadership. *Leadership Quarterly, 17,* 617–633.

Rosenthal, S. A., Hooley, J. M., Montoya, R. M., van der Linden, S. L., & Steshenko, Y. (2020). The narcissistic grandiosity scale: A measure to distinguish narcissistic grandiosity from high self-esteem. *Assessment, 27,* 487–507.

Roser, M. (2021). The argument for carbon price. Our World In Data.

Roseth, C. J., Johnson, D. W., & Johnson, R. T. (2008). Promoting early adolescents' achievement and peer relationships: The effects of cooperative, competitive, and individualistic goal structures. *Psychological Bulletin, 134,* 223–246.

Rossi, A. S., & Rossi, P. H. (1990). *Of human bonding: Parent-child relations across the life course.* Hawthorne, NY: Aldine de Gruyter.

Rossiter, J. R., & Smidts, A. (2012). Print advertising: Celebrity presenters. *Journal of Business Research, 65,* 874–879.

Ross, L., & Anderson, C. A. (1982). Shortcomings in the attribution process: On the origins and maintenance of erroneous social assessments. In D. Kahneman, P. Slovic, & A. Tversky (Eds.), *Judgment under uncertainty: Heuristics and biases.* New York: Cambridge University Press.

Ross, L., & Ward, A. (1995). Psychological barriers to dispute resolution. In M. P. Zanna (Ed.), *Advances in experimental social psychology* (Vol. 27). San Diego: Academic Press.

Ross, L. (1977). The intuitive psychologist and his shortcomings: Distortions in the attribution process. In L. Berkowitz (Ed.), *Advances in experimental social psychology* (Vol. 10). New York: Academic Press.

Ross, L. (1981). The "intuitive scientist" formulation and its developmental implications. In J. H. Havell & L. Ross (Eds.), *Social cognitive development: Frontiers and possible futures.* Cambridge, England: Cambridge University Press.

Ross, L. (1988). Situationist perspectives on the obedience experiments. Review of A. G. Miller's *The obedience experiments. Contemporary Psychology, 33,* 101–104.

Ross, L. (2018). From the fundamental attribution error to the truly fundamental attribution error and beyond: My research journey. *Perspectives on Psychological Science, 13,* 750–769.

Ross, L., Amabile, T. M., & Steinmetz, J. L. (1977). Social roles, social control, and biases in social-perception processes. *Journal of Personality and Social Psychology, 35,* 485–494.

Ross, M., & Fletcher, G. J. O. (1985). Attribution and social perception. In G. Lindzey & E. Aronson (Eds.), *The Handbook of social psychology* (3rd ed.). New York: Random House.

Roszell, P., Kennedy, D., & Grabb, E. (1990). Physical attractiveness and income attainment among Canadians. *Journal of Psychology, 123,* 547–559.

Rotge, J., Lemogne, C., Hinfray, S., Huguet, P., Grynszpan, O., Tartour, E., & . . . Fossati, P. (2015). A meta-analysis of the anterior cingulate contribution to social pain. *Social Cognitive and Affective Neuroscience, 10,* 19–27.

Rothbart, M., Fulero, S., Jensen, C., Howard, J., & Birrell, P. (1978). From individual to group impressions: Availability heuristics in stereotype formation. *Journal of Experimental Social Psychology, 14,* 237–255.

Rothgerber, H. (2020). Meat-related cognitive dissonance: A conceptual framework for understanding how meat eaters reduce negative arousal from eating animals. *Appetite, 146,* 104511.

Rothwell, J. (2023, October 13). Teens spend average of 4.8 hours on social media per day. Gallup.com.

Rotton, J., & Cohn, E. G. (2004). Outdoor temperature, climate control, and criminal assault: The spatial and temporal ecology of violence. *Environment and Behavior, 36,* 276–306.

Rotton, J., & Frey, J. (1985). Air pollution, weather, and violent crimes: Concomitant time-series analysis of archival data. *Journal of Personality and Social Psychology, 49,* 1207–1220.

Rotundo, M., Nguyen, D.-H., & Sackett, P. R. (2001). A meta-analytic review of gender differences in perceptions of sexual harassment. *Journal of Applied Psychology, 86,* 914–922.

Rovenpor, D. R., O'Brien, T. C., Roblain, A., De Guissme, L., Chekroun, P., & Leidner, B. (2019). Intergroup conflict self-perpetuates via meaning: Exposure to intergroup conflict increases meaning and fuels a desire for further conflict. *Journal of Personality and Social Psychology, 116,* 119–140.

Rowe, D. C., Almeida, D. M., & Jacobson, K. C. (1999). School context and genetic influences on aggression in adolescence. *Psychological Science, 10,* 277–280.

Royal Society, The. (2010, September). *Climate change: A summary of the science* [PDF file]. London: The Royal Society. https://royalsociety.org/~/media/Royal_Society_Content/policy/publications/2010/4294972962.pdf

Roy, M. M., Christenfeld, N. J. S., & McKenzie, C. R. M. (2005). Underestimating the duration of future events: Memory incorrectly used or memory bias? *Psychological Bulletin, 131,* 738–756.

Rubien-Thomas, E., Berrian, N., M. Rapuano, K., J. Skalaban, L., Cervera, A., Nardos, B., Cohen, A. O., Lowrey, A., M. Daumeyer, N., Watts, R., Camp, N. P., Hughes, B. L., Eberhardt, J. L., Taylor-Thompson, K. A., Fair, D. A., Richeson, J. A., & Casey, B. J. (2023). Uncertain threat is associated with greater impulsive actions and neural dissimilarity to black versus white faces. *Cognitive, Affective & Behavioral Neuroscience, 23,* 944–956.

Rubin, J. Z. (Ed.) (1981). *Third party intervention in conflict: Kissinger in the Middle East.* New York: Praeger.

Rubin, L. B. (1985). *Just friends: The role of friendship in our lives.* New York: Harper & Row.

Rubin, Z. (1973). *Liking and loving: An invitation to social psychology.* New York: Holt, Rinehart & Winston.

Ruddock, H. K., Brunstrom, J. M., & Higgs, S. (2021). The social facilitation of eating: Why does the mere presence of others cause an increase in energy intake? *Physiology & Behavior, 240.*

Ruddock, H. K., Brunstrom, J. M., Vartanian, L. R., & Higgs, S. (2019). A systemic review and meta-analysis of the social facilitation of eating. *American Journal of Clinical Nutrition, 110,* 842–861.

Rudert, S. C., Möring, J. N. R., Kenntemich, C., & Büttner, C. M. (2023). When and why we ostracize others: Motivated social exclusion in group contexts. *Journal of Personality and Social Psychology, 125,* 803–826.

Rudman, L. A., McLean, M. C., & Bunzl, M. (2013). When truth is personally inconvenient, attitudes change: The impact of extreme weather on implicit support for green politicians and explicit climate-change beliefs. *Psychological Science, 14,* 2290–2296.

Rudolph, U., Roesch, S. C., Greitenmeyer, T., & Weiner, B. (2004). A meta-analytic review of help-giving and aggression from an attributional perspective: Contributions to a general theory of motivation. *Cognition and Emotion,* 18, 815–848.

Ruiter, R. A. C., Abraham, C., & Kok, G. (2001). Scary warnings and rational precautions: A review of the psychology of fear appeals. *Psychology and Health, 16,* 613–630.

Ruiter, R. A. C., Kessels, L. T. E., Peters, G-J. Y., & Kok, G. (2014). Sixty years of fear appeal research: Current state of the evidence. *International Journal of Psychology, 49,* 63–70.

Ruiter, S., & De Graaf, N. D. (2006). National context, religiosity, and volunteering: Results from 53 countries. *American Sociological Review, 71*(2), 191–210.

Rule, B. G., Taylor, B. R., & Dobbs, A. R. (1987). Priming effects of heat on aggressive thoughts. *Social Cognition, 5,* 131–143.

Rule, N. (2014, May-June) Snap-judgment science. *APS Observer.* http://www.psychologicalscience.org/index.php/publications/observer/2014/may-june-14/snap-judgment-science.html.

Rule, N. O., Rosen, K. S., Slepian, M. L., & Ambady, N. (2011). Mating interest improves women's accuracy in judging male sexual orientation. *Psychological Science, 22,* 881–886.

Rupp, H. A., & Wallen, K. (2008). Sex differences in response to visual sexual stimuli: A review. *Archives of Sexual Behavior, 37,* 206–218.

Rusbult, C. E., Johnson, D. J., & Morrow, G. D. (1986). Impact of couple patterns of problem solving on distress and nondistress in dating relationships. *Journal of Personality and Social Psychology, 50,* 744–753.

Rusbult, C. E., Martz, J. M., & Agnew, C. R. (1998). The investment model scale: Measuring commitment level, satisfaction level, quality of alternatives, and investment size. *Personal Relationships, 5,* 357–391.

Rusbult, C. E., Morrow, G. D., & Johnson, D. J. (1987). Self-esteem and problem-solving behaviour in close relationships. *British Journal of Social Psychology, 26,* 293–303.

Rusbult, C. E., Olsen, N., Davis, J. L., & Hannon, P. A. (2001). Commitment and relationship maintenance mechanisms. In J. Harvey & A. Wenzel (Eds.), *Close romantic relationships: Maintenance and enhancement.* Mahwah, NJ: Erlbaum.

Rushton, J. P., & Campbell, A. C. (1977). Modeling, vicarious reinforcement and extraversion on blood donating in adults: Immediate and long-term effects. *European Journal of Social Psychology, 7,* 297–306.

Rushton, J. P. (1991). Is altruism innate? *Psychological Inquiry, 2,* 141–143.

Russell, A. M. T., Monds, L., Hing, N., Kroll, J., Russell, A. M., & Thorne, H. B. (2023). Social associations and alcohol consumption in an Australian community sample: An egocentric social network analysis. *Psychology of Addictive Behaviors.*

Russell, G. W. (1983). Psychological issues in sports aggression. In J. H. Goldstein (Ed.), *Sports violence.* New York: Springer-Verlag.

Russell, K. J., & Hand, C. J. (2017). Rape myth acceptance, victim blame attribution and just world beliefs: A rapid evidence assessment. *Aggression and Violent Behavior, 37,* 153–160.

Russell, N. J. C. (2011). Milgram's obedience to authority experiments: Origins and early evolution. *British Journal of Social Psychology, 50,* 140–162.

Russo, F. (2018, January). The toxic well of loneliness. *Scientific American,* pp. 64–69.

Ruva, C. L., & Coy, A. E. (2020). Your bias is rubbing off on me: The impact of pretrial publicity and jury type on guilt decisions, trial evidence interpretation, and impression formation. *Psychology, Public Policy, and Law, 26,* 22–35.

Ruva, C. L., & Guenther, C. C. (2015). From the shadows into the light: How pretrial publicity and deliberation affect mock jurors' decisions, impressions, and memory. *Law and Human Behavior, 39,* 294–310.

Ruva, C. L., & Guenther, C. C. (2017). Keep your bias to yourself: How deliberating with differently biased others affects mock-jurors' guilt decisions, perceptions of the defendant, memories, and evidence interpretation. *Law and Human Behavior, 41,* 478–493.

Ryan, R. (1999, February 2). Quoted by A. Kohn, In pursuit of affluence, at a high price. *The New York Times.* https://www.nytimes.com/1999/02/02/health/in-pursuit-of-affluence-at-a-high-price.html

Rydell, R. J., McConnell, A. R., & Beilock, S. L. (2009). Multiple social identities and stereotype threat: Imbalance, accessibility, and working memory. *Journal of Personality and Social Psychology, 96,* 949–966.

Rydell, R. J., Rydell, M. T., & Boucher, K. L. (2010). The effect of negative performance stereotypes on learning. *Journal of Personality and Social Psychology, 99,* 883–896.

Ryff, C. D., & Singer, B. (2000). Interpersonal flourishing: A positive health agenda for the new millennium. *Personality and Social Psychology Review, 4,* 30–44.

Saad, L. (2019, March 25). Americans as concerned as ever about global warming. *Gallup.* https://news.gallup.com/poll/248027/americans-concerned-ever-global-warming.aspx

Sabini, J., & Silver, M. (1982). *Moralities of everyday life.* New York: Oxford University Press.

Sacchetti, M., & Guskin, E. (2017, June 17). In rural America, fewer immigrants and less tolerance. *The Washington Post.* https://www.washingtonpost.com

Sachdeva, S., Iliev, R., and Medin, D. L. (2009). Sinning saints and saintly sinners: The paradox of moral self-regulation. *Psychological Science, 20,* 523–528.

Sacks, C. H., & Bugental, D. P. (1987). Attributions as moderators of affective and behavioral responses to social failure. *Journal of Personality and Social Psychology, 53,* 939–947.

Sadler, M. S., Correll, J., Park, B., & Judd, C. M. (2012). The world is not Black and White: Racial bias in the decision to shoot in a multiethnic context. *Journal of Social Issues, 68,* 286–313.

Safer, M. A., Bonanno, G. A., & Field, N. P. (2001). It was never that bad: Biased recall of grief and long-term adjustment to the death of a spouse. *Memory, 9,* 195–204.

Safer, M. A., Murphy, R. P., Wise, R. A., Bussey, L., Millett, C., & Holfeld, B. (2016). Educating jurors about eyewitness testimony in criminal cases with circumstantial and forensic evidence. *International Journal of Law and Psychiatry, 47,* 86–92.

Sagarin, B. J., Cialdini, R. B., Rice, W. E., & Serna, S. B. (2002). Dispelling the illusion of invulnerability: The motivations and mechanisms of resistance to persuasion. *Journal of Personality and Social Psychology, 83,* 526–541.

Sagarin, B. J., Rhoads, K. v. L., & Cialdini, R. B. (1998). Deceiver's distrust: Denigration as a consequence of undiscovered deception. *Personality and Social Psychology Bulletin, 24,* 1167–1176.

Sageman, M. (2004). *Understanding terror networks.* Philadelphia: University of Pennsylvania Press.

Said, C. P., & Todorov, A. (2011). A statistical model of facial attractiveness. *Psychological Science, 22,* 1183–1190.

Saks, M. J., & Hastie, R. (1978). *Social psychology in court* (p. 68). New York: Van Nostrand Reinhold.

Saks, M. J., & Marti, M. W. (1997). A meta-analysis of the effects of jury size. *Law and Human Behavior, 21,* 451–467.

Saks, M. J. (1974). Ignorance of science is no excuse. *Trial, 10*(6), 18–20.

Saks, M. J. (1996). The smaller the jury, the greater the unpredictability. *Judicature, 79,* 263–265.

Saks, M. J. (1998). What do jury experiments tell us about how juries (should) make decisions? *Southern California Interdisciplinary Law Journal, 6,* 1–53.

Saleem, M., Prot, S., Anderson, C. A., & Lemieux, A. F. (2017). Exposure to Muslims in media and support for public policies harming Muslims. *Communication Research, 44,* 841–869.

Salganik, M. J., Dodds, P. S., & Watts, D. J. (2006). Experimental study of inequality and unpredictability in an artificial cultural market. *Science, 311,* 854–856.

Salk, R. H., Hyde, J. S., & Abramson, L. Y. (2017). Gender differences in depression in representative national samples: Meta-analyses of diagnoses and symptoms. *Psychological Bulletin, 143,* 783–822.

Salman, J., Le Coz, E., & Johnson, E. (2016). Florida's broken sentencing system. *Sarasota Herald-Tribune.* http://projects.heraldtribune.com/bias/sentencing/

Salmela-Aro, K., & Nurmi, J-E. (2007). Self-esteem during university studies predicts career characteristics 10 years later. *Journal of Vocational Behavior, 70,* 463–477.

Salmivalli, C. (2009). Bullying and the peer group: A review. *Aggression and Violent Behavior, 15,* 112–120.

Salomon, E., Preston, J. L., & Tannenbaum, M. B. (2017). Climate change helplessness and the (de)moralization of individual energy behavior. *Journal of Experimental Psychology: Applied, 23,* 15–28.

Salovey, P., Mayer, J. D., & Rosenhan, D. L. (1991). Mood and healing: Mood as a motivator of helping and helping as a regulator of mood. In M. S. Clark (Ed.), *Prosocial behavior.* Newbury Park, CA: Sage.

Salvatore, J., Kuo, S. I., Steele, R. D., Simpson, J. A., & Collins, W. A. (2011). Recovering from conflict in romantic relationships: A developmental perspective. *Psychological Science, 22,* 376–383.

SAMHSA. (2023). *Key substance use and mental health indicators in the United States: Results from the 2022 National Survey on Drug Use and Health.* Washington, DC: Author.

Sanchez, C. A. (2012). Enhancing visiospatial performance through video game training to increase learning in visiospatial science domains. *Psychonomic Bulletin & Review, 19,* 58–65.

Sanchez, C., Jaguan, D., Shaikh, S., McKenney, M., & Elkbuli, A. (2020). A systematic review of the causes and prevention strategies in reducing gun violence in the United States. *American Journal of Emergency Medicine, 38*(10), 2169–2178.

Sanchez, D. T., Chaney, K. E., Manuel, S. K., Wilton, L. S., & Remedios, J. D. (2017). Stigma by prejudice transfer: Racism threatens white women and sexism threatens men of color. *Psychological Science, 28,* 445–461.

Sande, G. N., Goethals, G. R., & Radloff, C. E. (1988). Perceiving one's own traits and others': The multifaceted self. *Journal of Personality and Social Psychology, 54,* 13–20.

Sanders, G. S. (1981a). Driven by distraction: An integrative review of social facilitation and theory and research. *Journal of Experimental Social Psychology, 17,* 227–251.

Sanders, G. S. (1981b). Toward a comprehensive account of social facilitation: Distraction/conflict does not mean theoretical conflict. *Journal of Experimental Social Psychology, 17,* 262–265.

Sanders, G. S., Baron, R. S., & Moore, D. L. (1978). Distraction and social comparison as mediators of social facilitation effects. *Journal of Experimental Social Psychology, 14,* 291–303.

Sanderson, C. A., & Cantor, N. (2001). The association of intimacy goals and marital satisfaction: A test of four mediational hypotheses. *Personality and Social Psychology Bulletin, 27,* 1567–1577.

Sani, F., Herrera, M., Wakefield, J. R. H., Boroch, O., & Gulyas, C. (2012). Comparing social contact and group identification as predictors of mental health. *British Journal of Social Psychology, 51,* 781–790.

Sanislow, C. A., III, Perkins, D. V., & Balogh, D. W. (1989). Mood induction, interpersonal perceptions, and rejection in the roommates of depressed, nondepressed-disturbed, and normal college students. *Journal of Social and Clinical Psychology, 8,* 345–358.

Sanitioso, R., Kunda, Z., & Fong, G. T. (1990). Motivated recruitment of autobiographical memories. *Journal of Personality and Social Psychology, 59,* 229–241.

Santaella-Tenorio, J., Cerda, M., Villaveces, A., & Galea, S. (2016). What do we know about the association between firearm legislation and firearm-related injuries? *Epidemiologic Reviews, 38,* 140–157.

Santos, A., Meyer-Lindenberg, A., & Deruelle, C. (2010). Absence of racial, but not gender, stereotyping in Williams syndrome children. *Current Biology, 20,* R307–R308.

Santos, H. C., Varnum, M. E. W., & Grossman, I. (2017). Global increases in individualism. *Psychological Science, 28*(9), 1228–1239.

Sanz, V. (2017). No way out of the binary: A critical history of the scientific production of sex. *Signs, 43,* 1–27.

Sapadin, L. A. (1988). Friendship and gender: Perspectives of professional men and women. *Journal of Social and Personal Relationships, 5,* 387–403.

Sapolsky, R. (2005, December). Sick of poverty. *Scientific American,* pp. 93–99.

Sargent, R. H., & Newman, L. S. (2021). Pluralistic ignorance research in psychology: A scoping review of topic and method variation and directions for future research. *Review of General Psychology, 25,* 163–184.

Sarnoff, I., & Sarnoff, S. (1989). *Love-centered marriage in a self-centered world.* New York: Schocken Books.

Sar, S., & Rodriguez, L. (2019). The influence of mood and information processing strategies on recall, persuasion, and intention to get a flu vaccine. *Health Marketing Quarterly, 36,* 17–34.

Sartre, J-P. (1946/1948). *Anti-Semite and Jew.* New York: Schocken Books.

Sartre, J.-P. (1946). *No exit and three other plays.* Stuart Gilbert.

Sasaki, J. Y., & Kim, H. S. (2011). At the intersection of culture and religion: A cultural analysis of religion's implications for secondary control and social affiliation. *Journal of Personality and Social Psychology, 101,* 401–414.

Sassenberg, K., & Ditrich, L. (2019). Research in social psychology changed between 2011 and 2016: Larger sample sizes, more self-report measures, and more online studies. *Advances in Methods and Practices in Psychological Science, 2,* 107–114.

Sassenberg, K., Moskowitz, G. B., Jacoby, J., & Hansen, N. (2007). The carry-over effect of competition: The impact of competition on prejudice towards uninvolved outgroups. *Journal of Experimental Social Psychology, 43,* 529–538.

Satherley, N., Yogeeswaran, K., Osborne, D., & Sibley, C. G. (2018). If they say "yes," we say "no": Partisan cues increase polarization over national symbols. *Psychological Science, 29,* 1996–2009.

Sato, K. (1987). Distribution of the cost of maintaining common resources. *Journal of Experimental Social Psychology, 23,* 19–31.

Saucier, D. A., & Miller, C. T. (2003). The persuasiveness of racial arguments as a subtle measure of racism. *Personality and Social Psychology Bulletin, 29,* 1303–1315.

Saucier, D. A., Miller, C. T., & Doucet, N. (2005). Differences in helping Whites and Blacks: A meta-analysis. *Personality and Social Psychology Review, 9,* 2–16.

Saucier, G., Akers, L. G., Shen-Miller, S., Knežević, G., & Stankov, L. (2009). Patterns of thinking in militant extremism. *Perspectives on Psychological Science, 4,* 256–271.

Saucier, G., Thalmayer, A. G., & Bel-Bahar, T. S. (2014). Human attribute concepts: Relative ubiquity across twelve mutually isolated languages. *Journal of Personality and Social Psychology, 107,* 199–216.

Sauer, J., Brewer, N., Zweck, T., & Weber, N. (2010). The effect of retention interval on the confidence–accuracy relationship for eyewitness identification. *Law and Human Behavior, 34,* 337–347.

Savitsky, K., & Gilovich, T. (2003). The illusion of transparency and the alleviation of speech anxiety. *Journal of Experimental Social Psychology, 39,* 618–625.

Savitsky, K., Epley, N., & Gilovich, T. (2001). Do others judge us as harshly as we think? Overestimating the impact of our failures, shortcomings, and mishaps. *Journal of Personality and Social Psychology, 81,* 44–56.

Savitsky, K., Van Voven, L., Epley, N., & Wright, W. M. (2005). The unpacking effect in allocations of responsibility for group tasks. *Journal of Experimental Social Psychology, 41,* 447–457.

Sawyer, J., & Gampa, A. (2018). Implicit and explicit racial attitudes changed during Black Lives Matter. *Personality and Social Psychology Bulletin, 44,* 1039–1059.

Sax, L. J., Lindholm, J. A., Astin, A. W., Korn, W. S., & Mahoney, K. M. (2002). *The American freshman: National norms for fall, 2002.* Los Angeles: Cooperative Institutional Research Program, UCLA.

Sbarra, D. A., Law, R. W., & Portley, R. M. (2011). Divorce and death: A meta-analysis and research agenda for clinical, social, and health psychology. *Perspectives on Psychological Science, 6,* 454–474.

Scarr, S. (1988). Race and gender as psychological variables: Social and ethical issues. *American Psychologist, 43,* 56–59.

Schachter, S., & Singer, J. E. (1962). Cognitive, social and physiological determinants of emotional state. *Psychological Review, 69,* 379–399.

Schachter, S. (1951). Deviation, rejection and communication. *Journal of Abnormal and Social Psychology, 46,* 190–207.

Schacter, D. L., & Loftus, E. F. (2013). Memory and law: What can cognitive neuroscience contribute? *Nature Neuroscience, 16,* 119–123.

Schafer, R. B., & Keith, P. M. (1980). Equity and depression among married couples. *Social Psychology Quarterly, 43,* 430–435.

Schaffner, P. E. (1985). Specious learning about reward and punishment. *Journal of Personality and Social Psychology, 48,* 1377–1386.

Schaffner, P. E., Wandersman, A., & Stang, D. (1981). Candidate name exposure and voting: Two field studies. *Basic and Applied Social Psychology, 2,* 195–203.

Schaller, M., & Cialdini, R. B. (1988). The economics of empathic helping: Support for a mood management motive. *Journal of Experimental Social Psychology, 24,* 163–181.

Scheier, M. F., Swanson, J. D., Barlow, M. A., Greenhouse, J. B., Wrosch, C., & Tindle, H. A. (2021). Optimism versus pessimism as predictors of physical health: A comprehensive reanalysis of dispositional optimism research. *American Psychologist, 76,* 529–548.

Scherr, K. C., Redlich, A. D., & Kassin, S. M. (2020). Cumulative disadvantage: A psychological framework for understanding how innocence can lead to confession, wrongful conviction, and beyond. *Perspectives on Psychological Science, 15,* 353–383.

Schiffenbauer, A., & Schiavo, R. S. (1976). Physical distance and attraction: An intensification effect. *Journal of Experimental Social Psychology, 12,* 274–282.

Schimmack, U. (2021). Invalid Claims About the Validity of Implicit Association Tests by Prisoners of the Implicit Social-Cognition Paradigm. *Perspectives on Psychological Science, 16,* 435–442.

Schirmer, A., The, K., Wang, S., Vijayakumar, R., Ching, A., Nithianantham, D., Escoffier, N., & Cheok, A. (2011). Squeeze me, but don't tease me: Human and mechanical touch enhance visual attention and emotion discrimination. *Social Neuroscience, 6,* 219–230.

Schkade, D. A., & Kahneman, D. (1998). Does living in California make people happy? A focusing illusion in judgments of life satisfaction. *Psychological Science, 9,* 340–346.

Schkade, D. A., & Sunstein, C. R. (2003, June 11). Judging by where you sit. *The New York Times.* https://www.nytimes.com/2003/06/11/opinion/judging-by-where-you-sit.html

Schkade, D. A., Sunstein, C. R., & Hastie, R. (2007). What happened on deliberation day? *California Law Review, 95,* 915–940.

Schlenker, B. R., & Leary, M. R. (1982). Social anxiety and self-presentation: A conceptualization and model. *Psychological Bulletin, 92,* 641–669.

Schlenker, B. R., & Leary, M. R. (1985). Social anxiety and communication about the self. *Journal of Language and Social Psychology, 4,* 171–192.

Schlenker, B. R., & Weigold, M. F. (1992). Interpersonal processes involving impression regulation and management. *Annual Review of Psychology, 43,* 133–168.

Schlesinger, A., Jr. (1949). The statistical soldier. *Partisan Review, 16,* 852–856.

Schlesinger, A. M., Jr. (1965). *A thousand days.* Boston: Houghton Mifflin. Cited by I. L. Janis (1972) in *Victims of groupthink.* Boston: Houghton Mifflin.

Schmader, T., Johns, M., & Forbes, C. (2008). An integrated process model of stereotype threat effects on performance. *Psychological Review, 115,* 336–356.

Schmelz, M., Grueneisen, S., Kabalak, A., Jost, J., & Tomasello, M. (2018). Chimpanzees return favors at a personal cost. *PNAS, 114,* 7462–7467.

Schmiege, S. J., Klein, W. M. P., & Bryan, A. D. (2010). The effect of peer comparison information in the context of expert recommendations on risk perceptions and subsequent behavior. *European Journal of Social Psychology, 40,* 746–759.

Schmitt, D. P., & 12 others. (2004). Patterns and universals of adult romantic attachment across 62 cultural regions: Are models of self and of other pancultural constructs? *Journal of Cross-Cultural Psychology, 35,* 367–402.

Schmitt, D. P., & Allik, J. (2005). Simultaneous administration of the Rosenberg Self-Esteem Scale in 53 nations: Exploring the universal and culture-specific features of global self-esteem. *Journal of Personality and Social Psychology, 89,* 623–642.

Schmitt, D. P. (2003). Universal sex differences in the desire for sexual variety; tests from 52 nations, 6 continents, and 13 islands. *Journal of Personality and Social Psychology, 85,* 85–104.

Schmitt, D. P. (2005). Sociosexuality from Argentina to Zimbabwe: A 48-nation study of sex, culture, and strategies of human mating. *Behavioral and Brain Sciences, 28,* 247–311.

Schmitt, D. P. (2007). Sexual strategies across sexual orientations: How personality traits and culture relate to sociosexuality among gays, lesbians, bisexuals, and heterosexuals. *Journal of Psychology and Human Sexuality, 18,* 183–214.

Schmitt, D. P., Long, A. E., McPhearson, A., O'Brien, K., Remmert, B., & Shah, S. H. (2016). Personality and gender differences in global perspective. *International Journal of Psychology, 52*(1), 45–56.

Schmitt, D. P., Realo, A., Voracek, M., & Allik, J. (2008). Why can't a man be more like a woman? Sex differences in Big Five personality traits across 55 cultures. *Journal of Personality and Social Psychology, 94,* 168–182.

Schmitt, M. T., Branscombe, N. R., Postmes, T., & Garcia, A. (2014). The consequences of perceived discrimination for psychological well-being: A meta-analytic review. *Psychological Bulletin, 140,* 921–948.

Schnall, S., Roper, J., & Fessler, D. M. T. (2010). Elevation leads to altruistic behavior. *Psychological Science, 21,* 315–320.

Schneider, J., Rosman, T., Kelava, A., & Merk, S. (2022). Do open-science badges increase trust in scientists among undergraduates, scientists, and the public? *Psychological Science, 33,* 1588–1604.

Schneider, M. E., Major, B., Luhtanen, R., & Crocker, J. (1996). Social stigma and the potential costs of assumptive help. *Personality and Social Psychology Bulletin, 22,* 201–209.

Schoeler, T., Duncan, L., Cecil, C. M., Ploubidis, G. B., & Pingault, J.-B. (2018). Quasi-experimental evidence on short- and long-term consequences of bullying victimization: A meta-analysis. *Psychological Bulletin, 144,* 1229–1246.

Schofield, J. (1982). *Black and white in school: Trust, tension, or tolerance?* New York: Praeger.

Schofield, J. W. (1986). Causes and consequences of the colorblind perspective. In J. F. Dovidio & S. L. Gaertner (Eds.), *Prejudice, discrimination, and racism.* Orlando, FL: Academic Press.

Scholl, A., & Sassenberg, K. (2014). Where could we stand if I had . . . ? How social power impacts counterfactual thinking after failure. *Journal of Experimental Social Psychology, 53,* 51–61.

Scholten, S., Velten, J., & Margraf, J. (2018). Mental distress and perceived wealth, justice and freedom across eight countries: The invisible power of the macrosystem. *PLOS ONE, 13*(5), e0194642.

Schroeder, D. A., Dovidio, J. F., Sibicky, M. E., Matthews, L. L., & Allen, J. L. (1988). Empathic concern and helping behavior: Egoism or altruism: *Journal of Experimental Social Psychology, 24,* 333–353.

Schroeder, J., & Risen, J. L. (2014). Befriending the enemy: Outgroup friendship longitudinally predicts intergroup attitudes in a coexistence program for Israelis and Palestinians. *Group Processes and Intergroup Relations, 6,* 55–75.

Schroeder, J., Caruso, E. M., & Epley, N. (2016). Many hands make overlooked work: Over-claiming of responsibility increases with group size. *Journal of Experimental Psychology: Applied, 22,* 238–246.

Schroeder, J., Kardas, M., & Epley, N. (2017). The humanizing voice: Speech reveals, and text conceals, a more thoughtful mind in the midst of disagreement. *Psychological Science, 28*(12), 1745–1762.

Schuldt, J. P., Konrath, S. H., & Schwarz, N. (2011). "Global warming" or "climate change"? *Public Opinion Quarterly, 75,* 115–124.

Schultz, P. W., Nolan, J. M., Cialdini, R. B., Goldstein, N. J., & Griskevicius, V. (2018). The constructive, destructive, and reconstructive power of social norms: Reprise. *Perspectives on Psychological Science, 13,* 249–254.

Schulz-Hardt, S., Frey, D., Luthgens, C., & Moscovici, S. (2000). Biased information search in group decision making. *Journal of Personality and Social Psychology, 78,* 655–669.

Schulz, J. W., & Pruitt, D. G. (1978). The effects of mutual concern on joint welfare. *Journal of Experimental Social Psychology, 14,* 480–492.

Schuman, H., & Kalton, G. (1985). Survey methods. In G. Lindzey & E. Aronson (Eds.), *Handbook of Social Psychology* (Vol. 1). Hillsdale, NJ: Erlbaum.

Schuman, H., & Scott, J. (1989). Generations and collective memories. *American Sociological Review, 54,* 359–381.

Schumann, K., McGregor, I., Nash, K. A., & Ross, M. (2014). Religious magnanimity: Reminding people of their religious belief system reduces hostility after threat. *Journal of Personality and Social Psychology, 107,* 432–453.

Schwartz, H. A., Eichstaedt, J. C., Kern, M. L., Dziurzynski, L., Ramones, S. M., Agarwal, M., Shah, A., Kosinski, M., Stillwell, D., Seligman, M. E. P., & Ungar, L. H. (2013). Personality, gender, and age in the language of social media: The open-vocabulary approach. *PLOS ONE, 8*(9), e73791.

Schwartz, J. (2020, May 19). Americans see climate as a concern, even amid coronavirus crisis. *The New York Times.* https://www.nytimes.com/2020/05/19/climate/coronavirus-climate-change-survey.html

Schwartz, S. H., & Gottlieb, A. (1981). Participants' post-experimental reactions and the ethics of bystander research. *Journal of Experimental Social Psychology, 17,* 396–407.

Schwartz, S. H., & Rubel, T. (2005). Sex differences in value priorities: Cross-cultural and multimethod studies. *Journal of Personality and Social Psychology, 89,* 1010–1028.

Schwartz, S. H. (1975). The justice of need and the activation of humanitarian norms. *Journal of Social Issues, 31*(3), 111–136.

Schwarz, N., Sanna, L. J., Skurnik, I., & Yoon, C. (2007). Metacognitive experiences and the intricacies of setting people straight: Implications for debiasing and public information campaigns. *Advances in Experimental Social Psychology, 39,* 127–161.

Schwarz, S., & Baßfeld, L. (2019). Do men help only beautiful women in social networks? *Current Psychology: A Journal for Diverse Perspectives on Diverse Psychological Issues, 38,* 965–976.

Schwinger, M., Trautner, M., Pütz, N., Fabianek, S., Lemmer, G., Lauermann, F., & Wirthwein, L. (2022). Why do students use strategies that hurt their chances of academic success? A meta-analysis of antecedents of academic self-handicapping. *Journal of Educational Psychology, 114,* 576–596.

Schwinger, M., Wirthwein, L., Lemmer, G., & Steinmayr, R. (2014). Academic self-handicapping and achievement: A meta-analysis. *Journal of Educational Psychology, 106*(3), 744–761.

Schäfer, M., Haun, D. B. M., & Tomasello, M. (2015). Fair is not fair everywhere. *Psychological Science, 26,* 1252–1260.

Scobey-Thal, J. (2014, June 30). Third gender: A short history. *Foreign Policy.* https://foreignpolicy.com/2014/06/30/third-gender-a-short-history/

Scoboria, A., Wade, K. A., Lindsay, D. S., Azad, T., Strange, D., Ost, J., & Hyman, I. E. (2017). A mega-analysis of memory reports from eight peer-reviewed false memory implantation studies. *Memory, 25,* 146–163

Scorza, P., Duarte, C. S., Lee, S., Wu, H., Posner, J., Baccarelli, A., & Monk, C. (2023). Epigenetic intergenerational transmission: Mothers' adverse childhood experiences and dna methylation. *Journal of the American Academy of Child & Adolescent Psychiatry.*

Scott, B., Amel, E. L., Kroger, S. M., & Manning, C. (2015). *Psychology for sustainability* (4th ed.). New York: Psychology Press.

Sculley, J., & Watkins, C. D. (2022). The great porn experiment V2.0: Sexual arousal reduces the salience of familiar women when heterosexual men judge their attractiveness. *Archives of Sexual Behavior, 51,* 3071–3082.

Sczesny, S., & Kaufmann, M. C. (2018). Self-presentation in online professional networks: Men's higher and women's lower facial prominence in self-created profile images. *Frontiers in Psychology, 8.*

Seabrook, R. C., Ward, L. M., & Giaccardi, S. (2019). Less than human? Media use, objectification of women, and men's acceptance of sexual aggression. *Psychology of Violence, 9,* 536–545.

Sears, D. O. (1979). *Life stage effects upon attitude change, especially among the elderly.* Manuscript prepared for Workshop on the Elderly of the Future, Committee on Aging, National Research Council, Annapolis, MD, May 3–5.

Sears, D. O. (1986). College sophomores in the laboratory: Influences of a narrow data base on social psychology's view of human nature. *Journal of Personality and Social Psychology, 51,* 515–530.

Sebalo, I., Ball, L. J., Marsh, J. E., Morley, A. M., Richardson, B. H., Taylor, P. J., & Threadgold, E. (2023). Conspiracy theories: Why they are believed and how they can be challenged. *Journal of Cognitive Psychology, 35,* 383–400.

Sedikides, C. (1993). Assessment, enhancement, and verification determinants of the self-evaluation process. *Journal of Personality and Social Psychology, 65,* 317–338.

Sedikides, C., Gaertner, L., & Toguchi, Y. (2003). Pancultural self-enhancement. *Journal of Personality and Social Psychology, 84,* 60–79.

Sedikides, C., Gaertner, L., & Vevea, J. L. (2005). Pancultural self-enhancement reloaded: A meta-analytic reply to Heine (2005). *Journal of Personality and Social Psychology, 89,* 539–551.

Segal-Caspi, L., Roccas, S., & Sagiv, L. (2012). Don't judge a book by its cover, revisited: Perceived and reported traits and values of attractive women. *Psychological Science, 23,* 1112–1116.

Segall, M. H., Dasen, P. R., Berry, J. W., & Poortinga, Y. H. (1990). *Human behavior in global perspective: An introduction to cross-cultural psychology.* New York: Pergamon.

Segal, N. L., & Hershberger, S. L. (1999). Cooperation and competition between twins: Findings from a Prisoner's Dilemma game. *Evolution and Human Behavior, 20,* 29–51.

Segal, N. L. (1984). Cooperation, competition, and altruism within twin sets: A reappraisal. *Ethology and Sociobiology, 5,* 163–177.

Segerstrom, S., & Miller, G. E. (2004). Psychological stress and the human immune system: A meta-analytic study of 30 years of inquiry. *Psychological Bulletin, 130,* 601–630.

Segerstrom, S. C. (2001). Optimism and attentional bias for negative and positive stimuli. *Personality and Social Psychology Bulletin, 27,* 1334–1343.

Segerstrom, S. C., McCarthy, W. J., Caskey, N. H., Gross, T. M., & Jarvik, M. E. (1993). Optimistic bias among cigarette smokers. *Journal of Applied Social Psychology, 23,* 1606–1618.

Seibt, B., & Forster, J. (2004). Stereotype threat and performance: How self-stereotypes influence processing by inducing regulatory foci. *Journal of Personality and Social Psychology, 87*(1), 38–56.

Seidel, E., Eickhoff, S. B., Kellermann, T., Schneider, F., Gur, R. C., Habel, U., & Birgit, D. (2010). Who is to blame? Neural correlates of causal attribution in social situations. *Social Neuroscience, 5,* 335–350.

Selby, J. W., Calhoun, L. G., & Brock, T. A. (1977). Sex differences in the social perception of rape victims. *Personality and Social Psychology Bulletin, 3,* 412–415.

Seligman, M. (1994). *What you can change and what you can't.* New York: Knopf.

Seligman, M. E. P. (1991). *Learned optimism* (p. 78). New York: Knopf.

Seligman, M. E. P. (1998). The prediction and prevention of depression. In D. K. Routh & R. J. DeRubeis (Eds.), *The science of clinical psychology: Accomplishments and future directions.* Washington, DC: American Psychological Association.

Seligman, M. E. P. (2002). *Authentic happiness: Using the new positive psychology to realize your potential for lasting fulfillment.* New York: Free Press.

Sendén, M., Lindholm, T., & Sikström, S. (2014). Biases in news media as reflected by personal pronouns in evaluative contexts. *Social Psychology, 45,* 103–111.

Sen, S., & Lerman, D. (2007). Why are you telling me this? An examination into negative consumer reviews on the Web. *Journal of Interactive Marketing, 21,* 76–94.

Sentyrz, S. M., & Bushman, B. J. (1998). Mirror, mirror, on the wall, who's the thinnest one of all? Effects of self-awareness on consumption of fatty, reduced-fat, and fat-free products. *Journal of Applied Psychology, 83,* 944–949.

Sergent, K., & Stajkovic, A. D. (2020). Women's leadership is associated with fewer deaths during the COVID-19 crisis: Quantitative and qualitative analyses of United States governors. *Journal of Applied Psychology, 105,* 771–783.

Sezer, O., Gino, F., & Norton, M. I. (2018). Humblebragging: A distinct–and ineffective–self-presentation strategy. *Journal of Personality and Social Psychology, 114*(1), 52–74.

Shachnai, R., Kushnir, T., & Bian, L. (2022). Walking in her shoes: Pretending to be a female role model increases young girls' persistence in science. *Psychological Science, 33,* 1818–1827.

Shaffer, D. R., Pegalis, L. J., & Bazzini, D. G. (1996). When boy meets girls (revisited): Gender, gender-role orientation, and prospect of future interaction as determinants of self-disclosure among same- and opposite-sex acquaintances. *Personality and Social Psychology Bulletin, 22,* 495–506.

Shah, A. K., & Oppenheimer, D. M. (2008). Heuristics made easy: An effort-reduction framework. *Psychological Bulletin, 134,* 207–222.

Shakya, H. B., & Christakis, N. A. (2017). Association of Facebook use with compromised well-being: A longitudinal study. *American Journal of Epidemiology, 185,* 203–211.

Shapiro, D. L. (2010). Relational identity theory: A systematic approach for transforming the emotional dimension of conflict. *American Psychologist, 65,* 634–645.

Shariff, A. F., Willard, A. K., Andersen, T., & Norenzayan, A. (2016). Religious priming: A meta-analysis with a focus on prosociality. *Personality and Social Psychology Review, 20,* 27–48.

Sharma, A., Sanghvi, K., & Churi, P. (2022). The impact of Instagram on young adults' social comparison, colourism and mental health: Indian perspective. *International Journal of Information Management Data Insights, 2,* 100057.

Sharot, T., Fleming, S. M., Yu, X., Koster, R., & Dolan, R. J. (2012). Is choice-induced preference change long lasting? *Psychological Science, 23,* 1123–1129.

Sharot, T., Velasquez, C. M., & Dolan, R. J. (2010). Do decisions shape preference? Evidence from blind chance. *Psychological Science, 21,* 1231–1235.

Sharpe, D., & Faye, C. (2009). A second look at debriefing practices: Madness in our method? *Ethics and Behavior, 19,* 432–447.

Shaver, P. R., & Hazan, C. (1993). Adult romantic attachment: Theory and evidence. In D. Perlman & W. Jones (Eds.), *Advances in personal relationships* (Vol. 4). Greenwich, CT: JAI.

Shaver, P. R., & Hazan, C. (1994). Attachment. In A. L. Weber & J. H. Harvey (Eds.), *Perspectives on close relationships.* Boston: Allyn & Bacon.

Shaver, P. R., & Mikulincer, M. (2011). An attachment-theory framework for conceptualizing interpersonal behavior. In L. M. Horowitz & S. Strack (Eds.), *Handbook of interpersonal psychology: Theory, research, assessment, and therapeutic interventions.* Hoboken, NJ: Wiley.

Shaw, J., & Porter, S. (2015). Constructing rich false memories of committing crime. *Psychological Science, 26,* 291–301.

Shaw, J. (2020). Do false memories look real? Evidence that people struggle to identify rich false memories of committing crime and other emotional events. *Frontiers in Psychology, 11,* 650.

Shaw, J. S., III. (1996). Increases in eyewitness confidence resulting from postevent questioning. *Journal of Experimental Psychology: Applied, 2,* 126–146.

Shaw, M. E. (1981). *Group dynamics: The psychology of small group behavior.* New York: McGraw Hill.

Shayo, M., & Zussman, A. (2011). Judicial ingroup bias in the shadow of terrorism. *Quarterly Journal of Economics, 126,* 1447–1484.

Shedd, D., & Strandner, I. (2022, September 7). Waging psychological war against Russia. *Politico.*

Sheehan, B. E., & Lau-Barraco, C. (2019). A daily diary investigation of self-reported alcohol-related direct and indirect aggression. *Aggressive Behavior, 45,* 463–471.

Sheldon, K. M., & Niemiec, C. P. (2006). It's not just the amount that counts: Balanced need satisfaction also affects well-being. *Journal of Personality and Social Psychology, 91,* 331–341.

Sheldon, K. M., Elliot, A. J., Youngmee, K., & Kasser, T. (2001). What is satisfying about satisfying events? Testing 10 candidate psychological needs. *Journal of Personality and Social Psychology, 80,* 325–339.

Sheldon, K. M., Ryan, R. M., Deci, E. L., & Kasser, T. (2004). The independent effects of goal contents and motives on well-being: It's both what you pursue and why you pursue it. *Personality and Social Psychology Bulletin, 30,* 475–486.

Shell, R. M., & Eisenberg, N. (1992). A developmental model of recipients' reactions to aid. *Psychological Bulletin, 111,* 413–433.

Shelton, J. N., & Richeson, J. A. (2005). Intergroup contact and pluralistic ignorance. *Journal of Personality and Social Psychology, 88,* 91–107.

Shen, C., Sun, Q., Kim, T., Wolff, G., Ratan, R., & Williams, D. (2020). Viral vitriol: Predictors and contagion of online toxicity in World of Tanks. *Computers in Human Behavior, 108.*

Shen, H., Wan, F., & Wyer, R. S., Jr. (2011). Cross-cultural differences in the refusal to accept a small gift: The differential influence of reciprocity norms on Asians and North Americans. *Journal of Personality and Social Psychology, 100,* 271–281.

Sheppard, B. H., & Vidmar, N. (1980). Adversary pretrial procedures and testimonial evidence: Effects of lawyer's role and Machiavellianism. *Journal of Personality and Social Psychology, 39,* 320–322.

Sheppard, L. D. (2018). Gender Differences in Leadership Aspirations and Job and Life Attribute Preferences among U.S. Undergraduate Students. *Sex Roles, 79,* 565–577.

Shepperd, J. A. (2003). *Interpreting comparative risk judgments: Are people personally optimistic or interpersonally pessimistic?* Unpublished manuscript, University of Florida.

Shepperd, J. A., Arkin, R. M., & Slaughter, J. (1995). Constraints on excuse making: The deterring effects of shyness and anticipated retest. *Personality and Social Psychology Bulletin, 21,* 1061–1072.

Shepperd, J. A., Grace, J., Cole, L. J., & Klein, C. (2005). Anxiety and outcome predictions. *Personality and Social Psychology Bulletin, 31,* 267–275.

Shepperd, J. A., Klein, W. M. P., Waters, E. A., & Weinstein, N. D. (2013). Taking stock of unrealistic optimism. *Perspectives on Psychological Science, 8,* 395–411.

Shepperd, J. A., Waters, E., Weinstein, N. D., & Klein, W. M. P. (2015). A primer on unrealistic optimism. *Current Directions in Psychological Science, 24,* 232–237.

Shergill, S. S., Bays, P. M., Frith, C. D., & Wolpert, D. M. (2003). Two eyes for an eye: The neuroscience of force escalation. *Science, 301,* 187.

Sherif, M., & Sherif, C. W. (1969). *Social psychology.* New York: Harper & Row.

Sherif, M. (1935). A study of some social factors in perception. *Archives of Psychology, 187,* 60.

Sherif, M. (1937). An experimental approach to the study of attitudes. *Sociometry, 1,* 90–98.

Sherif, M. (1966). *In common predicament: Social psychology of intergroup conflict and cooperation.* Boston: Houghton Mifflin.

Sherman, A., & Barokas, G. (2023). The effect of name letter on market prices: Field experiments on seller behavior. *Journal of Behavioral and Experimental Economics, 106,* 1–10.

Sherman, D. K., Hartson, K. A., Binning, K. R., Purdie-Vaughns, V., Garcia, J., Taborsky-Barba, S., Tomassetti, S., Nussbaum, A. D., & Cohen, G. L. (2013). Deflecting the trajectory and changing the narrative: How self-affirmation affects academic performance and motivation under identity threat. *Journal of Personality and Social Psychology, 104,* 591–618.

Sherman, J. W. (1996). Development and mental representation of stereotypes. *Journal of Personality and Social Psychology, 70,* 1126–1141.

Sherman, J. W., Kruschke, J. K., Sherman, S. J., Percy, E. J., Petrocelli, J. V., & Conrey, F. R. (2009). Attentional processes in stereotype formation: A common model for category accentuation and illusory correlation. *Journal of Personality and Social Psychology, 96,* 305–323.

Sherman, J. W., Lee, A. Y., Bessenoff, G. R., & Frost, L. A. (1998). Stereotype efficiency reconsidered: Encoding flexibility under cognitive load. *Journal of Personality and Social Psychology, 75,* 589–606.

Sherrill, A. M., & Bradel, L. T. (2017). Contact sport participation predicts instrumental aggression, not hostile aggression, within competition: Quasi-experimental evidence. *Journal of Aggression, Conflict and Peace Research, 9*(1), 50–57.

Shewach, O. R., Sackett, P. R., & Quint, S. (2019). Stereotype threat effects in settings with features likely versus unlikely in operational test settings: A meta-analysis. *Journal of Applied Psychology, 104*(12), 1514–1534.

Shih, M., Pittinsky, T. L., & Ambady, N. (1999). Stereotype susceptibility: Identity salience and shifts in quantitative performance. *Psychological Science, 10,* 80–83.

Shiller, R. (2005). *Irrational exuberance* (2nd ed.). New York: Crown.

Shin, H., & Park, S. W. (2021). Perception of self-handicapping behavior in the workplace: Not that great. *Current Psychology: A Journal for Diverse Perspectives on Diverse Psychological Issues, 40,* 910–918.

Shin, H., Dovidio, J. F., & Napier, J. L. (2013). Cultural differences in targets of stigmatization between individual- and group-oriented cultures. *Basic and Applied Social Psychology, 35,* 98–108.

Shin, J., Suh, E. M., Li, N. P., Eo, K., Chong, S. C., & Tsai, M.-H. (2019). Darling, get closer to me: Spatial proximity amplifies Interpersonal liking. *Personality and Social Psychology Bulletin, 45,* 300–309.

Shipman, P. (2003). We are all Africans. *American Scientist, 91,* 496–499.

Shirazi, T. N., Self, H., Rosenfield, K. A., Dawood, K., Welling, L. L. M., Cárdenas, R., Bailey, J. M., Balasubramanian, R., Delaney, A., Breedlove, S. M., & Puts, D. A. (2022). Low perinatal androgens predict recalled childhood gender nonconformity in men. *Psychological Science, 33,* 343–353.

Shi, Z., Malki, A., Abdel-Salam, A.-S. G., Liu, J., & Zayed, H. (2020). Association between soft drink consumption and aggressive behaviour among a quarter million adolescents from 64 countries based on the Global School-Based Student Health Survey (GSHS). *Nutrients, 12,* 694.

Shostak, M. (1981). *Nisa: The life and words of a !Kung woman.* Cambridge, MA: Harvard University Press.

Shotland, R. L., & Stebbins, C. A. (1983). Emergency and cost as determinants of helping behavior and the slow accumulation of social psychological knowledge. *Social Psychology Quarterly, 46,* 36–46.

Shotland, R. L., & Straw, M. K. (1976). Bystander response to an assault: When a man attacks a woman. *Journal of Personality and Social Psychology, 34,* 990–999.

Showers, C., & Ruben, C. (1987). *Distinguishing pessimism from depression: Negative expectations and positive coping mechanisms.* Paper presented at the American Psychological Association convention, New York, NY.

Shrauger, J. S. (1975). Responses to evaluation as a function of initial self-perceptions. *Psychological Bulletin, 82,* 581–596.

Shrestha, N. R., Deason, R. G., Cordaro, M., Howard, K., & Haskard-Zolnierek, K. (2023). Evaluating the relationship of empathic concern to college students' responses to the covid-19 pandemic. *Journal of American College Health.*

Shriver, E. R., Young, S. G., Hugenberg, K., Bernstein, M. J., & Lanter, J. R. (2008). Class, race, and the face: Social context modulates the cross-race effect in face recognition. *Personality and Social Psychology Bulletin, 34,* 260–274.

Shteynberg, G., Bramlett, J. M., Fles, E. H., & Cameron, J. (2016). The broadcast of shared attention and its impact on political persuasion. *Journal of Personality and Social Psychology, 111,* 665–673.

Sidanius, J., Pratto, F., & Bobo, L. (1994). Social dominance orientation and the political psychology of gender: A case of invariance? *Journal of Personality and Social Psychology, 67,* 998–1011.

Siegel, M., Ross, C. S., & King, C. (2013). The relationship between gun ownership and firearm homicide rates in the United States, 1981–2010. *American Journal of Public Health, 103,* 2098–2105.

Sieverding, M., Decker, S., & Zimmerman, F. (2010). Information about low participation in cancer screening demotivates other people. *Psychological Science, 21,* 941–943.

Sigall, H. (1970). Effects of competence and consensual validation on a communicator's liking for the audience. *Journal of Personality and Social Psychology, 16,* 252–258.

Sigurdson, J. F., Wallander, J., & Sund, A. M. (2014). Is involvement in school bullying associated with general health and psychosocial adjustment outcomes in adulthood? *Child Abuse & Neglect, 38,* 1607–1617.

Silke, A. (2003). Deindividuation, anonymity, and violence: Findings from Northern Ireland. *Journal of Social Psychology, 143,* 493–499.

Silk, J. B., Alberts, S. C., & Altmann, J. (2003). Social bonds of female baboons enhance infant survival. *Science, 302,* 1231–1234.

Silva, K., Bessa, J., & de Sousa, L. (2012). Auditory contagious yawning in domestic dogs (*canis familiaris*): First evidence for social modulation. *Animal Cognition, 15,* 721–724.

Silver, L., & Huang, C. (2022, December 5). Key facts about China's declining population. Pew Research Center.

Silver, M., & Geller, D. (1978). On the irrelevance of evil: The organization and individual action. *Journal of Social Issues, 34,* 125–136.

Silverman, A. M., & Cohen, G. L. (2014). Stereotypes as stumbling-blocks: how coping with stereotypes threat affects life outcomes for people with physical disabilities. *Personality and Social Psychology Bulletin, 40,* 1330–1340.

Silver, N. (2023, February 27). Tweet. https://twitter.com/NateSilver538/status/1630279409759289349?lang=en

Silvia, P. J. (2005). Deflecting reactance: The role of similarity in increasing compliance and reducing resistance. *Basic and Applied Social Psychology, 27,* 277–284.

Simard, P., Simard, V., Laverdiere, O., & Descoteaux, J. (2023). The relationship between narcissism and empathy. *Journal of Research in Personality,* 104329.

Simons, D. J., & Chabris, C. F. (2011). What people believe about how memory works: A representative survey of the U.S. population. *Plos One, 6,* e22757.

Simonsohn, U. (2011a). Spurious? Name similarity effects (implicit egotism) in marriage, job, and moving decisions. *Journal of Personality and Social Psychology, 101*(1), 1–24.

Simonsohn, U. (2011b). Spurious also? Name-similarity effects (implicit egotism) in employment decisions. *Psychological Science, 22,* 1087–1089.

Simonton, D. K. (1994). *Greatness: Who makes history and why.* New York: Guilford.

Simpson, J. A. (1987). The dissolution of romantic relationships: Factors involved in relationship stability and emotional distress. *Journal of Personality and Social Psychology, 53,* 683–692.

Simpson, J. A., Gangestad, S. W., & Lerma, M. (1990). Perception of physical attractiveness: Mechanisms involved in the maintenance of romantic relationships. *Journal of Personality and Social Psychology, 59,* 1192–1201.

Simpson, J. A., Rholes, W. S., & Nelligan, J. S. (1992). Support seeking and support giving within couples in an anxiety-provoking situation: The role of attachment styles. *Journal of Personality and Social Psychology, 62,* 434–446.

Simpson, J. A., Rholes, W. S., & Phillips, D. (1996). Conflict in close relationships: An attachment perspective. *Journal of Personality and Social Psychology, 71,* 899–914.

Sinclair, S., Dunn, E., & Lowery, B. S. (2004). The relationship between parental racial attitudes and children's implicit prejudice. *Journal of Experimental Social Psychology, 41,* 283–289.

Singer, T., Seymour, B., O'Doherty, J. P., Stephan, K. E., Dolan, R. J., & Frith, C. D. (2006). Empathic neural responses are modulated by the perceived fairness of others. *Nature, 439,* 466–469.

Singh, D., & Randall, P. K. (2007). Beauty is in the eye of the plastic surgeon: Waist-hip ratio (WHR) and women's attractiveness. *Personality and Individual Differences, 43,* 329–340.

Singh, D. (1993). Adaptive significance of female physical attractiveness: Role of waist-to-hip ratio. *Journal of Personality and Social Psychology, 65,* 293–307.

Singh, D. (1995). Female judgment of male attractiveness and desirability for relationships: Role of waist-to-hip ratio and financial status. *Journal of Personality and Social Psychology, 69,* 1089–1101.

Singh, R., & Ho, S. J. (2000). Attitudes and attraction: A new test of the attraction, repulsion and similarity-dissimilarity asymmetry hypotheses. *British Journal of Social Psychology, 39,* 197–211.

SIPRI. (2023, accessed December 8). *Military expenditure.* Stockholm International Peace Research Institute. https://www.sipri.org/research/armaments/milex

Sittser, G. L. (1994, April). Long night's journey into light. *Second Opinion,* pp. 10–15.

Sivarajasingam, V., Moore, S., & Shepherd, J. P. (2005). Winning, losing, and violence. *Injury Prevention,11,* 69–70.

Six, B., & Eckes, T. (1996). Metaanalysen in der Einstellungs-Verhaltens-Forschung. *Zeitschrift fur Sozialpsychologie,* 7–17.

Skaalvik, E. M., & Hagtvet, K. A. (1990). Academic achievement and self-concept: An analysis of causal predominance in a developmental perspective. *Journal of Personality and Social Psychology, 58,* 292–307.

Skipper, Y., Jolley, D., & Reddington, J. (2023). 'But wait, that isn't real': A proof-of-concept study evaluating 'project real', a co-created intervention that helps young people to spot fake news online. *British Journal of Developmental Psychology.*

Skitka, L. J., & Tetlock, P. E. (1993). Providing public assistance: Cognitive and motivational processes underlying liberal and conservative policy preferences. *Journal of Personality and Social Psychology, 65,* 1205–1223.

Skitka, L. J. (1999). Ideological and attributional boundaries on public compassion: Reactions to individuals and communities affected by a natural disaster. *Personality and Social Psychology Bulletin, 25,* 793–808.

Skitka, L. J., Bauman, C. W., & Mullen, E. (2004). Political tolerance and coming to psychological closure following the September 11, 2001, terrorist attacks: An integrative approach. *Personality and Social Psychology Bulletin, 30,* 743–756.

Skitka, L. J., Bauyman, C. W., & Sargis, E. G. (2005). Moral conviction: Another contributor to attitude strength or something more? *Journal of Personality and Social Psychology, 88,* 895–917.

Slatcher, R. B., & Pennebaker, J. W. (2006). How do I love thee? Let me count the words: The social effects of expressive writing. *Psychological Science, 17,* 660–664.

Slavin, R. E., & Cooper, R. (1999). Improving intergroup relations: Lessons learned from cooperative learning programs. *Journal of Social Issues, 55,* 647–663.

Slavin, R. E., & Madden, N. A. (1979). School practices that improve race relations. *Journal of Social Issues, 16,* 169–180.

Slavin, R. E. (1985). Cooperative learning: Applying contact theory in desegregated schools. *Journal of Social Issues, 41*(3), 45–62

Slavin, R. E., Hurley, E. A., & Chamberlain, A. (2003). Cooperative learning and achievement: Theory and research. In W. M. Reynolds & G. E. Miller (Eds.), *Handbook of psychology: Educational psychology* (Vol. 7). New York: Wiley.

Slavin, R. E., Lake, C., & Groff, C. (2009). Effective programs in middle and high school mathematics: A best-evidence synthesis. *Review of Educational Research, 79,* 839–911.

Slepian, M. L., & Moulton-Tetlock, E. (2019). Confiding secrets and well-being. *Social Psychological and Personality Science, 10,* 472–484.

Slepian, M. L., Rule, N. O., & Ambady, N. (2012). Proprioception and person perception: Politicians and professors. *Personality and Social Psychology Bulletin, 38,* 1621–1628.

Slopen, N., Glynn, R. J., Buring, J., & Albert, M. A. (2010, November 23). Job strain, job insecurity, and incident cardiovascular disease in the Women's Health Study: Results from a 10-year prospective study. *PLOS ONE, 7*(7), e40512.

Slotow, R., Van Dyke, G., Poole, J., Page, B., & Klocke, A. (2000). Older bull elephants control young males. *Nature, 408,* 425–426.

Slotter, E. B., & Gardner, W. L. (2009). Where do you end and I begin? Evidence for anticipatory, motivated self-other integration between relationship partners. *Journal of Personality and Social Psychology, 96,* 1137–1151.

Slotter, E. B., Gardner, W. L., & Finkel, E. (2010). Who am I without you? The influence of romantic breakup on the self-concept. *Personality and Social Psychology Bulletin, 36,* 147–160.

Slovic, P., & Fischhoff, B. (1977). On the psychology of experimental surprises. *Journal of Experimental Psychology: Human Perception and Performance, 3,* 455–551.

Slovic, P., & Västfjäll, D. (2010). Affect, moral intuition, and risk. *Psychological Inquiry, 21,* 387–398.

Slovic, P. (2007). "If I look at the mass I will never act": Psychic numbing and genocide. *Judgment and Decision Making, 2,* 79–95.

Slovic, P., Västjfäll, D., Erlandsson, A., & Gregory, R. (2017). Iconic photographs and the ebb and flow of empathic response to humanitarian disasters. *PNAS, 114,* 640–644.

Smalarz, L., & Wells, G. L. (2014). Post-identification feedback to eyewitnesses impairs evaluators' abilities to discriminate between accurate and mistaken testimony. *Law and Human Behavior, 38,* 194–202.

Smalarz, L., & Wells, G. L. (2015). Contamination of eyewitness self-reports and the mistaken-identification problem. *Current Directions in Psychological Science, 24,* 120–124.

Smalarz, L., Yang, Y., & Wells, G. L. (2021). Eyewitnesses' free-report verbal confidence statements are diagnostic of accuracy. *Law and Human Behavior, 45,* 138–151.

Smedley, J. W., & Bayton, J. A. (1978). Evaluative race-class stereotypes by race and perceived class of subjects. *Journal of Personality and Social Psychology, 3,* 530–535.

Smeijers, D., Bulten, E., Franke, B., Buitelaar, J., & Verkes, R.-J. (2020). Associations of multiple trauma types and MAOA with severe aggressive behavior and MAOA effects on training outcome. *European Neuropsychopharmacology, 30,* 66–74.

Smelser, N. J., & Mitchell, F. (Eds.) (2002). *Terrorism: Perspectives from the behavioral and social sciences.* Washington, DC: National Research Council, National Academies Press.

Smith, A. (1776). *The wealth of nations.* Book 1. Chicago, IL: University of Chicago Press. (Republished, 1976), p. 18.

Smith, A. E., & Haney, C. (2011). Getting to the point: Attempting to improve juror comprehension of capital penalty phase instructions. *Law and Human Behavior, 35,* 339–350.

Smith, C., & Davidson, H. (2014). *The paradox of generosity: Giving we receive, grasping we lose.* New York: Oxford University Press.

Smith, C. M., Dzik, P., & Fornicola, E. (2019). Threatened suicide and baiting crowd formation: A replication and extension of Mann (1981). *Social Influence, 14,* 92–103.

Smith, C. T., De Houwer, J., & Nosek, B. A. (2013). Consider the source: Persuasion of implicit evaluations is moderated by source credibility. *Personality and Social Psychology Bulletin, 39,* 193–205.

Smith, D. E., Gier, J. A., & Willis, F. N. (1982). Interpersonal touch and compliance with a marketing request. *Basic and Applied Social Psychology, 3,* 35–38.

Smith, H. (1976) *The Russians.* New York: Balantine Books. Cited by B. Latané, K. Williams, & S. Harkins in "Many hands make light the work." *Journal of Personality and Social Psychology,* 1979, *37,* 822–832.

Smith, L. G. E., & Postmes, T. (2011). The power of talk: Developing discriminatory group norms through discussion. *British Journal of Social Psychology, 50,* 193–215.

Smith, M. (2023, July 3). Record number of Britons support same-sex marriage 10 years after key vote. YouGov.com.

Smith, M. H. (2017). A sample/population size activity: Is it the sample size of the sample as a fraction of the population that matters? *Journal of Statistics Education, 12,* 2.

Smith, P. B., & Tayeb, M. (1989). Organizational structure and processes. In M. Bond (Ed.), *The cross-cultural challenge to social psychology.* Newbury Park, CA: Sage.

Smith, P. B. (2005). Is there an indigenous European social psychology? *International Journal of Psychology, 40,* 254–262.

Smith, R. (2020, July 1). Do empty stadiums affect outcomes? The data says yes. *The New York Times.* https://www.nytimes.com/2020/07/01/sports/soccer/soccer-without-fans-germany-data.html

Smith, R. H., Turner, T. J., Garonzik, R., Leach, C. W., Urch-Druskat, V., & Weston, C. M. (1996). Envy and *Schadenfreude. Personality and Social Psychology Bulletin, 22,* 158–168.

Smith, S. G., Jackson, S. E., Kobayashi, L. C., & Steptoe, A. (2018). Social isolation, health literacy, and mortality risk: Findings from the English Longitudinal Study of Ageing. *Health Psychology, 37*(2), 160–169.

Smith, S. G., Zhang, X., Basile, K. C., Merrick, M. T., Wang, J., Kresnow, M., & Chen, J. (2018). *The National Intimate Partner and Sexual Violence Survey: 2015 Data Brief–Updated release* [PDF file]. National Center for Injury Prevention and Control, CDC. https://www.cdc.gov/violenceprevention/pdf/2015data-brief508.pdf

Smith, S. J., Axelton, A. M., & Saucier, D. A. (2009). The effects of contact on sexual prejudice: A meta-analysis. *Sex Roles, 61,* 178–191.

Smith, S. L., Pieper, K., & Choueiti, M. (2017, February). *Inclusion in the director's chair? Gender, race, & age of film directors across 1,000 films from 2007-2016.* Media, Diversity, & Social Change Initiative, University of Southern California Annenberg School for Communications and Journalism.

Smith, V. L. (1991). Prototypes in the courtroom: Lay representations of legal concepts. *Journal of Personality and Social Psychology, 61,* 857–872.

Smoreda, Z., & Licoppe, C. (2000). Gender-specific use of the domestic telephone. *Social Psychology Quarterly, 63,* 238–252.

Snodgrass, M. A. (1987). The relationships of differential loneliness, intimacy, and characterological attributional style to duration of loneliness. *Journal of Social Behavior and Personality, 2,* 173–186.

Snyder, C. R., & Smith, T. W. (1986). On being "shy like a fox": A self-handicapping analysis. In W. H. Jones et al. (Eds.), *Shyness: Perspectives on research and treatment.* New York: Plenum.

Snyder, C. R. (1980, March). The uniqueness mystique. *Psychology Today,* pp. 86–90.

Snyder, M., & Swann, W. B., Jr. (1976). When actions reflect attitudes: The politics of impression management. *Journal of Personality and Social Psychology, 34,* 1034–1042.

Snyder, M. (1984). When belief creates reality. In L. Berkowitz (Ed.), *Advances in experimental social psychology* (Vol. 18). New York: Academic Press.

Snyder, M. (1987). *Public appearances/private realities: The psychology of self-monitoring.* New York: Freeman.

Snyder, M. (1988). Experiencing prejudice firsthand: The "discrimination day" experiments. *Contemporary Psychology, 33,* 664–665.

Snyder, M., Tanke, E. D., & Berscheid, E. (1977). Social perception and interpersonal behavior: On the self-fulfilling nature of social stereotypes. *Journal of Personality and Social Psychology, 35,* 656–666.

Sofer, C., Dotsch, R., Wigboldus, D. H. J., & Todorov, A. (2015). What is typical is good: The influence of face typicality on perceived trustworthiness. *Psychological Science, 26,* 39–47.

Solano, C. H., Batten, P. G., & Parish, E. A. (1982). Loneliness and patterns of self-disclosure. *Journal of Personality and Social Psychology, 43,* 524–531.

Solberg, E. C., Diener, E., Wirtz, D., Lucas, R. E., & Oishi, S. (2002). Wanting, having, and satisfaction: Examining the role of desire discrepancies in satisfaction with income. *Journal of Personality and Social Psychology, 83,* 725–734.

Solnick, S., & Hemenway, D. (1998). Is more always better? A survey on positional concerns. *Journal of Economic Behaviour and Organization, 37,* 373–383.

Solnick, S. J., & Hemenway, D. (2012). The "Twinkie Defense": The relationship between carbonated non-diet soft drinks and violence perpetration among Boston high school students. *Injury Prevention, 18,* 259–263.

Solomon, H., & Solomon, L. Z. (1978). *Effects of anonymity on helping in emergency situations.* Paper presented at the Eastern Psychological Association convention.

Solomon, H., Solomon, L. Z., Arnone, M. M., Maur, B. J., Reda, R. M., & Rother, E. O. (1981). Anonymity and helping. *Journal of Social Psychology, 113,* 37–43.

Sommer, F., Leuschner, V., & Scheithauer, H. (2014). Bullying, romantic rejection, and conflicts with teachers: The crucial role of social dynamics in the development of school shootings—A systematic review. *International Journal of Developmental Science, 8,* 3–24.

Sommers, S. R., & Ellsworth, P. C. (2000). Race in the courtroom: Perceptions of guilt and dispositional attributions. *Personality and Social Psychology Bulletin, 26,* 1367–1379.

Sommers, S. R., & Ellsworth, P. C. (2001). White juror bias: An investigation of prejudice against Black defendants in the American courtroom. *Psychology, Public Policy, and Law, 7,* 201–229.

Sommers, S. R. (2006). On racial diversity and group decision making: Identifying multiple effects of racial composition on jury deliberations. *Journal of Personality and Social Psychology, 90,* 597–612.

Song, H., Hayeon, S., Anne, Z.-S., Jinyoung, K., Adam, D., Angela, V., . . . Mike, A. (2014). Does Facebook make you lonely?: A meta-analysis. *Computers in Human Behavior, 36,* 446–452.

Sonne, J., & Janoff, D. (1979). The effect of treatment attributions on the maintenance of weight reduction: A replication and extension. *Cognitive Therapy and Research, 3,* 389–397.

Sorhagen, N. S. (2013). Early teacher expectations disproportionately affect poor children's high school performance. *Journal of Educational Psychology, 105,* 465–477.

Sorokowska, A., Sorokowski, P., . . . Pierce, J. D. (2017). Preferred interpersonal distances: A global comparison. *Journal of Cross-Cultural Psychology, 48,* 577–592.

Sorokowski, P., et al. (2011). Attractiveness of leg length: Report from 27 nations. *Journal of Cross-Cultural Psychology, 42,* 131–139.

Sowislo, J. F., & Orth, U. (2013). Does low self-esteem predict depression and anxiety? A meta-analysis of longitudinal studies. *Psychological Bulletin, 139,* 213–240.

Sparkman, D. J., Eidelman, S., & Blanchar, J. C. (2016). Multicultural experiences reduce prejudice through personality shifts in openness to experience. *European Journal of Social Psychology, 46,* 840–853.

Sparkman, G., & Walton, G. (2017). Dynamic norms promote sustainable behavior, even if it is counternormative. *Psychological Science, 28,* 1663–1674.

Sparkman, G., & Walton, G. M. (2018). Dynamic norms promote sustainable behavior, even if it is counternormative. *Psychological Science, 28*(11), 1663–1674.

Sparrell, J. A., & Shrauger, J. S. (1984). *Self-confidence and optimism in self-prediction.* Paper presented at the American Psychological Association convention, Toronto, Ontario, Canada.

Spears, R., Ellemers, N., & Doosje, B. (2009). Strength in numbers or less is more? A matter of opinion and a question of taste. *Personality and Social Psychology Bulletin, 35,* 1099–1111.

Spector, P. E. (1986). Perceived control by employees: A meta-analysis of studies concerning autonomy and participation at work. *Human Relations, 39,* 1005–1016.

Speer, A. (1971). *Inside the Third Reich: Memoirs* (P. Winston & C. Winston, trans.). New York: Avon Books.

Spencer, B. D. (2007). Estimating the accuracy of jury verdicts. *Journal of Empirical Legal Studies, 4,* 305–329.

Spencer, C., Reed, R. G., Votruba-Drzal, E., & Gianaros, P. J. (2023). Psychological stress and the longitudinal progression of subclinical atherosclerosis. *Health Psychology.*

Spencer, S. J., Fein, S., Wolfe, C. T., Fong, C., & Dunn, M. A. (1998). Automatic activation of stereotypes: The role of self-image threat. *Personality and Social Psychology Bulletin, 24,* 1139–1152.

Spencer, S. J., Steele, C. M., & Quinn, D. M. (1999). Stereotype threat and women's math performance. *Journal of Experimental Social Psychology, 3,* 4–28.

Speth, J. G. (2008). Foreword. In A. A. Leiserowitz & L. O. Fernandez, *Toward a new consciousness: Values to sustain human and natural communities.* New Haven: Yale School of Forestry & Environmental Studies.

Speth, J. G. (2012, May/June). America, the possible: A manifesto, Part II. *Orion Magazine.* https://orionmagazine.org/article/america-the-possible-a-manifesto-part-ii/

Spielmann, S. S., MacDonald, G., & Wilson, A. E. (2009). On the rebound: Focusing on someone new helps anxiously attached individuals let go of ex-partners. *Personality and Social Psychology Bulletin, 35,* 1382–1394.

Spithoven, A. W. M., Cacioppo, S., Goossens, L., & Cacioppo, J. T. (2019). Genetic contributions to loneliness and their relevance to the evolutionary theory of loneliness. *Perspectives on Psychological Science, 14,* 376–396.

Spitzberg, B. H., & Hurt, H. T. (1987). The relationship of interpersonal competence and skills to reported loneliness across time. *Journal of Social Behavior and Personality, 2,* 157–172.

Spitz, H. H. (1999). Beleaguered *Pygmalion:* A history of the controversy over claims that teacher expectancy raises intelligence. *Intelligence, 27,* 199–234.

Spivak, B., Ogloff, J., Clough, J., Tinsley, Y., & Young, W. (2020). The impact of fact-based instructions on juror application of the law: Results from a Trans-Tasman field study. *Social Science Quarterly, 101,* 346–361.

Spivak, J. (1979). Hungary tries a bit of capitalism to cure some Communist ills. *The Wall Street Journal,* p. 1.

Spoelma, T. M. (2022). Counteracting the effects of performance pressure on cheating: A self-affirmation approach. *Journal of Applied Psychology, 107,* 1804–1823.

Sporer, S. L. (2008). Lessons from the origins of eyewitness testimony research in Europe. *Applied Cognitive Psychology, 22,* 737–757.

Sporer, S. L., Trinkl, B., & Guberova, E. (2007). Matching faces. Differences in processing speed of out-group faces by different ethnic groups. *Journal of Cross-Cultural Psychology, 38,* 398–412.

Sprecher, S., & Toro-Morn, M. (2002). A study of men and women from different sides of Earth to determine if men are from Mars and women are from Venus in their beliefs about love and romantic relationships. *Sex Roles, 46,* 131–147.

Sprecher, S. (1987). The effects of self-disclosure given and received on affection for an intimate partner and stability of the relationship. *Journal of Personality and Social Psychology, 4,* 115–127.

Sprecher, S., Aron, A., Hatfield, E., Cortese, A., Potapova, E., & Levitskaya, A. (1994). Love: American style, Russian style, and Japanese style. *Personal Relationships, 1,* 349–369.

Sprecher, S., Treger, S., & Sakaluk, J. K. (2013). Premarital sexual standards and sociosexuality: Gender, ethnicity, and cohort differences. *Archives of Sexual Behavior, 42,* 1395–1405.

Sprengholz, P., Tannert, S., & Betsch, C. (2023). Explaining boomerang effects in persuasive health communication: How psychological reactance to healthy eating messages elevates attention to unhealthy food. *Journal of Health Communication, 28,* 384–390.

Srivastava, S., McGonigal, K. M., Richards, J. M., Butler, E. A., & Gross, J. J. (2006). Optimism in close relationships: How seeing things in a positive light makes them so. *Journal of Personality and Social Psychology, 91,* 143–153.

Stack, L. (2016, June 8). In Stanford rape case, Brock Turner blamed drinking and promiscuity. *The New York Times.* https://nyti.ms/3tksSpa

Stack, S. (2000). Media impacts on suicide: A quantitative review of 293 findings. *Social Science Quarterly, 81,* 957–971.

Stack, S. (2003). Media coverage as a risk factor in suicide. *Journal of Epidemiology and Community Health, 57,* 238–240.

Stajkovic, A., & Luthans, F. (1998). Self-efficacy and work-related performance: A meta-analysis. *Psychological Bulletin, 124,* 240–261.

Stajkovic, A. D., Bandura, A., Locke, E. A., Lee, D., & Sergent, K. (2018). Test of three conceptual models of influence of the big five personality traits and self-efficacy on academic performance: A meta-analytic path-analysis. *Personality and Individual Differences, 120,* 238–245.

Stalder, D. R. (2008). Revisiting the issue of safety in numbers: The likelihood of receiving help from a group. *Social Influence, 3,* 24–33.

Stall, L. M., & Petrocelli, J. V. (2022). Countering conspiracy theory beliefs: Understanding the conjunction fallacy and considering disconfirming evidence. *Applied Cognitive Psychology.*

Stangor, C., Jonas, K., Stroebe, W., & Hewstone, M. (1996). Influence of student exchange on national stereotypes, attitudes and perceived group variability. *European Journal of Social Psychology, 26,* 663–675.

Stanley, D. J., & Spence, J. R. (2014). Expectations for replications: Are yours realistic? *Perspectives on Psychological Science, 9,* 305–318.

Stanley, M. L., Henne, P., Yang, B. W., & De Brigard, P. (2020). Resistance to position change, motivated reasoning, and polarization. *Political Behavior, 42,* 891–913.

Stanley, T. D., Carter, E. C., & Doucouliagos, H. (2018). What meta-analyses reveal about the replicability of psychological research. *Psychological Bulletin, 144,* 1325–1346.

Stanovich, K. E., West, R. F., & Toplak, M. E. (2013). Myside bias, rational thinking, and intelligence. *Current Directions in Psychological Science, 22,* 259–264.

Stanton, S. J., Beehner, J. C., Saini, E. K., Kuhn, C. M., & LaBar, K. S. (2009). Dominance, politics, and physiology: Voters' testosterone changes on the night of the 2008 United States Presidential election. *PLOS ONE, 4*(10), e7543.

Starks, T. J., & Parsons, J. T. (2014). Adult attachment among partnered gay men: Patterns and associations with sexual relationship quality. *Archives of Sexual Behavior, 43,* 107–117.

Starmans, C., Sheskin, M., & Bloom, P. (2017). Why people prefer unequal societies. *Nature Human Behavior, 1,* 0082.

Starr, D. (2019). The confession. *Science, 364,* 6445.

Stasser, G. (1991). Pooling of unshared information during group discussion. In S. Worchel, W. Wood, & J. Simpson (Eds.), *Group process and productivity.* Beverly Hills, CA: Sage.

Stasser, G., Kerr, N. L., & Bray, R. M. (1981). The social psychology of jury deliberations: Structure, process, and product. In N. L. Kerr & R. M. Bray (Eds.), *The psychology of the courtroom.* New York: Academic Press.

Statista. (2019). *Frequency of Facebook use in the United States as of February 2018, by gender.* https://www.statista.com/statistics/653014/frequency-usage-facebook-usa-gender/

Staub, E., & Bar-Tal, D. (2003). Genocide, mass killing, and intractable conflict. In D. Sears, L. Huddy, & R. Jervis (Eds.), *Handbook of political psychology.* New York: Oxford University Press.

Staub, E. (1989). *The roots of evil: The origins of genocide and other group violence.* Cambridge: Cambridge University Press.

Staub, E. (1996). Altruism and aggression in children and youth: Origins and cures. In R. Feldman (Ed.), *The psychology of adversity.* Amherst, MA: University of Massachusetts Press.

Staub, E. (1997). Blind versus constructive patriotism: Moving from embeddedness in the group to critical loyalty and action. In D. Bar-Tal & E. Staub (Eds.), *Patriotism in the lives of individuals and nations.* Chicago: Nelson-Hall.

Staub, E. (2003). *The psychology of good and evil: Why children, adults, and groups help and harm others.* New York: Cambridge University Press.

Staub, E. (2005a). The origins and evolution of hate, with notes on prevention. In R. J. Sternberg (Ed.), *The psychology of hate.* Washington, DC: American Psychological Association.

Staub, E. (2005b). The roots of goodness: The fulfillment of basic human needs and the development of caring, helping and nonaggression, inclusive caring, moral courage, active bystandership, and altruism born of suffering. In G. Carlo & C. P. Edwards (Eds.), *Moral motivation through the life span: Theory, research, applications. Nebraska Symposium on Motivation* (Vol. 51). Lincoln, NE: University of Nebraska Press.

Staub, E. (2015). *The roots of goodness and resistance to evil: Inclusive caring, moral courage, altruism born of suffering, active bystandership, and heroism.* New York: Oxford.

Staub, E. (2018). Preventing violence and promoting active bystandership and peace: My life in research and applications. *Peace and Conflict: Journal of Peace Psychology, 24*(1), 95–111.

Staub, E. (2019). Witnesses/bystanders: The tragic fruits of passivity, the power of bystanders, and promoting active bystandership in children, adults, and groups. *Journal of Social Issues, 75,* 1262–1293.

Stavrova, O., & Siegers, P. (2014, March 1). Religious prosociality and morality across cultures: How social enforcement of religion shapes the effects of personal religiosity on prosocial and moral attitudes and behaviors. *Personality and Social Psychology Bulletin, 40*(3), 315–333.

Steblay, N., Dysart, J. E., Fulero, S., & Lindsay, R. C. L. (2001). Eyewitness accuracy rates in sequential and simultaneous lineup presentations: A meta-analytic comparison. *Law and Human Behavior, 25,* 459–473.

Steblay, N. K., Wells, G. L., & Douglass, A. B. (2014). The eyewitness post-identification effect 15 years later: Theoretical and policy implications. *Psychology, Public Policy, and Law, 20,* 1–18.

Steblay, N. M., Besirevic, J., Fulero, S. M., & Jimenez-Lorente, B. (1999). The effects of pretrial publicity on juror verdicts: A meta-analytic review. *Law and Human Behavior, 23,* 219–235.

Steele, C. M., & Aronson, J. (1995). Stereotype threat and the intellectual test performance of African Americans. *Journal of Personality and Social Psychology, 69,* 797–811.

Steele, C. M. (1988). The psychology of self-affirmation: Sustaining the integrity of the self. In L. Berkowitz (Ed.), *Advances in experimental social psychology* (Vol. 21). Orlando, FL: Academic Press.

Steele, C. M. (1997). A threat in the air: How stereotypes shape intellectual identity and performance. *American Psychologist, 52,* 613–629.

Steele, C. M. (2010). *Whistling Vivaldi: And other clues to how stereotypes affect us.* New York: Norton.

Steele, C. M., Southwick, L. L., & Critchlow, B. (1981). Dissonance and alcohol: Drinking your troubles away. *Journal of Personality and Social Psychology, 41,* 831–846.

Steele, C. M., Spencer, S. J., & Aronson, J. (2002). Contending with group image: The psychology of stereotype and social identity threat. In Zanna, M. P. (Ed.), *Advances in experimental social psychology* (pp. 379–440). San Diego: Academic Press.

Steele, C. M., Spencer, S. J., & Lynch, M. (1993). Self-image resilience and dissonance: The role of affirmational resources. *Journal of Personality and Social Psychology, 64,* 885–896.

Steers, M. N., Wickham, R. E., & Acitelli, L. K. (2014). Seeing everyone else's highlight reels: How Facebook usage is linked to depressive symptoms. *Journal of Social and Clinical Psychology, 33,* 701–731.

Steffen, P. R., & Masters, K. S. (2005). Does compassion mediate the intrinsic religion-health relationship? *Annals of Behavioral Medicine, 30,* 217–224.

Stein, A. H., & Friedrich, L. K. (1972). Television content and young children's behavior. In J. P. Murray, E. A. Rubinstein, & G. A. Comstock (Eds.), *Television and social learning.* Washington, DC: Government Printing Office.

Steinbuch, Y. (2020, July 1). White man confronts Black woman driving in her own neighborhood: video. *The New York Post.* https://nypost.com/2020/07/01/white-man-confronts-black-woman-driving-in-her-neighborhood-video/

Steinhauer, J. (2015, January 2). Fight on guns is being taken to state ballots. *The New York Times.*

Stellar, J. E., Manzo, V. M., Kraus, M. W., & Keltner, D. (2012). Class and compassion: Socioeconomic factors predict responses to suffering. *Emotion, 12,* 449–459.

Stelter, B. (2008, November 25). Web suicide viewed live and reactions spur a debate. *The New York Times.* https://www.nytimes.com/2008/11/25/us/25suicides.html

Stelter, M., & Schweinberger, S. R. (2023). Understanding the mechanisms underlying the other-'race' effect: An attempt at integrating different perspectives. *British Journal of Psychology, 114,* 1–9.

Stelter, M., Essien, I., Sander, C., & Degner, J. (2022). Racial bias in police traffic stops: White residents' county-level prejudice and stereotypes are related to disproportionate stopping of Black drivers. *Psychological Science, 33,* 483–496.

Stelzl, M., Janes, L., & Seligman, C. (2008). Champ or chump: Strategic utilization of dual social identities of others. *European Journal of Social Psychology, 38,* 128–138.

Stendardi, D., Biscotto, F., Bertossi, E., & Ciaramelli, E. (2021). Present and future self in memory: The role of vmPFC in the self-reference effect. *Social Cognitive and Affective Neuroscience, 16,* 1205–1213.

Stenseng, F., Belsky, J., Skalicka, V., & Wichstrom, L. (2014). Preschool social exclusion, aggression, and cooperation: A longitudinal evalutation of the need-to-belong and the social-reconnection hypotheses. *Personality and Social Psychology Bulletin, 40,* 1637–1647.

Stephan, C. W., & Stephan, W. G. (1986). Habla Ingles? The effects of language translation on simulated juror decisions. *Journal of Applied Social Psychology, 16,* 577–589.

Stephan, W. G. (1986). The effects of school desegregation: An evaluation 30 years after *Brown.* In R. Kidd, L. Saxe, & M. Saks (Eds.), *Advances in applied social psychology.* New York: Erlbaum.

Stephan, W. G. (1987). The contact hypothesis in intergroup relations. In C. Hendrick (Ed.), *Group processes and intergroup relations.* Newbury Park, CA: Sage.

Stephan, W. G. (1988). *School desegregation: Short-term and long-term effects.* Paper presented at the national conference "Opening Doors: An Appraisal of Race Relations in America," University of Alabama.

Stephens-Davidowitz, S. (2014, January 18). Google, tell me. Is my son a genius? *The New York Times.* https://www.nytimes.com/2014/01/19/opinion/sunday/google-tell-me-is-my-son-a-genius.html

Stephens-Davidowitz, S. (2017). *Everybody lies: Big data, new data, and what the Internet can tell us about who we really are.* New York: Dey Street.

Stephens, N. M., Markus, H. R., & Townsend, S. S. M. (2007). Choice as an act of meaning: The case of social class. *Journal of Personality and Social Psychology, 93,* 814–830.

Sternberg, R. J., & Grajek, S. (1984). The nature of love. *Journal of Personality and Social Psychology, 47,* 312–329.

Sternberg, R. J. (1988). Triangulating love. In R. J. Sternberg & M. L. Barnes (Eds.), *The psychology of love.* New Haven, CT: Yale University Press.

Sternberg, R. J. (1998). *Cupid's arrow: The course of love through time.* New York: Cambridge University Press.

Sternberg, R. J. (2003). A duplex theory of hate and its development and its application to terrorism, massacres, and genocide. *Review of General Psychology, 7,* 299–328.

Stevenson, M. C., Lytle, B. L., Baumholser, B. J., & McCracken, E. W. (2017). Racially diverse juries promote self-monitoring efforts during jury deliberation. *Translational Issues in Psychological Science, 3,* 187–201.

Stevenson, M. C., McCracken, E., Watson, A., Petty, T., & Plogher, T. (2023). An attribution theory-based content analysis of mock jurors' deliberations regarding coerced confessions. *Law and Human Behavior, 47,* 348–366.

Stewart-Williams, S. (2007). Altruism among kin vs. nonkin: Effects of cost of help and reciprocal exchange. *Evolution and Human Behavior, 28,* 193–198.

Stinson, D. A., Cameron, J. J., Wood, J. V., Gaucher, D., & Holmes, J. G. (2009). Deconstructing the "reign of error": Interpersonal warmth explains the self-fulfilling prophecy of anticipated acceptance. *Personality and Social Psychology Bulletin, 35,* 1165–1178.

Stinson, D. A., Logel, C., Shepherd, S., & Zanna, M. P. (2011). Rewriting the self-fulfilling prophecy of social rejection: Self-affirmation improves relational security and social behavior up to 2 months later. *Psychological Science, 22,* 1145–1149.

Stinson, V., Devenport, J. L., Cutler, B. L., & Kravitz, D. A. (1996). How effective is the presence-of-counsel safeguard? Attorney perceptions of suggestiveness, fairness, and correctability of biased lineup procedures. *Journal of Applied Psychology, 81,* 64–75.

Stinson, V., Devenport, J. L., Cutler, B. L., & Kravitz, D. A. (1997). How effective is the motion-to-suppress safeguard? Judges' perceptions of the suggestiveness and fairness of biased lineup procedures. *Journal of Personality and Social Psychology, 82,* 211–220.

Stockdale, L., Morrison, R. G., Palumbo, R., Garbarino, J., & Silton, R. L. (2017). Cool, callous, and in control: Superior inhibitory control in frequent players of video games with violent content. *Social Cognition and Affective Neuroscience, 12,* 1869–1880.

Stocks, E. L., Lishner, D. A., & Decker, S. K. (2009). Altruism or psychological escape: Why does empathy promote prosocial behavior? *European Journal of Social Psychology, 39,* 649–665.

Stoet, G., & Geary, D. C. (2018). The gender-equality paradox in science, technology, engineering, and mathematics education. *Psychological Science, 29,* 581–593.

Stok, F. M., de Ridder, D. T. D., de Vet, E., & de Wit, J. B. F. (2014). Don't tell me what I should do, but what others do: The influence of descriptive and injunctive peer norms on fruit consumption in adolescents. *British Journal of Health Psychology, 19,* 52–64.

Stolzenberg, E. B., Aragon, M. C., Romo, E., Couch, V., McLennan, D., Eagan, M. K., & Kang, N. (2020). *The American Freshman: National Norms Fall 2019.* Los Angeles: Higher Education Research Institute.

Stolzenberg, E. B., Eagan, K., Aragon, M. C., Cesar-Davis, N. M., Jacobo, S., Couch, V., & Rios-Aguilar, C. (2019). *The American freshman: National norms fall 2017: Expanded version.* Los Angeles: Higher Education Research Institute.

Stone, A. L., & Glass, C. R. (1986). Cognitive distortion of social feedback in depression. *Journal of Social and Clinical Psychology, 4,* 179–188.

Stone, J. A., & Can, S. H. (2021). Gendered language differences in public communication? The case of municipal tweets. *International Journal of Information Management Data Insights, 1,* 100034.

Stone, J., Lynch, C. I., Sjomeling, M., & Darley, J. M. (1999). Stereotype threat effects on Black and White athletic performance. *Journal of Personality and Social Psychology, 77,* 1213–1227.

Stone, J., Quoted by Sharon Begley. (2000, November 6). The stereotype trap. *Newsweek.*

Stone, L. (1977). *The family, sex and marriage in England, 1500–1800.* New York: Harper & Row.

Stoner, J. A. F. (1961). *A comparison of individual and group decisions involving risk.* Unpublished master's thesis, Massachusetts Institute of Technology. Cited by D. G. Marquis in Individual responsibility and group decisions involving risk. *Industrial Management Review, 3,* 8–23.

Storms, M. D., & Thomas, G. C. (1977). Reactions to physical closeness. *Journal of Personality and Social Psychology, 35,* 412–418.

Storr, W. (2018, April 25). How scientists invented a test to measure hurt feelings. *The Cut.* https://amp.thecut.com/2018/04/book-excerpt-selfie-by-will-storr.html?__twitter_impression=true

Stouffer, S. A., Suchman, E. A., DeVinney, L. C., Star, S. A., & Williams, R. M., Jr. (1949). *The American soldier: Adjustment during army life* (Vol. 1.). Princeton, NJ: Princeton University Press.

Stout, J. G., Dasgupta, N., Hunsinger, M., & McManus, M. A. (2011). STEMing the tide: Using ingroup experts to inoculate women's self-concept in science, technology, engineering, and mathematics (STEM). *Journal of Personality and Social Psychology, 100,* 255–270.

Stoverink, A., Umphress, E., Gardner, R., & Miner, K. (2014). Misery loves company: Team dissonance and the influence of supervisor-focused interpersonal justice climate on team cohesiveness. *Journal of Applied Psychology, 99,* 1059–1073.

Stowell, J. R., Oldham, T., & Bennett, D. (2010). Using student response systems ("clickers") to combat conformity and shyness. *Teaching of Psychology, 37,* 135–140.

Strack, F., & Deutsch, R. (2004). Reflective and impulsive determinants of social behavior. *Personality and Social Psychology Review, 8*(3), 220–247.

Strack, F., Martin, L. L., & Stepper, S. (1988). Inhibiting and facilitating conditions of the human smile: A nonobtrusive test of the facial feedback hypothesis. *Journal of Personality and Social Psychology, 54,* 768–777.

Strack, S., & Coyne, J. C. (1983). Social confirmation of dysphoria: Shared and private reactions to depression. *Journal of Personality and Social Psychology, 44,* 798–806.

Strasser, A. A., Tang, K. Z., Romer, D., Jepson, C., & Cappella, J. N. (2012). Graphic warning labels in cigarette advertisements: Recall and viewing patterns. *American Journal of Preventative Medicine, 43,* 41–47.

Straus, M. A., & Gelles, R. J. (1980). *Behind closed doors: Violence in the American family.* New York: Anchor/Doubleday.

Strick, M., Holland, R. W., van Baaren, R. B., & van Kippenberg, A. (2012). Those who laugh are defenseless: How humor breaks resistance to influence. *Journal of Experimental Psychology: Applied, 18,* 213–223.

Strick, M., van Baaren, R. B., Holland, R. W., & van Knippenberg, A. (2009). Humor in advertisements enhances product liking by mere association. *Journal of Experimental Psychology: Applied, 15,* 35–45.

Stroebe, W., & Diehl, M. (1994). Productivity loss in idea-generating groups. In W. Stroebe & M. Hewstone (Eds.), *European review of social psychology* (Vol. 5). Chichester, UK: Wiley.

Stroessner, S. J., & Mackie, D. M. (1993). Affect and perceived group variability: Implications for stereotyping and prejudice. In D. M. Mackie & D. L. Hamilton (Eds.), *Affect, cognition, and stereotyping: Interactive processes in group perception.* San Diego: Academic Press.

Strong, S. R. (1968). Counseling: An interpersonal influence process. *Journal of Counseling Psychology, 17,* 81–87.

Strong, S. R. (1991). Social influence and change in therapeutic relationships. In C. R. Snyder & D. R. Forsyth (Eds.), *Handbook of social and clinical psychology.* New York: Pergamon.

Strong, S. R., Welsh, J. A., Corcoran, J. L., & Hoyt, W. T. (1992). Social psychology and counseling psychology: The history, products, and promise of an interface. *Journal of Personality and Social Psychology, 39,* 139–157.

Stroufe, B., Chaikin, A., Cook, R., & Freeman, V. (1977). The effects of physical attractiveness on honesty: A socially desirable response. *Personality and Social Psychology, 3,* 59–62.

Studdert, D. M., Zhang, Y., Holsinger, E. E., Prince, L., Holsinger, A. F., Rodden, J. A., Wintemute, G. J., & Miller, M. (2022). Homicide Deaths Among Adult Cohabitants of Handgun Owners in California, 2004 to 2016: A Cohort Study. *Annals of Internal Medicine, 175,* 804–811.

Stulp, G., Buunk, A. P., Pollet, T. V., Nettle, D., & Verhulst, S. (2013). Are human mating preferences with respect to height reflected in actual pairings? *PLOS ONE, 8*(1), e54186.

Sude, D. J., Knobloch-Westerwick, S., Robinson, M. J., & Westerwick, A. (2019). "Pick and choose" opinion climate: How browsing of political messages shapes public opinion perceptions and attitudes. *Communication Monographs, 86,* 457–478.

Sue, S., Smith, R. E., & Caldwell, C. (1973). Effects of inadmissible evidence on the decisions of simulated jurors: A moral dilemma. *Journal of Applied Social Psychology, 3,* 345–353.

Sugden, N. A., & Marquis, A. R. (2017). Meta-analytic review of the development of face discrimination in infancy: Face race, face gender, infant age, and methodology moderate face discrimination. *Psychological Review, 143,* 1201–1244.

Suits, D. (2021, June 24). Change to policy allows transgender Soldiers to serve openly. *Army News Service.*

Sullivan, D., Landau, M. J., Kay, A. C., & Rothschild, Z. K. (2012). Collectivism and the meaning of suffering. *Journal of Personality and Social Psychology, 103,* 1023–1039.

Suls, J., Dess, N., Iguchi, M., Howell, B., Mobley, M., & Widaman, K. (2019, October). APA task force report on violent video games. https://www.apa.org/science/leadership/bsa/report-violent-video-games.pdf

Sulzberger, A. G., & Meenan, M. (2010, April 25). Questions surround a delay in help for a dying man. *The New York Times.* https://www.nytimes.com/2010/04/26/nyregion/26homeless.html

Sun, C., Bridges, A., Wosnitzer, R., Scharrer, E., & Liberman, R. (2008). A comparison of male and female directors in popular pornography: What happens when women are at the helm? *Psychology of Women Quarterly, 32,* 312–325.

Sundie, J. M., Kenrick, D. T., Griskevicius, V., Tybur, J. M., Vohs, K. D., & Beal, D. J. (2011). Peacocks, porches, and Thorstein Veblen: Conspicuous consumption as a sexual signaling system. *Journal of Personality and Social Psychology, 100,* 664–680.

Sun, J., Harris, K., & Vazire, S. (2020). Is well-being associated with the quantity and quality of social interactions? *Journal of Personality and Social Psychology, 119*(6), 1478–1496.

Sunstein, C. (2016, January 15). How Facebook spreads falsehoods. *Bloomberg View* (reprinting in *Grand Rapids Press*).

Sunstein, C. R., & Hastie, R. (2008). *Four failures of deliberating groups.* Economics Working Paper Series, University of Chicago Law School (www.law.uchicago.edu).

Sunstein, C. R. (2007). Group polarization and 12 angry men. *Negotiation Journal, 23,* 443–447.

Sunstein, C. R. (2009). *Going to extremes: How like minds unite and divide.* New York: Oxford University Press.

Sunstein, C. R., Schkade, D., & Ellman, L. M. (2004). Ideological voting on federal courts of appeals: A preliminary investigation. *Virginia Law Review, 90,* 301–354.

Su, R., Rounds, J., & Armstrong, P. I. (2009). Men and things, women and people: A meta-analysis of sex differences in interests. *Psychological Bulletin, 135,* 859–884.

Suslow, T., Wildenauer, K., & Günther, V. (2019). Ruminative response style is associated with a negative bias in the perception of emotional facial expressions in healthy women without a history of clinical depression. *Journal of Behavior Therapy and Experimental Psychiatry, 62,* 125–132.

Sussman, N. M. (2000). The dynamic nature of cultural identity throughout cultural transitions: Why home is not so sweet. *Personality and Social Psychology Review, 4,* 355–373.

Svenson, O. (1981). Are we all less risky and more skillful than our fellow drivers? *Acta Psychologica, 47,* 143–148.

Swaab, R. I., Lount, R. B., Jr., Chung, S., & Brett, J. M. (2021). Setting the stage for negotiations: How superordinate goal dialogues promote trust and joint gain in negotiations between teams. *Organizational Behavior and Human Decision Processes, 167,* 157–169.

Swami, V., Chan, F., Wong, V., Furnham, A., & Tovée, M. J. (2008). Weight-based discrimination in occupational hiring and helping behavior. *Journal of Applied Social Psychology, 38,* 968–981.

Swann, W. B., Jr., & Predmore, S. C. (1985). Intimates as agents of social support: Sources of consolation or despair? *Journal of Personality and Social Psychology, 49,* 1609–1617.

Swann, W. B., Jr., & Read, S. J. (1981). Acquiring self-knowledge: The search for feedback that fits. *Journal of Personality and Social Psychology, 41,* 1119–1128.

Swann, W. B., Jr. (1996). *Self-traps: The elusive quest for higher self-esteem.* New York: Freeman.

Swann, W. B., Jr. (1997). The trouble with change: Self-verification and allegiance to the self. *Psychological Science, 8,* 177–180.

Swann, W. B., Jr., Buhrmester, M. D., Gómez, A., Jetten, J., Bastian, B., Vázquez, A., Zhang, A. (2014a). What makes a group worth dying for? Identity fusion fosters perception of familial ties, promoting self-sacrifice. *Journal of Personality and Social Psychology, 106,* 912–926.

Swann, W. B., Jr., Chang-Schneider, C., & Angulo, S. (2007). Self-verification in relationships as an adaptive process. In J. Wood, A. Tesser, & J. Holmes (Eds.), *Self and relationships.* New York: Psychology Press.

Swann, W. B., Jr., Gómez, Ý., Buhrmester, M. D., López-Rodríguez, L., Jiménez, J., & Vázquez, A. (2014b). Contemplating the ultimate sacrifice: Identity fusion channels pro-group affect, cognition, and moral decision making. *Journal of Personality and Social Psychology, 106,* 713–727.

Swann, W. B., Jr., Jetten, J., Gómez, Ý., Whitehouse, H., & Bastian, B. (2012). When group membership gets personal: A theory of identity fusion. *Psychological Review, 119,* 441–456.

Swann, W. B., Jr., Rentfrow, P. J., & Gosling, S. D. (2003). The precarious couple effect: Verbally inhibited men + critical, disinhibited women = bad chemistry. *Journal of Personality and Social Psychology, 85,* 1095–1106.

Swann, W. B., Jr., Sellers, J. G., & McClarty, K. L. (2006). Tempting today, troubling tomorrow: The roots of the precarious couple effect. *Personality and Social Psychology Bulletin, 32,* 93–103.

Swann, W. B., Jr., Stein-Seroussi, A., & Giesler, R. B. (1992a). Why people self-verify. *Journal of Personality and Social Psychology, 62,* 392–401.

Swann, W. B., Jr., Stein-Seroussi, A., & McNulty, S. E. (1992b). Outcasts in a white lie society. The enigmatic worlds of people with negative self-conceptions. *Journal of Personality and Social Psychology, 62,* 618–624.

Swann, W. B., Jr., Wenzlaff, R. M., Krull, D. S., & Pelham, B. W. (1991). Seeking truth, reaping despair: Depression, self-verification and selection of relationship partners. *Journal of Abnormal Psychology, 101,* 293–306.

Swanson, J. W. (2016). On thoughts, threats, and throwing the spear. *Schizophrenia Bulletin, 42,* 883–884.

Swap, W. C. (1977). Interpersonal attraction and repeated exposure to rewarders and punishers. *Personality and Social Psychology Bulletin, 3,* 248–251.

Sweeney, J. (1973). An experimental investigation of the free rider problem. *Social Science Research, 2,* 277–292.

Sweeney, P. D., Anderson, K., & Bailey, S. (1986). Attributional style in depression: A meta-analytic review. *Journal of Personality and Social Psychology, 50,* 947–991.

Sweeny, K., Melnyk, D., Miller, W., & Shepperd, J. A. (2010). Information avoidance: Who, what, when, and why. *Review of General Psychology, 14,* 340–353.

Swets, J. A., Dawes, R. M., & Monahan, J. (2000). Psychological science can improve diagnostic decisions. *Psychological Science in the Public Interest, 1,* 1–26.

Swift, A. (2017, May 22). In U.S., belief in creationist view of humans at new low. *Gallup.* https://news.gallup.com/poll/210956/belief-creationist-view-humans-new-low.aspx

Swim, J., Geiger, N., & Zawakzki, S. J. (2014). Psychology and energy-use reduction policies. *Policy Insights from the Behavioral and Brain Sciences, 1,* 180–188.

Swim, J. K., & Hyers, L. L. (1999). Excuse me—What did you just say?! Women's public and private reactions to sexist remarks. *Journal of Experimental Social Psychology, 35,* 68–88.

Swim, J. K. (1994). Perceived versus meta-analytic effect sizes: An assessment of the accuracy of gender stereotypes. *Journal of Personality and Social Psychology, 66,* 21–36.

Swim, J. K., Aviste, R., Lengieza, M. L., & Fasano, C. J. (2022). OK Boomer: A decade of generational differences in feelings about climate change. *Global Environmental Change Part A: Human & Policy Dimensions, 73.*

Swim, J. K., Cohen, L. L., & Hyers, L. L. (1998). Experiencing everyday prejudice and discrimination. In J. K. Swim & C. Stangor (Eds.), *Prejudice: The target's perspective.* San Diego: Academic Press.

Symons, D. (1979). *The evolution of human sexuality* (p. 253). New York: Oxford University Press.

Szymkow, A., Chandler, J., IJzerman, H., Parzuchowski, M., & Wojciszke, B. (2013). Warmer hearts, warmer rooms: How positive communal traits increase estimates of ambient temperature. *Social Psychology, 44,* 167–176.

Tafarodi, R. W., Lo, C., Yamaguchi, S., Lee, W. W-S., & Katsura, H. (2004). The inner self in three countries. *Journal of Cross-Cultural Psychology, 35,* 97–117.

Tajfel, H., & Billig, M. (1974). Familiarity and categorization in intergroup behavior. *Journal of Experimental Social Psychology, 10,* 159–170.

Tajfel, H. (1970, November). Experiments in intergroup discrimination. *Scientific American,* pp. 96–102.

Tajfel, H. (1981). *Human groups and social categories: Studies in social psychology.* London: Cambridge University Press.

Tajfel, H. (1982). Social psychology of intergroup relations. *Annual Review of Psychology, 33,* 1–39.

Tajfel, H., Turner, J. C., Austin, W. G., & Worchel, S. (1979). An integrative theory of intergroup conflict. *Organizational identity: A reader,* 56–65.

Takada, M., & Murata, K. (2014). Accentuation of bias in jury decision-making. *Group Processes & Intergroup Relations, 17,* 110–124.

Takahashi, K., Mizuno, K., Sasaki, A. T., Wada, Y., Tanaka, M., Ishii, A., & . . . Watanabe, Y. (2015). Imaging the passionate stage of romantic love by dopamine dynamics. *Frontiers in Human Neuroscience, 9,* 191.

Talhelm, T., Zhang, X., Oishi, S., Shimin, C., Duan, D., Lan, X., & Kitayama, S. (2014). Large-scale psychological differences within China explained by rice versus wheat agriculture. *Science, 344,* 603–608.

Talsma, K., Schüz, B., Schwarzer, R., & Norris, K. (2018). I believe, therefore I achieve (and vice versa): A meta-analytic cross-lagged panel analysis of self-efficacy and academic performance. *Learning and Individual Differences, 61,* 136–150.

Tamres, L. K., Janicki, D., & Helgeson, V. S. (2002). Sex differences in coping behavior: A meta-analytic review and an examination of relative coping. *Personality and Social Psychology Review, 6,* 2–30.

Tang, L., Jang, S., & Morrison, A. (2012). Dual-route communication of destination websites. *Tourism Management, 33,* 38–49.

Tang, S-H., & Hall, V. C. (1995). The overjustification effect: A meta-analysis. *Applied Cognitive Psychology, 9,* 365–404.

Tan, H. H., & Tan, M. L. (2008). Organizational citizenship behavior and social loafing: The role of personality, motives, and contextual factors. *Journal of Psychology, 142,* 89–108.

Tan, J. J. X., Kraus, M. W., Carpenter, N. C., & Adler, N. E. (2020). The association between objective and subjective socioeconomic status and subjective well-being: A meta-analytic review. *Psychological Bulletin, 146,* 970–1020.

Tankard, M. E., & Paluck, E. L. (2017). The effect of a Supreme Court decision regarding gay marriage on social norms and personal attitudes. *Psychological Science, 28,* 1334–1344.

Tannenbaum, M. B., Hepler, J., Zimmerman, R. S., Saul, L., Jacobs, S., Wilson, K., & Albarracín, D. (2015). Appealing to fear: A meta-analysis of fear appeal effectiveness and theories. *Psychological Bulletin, 141,* 1178–1204.

Tanner, R. J., Ferraro, R., Chartrand, T. L., Bettman, J. R., & Van Barren, R. (2008). Of chameleons and consumption: The impact of mimicry on choice and preferences. *Journal of Consumer Research, 34,* 754–766.

Tapp, J. L. (1980). Psychological and policy perspectives on the law: Reflections on a decade. *Journal of Social Issues, 36(2),* 165–192.

Tarabeih, H., Gilad, S., & Sheffield, J. (2022). The Sakhnin/Misgav land dispute: Using 3-D negotiation strategies to analyze conflict resolution in Israel. *Negotiation Journal, 38,* 537–572.

Tarrant, M., Branscombe, N. R., Warner, R. H., & Weston, D. (2012). Social identity and perceptions of torture: It's moral when we do it. *Journal of Experimental Social Psychology, 48,* 513–518.

Tarrant, M., Dazeley, S., & Cottom, T. (2009). Social categorization and empathy for outgroup members. *British Journal of Social Psychology, 48,* 427–446.

Tay, L., & Diener, E. (2011). Needs and subjective well-being around the world. *Journal of Personality and Social Psychology, 101,* 354–365.

Taylor, D. A., Gould, R. J., & Brounstein, P. J. (1981). Effects of personalistic self-disclosure. *Personality and Social Psychology Bulletin, 7,* 487–492.

Taylor, L. S., Fiore, A. T., Mendelsohn, G. A., & Cheshire, C. (2011). "Out of my league": A real-world test of the matching hypothesis. *Personality and Social Psychology Bulletin, 37,* 942–954.

Taylor, S. E. (1981). A categorization approach to stereotyping. In D. L. Hamilton (Ed.), *Cognitive processes in stereotyping and intergroup behavior.* Hillsdale, NJ: Erlbaum.

Taylor, S. E. (1989). *Positive Illusions: Creative Self-Deception and the Healthy Mind* (p. 214). New York: Basic Books.

Taylor, S. E. (2002). *The tending instinct: How nurturing is essential to who we are and how we live.* New York: Times Books.

Taylor, S. E., Crocker, J., Fiske, S. T., Sprinzen, M., & Winkler, J. D. (1979). The generalizability of salience effects. *Journal of Personality and Social Psychology, 37,* 357–368.

Taylor, S. E., Repetti, R. L., & Seeman, T. (1997). Health psychology: What is an unhealthy environment and how does it get under the skin? *Annual Review of Psychology, 48,* 411–447.

Taylor, S. E., Saphire-Bernstein, S., & Seeman, T. E. (2010). Are plasma oxytocin in women and plasma vasopressin in men biomarkers of distressed pair-bond relationships? *Psychological Science, 21,* 3–7.

Taylor, S. G., Eisenbarth, H., Sedikides, C., & Alicke, M. D. (2021). Explaining the better-than-average effect among prisoners. *Journal of Applied Social Psychology, 51,* 90–106.

Technical Working Group for Eyewitness Evidence. (1999). *Eyewitness evidence: A guide for law enforcement.* U.S. Department of Justice, Office of Justice Programs, National Institute of Justice.

Tedeschi, J. T., Nesler, M., & Taylor, E. (1987). *Misattribution and the bogus pipeline: A test of dissonance and impression management theories.* Paper presented at the American Psychological Association convention.

Teger, A. I. (1980). *Too much invested to quit.* New York: Pergamon.

Teigen, K. H. (1986). Old truths or fresh insights? A study of students' evaluations of proverbs. *British Journal of Social Psychology, 25,* 43–50.

Teigen, K. H., Evensen, P. C., Samoilow, D. K., & Vatne, K. B. (1999). Good luck and bad luck: How to tell the difference. *European Journal of Social Psychology, 29,* 981–1010.

Telch, M. J., Killen, J. D., McAlister, A. L., Perry, C. L., & Maccoby, N. (1981). *Long-term follow-up of a pilot project on smoking prevention with adolescents.* Paper presented at the American Psychological Association convention.

Tenney, E. R., MacCoun, R. J., Spellman, B. A., & Hastie, R. (2007). Calibration trumps confidence as a basis for witness credibility. *Psychological Science, 18,* 46–50.

Tennov, D. (1979). *Love and limerence: The experience of being in love.* New York: Stein and Day.

Tesser, A., Martin, L., & Mendolia, M. (1995). The impact of thought on attitude extremity and attitude-behavior consistency. In R. E. Petty & J. A Krosnick (Eds.), *Attitude strength: Antecedents and consequences.* Hillsdale, NJ: Erlbaum.

Tesser, A., Millar, M., & Moore, J. (1988). Some affective consequences of social comparison and reflection processes: The pain and pleasure of being close. *Journal of Personality and Social Psychology, 54,* 49–61

Tesser, A., Rosen, S., & Conlee, M. C. (1972). News valence and available recipient as determinants of news transmission. *Sociometry, 35,* 619–628.

Testa, M. (2002). The impact of men's alcohol consumption on perpetration of sexual aggression. *Clinical Psychology Review, 22,* 1239–1263.

Testa, R. J., Rider, G. N., Haug, N. A., & Balsam, K. F. (2017). Gender confirming medical interventions and eating disorder symptoms among transgender individuals. *Health Psychology, 36,* 927–936.

Tetlock, P. E. (1983). Accountability and complexity of thought. *Journal of Personality and Social Psychology, 45,* 74–83.

Tetlock, P. E. (1988). Monitoring the integrative complexity of American and Soviet policy rhetoric: What can be learned? *Journal of Social Issues, 44,* 101–131.

Tetlock, P. E. (2005). *Expert political judgment: How good is it? How can we know?* Princeton, NJ: Princeton University Press.

Thakar, M., & Epstein, M. (2011, November 16). *How love emerges in arranged marriages: A follow-up cross-cultural study.* Paper presented to the National Council on Family Relations.

Thaler, R. H., & Sunstein, C. R. (2021). *Nudge: The final edition.* New York: Penguin.

The New York Times. (2011, September 20). A grievous wrong. Editorial. https://www.nytimes.com/2011/09/21/opinion/a-grievous-wrong-on-georgias-death-row.html

Theroux, P. (1979, September 20). Paul Theroux, restless writer of the rails. Interview by Paul Hendrickson. *The Washington Post.*

Thomas, E. F., & McGarty, C. A. (2009). The role of efficacy and moral outrage norms in creating the potential for international development activism through group-based interaction. *British Journal of Psychology, 48,* 115–134.

Thomas, K. A., De Freitas, J., DeScioli, P., & Pinker, S. (2016). Recursive mentalizing and common knowledge in the bystander effect. *Journal of Experimental Psychology: General, 145,* 621–629.

Thompson, D. V., & Malaviya, P. (2013). Consumer-generated ads: Does awareness of advertising co-creation help or hurt persuasion? *Journal of Marketing, 77,* 33–47.

Thompson, L. L., & Crocker, J. (1985). *Prejudice following threat to the self-concept. Effects of performance expectations and attributions.* Unpublished manuscript, Northwestern University.

Thompson, L., Valley, K. L., & Kramer, R. M. (1995). The bittersweet feeling of success: An examination of social perception in negotiation. *Journal of Experimental Social Psychology, 31,* 467–492.

Thompson, W. C., Cowan, C. L., & Rosenhan, D. L. (1980). Focus of attention mediates the impact of negative affect on altruism. *Journal of Personality and Social Psychology, 38,* 291–300.

Thompson, W. C., Fong, G. T., & Rosenhan, D. L. (1981). Inadmissible evidence and juror verdicts. *Journal of Personality and Social Psychology, 40,* 453–463.

Thomson, R., & Murachver, T. (2001). Predicting gender from electronic discourse. *British Journal of Social Psychology, 40,* 193–208 (and personal correspondence from T. Murachver, May 23, 2002).

Thornton, B., & Maurice, J. (1997). Physique contrast effect: Adverse impact of idealized body images for women. *Sex Roles, 37,* 433–439.

Tice, D. M., Butler, J. L., Muraven, M. B., & Stillwell, A. M. (1995). When modesty prevails: Differential favorability of self-presentation to friends and strangers. *Journal of Personality and Social Psychology, 69,* 1120–1138.

Tideman, S. (2003). Announcement of Operationalizing Gross National Happiness conference, 2004, February 18–20. Distributed via the Internet.

Tidwell, N. D., Eastwick, P. W., & Finkel, E. J. (2013). Perceived, not actual, similarity predicts initial attraction in a live romantic context: Evidence from the speed-dating paradigm. *Personal Relationships, 20,* 199–215.

Tifferet, S. (2020). Gender differences in social support on social network sites: A meta-analysis. *Cyberpsychology, Behavior, and Social Networking, 23*(4), 199–209.

Tiffert, S., & Vilnai-Yavetz, I. (2014). Gender differences in Facebook self-presentation: An international randomized study. *Computers in Human Behavior, 35,* 388–399.

Tiihonen, J., Rautiainen, M., Ollila, H. M., Repo-Tiihonen, E., Virkkunen, M., Palotie, A., & . . . Paunio, T. (2015). Genetic background of extreme violent behavior. *Molecular Psychiatry, 20,* 786–792.

Tilcsik, A. (2011). Pride and prejudice: Employment discrimination against openly gay men in the United States. *American Journal of Sociology, 117,* 586–626.

Timeo, S., & Suitner, C. (2018). Eating meat makes you sexy: Conformity to dietary gender norms and attractiveness. *Psychology of Men and Masculinity, 19,* 418–429.

Timmermans, A. C., & Rubie-Davies, C. M. (2022). Gender and minority background as moderators of teacher expectation effects on self-concept, subjective task values, and academic performance. *European Journal of Psychology of Education.*

Timmerman, T. A. (2007). "It was a thought pitch": Personal, situational, and target influences on hit-by-pitch events across time. *Journal of Applied Psychology, 92,* 876–884.

Tindale, R. S., Davis, J. H., Vollrath, D. A., Nagao, D. H., & Hinsz, V. B. (1990). Asymmetrical social influence in freely interacting groups: A test of three models. *Journal of Personality and Social Psychology, 58,* 438–449.

Tissera, H., Mignault, M.-C., & Human, L. J. (2023). "Zooming" in on positive and accurate metaperceptions in first impressions: Examining the links with social anxiety and liking in online video interactions. *Journal of Personality and Social Psychology.*

Toburen, T., & Meier, B. P. (2010). Priming God-related concepts increases anxiety and task persistence. *Journal of Social and Clinical Psychology, 29,* 127–143.

Todd, A. R., Bodenhausen, G. V., Richeson, J. A., & Galinsky, A. D. (2011). Perspective taking combats automatic expressions of racial bias. *Journal of Personality and Social Psychology, 100,* 1027–1042.

Todd, A. R., Johnson, D. J., Lassetter, B., Neel, R., Simpson, A. J., & Cesario, J. (2021). Category salience and racial bias in weapon identification: A diffusion modeling approach. *Journal of Personality and Social Psychology, 120,* 672–693.

Todorov, A. (2011). Evaluating faces on social dimensions. In A. Todorov, S. T. Fiske, & D. A. Prentice (Eds.), *Social neuroscience: Toward understanding the underpinnings of the social mind.* New York: Oxford University Press.

Todorov, A., Mandisodza, A. N., Goren, A., & Hall, C. C. (2005). Inferences of competence from faces predict election outcomes. *Science, 308,* 1623–1626.

Tomasello, M. (2009). *Why we cooperate.* Boston: MIT Press.

Tomasello, M. (2014). The ultra-social animal. *European Journal of Social Psychology, 44,* 187–194.

Tong, Y. (2022, August 23). India's Sex Ratio at Birth Begins To Normalize. Pew Research Center.

Toronto News. (1977, July 26).

Totterdell, P., Kellett, S., Briner, R. B., & Teuchmann, K. (1998). Evidence of mood linkage in work groups. *Journal of Personality and Social Psychology, 74,* 1504–1515.

Touré-Tillery, M., & Fishbach, A. (2017). Too far to help: The effect of perceived distance on the expected impact and likelihood of charitable action. *Journal of Personality and Social Psychology, 112,* 860–876.

Towers, S., Gomez-Lievano, A., Khan, M., Mubayi, A., & Castillo-Chavez, C. (2015). Contagion in mass killings and school shootings. *PLOS ONE, 10*(7), e0117259.

Towers, S., Mubayi, A., & Castillo-Chavez, C. (2018). Detecting the contagion effect in mass killings; a constructive example of the statistical advantages of unbinned likelihood methods. *PloS One, 13*(5), e0196863.

Towson, S. M. J., & Zanna, M. P. (1983). Retaliation against sexual assault: Self-defense or public duty? *Psychology of Women Quarterly, 8,* 89–99.

Trail, T. E., Shelton, J. N., & West, T. V. (2009). Interracial roommate relationships: Negotiating daily interactions. *Personality and Social Psychology Bulletin, 35,* 671–684.

Tran, C. (2015, June 27). Revealed: Couple who shared THAT kiss in the middle of the street as riot police battled an angry mob in Vancouver are still an item and live together in Australia. *Daily Mail.* https://bit.ly/2P7P86A

Travis, L. E. (1925). The effect of a small audience upon eye-hand coordination. *Journal of Abnormal and Social Psychology, 20,* 142–146.

Tremblay, M.-P. B., Tuerk, C., Jackson, P. L., & Beauchamp, M. H. (2023). Social neuroscience. In G. G. Brown, B. Crosson, K. Y. Haaland, & T. Z. King (Eds.), *APA handbook of neuropsychology, Volume 2: Neuroscience and neuromethods., Vol. 2.* (pp. 177–195). American Psychological Association.

Trevor Project (2023). 2023 U.S. National Survey on the Mental Health of LGBTQ Young People. thetrevorproject.org.

Triandis, H. C. (1981). *Some dimensions of intercultural variation and their implications for interpersonal behavior.* Paper presented at the American Psychological Association convention.

Triandis, H. C. (1982). *Incongruence between intentions and behavior: A review.* Paper presented at the American Psychological Association convention.

Triandis, H. C. (1994). *Culture and social behavior.* New York: McGraw Hill.

Triandis, H. C. (2000). Culture and conflict. *International Journal of Psychology, 55,* 145–152.

Triplett, N. (1898). The dynamogenic factors in pacemaking and competition. *American Journal of Psychology, 9,* 507–533.

Trivedi, N., Haynie, D., Bible, J., Liu, D., & Simons-Morton, B. (2017). Cell phone use while driving: Prospective association with emerging adult use. *Accident Analysis and Prevention, 106,* 450–455.

Troianovski, A. (2022, March 17). Why Vladimir Putin invokes Nazis to justify his invasion of Ukraine. *New York Times.*

Trolier, T. K., & Hamilton, D. L. (1986). Variables influencing judgments of correlational relations. *Journal of Personality and Social Psychology, 50,* 879–888.

Tropp, L. R., & Barlow, F. K. (2018). Making advantaged racial groups care about inequality: Intergroup contact as a route to psychological investment. *Current Directions in Psychological Science, 27,* 194–199.

Tropp, L. R., & Pettigrew, T. F. (2005). Differential relationships between intergroup contact and affective and cognitive dimensions of prejudice. *Personality and Social Psychology Bulletin, 31,* 1145–1158.

Tropp, L. R., Okamoto, D. K., Marrow H., & Jones-Correa M. (2018). How contact experiences shape welcoming: Perspectives from U.S.-born and immigrant groups. *Social Psychology Quarterly, 81*(1), 23–47.

Tropp, L. R., White, F., Rucinski, C. L., & Tredoux, C. (2022). Intergroup contact and prejudice reduction: Prospects and challenges in changing youth attitudes. *Review of General Psychology, 26,* 342–360.

Trost, M. R., Maass, A., & Kenrick, D. T. (1992). Minority influence: Personal relevance biases cognitive processes and reverses private acceptance. *Journal of Experimental Social Psychology, 28,* 234–254.

Tsang, J-A. (2002). Moral rationalization and the integration of situational factors and psychological processes in immoral behavior. *Review of General Psychology, 6,* 25–50.

Tsioulcas, A. (2023, February 23). Harvey Weinstein will likely spend the rest of his life in prison after LA sentence. NPR.org.

Tukachinsky, R. (2020). Playing a bad character but endorsing a good cause: Actor-character fundamental attribution error and persuasion. *Communication Reports, 33,* 1–13.

Turliuc, M. N., Măirean, C., & Boca-Zamfir, M. (2020). The relation between cyberbullying and depressive symptoms in adolescence The moderating role of emotion regulation strategies. *Computers in Human Behavior, 109,* 106341.

Turner, B. L., Caruso, E. M., Dilich, M. A., & Roese, N. J. (2019). Body camera footage leads to lower judgments of intent than dash camera footage. *PNAS, 116,* 1201–1206.

Turner, C. W., Hesse, B. W., & Peterson-Lewis, S. (1986). Naturalistic studies of the long-term effects of television violence. *Journal of Social Issues, 42*(3), 51–74.

Turner, J. C. (1981). The experimental social psychology of intergroup behaviour. In J. Turner & H. Giles (Eds.), *Intergroup behavior.* Oxford, England: Blackwell.

Turner, J. C. (2000). Social identity. In A. E. Kazdin (Ed.), *Encyclopedia of Psychology* (p. 7). Washington, DC: American Psychological Association.

Turner, M. E., & Pratkanis, A. R. (1994). Social identity maintenance prescriptions for preventing groupthink: Reducing identity protection and enhancing intellectual conflict. *International Journal of Conflict Management, 5,* 254–270.

Turner, M. E., & Pratkanis, A. R. (1997). Mitigating groupthink by stimulating constructive conflict. In C. K. W. De Dreu & E. Van de Vliert (Eds.), *Using conflict in organizations.* London: Sage.

Turner, M. E., Pratkanis, A. R., Probasco, P., & Leve, C. (1992). Threat cohesion and group effectiveness: Testing a social identity maintenance perspective on groupthink. *Journal of Personality and Social Psychology, 63,* 781–796.

Turner, N., Barling, J., & Zacharatos, A. (2002). Positive psychology at work. In C. R. Snyder & S. J. Lopez (Eds.), *The handbook of positive psychology.* New York: Oxford University Press.

Tutu, D. (1999). *No future without forgiveness.* New York: Doubleday

Tversky, A., & Kahneman, D. (1974). Judgment under uncertainty: Heuristics and biases. *Science, 185(4157),* 1124–1131.

Tversky, A., & Kahneman, D. (1983). Extensional versus intuitive reasoning: The conjunction fallacy in probability judgment. *Psychological Review, 90,* 293–315.

Twenge, J. M., & Blake, A. B. (2020). Increased support for same-sex marriage in the U.S.: Disentangling age, period, and cohort effects. *Journal of Homosexuality.* Advance online publication. doi: 10.1080/00918369.2019.1705672

Twenge, J. M., & Cooper, A. B. (2020). The expanding class divide in happiness in the United States, 1972–2016. *Emotion.* Advance online publication. doi: 10.1037/emo0000774

Twenge, J. M., & Kasser, T. (2013). Generational changes in materialism and work centrality, 1976–2007: Associations with temporal changes in societal insecurity and materialistic role modeling. *Personality and Social Psychology Bulletin, 39,* 883–897.

Twenge, J. M., & Martin, G. N. (2020). Gender differences in associations between digital media use and psychological well-being: Evidence from three large datasets. *Journal of Adolescence, 79,* 91–102.

Twenge, J. M., & Spitzberg, B. H. (2020). Declines in non-digital social interaction among Americans, 2003–2017. *Journal of Applied Social Psychology, 50,* 363–367.

Twenge, J. M. (1997). Changes in masculine and feminine traits over time: A meta-analysis. *Sex Roles, 36,* 305–325.

Twenge, J. M. (2009). Change over time in obedience: The jury's still out, but it might be decreasing. *American Psychologist, 64,* 28–31.

Twenge, J. M. (2013). Teaching Generation Me. *Teaching of Psychology, 40,* 66–69.

Twenge, J. M. (2014). *Generation me: Why today's young Americans are more confident, assertive, entitled–and more miserable than ever before* (2nd ed.). New York: Atria.

Twenge, J. M. (2017). *iGen: Why today's super-connected kids are growing up less rebellious, more tolerant, less happy–and completely unprepared for adulthood.* New York: Atria Books.

Twenge, J. M. (2023). *Generations: The Real Differences between Gen Z, Millennials, Gen X, Boomers and Silents–and What They Mean for America's Future.* New York: Atria Books.

Twenge, J. M., Abebe, E. M., & Campbell, W. K. (2010). Fitting in or standing out: Trends in American parents' choices for children's names, 1880–2007. *Social Psychological and Personality Science, 1,* 19–25.

Twenge, J. M., Baumeister, R. F., Tice, D. M., & Stucke, T. S. (2001). If you can't join them, beat them: Effects of social exclusion on aggressive behavior. *Journal of Personality and Social Psychology, 81,* 1058–1069.

Twenge, J. M., Campbell, W. K., & Gentile, B. (2013). Changes in pronoun use in American books and the rise of individualism, 1960–2008. *Journal of Cross-Cultural Psychology, 44,* 406–415.

Twenge, J. M., Catanese, K. R., & Baumeister, R. F. (2002). Social exclusion causes self-defeating behavior. *Journal of Personality and Social Psychology, 83,* 606–615.

Twenge, J. M., Catanese, K. R., & Baumeister, R. F. (2003). Social exclusion and the deconstructed state: Time perception, meaninglessness, lethargy, lack of emotion, and self-awareness. *Journal of Personality and Social Psychology, 85,* 409–423.

Twenge, J. M., Dawson, L., & Campbell, W. K. (2016). Still standing out: Children's names in the United States during the Great Recession and correlations with economic indicators. *Journal of Applied Social Psychology, 46,* 663–670.

Twenge, J. M., Honeycutt, N., Prislin, R., & Sherman, R. A. (2016). More polarized but more Independent: Political party identification and ideological self-categorization among U.S. adults, college students, and late adolescents, 1970–2015. *Personality and Social Psychology Bulletin, 42,* 1364–1383.

Twenge, J. M., Martin, G. N., & Campbell, W. K. (2018). Decreases in psychological well-being among American adolescents after 2012 and links to screen time during the rise of smartphone technology. *Emotion, 18,* 765–780.

Twenge, J. M., Sherman, R. A., & Lyubomirsky, S. (2016). More happiness for young people and less for mature adults: Time period differences in subjective well-being in the United States, 1972–2014. *Social Psychological and Personality Science, 7,* 131–141.

Twenge, J. M., Sherman, R. A., & Wells, B. E. (2015). Changes in American adults' sexual behavior and attitudes, 1972–2012. *Archives of Sexual Behavior, 44*(8), 2273–2285.

Twenge, J. M., Spitzberg, B. H., & Campbell, W. K. (2019). Less in-person social interaction with peers among U.S. adolescents in the 21st century and links to loneliness. *Journal of Social and Personal Relationships, 36,* 1892–1913.

Twenge, J. M., Wells, B. E., & Le, J. (2023). Increases in LGB identification among us adults, 2014–2021. *Sexuality Research & Social Policy.*

Twenge, J. M., Zhang, L., Catanese, K. R., Dolan-Pascoe, B., Lyche, L. F., & Baumeister, R. F. (2007). Replenishing connectedness: Reminders of social activity reduce aggression after social exclusion. *British Journal of Social Psychology, 46,* 205–224.

Ty, A., Mitchell, D. V., & Finger, E. (2017). Making amends: Neural systems supporting donation decisions prompting guilt and restitution. *Personality and Individual Differences, 107,* 28–36.

Tykocinski, O. E., & Bareket-Bojmel, L. (2009). The lost e-mail technique: Use of an implicit measure to assess discriminatory attitudes toward two minority groups in Israel. *Journal of Applied Social Psychology, 39,* 62–81.

Tyler, J. M. (2012). Triggering self-presentation efforts outside of people's conscious awareness. *Personality and Social Psychology Bulletin, 38,* 619–627.

Tyler, J. M., McIntyre, M. M., Graziano, W. G., & Sands, K. J. (2015). High self-monitors' cognitive access to self-presentation-related information. *British Journal of Social Psychology, 54,* 205–219.

Tyler, T. R., & Lind, E. A. (1990). Intrinsic versus community-based justice models: When does group membership matter? *Journal of Social Issues, 46,* 83–94.

Uchino, B. N., Smith, T. W., & Berg, C. A. (2014). Spousal relationship quality and cardiovascular risk: Dyadic perceptions of relationship ambivalence are associated with coronary-artery calcification. *Psychological Science, 25,* 1037–1042.

Ugwuegbu, C. E. (1979). Racial and evidential factors in juror attribution of legal responsibility. *Journal of Experimental Social Psychology, 15,* 133–146.

Uleman, J. S. (1989). A framework for thinking intentionally about unintended thoughts. In J. S. Uleman & J. A. Bargh (Eds.), *Unintended thought: The limits of awareness, intention, and control.* New York: Guilford.

Uleman, J. S., Saribay, S. A., & Gonzalez, C. M. (2008). Spontaneous inferences, implicit impressions, and implicit theories. *Annual Review of Psychology, 59,* 329–360.

UMich. (2020, October). *Survey of consumers: Preliminary results for October, 2020.* University of Michigan. www.sca.isr.umich.edu

Unger, R. K. (1979). *Whom does helping help?* Paper presented at the Eastern Psychological Association convention, April.

United Nations (2019). Global Study on homicide, 2019 edition. https://www.unodc.org/unodc/en/data-and-analysis/global-study-on-homicide.html

United Nations. (2020). *United in science.* https://public.wmo.int/en/resources/united_in_science

Unkelbach, C., & Högden, F. (2019). Why does George Clooney make coffee sexy? The case for attribute conditioning. *Current Directions in Psychological Science, 28,* 540–546.

Unkelbach, C., & Memmert, D. (2010). Crowd noise as a cue in referee decisions contributes to the home advantage. *Journal of Sport & Exercise Psychology, 32,* 483–498.

Unkelbach, C., & Speckmann, F. (2021). Mere repetition increases belief in factually true COVID-19-related information. *Journal of Applied Research in Memory and Cognition, 10,* 241–247.

Unkelbach, C., Koch, A., Silva, R. R., & Garcia-Marques, T. (2019). Truth by repetition: Explanations and implications. *Current Directions in Psychological Science, 28,* 247–253.

UN News. (2019, June 12). *Understanding of LGBT realities "non-existent" in most countries, says UN expert.* https://news.un.org/en/story/2019/06/1040381

UNODC. (2023). Global study on homicide 2023. United Nations Office of Drugs and Crime. https://www.unodc.org/documents/data-and-analysis/gsh/2023/Global_study_on_homicide_2023_web.pdf

Unsworth, K. L., & McNeill, I. M. (2017). Increasing pro-environmental behaviors by increasing self-concordance: Testing an intervention. *Journal of Applied Psychology, 102,* 88–103.

Unsworth, N., Redick, T. S., McMillan, B. D., Hambrick, D. Z., Kane, M. J., & Engle, R. W. (2015). Is playing video games related to cognitive abilities? *Psychological Science, 26,* 759–774.

UN (United Nations). (2015). *The world's women: Trends and statistics.* United Nations Department of Economic and Social Affairs, pp. 1–232.

UN (United Nations). (2020). *The human cost of disasters—an overview of the last twenty years 2000-2019.* https://reliefweb.int/report/world/human-cost-disasters-overview-last-20-years-2000-2019

Upadhyaya, M., & Kozman, M. (2022). The Blue Whale Challenge, Social Media, Self-Harm, and Suicide Contagion. *The Primary Care Companion for CNS Disorders, 24*(5).

Urban, E. J., Charles, S. T., Levine, L. J., & Almeida, D. M. (2018). Depression history and memory bias for specific daily emotions. *PLOS ONE, 13*(9), e0203574.

U.S. Bureau of Economic Analysis. (2024). *Real disposable personal income: Per capita.* https://fred.stlouisfed.org/series/A229RX0#0

U.S. Census. (2019, November 19). One-person households on the rise. https://www.census.gov/library/visualizations/2019/comm/one-person-households.html

U.S. Department of Justice. (2017). *Eyewitness identification procedures for conducting photo arrays.* https://www.justice.gov/file/923201/download

Ušto, M., Drače, S., & Hadžiahmetović, N. (2019). Replication of the "Asch effect" in Bosnia and Herzegovina: Evidence for the moderating role of group similarity in conformity. *Psihologijske Teme, 28,* 589–599.

Uysal, A., Lin, H. L., & Knee, C. R. (2010). The role of need satisfaction in self-concealment and well-being. *Personality and Social Psychology Bulletin, 36,* 187–199.

Väänänen, A., Buunk, B. P., Kivimäke, M., Pentti, J., & Vahtera, J. (2005). When it is better to give than to receive: Long-term health effects of perceived reciprocity in support exchange. *Journal of Personality and Social Psychology, 89,* 176–193.

Vaillant, G. E. (1977). *Adaptation to life.* Boston: Little, Brown.

Vaillant, G. E. (2002). *Aging well: Surprising guideposts to a happier life from the landmark Harvard study of adult development.* Boston: Little, Brown.

Vala, J., Pereira, C., Oliveira Lima, M. E., & Leyens, J. (2012). Intergroup time bias and racialized social relations. *Personality and Social Psychology Bulletin, 38,* 491–504.

Valdesolo, P., & DeSteno, D. (2007). Moral hypocrisy: Social groups and the flexibility of virtue. *Psychological Science, 18,* 689–690.

Valdesolo, P., & DeSteno, D. (2008). The duality of virtue: Deconstructing the moral hypocrite. *Journal of Experimental Social Psychology, 44,* 1334–1338.

Valentine, T., & Mesout, J. (2009). Eyewitness identification under stress in the London Dungeon. *Applied Cognitive Psychology, 23,* 151–161.

Valentine, T., Pickering, A., & Darling, S. (2003). Characteristics of eyewitness identification that predict the outcome of real lineups. *Applied Cognitive Psychology, 17,* 969–993.

Vallone, R. P., Ross, L., & Lepper, M. R. (1985). The hostile media phenomenon: Biased perception and perceptions of media bias in coverage of the "Beirut Massacre." *Journal of Personality and Social Psychology, 49,* 577–585.

Vallone, R.P., Ross, L., Lepper, M.R. (1985). The hostile media phenonmenon: Biased perception and perceptions of media bias in coverage of the Beirut massacre. *Journal of Personality and Social Psychology,* 49, 3, 577–85.

Valor-Segura, I., Exposito, F., & Moya, M. (2011). Victim blaming and exoneration of the perpetrator in domestic violence: The role of beliefs in a just world and ambivalent sexism. *The Spanish Journal of Psychology, 14*(1), 195–206.

Van Assche, J., Roets, A., Van Hiel, A., & Dhont, K. (2019). Diverse reactions to ethnic diversity: The role of individual differences in authoritarianism. *Current Directions in Psychological Science, 28,* 523–527.

Van Assche, J., Swart, H., Schmid, K., Dhont, K., Al Ramiah, A., Christ, O., Kauff, M., Rothmann, S., Savelkoul, M., Tausch, N., Wölfer, R., Zahreddine, S., Saleem, M., & Hewstone, M. (2023). Intergroup contact is reliably associated with reduced prejudice, even in the face of group threat and discrimination. *American Psychologist, 78,* 761–774.

van Baaren, R. B., Holland, R. W., Kawakami, K., & van Knippenberg, A. (2004). Mimicry and prosocial behavior. *Psychological Science, 15,* 71–74.

van Baaren, R. B., Holland, R. W., Steenaert, B., & van Knippenberg, A. (2003). Mimicry for money: Behavioral consequences of imitation. *Journal of Experimental Social Psychology, 39,* 393–398.

Van Bavel, J. J., & Cunningham, W. A. (2012). A social identity approach to person memory: Group membership, collective identification, and social role shape attention and memory. *Personality and Social Psychology Bulletin, 38,* 1566–1578.

Van Bavel, J. J., Rathje, S., Harris, E., Robertson, C., & Sternisko, A. (2021). How social media shapes polarization. *Trends in Cognitive Sciences, 25,* 913–916.

Van Boven, L., Ehret, P. J., & Sherman, D. K. (2018). Psychological barriers to bipartisan public support for climate policy. *Perspectives on Psychological Science, 13,* 492–507.

VanDellen, M. R., Campbell, W. K., Hoyle, R. H., & Bradfield, E. K. (2011). Compensating, resisting, and breaking: A meta-analytic examination of reactions to self-esteem threat. *Personality and Social Psychology Review, 15,* 51–74.

Vandello, J. A., & Bosson, J. K. (2013). Hard won and easily lost: A review and synthesis of theory and research on precarious manhood. *Psychology of Men and Masculinity, 14,* 101–113.

Vandello, J. A., & Cohen, D. (1999). Patterns of individualism and collectivism across the United States. *Journal of Personality and Social Psychology, 77,* 279–292.

Vandello, J. A., Cohen, D., & Ransom, S. (2008). U.S. southern and northern differences in perceptions of norms about aggression: Mechanisms for the perpetuation of a culture of honor. *Journal of Cross-Cultural Psychology, 39,* 162–177.

van der Linden, S. (2023). *Foolproof: Why Misinformation Infects Our Minds and How to Build Immunity.* New York: W. W. Norton.

van der Linden, S., Leiserowitz, A., Rosenthal, S., & Maibach, E. (2017). Inoculating the public against misinformation about climate change. *Global Challenges, 1,* 1600008.

van der Meer, T. G. L. A., & Hameleers, M. (2022). I knew it, the world is falling apart! Combatting a confirmatory negativity bias in audiences' news selection through news media literacy interventions. *Digital Journalism, 10,* 473–492.

van der Meer, T. G. L. A., & Jin, Y. (2020). Seeking formula for misinformation treatment in public health crises: The effects of corrective Information type and source. *Health Communication, 35,* 560–575.

Vanderslice, V. J., Rice, R. W., & Julian, J. W. (1987). The effects of participation in decision-making on worker satisfaction and productivity: An organizational simulation. *Journal of Applied Social Psychology, 17,* 158–170.

Van Dessel, P., Mertens, G., Smith, C. T., & De Houwer, J. (2019). Mere exposure effects on implicit stimulus evaluation: The moderating role of evaluation task, number of stimulus presentations, and memory for presentation frequency. *Personality and Social Psychology Bulletin, 45,* 447–460.

Van de Vyver, J., Houston, D. M., Abrams, D., & Vasiljevic, M. (2016). Boosting belligerence: How the July 7, 2005, London bombings affected liberals' moral foundations and prejudice. *Psychological Science, 27,* 169–177.

van Dijk, W. W., Finkenauer, C., & Pollmann, M. (2008). The misprediction of emotions in track athletics: Is experience the teacher of all things? *Basic and Applied Social Psychology, 30,* 369–376.

van Dijk, W. W., Ouwerkerk, J. W., van Koningsbruggen, G. M., & Wesseling, Y. M. (2012). "So you wanna be a pop star?": Schadenfreude following another's misfortune on TV. *Basic & Applied Social Psychology, 34,* 168–174.

van Emmerik, A. A., Reijntjes, A., & Kamphuis, J. H. (2013). Writing therapy for post-traumatic stress: A meta-analysis. *Psychotherapy and Psychosomatics, 82,* 82–88.

van Hemmen, J., Veltman, D. J., Hoekzema, E., Cohen-Kettenis, P. T., Dessens, A. B., & Bakker, J. (2016). Neural activation during mental rotation in complete androgen insensitivity syndrome: The influence of sex hormones and sex chromosomes. *Cerebral Cortex, 26,* 1036–1045.

Van Lange, P. A. M., Manesi, Z., Meershoek, R. W. J., Yuan, M., Dong, M., & Van Doesum, N. J. (2018). Do male and female soccer players differ in helping? A study on prosocial behavior among young players. *PLOS ONE, 13*(12), e0209168.

van Meurs, E., Greve, J., & Strauss, B. (2022). Moving in the presence of others – a systematic review and meta-analysis on social facilitation. *International Review of Sport and Exercise Psychology.*

van Mulukom, V., Pummerer, L. J., Alper, S., Bai, H., Cavojova, V., Farias, J., Kay, C. S., Lazarevic, L. B., Lobato, E. J. C., Marinthe, G., Banai, I. P., Srol, J., & Zezelj, I. (2022). Antecedents and consequences of COVID-19 conspiracy beliefs: A systematic review. *Social Science and Medicine, 301,* 114912.

van Prooijen, J., Krouwel, A. P. M., Boiten, M., & Eendebak, L. (2015). Fear among the extremes: How political ideology predicts negative emotions and outgroup derogation. *Personality and Social Psychology Bulletin, 41,* 485–497.

Van Prooijen, J. W, & Acker, M. (2015). The influence of control on belief in conspiracy theories: Conceptual and applied extensions. *Applied Cognitive Psychology,* 29, 753–761.

van Prooijen, J.-W., & Krouwel, A. P. M. (2019). Psychological features of extreme political ideologies. *Current Directions in Psychological Science, 28,* 159–163.

Van Prooijen, J. W. (2019a). An existential threat model of conspiracy theories. *European Psychologist, 25,* 1–10.

Van Prooijen, J. W. (2019b). Belief in conspiracy theories: Gullibility or rational skepticism? In J. Forgas, & R. Baumeister (Eds.), *The social psychology of gullibility* (pp. 319–332). Routledge.

van Prooijen, J.-W., Etienne, T. W., Kutiyski, Y., & Krouwel, A. P. M. (2023). Conspiracy beliefs prospectively predict health behavior and well-being during a pandemic. *Psychological Medicine, 53,* 2514–2521.

van Schaik, J. E., & Hunnius, S. (2016). Little chameleons: The development of social mimicry during early childhood. *Journal of Experimental Child Psychology, 147,* 71–81.

van Straaten, I., Engels, R. C. M. E., Finkenauer, C., & Holland, R. W. (2009). Meeting your match: How attractiveness similarity affects approach behavior in mixed-sex dyads. *Personality and Social Psychology Bulletin, 35,* 685–697.

van Tuijl, L. A., Bennik, E. C., Penninx, B. W. J. H., Spinhoven, P., & de Jong, P. J. (2020). Predictive value of implicit and explicit self-esteem for the recurrence of depression and anxiety disorders: A 3-year follow-up study. *Journal of Abnormal Psychology, 129,* 788–798.

van Veluw, S. J., & Chance, S. A. (2014). Differentiating between self and others: An ALE meta-analysis of fMRI studies of self-recognition and theory of mind. *Brain Imaging and Behavior, 8,* 24–38.

Van Vugt, M., & Spisak, B. R. (2008). Sex differences in the emergence of leadership during competitions within and between groups. *Psychological Science, 19,* 854–858.

Vanwesenbeeck, I., Hudders, L., & Ponnet, K. (2020). Understanding the YouTube generation: How preschoolers process television and YouTube advertising. *Cyberpsychology, Behavior, and Social Networking, 23*(6), 426–432.

Van Yperen, N. W., & Buunk, B. P. (1990). A longitudinal study of equity and satisfaction in intimate relationships. *European Journal of Social Psychology, 20,* 287–309.

Van Zant, A. B., & Berger, J. (2020). How the voice persuades. *Journal of Personality and Social Psychology, 118,* 661–682.

Vargas, R. A. (2009, July 6). "City of Heroes" character "Twixt" becomes game's most hated outcast courtesy of Loyola professor. *The Times-Picayune.* www.nola.com

Vargas-Salfate, S., Paez, D., Liu, J. H., Pratto, F., & de Zúñiga, H. G. (2018). A comparison of social dominance theory and system justification: The role of social status in 19 nations. *Personality and Social Psychology Bulletin, 44,* 1060–1076.

Varnum, M. E. W., & Kitayama, S. (2011). What's in a name? Popular names are less common on frontiers. *Psychological Science, 22,* 176–183.

Varnum, M. E. W. (2012). Conformity effect sizes are smaller on the frontier. *Journal of Cognition and Cultures, 12,* 359–364.

Varnum, M. E. W. (2013). Frontiers, germs, and nonconformist voting. *Journal of Cross-Cultural Psychology, 44,* 832–837.

Vartanian, L. R., Spanos, S., Herman, C. P., & Polivy, J. (2015). Modeling of food intake: A meta-analytic review. *Social Influence, 10,* 119–136.

Vasquez, E. A., Denson, T. F., Pedersen, W. C., Stenstrom, D. M., & Miller, N. (2005). The moderating effect of trigger intensity on triggered displaced aggression. *Journal of Experimental Social Psychology, 41,* 61–67.

Vaughan-Johnston, T. I., & Jacobson, J. A. (2021). Naïve beliefs about self-esteem's importance. *Personality and Individual Differences, 173.*

Vaughan, K. B., & Lanzetta, J. T. (1981). The effect of modification of expressive displays on vicarious emotional arousal. *Journal of Experimental Social Psychology, 17,* 16–30.

Vedantam, S. (2012, May 9). Partisan psychology: Why do people choose political loyalties over facts? *NPR.* http://www.npr.org/blogs/itsallpolitics/2012/05/09/152287372/partisan-psychology-why-are-people-partial-to-political-loyalties-over-facts.

Veldhuis, J., Alleva, J. M., Bij de Vaate, A. J. D., Keijer, M., & Konijn, E. A. (2020). Me, my selfie, and I: The relations between selfie behaviors, body image, self-objectification, and self-esteem in young women. *Psychology of Popular Media, 9,* 3–13.

Verkuyten, M., & Yildiz, A. A. (2007). National (dis)identification and ethnic and religious identity: A study among Turkish-Dutch Muslims. *Personality and Social Psychology, 33,* 1448–1462.

Verplanken, B. (1991). Persuasive communication of risk information: A test of cue versus message processing effects in a field experiment. *Personality and Social Psychology Bulletin, 17,* 188–193.

Vescio, T. K., Gervais, S. J., Snyder, M., & Hoover, A. (2005). Power and the creation of patronizing environments: The stereotype-based behaviors of the powerful and their effects on female performance in masculine domains. *Journal of Personality and Social Psychology, 88,* 658–672.

Veysey, B. M., & Messner, S. F. (1999). Further testing of social disorganization theory: An elaboration of Sampson and Groves's "Community structure and crime." *Journal of Research in Crime and Delinquency, 36,* 156–174.

Vial, A. C., Brescoll, V. L., & Dovidio, J. F. (2019). Third-party prejudice accommodation increases gender discrimination. *Journal of Personality and Social Psychology, 117,* 73–98.

Vidmar, N., & Laird, N. M. (1983). Adversary social roles: Their effects on witnesses' communication of evidence and the assessments of adjudicators. *Journal of Personality and Social Psychology, 44,* 888–898.

Vidmar, N. (1979). The other issues in jury simulation research. *Law and Human Behavior, 3,* 95–106.

Viken, R. J., Treat, T. A., Bloom, S. L., & McFall, R. M. (2005). Illusory correlation for body type and happiness: Covariation bias and its relationship to eating disorder symptoms. *International Journal of Eating Disorders, 38,* 65–72.

Vilar, R., Liu, J. H., & Gouveia, V. V. (2020). Age and gender differences in human values: A 20-nation study. *Psychology and Aging, 35,* 345–356.

Viser, M., & Olorunnipa, T. (2020, August 21). As Trump prepares for GOP convention, Democrats plot their own counterprogramming. *The Washington Post.* https://www.washingtonpost.com/politics/republican-democratic-national-convention/2020/08/21/fdcf470a-e3bb-11ea-b69b-64f7b0477ed4_story.html

Visher, C. A. (1987). Juror decision making: The importance of evidence. *Law and Human Behavior, 11,* 1–17.

Visintainer, M. A., & Seligman, M. E. (1983, July/August). The hope factor. *American Health,* 59–61.

Visintainer, M. A., & Seligman, M. E. P. (1985). Tumor rejection and early experience of uncontrollable shock in the rat. Unpublished manuscript, University of Pennsylvania. See also M. A. Visintainer et al. (1982), Tumor rejection in rats after inescapable versus escapable shock. *Science, 216,* 437–439.

Visser, P. S., & Mirabile, R. R. (2004). Attitudes in the social context: The impact of social network composition on individual-level attitude strength. *Journal of Personality and Social Psychology, 87,* 779–795.

Vohs, K. D. (2015). Money priming can change people's thoughts, feelings, motivations, and behaviors: An update on 10 years of experiments. *Journal of Experimental Psychology: General, 144*(4), e86–e93.

Voigt, R., Camp, N. P., Prabhakaran, V., Hamilton, W. L., Hetey, R. C., Griffiths, C. M., . . . Eberhardt, J. L. (2017). Language from police body camera footage shows racial disparities in officer respect. *PNAS, 114,* 6521–6526.

Vollhardt, J. R. (2010). Enhanced external and culturally sensitive attributions after extended intercultural contact. *British Journal of Social Psychology, 49,* 363–383.

Vollrath, D. A., Sheppard, B. H., Hinsz, V. B., & Davis, J. H. (1989). Memory performance by decision-making groups and individuals. *Organizational Behavior and Human Decision Processes, 43,* 289–300.

von Hippel, W., Silver, L. A., & Lynch, M. B. (2000). Stereotyping against your will: The role of inhibitory ability in stereotyping and prejudice among the elderly. *Personality and Social Psychology Bulletin, 26,* 523–532.

von Soest, T., Luhmann, M., & Gerstorf, D. (2020a). The development of loneliness through adolescence and young adulthood: Its nature, correlates, and midlife outcomes. *Developmental Psychology, 56,* 1919–1934.

von Soest, T., Luhmann, M., Hansen, T., & Gerstorf, D. (2020b). Development of loneliness in midlife and old age: Its nature and correlates. *Journal of Personality and Social Psychology, 118,* 388–406.

Vorauer, J. D., & Quesnel, M. (2013). You don't really love me, do you? Negative effects of imagine-other perspective-taking on lower self-esteem individuals' relationship well-being. *Personality and Social Psychology Bulletin, 39,* 1428–1440.

Vorauer, J. D., & Ratner, R. K. (1996). Who's going to make the first move? Pluralistic ignorance as an impediment to relationship formation. *Journal of Social and Personal Relationships, 13,* 483–506.

Vorauer, J. D., & Sasaki, S. J. (2010). In need of liberation or constraint? How intergroup attitudes moderate the behavioral implications of intergroup ideologies. *Journal of Experimental Social Psychology, 46,* 133–138.

Vorauer, J. D., & Sasaki, S. J. (2011). In the worst rather than the best of times: Effect of salient intergroup ideology in threatening intergroup interactions. *Journal of Personality and Social Psychology, 101,* 307–320.

Vorauer, J. D., Main, K. J., & O'Connell, G. B. (1998). How do individuals expect to be viewed by members of lower status groups? Content and implications of meta-stereotypes. *Journal of Personality and Social Psychology, 75,* 917–937.

Vosoughi, S., Roy, D., & Aral, S. (2018). The spread of true and false news online. *Science, 359,* 1146–1151.

Vrij, A., Meissner, C. A., Fisher, R. P., Kassin, S. M., Morgan,Charles A., I.,II, & Kleinman, S. M. (2017). Psychological perspectives on interrogation. *Perspectives on Psychological Science, 12,* 927–955.

Vukasović, T., & Bratko, D. (2015). Heritability of personality: A meta-analysis of behavior genetic studies. *Psychological Bulletin, 141,* 769–785.

Vuletich, H. A., & Payne, B. K. (2019). Stability and change in implicit bias. *Psychological Science, 30,* 854–862.

Wade, K. A., Garry, M., & Pezdek, K. (2018). Deconstructing rich false memories of committing crime: Commentary on Shaw and Porter (2015). *Psychological Science, 29,* 471–476.

Wade, K. A., Green, S. L., & Nash, R. A. (2010). Can fabricated evidence induce false eyewitness testimony? *Applied Cognitive Psychology, 24,* 899–908.

Wade, L. (2017). *American hookup: The new culture of sex on campus.* New York: W. W. Norton.

Wadsworth, T. (2014). Sex and the pursuit of happiness: How other people's sex lives are related to our sense of well-being. *Social Indicators Research, 116,* 115–135.

Wagner, G. (2011). Going green but getting nowhere. *The New York Times.* https://www.nytimes.com/2011/09/08/opinion/going-green-but-getting-nowhere.html

Wagner, U., Tachtsoglou, S., Kotzur, P. F., Friehs, M.-T., & Kemmesies, U. (2020). Proportion of foreigners negatively predicts the prevalence of xenophobic hate crimes within German districts. *Social Psychology Quarterly, 83,* 195–205.

Walfish, S., McAlister, B., O'Donnell, P., & Lambert, M. J. (2012). An investigation of self-assessment bias in mental health providers. *Psychological Reports, 110,* 639–644.

Walker, M., & Keller, M. (2019). Beyond attractiveness: A multimethod approach to study enhancement in self-recognition on the Big Two personality dimensions. *Journal of Personality and Social Psychology, 117,* 483–499.

Walker, P. M., & Hewstone, M. (2008). The influence of social factors and implicit racial bias on a generalized own-race effect. *Applied Cognitive Psychology, 22,* 441–453.

Walker, R. (2004, December 5). The hidden (in plain sight) persuaders. *The New York Times Magazine.* www.nytimes.com

Wallace, D. B., & Kassin, S. M. (2012). Harmless error analysis: How do judges respond to confession errors? *Law and Human Behavior, 36,* 155–164.

Wallace, D. S., Paulson, R. M., Lord, C. G., & Bond, C. F., Jr. (2005). Which behaviors do attitudes predict? Meta-analyzing the effects of social pressure and perceived difficulty. *Review of General Psychology, 9,* 214–227.

Wallace, E., & Buil, I. (2023). Investigating trait antecedents of normative and deceptive Like-seeking on Instagram. *Personality and Individual Differences, 208,* 1–6.

Wallace, M. (1969, November 25). Transcript of interview of Vietnam War veteran on his role in alleged massacre of civilians at Songmy. *The New York Times.*

Waller, J. (2002). *Becoming evil: How ordinary people commit genocide and mass killing.* New York: Oxford University Press.

Walster (Hatfield), E., Aronson, V., Abrahams, D., & Rottman, L. (1966). Importance of physical attractiveness in dating behavior. *Journal of Personality and Social Psychology, 4,* 508–516.

Walster (Hatfield), E., Walster, G. W., & Berscheid, E. (1978). *Equity: Theory and research.* Boston: Allyn & Bacon.

Walter, K. V., Conroy-Beam, D., Buss, D. M., Asao, K., Sorokowska, A., Sorokowski, P., Aavik, T., Akello, G., Alhabahba, M. M., Alm, C., Amjad, N., Anjum, A., Atama, C. S., Atamtürk Duyar, D., Ayebare, R., Batres, C., Bendixen, M., Bensafia, A., . . . Bizumic, B. (2020). Sex differences in mate preferences across 45 countries: A large-scale replication. *Psychological Science, 31,* 408–423.

Walters, K., Christakis, D. A., & Wright, D. R. (2018). Are Mechanical Turk worker samples representative of health status and health behaviors in the U.S.? *PLOS ONE, 13*(6), e0198835.

Walther, E., Weil, R., & Düsing, J. (2011). The role of evaluative conditioning in attitude formation. *Current Directions in Psychological Science, 20,* 190–196.

Walton, G. M. (2014). The new science of wise psychological interventions. *Current Directions in Psychological Science, 23,* 73–82.

Walum, H., Westberg, L., Heinningsson, S., Neiderhiser, J. M., Reiss, D., Igl, W., Ganiban, J. M., Spotts, E. L., Pedersen, N. L., Eriksson, E., & Lichtenstein, P. (2008). Genetic variation in the vasopressin receptor 1a gene (*AVPR1A*) associates with pair-bonding behavior in humans. *PNAS, 105,* 14153–14156.

Wang, F., Gao, Y., Han, Z., Yu, Y., Long, Z., Jiang, X., Wu, Y., Pei, B., Cao, Y., Ye, J., Wang, M., & Zhao, Y. (2023). A systematic review and meta-analysis of 90 cohort studies of social isolation, loneliness and mortality. *Nature Human Behaviour, 7,* 1307–1319.

Wang, F. L., Galán, C. A., Lemery-Chalfant, K., Wilson, M. N., & Shaw, D. S. (2020). Evidence for two genetically distinct pathways to co-occurring internalizing and externalizing problems in adolescence characterized by negative affectivity or behavioral inhibition. *Journal of Abnormal Psychology, 129,* 633–645.

Wang, K.-Y., Bublitz, M. G., & Zhao, G. (Terry). (2021). Enhancing dieters' perseverance in adversity: How counterfactual thinking increases use of digital health tracking tools. *Appetite, 164.*

Wang, X., & Krumhuber, E. G. (2017). The love of money results in objectification. *British Journal of Social Psychology, 56,* 354–372.

Wang, X., Gao, L., Yang, J., Zhao, F., & Wang, P. (2020). Parental phubbing and adolescents' depressive symptoms: Self-esteem and perceived social support as moderators. *Journal of Youth and Adolescence, 49,* 427–437.

Wang, X., Zheng, L., Li, L., Zheng, Y., Sun, P., Zhou, F. A., & Guo, X. (2017). Immune to situation: The self-serving bias in unambiguous contexts. *Frontiers in Psychology, 8,* 822.

Wang, Y., Li, L., Cai, J., Li, H., & Wang, C. (2022). Incidental physical pain reduces brain activities associated with affective social feedback and increases aggression. *Social Cognitive and Affective Neuroscience, 18.*

Wang, Z. (2015). Examining big-fish-little-pond effects across 49 countries: A multilevel latent variable modeling approach. *Educational Psychology, 35,* 228–251.

Ward, W. C., & Jenkins, H. M. (1965). The display of information and the judgment of contingency. *Canadian Journal of Psychology, 19,* 231–241.

Warnick, D. H., & Sanders, G. S. (1980). The effects of group discussion on eyewitness accuracy. *Journal of Applied Social Psychology, 10,* 249–259.

Warr, P., & Payne, R. (1982). Experiences of strain and pleasure among British adults. *Social Science and Medicine, 16,* 1691–1697.

Washington, K. N., & Hans, J. D. (2013). Romantic attachment among young adults: The effects of parental divorce and residential instability. *Journal of Divorce & Remarriage, 54,* 95–111.

Waters, N. L., & Hans, V. P. (2009). A jury of one: Opinion formation, conformity, and dissent on juries. *Journal of Empirical Legal Studies, 6*(3), 513–540.

Watkins, D., Akande, A., & Fleming, J. (1998). Cultural dimensions, gender, and the nature of self-concept: A fourteen-country study. *International Journal of Psychology, 33,* 17–31.

Watkins, D., Cheng, C., Mpofu, E., Olowu, S., Singh-Sengupta, S., & Regmi, M. (2003). Gender differences in self-construal: How generalizable are Western findings? *Journal of Social Psychology, 143,* 501–519.

Watkins, E. R. (2008). Constructive and unconstructive repetitive thought. *Psychological Bulletin, 134,* 163–206.

Watson, D. (1982, November). The actor and the observer: How are their perceptions of causality divergent? *Psychological Bulletin, 92,* 682–700.

Watt, H., Hyde, J., Petersen, J., Morris, Z., Rozek, C., & Harackiewicz, J. (2017). Mathematics—a critical filter for STEM-related career choices? A longitudinal examination among Australian and U.S. adolescents. *Sex Roles, 77,* 254–271.

Watt, S. E., & Badger, A. J. (2009). Effects of social belonging on homesickness: An application of the belongingness hypothesis. *Personality and Social Psychology Bulletin, 35,* 516–530.

Watt, S. E., & Larkin, C. (2010). Prejudiced people perceive more community support for their views: The role of own, media, and peer attitudes in perceived consensus. *Journal of Applied Social Psychology, 40,* 710–731.

Waytz, A., Young, L. L., & Ginges, J. (2014). Motive attribution asymmetry for love vs. hate drives intractable conflict. *PNAS Proceedings of the National Academy of Sciences of the United States of America, 111,* 15687–15692.

Weary, G., Harvey, J. H., Schwieger, P., Olson, C. T., Perloff, R., & Pritchard, S. (1982). Self-presentation and the moderation of self-serving biases. *Social Cognition, 1,* 140–159.

Webb, C. E., Rossignac-Milon, M., & Higgins, E. T. (2017). Stepping forward together: Could walking facilitate interpersonal conflict resolution? *American Psychologist, 72,* 374–385.

Weber, A. L., & Harvey, J. (1994). *Perspective on close relationships.* Boston, MA: Allyn & Bacon.

Weber, N., Wells, G. L., & Semmler, C. (2004). Eyewitness identification accuracy and response latency: The unruly 10–12-second rule. *Journal of Experimental Psychology: Applied, 10,* 139–147.

Wegner, D. M., & Erber, R. (1992). The hyperaccessibility of suppressed thoughts. *Journal of Personality and Social Psychology, 63,* 903–912.

Wehr, P. (1979). *Conflict regulation.* Boulder, CO: Westview.

Weiler, S. M., Tetzlaff, B.-O., Herzberg, P. Y., & Jacobsen, T. (2021). When personality gets under the skin: Need for uniqueness and body modifications. *PLoS ONE, 16*(3).

Weiner, B. (1980). A cognitive (attribution)-emotion-action model of motivated behavior: An analysis of judgments of help-giving. *Journal of Personality and Social Psychology, 39,* 186–200.

Weiner, B. (1981). *The emotional consequences of causal ascriptions.* Unpublished manuscript, UCLA.

Weiner, B. (1985). "Spontaneous" causal thinking. *Psychological Bulletin, 97,* 74–84.

Weiner, B. (1995). *Judgments of responsibility: A foundation for a theory of social conduct.* New York: Guilford.

Weiner, B. (2008). Reflections on the history of attribution theory and research: People, personalities, publications, problems. *Social Psychology, 39,* 151–156.

Weiner, B. (2010). The development of an attribution-based theory of motivation: A history of ideas. *Educational Psychologist, 45,* 28–36.

Weiner, B., Osborne, D., & Rudoph, U. (2011). An attributional analysis of reactions to poverty: The political ideology of the giver and the perceived morality of the receiver. *Personality and Social Psychology Review, 15,* 199–213.

Weiner, J. (2017, October 6). The flagrant sexual hypocrisy of conservative men. *The New York Times.*

Weinstein, N., & Ryan, R. M. (2010). When helping helps: Autonomous motivation for prosocial behavior and its influence on well-being for the helper and recipient. *Journal of Personality and Social Psychology, 98,* 222–244.

Weinstein, N. D. (1980). Unrealistic optimism about future life events. *Journal of Personality and Social Psychology, 39,* 806–820.

Weinstein, N. D. (1982). Unrealistic optimism about susceptibility to health problems. *Journal of Behavioral Medicine, 5,* 441–460.

Weischelbaum, S., Lauinger, J., & Hutchinson, B. (2010, November 29). Brave local man makes it to work on time—after heroically saving man sprawled on No. 6 track. *New York Daily News.* https://www.nydailynews.com/new-york/brave-local-man-work-time-heroically-saving-man-sprawled-no-6-track-article-1.450738

Weis, R., & Cerankosky, B. C. (2010). Effects of video-game ownership on young boys' academic and behavioral functioning: A randomized, controlled study. *Psychological Science, 21,* 463–470.

Weitbrecht, E. M., & Whitton, S. W. (2020). College students' motivations for "hooking up": Similarities and differences in motives by gender and partner type. *Couple and Family Psychology: Research and Practice, 9*(3), 123–143.

Welborn, B. L., Gunter, B. C., Vezich, I. S., & Lieberman, M. D. (2017). Neural correlates of the false consensus effect: Evidence for motivated projection and regulatory restraint. *Journal of Cognitive Neuroscience, 29,* 708–717.

Welch, D. T., Ordonez, L. D., Snyder, D. G., & Christian, M. S. (2015). The slippery slope: How small ethical transgressions pave the way for larger future transgressions. *Journal of Applied Psychology, 100,* 114–127.

Welker, K. M., Baker, L., Padilla, A., Holmes, H., Aron, A., & Slatcher, R. B. (2014). Effects of self-disclosure and responsiveness between couples on passionate love within couples. *Personal Relationships, 21,* 692–708.

Wells, B. M., & Skowronski, J. J. (2012). Evidence of choking under pressure on the PGA tour. *Basic and Applied Social Psychology, 34,* 175–182.

Wells, G. L., & Bradfield, A. L. (1998). "Good, you identified the suspect": Feedback to eyewitnesses distorts their reports of the witnessing experience. *Journal of Applied Psychology, 83,* 360–376.

Wells, G. L., & Bradfield, A. L. (1999). Distortions in eyewitnesses' recollections: Can the postidentification-feedback effect be moderated? *Psychological Science, 10,* 138–144.

Wells, G. L., & Leippe, M. R. (1981). How do triers of fact enter the accuracy of eyewitness identification? Memory for peripheral detail can be misleading. *Journal of Applied Psychology, 66,* 682–687.

Wells, G. L., & Olson, E. A. (2001). The other-race effect in eyewitness identification: What do we do about it? *Psychology, Public Policy and the Law, 7,* 230–246.

Wells, G. L., & Petty, R. E. (1980). The effects of overt head movements on persuasion: Compatibility and incompatibility of responses. *Basic and Applied Social Psychology, 1,* 219–230.

Wells, G. L., & Smalarz, L. (2022). Lives destroyed by distorted recollections of fluency, attention, view, and confidence: A sin of bias in eyewitness identification. *Journal of Applied Research in Memory and Cognition, 11,* 461–464.

Wells, G. L. (1984). The psychology of lineup identifications. *Journal of Applied Social Psychology, 14,* 89–103.

Wells, G. L. (1993). What do we know about eyewitness identification? *American Psychologist, 48,* 553–571.

Wells, G. L. (2005). Helping experimental psychology affect legal policy. In N. Brewer & K. D. Williams (Eds.), *Psychology and law: An empirical perspective.* New York: Guilford.

Wells, G. L. (2008). Field experiments on eyewitness identification: Towards a better understanding of pitfalls and prospects. *Law and Human Behavior, 32,* 6–10.

Wells, G. L. (2020). Psychological science on eyewitness identification and its impact on police practices and policies. *American Psychologist, 75,* 1316–1329.

Wells, G. L., Ferguson, T. J., & Lindsay, R. C. L. (1981). The tractability of eyewitness confidence and its implications for triers of fact. *Journal of Applied Psychology, 66,* 688–696.

Wells, G. L., Kovera, M. B., Douglass, A. B., Brewer, N., Meissner, C. A., & Wixted, J. T. (2020). Policy and procedure recommendations for the collection and preservation of eyewitness identification evidence. *Law and Human Behavior, 44,* 3–36.

Wells, G. L., Lindsay, R. C. L., & Ferguson, T. (1979). Accuracy, confidence, and juror perceptions in eyewitness identification. *Journal of Applied Psychology, 64,* 440–448.

Wells, G. L., Lindsay, R. C. L., & Tousignant, J. P. (1980). Effects of expert psychological advice on human performance in judging the validity of eyewitness testimony. *Law and Human Behavior, 4,* 275–285.

Wells, G. L., Malpass, R. S., Lindsay, R. C. L., Fisher, R. P., Turtle, J. W., & Fulero, S. M. (2000). Mistakes in eyewitness identification are caused by known factors. Collaboration between criminal justice experts and research psychologists may lower the number of errors. *American Psychologist, 55,* 581–598.

Wells, G. L., Memon, A., & Penrod, S. D. (2006). Eyewitness evidence: Improving its probative value. *Psychological Science in the Public Interest, 7,* 45–75.

Wells, G. L., Olson, E. A., & Charman, S. D. (2002). The confidence of eyewitnesses in their identifications from lineups. *Current Directions in Psychological Science, 11,* 151–154.

Wells, G. L., Steblay, N. K., & Dystart, J. E. (2015). Double-blind photo lineups using actual eyewitnesses: An experimental test of a sequential versus simultaneous lineup procedure. *Law and Human Behavior, 39,* 1–14.

Welna, D. (2020, March 25). Commission issues verdict: Women, like men, should have to sign up for draft. *NPR.* https://www.npr.org/2020/03/25/821615322/commission-issues-verdict-women-like-men-should-have-to-sign-up-for-draft

Wenzlaff, R. M., & Prohaska, M. L. (1989). When misery prefers company: Depression, attributions, and responses to others' moods. *Journal of Experimental Social Psychology, 25,* 220–233.

Werner, C. M., Stoll, R., Birch, P., & White, P. H. (2002). Clinical validation and cognitive elaboration: Signs that encourage sustained recycling. *Basic and Applied Social Psychology, 24,* 185–203.

Wesselmann, E. D., & Williams, K. D. (2017). Social life and social death: Inclusion, ostracism, and rejection in groups. *Group Processes & Intergroup Relations, 20,* 693–706.

Westermann, C. J., & Coscia, M. (2022). A potential mechanism for low tolerance feedback loops in social media flagging systems. *PLoS ONE, 17*(5).

Westerwick, A., Johnson, B. K., & Knobloch-Westerwick, S. (2017). Confirmation biases in selective exposure to political online information: Source bias vs. content bias. *Communication Monographs, 84,* 343–364.

West, M. P., Wood, E. F., Casas, J. B., & Miller, M. K. (2017). The legal and methodological implications of death qualification operationalization. *Applied Psychology in Criminal Justice, 13,* 18–31.

West, S. G., & Brown, T. J. (1975). Physical attractiveness, the severity of the emergency and helping: A field experiment and interpersonal simulation. *Journal of Experimental Social Psychology, 11,* 531–538.

West, S. G., Whitney, G., & Schnedler, R. (1975). Helping a motorist in distress: The effects of sex, race, and neighborhood. *Journal of Personality and Social Psychology, 31,* 691–698.

Weyant, J. M., & Smith, S. L. (1987). Getting more by asking for less: The effects of request size on donations of charity. *Journal of Applied Social Psychology, 17,* 392–400.

Weyant, J. M. (1984). Applying social psychology to induce charitable donations. *Journal of Applied Social Psychology, 14,* 441–447.

Whang, W., Kubzansky, L, D., Kawachi, I., Rexrode, K. M., Kroenke, C. H., Glynn, R. J., Garan, H., & Albert, C. M. (2009). Depression and risk of sudden cardiac death and coronary heart disease in women. *Journal of the American College of Cardiology, 53,* 950–958.

Whatley, M. A., Webster, J. M., Smith, R. H., & Rhodes, A. (1999). The effect of a favor on public and private compliance: How internalized is the norm of reciprocity? *Basic and Applied Social Psychology, 21,* 251–261.

Whillans, A. V., Dunn, E. W., Smeets, P., Bekkers, R., & Norton, M. I. (2017). Buying time promotes happiness. *PNAS, 114*(32), 8523–8527.

Whisman, M. A., Gilmour, A. L., & Salinger, J. M. (2018). Marital satisfaction and mortality in the United States adult population. *Health Psychology, 37,* 1041–1044.

Whitechurch, E. R., Wilson, T. D., & Gilbert, D. T. (2011). "He loves me, he loves me not . . ."; Uncertainty can increase romantic attraction. *Psychological Science, 22,* 172–175.

White, C. J. M., Kelly, J. M., Shariff, A. F., & Norenzayan, A. (2019). Supernatural norm enforcement: Thinking about karma and God reduces selfishness among believers. *Journal of Experimental Social Psychology, 84,* 103797.

White, G. L., & Kight, T. D. (1984). Misattribution of arousal and attraction: Effects of salience of explanations for arousal. *Journal of Experimental Social Psychology, 20,* 55–64.

White, G. L. (1980). Physical attractiveness and courtship progress. *Journal of Personality and Social Psychology, 39,* 660–668.

White, J. W., & Kowalski, R. M. (1994). Deconstructing the myth of the nonaggressive woman. *Psychology of Women Quarterly, 18,* 487–508.

White, K., & Lehman, D. R. (2005). Culture and social comparison seeking: The role of self-motives. *Personality and Social Psychology Bulletin, 31,* 232–242.

White, K., Habib, R., & Hardisty, D. J. (2019). How to SHIFT consumer behaviors to be more sustainable: A literature review and guiding framework. *Journal of Marketing, 83,* 22–49.

White, L., & Edwards, J. (1990). Emptying the nest and parental well-being: An analysis of national panel data. *American Sociological Review, 55,* 235–242.

White, M. J., & Gerstein, L. H. (1987). Helping: The influence of anticipated social sanctions and self-monitoring. *Journal of Personality, 55,* 41–54.

White, S. R., & Bonnett, L. J. (2019). Biased sampling activity: An investigation to promote discussion. *Teaching Statistics, 41,* 8–13.

Whitley, B. E., Jr. (1987). The effects of discredited eyewitness testimony: A meta-analysis. *Journal of Social Psychology, 127,* 209–214.

WHO (World Health Organization). (2016). *Estimated rotavirus deaths for children under 5 years of age: 2013, 215,000.* https://www.who.int/immunization/monitoring_surveillance/burden/estimates/rotavirus/en/

WHO (World Health Organization). (2016). *Violence against women: Intimate partner and sexual violence against women.* Fact sheet No. 239. http://www.who.int/mediacentre/factsheets/fs239/en/

WHO (World Health Organization). (2021). *Violence against women.* https://www.who.int/news-room/fact-sheets/detail/violence-against-women

Wicker, A. W. (1969). Attitudes versus actions: The relationship of verbal and overt behavioral responses to attitude objects. *Journal of Social Issues, 25,* 41–78.

Widom, C. S. (1989). Does violence beget violence? A critical examination of the literature. *Psychological Bulletin, 106,* 3–28.

Wiegman, O. (1985). Two politicians in a realistic experiment: Attraction, discrepancy, intensity of delivery, and attitude change. *Journal of Applied Social Psychology, 15,* 673–686.

Wiesel, E. (1985, April 6). The brave Christians who saved Jews from the Nazis. *TV Guide,* pp. 4–6.

Wieselquist, J., Rusbult, C. E., Foster, C. A., & Agnew, C. R. (1999). Commitment, pro-relationship behavior, and trust in close relationships. *Journal of Personality and Social Psychology, 77,* 942–966.

Wike, R., Fetterolf, J., Fagan, M., & Moncus, J. J. (2023, April 6). Seven-in-ten Americans now see Russia as an enemy. Pew Research Center.

Wilcox, W. B. (2024). *Get married: Why Americans must defy the elites, forge strong families, and save civilization.* New York: Broadside.

Wilder, D. A., & Shapiro, P. (1991). Facilitation of outgroup stereotypes by enhanced ingroup identity. *Journal of Experimental Social Psychology, 27,* 431–452.

Wilder, D. A., & Shapiro, P. N. (1984). Role of out-group cues in determining social identity. *Journal of Personality and Social Psychology, 47,* 342–348.

Wilder, D. A., & Shapiro, P. N. (1989). Role of competition-induced anxiety in limiting the beneficial impact of positive behavior by out-group members. *Journal of Personality and Social Psychology, 56,* 60–69.

Wilder, D. A. (1977). Perception of groups, size of opposition, and social influence. *Journal of Experimental Social Psychology, 13,* 253–268.

Wilder, D. A. (1978). Perceiving persons as a group: Effect on attributions of causality and beliefs. *Social Psychology, 41,* 13–23.

Wilder, D. A. (1981). Perceiving persons as a group: Categorization and intergroup relations. In D. L. Hamilton (Ed.). *Cognitive processes in stereotyping and intergroup behavior.* Hillsdale, NJ: Erlbaum.

Wildschut, T., Insko, C. A., & Pinter, B. (2007). Interindividual-intergroup discontinuity as a joint function of acting as a group and interacting with a group. *European Journal of Social Psychology, 37,* 390–399.

Wildschut, T., Pinter, B., Vevea, J. L., Insko, C. A., & Schopler, J. (2003). Beyond the group mind: A quantitative review of the interindividual-intergroup discontinuity effect. *Psychological Bulletin, 129,* 698–722.

Wilford, J. N. (1999, February 9). New findings help balance the cosmological books. *The New York Times.*

Wilkes, J. (1987, June). Murder in mind. *Psychology Today,* pp. 27–32.

Wilkinson, G. S. (1990, February). Food sharing in vampire bats. *Scientific American, 262,* 76–82.

Wilkinson, R., & Pickett, K. (2009). *The spirit level: Why greater equality makes societies stronger.* London: Bloomsbury.

Wilkinson, R., & Pickett, K. (2011). *The spirit level: Why greater equality makes societies stronger.* Bloomsbury, Australia: Bloomsbury Publishing.

Wilkinson, R., & Pickett, K. (2017b). Inequality and mental illness. *The Lancet Psychiatry, 4,* 512–513.

Wilkinson, R. G., & Pickett, K. E. (2017a). The enemy between us: The psychological and social costs of inequality. *European Journal of Social Psychology, 47*(1), 11–24.

Willems, S., Dedonder, J., & Van der Linden, M. (2010). The mere exposure effect and recognition depend on the way you look! *Experimental Psychology, 57,* 185–192.

Willett, J., Saunders, C., Hackney, F., & Hill, K. (2022). The affective economy and fast fashion: Materiality, embodied learning and developing a sensibility for sustainable clothing. *Journal of Material Culture, 27,* 219–237

Williams, A. L., Grogan, S., Clark-Carter, D., & Buckley, E. (2013). Appearance-based interventions to reduce ultraviolent exposure and/or increase sun protection intentions and behaviours: A systematic review and meta-analyses. *British Journal of Health Psychology, 18,* 182–217.

Williams, D. K., Bourgeois, M. J., & Croyle, R. T. (1993). The effects of stealing thunder in criminal and civil trials. *Law and Human Behavior, 17,* 597–609.

Williams, E. F., & Gilovich, T. (2008). Do people really believe they are above average? *Journal of Experimental Social Psychology, 44,* 1121–1128.

Williams, J. E., & Best, D. L. (1990). *Measuring sex stereotypes: A multination study.* Newbury Park, CA: Sage.

Williams, J. E., Satterwhite, R. C., & Best, D. L. (1999). Pancultural gender stereotypes revisited: The Five Factor model. *Sex Roles, 40,* 513–525.

Williams, J. E., Satterwhite, R. C., & Best, D. L. (2000). *Five-factor gender stereotypes in 27 countries.* Paper presented at the XV Congress of the International Association for Cross-Cultural Psychology, Pultusk, Poland.

Williams, K. D., & Nida, S. A. (2009). Is ostracism worse than bullying? In M. J. Harris (Ed.), *Bullying, rejection, and peer victimization: A social cognitive neuroscience perspective* (pp. 279–296). New York: Springer Publishing Co.

Williams, K. D., & Nida, S. A. (2011). Ostracism: Consequences and coping. *Current Directions in Psychological Science, 20,* 71–75.

Williams, K. D., & Nida, S. A. (2022). Ostracism and social exclusion: Implications for separation, social isolation, and loss. *Current Opinion in Psychology, 47.*

Williams, K. D. (2001). *Ostracism: The power of silence.* New York: Guilford.

Williams, K. D. (2011, January/February). The pain of exclusion. *Scientific American Mind,* pp. 30–37.

Williams, K. D., Harkins, S., & Latané, B. (1981). Identifiability as a deterrent to social loafing: Two cheering experiments. *Journal of Personality and Social Psychology, 40,* 303–311.

Williams, K. D., Jackson, J. M., & Karau, S. J. (1992). In D. A. Schroeder (Ed.) *Social dilemmas: Perspectives on individuals and groups.* Westport, CT: Greenwood Publishing Group.

Williams, K. D., Nida, S. A., Baca, L. D., & Latané, B. (1989). Social loafing and swimming: Effects of identifiability on individual and relay performance of intercollegiate swimmers. *Basic and Applied Social Psychology, 10,* 73–81.

Williams, K. E. G., Krems, J. A., Ayers, J. D., & Rankin, A. M. (2021). Sex differences in friendship preferences. *Evolution and Human Behavior.*

Williams, M. J., & Eberhardt, J. L. (2008). Biological conceptions of race and the motivation to cross racial boundaries. *Journal of Personality and Social Psychology, 94,* 1033–1047.

Williams, M. J., & Tiedens, L. Z. (2016). The subtle suspension of backlash: A meta-analysis of penalties for women's implicit and explicit dominance behavior. *Psychological Bulletin, 142,* 165–197.

Willis, F. N., & Hamm, H. K. (1980). The use of interpersonal touch in securing compliance. *Journal of Nonverbal Behavior, 5,* 49–55.

Willis, J., & Todorov, A. (2006). First impressions: Making up your mind after a 100-ms exposure to a face. *Psychological Science, 17,* 592–598.

Willmott, D., Boduszek, D., Debowska, A., & Woodfield, R. (2018). Introduction and validation of the Juror Decision Scale (JDS): An empirical investigation of the Story Model. *Journal of Criminal Justice, 57,* 26–34.

Wilson, A. E., & Ross, M. (2001). From chump to champ: People's appraisals of their earlier and present selves. *Journal of Personality and Social Psychology, 80,* 572–584.

Wilson, D. S., & Wilson, E. O. (2008). Evolution for "the good of the group." *American Scientist, 96,* 380–389.

Wilson, D. S. (2015). *Does altruism exist? Culture, genes, and the welfare of others.* New Haven, CT: Yale University Press.

Wilson, E. O. (1978). *On human nature.* Cambridge, MA: Harvard University Press, p. 167.

Wilson, E. O. (2002, February). The bottleneck. *Scientific American, 286,* 83–91.

Wilson, G. (1994, March 25). Equal, but different. *The Times of London Higher Education Supplement.*

Wilson, J. P., & Petruska, R. (1984). Motivation, model attributes, and prosocial behavior. *Journal of Personality and Social Psychology, 46,* 458–468.

Wilson, J. P., & Rule, N. O. (2015). Facial trustworthiness predicts extreme criminal-sentencing outcomes. *Psychological Science, 26,* 1325–1331.

Wilson, J. P., Hugenberg, K., & Rule, N. O. (2017). Racial bias in judgments of physical size and formidability: From size to threat. *Journal of Personality and Social Psychology, 113,* 59–80.

Wilson, S. J., & Lipsey, M. W. (2005). *The effectiveness of school-based violence prevention programs for reducing disruptive and aggressive behavior.* Revised Report for the National Institute of Justice School Violence Prevention Research Planning Meeting, May 2005.

Wilson, T. D., & Gilbert, D. T. (2003). Affective forecasting. *Advances in Experimental Social Psychology, 35,* 346–413.

Wilson, T. D. (1985). Strangers to ourselves: The origins and accuracy of beliefs about one's own mental states. In J. H. Harvey & G. Weary (Eds.), *Attribution in contemporary psychology.* New York: Academic Press.

Wilson, T. D. (2002). *Strangers to ourselves: Discovering the adaptive unconscious.* Cambridge, MA: Harvard University Press.

Wilson, T. D., Dunn, D. S., Kraft, D., & Lisle, D. J. (1989). Introspection, attitude change, and attitude-behavior consistency: The disruptive effects of explaining why we feel the way we do. In L. Berkowitz (Ed.), *Advances in experimental social psychology* (Vol. 22). San Diego: Academic Press.

Wilson, T. D., Lindsey, S., & Schooler, T. Y. (2000). A model of dual attitudes. *Psychological Review, 107,* 101–126.

Wilson, W. R. (1979). Feeling more than we can know: Exposure effects without learning. *Journal of Personality and Social Psychology, 37,* 811–821.

Wilton, L. S., Apfelbaum, E. P., & Good, J. J. (2018). Valuing differences and reinforcing them: Multiculturalism increases race essentialism. *Social Psychological and Personality Science, 10,* 681–689.

Winquist, J. R., & Larson, J. R., Jr. (2004). Sources of the discontinuity effect: Playing against a group versus being in a group. *Journal of Experimental Social Psychology, 40,* 675–682.

Winter, F. W. (1973). A laboratory experiment of individual attitude response to advertising exposure. *Journal of Marketing Research, 10,* 130–140.

Wirth, J. H., Sacco, D. F., Hugenberg, K., & Williams, K. D. (2010). Eye gaze as relational evaluation: Averted eye gaze leads to feelings of ostracism and relational devaluation. *Personality and Social Psychology Bulletin, 36,* 869–882.

Wiseman, R. (1998, Fall). Participatory science and the mass media. *Free Inquiry,* pp. 56–57.

Wise, R. A., & Safer, M. A. (2010). A comparison of what U.S. judges and students know and believe about eyewitness testimony. *Journal of Applied Social Psychology, 40,* 1400–1422.

Wisman, A., & Koole, S. L. (2003). Hiding in the crowd: Can mortality salience promote affiliation with others who oppose one's worldviews? *Journal of Personality and Social Psychology, 84,* 511–526.

Wittenberg, M. T., & Reis, H. T. (1986). Loneliness, social skills, and social perception. *Personality and Social Psychology Bulletin, 12,* 121–130.

Wixon, D. R., & Laird, J. D. (1976). Awareness and attitude change in the forced-compliance paradigm: The importance of when. *Journal of Personality and Social Psychology, 34,* 376–384.

Wixted, J. T., & Wells, G. L. (2017). The relationship between eyewitness confidence and identification accuracy: A new synthesis. *Psychological Science in the Public Interest, 18,* 10–65.

Wixted, J. T., Mickes, L., Clark, S. E., Gronlund, S. D., & Roediger, H. I. (2015). Initial eyewitness confidence reliably predicts eyewitness identification accuracy. *American Psychologist, 70,* 515–526.

Wixted, J. T., Wells, G. L., Loftus, E. F., & Garrett, B. L. (2021). Test a witness's memory of a suspect only once. *Psychological Science in the Public Interest, 22*(1, Suppl), 1S–18S.

Wohl, M. J. A., Branscombe, N. R., & Reysen, S. (2010). Perceiving your group's future to be in jeopardy: Extinction threat induces collective angst and the desire to strengthen the ingroup. *Personality and Social Psychology Bulletin, 36,* 898–910.

Wojciszke, B., Bazinska, R., & Jaworski, M. (1998). On the dominance of moral categories in impression formation. *Personality and Social Psychology Bulletin, 24,* 1251–1263.

Wolfe, M. B., & Williams, T. J. (2018). Poor metacognitive awareness of belief change. *Quarterly Journal of Experimental Psychology, 71,* 1898–1910.

Wolfinger, N. (2019, May 28). *Are married people still happier?* Institute for Family Studies. https://ifstudies.org/blog/are-married-people-still-happier

Wolf, S., & Montgomery, D. A. (1977). Effects of inadmissible evidence and level of judicial admonishment to disregard on the judgments of mock jurors. *Journal of Applied Social Psychology, 7,* 205–219.

Wolf, W., Levordashka, A., Ruff, J. R., Kraaijeveld, S., Lueckmann, J.-M., & Williams, K. D. (2015). Ostracism online: A social media ostracism paradigm. *Behavior Research, 47,* 361–373.

Wollmer, M. A., & 18 others (2012). Facing depression with botulinum toxin: A randomized controlled trial. *Journal of Psychiatric Research, 46,* 574–581.

Wondergem, T. R., & Friedmeier, M. (2012). Gender and ethnic differences in smiling: A yearbook photographs analysis from kindergarten through 12th grade. *Sex Roles, 67,* 403–411.

Wong, E. M., Ormiston, M. E., & Haselhuhn, M. P. (2011). A face only an investor could love: CEOs' facial structure predicts their firms' financial performance. *Psychological Science, 22,* 1478–1483.

Wong, J. C. (2021, January 20). QAnon's 'Great Awakening' failed to materialize. What's next could be worse. *The Guardian.*

Wood, C., Conner, M., Miles, E., Sandberg, T., Taylor, N., Goldin, G., & Sheeran, P. (2016). The impact of asking intention or self-prediction questions on subsequent behavior: A meta-analysis. *Personality and Social Psychology Review, 20,* 245–268.

Wood, J. V., Perunovic, W., & Lee, J. W. (2009). Positive self-statements: Power for some, peril for others. *Psychological Science, 20,* 860–866.

Wood, O. (2012). How emotional tugs trump rational pushes: The time has come to abandon a 100-year-old advertising model. *Journal of Advertising Research, 52,* 31–39.

Wood, W., & Eagly, A. H. (2000). Once again, the origins of sex differences. *American Psychologist, 55,* 1062–1063.

Wood, W., & Eagly, A. H. (2002). A cross-cultural analysis of the behavior of women and men: Implications for the origins of sex differences. *Psychological Bulletin, 128,* 699–727.

Wood, W., & Eagly, A. H. (2007). Social structural origins of sex differences in human mating. In S. W. Gangestad & J. A. Simpson (Eds.), *The evolution of mind: Fundamental questions and controversies.* New York: Guilford.

Wood, W. (2017). Habit in personality and social psychology. *Personality and Social Psychology Review, 21,* 389–403.

Woodward, W., & Woodward, M. (1942, March 26). Not time enough. Editorial, *Bainbridge Review,* p. 1.

Woodzicka, J. A., & LaFrance, M. (2001). Real versus imagined gender harassment. *Journal of Social Issues, 57*(1), 15–30.

Woolley, A. W., Chabris, C. F., Pentland, A., Hasmi, N., & Malone, T. W. (2010). Evidence for a collective intelligence factor in the performance of human groups. *Science, 330,* 686–688.

Worchel, S., & Brown, E. H. (1984). The role of plausibility in influencing environmental attributions. *Journal of Experimental Social Psychology, 20,* 86–96.

Worchel, S., & Norvell, N. (1980). Effect of perceived environmental conditions during cooperation on intergroup attraction. *Journal of Personality and Social Psychology, 38,* 764–772.

Worchel, S., Andreoli, V. A., & Folger, R. (1977). Intergroup cooperation and intergroup attraction: The effect of previous interaction and outcome of combined effort. *Journal of Experimental Social Psychology, 13,* 131–140.

Worchel, S., Axsom, D., Ferris, F., Samah, G., & Schweitzer, S. (1978). Deterrents of the effect of intergroup cooperation on intergroup attraction. *Journal of Conflict Resolution, 22,* 429–439.

Worchel, S., Rothgerber, H., Day, E. A., Hart, D., & Butemeyer, J. (1998). Social identity and individual productivity within groups. *British Journal of Social Psychology, 37,* 389–413.

Word, C. O., Zanna, M. P., & Cooper, J. (1974). The nonverbal mediation of self-fulfilling prophecies in interracial interaction. *Journal of Experimental Social Psychology, 10,* 109–120.

Worden, R. E., McLean, S. J., Engel, R. S., Cochran, H., Corsaro, N., Reynolds, D., Najdowski , C. J. & Isaza, G. T. (2020). The Impacts of Implicit Bias Awareness Training in the NYPD. IACP/UC Center for Police Research and Policy & John F. Finn Institute for Public Safety.

Workman, E. A., & Williams, R. L. (1980). Effects of extrinsic rewards on intrinsic motivation in the classroom. *Journal of School Psychology, 18,* 141–147.

World Bank. (2019). *Global wage report 2018/19: What lies behind gender pay gaps.* https://www.ilo.org/global/research/global-reports/global-wage-report/WCMS_650568/lang–en/index.htm

World Meteorological Organization. (2017, October 30). *WMO greenhouse gas bulletin: The state of greenhouse gases in the atmosphere based on global observations through 2016.* Geneva: World Meteorological Organization. https://library.wmo.int/index.php?lvl=notice_display&id=20041

Worringham, C. J., & Messick, D. M. (1983). Social facilitation of running: An unobtrusive study. *Journal of Social Psychology, 121,* 23–29.

Wraga, M., Helt, M., Jacobs, E., & Sullivan, K. (2007). Neural basis of stereotype-induced shifts in women's mental rotation performance. *Social Cognitive and Affective Neuroscience, 2,* 12–19.

Wright, D. B., & Hall, M. (2007). How a "reasonable doubt" instruction affects decisions of guilt. *Basic and Applied Social Psychology, 29,* 91–98.

Wright, D. B., & Stroud, J. N. (2002). Age differences in lineup identification accuracy: People are better with their own age. *Law and Human Behavior, 26,* 641–654.

Wright, D. B., Memom, A., Skagerberg, E. M., & Gabbert, F. (2009). When eyewitnesses talk. *Current Directions in Psychological Science, 18,* 174–178.

Wright, E. F., Lüüs, C. A., & Christie, S. D. (1990). Does group discussion facilitate the use of consensus information in making causal attributions? *Journal of Personality and Social Psychology, 59,* 261–269.

Wright, G. S., Wilkinson, G. S., & Moss, C. F. (2020). Social facilitation in short-tailed fruit bats, Carollia perspicillata (Linnaeus). *Behaviour, 157,* 1193–1210.

Wright, P. J., Herbenick, D., & Paul, B. (2020). Adolescent condom use, parent-adolescent sexual health communication, and pornography: Findings from a US Probability sample. *Health Communication, 35,* 1576–1582.

Wright, P. J., Tokunaga, R. S., & Kraus, A. (2016). A meta-analysis of pornography consumption and actual acts of sexual aggression in general population studies. *Journal of Communication, 66,* 183–205.

Wright, R. (1998, February 2). Politics made me do it. *Time,* p. 34.

Wright, S. C., Tropp, L. R., & Mazziotta, A. (2017). Contact between groups, peace, and conflict. *Peace and Conflict: Journal of Peace Psychology, 23,* 207–209.

Wrzesniewski, A., & Schwartz, B. (2014b, July 4). The secret of effective motivation. *The New York Times.*

Wrzesniewski, A., Schwartz, B., Cong, X., Kane, M., Omar, A, & Kolditz, T. (2014a). Multiple types of motives don't multiply the motivation of West Point cadets. *PNAS, 111,* 10990–109905.

Wróbel, M., & Imbir, K. K. (2019). Broadening the perspective on emotional contagion and emotional mimicry: The correction hypothesis. *Perspectives on Psychological Science, 14,* 437–451.

Wu, B-P., & Chang, L. (2012). The social impact of pathogen threat: How disease salience influences conformity. *Personality and Individual Differences, 53,* 50–54.

Wu-Chung, E. L., Leal, S. L., Denny, B. T., Cheng, S. L., & Fagundes, C. P. (2022). Spousal caregiving, widowhood, and cognition: A systematic review and a biopsychosocial framework for understanding the relationship between interpersonal losses and dementia risk in older adulthood. *Neuroscience and Biobehavioral Reviews, 134.*

Wu, D., Cai, L., Liang, L., & Li, H. (2022). Patterns and predictors of code-switching in Singapore preschoolers: A corpus-based study. *International Journal of Bilingual Education and Bilingualism, 25,* 2933–2948.

Wuebbles, D.J., Fahey, D. W., Hibbard, K. A., DeAngelo, B., Doherty, S., Hayhoe, K., Horton, R., Kossin, J. P., Taylor, P. C., Waple, A. M., & Weaver, C.P. (2017). Executive summary. In D. J. Wuebbles, D. W. Fahey, K. A. Hibbard, D. J. Dokken, B. C. Stewart, & T. K. Maycock (Eds.), *Climate science special report: Fourth national climate assessment (Volume I).* Washington, DC: U.S. Global Change Research Program, pp. 12–34.

Wu, L., Wang, D., & Evans, J. A. (2019). Large teams develop and small teams disrupt science and technology. *Nature, 566,* 378–382.

Wu, S., Cheng, C. K., Feng, J., D'Angelo, L., Alain, C., & Spence, I. (2012). Playing a first-person shooter video game induces neuroplastic change. *Journal of Cognitive Neuroscience, 24,* 1286–1293.

Wu. S. J., & Cai. X. (2023). Adding Up Peer Beliefs: Experimental and Field Evidence on the Effect of Peer Influence on Math Performance. *Psychological Science.*

Wylie, R. C. (1979). *The self-concept (Vol. 2): Theory and research on selected topics.* Lincoln, NE: University of Nebraska Press.

Wynn, K., Bloom, P., Jordan, A., Marshall, J., & Sheskin, M. (2018). Not noble savages after all: Limits to early altruism. *Current Directions in Psychological Science, 27,* 3–8.

Xiao, Y. J., & Van Bavel, J. J. (2019). Sudden shifts in social identity swiftly shape implicit evaluation. *Journal of Experimental Social Psychology, 83,* 55–69.

Xie, Y., Chen, M., Lai, H., Zhang, W., Zhao, Z., & Anwar, C. M. (2016). Neural basis of two kinds of social influence: Obedience and conformity. *Frontiers in Human Neuroscience, 10,* 51.

Xi, J., Lee, M. T., Carter, J. R., & Delgado, D. (2022). Gender differences in purpose in life: The mediation effect of altruism. *Journal of Humanistic Psychology, 62,* 352–376.

Xu, H., Bègue, L., & Shankland, R. (2011). Guilt and guiltlessness: An integrative review. *Social and Personality Psychology Compass, 5,* 440–457.

Xu, M., & Petty, R. E. (2022). Two-sided messages promote openness for morally based attitudes. *Personality and Social Psychology Bulletin, 48,* 1151–1166.

Xu, Y., Farver, J. M., & Pauker, K. (2015). Ethnic identity and self-esteem among Asian and European Americans: When a minority is the majority and the majority is a minority. *European Journal of Social Psychology, 45,* 62–76.

Yair, O. (2021). The hostile mediator phenomenon: When threatened, rival partisans perceive various mediators as biased against their group. *Public Opinion Quarterly, 85,* 864–886.

Yamada, J., Kito, M., & Yuki, M. (2017). Passion, relational mobility, and proof of commitment: A comparative socio-ecological analysis of an adaptive emotion in a sexual market. *Evolutionary Psychology, 15*(4), Article 1474704917746056.

Yamagishi, T., Hashimoto, H., Cook, K. S., Kiyonari, T., Shinada, M., Mifune, N., Inukai, K., Takagishi, H., Horita, Y., & Li, Y. (2012). Modesty in self-presentation: A comparison between the USA and Japan. *Asian Journal of Social Psychology, 15,* 60–68.

Yamaguchi, S., Greenwald, A. G., Banaji, M. R., Murakami, F., Chen, D., Shiomura, K., Kobayashi, C., Cai, H., & Krendl, A. (2007). Apparent universality of positive implicit self-esteem. *Psychological Science, 18,* 498–500.

Yang, B. Z., Zhang, H., Ge, W., Weder, N., Douglas-Palumberi, H., Perepletchikova, F., Gelernter, J., & Kaufman, J. (2013). Child abuse and epigenetic mechanisms of disease risk. *American Journal of Preventative Medicine, 44,* 101–107.

Yang, F., Choi, Y-J., Misch, A., Yang, X., & Dunham, Y. (2018). In defense of the commons: Young children negatively evaluate and sanction free riders. *Psychological Science, 29,* 1598–1611.

Yang, K., & Girgus, J. S. (2019). Are women more likely than men are to care excessively about maintaining positive social relationships? A meta-analytic review of the gender difference in sociotropy. *Sex Roles: A Journal of Research, 81,* 157–172.

Yaniv, D. (2012). Dynamics of creativity and empathy in role reversal: Contributions from neuroscience. *Review of General Psychology, 16,* 70–77.

Yarmey, A. D. (2003a). Eyewitness identification: Guidelines and recommendations for identification procedures in the United States and in Canada. *Canadian Psychology, 44,* 181–189.

Yassine, J., & Tipton-Fisler, L. A. (2022). Independent contingency and token economy at recess to reduce aggression. *Contemporary School Psychology, 26,* 481–491.

Ybarra, M. L., Huesmann, L. R., Korchmaros, J. D., & Reisner, S. L. (2014). Cross-sectional associations between violent video and computer game playing and weapon carrying in a national cohort of children. *Aggressive Behavior, 40,* 345–358.

Ybarra, M. L., Mitchell, K. J., Hamburger, M., Diener-West, M., & Leaf, P. J. (2011). X-rated material and perpetration of sexually aggressive behavior among children and adolescents: Is there a link? *Aggressive Behavior, 37,* 1–18.

Yeager, D. S., Krosnick, J. A., Visser, P. S., Holbrook, A. L., & Tahk, A. M. (2019). Moderation of classic social psychological effects by demographics in the U.S. adult population: New opportunities for theoretical advancement. *Journal of Personality and Social Psychology, 117*(6), e84-e99.

Yelsma, P., & Athappilly, K. (1988). Marriage satisfaction and communication practices: Comparisons among Indian and American couples. *Journal of Comparative Family Studies, 19,* 37–54.

You, D., Maeda, Y., & Bebeau, M. J. (2011). Gender differences in moral sensitivity: A meta-analysis. *Ethics and Behavior, 21,* 263–282.

Younger, J., Aron, A., Parke, S., Chatterjee, N., & Mackey, S. (2010). Viewing pictures of a romantic partner reduces experimental pain: Involvement of neural reward systems. *PLOS ONE, 5*(10), e13309.

Young, L. (2009). Love: Neuroscience reveals all. *Nature, 457,* 148.

Young, S. G., Bernstein, M. J., & Hugenberg, K. (2010). When do own-group biases in face recognition occur? Encoding versus post-encoding. *Social Cognition, 28,* 240–250.

Youngstrom, E. A., Choukas-Bradley, S., Calhoun, C. D., & Jensen-Doss, A. (2015). Clinical guide to the evidence-based assessment approach to diagnosis and treatment. *Cognitive and Behavioral Practice, 22,* 20–35.

Yousif, Y., & Korte, C. (1995). Urbanization, culture, and helpfulness. *Journal of Cross-Cultural Psychology, 26,* 474–489.

Youyou, W., Stillwell, D., Schwartz, H. A., & Kosinski, M. (2017). Birds of a feather do flock together: Behavior-based personality-assessment method reveals personality similarity among couples and friends. *Psychological Science, 28,* 276–284.

Yovetich, N. A., & Rusbult, C. E. (1994). Accommodative behavior in close relationships: Exploring transformation of motivation. *Journal of Experimental Social Psychology, 30,* 138–164.

Yuan, J. P., Ho, T. C., Coury, S. M., Chahal, R., Colich, N. L., & Gotlib, I. H. (2022). Early life stress, systemic inflammation, and neural correlates of implicit emotion regulation in adolescents. *Brain, Behavior, and Immunity, 105,* 169–179.

Yu, F., Peng, T., Peng, K., Tang, S., Chen, C. S., Qian, X., & . . . Chai, F. (2016). Cultural value shifting in pronoun use. *Journal of Cross-Cultural Psychology, 47,* 310–316.

Yu, J., & McLellan, R. (2019). Beyond academic achievement goals: The importance of social achievement goals in explaining gender differences in self-handicapping. *Learning and Individual Differences, 69,* 33–44.

Yuki, M., & Schug, J. (2020). Psychological consequences of relational mobility. *Current Opinion in Psychology, 32,* 129–132.

Yukl, G. (1974). Effects of the opponent's initial offer, concession magnitude, and concession frequency on bargaining behavior. *Journal of Personality and Social Psychology, 30,* 323–335.

Yusupov, N., Dieckmann, L., Erhart, M., Sauer, S., Rex-Haffner, M., Kopf-Beck, J., Brückl, T. M., Czamara, D., & Binder, E. B. (2023). Transdiagnostic evaluation of epigenetic age acceleration and burden of psychiatric disorders. *Neuropsychopharmacology, 48,* 1409–1417.

Yzerbyt, V. Y., & Leyens, J-P. (1991). Requesting information to form an impression: The influence of valence and confirmatory status. *Journal of Experimental Social Psychology, 27,* 337–356.

Zaalberg, A., Nijman, H., Bulten, E., Stroosma, L., & van der Staak, C. (2010). Effects of nutritional supplements on aggression, rule-breaking, and psychopathology among young adult prisoners. *Aggressive Behavior, 36,* 117–126.

Zadro, L., Boland, C., & Richardson, R. (2006). How long does it last? The persistence of the effects of ostracism in the socially anxious. *Journal of Experimental Social Psychology, 42,* 692–697.

Zagefka, H., & Brown, R. (2005). Comparisons and perceived deprivation in ethnic minority settings. *Personality and Social Psychology Bulletin, 31,* 467–482.

Zagefka, H., Noor, M., Brown, R., De Moura, G. R., & Hopthrow, T. (2011). Donating to disaster victims: Responses to natural and humanly caused events. *European Journal of Social Psychology, 41,* 353–363.

Zainulbhai, H. (2016, March 8). Strong global support for gender equality, especially among women. *Pew Research Center.* https://www.pewresearch.org/fact-tank/2016/03/08/strong-global-support-for-gender-equality-especially-among-women/

Zajenkowski, M., Czarna, A. Z., Szymaniak, K., & Dufner, M. (2020). What do highly narcissistic people think and feel about (their) intelligence? *Journal of Personality, 88*(4), 703–718.

Zajonc, R. B. (1965). Social facilitation. *Science, 149,* 269–274.

Zajonc, R. B. (1968). Attitudinal effects of mere exposure. *Journal of Personality and Social Psychology, 9*(2), 1–27.

Zajonc, R. B. (1968). Attitudinal effects of mere exposure. *Journal of Personality and Social Psychology, 9,* Monograph Suppl. No. 2, part 2.

Zajonc, R. B. (1970, February). Brainwash: Familiarity breeds comfort. *Psychology Today,* pp. 32–35, 60–62.

Zajonc, R. B. (1980). Feeling and thinking: Preferences need no inferences. *American Psychologist, 35,* 151–175.

Zajonc, R. B. (1998). Emotions. In D. Gilbert, S. T. Fiske, & G. Lindzey (Eds.), *Handbook of social psychology,* (4th ed.). New York: McGraw Hill.

Zajonc, R. B. (2000). *Massacres: Mass murders in the name of moral imperatives.* Unpublished manuscript, Stanford University.

Zakaria, F. (2008). Do we need a wartime president? *Newsweek.* https://www.newsweek.com/do-we-need-wartime-president-91065

Zaki, J., Schirmer, J., & Mitchell, J. P. (2011). Social influence modulates the neural computation of value. *Psychological Science, 22,* 894–900.

Zak, P. J. (2008, June). The neurobiology of trust. *Scientific American,* pp. 88–95.

Zaragoza, M. S., & Mitchell, K. J. (1996). Repeated exposure to suggestion and the creation of false memories. *Psychological Science, 7,* 294–300.

Zarkadi, T., Wade, K. A., & Stewart, N. (2009). Creating fair lineups for suspects with distinctive features. *Psychological Science, 20,* 1448–1453.

Zebrowitz, L. A., Collins, M. A., & Dutta, R. (1998). The relationship between appearance and personality across the life span. *Personality and Social Psychology Bulletin, 24,* 736–749.

Zebrowitz, L. A., Olson, K., & Hoffman, K. (1993). Stability of babyfaceness and attractiveness across the life span. *Journal of Personality and Social Psychology, 64,* 453–466.

Zebrowitz, L. A., White, B., & Wieneke, K. (2008). Mere exposure and racial prejudice: Exposure to other-race faces increases liking for strangers of that race. *Social Cognition, 26,* 259–275.

Zebrowitz-McArthur, L. (1988). Person perception in cross-cultural perspective. In M. H. Bond (Ed.), *The cross-cultural challenge to social psychology.* Newbury Park, CA: Sage.

Zeigler-Hill, V., & Vrabel, J. K. (2023). Narcissistic personality features and contingencies of self-worth: What are the foundations of narcissistic self-esteem? *Self and Identity, 22,* 294–331.

Zella, S. (2017). Marital status transitions and self-reported health among Canadians: A life course perspective. *Applied Research in Quality of Life, 12,* 303–325.

Zell, E., Krizan, Z., & Teeter, S. R. (2015). Evaluating similarities and differences using metasynthesis. *American Psychologist, 70,* 10–20.

Zell, E., Strickhouser, J. E., Sedikides, C., & Alicke, M. D. (2020). The better-than-average effect in comparative self-evaluation: A comprehensive review and meta-analysis. *Psychological Bulletin, 146,* 118–149.

Zerjal, T. (2003). The genetic legacy of the Mongols. *The American Journal of Human Genetics, 72,* 717–721.

Zhang, A., & Rau, P.-L. P. (2022). She is my confidante! The impacts of social responsiveness and video modality on self-disclosure toward CG-based anthropomorphic agents in a smart home. *International Journal of Social Robotics, 14,* 1673–1686.

Zhang, D. D., Lee, H. F., Wong, C., Li, B., Pei, Q., Zhang, J., & An, Y. (2011). The causality analysis of climate change and large-scale human crisis. *PNAS, 108,* 17296–17301.

Zhang, H., & Lei, X. (2023). Effect of subjective sleep quality on aggression: A two-year longitudinal and fMRI pilot study. *Biological Psychology, 176,* 1–8.

Zhang, J. W., Chen, S., & Tomova Shakur, T. K. (2020). From me to you: Self-compassion predicts acceptance of own and others' imperfections. *Personality and Social Psychology Bulletin, 46,* 228–242.

Zhang, P., Zhang, Y., Mu, Z., & Liu, X. (2017). The development of conformity among Chinese children aged 9–15 years in a public choice task. *Evolutionary Psychology, 15*(4), 1474704917743637.

Zhang, S., & Kline, S. L. (2009). Can I make my own decision? A cross-cultural study of perceived social network influence in mate selection. *Journal of Cross-Cultural Psychology, 40,* 3–23.

Zhao, X., & Epley, N. (2022). Surprisingly happy to have helped: Underestimating prosociality creates a misplaced barrier to asking for help. *Psychological Science, 33,* 1708–1731.

Zhong, B. (2023). Going beyond fact-checking to fight health misinformation: A multi-level analysis of the Twitter response to health news stories. *International Journal of Information Management, 70.*

Zhong, C.-B., & Leonardelli, G. F. (2008). Cold and lonely: Does social exclusion literally feel cold? *Psychological Science, 19,* 838–842.

Zhong, C.-B., Bohns, V. K., & Gino, F. (2010). Good lamps are the best police: Darkness increases dishonesty and self-interested behavior. *Psychological Science, 21,* 311–314.

Zhou, S., Page-Gould, E., Aron, A., Moyer, A., & Hewstone, M. (2019). The Extended Contact hypothesis: A meta-analysis on 20 years of research. *Personality and Social Psychology Bulletin, 23,* 132–160.

Zhou, X., Sedikides, C., Wildschut, T., & Gao, D-G. (2008). Counteracting loneliness: On the restorative function of nostalgia. *Psychological Science, 19,* 1023–1029.

Zhu, L., Gigerenzer, G., & Huangfu, G. (2013). Psychological traces of China's socio-economic reforms in the ultimatum and dictator games. *PLOS ONE, 8,* e70769.

Zhu, N., & Chang, L. (2019). Evolved but not fixed: A life history account of gender roles and gender inequality. *Frontiers in Psychology, 10,* 1709.

Zhu, W. X., Lu, L., & Hesketh, T. (2009). China's excess males, sex selective abortion, and one child policy: Analysis of data from 2005 national intercensus survey. *British Medical Journal, 338,* b1211.

Zhu, Y., Zhang, L., Fan, L., & Han, S. (2007). Neural basis of cultural influence on self-representation. *NeuroImage, 34,* 1310–1316.

Ziano, I., & Wang, D. (2021). Slow lies: Response delays promote perceptions of insincerity. *Journal of Personality and Social Psychology, 120,* 1457–1479.

Zick, A., Pettigrew, T. F., & Wagner, U. (2008). Ethnic prejudice and discrimination in Europe. *Journal of Social Issues, 64,* 233–251.

Zillmann, D., & Weaver, J. B., III. (1999). Effects of prolonged exposure to gratuitous media violence on provoked and unprovoked hostile behavior. *Journal of Applied Social Psychology, 29,* 145–165.

Zillmann, D. (1988). Cognition-excitation interdependencies in aggressive behavior. *Aggressive Behavior, 14,* 51–64.

Zillmann, D. (1989). Aggression and sex: Independent and joint operations. In H. L. Wagner & A. S. R. Manstead (Eds.), *Handbook of psychophysiology: Emotion and social behavior.* Chichester, UK: Wiley.

Zimbardo, P. G. (1970). The human choice: Individuation, reason, and order versus deindividuation, impulse, and chaos. In W. J. Arnold & D. Levine (Eds.), *Nebraska symposium on motivation, 1969.* Lincoln: University of Nebraska Press.

Zimbardo, P. G. (2002, April). Nurturing psychological synergies. *APA Monitor, 5,* 38.

Zimbardo, P. G. (2004). A situationist perspective on the psychology of evil: Understanding how good people are transformed into perpetrators. In A. G. Miller (Ed.), *The Social Psychology of Good and Evil.* New York: Guilford.

Zimmer-Gembeck, M. J., Hawes, T., & Pariz, J. (2021). A closer look at appearance and social media: Measuring activity, self-presentation, and social comparison and their associations with emotional adjustment. *Psychology of Popular Media, 10,* 74–86.

Zitek, E. M., & Hebl, M. R. (2007). The role of social norm clarity in the influenced expression of prejudice over time. *Journal of Experimental Social Psychology, 43,* 867–876.

Zola-Morgan, S., Squire, L. R., Alvarez-Royo, P., & Clower, R. P. (1991). Independence of memory functions and emotional behavior. *Hippocampus, 1,* 207–220.

Zotto, M., & Pegna, A. J. (2017). Electrophysiological evidence of perceived sexual attractiveness for human female bodies varying in waist-to-hip ratio. *Cognitive, Affective & Behavioral Neuroscience, 17,* 577–591.

Zou, D., Jin, L., He, Y., & Xu, Q. (2014). The effect of the sense of power of Chinese consumers' uniqueness-seeking behavior. *Journal of International Consumer Marketing, 26,* 14–28.

Zubizarreta, A., Calvete, E., & Hankin, B. L. (2019). Punitive parenting style and psychological problems in childhood: The moderating role of warmth and temperament. *Journal of Child and Family Studies, 28,* 233–244.

Zuckerman, E. W., & Jost, J. T. (2001). What makes you think you're so popular? Self-evaluation maintenance and the subjective side of the "friendship paradox." *Social Psychology Quarterly, 64,* 207–223.

Zurbriggen, C. L. A., Jendryczko, D., & Nussbeck, F. W. (2021). Rosy or blue? Change in recall bias of students' affective experiences during early adolescence. *Emotion, 21,* 1637–1649.

Zuwerink, J. R., Monteith, M. J., Devine, P. G., & Cook, D. A. (1996). Prejudice toward blacks: With and without compunction? *Basic and Applied Social Psychology, 18,* 131–150.

Name Index

A

D

E

F

G

H

I

J

K

N

O

Q

R

S

T

W

X

Y

Z

Subject Index/Glossary

E

N

O

P

Q

R

S

T

U

V

W

Y